INDEX TO MARRIAGE NOTICES

IN

THE SOUTHERN CHURCHMAN

1835 — 1941.

Two Volumes in One

Prepared by:

The Historical Records Survey of Virginia,
Services Division
Work Projects Administration

JANAWAY PUBLISHING
Santa Maria, California

> *Notice*
>
> This book has been reproduced from carbon-copies of the original transcriptions of court records by the Works Progress Administration (WPA) in 1930s. In many instances, the resulting text is light, the documents are physically flawed, and foxing (or discoloration) occurs. The pages of this reprint have been digitally enhanced and, where possible, the flaws eliminated in order to provide clarity of content and a pleasant reading experience.

Index to Marriage Notices in Southern Churchman, 1835—1941.
Two Volumes in One

Prepared by:

The Historical Records Survey of Virginia,
Service Division
Works Projects Administration (WPA)
1942

Reprinted by:

Janaway Publishing, Inc.
732 Kelsey Ct.
Santa Maria, CA 93454
(805) 925-1038
www.JanawayGenealogy.com

2016

ISBN: 978-1-59641-374-0

Made in the United States of America

INDEX TO MARRIAGE NOTICES
IN
THE SOUTHERN CHURCHMAN
1835 - 1941

Prepared by

The Historical Records Survey of Virginia,
Service Division
Work Projects Administration

Sponsored by

The Virginia Conservation Commission

Volume I
A - K

Richmond, Virginia
The Historical Records Survey of Virginia
May 1942

The Historical Records Survey Projects

    Sargent B. Child, Director
    Kathleen Bruce, State Supervisor

Research and Records Programs

    Harvey E. Becknell, Director
    Milton W. Blanton, Regional Supervisor
    James A. McAleer, State Supervisor

Service Division

    Florence Kerr, Assistant Commissioner
    Blanche M. Ralston, Chief Regional Supervisor
    Ella G. Agnew, State Director

WORK PROJECTS ADMINISTRATION

    Howard O. Hunter, Commissioner
    Roy Schroder, Regional Director
    Russell S. Hummel, State Administrator

PREFACE

In January 1936 the Historical Records Survey, a nation-wide project of the Works Progress Administration now the Work Projects Administration, was organized by Dr. Luther H. Evans who served as director until March 1, 1940, when he was succeeded by Mr. Sargeant B. Child.

The survey began to function in Virginia in March 1936 as part of the Federal Writers' Project of which Dr. H. J. Eckenrode was State Director, and Dr. Lester J. Cappon of the University of Virginia part-time Technical Assistant. In November 1936, when the Historical Records Survey became independent of the Federal Writers' Project, Dr. Cappon was appointed part-time State Director. At the same time Miss Elizabeth B. Parker, a former supervisor of the Survey, was appointed Assistant State Director. On September 5, 1939, the Historical Records Survey of Virginia became a Statewide non-Federal project, with Miss Parker as State Supervisor.

The Historical Records Survey was consolidated with the Survey of Federal Archives in Virginia on January 1, 1940, to constitute a new Historical Records Survey project. Dr. Kathleen Bruce, who had been in charge of Federal Archives work in Virginia since September 16, 1936, was appointed State Supervisor and Miss Parker, Assistant State Supervisor. Miss Parker resigned from the Historical Records Survey on April 29, 1940. Mrs. Helen D. Bullock was appointed Assistant State Supervisor on June 24, 1940. Mrs. Bullock, who resigned on September 19, 1940, was succeeded on January 20, 1941, by Dr. Katharine Elizabeth Crane.

The Historical Records Survey of Virginia has published indexes to vital statistics as well as inventories of county, church, and Federal archives. The INDEX TO MARRIAGE NOTICES IN THE SOUTHERN CHURCHMAN is the third index to vital statistics, recorded in religious weeklies, which the project has published. The preceding volumes were the INDEX TO OBITUARY NOTICES IN THE RELIGIOUS HERALD, 1828-1938, December 1940, and the INDEX TO MARRIAGE NOTICES IN THE RELIGIOUS HERALD, Vol. I, A-L, August 1941, and Vol. II, M-Z, September 1941. The RELIGIOUS HERALD is a Baptist weekly published in Richmond. Indexes to vital statistics in religious papers have not commonly been undertaken by the Historical Records Survey projects; the volumes compiled in Virginia had to be specially authorized. The importance of making available to the public vital statistics in religious journals published in Virginia is better understood when one knows something of the history of the recording of marriages in Virginia and the fate of some of the older marriage records.

In the colonial period an official register of marriages, births, and deaths was kept in every Virginia parish, and copies of each registration were returned to the county clerk of the parish vestry and the head of the family. The official registrations of births and deaths ceased with the separation of Church and State in Virginia, not long after the establishment of the Commonwealth, and were not resumed until the middle of the nineteenth century. The official registration of marriages, however, never lapsed. This was because the Commonwealth made provision for maintaining the same sort of paper record as that which had been required under the colonial government, apart from the official register of marriages kept by the parish vestry. According to the State Bureau of Vital Statistics at Richmond, hundreds of these scraps of papers which testify to marriages celebrated in Virginia are still

i

Preface

extant, but it has not been determined whether they are the licenses that were required, or a marriage bond, or a combined license and marriage bond.

Under the code of 1849, the clerk of the county court and the clerk of the corporation court were required to register in books to be kept for that purpose every marriage license which they issued. These books are known as the registers of marriages. By an act of April 11, 1853, which became effective July 1, 1853, the clerk of the county court and the clerk of the corporation court were each required to "transmit to the auditor of public accounts a copy of his register of marriages during the preceding year, and on or before the first day of March in each year." In 1853, also, the General Assembly passed an act to take effect January 1, 1854, which ordered every minister to record every marriage celebrated by him and to return the certificate to the clerk of the county court or of the corporation court of the county or city in which the marriage was celebrated. At the same time, the clerk of the county court and the clerk of the corporation court were required to record in special volumes a note of the licenses which they issued, and to report to the commonwealth's attorney for prosecution any minister who failed to return the licenses. Finally in 1919 the marriage certificates and licenses were combined. Since then the note of licenses issued has been recorded in the marriage register, as is also the detailed information that is given in the combined marriage certificates and licenses. This information constitutes the permanent record of marriages.

Under the act effective July 1, 1853, which ordered the clerk of the county court and the clerk of the corporation court each to send annually to the auditor of public accounts a copy of his register of marriages, the first concentration of marriage records was brought about in Virginia. An act of 1918, approved March 9, 1918, required the auditor of public accounts to turn over to the newly created State Bureau of Vital Statistics all copies of the register of marriages which had been filed with him. Thereafter the clerk of the county court and the clerk of the corporation court were required to send copies of their registers of marriages direct to the State Bureau of Vital Statistics on or before March first in each year. An act of 1938, approved March 10, 1938, required that a duplicate of each combined license and certificate instead of a copy of each register of marriages be sent to the State Bureau of Vital Statistics. In this bureau are now concentrated the records of marriages celebrated in Virginia since June 30, 1853, although on account of inadequate storage, theft, fire, and other calamities which occured before the State Bureau of Vital Statistics was created, a number of these official records of marriages are missing. There is now being prepared under the sponsorship of the State Bureau of Vital Statistics an index to the marriage records dating from 1870 which are in its custody. In due course the index will probably be extended back to 1853. The Historical Records Survey has had no part in this index, which is not being constructed for publication but for use in the office of the State Bureau of Vital Statistics.

The INDEX TO MARRIAGE NOTICES IN THE SOUTHERN CHURCHMAN points to a recording of the marriages, over a period of 106 years, of approximately between six and seven thousand persons, most of whom were either members of the Protestant Episcopal Church in Virginia, or otherwise directly connected with it, or connected with it through descent from Virginia Episcopalians. The indexes to marriage notices published by the Historical Records Survey make amends in part for the lack of concentration of official records of marriages in Virginia prior to 1853. They provide a means for obtaining information on

Preface

some of the marriages celebrated from 26 to 33 years prior to 1861 in those eastern counties whose records were removed to the state courthouse at Richmond during the War for Southern Independence and destroyed when the courthouse was burned in the evacuation fire. Thus they point to substitute records for some of those early official marriage records dating from 1853 which are missing from the file of the State Bureau of Vital Statistics. The file of the SOUTHERN CHURCHMAN on which the index is based belongs, except the volume for 1900, to the Southern Churchman Publishing Company which maintains an office in the basement of the Mayo Memorial Church House, Richmond. That part of the file for the years, January 2, 1835-1893 and 1907 to 1942, was placed by the Company in the custody of the Virginia State Library. These volumes are available to searchers in the reading room of the State Library. Bound volumes for 1894-1899 and 1901-1906 are in the office of the Company, but steps are being taken to place them also in the custody of the State Library. Meanwhile they were made available to Historical Records Survey workers through the courtesy of Mrs. Tate Irvine, news editor of the weekly. Through the kindness of the family of the Rev. Meade Clark, D.D., rector of St. James' Church and editor of the SOUTHERN CHURCHMAN when he died in 1914, a project worker was permitted to collect the marriage notices in Dr. Clark's bound volume for 1900. Thus there are no gaps in the volumes for 1894-1906. Two workers specially assigned to the task checked the file in the custody of the Virginia State Library and found the following gaps: 1840-January 15, 1847; January 1, 8, 22, and 29, 1852; May 31-November 15, 1861 (apparently not published); March 14, 1862; June 10 and 24, 1864; July 8 and 22, 1864; August 5 and 19, 1864; September 2, 9, 16, and 30, 1864; October 7, 14, and 28, 1864; November 2, 1864; and March 22-August 24, 1865 (unknown whether any issues published). The number for November 4, 1842, and that for May 29, 1842, are in the SOUTHERN CHURCHMAN file of the College of William and Mary. The librarian, Dr. E. G. Swem, kindly had the marriage notices in these numbers copied for the Historical Records Survey.

In the volume January 17, 1850-January 6, 1853, in the custody of the State Library, the numbers for January 2 and 9, 1851, are bound immediately after the number for December 25, 1851, instead of at the beginning of 1851. Immediately following January 9, 1851, is January 15, 1852, then consecutively January 20 and 27, 1853. Then comes February 5, 1852. From this date, the numbers for 1852 are complete and are arranged in chronological order. As has already been stated in the list of gaps in the file, the numbers for January 1, 8, 22, and 29, 1852, are missing. These errors in binding are mentioned to save the time of students who are unfamiliar with the file.

Many workers by their alertness, their precision, and their energy have made it possible to complete the INDEX TO MARRIAGE NOTICES IN THE SOUTHERN CHURCHMAN before there becomes effective a reorganization of the Historical Records Survey with other statewide projects to form a clerical project under the War Services Program of the Work Projects Administration. The entry of the United States into the second World War caused a turnover of WPA workers so rapid that it is impracticable to list the names of all who took part in the work. The greater part of it on both Volume I and Volume II was checked, edited, and compiled under the supervision of Mrs. Neva Thompson. When Mrs. Thompson resigned on April 15, 1942, to accept a clerical position under the War Department, Mrs. Jennette A. Walls was assigned to take her post. The index was completed under the supervision of Mrs. Walls, who as a successful clerical worker is herself a product of the Historical Records Survey, since

Preface

she had never been trained or gainfully employed until she was assigned to the project's Richmond office. Mrs. Anne R. Morrison served as chief proofreader, and Mr. Ernest E. Williams as foreman of field work.

As in the INDEX TO MARRIAGE NOTICES IN THE RELIGIOUS HERALD, no attempt has been made to correct any name, spelling, date, or statement made in the printed notice except in the rare case of the spelling of the name of a well known rector, such, for instance, as the name Minnigerode, or in cases where names of Virginia counties were misspelled. In all other cases, names, dates, and statements have been reproduced exactly as they are printed in the SOUTHERN CHURCHMAN. When a second notice of the same marriage appeared, however, the notice which seemed to be the correct notice was indexed, and a reference to the other notice made in a footnote. This symbol * is also used to point out anything in an entry so unusual that it might appear to be an error of the copyist, the typist, or the editor. In certain cases, such as that of a parish for which no geographical location is cited, or of a name like "Big Lick", the settlement which later became the city of Roanoke, an explanatory footnote is given. In four major respects does editorial procedure depart from that employed in the INDEX TO MARRIAGE NOTICES IN THE RELIGIOUS HERALD. The first of these is the inclusion in each entry of the name of the paper immediately before the date of the issue in which the marriage notice appeared. The second is the inclusion of all facts given in the printed notice. The third is the inclusion of Marriage Announcements, A-K, in Volume I. The fourth is a cross reference printed under the maiden name of a widow to the entry which records her re-marriage. By citing "So. Ch." before the date of each issue, the possibility of one's assuming that the date cited is the date on which the marriage was celebrated is done away with. By citing all facts, it is believed that much additional pertinent information is furnished, such as the name of the domicile of the bride and of the groom before marriage, or the name of the place where the marriage was celebrated. In a number of cases the names of members of the families other than those of the parents are also cited. The advantage of having the marriage announcements, A-K, in Volume I and the cross references relative to widows does not have to be explained.

For clarity, as in the earlier index, a double entry is given for every marriage notice, one under the name of the groom, the other under the maiden name of the bride. In seeking a name, the searcher should be sure to look for the letter under "Addenda", if he has failed to find it under the letter alphabetically arranged in the body of the text. As all facts in the printed marriage notices are included in the entries, which number approximately between three thousand and thirty-five hundred, it was absolutely necessary to publish the index in two volumes.

The brief historical sketch which traces the founding of the weekly and the names and dates of service of its editors was written by Dr. Bruce.

Kathleen Bruce

Kathleen Bruce
State Supervisor
Historical Records Survey

Richmond, Virginia
May 29, 1942

Preface

some of the marriages celebrated from 26 to 33 years prior to 1861 in those eastern counties whose records were removed to the state courthouse at Richmond during the War for Southern Independence and destroyed when the courthouse was burned in the evacuation fire. Thus they point to substitute records for some of those early official marriage records dating from 1853 which are missing from the file of the State Bureau of Vital Statistics. The file of the SOUTHERN CHURCHMAN on which the index is based belongs, except the volume for 1900, to the Southern Churchman Publishing Company which maintains an office in the basement of the Mayo Memorial Church House, Richmond. That part of the file for the years, January 2, 1835-1893 and 1907 to 1942, was placed by the Company in the custody of the Virginia State Library. These volumes are available to searchers in the reading room of the State Library. Bound volumes for 1894-1899 and 1901-1906 are in the office of the Company, but steps are being taken to place them also in the custody of the State Library. Meanwhile they were made available to Historical Records Survey workers through the courtesy of Mrs. Tate Irvine, news editor of the weekly. Through the kindness of the family of the Rev. Meade Clark, D.D., rector of St. James' Church and editor of the SOUTHERN CHURCHMAN when he died in 1914, a project worker was permitted to collect the marriage notices in Dr. Clark's bound volume for 1900. Thus there are no gaps in the volumes for 1894-1906. Two workers specially assigned to the task checked the file in the custody of the Virginia State Library and found the following gaps: 1840-January 15, 1847; January 1, 8, 22, and 29, 1852; May 31-November 15, 1861 (apparently not published); March 14, 1862; June 10 and 24, 1864; July 8 and 22, 1864; August 5 and 19, 1864; September 2, 9, 16, and 30, 1864; October 7, 14, and 28, 1864; November 2, 1864; and March 22-August 24, 1865 (unknown whether any issues published). The number for November 4, 1842, and that for May 29, 1842, are in the SOUTHERN CHURCHMAN file of the College of William and Mary. The librarian, Dr. E. G. Swem, kindly had the marriage notices in these numbers copied for the Historical Records Survey.

In the volume January 17, 1850-January 6, 1853, in the custody of the State Library, the numbers for January 2 and 9, 1851, are bound immediately after the number for December 25, 1851, instead of at the beginning of 1851. Immediately following January 9, 1851, is January 15, 1852, then consecutively January 20 and 27, 1853. Then comes February 5, 1852. From this date, the numbers for 1852 are complete and are arranged in chronological order. As has already been stated in the list of gaps in the file, the numbers for January 1, 8, 22, and 29, 1852, are missing. These errors in binding are mentioned to save the time of students who are unfamiliar with the file.

Many workers by their alertness, their precision, and their energy have made it possible to complete the INDEX TO MARRIAGE NOTICES IN THE SOUTHERN CHURCHMAN before there becomes effective a reorganization of the Historical Records Survey with other statewide projects to form a clerical project under the War Services Program of the Work Projects Administration. The entry of the United States into the second World War caused a turnover of WPA workers so rapid that it is impracticable to list the names of all who took part in the work. The greater part of it on both Volume I and Volume II was checked, edited, and compiled under the supervision of Mrs. Neva Thompson. When Mrs. Thompson resigned on April 15, 1942, to accept a clerical position under the War Department, Mrs. Jennette A. Walls was assigned to take her post. The index was completed under the supervision of Mrs. Walls, who as a successful clerical worker is herself a product of the Historical Records Survey, since

Preface

she had never been trained or gainfully employed until she was assigned to the project's Richmond office. Mrs. Anne R. Morrison served as chief proofreader, and Mr. Ernest E. Williams as foreman of field work.

As in the INDEX TO MARRIAGE NOTICES IN THE RELIGIOUS HERALD, no attempt has been made to correct any name, spelling, date, or statement made in the printed notice except in the rare case of the spelling of the name of a well known rector, such, for instance, as the name Minnigerode, or in cases where names of Virginia counties were misspelled. In all other cases, names, dates, and statements have been reproduced exactly as they are printed in the SOUTHERN CHURCHMAN. When a second notice of the same marriage appeared, however, the notice which seemed to be the correct notice was indexed, and a reference to the other notice made in a footnote. This symbol * is also used to point out anything in an entry so unusual that it might appear to be an error of the copyist, the typist, or the editor. In certain cases, such as that of a parish for which no geographical location is cited, or of a name like "Big Lick", the settlement which later became the city of Roanoke, an explanatory footnote is given. In four major respects does editorial procedure depart from that employed in the INDEX TO MARRIAGE NOTICES IN THE RELIGIOUS HERALD. The first of these is the inclusion in each entry of the name of the paper immediately before the date of the issue in which the marriage notice appeared. The second is the inclusion of all facts given in the printed notice. The third is the inclusion of Marriage Announcements, A-K, in Volume I. The fourth is a cross reference printed under the maiden name of a widow to the entry which records her re-marriage. By citing "So. Ch." before the date of each issue, the possibility of one's assuming that the date cited is the date on which the marriage was celebrated is done away with. By citing all facts, it is believed that much additional pertinent information is furnished, such as the name of the domicile of the bride and of the groom before marriage, or the name of the place where the marriage was celebrated. In a number of cases the names of members of the families other than those of the parents are also cited. The advantage of having the marriage announcements, A-K, in Volume I and the cross references relative to widows does not have to be explained.

For clarity, as in the earlier index, a double entry is given for every marriage notice, one under the name of the groom, the other under the maiden name of the bride. In seeking a name, the searcher should be sure to look for the letter under "Addenda", if he has failed to find it under the letter alphabetically arranged in the body of the text. As all facts in the printed marriage notices are included in the entries, which number approximately between three thousand and thirty-five hundred, it was absolutely necessary to publish the index in two volumes.

The brief historical sketch which traces the founding of the weekly and the names and dates of service of its editors was written by Dr. Bruce.

Kathleen Bruce

Kathleen Bruce
State Supervisor
Historical Records Survey

Richmond, Virginia
May 29, 1942

THE SOUTHERN CHURCHMAN

The SOUTHERN CHURCHMAN, a weekly, representing the evangelical thought within the Protestant Episcopal Church in the United States of America, is published in Richmond, Virginia, by the Southern Churchman Publishing Company, an independent, unincorporated company. The paper was founded, however, by an individual, one hundred and six years ago. The founder was the Rev. William Fitzhugh Lee, rector of St. John's Church, Richmond, September 1828-December 21, 1829, and afterward rector of Christ Church, Richmond.

According to the bishop of the Protestant Episcopal Church in Virginia who was the assistant bishop in 1835, William Fitzhugh Lee through his mother, Sally Lee, who married Edmund I. Lee of Alexandria, was the grandson of Richard Henry Lee of Chantilly, Westmoreland County, one of the outstanding Virginians of the American Revolution (Bishop /William/ Meade, OLD CHURCHES, MINISTERS, AND FAMILIES OF VIRGINIA, 1857, II, 143). Young Lee was compelled to give up his rectorship on account of his health. "As to body", wrote Bishop Meade, "Mr. Lee being little more than thin air, or a light feather ... his horse felt not the rider on his back but the people felt the weight and power of a strong mind ... he devoted himself to the press, and was the first editor of the Southern Churchman, establishing it at Richmond. He continued to edit the same until his part of the work was performed. When lying on a sick-bed, his proof sheets corrected, his selections made and editorials written, while propped up with bolsters and pillows thus to the last spending and being spent ..." (IBID, I, 460-61). Lee published the first issue of the SOUTHERN CHURCHMAN on January 2, 1835. He was only in his thirty-third year when he died on Friday, May 19, 1837, in Alexandria which was then in the District of Columbia. The weekly issue due on the day he died and on Friday, May 26, 1837, appeared as usual. Lee's indomitable spirit, his mind, and his energy had triumphed. He had established a journal which would live.

There was no break in the immediately succeeding issues. Beginning on June 2, and running through September 1, 1837, the space in which "William F. Lee, editor", had formerly been printed carried "Rev. Lucius M. Purdy, editor." Beginning with the issue of September 8, however, the space for the editor's name is blank until November 17, 1837, when "Rev. Z. Meade, editor", fills the blank. On leaving his congregation in Boston, Meade sought the restoration of his health "in the milder climate of Richmond and in the editorial chair" (IBID, II, 53). Without a break also, the paper is headed "Richmond", and the Richmond office address is given through December 31, 1839, although it has been said that when Lee left Richmond for Alexandria, he "moved his office with him" (The Editors ...", SO. CH., Jan. 5, 1935).

Because of a gap, 1840-January 15, 1847, in the only available files of this paper, the change in editors during these years, and the date of the removal of the office of the editor from Richmond could not be traced. The next available issue is dated January 22, 1847; it is headed "Alexandria, Va.", and the usual space for the editor's name shows "Rev. E. R. Lippitt, editor." Nine years later Lippitt was advertizing in the SOUTHERN CHURCHMAN (Sept. 26, 1856) his "Family School for Boys" in Alexandria. In 1846 the United States Government had retroceded to Virginia the territory in the District of Columbia which the General Assembly by an act of December 3, 1789, had ceded

The SOUTHERN CHURCHMAN

to the United States for the permanent seat of the Government. Lippitt's name as that of editor of the SOUTHERN CHURCHMAN appears for the last time in the issue of Friday, March 31, 1848. The issue of April 7, cites no editor's name but gives the names of the printers. In the issue of June 2, 1848, the "Rev. George A. Smith, editor", is recorded. Meanwhile, Bishop Meade wrote in the issue of May 26, 1848, "The editorial care of the Southern Churchman, our Diocesan paper, has recently, as you all know, been transferred to another editor. The Rev. George A. Smith, one of our esteemed ministers, has undertaken the charge of it." The significance of the paper for the diocese is implied in the bishop's words, "our Diocesan paper."

Smith edited the SOUTHERN CHURCHMAN for seven years; he published his farewell editorial in the issue of September 27, 1855. But the Rev. D. Francis Sprigg was to edit it for forty-four years. At the head of the issue of Friday, October 5, 1855, appears the new editor's motto, carried thereafter under his editorship, "Nisi Dominus Frustra" which he explained were "the first words of the 127th Psalm in the Vulgate version. The whole verse reads: 'Except the Lord build the house, they labor in vain that build it: except the Lord keep the city, the watchman waketh but in vain.'"

Having taken charge in 1855, Sprigg was editor of the SOUTHERN CHURCHMAN during the War for Southern Independence. When United States troops occupied Alexandria, he moved the paper to Richmond. No issue appeared after that which is headed Alexandria, May 24, 1861, until that of November 22, 1861, which was the earliest war issue printed in Richmond. The last known issue which appeared during the war is dated March 15, 1865. Each war issue printed in Richmond was cut to a single sheet until November 9, 1864, when the single sheet which had been shortened on April 8, 1864, was folded over, thus making two small sheets. When the war ended Sprigg returned to Alexandria, and started afresh with "New Series, Vol. I, No. 1," August 31, 1865. The paper was printed in Alexandria until he was called to Richmond in 1879 to be rector of the Moore Memorial Church, the forerunner of the present Grace and Holy Trinity. Sprigg moved the paper with him, and the first issue of the new series to be headed Richmond appeared on April 17, 1879. The office of the SOUTHERN CHURCHMAN remained thereafter in Richmond. In the issue of September 28, 1899, Sprigg wrote: "With this number of the Southern Churchman my connection with it ceases. I have no pecuniary interest in it, or responsibility; no editorial management of it. Its good-will has been bought by the 'Protestant Episcopal Churchman Company' who have appointed Rev. William Meade Clark of St. James' Church, Richmond, its editor. In taking leave of its subscribers, some of whom are my friends and have been, I do so with more or less sorrow. I have been connected with it for forty-four years."

The name of the editor and that of the publishing company is not printed in the issues of 1899. Beginning with the issue of March 3, 1900, the Southern Churchman Publishing Company is cited as the publisher.

The Rev. Meade Clark served as editor until his death in 1914. His successors were the Rev. Edward L. Goodwin, D.D., 1914-1920, the Rev. W. Russell Bowie, D.D., 1920-1923, the Rev. Joseph B. Dunn, D.D., 1924-1927, Langbourne M. Williams, 1927-1931, the first layman to serve as editor, the Rev. Charles W. Sherrin, D.D., 1931-September 10, 1938, the Rev. Samuel B. Chilton, September 10, 1938-May 1940, and the Rev. Beverley M. Boyd, May 1940---.

ABBREVIATIONS

Com.	Commodore
Co.	County
d. of	daughter of
gr.d.	granddaughter
gr.s.	grandson
Rev.	Reverend
Rt. Rev.	Right Reverend
s. of	son of
So. Ch.	Southern Churchman
Ven.	Venerable

CONTENTS

	Page
Preface	i
The Southern Churchman	v
Abbreviations	vii
Letter A	1
Letter B	20
Letter C	78
Letter D	123
Letter E	149
Letter F	159
Letter G	178
Letter H	208
Letters IJ	261
Letter K	282
Addenda: letters A - K	295
Announcements of Approaching Marriages, 1915 - 1940	519

INDEX TO MARRIAGE NOTICES
IN
THE SOUTHERN CHURCHMAN
1835 - 1941

AARON
    John Ponniah (The Rev.), and Grace Azariah, second d. of the Bishop of Dornakal. So. Ch., Dec. 1, 1934

ABBOT
    Nannie Lee, formerly of Georgetown, U.S., and Maj. Wm. G. Bently of Richmond, by the Rev. Geo. W. Dame, in the Church of the Epiphany, Danville. So. Ch., June 19, 1863

ABBOTT
    Virginia T., d. of the late J. B. Abbott, and Claiborne Watkins, all of Richmond, by the Rev. Joshua Peterkin, in St. James' Church, Richmond. So. Ch., Mar. 14, 1856

ABELL
    John H., of St. Mary's Co., Md., and Evelina W. Tompkins, by the Rev. J. E. Poindexter, at Ormsby, Caroline Co., Va. So. Ch., Sept. 28, 1882
    Mary, of Martinsburg, and Samuel Paul of Springfield, Mo., by the Rev. Henry Thomas, in Trinity Church, Martinsburg. So. Ch., May 2, 1889

ABRAMS
    Wm. J., and Eloise Duval, by the Rev. J. Hervey Hundley, D.D., in Salem M. E. Church, Gloucester Co., Va. So. Ch., Feb. 2, 1893

ACHESON
    Mary J., of Wheeling, Va., and David Lynn of Cumberland, Md., by the Rev. E. T. Perkins, at the residence of the bride's father. So. Ch., Jan. 11, 1861

ACHREE
    J. Alice, of Bedford, and David C. Tinsley of Amherst, by the Rev. R. J. McBryde, at Forest Home, Bedford Co. So. Ch., Dec. 23, 1869

ADAMS
    Albert R., and Marianna Ferguson, by the Rev. A. Wade, at Longwood, Charles City Co., Va. So. Ch., Dec. 3, 1874
    Bettie D., and Robert B. Clements of Gloucester Co., Va., by the Rev. William B. Lee, at the residence of the bride's mother in Mathews Co., Va. So. Ch., Jan. 8, 1891
    Chas. M. (Dr.), of Madison Co., and Sallie A. Hester, by the Rev. Mr. Woodall, at Rest Easy, near Jackson, Miss. So. Ch., June 17, 1864
    E. F., of Memphis, Tenn., and Nannie M., second d. of W. B. and S. M. Weisiger formerly of Virginia, by the rector, the Rev. D. Sessums, in Calvary Church, Memphis, Tenn. So. Ch., Sept. 10, 1885
    Elvira, d. of the late Dr. John Adams of Richmond, Va., and David Minge of Alabama, by the Rev. Wm. H. Hart, at Richmond, Va. So. Ch., Oct. 13, 1837
    Joel T., of Algomia, W.Va., and Kate C., d. of David R. Snow, Esq., by the Rev. C. O. Pruden, at Snowden, the home of the bride's father, Pittsylvania Co., Va. So. Ch., Apr. 14, 1892
    Joseph M., of Rockbridge Co., Va., and Sarah G., d. of the

MARRIAGE NOTICES IN THE SOUTHERN CHURCHMAN WITH DATES OF PUBLICATION

late George B. Richards, by the Rev. R. H. Mason, at Jay Cliff, near Warm Springs, Va. So. Ch., July 9, 1868

Mary Frances, of Weston, Mo., and Wm. H. Miller, Esq., Attorney at Law, Parkville, Mo., by the Rev. W. Norman Irish, at Weston, Mo. So. Ch., Nov. 9, 1855

Nannie E., and Philip F. Brown, by the Rev. Churchill J. Gibson, in Christ Church, Smithfield, Va. So. Ch., July 18, 1867

Rebecca A., and George W. Hunton, M.D., both of Fauquier Co., Va., by the Rev. George W. Nelson, at Warrenton, Va. So. Ch., Jan. 1, 1885

Richard H. (Capt.), and Lizzie C., d. of Dr. John B. Radford, all of Montgomery Co., Va., by the Rev. Edward H. Ingle, at "Arnheim", the residence of the bride's father. So. Ch., Nov. 9, 1871

Thomas D., and Mrs. Laura A. Culver, by the Rev. H. L. Derby, at Lancaster, Va. So. Ch., Feb. 19, 1880

Virgie, oldest d. of William Adams, Esq., of Charles City Co., Va., and J. Bollie Brockwell, Esq., by the Rev. John P. Tyler, in Salem M. E. Church, Charles City Co., Va. So. Ch., Dec. 4, 1890

Wm. W., of Petersburg, and E. Sherrod, d. of Col. James M. Wilcox of Charles City Co., Va., by the Rev. Dr. Wade, at Buckland, residence of bride's father. So. Ch., Nov. 14, 1872

ADAMSON
Catherine M., d. of Emma G. and the late Capt. Wm. Adamson of Dundee, Scotland, and Charles R. Limestrong late of England, by the Rev. A. P. Gray, in Trinity Church, Manassas. So. Ch., Oct. 2, 1884

Ethel, and Thomas H. Lion, by the Rev. A. P. Gray, in Trinity Church, Manassas. So. Ch., June 28, 1888

Ronald J., and Annie E. Merchant, by the Rev. A. P. Gray, in Trinity Church, Manassas. So. Ch., Oct. 2, 1884

Weatherly J., formerly of Scotland, and Mattie T., d. of George Dent of Prince George's, Md., by the Rev. A. P. Gray, in Trinity Church, Manassas. So. Ch., June 28, 1888

ADDINGTON
Richard D. (Dr.), and Hannah Elizabeth, d. of Joseph A. Weed, all of Richmond, Va., in Monumental Church, Richmond, Va. So. Ch., Nov. 9, 1855

ADDISON
John, of Richmond, and Rebecca F., d. of the late Col. S. M. Ball of Virginia, by the Rev. R. H. McKim, in Christ Church, Alexandria, Va. So. Ch., Jan. 2, 1873

Marie E., d. of Thos. B. Addison, Esq. of Georgetown, and the Rev. Thomas G. Addison, by the Rev. N. P. Tillinghast, in St. John's Church, Georgetown, D.C. So. Ch., Apr. 25, 1856

May, d. of the late Wm. Meade Addison of Baltimore, Md., and John H. Chew of Washington, D.C., by the Rev. Joshua Peterkin, D.D., at the residence of John Addison, Richmond. So. Ch., Feb. 16, 1888

Nellie C., and Robert G.

MARRIAGE NOTICES IN THE SOUTHERN CHURCHMAN WITH DATES OF PUBLICATION

Rennolds, both of Richmond, by the Rev. Dr. Peterkin, in St. James Church. So. Ch., Jan. 22, 1885

Rebecca C., d. of the late William Meade Addison, Esq., and J. Lowrie Ingle, M.D. all of Baltimore, by the Rev. Edward H. Ingle assisted by the Rev. Campbell Fair, D.D., in Church of the Ascension, Baltimore. So. Ch., Oct. 31, 1878

Thomas D., of Fairfax Co., and Mary Brockenbrough, d. of the late Dr. John Philip Smith of Clarke Co., by the Rev. John B. Newton, in Monumental Church, Richmond, Va. So. Ch., Feb. 24, 1887

Thomas G. (The Rev.), and Marie E., d. of Thos. B. Addison, Esq. all of Georgetown, by the Rev. N. P. Tillinghast, in St. John's Church, Georgetown, D. C. So. Ch., Apr. 25, 1856

Walter D., of New York, formerly of Alexandria, and Mary Grafton, d. of the Rev. H. S. Kepler of Richmond, by the Rev. Dr. Peterkin, in St. James Church, Richmond. So. Ch., June 20, 1867

Watkins, Jr., and Margaret D. Dodge, both of Georgetown, by the Rev. J. Vaughn Lewis, in St. John's (Episcopal) Church, Georgetown. So. Ch., Sept. 25, 1873

ADGER
Margaret C., d. of the late Wm. Adger, Esq. of Charleston, and Wm. L. Manning of Clarendon, by the Rev. G. R. Brackett, in Second Presbyterian Church. So. Ch., Feb. 22, 1877

ADIE
Geo. (The Rev.), rector of Shelburn Parish,*and Mrs. Mary E. Powell, by the Rev. C. W. Andrews, at Longholler, Loudoun Co., Va. So. Ch., Jan. 8, 1836

Margaret, d. of the late Rev. Geo. Adie of Leesburg, Loudoun Co., Va., and James Turner Pope of Brunswick, by the Rev. James Grammer, at the residence of Mrs. B. H. Harrison in Cumberland Co. So. Ch., Oct. 21, 1864

AGEE
Ella C., and J. Warner Kyle, by the Rev. Mr. Burwell, near Columbia, Va., residence of B. H. Agee, Esq., father of bride. So. Ch., Oct. 23, 1884

AGLIONBY
Francis K. (The Rev.), A.M., s. of Charles Aglionby, Esq. of Jefferson Co., W. Va., and Amy, d. of the officiating clergyman, the Rev. E. A. Bickerstith, assisted by the Rev. E. Bickerstith and the Rev. F. T. Charasse, in Christ's Church, Hampstead, London, N. W. So. Ch., Sept. 14, 1876

AIKEN
Archibald M., and Mary Ella, d. of Lewis A. Yates, all of Danville, by the Rev. Geo. W. Dame, at the residence of the bride's father, Danville, Va. So. Ch., Jan. 12, 1882

AINSWORTH
Maria, and John W. Hooff, both of Blue Ridge, Jefferson Co., W. Va., by the Rev. P. D. Thompson, in Wickliffe rectory. So. Ch., Apr. 13, 1893

* Shelburn Parish is in Loudoun County, Virginia (Journal ... Diocese of Virginia, Richmond, 1941)

MARRIAGE NOTICES IN THE SOUTHERN CHURCHMAN WITH DATES OF PUBLICATION

ALBERT
   Ellen, and John S. Blair, by
     the Rev. William H. Laird,
     in St. John's Church, Washington, D. C. So. Ch.,
     July 13, 1893
   Jacob, of Baltimore, and
     Virginia, d. of J. Henry
     Greenway of Harford Co.,
     Md., by the Rt. Rev. T. B.
     Lyman, D.D., Bishop of North
     Carolina, assisted by the Rev.
     Chauncey B. Brewster, in Grace
     Church, Baltimore. So. Ch.,
     Dec. 31, 1885

ALCOCK
   Caroline Fisher, and Louis H.
     Claggett, Esq., by the Rev.
     John C. McCabe, rector of the
     Church of the Ascension, at
     Baltimore. So. Ch., July
     10, 1857
   Sarah E. C., and John Thomas
     Ireland, Esq., by the Rev.
     John C. McCabe, rector of the
     Church of the Ascension,
     Baltimore, at Baltimore.
     So. Ch., July 10, 1857

ALCOMBE
   John Roy, Esq., and Matilda T.,
     only d. of Lt. John Hite
     Lee, U.S. Navy, deceased,
     by the Rev. Wm. H. Kinckle,
     at Lynchburg, Va. So. Ch.,
     Jan. 4, 1856

ALDER
   Ida J., and Charles Henry
     Fauver, both of Blue Ridge,
     Jefferson Co., W. Va., by
     the Rev. P. D. Thompson, in
     Christ Church, Blue Ridge.
     So. Ch., June 22, 1893

ALEXANDER
   Edward P. (Lt.), U.S. Army,
     and Bettie S., d. of the
     late Dr. Alexander H. Mason,
     by the Rev. T. E. Locke, at
     Cleveland, King George Co.
     So. Ch., Apr. 13, 1860
   Elizabeth (Mrs.), and Col.
     Gerard Alexander, by the Rt.
     Rev. Bishop Ives, at Edenton,
     N. C. So. Ch., Mar. 24, 1837
   Elizabeth C., d. of Mark Alexander, Jr., Esq. of Mecklenburg, and Col. James R. Herbert of Baltimore, by the Rev.
     John T. Clark, at "Chester", the
     residence of John Coleman, Esq.
     of Halifax, gr. f. of bride.
     So. Ch., Nov. 26, 1868
   Florine, d. of Capt. John and
     Mrs. Eleanor Alexander, and
     Wm. Follit of England, by
     the Rev. Wm. J. Morton of
     Richmond, Va., at South
     Warren, Albemarle Co., Va.
     So. Ch., June 22, 1893
   George (Col.), of New York
     City, and Anna Beckwith, d.
     of the late Rev. Charles M.
     Callaway, by the Rev. Julius
     Sams, D.D., at the residence
     of the bride's mother, Baltimore. So. Ch., July 26, 1883
   Gerard (Col.), and Mrs. Elizabeth
     Alexander, by the Rt. Rev.
     Bishop Ives, at Edenton, N. C.
     So. Ch., Mar. 24, 1837
   Helen S., and Thomas Brawner
     of Prince George's, Md., by
     the Rev. A. P. Gray, at
     "Millford," Prince William
     Co., Va. So. Ch., Oct. 23, 1879
   Joseph G. (Dr.), of Church Hill,
     Tenn., and Lucie R., d. of the
     late J. B. Gray, by the Rev.
     Dr. Murdaugh, at "Travellers
     Rest." So. Ch., Dec. 2, 1875
   Mariette, d. of Gustavus B.
     Alexander, Esq., and the Rev.
     William McGuire of Westmoreland, by the Rev. B. B. Leacock, in St. Paul's Church,
     King George Co., Va. So. Ch.,
     Mar. 25, 1852
   Marion S., of King George Co.,
     Va., and John W. Jones, Esq.
     of Botetourt Co., by the Rev.
     Wm. McGuire, in Trinity Church,

MARRIAGE NOTICES IN THE SOUTHERN CHURCHMAN WITH DATES OF PUBLICATION

Buchanan, Botetourt Co. So. Ch., Mar. 13, 1863

Martha S. of Bonham, and Geo. A. Preston recently of Va., by the Rev. Francis R. Starr, at Bonham, Fannin Co., Texas. So. Ch., Oct. 24, 1872

Mary, d. of John Alexander of Albemarle Co., Va., and Frank C. Morgan of the Channel Islands, by the Rev. William J. Morton of Richmond, Va., at Warren, Albemarle Co., Va. So. Ch., Dec. 15, 1892

ALFORD
Jennie M. (Mrs.), and E. Macon Jones of Huntington, W. Va., by the Rev. John S. Gibson, at the residence of the bride in Hamlin, Lincoln Co., W. Va. So. Ch., Mar. 16, 1893

ALFRIEND
Johnnie E., youngest d. of the late John W. Alfriend of Dinwiddie Co., and the Rev. S. Moylan Bird, by the Rev. W. H. Platt and the Rev. C. J. Gibson, in Calvary Church, Dinwiddie Co. So. Ch., June 5, 1863

ALLAN
William (Col.), of Baltimore, and E. R., d. of Col. J. T. L. Preston of Lexington, Va., by the Rev. Thomas L. Preston, D.D., at Lexington, Va. So. Ch., June 4, 1874

ALLEN
Alva May, of Windsor, Ont., and the Rev. David T. Davies, Missionary in charge of Emmanuel Church, Detroit, by the Rev. M. C. Davies, rector of St. George's Church, the Rt. Rev. Herman Page, D.D., Bishop of the Diocese, and the Rev. Leonard Hagger, Archdeacon, assisted in the celebration of Holy Communion, in St. George's Church, Walkerville, Ont. So. Ch., July 7, 1935

Charles, and Florence, third d. of Jas. S. Kelley, all of Hanover, by the Rev. S. S. Hepbron, at the residence of the bride's parents. So. Ch., Dec. 20, 1888

Elizabeth Denison (Mrs.), gr. d. of President Tyler, and d. of the late Rev. Henry Denison, and the Rev. James H. Williams of Nashville, formerly rector of Grace Church, Lynchburg, by the Rev. Mr. Hubard of Salem, assisted by the Rev. Mr. Hullihen, in Trinity Church, Staunton. So. Ch., Apr. 27, 1893

Emma, youngest d. of Wm. T. Allen of Clarke Co., Va., and Bushrod C. Washington, Jr. of Charlestown, W. Va., by the Rev. P. P. Phillips, rector of Grace Church, Berryville, Va., at Balclutha, Clarke Co., Va. So. Ch., Oct. 20, 1887

Emma B., youngest d. of the late Robt. Allen, and Pugh B. Houston, C. E., by the Rev. L. B. Johnston, at the residence of Dr. O. W. Kean, Goochland Co., Va. So. Ch., Oct. 31, 1878

Evy, and Dr. Edwin Wood, by the Rev. Pendleton Brooke, at the residence of the bride's mother, Botetourt Co., Va. So. Ch., Jan. 22, 1874

Fannie J., d. of the late Hon. Robert Allen, and Dr. O. W. Kean of Goochland Co., by the Rev. J. A. Wharton, at Mt. Prospect, Bedford Co., Va. So. Ch., Mar. 18, 1864

Hugh P., and Fanny, only d. of the late R. D. and Elizabeth Stockton Shepherd, by the Rev. L. R. Mason, in Trinity Church, Shepherdstown. So. Ch., Feb. 2, 1888

MARRIAGE NOTICES IN THE SOUTHERN CHURCHMAN WITH DATES OF PUBLICATION

James W., of Bedford, and Julia Nelson, only d. of Hugh N. Pendleton of Jefferson, by the Rev. Mr. Pendleton, at Westwood. So. Ch., Mar. 28, 1856

Josephine, d. of Jos. Allen, Esq. of Richmond, and Thomas Marshall Hewitt, by the Rev. Joshua Peterkin, at Richmond. So. Ch., Apr. 16, 1858

Julia D. (Mrs.), youngest d. of Wm. D. Roberts, Esq. of Norfolk City, and John H. Riddick, Esq. of Suffolk, by the Rev. Dr. Minnigerode, in Norfolk. So. Co., Jan. 18, 1856

Maria D., of Jefferson Co., W. Va., and H. P. Morris of Richmond, Va., by the Rev. A. J. Willis, in the Church of the Holy Spirit, Summit Point, Jefferson Co., W. Va. So. Ch., Dec. 22, 1892

Mary B., d. of Wm. F. Allen, and J. Elliott Brayarly, all of Clarke Co., by the Rev. P. P. Phillips, at Balclutha, the residence of the bride's father. So. Ch., Sept. 11, 1884

Mary Watts, d. of Judge John J. Allen of Botetourt Co., Va., and Edward A. Moore of Rockbridge Co., Va., by the Rev. Edward H. Ingle, at "Beaver Dam", the residence of the bride's father. So. Ch., Dec. 6, 1877

Maude, youngest d., of Mr. and Mrs. F. L. Allen of Amherst, and David Hall Holmes of Baltimore, by the Rev. A. P. Gray, of Ascension Church, in the home of the bride's parents. So. Ch., Oct. 13, 1892

O. S., and Virginia, d. of Richard Archer, Esq. of Amelia Co., by the Rev. A. B. Tizzard, in Christ Church, Amelia Court House, Va. So. Ch., Dec. 26, 1889

R. Owen, and Edith Howard, both of Clarke Co., Va., by the Rev. John McGill, rector of Piedmont Parish, Fauquier Co., Va., near Frederick, Md. So. Ch., Dec. 27, 1866

Robert E., and Anna L., d. of the late John S. Wilson, all of Buchanan, by the Rev. Edward H. Ingle, in Trinity Church, Buchanan. So. Ch., Nov. 15, 1877

Thomas H. (Maj.), of Charlotte, N. C., and Laura E., d. of the late Dr. Edward Porcher of Charleston, S. C., by the Rev. Edward H. Ingle, in St. Paul's Chapel, Salom. So. Ch., July 16, 1874

ALLSTON
Louisa Porcher, d. of Joseph Blyth Allston and the Rev. Wm. Nelson Meade of Virginia, by the Rev. Benjamin Allston, at Badwell, Abbeville Co., S. C. So. Ch., Oct. 13, 1887

ALMY
Annie, d. of Rear Admiral John J. Almy, U.S. Navy, and Lt. John Taylor Haines, Fifth Calvary, U.S. Army, by the Rev. David Barr, in the Church of the Epiphany, Washington, D.C. So. Ch., June 27, 1889

ALRICH
Wm. A. (The Rev.), rector of St. Martins Parish, Hanover Co., Va., and Mary J., d. of Thomas R. Love, Esq. of Fairfax Courthouse, by the Rev. O. A. Kinsolving, at the residence of the bride's father. So. Ch., May 13, 1869

William Augustus (The Rev.), rector of Emmanuel Church, Pittsylvania, and Mary Latane Berkeley of Hanover Co., Va., by the Rev. Robt. Douglas Roller, in the

MARRIAGE NOTICES IN THE SOUTHERN CHURCHMAN WITH DATES OF PUBLICATION

"White House", St. Martin's Parish,* So. Ch., Jan. 3, 1878

ALSTON
  Philip Wm. (The Rev.), rector of Calvary Church, Memphis, [name of bride and officiating minister omitted], at Mercer Hall, Tenn., residence of Bishop Otey. So. Ch., July 16, 1847

AMBLER
  Annie Gordon, d. of Marshall Ambler, Esq. of Lakeland, Louisa Co., Va., and Dr. George W. Fleming, Jr. of Chantilly, by the Rev. Curtis Grubb, in the Church of Our Savior, St. Martin's Parish, Hanover Co., Va. So. Ch., May 3, 1883
  B. Mason, Esq., of Parkersburg, W. Va., and Nannie L., d. of C. S. Baker, Esq. of Winchester, Va., by the Rev. John Ambler assisted by the Rev. L. R. Mason, at the residence of the bride's father. So. Ch., Nov. 25, 1875
  Bessie Barbour, d. of John Jacquelin Ambler, and Robert Ellis Gish of Lynchburg, Va., by the Rev. A. P. Gray, at "Glen Ambler", Amherst Co., Va. So. Ch., Dec. 5, 1889
  Beverly Landon, of Amherst, Va., and Isaltta Carter Hubard of Arrington, Nelson Co., Va., in the Church of the Advent, Spartansburg, S.C. So. Ch., Feb. 5, 1916
  Charles E. (The Rev.), rector of St. Ann's Church, Albemarle Co., Va., and Betty Burnet, d. of the Rev. Dr. E. C. McGuire, in St. George's Church, Fredericksburg. So. Ch., Aug. 7, 1851
  Charles E. (The Rev.), of Charles Town, and Susan W. Keyes, by the Rev. Walter Williams of Leesburg, at the residence of the bride's father, H. Keyes, Esq. of Charles Town, Va. So. Ch., Sept. 21, 1860
  Edward B., of Monroe, Va., and Agnes Cabell, only d. of Capt. Walter Coles, by the Rev. Dr. C. O. Pruden, at Coles Hill, Pittsylvania Co., Va. So. Ch., Nov. 23, 1907
  Eliza Chew, youngest d. of the officiating clergyman, and Launcelot Minor Blackford, Principal of the Episcopal High School, by the Rev. John Ambler assisted by the Rt. Rev. Alfred M. Randolph, D.D., LL.D., in the Chapel of the Theological Seminary, near Alexandria, Va. So. Ch., Aug. 14, 1884
  Ella E., d. of the late Col. John Ambler, and Francis E. Brooke, Esq., s. of the Hon. Judge Brooke of the Court of Appeals, by the Rt. Rev. Bishop Moore. So. Ch., Dec. 1, 1837
  James Murray, of Baltimore, and Eliza Llewellyn Randolph, eldest d. of the officiating clergyman, the Rt. Rev. A. M. Randolph, D.D., in St. Paul's Church, Richmond, Va. So. Ch., Jan. 21, 1886
  Jeannie K., d. of Mrs. Susan W. and the late Rev. Charles E. Ambler, and John Augustine Washington, by the Rev. Dallas Tucker, at the residence of the bride's mother, Charles Town, W. Va. So. Ch., Dec. 18, 1890
  John, Jr., Esq., of Glen-

---

* St. Martin's Parish is in Hanover County, Virginia (Journal ... Diocese of Virginia, Richmond, 1941)

MARRIAGE NOTICES IN THE SOUTHERN CHURCHMAN WITH DATES OF PUBLICATION

Ambler, and Laura B., only d. of Beverly Davies, dec'd., of Amherst Co., by the Rev. R. W. Nowlin, at Sunny Side, residence of Dr. H. L. Davies. So. Ch., Feb. 27, 1857

John, of Louisa Co., Va., and Mary O. Schooler, of Hanover Co., Va., at Shantilly,* Hanover Co., Va. So. Ch., Jan. 3, 1884

John Cary, (lately in charge of Emmanuel Church, Middleburg, and now attached to the Japan Mission), and Nannie Lou, only d. of Mrs. M. H. Johnson of Boydton, by the Rev. P. M. Boyden assisted by the Rev. John Ambler, in St. James Church, Boydton, Mecklenburg Co., Va. So. Ch., June 27, 1889

John Nicholas, of Buckingham Co., Va., and Anna Rockwell Neal of Marion, N. C., by the Rev. R. L. Abernathy, D.D., in the Methodist Episcopal Church, Marion, N. C. So. Ch., July 14, 1892

Katherine, d. of the late P. St. George Ambler, and Thos. Deane Jellis of Lynchburg, by the Rev. J. P. Lawrence, at St. Moor, residence of the bride's mother, So. Ch., Jan. 31, 1878

Laura Carter, eldest d. of J. J. Ambler, Esq. and gr. d. of the late Hon. Philip Pendleton Barbour, for many years associate Justice of the Supreme Court of the U.S., and Lafayette Penn Rodes, brother of the late Major Gen. R. E. Rodes, C. S. A., by the Rev. E. S. Gregory, rector of the Church of the Epiphany, at the residence of the bride's parents, Lynchburg, Va. So. Ch., July 19, 1883

Lucy, eldest d. of the Rev. John Ambler, and the Rev. L. R. Mason, by the Rt. Rev. John Johns, assisted by the Rev. R. R. Mason, at Clarens, residence of the late Hon. James M. Mason, near Alexandria, Va. So. Ch., Nov. 25, 1875

Mary Cary, d. of Maj. Thos. M. Ambler, and Dr. Robt. M. Stribling, Jr., by the Rev. Thos. E. Duncan, at St. Morven, Fauquier. So. Ch., Sept. 4, 1857

Mary Cary, d. of the Rev. T. M. Ambler of Wilmington, N. C., and Thomas H. Willcox, by the Rev. A. S. Lloyd assisted by the Rev. R. R. Claiborne, in St. Luke's Church, Norfolk, Va. So. Ch., Nov. 12, 1885

R. J., of Fauquier, and Annie M., d. of Thomas H. Wills, by the Rev. Charles E. Ambler, at Rock Hall, Jefferson Co. So. Ch., Aug. 21, 1857

T. M. (The Rev.), rector of St. Paul's Church, Wilmington, N. C., and Bettie F., third d. of James W. Curtis, Esq. of Williamsburg, Va., by the Rev. Geo. T. Wilmer, D.D., assisted by the Rev. L. B. Wharton, in Bruton Parish Church, Williamsburg, So. Ch., Oct. 30, 1873

Thomas M. (The Rev.), and Anna Bland, youngest d. of Robert Bolling, Esq. of Brunswick, by the Rev. Churchill J. Gibson, in Grace Church, Petersburg, So. Ch., May 30, 1856

Thomas M. (The Rev.), and Virginia M., d. of W. W.

* Given as printed

MARRIAGE NOTICES IN THE SOUTHERN CHURCHMAN WITH DATES OF PUBLICATION

Sharp, Esq., of Norfolk, by the Rev. E. M. Rodman assisted by the Rev. J. J. Sams, in Christ Church, Norfolk. So. Ch., Oct. 26, 1860

AMES
George L. (Dr.), and Gabriella S. Mapp, by the Rev. Henry L. Derby, in St. George's Church, Pungoteague, Accomac, Va. So. Ch., Dec. 14, 1893

Lizzie M., d. of George C. Ames, Esq., of Washington, and the Rev. Charles H. Hall, rector of the Church of the Epiphany, by the Rev. G. D. Cummins, D.D. So. Ch., Sept. 18, 1857

AMISS
Cora DeSoissolle, and J. Paul Fletcher, by the Rev. W. T. Roberts, rector, assisted by the Rev. L. B. Johnston, in Emmanuel Church, Harrisonburg, Va. So. Ch., Jan. 28, 1892

Elvira Spindle, d. of Elijah Amiss of Rappahannock Co., and Dr. Robert Holliday of Caroline Co., by the Rev. P. Slaughter, at Molville, the seat of John Minor Leavell, So. Ch., Jan. 25, 1866

AMMEN
A. Eliza, d. of Col. D. Ammen of Botetourt Co., Va., and James Goodwin of Baltimore, Md., by the Rev. Edmund W. Hubard, in St. Mark's Church, Fincastle. So. Ch., Dec. 15, 1870

ANCELL
Benjamin L. (The Rev.), of the Episcopal Church Mission, Yangchow, China, s. of the late Capt. John J. Ancell of Fluvanna Co., and Frances Fenton Cattell, M.D., d. of the late Rev. Thomas W. Cattell of New Jersey, by the Rev. H. St. George Tucker, at Yokahama, Japan. So. Ch., Aug. 20, 1910

Virginia Adeline, and Sidney Willard Pace of Fluvanna Co., Va., by the Rev. T. E. Locke, in the rectory of St. Anne's Parish, Albemarle Co., Va. So. Ch., Jan. 1, 1885

ANDERSON
Alvernon H., d. of Daniel Anderson, Esq., and George M. Lamon, all of Berkely Co., Va., by the Rev. Wm. McGuire, at the residence of Franklin Bowley, Esq. So. Ch., Apr. 8, 1859

Edwin J. (The Rev.), priest-in charge of St. Aidan's Church, Blue Island, Ill., and Phyllis Fraser. So. Ch., Sept. 17, 1938

Ellen L.,* d. of Gen. Joseph R. Anderson of Richmond, and William A. Anderson, Esq. of Lexington, Va., by the Rev. Charles Minnigerode, D.D., in St. Paul's Church, Richmond, Va. So. Ch., Aug. 3, 1871

F. T., of Howardsville, Albemarle Co., Va., and Mary G. Lewis, d. of Z. R. Lewis, Esq. of Nelson Co., Va., by the Rev. G. S. Somerville, in Christ Church, Norwood, Nelson Co., Va. So. Ch., Feb. 26, 1891

Frederick, and Cora, d. of Philip Harrison, Esq., by the Rt. Rev. Richard C. Moore, in Richmond, Va. So. Ch., Nov. 6, 1835

George B., of Texas, and Maria B. only d. of Addison B. Carter of Winchester, Va., by the Rev. Dr. Hubard, in Christ Church, Winchester, Va. So. Ch., Jan. 8, 1880

John F. T., and Lizzie Campbell, eldest d. of Dr.

* Given as printed, but should be "G"

MARRIAGE NOTICES IN THE SOUTHERN CHURCHMAN WITH DATES OF PUBLICATION

J. S. D. Cullen, by the Rev. Dr. Preston assisted by the Rev. Dr. Minnigerode, in the First Presbyterian Church. So. Ch., Dec. 30, 1880

Joseph K., of Montgomery Co., Va., and V. C., only d. of Mrs. C. H. Tebault of New Orleans, La., by the Rev. J. P. Lawrence, at Oak Grove, Amherst Co., Va., the residence of Mrs. Col. E. R. Long. So. Ch., Dec. 2, 1886

Jos. R. (Gen.), of Richmond, Va., and Mary E., d. of the late Gen. James W. Pegram, by the Rev. William Dame, at the residence of Col. D. G. McIntosh, Towsontown. So. Ch., Nov. 9, 1882

Joseph W., of the Co. of Botetourt, and Sue W., d. of Mrs. Anne C. Morris of Charlottesville, by the Rev. R. K. Meade, in Christ Church, Charlottesville. So. Ch., July 8, 1859

Julius L., of Ironton, Ohio, and Juliet T. Savage of Mason Co., Ky., by the Rev. J. B. Craighill, near Maysville. So. Ch., Nov. 2, 1871

M. C., eldest d. of R. G. Anderson of Amelia Co., and Beverley B. Carter, by the Rev. P. F. Berkeley, at Selma, the residence of the bride's father. So. Ch., Nov. 11, 1875

Mary Bruce, and Thomas Seddon Bruce, by the Rev. Dr. Charles Minnigerode, at Richmond, the residence of Gen. Joseph R. Anderson. So. Ch., Apr. 22, 1875

Richard W. (The Rev.), youngest s. of the late Meriwether L. Anderson of "Pant-Ops", Albemarle Co., Va., and rector of St. James' Church, Texarkana, Tex., and Mary A. Beatty, youngest d. of Dr. W. H. Beatty of Birmingham, by the Rev. Thos. J. Beard, in the Church of the Advent, Birmingham, Ala. So. Ch., Apr. 30, 1891

Robert A., of Edinburgh, Scotland, and Mary Talcott, d. of the late Rev. E. C. Hutchinson of St. Louis, niece of Dr. Randolph of Millwood, by the Rev. Joseph R. Jones, in Christ Church, Millwood, Clarke Co., Va. So. Ch., Apr. 22, 1880

Robert N., and Nannie Gardner, by the Rev. T. G. Dashiell, at Hunter's Hill, Louisa Co., the residence of Geo. J. Gardner So. Ch., Dec. 3, 1868

Thomas, Esq. (Vestryman), and Martha, d. of the late Dr. Turner Wootton and Mrs. Caroline Wootton, by the Rev. W. A. Avirett, in Christ Church, Rockville, Montgomery Co., Md. So. Ch., Feb. 20, 1873

Virginia, of Bath Co., Va., and Joseph McAllister of Covington, Va., by the Rev. L. R. Combs assisted by the Mr. White (Presbyterian), in Grace Church, Warm Springs, Bath Co., Va. So. Ch., Apr. 27, 1893

William A., Esq., of Lexington, and Ellen L.,* d. of Gen. Joseph R. Anderson of Richmond, by the Rev. Charles Minnigerode, D.D., in St. Paul's Church, Richmond, Va. So. Ch., Aug. 3, 1871

ANDRAS

Elizabeth, d. of John Andras,

* Given as printed, but should be "G"

MARRIAGE NOTICES IN THE SOUTHERN CHURCHMAN WITH DATES OF PUBLICATION

Esq. of Bath (England), and the Rev. Edward Winthrop, Prof. of Sacred Literature in the Theological Seminary of Kentucky, by the Rev. Jno. Ward, at Lexington [no state indicated]. So. Ch., June 28, 1839

ANDREWS
Annie, d. of the Rev. C. W. Andrews, D.D., and Geo. R. Robinson, by the Rev. C. W. Andrews, D.D., in the Episcopal Church, Shepherdstown. So. Ch., Oct. 5, 1855

Carolyn Snowden, d. of R. Snowden Andrews, and Gibson Fahnestock of New York, by the Rev. J. H. Eccleston, D.D., in Emmanuel Church, Baltimore. So. Ch., June 12, 1884

Charles W., of Shepherdstown, and Jane Morrison Quigley, at the residence of Henry C. Page, Charles Town, W. Va. So. Ch., May 8, 1909

Elizabeth, and the Rev. John Oliver Patterson, priest-in-charge of St. Ansgarious Church, Chicago. So. Ch., Aug. 15, 1936

Garnett (Col.), of Yazoo City, Miss., and Rosalie Champ, d. of Andrew Beirne, Esq., by the Rev. Wm. McGuire, at Linden Grove, Monroe Co., W. Va. So. Ch., Sept. 5, 1867

Lila, d. of the officiating clergyman, and the Rev. Magruder Maury, rector of St. George's Church, Fredericksburg, by the Rev. C. W. Andrews, D.D., in Trinity Church, Shepherdstown. So. Ch., Nov. 2, 1865

ANNAN
Fannie S., and Chas. Andrews Robinson, both of St. Louis, by the Rev. P. G. Robert, at St. Louis, Mo. So. Ch., Jan. 15, 1885

Roger P., and Adelaide S. Hall, both of Clarke Co., Va., by the Rev. T. F. Martin, at the residence of Mrs. Catharine V. Hall. So. Ch., Nov. 7, 1867

ANSHUTZ
Rebecca, second d. of the late C. P. Anshutz, and John Mitchell, Esq. of Des Moines, Iowa, by the Rev. Wm. F. M. Jacobs, at Moundsville. So. Ch., Jan. 14, 1859

ANTHONY
Ann E., d. of the late Samuel Anthony, Esq., and Capt. Wm. C. Whittle, U.S. Navy, by the Rev. T. M. Ambler, at the residence of her uncle, Buchanan. So. Ch., Aug. 12, 1859

Deborah Couch, d. of the late William H., and Mary D. Anthony of Botetourt Co., Va., and Dr. Edward McCarthy of Richmond, by the Rev. Joshua Peterkin assisted by the Rev. L. W. Burton, in St. James' Church. So. Ch., Oct. 23, 1890

Julia Gilmer, youngest d. of Col. Wm. H. Anthony, and Dr. Evan W. Warfield of Maryland, by the Rt. Rev. A. M. Randolph, at the home of the bride, No. 403 E. Main St., Richmond, Va. So. Ch., July 10, 1890

Julia M., and Gilmer P. Breckenridge, both of Botetourt, by the Rev. T. M. Ambler, at the residence of G. Anthony, the bride's uncle, Buchanan. So. Ch., Jan. 27, 1860

Mary F., d. of William H. and M. V. Anthony of Botetourt Co., Va., and James E. Mason of Richmond, Va., by the Rev. C. C. Randolph, in Trinity Church, Buchanan. So. Ch., Jan. 8, 1885

S. T., d. of Wm. H. and Mrs. Mary V. Anthony, and the Rev.

MARRIAGE NOTICES IN THE SOUTHERN CHURCHMAN WITH DATES OF PUBLICATION

C. C. Randolph, by the Rev. H. M. Jackson, in Trinity Church, Buchanan, Botetourt Co., Va. So. Ch., Oct. 23, 1879

APPERSON
Allen, of Richmond, Va., and Lizzie Moore, by the Rev. A. Wade, at Kittawan, the residence of the bride's father. So. Ch., Mar. 19, 1874

James R., and Mary V., only d. of H. G. Lipscomb, both of New Kent, by the Rev. B. S. Hepbron, in St. Peter's Church. So. Ch., Dec. 1, 1888

R. A. (Mrs.), of Richmond, and James W. Taylor of Ashland, by the Rev. T. G. Dashiell, at the residence of P. P. Winston. So. Ch., Aug. 7, 1884

APPLETON
Edward Webster (The Rev.), of St. John's Church, and Sarah Nowell, youngest d. of the late George Louis Mayor, Esq., all of Lancaster, by the Rt. Rev. Samuel Bowman, D.D., assistant Bishop of the Diocese in St. John's (Free) Church, Lancaster. So. Ch., Oct. 15, 1858

Samuel G. (The Rev.), and Sarah Ann, d. of the late Sylvester Gardner, Esq., both of Manlius, N. Y., by the Rev. S. C. Millett, at Manlius, N. Y. So. Ch., Oct. 11, 1839

ARAKI
Iyo (Miss), and Dr. Tokutaro Kubo, chief of staff in St. Luke's Hospital, Tokyo, in Trinity Cathedral, Tokyo. So. Ch., Dec. 8, 1934

ARCHER
Bessie M., of Vinita, Va., and Minor C. Horner of Midlothian, Va., by the Rev. John G. Scott, rector of Manakin Church, Powhatan Co., Va., in Manakin Church, Powhatan Co., Va. So. Ch., Jan. 28, 1922

Cadmus, of Chesterfield, and Maggie C., d. of George W. Feild, Esq. of Greensville, Va., by the Rev. G. W. S. Parham. So. Ch., May 23, 1878

Carthous, of Henrico, and Maria, d. of the late T. C. Willson of Amelia Co., Va., by the Rev. P. F. Beckeley, at Selma, the residence of Richard Anderson of Amelia Co. So. Ch., Oct. 29, 1868

Frances W., d. of Robert S. Archer, Esq., and Andrew H. Christian, Jr., by the Rev. Hartley Carmichael assisted by the Rev. Robert P. Kerr, D.D., in St. Paul's Church, Richmond, Va. So. Ch., Sept. 11, 1890

Mary F., d. of Dr. Robert Archer of the U.S. Army, and the Rev. Frederick Goodwin, rector of Trinity Church, Staunton, Va., by the Rev. Mr. Cheevers, at Fort Monroe, Va. So. Ch., Nov. 10, 1837

Mattie E., d. of William S. Archer, and John D. Blair, by the Rev. Landon R. Mason, at 806 Park Ave., Richmond, residence of the bride's father. So. Ch., Oct. 1, 1891

P. Jefferson, Esq., of Richmond, and Lucy A. Pulliam of Powhatan Co., by the Rev. Andrew Fisher, in St. Luke's Church, Powhatan Co. So. Ch., Jan. 8, 1858

Richard (Capt.), C.S. Army, and Virginia Page, d. of the late Thomas L. Hobson, Esq. all of Powhatan, by the Rev. J. D. Powell, in Emmanuel Church, Powhatan. So. Ch., Feb. 19, 1864

MARRIAGE NOTICES IN THE SOUTHERN CHURCHMAN WITH DATES OF PUBLICATION

Richard F., and Susan, d. of the late Mrs. Mary T. Moseley of Powhatan Co., by the Rev. A. B. Tizzard, in St. James' Church, Richmond. So. Ch., Feb. 2, 1871

Robert S., and Ann Virginia, d. of the late Dr. Geo. Watson, all of Richmond, by the Rev. F. D. Goodwin, in St. Paul's Church, Richmond, Va. So. Ch., Dec. 5, 1856

Stephen, and Laura A. Clark, by the Rev. A. B. Tizzard, at Mantua, Chesterfield Co., Va. So. Ch., Nov. 19, 1885

Susan V., d. of Dr. Robert Archer, and Dr. Levin S. Joynes, by the Rev. Charles Minnigerode, at Richmond. So. Ch., June 11, 1858

Virginia, d. of Richard Archer, Esq. of Amelia Co., and O. S. Allen, by the Rev. A. B. Tizzard, in Christ Church, Amelia Court House, Va. So. Ch., Dec. 28, 1889

Wister (Prof.), of Abbeville, S.C., and Rose Garland Ellis of Amherst C.H., Va., by the Rev. W. M. Clark, in Ascension Church, Amherst C.H., Va. So. Ch., Dec. 3, 1885

ARCHIBALD
Marietta Atkinson, d. of the Hon. Archibald of Smithfield, and George D. Wise, Esq. of Accomac Co., by the Rev. Henry A. Wise, at Smithfield, Isle of Wight Co. So. Ch., Dec. 23, 1859

ARLIENDT
Wm. (Dr.), and Adele Tyler, by the Rev. R. S. Barrett, in Trinity Church, Owensboro, Ky. So. Ch., Feb. 21, 1884

ARMISTEAD

Bowles E., and Elizabeth Lewis, d. of Henry M. Marshall, by the Rev. Kinloch Nelson, at Fairfield, Fauquier Co. So. Ch., Dec. 7, 1871

Bowles Ed., and Susan Lewis Marshall, by the Rev. Jno. McGill, at "Ivanhoe", residence of bride's father. So. Ch., Oct. 31, 1867

Fannie Allen, of Farmville, Va., and John H. Lowman of Roanoke, Va., by the Rev. Dr. Harding, in the Presbyterian Church, Farmville, Va. So. Ch., Oct. 20, 1892

John R., of Petersburg, Va., and Elizabeth E., d. of William Edloe, Esq. of Williamsburg, by the Rev. Wm. Hodges. So. Ch., Dec. 22, 1837

John R., of Charles City Co., Va., and Gutrude* H., d. of P. H. Hoof of Alexandria, Va., by the Rev. Wm. A. Stickney, at Weyanoke, Marengo Co., Ala., the residence of Mrs. Mary H. Minge. So. Ch., Dec. 6, 1883

Louis A. (Brevet Maj.), U.S.A., and Mrs. Cornelia L. T. Jameson, d. of the late Wm. Taliaferro, Esq. Westmoreland Co., Va., by the Rev. C. B. Dana, in Christ Church, Alexandria, Va. So. Ch., Apr. 7, 1853

Louisa G., of Fauquier Co., and the Rev. Chas. C. Taliaferro, rector of Cumberland Parish, Lunenburg Co., Va., by the Rev. C. W. Andrews, near Upperville, Fauquier Co. So. Ch., June 3, 1836

Lucy F., and John E. Welbourn of Baltimore City, by the Rev. Dr. A. Wade, at Tommahind, Charles City Co., Va. So. Ch., Feb. 12, 1874

ARMSTRONG
Bessie O. G., d. of the late Capt. James Welby Armstrong,

* Given as printed

MARRIAGE NOTICES IN THE SOUTHERN CHURCHMAN WITH DATES OF PUBLICATION

gr. d. of the late Wm. A. Stephenson, Esq. of Lipperville, Fauquier Co., Va., and L. L. Booker of Los Vegas, Hot Springs, N.M., formerly of Va., by the Rev. Stephen H. Greene of St. John's Church, St. Louis, Mo., at the residence of T. H. Simpson, Logansport, Ind. So. Ch., Dec. 23, 1886

Charles O'Reilly, and Mary Cornelia Briscoe Martin, third d. of the officiating clergyman, by the Rev. T. F. Martin, rector of the Church, assisted by the Rt. Rev. C. T. Quintard, in St. Ann's Church, Nashville. So. Ch., Jan. 23, 1890

Ella F., and T. E. Friend, Esq., by the Rev. Edward Valentine Jones, in St. John's Church, City Point, Va. So. Ch., Jan. 20, 1876

Emma Florence, and Richard R. Johnson, both of Albemarle Co., by the Rev. T. E. Locke. So. Ch., Oct. 15, 1885

Ethel, of Shelbyville, Ky., and the Rev. M. R. Worsham, by the Rev. Dr. John K. Mason, in St. Andrew's Church, Louisville, Ky. So. Ch., May 9, 1908

Miriam M., and Hon. Wm. C. Glenn, by the Rev. R. S. Barrett, in St. Luke's Cathedral, Atlanta, Ga. So. Ch., Dec. 19, 1889

Robert L., of Baltimore, and Cassie M., d. of Col. Nat. Tyler formerly of Richmond, Va., by the Rev. Wm. Kirkus, in the Church of Saint Michael's*

and All Angels. So. Ch., July 8, 1880

ARNEST
A. E., and Robert Newton, both of Westmoreland, by the Rev. D. M. Wharton, in Westmoreland Co., Va. So. Ch., May 7, 1868

ARNOLD
Thomas (Dr.), and Mary R. Brockenbrough, by the Rev. Andrew Fisher, at the residence of Col. John M. Brockenbrough. So. Ch., June 30, 1870

ARRINGTON
John White, and Mary Carter Sublett, by the Rev. J. J. Clopton, in Meade Memorial Church, Manchester, Va. So. Ch., May 30, 1889

ASHBROOK
Cornelia Letcher, d. of Mr. and Mrs. L. L. Ashbrook formerly of St. Louis, now of Manhattan, and Richard J. Compton, Jr. of St. Louis, Mo., by the Rev. Pendleton Brooke, in St. Paul's Church, Manhattan, Kan. So. Ch., Nov. 27, 1880

ASHBURNER
Harriet E., d. of the late Algernon E. Ashburner of Philadelphia, and the Rev. Dallas Tucker, by the Rev. L. S. Osborne, in the Trinity Church, West Philadelphia. So. Ch., July 1, 1880

ASHBY
Alice, and Robert McGill Mackall, by the Rev. Jno. McGill, at "Sunny Side", the residence of the bride's father in Fauquier Co., Va. So. Ch., Jan. 30, 1868

Blanche, d. of Sam'l T. Ashby, Esq. of Culpeper Co., Va., and Maurice W. Lambire of George-

* Given as printed

MARRIAGE NOTICES IN THE SOUTHERN CHURCHMAN WITH DATES OF PUBLICATION

town, D.C., by the Rev. Jno.
S. Lindsay, in St. Stephen's
Church, Culpeper C.H., Va.
So. Ch., Dec. 25, 1873
Edith T., and Hubert Snowden,
by the Rev. H. Suter, in
Christ Church, Alexandria.
So. Ch., June 19, 1879
Eloise Bartleman, d. of the late
F. Westwood Ashby, and Dr.
William Reginald Purvis, by
the Rev. Dr. Suter, in Christ
Church, Alexandria, Va. So.
Ch., June 23, 1892
Estelle V., third d. of the
late Capt. Samuel T. Ashby,
and I. L. Johnson of Union-
town, Penn., by the Rev.
John McGill, at the res-
idence of the Misses
Kirkman, Culpeper, Va. So.
Ch., Jan. 11, 1883
J. Washington (Dr.), and
Agness Marion, d. of the
late Dr. John Taylor of
Caroline Co., by the Rev.
John Cole, at the residence
of her brother in Culpeper
Co. So. Ch., May 13, 1859
James, and Mary B., d. of R. C.
L. Moncure, Jr., by the Rev.
J. M. Meredith, in Aquia
Church, Stafford Co., Va.
So. Ch., Jan. 2, 1879
Janet McG., d. of Col. T. W.
Ashby, and the Rev. C. E.
Woodson of Franklin, Va.,
by the Rev. Dr. Suter
assisted by the Rev. Dr.
Walker, in Christ Church,
Alexandria, Va. So. Ch.,
Nov. 27, 1890
Lucy, and C. C. Carmichael,
by the Rev. A. P. Saunders,
Fredericksburg, Va. So. Ch.,
Jan. 5, 1893
Norman, and Mary, d. of D. P.
Stallard, both of Culpeper,
Va., by the Rev. J. Green
Shackelford and the Rev.

Wm. T. Roberts, in Ascension
Church, Washington, D.C.
So. Ch., Nov. 12, 1885
Roberta S., d. of the late
John Ashby, Esq., and
Erasmus Taylor, by the Rev.
J. Earnest, at Mount
Independence, in Fauquier
Co. So. Ch., Jan. 15, 1852
ASHE
William S., Esq., Attorney at
Law, and Sarah Ann Green,
by the Rev. Thomas F.
Davis, Jr., in Washington.
So. Ch., Jan. 22, 1836
ASHFORD
F. A. (Dr.) formerly of the 17th
Va. Infantry, and Belle, d. of
Moses Kelly, Esq., cashier of the
National Metropolitan Bank of
Washington, in Washington, So.
Ch., Dec. 5, 1872
ASHLIN
Gunnell H., of Fluvanna, and Eliza-
beth H. Scott of Buckingham Co.,
by the Rev. Wm. M. Nelson, in
Buckingham Co. So. Ch., Oct.
19, 1855
Robt. W. (Col.), and Mrs.
Mary E. Leo Graham, both of
Fluvanna Co., by the Rev.
S. C. Roberts, at Rivanna
Mills, Fluvanna Co., Va. So. Ch.,
Mar. 9, 1871
Sarah A., d. of Col. Robert
W. Ashlin of Fluvanna Co.,
and John W. Rison of Rich-
mond, by the Rev. S. C.
Roberts, at Rivanna Hall,
Fluvanna Co., Va. So. Ch.,
Feb. 24, 1870
ASHTON
Chas. H., of King George Co.,
and Ida B. Welch, by the
Rev. Jno. McGill, at the
residence of the bride's
father, S. Welch, near "The
Plains", Fauquier Co. So. Ch.,
Dec. 16, 1869
Ella, d. of the late Wm. A. H.

MARRIAGE NOTICES IN THE SOUTHERN CHURCHMAN WITH DATES OF PUBLICATION

Ashton of King George Co., and William P. Berry, Esq. of Eden, King George Co., Va., by the Rev. Henry Wall, at Marmion. So. Ch., Dec. 7, 1865

Ellen, youngest d. of H. W. Ashton, and Robt. L. Horner, all of Fauquier, by the Rev. O. S. Barton, at "North Wales", residence of the bride's father. So. Ch., Sept. 21, 1865

Gissie Stuart, second d. of Dr. Horace Ashton of King George Co., Va., and Thomas W. Franklin, Esq. of Stafford Co., by the Rev. James W. Shields, at "Bleak Hill", residence of the bride's father. So. Ch., Jan. 17, 1878

J. T. of King George, and Hannah More Wiatt of Spotsylvania Co., Va., by the Rev. A. M. Randolph, in Spotsylvania Co., Va. So. Ch., Nov. 25, 1859

J. W., of Portsmouth, and Bettie, d. of the late Dr. Wm. Cole of Prince George Co., Va., by the Rev. Dr. Gibson, at the residence of the bride's uncle, John Cole, in Petersburg. So. Ch., Nov. 30, 1871

Lewis A., Esq., and Mary B., d. of the late Abram B. Hooe of King George, by the Rev. E. B. McGuire, at St. Paul's Church, King George Co. So. Ch., Dec. 8, 1870

Mattie T., d. of Dr. Horace D. Ashton, and H. C. Grymes of King George Co., by the Rev. Edward McGuire, at "Bleak Hill", the residence of the bride's father, in King George Co. So. Ch., Dec. 9, 1880

Robert (The Rev.), rector of Holy Trinity Parish, Dio Marquette, Iron Mountain, Mich., and May Dawkins of Jacksonville, Fla. by the Rev. L. Fitz-James Hindry, in Trinity Church, St. Augustine, Fla. So. Ch., July 20, 1929

Stuart T. (Dr.), and Nina F., d. of John H. Barnes, Esq., by the Rev. Frank Page, at the residence of the bride's parents, near Fairfax C.H., Va. So. Ch., Dec. 20, 1888

ASPINWALL
Helen Lloyd, d. of Mrs. J. L. Aspinwall of Barrytown, N.Y., and Francis E. Shober, Jr. of North Carolina, by the Rev. J. T. Wheat, D.D. assisted by the Rev. G. B. Hopson, at the residence of the bride's mother. So. Ch., May 4, 1882

ASSHETON
Eleanor Louise, youngest d. of William Assheton, Esq., and Walter Montague Luard, s. of the Rev. C. Luard, rector of Aunsby, Lincolnshire, England, by the Rev. Herbert Asshoton, at Rockspring, Fauquier Co., Va. So. Ch., Jan. 11, 1883

ASTELL
William W., and Rosa M. Blacker, by the Rev. P. F. Berkeley, at Haw Branch, the residence of the bride's parents, in Amelia Co. So. Ch., June 30, 1881

ATKINS
Addison B. (The Rev.), rector of Christ Church, Germantown, Philadelphia, and Ellen Calvert, second d. of the late C. C. Stuart, Esq., by the Rev. R. T. Brown, rector of Zion Church,

MARRIAGE NOTICES IN THE SOUTHERN CHURCHMAN WITH DATES OF PUBLICATION

Fairfax C.H., at Chantilly, Fairfax Co., Va. So. Ch., Nov. 30, 1854
Addison Butler, s. of the officiating clergyman, and Helen R. Oliffe, by the Rev. A. B. Atkins, D.D., rector of St. John's Church, Yonkers, in New York, at the residence of the bride's mother. So. Ch., Feb. 13, 1879
Nellie Prior, and Richard Hardaway Meade, both of Richmond, Va., by the Rev. Moses D. Hoge, pastor of Second Presbyterian Church, and the Rev. J. B. Newton, rector of Monumental Church, in the Second Presbyterian Church, Richmond, Va. So. Ch., Nov. 23, 1893

ATKINSON
Anne Eliza, and H. Clay Pleasants of Clinton, Texas, formerly of Goochland Co., Va., by the Rev. Mr. Jones of the Episcopal Church, near Gonzales, Texas. So. Ch., Feb. 5, 1858
Belle, and John W. Lockett, Esq., by the Rev. J. Maxwell Pringle, at the residence of the bride's father, John C. Atkinson, Esq., in Henderson, Ky. So. Ch., Dec. 3, 1874
Eliza W., d. of Roger B. Atkinson of Lunenburg Co., Va., and the Rev. Henry C. Lay, by the Rev. Edmund Withers, at Sherwood. So. Ch., May 28, 1847
Emmett F., d. of the late James Atkinson of Alexandria, Va., and Richard Stonnell, Esq. of Prince William Co., Va., by the Rev. Dr. R. H. McKim, in Christ Church, Alexandria, Va. So. Ch., Nov. 26, 1874
Geo. R., of Prince William Co., and Jennie B., youngest d. of the late Dr. Oliver Jones of Fairfax Co., by the Rev. Dr. Addison, in Washington, D.C. So. Ch., Nov. 4, 1875
Louisa W., d. of Roger B. Atkinson, Esq., and Orlando Smith, Esq. of Lunenburg C.H., by the Rev. Henry Wall assisted by the Rt. Rev. Henry C. Lay, D.D., brother-in-law of the bride, at Sherwood, Lunenburg Co., Va. So. Ch., May 4, 1860
Mary Carleton, eldest d. of the late Guy Atkinson, Esq. of Alexandria, D.C., and Joseph R. Somers of Fairfax Co., Va., by the Rev. E. R. Lippet, at Alexandria. So. Ch., Oct. 5, 1837
Mary D., and R. H. Cunningham, both of Henderson, Ky., by the Rev. J. M. Pringle, at residence of the bride's father. So. Ch., Nov. 18, 1875
Mary Mayo, d. of the Bishop, and the Rev. D. Hillhouse Buel, by the Bishop of North Carolina, in St. James' Church, Wilmington. So. Ch., July 17, 1857
Mary T., second d. of Roger B. Atkinson, Esq., and the Rev. Lewis Walke, by the Rev. F. M. Baker, at Sherwood, Lunenburg Co., Va. So. Ch., Oct. 8, 1858
Roger B., Esq., of Sherwood, and Mrs. Ann N. Toler, d. of the late George N. Grymes of King George Co., Va., by the Rev. C. J. Gibson, at Kinderwood, Lunenburg Co. So. Ch., June 15, 1860

MARRIAGE NOTICES IN THE SOUTHERN CHURCHMAN WITH DATES OF PUBLICATION

Susie H., d. of Dr. Robert Atkinson of Baltimore, and Thomas M. Nelson of Clarke Co., Va., by the Rev. Jos. R. Jones, rector of Christ Church, Millwood, Va., in Grace Church, Baltimore. So. Ch., Jan. 3, 1878

Thomas, Esq., of Baldwin Co., Ala., and Agnes Almeda White of Isle of Wight Co., Va.; by the Rev. James Chisholm, at Smithfield, Va. So. Ch., Jan. 19, 1854

Thomas, Jr., and Ida Louise, d. of the late Fred'k Wm. Hanewinckle of Richmond, by the Rt. Rev. Bishop of North Carolina, gr.f. of the groom, in St. James' Church, Richmond, Va. So. Ch., Feb. 5, 1880

ATWELL
Sam'l, and Ella Marshall, both of King George Co., Va., by the Rev. T. E. Locke, at Shiloh, King George Co. So. Ch., Sept. 7, 1860

AUGUR
Cassius, and Juaniata E., eldest d. of John R. Barnes, Esq., all of Fairfax Co., by the Rev. Jno. McGill. So. Ch., Apr. 24, 1873

AUGUST
Sarah Cabell, d. of James A. August of Hot Springs, Va., and Dr. Philip Percey, eldest s. of R. L. Parrish of Covington, Va., by the Rev. L. R. Combs, in the Episcopal Church, at Warm Springs, Va. So. Ch., Oct. 19, 1893

AULD
Elizabeth (Mrs.), and Thomas Sheppard, both of Richmond, by the Rev. R. S. Barrett, in Richmond. So. Ch., June 3, 1880

AUSTIN
P. M., and Mrs. Sarah A. Burton, by the Rev. J. B. Craighill, at Maysville, Ky. So. Ch., Apr. 18, 1872

AVENT
Lizzie, eldest d. of Maj. Wm. F. Avent of Oxford, Miss., and John H. Wilson, Esq., Commonwealth's Attorney, Greensville Co., by the Rev. David Barr, at the residence of Tamlin Avent (bride's gr.f.) Greensville Co. So. Ch., Oct. 3, 1872

AVERETT
Mary E. (Mrs.), of Gainsville, Ala., and the Rev. Wm. D. Christian, rector of Grace Church, Lake Providence, La., by the Rt. Rev. Wm. M. Green, D.D., at Meridian, Miss. So. Ch., Nov. 25, 1875

AVERITT
Jas. A. (The Rev.), of Alabama, and Mary L. D., d. of Philip Williams, Esq. of Winchester, by the Rev. Mr. Meredith, in Christ Church, Winchester. So. Ch., Mar. 14, 1862

AVERY
Preston Stoddard, of Pensacola, Fla., and Judith Fauntleroy Miller, by the Rev. K. J. Hammond, in Trinity Episcopal Church, Washington, Va. So. Ch., Nov. 6, 1920

William, and Minnie Lee Woodhouse, by the Rev. John C. Cornick, in Eastern Shore Chapel, Princess Anne Co., Va. So. Ch., Sept. 17, 1891

AYCOCK
Gaston Lake, of Louisburg, N. C., and Mary Campbell, d. of Capt. and Mrs. J. A.

MARRIAGE NOTICES IN THE SOUTHERN CHURCHMAN WITH DATES OF PUBLICATION

Goodwyn, by the Rev. J. C. Norton, rector of Emmanuel Church, Warrenton, N.C., at Elberon, N.C. So. Ch., Jan. 22, 1910

AYLETT
Pattie Waller, d. of Col. W. R. Aylett of King William Co., Va., and Dr. George Carrington Callaway of Nelson Co., by the Rev. S. S. Hepbron, in St. David's Church, King William Co. So. Ch., June 21, 1888

Sallie B., eldest d. of Col. W. R. Aylett of King William Co., and R. T. Goodwyn of Nottoway Co., Va., by the Rev. S. S. Hepburn*, at Montville, the residence of the bride's father. So. Ch., July 9, 1891

William R., of King William Co., and Alice R. Brockenbrough, by the Rev. Andrew Fisher, at Bellville, Richmond Co. So. Ch., Aug. 17, 1860

AYRE
Bettie R., d. of William Ayre, and Recton F. Thomas, Esq., by the Rev. W. A. Alrich, at the residence of the bride's father in Fairfax Co. So. Ch., Feb. 27, 1868

Ida De Vere, youngest d. of Wm. Ayre of "Buena Vista", and George F. Harrison, all of Fairfax Co., by the Rev. A. P. Gray, in St. John's Church, Centreville. So. Ch., Sept. 9, 1880

M. Lucretia, d. of William and Martha Ayre, and Richard B. Dorsey, all of Fairfax, by the Rev. A. P. Gray, in St. John's Church, Centreville. So. Ch., Feb. 3, 1881

Mary W., eldest d. of Wm. Ayre of Fairfax Co., Va., and Robt. D. Woolf, by the Rev. Jno. McGill, at Buena Vista. So. Ch., Feb. 12, 1874

William, Jr., and Florence O., eldest d. of Thomas H. Walker, Esq., all of Fairfax Co., by the Rev. John McGill, at the residence of the bride's parents. So. Ch., Feb. 7, 1878

AYRES
Bena, d. of Col. E. W. Ayres, the well known Washington correspondent, and Cabell Whitehead, assistant assayer of the United States Mint at Boise City, Idaho, by the Rev. Dr. Mott, assistant rector of Epiphany Church, Washington, D.C. So. Ch., Oct. 11, 1888

Charlotte, d. of Henry Ayres, Esq., and Capt. Alfred Maddox of Balto.*, by the Rev. J. B. Craighill, at "Salt Grove", Northampton Co., Va. So. Ch., Jan. 27, 1870

Edward F., of Philadelphia, and Agnes Dade (Daisy), eldest d. of Capt. R. H. and Mrs. Agnes M. Fitzhugh formerly of Virginia, by the Rev. E. H. Ward, rector of Christ Church, at the residence of the bride's parents, Lexington, Ky. So. Ch., Feb. 2, 1893

James K., and Sallie Upshur Hack, by the Rev. J. M. Chevers, at Fairview, Accomac Co. So. Ch., Dec. 5, 1856

AZARIAH
Grace, second d. of the Bishop of Dornakal, and the Rev. John Ponniah Aaron. So. Ch., Dec. 1, 1934

* Given as printed

-B-

BACKUS
  Jean Wallace, d. of Mrs. Eliza Burton Backus of Cleveland, Ohio, and the late Rev. Arthur Mann Backus, and Archibald Nail Dawson, M.D. of Cleveland, Ohio, by the Bishop of Lexington, the bride's uncle, assisted by the Bishop of Ohio and the rector of St. Paul's Church, in St. Paul's Church, Cleveland, Ohio. So. Ch., Dec. 3, 1910

BACON
  Susie Stanford, only child of James T. and Susan S. Bacon of Stanford Hall, Albemarle Co., Va., and Elder Ernle George, s. of the late Wm. Taylor Money of the Madras army, by the Rev. Edward Valentine Jones, in Grace Church, Albemarle Co., Va. So. Ch., Oct. 22, 1891

  Susy, of Richmond, Va., and Dr. Robert H. Thornton of Newport, Ky., by the Rev. Mr. Graighill, in the Episcopal Church, Dalton, Ga. So. Ch., Nov. 19, 1891

BACOT
  Emma Cecilia, and the Rev. Thos. Richey, by the Rev. Dr. Mahan, in Grace Church, Jersey City. So. Ch., Oct. 22, 1858

BADEN
  Zelia R., and Philip DeCatesby Lee, both of Fairfax Co., by the Rev. R. A. Castleman, at the residence of Mr. Yates, near Chantilly, Va. So. Ch., Oct. 26, 1893

BAGBY
  Susan M., and Robert O. Cralle, both of Powhatan Co., by the Rev. Andrew Fisher, at the residence of Bennett M. Bagby. So. Ch., Dec. 19, 1856

  Virginia, eldest d. of the late Dr. George W. Bagby, and Henry Taylor, Jr., by the Rev. Joshua Peterkin assisted by the Rt. Rev. A. M. Randolph. So. Ch., June 17, 1886

  William C., and Alice Catlett of Port Royal, Va., by the Rev. S. S. Ware, in St. Peter's Church, Port Royal, Va. So. Ch., June 27, 1889

BAGGOTT
  Martha L., and James W. Spilman, by the Rev. Edw. C. McGuire. So. Ch., Sept. 13, 1839

BAGLEY
  H. M., lately from Virginia, and Louisa Towles, by the Rev. R. S. Barrett, at the residence of the bride's mother in Henderson Co., Ky. So. Ch., Feb. 21, 1884

BAGLY
  Colin S., and Clara R. Neblett, by the Rev. L. J. Sothoron, in St. John's Church, Cumberland Parish.* So. Ch., Nov. 27, 1879

BAGNALL
  Annie D., of Onancock, Accomac Co., Va., and Dr. D. Claude Handy of Annapolis, Md., by the Rev. J. B. Craighill, in St. James' Church, Drummondtown. So. Ch., Dec. 2, 1869

BAGWELL
  Elizabeth M., d. of Dr. T. P. Bagwell, and Dr. Edward R. Leatherbury, by the Rev. J. M. Chevers, in Onancock. So. Ch., Dec. 23, 1855

  Lillian W., of Onancock, and Armistead L. Capehart of Kittrell, N.C., by the Rev. Henry L. Derby, in Trinity Church,

---

* Cumberland Parish is in Lunenburg County, Virginia (*Journal ... Diocese of Southern Virginia*, Portsmouth, Va., 1941)

MARRIAGE NOTICES IN THE SOUTHERN CHURCHMAN WITH DATES OF PUBLICATION

Onancock. So. Ch., July 28, 1892
Sally W., d. of Dr. T. P. Bagwell, and Thomas R. Joynes, Jr., by the Rev. J. M. Chevers, in Onancock. So. Ch., Dec. 28, 1855

BAILEY
Alice Cabell, d. of the late Samuel M. Bailey, and William Sandford Garbey, all of Covington, Ky., by the Rev. Frank Woods Baker assisted by the Rev. Robert A. Gibson of Cincinnati. So. Ch., Dec. 15, 1887
Mary Thomazine, second d. of D. M. Bailey, Esq., cashier, National Exchange Bank of Weston, and Maj. Thomas Pettigrew, formerly of North Carolina, now of West Virginia, by the Rev. T. H. Lacy, at the residence of the bride's parents. So. Ch., Feb. 5, 1891
Sarah White, d. of the late Samuel M. Bailey, and Victor James Robertson of San Francisco, Cal., by the Rev. Frank Woods Baker, at Covington, Ky. So. Ch., Oct. 31, 1889
Wm. C., and Mary Gertrude Stevens, by the Rev. A. E. Evison, in Trinity Church, Edisto Island, S.C. So. Ch., Sept. 14, 1907

BAINBRIDGE
Mary Wallace, of Fredericksburg, and Hamilton Cassard of Baltimore, by the Rev. Edward C. Murdaugh, in Trinity Church, Fredericksburg, Va. So. Ch., Dec. 4, 1879

BAKER
E. Folsom (The Rev.), and Frances H., d. of the late Abraham N. Wagener, Esq., of Pen Yan, by the Rev. Dr. Mahan, in St. Stephen's Church, Olean, N.Y. So. Ch., Oct. 22, 1858
Elizabeth Lovejoy, d. of Mr. and Mrs. Wm. L. Baker of Sioux Falls, S.D., and the Rev. Robert Talbot Dickerson of Wilmington, Del., now on furlough from Liberia, by the Rev. Elwood Haines, in Christ Church, Glendale, Ohio. So. Ch., Apr. 29, 1933
Ella, eldest d. of W. B. Baker, Esq. of Winchester, Va., and the Rev. C. B. Page, rector of Trinity Church, Danville, Ky., by the Rev. George W. Peterkin, rector of Memorial Church, Baltimore, Md., assisted by the Rev. Mr. Gilbert, at the residence of the bride's father. So. Ch., Dec. 3, 1875
Emily Eyre, youngest d. of Judge Richard H. Baker, and Theodore S. Garnett, by the Rev. N. A. Okeson, at the residence of R. H. Baker, Esq., Norfolk, Va. So. Ch., Nov. 13, 1873
Francis M. (The Rev.), rector of Grace Church, and Mrs. Maria F. Gassaway, eldest d. of Samuel C. Greenhow, Esq. of Alexandria, Va., by the Rev. Dr. Peterkin, in St. James' Church, Richmond, Va. So. Ch., Nov. 30, 1871*
Henry, and Susan Randolph Meade, d. of J. J. Hite, all of Nelson Co., by the Rev. Edmund Withers, at the residence of Mrs. Hopkins. So. Ch., Jan. 28, 1869
Lucy J., d. of the late Thomas Baker, and Morgan M. Brannon, all of Winchester, by the Rev. C. Walker, in Christ Church, Winchester, Va. So. Ch., Nov. 2, 1855
Nannie L., d. of C. S. Baker, Esq., of Winchester, Va., and B. Mason Ambler, Esq. of

---

* A notice appears in the issue of Nov. 16, 1871, identical with this except that "Greenhow" is written "Greenwood"

MARRIAGE NOTICES IN THE SOUTHERN CHURCHMAN WITH DATES OF PUBLICATION

Parkersburg, W.Va., by the Rev. John Ambler assisted by the Rev. L. R. Mason, at the residence of the bride's father. So. Ch., Nov. 25, 1875
Richard H., Jr., and Nannie Mallory Hope, youngest d. of James Barron Hope, Esq., by the Rev. Beverly D.. Tucker, in St. Paul's Church, Norfolk. So. Ch., Nov. 5, 1885
T. Roberts, of Richmond, Va., and Maria G., only d. of Henry K. Burgwyn, Esq. of North Carolina, by the Rev. Dr. Bowles, rector, assisted by the Rev. F. M. Baker of Richmond, Va., in the Church of the Advent, Boston, Mass. So. Ch., Nov. 12, 1868

BALCH
Alexandrine Macomb, youngest d. of L. P. W. Balch, Esq., and the Rev. George D. Cummins, rector of Christ Church, Norfolk, Va., by the Rev. Richard T. Brown, in Leetown, Jefferson Co. So. Ch., July 2, 1847
Augusta, eldest d. of the Rev. Dr. Balch, and John Neilson, Esq. of New York, by the Rev. Dr. Balch assisted by the Rt. Revs. the Bishops of Vermont and Delaware, in Newport, R.I. So. Ch., Feb. 15, 1861
Lewis F. W. (The Rev.), rector of St. Bartholmew's Church, N.Y., and Anna, eldest d. of Hon. William Jay, by the Rt. Rev. Bishop Underdonk of New York Diocese. So. Ch., Apr. 19, 1839

BALDWIN
Cornelia Lee, d. of Dr. R. T. Baldwin, and J. Peyton Clark, Esq., all of Winchester, Va., by the Rev. C. Walker, in Winchester, Va. So. Ch., Aug. 8, 1856
Kate M., of Winchester, and Barton Myers of Norfolk, by the Rev. James Hubard assisted by the Rev. Walter Q. Hullihen, in Winchester, Va. So. Ch., Jan. 11, 1883
M. W. (Mrs.), and the Rev. C. H. Shield, by the Rev. C. E. Ambler, in Springfield. So. Ch., Oct. 13, 1870
Oliver P., Esq., and Eliza Lee Sheffey, by the Rev. Mr. Boyden, Staunton. So. Ch., June 28, 1839
Wm. Ludwell, of Frederick Co., and Lizzie, d. of the late Dr. Randolph Kownslar of Berryville, Clarke Co., Va., by the Rev. P. P. Phillips, in Grace Church, Berryville. So. Ch., July 15, 1880

BALL
Charlotte C., formerly of Washington, D.C., and Edward Landon Carter of Va., by the Rev. J. H. Chew, in St. Alban's Church, Washington, D. C. So. Ch., Aug. 24, 1871
Fannie J., d. of Dr. Athwell Ball of Mississippi, and Hopkins Harding of Northumberland Co., Va., by the Rev. H. L. Derby, at "Bewdley", Lancaster, Va., the residence of Capt. James Ball. So. Ch., Dec. 28, 1876
Geo. P., formerly of Spottsylvania Co., and Fannie, eldest d. of Dr. J. W. White, by the Rev. Geo. W. Dame, at the residence of the bride's father, near Laurel Grove, Spottsylvania Co.

MARRIAGE NOTICES IN THE SOUTHERN CHURCHMAN WITH DATES OF PUBLICATION

So. Ch., Jan. 11, 1877
James K., and Fannie M., d. of James V. Sullivan of Lancaster Co., Va., by the Rev. H. L. Derby assisted by the Rev. John Moncure, at "Riverside", Lancaster, Va. So. Ch., Dec. 15, 1881

Landonia M., d. of Maj. Ball, lately of Casanova, Fauquier Co., Va., and William Pill of Henderson, N.C., by the Rev. David Barr of Epiphany Parish, Washington, at the bride's home, 2325 Pennsylvania Ave., Washington, D.C. So. Ch., Sept. 4, 1890

Loula A., d. of the late John T. Ball of Meridian, Miss., and O. Edward Wilkins, cashier of the Henrietta Mills, by the Rev. E. A. Osborne of Charlotte, at the residence of Fred S. Mosher, Supt. of Henrietta Mills, Rutherford Co., N.C. So. Ch., Oct. 2, 1890

M. Dulany, Esq. of Fairfax Co., Va., and Sallie U. Wright of Williamsburg, by the Rev. R. T. Brown, in the Chapel of William and Mary College. So. Ch., Oct. 26, 1860

Martha C. T., d. of the late W. W. Ball of Fairfax Co., Va., and William Selwyn Ball, by the Rev. W. E. Judkins, at Langley, Fairfax Co., Va. So. Ch., Dec. 18, 1879

Mary E., and John W. Chowning, by the Rev. H. L. Derby, in Lancaster Co., Va. So. Ch., Dec. 12, 1878

Mary P., formerly of Mississippi, and Alfred Hudnall of Northumberland Co., by the Rev. H. L. Derby, in Grace Church, Lancaster, Va. So. Ch., June 26, 1879

Mary Stuart, d. of Col. M. D. Ball of Alaska, formerly of Alexandria, and James C. Gillmore, U.S.N., at "The Castle", Sitka, Alaska. So. Ch., June 9, 1881

Mary V., of Norfolk Co., Va., and the Rev. N. F. Marshall, by the Rev. A. S. Lloyd, in St. Luke's Church, Norfolk. So. Ch., Dec. 23, 1886

Nannie Lee, d. of James Flexmer and Mariah Ball, and Robert Conway Sanford of Westmoreland Co., by the Rev. H. L. Derby, at the residence of the bride's parents, Ditchley, Northumberland Co., Va. So. Ch., Mar. 27, 1884

Rebecca F., d. of the late Col. S. H. Ball of Virginia, and John Addison of Richmond, by the Rev. R. H. McKim, in Christ Church, Alexandria, Va. So. Ch., Jan. 2, 1873

Sarah A., and Logan Hunter, by the Rev. W. A. Alrich, at the residence of the bride's father near Buckland, Va. So. Ch., Apr. 8, 1869

Thomas, and Maria Louisa, d. of the late James Hurst of Northumberland, by the Rev. E. Adams, in Northumberland Co. So. Ch., Dec. 11, 1835

Warner, of Northumberland, and "Lelia"*, d. of A. L.

---

* Given as printed

MARRIAGE NOTICES IN THE SOUTHERN CHURCHMAN WITH DATES OF PUBLICATION

and Mary D. Carter, by the Rev. H. L. Derby, at the residence of the bride's father, Midway, Lancaster, Va. So. Ch., Nov. 25, 1875
William Selwyn, and Martha C. T., d. of the late W. W. Ball of Fairfax Co., Va., by the Rev. W. E. Judkins, at Langley, Fairfax Co., Va. So. Ch., Dec. 18, 1879

BALLARD
Mary E., d. of the late Garland Ballard of Orange, and John S. Hansbrough, by the Rev. J. Earnest, at Orange C. H. So. Ch., Aug. 15, 1856
William H. (Dr.), of Louisiana, and Lizzie P. Griffin, by the Rev. Edwin A. Penick, at the residence of Dr. John H. Griffin, Salem, Roanoke Co., Va. So. Ch., Jan. 16, 1879

BANISTER
Euretta B., d. of the late John Munro Banister, and Charles L. Stickny of Greensboro, Ala., by the Rev. Mr. Platt, in St. Paul's Church, Petersburg, Va. So. Ch., Oct. 5, 1860
Helen T., youngest d. of the late John Monro* Banister, Esq., and Robert L. Madison, M.D., of Lexington, Va., by the Rev. Mr. Platt, in St. Paul's Church, Petersburg, Va. So. Ch., Feb. 10, 1860
John M., rector of Bath Parish, Dinwiddie Co., and Mary Louisa, d. of the late Gen. Wm. H. Brodnax, by the Rev. Edmund Withers, at Kingston, Dinwiddie Co., Va. So. Ch., Feb. 11, 1848

BANKHEAD
Bettie, d. of Dr. Wm. Bankhead of Orange, and B. L. Winston of Hanover, by the Rev. Joseph Earnest, in Edgemont, Orange Co. So. Ch., June 11, 1858
Charles L., of Harrisonburg, and Mary W., d. of Dr. Wm. Bankhead of Orange Co., Va., by the Rev. Joseph Earnest, in Edgemont, Orange Co., Va. So. Ch., Oct. 5, 1855
Ellen M., d. of Dr. William Bankhead of Orange, and Jaqueline M. Meredith of Stafford Co., by the Rev. Joseph Earnest, in Edgemont, Orange Co. So. Ch., Jan. 15, 1858
Mary Enor, of Virginia, and John Banks of Kentucky, by the Rev. John S. Hansbrough, at the residence of Charles Bankhead, Orange Co., Va. So. Ch., Aug. 31, 1882
Mary W., d. of Dr. Wm. Bankhead of Orange Co., Va., and Charles L. Bankhead of Harrisonburg, by the Rev. Joseph Earnest, in Edgemont, Orange Co., Va. So. Ch., Oct. 5, 1855
Nora, youngest d. of Dr. Wm. Bankhead of Caroline Co., and Maj. John M. Lee, by the Rev. B. E. Habersham, at Signal Hill, Hanover Co., the residence of B. L. Winston, Esq. So. Ch., Nov. 16, 1871
Rosalie Stuart, d. of Dr. Wm. Bankhead of Orange Co., and Richard M.

* Given as printed

MARRIAGE NOTICES IN THE SOUTHERN CHURCHMAN WITH DATES OF PUBLICATION

Winston of Hanover, by
the Rev. Joseph Earnest,
at Edgemont. So. Ch.,
Nov. 20, 1857

BANKS
Jabez, and Sarah Chambers,
both of New Castle Co., by
the Rev. W. D. Hanson, in
Faulkland, Del. So. Ch.,
Mar. 29, 1883

John., of Kentucky, and Mary
Minor Bankhead of Virginia, by
the Rev. John S. Hansbrough,
at the residence of Charles
Bankhead, Orange Co., Va.
So. Ch., Aug. 31, 1882

Richard R., and Clara B.
Swann, both of Wilmington,
Del., by the Rev. W. D.
Hanson, in Wilmington, Del.
So. Ch., Aug. 28, 1884

Robert A. (Col.), and Louisa
J., d. of William Finks, Esq.,
all of Madison Co., by the
Rev. J. Earnest, at Madison
C. H. So. Ch., May 7, 1847

BANNER
Pattie Helen, d. of the late
Lewis B. Banner, Esq., and
the Rev. George Badger Wetmore,
D.D., by the Rev. James A.
Weston, at Banner Elk,
Watauga Co., N.C. So. Ch.,
Apr. 16, 1885

BANNISTER
Monro (Dr.), and Fanny
Peyton, eldest d. of the
late William J. Barks-
dale, all of Amelia Co.,
by the Rev. P. F. Berkeley,
at Clay Hill. So. Ch.,
Apr. 27, 1860

T. Lewis (The Rev.), rector of
St. Thomas' Church, Green-
ville, Ala., and Louisa E.,
d. of the Rev. Wellington
E. Webb, by the rector
of St. Paul's Church,
Bergen, N.J., in St. Paul's
Church, Bergen, N.J. So.
Ch., Nov. 16, 1871

BANTA
Mary D., and Llewellyn B.
Marshall, by the Rev.
Henry T. Sharp, in the
Church of the Ascension,
Frankfort, Ky. So. Ch.,
Dec. 23, 1875

BANTON
Emerline* J., of Richmond, and
Charles Mann, by the Rev.
W. H. Kinckle. So. Ch.,
June 27, 1856

BAPTIST
Sallie G., eldest d. of the Rev.
E. L. Baptist, and Wm. G.
Moss, by the Rev. P. M.
Boyden, at the residence
of the bride's father,
Mecklenburg Co., Va. So.
Ch., Mar. 31, 1892

BARBEE
Kate, and John A. M'Culloch,
both of Mason Co., W.Va.,
by the Rev. T. H. Lacy, at
the residence of the bride's
father, Dr. Andrew Barbee,
in Point Pleasant, W.Va.
So. Ch., Nov. 1, 1877

BARBER
Edward B., of London,
and Mrs. Sarah Shadgett
of Quebec, Canada, by
the Rev. Dr. Empie, in
Richmond, Va. So. Ch.,
Dec. 1, 1837

Merrill Phillip, and Helen
Meredith, d. of C. D. S.
and Helen Joliffe Clark-
son, late of Haymarket, Va.,
at Vero Beach, Fla. So.
Ch., Mar. 21, 1931

BARBOUR
Elsie C., youngest d. of
B. Johnson Barbour, Esq.,
and J. C. Graves, by the
Rev. F. G. Scott, at the
residence of the bride's
father, Orange Co., Va.
So. Ch., July 31, 1890

* Given as printed

MARRIAGE NOTICES IN THE SOUTHERN CHURCHMAN WITH DATES OF PUBLICATION

BARCLAY
    Lucy Eleanor, second d. of D. Robert Barclay, Esq., and Edmond L. McClelland of the Episcopal High School, near Alexandria, Va., by the Rev. George C. Betts, rector, in Trinity Church, St. Louis. So. Ch., July 20, 1882

BARHAM
    Chas. A. W., formerly of Durham, N.C., and Mary Hannah, d. of E. Wilkinson, Esq., Mayor of West Point, by the Rev. Pendleton Brooke, in St. John's Church, West Point, Va. So. Ch., Mar. 7, 1889

    W. B. (Dr.), of Newsoms, Southampton Co., Va., and Fanny, d. of the late Edmund Berkeley, Esq. of Hanover Co., by the Rev. W. A. Alrich, at the "White House", Hanover Co., Va. So. Ch., May 12, 1881

BARKER
    Charles M., of Clarksville, Tenn., and Virginia M., d. of Thomas S. Watson, by the Rev. J. M. Rawlings, at Brackett's, Louisa Co., Va. So. Ch., Dec. 25, 1879

    Thomas M., of Christian Co., Ky., and Mary Love, d. of Col. John D. Morris, by the Rev. Mr. Ringgold, in Clarksville, Tenn/ So. Ch., Jan. 24, 1867

BARKSDALE
    Caroline C., of Albemarle, and T. J. D. Eddins of Green Co., by the Rev. R. K. Meade. So. Ch., Dec. 20, 1839

    Conway, and Augusta, youngest d. of the late John Peachy, all of Amelia Co., by the Rev. P. F. Berkeley, in the Parish Church of Raleigh Parish.* So. Ch., May 4, 1860

    Conway, and Maud Eggleston, by the Rev. A. B. Tizzard, in St. John's (Grub Hill) Church, Amelia Co. So. Ch., Sept. 16, 1886

    Elizabeth Read, and the Rev. Giles Buckner Palmer, by the Rev. Giles B. Cooke, uncle of the groom, in Durham, N.C. So. Ch., Oct. 24, 1914

    Elsie W., d. of George A. Barksdale, Esq. of Richmond, Va., and Henry T. Wickham of Hanover Co., Va., by the Rev. Charles Minnigerode, D.D., in St. Paul's Church, Richmond, Va. So. Ch., Dec. 24, 1885

    Fanny Peyton, d. of the late William T. Barksdale, and Dr. Monroe Bannister, all of Amelia Co., by the Rev. P. F. Berkeley, at Clay Hill. So. Ch., Apr. 27, 1860

    Geo. A., and Elsie Florence, eldest d. of A. Warwick, all of Richmond, by the Rev. Chas. Minnigerode, at the residence of the bride's father. So. Ch., Jan. 27, 1860

    George A., and E. C. Powers, both of Richmond, by the Rev. Pike Powers assisted by the Rev. W. H. H. Powers of Md., in St. Andrew's

---

* Raleigh Parish is in Amelia County, Virginia (Journal ... Diocese of Southern Virginia, Portsmouth, Va., 1941)

MARRIAGE NOTICES IN THE SOUTHERN CHURCHMAN WITH DATES OF PUBLICATION

Church, in Richmond. So. Ch., Oct. 12, 1882

Mariana Tabb, d. of Dr. Randolph Barksdale, and Benj. H. Heyward of Charleston, S.C., by the Rev. Dr. Charles Minnigerode. So. Ch., Dec. 18, 1884

Nannie E., of Charlotte, and William Townes, Jr. of Mecklenburg, by the Rev. H. A. Brown, at the residence of Henry E. Edmunds, Charlotte Co., Va. So. Ch., Dec. 14, 1864

Randolph (Dr.), and Elizabeth B., d. of Wm. H. Macfarland, Esq., all of Richmond, by the Rev. Chas. Minnigerode, in St. Paul's Church, Richmond. So. Ch., June 11, 1858

Sallie C., and James B. Boker, of Middleburg, Loudoun Co., by the Rev. Geo. W. Dame, at Whitlock, Halifax Co. So. Ch., July 15, 1869

Zella Maud, d. of John J. and Elizabeth M. Barksdale, and John B. Spencer of Halifax Co., Va., by the Rev. C. O. Pruden, at the home of the bride's parents, "Little Nook" farm, near Mt. Airy, Pittsylvania Co., Va. So. Ch., Dec. 6, 1888

BARNES

Harriet V., d. of the late Henry Barnes of Madison Co., Va., and Hudson Shackleford of Albemarle, by the Rev. James T. Johnston, in St. Paul's Church. So. Ch., May 29, 1857

Helena J. (Mrs.) [colored], of Lynchburg, Va., and the Rev. Charles L. Somers [colored, rector of colored churches in Lynchburg, Belford, and Roanoke], by the Rev. Robert A. Magill, rector of St. John's Episcopal Church, Lynchburg, in Lynchburg, Va. So. Ch., Jan. 18, 1936

Juaniata E., eldest d. of John R. Barnes, Esq., and Cassius Augur, all of Fairfax Co., by the Rev. Jno. McGill. So. Ch., Apr. 24, 1873

Julia A., d. of the late Henry Barnes of Madison Co., and Gibbon S. Conway of Madison Co., by the Rev. James T. Johnston, in St. Paul's Church. So. Ch., May 29, 1857

Lillie, second d. of John S. Barnes, and Wm. H. Palmer, all of Fairfax Co., by the Rev. Jno. McGill, in Zion Church, Fairfax Courthouse. So. Ch., Feb. 8, 1877

Nina F., d. of John H. Barnes, Esq., and Dr. Stuart T. Ashton, by the Rev. Frank Page, at the residence of the bride's parents, near Fairfax C. H., Va. So. Ch., Dec. 20, 1888

BARNETT

Gertrude Guerry, and the Rev. Edgar L. Pennington, rector of Holy Cross Church, Miami, Fla., by Bishop Wing of South Florida, in St. Barnabas' Church, DeLand, Fla. So. Ch., July 6, 1940

Mary Elizabeth, d. of John L. Barnett, Esq. of Salem, Va., and Benjamin Arthur Middleton, M.D. of Richmond Co., Va., by the Rev. E. C. Gordon, in Salem, Va. So. Ch., Dec. 29, 1881

MARRIAGE NOTICES IN THE SOUTHERN CHURCHMAN WITH DATES OF PUBLICATION

Sidney, and E. Katie, third d. of Dr. Mix, all of Albemarle Co., by the Rev. T. E. Locke. So. Ch., Oct. 15, 1885

BARNEY
Carrie, of Richmond, and Thomas R. Borland of Norfolk, by the Rev. Charles Minnigerode, in St. Paul's Church, Richmond. So. Ch., Jan. 1, 1880

Charles R., and Mary Ann, d. of Robert T. Gwathmey, Esq. of Richmond, by the Rt. Rev. Bishop Moore. So. Ch., June 7, 1839

Wm. H., of Mobile, Ala., and Sallie R. Norvell of Lynchburg, by the Rev. W. H. Pendleton, in St. Stephen's Church, Bedford, Va. So. Ch., Oct. 31, 1867

BARNS
Marcellus N., and Manie F. Watson, both of Fairmont, by the Rev. G. A. Gibbons, in Christ Church, Fairmont, W. Va. So. Ch., Jan. 2, 1879

BARNWELL
Elizabeth Marshall, d. of Mr. and Mrs. Henry Barnwell of Adams Run, and Henry Flinn Dargan of Darlington, S.C., by the Rev. Thomas P. Baker, in Christ Church, Adams Run, S.C. So. Ch., Oct. 1, 1910

Stephen Elliott (The Rev.), of Beaufort, S.C., and Matilda R., d. of the late Alonzo R. Cushman of New York, by the Rev. John P. Lundy, in the Church of the Holy Apostles, N.Y. So. Ch., Oct. 16, 1873

BARR
Beverley Ray, d. of the late Rev. and Mrs. David Barr of Washington, D.C., and George Eugene Clancey of Manila, formerly of Sioux City, Iowa, at Manila, Philippine Islands. So. Ch., Jan. 1, 1910

David (The Rev.), rector of Meherin Parish, Greenville Co., Va., and Jeanie, d. of Com. Wm. C. Whittle of Buchanan, by the Rev. Pendleton Brooks, in Trinity Church, Buchanan, Va. So. Ch., Feb. 13, 1873

Oscar O., of Edgefield, and Mollie M. Haile of Essex Co., Va., by the Rev. E. T. Walker, at the residence of M. L. Holson, the bride's brother-in-law, in Edgefield, S.C. So. Ch., Jan. 6, 1881

W. A. (The Rev.), and Ida Herndon Stringfellow, by the Rev. F. Stringfellow, the bride's father, in the rectory, Martinsville, Va. So. Ch., Feb. 9, 1893

BARRACK
Richard H., and Martha Jane Edmunis, both of Westmoreland Co., Va., by the Rev. T. E. Locke. So. Ch., Sept. 7, 1860

BARRET
Marcella C., of Goochland Co., Va., and W. A. Hankins of Surry Co., Va., by the Rev. P. M. Boyden, at Mt. Bernard, in Goochland Co. So. Ch., Jan. 27, 1881

T. T., and Clara A., d. of the officiating clergyman, both of Henderson, Ky., by the Rev. J. M. Pringle, in St. Paul's Church, Henderson, Ky. So.

MARRIAGE NOTICES IN THE SOUTHERN CHURCHMAN WITH DATES OF PUBLICATION

Ch., Dec. 14, 1876
BARRETT
  Annie, of Wytheville, and
  Dr. Henry Dodson of
  Millen, N.C., by the
  Rev. R. S. Barrett of
  Kentucky, and the Rev.
  Mercer P. Logan, the
  rector, in St. John's
  Church, Wytheville,
  Va. So. Ch., Oct. 11, 1883
  Bettie Y., and J. Syme
  Fleming, both of Goochland
  Co., Va., by the Reb. P. M.
  Boyden, at Mt. Bernard,
  Goochland Co., Va. So.
  Ch., Dec. 2, 1880
  Richard Rice, of Concord, Mass.,
  and Anne Camden, eldest d.
  of Mr. and Mrs. Baldwin D.
  Spilman of "Elway Hall",
  at Warrenton, Va. So.
  Ch., Jan. 25, 1913
  William Herndon, and Henrietta,
  d. of George F. Harrison
  of Goochland Co., Va.,
  by the Rev. R. A. Goodwin,
  the bride's brother-in-law
  and rector of the church,
  in St. John's Church,
  Petersburg, Va. So. Ch.,
  Feb. 9, 1893
BARRINGER
  Paul B. (Lt.), of Virginia, and
  Lucy Landon, d. of Dr.
  Charles L. and Mary
  Venable Minor, by the Rev.
  W. G. Clark, in Trinity
  Church, Asheville, N.C.
  So. Ch., Dec. 22, 1917
BARROLL
  Anna Matilda, and the Rev. John
  Payne of King George Co.,
  Va., Missionary appointed
  by the Episcopal Church
  to Cape Palmas, Africa,
  by the Rev. C. F. Jones,
  Chestertown, Md. So. Ch.,
  Apr. 21, 1837
BARRON
  Samuel, Jr. (Capt.), and
  Agnes M. Smith, all of
  Richmond Co., by the rector,
  in St. John's Church, Lunen-
  burg Parish, Richmond Co.
  So. Ch., May 20, 1869
BARROW
  David Crenshaw, Jr., and
  Fannie Ingle, d. of A. K.
  Childs, Esq., all of Athens,
  by the Rev. Edward H. Ingle,
  in Emmanuel Church, Athens,
  Ga. So. Ch., Feb. 13, 1879
  M. Louise, of Woodbridge,
  and Charles D. Fredricks
  of New York, by the Rev. A.
  G. Shears of New Haven, at
  Woodbridge, N.J. So. Ch.,
  Nov. 13, 1857
BARTLETT
  A. E. J. (Mrs.), and George
  Gibson, Esq., by the Rev.
  C. Gibson, in Grace Church,
  Petersburg, Va. So. Ch.,
  Aug. 29, 1856
  Helen S., d. of the late
  Rev. Hobart M. Bartlett,
  and Dr. R. N. Hudson of
  Louisa Co., Va., by the
  Rev. T. G. Dashiell, at
  the residence of P. H.
  Gibson, Esq., Richmond, Va.
  So. Ch., Oct. 13, 1881
BARTLEY
  Wm. M., one of the principals
  of the Virginia and Tenn-
  essee College Institute*,
  and C. Amalia T. Henri-
  ques, both of Bristol,
  by the Rev. F. T. Goodwin,
  Bristol, Va. So. Ch., Oct.
  2, 1857
BARTON
  C. Marshall of Fredrick,*
  Va., and Ellen H. of
  Fauquier, d. of the late
  Dr. Jaqueline A. Marshall,
  by the Rev. Ch. H. Sheilds*,
  Prospect Hill, Fauquier Co.
  So. Ch., Oct. 7, 1859

* Given as printed

MARRIAGE NOTICES IN THE SOUTHERN CHURCHMAN WITH DATES OF PUBLICATION

Charles B., s. of the late Gen. Charles J. Barton of the English Army, and Fanny Tebault, d. of the late Col. Edward James of Princess Anne, by the Rev. William R. Savage, at the residence of the bride's mother in Princess Anne Co., Va. So. Ch., Feb. 19, 1885

George L., formerly of Maryland, and Mariana Prentis Causey, by the Rev. Henry L. Derby, at Suffolk, Va. So. Ch., Nov. 6, 1890

Hugh, s. of the late Gen. Charles J. Barton of the English Army, and Anna, d. of John A. Mayer, Esq. of Norfolk Co., by the Rev. W. R. Savage, in Emmanuel Church, Kempsville, Va. So. Ch., June 14, 1888

Joseph M., of Frederick Co., Va., and Mary Neill of Clarke Co., by the Rev. F. M. Whittle. So. Ch., Feb. 27, 1857

Mary D., d. of Ellen H. and the late Charles H. Barton, and Richard H. Smith, by the Rev. H. B. Lee, at the residence of the bride's mother, Markham, Fauquier Co., Va. So. Ch., Nov. 2, 1882

R. T., Esq., of Winchester, and Katie, d. of Wm. Knight, Esq. of Cecil Co., Md., by the Rev. C. H. Shield, at "Essex Lodge." S. Ch., Mar. 5, 1868

Susan Catharine, d. of Judge and Mrs. W. S. Barton, and Dr. Alfred Copeland Palmer of Norfolk, by the Rev. J. Green Shackelford, the rector, in Trinity Church, Fredericksburg. So. Ch., Dec. 8, 1887

BASKERVILL
H. E. C., of Richmond, Va., and Mrs. Margaret A. Humphreys of Springfield, Ill., in Springfield, Ill. So. Ch., Sept. 7, 1876

BASKERVILLE
P. Hamilton, and E. M. d. of Dr. John C. Skelton, all of Richmond, by the Rev. George Woodbridge assisted by the Rev. Charles Minnigerode, in Monumental Church, Richmond, Va. So. Ch., June 24, 1875

BASS
Montese, and Richard H. Bruce, both of Chesterfield Co., Va., by the Rev. A. B. Tizzard, in Trinity Church, Dale Parish, Chesterfield Co., Va. So. Ch., May 29, 1890

BASSET
Henry S., and Lillian A. Finegan, both of Nashville, Tenn., by the Rev. T. F. Martin, rector of St. Anne's Church, at the residence of the bride's aunt, Mrs. Susan Brandon. So. Ch., Nov. 22, 1888

BASSETT
Benjamin Harrison, Esq., of Brenham, Texas, and Mary Burnet, d. of G. W. Bassett, Esq., by the Rev. Mr. Carraway, at Clover Lea, Hanover Co., Va. So. Ch., Jan. 11, 1861

Ella M., d. of G. W. Bassett, Esq., and Col. L. W. Washington of Jefferson Co., Va., by the Rev. G. S. Carraway, at Clover Lea, Hanover Co., Va. So. Ch.,

MARRIAGE NOTICES IN THE SOUTHERN CHURCHMAN WITH DATES OF PUBLICATION

Nov. 16, 1860
Frances Carter, d. of G. W. Bassett, Esq., and Charles T. Mitchell, Esq. of Charleston, S.C., by the Rev. Mr. Carraway, at "Clover Lea", the residence of the bride's father, in Hanover. So. Ch., Dec. 11, 1863

Jefferson (Lt.), of Texas, and Lucy Gilmer, d. of Cary Breckinridge, by the Rev. Wm. McGuire, at Grove Hill, Botetourt Co., Va. So. Ch., Feb. 8, 1865

Mary Burnet, d. of G. W. Bassett, Esq., and Benjamin Harrison Bassett, Esq. of Brenham, Tex., by the Rev. Mr. Carraway, at Clover Lea, Hanover Co., Va. So. Ch., Jan. 11, 1861

BASSINGER
William (Maj.), of Savannah, and M. Garnett of Virginia, by the Rev. P. F. Berkeley*, in Prince Edward Co. So. Ch., Nov. 29, 1866

BASSITT
Annette Lewis, d. of G. W. Bassitt, Esq. of Hanover Co., and Julian E. Ingle of Westmoreland, Md., by the Rev. B. E. Habersham assisted by the Rev. E. A. Dalrymple, at Clover Lea, Hanover Co., Va. So. Ch., Feb. 13, 1873

BASTABLE
G. M., Jr., of Fauquier Co., Va., and Mary Anna, d. of D. R. Semmes, Esq., by the Rev. H. Suter, in Christ Church, Alexandria, Va. So. Ch., Dec. 13, 1883

Mary, and Alfred Thornton Forbes, both of Fauquier, by the Rev. John Lindsay, D.D., at "Montevideo", Fauquier Co., Va. So. Ch., Nov. 5, 1885

BATCHELOR
Adelaide, and Joshua B. Callahan, both of Montgomery Co., Md., by the Rev. John S. Lindsay, D.D., in Georgetown, D.C. So. Ch., Dec. 16, 1886

BATTE
Richard D., and Mattie J. Fulton, by the Rev. J. Y. Downman, in All Saints' Church, Richmond. So. Ch., Nov. 3, 1892

Robert B., of Prince George Co., and Helen Bland, d. of Col. S. Bassett French of Whitby, Chesterfield Co., by the Rev. Churchill J. Gibson, rector of Grace Church, Petersburg, in Meade Memorial Church, Manchester. So. Ch., Dec. 25, 1873

BATTLE
Joseph D., formerly of North Carolina, and Clara Bell Withrow, by the Rev. Mr. Bird of Trinity Church, at the residence of the bride's mother, in Galveston, Tex. So. Ch., Sept. 23, 1886

BAUDER
Fannie Care, second d. of Prof. Eszra* and Julia C. Bauder, and J. Bankhead T. Thornton, all of Brentsville, by the Rev. A. P. Gray, in St. James' Church, Brentsville. So. Ch., Nov. 19, 1885

M. Louise, eldest d. of Prof. Ezra and Julia C. Bauder, and Chas. Edgar Nicol, by the Rev. A. P.

* Given as printed

MARRIAGE NOTICES IN THE SOUTHERN CHURCHMAN WITH DATES OF PUBLICATION

Gray, at the residence of the bride's parents, Brentsville, Va. So. Ch., Nov. 25, 1880

BAYLISS
Robert L., and Lucie C., d. of George T. Darracott, Esq. of Hanover Co., Va., by the Rev. S. S. Hepburn*, at the residence of the bride's father, (The Glympre). So. Ch., Dec. 11, 1890

BAYLOR
Henry B., and Annie, d. of George Shirley, all of Jefferson Co., by the Rev. J. W. Blake, in Grace Church, Smithfield, Jefferson Co., W.Va. So. Ch., Nov. 4, 1880

J. R., Jr., of Albemarle Co., Va., and Julia L., d. of P. F. Howard of Richmond, Va., by the Rev. C. H. Read assisted by the Rev. Thomas Drew, at the residence of the bride's brother-in-law, A. C. Bruce, in Charlotte Co., Va. So. Ch., Dec. 6, 1883

James B., of the U.S. Coast and Geodetic Survey, and Ellen C., d. of Charles Bruce, Esq., by the Rev. Thomas Drew, at Staunton Hill, Charlotte Co., Va. So. Ch., Jan. 13, 1881

John C. (Dr.), of Norfolk, Va., and Pattie, d. of Gen. John C. Pemberton of Fauquier Co., Va., by the Rev. John S. Lindsay, in St. James' Church, Warrenton, Va. So. Ch., Jan. 15, 1874

Kate Brooke, d. of the late Richard Baylor, Esq. of Essex Co., Va., and William A. Thom, Jr., by the Rev. B. D. Tucker assisted by the Rev. Arthur Lloyd, in St. Paul's Church, Norfolk, Va. So. Ch., Jan. 20, 1887

T. G., and Sallie M. Beckwith, by the Rev. J. H. W. Blake, at the residence of the bride's father, Jefferson Co., W.Va. So. Ch., Jan. 13, 1881

Thomas G., and Margaret E., only d. of Col. Giles B. Cooke of Borough, Va., by the Rev. Mr. Parks. So. Ch., Nov. 29, 1839

BAYLY
Mary P., and Dr. Arthur W. Downing, by the Rev. Aristides S. Smith of the Presbyterian Church, at Bellevue, Accomack Co., Va. So. Ch., Nov. 24, 1837

Sally C., second d. of Thomas M. Bayly, and Dr. P. F. Browne of Williamsburg, by the Rev. H. M. Bartlett, in Accomac. So. Ch., Nov. 29, 1839

BEADLES
Mary Wilson, of Richmond, and the Rev. Wm. McGuire of Essex Co., Va., by the Rev. Joshua Peterkin, D.D., in St. James' Church, Richmond, Va. So. Ch., Oct. 11, 1883

BEAGEN
H. J. (The Rev.), of Norfolk, Va., and Blanche H. Nicklin of Alexandria, Va., by the Rev. George H. Norton, D.D., in St. Paul's Church, Alexandria, Va. So. Ch., Nov. 1, 1888

BEAL
Richard Henry (The Rev.), and Catharine M., d. of Thomas Flint, Esq. of Baltimore, by the Rev. J. M. Jennings, in St. John's

---

* Given as printed

MARRIAGE NOTICES IN THE SOUTHERN CHURCHMAN WITH DATES OF PUBLICATION

BEALE
Church. So. Ch., Apr. 5, 1839
Fanny Bruce, and Charles I. Sale of Tappahannock, Va., in St. George's Church, Fredericksburg, Va. So. Ch., Oct. 17, 1914
J. L. (Dr.), of Washington, D.C., and Fannie S., d. of the late Rev. J. Sommerville Marbury of Alabama, by the Rev. C. K. Nelson, D.D., at the residence of the bride's grandfather, John Marbury, Esq., in Georgetown, D.C. So. Ch., Dec. 11, 1873
Louisa U., d. of the late Rev. Upton Beale of Norfolk, and Augustine T. Brooke of Maryland, by the Rev. Dr. Goodrich of N.O.*, at the residence of Col. E. T. Tayloe, Powhatan, King George Co. So. Ch., Dec. 9, 1869
Marguerite M., of Savannah, Ga., and the Very Rev. Herbert L. Johnson, Dean of St. Paul's Cathederal, Detroit, by the Rt. Rev. Herman Page, D.D. assisted by the Rev. R. W. Woodroofe, rector of St. John's Church, Detroit. So. Ch., Aug. 11, 1928
R. Channing, of Corsicana, Tex., and Emma B. Garnett, by the Rev. G. W. Beale, in King George Co., Va. So. Ch., Feb. 19, 1874
See also MURDOCK Catharine M. (Mrs.)

BEALL
A. Brooke, of Norfolk, and Mattie B., d. of the late John Hooff of Alexandria, Va., by the Rev. A. M. Randolph, in Emmanuel Church, Baltimore. So. Ch., May 8, 1873
Horace, and Cornelia A. Richardson of Clarke Co., Va., by the rector, the Rev. P. P. Phillips, in Grace Church, Berryville, Va. So. Ch., Oct. 27, 1881
Lizzie Alston, d. of L. J. Beall, and William Mitchell, all of Richmond, by the Rev. Joshua Peterkin, in St. James' Church, Richmond. So. Ch., Dec. 2, 1875
Upton (The Rev.), and Louisa, d. of Benj. Ogle, Esq., by the Rev. Dr. Marbury, at Bel-Air, Prince George's Co., Md. So. Ch., Oct. 27, 1837

BEAMAN
Richard, of Nansemond Co., Va., and Eliza Mary Stanwood, by the Rev. Douglass Hooff, at the residence of the bride, Portsmouth. So. Ch., Dec. 27, 1883

BEAN
Henry H. (The Rev.), rector of St. Stephen's Church, Harrisburg, Pa., and Harriet Seton, youngest d. of the late Martin Hoffman, Esq. of New York, by the Rev. J. T. Cushing, at Goshen, N.H. So. Ch., Oct. 14, 1852

BEAR
D. Newton, and Mattie Glenn, d. of Abner Shacklett, all of Harrisonburg, by the Rev. O. S. Bunting, in Emmanuel Church, Harrisonburg, Va. So. Ch., Dec. 28, 1882
Decatur B., of Rockingham Co., Va., and Anna V. Gibboney, both deaf mutes, by the Rev. Job

---
* Given as printed

MARRIAGE NOTICES IN THE SOUTHERN CHURCHMAN WITH DATES OF PUBLICATION

Turner assisted by the Rev. Mr. Preston as interpreter, in Wytheville, Va. So. Ch., Feb. 25, 1886

BEASLEY
Richard H. (The Rev.), of Lynchburg, Va., rector of Emmanuel Church, Bristol, Va., and Carrie Mae, d. of Mr. and Mrs. H. H. Bemis of Como, Miss., in Holy Innocents' Episcopal Church, Como, Miss. So. Ch., Sept. 25, 1937

Sallie Upshur, d. of the officiating clergyman, and W. F. C. Morsell, by the Rev. Dr. Beasley assisted by the Rev. Dr. Morsell, in All Saints' Church, Torresdale, Philadelphia. So. Ch., July 10, 1873

BEATTIE
Charles J., of "Marlboro", S.C., and Telia H. Wilkinson of Powhatan Co., Va., by the Rev. R. N. Pratt, at "Belone", S.C. So. Ch., Mar. 19, 1885

BEATTY
Mary A., youngest d. of Dr. W. H. Beatty of Birmingham, and the Rev. Richard W. Anderson, youngest s. of the late Meriwether L. Anderson of "Pants-Ops", Albemarle Co., Va., and rector of St. James' Church, Texarkana, Tex., by the Rev. Thos. J. Beard, in the Church of the Advent, Birmingham, Ala. So. Ch., Apr. 30, 1891

BEAUCLERK
Charles St. John, and Kate Lee Coleman, both of Amelia Co., Va., by the Rev. W. J. Page, in Christ Church, Amelia C.H., Va. So. Ch., Feb. 5, 1885

BEAUFORT
Fannie Claiborne, youngest d. of the late Capt. Charles B. Beaufort, U.S. R.S., and the Rev. Charles J. Kilgour of Frederick Co., Md., by the Rev. A. P. Stryker, in St. Barnabas' Church, Baltimore. So. Ch., Nov. 4, 1875

BEAVEN
W. Y. (The Rev.), rector of the parish, and Annie H., d. of J. Thomas Kirby of Talbot, by the Rev. George F. Beaven, father of the groom, assisted by the Revs. E. F. Dashiell, D.D., of St. Michael's, Albert Ware of Wye, and Geo. S. Gassner of Trinity Church, in All Saints' Church, Talbot Co., Md. So. Ch., Feb. 5, 1885

BEAVERS
Ann Eliza, and Harrison Lloyd, by the Rev. F. M. Whittle. So. Ch., Aug. 3, 1854

BECK
Dora, of Roanoke, and W. A. Willmeth of Roanoke, by the Rev. D. M. Wood, in Roanoke, Va. So. Ch., Dec. 3, 1885

BECKWITH
Catherine Devereux, d. of Dr. John Beckwith of Petersburg, and Henry F. Spaulding, Esq., of New York, by the Rev. John Beckwith of the Diocese of Maryland, in St. Paul's Church, Petersburg. So. Ch., July 3, 1857

Charles M. (The Rev.), of St. Luke's Cathedral, Atlanta, Ga., and Susan Rainsford,

MARRIAGE NOTICES IN THE SOUTHERN CHURCHMAN WITH DATES OF PUBLICATION

d. of George R. Fairbanks, Esq. of Fernandina, Fla., by the Rt. Rev. J. W. Beckwith, Bishop of Georgia assisted by the Rt. Rev. Wm. M. Green, Bishop of Mississippi, in St. Augustine's Chapel, University of the South, Sewanee, Tenn. So. Ch., Nov. 5, 1884

Sallie M., and T. G. Baylor, by the Rev. J. H. W. Blake, at the residence of the bride's father, Jefferson Co., W.Va. So. Ch., Jan. 13, 1881

T. S., of Petersburg, Va., and Emma, d. of Dr. S. B. Cary, by the Rev. Charles Mann, in Abingdon Church, Gloucester Co., Va. So. Ch., Nov. 26, 1868

BEDINGER
Henrietta, d. of the late Daniel Bedinger, and Edmund J. Lee, Jr., Esq., by the Rev. E. Cornwall, in Southport, Conn. So. Ch., Sept. 18, 1835

Henry (The Rev.), of Greenport, L.I., and Ada, d. of N. W. Doughty, by the Rev. J. Carpenter Smith, S.T. D., in St. George's Church, Flushing, L.I. So. Ch., May 4, 1876

BEDSU
James, of England, and S.S. Warriner, by the Rev. P. F. Berkeley, at Oaklevel, the residence of the bride, in Amelia Co. So. Ch., Mar. 25, 1880

BEELER
Fannie Lee, youngest d. of Joseph Beeler, Esq. of Washington Co., Md., and Capt. Wm. T. Chase of Lancaster, Va., by the Rev. Mr. Mitchell, at Silver Lawn, the residence of the bride's father. So. Ch., Jan. 16, 1873

BEEMAN
Henry (The Rev.), of New Lexington, Ohio, and Hortensia H., d. of Judge Lee of New Lexington, Ohio, by the Rev. Pendleton Brooke, at Clarksburg, W.Va. So. Ch., Oct. 20, 1870

BEERS
Elizabeth Louise, d. of the late Daniel G. and Arabella Fitch Beers of Newton, and Frederick Foote Johnson, Bishop coadjutor of Missouri, by the Rev. James H. George, rector, assisted by the Rev. Charles J. Griffen, of South Lee, Mass., in Trinity Church, Newtown, Conn. So. Ch., July 10, 1915

BEHLING
Elizabeth, and Chester Lee Smoak, by the Rev. Thomas P. Baker, at the residence of the bride's parents, near Meggett, S.C. So. Ch., Mar. 23, 1912

BEIRNE
Mary Gray, d. of Andrew Beirne, Esq., and Thomas Allston Middleton, Esq. of Charleston, S.C., by the Rev. Wm. McGuire, at Linden Grove, Monroe Co., W.Va. So. Ch., July 26, 1866

Oliver, of Virginia, and Sally C., d. of Daniel Sprigg, by the Rev. D. F. Sprigg, at the residence of the bride's father, Baltimore, Md. So. Ch., Jan. 7, 1869

Richard F., of Lewisburg, W.Va., and Clara M. Grundy, by the Rev. Charles Morris, at the

MARRIAGE NOTICES IN THE SOUTHERN CHURCHMAN WITH DATES OF PUBLICATION

residence of the bride's father, J. B. Grundy, Ashland, Va. So. Ch., July 5, 1877

Rosalie Champ, d. of Andrew Beirne, Esq., and Col. Garnett Andrews of Yazoo City, Miss., by the Rev. Wm. McGuire, at Linden Grove, Monroe Co., W.Va. So. Ch., Sept. 5, 1867

BELCHES

Lucy Berkeley, and Stuart Breese, both of Virginia, by the Rev. E. G. Cobb, at East Hampton, Mass. So. Ch., Jan. 16, 1909

Richard, Esq., formerly of Plymouth, England, now of Prince William Co., and Fannie C., eldest d. of Col. Edward Berkeley, by the Rev. R. T. Brown, at the residence of the bride's father. So. Ch., Sept. 19, 1872

BELFIELD

Frances Merriweather, and G. M. Muse, by the Rev. D. M. Wharton, at the residence of the bride's father. So. Ch., Jan. 21, 1869

BELL

Abbie, and James M. Berry, both of Liberty, Va., by the Rev. John K. Mason, at the residence of O. P. Bell, Liberty, Va. So. Ch., June 15, 1882

C. H. (Miss), of Mathews, and L. B. White of Norfolk, by the Rev. Jno. McGill, at Trinity Church, Mathews Co. So. Ch., Jan. 13, 1870

Edwin D., Esq., of Staunton, and Mary L., d. of Dr. John N., deceased, and Henrietta Vaughan, by the Rev. C. J. Gibson, at "Virginia Villa", the residence of Mrs. Dr. Vaughan, near Petersburg, So. Ch., Nov. 12, 1885

Eliza Amelia, d. of Judge John W. and M. C. Bell of Culpeper, Va., and Otis Bowyer of Baird. Tex., by the Rev. Wm. T. Roberts, in St. Stephen's Church, Culpeper, Va. So. Ch., Dec. 15, 1887

Emeline, d. of Squire Bell of Clarke Co., Va., and James E. Hesser of Loudoun, by the Rev. F. M. Whittle, Clarke Co., Va. So. Ch., Jan. 13, 1853

George, and Julia, d. and sister of the officiating clergymen, by the Rev. Dr. Wall assisted by his s., the Rev. Edward Wall, in St. Paul's Church, Kent Co., Md. So. Ch., Dec. 25, 1884

H. M. (Maj.), of Staunton, Va., and Mrs. Martha V. Timberlake, nee Crane of Jefferson Co., W. Va., by the Rev. Dallas Tucker, rector of Zion Church, Charles Town, assisted by the Rev. Walter O. Hullihen, rector of Trinity Church, Staunton, Va., at the residence of the bride's mother, Mrs. Margaret S. Crane, near Charles Town, Jefferson Co., W.Va. So. Ch., Nov. 11, 1886

James C., and C. Inez Harllee, by the Rev. Henry L. Derby, Suffolk, Va., at the residence of the bride's mother. So. Ch., Feb. 26, 1891

Margaret Soutter, only d. of the late Alexander Bell of Norfolk, and Walter F. Irvine of New Orleans, by the Rev. O. S. Barten, in Christ Church. So. Ch., Nov. 19, 1868

Mary Miller Northana, youngest d. of Capt. James M. Bell, and James M. Smith, Esq., by the Rev. Mr.

MARRIAGE NOTICES IN THE SOUTHERN CHURCHMAN WITH DATES OF PUBLICATION

Lamon. So. Ch., Jan. 9, 1835
Orville Clifton, and Gretchen Parr, both of Bedford City, by the Rev. T. W. Jones, in St. John's*, Bedford City, Va. So. Ch., Nov. 6, 1890
Rosalie M., of Charles City, Va., and Herbert S. Saunders formerly of Richmond, Va., by the Rev. John P. Tyler, at the Glebe, Charles City Co., Va. So. Ch., Nov. 21, 1889
W. Pierce, of Washington, D. C., and Julia C., d. of the late Rev. Geo. Woodbridge, D.D., by the Rt. Rev. Wm. Pinkney* assisted by the Rev. Dr. Elliott of Washington, D.C., in Richmond, at the residence of the bride's mother. So. Ch., Feb. 27, 1879
William P., and Margaret D. Blackstone, by the Rev. John McNabb, in St. James' Church, Accomac C. H., Va. So. Ch., Nov. 10, 1887

BELLEN
Reuben A., and Adella J. Wilson, both of Nansemond Co., Va., but originally from Schoharie Co., N.Y., by the Rev. J. B. Craighill, in the Rectory of St. Paul's Church, Suffolk. So. Ch., Jan. 11, 1877

BELLINGER
Emily Shaffer, and Samuel Elmore Boney of Laurens, S.C., by the Rev. Thomas P. Baker, Walterboro, S. C. So. Ch., Jan. 16, 1909

BEMIS
Carrie Mae, d. of Mr. and Mrs. H. H. Bemis of Como, Miss., and the Rev. Richard H. Beasley of Lynchburg, Va., rector of Emmanuel Church, Bristol, Va., in Holy Innocents' Episcopal Church, Como, Miss. So. Ch., Sept. 25, 1937

BEMISS
Eli Lockert, of New Orleans, and Cyane Dandridge Williams of Alexandria, Va., by the Rev. T. G. Dashiell assisted by the Rev. Joshua Peterkin, in St. James' Church, Richmond. So. Ch., Jan. 16, 1890

BENDERT
Mary, of Kent Island, Md., and Henry Eckstorm, by the Rev. P. D. Thompson, at the residence of Mr. Frederick Fondelheight, Kent Island, Md. So. Ch., Jan. 12, 1888

BENEDICT
Lucy V., and the Rev. Charles D. Williams, by the Rev. Dr. Benedict, father of the bride and rector of St. Paul's assisted by the Rev. Dr. Pise and the Rev. Dr. Jaeger, formerly of Gambier, in St. Paul's Church, Cincinnati. So. Ch., Oct. 21, 1886

BENNET
Laura Dillon, eldest d. of William Bennet, Esq. of Burke Co., Ga., and Joseph Packard, Jr. of Virginia, by the Rt. Rev. John W. Beckwith, D.D., in Savannah. So. Ch., Apr. 23, 1868

BENNETT
Gertrude, eldest d. of the late Hon. J. M. Bennett of Weston, formerly Auditor of Virginia and Dr. Fleming Howell of Clarksburg, by the Rev. T. H. Lacy, in St. Paul's Church, Weston, W.Va. So. Ch., Oct. 8, 1891
James W., of Middlesex Co., Va., and Ellen T., d. of Yancey Sleet of Mathews Co., Va., by the Rev.

* Given as printed

MARRIAGE NOTICES IN THE SOUTHERN CHURCHMAN WITH DATES OF PUBLICATION

Peregrine Wroth, at Mathews C. H., Va. So. Ch., Mar. 18, 1875

Lorenzo T. (The Rev.), assistant minister of the Parish of Trinity Church, and Marina Bishop, d. of the late Jacob Smith, Esq. of East Haven, by the Rev. Dr. Croswell, New Haven, Conn. So. Ch., Aug. 9, 1839

Lucie V., and Dr. Frank Boyette of Clinton, N.C., by the Rev. C. O. Pruden, at the residence of the bride's mother, Mrs. M. A. Bennett, Chatham, Va. So. Ch., Jan. 5, 1888

Mary Lee, youngest d. of the late Hon. Jonathan M. and Margaret E. Bennett of Weston, W.Va., and William Duckett Bowie, s. of ex-Governor Bowie of Prince George's Co., Md., by the Rev. T. H. Lacy, at the residence of the bride's brother, Hon. Louis Bennett, Weston, W.Va. So. Ch., Nov. 27, 1890

W. G., and Alice Brannon, both of Weston, Lewis Co., W.Va., by the Rev. Andrew Fisher, in St. Paul's Church, Weston. So. Ch., Apr. 4, 1872

BENTLEY
Elizabeth Gay, d. of Efford B. and Lucy W. Bentley of Richmond, and the Rev. Frank J. Brooke of Philippi, W.Va., formerly of Richmond, by the Rev. Charles Minnigerode, D.D., in St. Paul's Church, Richmond, Va. So. Ch., Dec. 2, 1880

Elizabeth Logan, only d. of Mr. and Mrs. William C. Bentley, and Lt. Charles R. Irving of the First Virginia Medical Corps, by the Rev. W. Russell Bowie, D.D., rector of St. Paul's Church, at the residence of the bride's parents, 2417 Park Ave., Richmond, Va. So. Ch., Sept. 29, 1917

William Chamberlayne of Richmond, Va., and Lulu, youngest d. of the late Joseph Logan of Louisiana, by the Rev. Nowell Logan of Vicksburg, Miss., at Algoma*, Buckingham Co., Va., at the country residence of the bride's uncle, Gen. T. M. Logan. So. Ch., Dec. 10, 1891

BENTLY
Mary Amanda, youngest d. of Mrs. Lucy W. and the late E. B. Bently of Richmond, and Dr. Richard Heath Dabney, Prof. of History, University of Indiana, Bloomington, formerly of Virginia, by the Rev. Charles Minnigerode, D.D., in St. Paul's Church, Richmond, Va. So. Ch., June 28, 1888

Wm. G. (Maj.), of Richmond, and Nannie Lee Abbot, formerly of Georgetown, U. S., by the Rev. Geo. W. Dame, in the Church of the Epiphany, Danville. So. Ch., June 19, 1863

BENTON
George (The Rev.), Missionary to Crete, and Caroline, d. of Reuben Spencer of Richmond, Va., by the Rev. Bird Wilson, D.D., in St. Peter's Church. So. Ch., Sept. 9, 1836

BERGER
Mary, eldest d. of Mrs. M. A. and the late Rev. A. J. Berger of Rolling Side, Catonsville, Md., and John Caile Harrison, by

* Given as printed

MARRIAGE NOTICES IN THE SOUTHERN CHURCHMAN WITH DATES OF PUBLICATION

the Rev. J. S. B. Hodges, D.D., in St. Paul's Church, Baltimore. So. Ch., May 8, 1890

BERKELEY
Cornelia L., d. of the officiating clergyman, and S. H. Hackett, by the Rev. P. F. Berkeley, in Amelia Co., Va. So. Ch., Jan. 21, 1875

Edmonia, and B. Howson Hooe of Manassas, Va., by the Rev. W. A. Alrich, at the "White House", Hanover Co., Va. So. Ch., Oct. 7, 1880

Edmonia, fourth d. of the late Wm. H. Berkeley of King and Queen Co., Va., and the Rev. J. P. Lawrence, by the Rev. H. M. Jackson assisted by the Rev. Pike Powers, in Grace Church, Richmond, Va. So. Ch., Jan. 5, 1888

Edmund, late of Virginia, and Julia L., d. of G. H. Ramsey of Jackson, Tenn., by the Rev. N. B. Jones, in Jackson, Tenn. So. Ch., Oct. 23, 1879

Edmund, of Hanover Co., Va., and Lottie C. Breathed of Lynchburg, Va., by the Rev. T. M. Carson, at the residence of the bride's parents. So. Ch., Mar. 22, 1888

Edward F. (The Rev.), minister of Christ Church, Lexington, Ky., and Sarah Ann S., only d. of the late Francis F. Maury, by the Rev. M. F. Maury, in Bath Co., Ky. So. Ch., May 24, 1839

Fannie, d. of the late Edmund Berkeley, Esq. of Hanover Co., and Dr. W. B. Barham of Newsoms, Southampton Co., Va., by the Rev. W. A. Alrich, at the "White House", Hanover Co., Va. So. Ch., May 12, 1881

Fannie C., eldest d. of Col. Edward Berkeley of Prince William Co., and Richard Belches, Esq., formerly of Plymouth, England, now of Prince William Co., by the Rev. R. T. Brown, at the residence of the bride's father. So. Ch., Sept. 19, 1872

Frances A. T., d. of the late Dr. Berkeley of Frederick Co., Va., and Lt. James S. Davis of the U.S. Army, by the Rev. Philip Slaughter, at Berea, Prince William Co. So. Ch., Jan. 15, 1836

Frances Callender, youngest d. of the late Maj. William N. Berkeley of the University of Virginia, formerly of Aldie, Loudoun Co., and the Rev. Henry Horton Williams of Charlottesville, Va., formerly of Birkenhead, England, by the Rev. W. R. Mason. So. Ch., Oct. 9, 1909

Frances Campbell, only d. of Mr. and Mrs. Robert Carter Berkeley, and Dr. Karl Young of the University of Wisconsin, by the Rev. G. MacLaren Brydon, rector of Trinity Church, at Ellembrie, the residence of the bride's father, in Morgantown, W.Va. So. Ch., Aug. 26, 1911

Kate Spotswood, d. of the late Dr. E. Berkeley of Staunton, and Lt. W. T. Iglehart, C.S.A., of Annapolis, Md., by the Rev. J. A. Latane, at the residence of the bride's mother, in Staunton, Va. So. Ch., Aug. 7, 1863

Katherine Noland, youngest

MARRIAGE NOTICES IN THE SOUTHERN CHURCHMAN WITH DATES OF PUBLICATION

d. of Col. Edmund Berkeley of Prince William Co., and Capt. J. A. V. Feltus of Mississippi, by the Rev. B. T. Turner, in St. Paul's Church, Haymarket, Va. So. Ch., Oct. 13, 1892

L. A., third d. of the late Wm. H. Berkeley of King and Queen, and W. E. Briggs of Surry Co., by the Rev. Dr. Newton, at Wanderer's Rest. So. Ch., Nov. 13, 1873

Lavinia, d. of Dr. E. Berkeley of Staunton, Va., and Norborne Berkeley of Aldie, Loudoun Co., by the Rev. T. T. Castleman, at Staunton, Va. So. Ch., Dec. 20, 1849

Lucy Beverley, d. of Maj. William N. Berkeley of Albemarle Co., formerly of Loudoun, and Alexander B. Moore of Loudoun, by the Rev. J. S. Hanckle, D.D., in Christ Church, Charlottesville, Va. So. Ch., Feb. 24, 1881

Lulie T., d. of the officiating clergyman, and T. C. Haskins of Brunswick Co., by the Rev. P. F. Berkeley, at Airwell, Amelia Co., Va. So. Ch., Sept. 28, 1882

Margaret W., d. of Mary W. and Edmund Berkeley of Prince William Co., Va., and Addington G. Nance of Mississippi, by the Rev. A. P. Gray, at "Evergreen", the residence of the bride's parents. So. Ch., Sept. 25, 1884

Maria H., d. of the late Wm. H. Berkeley of King and Queen Co., Va., and Wm. P. Christian of Hanover Co., Va., by the Rev. Edward H. Ingle, rector, in St. John's Church, Big Lick. So. Ch., Nov. 15, 1877

Mary Latane, of Hanover Co., Va., and the Rev. William Augustus Alrich, rector of Emmanuel Church, Pittsylvania, by the Rev. Robt. Douglas Roller, at the "White House", St. Martin's Parish.**So. Ch., Jan. 3, 1878

Mary M., d. of Col. Edmund and Mary Berkeley of Prince William Co., Va., and Capt. J. S. McNeiley of Greenville, Miss., by the Rev. A. P. Gray assisted by the Rev. H. T. Sharp, at "Evergreen." So. Ch., June 30, 1881

Nannie C., of Staunton, Va., and John F. Brooke of Chicago, Ill., by the Rev. A. S. Berkeley, at the residence of Mrs. M. R. S. Berkeley, Staunton, Va. So. Ch., Sept. 3, 1874

Nannie R., eldest d. of William H. Berkeley of King and Queen Co., and Lancy Jones, Jr. of Hanover, by the Rev. Mr. Habersham, at Wanderer's Rest. So. Ch., Jan. 5, 1871

Norborne, of Aldie, Loudoun Co., and Lavinia, d. of Dr. E. Berkeley of Staunton, Va., by the Rev. T. T. Castleman, at Staunton, Va. So. Ch., Dec. 20, 1849

P. F. (The Rev.), and Mary Eppes, second d. of the late Richard N. Thweate*, by the Rev. Wm. V. Bowers, at Mantua in Chesterfield Co., Va. So. Ch., Sept. 15, 1837

P. J., and Mary, d. of the late John Y. Mason and gr. d. of Judge John Y. Mason, former Minister to

* Given as printed
** St. Martin's Parish is in Hanover County, Virginia (Journal ... Diocese of Virginia, Richmond, 1941)

MARRIAGE NOTICES IN THE SOUTHERN CHURCHMAN WITH DATES OF PUBLICATION

France, by the Rev. P. F. Berkeley, in St. John's Church, Grub Hill, Amelia Co., Va. So. Ch., Nov. 10, 1881

Richard F., and Sallie W. Scott of Gordonsville, by the Rev. L. R. Combs, at the residence of the bride's brother, J. W. Scott, M.D., Gordonsville, Va. So. Ch., Nov. 26, 1885

Robert C., of Hanover Co., and Fanny C., eldest d. of Lancelot Minor, Esq. of Amherst, by the Rev. Wm. H. Kinckle of Lynchburg, at "Briery Knowe", Amherst Co., Va. So. Ch., May 8, 1863

Wm. W., of King and Queen Co., and Bettie Sims, d. of the late Thomas C. Read of Roanoke Co., Va., by the Rev. L. B. Wharton, at Alta Monte, the residence of Mrs. Walter Preston. So. Ch., Sept. 8, 1870

BERKELY

Landon C., of Danville, and Annie P. Harrison of Hanover, by the Rev. Robert R. Claiborne, in Fork Church, Hanover Co., Va. So. Ch., Sept. 30, 1880

BERNARD

Alfred N., Esq., and Margaret B., d. of W. R. Mason, Esq., by the Rev. Mr. Friend, at Cleveland, King George Co., Va. So. Ch., Nov. 23, 1855

D. Meade, Jr., Esq., and Lucia B. Morrison, by the Rev. Dr. J. H. Morrison and the Rev. Otis A. Glazebrook, in St. Andrew's Church, Brunswick Co., Va. So. Ch., Jan. 26, 1871

Eliza Frances, d. of the late William Bernard, Jr., Esq. of Belle Grove, King George Co., Va., and Thomas Semmes of Alexandria, D.C., by the Rev. Mr. Friend, at Port Royal, Va. So. Ch., Dec. 6, 1839

George S., and Fanny, d. of Samuel J. Rutherfoord of Amelia Co., by the Rev. P. F. Berkely, at Cassels, the residence of the bride's father. So. Ch., June 30, 1870

BERRY

Frances Miriam, d. of Lewis Berry, Esq. of Whitesborough, and the Rev. Benjamin W. Whitcher, rector of St. Peter's Church, Oriskany, by the Rev. Mr. Hull, in St. Peter's Church, Oriskany. So. Ch., Jan. 29, 1847

H. Thacker, and Nannie Atkinson Grymes, by the Rev. John McNabb, Woodstock, King George Co., Va. So. Ch., Jan. 12, 1893

Helen J., second d. of Hon. Taylor Berry of Amherst, and Holbrook Rion, Esq. of Winnsboro, S.C., by the Rev. Wm. Meade Clark, in Ascension Church, Amherst C.H., Va. So. Ch., May 21, 1885*

James M., and Abbie Bell, both of Liberty, Va., by the Rev. John K. Mason, at the residence of O. P. Bell, Liberty, Va. So. Ch., June 15, 1882

John T., of Paris, Tex., and Ellen Dupuy, youngest d. of the late Thomas McKinney of Lynchburg, Va., by the Rev. George Beckett, in St. Peter's Church, Columbia, Tenn. So. Ch., Nov. 21, 1872

Mildred, d. of Hon. Taylor Berry, and Dr. C. R. Harding, Prof. of Greek

---

* A notice appears in the issue of May 14, 1885 identical with this, except that "Holbrook" is written "Holbrooke"

MARRIAGE NOTICES IN THE SOUTHERN CHURCHMAN WITH DATES OF PUBLICATION

at Davidson College, N. C., by the Rev. Dr. Harding, at Edgewood, the residence of the bride's parents, Amherst, Va. So. Ch., Sept. 13, 1888

Rosalie T., d. of Henry Berry, Esq. of Shepherdstown, Va., and Dr. John C. Vanwyck of Baltimore, by the Rev. Dr. Andrews. So. Ch., Apr. 23, 1858

Rose, eldest d. of Taylor Berry, Esq. of Amherst C. H., Va., and Charles Lunsford of Petersburg, Va., by the Rev. O. S. Bunting, at the residence of the bride's father. So. Ch., May 12, 1881

William P., Esq., of Eden, King George Co., Va., and Ella, d. of the late Wm. A. H. Ashton of King George Co., by the Rev. Henry Wall, Marmion. So. Ch., Dec. 7, 1865

BERRYMAN
John Strother, and Eliza Lane, d. of Judge Montgomery Slaughter, by the Rev. Dr. E. C. Murdaugh, in Trinity Church, Fredericksburg, Va. So. Ch., Feb. 21, 1884

BETTICHER
Charles E. (The Rev.), Associate Editor of the Spirit of Missions, and Margaret Copeland, d. of the late Mr. and Mrs. William B. Graves of Baltimore, by the Rev. Hobart Smith, rector, in St. Thomas' Church, Garrison Forest, Md. So. Ch., May 4, 1918

BEVAN
Archibald Buchanan, and Mary Mann Meade, both of Clarke Co., Va., by the Rev. Edward H. Ingle, in the Church of the Epiphany, Washington, D.C. So. Ch., Feb. 6, 1909

BEVERLEY
Maria, and Walter Johnson, by the Rev. L. B. Combs, at the colored mission chapel near Gordonsville. So. Ch., Dec. 3, 1885

Robert, Jr., and Richardetta E., fifth d. of Maj. Richard H. Carter, by the Rev. John McGill, at Glenwelby, Fauquier Co., Va., residence of the bride's parents. So. Ch., Dec. 13, 1879

BEVERLY
Carter (The Rev.), rector of the church at Ivy, Va., and Emily Tiffany, by the Rt. Rev. H. St. George Tucker, D.D., Bishop of Virginia, at Warrenton, Va. So. Ch., Sept. 24, 1932

Frances Susan (Mrs.), of Nottoway Co., and Francis W. Epes, Esq., by the Rev. Thomas E. Locke, Lunenburg, Va. So. Ch., Sept. 20, 1839

Harry Stanard, and Florence Lacy Tuggle, by the Rev. T. P. Eppes assisted by the Rev. W. H. Milton, at "The Grove", the residence of the bride's father, in Nottoway Co., Va. So. Ch., Dec. 28, 1893

Virginia, third d. of Robt. Beverly, Esq. of Fauquier Co., and the Rev. John McGill, by the Rev. R. M. McKim, in

MARRIAGE NOTICES IN THE SOUTHERN CHURCHMAN WITH DATES OF PUBLICATION

the Episcopal Church, The Plains, Fauquier Co. So. Ch., July 3, 1873

BIBB
C. Belle, of Nelson Co., Va., and John A. Page of Roanoke, Va., by the Rev. Davis M. Wood, in Trinity Church, Nelson Co., Va. So. Ch., Dec. 16, 1886

Mary F., d. of B. C. Bibb, Esq. of Baltimore, and Dr. Walton Saunders of Essex Co., Va., by the Rev. A. M. Randolph, at the residence of the bride's parents, in Baltimore. So. Ch., Nov. 16, 1882

BICKERSTITH
Amy, d. of the first mentioned divine [the Rev. E. A. Bickerstith], and the Rev. Francis K. Aglionby, A.M., s. of Charles Aglionby, Esq. of Jefferson Co., W. Va., by the Rev. E. A. Bickerstith assisted by the Rev. E. Bickerstith and the Rev. F. T. Charasse, in Christ Church, Hampstead, London, N.W. So. Ch., Sept. 14, 1876

BIDGOOD
John W., and Minnie S. Gary, by the Rev. J. B. Craighill, at Suffolk, Va. So. Ch., Jan. 21, 1875

BIGGS
Fannie Chase, and James Grist Staton, by the Rt. Rev. Robert Strange, Bishop of East Carolina, in the Church of the Advent, Williamston, N.C. So. Ch., Sept. 12, 1908

BILLOPP

Nellie, d. of the Rev. Thomas F. Billopp, and George W. Brooke, Esq., all of Prince George's Co., Md., by the Rev. Dr. Lewin, in the Brick Church, Queen Anne Parish. So. Ch., Apr. 22, 1875

BILLUPS -
Mary Adelaide, of Mathews Co., Va., and Thos. S. Tabb, Esq. of Taddsburg, Gloucester Co., Va., by the Rev. Mr. Carraway, in Trinity Church, Kingston Parish.* So. Ch., Nov. 23, 1854

BINFORD
Bertie, of Bedford, and Pleasant Dawson of Amherst, by the Rev. R. J. McBryde, at Forest Home, Bedford Co. So. Ch., Dec. 23, 1869

BIRCHETT
Laura Townes, only d. of the late Robert Birchett of Petersburg, and Dr. John M. Pleasants of Dinwiddie Co., by the Rev. C. J. Gibson, in Grace Church, Petersburg. So. Ch., July 3, 1857

BIRD
Benjamin L. (Dr.), and Nannie Ogle, d. of John Hodges, Esq., by the Rev. Wm. Hodges, at Omaha, Prince George's Co., Md. So. Ch., June 25, 1868

Gilbert Bonham, s. of the late Robert Bird, deputy Surgeon General of the East India Medical Service, and Mary Bowdoin, youngest d. of Carter H. and Lelia G. Page of Albemarle Co., Va., by the Rev. J. S. Hanckel assisted by the Rev. H. B. Lee, at the residence of the bride's father. So. Ch., Mar. 10, 1892

Henry Buchanan, of

---

* Kingston Parish is in Mathews County, Virginia (Journal ... Diocese of Virginia, Richmond, 1941)

MARRIAGE NOTICES IN THE SOUTHERN CHURCHMAN WITH DATES OF PUBLICATION

Del., and Hannah Maria, third d. of Allen Williams, Esq., by the Rev. F. M. Whittle, at Mount Hebron, Clarke Co., Va. So. Ch., Feb. 8, 1855

J. Edward, and Jennie C. Herman, both of Baltimore, by the Rev. Julius E. Grammer, D.D., in Baltimore. So. Ch., Nov. 13, 1884

Jas. A., of Baltimore, and Judith Eleanor Ewbank*, by the Rev. Edmund Withers, South Hill, Essex Co. So. Ch., Dec. 24, 1858

S. Moylan (The Rev.), and Johnnie E., youngest d. of the late John W. Alfriend of Dinwiddie Co., by the Rev. W. H. Platt and the Rev. C. J. Gibson, in Calvary Church, Dinwiddie Co. So. Ch., June 5, 1863

William, and M. E., d. of E. C. Taylor, by the Rev. P. F. Berkeley, at Greenwood, Hanover Co. So. Ch., Nov. 29, 1866

BIRKETT
James W., of England, and Edna Vaulx, d. of Edgar V. and Eugenia A. Weir of Prince William Co., Va., by the Rev. A. P. Gray, in Trinity Church, Manassas, Va. So. Ch., Dec. 29, 1881

BISHOP
Fannie A., and John W. Durham, both of Albemarle, by the Rev. Thomas E. Locke, at the residence of Shadrack Bishop. So. Ch., June 17, 1886

Joseph, of Albemarle, and Fanny McGrath of Ireland, by the Rev. Wm. M. Nelson, at the residence of the Rev. Joseph Wilmer, Albemarle Co. So. Ch., Nov. 5, 1858

BISSELL
Martha E. Patterson, d. of the Rt. Rev. Dr. Bissell of Burlington, Vt., and Willard S. Pope, by the Rev. Rufus Clarke, Jr., rector of St. Paul's Church, in Detroit, Mich. So. Ch., Nov. 2, 1882

S. B. S. (The Rev.), and Frances M., d. of Rensselaer Havens, Esq., by the Rev. Dr. Spring, in the City of New York. So. Ch., Dec. 20, 1839

BIXBY
Mary Pelia, of Lock Haven, and the Rev. Samuel B. Dalrymple, rector of the parish, by the Rev. Robert B. Heet, in St. Paul's Church, Lock Haven. So. Ch., June 3, 1859

BLACK
J. Thomas, of Bastross Co., Tex., and Maida W., eldest d. of O. P. Winston formerly of Louisa Co., Va., by the Rev. J. W. Phillips of Austin, in Bastross Co., Tex. So. Ch., Feb. 18, 1875

Wm. J., and Virginia F. Price, both of Lynchburg, by the Rev. T. M. Garson, in St. Paul's Church, Lynchburg. So. Ch., Mar. 14, 1872

BLACKBURN
Charlotte Moncure, of Alexandria, Va., and Thomas Martin Shepherd of Batopilas, Mexico, by the Rev. Henry Easter, at El Paso, Tex., in St. Clement's Episcopal

---

* Given as printed

MARRIAGE NOTICES IN THE SOUTHERN CHURCHMAN WITH DATES OF PUBLICATION

Church. So. Ch., Jan. 8, 1910
Ellen T., d. of the late Dr. R. S. Blackburn of Clarke Co., Va., and Thomas B. Washington of Jefferson Co., W.Va., by the Rev. Dr. G. H. Norton, D.D., in Alexandria. So. Ch., Nov. 12, 1874
Isabella M., of Volcano, and John Salisbury of Pittsburgh, Pa., by the Rev. S. D. Tomkins, in Emmanuel Church, Volcano, Wood, W.Va. So. Ch., Sept. 17, 1874
Jane W., d. of the late Dr. R. S. Blackburn of Clarke Co., Va., and F. Berger Moran of Charlottesville, formerly of New York, by the Rev. T. F. Martin assisted by the Rev. H. Suter, at Weehaw, the residence of the bride's mother. So. Ch., July 13, 1871
Kate M., d. of Mrs. Elizabeth H. Blackburn of Bowling Green, and the Rev. G. C. Waller, rector of Zion Church, Louisville, by the Rev. E. T. Perkins, D.D., rector of St. Paul's Church, Louisville, in Christ Church, Bowling Green, Ky. So. Ch., Mar. 16, 1876
Sarah E., and W. B. Harris, Esq., both of Clarke Co., Va., by the Rev. Dr. Norton, in Alexandria. So. Ch., June 18, 1874
Virginia E., and John R. Marchant, by the Rev. J. Hervey Hundley, at "Barn Elms", Middlesex Co., Va. So. Ch., Feb. 29, 1872

BLACKER
Annabella Elizabeth, d. of Mr. and Mrs. M. M. Blacker, and Walter Frank Gustave Degacher, all of Amelia Co., Va., but recently of England, by the Rev. P. F. Berkeley, at Hawbranch*, the residence of the bride's parents. So. Ch., Apr. 26, 1877
Rosa M., and William W. Astell, by the Rev. P. F. Berkeley, at Haw Branch*. the residence of the bride's parents, Amelia Co. So. Ch., June 30, 1881
Theodosia Violet, d. of M. M. and Mrs. F. Blacker, and Stannus Henry Handcock, all of Amelia Co., Va., by the Rev. P. F. Berkeley, in St. John's Church, Grubb Hill, Amelia Co., Va. So. Ch., Oct. 4, 1883

BLACKFORD
B. Lewis, of Washington City (late of Virginia), and Nannie Beirne, youngest d. of the late J. B. Steenbergen of Virginia, by the Rt. Rev. H. C. Lay, D.D., Bishop of Easton, in St. Paul's Church, Baltimore. So. Ch., July 29, 1869
Benjamin (Dr.), of Lynchburg, Va., and Mrs. Emily Byrd, d. of the late Robert Neilson of Baltimore, by the Rev. Thomas U. Dudley, in

* Given as printed

MARRIAGE NOTICES IN THE SOUTHERN CHURCHMAN WITH DATES OF PUBLICATION

Christ Church, Baltimore. So. Ch., Jan. 26, 1871*

Charles M., of Lynchburg, and Susan Leigh, d. of the late Thomas M. Colston of Loudoun, by the Rev. D. C. T. Davis, at "Hill and Dale", the residence of Raleigh Colston, Esq. of Albemarle. So. Ch., Feb. 29, 1856

Emily Chapman, only d. of Col. Eugene Blackford of Baltimore Co., Md., and Arthur E. Poultney of Baltimore, by the Rev. E. Lawrence, rector, assisted by the Rev. J. S. Lindsay, D.D. of Boston, Mass., in St. Mark's Church, Pikesville, Md. So. Ch., June 16, 1892

Eugene, of Lynchburg, Va., and Rebecca C., d. of John M. Gordon, Esq. of Baltimore, by the Rev. Randolph H. McKim of Portsmouth assisted by the Rev. George Leeds, D.D., in Grace Church, Baltimore. So. Ch., July 4, 1867

Launcelot Minor, principal of the Episcopal High School, and Eliza Chew Ambler, youngest d. of the officiating clergyman, the Rev. John Ambler assisted by the Rt. Rev. Alfred M. Randolph, D.D., LL.D., in the Chapel of the Theological Seminary, near Alexandria, Va. So. Ch., Aug. 14, 1884

Lizzie Robertson, and Arthur Selden Lloyd, by the Rev. John J. Lloyd assisted by the Rev. Wm. M. Clark, in St. Thomas' Church, Abingdon, Va. So. Ch., July 15, 1880

Nannie C., only d. of Charles M. Blackford, Esq., and Samuel T. Withers, all of Lynchburg, Va., by the Rev. T. M. Carson, in St. Paul's Church, Lynchburg, Va. So. Ch., Feb. 22, 1883

William (formerly of Lynchburg), and Alice B. Potter, d. of the late J. B. Steenbergen of Virginia, by the Rev. M. Mahan, D.D., in St. Paul's Church, Baltimore. So. Ch., Oct. 14, 1869

Wm. W., and Mary, eldest d. of Wyndham Robertson, Esq., by the Rev. Mr. Woodbridge, in St. Paul's Church, Richmond, Va. So. Ch., Jan. 18, 1856

BLACKIE

Marion Grieve, d. of the late Dr. George S. Blackie of Nashville, Tenn., and S. Malone Gibson of Galveston, Tex., by the Rev. M. Cabell Martin, in St. Peter's Church, Nashville, Tenn. So. Ch., Dec. 2, 1886

Robt. (publisher), of Glasgow, Scotland, and Lucy, third d. of Brodie Strachan Herndon, M.D., of Savannah, by the Rev. Thos. Boone, rector of Christ Church, at the residence of Capt. Mercer, Savannah, Ga. So. Ch., Nov. 29, 1877

BLACKISTON

James W., and Mary L. Thomas, both of Kent Island, Queen Anne's Co., by the Rev. P. D. Thompson, in Kingsley Chapel, Kent Island, Md. So. Ch., Oct. 8,

---

* This notice appears in issue of Jan. 19, 1871, with the exception that "Neilson" is written "Nelson"

MARRIAGE NOTICES IN THE SOUTHERN CHURCHMAN WITH DATES OF PUBLICATION

1885
BLACKSTONE
  Margaret D., and William P. Bell, by the Rev. John McNabb, in St. James' Church, Accomac C.H., Va. So. Ch., Nov. 10, 1887
BLACKWELL
  Daphne Jean, and Richard Cary Horner of Bristol, Tenn., formerly of Fauquier Co., Va., in the Presbyterian Church in Vicksburg, Miss. So. Ch., Feb. 6, 1909
  Edgar, and Sarah A. Harding, both of Northumberland Co., Va., by the Rev. H. T. Bacon assisted by the Rev. H. L. Derby, in "Rehoboth Church." So. Ch., Dec. 16, 1880
  Edwin, professor in Bethel Academy, and Nannie S. Leavell, by the Rev. W. T. Leavell assisted by the Rt. Rev. Bishop Peterkin, in St. Stephen's Church, Culpeper C.H. So. Ch., Nov. 28, 1878
  Elias E., and Fannie G. Blackwell, both of Fauquier Co., by the Rev. George W. Nelson, in St. James' Church, Warrenton, Va. So. Ch., Feb. 9, 1882
  Fannie G., and Elias E. Blackwell, both of Fauquier Co., by the Rev. George W. Nelson, in St. James' Church, Warrenton, Va. So. Ch., Feb. 9, 1882
  Joseph H., of Charlottesville, and Mary Saunders, by the Rev. J. Y. Downman, at the residence of the bride's brother-in-law, Charles W. Green. So. Ch., May 2, 1889
  Mary Eliza, d. of the late Robert Blackwell, and Opie D. Jordan, all of Isle of Wight Co., by the Rev. David Barr, in Isle of Wight Co., Va. So. Ch., May 23, 1889
  Mary J., and Dr. Thomas W. Smith, both of Fauquier Co., by the Rev. G. W. Nelson, at the home of the bride. So. Ch., Sept. 23, 1886
BLAIN
  Daniel (The Rev.), and Mary Louisa, d. of Dr. John C. Mercer, by the Rev. S. W. Blain, in Williamsburg, Va. So. Ch., Feb. 7, 1867
BLAIR
  Claudia M., d. of the late Wm. T. and Mrs. Jane R. Blair, and J. Osborn Haw, by the Rev. Joshua Peterkin, at the residence of Charles W. Goddin, 605 West Grace Street, Richmond, Va. So. Ch., Apr. 26, 1883
  Heningham E., d. of Col. Walter D. Blair of Richmond, and Maj. John H. Claiborne, by the Rev. Dr. J. Peterkin. So. Ch., Sept. 17, 1868
  John D., and Mattie E., d. of William S. Archer, by the Rev. Landon R. Mason, at the residence of the bride's father, 806 Park Ave., Richmond. So. Ch., Oct. 1, 1891
  John S., and Ellen Albert, by the Rev. William H. Laird, in St. John's Church, Washington, D.C. So. Ch., July 13, 1893
BLAKE
  Hannah G., and Col. Wm. E. Gaskins, both of Fauquier

MARRIAGE NOTICES IN THE SOUTHERN CHURCHMAN WITH DATES OF PUBLICATION

Co., Va., by the Rev. Jno. S. Lindsay, at the bride's residence. So. Ch., Dec. 25, 1873

BLAKEY
Maria Ann, d. of Capt. W. P. Blakey of Richmond, Va., and Blanchard C. Miller of Grayson, Carter Co., Ky., by the Rev. T. G. Dashiell, at the residence of the bride's father. So. Ch., Dec. 23, 1880

BLAND
Emma Randolph, second d. of John B. Bland, and Samuel M. Selden of Lynchburg, Va., by the Rev. J. C. Dinwiddie, at the residence of the bride's father at Orange C.H. So. Ch., July 10, 1873

BLANKENSHIP
Hattie Cabell, d. of the late Thomas H. Blankenship of Richmond, and Theodore Hacker of New York, N.Y., by the Rev. Mr. Strong, in St. John's Episcopal Church, Savannah, Ga. So. Ch., Dec. 18, 1890

BLANKINGSHIP
Nannie, d. of the late Thos. O. Blankingship of Manchester, and John H. Huston of Comanche, Texas, by the Rev. J. J. Clopton, at Manchester, Va. So. Ch., Oct. 2, 1884

BLANTON
Benj. W. B., of Cumberland Co., and Virginia L. of Richmond, d. of the late Col. Francis Wicker, by the Rev. H. S. Kepler, rector of St. John's Church, Richmond. So. Ch., Feb. 22, 1856

C. W., and Martha K., eldest d. of Charles Bugg, Esq., all of Farmville, Va., by the Rev. A. S. Lloyd, in John's Memorial Church, Farmville. So. Ch., Sept. 25, 1884

Rosalie, d. of J. C. and S. E. Blanton of Cumberland Co., Va., and B. I. Grigg, by the Rev. F. Stringfellow, in Grace Church, Ca Ira, Va. So. Ch., May 20, 1880

BLEDSOE
Anna, youngest d. of the late Dr. Albert T. Bledsoe of Alexandria, and Edgar E. Dinwiddie, by the Rev. H. Suter, in Christ Church, Alexandria. So. Ch., Feb. 17, 1881

Emily Albertine, d. of Prof. Bledsoe of the University of Virginia, and Wm. Dinwiddie of Greenwood, Albemarle Co., by the Rev. R. K. Meade, at the University of Virginia. So. Ch., July 15, 1864

Lillie M., d. of Dr. A. T. Bledsoe of Baltimore, and J. F. Wayland of Albemarle Co., Va., by the Rev. T. U. Dudley, in Baltimore. So. Ch., July 21, 1870

Sophia, d. of Dr. A. T. Bledsoe of the University of Virginia, and James B. Herrick, by the Rev. Dr. William Sparrow, in Christ Church, Charlottesville, Va. So. Ch., July 6, 1860

Thomas A., Esq., of Staunton, Va., and Edmonia R., youngest d. of the late E. R. Page, Esq. of

MARRIAGE NOTICES IN THE SOUTHERN CHURCHMAN WITH DATES OF PUBLICATION

Campbell C.H., Va., by the Rev. R. A. Cobbs, at "Austed", near "Hawks Nest", Fayette Co., W.Va. So. Ch., May 1, 1879

BLEIGHT
A. C., of Fauquier Co., and Grace A., second d. of F. A. C. Terrett of Fairfax Co., by the Rev. John McGill, in Zion Church, Fairfax Co. So. Ch., Oct. 4, 1877

BLINCOE
Bettie, d. of the late Samson Blincoe, Esq. of Leesburg, Loudoun Co., Va., and Philip H. Hooff of Alexandria, Va., by the Rev. George Adie. So. Ch., Feb. 19, 1847

Mary, and the Rev. William N. Ward of Bowling Green, Caroline Co., Va., by the Rev. George Adie, in Leesburg, Va. So. Ch., Aug. 26, 1836

BLISS
See also WASHINGTON
Martha B. (Mrs.)

BLODGETT
Edward W., of Pawtucket, R. I., and Caroline A. Morgan of Fauquier Co., Va., by the Rev. George W. Nelson, in St. James' Church, Warrenton, Va. So. Ch., Mar. 3, 1887

BLOSCHAM
Wm. D., of Tallahassee Fla., and Mary C. Davis of Tallahassee, Fla., by the Rev. T. E. Locke, in St. Paul's Church, Lynchburg, Va. So. Ch., Nov. 7, 1856

BLOW
Jennie, d. of Judge George Blow of Norfolk, and E. W. Hoff, by the Rev. Dr. Barton, in Christ Church, Norfolk, Va. So. Ch., Sept. 28, 1882

William, and Lavinia Cargill, by the Rev. Henry C. Lay, Norfolk, Va. So. Ch., Apr. 9, 1847

BLUM
Ernest, of Richmond, and Mary E., eldest d. of Maj. Jno. D. Richardson of Clarke Co., Va., by the Rev. T. F. Martin, at the residence of the bride's father, Fairfield. So. Ch., Apr. 8, 1869

BLUME
John A., of Bath Co., Va., and Ada C., d. of Dr. John H. Freeman of Rockbridge Co., Va., by the Rev. Dr. W. N. Pendleton, at Spring Bower, the residence of the bride's father. So. Ch., Nov. 9, 1871

John A., and Eleanor Conrad, eldest d. of S. J. Campbell, all of Lexington, Va., by the Rev. W. S. Campbell of London, Ohio, in Grace Memorial Church, Lexington, Va. So. Ch., Nov. 6, 1884

Louise H., and George D. Moore, both of Charles Town, W.Va., by the Rev. R. J. McBryde, D.D., at St. George's Rectory, Fredericksburg, Va. So. Ch., June 8, 1907

BLUNT
Elizabeth, and George Dillard, both of Hanover Co., Va., by the Rev. Curtis Grubb, at the residence of the bride. So. Ch., Feb. 15, 1883

BOCOCK
Rosa, and Henry Gibbs, all

MARRIAGE NOTICES IN THE SOUTHERN CHURCHMAN WITH DATES OF PUBLICATION

of Albemarle, by the Rev.
T. E. Locke, at Woodstock,
the residence of the bride's
mother. So. Ch., Sept.
26, 1889

BOGARDUS
Ellen Haile, d. of the late
John J. Haile, Esq. of
Plattsburg, N.J., and the
Rev. George S. Mallory,
D.D., by the Rev. J. H.
Chesley, in St. John's
Church, Hampton, Va. So.
Ch., Dec. 21, 1882

BOGART
Anna Wilhelmina, eldest d.
of Wm. S. Bogart, and
Robert H. Walthour, all of
Savannah, by the Rev.
Charles H. Strong, in St.
John's Church, Savannah,
Ga. So. Ch., Mar. 1,
1883

BOGGS
Bessie M'C., elder d. of
Gen. Wm. R. Boggs of
the Virginia Agricultural
and Mechanical College,
and Wm. B. Taylor of
Richmond, by the Rev.
Nelson P. Dame, in the
Episcopal Church in
Blacksburg, Va. So. Ch.,
Dec. 18, 1879

Clara L., and James L.
Rawlins, both of Spotsyl-
vania Co., Va., by the
Rev. Wm. W. Greene, at
"Livingston", Spotsyl-
vania Co. So. Ch., Feb.
15, 1872

Eliza H., d. of Lewis A.
Boggs, Esq., and Lt.
Valentine M. Johnson of
Marion, Ala., by the Rev.
William W. Greene, at
Livingston, Spotsylvania
Co., Va. So. Ch., May 10,
1861

BOKER

James B., of Middleburg,
Loudoun Co., and Sallie C.
Barksdale, by the Rev. Geo.
W. Dame, at Whitlock,
Halifax Co. So. Ch.,
July 15, 1869

BOLLING
Anna Bland, youngest d. of
Robert Bolling, Esq. of
Brunswick, and the Rev.
Thomas M. Ambler, by the
Rev. Churchill J. Gibson,
in Grace Church, Petersburg.
So. Ch., May 30, 1856

Bartlett, of Petersburg,
and Meta, d. of the late
Col. Charles Stuart of
Alexandria, by the Rev.
Henderson Suter, in Christ
Church, Alexandria. So.
Ch., June 23, 1881

Jane Rolfe, d. of the late
Col. Wm. Bolling, and
Robert Skipwith, by the
Rev. J. P. B. Wilmer,
at Bolling Hall, Goochland
Co., Va. So. Ch., July
16, 1847

John M., of New York City,
and Margaret P., d. of the
late Judge Richard W.
Walker, by the Rev. J. M.
Bannister, D.D., at the
residence of the bride's
mother at Huntsville,
Ala. So. Ch., Nov. 24,
1881

Julia C., eldest d. of
Thomas Bolling, Esq. of
Goochland Co., Va., and
P. B. Cabell of Nelson
Co., by the Rev. T. F.
Martin, at Bolling's
Island. So. Ch., Mar.
8, 1861

Pocahontas, d. of Robert
Bolling, Esq. of Bucking-
ham Co., Va., and the Rev.
W. C. Meredith, by the
Rev. Olcott Bulkley, at

MARRIAGE NOTICES IN THE SOUTHERN CHURCHMAN WITH DATES OF PUBLICATION

Chellow. So. Ch., June 11, 1847
Samuel M., of Fauquier Co., and Elizabeth B., d. of Hon. James P. Holcombe of Bedford Co., Va., by the Rev. Edward H. Ingle of Roanoke, at "Bellvue", the residence of the bride's father. So. Ch., Sept. 12, 1872

BOLTON
Cornelius Winter (The Rev.), rector of Christ Church, Pelham, and Cornelia, eldest d. of Cornelius G. Van Rensselaer of Greenbush, by the Rev. Alexander Dickson, at Greenbush. So. Ch., Sept. 26, 1856

BOND
Ronald Moore, of Port Deposit, Md., and Lucy Calvert, d. of Thomas Chandler and Lucy Walke Cruikshank, by the Rev. Roger Atkinson Walke of Tokio, Japan, in St. Stephen's Chapel, Cecilton, Md. So. Ch., Oct. 23, 1909

BONEY
Samuel Elmore, of Laurens, S.C., and Emily Shaffer Bellinger, by the Rev. Thomas P. Baker, at Walterboro, S.C. So. Ch., Jan. 16, 1909

BONNER
J. W. (Prof.), of Marion Co., W.Va., and Mary W. of Weston, d. of Mrs. S. A. V. Smith and the late Isaac Smith of Williamsburg, Va., and niece of Hon. W. E. Lively of Weston, by the Rev. T. H. Lacy, in St. Paul's Church, Weston, W. Va. So. Ch., June 28, 1888

BONNEY
George L., and Nellie L. Woodhouse, both of Princess Anne, by the Rev. W. R. Savage, in Eastern Shore Chapel, Princess Anne Co., Va. So. Ch., Jan. 28, 1886

BONSAL
Fannie L., d. of Stephen Bonsal, and Walter B. Brooks, Jr., by the Rev. J. S. B. Hodges, D.D., in St. Paul's Church, Baltimore. So. Ch., Dec. 27, 1883

BOOKER
Betty, and David Leary, both of Amelia Co., Va., by the Rev. P. F. Berkeley, at the residence of the bride's mother. So. Ch., Dec. 12, 1872

Carrie, d. of the late George T. Booker, of Richmond, and the Rev. Robert Douglas Roller of St. Martin's Parish, Hanover Co., Va. (formerly of Rockingham Co., Va.), by the Rev. Charles Minnigerode, D.D., at the residence of the bride's father, in Richmond. So. Ch., Nov. 1, 1877

Henry Wise, and Fannie, d. of Maj. Baker P. Lee, by the Rev. J. J. Gravatt, in St. John's Church, Hampton, Va. So. Ch., June 29, 1882

John, of Prince Edward, and Nannie, d. of Josiah Shepperson, Esq. of Campbell Co., by the Rev. T. E. Locke, at Cottage Hill, Charlotte Co. So. Ch., June 26, 1857

Judson H. (M.D.), of Northumberland Co., and Grace

MARRIAGE NOTICES IN THE SOUTHERN CHURCHMAN WITH DATES OF PUBLICATION

A., d. of George C. Thomas of Berryville, Va., by the Rev. P. P. Phillips, at Berryville, Va. So. Ch., Dec. 10, 1885

L. L., of Las Vegas, Hot Springs, N.M., formerly of Virginia, and Bessie O. G., d. of the late Capt. James Welby Armstrong and gr.d. of the late Wm. A. Stephenson, Esq. of Upperville, Fauquier Co., Va., by the Rev. Stephen H. Greene of St. John's Church, St. Louis, Mo., at the residence of T. H. Simpson, Logansport, Ind. So. Ch., Dec. 23, 1886

Thomas H., and Alice Worsham, both of Amelia Co., Va., by the Rev. P. F. Berkeley, at the bride's residence. So. Ch., Dec. 12, 1872

Y. Evens, and Sallie W., d. of the late Dr. F. Evens, all of Amelia Co., by the Rev. P. F. Berkeley, at the residence of the bride's uncle, George Wiley, Amelia Co. So. Ch., June 5, 1884

BOOL
P. H., and Mary A. Ward, by the Rev. J. B. Craighill, at the residence of Mrs. Tabitha Ward, Northampton Co., Va. So. Ch., Apr. 22, 1869

BOON
Virginia Kent, niece of Charles Boon of Luke, Md., and Simon Casady III, s. of the officiating clergyman, the Rt. Rev. Thomas Casady, D.D., Bishop of Oklahoma, in Oklahoma City, Okla. So. Ch., July 1, 1933

BOONE
Caroline Wilding, and Mr. Jan-Rhein, Charge d'affaires for the Netherlands, by the Rt. Rev. William J. Boone, D.D., father of the bride, at the Netherlands Consulate, Shanghai, China, and later in St. John's Memorial Church. So. Ch., June 26, 1890

Thomas (The Rev.), rector of Christ Church, Savannah, Ga., and Anna Sterges, second d. of the late Hon. John Henry Hedley of Clifton, Staten Island, N.Y., by the Rev. John C. Eccleston, the rector of the parish, in St. John's Church, Clifton, Staten Island. So. Ch., Mar. 4, 1886

Wm. J. (The Rev.), of Eufaula, Ala., and Mary Caroline, d. of Charles A. De Saussure, Esq., by the Rev. C. P. Gadsden, in St. Luke's Church, Charleston, S.C. So. Ch., Feb. 4, 1869

William J. (The Rev.), and Henrietta F., d. of the late John R. Harris of Brooklyn, N.Y., by the Rev. Elliot H. Thomson, in the Chapel of the Nativity, at Wuchang, China. So. Ch., Aug. 23, 1877

BOOTES
Elizabeth, d. of Samuel Bootes, and Cantwell Clark of Newcastle Co., Del., by the Rev. John Johns of Baltimore, in Georgetown. So. Ch., Dec. 22, 1837

BOOTH
Edwin G. (Dr.), of Nottoway Co., Va., and Clara H., d.

MARRIAGE NOTICES IN THE SOUTHERN CHURCHMAN WITH DATES OF PUBLICATION

of John A. Thomson, Esq. of Jefferson Co., W.Va., by the Rev. T. F. Martin, in Grace Church, Berryville, Va. So. Ch., Oct. 20, 1870

BORLAND
Thomas R., of Norfolk, and Carrie Barney of Richmond, by the Rev. Charles Minnigerode, in St. Paul's Church, Richmond. So. Ch., Jan. 1, 1880

BOSSIEUX
Cyrus, and M. Parker, youngest d. of the late Nathaniel L. Savage of New Kent Co., Va., by the Rev. Wm. Norwood, D.D., in Richmond, Va. So. Ch., Aug. 10, 1871

Virginius, and Mrs. Delia E. Bradley, both of Henrico Co., by the Rev. Henry Wall, D.D. So. Ch., Jan. 5, 1871

BOSTON
Susan V. (Mrs.), of Fluvanna Co., Va., and Capt. Richard M. Graves, C.S.A., by the Rev. Wm. McGuire, at Buchanan, Botetourt Co. So. Ch., Dec. 4, 1863

BOSWELL
Thomas T. (Col.), of Mecklenburg Co., and Amanda M. Hundley of Halifax, by the Rev. John T. Clark, at Mount Laurel. So. Ch., Nov. 22, 1866

BOTELER
Angelica Peale, d. of Hon. A. R. Boteler, and Henry Didier of Baltimore, by the Rev. Dr. Andrews, at Fountain Rock, near Shepherdstown. So. Ch., Oct. 5, 1860

Helen M., d. of the Hon. Alexander R. Boteler, and Capt. Dudley D. Pendleton, by the Rev. Charles W. Andrews, D.D., in Trinity Church, Shepherdstown. So. Ch., May 3, 1866

Mary M., and John G. Mason, Esq. of Fredericksburg, by the Rev. C. W. Andrews, D.D. and the Rev. C. R. Hains, in Trinity Church, Shepherdstown. So. Ch., Mar. 24, 1870

Wm. H., and Elizabeth Martin, both of Fauquier Co., Va., by the Rev. Geo. Lemmon. So. Ch., Oct. 6, 1837

BOTTS
Henry T., Esq., and Betty Hull, d. of Dr. B. S. Herndon, by the Rev. A. M. Randolph, in St. George's Church, Fredericksburg. So. Ch., July 27, 1860

Mary Berkley, only d. of the late Gen. Thos. H. Botts of Frederick Co., and David Howell, Jr. of Charles Town, W.Va., by the Rev. Magruder Maury, at the residence of T. B. Barton, Esq. So. Ch., Nov. 19, 1868

BOULDIN
Alice H., d. of the late Judge Wood Bouldin of the Court of Appeals, and Boylan Green, Esq., s. of Col. Wm. E. Green of Charlotte Co., by the Rev. Davis M. Wood, at "Cleft Oak", Charlotte Co., Va. So. Ch., Sept. 15, 1881

Mattie D., and Dr. David Flournoy, by the Rev. H. A. Brown, at the residence of Wood Bouldin, Esq., Roanoke, Charlotte Co., Va. So. Ch., Nov. 4, 1869

MARRIAGE NOTICES IN THE SOUTHERN CHURCHMAN WITH DATES OF PUBLICATION

BOULTON
　Emily, d. of John Boulton, Esq. of Philadelphia, and the Rev. William A. Newbold, assistant minister of St. Andrew's Church, Wilmington, Del., by the Rt. Rev. Alfred Lee, D.D., in the Church of the Epiphany. So. Ch., Oct. 15, 1858

BOULWARE
　Aubin L., of Richmond, and Jane Grace, d. of the late Gov. W. Ballard Preston of Virginia, by the Rev. Nelson P. Dame, at Smithfield, residence of the bride's mother, Montgomery Co. So. Ch., Nov. 21, 1878

BOWDEN
　Upton B. (The Rev.), rector of MacComb City, Miss., and Henrietta P., d. of the Rev. W. K. Douglas, D.D., rector of Calvary Church, New Orleans, by the Rt. Rev. Bishop of Louisiana, the Bishop of Mississippi assisting and pronouncing the benediction, in Calvary Church, New Orleans. So. Ch., Nov. 30, 1882

BOWDOIN
　Louisa, d. of George E. Bowdoin of Baltimore, and Murray Rush of Philadelphia, by the Rt. Rev. John Johns, in Christ Church, Baltimore. So. Ch., Jan. 13, 1876
　Louisa (Mrs.), and Theodore S. Garnett, at Oak Grove, Northampton Co., Va. So. Ch., Aug. 13, 1885

BOWEN
　Isabella, d. of Bishop Bowen, and Joseph W. Faber, Esq., by the Rev. W. W. Spear, assistant minister, St. Michael's Church, Charleston, S.C. So. Ch., Apr. 21, 1837
　J. Pollard, of Galveston, Texas, and Edmonia, second d. of the late H. E. Evans of Clarke Co., Va., by the Rev. Jas. R. Jones, in Christ Church, Millwood, Clarke Co. So. Ch., Oct. 2, 1873
　James (Gen.), of Hastings upon Hudson, and Athenia, d. of the late Anthony Rutgers Livingston, by the Rev. Wm. Paret, D.D., in the Church of the Epiphany, Washington, D.C. So. Ch., Apr. 3, 1879
　James R., Esq., of Bedford Co., Va., and Mary S. eldest d. of the late Elverton A. Shands of Harrisonburg, Va., by the Rev. T. U. Dudley, in Harrisonburg, Va. So. Ch., June 11, 1868
　Rees T. (Hon.), of Tazewell Co., Va., and Lucie J., d. of Dr. John J. Gravatt, by the Rev. James E. Poindexter, at the residence of the bride's father, Port Royal, Va. So. Ch., Sept. 16, 1875
　Wm. B. (Dr.), and E. L. Sommerville, by the Rev. Joseph R. Jones, in Meade Memorial Church, White Post, Va. So. Ch., Oct. 20, 1881

BOWERS
　A. S., and Kate J., eldest d. of Robert Bowman, all of Culpeper Co., Va., by the Rev. John McGill, at the residence of the bride's parents. So. Ch., Nov. 27, 1884
　Annie M., and Samuel G. Brown, by the Rev. W. D.

MARRIAGE NOTICES IN THE SOUTHERN CHURCHMAN WITH DATES OF PUBLICATION

Hanson, at Faulkland, Del. So. Ch., Mar. 16, 1882

Fannie C., of Philadelphia, and the Rev. W. C. Gray of Bolivar, Tenn., by the Rev. William V. Bowers, father of the bride, assisted by the Rev. Dr. Beaseley of Torresdale, in St. Andrew's Church, Philadelphia. So. Ch., Aug. 16, 1877

BOWIE

J. Wilson, and Mary L., l. of Dr. W. G. West of Loudoun Co., Va., by the Rev. S. S. Ware, in Christ Church, Loudoun Co., Va. So. Ch., Jan. 8, 1880

John M., and Sarah B., d. of the officiating clergyman, the Rev. James J. Page, in Holy Trinity Church, Prince George's Co., Md. So. Ch., Nov. 1, 1888

Thomas C., of Tensas Parish, La., and Maria Vidal, d. of Dr. Wm. Byrd Page of Natchez, Miss., formerly of Virginia, by the Rev. Dr. Dana, rector of Trinity Church, Natchez, Miss. So. Ch., June 7, 1866

Walter Russell, and Elizabeth Halsted Branch, both of Richmond, by the Rev. Dr. Minnigerode assisted by the Rev. Dr. McDonald, in St. Paul's Church, Richmond. So. Ch., Dec. 1, 1881

William Duckett, s. of ex-Governor Bowie of Prince George's Co., Md., and Mary Lee, youngest d. of the late Hon. Jonathan M. and Margaret E. Bennett of Weston, W.Va., by the Rev. T. H. Lacy, at the residence of the bride's brother, Hon. Louis Bennett, Weston, W.Va. So. Ch., Nov. 27, 1890

BOWLER

Mary, d. of Henry Bowler, of Richmond, Va., and Henry J. Going, Esq., s. of the Venerable Archdeacon Going of Killaloe Co., Tipperary, Ireland, by the Rev. T. G. Dashiell, at the home of the bride's father, in Richmond. So. Ch., Nov. 19, 1874

BOWMAN

Isaac, and Margaret M. Reed, both of Berryville, Clarke Co., Va., by the Rev. T. F. Martin, at the residence of Mr. Leiday. So. Ch., Feb. 20, 1868

Kate J., eldest l. of Robert Bowman, and A. S. Bowers, all of Culpeper Co., Va., by the Rev. John McGill, at the residence of the bride's parents. So. Ch., Nov. 27, 1884

BOWYER

Charles C., Esq., and Kittie Bell Parsons, by the Rev. T. H. Lacy, in Christ Church, Point Pleasant, W. Va. So. Ch., Oct. 9, 1879

James H. (Dr.), and Eliza K. Nelson, by the Rev. W. H. Pendleton, at Elk Hill, the residence of Dr. Thos. H. Nelson, Bedford Co. So. Ch., Sept. 21, 1860

Otis, of Baird, Texas, and Eliza Amelia, d. of Judge John W. and M. C. Bell of Culpeper, Va., by the Rev. W. T. Roberts, in St. Stephen's Church, Culpeper, Va. So. Ch., Dec. 15, 1887

Woodville, of Fincastle, and E. Ann, l. of Ferdinand Woltz, Esq., clerk of Botetourt County Court, by the Rev. T. F. Martin of Nelson Co., in Fincastle. So. Ch., Oct. 29, 1858

See also MEREDITH, Lewly (Mrs.)

BOYCE

MARRIAGE NOTICES IN THE SOUTHERN CHURCHMAN WITH DATES OF PUBLICATION

Geo. W., and Elizabeth H. Ginnelley, by the Rev. Thos. Deane Lewis, at the residence of the bride's parents, Fairfax Court House, Va. So. Ch., Dec. 14, 1893

Katharine Lawrence, d. of Col. N. L. Boyce of Clarke Co., Va., and Robert Lee Jones of Taylor, Texas, by the Rev. Jos. R. Jones, father of the groom, assisted by John P. Tyler, rector, in Christ Church, Millwood, Va. So. Ch., Oct. 29, 1891

BOYD

George H. (The Rev.), rector of historic St. Peter's Church, Perth Amboy, N.J., and Esther Murdock, by the Rt. Rev. Francis M. Taitt, Bishop of Pennsylvania, assisted by the Rev. John R. McCrory, rector of St. Bartholomew's Episcopal Church, Wissisnoming.* So. Ch., July 7, 1935

James G. S., and Mary Susan, d. of the late James Cocke, Esq., by the Rev. A. B. Tizzard, at the residence of Dr. Richard Taylor, Amelia Co. So. Ch., Jan. 18, 1856

Lizzie Bright, d. of Col. Thos. J. Boyd, and John Stuart Crockett, Esq., Commonwealth's attorney, all of Wytheville, by the Rev. Robb White, at the residence of the bride's father, Wytheville, Va. So. Ch., Sept. 21, 1876

Mary, d. of the late James M. Boyd of Lynchburg, and Capt. F. B. Clopton of Richmond, by the Rev. W. H. Kinckle. So. Ch., Dec. 17, 1858

Wm. Robert, Esq., of Ala., and Margaret Farlie Smith of Hanover Co., Va., by the Rev. G. S. Carraway, in Immanuel Church, Hanover Co., Va. So. Ch., Oct. 28, 1859

BOYDEN

John L., and Cornelia C., d. of Col. Samuel S. Payne, by the Rev. P. M. Boyden assisted by the Rev. Oscar Bunting, at Mountain Home, Amherst Co., Va. So. Ch., Sept. 11, 1879

P. M. (The Rev.), rector of St. James' Parish, Northam, and Ella W., d. of the late William M. Smith, M.D., by the Rev. Frank Stringfellow, at Hebron Church, Goochland Co. So. Ch., Sept. 4, 1879

BOYETTE

Frank (Dr.), of Clinton, N.C., and Lucie V. Bennett, by the Rev. C. O. Pruden, at the residence of the bride's mother, Mrs. M. A. Bennett, Chatham, Va. So. Ch., Jan. 5, 1888

BOYKIN

Anthony R. (Dr.), of Smithfield, and Lillian S., youngest d. of the late Rich. H. Riddick, Esq., by the Rev. J. B. Craighill, at the residence of the bride's mother, in Isle of Wight Co., Va. So. Ch., Oct. 12, 1876

Christopher C., of Buchanan, Va., and Florence G. Jeffries of West Point, by the Rev. E. Meade, in St. John's Church. So. Ch., Aug. 8, 1889

Richard Elliott, Esq., of Smithfield, Va., and Minnie Pegram Wilson, by the Rev. J. W. Keeble, at Mantura, Surry Co., Va. So. Ch., Nov. 22, 1877

* Possibly the Philadelphia suburb

MARRIAGE NOTICES IN THE SOUTHERN CHURCHMAN WITH DATES OF PUBLICATION

Richard S., of Southampton Co., and Susan E., eldest d. of R. Henley Pretlow of "Little Surry", Va., by the Rev. David Barr, in the Church of Our Saviour, Ivor, Va. So. Ch., Apr. 14, 1887

Sarah, d. of the late Dr. Francis Boykin, and Dr. F. T. Fry, by the Rev. Dr. Peterkin, in St. James' Church, Richmond. So. Ch., Dec. 2, 1875

BRACKETT
Jeffrey R., of Massachusetts, and Susan Katherine, d. of W. Strother Jones of Virginia, by the Rev. J. S. B. Hodges, S.T.D., in St. Paul's Church, Baltimore. So. Ch., June 24, 1886

BRADEN
R. Walter, of Loudoun Co., Va., and Katie, d. of the late Dr. J. D. Heaton, by the Rev. S. S. Ware, in St. Paul's Church, Hamilton, Va. So. Ch., Feb. 3, 1881

BRADFORD
Flora, d. of Col. S. S. Bradford, and Travers Daniel of Richmond, in St. Stephen's Episcopal Church, Culpeper. So. Ch., Jan. 17, 1878

Rosa W., of Clarke Co., Va., and William J. Manning of Winchester, Va., by the Rev. Jas. R. Hubard assisted by the Rev. John P. Tyler, at "Abbeyville", Clarke Co., Va. So. Ch., May 19, 1892

Sydney, of Norfolk, Va., and Kate S., d. of the late John S. Braxton of Fredericksburg, Va., by the Rev. R. J. McBryde, at Fredericksburg. So. Ch., Dec. 2, 1880

BRADLEY
Alice, youngest d. of Joseph H. Bradley, Esq., of Washington, and the Rev. Walter Williams of Leesburg, Va., by the Rev. George D. Cummins, D.D., of Baltimore, in Trinity Church. So. Ch., Mar. 4, 1859

Delia E. (Mrs.), and Virginius Bossieux, both of Henrico Co., by the Rev. Henry Wall, D.D. So. Ch., Jan. 5, 1871

Edwin B., Esq., of Baltimore, and Lucy W., d. of the late Hay Taliaferro of Orange, Va., by the Rev. J. Earnest, in St. Thomas' Church, Orange Court House. So. Ch., Sept. 16, 1859

Sarah A. (Mrs.), and John Viles, by the Rev. H. Wall, D.D. So. Ch., Mar. 16, 1871

BRADY
Alfred F., of New Orleans, La., and Minna J., d. of the late Wm. A. Scott of Buckingham Co., Va., by the Rev. B. M. Wales, So. Ch., Oct. 8, 1874

Louisa L., of Wheeling, Va., and John Horsley of Buckingham Co., Va., by the Rev. E. T. Perkins, in St. Matthew's Church, Wheeling. So. Ch., Jan. 11, 1861

BRAMBLE
Flora, and Samuel Johnson, both of Dorchester, Co., Md., by the Rev. Wm. W. Greene, at Church Creek. So. Ch., Feb. 17, 1881

BRAMHALL

MARRIAGE NOTICES IN THE SOUTHERN CHURCHMAN WITH DATES OF PUBLICATION

Frank J. (Col), and S. Jennie Nichols, by the Rev. John McNabb, at the residence of the bride's parents. So. Ch., June 14, 1877

BRAMHAM
Lucy E., of Albemarle, and Wm. T. Childress of Nelson Co., by the Rev. T. E. Locke, at the residence of David R. Bramham. So. Ch., June 6, 1889

BRANCH
Christophine McC., eldest d. of D. H. Branch, Esq. of Petersburg, and John Clay, Esq. of Chesterfield, by the Rev. C. J. Gibson, at Petersburg, Va. So. Ch., Oct. 26, 1855

Elizabeth Halsted, and Walter Russell Bowie, both of Richmond, by the Rev. Dr. Minnigerode assisted by the Rev. Dr. McDonald, in St. Paul's Church, Richmond. So. Ch., Dec. 1, 1881

Jas. R., of Petersburg, and Mattie L., d. of Dr. Wm. Patterson of Richmond, by the Rev. Horace Stringfellow, in St. Paul's Church, Richmond. So. Ch., Dec. 12, 1856

James R., Jr., and Mary Lilian Hubball, by the Rev. W. L. Gravatt, in St. Paul's Church, Richmond, Va. So. Ch., Nov. 5, 1885

Wm. J., and Lina G., d. of the late Ambrose Carlton of Richmond, by the Rev. Dr. Minnigerode, in St. Paul's Church. So. Ch., July 3, 1884

BRANDER
Thos. A. (Capt.), P.A.C.S., and Elizabeth L., eldest d. of the Rev. Lewis Walke, by the Rev. F. M. Baker, in St. Luke's Church, Powhatan Co., Va. So. Ch., Feb. 15, 1865

BRANNON
Alice, and W. G. Bennett, both of Weston, Lewis Co., W. Va., by the Rev. Andrew Fisher, in St. Paul's Church, Weston. So. Ch., Apr. 4, 1872

Morgan M., and Lucy J., d. of the late Thomas Baker, all of Winchester, by the Rev. C. Walker, in Christ Church, Winchester, Va. So. Ch., Nov. 2, 1855

BRANON
Florence, d. of Judge John Branon of Weston, and the Rev. A. A. McDonough, by the Rev. J. F. Woods, in Weston, W.Va. So. Ch., June 29, 1876

BRAWNER
Charles E., and Josephine T., only child and d. of J. J. Cockrell, by the Rev. John McGill, at the residence of the bride's father, in Prince William Co. So. Ch., Nov. 13, 1873

Thomas, of Prince George's, Md., and Helen S. Alexander, by the Rev. A. F. Gray, at "Milford", Prince William Co., Va. So. Ch., Oct. 23, 1879

BRAXTON
Bettie H., eldest d. of the late Dr. W. T. Braxton of Hanover, and Dr. W. W. Dew of Russell Co., by the Rev. S. S. Hepbron, in Immanuel Church. So. Ch., June 20, 1889

Eliza Marshall, d. of Hon. E.

MARRIAGE NOTICES IN THE SOUTHERN CHURCHMAN WITH DATES OF PUBLICATION

M. Braxton, and John L. Brockenborough, by the Rev. R. J. McBryde, in St. George's Church, Fredericksburg. So. Ch., Feb. 19, 1880

Kate S., d. of the late John Braxton of Fredericksburg, Va., and Sydney Bradford of Norfolk, Va., by the Rev. R. J. McBryde, at Fredericksburg. So. Ch., Dec. 2, 1880

Lily, d. of the late John S. Braxton of Norfolk, Va., and Marshall Carter Hall, by the Rev. R. J. McBryde, in St. George's Church, Fredericksburg, Va. So. Ch., Dec. 8, 1881

Maria G., d. of John S. and Oliva J. Braxton, and Oscar M. Lemoine, all of Emmerton, Va., by the Rev. A. M. Randolph, in Emmanuel Church, Baltimore. So. Ch., Aug. 3, 1876

Muse, and Janet Potter, d. of Judge Thomas C. Fuller, by the Rev. Dr. Daniel Elliott, at the residence of the bride's parents, Raleigh, N.C. So. Ch., Nov. 9, 1893

Susie G., d. of the late Dr. W. P. Braxton, of Hanover, and George W. West of Richmond, by the Rev. S. S. Hepbron, in Immanuel Church, Hanover Co. So. Ch., Oct. 16, 1890

Tomlin (Dr.), of King William, and Mary, d. of Allen T. Caperton, Esq. of Monroe Co., by the Rev. R. H. Phillips, at Elmwood, the residence of the bride's father. So. Ch., Jan. 18, 1861

BREATHED
Francis, of Goochland Co., Va., and Eleanor A., d. of D. R. Shelton of Louisa Co., Va., by the Rev. H. P. R. McCoy, at Roseneath, the residence of the bride's father. So. Ch., Mar. 11, 1880

Lottie C., of Lynchburg, Va., and Edmund Berkeley of Hanover Co., Va., by the Rev. T. M. Carson, at the residence of the bride's parents. So. Ch., Mar. 22, 1888

BRECKENRIDGE
Bettie T., of Staunton, Va., and Nathaniel P. Catlett of Staunton, Va., by the Rev. P. Slaughter, in Trinity Church, Staunton, Va. So. Ch., Nov. 28, 1856

BRECKINRIDGE
A. N., of Staunton, and Bettie C., d. of the late Col. Robt. L. Wright of Loudoun Co., Va., by the Rev. J. R. Hubard, in Christ Church, Winchester, Va. So. Ch., June 15, 1876

Cary (Col.), of Botetourt, Va., and Mary Virginia Caldwell of Greenbrier Co., W.Va., by the Rev. Peter Tinsley. So. Ch., July 19, 1866

Lucy Gilmer, d. of Cary Breckinridge, and Lt. Jefferson Bassett of Texas, by the Rev. Wm. McGuire, at Grove Hill, Botetourt Co., Va. So. Ch., Feb. 8, 1865

Nannie A., d. of Mrs. Peachy Gilmer Breckinridge, of

MARRIAGE NOTICES IN THE SOUTHERN CHURCHMAN WITH DATES OF PUBLICATION

Botetourt Co., Va., and Wm. Gordon Robertson of Roanoke, Va., by the Rev. C. C. Randolph, at Grove Hill, Botetourt Co., Va. So. Ch., Nov. 23, 1882

P. Gilmer, and Julia M. Anthony, both of Botetourt, by the Rev. T. M. Ambler, at the residence of G. Anthony, the bride's uncle, in Buchanan. So. Ch., Jan. 27, 1860

BREMHE
Ottomar, Esq., of Baltimore, and Mary, d. of Thomas J. Hall, Esq. of Anne Arundel Co., Md., by the Rev. John C. McCabe, D.D., in St. James' Church, West River, Md. So. Ch., Nov. 16, 1860

BRENNER
John E., of Middleburg, Loudoun Co., and Jennie M., only d. of G. W. Dear of Centreville, Va., by the Rev. John McGill, at the residence of the bride's father. So. Ch., Sept. 17, 1874

BRENT
Lucy C. (Mrs.), of Fredericksburg, Va., and Frederick W. Page of Albemarle Co., Va., by the Rev. G. L. Petrie, at the residence of Prof. Dennington, at University of Virginia. So. Ch., Dec. 6, 1883

Randolph S., and Laura, d. of Maj. Henry C. DeShields, all of Northumberland, by the Rev. H. L. Derby, at "Summerfield", Northumberland Co., Va. So. Ch., Jan. 11, 1883

BREESE*
Stuart, and Lucy Berkeley Belches, both of Virginia, by the Rev. E. G. Cobb, at East Hampton, Mass. So. Ch., Jan. 16, 1909

BRESEE
May, and H. B. Nalle, by the Rev. R. R. Claiborne, in Emmanuel Church, Rapidan. So. Ch., Dec. 18, 1884

BREWSTER
R. J. Walker, and Leila Shoemaker, by the Rev. John Lindsay, D.D., in West Washington, D.C. So. Ch., Nov. 5, 1885

BRIAN
Phoebe, and Springer L. Grubb, both of Newport, Del., by the Rev. W. D. Hanson. So. Ch., June 5, 1879

BRIDGEMAN
Victor M. (Lt.), U.S.A., and Ida, d. of John F. and the late Violetta Pickrell, by the Rev. J. B. Perry, in Washington, D.C. So. Ch., Oct, 6, 1887

BRIDGES
Irene S., d. of R. M. Bridges, Esq. of Culpeper Co., Va., and W. Winston Jones, Jr. of New Kent Co., Va., by the Rev. C. Y. Steptoe, in Culpeper Co., Va. So. Ch., Jan. 11, 1872

Wm. M. (Capt.), and Lucy C., d. of the late Gen. Philip St. George Cocke, by the Rev. J. H. Morrison, D.D., at "Belmead", Powhatan Co. So. Ch., Apr. 27, 1871

BRIGGS
Marian J., of Clarke Co., Va., and Hugh T. Douglass of Zanesville, Ohio, by the Rev. F. M. Whittle,

* Given as printed

MARRIAGE NOTICES IN THE SOUTHERN CHURCHMAN WITH DATES OF PUBLICATION

in Clarke Co., Va. So.
Ch., July 7, 1853
Robert W., of Clarke Co.,
Va., and Minnie, d. of the
late Joel Z. Harper, by the
Rev. O. A. Kinsolving, at
"Rock Cliff", Fauquier Co.,
Va. So. Ch., Dec. 5, 1887
W. E., of Surry Co., and L.
A. Berkeley, third d. of
the late Wm. H. Berkeley
of King and Queen, by the
Rev. Dr. Newton, at
Wanderer's Rest. So. Ch.,
Nov. 13, 1873
Wm. H. (Capt.), and Hart,
eldest d. of the late Jas.
W. Cook of Greensville
Co., Va., by the Rev.
David Barr, at "Midfield",
near Hicksford, Greensville
Co., Va. So. Ch., June
16, 1870
BRIGHTWELL
Ann E., and F. Y. Naylor,
both of District of
Columbia, by the Rev. Wm.
Pinkney.* So. Ch., Dec.
22, 1837
Bettie, and Benjamin F.
Jenkins, both of Spotsyl-
vania Co., Va., by the
Rev. Wm. W. Greene. So.
Ch., Apr. 2, 1868
BRINKLEY
Annie May, of Suffolk, Va.,
and James Harry Newton
formerly of England, by
the Rev. Henry L. Derby,
in St. Paul's Church,
Suffolk, Va. So. Ch.,
Nov. 28, 1889
BRITTINGHAM
Jacob (The Rev.), of
Parkersburg, and Florence
V. Shearer of Moorefield,
W.Va., by the Rt. Rev.
George W. Peterkin, in
Immanuel Church, Moore-
field, W.Va. So. Ch.,

Sept. 21, 1882
Maggie A., of Northampton
Co., Va., and J. L. D.
Butt of Memphis, Tenn.,
by the Rev. J. B. Craig-
hill, in Christ Church,
Eastville. So. Ch., Dec.
16, 1869
BRITTON
Elizabeth Alexander Ware
(Mrs.), d. of the late
Josiah W. Ware, Esq. of
Berryville, Va., and James
Mercer Garnett McGuire,
M.D., of Berryville, Va.,
by the Rev. Horace Edwin
Hayden assisted by the
Rev. Henry L. Jones, at
Plymouth, Pa. So. Ch.,
May 8, 1884
J. Blodget, of Philadelphia,
and Fanny Baylor, d. of
Joseph Horner, Esq., by
the Rev. John S. Lindsay,
in St. James' Church,
Warrenton, Va. So. Ch.,
Oct. 8, 1874
John R., of Trenton, N.J.,
and Carolyn Peyton, d. of
the late Rev. George
Washington Nelson, by the
Rev. E. S. Hinks, in St.
James' Church, Warrenton,
Va. So. Ch., Sept. 24,
1910
BROADDUS
Roland F., Esq., and Bessie
C., second d. of Mrs. L.
M. Ruffin, both of Hanover,
by the Rev. S. S. Hepbron,
in Immanuel Church,
Hanover. So. Ch., May
2, 1889
BROADNAX
W. M. A. (The Rev.), rector
of St. Paul's Church,
Lee Center, and Matilda
F. Smedly of Chicago,
by the Rev. H. N.
Shenck, in Trinity

* Given as printed

MARRIAGE NOTICES IN THE SOUTHERN CHURCHMAN WITH DATES OF PUBLICATION

Church, Chicago. So. Ch., June 17, 1859

BROCK
  Elizabeth T., and Edwin L. Hewitt, by the Rev. J. Y. Downman, at the residence of the bride's father, Dr. C. W. P. Brock. So. Ch., May 2, 1889

  Henry C. (Prof.), of Kenmore University High School, and Mary Carter Irving, by the Rev. R. J. McBryde, at the residence of R. K. Irving, near Buckingham C.H. So. Ch., Sept. 9, 1875

  Virginia Allen, d. of Dr. C. W. P. Brock of Richmond, Va., and Floyd Hughes, Esq. of Norfolk, Va., by the Rev. J. Y. Downman assisted by the Rev. Dr. O. S. Barten, in All Saints' Church, Richmond, Va. So. Ch., Nov. 23, 1893

BROCKENBOROUGH
  John B. (Maj.), of Bedford Co., Va., and Roberta, eldest d. of Judge Robert Johnson of Harrisonburg, Va., by the Rev. O. S. Bunting, in Emmanuel Church, Harrisonburg, Va. So. Ch., Jan. 24, 1884

  John L., and Eliza Marshall, d. of Hon. E. M. Braxton, by the Rev. R. J. McBryde, in St. George's Church, Fredericksburg. So. Ch., Feb. 19, 1880

BROCKENBROUGH
  Alice R., and William R. Aylett of King William Co., by the Rev. Andrew Fisher, at Bellville, Richmond Co. So. Ch., Aug. 17, 1860

  Betty, of Essex, and Samuel F. Harwood, Esq. of King and Queen Co., by the Rev. H. W. L. Temple, in St. John's Church, Tappahannock, Essex Co., Va. So. Ch., Apr. 8, 1869

  Branch, of Richmond Co., Va., and Robert H. Montgomery of King George Co., by the Rev. Beverly Tucker, at Waveland. So. Ch., Dec. 27, 1877

  Etta, youngest d. of the late Col. M. F. Brockenbrough of Richmond Co., Va., and Robt. T. Knox of Fredericksburg, by the Rev. Andrew Fisher, in St. John's Church, Warsaw, Richmond Co., Va. So. Ch., Nov. 19, 1868

  Littleton, of Baltimore, and Emma, d. of the late E. H. Chamberlayne of Richmond, Va., by the Rev. Edward Wall, in St. Mark's Rectory, Petersville, Md. So. Ch., Dec. 3, 1885

  Loula Gray, d. of the late George L. Brockenbrough of Florida, and James C. Lamb, Esq. of Richmond, by the Rev. Everard Meade, at the residence of Thomas W. Brockenbrough of Richmond Co. So. Ch., Mar. 3, 1881

  Loula S., d. of Capt. Wm. A. Brockenbrough, and Douglas H. Knox of Fredericksburg, Va., by the Rev. A. B. Kinsolving, at Waveland, Richmond Co., Va. So. Ch., May 26, 1887

  Mary R., of Richmond Co., and Dr. Thomas Arnold, by the Rev. Andrew Fisher, at the residence of Col. John M. Brockenbrough. So. Ch., June 30, 1870

MARRIAGE NOTICES IN THE SOUTHERN CHURCHMAN WITH DATES OF PUBLICATION

Saide, eldest d. of Wm. F. Brockenbrough, Esq. of "Belleville", Richmond Co., Va., and Jas. C. Lamb of Richmond, Va., by the Rev. A. Johnson assisted by the Rev. B. D. Tucker of Norfolk, Va., in St. John's Church, Warsaw, Va. So. Ch., Jan. 7 and 14, 1886

Sallie Maxwell, d. of Thomas W. Brockenbrough of Richmond, and Capt. William A. Brockenbrough of Richmond Co., by the Rev. Everard Meade, at the residence of the bride's father. So. Ch., Mar. 3, 1881

William A. (Capt.), of Richmond Co., and Sallie Maxwell, d. of Thomas W. Brockenbrough of Richmond, by the Rev. Everard Meade, at the residence of the bride's father. So. Ch., Mar. 3, 1881

BROCKINTON
Mollie, and Washington Peace, Jr. of Watha, N.C., at West Andrews, S.C. So. Ch., June 4, 1910

BROCKWELL
J. Bollie, Esq., and Virgie, eldest d. of William Adams, Esq. of Charles City Co., Va., by the Rev. John P. Tyler, in Salem M. E. Church, Charles City Co., Va. So. Ch., Dec. 4, 1890

BRODIE
Walter J., of Forfarshire, Scotland, and Nannie S., d. of Dr. L. W. Mayo of Bedford Co., Va., by the Rev. G. A. Gibbons, at the residence of the bride's father. So. Ch., Jan. 14, 1875

BRODNAX
Mary Louisa, d. of the late Gen. Wm. H. Brodnax, and John M. Banister, rector of Bath Parish, Dinwiddie Co., by the Rev. Edmund Withers, in Kingston, Dinwiddie Co., Va. So. Ch., Feb. 11, 1848

BROGDEN
William T., of Richmond Co., N.C., and Julia F. Hicks of Oxford, N.C., by the Rev. P. D. Thompson, at the residence of the bride's father, E. H. Hicks. So. Ch., June 18, 1874

BRONAUGH
Mary M., eldest d. of John C. and Sarah Bronaugh, and Sidney, s. of the late Francis Taylor, U.S.A., of Cumberland, Md., by the Rev. A. P. Gray, at the residence of the bride's sister, Prince William Co. So. Ch., Mar. 13, 1884

N. L., of Nicholasville, Ky., and Marguerite Robertson, d. of Mrs. Anna Meade and the late Dr. Robert P. Letcher of Henderson, and gr.d. of the late Hon. Tucker Woodson of "Churchland", Jessamine Co., Ky., by the Rev. Russell Cecil. So. Ch., Jan. 1, 1885

BROOKE
A. M. C. (Mrs.), d. of the late Hon. Daniel R. Clymer of Reading, Pa., and the Rev. Randolph Harrison McKim, D.D., by the Rt. Rev. Wm. Paret, D.D., Bishop of

- 64 -

MARRIAGE NOTICES IN THE SOUTHERN CHURCHMAN WITH DATES OF PUBLICATION

Maryland assisted by the Rev. Halstead McKim, in St. Thomas' Church, N.Y. So. Ch., July 31, 1890

Agnes T., formerly of Fauquier Co., Va., and Dr. John C. Wise, United States Navy, by the Rev. A. Y. Hundley, in Abingdon Church, Gloucester Co., Va. So. Ch., May 15, 1879

Augustine T., of Md., and Louisa U., d. of the late Rev. Upton Beale of Norfolk, by the Rev. Dr. Goodrich, of N. O.*, at the residence of Col. E. T. Tayloe, Powhatan, King George Co. So. Ch., Dec. 9, 1869

Francis E., Esq., s. of the Hon. Judge Brooke of the Court of Appeals, and Ella B. Ambler, d. of the late Col. John Ambler, by the Rt. Rev. Bishop Moore. So. Ch., Dec. 1, 1837

Francis S. (Dr.), of Spotsylvania Co., and Harriet A., d. of John B. Lightfoot, Esq. of Port Royal, by the Rev. William Friend, in St. Peter's Church, Port Royal, Va. So. Ch., Nov. 7, 1867

Frank J. (The Rev.), of Philippi, W.Va., formerly of Richmond, and Elizabeth Gay, d. of Efford B. and Lucy W. Bentley of Richmond, by the Rev. Charles Minnigerode, D.D., in St. Paul's Church, Richmond. So. Ch., Dec. 2, 1880

George W., Esq., and Nellie, d. of the Rev. Thomas F. Billopp, all of Prince George Co., Md., by the Rev. Dr. Lewin, in the Brick Church, Queen Anne Parish. So. Ch., Apr. 22, 1875

John F., of Chicago, Ill., and Nannie C. Berkeley of Staunton, Va., by the Rev. A. S. Berkeley, at the residence of Mrs. M. R. S. Berkeley, Staunton, Va. So. Ch., Sept. 3, 1874

John M. (Capt.), of Virginia Military Institute, and Mrs. Kate C. Pendleton, by the Rev. M. Maury, in St. George's Episcopal Church, Fredericksburg, Va. So. Ch., Mar. 30, 1871

Lily T. Marshall, d. of Mrs. Martin P. Brooke, and Moses M. Green, Esq., all of Warrenton, by the Rev. John S. Lindsay, in St. James' Church, Warrenton, Va. So. Ch., Jan. 23, 1879

Louisa, d. of the Bishop of Oklahoma, and Mrs. Francis Key Brooke, and Thomas Catesby Jones of New York, by the Rev. H. Percy Silver, chaplain of the Military Academy, West Point, assisted by the bride's father, in St. Saviour's Chapel, Cathedral of St. John the Divine, New York City. So. Ch., Sept. 9, 1916

Mary Baldwin, of Guthrie, Okla., and Ernest Trowbridge Gregory of Brookline, Mass., by the Rt. Rev. Francis K. Brooke, father of the bride, and the Rev. Dr. George F. Smythe, in the Church of the Holy Spirit, Gambier, Ohio. So. Ch., Sept. 14, 1907

Mary Urquhart, d. of

---

* Given as printed

MARRIAGE NOTICES IN THE SOUTHERN CHURCHMAN WITH DATES OF PUBLICATION

Mr. and Mrs. William Throckmorton Brooke, gr. d. of the late Hon. John Goode of Virginia, and James Benton of Denver, Col., s. of the late James Benton Grant, ex-Governor of Colorado, by the Rev. David W. Howard, in St. Luke's Church, Norfolk, Va. So. Ch., May 9, 1914*

Olive Dunbar, d. of the Rev. Robert D. Brooke of Iowa, and Malcolm McLean of Alexandria, Va., by the Rev. R. H. McKim, in Christ Church, Alexandria, Va. So. Ch., Nov. 20, 1873

Pendleton (The Rev.), of Botetourt Co., and Carrie Lindsay, d. of J. Bunting, Esq. of Bristol, Goodson, Tenn., and Virginia,** by the Rev. Jno. S. Lindsay of Warrenton, in Emmanuel Church, Goodson, Va. So. Ch., May 1, 1873

R. B., and Ella C. Harrison, by the Rev. H. L. Derby, in White Chapel Church, Lancaster, Va. So. Ch., Nov. 25, 1886

Robert D. (The Rev.), of Dubuque, Iowa, and Mary W., d. of the Rev. George A. Smith of Clarens, Fairfax Co., by the Rev. C. B. Dana. So. Ch., Oct. 24, 1850

Ruth Sheldon, d. of the Bishop of Oklahoma, and Mrs. Francis Key Brooke, and Edward Henry Lee of Chicago, by the Rt. Rev. Dr. Daniel Sylvester Tuttle, Presiding Bishop of the church, in the Chapel of St. Luke's Church, Evanston, Ill. So. Ch., Oct. 7, 1916

Samuel, of Prince George's Co., Md., and Mary C. Hoxton, gr.d. of the Rev. Dr. Minnigerode, by the Rev. Dr. Minnigerode and the Rev. Buckner Randolph, in St. Paul's Church, Alexandria. So. Ch., Oct. 26, 1893

Warner L., of Norfolk, Va., and Maria Shelby Fassmann, gr.d. of Mrs. Judge Phelan of "Fatherland", near Nashville, Tenn., by the Rev. T. F. Martin, in St. Ann's Church, Nashville. So. Ch., Mar. 6, 1884

BROOKS
George D., and Ruth, d. of the late William H. Irwin of Alexandria, Va., by the Rev. H. Suter assisted by the Rev. G. H. Norton, D. D., in Christ Church, Alexandria, Va. So. Ch., Dec. 1, 1881

Daniel A., Jr., and Mrs. A. Newton Wall, by the Rev. Henry T. Sharp, in St. Paul's Church, Caseyville, Ky. So. Ch., Mar. 2, 1871

James, and Sarah J. Butt, both of Berkeley Co., W. Va., by the Rev. George S. May, near Hedgesville. So. Ch., Apr. 2, 1874

Jas. G., of Richmond, and Mary M. Tunstall of Lynchburg, by the Rev. W. H. Kinckle, in St. Paul's Church, Lynchburg. So. Ch., June 12, 1857

Mary L., of Caroline Co., Va., and Walter S. Stone of Hanover Co., Va., by the Rev. Curtis Grubb, in

---

* A notice appeared in the May 2, 1914 issue identical with this except that the groom's name was given as James Benton Grove, and he was not cited as the son of ex-governor Grant of Colorado.

** Given as printed

MARRIAGE NOTICES IN THE SOUTHERN CHURCHMAN WITH DATES OF PUBLICATION

St. Martin's Church, Hanover Co., Va. So. Ch., Jan. 11, 1883

Walter B., Jr., and Fannie L., d. of Stephen Bonsal, by the Rev. J. S. B. Hodges, D.D., in St. Paul's Church, Baltimore. So. Ch., Dec. 27, 1883

William F., of Alexandria, Va., and Florence Powell of Richmond, by the Rev. J. D. Powell, at the residence of Col. D. Lee Powell, in Richmond. So. Ch., Jan. 26, 1871

Wm. H. (The Rev.), minister of St. Thomas' Church, Newark, Del., and Ellen C. Gray of Boston, by the Rev. W. T. Smithett, in Trinity Church, Boston. So. Ch., Aug. 26, 1852

BROOME
Roger G. B. (Dr.), of Louisa Co., Va., and Sallie R. Poindexter, sister of the officiating minister, by the Rev. James E. Poindexter, in St. Peter's Church, Port Royal, Caroline Co. So. Ch., Dec. 18, 1884

BROTBECK
John Herbert, and Isabelle Dudley Vance, by the Rev. Joseph Baker, in Mapisco Church, Va. So. Ch., Feb. 28, 1914

BROUN
Ann Conway, d. of Maj. Thomas L. and Mary M. Broun, and Philip S. Powers of Richmond, by Bishop Peterkin and the Rev. R. D. Roller, rector of the church, in St. John's Church, Charleston, Kanawha Co., W. Va. So. Ch., Oct. 1, 1891

Louise Fontaine, d. of Maj. Thomas L. and Mary M. Broun, and Malcolm Jackson, by Bishop Peterkin and the Rev. R. D. Roller, rector of the church, in St. John's Church, Charleston, Kanawha Co., W. Va. So. Ch., Oct. 1, 1891

Margaretta Moss, d. of the late Dr. J. C. Broun, and Dawson McCormick, all of Clarke Co., Va., by the Rt. Rev. R. H. Wilmer, D. D., Bishop of Alabama, and the Rev. P. P. Philips, rector, in Grace Church, Berryville, Va. So. Ch., Sept. 13, 1883

Mary Lewis, d. of Prof. Wm. LeRoy Broun of Vanderbilt University, and Charles F. Ordway of Nashville, Tenn., by the Rev. Wm. Graham, rector of Christ Church, at the residence of the bride's father. So. Ch., July 21, 1881

W. LeRoy, of Albemarle Co., and Sallie J., d. of Dr. Geo. Fleming of Hanover, by the Rev. C. C. Bitting, at Chantilly, Hanover Co., Va. So. Ch., Nov. 18, 1859

BROUSE
See also POYTHERESS, Marie Josephine (Mrs.)

BROWER
George, Esq., of Baltimore, Md., and Lucy H., d. of the late Thomas Tabb of Toddsburg, Gloucester Co., Va., by the Rev. C. Mann, at Exchange, the residence of James K. Dabney, Esq. So. Ch., Mar. 19, 1858

MARRIAGE NOTICES IN THE SOUTHERN CHURCHMAN WITH DATES OF PUBLICATION

BROWN
- Alexander, and Sallie Randolph Cabell, by the Rev. Byrd Thornton Turner, at Union Hill, Nelson Co., Va. So. Ch., May 6 and June 10, 1886
- Alice, youngest d. of the late Chas. Brown, Esq. of Mt. Holly, N.J., and the Rev. Lucien Lee Kinsolving of Porto Alegre, Brazil, by the Rev. Prof. Angus Crawford of The Virginia Theological Seminary, brother-in-law of the bride, assisted by the Rev. O. A. Kinsolving, D.D. of the Diocese of Virginia, father of the groom, in Trinity Church, Mt. Holly, N.J., (the Rev. Martin Tignor, rector.) So. Ch., Jan. 21, 1892
- Annie, eldest d. of John Brown, Esq. of Memphis, Tenn., and Wm. B. Weisiger, Jr., recently of Virginia, by the Rev. Mr. Taylor; in Court Street Presbyterian Church. So. Ch., Oct. 22, 1874
- B. Frank, and Lillie B., eldest d. of John N. Murphy, Esq., all of Westmoreland Co., Va., by the Rev. Wm. Dame, in Baltimore, Md. So. Ch., June 17, 1886
- Benjamin R., and Mary E., d. of Mrs. S. H. Taylor, all of Norfolk, Va., by the Rev. A. S. Lloyd, in St. Luke's Church, Norfolk, Va. So. Ch., Jan. 13, 1887
- Chas. T., of Madison Co., and Fannie Hester, by the Rev. Dr. Savage, at Rest Easy, the residence of the bride's father, near Jackson, Miss. So. Ch., June 17, 1864
- E. M., and J. W. Sims, Esq., by the Rev. A. B. Tizzard, in Chesterfield Co., Va. So. Ch., Oct. 17, 1872
- Fannie Washington, and George J. Torrence, by the Rt. Rev. A. M. Randolph assisted by the Rev. J. Lumbley Lough, in Emmanuel Church, Baltimore. So. Ch., Nov. 8, 1883
- Felix E. (Dr.), of Baltimore, Md., and Marian A. Sullivan of Lancaster Co., by the Rev. H. L. Derby, at River Side, Lancaster Co. So. Ch., Aug. 24, 1882
- Forrest W., Commonwealth's attorney of Charles Town, W. Va., and Emma Beverly, d. of the late David H. Tucker of Richmond, Va., by the Rev. Dallas Tucker, in Zion Church, Charles Town, W.Va. So. Ch., June 25, 1885
- J. (Doct.)*, of Gerrardstown, and Mary Ellen, youngest d. of Thomas Gill of Berkeley Co., by the Rev. J. E. Jackson of Winchester. So. Ch., Dec. 8, 1837
- J. Thompson, and Cassie D. Tucker, both of Virginia, by the Rev. Dallas Tucker, in St. James' Episcopal Church, Wooster, Ohio. So. Ch., Oct. 26, 1882
- John F., of Minneapolis, and Sophie D. Littlejohn of Oxford, N.C., by the Rev. P. D. Thompson, at the residence of the bride's father, Maj. J. T. Littlejohn. So. Ch., July 2, 1874
- John Peyton, and Elizabeth,

---
* Given as printed

MARRIAGE NOTICES IN THE SOUTHERN CHURCHMAN WITH DATES OF PUBLICATION

d. of Robert Fulton, all of Charles Town, by the Rev. Alex. Jones. So. Ch., Dec. 15, 1837

Lewis B., of Madison Co., and Emily Virginia, d. of Dr. L. Millan of Rappahannock Co., by the Rev. R. T. Brown, at Woodville, Va. So. Ch., Apr. 21, 1870

Lizzie, and William Mayo, both of Westmoreland, by the Rev. D. M. Wharton, at the residence of the bride's father, Col. Thomas Brown. So. Ch., Jan. 16, 1873

Margaret Ann Barclay, d. of the late John D. Brown, and the Rev. William C. Russell, rector of St. Andrew's Church, Wilmington, Del., by the Rev. James T. Johnston, in Alexandria, D.C. So. Ch., Dec. 3, 1835

Martha A., second d. of Richard L. Brown, Esq., and E. A. Saunders, Jr., by the Rev. L. W. Burton, in St. John's Church, Richmond, Va. So. Ch., May 1, 1884

Mary, d. of B. P. Brown, M.D., of Cleveland, and the Rev. R. Rush Swope, rector of St. Matthew's Church, Wheeling, W.Va., by the Rev. J. W. Brown, D.D. assisted by the Rev. G. W. Hinkle, in Trinity Church, Cleveland, Ohio. So. Ch., Jan. 30, 1879

Mary Eliza (Lily), d. of Benjamin and Sarah P. Brown, and Joseph Gales Holcombe of Washington, D.C., by the Rev. A. P. Gray, in Ascension Church, Amherst. So. Ch., Dec. 18, 1890

Mary L., d. of Geo. Fred. and M. Fenton Brown, and John Murphy, Esq. of Westmoreland, Va., by the Rev. John M. Rogers of N. J., at St. Peckatone, the residence of the bride's father. So. Ch., Nov. 30, 1860

Mary R., d. of the Rt. Rev. Dr. Wm. A. Brown, and Warren Channel of Portsmouth, Va., by the Bishop assisted by the Rev. Roderick H. Jackson, rector of St. John's, in St. John's Church, Portsmouth. So. Ch., Nov. 1, 1941

Philip F., and Nannie E. Adams, by the Rev. Churchill J. Gibson, in Christ Church, Smithfield, Va. So. Ch., July 18, 1867

Samuel G., and Annie M. Bowers, by the Rev. W. D. Hanson, at Faulkland, Del. So. Ch., Mar. 15, 1882

Thomas, Jr., and Lottie E., youngest d. of the late R. A. Claybrook, by the Rev. F. W. Claybrook, in Yeocomico Church, Westmoreland Co. So. Ch., Jan. 20, 1876

William Ambrose (The Rt. Rev.), D.D., LL.D., Bishop of Southern Virginia, and Winifred Washington, d. of Judge Legh Richmond and Mrs. Mattie Peters Watts of Portsmouth, Va., by the Rt. Rev. Robert C. Jett, D.D., retired Bishop of Southwestern Virginia, assisted by Philip DuMond Davis, in St. John's Church, Portsmouth. So. Ch., Sept.

MARRIAGE NOTICES IN THE SOUTHERN CHURCHMAN WITH DATES OF PUBLICATION

16, 1939
William Cabell (The Rev.), of Nelson Co., Va., and Ida Mason Dorsey, by the Rev. A. R. Stuart, D.D., in Christ Church, Georgetown, D.C. So. Ch., Aug. 13, 1891
Wingfield L., of Montana, and Sallie Perkins Lewis of Nelson Co., Va., by the Rev. T. E. Locke, at Avon Hill, the residence of Z. R. Lewis. So. Ch., Jan. 26, 1888
See also STEPHENSON, Sarah (Mrs.)

BROWNE
Andrew S., of Norfolk, Va., and Mary Minor, d. of Jno. R. Segar, Esq., by the Rev. J. Hervey Hundley, at the residence of the bride's father in Middlesex Co., Va. So. Ch., Oct. 6, 1887
Granville S. P., of N.C., and Cornelia R. Goodloe, by the Rev. Henry L. Derby, at the residence of the bride's mother in Suffolk, Va. So. Ch., Apr. 23, 1891
Josephine, eldest d. of Dr. P. T. Browne of Accomac Co., Va., and the Rev. T. A. Tidball, rector of Trinity, Portsmouth, by the Rev. Alexander S. Berkeley, in St. James' Church, Drummondtown. So. Ch., Oct. 31, 1872
Orris A., of Cape Charles City, and Nannie Bruce Howard of Richmond, Va., by the Rev. Thomas Tidball, D.D. of Camden, N.J. assisted by the Rev. Landon R. Mason, rector of the church, in Grace Church, Richmond, Va. So. Ch., Dec. 17, 1891
P. F. (Dr.), of Williamsburg, and Sally C., second d. of Thomas M. Bayly, by the Rev. H. M. Bartlett, in Accomac Co. So. Ch., Nov. 29, 1839
Wm. P. (The Rev.), and Mary Brown, d. of R. B. Johnson, M.D., and gr.d. of the late Gov. McWillie, by the rector, the Rev. W. Presbury, assisted by the Rev. V. B. Bowden, in St. Philip's Church, Kirkwood, Miss. So. Ch., Aug. 23, 1883
Willie A., d. of Dr. P. F. Browne of Accomac, and Geo. S. Stokes of Danville, by the Rev. T. A. Tidball, in St. James' Church, Drummondtown, Va. So. Ch., June 20, 1872

BROWNING
Belle Fauntleroy, eldest d. of John A. Browning, Esq. of Greenfield, Rappahannock Co., Va., and Dangerfield Lewis, Esq. of Cleve, King George Co., Va., by the Rev. James Carmichael, D.D. assisted by the Rev. John McGill, in Trinity Church, Bloomfield Parish,*Va. So. Ch., Nov. 18, 1880

BROWSE
Frances Louise, and the Rev. Peerce Naylor McDonald of Anchorage, Ky., by the Rt. Rev. George Peterkin assisted by the Rev. J. L. Fish of Sistersville, at Raven Rock, the residence of the bride's mother, Mrs. Robert Browse, Pleasants Co., W.Va. So. Ch., July 2, 1910
Mary E., and Edmund Holdren, by the Rev. Jacob Brittingham, at Grape Island, W Va. So. Ch., Feb. 23,

---

* Bloomfield Parish was in Rappahannock County, Virginia. In 1881 the name "Bloomfield" was changed to "Bromfield" (<u>Journals ... Diocese of Virginia</u> 1880, 1881 and 1941)

- 70 -

MARRIAGE NOTICES IN THE SOUTHERN CHURCHMAN WITH DATES OF PUBLICATION

1882
Robert Thomas, and Mary Aglionby McDonald, by the Rev. P. N. McDonald and the Rev. J. S. Alfriend, at "Media", near Charles Town, W.Va. So. Ch., Nov. 11, 1911

BRUCE
Albert C., of Charlotte Co., and Mary E., d. of Philip F. Howard, by the Rev. Charles H. Read, D.D., at the residence of the bride's father, in Richmond, Va. So. Ch., Dec. 10, 1874

Annie* Seddon, d. of Charles Bruce, Esq. of Charlotte Co., Va., and Thos. Nelson Page of Richmond, by the Rev. Frank Page, at Staunton Hill. So. Ch., Aug. 12, 1886

Callie, d. of Edward C. Bruce of Winchester, and Charles Russell Oldham of Moundsville, W.Va., by the Rev. Nelson P. Dame, in Christ Church, Winchester. So. Ch., July 5, 1888

Ellen C., d. of Charles Bruce, Esq., and James B. Baylor of the U.S. Coast and Geodetic Survey, by the Rev. Thomas Drew, at Staunton Hill, Charlotte Co., Va. So. Ch., Jan. 13, 1881

J. Douglas (Col.), of Clarke Co., and M. Claiborne, d. of the late James R. Hubard of Norfolk, in Winchester. So. Ch., Nov. 5, 1868

Mary Hubbard, d. of Edward C. Bruce, Esq. of Winchester, and the Rev. Jefferson Randolph Taylor, rector of Trinity Church, Moundsville, W. Va., by the Rev. Nelson P. Dame, rector of the parish, in Christ Church, Winchester, Va. So. Ch., Jan. 29, 1891

Richard, Esq., of Halifax Co., Va., and Mary E., eldest d. of A. J. Lowry of Madison Parish, La., by the Rev. C. K. Marshall, Madison Parish, La. So. Ch., Feb. 27, 1857

Richard H., and Montese Bass, both of Chesterfield Co., Va., by the Rev. A. B. Tizzard, in Trinity Church, Dale Parish, Chesterfield Co., Va. So. Ch., May 29, 1890

Sophie C., of South Bend, Halifax Co., and Matthew Fontaine Maury of Richmond, by the Rev. C. B. Bryan assisted by the rector, the Rev. Dr. G. W. Dame, in the Church of the Epiphany, in Danville. So. Ch., June 23, 1892

Thomas Seddon, and Mary Bruce Anderson, by the Rev. Charles Minnigerode, at the residence of Gen. Joseph R. Anderson, at Richmond. So. Ch., Apr. 22, 1875

BRUGH
Louisa D., of Botetourt, and Richard Cogdell of Georgia, by the Rev. E. W. Hubard, at Oak Grove. So. Ch., June 23, 1870

BRUNE
Frederick William, and Blanche, d. of Augusta C. E. and the late Samuel M. Shoemaker, by

---

* Given as printed. Should be Anne

MARRIAGE NOTICES IN THE SOUTHERN CHURCHMAN WITH DATES OF PUBLICATION

the Rev. J. H. Eccleston, D.D., in Emmanuel Church, Baltimore, Md. So. Ch., May 7, 1885

BRYAN
C. B. (The Rev.), of Virginia, and Mary, d. of Dr. W. W. Scott of Lenoir, N.C., by the Rev. F. L. Bush. So. Ch., Mar. 9, 1882

Georgia I., second d. of John R. Bryan, Esq., and Doct.* A. S. Grinnan of Madison Co., by the Rev. C. Mann, at Eagle Point, Gloucester Co., Va. So. Ch., July 1, 1859

Joseph, Esq., of Richmond, and Isabel Lamont, second d. of John Stewart, Esq. of Brook Hill, by the Rev. Wm. Norwood, D.D., in Emmanuel Church, Henrico Co. So. Ch., Feb. 16, 1871

Malcolm Wright, of Roanoke, Va., and Mary Anne, d. of the late Charles E. de Haven, by the Rev. C. George Currie, D.D., in St. Luke's Church, Philadelphia. So. Ch., Dec. 31, 1885

BRYANT
Addie, and Peter Epps, Esq., by the Rev. James Walter Keeble, at the residence of the bride's father, Prince George Co., Va. So. Ch., Sept. 14, 1876

Jonathan, and Charlotte Killman, both of Westmoreland, by the Rev. D. M. Wharton. So. Ch., Dec. 31, 1868

W. S., of Baltimore, Md., and Julia B. Eggleston, by the Rev. W. M. Walters, at the residence of the bride's father in Giles Co., Va. So. Ch., Jan. 11, 1883

William (The Rev.), and Emma, d. of John C. Herbert, Esq. of Prince George's Co., Md., by the Rev. William Pinkney, in Prince George's Co., Md. So. Ch., Dec. 1, 1837

BRYARLY
J. Elliott, and Mary B., d. of Wm. T. Allen, all of Clarke Co., by the Rev. F. P. Phillips, at Balclutha, the residence of the bride's father. So. Ch., Sept. 11, 1884

Mary, d. of the late Robt. P. Bryarly, and Jacob Van Doran, Jr., by the Rev. Wm. McGuire, at Federal Hill, Berkeley Co. So. Ch., Oct. 9, 1857

BUCHANAN
Anselan (The Rev.), rector of St. John's P. E. Church, Bayonne, N.J., and Willia, d. of Mrs. E. H. Thompson of Louisville, and the late William Henry Thompson, U.S. Navy, by the Rev. Dr. Craik, in Christ Church. So. Ch., July 1, 1875

BUCK
Charles E., and Emily Chesley, d. of the officiating clergyman, the Rev. J. W. Chesley, in All Faith Church, St. Mary's Co., Md. So. Ch., June 28, 1877

R. Carey, M.D., of Fauquier Co., and Mary Lewis, d. of J. T. Leachman of Prince William Co., Va., by the Rev. Arthur P. Gray, at the residence of the bride's parents. So. Ch., Dec. 1, 1881

* Given as printed

MARRIAGE NOTICES IN THE SOUTHERN CHURCHMAN WITH DATES OF PUBLICATION

BUCKINGHAM
    Olive, youngest d. of the late E. F. Buckingham Washington, D.C., and B. W. Leigh, Martinsburg, W. Va., by the Rev. Wallace Cornahan, Little Rock, Ark., at the home of Mr. and Mrs. Warren Taylor, Bastrop, La. So. Ch., Oct. 5, 1893

BUCKNER
    C. C., Esq., of Alexandria, and Louisa F. Dickinson of Caroline Co., Va., by the Rev. Henry Wall. So. Ch., Dec. 1, 1853

    Martha Bull, d. of Aylette Harris Buckner of Rappahannock Co., Va., and William Meade Fletcher of Rappahannock Co., at the Raleigh Hotel, Washington, D.C. So. Ch., Oct. 10, 1914

    Mary Elizabeth, eldest d. of John S. Buckner of Rappahannock Co., and Richard Percy Spiers of Halifax, N.C., by the Rev. R. T. Brown, near Sperryville, Va. So. Ch., Feb. 9, 1871

    Simon Bolivar (Gen.), of Hart Co., Ky., and Delia Hayes, eldest d. of Maj. John H. Claiborne, by the Rev. Joshua Peterkin, D.D., at the residence of the bride's uncle, Herbert A. Claiborne, Esq. So. Ch., June 25, 1885

BUEL
    D. Hillhouse (The Rev.), and Mary Mayo Atkinson, d. of the Bishop, by the Bishop of North Carolina, in St. James' Church, Wilmington. So. Ch., July 17, 1857

BUFFINGTON
    John N. (Dr.), of Cabell Co., and Maria Farley, d. of the late John Thompson, Esq. of Culpeper C.H., by the Rev. John Cole, in Culpeper Co. So. Ch., Mar. 20, 1857

BUFORD
    Bettie, and James Phillips, Esq. of Greensville Co., Va., by the Rev. Otis A. Glazebrook, at the residence of the bride's mother in Brunswick. So. Ch., May 4, 1871

    Thomas M., of Petersburg, Va., and Maria Louisa, d. of Jabez Smith of Chesterfield Co., by the Rev. Andrew Syme, Petersburg, Va. So. Ch., Dec. 1, 1837

BUGG
    Martha K., eldest d. of Charles Bugg, Esq., and C. W. Blanton, all of Farmville, Va., by the Rev. A. S. Lloyd, in John's Memorial Church, Farmville. So. Ch., Sept. 25, 1884

BULL
    John Elliot, and Jessie Bryan, d. of the Rev. John B. Williams, rector of the parish, by the Rev. Dr. Ellison Capers, in Prince George's Winjah, Episcopal Church, Georgetown, S.C. So. Ch., Jan. 12, 1893

BUNTING
    Carrie Lindsay, d. of J. Bunting, Esq. of Bristol, Goodson, Tenn., and Virginia,* and the Rev. Pendleton Brooke of Botetourt Co., by the Rev. Jno. S. Lindsay of Warrenton, in Emmanuel Church, Goodson, Va. So. Ch., May 1, 1873

    Chambers L. (Dr.), and Fannie K. Keebler, both of Bristol - Goodson,* by the

* Given as printed

MARRIAGE NOTICES IN THE SOUTHERN CHURCHMAN WITH DATES OF PUBLICATION

Rev. O. S. Bunting, at Bristol - Goodson, Va. - Tenn.* So. Ch., Dec. 15, 1887

J., Jr., of Roanoke, Va., and Margaret Douglass, d. of Col. W. H. Fry, proprietor of Coyners Springs, by the Rev. O. S. Bunting, at the residence of the bride's father. So. Ch., Nov. 17, 1887

Minnie, of Bristol - Goodson, and Edward T. Jones, Esq. of Abingdon, by the Rev. O. S. Bunting, in Emmanuel Church, Bristol - Goodson, Va.* So. Ch., Dec. 25, 1884

Oscar S., of Amherst Co., Va., and Mary P., eldest d. of Dr. S. G. Harriss of Boydton, Va., by the Rev. P. M. Boyden assisted by the Rev. R. A. Goodwin. So. Ch., Nov. 13, 1879

BURCH
Anna E., eldest d. of James Burch of Essex Co., Va., and Samuel L. Sparrow of Middlesex Co., by the Rev. J. H. Hundley, at the residence of the bride's father. So. Ch., Oct. 31, 1889

F. M. (The Rev.), and Mary C. Smoot, by the Rev. W. Strother Jones assisted by the Rev. James H. Williams, at the residence of the bride's father, J. H. D. Smoot, Alexandria, Va. So. Ch., Nov. 16, 1882

BURCHER
Sallie J., d. of James Burcher, Esq., and Charles J. Ost, Esq., by the Rev. John C. McCabe, in Hampton. So. Ch., Dec. 28, 1855

BURGIE
Josephine, and Thomas Willoughby Cole of Virginia, in Trinity Church, Chicago, Ill. So. Ch., Jan. 15, 1885

BURGWIN
Hill, Esq., of the city of Pittsburgh, and Susan Nash Wooster, d. of the Hon. Henry K. Nash, by the Rev. Joseph W. Murphy, in Hillsboro, N.C. So. Ch., Nov. 1, 1888

BURGWYN
Collinson P. E., and Rosa Bayly, d. of E. G. Higginbotham of Ravenswood, Henrico Co., by the Rev. Green Shackelford assisted by the Rev. Dr. Minnigerode, at the residence of the bride's gr. mother, Mrs. Jane O. Bayly, 203 W. Franklin St., Richmond. So. Ch., Oct. 23, 1884

Maria G., only d. of Henry K. Burgwyn of North Carolina, and T. Robert Baker of Richmond, by the Rev. Dr. Bowles, rector, assisted by the Rev. F. M. Baker of Richmond, Va., in the Church of the Advent in Boston, Mass. So. Ch., Nov. 12, 1868

Wm. H. S., Esq., of Baltimore, Md., and Margaret Carlisle, d. of the late James and Mrs. Ann Dent Dunlop of Richmond, by the Rev. Dr. Minnigerode, in St. Paul's Church, Richmond, Va. So. Ch., Nov. 30, 1876

* Given as printed

MARRIAGE NOTICES IN THE SOUTHERN CHURCHMAN WITH DATES OF PUBLICATION

BURKE
　Julian T., and Esther D., d. of Charles S. Taylor, Esq., all of Alexandria, by the Rev. D. F. Sprigg, in St. Paul's Church, Alexandria. So. Ch., Oct. 25, 1877

BURKHARDT
　William Hullihen (The Rev.), of the Diocese of West Virginia, and Janie Carr, d. of W. M. S. and Bettie I. Dunn, by the Rev. Walter I. Hullihen of Staunton, at Midway, Va. So. Ch., July 6, 1893

BURKHART
　Bessie Keyes, and Robort* Lamon, both of Martinsburg, by the Rev. Henry Thomas assisted by the Rev. Walter I. Hullihen, in Trinity Church, Martinsburg. So. Ch., May 2, 1889

BURKS
　Josephine F., and Robert W. Withers of Alabama, by the Rev. John K. Mason, at the residence of O. P. Bell, Liberty, Va. So. Ch., June 15, 1882
　Rowland, of Liberty, Va., and Eliza F., d. of the late John J. Lloyd of Alexandria, Va., by the Rev. Arthur S. Lloyd, in Farmville, Va. So. Ch., Feb. 17, 1881

BURMLEY
　Annie Lewis, of Albemarle Co., Va., and Peachy H. Early of Campbell Co., by the Rev. W. W. Kimball, at the residence of the bride's parents. So. Ch., Aug. 14, 1884

BURNETT
　J. R., of Livingston, N.J., and Phoebe Osborne of Castile, Genessee Co., N. Y., (a pupil of the Institution for the Deaf and Dumb), by the Rev. Dr. Milnor, President of the Institution, at the Institution for the Deaf and Dumb, Richmond, Va. So. Ch., Aug. 16, 1839

BURNHAM
　Michael, of New York, and Jane Carter, d. of Charles Sigourney, Esq. of Hartford, by the Rt. Rev. Bishop Griswold, in Boston. So. Ch., Oct. 18, 1839
　Robert, and Lottie Marshall, by the Rev. Robb White, in Grace Church, Albemarle Co., Va. So. Ch., Jan. 10, 1884

BURNS
　Lillie, d. of A. P. Burns, of Baltimore, and Charles L. Turner of Prince George's Co., Md., by the Rev. J. B. Perry, in St. Andrew's Church, Washington, D.C. So. Ch., July 30, 1885
　Minnie R., d. of Dr. A. P. Burns of Maryland, and Wm. Everett Harman, of Chicago, Ill., by the Rev. Fritz Simons**, in Chicago. So. Ch., Jan. 26, 1888
　Virginia Isabella, d. of David W. Burns, and Thomas M. Tiller, all of Richmond, by the Rev. Mt. Peterkin, in St. James' Church, Richmond, Va. So. Ch., Nov. 28, 1856
　Virginia R., d. of Dr. A. P. Burns of Baltimore, and J. C. Bush of Philadelphia,

---

* Given as printed
** A notice appears in the issue of Jan. 19, 1888 identical with this, except that "Fritz Simons" is written "Fitz Simons"

MARRIAGE NOTICES IN THE SOUTHERN CHURCHMAN WITH DATES OF PUBLICATION

by the Rev. Dr. A. M.
Randolph, in Baltimore.
So. Ch., Feb. 3, 1881

BURR
Peter P., of Fredericksburg, and Maria S. Wiatt,
by the Rev. W. W. Green,
at the residence of the
bride's brother-in-law,
Spotsylvania Co. So.
Ch., Dec. 18, 1863

BURROUGHS
J. R. Freeman, of Lynchburg, and Lucy Whiting
Davies, by the Rev. Wm.
H. Pendleton, at the
residence of Mayo Davies,
Esq., Bedford Co., Va.
So. Ch., Jan. 20, 1860

BURRUSS
S. G. (Mrs.), of New Kent
Co., Va., and G. W.
Harrison of Marion,
Ala., by the Rev. S. S.
Hepbron, at Farmington,
the residence of W. H.
Macon, Esq. So. Ch.,
Jan. 31, 1889

BURTON
Dora, of Hanover Co., Va.,
and Harvey S. Comery, of
Thomaston, Me., by the
Rev. S. S. Hepbron. So.
Ch., Dec. 11, 1884
Sarah A. (Mrs.), and P. M.
Austin, by the Rev. J. B.
Craighill, at Maysville,
Ky. So. Ch., Apr. 18,
1872
Sarah Louise, d. of the Rt.
Rev. and Mrs. Lewis
Burton of Lexington, and
Henry Kavanaugh, s. of
Mrs. Kate Adams and the
late Col. Hubbard Kavanaugh
Milward of Lexington,
Ky., by the Bishop of
Lexington assisted by
the Very Rev. W. T.
Capers, Dean of the
Cathedral, in Christ
Church Cathedral, Lexington,
Ky. So. Ch., July 9, 1910

BURWELL
Evelyn Carter, and E. Wickham, both of Clarke Co.,
Va., by the Rev. John P.
Tyler, rector, in Christ
Church, Millwood, Va. So.
Ch., June 30, 1892
George H., of Richmond, and
Laura D., d. of Maj.
Charles H. Lee of Loudoun
Co., by the Rev. W. H.
Johnson, at "Dumbarton",
the residence of the
bride's father. So. Ch.,
Oct. 4, 1877
Lucy C., d. of Col. Thos. N.
Burwell of Botetourt Co.,
Va., and Dr. P. Trent of
Richmond, Va., by the Rev.
F. M. Baker, at Rustic
Lodge. So. Ch., Oct. 26,
1855
Nannie W., and Dr. Wilson G.
Hunter of Norfolk, by the
Rev. G. W. Dame, in Danville. So. Ch., Apr. 17,
1863
Nelson Chancellor, s. of Dr.
William Burwell of
Perkersburg, W.Va., and
Katharine Lomax, youngest
d. of Mrs. Kate Lomax Reed
and the late Rev. Theodore
Reed, rector of the Church
at Bladenburg and Hyattsville, Md., by the Rev. R.
P. Williams, in Trinity
Chapel, Washington, D.C.
So. Ch., Jan. 30, 1909
Thomas H., of Virginia, and
Virginia, d. of the late
Jesse Sharpe, Esq., by the
Rev. Dr. H. B. Martin, at
Wilmington, Del. So. Ch.,
Nov. 16, 1882
See also HENRY, Susan R.
(Mrs.)

MARRIAGE NOTICES IN THE SOUTHERN CHURCHMAN WITH DATES OF PUBLICATION

BUSH
    J. C., of Philadelphia, and Virginia R., d. of Dr. A. P. Burns, by the Rev. Dr. A. M. Randolph, in Baltimore. So. Ch., Feb. 3, 1881

BUTLER
    Chas. T. (Dr.), of Maryland, and Bettie L., d. of Wm. N. Craighill, Esq. of Baltimore, by the Rev. James B. Craighill assisted by the Rev. J. H. Williams, at Lynchburg, Va. So. Ch., Sept. 10, 1874

    Charlotte F., of Harrisonburg, Va., and Clifford M. Maddox of Baltimore, Md., by the Rev. D. M. Wood, at the residence of the bride's brother, Dr. W. S. Butler, Roanoke City, Va. So. Ch., Apr. 23, 1885

    Clement M. (The Rev.), of Syracuse, N.Y., and Frances L., d. of the Rev. Wm. H. Hart of Richmond, by the Rt. Rev. Bishop Moore. So. Ch., Apr. 21, 1837

    Geo. G., of Washington, and Adie, d. of the late Edward Ingle of Washington City, by the Rev. Wm. Hodges, in Christ Church, Washington, D.C. So. Ch., Aug. 3, 1854

    Jenny V., d. of the late John H. Butler of Norfolk, Va., and Lt. Wilkinson Penrose, C.S.A. of New Orleans, by the Rev. Wm. C. Butler, in Norfolk, Va. So. Ch., Mar. 7, 1862

    Mattie A., of Jackson, Tenn., and Dr. Charles W. Chancellor of Memphis, by the Rt. Rev. J. P. B. Wilmer, Bishop of Louisiana, in New Orleans. So. Ch., Mar. 21, 1867

    Nannie E., d. of the late John H. Butler of Norfolk, Va., and H. O. Rawles of Baltimore, by the Rev. Wm. C. Butler, in the Church of the Holy Innocents, Henderson, N. C. So. Ch., Jan. 15, 1864

    W. W. S. (Dr.), of Staunton, Va., and Agnes Alexander Jones, sister of the officiating clergyman, the Rev. W. Strother Jones, in Emmanuel Church, Fauquier Co., Va. So. Ch., Nov. 30, 1882

    Wm. C. (The Rev.), of Halifax C. H., Va., and Fanny Woods of Albemarle Co., Va., by the Rev. R. K. Meade, in Christ Church, Charlottesville. So. Ch., Dec. 30, 1859

BUTT
    J. L. D., of Memphis, Tenn., and Maggie A. Brittingham of Northampton Co., Va., by the Rev. J. B. Craighill, in Christ Church, Eastville. So. Ch., Dec. 15, 1869

    Sarah J., and James Brooks, both of Berkeley Co., W.Va., by the Rev. George S. May, near Hedgesville. So. Ch., Apr. 2, 1874

BUXTON
    Catherine Cameron, and Joseph H. McRee of Wilmington, N.C., by the Rev. J. Buxton, D. D. assisted by the Rev. D. Hillhouse Buel, at Ashville, N.C. So. Ch.,

MARRIAGE NOTICES IN THE SOUTHERN CHURCHMAN WITH DATES OF PUBLICATION

Nov. 11, 1875
BYERS
  Cordelia Agnes, d. of the late John A. Byers, C.E. of Hancock, Md., and John McCulloch, Jr. of Point Pleasant, by the Rev. Horace Edwin Hayden, rector of St. John's Church, West Brownsville, Pa., assisted by the Rev. T. Hugo Lacy, rector of the parish, in Christ Church, Point Pleasant, W.Va. So. Ch., Nov. 13, 1873

  Hattie A., d. of J. A. Byers, Esq. of Hancock, Md., and Sam'l M. Stephens of Baltimore, by the Rev. Horace E. Hayden, at the residence of Talliaferro Stribling, Esq., Point Pleasant, W. Va. So. Ch., Dec. 26, 1867

  Kate Elizabeth, d. of John A. Byers, Esq., and the Rev. Horace Edwin Hayden, all of Md., by the Rev. Joseph A. Nock, Point Pleasants, W. Va. So. Ch., Dec. 10, 1868

BYRD
  Courtney B., and the Rev. Joseph R. Jones, rector of Christ Church, Millwood, by the Rev. Dr. Andrews, in Trinity Church, Shepherdstown, So. Ch., Oct. 5, 1860

  E. Wickham, and Evelyn Carter Burwell, both of Clarke Co., Va., by the Rev. John P. Tyler, rector, in Christ Church, Millwood, Va. So. Ch., June 20, 1892

  Emily (Mrs.), d. of the late Robert Neilson, of Baltimore, and Dr. Benjamin Blackford of Lynchburg, Va., by the Rev. Thomas U. Dudley, in Christ Church, Baltimore. So. Ch., Jan. 26, 1871*

  Geo. H., of Baltimore, and Lucy Carter, d. of the late E. F. Wickham, by the Rev. Mr. Peterkin, at the residence of W. F. Wickham, Hanover Co. So. Ch., Feb. 6, 1857

  Rebecca M., and Robinson Nottingham, both of Northampton Co., Va., by the Rev. Dr. Colton, in Christ Church, Eastville, Va. So. Ch., Nov. 23, 1860

  Robert W., of Roanoke City, and Frances Minor, only d. of John T. McDaniel, by the Rev. John McGill, at the residence of the bride's parents, Montgomery Co., Va. So. Ch., Feb. 16, 1893

BYUS
  Annie E., and Jesse C. Richardson, both of Church Creek, Dorchester Co., Md., by the Rev. Wm. W. Greene. So. Ch., Apr. 7, 1881

* This notice appears in the issue of Jan. 19, 1871, except that "Neilson" is written "Nelson"

C

CABELL

Annie Woolsten, d. of George W. Cabell, Esq. of Inglewood, Nelson Co., and Dr. Henry L. Cabell, by the Rev. F. D. Goodwin. So. Ch., July 5, 1855

Ella Bruce, d. of the late Mayo Cabell, Esq., and Thos. A. Seddon of Fredericksburg, Va., by the Rev. Edmund Withers, at Union Hill, Nelson Co., Va. So. Ch., Jan. 6, 1876

Henry L. (Dr.), and Annie Woolsten, d. of George W. Cabell, Esq. of Inglewood, Nelson Co., by the Rev. F. D. Goodwin. So. Ch., July 5, 1855

James L. (Prof.), and Margaret N. Gibbons, by the Rev. R. K. Meade, at University of Virginia. So. Ch., Feb. 15, 1839

Jessie, of Norwood, Nelson Co., and the Rev. George Braxton Taylor of Chapel Hill, N. C., by the Rev. J. B. Taylor, D.D. assisted by the Rev. Davis M. Wood, in Christ Church, Norwood. So. Ch., Jan. 3, 1889

Kate Hamilton, and Herbert A. Claiborne, by the Rev. Melville Jackson, at the residence of the bride's father, Col. H. Coalter Cabell. So. Ch., Feb. 16, 1882

Lizzie Caskie, d. of Dr. Robert G. Cabell of Richmond, Va., and Albert Ritchie of Baltimore, by the Rev. Thomas G. Addison, D. D. assisted by the Rev. Charles Minnigerode, D. D., in St. Paul's Church, Richmond, Va. So. Ch., Nov. 18, 1875

Mary Cornelia, d. of Wm. D. Cabell, and Wm. Stephenson of Washington, Penn., by the Rev. Mayo Cabell Martin, rector of the Church of the Holy Trinity, Nashville, Tenn., at the home of the bride's father, Norwood, Nelson Co., Va. So. Ch., Aug. 11, 1887

P. B., of Nelson Co., and Julia C., oldest d. of Thomas Bolling, Esq. of Goochland Co., Va., by the Rev. T. F. Martin, at Bolling's Island. So. Ch., Mar. 8, 1861

Richard H., of Lovingston, and Louisa, youngest d. of the late Rev. Edmund Withers, by the Rev. B. T. Turner, in Christ Church, Norwood. So. Ch., July 3, 1884

Sallie Randolph, and Alexander Brown, by the Rev. Byrd Thornton Turner, at Union Hill, Nelson Co., Va. So. Ch., May 6 and June 10, 1886

See also EPES, Sallie Cabell (Mrs.)

CALDWELL

Ella, of Fredericksburg, Va., and Samuel L. Dedman of Fulton, Mo., by the Rev. John K. Mason, at Fredericksburg, Va. So. Ch., Sept. 11, 1884

Ellen D., d. of the late Rev. David Caldwell, and the Rev. J. R. McBryde of Amherst, by the Rev. Edmund Withers assisted by the Rev. Henderson Suter, at Hazlewood, Nelson Co. So. Ch., June 8, 1871

J. North, of Greenbrier Co., W. Va., and Caroline S., d. of Withers Waller, by the Rev.

MARRIAGE NOTICES IN THE SOUTHERN CHURCHMAN WITH DATES OF PUBLICATION

T. C. Page, in Clifton Chapel, Stafford Co. So. Ch., May 5, 1887

James E., Esq., and Mary A. M. Lee, all of Petersburg, Va., by the Rev. C. J. Gibson, in Grace Church, Petersburg, Va. So. Ch., Dec. 12, 1856

Joseph Eager, of Wytheville, Va., and Virginia Craddock Warner of Portsmouth, Va., by the Rev. Braxton Bryan, in Grace Church, Petersburg, Va. So. Ch., May 22, 1915

Mary Virginia, of Greenbrier Co., W. Va., and Col. Cary Breckinridge of Botetourt, Va., by the Rev. Peter Tinsley. So. Ch., July 19, 1866

CALHOUN

James Grant, of Maryland, and Edmonia Churchill Harrison of Danville, formerly of Hanover Co., Va., by the Rev. Geo. W. Dame, D. D., assisted by the Rt. Rev. A. M. Randolph, Assistant Bishop of Virginia, and the Rev. J. Y. Downman, in the Church of the Epiphany, Danville, Va. So. Ch., Sept. 23, 1886

Louise C., d. of P. Calhoun, Esq, of Bridgeport, and George Woodville Latham of Lynchburg, Va., by the Rev. G. S, Coit, D. D., at Bridgeport, Conn. So. Ch., Sept. 30, 1859

CALLAHAN

Joseph B., and Adelaide Batchelor, both of Montgomery Co., Md., by the Rev. John S. Lindsay, D. D., in Georgetown, D. C. So. Ch., Dec. 16, 1886

CALLAWAY

Anna Beckwith, d. of the late Rev. Charles M. Callaway, and Col. George Alexander of New York City, by the Rev. Julius Sams, D. D., at the residence of the bride's mother in Baltimore. So. Ch., July 26, 1882

Charles McK. (The Rev.), and M. M. Holtzman of Virginia, by the Rev. Mr. Clark, in Christ Church, Alexandria. So. Ch., July 18, 1850

George Carrington (Dr.), of Nelson Co., and Pattie Waller, d. of Col. W. R. Aylett of King William Co., Va., by the Rev. S. S. Hepbron, in St. David's Church, King William Co. So. Ch., June 21, 1888

Lila C., eldest d. of Dr. P. C. Callaway, and Wm. B. Hubard, all of Nelson Co., Va., by the Rev. T. F. Martin, at the residence of the bride's father. So. Ch., Feb. 8, 1865

Sallie K., of Spotsylvania Co., Va., and Geo. W. Meade, Esq. formerly of Clarke Co., Va., by the Rev. C. M. Callaway, at Topeka, Kan. So. Ch., June 4, 1858

Sarah B., d. of Dr. P. Carrington Callaway of Nelson, and Francis Key Meade of Clarke, an associate principal of Norwood School, by the Rev. Edmund Withers, at Montezuma, Nelson Co., Va. So. Ch., Sept. 24, 1874

CALLENDER

Virginia C., d. of Rev. and Mrs. William E. Callender (secretary of the Seaman's Institute of America), and James B. Johnston, by the Rt. Rev. B. D. Tucker,

MARRIAGE NOTICES IN THE SOUTHERN CHURCHMAN WITH DATES OF PUBLICATION

CAMDEN
    Jessie, only d. of Dr. T. B. Camden of Wheeling, and Dr. J. S. Lewis, of Weston, by the Rev. R. R. Swope, in St. Mathews Church. So. Ch., Feb. 15, 1883
    Richard P., Esq., and Flora Davisson, by the Rev. Henry T. Sharp, in St. Paul's Church, Weston, W. Va. So. Ch., June 9, 1870

CAMERON
    Benneham, of North Carolina, and Sallie Taliaferro, d. of Mr. and Mrs. P. H. Mayo, in All Saints Church, Richmond, Va. So. Ch., Nov. 19, 1891
    Helen Miller, and the Rev. Everett H. Jones, rector of St. Marks Church, in St. Marks Church, San Antonio, Tex. So. Ch., Dec. 7, 1940
    John A., of Canada, and Kate S. Crewe, third d. of Wm. and Sarah Crewe of Prince William Co., Va., formerly of England, at "Chestnut Hill," the residence of the bride's father. So. Ch., July 17, 1884

CAMMACK
    Caroline M., d. of Robt. Cammack, Esq. of Spotsylvania Co., Va., and Robert C. Duerson, Esq., by the Rev. J. W. Woodville. So. Ch., Oct. 25, 1839

CAMP
    Emma B., of Norfolk, and David S. Read of Roanoke Co., by the Rev. O. S. Barten, D. D., rector, in Christ Church, Norfolk. So. Ch., Aug. 18, 1870

CAMPBELL
    Ann E., and A. J. West, both of Jefferson, by the Rev. J. D. Powell. So. Ch., Feb. 15, 1856
    Annie, and Joseph D. Tulloss, by the Rev. Jno. McGill, at the residence of S. Welsh, the bride's uncle. So. Ch., Dec. 9, 1869
    Eleanor Conrad, eldest d. of S. J. Campbell, and John A. Blume, all of Lexington, Va., by the Rev. W. S. Campbell of London, Ohio, in Grace Memorial Church, Lexington, Va. So. Ch., Nov. 6, 1884
    George, s. of Mr. and Mrs. J. G. Campbell of Mobile, Ala., and Virginia Duncan, d. of Mr. and Mrs. F. W. Nelson, by the Rev. Robert B. Nelson, a cousin of the bride, in Richmond. So. Ch., Sept. 25, 1920
    Helen Barton, d. of the late Robert Campbell, Esq. of Philadelphia, Pa., and Jay Cooke of Washington City, by the Rev. Dr. Lindsay of Georgetown, in St. Mark's Church, Berkeley Springs, Morgan Co., W. Va. So. Ch., Nov. 9, 1882
    J. Harmond (Dr.), of Athens, Ga., and Mattie Paxton, d. of J. P. Steele, Esq., by the Rev. Mr. Irwin, of the Presbyterian church, in Lexington, Va. So. Ch., Jan. 4, 1883
    John P. (Dr.), of the University of Georgia, Athens, and Martha Forest, d. of Maj. R. W. Hunter, by the Rev. Nelson P. Dame, in Christ Church, Winchester. So. Ch., Feb. 18, 1892
    Phebe K., d. of J. Mason Campbell, Esq. of Baltimore, and the Rev. A. P. Stryker, by the Rt. Rev.

MARRIAGE NOTICES IN THE SOUTHERN CHURCHMAN WITH DATES OF PUBLICATION

W. R. Whittingham, D. D., in Grace Church, Baltimore, Md. So. Ch., Oct. 12, 1865

Philip S., and Lizzie, d. of the late John and Louisa A. Milton, by the Rev. John L. McKee, at the residence of Mr. R. M. Cunningham, in Louisville, Ky. So. Ch., Oct. 20, 1870

Sallie Mitchell, and the Rev. Thomas Walker Jones, rector of All Saints Church, Grenada, Miss., in Christ Church, Roanoke, Va. So. Ch., Sept. 18, 1915

Sarah A. (Mrs.), and Chas. O. Padgett, by the Rev. W. H. Pendleton, at the residence of the bride's mother in Bedford Co. So. Ch., Feb. 20, 1868

Wm., and Janet R. R. Latane, both of Essex Co., Va., by the Rev. H. W. L. Temple, in Essex Co. So. Ch., Jan. 2, 1868

Wm., of Charlestown, W. Va., and Ellen M., d. of the late Robert Rollins Fowle of Fairfax Co., Va., by the Rev. S. A. Wallis, in St. Paul's Church, Alexandria, Va. So. Ch., June 12, 1890

Wm. A., and Georgie T. Locke, d. of Capt. J. M. Locke, all of Berryville, Va., by the Rev. P. P. Phillips, in Grace Church, Berryville, Va. So. Ch., Apr. 26, 1888

Wm. P., of Bethany, Va., and Nannie, only d. of Dr. P. H. Cochrane, by the Rev. A. Buchanan, in St. Paul's Church, Louisville, Ky. So. Ch., July 21, 1870

William Stevens (The Rev.), of Trinity Church, Bellaire, and Virginia, d. of W. C. Stewart, by the Rev. J. M. Kendrick, D. D., at the residence of the bride's parents in Bellaire, Ohio. So. Ch., Aug. 16, 1888

CANNON
Mallory King, and Jessie Tredway Purnell, both of Charlotte, N. C., by the Rev. Willis Gaylord Clark, rector, in St. Peter's Episcopal Church, Charlotte, N. C. So. Ch., June 5, 1937

CANTHORN
M. A., Esq., of Danville, and Mary A. Hurley, by the Rev. George W. Dame, at Pittsylvania C.H. So. Ch., Dec. 29, 1870

CAPEHART
Armistead L., of Kittrell, N. C., and Lillian W. Bagwell of Onancock, by the Rev. Henry L. Derby, in Trinity Church, Onancock. So. Ch., July 28, 1892

Cadmus, of Norfolk, and Mary Martin, youngest d. of G. W. Capehart, by the Rev. Edward Wootten, at "Scotch Hall," Bertie Co., N. C. So. Ch., Jan. 14, 1869

Mary Martin, youngest d. of G. W. Capehart, and Cadmus Capehart of Norfolk, by the Rev. Edward Wooten, at "Scotch Hall," Bertie Co., N. C. So. Ch., Jan. 14, 1869

CAPERS
Charlotte P., d. of Mrs. John G. Capers of Washington, D.C., and Maj. Ralph Stover Keyser, United States Marine Corps, s. of Mr. and Mrs. Charles Eugene Keyser, by

MARRIAGE NOTICES IN THE SOUTHERN CHURCHMAN WITH DATES OF PUBLICATION

the Rev. Walter B. Capers, the paternal uncle of Miss Capers, at the residence of Mrs. John G. Capers, Washington, D.C. So. Ch., Sept. 11, 1920

Wm. Theodotus (The Rt. Rev.), D.D., Bishop of West Texas, and Mrs. Louis Cash Myers of Memphis, Tenn., by the Rev. Dr. Walter B. Capers, brother of the groom and rector of St. Andrew's Church, Jackson, Miss., assisted by the Rev. W. D. Britton, in Grace Church, Memphis. So. Ch., June 13, 1936

CAPERTON

Harriet, d. of Hon. A. T. Caperton, and W. A. Gordon of Georgetown, D.C., by the Rev. Mr. Mason, at Union, W. Va. So. Ch., Jan. 21, 1875

Lelia, d. of Hon. A. T. Caperton, and Robert Stiles of Richmond, by the Rev. Mr. Phillips of Staunton, at the residence of the bride's father, near Union, Monroe Co., W.Va. So. Ch., July 23, 1874

Mary, d. of Allen T. Caperton, Esq. of Monroe Co., and Dr. Tomlin Braxton of King William, by the Rev. A. H. Phillips, at Elmwood, the residence of the bride's father. So. Ch., Jan. 18, 1861

CARDWELL

W. D., s. of Hon. R. H. Cardwell, and Jane T., d. of the late Dr. Thomas L. Gregory, all of Hanover Co., Va., by the Rev. S. S. Hepburn,* at Blenheim, the residence of the bride's mother. So. Ch., May 15, 1890

CAREY

Gill A., Esq., of Hampton, Va., and Jennie L. Smith, d. of the officiating clergyman, the Rev. John C. McCabe, rector of the Church of the Ascension, in Baltimore. So. Ch., Oct. 3, 1856

N. R. (Dr.), and Susan, d. of Miers W. Fisher, Esq., by the Rev. J. M. Chevers, in Northampton Co. So. Ch., Dec. 28, 1855

Samuel B.(Dr.), of Gloucester, and Winifred E. McCarty of Middlesex Co., Va., by the Rev. Mr. Carraway, in Christ Church [location not given] So. Ch., Feb. 1, 1856

CARGILL

Lavinia, and William Blow, by the Rev. Henry C. Lay, at Norfolk, Va. So. Ch., Apr. 9, 1847

Mary Blanche, eldest d. of George W. Cargill, Esq., of Winfield, Putnam Co., W.Va., and William Walter Pendleton, Esq., of Clifton Forge, Va., formerly of Louisa Co., by the Rev. R. A. Cobbs of Charleston, at the residence of the bride's father. So. Ch., Nov. 13, 1884

Wm. E., of New York, and Pattie Hughes of Halifax, Va., by the Rev. O. A. Kinsolving, at the residence of the bride's mother. So. Ch., Sept. 8, 1870

CARLETON

V. S., and Emma Rahm, both of Richmond, Va., by the Rt. Rev. F. M. Whittle, in Trinity Church, Rocky Mount, Va. So. Ch., Nov. 30, 1876

CARLTON

* Given as printed

MARRIAGE NOTICES IN THE SOUTHERN CHURCHMAN WITH DATES OF PUBLICATION

Ling G., d. of the late Ambrose Carlton of Richmond, and Wm. J. Branch, by the Rev. Dr. Minnigerode, in St. Paul's Church. So. Ch., July 3, 1884

CARMICHAEL

C. C., and Lucy Ashby, by the Rev. A. P. Saunders, at Fredericksburg, Va. So. Ch., Jan. 5, 1893

James, and Lucilla, d. of Dr. John H. Wallace of Fredericksburg, by the Rev. A. M. Randolph, at Fredericksburg. So. Ch., Dec. 13, 1861

William, Esq., of Maryland, and Harriett H., d. of Dr. F. W. Powell of Middleburg, Va., by the Rev. O. A. Kinsolving. So. Ch., Nov. 9, 1860

CARNAHAN

Wallace (The Rev.), of San Marcos, Tex., and Frances E. Gillespie of Jackson, Miss., at Jackson, Miss. So. Ch., Nov. 23, 1907

CARNEAL

Argyle, of Richmond, and Lottie Leigh of Ayletts, King William Co., Va., by the Rev. W. T. Roberts, at the residence of the bride's mother. So. Ch., Jan. 3, 1889

CARPENDER

Charles S., of New Brunswick, N.J., and Alice B. Robinson, niece of Mrs. Haxall, by the Rev. Charles Minnigerode, at the residence of W. H. Haxall, Richmond. So. Ch., June 24, 1875

CARPENTER

Mary, only d. of W. J. Carpenter of Ashland, Va., and James G. White of Albemarle Co., Va., by the Rev. John McGill, at the residence of the bride's parents. So. Ch., Dec. 15, 1887

William L., of Albemarle, and Annie E., d. of the late Thos. W. Terry, by the Rev. Robt. Douglas Roller, at the residence of H. C. Doswell, Hanover Co., Va. So. Ch., Nov. 9, 1876

CARPER

J. J., of Franklin Co., Va., and Mary E. Wilson of Botetourt Co., Va., by the Rev. E. W. Hubard, in St. Mark's Church, Fincastle. So. Ch., Dec. 28, 1871

Phillip W., and Minnie, d. of James Cockerille, all of Loudoun Co., by the Rev. Frank Page, at the residence of the bride's father. So. Ch., Dec. 26, 1878

Placie A., of Botetourt, and Geo. E. Johnson of Lynchburg, by the Rev. E. W. Hubard, in Fincastle. So. Ch., June 22, 1871

CARR

Betsy Breckinridge, d. of Col. G. W. Carr of "Hawksdale", Roanoke Co., Va., and Donald McDonald of Louisville, Ky., by the Rev. W. H. Meade, D.D., in St. John's P. E. Church, Roanoke. So. Ch., Nov. 3, 1887

Charlotte, d. of Dr. W. G. Carr, and Dr. John Henry Cochran of Middleburg, Va., by the Rev. T. U. Dudley, at Bentivar, Albemarle Co., Va. So. Ch., Oct. 10, 1867

Geo. Watson (Lt.), 9th Infantry, U.S.A., and Emma Gilmer, d. of the late Gen. Edward Watts, by the Rev. P. Tinsley, in St. John's Church, Roanoke Co. So. Ch., Dec. 7, 1860

MARRIAGE NOTICES IN THE SOUTHERN CHURCHMAN WITH DATES OF PUBLICATION

Gertrude M., and Joseph G. Mason of Clarke Co., Va., by the Rev. Pendleton Brooke, at the residence of the bride's father, Dr. J. L. Carr, Clarksburg, W.Va. So. Ch., Nov. 25, 1869

Lucie Laurie, d. of Wm. G. Carr of Albemarle Co., Va., and E. L. Stuart of Alexandria, Va., by the Rev. J. Stuart Hanckle, D.D., at Bonivar, the residence of the bride's father. So. Ch., July 1, 1873

CARRINGTON

Agnes G., d. of Henry Carrington, Esq., and Joel W. Marshall, by the Rev. J. A. Mitchell, at Ingleside, Charlotte Co., Va. So. Ch., Dec. 14, 1865

Bessie L., d. of the late Wm. C. and Mrs. Maria L. Carrington, and James N. Dunlop, all of Richmond, by the Rev. Mr. Minnigerode, at the residence of the bride's mother. So. Ch., Mar. 30, 1876

Elizabeth C., d. of Henry Carrington, Esq. of Charlotte Co., Va., and Judge George H. Gilmer, by the Rev. T. E. Locke, at Ingleside. So. Ch., Dec. 26, 1856

Emma, of Charlotte Co., Va., and John W. Riely of Fredericksburg, by the Rev. James A. Mitchell, at "Ingleside", the residence of the bride's father. So. Ch., Nov. 7, 1867

Eugene, and Cora, d. of Capt. Charles Dimmock, all of Richmond, Va., by the Rev. Mr. Marvell, in Washington. So. Ch., Apr. 22, 1859

Henry A., of Charlotte, and Lottie E., d. of Dr. John Cullen of Richmond, by the Rev. W. H. Kinckle, in St. Paul's Church, Richmond. So. Ch., Feb. 8, 1856

John Mattaner, and Sally F. Toot, by the Rev. Albert R. Walker, in St. John's Church, Halifax Courthouse, Va. So. Ch., Mar. 10, 1870

Loisa* A., d. of the late Dr. Carrington of Richmond, and Dr. G. W. Jones, by the Rev. Joshua Peterkin, in the city of Richmond. So. Ch., June 13, 1856

Louise C., and Wm. Leigh of Halifax C.H., Va., by the Rev. D. M. Wood, at the residence of the bride's father, Col. H. A. Carrington. So. Ch., Oct. 11, 1883

Richard A., formerly of Virginia, and Emilie C., d. of Hon. William Crooks, by the Rev. E. S. Thomas, in St. Paul's Church, St. Paul, Minn. So. Ch., Mar. 30, 1882

CARROLL

Bettie J. (Mrs.), of Oxford, N.C., and Alexander Cooper, by the Rev. P. D. Thompson, in St. Stephen's Church, Oxford, N.C. So. Ch., June 18, 1874

Everallan,* and John W. Todd, both of Smithfield, Isle of Wight Co., Va., by the Rev. Edw. W. Vnoth,* in Christ Church, Smithfield, Va. So. Ch., Jan. 11, 1877

Jas. R., of Warren Co., N.C., and Laura, d. of the late Hon. Joel Holloman of Isle of Wight Co., Va., by the Rev. John Wingfield, in Christ Church, Hicksford,

* Given as printed

MARRIAGE NOTICES IN THE SOUTHERN CHURCHMAN WITH DATES OF PUBLICATION

Va. So. Ch., Mar. 8, 1865
John N., of the "Caves", Baltimore Co., and Mary R., d. of Dr. J. Hanson Thomas of Baltimore, by the Rev. Dr. Mahan, in Grace Church, Baltimore. So. Ch., Apr. 28, 1870
Julia W. (Mrs.), and Maj. Everard M. Todd, both of Smithfield, Va., by the Rev. David Barr, in Christ Church, Norfolk, Va. So. Ch., Nov. 3, 1887
Mary Sterett, d. of Henry Hill Carroll of Baltimore Co., Md., and the Rev. Duncan McCulloch, by the Rev. Landon R. Mason, at Clymalora Manor. So. Ch., Jan. 5, 1888

CARSON
Cyrus, and Lydia A. Swann, both of Caroline Co., Va., by the Rev. W. W. Greene. So. Ch., Feb. 1, 1861
Maud Lee, d. of the officiating clergyman, and William Minor Lile, by the Rev. T. M. Carson, in St. Paul's Church, Lynchburg. So. Ch., Feb. 2, 1888

CARTER
A. Rosalie, of Gloucester, and Wm. R. Smart, by the Rev. Edmund Withers, in White Chapel Church,* Lancaster Co., Va. So. Ch., Sept. 18, 1857
Anne Campbell, youngest d. of Hill Carter, Esq., and Chapman Johnson Leigh of New York City, by the Rev. A. M. Randolph, at Shirley, Charles City Co., Va. So. Ch., June 29, 1860
Beverley B., and M. C., eldest d. of R. G. Anderson of Amelia Co., by the Rev. P. F. Berkeley, at Selma, the residence of the bride's father. So. Ch., Nov. 11, 1875
Cassius (Dr.), of Fairfax, and Jane A., d. of the late Rev. Charles Taliaferro, by the Rev. J. Earnest, at Mount Sharon, in Orange, Va. So. Ch., June 27, 1856
Charlotte A., d. of G. M. Carter, Esq., and S. B. Greenlaw, all of Westmoreland Co., by the Rev. T. E. Locke, at the residence of the bride's father. So. Ch., Aug. 19, 1869
Charlotte P., only d. of William Carter, Esq. of Hanover Co., and George Wickham, s. of the late John Wickham, Esq., by the Rt. Rev. R. C. Moore, at Richmond, Va. So. Ch., Oct. 25, 1839
D. D. (Dr.), of Hancock, Md., and Addie, d. of Garrett Wynkoop of Hedgesville, Va., by the Rev. W. D. Hanson, in Mount Zion Church, Hedgesville. So. Ch., Oct. 28, 1869
Edward (Capt.), and Jeanie Turner, by the Rev. John McGill. So. Ch., Sept. 26, 1867
Edward Landon, of Virginia, and Charlotte C. Ball, formerly of Washington, D.C., by the Rev. J. H. Chew, in St. Alban's Church, Washington, D.C. So. Ch., Aug. 24, 1871
Edward Stuart, s. of Mr. and Mrs. Stuart Carter of Prince William Co., Va., and Frances Anne Casemove,** d. of the late Rev. Andrew Glassell Grinnan and his

---

* White Chapel Church is in Christ Church Parish, Lancaster Co., Virginia
** Given as printed. Possibly "Casenove".

MARRIAGE NOTICES IN THE SOUTHERN CHURCHMAN WITH DATES OF PUBLICATION

wife, Anne Casemore* Minor, by the Rev. R. Bryan Grinnan, at the home of the bride's aunt, Miss Nina S. Grinnan, Brampton, near Orange, Va. So. Ch., Aug. 7, 1926

Elizabeth Hill, eldest d. of Hill Carter, Esq. of Charles City and John Wickham of Henrico, by the Rev. Dr. Okesen, at Shirley. So. Ch., Dec. 9, 1859

Ellen H., and Wm. B. Hurt, by the Rev. Geo. W. Dame, at Pittsylvania C.H. So. Ch., Feb. 10, 1870

Evelyn V., of Nelson Co., Va., and F. G. Thorp of Henrico Co., by the Rev. Edmund Withers, at the residence of Wm. Carter of Nelson Co. So. Ch., Dec. 5, 1867

Florence Ida, d. of Geo. M. Carter, and Wm. P. Taylor, by Bishop Payne, at Oak Grove, Westmoreland Co., Va. So. Ch., May 15, 1873

George H., of Frederick Co., Va., and E. Carroll Castleman of Clarke Co., by the Rev. P. P. Phillips, in Grace Church, Berryville. So. Ch., Oct. 27, 1881

H. L. (Lt.), of the 53rd Virginia Regiment, and Eliza G. Poindexter, by the Rev. George T. Wilmer, D. D., at Pittsylvania C. H. So. Ch., Feb. 27, 1863

Hattie S. (Mrs.), and S. D. Wainwright, both of Norwood, Nelson Co., Va., by the Rev. Davis M. Wood, at Norwood, Va. So. Ch., Nov. 22, 1888

Lavinia, and Edward Mortimer Harrison, by the Rev. Joseph Baker, rector of Westover, in Grace Church, Granville, Va. So. Ch., Feb. 28, 1914

Lelia, d. of A. L. and Mary D. Carter, and Warner Ball of Northumberland, by the Rev. H. L. Derby, at the residence of the bride's father, Midway, Lancaster, Va. So. Ch., Nov. 25, 1875

Louisa T., d. of Geo. F. Carter, and Robert Carter, all of Fairfax, by the Rev. Frank Page, in Subley Church. So. Ch., June 22, 1882

Maria B., only d. of Addison B. Carter of Winchester, Va., and George B. Anderson of Texas, by the Rev. Dr. Hubard, in Christ Church, Winchester, Va. So. Ch., Jan. 8, 1880

Nonie, and John H. Pritchett, by the Rev. H. L. Derby, at the residence of the bride's mother, in Lancaster, Va. So. Ch., July 22, 1880

Richardetta E., fifth d. of Maj. Richard H. Carter, and Robert Beverley, Jr., by the Rev. John McGill, at Glenwelby, Fauquier Co., Va. So. Ch., Dec. 18, 1879

Robert, and Louisa T., d. of Geo. F. Carter, all of Fairfax, by the Rev. Frank Page, in Sudley Church. So. Ch., June 22, 1882

Robert S. (The Rev.), of Virginia, and Bessie Lloyd, d. of the late Maj. Burr P. Noland, by the Rev. T. W. Dudley, D. D., in Immanuel Church, Middleburg, Loudoun

---

* Given as printed. Possibly "Cazenove"

MARRIAGE NOTICES IN THE SOUTHERN CHURCHMAN WITH DATES OF PUBLICATION

Co. So. Ch., Sept. 10 and 17, 1891
Ross, and Sallie C. Lucke, by the Rev. Geo. W. Dame assisted by the Rev. Wm. Hoxton, at Pittsylvania Courthouse. So. Ch., July 15, 1869
Sally H., and Dr. A. A. Edwards, by the Rev. Edmund Withers, at Fleet's Bay, Lancaster Co., Va. So. Ch., Aug. 18, 1853
Seignora C., d. of Winston Carter of Prince William Co., and John G. White of Fauquier, by the Rev. R. T. Brown, in St. Paul's Church, Haymarket. So. Ch., Nov. 21, 1872
Selina D., third d. of Maj. Richard H. Carter, and John H. Washington, all of Fauquier Co., Va., by the Rev. Jno. McGill, at "Glenn Welby", the residence of the bride's father. So. Ch., Nov. 16, 1871
Susan Elwood (Ellie), of Chatham, and the Rev. E. Sterling Gunn of Halifax Co., Va., by the Rev. C. O. Pruden assisted by the Rev. Mr. Amiss, Presiding Elder of the Methodist Church, Danville district, in Emmanuel Church, Chatham, Va. So. Ch., Jan. 1, 1891
Thomas, Esq., and Ann Willing, d. of the late William Byrd Page, by the Rev. Mr. Stringfellow, at Page-Brook, the residence of Jno. Page, Esq. So. Ch., Dec. 11, 1835
Thomas H. (Dr.), of King William Co., Va., and Susan, d. of Wm. H. Roy, Esq. of Mathews Co., Va., by the Rev. Mr. Carraway, at Green Plains. So. Ch., Dec. 14, 1855
Thomas Nelson, and Agnes Atkinson Mayo, by the Rev. Robert A. Mayo assisted by the Rev. John B. Newton, in Monumental Church, Richmond. So. Ch., Dec. 8, 1887
V. Betty, d. of Capt. R. D. Carter of Fleets Bay, Northumberland, and Cyrus Harding of Snowden Park, Northumberland, by the Rev. Edmund Withers, in Christ Church, Lancaster Co., Va. So. Ch., Dec. 14, 1855
William F., and Augusta E. Dodson, by the Rev. H. L. Derby, at Lancaster, Va. So. Ch., Apr. 15, 1880
William F. (Dr.), U.S.A., and Anna H., d. of the late Dr. Wm. A. Christian of Hanover Co., Va., by the Rev. Dr. E. C. Murdaugh of Fredericksburg, Va., in St. John's Church, Richmond, Va. So. Ch., Oct. 25, 1883

CARTWRIGHT
Clara F., of Mason Co., W.Va., and John M'Quisten Morris, of Portsmouth, Ohio, by the Rev. T. H. Lacy, at the residence of Judge John Cartwright, the bride's father, near Mason City, Mason Co., W.Va. So. Ch., Sept. 18, 1879

CARUTHERS
Lalivesia* H. P., d. of the late Col. Wm. A. Caruthers formerly of Lexington, Va., and George H. Packwood of Maitland, Fla., by the Rev. Wm. W. Greene, at the residence of the bride's mother, in Nottoway Co., Va. So. Ch.,

---

* Given as printed

MARRIAGE NOTICES IN THE SOUTHERN CHURCHMAN WITH DATES OF PUBLICATION

CARY
    Charles E., of Gloucester, Va., and Virginia C., d. of the late Col. George Willis, by the Rev. John S. Hansbrough, at Wood Park, Orange Co., Va. So. Ch., June 11, 1885
    Emma, d. of Dr. S. B. Cary, and T. S. Beckwith of Petersburg, Va., by the Rev. Charles Mann, in Abingdon Church, Gloucester Co., Va. So. Ch., Nov. 26, 1868
    James, Jr., of Baltimore, Md., and Martha, d. of the Rev. Wm. N. Ward, at Bladensfield, Richmond Co., Va. So. Ch., July 1, 1869
    Richard M., Esq., of Petersburg, and Hannah E. Whiting of Hampton, by the Rev. John C. McCabe, at Hampton. So. Ch., Aug. 30, 1855
    Sallie E., d. of the late Dr. N. B. Cary, and William S. Graves of Liberty, Va., by the Rev. Dr. Minnigerode, at the residence of the bride's uncle, Col. John B. Cary, Richmond, Va. So. Ch., Sept. 27, 1883
    Virgie A., d. of E. B. S. Cary, Esq., and Richard H. Horner, by the Rev. Charles Mann, at "Secluseval", Gloucester Co., Va. So. Ch., Jan. 25, 1872

CASADY
    Phineas McCray (The Rev.), Vicar of St. Paul's Church, Clinton, Okla., eldest s. of the Bishop of Oklahoma, and Myra Shelby, d. of John H. Frederickson of Oklahoma City, by the Rt. Rev. Thomas Casady, S.T.D., in St. Paul's Cathedral, Oklahoma City. So. Ch., June 22, 1935
    Simon, III, s. of the officiating clergyman, and Virginia Kent Boon, niece of Charles Boon of Luke, Md., by the Rt. Rev. Thomas Casady, D.D., Bishop of Oklahoma, at Oklahoma City, Okla. So. Ch., July 1, 1933

CASKIE
    John S., Esq., of Richmond, and Fannie, d. of the late Col. Wm. R. Johnson of Oakland, Chesterfield Co., Va., by the Rev. A. B. Tizzard. So. Ch., Oct. 4, 1849

CASSARD
    Hamilton, of Baltimore, and Mary Wallace Bainbridge of Fredericksburg, by the Rev. Edward C. Murdaugh, in Trinity Church, Fredericksburg, Va. So. Ch., Dec. 4, 1879

CASTLE
    Henry Northrup, and Sallie Taylor Hubard, both of Norfolk, Va., by the Rev. Arthur Selden Lloyd, D.D., of Virginia, in New York City. So. Ch., Mar. 7, 1908

CASTLEMAN
    Alleyne (Mrs.), and Phillip Powers Page, by the Rev. C. T. Page, father of the groom, of Altavista, Va., in Chicago, Ill. So. Ch., Feb. 18, 1922
    E. Carrol, of Clarke Co., and George H. Carter of Frederick Co., Va., by the Rev. P. P. Phillips, in Grace Church, Berryville. So. Ch., Oct. 27, 1881

MARRIAGE NOTICES IN THE SOUTHERN CHURCHMAN WITH DATES OF PUBLICATION

Eloisa M., and Charles H. Green, Esq. of Warren Co., Va., by the Rev. F. M. Whittle, at Prospect Hill, the residence of the bride's mother, in Clarke Co., Va. So. Ch., June 13, 1856

Emeline F., d. of Wm. A. Castleman, Esq., and James T. Louthan, all of Clarke Co., Va., by the Rev. F. M. Whittle. So. Ch., Apr. 17, 1857

Robert A. (The Rev.), and Mary Morrison, d. of the late Rev. Wm. F. Lee, by the Rev. Dr. Sparrow, in the chapel of the Theological Seminary of Virginia. So. Ch., July 29, 1852.

Robert Allen (The Rev.), and Fannie S., d. of Col. Oliver R. and Mary Funsten of Clarke Co., Va., by the Rev. J. B. Funsten assisted by the Rev. George S. Somerville, at Mirador, near Greenwood Depot, Albemarle Co., Va. So. Ch., Dec. 26, 1886

CATLETT
Alice, of Port Royal, and William C. Bagby, by the Rev. S. S. Ware, in St. Peter's Church, Port Royal, Va. So. Ch., June 27, 1889

Charles, Jr., of Gloucester, Va., and Deborah Powell Cockey, at Norfolk, Va. So. Ch., Sept. 6, 1913

Nathaniel P., and Bettie T. Breckinridge, both of Staunton, Va., by the Rev. P. Slaughter, in Trinity Church, Staunton, Va. So. Ch., Nov. 28, 1856

CATLIN
Wm., and Mrs. Martha Christian, by the Rev. Dr. A. Wade, at Milton, Charles City Co., Va. So. Ch., Feb. 9, 1871

CATON
George C., of Fauquier Co., Va., and Sarah L. Stephens of "Oakwood", Theological Seminary, formerly of Fauquier Co., by the Rev. Samuel A. Wallis, at "Oakwood", Theological Seminary, Va. So. Ch., Jan. 8, 1916

CATTELL
Frances Fenton, M.D., d. of the late Rev. Thomas W. Cattell of New Jersey, and the Rev. Benjamin L. Ancell of the Episcopal Church Mission, Yangchow, China, s. of the late Capt. John J. Ancell of Fluvanna Co., by the Rev. H. St. George Tucker, at Yokahama, Japan. So. Ch. Aug. 20, 1910

CAUSEY
Beverley Douglas, and M. Catherine Paul, in Christ Church, LaCrosse, Wis. So. Ch., July 25, 1908

J. C., of Baltimore, Md., and Evelyn Spottswood, second d. of the late Hon. B. B. Douglas, by the Rev. J. Hervey Hundley, at Cownes, King William Co., Va. So. Ch., Mar. 6, 1879

Mariana Prentis, and George L. Barton, formerly of Maryland, by the Rev. Henry L. Derby, at Suffolk, Va. So. Ch., Nov. 6, 1890

CAVITT
Clarence V., of Texas, and Bessie Carr, second d. of George F. Harrison, gr.d. of the late D. Holmes Conrad, of Martinsburg, W.Va.

MARRIAGE NOTICES IN THE SOUTHERN CHURCHMAN WITH DATES OF PUBLICATION

by the Rev. Mr. McCoy of the Presbyterian church assisted by the Rev. P. M. Boyden, at Longwood, Goochland Co., Va. So. Ch., May 22, 1879

CAZENOVE
Fanny A., eldest d. of the late Louis A. Cazenove of Alexandria, and Charles L. C. Minor of Hanover Co., by the Rev. C. Walker, D.D., at Alexandria. So. Ch., Jan. 18, 1861

CHAFFIN
Richard B. (Lt.), late of the C. S. Army, and Sarah H., d. of Dr. John B. Harvie of Powhatan Co., by the Rev. Mr. Powell, at Fighting Creek, Powhatan Co. So. Ch., Nov. 29, 1866

CHALMERS
Christopher C., and Mrs. Ellen M. Jordan, by the Rev. David Barr, at Smithfield, Va. So. Ch., Oct. 22, 1885

Daisye Edmunds, d. of Mr. and Mrs. Joseph Williams Chalmers, and Henry Edmunds Coleman of Louisville, Ky., by the Rev. Flournoy Bouldin, Houston, Va., at the home of the bride's parents. So. Ch., Sept. 19, 1908

David, Esq., of Halifax Co., and Mrs. Anna Maria Mead of Richmond, by the Rev. George Woodbridge, in St. Paul's Church. So. Ch., Jan. 18, 1856

Elizabeth Anne, d. of David Chalmers, Esq., and the Rev. John Cosby of St. James' Parish, Mecklenburg, Va., by the Rev. Walter Williams, at Springfield, Halifax, Va. So. Ch., Oct. 22, 1858

H. C. (Dr.), of Charlotte Co., Va., and Isobel Gordon, d. of Mr. and Mrs. William H. Seaman, at the residence of Maj. and Mrs. Owen, Washington, D.C. So. Ch., Dec. 25, 1915

Margaret, of Smithfield, and Frank C. Watson of Jacksonville, Fla., by the Rev. David Barr, in Christ Church, Smithfield, Va. So. Ch., Dec. 2, 1886

Wm. M., Esq., of Lynchburg, and Emma N. Radford of Bedford, by the Rev. W. H. Pendleton, at Ashwood, Bedford Co., Va. So. Ch., Dec. 17, 1868

CHAMBERLAYNE
Emma, d. of the late E. H. Chamberlayne of Richmond, Va., and Littleton Brockenbrough of Baltimore, Md., by the Rev. Edward Wall, in St. Mark's rectory, Petersville, Md. So. Ch., Dec. 3, 1885

J. H. (Capt.), of the Norfolk "Virginian", and Mary Walker, d. of the Rev. Churchill Gibson the officiating clergyman, assisted by the Rev. Robert Gibson, in Grace Church, Petersburg, Va. So. Ch., Oct. 30, 1873

Martha Dabney, d. of John Hampden Chamberlayne, gr.d. of the Rev. Churchill J. Gibson, D.D., and Edward Pleasants Valentine of Richmond, Va., by the Rev. Robert A. Gibson, rector of Christ Church, Cincinnati, Ohio, in Grace Church, Petersburg, Va. So. Ch., Nov. 23, 1893

Mary S., d. of E. H. Chamberlayne, and Rev. Edward Wall,

MARRIAGE NOTICES IN THE SOUTHERN CHURCHMAN WITH DATES OF PUBLICATION

all of Richmond, by the Rev. J. Peterkin, D.D. So. Ch., May 11, 1876

CHAMBERS
Maria, and N. L. Davis, by the Rev. Olcott Bulkley, at the residence of Dr. Chambers, Dover, Lafayette Co., Mo. So. Ch., July 9, 1858

Sarah, and Jabez Banks, both of New Castle Co., by the Rev. W. D. Hanson, at Faulkland, Del. So. Ch., Mar. 29, 1883

W. S., of Caroline Co., and C. C. Redding of King George Co., Va., by the Rev. Dr. W. A. Baynham, at the residence of J. M. Garret. So. Ch., Mar. 1, 1883*

CHANCELLOR
Ana Randolph, youngest d. of the Hon. Wm. Nelson Chancellor, and Harry Parker Moss, by the Rev. S. Scollay Moore, at Parkersburg, W.Va. So. Ch., May 8, 1890

Charles W. (Dr.), of Memphis, and Mattie A. Butler of Jackson, Tenn., by the Rt. Rev. J. P. B. Wilmer, Bishop of Louisianna, at New Orleans. So. Ch., Mar. 21, 1867

Leah Seddon, d. of C. W. Chancellor, M.D. of Baltimore, gr.d. of the late Gen. A. G. Taliaferro and Mrs. A. H. M. Taliaferro of "Annandale", Culpeper Co., Va., and Henry G. Willis of Orange Co., by the Rev. George Murray, the rector, in Emmanuel Church, Culpeper Co. So. Ch., Dec. 15, 1887

Rush W. (Dr.), of Virginia, and Lilly, d. of the late Thomas Ellzey, Esq., by the Rev. John McGill, at Westwood Grove, Loudoun Co., Va. So. Ch., Nov. 30, 1876

CHANDLER
Allan M., and Ada S. Fairfax, by the Rev. R. M. Chandler, at the residence of W. H. Musser, near Germantown, Montgomery Co., Md. So. Ch., Oct. 27, 1892

John W., of Richmond, and Ella M., d. of Col. John K. Cooke formerly of Portsmouth, Va., by the Rev. A. B. Tizzard, at the residence of the bride's father in Chesterfield Co. So. Ch., Apr. 22, 1864

Lucy Penelope, of Westmoreland, Va., and Col. Francis Dent of St. Mary's Co., Md., by the Rev. W. C. Latane assisted by the Rev. E. F. Saumenig, at Windsor, Westmoreland Co., Va. So. Ch., Dec. 28, 1893

Mary J., d. of the late John R. Chandler, M.D., U.S.N., and the Rev. John H. D. Wingfield, by the Rev. John H. Wingfield, in Trinity Church, Portsmouth, Va. So. Ch., Sept. 2, 1859

CHANLER
John Armstrong, and Amelie, d. of Alfred Landon and S. C. Rives, by the Rev. E. L. Goodwin, at Castle Hill, Albemarle Co., Va. So. Ch., June 21, 1888

CHANNEL
Warren, of Portsmouth, Va., and Mary ., d. of the Rt. Rev. Dr. Wm. A. Brown, by the Bishop assisted by the Rev. Roderick H. Jackson, rector of St. John's Church, in St. John's Church, Ports-

---

* It is impossible to discern in this case which is the husband and which the wife, except by the custom of the editor of the Southern Churchman to publish the name of the husband first, which would make the husband C. C. Redding

MARRIAGE NOTICES IN THE SOUTHERN CHURCHMAN WITH DATES OF PUBLICATION

mouth. So. Ch., Nov. 1, 1941

CHAPIN
M. V., and the Rev. Thomas S. Savage, M.D., at Cape Palmas, Western Africa. So. Ch., Nov. 4, 1842

CHAPMAN
Alfred, of Orange Co., and Mary E., d. of Wm. Kinney, Esq. of Staunton, Augusta Co., Va., by the Rev. F. D. Goodwin, at Staunton, Va. So. Ch., Dec. 15, 1837

Felicia C., d. of Gov. Chapman of Alabama, and Bolling Hubard of Buckingham, Va., by the Rev. J. M. Banister, D.D., at Huntsville. So. Ch., Mar. 5, 1874

Louise, niece of Gen. B. Cheatham, and Howard Angus Kennedy of Montreal, nephew of Prof. John Blackie of Edinburgh, by the Rev. William Graham, D.D., rector of Christ Church, assisted by the Rev. M. Cabell Martin, rector of St. Peter's Church, in St. Peter's Church, Nashville, Tenn. So. Ch., June 17, 1886

Pearson (Dr.), of Md., and Eddie K., d. of the officiating minister, the Rev. Wm. N. Ward, at Bladensfield, Westmoreland Co., Va. So. Ch., Nov. 30, 1876

CHASE
Emma, d. of Capt. W. M. Chase, and Guthrie R. Dunton, all of Lancaster Co., Va., by the Rev. H. L. Derby assisted by the Rev. John Moncure and the Rev. John Y. Downman, in Grace Church, Lancaster Co., Va. So. Ch., Nov. 23, 1882

Wm. T. (Capt.), of Lancaster Va., and Fannie Lee, youngest d. of Joseph Beeler, Esq. of Washington Co., Md., by the Rev. Mr. Mitchell, at Silver Lawn, the residence of the bride's father. So. Ch., Jan. 16, 1873

CHEADLE
Hattie, and Wm. E. Whitehead, all of Appomattox Co., Va., by the Rev. A. S. Lloyd, at the home of the bride's father. So. Ch., Dec. 28, 1882

CHEATWOOD
Sally P., of Russell Parish, Bedford Co., Va., and George R. Smith of Scotland, by the Rev. Albert Ware, at the residence of the bride's father. So. Ch., Oct. 26, 1876

CHENEY
Chas. Edward (The Rev.), rector of Christ Church, Chicago, and C. Emma Griswold, d. of Dr. Alexander Fisher, by the Rev. N. H. Schenck, rector of Emmanuel Church, Baltimore, in Trinity Church, Chicago. So. Ch., May 4, 1860

CHESLEY
Emily, d. of the officiating clergyman, and Charles E. Buck, by the Rev. J. W. Chesley, in All Faith Church, St. Mary's Co., Md. So. Ch., June 28, 1877

J. Harry (The Rev.), of Maryland, and Caludia W., d. of Margaret L., and the late Maj. J. Thomas Smith of Fauquier Co., Va., by the Rev. J. W. Chesley assisted by the Rev. C. Walker, D.D.,

MARRIAGE NOTICES IN THE SOUTHERN CHURCHMAN WITH DATES OF PUBLICATION

at the residence of the bride's mother, on Seminary Hill. So. Ch., July 25, 1878

Wm. F., Esq., and Mollie, only d. of Wm. S. Lyon, Esq., all of St. Mary's Co., Md., by the Rev. J. W. Chesley, at "The Heights", St. Mary's Co., Md. So. Ch., July 25, 1878

CHESTNUTT
Mary Alice, and Dr. Wm. L. Nuttall, by the Rev. Henry T. Sharp, in the Church of the Ascension, Frankfort, Ky. So. Ch., May 11, 1876

CHETWOOD
Hobart (The Rev.), rector of Burlington College, and Annie P., second d. of the late Rev. P. Parke, D.D., by the Rev. Lewis Walke, in Christ Church, Norfolk. So. Ch., May 1, 1857

CHEVALLIE
Mary Gallego, youngest d. of the late Peter J. Chevallie, and Edward L. Handy, Commander, U.S.N., by the Rev. George Woodbridge, in St. Paul's Church, Richmond, Va. So. Ch., Apr. 18, 1856

CHEW
John H., of Washington, D.C., and May, d. of the late Wm. Meade Addison of Baltimore, Md., by the Rev. Joshua Peterkin, D.D., at the residence of John Addison, Richmond. So. Ch., Feb. 16, 1888

S. C. (Dr.), and Agnes Robb, d. of the late Alexander Marshall, by the Rev. Mr. Paine, in Mount Calvary Church, Baltimore. So. Ch., June 12, 1884

Thomas J., formerly of Maryland, and Phoebe Pemberton, d. of Caroline Nourse and the late Com. Bladen Dulaney, by the Rev. A. P. Gray, at "Cloverland". So. Ch., Nov. 1, 1883

CHICHESTER
D. Conway, of Fairfax, and Julia Sully of Alexandria, Va., by the Rev. C. B. Dana, in Christ Church, Alexandria, Va. So. Ch., May 4, 1860

J. Conway, and Virginia Corse, both of Fairfax Co., by the Rev. R. T. Brown, in the chapel of the Theological Seminary. So. Ch., Aug. 10, 1860

Jonny P., youngest d. of the late Capt. George Chichester of Fairfax Co., and James S. Hereford, of Dallas, Tex., by the Rev. John McGill, in St. Paul's Church, Alexandria. So. Ch., Feb. 5, 1874

Madge, d. of Maj. John H. Chichester, and James M. Mason, by the Rev. Kinloch Nelson, D.D., in old Falls Church, Fairfax Co., Va. So. Ch., Oct. 30, 1884

Minnie, d. of the late Maj. John H. Chichester of Fairfax Co., and John C. Davidson, of Washington, D.C., by the Rev. Frank Page, in Fall's Church, Fairfax Co., Va. So. Ch., Dec. 5, 1889

Richard M., and Nannie Lee, d. of Judge R. H. Cockerille, all of Fairfax Co., by the Rev. Jno. McGill, in Christ Church, Fairfax Co. So. Ch., May 11, 1876

Sallie C., of Fauquier Co., Va., and Wm. A. Linton of Washington, D.C., by the Rev. George W. Nelson, in

MARRIAGE NOTICES IN THE SOUTHERN CHURCHMAN WITH DATES OF PUBLICATION

"Baldwins Ridge" Church. So. Ch., Mar. 4, 1886

CHILDRESS
Wm. T., of Nelson Co., and Lucy E. Branham of Albemarle, by the Rev. T. E. Locke, at the residence of David R. Branham. So. Ch., June 6, 1889

CHILDS
Allen, of Philadelphia, and Kate B., d. of the late Col. John D. Kurtz, United States Engineers, by the Rev. Dallas Tucker assisted by the Rev. D. B. Knickerbacker, D.D., in Gethsemane Church, Minneapolis, Minn. So. Ch., Oct. 10, 1878

Fannie Ingle, d. of A. E. Childs, Esq., and David Crenshaw Barrow, Jr., all of Athens, by the Rev. Edward H. Ingle, in Emmanuel Church, Athens, Ga. So. Ch., Feb. 13, 1879

Janet Sayce, d. of Allen Childs, and The Rev. Paul Micou, by the Rev. Louis C. Washburn, rector, and the Rev. Dr. William E. Gardner, in Old Christ Church, Philadelphia. So. Ch., Dec. 24, 1921

CHILTON
Lucy S., of Warrenton, Va., and A. L. Ellett, Jr. of Richmond, Va., by the Rev. George W. Nelson. So. Ch., Jan. 31, 1884

Samuel Blackwell (The Rev.), rector of St. Paul's Parish, Hanover, Va., and Harriet Harrington, d. of the Rev. and Mrs. Alexander McMillan of Carlisle, Pa., in St. John's Church, Carlisle, Pa. So. Ch., Sept. 26, 1925

Susan J. (Mrs.), of Lancaster, and John M. McCarty of Richmond Co., by the Rev. H. L. Derby, at Norwood, Lancaster, Va. So. Ch., Nov. 18, 1875

CHINN
Joseph W., and Josephine J. Lane, both of Richmond Co., by the Rev. Campbell Fair, D.D., at 384 Lanvale St., Baltimore, Md. So. Ch., Oct. 1, 1885

Lucy J., d. of the late John L. Chinn, Esq., and J. Baily Jett of Westmoreland Co., by the Rev. E. C. McGuire, D.D. So. Ch., Feb. 15, 1856

Sallie S., and Capt. Robert H. Tyler, both of Prince William Co., Va., by the Rev. H. W. L. Temple, at Tappahannock, Essex. So. Ch., Feb. 27, 1863

CHISHOLM
Jas. (The Rev.), rector of Norborne Parish, Berkeley Co., and Jane Byrd, d. of John W. Page, Esq. of Clarke Co., Va., by the Rev. Wm. G. H. Jones, in Christ Church, Millwood. So. Ch., Sept. 3, 1847

CHOWNING
John W., and Mary E. Ball, by the Rev. H. L. Derby, in Lancaster Co., Va. So. Ch., Dec. 12, 1878

Sophronia Elizabeth, youngest d. of Col. John Chowning, and John Towles, by the Rev. Ephraim Adams, in White Chapel, Lancaster Co. So. Ch., Aug. 21, 1835

CHRISMAN
Elizabeth H., and the Rev. C. L. Rodgers of Osmond, Neb. (formerly of North Carolina), by the Rev. Wilson P. Chrisman of Moundsville, W.Va., brother of the bride, at the

- 95 -

MARRIAGE NOTICES IN THE SOUTHERN CHURCHMAN WITH DATES OF PUBLICATION

home of the bride in Martinsburg, W.Va. So. Ch., Jan. 12, 1907

CHRISTIAN

Andrew H., Jr., and Frances W., d. of Robert S. Archer, Esq., by the Rev. Hartley Carmichael assisted by the Rev. Robert P. Kerr, D.D., in St. Paul's Church, Richmond, Va. So. Ch., Sept. 11, 1890

Anna H., d. of the late Dr. Wm. A. Christian of Hanover Co., Va., and Dr. William F. Carter, U.S.A., by the Rev. Dr. E. C. Murdaugh of Fredericksburg, Va., in St. John's Church, Richmond, Va. So. Ch., Oct. 25, 1883

Edmund O. (Dr.), of New Kent Co., and Elizabeth Christian of Greenway, Charles City Co., by the Rev. W. T. Leavell, at Greenway, Charles City Co. So. Ch., July 25, 1850

Edward, and Agnes Roy Pendleton, by the Rev. E. Meade, in St. John's Church, Tappahannock, Va. So. Ch., Jan. 7, 1886

Elizabeth, of Greenway, Charles City Co., and Dr. Edmund O. Christian of New Kent Co., Va., by the Rev. W. T. Leavell, at Greenway, Charles City Co. So. Ch., July 25, 1850

Louisa W., d. of Prof. J. Heath Christian, and the Rev. Reverdy Estill, rector of Trinity Church, Portsmouth, Va., by the Rev. G. W. Dame, in Memorial Church, Baltimore. So. Ch., Dec. 7, 1882

Martha (Mrs.), and Wm. Catlin, by the Rev. Dr. A. Wade, at Milton, Charles City Co., Va. So. Ch., Feb. 9, 1871

Mattie M., d. of the late Judge John B. Christian of Virginia, and the Rev. John M. Mitchell, rector of St. John's Church, Montgomery, Ala., by the Rt. Rev. Richard H. Wilmer, D.D., at Wakefield, Perry Co., Ala. So. Ch., Dec. 26, 1862

Walter, of Richmond, Va., and Kate B. Newton, by the Rev. John B. Newton assisted by the Rev. S. S. Hepbron, at Summer Hill, Hanover Co., Va. So. Ch., Dec. 4 and 11, 1884

William (The Rev.), of Washington, D.C., and Elizabeth Marshall Marbury of Prince George's Co., Md., by the Rev. Dr. Pinckney, in St. Luke's Church, Bladensburg, Md. So. Ch., Oct. 1, 1858

Wm. A., of Alabama, and Anna M., d. of the late Wm. Harrison, Esq. of Maycox, James River, by the Rev. Mr. Norwood, at Evergreen, seat of Lt. Cocke of the U.S.N. So. Ch., Aug. 2, 1839

Wm. D. (The Rev.), rector of Grace Church, Lake Providence, La., and Mary E. Averett of Gainesville, Ala., by the Rt. Rev. Wm. M. Greene, D.D., at Meridian, Miss. So. Ch., Nov. 25, 1875

Wm. P., of Hanover Co., Va., and Maria H., d. of the late Wm. H. Berkeley of King and Queen Co., Va., by the Rev. Edward H. Ingle, rector, in St. John's Church, Big Lick.* So. Ch., Nov. 15, 1877

---

* Probably Big Lick, Va., which developed into the city of Roanoke

MARRIAGE NOTICES IN THE SOUTHERN CHURCHMAN WITH DATES OF PUBLICATION

CHUNN
    Bertha, d. of Andrew J. and Belle Chunn, and Lloyd O. Gold of Florida, by the Rev. H. B. Lee, in Emmanuel Church, Fauquier Co., Va. So. Ch., Nov. 2, 1882
    Mabel, only d. of the late Dr. James Chunn, and Robert T. Wilson, M.D., all of Baltimore, by the Rt. Rev. Alfred Randolph, D.D., in Emmanuel Church, Baltimore. So. Ch., Jan. 17, 1884

CHURCH
    Joseph B., and Laura V., d. of W. C. Murdock, all of Washington, by the Rev. Edward H. Ingle, in the Church of the Ascension, Washington, D.C. So. Ch., June 15, 1882

CLAGETT
    Adaline,*d. of the late Thomas Clagett, and the Rev. Henry Inglesby Kershaw, rector of the parish, by Bishop Pinckney assisted by the Rev. Dr. Sewin, the Rev. T. F. Billipp, and the Rev. R. S. Gordon, in Trinity Church, Upper Marlboro, Md. So. Ch., Dec. 24, 1874
    Edith, d. of H. B. Clagett of Alexandria, and the Rev. Reverdy Estill of Atlanta, Ga., by the Rev. R. H. McKim, D.D., in Christ Church, Alexandria. So. Ch., Sept. 24, 1874
    Julia, only d. of Dr. Thomas H. Clagett, and Alexander H. Rogers, all of Loudoun Co., Va., by the Rev. O. A. Kinsolving, at Leesburg. So. Ch., Nov. 5, 1858
    Rachel, d. of Thomas Clagett, Esq. of Prince George's Co., Md., and Chas. J. Kinsolving of Washington, by the Rev. O. A. Kinsolving of Virginia, in Trinity Church, Upper Marlboro. So. Ch., July 21, 1870

CLAGGETT
    Louis H., Esq., and Caroline Fisher Alcock, by the Rev. John C. McCabe, rector of the Church of the Ascension, at Baltimore. So. Ch., July 10, 1857
    Sarah Genevieve, d. of the late Elizabeth West and Samuel Claggett and great gr.d. of Bishop Thomas Claggett, and John M. Kopper, s. of Mr. and Mrs. Henry Kopper of Madison, N.J., gr.s. of Gen. Thomas Trueman Wheeler of Maryland, by Archdeacon E. T. Helfenstein and the Rev. C. L. Atwater, at "The Merryland Tract", the home of the bride's brother, Dr. Samuel Claggett, Oakland, Md. So. Ch., May 20, 1911

CLAIBORNE
    Delia Hayes, eldest d. of Maj. John H. Claiborne, and Gen. Simon Bolivar Buckner of Hart Co., Ky., by the Rev. Joshua Peterkin, D.D., at the residence of the bride's uncle, Herbert A. Claiborne, Esq. So. Ch., June 25, 1885
    George, Esq., and Virginia, d. of R. D. Turnbull, Esq., all of Brunswick Co., by the Rev. R. A. Castleman, at Lawrenceville, Brunswick Co., Va. So. Ch., Feb. 6, 1863
    Herbert A., and Kate Hamilton Cabell, both of Richmond, by the Rev. Melville Jackson,

* Given as printed

MARRIAGE NOTICES IN THE SOUTHERN CHURCHMAN WITH DATES OF PUBLICATION

at the residence of the bride's father, Col. H. Coalter Cabell. So. Ch., Feb. 16, 1882

Jennie, and Eugene M. Redd of Hanover Co., Va., by the Rev. Oscar S. Bunting, at Geddes, Amherst Co., Va. So. Ch., Jan. 1, 1880

John H. (Maj.), and Honingham E., d. of Col. Walter D. Blair of Richmond, by the Rev. Dr. J. Peterkin. So. Ch., Sept. 17, 1868

Mattie A., d. of Dr. Wm. S. Claiborne, and Thomas W. Willcox, Esq. of Charles City Co., by the Rev. J. D. Powell, in St. Mark's Church, Now Glasgow. So. Ch., Dec. 17, 1858

R. R., rector of Emmanuel Church, Rapidan, and Jane, d. of E. Goss, by the Rev. J. S. Hansbrough of Orange, at the residence of the bride's father. So. Ch., Oct. 26, 1882

CLANCEY

George Eugene, of Manila, formerly of Sioux City, Ia., and Beverley Ray, d. of the Rev. and Mrs. David Barr of Washington, D.C., at Manila, Phillipine Islands. So. Ch., Jan. 1, 1910

CLARK

Cantwell, of Newcastle Co., Del., and Elizabeth, d. of Samuel Bootes, by the Rev. John Johns of Baltimore, at Georgetown. So. Ch., Dec. 22, 1837

Colin D., of Baltimore, and Bettie B., eldest d. of the Rev. John Cooke, by the Rev. Horace Stringfellow, at Dewberry, Hanover Co., Va. So. Ch., Nov. 16, 1855

Edwin Spottswood, formerly of The Plains, Va., and Lucy Arline, d. of Edwin J. Sweet of Washington, D.C., by the Rev. David Barr, at the Church of the Epiphany, Washington, D.C. So. Ch., Sept. 12, 1889

Eliza C., d. of William H. Clark, Esq. of Halifax Co., Va., and A. W. Shields, Esq. of Richmond, by the Rev. John T. Clark, at Banister Lodge. So. Ch., Dec. 5, 1867

Fannie Walker, d. of Dr. E. P. Clark of The Plains, Fauquier Co., Va., and Dr. William R. Tulloss of Haymarket, Prince William Co., Va., by the Rev. David Barr, at Washington, D.C. So. Ch., Feb. 9, 1907

J. Peyton, Esq., and Cornelia Lee, d. of Dr. R. T. Baldwin, all of Winchester, by the Rev. C. Walker, at Winchester, Va. So. Ch., Aug. 8, 1856

Joseph Trueman, of Prince Edward Co., and Sallie Nelson, d. of William H. McGuire, gr.d. of the late Woodson Hughes, Esq. of Halifax C.H., Va., by the Rev. Dr. O. A. Kinsolving, in St. John's Church, Halifax C. H., Va. So. Ch., Feb. 7, 1889

Julia, d. of the late William L. Clark, Esq. of Winchester, Va., and Capt. Thomas S. B. Tucker of Williamsburg, Va., by the Rev. William C. Meredith, at Carysbrook, Frederick Co., Va. So. Ch., Dec. 20, 1866

MARRIAGE NOTICES IN THE SOUTHERN CHURCHMAN WITH DATES OF PUBLICATION

Laura A., and Stephen Archer, by the Rev. A. B. Tizzard, at Mantua, Chesterfield Co., Va. So. Ch., Nov. 19, 1885

Lemuel, Esq., of Baltimore, and Kate Hyatt, d. of Reuben Middleton, Esq., by the Rev. John Collins McCabe, D.D., at Hyattsville, near Bladensburg, Md. So. Ch., May 31, 1866

Priscilla S., of Martinsville, Va., and Geo. E. Lemmon of Lynchburg, by the Rev. J. T. Clark assisted by the Rev. W. M. Clark and the Rev. Thomas J. Packard, in St. Luke's Church, Clover. So. Ch., Feb. 7, 1884

Rosa, of Halifax, and William W. Wilkins of Brunswick Co., by the Rev. John T. Clark, at Banister Lodge. So. Ch., Nov. 22, 1866

W. M. (The Rev.), rector of the parish, and Nannie Douglas Tapscott of Amherst C. H., Va., by the Rev. John T. Clark of North Carolina assisted by the Rev. A. S. Lloyd of St. Luke's Church, Norfolk, in Ascension Church, Amherst C. H., Va. So. Ch., Oct. 15, 1885

CLARKE

Amelia R., and Jacob Faulcon, Esq., by the Rev. William Hodges, in Surry Co., Va. So. Ch., Apr. 30, 1847

Edmond, and Emma Worsham, both of West Point, Va., by the Rev. Pendleton Brooke, at the residence of the bride's father.
So. Ch., Sept. 6, 1888

John, and Bettie Sims, oldest d. of Dr. E. A. Coleman, all of Halifax Co., Va., by the Rev. John Grammer. So. Ch., Nov. 13, 1857

John J., Civil Engineer, Rockingham Co., N.C., and Lucy S. of Richmond, Va., d. of the late Miles Macon, Esq., by the Rev. H. S. Kepler. So. Ch., Apr. 13, 1860

Loulie, d. of Hon. W. E. Clarke of Demopolis, and W. Douglas Mason of Virginia, by the Rev. R. W. Barnwell, in Trinity Church, Demopolis, Ala. So. Ch., June 17, 1880

Maurice (The Rev.), of England, and Sheldena Macrae of Upperville, Fauquier Co., Va., by the Rev. R. W. Trapnell, at St. Andrews-on-the-Mountain, near Charles Town, W.Va. So. Ch., June 22, 1907

William E., Esq., of Baltimore, and Anna, d. of the late Col. Thomas Mason of Albemarle Co., by the Rev. Richard K. Meade, at Tafton. So. Ch., Nov. 28, 1867

Wm. L., Jr. (Capt.), of Winchester, and Mary Johnson Stuart of Staunton, by the Rev. Mr. Baker, at Staunton, Va. So. Ch., May 16, 1862

Wm. Meade (The Rev.), of Mecklenburg Co., Va., and Laura M. Walker, by the Rev. John T. Clarke assisted by the Rev. C. Walker, D.D., in the Seminary Chapel, near Alexandria, Va. So. Ch., June 16, 1881

CLARKSON

Charles Dana Sayres, of Haymarket, and Helen Meredith,

MARRIAGE NOTICES IN THE SOUTHERN CHURCHMAN WITH DATES OF PUBLICATION

    d. of the late Wm. H.
Jolliffe of Baltimore,
Md., by the Rev. Cary
Gamble, in St. Paul's
Church, Haymarket, Va.
So. Ch., Dec. 14, 1907
Helen Meredith, d. of C.
D. S. and Helen Joliffe Clarkson late of
Haymarket, Va., and
Merrill Phillip Barber,
at Vero Beach, Fla. So.
Ch., Mar. 21, 1931
Henry M. (Dr.) (Surgeon
P. A. C. S.), of South
Carolina, and Jeanie
Irvin, youngest d. of
the late John J. Sayrs,
of Alexandria, Va., by
the Rev. R. R. Mason, in
Fluvanna Co., Va., at the
residence of the bride's
brother-in-law, W. S. Boswell, Esq. So. Ch., Oct.
2, 1863

CLAY
    Cyrus B., and Mary C., d.
of James A. Meriwether,
all of Bedford, by the
Rev. R. H. Wilmer. So.
Ch., Dec. 21, 1855
John, Esq., of Chesterfield,
and Christophine McC., d.
of D. H. Branch, Esq.
of Petersburg, by the Rev.
C. J. Gibson, at Petersburg, Va. So. Ch., Oct.
26, 1855
John B., of Newport News,
and Lottie J. Tilford of
Hampton, Va., by the Rev.
J. J. Gravatt in St. John's
Church, Hampton, Va. So.
Ch., Jan. 12, 1882
Joseph, Esq., of Georgia,
and Mary E., d. of Dr. B. S.
Herndon, by the Rev. M.
Maury, at Fredericksburg.
So. Ch., Dec. 7, 1865
Lafayette Henry, and Susan
Norfleet, d. of the late
Daniel Eppes, Esq., all
of Prince George Co., by
the Rev. W. F. Gardiner,
at Hickory Grove, Prince
George Co. So. Ch., Jan.
11, 1872
Paul A. (Capt.), of Bedford
Co., and Mary L., d. of
Edward O. Watkins, Esq.,
by the Rev. William H.
Hart, at Presque Isle,
Chesterfield Co., Va. So.
Ch., Dec. 1, 1837

CLAYBROOK
    Edwin C., and Judith W. Newton, by the Rev. Andrew
Fisher, at the residence
of the bride's father, Linden,
Westmoreland Co. So. Ch.,
Jan. 31, 1867
Lottie E., youngest d. of the
late R. A. Claybrook, and
Thomas Brown, Jr., by the
Rev. F. W. Claybrook, in
Yeocomico Church, Westmoreland Co., Va. So. Ch., Jan.
20, 1876

CLAYTER
    Evelynn, d. of Robert and
Mary Clayter of Bedford
City, Va., and Samuel, s.
of Judge MacRae of North
Carolina, by the Rev. T. W.
Jones, in St. John's Church,
Bedford City, Va. So. Ch.,
Dec. 25, 1890

CLAYTOR
    Alexander R., of West River
and Lizzie B. Robinson
formerly of Baltimore Co.,
by the Rev. William F.
Gardner, at "Clifton". So.
Ch., Nov. 13, 1884
Mary R., of Lynchburg, and
Col. Edward J. Steptoe
of the U.S. Army, by the
Rev. W. H. Kinckle, at
Lynchburg. So. Ch., Jan.
27, 1860

MARRIAGE NOTICES IN THE SOUTHERN CHURCHMAN WITH DATES OF PUBLICATION

CLEMENS
J. J. (The Rev.), of Eastville, Va., and Sue G., youngest d. of the late John F. Scott, by the Rev. A. M. Randolph, at the residence of the bride's mother, Fredericksburg, Va. So. Ch., Sept. 21, 1871

CLEMENTS
Robert B., of Gloucester Co., Va., and Bettie D. Adams, by the Rev. William B. Lee, at the residence of the bride's mother in Mathews Co., Va. So. Ch., Jan. 8, 1891

CLEMMITT
Alys Landon, d. of Mrs. Annie Guy Clemmitt, and Julian Moseley, s. of Calvin Wilson, by the Rev. G. Freeland Peter assisted by the Rev. J. Calvin Stewart, at the home of the bride's mother, Richmond, Va. So. Ch., Jan. 27, 1917

CLEMSON
John B. (The Rev.), rector of the Church of the Ascension, Philadelphia, and Phoebe Waln, d. of David Lewis, Esq., by the Rev. John Coleman. So. Ch., Aug. 2, 1839

CLEVELAND
Ella M., d. of Richard M. Cleveland, of Albemarle Co., Va., and George W. Lockie of Rockbridge Co., by the Rev. T. E. Locke, at the residence of the bride's father. So. Ch., Apr. 18, 1889

Martha B., d. of William Cleveland, Esq., and Prof. Reuel Keith, U.S.N., by the Rev. Thomas S. Savage, in Trinity Church, Pass Christian, Miss. So. Ch., Nov. 27, 1851

Sarah J., of Huntsville, d. of the late Wm. Cleveland of Jefferson Co., Va., and Franklin Edwards of Springfield, Ill., by the Rev. Mr. McMasters, in Huntsville, Mo. So. Ch., June 5, 1857

CLINGMAN
Robert C. (The Rev.), rector of St. Peter's Church, Akron, Ohio, and Joy Loree Hardgrove of Westfield, N.J., by the groom's father, the Bishop of Kentucky, at the residence of the bride. So. Ch., July 5, 1941

CLOAK
Fredrica, and Christopher Hager, both of Richmond, by the Rev. Mr. Hawley, at Washington, D.C. So. Ch., Dec. 22, 1837

CLOPTON
F. B. (Capt.), of Richmond, and Mary, d. of the late James M. Boyd of Lynchburg, by the Rev. W. H. Kinckle. So. Ch., Dec. 17, 1858

John J. (The Rev.), rector of Meade Memorial Church, Manchester, Va., and Irene Cooper Horsoley, by the Rev. George S. Somerville, in Trinity Church, Nelson Co., Va. So. Ch., Dec. 10, 1891

Susan Latane, d. of E. A. J. Clopton, Esq., and Jackson Turpin, Esq., by the Rev. Henry Wall, D.D., in St. John's Church, Richmond, Va. So. Ch., June 1, 1871

Wm. D. (Maj.), of Cumberland, and Lucie Perkins, d. of Chastain Shores, deceased, by the Rev. Wm. C. Meredith, at Seven Islands in Buckingham Co. So. Ch., Aug. 27, 1858

MARRIAGE NOTICES IN THE SOUTHERN CHURCHMAN WITH DATES OF PUBLICATION

CLOSE
  Elvira R., d. of the late S. Close of New York, and the Rev. Charles Dana, D.D. of Alexandria, Va., by the Rt. Rev. Bishop John's, in Christ Church, Alexandria. So. Ch., July 27, 1860

CLYMER
  See BROOKE, A. M. C. (Mrs.)

COAKLEY
  William, and Lillie J. Hutt, by the Rev. D. H. Wharton, at the residence of the bride's father in Westmoreland Co., Va. So. Ch., Jan. 15, 1880

COBB
  Meta Eugenia, and L. Holmes Ginn, both of Clarke Co., Va., by the Rev. John P. Tyler, rector, in Christ Church, Millwood, Va. So. Ch., May 19, 1892

COBBS
  R. A. (The Rev.), rector of the parish, and Betty P. Storrs of Marengo Co., by the Rev. N. H. Cobbs, D.D., in the Church of the Holy Cross, Union Town, Ala. So. Ch., Sept. 17, 1858
  Virginia L., d. of John L. Cobbs, Esq. of Bedford, and Charles W. Price, Esq. of Missouri, by the Rev. O. A. Kinsolving, in Bedford Co., Va. So. Ch., Nov. 23, 1848

COCHRAN
  Anna Elizabeth, d. of Col. James C. and Elizabeth Brooke Cochran of Folly, Augusta Co., Va., and gr.d. of the late Judge Brooke of St. Julien, Spotsylvania Co., Va., and Lionel Seymour Rawlinson, of Herringstone, Augusta Co., Va., s. of Canon Rawlinson of Canterbury, England, by the Rev. W. Q. Hullihen, in Trinity Church, Staunton, Va. So. Ch., June 22, 1893
  Charlotte Carr, d. of Dr. J. H. Cochran, and Robert S. Cochran of The Plains, by the Rt. Rev. Thomas U. Dudley, Bishop of Kentucky, assisted by the Rev. John Norwood, rector of the parish, in Trinity Church, "The Plains". So. Ch., Dec. 7, 1893
  Fannie R., d. of William A. Cochran, Esq., and Richard R. Cochran, Esq., by the Rev. Jno. Collins McCabe, D.D., at "Spring Valley", the residence of the bride's father, near Middletown, Del. So. Ch., Oct. 21, 1869
  Fanny B., d. of Dr. William Cochran of Middleburg, and Thomas U. Dudley, Jr. of Richmond, by the Rev. O. A. Kinsolving, in Emanuel Church, Middleburg. So. Ch., July 22, 1859
  H. P., of Richmond, Va., and Jenny Lewis, d. of Col. Joseph F. Kent, at "Bellefield", Wythe Co., Va. So. Ch., Jan. 22, 1880
  John Henry (Dr.), of Middleburg, Va., and Charlotte, d. of Dr. W. G. Carr, by the Rev. T. U. Dudley, at Bentivar, Albemarle Co., Va. So. Ch., Oct. 10, 1867
  John L. (Capt.), and Mrs. Mary Massie, both of Charlottesville, by the Rev. Edmund Withers, at the residence of P. C. Massie, Nelson Co. So. Ch., Sept. 17, 1868
  I. H. (Capt.), Coast Artillery

MARRIAGE NOTICES IN THE SOUTHERN CHURCHMAN WITH DATES OF PUBLICATION

Corps, U.S.A., and Mary Welby Turner, at Grace Church, The Plains, Va. So. Ch., Oct. 27, 1917

Mildred Woodword, and the Rev. Mr. Wright, by Bishop Jett, the Rev. David Cady Wright, of Christ Church, Savannah, and the Rev. Dr. John J. Gravatt, rector of Trinity Church, in Trinity Church, Staunton, Va. So. Ch., Sept. 23, 1933

Richard R., Esq., and Fannie R., d. of William A. Cochran, Esq., by the Rev. Jno. Collins McCabe, D.D., at "Spring Valley", the residence of the bride's father, near Middletown, Del. So. Ch., Oct. 21, 1869

Robert S., of The Plains, and Charlotte Carr, d. of Dr. J. H. Cochran, by the Rt. Rev. Thomas U. Dudley, Bishop of Kentucky, assisted by the Rev. John Norwood, rector of the parish, in Trinity Church, "The Plains". So. Ch., Dec. 7, 1893

COCHRANE

Nannie, only d. of Dr. P. H. Cochrane, and Wm. P. Campbell, of Bethany, Va., by the Rev. A. Buchanan, at St. Paul's Church, Louisville, Ky. So. Ch., July 21, 1870

COCKE

Blanche B., d. of the late Wm. Ronald Cocke, and Arthur Orr Venable, of Atlanta, Ga., by the Rev. Edward Valentine Jones, at Red Hills, Fluvanna Co., Va. So. Ch., June 18, 1890

Edmund Randolph (Capt.), of Oaklands, Cumberland Co., Va., and Lucia Cary Harrison, by the Rev. Edmund C. Murdaugh, D.D., at Lower Brandon, James River. So. Ch., May 30, 1878

Effie, d. of Woodson S. Cocke, deceased, and Charles Farson, of the law firm of Holden and Farson, by the Rev. Mr. Tupper, in Chicago. So. Ch., Feb. 24, 1881

James, of New York, and Martha Cocke of Prince George, Va., by the Rev. R. E. Northam. So. Ch., Jan. 11, 1839

John H., of Fluvanna Co., Va., and Ruth A. Howell, by the Rev. Wm. H. Meade, at Zion Church, Charles Town, W.Va. So. Ch., Nov. 30, 1882

Louisiana B., d. of Col. Philip St. Geo. Cocke, and Richard B. Kennon of Richmond, by the Rev. J. D. Powell, at "Belmead", the residence of the bride's father, Powhatan Co. So. Ch., June 29, 1860

Lucy C., d. of the late Gen. Philip St. George Cocke, and Capt. Wm. M. Bridges, by the Rev. J. H. Morrison, D.D., at "Belmead", Powhatan Co. So. Ch., Apr. 27, 1871

Martha, of Prince George, Va., and James Cocke of New York, by the Rev. R. E. Northam. So. Ch., Jan. 11, 1839

Mary Elizabeth, and Virgil Holman Richardson, all of Columbia, Fluvanna Co., Va., by the Rev. J. H. Morrison, D.D., in St. John's Church, Columbia, Va. So. Ch., July 20, 1876

Mary Susan, d. of the late James Cocke, Esq., and James G. S. Boyd, by the Rev. A. B. Tizzard, at the residence of Dr. Richard

MARRIAGE NOTICES IN THE SOUTHERN CHURCHMAN WITH DATES OF PUBLICATION

Taylor, Amelia Co. So. Ch., Jan. 18, 1856
Sallie B., d. of the late Gen. Philip St. George Cocke of Powhatan, and Samuel M. Wilson, Esq. of Norfolk Co., by the Rev. J. D. Powell, at "Belmead", Powhatan Co. So. Ch., Mar. 1, 1866
Thomas L. P., of Powhatan Co., and Mary B., d. of the late C. C. Curtis of Gloucester Co., Va., by the Rev. Dr. Peterkin, at the residence of J. W. Cringan. So. Ch., Apr. 30, 1874

COCKERILLE
Hattie L., second d. of Hon. R. H. Cockerille of Fairfax Co., and Lewis H. Freeman of Loudoun Co., by the Rev. John McGill, at "Avon", the residence of the bride's father. So. Ch., Sept. 20, 1877
James F., of Loudoun, and Sarah A. Cole of Fairfax, by the Rev. Frank Page, at St. Timothy's Church, Herndon. So. Ch., July 22, 1880
Minnie, d. of James Cockerille, and Phillip W. Carper, all of Loudoun Co., by the Rev. Frank Page, at the residence of the bride's father. So. Ch., Dec. 26, 1878
Nannie Lee, d. of Judge R. H. Cockerille, and Richard M. Chichester, all of Fairfax Co., Va., by the Rev. Jno. McGill, in Christ Church, Fairfax Co. So. Ch., May 11, 1876

COCKEY
Deborah Powell, and Charles Catlett, Jr. of Gloucester, in Norfolk, Va. So. Ch., Sept. 6, 1913
William Warfield, and Lizzie Lee Jones, by the Rev. Henry L. Derby, at the residence of the bride in Suffolk, Va. So. Ch., Sept. 5, 1889

COCKRELL
Josephine T., only child and d. of J. J. Cockrell, and Charles E. Brawner, by the Rev. John McGill, at the residence of the bride's father in Prince William Co. So. Ch., Nov. 13, 1873

COCKRILL
Nancy, third d. of Thos. Cockrill, Esq., and Edwin Cook Glascock, all of Fauquier Co., Va., at the home of the bride's father. So. Ch., Feb. 22, 1872

COFER
James M. (The Rev.), rector of Tillotson Parish, Buckingham Co., Va., and Mary E., d. of the late George Duncan of Buckingham Co., by the Rev. Nicholas H. Cobbs. So. Ch., Mar. 3, 1837

COGDELL
Richard, of Georgia, and Louisa D. Brugh of Botetourt, by the Rev. E. W. Hubard, at Oak Grove. So. Ch., June 23, 1870

COGGILL
Ella Virginia, d. of the late Frederick Coggill of New York City, and Levin Joynes of Richmond, Va., by the Rev. D. Houghton, at the Church of the Transfiguration, New York City. So. Ch., Nov. 25, 1886

COGHILL
H. E. (Miss), of King George, and F. G. South of Colorado,

MARRIAGE NOTICES IN THE SOUTHERN CHURCHMAN WITH DATES OF PUBLICATION

by the Rev. A. J. Willis, at "Lothian", the residence of the bride's father, King George Co., Va. So. Ch., Mar. 17, 1877

COIT
Henry A. (The Rev.), of Concord, N.H., and Mary Bowman, d. of Charles Wheeler, Esq., by the Rev. Dr. Bowman, at the Church of the Epiphany, Philadelphia. So. Ch., Apr. 11, 1856

COKE
Addie C., second d. of the late W. W. Coke of Princess Anne Co., Va., and Lewis Stirling Smith, by the Rt. Rev. Alexander Garrett, in St. Matthews Cathedral, Dallas, Tex. So. Ch., Oct. 22, 1891

Eliza Alice, d. of the late W. W. Coke of Norfolk, Va., and I. T. Howard, by the Rev. Gabriel Johnson, in Dallas, Tex. So. Ch., Nov. 14, 1889

COLE
Bettie, d. of the late Dr. Wm. Cole of Prince George Co., Va., and J. W. Ashton of Portsmouth, by the Rev. Dr. Gibson, at the residence of the bride's uncle, John Cole, in Petersburg. So. Ch., Nov. 30, 1871

Catherine B., d. of Dr. Jessie Cole, and Charles Friend, Esq., by the Rev. Mr. Hodges, at Williamsburg. So. Ch., June 14, 1849

George R., of Piedmont, W.Va., and Barbara Ellen Toney of Westernport, by the Rev. W. Herbert Asshoton, at Westernport, Md. So. Ch., Jan. 11, 1883

George Washington (The Rev.), of Tecumseh, Mich., and Harriet Amelia, youngest d. of James Guion, Esq. of Westchester, N.Y., by the Rev. Dr. Milnor, in New York. So. Ch., Oct. 11, 1839

J. Thompson, of the Japan Mission, and Annie E., youngest d. of Cassius F. Lee, Esq. of Fairfax Co., by the Rev. William F. Gardner assisted by the Rt. Rev. George W. Peterkin, D.D., in the chapel of the Theological Seminary near Alexandria, Va. So. Ch., May 6, 1886

John (The Rev.), rector of St. Stephen's Church, Culpeper Co., and Fanny E., d. of the late John Thompson of Culpeper Co., by the Rev. Wm. F. Lockwood, rector of St. Thomas' Parish, Md., at Culpeper Court House, Va. So. Ch., Apr. 19, 1855

John T., and Henrietta, d. of Dr. William Gibson, all of Alexandria, by the Rev. Nathaniel L. Briggs, in the parsonage of Emmanuel P. E. Church, Philadelphia. So. Ch., Feb. 8, 1883

Sarah A., of Fairfax, and James F. Cockerille of Loudoun, by the Rev. Frank Page, in St. Timothy's Church, Herndon. So. Ch., July 22, 1880

Thomas L. (The Rev.), of Rhinecliff, N.Y., and Jessie D., d. of the late Thomas D. Savage of New York, by the Rev. J. H. Eccleston, D.D. assisted by the Rev. Samuel A. Wallis, in Emmanuel Church, Baltimore. So. Ch., July 3, 1884

MARRIAGE NOTICES IN THE SOUTHERN CHURCHMAN WITH DATES OF PUBLICATION

Thomas Willoughby, of Virginia, and Josephine Burgie, in Trinity Church, Chicago, Ill. So. Ch., Jan. 15, 1885

COLEMAN

Bettie Sims, eldest d. of Dr. E. A. Coleman, and John Clarke, all of Halifax Co., Va., by the Rev. John Grammer. So. Ch., Nov. 13, 1857

Betty Ann (Mrs.), and James P. Coleman, by the Rev. C. Walker, at Strawberry Hill, Amherst Co., Va. So. Ch., Mar. 26, 1847

Henry Edmunds, of Louisville, Ky., and Daisye Edmunds, d. of Mr. and Mrs. Joseph Williams Chalmers, by the Rev. Flournoy Bouldin, Houston, Va., at the home of the bride's parents. So. Ch., Sept. 19, 1908

James P., and Mrs. Betty Ann Coleman, by the Rev. C. Walker, at Strawberry Hill, Amherst Co., Va. So. Ch., Mar. 26, 1847

John C. (Dr.), and Nannie L., d. of Mrs. Mildred L. and John R. Edmunds, Esq., by the Rev. John Grammer, at Redfield, Halifax Co. So. Ch., Feb. 15, 1861

John Mabry, and Evelyn Byrd, d. of Frederick W. Page, Esq. of Albemarle Co., Va., by the Rev. O. A. Kinsolving, in Grace Church, Halifax Co., Va. So. Ch., July 27, 1882

Kate Lee, and Charles St. John Beauclerk, both of Amelia Co., Va., by the Rev. W. J. Page, in Christ Church, Amelia C. H. So. Ch., Feb. 5, 1885

Mary E., eldest d. of Thompson Coleman, Esq., and Wm. P. Logue of Jackson, Tenn., by the Rev. Geo. W. Dame, in Pittsylvania. So. Ch., Aug. 1, 1862

Mary Frances, youngest d. of the late Maj. Reuben Coleman of Amherst, and William Thomas Higginbotham of Petersburg, by the Rev. Cleland Nelson. So. Ch., Sept. 6, 1839

Nannie T., d. of the late William E. Coleman of Virginia, and Geo. Y. Worthington, Jr., of Fauquier Co., Va., by the Rev. W. C. Williams, in Summerville, Ga. So. Ch., Nov. 28, 1878

Nathaniel R., Esq., of Halifax Co., Va., and Annie Nelson, d. of Frederick W. Page, Esq. of Albemarle Co., Va., by the Rev. E. Boyden, in Grace Church, Walker's Parish, Albemarle Co., Va. So. Ch., Jan. 21, 1875

R. T. (Dr.), of Richmond, and Millie Rose Irving, by the Rev. T. F. Martin, at Bellvette, Nelson Co., Va. So. Ch., Nov. 9, 1855

Richard, and Theckla, d. of Carl Roeser, by the Rev. Frank Page, at the residence of the bride's father near Dranesville.* So. Ch., Feb. 8, 1883

Richard F., of Richmond, Va., and Maude M. Jerdone of Charles City Co., Va., by the Rev. John P. Tyler, at "Sterling", the home of the bride, in Charles City Co., Va. So. Ch., Dec. 4,

---

* Given as printed

MARRIAGE NOTICES IN THE SOUTHERN CHURCHMAN WITH DATES OF PUBLICATION

1890
Sallie Ann, second d. of Thompson Coleman, Esq., and Felix A. Luck, by the Rev. Geo. W. Dame, near Ringgold in Pittsylvania. So. Ch., Mar. 18, 1864

T. Gordon, Jr., of Halifax Co., and Isabella, d. of Alexander Rives, Esq. of Albemarle, by the Rev. R. K. Meade, at Carlton. So. Ch., Dec. 12, 1856

COLES
Agnes Cabell, only d. of Capt. Walter Coles, and Edward B. Ambler of Monroe, Va., by the Rev. Dr. C. O. Pruden, at Coles Hill, Pittsylvania Co., Va. So. Ch., Nov. 23, 1907

J. Thompson, and Blanche Leftwich, both of Pittsylvania Co., Va., by the Rev. C. O. Pruden, at "Forest Grove", the residence of the bride's mother, Mrs. M. B. Coles, in Pittsylvania Co., Va. So. Ch., Feb. 5, 1885

Julia Stricker, only d. of Peyton S. Coles of Albemarle Co., and Edmund Lyons Mackenzie, by the Rev. T. E. Locke assisted by the Rev. Robert Coles, in Christ Church, St. Anne's Parish, Albemarle Co., Va. So. Ch., July 26, 1888

Sarah, of Lancaster, and Chas. B. Whitney of Campbell Court House, by the Rev. Edmund Withers, at Locust Green, Lancaster Co., Va. So. Ch., May 16, 1856

Walter (Dr.), of St. Louis, and Lizzie C., d. of Col.

Edmund Pendleton, by the Rev. E. W. Hubard, in Trinity Church, Buchanan, Va. So. Ch., July 18, 1872

COLHOUN
J. B. (The Rev.), and Elizabeth Jane Moore of Princess Anne, by the Rev. James Moore, father of the bride, and the Rev. Meyer Lewin, in St. Andrew's Church, Princess Anne, Somerset Co., Md. So. Ch., Oct. 22, 1858

COLLINGS
Edward, Esq., of Illinois, and Rebecca C., d. of J. B. Fenimore, by the Rev. Jno. Collins McCabe, D.D., at Middletown, Del. So. Ch., Oct. 21, 1869

COLLINS
Annie M., d. of J. Preston Collins, and John H. G. Hughes, all of Albemarle, Va., by the Rev. T. E. Locke. So. Ch., Apr. 21, 1892

Jennie Lynd, and Byron A. Pugin, all of Albemarle, by the Rev. T. E. Locke, at the residence of Wm. Collins. So. Ch., Nov. 12, 1885

Joseph S. (The Rev.), of Alexandria, Va., and Mrs. Dorotha W. Mopps of Baltimore, by the Rev. T. B. Lemon. So. Ch., Jan. 3, 1850.

COLSTON
E. F., d. of Raleigh Colston, Esq., of Albemarle, Va., and Prof. B. L. Gildersleeve, by the Rev. Wm. N. Nelson, at Hillandale,* Albemarle Co., Va. So. Ch., Oct. 4, 1866

J. Annie, d. of the late Col. Edward Colston of Berkeley Co., Va., and Dr. Theodore

* Given as printed

MARRIAGE NOTICES IN THE SOUTHERN CHURCHMAN WITH DATES OF PUBLICATION

A. Michie of Charlottesville, Albemarle Co., Va., by the Rev. R. D. Roller, in Trinity Church, Martinsburg, W. Va. So. Ch., Oct. 23 and Nov. 6, 1884

Laura Holmes, youngest d. of Raleigh Colston, and W. R. Royall, all of Richmond, Va., by the Rev. Dr. Peterkin assisted by the Rev. Dr. Kerr, in St. James' Church. So. Ch., Feb. 24, 1887

Lucy, d. of the late Edward Colston of Honeywood, Berkeley Co., Va., and Bennett Taylor of Albemarle Co., Va., by the Rev. W. D. Hanson. So. Ch., July 12, 1866

Mary White, d. of the late Edward Colston, Esq., and Williams Leigh, by the Rev. D. Francis Sprigg, at Honeywood, Berkeley Co., Va. So. Ch., Nov. 23, 1854

Nannie F., d. of the late Thomas M. Colston of Fauquier, and Prof. John B. Minor of the University of Virginia, by the Rev. D. C. T. Davis, at the residence of Raleigh Colston, Esq., Hillandale.* So. Ch., Mar. 11, 1859

Susan Leigh, d. of the late Thomas M. Colston of Loudoun, and Charles M. Blackford of Lynchburg, by the Rev. D. C. T. Davis, at "Hill and Dale" the residence of Raleigh Colston, Esq., in Albemarle. So. Ch., Feb. 29, 1856

Wm. B. (Capt.), of the "Stonewall Brigade", and Minnie, d. of Dr. R. Summers of Martinsburg, Va., by the Rev. W. D. Hanson. So. Ch., July 12, 1866

COLTON
Hannah Maria, of Richmond, Va., and Patrick Henry Fitzhugh of Gloucester Co., by the Rev. Wm. H. Hart. So. Ch., Nov. 3, 1837

COLVIN
Frances L., of Suffolk, Va., and Johnson M. Mundy of Rochester, N.Y., by the Rev. Douglass Hooff, in Trinity Church, Portsmouth, Va. So. Ch., Oct. 9 and 16, 1884

COMBS
Elizabeth Edmington, and Dr. C. T. Peirce of Lancaster Co., by the Rev. L. R. Combs, father of the bride, assisted by the Rev. W. H. Clark of St. James' Church, Richmond, in Trinity Church, Lancaster Co., Va. So. Ch., Mar. 23, 1907

Lawrence R. (The Rev.), of Gordonsville (formerly of Stafford Co., Va.), and Minnie R., d. of the late W. F. H. Jacobs of Fairfax Co., Va., by the Rev. Frank Stringfellow, in the Seminary Chapel. So. Ch., Dec. 20, 1883

COMER
M. Elizabeth, and Capt. George F. Wiese, by the Rev. J. Jacquelin Ambler, Jr., in St. Mark's Church, Dante, Va. So. Ch., May 9, 1931

COMERY
Harvey S., of Thomaston, Me., and Dora Burton of Hanover Co., by the Rev. S. S.

* Given as printed

MARRIAGE NOTICES IN THE SOUTHERN CHURCHMAN WITH DATES OF PUBLICATION

Hepbron. So. Ch., Dec. 11, 1884

COMPTON
Frances Gertrude, and George Hunter Ott, both of Harrisonburg, Va., by the Rev. Dr. Addison, at Washington City. So. Ch., Nov. 7, 1889

Key, of Norfolk, and Sallie, d. of Henry A. Tayloe, Esq., by the Rev. A. B. Kinsolving, at "Mount Airy", Richmond Co., Va. So. Ch., Nov. 22, 1888

Richard J., Jr., of St. Louis, Mo., and Cornelia Letcher, d. of Mr. and Mrs. L. L. Ashbrook of Manhattan, formerly of St. Louis, by the Rev. Pendleton Brooke, in St. Paul's Church, Manhattan, Kan. So. Ch., Nov. 27, 1890

CONDIT
Elizabeth Ann, d. of Ichabod Condit, and Rev. James A. Williams, rector of St. Mark's Church, both of Orange, N.J., by the Rev. Richard Cox, at Orange, N.J. So. Ch., Oct. 27, 1837

Martha, d. of Israel D. Condit, and Edward T. Whittingham, M.D., all of Millburn, by the Bishop of Maryland assisted by the Bishop of New Jersey, in St. Stephen's Church, Millburn, N.J. So. Ch., Jan. 21, 1859

CONKLIN
Margaret F., d. of Henry N. Conklin, Esq., and the Rev. A. M. Wylie, all of Brooklyn, by the Rev. B. C. Cutler, D.D., at the residence of the bride's parents. So. Ch., Dec. 21, 1860

CONRAD
Frank E., and Mary J., d. of the late Henry T. Harrison, all of Leesburg, by the Rev. R. T. Davis, D.D., at home. So. Ch., Nov. 15, 1883

CONSTANTINE
Nicholas, of Norfolk, Va., formerly of Satista, Greece, and Martha L. Randolph of Suffolk, Va., by the Rev. H. L. Derby, in St. Paul's Church, Suffolk, Va. So. Ch., June 6, 1889

CONWAY
Gibbon S., and Julia A., d. of the late Henry Barnes, all of Madison Co., by the Rev. James T. Johnston, in St. Paul's Church. So. Ch., May 29, 1857

Maggie E., and Joseph A. Pate, by the Rev. R. S. Barrett, at Richmond, Va. So. Ch., July 1, 1880

COOK
Catherine T., and William A. Deahl, s. of A. W. Deahl, by the Rev. Father O'Kane, at the residence of the bride's mother, 313 N. Pitt St., Alexandria, Va. So. Ch., Dec. 25, 1890

Elizabeth C., and William F. Speer, by the Rev. Dr. Andrew Symm, all of Petersburg, Va. So. Ch., Nov. 3, 1837

Geo. E., of Clarksville, Tenn., and Caroline Homozelle Thompson of Kanawha Co., W.Va., by the Rev. W. G. Stewart, at Belleville,

MARRIAGE NOTICES IN THE SOUTHERN CHURCHMAN WITH DATES OF PUBLICATION

the residence of the late Col. Frank Thompson. So. Ch., Jan. 2, 1868

Hart, eldest d. of the late Jas. W. Cook of Greensville Co., Va., and Capt. Wm. H. Briggs, by the Rev. David Barr, at "Midfield", near Hicksford, Greensville Co., Va. So. Ch., June 16, 1870

Kate, and Capt. F. John Jones, by the Rev. P. D. Thompson, in Christ Church, Kent Island, Md. So. Ch., Jan. 4, 1883

Mary Allen, d. of the late Lt. John A. Cook formerly of the U.S.N., and Frederick Fairfax, all of Washington, D.C., by the Rev. Isaac Cole, in Baltimore. So. Ch., Jan. 21, 1869

COOKE
Bettie B., eldest d. of the Rev. John Cooke, and Colin D. Clark of Baltimore, by the Rev. Horace Stringfellow, at Dewberry, Hanover Co., Va. So. Ch., Nov. 16, 1855

Edmonia Churchill, youngest d. of Mr. and Mrs. James Churchill Cooke, and James Edward Stansbury of Baltimore, Md., by the Rev. J. Y. Downman, D.D. of All Saint's Church, Richmond, at Foxleigh, the residence of Mr. and Mrs. James Churchill Cooke. So. Ch., Dec. 24, 1910

Ella M., d. of Col. John K. Cooke formerly of Portsmouth, Va., and John W. Chandler of Richmond, by the Rev. A. B. Tizzard, at the residence of the bride's father in Chesterfield Co. So. Ch., Apr. 22, 1864

Fannie, youngest d. of the Rev. John Cooke, and John P. Harrison of Richmond, by the Rev. Horace Stringfellow, at Dewberry, Hanover Co., Va. So. Ch., Nov. 16, 1855

J. Addison, of Staunton, Va., and Mary Lewis Sams of Baltimore, by the Rev. Dr. J. J. Sams, at Holy Trinity Church, Baltimore. So. Ch., May 8, 1890

James W. (The Rev.), assistant minister of St. George's Church, New York, and Emily, d. of the late Crooke Stevenson, Esq. Of Philadelphia, by the Rev. Stephen H. Tyng, D.D., in Philadelphia. So. Ch., Aug. 23, 1839

Jay, of Washington City, and Helen Barton, d. of the late Robert Campbell, Esq. of Philadelphia, by the Rev. Dr. Lindsay of Georgetown, in St. Mark's Church, Berkeley Springs, Morgan Co., W.Va. So. Ch., Nov. 9, 1882

Margaret E., only d. of Col. Giles B. Cooke of Borough, Va., and Thomas G. Baylor, by the Rev. Mr. Parks. So. Ch., Nov. 29, 1839

Maria Elizabeth, d. of the late Dr. Thomas Alfred Cooke (formerly of Gloucester Co., Va.), and Fanny Pennill, his wife, both of St. Landry Parish, La., and

MARRIAGE NOTICES IN THE SOUTHERN CHURCHMAN WITH DATES OF PUBLICATION

the Rev. Herbert Cope Duncan, rector of St. James Church, Alexandria, La., by the Rt. Rev. the Bishop of Louisiana, in St. John's Church, Washington, La. So. Ch., Feb. 1, 1883

Mary Gatlin, eldest d. of Chas. Cooke, and Huling P. Robertson of Salado, Bell Co., Tex., in Gainesville, Sumter Co., Ala. So. Ch., Mar. 5, 1885

Robert, Esq., late of the state of Louisiana, and Virginia Ann, only d. of the late Thomas C. Russell, Esq., by the Rev. John C. McCabe, rector of St. John's Church, Hampton, at "Half-way-House", York Co., Va. So. Ch., Feb. 2, 1854

Susan Randolph, and the Rev. Charles Henry Lee, Jr., by the Rev. John P. Tyler and the Rev. William R. Lee, in Christ Church, Millwood, Clarke Co., Va. So. Ch., Oct. 5, 1893

Thomas P., of Gloucester Co., and Susan E., d. of the late Francis Waldron of Berryville, Va., by the Rev. P. P. Phillips, rector of Grace Church, in Berryville, Va. So. Ch., Jan. 29, 1891

COOKLEY
Virginia B., d. of the late Horace Cookley of Fredericksburg, Va., and Anthony B. Patton, by the Rev. R. J. McBryde, at the residence of the bride's mother. So. Ch., Jan. 19, 1882

COOPER
Alexander, and Mrs. Bettie J. Carroll of Oxford, N.C., by the Rev. P. D. Thompson, in St. Stephen's Church, Oxford, N.C. So. Ch., June 18, 1874

George E. (Dr.), U.S. Army, and Elva M. Jones, by the Rev. M. L. Chevers. So. Ch., Oct. 5, 1860

Mary J., and Charles H. Patterson, by the Rev. Henry T. Sharp, in St. John's Church, Uniontown, Ky. So. Ch., Nov. 28, 1872

Sarah Ann, only d. of the late B. B. Cooper, Esq., and the Rev. Francis P. Lee, by the Rev. John Woart, in Camden. So. Ch., Oct. 27, 1837

Virginia Mason, d. of Gen. Samuel Cooper of Virginia, and Nicholas Dawson of Baltimore, by Bishop Johns assisted by the Rev. Arthur Johns, in the chapel of the Theological Seminary, Fairfax Co., Va. So. Ch., Nov. 6, 1873

Wm. B. (The Rev.), of the Protestant Episcopal Mission, Yedo, and Alice Minnette, d. of the Rev. R. S. Maclay, D.D., of Yokohama, by the Rt. Rev. C. M. Williams, D.D., in Christ Church, Yokahama, Japan. So. Ch., Apr. 12, 1877

COPPRIDGE
Malissa T., of Pittsylvania Co., Va., and N. A. Wilkinson of Rockingham Co., N.C., by the Rev. C. O. Pruden, at the residence of the bride's mother in Pittsylvania. So. Ch.,

MARRIAGE NOTICES IN THE SOUTHERN CHURCHMAN WITH DATES OF PUBLICATION

Jan. 1, 1885

CORBELL
Samuel V., and Agnes, d. of Edward T. Thruston, Esq., all of Gloucester Co., by the Rev. Wm. B. Lee, in Abingdon Church, Gloucester Co., Va. So. Ch., Oct. 22, 1885

CORBIN
James Parke (Maj.), of Mossneck, and Eliza Lewis, oldest d. of Richard B. Hoomes of Virginia, by the Rev. Thos. Addison, at Belle Hill, the residence of J. Edward Dickinson, Esq. So. Ch., Aug. 29, 1856

James Parke, of Caroline, and Edmonia FitzHugh, d. of the late J. B. Ficklen,* Esq. of Bolmont, Stafford Co., Va., by the Rev. E. C. Murdaugh, D.D., in St. George's Church, Fredericksburg, Va. So. Ch., Feb. 22, 1877

Nannie Maury, d. of S. Wellford and Nannie Maury Corbin of Farley Vale, King George Co., Va., and Thomas Richie Marshall of Richmond, by the Rev. J. K. Mason, in St. George's Church, Fredericksburg, Va. So. Ch., July 8, 1886

CORDOZA
Ed. S., of Richmond, Va., and Elizabeth Wormely, d. of John B. and Alice Norris, by the Rev. J. E. Hammond, in Memorial Church, Manchester. So. Ch., Dec. 14, 1871

CORNELL
Lucy Ogden, nurse in the Hudson Stuck Memorial Hospital at Fort Yukon, Alaska, d. of the late Dr. William P. Cornell of Charleston, S.C., and of Mrs. William P. Cornell, Executive Secretary of the Diocese of Florida, and the Rev. Merritt F. Williams, priest in charge of St. Stephen's Mission, Fort Yukon, Alaska, s. of Mr. and Mrs. Leonard O. Williams, of St. Louis, Mo., by the Rt. Rev. John Boyd Bentley, Bishop Suffragan of Alaska, at Fort Yukon, Alaska. So. Ch., Aug. 6, Dec. 3 and 10, 1932

CORNER
Carrie J., and Charles D. Ridout, by the Rev. Samuel Ridout, in St. Margaret's Church, Anne Arundel Co., Md. So. Ch., Nov. 29, 1883

CORNICK
Fannie F., d. of Dr. and Mrs. Cornick of Powhatan Co., Va., and Thos. H. Dunn, by the Rev. P. F. Berkeley, in Grace Church, Gonito Parish, Powhatan Co. So. Ch., Oct. 2, 1873

John (The Rev.), and Annie L., d. of E. B. Macon of Princess Anne. by the Rev. Mr. Lloyd and the Rev. Mr. Anson, rector, in the old chapel in Princess Anne. So. Ch., Nov. 2, 1893

CORNING
Erastus, Jr., of Albany, and Grace Fitz-Randolph, d. of the Rev. Dr. Schenck, by the Bishop of Albany and the Bishop of Long Island, in St. Ann's Church, Brooklyn. So. Ch., Jan. 23, 1879

CORNNELL
Hiram T., Esq., and Susan Ida McDonald, both of Clarke Co., Va., by the Rev. John P. Tyler, rector, in Christ Church, Millwood, Va. So. Ch., Dec. 31, 1891

CORNWALL
Helen, eldest d. of Charles W.

* Given as printed

MARRIAGE NOTICES IN THE SOUTHERN CHURCHMAN WITH DATES OF PUBLICATION

Cornwall, Esq., and the Rev. M. T. McCormick of Petersburg, Va., by the Rev. John Downie, M.A., at Colchester, Ontario, Canada. So. Ch., Oct. 2, 1873

CORRELL
Thomas A. (Dr.), and Annie F., d. of Dr. Washington A. Smith of Taylor's Island, by Dr. Wm. W. Greene, in Grace Church, Taylor's Island, Dorchester, Md. So. Ch., Dec. 25, 1879

CORSE
J. D., and Lucy E., d. of the Rev. George A. Smith, by the Rev. R. D. Brooke, in Christ Church, Alexandria. So. Ch., June 21, 1855

Virginia, and J. Conway Chichester, both of Fairfax Co., by the Rev. R. T. Brown, in the chapel of the Theological Seminary. So. Ch., Aug. 10, 1860

COSBY
Annie, of Hanover, and G. A. Rogers of Richmond, Va., by the Rev. R. S. Barrett, in Hanover Co. So. Ch., June 3, 1880

Chas. E., of Halifax, and Mrs. Hallie W. Shelton, d. of Jos. H. Turner, Esq., by the Rev. John Cosby, in Columbia, Fluvanna Co., Va. So. Ch., July 29, 1869

Cornelia C., of Halifax Co., Va., and Capt. J. D. Van Benthuysen of New Orleans, by the Rev. John Cosby, at "Woodside", the residence of the bride's father. So. Ch., Dec. 19, 1867

John (The Rev.), of St. James Parish, Mecklenburg, Va., and Elizabeth Anne, d. of David Chalmers, Esq., by the Rev. Walter Williams, at Springfield, Halifax, Va. So. Ch., Oct. 22, 1858

M. Loulie, d. of Dabney Cosby, Sr., Esq., and Robert H. Edmondson, by the Rev. O. A. Kinsolving, D.D., in St. John's Church, Halifax, C.H. So. Ch., Oct. 23, 1884

William H., and Kate Hull Hayden, both of Baltimore, by the Rev. Horace Edwin Hayden assisted by the Rev. J. Everest Cathell, rector of the Church of the Ascension, in the Church of the Ascension, Baltimore. So. Ch., June 11, 1874

COSTIN
Catherine, d. of Robert and Catherine Costin, and Madison, s. of Richard H. Rush of Philadelphia, by the Rev. George W. Easter, at Kendall Grove, the residence of the bride's parents, Eastville, Va. So. Ch., Oct. 9, 1884

COTTON
Nannie M., second d. of Dr. John T. Cotton, and Frank Woodman, all of Charleston, by the Rev. R. A. Cobbs, at the residence of the bride's father. So. Ch., Oct. 30, 1884

COTTRILL
Michael D., and Minnie L., d. of John F. Jordan, both of Lewis Co., by the Rev. T. H. Lacy, at St. Paul's Rectory, Weston, W.Va. So. Ch., Oct. 13, 1887

MARRIAGE NOTICES IN THE SOUTHERN CHURCHMAN WITH DATES OF PUBLICATION

COULTER
  Lee A., and Lucy Page, youngest d. of Wm. B. and Sally N. Weisiger, by the Rev. Davis Sessums, in Calvary Church, Memphis, Tenn. So. Ch., June 25, 1885

COUNSELMAN
  Minnie, eldest d. of L. W. and M. A. Counselman of Baltimore, and the Rev. Peregrine Wroth, by the Rt. Rev. Wm. Pinkney,* D.D., in the Church of the Messiah, Baltimore, Md. So. Ch., Feb. 26, 1880

COURTNEY
  Bushrod E., and Georgianna Unruh, by the Rev. T. Grayson Dashiell, in Yeocomico Church. So. Ch., Dec. 17, 1858

  Carrie, and John Stanhope of Hagerstown, Md., by the Rev. Dr. Hodges of St. Paul's Church, Baltimore. So. Ch., Nov. 27, 1884

  Rosa, youngest d. of the late Thomas Courtney of King and Queen Co., Va., and S. Smith Shepherd, by the Rev. J. Hervey Hundley, at the residence of Mr. Bird Courtney. So. Ch., Dec. 20, 1888

COVINGTON
  Anna Laura, of Bridgewater, and Jas. P. Gott of Montgomery Co., Md., by the Rev. O. S. Bunting, at the Baptist Church, Bridgewater, Rockingham Co. So. Ch., Nov. 11, 1886

COWAN
  James S., of Baltimore, and Ellen C., d. of James M. Wright, Esq., by the Rev. Jno. Collins McCabe, D.D., rector of St. Luke's Church, Bladensburg, in Prince George's Co., Md. So. Ch., July 4, 1867

  Jennie D., and Platt D. Cowan of South Carolina, by the Rev. Dr. Sprigg, in Richmond. So. Ch., Feb. 11, 1886

  Louisa Antoinette, d. of Jacob N. Cowan,* Esq., and Frank J. Manning, Esq. of Jefferson Co., Va., by the Rev. T. U. Dudley, at "Belmont", Rockingham Co., Va. So. Ch., Jan. 30, 1868

  Platt D., of South Carolina, and Jennie D. Cowan, by the Rev. Dr. Sprigg, in Richmond. So. Ch., Feb. 11, 1886

COWARD
  Benjamin R., and Roberta B., d. of John R. and Sallie E. Taylor, by the Rev. Curtis Grubb, at the residence of the bride's parents, Taylorsville, Hanover Co., Va. So. Ch., Feb. 15, 1883

COWCHER
  Mary Ann E., d. of the late Edward Cowcher of Dartmouth, England, and the Rev. Jas. Bryant Purcell, rector of St. John's Church, Mount Washington, Baltimore Co., by the Rev. A. M. Randolph, D.D., rector, assisted by the Rev. Dr. Dalrymple, in Emmanuel Church, Baltimore, Md. So. Ch., Nov. 28, 1878

COWDERY
  Fannie P., d. of Dr. G. W. Cowdery, and John P. Leigh, Jr., all of Norfolk, by the Rev. N. A. Oakeson, in St.

* Given as printed

MARRIAGE NOTICES IN THE SOUTHERN CHURCHMAN WITH DATES OF PUBLICATION

Paul's Church. So. Ch., May 3, 1861

COWEN
Annie L., oldest d. of J. N. Cowen* of Rockingham Co., Va., and Eugene West from Frederick Co., Md., of Company G, 7th Virginia Cavalry, Rosser's Brigade, by the Rev. J. C. Wheat, at Belmont Hall, the residence of the bride's father. So. Ch., Apr. 29, 1864

COWHERD
Susan Emma, d. of E. Festus Cowherd, Esq., and William C. Scott, Jr., by the Rev. F. G. Scott, at the residence of the bride's father near Gordonsville, Va. So. Ch., June 1, 1876

COWLING
R. C. (The Rev.), of Wickliffe, Va., and Elizabeth C. Thompson, d. of the rector of Leeds Church, by the Rev. P. D. Thompson assisted by the Rev. E. W. Cowling, in Leeds Church, Fauquier Co., Va. So. Ch., Aug. 14, 1909

COX
Emma D. (Mrs.), of Chesterfield Co., Va., and Henry C. Cox, Esq., by the Rev. A. B. Tizzard, at the residence of the bride. So. Ch., Feb. 18, 1886

Geo. H., of Buckingham, and Susan A. S. Slaughter, by the Rev. R. H. Wilmer, at the residence of J. A. Clay, Esq., of Bedford Co., Va. So. Ch., Apr. 4, 1856

Geo. W. (Dr.), and Cordelia Stem, both of Lunenburg Co., by the Rev. Henry Wall, at the residence of G. W. Gee. So. Ch., Apr. 6, 1860

Gilbert Jefferson, of Alexandria, Va., and Ella Lawrence, d. of Thomas N. Murphy, Esq. of Iowa, by the Rev. R. A. Castleman, at Cople Chapel, Westmoreland Co., Va. So. Ch., Jan. 7, 1892

Henry C., Esq., and Mrs. Emma D. Cox of Chesterfield Co., Va., by the Rev. A. B. Tizzard, at the residence of the bride. So. Ch., Feb. 18, 1886

Homoiselle R., of Heathsville, Northumberland Co., and Wm. G. Moss of Westmoreland Co., by the Rev. H. L. Derby, in St. Stephen's Church, Heathsville, Northumberland Co., Va. So. Ch., Sept. 7, 1882

John T., and Annie C. Donohoe of Loudoun Co., Va., by the Rev. R. T. Davis assisted by the Rev. Henry T. Sharp, D.D., of Grace Church, Alexandria, Va., in St. James Church, Leesburg, Va. So. Ch., Jan. 31, 1884

John Wentworth (Lt.), U.S.N., and Emma Matilda, d. of the late William T. Stockton, Esq. of Pennsylvania, by the Rev. Mr. Meade, in Albemarle Co. So. Ch., Nov. 24, 1837

Lewis Berkeley, of Portland, Ore., and Elinor Jackson, d. of the officiating clergyman, the Rev. William F. Junkin, at the First Presbyterian Church, Montclair, N.J. So. Ch., July 17, 1890

Mary Jane, and Samuel R. Wortham, both of Amherst, by the Rev. W. H. Kinkle*

* Given as printed

MARRIAGE NOTICES IN THE SOUTHERN CHURCHMAN WITH DATES OF PUBLICATION

So. Ch., Nov. 9, 1855
Sarah S., d. of the late James Cox of Pleasants Co., Va., formerly of Hedgesville, Berkeley Co., Va., and John B. Triplett, by the Rev. W. L. Hyland, at the residence of the bride's brother in Pleasants Co., Va. So. Ch., Mar. 29, 1861

COXE
Mary F. M., d. of the late R. S. Coxe, Esq. of Richmond, Va., and gr.d. of the late Dr. Wm. Smith Coxe of Burlington, N.J., and William T. Lawrence, by the Rev. R. S. Barrett, at the residence of the bride's mother in Henrico Co., Va. So. Ch., Feb. 26, 1880

COYLE
Mary Farr, d. of the late Fitzhugh Coyle, and Dr. Edmund Kennedy Goldsborough, all of Washington, D.C., by the Rev. John B. Morgan, in the Church of the Holy Trinity, Paris, France. So. Ch., Sept. 26, 1878

Randolph, and Jane T., d. of Alexander Moore, Esq. of Alexandria, by the Rev. Mr. Dana, at Alexandria, D.C. So. Ch., Dec. 22, 1837

COYNER
Julius Jackson, of Basic City, Va., and Mary Louisa, third d. of Dr. John and Mrs. Sallie G. Ligon of Pocahontas Co., W.Va., by the Rev. T. H. Lacy, in Emmanuel Church, Clover Lick, Pocahontas Co., W.Va. So. Ch., Oct. 1, 1891

CRABB
Robert W., and Betty Edwards, only d. of Judge S. D. Delaney, by the Rev. Henry T. Sharp, in St. John's Church, Uniontown, Ky. So. Ch., Feb. 11, 1875

Tasker Carter, and Mildred Edmonia Pendleton, by the Rev. Andrew Fisher, at Warsaw, Richmond Co. So. Ch., Oct. 31, 1867

CRADDOCK
John W., of Baltimore, Md., and M. Peachy Gilmer of Chatham, Va., by the Rev. C. O. Pruden, rector, in Emmanuel Church, Chatham, Va. So. Ch., Dec. 30, 1886

CRAFT
Virginia, and the Rev. John Letcher Showell, gr.s. of the late ex-Governor John Letcher of Virginia, by the Rt. Rev. William Forbes Adams, D.D., LL.D., D.C.L., assisted by the rector of the parish, at Vienna, Md. So. Ch., Sept. 27, 1913

CRAFTON
Adelaide, of Essex Co., Va., and Thos. Hudgins of New York, by the Rev. J. Harvey* Hundley, at the home of the bride. So. Ch., Jan. 10, 1884

Cary Marcellus, of Orange, and Mary Jane, d. of Mr. and Mrs. Edmund Willis Scott, by the Rev. F. G. Scott, D.D., of Petersburg, uncle of the bride, in Epiphany Chapel, Somerset, Va. So. Ch., June 14, 1913

CRAIGHILL
Bessie Rutherford, d. of Col. Wm. P. Craighill, U.S. Army, and the Rev.

---

* Given as printed

MARRIAGE NOTICES IN THE SOUTHERN CHURCHMAN WITH DATES OF PUBLICATION

Hunter Davidson, Diocese of Easton, Protestant Episcopal Church, by the Rev. Dallas Tucker, at Charles Town, Jefferson Co., W.Va. So. Ch., July 24, 1890

Bettie L., d. of Wm. N. Craighill, Esq. of Baltimore, and Dr. Chas. T. Butler of Maryland, by the Rev. James B. Craighill assisted by the Rev. J. H. Williams, at Lynchburg, Va. So. Ch., Sept. 10, 1874

Carrie T., eldest d. of Robert T. and Edlie* H. Craighill, and H. H. S. Handy, all of Lynchburg, by the Rev. T. M. Carson, rector of St. Paul's, at the residence of the bride's father in Lynchburg, Va. So. Ch., Jan. 14, 1886

E. A. (Dr.), of Lynchburg, and Mattie A., d. of J. V. Hobson, by the Rev. J. B. Craighill, in St. James' Church, Richmond. So. Ch., Apr. 23, 1874

George P., and Lydia Langhorne, both of Lynchburg, by the Rev. James P. Craighill and the Rev. T. M. Carson, in St. Paul's Church, Lynchburg, Va. So. Ch., Oct. 28, 1875

James B. (The Rev.), of Maysville, Ky., and Maggie S., d. of Dr. G. W. Smith of "Ingleside", Eastville, Va., by the Rev. J. J. Clemens, in Christ Church, Northampton Co., Va. So. Ch., Dec. 8, 1870

Mary, d. of Col. W. P. Craighill, and Dr. W. F. Lippitt, Jr. of Charles Town, Jefferson Co., W.Va., by the Rev. Dallas Tucker. So. Ch., Aug. 11, 1887

Robt. E. (Capt.), and Nannie Scott Hunter, both of Lynchburg, by the Rev. T. M. Carson, rector, in St. Paul's Church, Lynchburg, Va. So. Ch., Nov. 23, 1893

W. P. (Col.), U.S.A., and Rebecca Churchill, d. of the late Rev. Alexander Jones, D.D., by the Rev. Joseph B. Jones of Virginia, in St. John's Church, Baltimore Co., Md. So. Ch., Oct. 1, 1874

CRALLE

Alice Fleming, d. of Richard K. Cralle, Esq., and the Rev. Thos. Ward White, by the Rev. T. V. Moore, D.D., in First Presbyterian Church, Richmond, Va. So. Ch., Oct. 24, 1862

Bettie M., and Capt. W. G. Williamson, all of Virginia, by the Rev. Edward Valentine, at Huntington, W.Va. So. Ch., Oct. 24, 1872

Robert O., and Susan M. Bagby, both of Powhatan Co., by the Rev. Andrew Fisher, at the residence of Bennett M. Bagby. So. Ch., Dec. 19, 1856

CRALLIS

G. T., and Eliza G., youngest d. of the late Thos. C. Wilson, by the Rev. P. F. Berkeley, at Selma, Amelia Co. So. Ch., Mar. 29, 1866

CRAMER

Julia M., and James B. Stevenson, both of Harrison-

---

* Given as printed

MARRIAGE NOTICES IN THE SOUTHERN CHURCHMAN WITH DATES OF PUBLICATION

burg, Va., by the Rev. O. S. Bunting. So. Ch., Nov. 20, 1884

CRANE

A. Judson, of Richmond, and Sarah Ellen Smith, by the Rev. Mr. Temple, in King and Queen Co. So. Ch., Dec. 21, 1855

Charles L., s. of Mrs. Joseph Minor Crane of Charles Town, W.Va., and Ann Megguire Lionberger of Pilot Grove, Mo., d. of Lt. John Lionberger, deceased (originally of Virginia), at the residence of the bride's sister Mrs. R. R. Kimball, Ormond, Fla. So. Ch., May 8, 1909

Heber O. (The Rev.), and Bettie Wharton of Mississippi, by the Rev. J. Francis Girault, rector of St. Anna's Church, New Orleans, at the residence of Gen. J. Wharton, brother of the bride, in New Orleans. So. Ch., Mar. 23, 1876

Henry W., of Baltimore, and Mary B. Gresham of King and Queen Co., Va., at Walkerton, King and Queen Co., Va. So. Ch., Dec. 6, 1888

James C., of Jefferson Co., W.Va., and Willie Leith of Loudoun Co., Va., by the Rev. T. F. Martin, at the residence of Dr. Plaster, Snickersville. So. Ch., June 5, 1873

James C., of Baltimore, and Virginia, d. of Thomas I. Hall, Esq., by the Rev. Theodore Gambrall, in St. James' Church, Anne Arundel Co., Md. So. Ch., Apr. 29, 1875

See also TIMBERLAKE, Martha V. (Mrs.)

CRAVEN

George W., and Susan Ann, d. of A. St.C. Heiskell of Charlottesville, by the Rev. R. K. Meade, at Penn Park. So. Ch., Nov. 24, 1837

CRAWFORD

John E., of Lynchburg, and Laura L. Nicholson of Salem, Roanoke Co., Va., by the Rev. W. H. Pendleton, at Salem, Roanoke Co., Va. So. Ch., Feb. 15, 1855

CREERY

J. Edward, and Leonora Peroe, both of Richmond, in Christ Church, Richmond. So. Ch., May 3, 1877

CREIGHTON

Jane, eldest d. of the Rev. Wm. Creighton, D.D., and the Rev. Edward N. Mead, rector of St. Paul's Church, Sing Sing, by the Rt. Rev. Benj. T. Onderdonk, D.D., at Mount Pleasant, Westchester Co., N.Y. So. Ch., Jan. 11, 1839

CRENSHAW

Eliza M., d. of Col. John Crenshaw, deceased, and William V. Jordan, Esq., by the Rev. John A. Wharton. So. Ch., Oct. 4, 1866

Miles K., of Charles City Co., Va., and Antoinette Virginia, d. of N. A. Thornton, Esq. of Richmond, by the Rev. Mr. Minnigerode, in St. Paul's Church, Richmond, Va. So. Ch., Nov. 28, 1856

MARRIAGE NOTICES IN THE SOUTHERN CHURCHMAN WITH DATES OF PUBLICATION

CREWE
    Kate S., third d. of Wm. and Sarah Crewe of Prince William Co., Va., formerly of England, and John A. Cameron of Canada, by the Rev. A. P. Gray, at "Chestnut Hill", the residence of the bride's father. So. Ch., July 17, 1884

CRICHTON
    Anna E., of Brunswick Co., Va., and Dr. Jas. W. Oliver of Mecklenburg, by the Rev. Theo. Pryor, D.D., at the residence of the bride's father. So. Ch., June 13, 1867

CRISP
    W. Benton, of Baltimore, and Mary N., d. of the late Cornelius Van Devanter of Clarke Co., Va., by the rector, the Rev. P. P. Phillips, in Grace Church, Berryville, Va. So. Ch., Aug. 5, 1886

CRITCHLER
    John, Esq., of Westmoreland Co., Va., and Lizzie, second d. of Kenon* Whiting, Esq., by the Rev. E. H. Harlow, at Hampton, Elizabeth City Co. So. Ch., Nov. 20, 1857

CROCKETT
    Eugene W., of Wythe Co., Va., and Bettie F., d. of L. F. Johnson, Esq., by the Rev. Pendleton Brooke, in Bristol. So. Ch., Sept. 9, 1875

    John Stuart, Esq., Commonwealth's Attorney, and Lizzie Bright, d. of Col. Thos. J. Boyd, all of Wytheville, by the Rev. Robb* White, at the residence of the bride's father, Wytheville, Va. So. Ch., Sept. 21, 1876

CROFT
    Fred A. (The Rev.), vicar of St. John's Church, Durant, Okla., and Pauline Flint of Madill, Okla., by the Rt. Rev. Thomas Cassady, D.D., Bishop of Oklahoma, in the Bishop's Chapel. So. Ch., Apr. 21, 1934

CROOKS
    Emilie C., d. of Hon. William Crooks, and Richard A. Carrington formerly of Virginia, by the Rev. E. S. Thomas, in St. Paul's Church, St. Paul, Minn. So. Ch., Mar. 30, 1882

CROSDALE
    Edmund, and Julianna M. J., d. of the Rev. Wm. G. H. Jones, rector of St. George's Parish, Accomac Co., Va., by the Rev. William G. H. Jones, at Somerset Co., Md. So. Ch., Feb. 22, 1849

CROSS
    A. L., of Centreville, and Ida J. Grinnelly, by the Rev. R. A. Castleman, at the residence near Fairfax C.H., Va. So. Ch., Feb. 23, 1893

CROSSON
    James Cope (The Rev.), former rector of St. Jude and the Nativity, Philadelphia, and Dagmar Johnson, by the Rev. Charles B. Dubell, rector of St. Simeon's, Philadelphia, and the Rev. Charles A. Jessup, Dean of St. Paul's Cathedral, Buffalo, N.Y. So. Ch., Oct. 24, 1925

    Richard C., and Sarah A. Lynn, both of Loudoun Co., by the

---

* Given as printed

MARRIAGE NOTICES IN THE SOUTHERN CHURCHMAN WITH DATES OF PUBLICATION

Rev. F. M. Whittle. So. Ch., Apr. 17, 1857

CROUCH
John H., and Catharine A. Devine, both of Newcastle Co., by the Rev. W. D. Hanson, at Faulkland, Del. So. Ch., Mar. 8, 1883

CROW
C. Eugenia, d. of the late Thos. H. Crow of Berryville, Clarke Co., Va., and John B. Glover, by the Rev. T. F. Martin, in Grace Church, Berryville. So. Ch., Nov. 26, 1868

George B., of Jackson Co., and Eliza Margaret, d. of the Hon. Daniel Polsley of Point Pleasant, by the Rev. Horace Edward Hayden, at Point Pleasant, W.Va. So. Ch., Apr. 28, 1870

John F., of Baltimore, and Sue W., only d. of the late Hon. Edmund W. Hubard, by the Rev. Arthur Lloyd, at Saratoga, the home of the bride in Buckingham Co., Va. So. Ch., Feb. 10, 1881

CROWN
John O., editor of "Clarke Courier", and Sadie J. Smith, all of Berryville, by the Rev. T. F. Martin, in Grace Church, Berryville. So. Ch., Oct. 30, 1873

CROXTON
E. C., of Tappahannock, Va., and James R. Gordon of Richmond. By the Rev. J. B. Newton, in St. John's Church, Tappahannock. So. Ch., Apr. 2, 1874

Mary Louisa, and J. W. McDaniel, both of Tappahannock, by the Rev. H. W. L. Temple, at Tappahannock, Essex Co. So. Ch., Jan. 2, 1868

CROZET
Claudia, only d. of Col. Crozet, and Charles S. Mills, M.D., by the Rev. Dr. Empie, at Richmond, Va. So. Ch., Oct. 25, 1839

CRUIKSHANK
Lucy Calvert, d. of Thomas Chandler and Lucy Walke Cruikshank, and Ronald Moore Bond of Port Deposit, Md., by the Rev. Roger Atkinson Walke of Tokio, Japan, in St. Stephen's Chapel, Cecilton, Md. So. Ch., Oct. 23, 1909

Thomas C., Jr., and Lucy H., d. of the Rev. Lewis Walke, by the Rev. Lewis Walke assisted by the Rev. F. M. Baker, in St. Stephen's Church, Cecil Co., Md. So. Ch., Dec. 23, 1875

CRUMP
Beverley T., of Richmond, and Etta O., d. of Henry A. Taylor, Esq., by the Rev. M. Johnson, at "Mount Airy", Richmond Co., Va. So. Ch., Oct. 23, 1884

Elizabeth, and Joseph Rogers, in Richmond, Va. So. Ch., Jan. 9, 1835

Fanny B., youngest d. of Judge William W. Crump of Richmond, and J. Randolph Tucker of Charleston, W.Va., by the Rev. Dr. Minnigerode assisted by the Rev. Dallas Tucker, in Richmond. So. Ch., May 15, 1873

George (Dr.), of Vicksburg, Miss., formerly of Fredericksburg, Va., and Fanny, d.

MARRIAGE NOTICES IN THE SOUTHERN CHURCHMAN WITH DATES OF PUBLICATION

of John S. Green, Esq. of
Rappahannock, Va., by the
Rev. Mr. Woodville. So.
Ch., Sept. 22, 1837
J. T., and Mrs. Sue A.
Purdie of Chesterfield Co.,
Va., by the Rev. A. B.
Tizzard, at Clover Hill,
Chesterfield Co., Va.
So. Ch., Jan. 10, 1889
Lucy A., d. of the late
John P. Crump of Din-
widdie Co., Va., and
John M. Patton of Vir-
ginia, by the Rev. Wil-
liam M. Dame, in Memorial
Church, Baltimore. So.
Ch., Oct. 24, 1878
Sallie C., d. of the late
Dr. William Crump of Cul-
peper, and the Rev. R. A.
Goodwin of Boydton, Va.,
by the Rev. James G. Minni-
gerode, in St. Stephen's
Church, Culpeper, Va.
So. Ch., Nov. 1, 1877

CRUTCHFIELD
Bettie, and Frank Merritt,
both of Tazewell Co., by
the Rev. W. R. Savage,
in Stras Memorial Church,
Tazewell C. H. So. Ch.,
May 25, 1893

CRUTE
J. N., and Hattie, d. of Wm.
E. Gannaway, Esq., all of
Buckingham Co., Va., by
the Rev. A. S. Lloyd, in
St. Peter's Church, Curds-
ville, Va. So. Ch., Dec.
20, 1883

CULLEN
George, and Mary E., d. of
Dr. Edmund P. Taliaferro,
all of Orange Courthouse,
Va., by the Rev. J. Earnest,
rector of Zion Parish,
Prince George's Co., Md.,
in Emmanuel Church, Baltimore.
So. Ch., Dec. 13, 1866

Lizzie Campbell, eldest d.
of Dr. J. S. D. Cullen,
and John F. T. Anderson,
by the Rev. Dr. Preston
assisted by the Rev. Dr.
Minnigerode, in the First
Presbyterian Church. So.
Ch., Dec. 30, 1880
Lottie E., d. of Dr. John
Cullen of Richmond, and
Henry A. Carrington of
Charlotte, by the Rev.
W. H. Kinckle, in St.
Paul's Church, Richmond.
So. Ch., Feb. 8, 1856

CULVER
Laura A. (Mrs.), and Thomas
D. Adams, by the Rev.
H. L. Derby, at Lancaster,
Va. So. Ch., Feb. 19,
1880

CUMMINGS
Charles A. (The Rev.), of
Duluth, Minn., and Ada F.
Earhart, by the Rt. Rev. H.
B. Whipple, D.D., Bishop of
Minnesota, at Worthington, Pa.
So. Ch., Nov. 2, 1882

CUMMINS
George D. (The Rev.), rector
of Christ Church, Norfolk,
Va., and Alexandrine Macomb,
youngest d. of L. P. W.
Balch, Esq., by the Rev.
Richard T. Brown, at Lee-
town, Jefferson Co. So.
Ch., July 2, 1847

CUNINGHAM
Mattie, d. of John W. Cuningham, Esq., of Person Co.,
N.C., and the Rev. Thomas
J. Packard of Halifax Co.,
Va., by the Rev. O. A. Kinsolving, D.D., assisted
by the Rev. B. S. Bronson,
in Cuningham Chapel, North
Carolina. So. Ch., June 11,
1885

CUNNINGHAM
Edward, Jr., of St. Louis,

MARRIAGE NOTICES IN THE SOUTHERN CHURCHMAN WITH DATES OF PUBLICATION

and Nina, second d. of Chas. A. Thornton, Esq., of Mississippi, by the Rev. Aristides Smith, at the residence of P. B. Key, Esq., Enfield, N. C. So. Ch., Jan. 4, 1877

John A., of Richmond, and Mattie M. Eggleston, by the Rev. John McGill, at Bell Pre, the residence of the bride's parents. So. Ch., Apr. 10, 1884

John M., of Nashville, Tenn., and Roberta W., d. of George Hamilton of Culpeper Co., Va., by the Rev. C. Y. Steptoe, in Christ Church. So. Ch., Oct. 1, 1874

Pattie, d. of the late Alec. Cunningham, Esq., and Benj. F. Garrett, by the Rev. Geo. W. Dame, D.D., at Okolona, Pittsylvania Co. So. Ch., Dec. 12, 1889

R. H., and Mary D. Atkinson, both of Henderson, Ky., by the Rev. J. M. Pringle, at the residence of the bride's father, So. Ch., Nov. 18, 1875

CURD
J. L., and L. B. Wombwell, Esq. of Florida, by the Rev. Lewis W. Burton of St. John's Church, at the residence of the bride's parents, 1920 E. Broad St., Richmond. So. Ch., Dec. 27, 1888

CURRIE
Louisa, d. of the late Dr. E. A. Currie, and E. G. Hall, by the Rev. Henry L. Derby, at "Verville", the residence of the bride's mother, in Lancaster Co., Va. So. Ch., Dec. 29, 1881

CURTIS
Alice May, and O. M. Etheridge, by the Rev. John B. Newton, at the residence of Dr. Etheridge, Norfolk Co., Va. So. Ch., June 19, 1884

J. (The Rev.), pastor of St. Paul's Church, and Landonia, d. of John Lorentz of Lewis Co., W.Va., by the Rev. D. Greer of Clarksburg, in St. Paul's Church, Weston, W.Va. So. Ch., Apr. 23, 1868

Mary B., d. of the late C. C. Curtis of Gloucester Co., Va., and Thomas L. P. Cocke of Powhatan Co., by the Rev. Dr. Peterkin, at the residence of J. W. Cringan. So. Ch., Apr. 30, 1874

CUSHMAN
Betty Hanson, d. of the late J. P. Cushman, former president of Hampton Sidney College, and the Rev. Wm. C. Meredith, by the Rev. Geo. W. Dame, at the Fork, residence of Mrs. Carter Page in Cumberland Co. So. Ch., Jan. 27, 1860

Matilda R., d. of the late Alonzo R. Cushman of New York, and the Rev. Stephen Elliott Barnwell of Beaufort, S.C., by the Rev. John P. Lundy, in the Church of the Holy Apostles, New York. So. Ch., Oct. 16, 1873

CUSTIS
Bettie F., third d. of James W. Custis, Esq., of Williamsburg, Va., and the Rev. T. M. Ambler, rector of St.

MARRIAGE NOTICES IN THE SOUTHERN CHURCHMAN WITH DATES OF PUBLICATION

Paul's Church, Wilmington, N.C., by the Rev. Geo. T. Wilmer, D.D. assisted by the Rev. L. B. Wharton, in Bruton Parish Church, Williamsburg, Va. So. Ch., Oct. 30, 1873
John T. W., and Eliza Waddey, all of Northampton Co., Va., by the Rev. John M. Chevers, in Christ Church, Eastville. So. Ch., June 5, 1857

CUTCHINS
Louis E., s. of Col. and Mrs. Sol. Cutchins of Richmond, Va., and Cary, d. of Mr. and Mrs. Mann S. Valentine, Jr., by the Rev. Robert Williams. So. Ch., Jan. 22, 1910

CUTTER*
Raymonde Virginia, d. of Mrs. Mildred Middleton and the late Ralph Hastings Cutter of Savannah, Ga., and Frederick Charles Smutzger* of Denver, Col., by the Rev. Percy Grant, in the Church of Ascension, Fifth Avenue, New York City. So. Ch., Feb. 15, 1908

CUTTS
Samuel H., Esq., of Washington, D.C., and Maria S. DeKrafft, by the Rev. Mr. Powell, in Goochland Co. So. Ch., Nov. 29, 1866

* A notice appears in the issue of Feb. 1, 1908, identical with this except that "Cutter" is written "Cutler" and "Smutzger" is written "Sweetzer"

DABNEY
- Catharine M., d. of Capt. George Dabney, and Hon. Seaton Grantland, member of Congress from Georgia, by the Rev. George Woodbridge, at Hanover Co. So. Ch., Oct. 30, 1835
- Chiswell, of Pittsylvania, and Lucy D., d. of the late Col. Edmund Fontaine of Beaverdam, by the Rev. W. A. Alrich, at Beaverdam, Hanover Co., Va. So. Ch., Apr. 10, 1873
- Emmeline, d. of Thos. S. Dabney of Burleigh, and B. H. Greene of New Orleans, by the Rt. Rev. J. P. B. Wilmer of the Diocese of Louisiana assisted by the rector, the Rev. H. C. Harris, at Dry Grove, Miss., in the Church of the Holy Comforter. So. Ch., Nov. 18, 1869
- James B., of Caroline C., Va., and Ella J. Smith of Spotsylvania, by the Rev. Wm. W. Greene, at the residence of the bride's father, So. Ch., Feb. 8, 1872
- Kitty M., d. of Chiswell Dabney, Esq., and Dr. Thomas L. Walker, all of Lynchburg, by the Rev. W. H. Kinckle, in St. Paul's Church. So. Ch., Aug. 22, 1856
- Lelia Madison, eldest d. of Judge Wm. Pope Dabney, and Wm. Marshall Taylor, by the Rev. Frank Stringfellow, in Powhatan Co., Va. So. Ch., Oct. 19, 1882
- Lucy Tabb, d. of James K. Dabney of Gloucester Co., and James F. Duncan of Norfolk, by the Rev. Mr. Robertson, in Ware Church, Gloucester Co. So. Ch.; Mar. 3, 1881
- Richard Heath (Dr.), Prof. of History, University of Indiana, Bloomington, formerly of Virginia, and Mary Amanda, youngest d. of Mrs. Lucy W. and the late E. B. Bently of Richmond, by the Rev. Charles Minnigerode, D.D., in St. Paul's Church, Richmond, Va. So. Ch., June 28, 1888
- T. T., of Gloucester Co., and Marie L., d. of Hugh Perry Keane, Esq., by the Rev. T. G. Dashiell, in St. Mark's Church, Richmond, Va. So. Ch., Dec. 6, 1888
- Virginius, Esq., and Anna W., d. of Maj. Burr P. Noland of Middleburg, by the Rev. O. A. Kinsolving. So. Ch., Feb. 28, 1867
- Walter D., and Mary B., d. of Archibald N. Douglas, all of Albemarle Co., Va., by the Rev. J. S. Hanckel, at Rose Valley, residence of the bride's father. So. Ch., Nov. 21, 1878
- William Albert, Esq., of Lynchburg, Va., and Emily Goggin, d. of the late Dr. Thomas N. Nelson of Bedford, by the Rev. Albert Ware, at the residence of the bride's mother, Elk Hill, Bedford Co., Va. So. Ch., Nov. 8 and 29, 1877
- Wm. Pope, of Powhatan, and Leila B., youngest d. of the late Ambrose Madison of

MARRIAGE NOTICES IN THE SOUTHERN CHURCHMAN WITH DATES OF PUBLICATION

Madison, by the Rev. J.
Earnest, at Woodbury
Forest, Madison Co., Va.
So. Ch., Jan. 16, 1857

DADE
William A., and Julia B.
Russell, by the Rev.
Curtis Grubb, in St.
John's Church, Pittman,
Lake Co., Fla . So. Ch.,
May 26, 1892

DAILY
William A., Esq., of
Alleghany Co., Md., and
Jean K. Jamisson, by the
Rev. W. A. Alrich, at
Centreville, Fairfax,
Co., Va. So. Ch., Feb.
27, 1868

DAINGERFIELD
Adela Carter, d. of Mr.
and Mrs. John Haigh Daingerfield of Norfolk, and the
Rev. James De Wolf, Jr., s.
of the Rt. Rev. James De
Wolf Perry of the diocese
of Rhode Island, by the
bridegroom's father assisted
by the rector, the Rev.
W. Taylor Willis, in Christ
and St. Luke's Church. So.
Ch., Oct. 7, 1939

Algernon Gray, of Harrisonburg,
Va., and Lizzie W. Thomas
of Richmond, by the Rev. T.
G. Addison, D.D., in the
rectory of Trinity Church,
219 C. St., N. W., Washington, D.C. So. Ch., Sept.
2, 1886

Foxall A., 11th Regiment
Virginia Cavalry, and
Henrietta, d. of A. S.
Gray of Harrisonburg, by
the Rev. J. E. Latane, in
the Presbyterian Church in
Harrisonburg. So. Ch., Nov.
20, 1863

Lilly, eldest d. of L. P.
Daingerfield, Esq., and
Edward H. Fisher of Richmond, Va., by the Rev.
Richard H. Mason, uncle of
the bride, at the residence of the bride's father
in Augusta Co. So. Ch.,
Apr. 23, 1885

Mary H., d. of John B.
Daingerfield, and Phillip
B. Hooe, all of Alexandria,
Va., by the Rev. George H.
Norton, at Alexandria, Va.
So. Ch., Oct. 24, 1867

Virginia, and Charles O.
Groome, Esq., by the Rev.
John C. McCabe, rector of
the Church of the Ascension,
in St. Peter's Church,
Baltimore. So. Ch., Dec. 3,
1858

William B., of Alexandria,
and Hattie M. Taylor of
Fredericksburg, by the Rev.
Dr. Murdaugh, in St.
George's Church, Fredericksburg, Va. So. Ch., Oct.
22, 1874

DAINGERGELD
Edward Lonsdale, and Sallie
V. Smith, by the Rev. Dr.
Norton, at the residence of
the bride's father, F. L.
Smith, Esq. So. Ch., Oct.
21, 1875

DALRYMPLE
Samuel B. (Rev.), rector of
the parish, and Mary Pelia
Bixby of Lock Haven, by
the Rev. Robert B. Heet,
in St. Paul's Church, Lock
Haven. So. Ch., June 3,
1859

DALTON
Ella J., and James W. Motley,
by the Rev. C. O. Pruden, in
St. John's P. E. Church, Mt.
Airy, Pittsylvania Co., Va.
So. Ch., July 14, 1892

DAME
Dorothy, d. of Mr. and Mrs.

MARRIAGE NOTICES IN THE SOUTHERN CHURCHMAN WITH DATES OF PUBLICATION

Eugene Cushing Dame of Richmond, Va., and Norman Randolph Watt, by the Rev. Wm. M. Clark, D.D., in St. James' Church, Richmond, Va. So. Ch., June 29, 1912

E. C., of Covington, Ky., and Minnie E. Saunders, by the Rev. Dr. George Dame assisted by the Rev. George W. Dame, in Richmond, at the residence of Mrs. William O. Saunders, on South Pine St. So. Ch., Sept. 15, 1887

George W., Jr. (The Rev.), assistant minister of the Church of the Ascension, and Lavinia Hinks, of Baltimore, by the Rev. George W. Dame, Sr., assisted by the Rev. W. M. Dame and the Rev. Nelson Dame, in Memorial Church, Baltimore. So. Ch., June 12, 1884

Lucy Carter, oldest d. of the officiating clergyman, and the Rev. P. D. Thompson of Halifax, by the Rev. Geo. W. Dame, in the Church of the Ephiphany* in Danville, Va. So. Ch., Apr. 8, 1864

Nelson P. (The Rev.), of Blacksburg, Va., and Mary N., d. of the Rev. C. Walker, D.D., of the Theological Seminary of Virginia, by the Rev. George W. Dame assisted by the Rev. W. W. Walker, in the Chapel on Seminary Hill. So. Ch., July 4, 1878

W. M. (Rev.), and Susie M., d. of the late Col. David Funsten, by the Rev. G. H. Norton, in the Chapel of the Episcopal Theological Seminary, near Alexandria, Va. So. Ch., Oct. 14, 1869

DAMERON
Fannie Scott, d. of George H. Dameron of Amherst Co., Va., and Benjamin N. Upham of Vermont, by the Rev. J. P. Lawrence, at the residence of the bride's father. So. Ch., Nov. 7, 1878

DANA
Charles B. (Rev.), D.D., of Alexandria, Va., and Elvira R., d. of the late S. Close, Esq. of New York, by the Rt. Rev. Bishop Johns, in Christ Church, Alexandria. So. Ch., July 27, 1860

DANCE
Henrietta H., and the Rev. Wm. W. Greene of Spotsylvania, Co., Va., by the Rev. John Cosby, in Lunenburg, Co., Va., at the residence of the bride's mother. So. Ch., Oct. 26, 1860

Stuart Lee, of Richmond, Va., and Alice Leigh, d. of Maj. Charles and Anne C. Old of Powhatan Co., by the Rev. C. O. Prudon, in Emmanuel Church, Powhatan Co., Va. So. Ch., Jan. 1, 1891

DANDRIDGE
Edmund Pendleton (The Rev.), and Mary Robertson, d. of Arthur Seldon and Lizzie Robertson Blackford Lloyd, by the Rev. A. S. Lloyd, D.D., and the Bishop of West Virginia, in Christ Church, Alexandria, Va. So. Ch., Oct. 16, 1909

Sallie Pendleton, d. of A. S. Dandridge, Esq., and Blackburn Hughes of Martinsburg, by the Rev. James Grammer, at "The Bower",

---

* Given as printed

MARRIAGE NOTICES IN THE SOUTHERN CHURCHMAN WITH DATES OF PUBLICATION

Jefferson Co., W. Va. So. Ch., Oct. 2, 1873

DANEHOWER
Washington, and Fanny, d. of J. Rector Smoot, Esq., by the Rev. Mr. Suter, at the residence of the bride's father in Alexandria, Va. So. Ch., Oct. 25, 1883

DANIEL
Anna T., of Cumberland, and M. Lewis Randolph, Esq. of Albemarle, by the Rev. R. J. McBryde, in St. Paul's, Lynchburg. So. Ch., Feb. 10, 1870

D. K., and Franklin A. Kinckle of Lynchburg, by the Rev. E. W. Hubard, at Union Hill, Cumberland Co., Va. So. Ch., Dec. 16, 1869

Isabelle B., gr.d. of Hon. A. W. Venable of North Carolina, and Dr. A. Strachan Jones of Warren Co., by the Rev. Taylor Martise, at the residence of the bride's grandfather. So. Ch., Dec. 28, 1871

John Moncure, Esq., of Louisville, Ky., and Anne E. Leavell of Jefferson Co., W.Va., by the Rev. W. H. Meade assisted by the Rev. C. E. Ambler and the Rev. W. T. Leavell, at Media, Jefferson Co., W.Va. So. Ch., Nov. 5, 1874

John Moncure, Jr., and Margaret Micou, by the Rev. R. W. Micou, father of the bride, in the Chapel of the Theological Seminary. So. Ch., Dec. 26, 1908

John W., of Salisbury, N.C., and Betty Ambler, d. of the late William H. Fitzhugh, Esq., by the Rev.

John K. Mason assisted by the Rev. R. J. McBryde, D.D., in St. George's Church, Fredericksburg, Va. So. Ch., Oct. 2, 1884

Kate M., and Charles B. Williams, both of Culpeper Co., by the Rev. John B. McGill, at the residence of the bride's mother. So. Ch., Dec. 28, 1882

Samuel Pride, of Charlotte Co., Va., and Mattie Wright, d. of Mattie W. and J. Emmett Guy, in St. John's Church, Marion, N.C. So. Ch., May 4, 1907

Travers, of Richmond, and Flora, d. of Col. S. S. Bradford, in St. Stephen's Episcopal Church, Culpeper. So. Ch., Jan. 17, 1878

William, and Sallie Evelyn, d. of Edwin W. and Indiana V. Rives of Sussex Co., Va., by the Rev. Richard McIlwain, in the Presbyterian Church, Farmville. So. Ch., Nov. 23, 1865

William S., of Richmond, and Lizzie J., d. of the late John G. Lane, by the Rev. W. M. Clark, at the residence of the bride's brother, H. B. Lane, Fredericksburg, Va. So. Ch., Oct. 22, 1891

DARDEN
Annie J., eldest d. of A. S. Darden, Esq., of Suffolk, Va., and Joseph P. Webb, by the Rev. James Murray, at the residence of the bride's father. So. Ch., Feb. 10, 1881

Romine, and J. N. Sebrell, by the Rev. H. L. Derby, at Jerusalem, Southampton, Va. So. Ch., Apr. 18, 1872

MARRIAGE NOTICES IN THE SOUTHERN CHURCHMAN WITH DATES OF PUBLICATION

DARGAN
  Henry Flinn, of Darlington, S.C., and Elizabeth Marshall, d. of Mr. and Mrs. Henry Barnwell of Adams Run, by the Rev. Thomas P. Baker, in Christ Church, Adams Run, S.C. So. Ch., Oct. 1, 1910
DARLEY
  George, and Ellen Harrison, by the Rev. H. T. Sharp, in Grace Church, Alexandria, Va. So. Ch., Jan. 29, 1880
DARRACOTT
  Lucie C., d. of George F. Darracott, Esq. of Hanover Co., Va., and Robert L. Bayliss, by the Rev. S. S. Hepbron, at the residence of the bride's father (The Glympre). So. Ch., Dec. 11, 1890
DARST
  James Chandler, formerly of Salem, Va., and Marie Josephine Poythcress (nee Brouse), by the Rev. W. R. Savage assisted by the Rev. W. H. Burkhardt of Bluefield, W.Va., in Stras Memorial Church, Tazewell C.H. So. Ch., May 25, 1893
DASHIELL
  Julius M. (The Rev.), vice rector of the college of St. James', Maryland, and Mary Thornton, second d. of Robert S. Voxx, Esq., by the Rev. Dr. Kerfoot, at Hawthrone, the residence of the bride's father, Rappahannock Co., Va. So. Ch., Aug. 26, 1859
  T. G. (The Rev.), of Richmond, and Kate, d. of the officiating clergyman, by the Rev. Wm. Sparrow, D.D., at Staunton. So. Ch.,
Jan. 11, 1865
  T. Grason* (The Rev.), and Wilhelmina, d. of the Rev. Dr. Sparrow, by the Rev. Dr. Sparrow, in the Chapel of the Theological Seminary of Virginia [in Alexandria]. So. Ch., July 27, 1854
  William S., and Landonia R., second d. of the late Capt. Robert D. Minor, all of Richmond, Va., by the Rev. T. G. Dashiell assisted by the Rev. Dr. Peterkin, at Richmond. So. Ch., Dec. 20, 1883
DASHNER
  John J., of Monroe C., Mo., and Margaret E. F., d. of Charles C. Miller, Esq. of Mason Co., W.Va., by the Rev. Horace E. Hayden, at the residence of the bride's father. So. Ch., Oct. 8, 1868
DAVENPORT
  Charles, and Ellen T., d. of Dr. J. B. McCaw, all of Richmond, Va., by the Rev. Dr. Minnigerode, at the residence of the bride's father. So. Ch., Dec. 11, 1879
  Willis W., and Lou Glascock, both of Lancaster Co., Va., by the Rev. H. L. Derby, at Lancaster Court House, Va. So. Ch., Nov. 17, 1881
DAVIDSON
  Alfred Francis, London, Eng., and Mary Elizabeth Skelding of Alleghany Co., Va., by the Rev. L. R. Combs, at the residence of her brother-in-law, Dr. O. L. Rogers, Covington, Va. So. Ch., Apr. 27, 1893
  Henry G. (Dr.), resident physician at the Rockbridge Alum Springs, and Kate Banks, d. of the late Rix Jordan, Esq.

* Given as printed

MARRIAGE NOTICES IN THE SOUTHERN CHURCHMAN WITH DATES OF PUBLICATION

of Hampton, Va., by the Rev. Edwin H. Harlow, in St. John's Church, Hampton, Va. So. Ch., June 25, 1858

Hunter (The Rev.), diocese of Easton, Protestant Episcopal Church, and Bessie Rutherford, d. of Col. Wm. P. Craighill, U.S. Army, by the Rev. Dallas Tucker, at Charles Town, Jefferson Co., W.Va. So. Ch., July 24, 1890

John C., of Washington, D.C., and Minnie, d. of the late Maj. John H. Chichester of Fairfax Co., by the Rev. Frank Page, at Fall's Church, Fairfax Co., Va. So. Ch., Dec. 5, 1889

Robert James, of Liverpool, Eng., and Anna Maria McBride, by the Rev. John McGill, at the residence of the bride's father, Blacksburg, Va. So. Ch., May 12, 1892

Sallie B., d. of the late Dr. H. G. Davidson of Lexington, and Dr. J. J. Kirkbride, by the Rev. R. J. McBryde, D.D., at the residence of the bride's mother. So. Ch., June 18, 1885

DAVIES

Catharine M., d. of Dr. Henry L. Davies of Amherst, and Calvin D. Jones of Lynchburg, by the Rev. Mr. Martin. So. Ch., Feb. 29, 1856

David T. (The Rev.), Missionary-in-Charge of Emmanuel Church, Detroit, and Alva May Allen of Windsor, Ont., by the Rev. M. C. Davies, rector of St. George's, the Rt. Rev. Herman Page, D.D., Bishop of the Diocese, and the Ven. Leonard Hagger, Archdeacon, assisting in the celebration of Holy Communion, in St. George's Church, Walkerville, Ont. So. Ch., July 7, 1935

James J., and Mildred H., eldest d. of Maj. W. W. Thornton of Brentsville, Va., by the Rev. Jno. McGill, at the residence of the bride's father. So. Ch., Apr. 17, 1873

Laura B., only d. of Beverly Davies, deceased, of Amherst Co., and John J. Ambler, Jr., Esq., of Glen-Ambler, by the Rev. R. W. Nowlin, at Sunny Side, residence of Dr. H. L. Davies. So. Ch., Feb. 27, 1857

W. W., of Richmond, Va., and Maria Louisa, youngest d. of the late Charles Middleton, Esq. of England, by the Rev. A. B. Tizzard, at Eppington, Chesterfield Co., Va. So. Ch., Dec. 22, 1887

DAVIS

Alice S., and Daniel H. Somers of Brooklyn, N.Y. formerly of Virginia, by the Rev. Henderson Suter, at the residence of the bride's father, Lynchburg, Va. So. Ch., Nov. 19, 1868

Ashby L., Esq., of Lunenburg, and Mrs. Sallie Cabell Epes, d. of the late Gen. B. W. Cabell, by the Rev. Thomas Ward White, at Bridgewater, Pittsylvania, Va. So. Ch., Jan. 29, 1864

Edward (First Lt.), Eleventh Cavalry, U.S. Army, and Alice Lawrason, d. of the Ven. W. W. Steel, archdeacon of Havanna, in Holy Trinity Chapel, Havana, Cuba. So.

MARRIAGE NOTICES IN THE SOUTHERN CHURCHMAN WITH DATES OF PUBLICATION

Ch., Nov. 30, 1907

Ilicia W., d. of Dr. James M. Davis, and the Rev. John L. Gibson of Bellaire, Ohio, by the Rev. Isaac Gibson assisted by the Rev. Wm. H. Neilson Jr. and the Rt. Rev., the Bishop of the diocese of New Jersey, at the residence of the bride's mother, Trenton. So. Ch., Jan. 20, 1880

J. W., and Eliza A. Elliott, both of Pittsylvania Co., Va., by the rector, the Rev. C. O. Pruden, in Emmanuel Church, Chatham, Va. So. Ch., Mar. 25, 1886

James M. M., of Richmond, Va., and Alice F., d. of Maj. Robert C. Saunders, by the Rev. Wm. W. Greene, in the Church of the Good Shepherd, Campbell Co., Va. So. Ch., Jan. 15, 1874

James S. (Lt.), of the U.S. Army, and Frances A. T., d. of the late Dr. Berkeley of Frederick Co., Va., by the Rev. Philip Slaughter, at Berea, Prince William Co. So. Ch., Jan. 15, 1836

John G., and Elizabeth A., only d. of Wm. E. Hicks of Mathews Co., Va., by the Rev. Peregrine Wroth, at the residence of the bride's father. So. Ch., Feb. 6, 1873

Kate, of Essex Co., Va., and C. Henry Tilden of Philadelphia, by the Rev. Mr. Koeble, in St. John's, Tappahannock. So. Ch., Aug. 10, 1876

Lucy Whiting, and Freeman J. R. Burroughs of Lynchburg, by the Rev. Wm. H. Pendleton, at the residence of Mayo Davies, Esq., Bedford Co., Va. So. Ch., Jan. 20, 1860

M. Virginia, and Philip A. Krise, by the Rev. Henderson Suter, at the residence of the bride's father, Lynchburg, Va. So. Ch., Nov. 19, 1868

Mary C., and Wm. D. Bloscham, both of Tallahassee, Fla., by the Rev. T. E. Locke, in St. Paul's Church, Lynchburg, Va. So. Ch., Nov. 7, 1856

Mary Jane, eldest d. of Prof. John S. Davis, and James P. Harrison of Danville, by the Rev. J. S. Hanckel, D.D., at the University of Virginia. So. Ch., Feb. 20, 1879

N. L., Esq., and Maria Chambers, by the Rev. Olcott Bulkley, at the residence of Dr. Chambers, Dover, Lafayette Co., Mo. So. Ch., July 9, 1858

R. T. (The Rev.), rector of St. James' Parish, Leesburg, and Louisa T. Frost of Orange, by the Rev. Theodore Carson, at "Mt. Sharon", residence of Mrs. Taliaferro, in Orange Co., Va. So. Ch., Oct. 21, 1869

Robert H., Esq., of St. Louis, and Mary Cornelia Newsom of Petersburg, by the Rev. W. H. Platt, at Petersburg, Va. So. Ch., Feb. 13, 1857

Theodore, of Globe, Ariz., and Josephine, eldest d. of the late Elizabeth Randolph and David Randolph Meade of Virginia, by the Rev. Henry Easter, in St. Clement's Church, El Paso, Tex. So. Ch., July 31, 1909

W. G., of Fauquier Co., Va.,

MARRIAGE NOTICES IN THE SOUTHERN CHURCHMAN WITH DATES OF PUBLICATION

and Edrina C., d. of Mrs. S. D. and the late C. B. Haddox, by the Rev. H. B. Lee, at "Hillsboro", the residence of the bride's mother in Rappahannock Co. So. Ch., Jan. 1, 1885

Wm. Blackford (Assist. Surgeon), U.S.N., and Kontie, d. of the late W. J. Howland, by the Rev. J. D. Powell assisted by the Rev. J. S. Lindsay, at Portsmouth, Va. So. Ch., May 11, 1871

DAVISON
Eleanor Drusilla (Fleming) (Mrs.), of Braxton Co., and Wm. G. Harrison, Clerk of the Circuit Court of Lewis Co., by the Rev. T. H. Lacy, in the Church at Burnsville, Braxton Co., W.Va. So. Ch., Nov. 10, 1887

W. F. (Dr.), formerly of Richmond, Va., and Lonnelle Glovers of Smithfield, by the Rev. David Barr, at Smithfield, Va. So. Ch., Dec. 2, 1886

DAVISSON
Edwin George, and Anna Maybury, third d. of Hon. M. W. and Mrs. Sarah Eliza Harrison, by the Rev. T. H. Lacy, rector of St. Paul's Church, at the residence of the Hon. Matthew W. Harrison, Weston, W.Va. So. Ch., Dec. 29, 1892

Flora, and Richard P. Camden, Esq., by the Rev. Henry T. Sharp, in St. Paul's Church, Weston, W.Va. So. Ch., June 9, 1870

DAWKINS
May, of Jacksonville, Fla., and the Rev. Robert Ashton, rector of Holy Trinity Parish, Dio Marquette, Iron Mountain, Mich., by the Rev. L. Fitz-James Hindry, in Trinity Church, St. Augustine, Fla. So. Ch., July 20, 1929

DAWSON
Archibald Nail, M.D., of Cleveland, Ohio, and Jean Wallace, d. of Mrs. Eliza Burton Backus of Cleveland, O., and the late Rev. Arthur Mann Backus, by the bride's uncle, the Bishop of Lexington, assisted by the Bishop of Ohio and the rector of St. Paul's, in St. Paul's Church, Cleveland, Ohio. So. Ch., Dec. 3, 1910

Eldon, and Margaret Douglas, d. of C. J. Meriwether, by the Rev. A. Ware, at Broadview, the residence of the bride's father, Bedford Co., Va. So. Ch., Jan. 29, 1880

Mary Ann, d. of the late Capt. Pleasant Dawson, and Z. D. Tinsley, Esq. of Amherst Co., by the Rev. Mr. Cofer, in Bedford Co. So. Ch., Nov. 24, 1837

Nicholas, of Baltimore, and Virginia Mason, d. of Gen. Samuel Cooper of Virginia, by Bishop Johns assisted by the Rev. Arthur Johns, in the Chapel of the Theological Seminary, Fairfax Co., Va. So. Ch., Nov. 6, 1873

Philip, of Lynchburg, s. of the late Nicholas Dawson of Fairfax Co., Va., and Louisa Fontaine Washington, by the Rt. Rev. B. D. Tucker of Southern Virginia, uncle of the bride, and the Rev. William G. Pendleton, D.D., rector of the Virginia Episcopal School, and brother-in-law of the groom, at Washington,

MARRIAGE NOTICES IN THE SOUTHERN CHURCHMAN WITH DATES OF PUBLICATION

D.C., the home of the bride's mother, Mrs. Lawrence Washington. So. Ch., July 9, 1921
Pleasant, of Amherst, and Bertie Binford of Bedford, by the Rev. R. J. McBryde, at Forest Home, Bedford Co. So. Ch., Dec. 23, 1869
Samuel Cooper, and Edna French (d. of the late Richard F. Horner of Fauquier), all of Alexandria, by the Rev. Professor Berryman Green, D.D., at Alexandria, Va. So. Ch., Apr. 13, 1907

DAY
Dwight Harvey (Lt.), U.S.N., s. of Mr. and Mrs. Carlyle Harwood Day of St. Paul, Minn., and Alice Dandridge, d. of the Rev. Dr. and Mrs. Charles H. Lee, by the Rev. David Cady Wright, D.D., rector of Christ Church, Savannah, Ga., assisted by the Rev. Robb White, Jr., rector of St. Thomas' Church, Thomasville, Ga., in the old historic Christ Church, Frederica, St. Simon's Island, Ga. So. Ch., Aug. 4, 1934
Fannie Lee, d. of the late Richard H. B., and Martha J. Day of Buckingham, W.Va., and Alexander Brown of Roanoke, Va., s. of the Rev. R. K. Meade of Virginia and gr.s. of Bishop Meade by the Rev. T. H. Lacy, in the Church of the Transfiguration, Buckhannon, W.Va. So. Ch., Nov. 13, 1890
Henry Coit, of Georgia, and Janie A., d. of the late Rev. C. C. Taliaferro of Virginia, by the Rev. Mr. Kinsbrough, at Mt. Sharon, Va.

So. Ch., Sept. 29, 1870
Henry Fenton, and Mary Elsie Saunders, by the Rev. C. C. Randolph, in the Church of the Good Shepherd, Campbell Co., Va. So. Ch., July 5, 1913
Henry M., Esq., of New York City, and Emily D. Garrett of Putnam Co., W.Va., by the Rev. T. H. Lacy, at Buffalo, W.Va. So. Ch., Apr. 26, 1877
Lee Garnett, and Nancy Nye Sayles, by the Rev. Frederic S. Penfold, at Pawtucket, R.I. So. Ch., Oct. 3, 1925

DAYTON
Caroline Kirkham, and the Rev. Kline d'Aurandt Engle, Curate of St. John's, York, Pa., by the Rt. Rev. Wyatt Brown, D.D., assisted by Canon Paul S. Atkins, rector of St. John's, York, Pa., and the Very Rev. Hiram R. Bennett, Dean of St. John's Cathedral, Wilmington, Del., in the Chapel of the Holy Spirit, Bishopscourt, Harrisburg, Pa. So. Ch., Dec. 7, 1935

DEAHL
Charles J., and Phebe J. Stoutenburgh, by the Rev. H. T. Sharp, at Alexandria. So. Ch., Oct. 18, 1888
Lucie C., d. of the late William Deahl of Berryville, Clarke Co., Va., and Dr. L. S. Hill of South Carolina, by the Rev. A. E. Cornish, at the residence of Capt. Clinton Ward, Edgefield Co., S.C. So. Ch., Aug. 14, 1890
William A., s. of A. W. Deahl, and Catherine T. Cook, by the Rev. Father O'Kane, at the residence of the bride's

MARRIAGE NOTICES IN THE SOUTHERN CHURCHMAN WITH DATES OF PUBLICATION

mother, 313 N. Pitt St., Alexandria, Va. So. Ch., Dec. 25, 1890

DEANS
Bettie Carter, d. of the late Josiah L. Deans of Gloucester Co., Va., and the Rev. D. Watson Winn of Richmond, Va., by the Rev. R. H. Paine, in Mt. Calvary Church, Baltimore, Md. So. Ch., Jan. 6, 1887

Lizzie, eldest d. of Josias Deans, Esq., and Dr. Chas. F. Fahs, U.S.N., by the Rev. C. Mann, at Rosewell, Gloucester Co., at the residence of the bride's father. So. Ch., July 1, 1859

Rosa Burnet, of Gloucester Co., Va., and Virgil Gardner Weaver of Selma, Ala., by the Rev. A. Y. Hundley, in Abingdon Church, Gloucester Co., Va. So. Ch., July 22, 1875

DEAR
Jennie M., only d. of G. W. Dear of Centreville, Va., and John E. Brenner of Middleburg, Loudoun Co., by the Rev. John McGill, at the residence of the bride's father. So. Ch., Sept. 17, 1874

Richard B., of Duluth, Minn., (formerly of **Virginia**), and **Ridie L., youngest d. of the late M. M. Jamesson, Esq. of** Fairfax Co., Va., by the Rev. C. P. Caucett, in La Cross, Wis., at the residence of the bride's brother, Wm. Skeffington Jamesson. So. Ch., Dec. 23, 1886

DEARBORN
Alexander R., of Atlanta, Ga., and Mary H. Patton of Richmond, by the Rev. Dr. Eccleston of Baltimore, in St. James' Church, Richmond, Va. So. Ch., July 8, 1886

DEATLEY
William B., of Westmoreland Co., and Mary M. Jones of King George Co., by the Rev. T. E. Locke, at Peach Hill, King George Co., Va. So. Ch., Nov. 19, 1868

DECATUR
Maria S., d. of Com. Stephen Decatur, United States Navy, and Capt. Wyndham R. Mayo of Virginia, by the Rev. Pelham Williams, in the Church of Messiah, Boston, Mass. So. Ch., Apr. 30, 1874

DECKER
Lowell Laurence, of New York, and Mary Scollay, d. of the late Rev. George W. and Mary Scollay Nelson, in Saint James' Church, Warrenton, Va. So. Ch., Oct. 19, 1912

DEDMAN
Samuel L., of Fulton, Mo., and Ella Caldwell of Fredericksburg, Va., by the Rev. John K. Mason, at Fredericksburg, Va. So. Ch., Sept. 11, 1884

DEFOREST
Eunice Amarida, of Dover, Dutchess Co., N.Y., and the Rev. Solon G. Putnam of Guilford, Chenango Co., by the Rev. Mr. Kellogg, at Clinton, Oneida Co., N.Y. So. Ch., Jan. 11, 1839

DEGACHER
Walter Frank Gustave, and Annabella Elizabeth, d. of Mr. and Mrs. M. M. Blacker, all of Amelia Co., Va., but recently of England, by the Rev. P. F. Berkeley, at Hawbranch, residence of the bride's parents. So. Ch.,

MARRIAGE NOTICES IN THE SOUTHERN CHURCHMAN WITH DATES OF PUBLICATION

Apr. 26, 1877

DEHAVEN
Mary Anne, d. of the late Charles E. deHaven, and Malcolm Wright Bryan of Roanoke, Va., by the Rev. C. George Currie, D.D., in St. Luke's Church, Philadelphia. So. Ch., Dec. 31, 1885

DEKRAFFT
Maria S., and Samuel H. Cutts, Esq. of Washington, D.C., by the Rev. Mr. Powell, at Goochland Co. So. Ch., Nov. 29, 1866

DELANEY
Betty Edwards, only d. of Judge S. D. Delaney, and Robert W. Crabb, by the Rev. Henry T. Sharp, in St. John's Church, Uniontown, Ky. So. Ch., Feb. 11, 1875

DELAPLANE
Fanny B., only d. of the late Rev. John Delaplane, and the Rev. William D. Hanson, by the Rev. Charles W. Andrews, D.D., in Trinity Church, Martinsburg. So. Ch., May 10, 1866

DELK
Ann E. (Mrs.), and Thomas N. Urquhart, both of Isle of Wight Co., Va., by the Rev. David Barr assisted by the Rev. Mr. Pearson, at Smithfield, Va. So. Ch., Dec. 30, 1886

J. E. L., M.D., and Margaret Ada Urquhart, both of Isle of Wight Co., Va., by the Rev. E. W. Wroth, in the Church of Our Saviour, Ivor, Va. So. Ch., May 10, 1877

DELONY
Laura Virginia, and Richard Lee Walton of Norfolk, Va., by the Rev. R. T. Davis, D.D., at the residence of the bride's uncle, Maj. Charles H. Lee, of Leesburg, Va. So. Ch., Apr. 11, 1889

DEMENT
Noble, of Charles Co., Md., and Kate K. Pickrell of Alexandria, Va., by the Rev. J. T. Johnston. So. Ch., Jan. 11, 1856

DENISON
Annie V., and Theodore Stanwood Rumney, d. and s. of the officiating clergyman, by the Rev. Dr. Denison and the Rev. Dr. Rumney, in the Church of the Heavenly Rest, New York. So. Ch., Apr. 18, 1872

Henry Mandeville (The Rev.) of Brooklyn, N.Y., and Alice, d. of ex-President Tyler of Sherwood Forest, Charles City Co., by the Rev. W. T. Leavell, at Sherwood Forest, Charles City Co., Va. So. Ch., July 18, 1850

See also ALLEN, Elizabeth Denison (Mrs.)

DENNIS
Ferdinand, and Kate Fristoe, both of Rappahannock Co., by the Rev. R. T. Brown, of the Episcopal Church, at Sperryville, Rappahannock Co., Va. So. Ch., Feb. 20, 1868

Samuel, of Albemarle, and Judith, d. of P. J. Harkins of Powhatan Co., by the Rev. P. F. Berkeley, at the residence of the bride's father. So. Ch., Oct. 29, 1868

V. R., d. of Dr. Benjamin and Charlotte W. Dennis of Amelia Co., Va., and Creed Haskins of Powhatan Co., by

MARRIAGE NOTICES IN THE SOUTHERN CHURCHMAN WITH DATES OF PUBLICATION

the Rev. P. F. Berkeley, at Vauxcluse in Amelia Co. So. Ch., Feb. 20, 1868

DENNY
George H., of Boone Co., Mo., and Ellen C. Jarvis of Loudoun Co., Va., by the Rev. Theodore Reed, in St. James' Church, Leesburg. So. Ch., Nov. 16, 1876

John W., and Annie E. Kirwan, both of Dorchester Co., Md., by the Rev. Wm. W. Greene, at Church Creek. So. Ch., Jan. 4, 1883

DENT
John Francis (Col.), of St. Mary's Co., Md., and Lucy Penelope Chandler of Westmoreland, Va., by the Rev. W. C. Latane assisted by the Rev. E. F. Saumenig, at Windsor, Westmoreland Co., Va. So. Ch., Dec. 28, 1893

Mattie T., d. of George Dent of Prince George's, Md., and Weatherly J. Adamson formerly of Scotland, by the Rev. A. P. Gray, in Trinity Church, Manassas. So. Ch., June 28, 1888

DEPAUW
Jane, d. of Col. Nowland T. DePauw, and Harold J. Gates of Louisville, Ky., by the Rev. E. S. Hinks, at the home of the bride, "Waverley Farms", Haymarket, Va. So. Ch., Dec. 28, 1912

Nowland G., of Haymarket, Va., and Harriet Hairston, d. of the late Sarah Knight Callaway and William Washington Meade, by the Rev. A. G. Grinnan, at the home of the bride's brother, Stasius Meade, Braddock Heights, Alexandria, Va. So. Ch., May 6 and 13, 1911

DERBY
C. A. (Maj.), of the Georgia Military Institute, and Clara Jane, d. of Hon. Wm. H. Hunt of Marietta, Ga., by the Rev. B. E. Habersham, So. Ch., Nov. 2, 1854

Elizabeth Stuart, youngest d. of the late Rev. Henry L. Derby, one time rector of St. Andrew's, and the Rev. Arthur P. Gray, Jr., rector of St. Andrew's Church, Lawrenceville, Va., by the Rev. Arthur P. Gray, Sr., the Rev. Jeff. Ran. Taylor assisting, in the Episcopal Church, Accomac. So. Ch., Oct. 14, 1911

Mattie A., and Julian F. Snow, by the Rev. B. D. Tucker assisted by the Rev. H. L. Derby, in Grace Church, Lancaster, Va. So. Ch., Feb. 13, 1879

DERICKSON
Mary Henrietta, d. of Levin Derickson, and Thomas W. McNeely, by the Rev. Geo. S. Fitzhugh, in St. Paul's Church, Berlin, Md. So. Ch., Dec. 12, 1872

DERR
Oscar D., Esq., of Roanoke, Va., and Bessie Allen, youngest d. of Capt. George and Mary R. Lawrence of Goochland C.H., by the Rev. P. H. Boyden, in Grace Episcopal Church, Goochland C.H., Va. So. Ch., June 17, 1886

DERRICK
Annie P., of Houston, Va., and Edward A. Holmes of Chatham Hill, Smyth Co., Va., by the Rev. Mr. Raymond, at the home of her brother, G. H. Derrick, Pulaski, Va. So. Ch.,

MARRIAGE NOTICES IN THE SOUTHERN CHURCHMAN WITH DATES OF PUBLICATION

Aug. 26, 1911
DERRIEUX
Emma S., and Thos. B. Skipwith, both of Powhatan Co., Va., by the Rev. P. F. Berkeley, at Edge Hill, the residence of M. L. Waring. So. Ch., Dec. 7, 1871

DE SAUSSURE
Mary Caroline, d. of Charles A. De Saussure, Esq., and the Rev. Wm. J. Boone of Eufaula, Ala., by the Rev. C. P. Gadsen, in St. Luke's Church, Charleston, S.C. So. Ch., Feb. 4, 1869

DESHIELD
Ella, d. of Maj. Henry Deshield of Northumberland Co., Va., and William C. Snow formerly of Northumberland, but now of Greensboro, N.C., by the Rev. John Moncure assisted by the Rev. H. L. Derby, in St. Stephen's Church, Heathsville, Va. So. Ch., Dec. 8, 1881

DESHIELDS
Laura, d. of Maj. Henry C. Deshields, and Randolph S. Brent, all of Northumberland, by the Rev. H. L. Derby, at "Summerfield", Northumberland Co., Va. So. Ch., Jan. 11, 1883

DESHON
Estelle, d. of C. M. Deshon, Esq. of Baltimore, and Benjamin* Maitland, Jr., Esq., by the Rev. Jno. C. McCabe, D.D., rector of the Church of the Ascension, at Baltimore. So. Ch., Aug. 17, 1860

DESHONG
Louisa, d. of John O. Deshong, and J. Edwards Woodbridge, by the Rev. Geo. Woodbridge, D.D. of Richmond, assisted by the Rev. Henry Brown, at Chester, Pa. So. Ch., June 8, 1876

DEUEL
Eleanor, and the Rev. Willis Gerhart, rector of the Church of the Heavenly Rest, Abilene, Tex., by the Rt. Rev. E. Cecil Seaman, in Grace and Holy Trinity Cathedral, Kansas City. So. Ch., Nov. 16, 1940

DEVERE
M. Schele (Prof.), of the University of Virginia, and Lucy B., d. of Alexander Rives, Esq., by the Rev. R. K. Meade, at Carlton, near Charlottesville. So. Ch., Mar. 30, 1860

DEVINE
Catharine A., and John H. Crouch, both of Newcastle Co., by the Rev. W. D. Hanson, at Faulkland, Del. So. Ch., Mar. 8, 1883

DEVOE
Ann, of Parkersburg, and James Todd of Wheeling, by the Rev. E. T. Perkins. So. Ch., Aug. 11, 1848

DEW
W. W. (Dr.), of Russell Co., and Bettie H., eldest d. of the late Dr. W. T. Braxton of Hanover, by the Rev. S. S. Hepbron, in Immanuel Church. So. Ch., June 20, 1889

DEWITT
Clinton, Esq., and Octavia Oley, both of Alexandria, Va., by the Rev. T. M. Carson, in St. Paul's Church, Lynchburg. So. Ch., Aug. 27, 1874

* Given as printed

MARRIAGE NOTICES IN THE SOUTHERN CHURCHMAN WITH DATES OF PUBLICATION

See also M'COLLOUGH, S. E. (Mrs.)
Wm., and Elizabeth F., youngest d. of Jesse Jones, both of Bedford, by the Rev. N. Sale. So. Ch., Dec. 22, 1837

DEY
William Morton, and Ellen Alice, d. of William W. Old and Alice Herbert, his wife, by the rector, the Rev. Francis C. Steinmetz, S. T. D., in Christ Church, Norfolk, Va. So. Ch., Jan. 7, 1911

DICKENS
Francis A., Jr., and Dora B., d. of the late Branton Garlick, by the Rev. J. J. Anderson, at Waterloo, New Kent Co., Va. So. Ch., Jan. 10, 1878

DICKENSEN
James M., and Lucy M. Jeffries, gr.d. of the late Judge James M. Jeffries, by the Rev. J. Hervey Hundley, in Bethel Methodist Church, Middlesex Co., Va. So. Ch., Oct. 29, 1891

DICKENSON
Margaret Gray, and Wm. Randolph Madison, by the Rev. J. K. Mason, in St. George's Church, Fredericksburg, Va. So. Ch., Oct. 9, 1890

William, and Margarett Gray by the Rev. Mr. Randolph, at Traveller's Rest. So. Ch., Aug. 14, 1863

DICKERSON
Robert Talbot (The Rev.), of Wilmington, Del., now on furlough from Liberia, and Elizabeth Lovejoy, d. of Mr. and Mrs. Wm. L. Baker of Sioux Falls, S.D., by the Rev. Elwood L. Haines, in Christ Church, Glendale, Ohio. So. Ch., Apr. 29, 1933

DICKINSON
Ella R., of Houston, and G. R. Scott of Corpus Christi, Tex., by the Rev. J. J. Clemens, in Christ Church, Houston, Tex. So. Ch., May 12, 1881

Jane H., d. of Wm. I. Dickinson, and Thomas I. Yerby, both of Spotsylvania, by the Rev. Mr. Friend, at "Nottingham", residence of the bride's father in Spotsylvania Co. So. Ch., July 27, 1860

Kate C., of "Moss Side", and J. L. Marye, Jr. of Newport News, Va., by the rector of the parish, in Grace Church, Caroline Co., Va. So. Ch., Dec. 25, 1890

Louisa F., of Caroline Co., Va., and C. C. Buckner, Esq. of Alexandria, by the Rev. Henry Wall. So. Ch., Dec. 1, 1853

Sopha B., of King George Co., Va., and Achille Murat Willis of Rappahannock Co., Va., by the Rev. A. J. Willis, at Berry Plain, King George Co., Va., the residence of the bride's father. So. Ch., Mar. 19, 1885

DICKSON
Jemima, d. of John Dickson formerly of Scotland, now of Albemarle Co., Va., and George Napier Thomson of Richmond, by the Rev. T. D. Bell, pastor of the Presbyterian Church in Scottsville, assisted by the Rev. T. E. Locke, rector of St. Anne's parish, at Oakland Grove, Albemarle Co. So.

MARRIAGE NOTICES IN THE SOUTHERN CHURCHMAN WITH DATES OF PUBLICATION

Ch., Oct. 24, 1878
Marion Hamilton, d. of Wm. Dickson formerly of Scotland, now of Albemarle Co., Va., and Allen Reid of Owensboro, Ky., by the Rev. T. E. Locke, at Oakland Grove, Albemarle Co., Va. So. Ch., Dec. 2, 1886

DIDIER
Edmund, Esq., late of Baltimore, and Katherine E. Kent of Roanoke, Va., by the Rev. D. M. Wood. So. Ch., Aug. 14, 1884
Henry, of Baltimore, and Angelica Peale, d. of Hon. A. R. Boteler, by the Rev. Dr. Andrews, at Fountain Rock, near Shepherdstown. So. Ch., Oct. 5, 1860

DIETTERICK
Phyllis G., of Berwick, Pa., and the Rev. Kenneth M. Gearhart, rector of Christ Church, Danville, Pa., by Canon Clifford W. French, in Keferstein Memorial Chapel of the Holy Spirit, Bishopcourt, Harrisburg. So. Ch., Jan. 23, 1937

DIGGES
Anna E., of Warrenton, Va., and James Vass of Culpeper Co., Va., by the Rev. George W. Nelson, in St. James' Church, Warrenton, Va. So. Ch., Nov. 23, 1882

DIGGS
Julia C., and Dr. Hazeal Williams, both of Virginia, by the Rev. H. M. Wharton, So. Ch., Apr. 13, 1882
Mary E., of Mathews Co., Va., and J. J. Freeman of North Carolina, by the Rev. Mr. Carraway, at Oakland. So. Ch., Feb. 1, 1856

DILLARD
Anna J. (Mrs.), formerly of Gloucester, and Dr. John S. Tribble of Essex Co., by the Rev. H. L. Derby, at "Midway", Lancaster Co., Va. So. Ch., Mar. 1, 1877
George, and Elizabeth Blunt, both of Hanover Co., Va., by the Rev. Curtis Grubb, at the residence of the bride. So. Ch., Feb. 15, 1883
Henrietta E. Anthony, d. of George H. Dillard, Esq. of Sussex Co., Va., and Murdock M. Urquhart of Southampton Co., by the Rev. C. J. Gibson, at "Inglewood". So. Ch., Dec. 30, 1875
Joseph J., and Mary E. Tunstill, by the Rev. H. L. Derby, at "Spring Hill", Sussex, Va. So. Ch., Sept. 4, 1873
Ruffin, of North Carolina, and Bessie A. Moorman of Campbell Co., Va., by the Rev. W. W. Kimball, at the home of the bride. So. Ch., Oct. 6, 1881
William (Judge), and Mary F. Evans, all of Amherst Co., Va., by the Rev. A. P. Gray, at "Grand Oaks", Amherst Co., the residence of the bride's father. So. Ch., Mar. 24, 1892

DILLON
Agnes, of Savannah, Ga., and Wm. L. Randolph, Esq. of Albemarle Co., by the Rev. J. D. Powell, at "Oakland", Cumberland Co. So. Ch., Mar. 1, 1866

DIMICK
Adeline C., d. of Col. J. Dimick, U.S.A., and Capt. Joseph Roberts, U.S.A., by the Rev. M. L. Chevers, in the Centurion Church, Old

MARRIAGE NOTICES IN THE SOUTHERN CHURCHMAN WITH DATES OF PUBLICATION

Point. So. Ch., Oct. 19, 1860

DIMMOCK
Cora, d. of Capt. Charles Dimmock, and Eugene Carrington, all of Richmond, by the Rev. Mr. Marvell, at Washington. So. Ch., Apr. 22, 1859

Emily Moale, d. of the late Charles H. Dimmock of Richmond, Va., and C. Taylor Jenkins of Baltimore, by the Rev. A. Y. Hundley, at "Sherwood", Gloucester Co., Va. So. Ch., Dec. 9, 1880

Marion J., of Richmond, Va., and Sophia Chinn, second d. of the late William Y. Downman, by the Rev. J. Y. Downman, brother of the bride, assisted by the Rev. Wm. M. Clark, in St. George's Church, Fredericksburg, Va. So. Ch., Oct. 20, 1892

William Courtney, of Richmond, Va., and Mary Byrd, second d. of R. C. and C. W. Selden, by the Rev. A. Y. Hundley, at Sherwood, Gloucester Co., Va. residence of the bride's father. So. Ch., Dec. 10, 1874

DINWIDDIE
Edgar E., and Anna, youngest d. of the late Dr. Albert T. Bledsoe of Alexandria, by the Rev. H. Suter, at Christ Church, Alexandria. So. Ch., Feb. 17, 1881

Wm., of Greenwood, Albemarle Co., and Emily Albertine, d. of Prof. Bledsoe of the University of Virginia, by the Rev. R. K. Meade, at the University of Virginia. So. Ch., July 15, 1864

DIRDING
Lemuel L., and Ruth R. Robins, both of Berkeley Co., W.Va., by the Rev. W. T. Leavell, rector of Mt. Zion Church, Hedgesville, Va., at North Mountain, Berkeley Co., W.Va. So. Ch., Jan. 4, 1883

DITTY
Mary Eliza, d. of Dr. Thomas R. Ditty of Westmoreland Co., Va., and John Manning of Prince George's Co., Md., by the Rev. T. E. Locke, at Eltham, Westmoreland Co., Va. So. Ch., June 18, 1858

DIX
Morgan, S. T. D. (The Rev.), rector of Trinity Church, and Emily Woolsey, by the Rt. Rev. H. Potter, D.D., in New York, at the residence of the bride's mother. So. Ch., June 11, 1874

DIXION
Emily E., and J. J. Wheat, by the Rev. James T. Johnston, in St. Paul's Church. So. Ch., Nov. 4, 1842

DIXON
Ella, d. of John A. Dixon of Alexandria, and Robert J. Thomas of Louisville, Ky., by the Rev. G. H. Norton, D.D., at the residence of the bride's parents. So. Ch., June 1, 1871

Joseph D., of Lancastershire, England, and Mrs. Joan D. Weir (nee Douglas), by the Rev. A. P. Gray, at "Liberia", Prince William Co., Va. So. Ch., Oct. 23, 1879

Julia, and Edwin Francis Tatsapaugh, by the Rev. John Aikon. So. Ch., Nov. 16, 1848

DOBBIN

MARRIAGE NOTICES IN THE SOUTHERN CHURCHMAN WITH DATES OF PUBLICATION

Mary Grace, d. of Nimrod M. Dobbin and Mary Ducke Hardin, his wife, of Watauga Co., N.C., and Roscoe R. Griggs of Macon Co., N.C., by the Rev. Hugh A. Dobbin of Valle Crucis, in Saint Matthew's Church, Todd, N.C. So. Ch., Sept. 30, 1911

Mary M., d. of Jas. H. Dobbin, and John S. Finley, by the Rev. Robert A. Gibson, at the residence of the bride's father in Nottoway Co. So. Ch., Jan. 19, 1871

DOBYNS
Edgar S., and Lorena Hundley, by the Rev. H. L. Derby, at the residence of Urban Dunaway, Northumberland Co., Va. So. Ch., Jan. 25, 1883

DODD
David H., and M. Virginia Shaffer, both of Berkeley Co., W.Va., by the Rev. W. T. Leavell, in Mt. Zion Church, Hedgesville. So. Ch., July 7, 1892

Mason B., and Maria F. Kirkpatrick, by the Rev. John McGill, in Fauquier Co., Va. So. Ch., Apr. 4, 1867

Nannie L., and Robert C. Weaver of Warren Co., Va., by the Rev. Mr. Turbin, at the residence of the bride's father near Bealton, Fauquier Co., Va. So. Ch., Nov. 8, 1883

DODGE
Anson G. P., Jr. (The Rev.), rector of Christ Church, Frederica, St. Simon's Island, Ga., and Anna D., d. of the late Horace Gould, of St. Simon's Island, by the Rev. Henry E. Lucas, rector, in St. Mark's Church, Brunswick, Ga. So. Ch., June 12, 1890

Margaret D., and Watkins Addison, Jr., both of Georgetown, by the Rev. J. Vaughn Lewis, in St. John's (Episcopal) Church, Georgetown. So. Ch., Sept. 25, 1873

DODSON
Augusta E., and William F. Carter, by the Rev. H. L. Derby, at Lancaster, Va. So. Ch., Apr. 15, 1880

Henry (Dr.), of Millon, N.C., and Annie Barrett of Wytheville, by the Rev. R. S. Barrett of Kentucky, and the Rev. Mercer P. Logan, the rector, in St. John's Church, Wytheville, Va. So. Ch., Oct. 11, 1883

DOGGETT
Eugenia S., and George N. Doggett of Chicago, by the Rev. John K. Mason, at the residence of the bride's father, Lee B. Doggett, Fredericksburg, Va. So. Ch., Mar. 18, 1886

George N., Chicago, and Eugenia S. Doggett, by the Rev. John K. Mason, at the residence of the bride's father, Lee B. Doggett, Fredericksburg, Va. So. Ch., Mar. 18, 1886

DOLL
John Harlan, and Mary Louisa, youngest d. of the late Col. Edmund P. Hunter, by the Rev. Henry Thomas, in Trinity Church, Martinsburg, W.Va. So. Ch., July 16, 1891

DONALDSON
Frank, Jr., and Nannie Beirne, d. of the late William H. McFarland of Richmond, Va., by the Rev. Dr. C. W.

MARRIAGE NOTICES IN THE SOUTHERN CHURCHMAN WITH DATES OF PUBLICATION

Rankin, in St. Paul's Church, Baltimore. So. Ch., Apr. 29, 1880

DONNELL
Elizabeth, d. of William Donnell, Esq. and Charles H. Tilghman, of Talbot Co., Md., by the Rev. A. M. Randolph, D.D., at the residence of the bride's father, in Baltimore. So. Ch., Dec. 8, 1881

Mary C., d. of the late Wm. Donnell, and C. Howard Lloyd, by the Rev. Dr. J. H. Eccleston, in Baltimore, at the residence of her mother. So. Ch., Nov. 29, 1888

John, of Washington City, and Mary Cotent Lamb, by the Rev. Thos. Gallaudet, of St. Ann's, New York, assisted by the Rev. B. D. Tucker, at the residence of the bride's brother, Col. William Lamb, Norfolk. So. Ch., Apr. 28, 1887

William, Esq., and Mary Elizabeth, d. of D. Sprigg, Esq., all of Baltimore, by the Rev. D. F. Sprigg, in Emanuel Church, Baltimore. So. Ch., Apr. 1, 1859

DONOHOE
Annie C., of Loudoun Co., Va., and John T. Cox of Alexandria, Va., by the Rev. R. T. Davis, D.D., assisted by the Rev. Henry T. Sharp, D.D., in St. James Church, Leesburg, Va. So. Ch., Jan. 31, 1884

S. Rozell, ed. of the Fairfax Herald, and Susan Lindsay, d. of Thomas Moore, by the Rev. Frank Page, in Zion Church, Fairfax C. H., Va. So. Ch., May 29, 1884

DORNIN
Thomas A. (Lt.), commanding U.S. Ship Relief (an exploring vessell), and Ann M. Thorburn, d. of Samuel Howison, Esq. of Fredericksburg, Va., by the Rev. Mr. Wingfield, in Christ Church, Norfolk, Va. So. Ch., Aug. 4, 1837

DORR
C. P. (Hon.), of Webster Co., and Belle G., eldest d. of Dr. John and Mrs. Sallie G. Ligon, by the Rev. T. H. Lacy, at Clover Lick, Pocohontas Co., W.Va. So. Ch., Oct. 1, 1885

DORSEY
Ida Mason, and the Rev. William Cabell Brown of Nelson Co., Va., by the Rev. A. R. Stuart, D.D., in Christ Church, Georgetown, D.C. So. Ch., Aug. 13, 1891

Margaret Warfield, d. of Joshua W. Dorsey of Ellicott City, Md., and Robert Harris Woods of Albemarle Co., Va., by the Rev. R. A. Poole, in St. Stephen's Church, Ellicott City, Md. So. Ch., Nov. 29, 1888

Millie Goodwin, eldest d. of Mrs. Kate C. Dorsey, and Bernard Hooe Fowle, by the Rev. A. R. Stuart, D.D., at the residence of the bride's mother, Georgetown, D.D. So. Ch., Nov. 7 and 28, 1889

Owen J. (The Rev.), of Maryland, and C. Virginia, d. of Garrett Wyncoop* of Hedgesville, by the Rev. John W. Lea, at Hedgesville, W.Va. So. Ch., Apr. 27, 1876

* Given as printed

MARRIAGE NOTICES IN THE SOUTHERN CHURCHMAN WITH DATES OF PUBLICATION

Richard B., and M.
Lucretia, d. of William
and Martha Ayre, all of
Fairfax, by the Rev. A. P.
Gray, in St. John's Church,
Centreville. So. Ch., Feb.
3, 1881

DORTCH
Wm. T. (Col.), of Goldsborough,
N.C., and Hattie, d. of
Allen Williams, Esq. of
Clarke Co., Va., by the Rev.
J. F. Martin, at the residence of the bride's
father. So. Ch., Jan. 11,
1872

DOSWELL
T. Bernard, of Hanover Co.,
and Ellen B. Morris of
Caroline Co., Va., by the
Rev. Curtis Grubb, in St.
Martin's Church, Hanover
Co., Va. So. Ch., Dec. 25,
1884

DOUGHERTY
Frances Henrietta, d. of W. W.
Dougherty, Esq., and the Rev.
James D. Nicholson of Maryland, by the Rev. John M.
Forbes, in St. Luke's Church,
New York. So. Ch., Apr. 21,
1837

DOUGHTY
Ada, d. of N. W. Doughty, and
the Rev. Henry Bedinger of Greenport, L.I., by the Rev. J.
Carpenter Smith, S. T. D., in
St. George's Church, Flushing,
L. I. So. Ch., May 4, 1876

DOUGLAS
Bessie, d. of the late Hon. B.
B. Douglas, and Travers D.
Moncure, by the Rev. E.
Meade, at "Cownes", King
William Co., Va. So. Ch.,
July 20, 1882
Evelyn Spottswood, second d.
of the late Hon. B. B.
Douglas, and J. C. Causey
of Baltimore, Md., by the
Rev. J. Hervey Hundley, at
Cownes, King William Co.,
Va. So. Ch., Mar. 6, 1879
Henrietta P., d. of the Rev.
W. K. Douglas, D.D., rector
of Calvary Church, New
Orleans, and the Rev. Upton
B. Bowdon, rector of MacComb
City, Miss., by the Rt. Rev.
Bishop of Louisianna, the
Bishop of Mississippi,
assisting and pronouncing
the benediction. in Calvary
Church, New Orleans. So.
Ch., Nov. 30, 1882
Mary B., d. of Archibald N.
Douglas, and Walter D.
Dabney, all of Albemarle
Co., Va., by the Rev. J.
S. Hanckel, at Rose Valley,
residence of the bride's
father. So. Ch., Nov. 21,
1878
Wm. Taylor (The Rev.) rector of
Grace Church, Lake Providence,
La., and Anna Prophet of
New Orleans, by the Rev. Wm.
K. Douglas, D.D., assisted
by the Rev. C. S. Hedges,
D.D., the Bishop of Louisiana
pronouncing the blessing,
in Calvary Church, New
Orleans. So. Ch., Feb. 26,
1885
See also WEIR, Joan D. (Mrs.)

DOUGLASS
Elizabeth Joan, of Williamsburg, and Walter Weir of
Prince William Co., by the
Rev. Andrew Fisher, at Zoar,
King William Co. So. Ch.,
Oct. 24, 1867
Hugh T., of Zanesville, Ohio,
and Marian J. Briggs of
Clarke Co., Va., by the Rev.
F. M. Whittle, at Clarke
Co., Va. So. Ch., July 7,
1853
James T., Esq., of Bedford Co.,
Va., and Mrs. Lewly Meredith,

MARRIAGE NOTICES IN THE SOUTHERN CHURCHMAN WITH DATES OF PUBLICATION

d. of H. M. Bowyer, Esq. of Botetourt Co., Va., by the Rev. Pendleton Brooke, at Valveide, the residence of Col. R. W. Hughes. So. Ch., Apr. 6, 1871

Mary Ellen, youngest d. of the late Hon. Beverly Douglass of King William Co., and William Weathers of Kentucky, by the Rev. S. S. Hepbron, at Coons, King William Co. So. Ch., Nov. 5, 1891

Walter C., and Ellen, youngest d. of Hon. Jas. F. Johnson, by the Rev. T. W. Hooper, at the residence of the bride's father, Liberty, Va. So. Ch., Jan. 6, 1870

DOUHTAT*

Mary, d. of Maj. R. Douhtat, of Charles City Co., and Dr. Jakqueline* Marshall, of Fauquier Co., Va., by the Rev. A. Wade, at "Lower Weyanoke". So. Ch., Dec. 16, 1869

DOUTHAT

Agnes, d. of Maj. R. Douthat, and Col. R. Stribling of Fauquier Co., by the Rev. A. Wade, at Wyanoke, Charles City Co. So. Ch., Sept. 1, 1870

Carrie Harrison, of Charles City Co., and James P. Harrison of Danville, by the Rev. John P. Tyler, rector, in Westover Church. So. Ch., Oct. 30, 1890

Jaquelin Marshall, of Danville, Va., and Carrie Rivers, youngest d. of the late W. M. Harrison of Charles City Co., Va., at Westover, the residence of the bride's brother-in-law. So. Ch., Nov. 20, 1879

Mildred Carter, d. of Maj. Robt. Douthat, and Charles Morton Riddle of Petersburg, Va., at "Westbury", residence of the bride's parents, Charles City Co., Va. So. Ch., July 6, 1893

Robert, Jr., and Rebecca P., d. of J. A. and Rebecca Marshall, all of Fauquier Co., Va., by the Rev. H. B. Lee, at "The Craig", the residence of the bride's parents, So. Ch., Jan. 3, 1884

DOWNER

J. W. (Dr.), of Charles Town, and Eliza T., d. of Maj. I. Greene, by the Rev. T. F. Martin, at the residence of E. C. Marshall, Berryville, Clarke Co., Va. So. Ch., May 8, 1879

DOWNING

Alice, d. of Dr. A. W. Downing, and Levin W. Nottingham, by the Rev. J. B. Craighill, at "Chatham", Northampton Co. So. Ch., May 12, 1870

Arthur W. (Dr.), and Mary P. Bayly, by the Rev. Aristides S. Smith of the Presbyterian Church, at Bellevue, Accomac Co., Va. So. Ch., Nov. 24, 1837

Maggie H., and Frederick Waddy, both of Northampton Co., Va., by the Rev. J. B. Craighill, at Chatham, residence of the bride's father. So. Ch., Apr. 29, 1869

DOWNMAN

Hariot J., of Warrenton, Va., and R. B. L. Fleming of Fauquier Co., by the Rev. George W. Nelson, in St. James' Church, Warrenton, Va.

* Given as printed

MARRIAGE NOTICES IN THE SOUTHERN CHURCHMAN WITH DATES OF PUBLICATION

So. Ch., Jan. 12, 1882
Joseph, Esq., of Layton Stone, and Isabella H., only d. of Dr. Hugh Hamilton, by the Rev. Mr. Cole, at Oak Farm, Fauquier Co. So. Ch., Dec. 23, 1859
Nannie H., d. of the late W. Yates Downman, and R. Innes Taylor, of Spotsylvania Co., Va., by the Rev. E. C. Murdaugh, D.D., at Idlewild, near Fredericksburg, the residence of the bride's mother. So. Ch., Oct. 26, 1876
Robert H., and Fanny Scott, d. of Dr. Frederick Horner, by the Rev. G. H. Norton, at Warrenton. So. Ch., May 23, 1856
Sophia Chinn, second d. of the late William Y. Downman, and Marion J. Dimmock, of Richmond, Va., by the Rev. J. Y. Downman, brother of the bride, assisted by the Rev. Wm. M. Clark, in St. George's Church, Fredericksburg, Va. So. Ch., Oct. 20, 1892

DOYLE
Mary Francis, d. of Ida C. and the late George W. Doyle, of Wilmington, N.C., and Charles Martin Niles, D.D., by the Rev. Edmund Banks Smith, chaplain U.S.A., headquarters, Governor's Island, N. Y., in the Church of the Saviour, Philadelphia, Pa. So. Ch., Oct. 24, 1908

DRANE
Frederick Blount (The Rev.), Archdeacon of Alaska, and Rebecca Bennehan Wood, of Edenton, N.C., at Seattle, Wash. So. Ch., Oct. 11, 1924

DRAPER
John S., of Pulaski, Va., and Janie, second d. of Dr. G. S. Hairston, deceased, of Henry Co., Va., by the Rev. J. R. Lee, at Marrowbone, Henry Co., Va. So. Ch., May 11, 1871*

DREW
Horace, of Jacksonville, Fla., and Gertrude, second d. of G. R. Fairbanks, Esq., by the Rt. Rev. H. B. Whipple, D.D., Bishop of Minnesota, assisted by the Rt. Rev. W. M. Green, D.D., Bishop of Mississippi and the Rev. W. P. DuBose, D.D., in St. Augustine Chapel, University of the South, Sewanee, Tenn. So. Ch., Oct. 21, 1875

DREWRY
Major A., and Mary, d. of the late Wm. M. Harrison, by the Rev. A. Wade, assisted by the Rev. Joshua Peterkin, in Westover Church, Charles City Co., Va. So. Ch., Feb. 24, 1870

DUANE
Alexander (Dr.), of New York City, and Susan W., d. of William R. Galt, Esq., by the Rev. Beverly D. Tucker assisted by the Rev. Alexander Galt, brother of the bride, at the residence of the bride's parents. So. Ch., July 30, 1891
Richard B. (The Rev.), rector of Grace Church, Honesdale, Penn., and Margaret A., eldest d. of Sampson Tams, Esq., by the Rev. J. B. Fowles, in St. Andrews Church, Philadelphia. So. Ch., Oct. 24, 1850

DUBOIS

---

* The original incorrect notice of this marriage published in the Southern Churchman May 4, 1871, and later corrected by the editor in the May 11th issue, is omitted from this volume.

MARRIAGE NOTICES IN THE SOUTHERN CHURCHMAN WITH DATES OF PUBLICATION

Redir Madeleine, second d. of Maj. D. DuBois, and Thomas E. Jefferies, all of Charleston, W.Va., by the Rev. R. A. Cobbs in St. John's Church, Charleston, W.Va. So. Ch., Oct. 30, 1884

DUBOSE
William Porcher (The Rev.), S. T. D., Prof. of Exegesis, and Chaplain in the University of the South, and Mrs. Maria Louisa Yerger, by the Rt. Rev. the assistant Bishop of Kentucky, at Moffat, Tenn. So. Ch., Jan. 30, 1879

DUCKWORTH
James A., of Mossly Hill, England, and Emsie Minnigerode of Richmond, by the Rev. Charles Minnigerode, D.D., father of the bride, in St. Paul's Church, Richmond, Va. So. Ch., May 19, 1881

DUDLEY
Alice Harrison, third d. of the Rt. Rev. Thomas Underwood Dudley, D.D., and William Adair McDowell, Esq., of Clay City, Ky., by the Bishop of the Diocese of Kentucky, in Calvary Church, Louisville, Ky. So. Ch., Nov. 3, 1887

Deborah Davis, d. of the late Peter Dudley of Lynchburg, Va., and the Rev. Wm. H. Kinckle, pastor of St. Paul's Church, by the Rt. Rev. Bishop Johns, in St. Paul's Church, Lynchburg. So. Ch., Oct. 26, 1865

Fanny Berkeley Cochran, d. of the Rt. Rev. Thomas Underwood Dudley, D.D., and Harry Reamer Woodward, Esq. of New Albany, Ind., by the Rt. Rev. the Bishop of Kentucky and Louisiana, in Calvary Church, Louisville, Ky. So. Ch., June 10, 1886

Harriet Gardner, d. of the Rt. Rev. Thomas Underwood Dudley, D.D., and Tevis Goodloe, Esq. of Louisville, Ky., by the Rt. Rev., the Bishop of Kentucky assisted by the Rev. William F. Gardner of Maryland, in Calvary Church, Louisville, Ky. So. Ch., Jan. 19, 1893

Thomas U., Jr., of Richmond, and Fanny B., d. of Dr. William Cochran of Middleburg, by the Rev. O. A. Kinsolving, in Emanuel Church, Middleburg. So. Ch., July 22, 1859

Thos. U., rector of Christ Church, Baltimore, and Virginia, second d. of John H. Rowland, Esq., by the Rev. O. S. Barton, in Christ Church, Norfolk, Va. So. Ch., Apr. 15, and May 13, 1869

DUER
A. Adgate, of Baltimore, and Madge L., d. of the late Col. Thomas Marshall of Fauquier Co., Va., by the Rev. Wm. Meredith, at Springdale, Va. So. Ch., Nov. 7, 1872

DUERSON
Robert C., Esq., and Caroline M., d. of Robt. Cammack, Esq., by the Rev. J. W. Woodville. So. Ch., Oct. 25, 1839

DUFFEY
Edward S., and Amanda M., d. of A. G. Smith of Middleburg, by the Rev. O. A. Kinsolving. So. Ch., Mar. 18, 1869

DUFFIELD
Charles B., Esq., of Drummondtown, and Sarah E., d. of Thomas R. Joynes of

MARRIAGE NOTICES IN THE SOUTHERN CHURCHMAN WITH DATES OF PUBLICATION

Montpelia, Accomac Co., Va., by the Rev. Enoch Reed of Aberdeen. So. Ch., Aug. 18, 1853

DULANEY
Phoebe Pemberton, d. of Caroline Nourse and the late Com. Bladen Dulaney, and Thomas J. Chew formerly of Maryland, by the Rev. A. P. Gray, at "Cloverland". So. Ch., Nov. 1, 1883

DULANY
Bladen T., late of Fauquier Co., and Jane M., d. of T. R. Love, Esq. of Fairfax Court House, by the Rev. R. T. Brown, pastor of Zion Church, Fairfax C.H., Va., in Trinity Church, Washington, D.C. So. Ch., Apr. 15, 1859

Henry Grafton, and Ida, d. of the late George Cuthbert Powell of Loudoun Co., Va., by the Rev. O. A. Kinsolving, in Emanuel Church, Middleburg. So. Ch., June 14, 1855

R. H., Jr., and Eva F. Randolph, both of Loudoun Co., by the Rev. W. H. Johnson, in Trinity Church, Upperville. So. Ch., Oct. 4, 1877

DUMAURIER*
Eugenie, and Clyde Robe Meredith, by the Rev. Page Dame, D.D., in Memorial Church Rectory, Baltimore, Md. So. Ch., Oct. 17, 1925

DUNBAR
Helen M., and the Rev. Samuel R. Slack, both of Weymouth, by the Rev. John Wright, rector of St. Matthew's Church, Boston, in Trinity Church, Weymouth, Mass. So. Ch., Jan. 18, 1877

DUNCAN
Fannie C., youngest d. of the late Stephen Duncan of Louisiana, and W. Taylor Milton of Clarke Co., by the Rev. T. F. Martin, in Grace Church, Berryville, Va. So. Ch., Nov. 14, 1867

Herbert Cope (The Rev.), rector of St. James' Church, Alexandria, La., and Maria Elizabeth, d. of the late Dr. Thomas Alfred Cooke formerly of Gloucester Co., Va., and Fanny Pennill, his wife, both of St. Landry Parish, La., by the Rt. Rev., the Bishop of Louisiana, in St. John's Church, Washington, La. So. Ch., Feb. 1, 1883

J. J., and Maud, d. of Judge Geo. H. Lee, by the Rev. J. F. Woods, at Clarksburg, W.Va. So. Ch., Nov. 2, 1871

James F., of Norfolk, and Lucy Tabb, d. of James K. Dabney of Gloucester Co., by the Rev. Mr. Robertson, in Ware Church, Gloucester Co. So. Ch., Mar. 3, 1881

Mary E., d. of the late George Duncan, and the Rev. James M. Cofer, rector of Tillotson Parish, both of Buckingham Co., Va., by the Rev. Nicholas H. Cobbs, So. Ch., Mar. 3, 1837

Thomas (The Rev.), of Fauquier, and Maria L., d. of the late Com. Morris of Washington, D.C., by the Rev. Geo. D. Cummins, in Trinity Church, Washington, D.C. So. Ch., June 12, 1857

DUNKIN
Eliza Huger, and Mercer P. Logan, D.D., by the Rt. Rev. William A. Guerry, D.D., in St. Paul's Church,

---

* Written "duMaurier" in Southern Churchman

MARRIAGE NOTICES IN THE SOUTHERN CHURCHMAN WITH DATES OF PUBLICATION

Radcliffeboro, Charleston, S.C. So. Ch., Oct. 22, 1921

DUNKLIE
Frank, of Giles Co., Va., and Nannie H., d. of Capt. E. Peachy Williams formerly of Clarke Co., Va., by the Rev. Woodson Walker of Mt. Jackson, Shenandoah Co., Va., in Grace Church, Berryville. So. Ch., May 19, 1881

DUNLOP
Amanda Pamela, d. of the late James and Ann Dent Dunlop of Richmond, Va., and the Rev. Julian Edward Ingle of Henderson, N.C., by the Rev. Hartley Carmichael, in St. Paul's Church. So. Ch., May 19, 1892

Ann Dent, d. of the late James and Ann Dent Dunlop, and James Madison Wise, all of Richmond, by the Rev. Dr. Minnigerode, in St. Paul's Church, Richmond, Va. So. Ch., Dec. 2, 1880

Geo. T., of Maryland, and Emily R., d. of James B. Kirk, Esq. of Culpeper Co., Va., by the Rev. R. H. Phillips, at the residence of the bride's father. So. Ch., Dec. 26, 1867

James N., and Bessie L., d. of the late Wm. C., and Mrs. Maria L. Carrington, all of Richmond, by the Rev. Mr. Minnigerode, at the residence of the bride's mother. So. Ch., Mar. 30, 1876

Margaret Carlisle, d. of the late James and Mrs. Ann Dent Dunlop of Richmond, and Wm. H. S. Burgwyn, Esq. of Baltimore, Md., by the Rev. Dr. Minnigerode, in St. Paul's Church, Richmond, Va. So. Ch., Nov. 30, 1876

Susan Elizabeth, eldest d. of James Dunlop of Little Rock, Ark., and the Rev. Andrew F. Freeman, rector of Christ Church, Little Rock, Ark., by the Rev. C. J. Gibson, at the residence of James Dunlop, Esq. So. Ch., July 23, 1858

DUNN
Emmett Clarke, and Mary Cassandra, d. of Col. L. Wilber Reid, by the Rev. William Hullihen Burkhardt, brother-in-law of the groom, in St. Paul's Church, Alexandria, Va. So. Ch., Nov. 23, 1893

Fanny L., of Powhatan Co., Va., and William D. Wren of Richmond, by the Rev. F. Stringfellow, in Immanuel Church, Powhatan Co. So. Ch., Nov. 16, 1876

J. (The Rev.), rector of St. Mary's Church, Fayette, Mo., and Ann Maria, eldest d. of William Howard, Esq. of Cooper Co., Mo., by the Rev. J. A. Harrison, in Christ Church, Boonville, Mo. So. Ch., Jan. 6, 1853

Janie Carr, d. of W. M. S. and Bettie I. Dunn, and the Rev. William Hullihen Burkhardt of the Diocese of West Virginia, by the Rev. Walter Q. Hullihen, of Staunton, at Midway, Va. So. Ch., July 6, 1893

Thos. H., and Fannie F., d. of Dr. Wm. Cornick of Powhatan Co., Va., by the Rev. P. F. Berkeley, in Grace Church, Genito Parish, Powhatan Co. So. Ch., Oct. 2, 1873

Virginia C., and George Keller, Jr., by the Rev. Pendleton

MARRIAGE NOTICES IN THE SOUTHERN CHURCHMAN WITH DATES OF PUBLICATION

Brooke, at the residence of the bride's uncle in Abingdon, Va. So. Ch., Nov. 30, 1871

DUNSTEN
F. T., of Richmond, and Charlotte A., d. of J. T. Moss of Powhatan, by the Rev. A. B. Tizzard, at Manikintown. So. Ch., Jan. 25, 1861

DUNTON
Geo. F., and Lizzie M. Kellam, by the rector of the parish, in Christ Church, Eastville. So. Ch., Jan. 27, 1870

Guthrie R., and Emma, d. of Capt. Wm. Chase, all of Lancaster Co., Va., by the Rev. H. L. Derby assisted by the Rev. John Moncure and the Rev. John Y. Downman, in Grace Church, Lancaster Co., Va. So. Ch., Nov. 23, 1882

DUPONT*
Marguerite L., youngest d. of the late E. Irenie duPont of Brandywine, and Cazenove G. Lee of Fairfax Co., Va., by the Rt. Rev. G. W. Peterkin of West Virginia, assisted by the Rev. D.D. Smith, in Christ Church, Brandywine, Del. So. Ch., Sept. 29, 1881

DUPREE
Mildred, d. of the late Lewis Dupree, Esq., and Dr. J. G. P. Roulhac of Hickman, Ky., by the Rev. P. G. Robert, at Retirement, Southampton Co. So. Ch., Mar. 20, 1857

DURHAM
John W., and Fannie A. Bishop, both of Albemarle, by the Rev. Thomas E. Locke, at the residence of Shadrak Bishop. So. Ch., June 17, 1886

DURRETT
Bessie Gantt, d. of Robt. and Eva W. Durrett of Albemarle Co., Va., and Roy W. Follit, by the Rev. T. E. Locke, at Rock Castle. So. Ch., Dec. 7, 1893

DUVAL
Alexander, Esq., and Eliza M., d. of Wm. M. Waller, Esq., by the Rev. Mr. Sale, at Forest Hill, Amherst Co., Va. So. Ch., May 10, 1839

Eloise, and Wm. J. Abrams, by the Rev. J. Hervey Hundley, D.D., in Salem M.E. Church, Gloucester Co., Va. So. Ch., Feb. 2, 1893

James D., and Anna Mills, d. of Capt. Camm Patteson, by the Rev. T. E. Locke, at Sunnyside, Buckingham Co., Va. So. Ch., May 31, 1888

Lucy Waller, and P. Lightfoot Wormely, by the Rev. Dr. Peterkin, in St. James' Church, Richmond, Va. So. Ch., Oct. 23, 1873

Sarah C., d. of Maj. William Duval of Buckingham Co., and Dr. William H. Howard of Hanover, by the Rev. Nicholas H. Cobbs. So. Ch., Nov. 24, 1837

DUVALL
John B., of Charles City Co., and Alice, d. of the late Fendall Gregory, Esq. of Piping Tree, King William Co., by the Rev. S. S. Hepbron, in Acquintan Church, King William Co. So. Ch., Feb. 13, 1890

Mary E., d. of Henry Duvall, Esq., and the Rev. Fleming James, rector of St. Mark's

---

* Written "duPont" in Southern Churchman

MARRIAGE NOTICES IN THE SOUTHERN CHURCHMAN WITH DATES OF PUBLICATION

Church, all of Baltimore, by
the Rev. A. M. Randolph
assisted by the Rev. T. U.
Dudley, in St. Mark's Church,
Baltimore. So. Ch., May 9,
1872

DYKE

Mattie, d. of Thomas L.
Dyke of King and Queen
Co., Va., and Charles
Oliver, by the Rev. J. H.
Hundley, at the residence
of the bride's father.
So. Ch., Feb. 6, 1890

E

EARHART
Ada F., and the Rev. Charles A. Cummings of Duluth, Minn., by the Rt. Rev. H. B. Whipple, D.D., Bishop of Minnesota, at Worthington, Pa. So. Ch., Nov. 2, 1882

EARLE
Fanny Shepherd, only d. of Mrs. William B. Earle and Henry Ennels Wright, all of Queen Anne's Co., Md., by the Ven. R. Bowden Shepherd, Archdeacon of the Diocese of New Jersey, in St. Paul's Church, Centreville, Md. So. Ch., Jan. 25, 1913

EARLY
Peachy H., of Campbell Co., and Annie Lewis Burnley of Albemarle Co., Va., by the Rev. W. W. Kimball, at the residence of the bride's parents. So. Ch., Aug. 14, 1884

EARNEST
Joseph (The Rev.), rector of St. Thomas', and Bettie F., d. of the late Dr. Edward P. Taylor, by the Rev. E. Boyden, in St. Thomas' Church, Orange, Va. So. Ch., Jan. 15, 1852

EASLEY
Bettie R., and Dr. A. Judson Thompson of South Carolina, by the Rev. O. A. Kinsolving, D.D., at "Wilbon", near South Boston, Halifax Co., Va. So. Ch., Oct. 8, 1885

Louisa, and Maurice P. Penick, by the Rev. O. A. Kinsolving, D.D., at "Wilbon", near South Boston, Halifax Co., Va. So. Ch., Oct. 8, 1885

Mattie H., d. of the late Dr. Henry Easley of Halifax, and Wm. E. Owen, by the Rev. O. A. Kinsolving, D.D., in the Presbyterian Church, Black Walnut, Halifax Co., Va. So. Ch., Oct. 23, 1884

R. Holt, of Halifax C.H., and Louise E., eldest d. of the late Judge George H. Gilmer, by the Rev. W. A. Alrich, in Emmanuel Church, Chatham, Pittsylvania Co., Va. So. Ch., Nov. 20, 1879

EAST
Carrie E., of Norfolk, and the Rev. John T. Foster of North Danville, by the Rev. Dr. Barten assisted by the Rev. A. S. Lloyd in St. Luke's Church, Norfolk, Va. So. Ch., Dec. 5, 1889

EASTBURN
Manton (The Rt. Rev.), D.D., Bishop of Massachusetts, and Mary J., d. of George E. Head, Esq., by the Rev. John Cotton Smith, in Trinity Church, Boston, Mass. So. Ch., Feb. 8, 1856

EASTER
Geo. W. (The Rev.), of Baltimore, Md., and Rosa MacMurdo of Richmond, Va., by the Rev. Geo. Woolbridge, D.D., at Ashland, Hanover Co., Va. So. Ch., Mar. 21, 1867

Geo. W. (The Rev.), rector of Hungars Parish, Northampton Co., Va., and Olivia, d. of Joseph H. Harrison of Talbot Co., Md.

MARRIAGE NOTICES IN THE SOUTHERN CHURCHMAN WITH DATES OF PUBLICATION

by the Rev. Ernest McGill, in Christ Church, St. Michael's, Talbot Co., Md. So. Ch., Oct. 20, 1887

EASTMAN
Alice L., only d. of the Hon. C. Eastman, and E. B. Jones of Washington, Rappahannock Co., Va., by the Rev. C. C. Pearson, near Point Pleasant, W.Va. So. Ch., Dec. 10, 1891

EASTWOOD
Cora Maupin, of Portsmouth, Va., and Leigh Powell of Richmond, s. of the officiating clergyman, the Rev. J. D. Powell, assisted by the Rev. O. S. Barton, D.D., in St. John's Church, Portsmouth. So. Ch., Nov. 2, 1882

ECHOLS
M. Alice, d. of the late Capt. Edward Echols of Rockbridge Co., Va., and Arthur E. Sherwood of Clifton Forge, Va., formerly of Derbyshire, England, by the Rev. D. W. Shanks, at Mountain Home, Va. So. Ch., Jan. 8, 1880

ECKSTORM
Henry, and Mary Bendert of Kent Island, Md., by the Rev. P. D. Thompson, at the residence of Frederick Fondelheight, Kent Island, Md. So. Ch., Jan. 12, 1888

EDDINS
T. J. D., of Greene Co., and Caroline C. Barksdale of Albemarle, by the Rev. R. K. Meade. So. Ch., Dec. 20, 1839

EDEY
Arthur H., of South Carolina, and Elvira A. Wheatly of Virginia, by the Rev. C. Y. Steptoe, in Christ Church, Culpeper Co., So. Ch., Aug. 21, 1873

EDLOE
Elizabeth E., d. of William Edloe, Esq. of Williamsburg, Va., and John R. Armistead of Petersburg, Va., by the Rev. Wm. Hodges. So. Ch., Dec. 22, 1837

EDMISTON
Matthew (Dr.), and Ella Bennett, d. of the late Col. Alfred Jackson of C.S.A., and Mrs. Mary Jackson, by the Rev. T. H. Lacy, in St. Paul's Church, Weston, W.Va. So. Ch., May 15, 1890

EDMISTONE
Fannie, d. of Judge Edmistone of Weston, W.Va., and the Rev. George M. Fleming of the Presbyterian Church, by the Rev. W. H. H. Powers, in St. Paul's Church, Weston, W.Va. So. Ch., Dec. 25, 1879

EDMOND
Julia W., d. of the late Horace P. Edmond, and Dinwiddie Johnston Luckett of Rockville, Md., by the Rev. James W. Morris, at the residence of her aunt, Miss Woodbridge. So. Ch., June 24, 1911

Martha A., youngest d. of Robert Edmond, Esq., and Geo. N. Woodbridge, by the Rev. George Woodbridge, in the Monumental Church, Richmond, Va. So. Ch., Dec. 15, 1870

EDMONDS
Helen M., and Eliss Gray, both of Fauquier, by the Rev. Jno. Lindsay, rector of St. James' Church, Warrenton, in Fauquier Co., Va. So. Ch., Dec. 7, 1871

MARRIAGE NOTICES IN THE SOUTHERN CHURCHMAN WITH DATES OF PUBLICATION

Philip M., of Fauquier Co., and Selina M. Slade of Fairfax Co., by the Rev. Jno. McGill, at "The Falls" Church. So. Ch., Nov. 1, 1877

Tazwell, and C. B. Shearman, all of Lancaster, by the Rev. H. L. Derby, at the residence of Thomas Smither, Kilmarnock, Lancaster, Va. So. Ch., Jan. 31, 1878

EDMONDSON
Robert H., and M. Loulie Cosby, d. of Dabney Cosby, Sr., Esq., by the Rev. O. A. Kinsolving, D.D., in St. John's Church, Halifax C. H. So. Ch., Oct. 23, 1884

Sue H., d. of Maj. H. A. Edmondson, and Henry Edmunds, by the Rev. O. A. Kinsolving, in St. John's Church, Halifax C. H., Va. So. Ch., Oct. 18, 1883

EDMUND
Horace P., and Sarah E. Woodbridge, eldest d. of the officiating clergyman, by the Rev. Geo. Woodbridge, D.D., in Monumental Church, Richmond. So. Ch., Nov. 19, 1858

EDMUNDS
Henry, and Sue H., d. of Maj. H. A. Edmondson, by the Rev. O. A. Kinsolving, in St. John's Church, Halifax C. H., Va. So. Ch., Oct. 18, 1883

Martha Jane, and Richard H. Barrack, all of Westmoreland Co., Va., by the Rev. T. E. Locke. So. Ch., Sept. 7, 1860

Nannie L., d. of Mrs. Mildred L. and John R. Edmunds, Esq., and Dr. John C. Coleman, by the Rev. John Grammer, at Redfield, Halifax Co. So. Ch., Feb. 15, 1861

Sally, d. of John R. Edmonds of Halifax Co., Va., and Robert Hubard, Jr. of Buckingham Co., Va., by the Rev. Edmund W. Hubard, at Redfield. So. Ch., Nov. 10, 1870

EDWARDS
A. A. (Dr.), and Sally H. Carter, by the Rev. Edmund Withers, at Fleet's Bay, Lancaster Co., Va. So. Ch., Aug. 18, 1853

Chas. G. (Dr.), of Leesburg, Va., and Ida A. Perkins of Louisville, d. of the officiating minister, the Rev. E. T. Perkins, D.D., in St. Paul's Church, Louisville, Ky. So. Ch., Dec. 19, 1872

Elizabeth Wilmer Wilson, and the Rev. J. H. Townsend, rector of St. John's Church, Camden, N.J., by the Rev. W. T. Snyder, rector of the Church of the Incarnation, at the residence of the bride's brother, Admiral Henry B. Wilson, Washington, D.C. So. Ch., Nov. 10, 1917

Franklin, of Springfield, Ill., and Sarah J. Cleveland of Huntsville, d. of the late Wm. Cleveland of Jefferson Co., Va., by the Rev. Mr. McMasters, at Huntsville, Mo. So. Ch., June 5, 1857

George H. (The Rev.), of New Jersey, and Hariot Taylor, d. of the late D. Boyd Smith of Alexandria, by the Rev. D. J. Edwards, in St. Paul's Church, Alexandria. So. Ch., Nov. 16, 1882

James K., of Washington City, and Sallie M. Hoge of Prince George's Co., Md., by the Rev. W. L. Hyland, D.D., rector assisted by the Rev. J. M. E. McKee of Anacostia

MARRIAGE NOTICES IN THE SOUTHERN CHURCHMAN WITH DATES OF PUBLICATION

Parish, D.C., in St. Barnabas' Chapel, St. John's Parish, Prince George's Co., Md. So. Ch., Aug. 31, 1882

John L., Esq., of Washington, D.C., and Carrie Seymour, d. of the officiating clergyman, the Rev. Dr. Hodges, at Warrenton, N.C. So. Ch., Oct. 18, 1866

Maria Theresa, d. of the late Wm. N. Edwards, Esq., and Dr. Richard W. J'anson of Surry, by the Rev. Edward Valentine Jones, at Rosewood, the residence of Wm. Henry Harrison, Prince George Co., Va. So. Ch., Jan. 20, 1896

Martha A., and Thomas W. Griffith of Loudoun, by the Rev. F. M. Whittle, at the residence of the bride's father in Clarke Co. So. Ch., Feb. 15, 1856

Robert A., Esq., sheriff of Isle of Wight County, and Eva Wills, eldest d. of Henry R. Parker, Esq. of Smithfield, by the Rev. David Barr, in Christ Church, Smithfield. So. Ch., Feb. 2, 1888

Thos. W., Jr., and Lily Southgate Rust, all of Loudoun Co., by the Rev. H. B. Lee assisted by the Rev. R. T. Davis, D.D., at Rockland, the home of the bride, near Leesburg, Va. So. Ch., Sept. 19, 1889

EELS
Annie Powers, d. of the Rev. Edward Eels, and Stanislaus P. Franchot, by the Rev. Edward Eels assisted by the Rev. David Barr, in St. Mark's Church, St. Albans, W. Va. So. Ch., May 14, 1874

EFFINGER
Lula L., d. of the late Jacob P. Effinger of Harrisonburg, Va., and Wm. B. Hancock of Winchester, Va., by the Rev. O. S. Bunting, in Emmanuel Church, Harrisonburg, Va. So. Ch., July 5, 1888

EGERTON
Aloerda Stuart, d. of Bessie Stuart and the late R. O. Egerton, and John Stevens Jones, by the Rev. Pembroke W. Reed, rector, in St. John's Church, Petersburg, Va. So. Ch., Feb. 24, 1912

R. O., of Petersburg, Va., and Bessie Stuart Hall, by the Rev. J. K. Mason, at Fredericksburg, Va., at the residence of the bride's father, Horace B. Hall, Esq. So. Ch., May 1, 1884

EGGLESTON
Helen Josephine, eldest d. of Col. W. C. Eggleston of Yallabusha Co., Miss., and Henry R. Jones, formerly of Richmond, Va., by the Rev. E. A. Taylor, at Grenada, Miss. So. Ch., July 28, 1881

Julia B., and W. S. Bryant, of Baltimore, Md., by the Rev. W. M. Walters, at the residence of the bride's father, in Giles Co., Va. So. Ch., Jan. 11, 1883

Louis T., of Giles Co., and Kate L., youngest d. of the late Capt. Winston Radford, by the Rev. E. W. Hubbard, at Ashwood, Bedford Co., Va. So. Ch., Dec. 1, 1887

Mattie, and John A. Cunningham of Richmond, by the Rev. John McGill, at Bell Pre, the residence of the bride's parents. So. Ch., Apr. 10, 1884

Maud, and Conway Barksdale, by the Rev. A. B. Tizzard, in St. John's (Grubb Hill)

MARRIAGE NOTICES IN THE SOUTHERN CHURCHMAN WITH DATES OF PUBLICATION

Church, Amelia Co. So. Ch., Sept. 16, 1886
Wm. M. (Dr.), and Sallie Stuart, d. of the late Gen. Wm. E. Starke of New Orleans, by the Rt. Rev. Bishop Adams, in the Church of the Holy Trinity, Vicksburg, Miss. So. Ch., Dec. 29, 1881

EGLIN
Benjamin, of Washington City, and Nanny, eldest d. of Judge H. W. Thomas, by the Rev. John McGill, at Fairfax Court House. So. Ch., Jan. 2, 1873

EICHELBERGER
Mary Daniels, and Harry Slicer Hedges, M.D., of Moorefield, W.Va., by the Rev. Robt. Douglas Roller, rector at Martinsburg, W.Va. So. Ch., Nov. 6, 1884

ELAM
Kate, youngest d. of A. G. Elam, Esq., of Chesterfield Co., Va., and Samuel R. Perkins of Richmond, by the Rev. A. B. Tizzard, at the residence of the bride's parents. So. Ch., Sept. 9, 1880

ELEY
Nannie T., d. of Benjamin C. Eley, and Arthur J. Pinner, all of Chuckatuck, Va., by the Rev. Douglass Hooff, at the residence of the bride's father. So. Ch., Dec. 27, 1883

ELIASON *
Mary M., and Dr. Augustine S. Mason, of Famouth*, Va., by the Rev. O. A. Kinsolving, at "Oakley", Fauquier Co., the residence of Henry G. Dulaney, Esq. So. Ch., Nov. 12, 1858

ELLERSLIE
Agnes Spottiswoode, only d. of the Hon. Anthony Kennedy Ellerslie, Baltimore Co., Md., late United States Senator from Maryland, and the Rev. Hall Harrison, of St. Paul's School, Concord, by the Rt. Rev. The Bishop of Pittsburg, in St. Paul's Church, Baltimore, Md. So. Ch., Nov. 18, 1875

ELLET
Cornelia Daniel, youngest d. of the late Col. Charles Ellet of Pennsylvania, and A. Moore, Jr., of Clarke Co., by the Rev. Edmund Withers, at Norwood, Nelson Co., Va. So. Ch., Sept. 18, 1873

ELLETT
A. L., Jr., of Richmond, Va., and Lucy S. Chilton of Warrenton, Va., by the Rev. George W. Nelson. So. Ch., Jan. 31, 1884
A. L., and Mary S. Fourqurean, by the Rev. A. B. Tizzard, at Winterpock, Chesterfield Co. So. Ch., Sept. 16, 1886

ELLICOTT
Adele, d. of W. H. Ellicott of Baltimore, and the Rev. Isaac Nicholson, rector of St. Mark's Church, Philadelphia, by the Rev. J. S. B. Hodges, in St. Paul's Church, Baltimore. So. Ch., Apr. 29, 1880

ELLIOT
Adam (The Rev.), missionary to the Six Nations Indians, Upper Canada, and Eliza Beulah, third d. of Henry Charles Howells, Esq., formerly of Bristol, England, by the Rev. Dr. Upfold, in Pittsburgh. So. Ch., June 28, 1839

ELLIOTT
Charlotte Barnwell, and Charles

* Given as printed

MARRIAGE NOTICES IN THE SOUTHERN CHURCHMAN WITH DATES OF PUBLICATION

McD. Puckette, by the Rt. Rev. R. W. B Elliott, Bishop of Western Texas, assisted by the Rt. Revs. the Bishop of Tennessee and Mississippi, in St. Paul's-on-the-Mountain, Sewanee, Tenn. So. Ch., Jan. 17, 1884

Eliza A., and J. W. Davis, both of Pittsylvania Co., Va., by the rector, the Rev. C . O. Pruden, in Emmanuel Church, Chatham, Va. So. Ch., Mar. 25, 1886

Grace Hamilton, youngest d. of the late S. C. Elliott of Norfolk, Va., and the Rev. James W. Shields of Richmond, Va., by the Rev. Wm. M. Dame assisted by the Rev. O. S. Barton, in St. Luke's Church, Norfolk, Va. So. Ch., July 22, 1875

Mary, eldest d. of the late John and Catharine Elliott, of Baltimore, and the Rev. Samuel McElwee of Dover, Del. (formerly of Washington, D.C.), by the Rt. Rev. Alfred Lee, D.D., at Wilmington, Del. So. Ch., Dec. 14, 1871

W. Nevin (The Rev.), rector of St. James' Church, Exchange, Penn., s. of Mary C. Elliott, and Hannah Hower Kirkham, by the Rev. J. Henry Lehn, rector of St. John's Church and a classmate of the groom, in St. John's Church, Ashland, Penn. So. Ch., July 30, 1932

ELLIS

Charles, and Mary E., d. of Dr. T. J. Harly, all of Berkeley Co., W.Va., by the Rev. George S. May, at Hedgesville. So. Ch., Nov. 26, 1874

Millie J., d. of the late Col. Thomas J. Ellis, 19th Virginia Infantry, and H. A. Strode, Principal of University High School, by the Rev. H. J. McBryde, in Ascension Church, Amherst C.H., Va. So. Ch., Oct. 31, 1872

Minnie M., and Judge Alexander Stuart Hall, in the Ellis home, "Afton", Buckingham Co., Va. So. Ch., Mar. 14, 1908

Pattie Waller, d. of Charles L. Ellis, and John E. Jackson, by the Rev. A. P. Gray, in Ascension Church, Amherst C.H. So. Ch., Nov. 14, 1889

Rose Garland, of Amherst C. H., Va., and Prof. Wister Archer, by the Rev. W. M. Clark, in Ascension Church, Amherst C. H., Va. So. Ch., Dec. 3, 1885

Wm. T., Esq., of Vicksburg, Miss., and Emily M., d. of C. J. Thompson, Esq. of Louisa Co., Va., by the Rev. J. D. Powell, at "Edgwood", Louisa Co., Va. So. Ch., Sept. 27, 1866

ELLSWORTH

Julie, eldest d. of P. W. Ellsworth, Esq., M.D., and great gr. d. of the late Chief Justice Ellsworth of the U.S. Supreme Court, and Augustus Julian Lyman of Asheville, N.C., youngest s. of the Rt. Rev. Theodore B. Lyman, Bishop of North Carolina, and gr. s. of the late Jacob Albert Merchant of Baltimore, by the Rt. Rev. John Williams, Bishop of Con-

MARRIAGE NOTICES IN THE SOUTHERN CHURCHMAN WITH DATES OF PUBLICATION

necticut, assisted by the father of the bridegroom, at the residence of the bride's father, Hartford, Conn. So. Ch., Dec. 28, 1882

ELLZEY
Alice, third d. of Thomas Ellzey, Esq., and John O. Jordan, Esq. of Richmond, Va., by the Rev. R. T. Davis, at Middleton, Loudon Co., Va. So. Ch., Nov. 6, 1873

Lilly, d. of the late Thomas Ellzey, Esq., and Dr. Rush W. Chancellor of Virginia, by the Rev. John McGill, at Westwood Grove, Loudoun Co., Va. So. Ch., Nov. 30, 1876

Mary, d. of the late Thomas L. Ellzey, and Lyman W. Shepard of Ontario, Canada, by the Rev. R. T. Davis, D.D., at Westwood Grove, Loudoun Co., Va. So. Ch., Oct. 9, 1879

ELY
Annie L., of W. Carrianna, Fla., and E. Winston Henry, Jr. of Charlotte Co., Va., by the Rev. W. T. Saunders of the Episcopal Church, at W. Carrianna, Fla. So. Ch., Jan. 17, 1867

EMERY
Mary Abbot, eldest d. of Charles Emery, Esq. of Dorchester, and the Rev. A. T. Twing, D.D. of New York City, by the Rt. Rev., the Bishop of the Diocese, in St. Mary's Church, Dorchester, Mass. So. Ch., June 22, 1876

EMMEL
Ferdinand, Esq., and Zillah M. Whittle, d. of L. N. Whittle, Esq., by the Rev. Benjamin Johnson, in Christ Church, Macon, Ga. So. Ch., Apr. 23, 1874

ENDERS
Jacob, of Clarke, and Catharine Luke of Snickersville, Loudoun Co., Va., by the Rev. F. M. Whittle, at Snickersville, Loudoun Co., Va. So. Ch., July 7, 1853

ENGLAND
Augusta, d. of the late Joseph T. England, and Charles E. Grimes, Jr., all of Baltimore, by the Rev. Edward H. Ingle, in St. Bartholomew's Church, Baltimore. So. Ch., Feb. 17, 1887

ENGLE
Kline N. d'Aurandt (The Rev.), curate of St. John's, York, Pa., and Caroline Kirkham Dayton, by the Rt. Rev. Wyatt Brown, D.D., Bishop of Harrisburg, assisted by Canon Paul S. Atkins, rector of St. John's, York, Pa., and the Very Rev. Hiram R. Bennett, Dean of St. John's Cathedral, Wilmington, Del., in the Chapel of the Holy Spirit, Bishopscourt, Harrisburg, Pa. So. Ch., Dec. 7, 1935

ENGLISH
W. O., and Jessie Gordon, by the Rev. Grayson Dashiell, at Richmond, Va. So. Ch., Sept. 11, 1879

Wm. O., of Westmoreland, and Bettie, d. of Dr. Wm. F. Gooch of Albemarle, by the Rev. D. C. T. Davis, in the Episcopal Church, Charlottesville. So. Ch., Aug. 12, 1859

ENSLEY
Harriette Saunders, d. of Enoch Ensley of Memphis, and Dr. John Hamilton Potter Hodgson, by the Rev. Telfair Hodgson, in Calvary Church, Memphis, Tenn. So. Ch., Oct. 30, 1890

ENTWISLE
G. Edwin, of Alexandria, and

MARRIAGE NOTICES IN THE SOUTHERN CHURCHMAN WITH DATES OF PUBLICATION

Augusta Skipper of Baltimore Co., Md., by the Rev. D. F. Sprigg, in Grace Church, Alexandria. So. Ch., Dec. 9, 1869
Priscila Richards, d. of James Entwisle, Sr. of Alexandria, Va., and William T. Payne of Georgetown, D.C., by the Rev. D. F. Sprigg, in Grace Church. So. Ch., Dec. 17, 1858

EOFF
John Ravenscroft, Esq., of Hampton, Va., and Eloise Hepburn, eldest d. of the Rev. J. D. Powell, by the Rev. J. D. Powell, rector, in St. John's Church, Portsmouth, Va. So. Ch., June 27, 1889

EPES
Francis W., Esq., and Mrs. Frances Susan Beverly of Nottoway Co., by the Rev. Thomas E. Locke, at Lunenburg, Va. So. Ch., Sept. 20, 1839
Mary R. F., d. of the late Robert Epes, Prince George Co., and John A. Peterson, Jr. of Prince George Co., by the Rev. A. B. Tizzard, at Petersburg, Va. So. Ch., May 18, 1854
Rosa B., d. of Isaac O. Epes, Esq., and William S. Gregory of Lunenburg Co., Va., by the Rev. William Herbert Assheton, at Bellefonte, Nottoway Co., Va. So. Ch., Feb. 16, 1882
Sallie Cabell (Mrs.), d. of the late Gen. B. W. Cabell, and Ashby L. Davis, Esq. of Lunenburg, by the Rev. Thomas Ward White, at Bridgewater, Pittsylvania, Va. So. Ch., Jan. 29, 1864
Thomas G., and Belle G. Neblett, d. of Colin Neblett, Esq., all of Lunenburg Co., Va., by the Rev. L. J. Sothoron, at the residence of the bride's father. So. Ch., June 17, 1875

EPPES
George, of Richmond, and Lizzie R., d. of Mrs. Georgeanna Pollard of King William Co., Va., by the Rev. S. S. Hepbron, at Octogon, the residence of the bride's mother. So. Ch., Nov. 26, 1891
Susan Norfleet, d. of the late Daniel Eppes, Esq., and Lafayette Henry Clay, all of Prince George Co., by the Rev. W. F. Gardiner, Hickory Grove, Prince George Co. So. Ch., Jan. 11, 1872
Tempe W., youngest d. of Dr. W. Eppes, and Price P. Gantt, Esq., by the Rev. S. Ridout, M.D., in Christ Church, St. Ann's Parish, Albemarle Co. So. Ch., Sept. 12, 1867

EPPS
Peter, Esq., and Addie Bryant, by the Rev. James Walter Keeble, at the residence of the bride's father, Prince George Co., Va. So. Ch., Sept. 14, 1876

ESTILL
Reverdy (The Rev.), of Atlanta, Ga., and Edith, d. of F. B. Clagett of Alexandria, by the Rev. R. H. McKim, D.D., in Christ Church, Alexandria. So. Ch., Sept. 24, 1874
Reverdy (The Rev.), rector of Trinity Church, Portsmouth, Va., and Louisa W., d. of Prof. J. Heath Christian, by the Rev. G. W. Dame, in Memorial Church, Baltimore. So. Ch., Dec. 7, 1882

ETHERIDGE
O. M., and Alice May Curtis, by the Rev. John B. Newton,

MARRIAGE NOTICES IN THE SOUTHERN CHURCHMAN WITH DATES OF PUBLICATION

at the residence of Dr. Etheridge, Norfolk Co., Va. So. Ch., June 19, 1884

EUBANK
Arthur Lawrence, of Greensville Co., and Martha Webb Logan, by the Rev. F. A. Juhan, in Greenville, S.C. So. Ch., Feb. 23, 1918
Llewellyn Johnson (Mrs.), of Waco, Tex., and Charles M. Langhorne of Richmond, Va., at Roanoke, Va. So. Ch., Oct. 21, 1911

EUSTACE
Wm. C., of Lancaster Co., and Mary L. Tomlin, d. of the late Williamson Tomlin, Esq., by the Rev. E. C. McGuire. So. Ch., Dec. 15, 1837

EVANS
Annie H., and John H. Farmer, by the Rev. John McNabb, at Onancock, Va. So. Ch., Nov. 1, 1888
DeLancy, of Washington, N.C., and Lizzie M. Jordon of Warrenton, Va., by the Rev. George W. Nelson, in Warrenton, Va. So. Ch., Jan. 1, 1885
Edmonia, second d. of the late H. E. Evans of Clarke Co., Va., and J. Pollard Bowin of Galveston, Tex., by the Rev. Jas. R. Jones, in Christ Church, Millwood, Clarke Co. So. Ch., Oct. 2, 1873
James, Surgeon C.S.A., of Marion Dist., So. Ca.,*and M. Antoinette, d. of Wm. A. Powell, Esq. of Leesburg, Va., by the Rev. J. D. Powell, at Richmond City. So. Ch., Jan. 11, 1865

James Daniel, of Philadelphia, and Helen Lowndes, youngest d. of the late Dr. St. Julian Revenel, by the Rev. John Kershaw, D.D., rector of St. Michael's Church, at home, Charleston, S. C. So. Ch., Apr. 27, 1907
Mary F., and Judge William Dillard, both of Amherst Co., Va., by the Rev. A. P. Gray, at "Grand Oaks", the residence of the bride's father, Amherst Co. So. Ch., Mar. 24, 1892
Otto L., of Amherst Courthouse, and Mary E., d. of the late Maj. Peyton Randolph, by the Rev. G. H. Norton of Alexandria. So. Ch., Dec. 17, 1891
Victoria Ellen, and Edwin Augustus Morse, by the Rev. R. A. Castleman, at Cople Rectory, Hague, Westmoreland Co., Va. So. Ch., Mar. 3, 1892

EVENS
Sallie W., d. of the late Dr. F. Evens, and Y. Evens Booker, all of Amelia Co., by the Rev. P. F. Berkeley, at the residence of the bride's uncle, George Wiley, in Amelia Co. So. Ch., June 5, 1884

EVERETT
Louise Montague, and Charles Landon Scott, all of Albemarle, by the Rev. W. H. Williams, at Belmont, the residence of the bride's mother. So. Ch., Oct. 16, 1879
S. W. (Dr.), of Quincy, Ill., and Mary, d. of the late Dr. Sidney W. Smith, by the Rev. C. B. Dana, at Alexandria. So. Ch., July 16, 1858

* Given as printed

MARRIAGE NOTICES IN THE SOUTHERN CHURCHMAN WITH DATES OF PUBLICATION

William B., III, of Marshall, Va., and Anne D. White of Washington, D.C., by Dean Powell and the Rev. B. D. Chambers, cousin of the bride, in Bethlehem Chapel of the National Cathedral. So. Ch., Apr. 27, 1940

EWART
Terrance J., of Topeka, Kans., and Mary Meade, eldest d. of John Mackey Meade of Topeka, by the Rev. Bishop F. R. Millspaugh assisted by Dean Kay [Miss Meade belongs to the Virginia family and finished her education at Winchester, Va., at the Episcopal Female Institute], in Grace Cathedral, Topeka, Kans. So. Ch., July 24, 1909

EWBANK*
Judith Eleanor, and Jas. A. Bird of Baltimore, by the Rev. Edmund Withers, at South Hill, Essex Co. So. Ch., Dec. 24, 1858
Sarah Virginia*, d. of Joseph Ewbank, and Edgar B. Montague, by the Rev. Edmund Withers, at Nesting, Middlesex Co. So. Ch., Dec. 24, 1858

EWELL
Helen Wood, eldest d. of John S. and Alice J. Ewell of Prince William Co., and Greer R. Gulick of Loudoun Co., by the Rev. A. P. Gray, at "Edge Hill", the residence of the bride's parents. So. Ch., Mar. 18, 1884

EWING
James Alfred, and Anne Maria, d. of the late Thomas Blackburn Washington, Esq. of Claymont, Jefferson Co., W.Va., U.S.A., by the Rev. John Piper assisted by the Rev. E. W. Syle, D.D., at the British Legation, Yedo, Japan, before Sir Harry Parkes, K.C.B. So. Ch., June 19, 1879

EYLER
Armand Tice (The Rev.), Vicar of Christ Church, Valdosta, and St. James' Church, Quitman, Ga., and Mary Adeline, d. of William F. Sheppard of Savannah, Ga., by the Rev. Bishop Reese and the Rev. C. C. J. Carpenter, rector of St. John's Church, in St. John's Church, Savannah, Ga. So. Ch., Mar. 4, 1933

EYSTER
Anne Ambler (Mrs.), and Robert Braden Wright of Williamsport, Md., by her rector, the Rev. Conrad Goodwin, and the Rev. F. W. Ambler of Summerville, S.C., brother of the bride, at the home of the bride, Charles Town, W.Va. So. Ch., Sept. 3, 1921

* Given as printed

-F-

FABER
    Joseph W., Esq., and Isabella, d. of Bishop Bowen, by the Rev. W. W. Spear, assistant minister, St. Michael's Church, Charleston, S.C. So. Ch., Apr. 21, 1837

FAHNESTOCK
    Gibson, of New York, and Carolyn Snowden, d. of R. Snowden Andrews, by the Rev. J. H. Eccleston, D.D., Emmanuel Church, Baltimore. So. Ch., June 12, 1884

FAHS
    Chas. F. (Dr.), U.S.N., and Lizzie, eldest d. of Josias Deans, Esq., by the Rev. C. Mann, at Rosewell, the residence of the bride's father, Gloucester Co. So. Ch., July 1, 1859

FAIRBANKS
    Gertrude, second d. of G. R. Fairbanks, Esq., and Horace Drew of Jacksonville, Fla., by the Rt. Rev. H. B. Whipple, D.D., Bishop of Minnesota, assisted by the Rt. Rev. W. M. Green, D.D., Bishop of Mississippi, and the Rev. W. P. DuBose, D.D., in St. Augustine Chapel, University of the South, Sewanee, Tenn. So. Ch., Oct. 21, 1875

    Susan Rainsford, d. of George R. Fairbanks, Esq. of Fernandina, Fla., and the Rev. Charles M. Beckwith of St. Luke's Cathedral, Atlanta, Ga., by the Rt. Rev. J. W. Beckwith, Bishop of Georgia, assisted by the Rt. Rev. Wm. M. Green, Bishop of Mississippi, in St. Augustine's Chapel, University of the South, Sewanee, Tenn. So. Ch., Nov. 6, 1884

FAIRFAX
    A. Carlyle, and Virginia Caroline, d. of Wm. H. Redwood, Esq., all of Baltimore, by the Rev. A. S. Randolph, in Emmanuel Church, Baltimore. So. Ch., May 8, 1873

    Ada S., and Allan M. Chandler, by the Rev. R. M. Chandler, at the residence of W. H. Musser, near Germantown, Montgomery Co., Md. So. Ch., Oct. 27, 1892

    Arthur Percy, youngest s. of the late Capt. Archibald Blair Fairfax, U.S.N., and Nancy Hunter, only d. of Judge John Blair Hoge of Martinsburg, W.Va., by the Rev. Douglas F. Forrest, D.D., in Trinity Church, Washington, D.C. So. Ch., Feb. 9, 1882

    Edith, d. of Dr. Orlando Fairfax, and Dr. J. Jacquelin Moncure, all of Richmond, at the residence of the bride's father, in Richmond. So. Ch., Nov. 15, 1877

    Ella Louise, and Capt. E. L. Wharton, both of Westmoreland, Va., by the Rev. D. M. Wharton. So. Ch., Jan. 13, 1881

MARRIAGE NOTICES IN THE SOUTHERN CHURCHMAN WITH DATES OF PUBLICATION

Emily C., eldest d. of W. M. C. Fairfax, Esq., and the Rev. Francis M. Whittle of Kanawha Co., Va., by the Rev. C. M. Butler, D.D., in Washington, D.C. So. Ch., June 23, 1848

F. (Dr.), of King George Co., and Mary J., d. of James Jett, Esq. of Westmoreland Co., by the Rev. Mr. Dashiell, at Loch Harbour, Westmoreland Co., Va. So. Ch., Dec. 7, 1855

Frederick, and Mary Allen, d. of the late Lt. John A. Cook formerly of the U.S. N., all of Washington, D.C., by the Rev. Isaac Cole, in Baltimore. So. Ch., Jan. 21, 1869

Mary Jett, and Wm. H. Musser of Maryland, by the Rev. D. M. Wharton, in St. James' Church, Westmoreland. So. Ch., June 14, 1883

Wm. F. (Dr.), of Tipton Co., Tenn., and Eleanor Griffith, at Locust Farm, Westmoreland Co. So. Ch., Mar. 14, 1867

FALCONER
J. W., and Carrie C. Jones, both of Tappahannock, Va., by the rector, the Rev. T. W. Roberts, in St. John's Church, Tappahannock, Va. So. Ch., Jan. 3, 1889

FANT
Mary Gertrude, d. of Edward Fant of Fauquier, and Hambleton Shepherd of Irvington, Ga., by the Rev. O. S. Barten, in the Episcopal Church, in Warrenton. So. Ch., Dec. 23, 1859

FARINHOLT
William H., and Eliza Boothe, d. of the Rev. J. Hervey Hundley, rector of Christ Church and St. David's, by the Rev. Beverly D. Tucker assisted by the father of the bride, at Rose Hill, Essex Co., Va. So. Ch., May 4, 1876

FARLAND
Margaret F., d. of Mrs. E. Douglas Farland of Tappahannock, Va., and J. Leslie Hall, Prof. of English and History in the College of William and Mary, in St. John's Church, Tappahannock. So. Ch., June 13, 1889

FARMER
John H., and Annie H. Evans, by the Rev. John McNabb, at Onancock, Va. So. Ch., Nov. 1, 1888

Newton J., of Campbell Co., and Fannie B. Murrell of Bedford Co., by the Rev. W. W. Kimball, near New London, Bedford Co., Va. So. Ch., Mar. 2, 1882

FARNEY
See also RICE, Emma E. (Mrs.)

FARRA
Virginia G., of Mt. Jackson, and Frank P. Irwin of Oil City, Pa., by the Rev. John K. Mason, in St. Andrew's Church, Mt. Jackson, Va. So. Ch., Dec. 5, 1878

FARRAR
Bell, and Robert Montgomery, Esq., both of Point Coupee Parish, La., by the Rev. Jno. R. Lee, at Bleak Hill, the residence of Peter Saunders, Jr., Esq., Franklin Co., Va. So. Ch., Jan. 6,

MARRIAGE NOTICES IN THE SOUTHERN CHURCHMAN WITH DATES OF PUBLICATION

1870
Laura M., d. of B. J. Farrar of Nashville, Tenn., and the Rev. Mayo Cabell Martin, rector of St. Clement's Church, El Paso, Tex., by the Rev. T. F. Martin assisted by the Rev. James R. Winchester and the Rev. W. C. Gray, D.D., in Woodland Street Presbyterian Church, Nashville. So. Ch., Nov. 17, 1892

FARSON
Charles, of the law firm of Holden & Farson, and Effie, d. of Woodson S. Cocke, deceased, by the Rev. Mr. Tupper, in Chicago. So. Ch., Feb. 24, 1881

FASSMAN
Anna W., gr.d. of Mrs. Judge Phelan of "Fatherland Place", East Nashville, and the Rev. J. Green Shackelford, rector, of Trinity Church, Fredericksburg, Va., by the Rev. T. F. Martin, rector assisted by the Rev. M. Cabell Martin, in St. Ann's Church, Nashville, Tenn. So. Ch., Nov. 10, 1887

Maria Shelby, gr. d. of Mrs. and Judge Phelan of "Fatherland", near Nashville, Tenn., and Warner L. Brooke of Norfolk, Va., by the Rev. T. F. Martin, in St. Ann's Church, Nashville. So. Ch., Mar. 6, 1884

FAULCON
Jacob, Esq., and Amelia R. Clarke, by the Rev. William Hodges, in Surry Co., Va. So. Ch., Apr. 30, 1847

FAULCONER
Mabel C., of Low Moor, Va., and Dr. William Lee Meadon of Fauquier Co., Va., by the Rev. P. N. McDonald, at Mont Carbon, W. Va. So. Ch., June 5, 1909

FAULKNER
Charles James, and Susie A., d. of Mr. and Mrs. William H. Harrison, by the Rev. P. F. Berkeley, at the Wigwam, Amelia Co. So. Ch., Oct. 2, 1873

Mai Boyd, of Martinsburg, and H. Douglas Fuller of Winchester, by the Rev. Henry Thomas assisted by the Rev. N. P. Dame, in Trinity Church, Martinsburg, W. Va. So. Ch., May 2, 1889

FAUNT-LE-ROY
Lizzie Randolph, eldest d. of Dr. John Faunt-Le-Roy formerly of Clarke Co., and Dr. S. McGill of Fauquier Co., by the Rev. John McGill, assist. minister at St. James' Church, and the Rev. Richard T. Davis, in St. James' Church, Leesburg. So. Ch., May 11, 1871

FAUNT LE ROY
Sallie E., and Charles E. Sears, at Oakenham, Middlesex Co., Va. So. Ch., July 20, 1876

FAURE
John P., of New York, and Lucy J., d. of the late Gen. Charles G. Halpine, by the Rev. J. B. Perry, in Washington. So. Ch., Oct. 11, 1878

FAUVER
Charles Henry, and Ida J. Alder, both of Blue Ridge,

MARRIAGE NOTICES IN THE SOUTHERN CHURCHMAN WITH DATES OF PUBLICATION

    Jefferson Co., W.Va., by
the Rev. P. D. Thompson,
in Christ Church, Blue
Ridge. So. Ch., June 22,
1893
FAWCETT
    Edward S., and Mary Goulding,
d. of J. Wallace Hooff
of Alexandria, Va., by
the Rev. Geo. H. Norton,
D.D., in St. Paul's
Church, Alexandria, Va.
So. Ch., Oct. 28, 1875
FEARNEYHOUGH
    Sarah E. Lane, d. of Edward
Fearneyhough, Esq. of
Albemarle Co., and
Benjamin Franklin McVeigh
of Alexandria, by the
Rev. S. R. Slack, at
Mt. Airy, Albemarle Co.,
Va. So. Ch., Mar. 3,
1853
FEILD
    Maggie C., d. of George
W. Field, Esq. of
Greenville, Va., and
Cadmus Archer of
Chesterfield, by the
Rev. G. W. S. Parham.
So. Ch., May 23, 1878
    Robert R., and Mary W.,
youngest d. of the
late Maj. John F.
Wren, by the Rev. Dr.
Peterkin, in St.
James' Church, Richmond. So. Ch., Dec.
17, 1885
FELIX
    Francis* Agustie, of San
Andres, Island of Cuba,
and the Rev. Francis
Peck, by the Rev. Mr.
Guion, at Kensington, Conn.
So. Ch., Sept. 17, 1847
FELL
    John H., and Anna,
youngest d. of the late
Bishop Gadsden, by the Rev.
T. F. Gadsden, in Grace
Church, Anderson, S.C.
So. Ch., Sept. 23, 1880
FELTUS
    J. A. V. (Capt.), of Mississippi, and Katherine
Noland, youngest d. of Col.
Edmund Berkeley of Prince
William Co., by the Rev.
B. T. Turner, in St. Paul's
Church, Haymarket, Va. So.
Ch., Oct. 13, 1892
FENDALL
    Benjamin T., of Maryland, and
Florence P. Mason formerly
of Virginia, by the Rev.
W. A. Leonard, D.D., in St.
John's Church, Washington,
D.C. So. Ch., May 12,
1887
    Nannie, d. of T. D. Fendall,
Esq., and John F. Tackett,
all of Alexandria, Va., by
the Rev. J. B. Perry, in
St. Paul's Church, Alexandria, Va. So. Ch., Oct.
25, 1883
FENDLEY
    Harrison W., and Bettie F.
Preston, by the Rev. Henry
Wall, D.D., in St. John's
Church, Richmond. So. Ch.,
Nov. 10, 1870
    Thomas M., of Chesterfield
Co., and Cora Virginia
Lacy of Lynchburg, by the
Rev. T. M. Carson, in St.
Paul's Church, Lynchburg.
So. Ch., Apr. 28, 1870
FENIMORE
    Rebecca C., d. of J. B.
Fenimore, and Edward
Collings, Esq. of Illinois, by the Rev. Jno.
Collins McCabe, D.D., at
Middletown, Del. So. Ch.,
Oct. 21, 1869
FEREBEE
    Nelson McP. (Dr.), U.S.N.,
and Martha T. Gregory, by

* Given as printed

MARRIAGE NOTICES IN THE SOUTHERN CHURCHMAN WITH DATES OF PUBLICATION

the Rev. P. D. Thompson, in Granville Co., N.C. So. Ch., Nov. 28, 1872

FERGUSON
Elizabeth, d. of Austin Ferguson,*Esq., and Mr. Shaw, of Texas, by the Rev. Dr. A. Wade, at Northwood, Charles City Co. So. Ch., Feb. 9, 1871

J. Dudley (The Rev.), rector of Trinity Church, Canaseraga, diocese of Western New York, and Mary, youngest d. of Robert H. Leathem, Esq., by the Rev. Erskine M. Rodman, D.D., rector of Grace Church, Plainfield, N.J. and Dean of Convocation. So. Ch., July 6, 1882

Marianna, and Albert R. Adams, by the Rev. A. Wade, at Longwood, Charles City Co., Va. So. Ch., Dec. 3, 1874

FERGUSSON
Hester V. T., d. of Austin Fergusson,*Esq., and Phillip Tabb of Baltimore by the Rev. A. Wade, at Northwood, Charles City Co., Va. So. Ch., Feb. 24, 1870

FERNALD
Wm. L. (Lt.), of Danville, and J. Alberta, youngest d. of B. F. Gravely, Esq., by the Rev. Geo. W. Dame, at Leatherwood, Henry Co. So. Ch., Mar. 1, 1877

FERRALL
Jennie D., of Prince George, and Charles D. Leiberman of Washington, D.C., by the Rev. Jno. Collins McCabe, D.D., at the residence of the bride's grandfather,

Robert Clark, Esq., in Prince George's Co., Md. Nov. 7, 1867

FERRELL
Chiles Mason, and Katherine Douglas White, by the Rev. D. A. Cunningham, D.D., in the First Presbyterian Church, Wheeling, W.Va. So. Ch., Mar. 12, 1891

FERRIS
Edson E., of New York, and Emily C. B. Magruder of Prince George's Co., Md., by the Rev. J. H. Elliott, D.D., in Ascension Parsonage, Washington, D.C. So. Ch., Jan. 31, 1889

FESSENDEN
John M. (Col.), of Boston, and Mrs. Sarah Richards of Washington, D.C., by the Rev. D. M. Wharton, at Spring Grove, the residence of the bride's mother, Westmoreland, Va. So. Ch., July 16, 1868

FEWELL
Margaret L., and Charles H. Whittington, by the Rev. Jno. McGill, at Manassas. So. Ch., Dec. 21, 1871
See also KENTER, Kate (Mrs.)

FICKLEN
Edmonia Fitz Hugh, d. of the late J. B. Ficklen,*Esq. of Belmont, Stafford Co., Va., and James Parke Corbin of Caroline, by the Rev. E. C. Murdaugh, D.D., in St. George's Church, Fredericksburg, Va. So. Ch., Feb. 22, 1877

Susan M., and Dr. E. J. Harrison of Cumberland Co., Va., at Redhouse, the residence of James B. Ficklen, Buckingham Co. So. Ch., June 11, 1868

FICKLIN

* Given as printed

MARRIAGE NOTICES IN THE SOUTHERN CHURCHMAN WITH DATES OF PUBLICATION

Nannie E., d. of the late J. B. Ficklin,*Esq. of Falmouth, and Daniel Murray Lee, by the Rev. Dr. Murdaugh, in St. George's Church, Fredericksburg, Va. So. Ch., Oct. 21, 1875

William F., Esq., and Julia Bell, second d. of Capt. John L. Stansbury of Snowden, near Fredericksburg, by the Rev. E. C. Murdaugh, D.D., in St. George's Church, Fredericksburg, Va. So. Ch., Oct. 28, 1874

FIELD

Henry (Mrs.), of Chicago, and Thos. Nelson Page of Virginia, by the Rev. Frank Page of Waco, Tex., assisted by the Rev. Mr. Anderson of Elmhurst, Ill. So. Ch., June 15, 1893

Sallie T., of Port Royal, and Hugh Morson of Raleigh, N.C., by the Rev. James E. Poindexter, in St. Peter's Church, Port Royal, Va. So. Ch., May 15, 1879

Sally B., and E. Randolph Phelps, by the Rev. Everard Meade, at Walnut Grove, Greensville Co., Va. So. Ch., Nov. 17, 1892

William P., and Bell F. Jewett, by the rector, in Moore Memorial Church, Richmond. So. Ch., May 2, 1889

FINCH

Elizabeth M., d. of Jas. M. Finch, Esq., and Mann S. Valentine, by the Rev. Preston Nash, at Belle Nemus, Powhatan Co., Va. So. Ch., Dec. 8, 1887

Sally Cary, d. of James M. Finch, Esq., and Mann S. Valentine, Jr. of Richmond, Va., by the Rev. Frank Stringfellow, at Belle Nemus, Powhatan Co., Va. So. Ch., Mar. 23, 1882

FINEGAN

Lillian A., and Henry S. Basset, both of Nashville, Tenn., by the Rev. T. F. Martin, rector of St. Ann's Church, at the residence of the bride's aunt, Mrs. Susan Brandon. So. Ch., Nov. 22, 1888

FINKS

Louisa J., d. of William Finks, Esq., and Col. Robert A. Banks, all of Madison Co., by the Rev. J. Earnest, at Madison Court House. So. Ch., May 7, 1847

FINLEY

John S., and Mary M., d. of Jas. H. Dobbin, by the Rev. Robert A. Gibson, at the residence of the bride's father, in Nottaway Co. So. Ch., Jan. 19, 1871

FISCHER

J. M. (Prof.), of Washington, Ga., and Kate P., d. of Wm. H. McKnight, Esq. of Alexandria, Va., by the Rev. D. F. Sprigg, at Alexandria, Va. So. Ch., Apr. 26, 1866

FISHBURNE

Margaret Lynn, d. of Dr. and Mrs. R. B. Fishburne, and the Rev. John Armstead Welbourn of Tokyo, Japan, by the Rev. Hullihen Burkhardt assisted by the Rev. Edwin B. Niver, D.D., in St. James' Church, Lees-

---

* Given as printed

MARRIAGE NOTICES IN THE SOUTHERN CHURCHMAN WITH DATES OF PUBLICATION

burg, Va. So. Ch., Jan. 2, 1915

FISHER
Andrew C., and Mary A. Washington, by the Rev. Wm. C. Latane, in St. Peter's Church, Oak Grove, Va. So. Ch., Oct. 6, 1881

C. Emma Griswold, d. of Dr. Alexander Fisher, and the Rev. Chas. Edward Cheney, rector of Christ Church, Chicago, by the Rev. N. H. Schenck, rector of Emmanuel Church, Baltimore, in Trinity Church, Chicago. So. Ch., May 4, 1860

Edward H., of Richmond Va., and Lilly, eldest d. of L. P. Daingerfield, Esq., by the Rev. Richard H. Mason, uncle of the bride, at the residence of the bride's father, in Augusta Co. So. Ch., Apr. 23, 1885

Margaret J., d. of James Fisher, Jr. of Richmond and the Rev. Cornelius Walker, by the Rev. Andrew Fisher. So. Ch., Dec. 24, 1847

Mollie L., of Northampton Co., Va., and Dr. James M. McNutt of Bedford, by the Rev. J. B. Craighill, in Christ Church, Eastville. So. Ch., Mar. 24, 1870

Susan, d. of Miers W. Fisher, Esq., and Dr. N. R. Carey, by the Rev. J. M. Chevers, in Northampton Co. So. Ch., Dec. 28, 1855

William H., and Edith, d. of J. Randolph Ridgely, by the Rev. J. H. Eccleston, D.D., in Emmanuel Church, Baltimore. So. Ch., Nov. 27, 1884

FITCHETT
Margaret, and Jno. A. Green, both of Warwick Co., Va., by the Rev. Henry Wall, D.D. So. Ch., Jan. 5, 1871

FITCHETTE
J, Otis, and Mary L. Walker, by the Rev. T. W. Jones, in the Episcopal rectory, Liberty, Va. So. Ch., May 24, 1888

FITZHUGH
Agnes Dade (Daisy), eldest d. of Capt. R. H. and Mrs. Agnes M. Fitzhugh formerly of Virginia, and Edward F. Ayres of Philadelphia, by the Rev. E. H. Ward, rector of Christ Church, at the residence of the bride's parents, Lexington, Ky. So. Ch., Feb. 2, 1893

Betty Ambler, d. of the late William H. Fitzhugh, Esq., and John W. Daniel of Salisbury, N.C., by the Rev. John K. Mason assisted by the Rev. R. J. McBryde, D.D., in St. George's Church, Fredericksburg, Va. So. Ch., Oct. 2, 1884

Catlett C., and Florence R. Grubb, at Cool Water, the residence of the bride's parents, J. F. and K. F. Grubb, Hanover Co. So. Ch., Oct. 26, 1907

Eliza W., d. of the late George Fitzhugh, Esq., and Washington Pearce, Esq., by the Rev. J. Cole, at Milton, Culpeper Co., Va. So. Ch., June 27, 1856

Elizabeth M., and Sanford M. Hutchison, both of Fairfax Co., Va., by the Rev. Frank Page, at the resi-

MARRIAGE NOTICES IN THE SOUTHERN CHURCHMAN WITH DATES OF PUBLICATION

dence of the bride's mother. So. Ch., Jan. 20, 1881

Geo. Warren, and Bettie F. Gray, both of Fauquier, by the Rev. Jno. Lindsay, rector of St. James' Church, Warrenton. So. Ch., Dec. 7, 1871

Georges (The Rev.), and Angeline B. Purnell, by the Rt. Rev. Henry C. Lay, D.D., LL.D., in St. Paul's Church, Berlin, Worcester Co., Md. So. Ch., June 18, 1874

Henry B., Esq., of Sherwood Forest, Stafford Co., Va., and Mary B., d. of John B. Lewis, Esq., by the Rev. Henry Wall, at "Shellfield", Westmoreland Co., Va. So. Ch., Feb. 21, 1867

Jane C. W., d. of Austin Fitzhugh, Esq., and George Turner, all of King George Co., by the Rev. E. B. McGuire, at Mill Bank, the residence of the bride's father. So. Ch., May 30, 1872

Jane Elizabeth, d. of Henry Fitzhugh, Esq., and John Tayloe, Jr., Esq. of "Cloverdale", King George Co., Va., by the Rev. Henry Wall, at "Sherwood Forest", Stafford Co., Va. So. Ch., Jan. 17, 1867

Lola H., d. of Henry Fitzhugh, Esq. of Sherwood Forest, and L. C. Mitchell of Lancaster Co., Va., by the Rev. R. J. McBryde, at the residence of John Taylor, Esq., Fredericksburg, Va. So. Ch., Jan. 11, 1883

Lucretia, d. of the late Norman R. Fitzhugh of Alexandria, and John Marshall of Markham, by the Rev. James T. Johnson, in St. Paul's Church, Alexandria, Va. So. Ch., Feb. 16, 1854

Mary Francis, d. of the late Dr. George Fitzhugh of King George Co., Va., and John Seib, U.S. Topographical Engineer, by the Rev. E. C. McGuire, D.D. So. Ch., Nov. 23, 1854

Nannie M. Baron, of Culpeper, Va., and Washington F. Peace of Warrenton, Va., by the Rev. C. O. Pruden, at the residence of the bride's brother, Wm. F. Fitzhugh, in Pittsylvania Co., Va. So. Ch., Feb. 19, 1885

Nannie Mayo, d. of R. H. and Agnes Dade Fitzhugh, and W. L. Maclean, at the residence of the bride's father, in Lexington, Ky. So. Ch., Sept. 28, 1893

Parke, of Pittsylvania Co., Va., and Elizabeth, d. of L. W. T. Wickham of Henrico Co., Va., by the Rev. Green Shackelford, at the residence of the bride's father. So. Ch., Jan. 24, 1884

Patrick Henry, of Gloucester Co., and Hannah Maria Colton of Richmond, Va., by the Rev. Wm. H. Hart. So. Ch., Nov. 3, 1837

Sallie, eldest d. of Maj. N. Fitzhugh, and A. A. Preston, Esq. of Charleston, W.Va., by the Rev. C. M. Callaway, rector, assisted by the Rev. Edward Valentine Jones, in

MARRIAGE NOTICES IN THE SOUTHERN CHURCHMAN WITH DATES OF PUBLICATION

burg, Va. So. Ch., Jan. 2, 1915

FISHER

Andrew C., and Mary A. Washington, by the Rev. Wm. C. Latane, in St. Peter's Church, Oak Grove, Va. So. Ch., Oct. 6, 1881

C. Emma Griswold, d. of Dr. Alexander Fisher, and the Rev. Chas. Edward Cheney, rector of Christ Church, Chicago, by the Rev. N. H. Schenck, rector of Emmanuel Church, Baltimore, in Trinity Church, Chicago. So. Ch., May 4, 1860

Edward H., of Richmond Va., and Lilly, eldest d. of L. P. Daingerfield, Esq., by the Rev. Richard H. Mason, uncle of the bride, at the residence of the bride's father, in Augusta Co. So. Ch., Apr. 23, 1885

Margaret J., d. of James Fisher, Jr. of Richmond and the Rev. Cornelius Walker, by the Rev. Andrew Fisher. So. Ch., Dec. 24, 1847

Mollie L., of Northampton Co., Va., and Dr. James M. McNutt of Bedford, by the Rev. J. B. Craighill, in Christ Church, Eastville. So. Ch., Mar. 24, 1870

Susan, d. of Miers W. Fisher, Esq., and Dr. N. R. Carey, by the Rev. J. M. Chevers, in Northampton Co. So. Ch., Dec. 28, 1855

William H., and Edith, d. of J. Randolph Ridgely, by the Rev. J. H. Eccleston, D.D., in Emmanuel Church, Baltimore. So. Ch., Nov. 27, 1884

FITCHETT

Margaret, and Jno. A. Green, both of Warwick Co., Va., by the Rev. Henry Wall, D.D. So. Ch., Jan. 5, 1871

FITCHETTE

J. Otis, and Mary L. Walker, by the Rev. T. W. Jones, in the Episcopal rectory, Liberty, Va. So. Ch., May 24, 1888

FITZHUGH

Agnes Dade (Daisy), eldest d. of Capt. R. H. and Mrs. Agnes M. Fitzhugh formerly of Virginia, and Edward F. Ayres of Philadelphia, by the Rev. E. H. Ward, rector of Christ Church, at the residence of the bride's parents, Lexington, Ky. So. Ch., Feb. 2, 1893

Betty Ambler, d. of the late William H. Fitzhugh, Esq., and John W. Daniel of Salisbury, N.C., by the Rev. John K. Mason assisted by the Rev. R. J. McBryde, D.D., in St. George's Church, Fredericksburg, Va. So. Ch., Oct. 2, 1884

Catlett C., and Florence R. Grubb, at Cool Water, the residence of the bride's parents, J. F. and K. F. Grubb, Hanover Co. So. Ch., Oct. 26, 1907

Eliza W., d. of the late George Fitzhugh, Esq., and Washington Pearce, Esq., by the Rev. J. Cole, at Milton, Culpeper Co., Va. So. Ch., June 27, 1856

Elizabeth M., and Sanford M. Hutchison, both of Fairfax Co., Va., by the Rev. Frank Page, at the resi-

MARRIAGE NOTICES IN THE SOUTHERN CHURCHMAN WITH DATES OF PUBLICATION

dence of the bride's mother. So. Ch., Jan. 20, 1881

Geo. Warren, and Bettie F. Gray, both of Fauquier, by the Rev. Jno. Lindsay, rector of St. James' Church, Warrenton. So. Ch., Dec. 7, 1871

Georges (The Rev.), and Angeline B. Purnell, by the Rt. Rev. Henry C. Lay, D.D., LL.D., in St. Paul's Church, Berlin, Worcester Co., Md. So. Ch., June 18, 1874

Henry B., Esq., of Sherwood Forest, Stafford Co., Va., and Mary B., d. of John B. Lewis, Esq., by the Rev. Henry Wall, at "Shellfield", Westmoreland Co., Va. So. Ch., Feb. 21, 1867

Jane C. W., d. of Austin Fitzhugh, Esq., and George Turner, all of King George Co., by the Rev. E. B. McGuire, at Mill Bank, the residence of the bride's father. So. Ch., May 30, 1872

Jane Elizabeth, d. of Henry Fitzhugh, Esq., and John Tayloe, Jr., Esq. of "Cloverdale", King George Co., Va., by the Rev. Henry Wall, at "Sherwood Forest", Stafford Co., Va. So. Ch., Jan. 17, 1867

Lola H., d. of Henry Fitzhugh, Esq. of Sherwood Forest, and L. C. Mitchell of Lancaster Co., Va., by the Rev. R. J. McBryde, at the residence of John Taylor, Esq., Fredericksburg, Va. So. Ch., Jan. 11, 1883

Lucretia, d. of the late Norman R. Fitzhugh of Alexandria, and John Marshall of Markham, by the Rev. James T. Johnson, in St. Paul's Church, Alexandria, Va. So. Ch., Feb. 16, 1854

Mary Francis, d. of the late Dr. George Fitzhugh of King George Co., Va., and John Seib, U.S. Topographical Engineer, by the Rev. E. C. McGuire, D.D. So. Ch., Nov. 23, 1854

Nannie M. Baron, of Culpeper, Va., and Washington F. Peace of Warrenton, Va., by the Rev. C. O. Pruden, at the residence of the bride's brother, Wm. F. Fitzhugh, in Pittsylvania Co., Va. So. Ch., Feb. 19, 1885

Nannie Mayo, d. of R. H. and Agnes Dade Fitzhugh, and W. L. Maclean, at the residence of the bride's father, in Lexington, Ky. So. Ch., Sept. 28, 1893

Parke, of Pittsylvania Co., Va., and Elizabeth, d. of L. W. T. Wickham of Henrico Co., Va., by the Rev. Green Shackelford, at the residence of the bride's father. So. Ch., Jan. 24, 1884

Patrick Henry, of Gloucester Co., and Hannah Maria Colton of Richmond, Va., by the Rev. Wm. H. Hart. So. Ch., Nov. 3, 1837

Sallie, eldest d. of Maj. N. Fitzhugh, and A. A. Preston, Esq. of Charleston, W.Va., by the Rev. C. M. Callaway, rector, assisted by the Rev. Edward Valentine Jones, in

MARRIAGE NOTICES IN THE SOUTHERN CHURCHMAN WITH DATES OF PUBLICATION

St. John's Church, Charleston, W.Va. So. Ch., Dec. 5, 1872

Sallie R., and James T. Omohundro, both of Pittsylvania Co., Va., by the Rev. C. O. Pruden, in Pittsylvania Co., Va. So. Ch., Jan. 1, 1885

Sarah E., d. of the late Wm. M. Fitzhugh, and Cooke F. Slade, all of Fairfax, Va., by the Rev. Frank Page, in Zion Church, Fairfax Court House. So. Ch., July 21, 1887

Sarah N., d. of Austin W. Fitzhugh, Esq., and the Rev. Edward B. McGuire, by the Rev. T. E. Locke, at Mill Bank, King George Co. So. Ch., July 15, 1869

Wm. H., Jr., Esq., of Fredericksburg, and Mary A., d. of the late Carter H. Harrison of Cumberland, by the Rev. A. M. Randolph, at "Longwood", the residence of the bride's brother, George F. Harrison, Goochland Co., Va. So. Ch., Apr. 1, 1859

FITZSIMONS
Amy Perry, and James Pickens Walker of Barbour Co., W. Va., by the Rev. Thos. P. Baker, at Adam's Run, S.C. So. Ch., Oct. 31, 1908

FLEET
J. Ryland, of King and Queen Co., Va., and Anna, d. of the late William Rutherfoord of Richmond, Va., by the Rev. Joshua Peterkin, D.D., at Richmond, Va. So. Ch., Feb. 12, 1880

FLEMING
A. Walton, of Washington D.C., and Gay Bernard Robertson, by the Rev. S. S. Ware, in St. Peter's Church, Port Royal. So. Ch., Nov. 28, 1891

Charlotte I., and the Rev. William M. Green, by the Rev. Philip B. Wiley, in St. Matthews* Church, Pittsborough. So. Ch., Jan. 8, 1836

George M. (The Rev.), of the Presbyterian Church, and Fannie, d. of Judge Edmistone of Weston, W. Va., by the Rev. W. H. H. Powers, in St. Paul's Church, Weston, W. Va. So. Ch., Dec. 25, 1879

George W., Jr. (Dr.), of Chantilly, and Annie Gordon, d. of Marshall Ambler, Esq. of Lakeland, Louisa Co., Va., by the rector, the Rev. Curtis Grubb, in the Church of Our Savior, St. Martin's Parish, Hanover Co., Va. So. Ch., May 3, 1883

J. Syme, and Bettie Y. Barrett, both of Goochland Co., Va., by the Rev. P. M. Boyden, at Mt. Bernard, Goochland Co., Va. So. Ch., Dec. 2, 1880

R. B. L., of Fauquier Co., and Hariot J. Downman of Warrenton, Va., by the Rev. George W. Nelson, in St. James' Church, Warrenton, Va. So. Ch., Jan. 12, 1882

Sallie E., youngest d. of Tarlton Fleming, Esq. of Mannsville, Goochland Co., Va., and Jesse H. Heath of Petersburg, by the Rev. A. B. Tizzard. So. Ch.,

* Given as printed

MARRIAGE NOTICES IN THE SOUTHERN CHURCHMAN WITH DATES OF PUBLICATION

Dec. 1, 1853
Sallie J., d. of Dr. Geo. Fleming of Hanover, and W. LeRoy Brown of Albemarle Co., by the Rev. C. C. Bitting, at Chantilly, Hanover Co., Va. So. Ch., Nov. 18 1859

T. M. (Dr.), and Anna, d. of the officiating clergyman, the Rev. J. H. Morrison, D.D., at the Rectory, Goochland Co. So. Ch., Jan. 19, 1871

Thomas, and Grace Irwin, at the residence of the bride's father at Alexandria. So. Ch., Dec. 9, 1880

Thomas Mann, M.D., and Virginia K. Hobson, d. of the late John B. Pemberton, all of Goochland Co., Va., by the Rev. Erskine M. Rodman, at Clover Forest. So. Ch., Mar. 13, 1857

FLETCHER
Emily, and Joseph Skelding, at Low Moor, the residence of the bride. So. Ch., Nov. 14, 1889

H. S., of Rappahannock Co., Va., and Mary C., second d. of Col. O.R. Funsten, by the Rev. Jos. R. Jones, at "The Highlands", Clarke Co., Va. So. Ch., Apr. 15, 1869

Indiana, of Amherst, Va., and the Rev. James Henry Williams of New York City, by the Rev. Wm. H. Kinckle, in St. Paul's Church, Lynchburg, Va. So. Ch., Sept. 14, 1865

J. Paul, and Cora De Soisselle Amiss, by the Rev. W. T. Roberts, rector, assisted by the Rev. L. B. Johnston, in Emmanuel Church, Harrisonburg, Va. So. Ch., Jan. 28, 1892

James W., of Rappahannock Co., and Catharine Mackey, eldest d. of John N. Meade, Esq. of Frederick Co., Va., by the Rev. Wm. C. Meredith, at Shady Oak, the residence of the bride's father. So. Ch., Feb. 3, 1870

Mary O., and George W. Kinsey, both of Rappahannock Co., Va., by the Rev. Walter P. Griggs, at "Rose Hill", the residence of the bride's parents. So. Ch., Nov. 29, 1888

William Meade, of Rappahannock Co., and Martha Ball, d. of Aylette Harris Buckner of Rappahannock Co., Va., at the Raleigh Hotel, Washington, D.C. So. Ch., Oct. 10, 1914

FLINT
Catharine M., d. of Thomas Flint, Esq. of Baltimore, and the Rev. Richard Henry Beal, by the Rev. J. M. Jennings, in St. John's Church. So. Ch., Apr. 5, 1839

Pauline, of Madill, Okla., and the Rev. Fred A. Croft, vicar of St. John's Church, Durant, Okla., by the Rt. Rev. Thomas Casady, D.D., Bishop of Oklahoma, in the Bishop's Chapel. So. Ch., Apr. 21, 1934

FLIPPEN
F. P., of Cumberland Co., Va., and Alice S., d. of the late Rev. J. H.

MARRIAGE NOTICES IN THE SOUTHERN CHURCHMAN WITH DATES OF PUBLICATION

Morrison, D.D., of Virginia by Chaplain Wm. F. Morrison, U.S.N., assisted by the Rev. Henry Thomas in St. Peter's Church, Poolesville, Md. So. Ch., Jan. 20, 1887

FLOOD
Mary Walker (Mrs.), and Maj. T. P. Taylor, by the Rev. W. H. Pendleton, in St. Paul's Church, Lynchburg. So. Ch., Apr. 14, 1870

FLOURNOY
David (Dr.), and Mattie D. Bouldin, by the Rev. H. A. Brown, at Roanoke, the residence of Wood Bouldin, Esq., Charlotte Co., Va. So. Ch., Nov. 4, 1869

FLOYD
Mary A., and James A. Wiggins, Madison Co., Ala., by the Rev. Geo. W. Dame, Brookfield, Campbell Co. So. Ch., Sept. 24, 1858

FLYNN
Martha, and James Hulett, by the Rev. Henry F. Sharp, in Frankfort, Ky. So. Ch., Aug. 27, 1874

FOARD
Ella A. B., d. of the late Richard J. Foard, Esq. of Bohemia Manor, and Franklin Platt, Esq. of Newark, Del., by the Rev. Jno. Collins McCabe, D.D., rector of St. Ann's Church, Middletown, Del., in St. Augustine Church, Bohemia Manor, Md. So. Ch., Feb. 3, 1870

FOGG
T. J., and Miss V. M. Lumpkin, both of Essex Co., Va., by the Rev. H. H. Jones. So. Ch., Oct. 29, 1885

FOLLIT
John Lucas, and Bettie Lewis, eldest d. of Dr. Mix, by the Rev. T. E. Locke, at the residence of Dr. Oscar Gunnell Mix, near Warren, Albemarle Co., Va. So. Ch., June 21, 1888

Roy W., and Bessie Gantt, d. of Robt., and Eva W. Durrett of Albemarle Co., Va., by the Rev. T. E. Locke, at Rock Castle. So. Ch., Dec. 7, 1893

Wm., of England, and Florine, d. of Capt. John and Mrs. Eleanor Alexandria, by the Rev. Wm. J. Morton of Richmond, Va., at South Warren, Albemarle Co., Va. So. Ch., June 22, 1893

FONES
George Hamilton, and Mary Susan Reynolds, both of Westmoreland, by the Rev. R. A. Castleman, at Cople Rectory, Hague, Westmoreland Co., Va. So. Ch., Jan. 23, 1890

FONTAINE
Charles H., and Nannie J. North, by the Rev. Albert Walker, at Oak Grove, the residence of Mrs. Parham Moon, in Halifax Co., Va. So. Ch., Apr. 2, 1868

Emilie (Mrs.), and Cyrus S. Gilbert of Newark, Ohio, by the Rev. Francis M. Whittle, at Pocahontas, Goochland Co., Va. So. Ch., July 10, 1851

Lucy D., d. of the late Col. Edmund Fontaine of Beaverdam, and Chiswell Dabney of Pittsylvania, by the Rev. W. A. Alrich, at Beaverdam, Hanover Co., Va. So. Ch., Apr. 10, 1873

MARRIAGE NOTICES IN THE SOUTHERN CHURCHMAN WITH DATES OF PUBLICATION

Richard Morris, and Kate Meade, third d. of the late Lucius H. Minor, all of Hanover Co., Va., by the Rev. W. A. Alrich, in Trinity Church, St. Martin's Parish, Hanover. So. Ch., June 4, 1874

Susan W., d. of the late James Fontaine, Esq. of Hanover, and Berkely Minor, by the Rev. George W. Nelson, at Rock Castle, Hanover Co., Va. So. Ch., Sept. 16, 1875

FOOTE
Jeannie, d. of Frederick Foote, Esq. of Prince William Co., Va., and Dr. R. Stuart Lomax of King George, by the Rev. John Fowles, at Waverley. So. Ch., Dec. 7, 1855

M. Dora, d. of the late Frederick Foote, and Wm. L. Heuser, all of Prince William Co., Va., by the Rev. A. P. Gray, at Waverly, the residence of the bride's family. So. Ch., Jan. 4, 1883

FORBES
Alfred Thornton, and Mary Bastable, both of Fauquier, by the Rev. John Lindsay, D.D., at "Montevideo", Fauqier Co., Va. So. Ch., Nov. 5, 1885

Kate Ramsay, d. of John Murray Forbes, Esq. of Fauquier, and Otto Wittichen late of Germany, now of Prince William Co., Va., by the Rev. Philip Slaughter, D.D. assisted by the Rev. John S. Lindsay, in St. James' Church, Warrenton, Va. So. Ch., Nov. 28, 1878

Laura V., d. of Dr. J. T. Forbes, and Harrison Robertson, Esq. of Danville, Va., by the Rev. Wm. M. Dame, at the residence of the bride's father, Baltimore, Md. So. Ch., Nov. 18, 1880

FORCTER
Charles W., of South Carolina, and Fairinda C. Payne, by the Rev. Dr. Pendleton, in Grace Church, Lexington, Va. So. Ch., Nov. 27, 1879

FORD
Lizzie Allen, d. of the late N. W. Ford, Esq., and George V. Moncure, Jr., all of Stafford Co., Va., by the Rev. John Moncure assisted by the Rev. G. H. Appleton, in Aquia Church, Va. So. Ch., Jan. 11, 1883

FOREMAN
Margaret (Mrs.), and Grafton Hilliard, both of Smithfield, by the Rev. Alex. Jones. So. Ch., Dec. 15, 1837

FORREST
Agnes Lyle, d. of the late Samuel Forrest, Purser U. S. Navy, and John Montgomery Macfarland, by the Rev. Wm. H. Meado, at the residence of the bride's mother, in Charlestown, W.Va. So. Ch., Jan. 2, 1879

Douglas French (The Rev.), and Sallie W., d. of William Rutherford, Esq. of Richmond, Va., by the Rev. J. Peterkin, D.D., at the residence of the bride's father. So. Ch., Jan. 30, 1873

FORSYTH

MARRIAGE NOTICES IN THE SOUTHERN CHURCHMAN WITH DATES OF PUBLICATION

Robert W. (The Rev.), and Madge W., d. of Mrs. M. L. Smith, by the Rev. Dr. Walker assisted by the Rev. Peregrine Wroth, in Emmanuel Church, Theological Seminary of Virginia. So. Ch., Dec. 20, 1883

FOSTER
Anna S., second d. of Thomas Foster, and Philip Rahm, all of Richmond, by the Rev. Geo. Woodbridge, in Monumental Church. So. Ch., Mar. 1, 1861

Corrie G., and Robert E. Peyton, Jr., by the Rev. Jno. McGill, in Trinity Church, Salem, Fauquier. So. Ch., Apr. 28, 1870

Elleanor, d. of Dr. Patrick H. Foster, and Dr. John T. Jackson of Prince Edward, by the Rev. J. T. Clark, at Red Level, Halifax Co., Va. So. Ch., Mar. 21, 1856

James J., of Richmond, Va., and Rebecca Porterfield, second d. of Edwin M. Taylor, Esq., by the Rev. James A. Latane, at the residence of the bride's father, Staunton, Va. So. Ch., Dec. 5, 1867

John H., and Lizzie, d. of Mrs. Mildred and the late Dr. Wm. C. Stribling, all of Fauquier Co., by the Rev. H. B. Lee, at "Hartlands", Fauquier Co. So. Ch., June 30, 1881

John T. (The Rev.), of North Danville, and Carrie E. East of Norfolk, by the Rev. Dr. Barten assisted by the Rev. A. S. Lloyd, in St. Luke's Church, Norfolk. So. Ch., Dec. 5, 1889

Richard F., of Richmond, and Fannie C., d. of Dr. F. Stribling of Staunton, Va., by the Rev. Mr. Latane, at the residence of the bride's father. So. Ch., Mar. 2, 1860

Robert B., of Charlotte Co., Va., and Martha E., d. of Thos. A. Spears, Esq. of Powhatan Co., by the Rev. A. B. Tizzard, at Alexandria, Va. So. Ch., Nov. 7, 1856

FOURQUREAN
Joseph M., of Richmond, Va., and Martha C. Pendleton, formerly of Richmond, by the Rev. Robert Lowry, in Trinity Church, Elizabeth, N.J. So. Ch., Mar. 2, 1871

Mary S., and A. L. Ellett, by the Rev. A. B. Tizzard, at Winterpock, Chesterfield Co. So. Ch., Sept. 16, 1886

FOWLE
Bernard Hooe, and Millie Goodwin, eldest d. of Mrs. Kate C. Dorsey, by the Rev. A. R. Stuart, D.D., at the residence of the bride's mother, Georgetown, D.C. So. Ch., Nov. 7 and 28, 1889

Ellen Bernard, d. of the late George D. Fowle of Alexandria, and Gen. Fitzhugh Lee, of Richlands, Va., by the Rev. Geo. H.

MARRIAGE NOTICES IN THE SOUTHERN CHURCHMAN WITH DATES OF PUBLICATION

Norton, D.D., at the residence of the bride's uncle, Philip B. Hooe, Esq. So. Ch., Apr. 27, 1871

Ellen M., d. of the late Robert Rollins Fowle of Fairfax Co., Va., and Wm. Campbell of Charles Town, W.Va., by the Rev. S. A. Wallis, in St. Paul's Church, Alexandria, Va. So. Ch., June 12, 1890

Fannie Lightfoot, d. of William H. Fowle, Esq. of Alexandria, and Bladen Tasker Tayloe of King George, by the Rev. D. Francis Sprigg, rector of Grace Church. So. Ch., May 6, 1859

FOWTHES
Solomon, and Sophia Johnson, both of Petersburg, Va., by the Rev. Luther W. Doggett, at the residence of Joseph Carr. So. Ch., Oct. 3, 1889

FOX
Elizabeth, d. of John Fox, Sr., and Dr. Wm. Cabell Moore of Washington City, at the home of the bride's parents at Big Stone Gap, Va. So. Ch., Sept. 21, 1907

James McCaw, and Jennie D. Hall, both of Richmond, Va., by the Rev. D. F. Sprigg assisted by the Rev. Joshua Peterkin, D.D., in Moore Memorial Church. So. Ch., Sept. 27, 1883

FRANCE
Minnie H., and Henry F. Vass, by the Rev. Geo. W. Dame, in the Church of the Epiphany, Danville. So. Ch., Feb. 13, 1879

FRANCHOT
Stanislaus P., and Annie Powers, d. of the officiating clergyman, the Rev. Edward Eells, assisted by the Rev. David Barr, in St. Mark's Church, St. Albans, W.Va. So. Ch., May 14, 1874

FRANCIS
John T. (Dr.), of Norfolk, and Mildred, d. of the late Charles Carter Lee of Windsor, Powhatan Co., by the Rev. Martin Johnson, in St. Luke's Church, Powhatan Co. So. Ch., Feb. 23, 1888

Lewis, of Edina, and Susanna Freeman, by the Rev. John Seys, in Richmond, Va. So. Ch., Sept. 9, 1836

FRANKLIN
B. (The Rev. Dr.), of Shrewsbury, N.J., and Lucy M. Shiff of Baltimore, by the Rt. Rev. John Scarborough, D.D., Bishop of New Jersey, assisted by the Rev. William Kirkus of Baltimore, in Grace Church, Baltimore. So. Ch., Sept. 23, 1886

Thomas W., Esq., of Stafford Co., and Gissie Stuart, second d. of Dr. Horace Ashton of King George Co., Va., by the Rev. James W. Shields, at "Bleak Hill", the residence of the bride's father. So. Ch., Jan. 17, 1878

FRASER
Phyllis, and the Rev. Edwin J. Anderson, priest-in-charge of St. Aidan's Church, Blue Island, Ill. So. Ch., Sept. 17, 1938

FRAZER
Louisa A., and Lawrence Sanford, both of Spotsylvania Co., Va., by the Rev. Wm. W. Greene. So.

MARRIAGE NOTICES IN THE SOUTHERN CHURCHMAN WITH DATES OF PUBLICATION

Ch., Nov. 27, 1863

FREAR
  Dennis H., of Dinwiddie, and Ann E., d. of B. W. Johnson, by the Rev. Mr. Ambler, in Brunswick. So. Ch., Jan. 18, 1856

FRED
  Frank L., of Indian Territory, and Eugenia C., d. of the late George D. Smith of Loudoun Co., Va., by the Rev. Carter Page, at Locust Grove, the home of the bride. So. Ch., Oct. 20, 1887

FREDRICKS
  Charles D., of New York, and M. Louise Barrow of Woodbridge, by the Rev. A. G. Shears of New Haven, at Woodbridge, N. J. So. Ch., Nov. 13, 1857

FREDERICKSON
  Myra Shelby, d. of John H. Frederickson of Oklahoma City, and the Rev. Phineas McCray Casady, vicar of St. Paul's Church, Clinton, Okla., eldest s. of the Bishop of Oklahoma, by the Rt. Rev. Thomas Casady, S.T.D., in St. Paul's Cathedral, Oklahoma City. So. Ch., June 22, 1935

FREELAND
  Carter Penn, third d. of John Freeland, Esq. of Richmond, Va., and H. L. D. Lewis, Esq. of Clarke Co., Va., by the Rev. Dr. Minnigerode, in St. Paul's Church, Richmond, Va. So. Ch., May 11, 1871

FREEMAN
  Ada C., d. of Dr. John H. Freeman of Rockbridge Co., Va., and John A. Blume of Bath Co., Va., by the Rev. Dr. W. N. Pendleton, at Spring Bower, the residence of the bride's father. So. Ch., Nov. 9, 1871

  Andrew F. (The Rev.), rector of Christ Church, Little Rock, Ark., and Susan Elizabeth, eldest d. of James Dunlop of Little Rock, Ark., by the Rev. C. J. Gibson, at the residence of James Dunlop, Esq. So. Ch., July 23, 1858

  De Graphen, of West Point, Miss., and Jane Seymore Koon of Falls Church, by the Rev. J. C. Koon, at the residence of the bride's mother, near Falls Church, Va. So. Ch., Oct. 7, 1886

  J. J., of North Carolina, and Mary E. Diggs of Mathews Co., Va., by the Rev. Mr. Carraway, at Oakland. So. Ch., Feb. 1, 1856

  Jennie H., d. of the Hon. A. A. Freeman, and Abram L. Koon, by the Rev. Frank Page assisted by the Rev. John C. Fair, in Old Falls Church, Fairfax Co., Va. So. Ch., Apr. 24, 1884

  Lewis H., of Loudoun Co., and Hattie L., second d. of Hon. R. H. Cockerille of Fairfax Co., by the Rev. John McGill, at "Avon", the residence of the bride's father. So. Ch., Sept. 20, 1877

  Methven T., of Macon, Ga., and Elizabeth Kendall, eldest d. of

- 174 -

MARRIAGE NOTICES IN THE SOUTHERN CHURCHMAN WITH DATES OF PUBLICATION

the late John M. Strother, by the Rev. Joshua Peterkin, D.D., in St. James' Church, So. Ch., Feb. 4, 1886
Susanna, and Lewis Francis of Edina, by the Rev. John Seys, in Richmond, Va. So. Ch., Sept. 9, 1836
Wm. M., and Mrs. Jane E. Quillen, both of Berlin, Worcester Co., Md., by the Rev. George S. Fitzhugh. So. Ch., Jan. 15, 1874

FRENCH
Helen Bland, d. of Col. S. Bassett French of Whitby, Chesterfield Co., and Robert B. Batte of Prince George Co., by the Rev. Churchill J. Gibson, rector of Grace Church, Petersburg, in Meade Memorial Church, Manchester. So. Ch., Dec. 25, 1873
Mary E., and R. M. Jones, Esq., both of Stafford Co., Va., by the Rev. J. M. Meredith, at the residence of the bride's father. So. Ch., Feb. 1, 1872

FRETWELL
V. L. (Mrs.), of Albemarle, and David Hansbrough, by the Rev. Wm. N. Nelson assisted by the Rev. D. T. C. Davis. So. Ch., Mar. 14, 1862

FRIEND
Charles, Esq., and Catherine B., d. of Dr. Jesse Cole, by the Rev. Mr. Hodges, at Williamsburg. So. Ch., June 14, 1839
Jane Minge, second d. of the late Charles Friend, Esq. of Prince George Co., Va., and the Rev. Philip D. Stephenson, pastor of the Presbyterian Church, Trenton, Tenn, by the Rev. Churchill J. Gibson, in the Chapel of the Union Theological Seminary, Prince Edward Co. So. Ch., Jan. 13, 1876
Nannie C. (Mrs.), of Port Royal, Va., and Maj. W. J. Johnson of Richmond, by the Rev. Geo. Woodbridge, D.D. of Richmond, Va., at the residence of Mrs. Tiffey, Washington, D.C. So. Ch., Oct. 26, 1876
Natalie Churchill, d. of the late Charles Friend, Esq. of Petersburg, Va., and James Henderson Smith, by the Rev. Churchill J. Gibson, D.D., of Petersburg, at the residence of the bride's great uncle, the Rev. J. M. Atkinson, D.D., Hampden Sidney* College, Va. So. Ch., Dec. 26, 1878
T. E., Esq., and Ella F. Armstrong, by the Rev. Edward Valentine Jones, in St. John's Church, City Point, Va. So. Ch., Jan. 20, 1876
Wm. (The Rev.), of Port Royal, and Anna C., d. of Richard V. Tiffey, Esq., by the Rev. George Woodbridge of Richmond, at Office Hall, King George Co. So. Ch., Feb. 27, 1857

FRISTOE
Kate, and Ferdinand Dennis, both of Rappahannock Co., by the Rev. R. T. Brown, of the Episcopal Church,

* Given as printed

MARRIAGE NOTICES IN THE SOUTHERN CHURCHMAN WITH DATES OF PUBLICATION

at Sperryville, Rappahannock Co., Va. So. Ch., Feb. 20, 1868

FROST
Louisa T., of Orange, and the Rev. R. T. Davis, rector of St. James' Parish, Leesburg, by the Rev. Theodore Carson, at "Mt. Sharon", the residence of Mrs. Taliaferro, in Orange Co., Va. So. Ch., Oct. 21, 1869

FRY
F. T. (Dr.), and Sarah, d. of the late Dr. Francis Boykin, by the Rev. Dr. Peterkin, in St. James' Church, Richmond. So. Ch., Dec. 2, 1875

Margaret Douglas, d. of Col. W. H. Fry, proprietor of Coyners Springs, and J. Bunting Jr., by the Rev. O. S. Bunting, at the residence of the bride's father. So. Ch., Nov. 17, 1887

Philip, of Orange Court House, and Mary Oden of Martinsburg, by the Rev. R. R. Mason assisted by the Rev. W. C. Meredith, D.D., in Christ Church, Winchester, Va. So. Ch., Aug. 21, 1873

FUGITT
J. Preston (The Rev.), and Mary H. Williams, d. of the late Col. Ruffin of North Carolina, by the Rt. Rev. W. R. Whittingham, Bishop of Maryland, in Mt. Calvary Church, Baltimore City. So. Ch., Sept. 30, 1859

FULLER
H. Douglas, of Winchester, and Mai Boyd Faulker of Martinsburg, by the Rev. Henry Thomas assisted by the Rev. N. P. Dame, in Trinity Church, Martinsburg, W.Va. So. Ch., May 2, 1889

Janet Potter, d. of Judge Thomas C. Fuller, and Muse Braxton, by the Rev. Dr. Daniel Elliott, at the residence of the bride's parents, Raleigh, N.C. So. Ch., Nov. 9, 1893

FULLERTON
George H. (The Rev.), of Philadelphia, and Rebekah Daingerfield, d. of the late Daniel Boyd Smith of Alexandria, Va., by the Rev. George H. Norton, at the residence of the bride's father. So. Ch., Jan. 3, 1884

Rosa, and the Rt. Rev. Peter Trimble Rowe, D.D., Bishop of Alaska, by the Rev. E. V. Shayler, in St. Mark's Church, Seattle, Wash. So. Ch., Nov. 20, 1915

FULTON
Elizabeth, d. of Robert Fulton, and John Peyton Brown, all of Charlestown, by the Rev. Alex Jones. So. Ch., Dec. 15, 1837

J. Mattie, and Richard D. Batte, by the Rev. J. G. Downman, in all Saints' Church, Richmond. So. Ch., Nov. 3, 1892

John H. (Judge), and Cynthia, d. of the late Ephraim McGavock, all of Wytheville, Va., by the Rev. Robb White, at the residence of the bride's mother. So. Ch., June 15, 1876

FUNKHAUSER
Albertus A., and Annie M., d. of Dr. P. H. H. Koontz, all of Shenandoah Co., by the

MARRIAGE NOTICES IN THE SOUTHERN CHURCHMAN WITH DATES OF PUBLICATION

Rev. W. W. Walker, at the residence of the bride's father, Mt. Jackson, Va. So. Ch., Jan. 6, 1881

FUNSTEN

Annie, youngest d. of the late Col. Oliver R. Funsten, and Robert C. Jett of Mount Jackson, Va., by the Rev. R. Allen Castleman assisted by the Rev. James B. Funsten, in Emmanuel Church, Greenwood. So. Ch., Nov. 20, 1890

Cary, d. of the late Col. David Funsten, of Alexandria, Va., and J. A. Slaughter of Little Rock, Ark., by the Rev. Wm. M. Dame, in St. Luke's Church, Norfolk. So. Ch., Dec. 24, 1874

Fannie S., d. of Col. Oliver R. and Mary Funsten of Clarke Co., Va., and the Rev. Robert Allen Castleman, by the Rev. J. B. Funsten assisted by the Rev. George S. Somerville, at Mirador, near Greenwood Depot, Albemarle Co., Va. So. Ch., Dec. 23, 1886

J. B. (The Rev.), and Ida Vivian, youngest d. of W. C. and Eliza Pratt, by the Rov. J. E. Poindexter, at Camden, near Port Royal, Caroline Co., Va. So. Ch., Dec. 23, 1886

Lizzie Lee, d. of the late Col. David Funsten, and Edwin S. Hinks of Baltimore, by the Rev. W. M. Dame assisted by the Rev. George M. Funsten, in Memorial Church, Baltimore. So. Ch., May 8, 1884

Margaret Byrd, d. of Col. O. R. Funsten, and Thomas Semmes of Alexandria, Va., by the Rev. James B. Funsten, at "Mirador", Albemarle Co., Va. So. Ch., June 9, 1887

Mary C., second d. of Col. O. R. Funsten, and H. S. Fletcher of Rappahannock Co., Va., by the Rev. Jos. R. Jones, at "The Highlands", Clarke Co., Va. So. Ch., Apr. 15, 1869

Oliver Ridgeway, of Clarke Co., and Lucy Pratt, d. of Geo. W. Lewis of Westmoreland Co., Va., by the Rev. T. E. Locke, at Claymont, the residence of the bride's father. So. Ch., June 18, 1868

Susie M., d. of the late Col. David Funsten, and the Rev. W. M. Dame, by the Rev. G. H. Norton, in the Chapel of the Episcopal Theological Seminary, near Alexandria, Va. So. Ch., Oct. 14, 1869

William Pratt, and Margaret Louise Gildey, by the Rt. Rev. James Bowen Funsten, Bishop of Idaho, in St. John's Episcopal Church, Washington, D.C. So. Ch., Aug. 10, 1918

FURR

Ann Maria, and Samuel T. Marts, both of Clarke Co., Va., by the Rev. F. M. Whittle. So. Ch., Aug. 3, 1854

FYFFE

Elizabeth, and Henry C. Tolle, by the Rev. T. E. Locke, in St. John's

MARRIAGE NOTICES IN THE SOUTHERN CHURCHMAN WITH DATES OF PUBLICATION

Church, Scottsville, Va.
So. Ch., Nov. 27, 1890
Mary Gertrude, of Pooles-
Ville, and Benjamin
Franklin Pope of

Baltimore, by the Rev.
Walter P. Griggs, in St.
Peter's Church, Poolesville,
Md. So. Ch., June 30,
1892

-G-

GADSEN
Anna, youngest d. of the late Bishop Gadsen, and John H. Fell, by the Rev. T. F. Gadsen, in Grace Church, at Anderson, S.C. So. Ch., Sept. 23, 1880

Edward Miles, of Washington, D.C., and Lella Page, d. of the late Rev. Dr. Pentleton, by the Rev. Frank Page and the Rev. Robert J. McBryde, D.D., rector of the parish, at the residence of the bride's family, Lexington, Va. So. Ch., Feb. 19, 1885

Jane D., d. of the late Rev. C. E. Gadsen, and Wm. Sayre formerly of Virginia, by the Rev. T. F. Gadsden, at Mt. Pleasant, Charleston, S.C. So. Ch., Nov. 28, 1872

GAILLARD
Arthur P., of South Carolina, and Leize Palmer of Richmond, Va., by the Rev. J. Peterkin, at the residence of W. Fletcher Richardson. So. Ch., Jan. 23, 1890

Margaret E., d. of the late Theodore Gaillard of St. John's Berkley,*and the Rev. J. Mercier Green, rector of Christ Church, Charleston, by the Rev. W. B. W. Howe, in St. Philip's Church, Charleston. So. Ch., Nov. 11, 1859

GAIN
John Henry, of Loudoun, and Euphemia Kate Mutter of Scotland, by the Rev. A. B. Tizzard, at Mantua, Chesterfield Co., Va. So. Ch., Mar. 13, 1879

* Located in South Carolina

GAINES
Anderson Q., and Margaret T. Nolan, by the Rev. Henry T. Sharp, at Frankfort, Ky. So. Ch., Sept. 3, 1874

Grenville, and Elizabeth T. Harris, both of Warrenton, Va., by the Rev. George W. Nelson, in St. James' Church, Warrenton, Va. So. Ch., Nov. 23, 1882

GALATTI
Edward, Esq., of Louisville, Ky., and Lucy H., only d. of James H. Rogers, Esq. of Charleston, by the Rev. R. A. Cobbs, rector, in St. John's Church, Charleston, W.Va. So. Ch., Mar. 26, 1885

GALE
Wm. B., and V. Clarissa, d. of Charles H. Kehr, all of Abingdon, by the Rev. Edward H. Ingle, at Abingdon. So. Ch., Aug. 9, 1866

William D., of Tennessee, and Catherine of New Orleans, second d. of the Rt. Rev. L. Polk, D.D., Bishop of Louisiana, by the Rt. Rev. L. Polk, D.D., Bishop of Louisiana, in Trinity Church, New Orleans. So. Ch., Jan. 14, 1859

GALLAGHER
Fannie, of Mason Co., W.Va., and Francis Radford, Esq. of Meigs Co., Ohio, by the Rev. T. H. Lacy, at the residence of the bride's mother, West Columbia, W.Va. So. Ch., Feb. 1, 1877

GALLOWAY
Lucinda Louisa, youngest d.

MARRIAGE NOTICES IN THE SOUTHERN CHURCHMAN WITH DATES OF PUBLICATION

of Thos. S. Galloway, Esq. of Rockingham Co., N.C., and Dr. A. B. Johns, Jr., by the Rev. Jno. R. Lee, at Mount Vue. So. Ch., Nov. 18, 1869

GALT
Jean Malcolm, d. of the late Wm. Galt of Glenarvon, Fluvanna Co., and Alexander F. Kinney of Staunton, by the Rev. Mr. Latane, in Trinity Church, Staunton. So. Ch., Nov. 5, 1858

Lucy M., d. of the late William Galt, Esq. of Fluvanna, and Capt. Wm. H. Holman of Buckingham, by the Rev. James A. Latane, at Staunton. So. Ch., July 15, 1864

Susan W., d. of William R. Galt, Esq., and Dr. Alexander Duane of New York City, by the Rev. Beverly D. Tucker assisted by the Rev. Alexander Galt, brother of the bride, at the residence of the bride's parents. So. Ch., July 30, 1891

GALUSHA
John W., and Kate Hunt, by the Rev. Robert R. Claiborne, at the residence of the bride's father, in Sussex Co. So. Ch., Jan. 1, 1880

M. H. (The Rev.), and Sallie A., only d. of the late John Hardaway, Esq., by the Rev. W. H. Platt and the Rev. C. J. Gibson, at Mt. Pleasant, Dinwiddie Co., Va., the residence of the bride's relatives. So. Ch., July 6, 1860

GAMBLE
George Peterkin, and Mary Lyon, d. of Judge and Mrs. David Gardiner Tyler, by the Rev. Cary Gambel of the Church of the Nativity, Huntsville, Ala., and the Rev. E. W. Gamble of St. Paul's Church, Selma, Ala., father and uncle of the groom, at "Sherwood Forest", the home of the bride's parents, in Charles City Co., Va. So. Ch., Oct. 23, 1926

Richard W., of Savannah, Ga., and Mary Louisa, d. of Maj. R. C. Taylor of Norfolk, Va., by the Rev. A. S. Lloyd, rector of St. Luke's Episcopal Church, Norfolk, Va. So. Ch., June 16, 1892

GAMBRILL
Philip Doddridge, Esq., of Marysville, Ky., and Jane, youngest d. of the late George Kincheloe of Parkersburg, Va., by the Rev. W. L. Hyland, rector of Trinity Parish, Wood Co., Va. So. Ch., Dec. 28, 1860

GANNAWAY
Hattie, d. of Wm. E. Gannaway, Esq., and J. N. Crute, all of Buckingham Co., Va., by the Rev. A. S. Lloyd, in St. Peter's Church, Curdsville, Va. So. Ch., Dec. 20, 1883

GANTT
Fannie P., d. of Dr. John Gantt of Albemarle Co., and John R. Mitchell, Esq. of Washington, by the Rev. Wm. N. Nelson, at Albemarle Co., Va. So. Ch., Oct. 26, 1854

Price P., Esq., and Tempe W., youngest d. of Dr. W. Eppes, by the Rev. S. Ridout, M.D., in Christ Church, St. Ann's Parish, Albemarle Co. So. Ch., Sept. 12, 1867

MARRIAGE NOTICES IN THE SOUTHERN CHURCHMAN WITH DATES OF PUBLICATION

Thomas P., and Nannie P. Horseley, by the Rev. George Somerville, in Christ Church, Norwood, Nelson Co. So. Ch., July 9, 1891

Thomas Perkins, and Lizzie Rose, eldest d. of the late Charles Scott, all of Albemarle Co., by the Rev. T. E. Leake. So. Ch., Nov. 19, 1874

GARBEE
Robert E., and Jannet T. Withers, both of Campbell Co., Va., by the Rev. W. W. Kimball, at the home of the bride. So. Ch., Oct. 6, 1881

GARBER
William H., Esq., of Staunton, and Sallie Tyler Tebbs of Loudoun Co., by the Rev. O. A. Kinsolving, in Emanuel Church, Middleburg. So. Ch., Nov. 23, 1854

GARBEY
William Sandford, and Alice Cabell, d. of the late Samuel M. Bailey, all of Covington, Ky., by the Rev. Frank Woods Baker assisted by the Rev. Robert A. Gibson, of Cincinnati. So. Ch., Dec. 15, 1887

GARDNER
Albert G., of Alexandria Co., and Louisa V. McRae of Fairfax Co., by the Rev. W. F. Lockwood, in the Chapel of the Theological Seminary of Virginia. So. Ch., Jan. 18, 1851

Delaware B., and Omega, eldest d. of John A. McMinn of Hanover Co., by the Rev. S. S. Hepbron, at the residence of the bride's father. So. Ch., Dec. 1, 1887

J. F. (Dr.), and Alice J., eldest d. of John W. Mosby, Esq., all of Nelson Co., Va., by the Rev. T. F. Martin, at "Valley Farm", Nelson Co., Va. So. Ch., Jan. 24, 1867

John F. (Dr.), of Richmond, and Isabella C., d. of F. K. Nelson, Esq., by the Rev. E. Borden, at Clover Fields, Albemarle Co. So. Ch., Oct. 31, 1856

Nannie, and Robert N. Anderson, by the Rev. T. G. Dashiell, at Hunter's Hill, the residence of Geo. Gardner, Louisa Co. So. Ch., Dec. 3, 1868

Nina Nelson, and Clare H. Walpole, by the Rev. Mr. Clark, at Meadowbrook, Nelson Co., Va. So. Ch., Sept. 18, 1884

Sarah Ann, d. of the late Sylvester Gardner, Esq., both of Manlius, N.Y., and the Rev. Samuel G. Appleton, by the Rev. S. C. Millett, at Manlius, N.Y. So. Ch., Oct. 11, 1839

W. F. (The Rev.), and Harriet C., d. of John H. Rowland, Esq., of Norfolk, by the Rev. Mr. Barton, in Christ Church, Norfolk, Va. So. Ch., Apr. 30, 1868

GARLAND
Anne (Mrs.), and the Rev. J. H. D. Wingfield, D.D., in St. Paul's Church, Petersburg. So. Ch., June 25, 1874

Ella Rose, d. of S. Meredith Garland, Esq., of Amherst C. H., and Henry W. Mills, Esq. of Nelson Co., by the Rev. J. D. Powell, at the residence of her father. So. Ch., Aug. 6, 1858

MARRIAGE NOTICES IN THE SOUTHERN CHURCHMAN WITH DATES OF PUBLICATION

James V., and Nannie T., only
d. of Samuel Lyell, Esq.,
all of Richmond Co., Va.,
by the Rev. Beverly D.
Tucker, at Forest Home, residence of the bride's father.
So. Ch., Dec. 28, 1876

Mary Shepherd, third d. of
William H. Garland, and
John Hattersley of the
Albemarle Soap Stone
Company, by the Rev.
Thomas E. Locke, at Ivy
Hill. So. Ch., Oct. 28,
1886

GARLICK
Dora B., d. of the late
Branton Garlick, and
Francis A. Dickens, Jr.,
by the Rev. J. J. Anderson,
at Waterloo, New Kent Co.,
Va. So. Ch., Jan. 10,
1878

GARNER
Robert, and Mary Ann Ingram,
both of Lancaster Co., by
the Rev. H. L. Derby, at
the residence of William
M. Kirk, Lancaster, Va. So.
Ch., Aug. 5, 1875

GARNETT
B., Esq., of Essex, Va., and
Ann E. Gatewood, by the
Rev. Mr. Carraway, at Linden
Hall, the residence of the
bride's father, Middlesex.
So. Ch., Dec. 4, 1863

Edith G., and D. F. Goss, by
the Rev. Everard Meade, in
St. John's Church, Tappahannock, Essex Co., Va. So.
Ch., Nov. 25, 1880

Emily D., of Putnam Co., W.Va.,
and Henry M. Day, Esq.
of New York City, by the
Rev. T. H. Lacy, at Buffalo,
W.Va. So. Ch., Apr. 26,
1877

Emma B., and R. Channing
Beale of Corsicana, Tex.,
by the Rev. G. W. Beale,
in King George Co., Va.
So. Ch., Feb. 19, 1874

James M., Pres. of St.
John's College, Annapolis,
Md., and Kate Huntington,
second d. of Maj. Burr P.
Noland of Loudoun, by the
Rev. Wm. M. Dame, at
Middleburg, Va. So. Ch.,
Apr. 27, 1871

Louis A., of San Francisco,
Cal., and Maria Champe,
d. of Muscoe Garnett, Esq.
of Essex Co., Va., by the
Rev. C. B. Dana, in Christ
Church, Alexandria, Va.
So. Ch., Mar. 31, 1853

M., of Virginia, and Maj. William Bassinger of Savannah,
by the Rev. P. F. Berkeley,*
in Prince Edward Co. So.
Ch., Nov. 29, 1866

Maria Champe, d. of Muscoe
Garnett, Esq. of Essex
Co., Va., and Louis A.
Garnett of San Francisco,
Cal., by the Rev. C. B.
Dana, in Christ Church,
Alexandria, Va. So. Ch.,
Mar. 31, 1853

Mary Champe, d. of Edgar H.
Garnett, and William Mason
McCarty, all of Richmond,
Va., by the Rev. Joshua
Peterkin, D.D. So. Ch.,
Aug. 18, 1881

Nannie D., and James C.
Henly, by the Rev. E.
Meade, in Rappahannock
Church, Essex Co., Va. So.
Ch., Jan. 8, 1885

S. B., of King George Co.,
Va., and Robert L. Randolph
of Baltimore, by the Rev.
Percy Gordon, D.D., of
Alabama, at the residence
of the bride's mother. So.
Ch., Jan. 22, 1880

Theodore S., and Emily Eyre,

* Given as printed

MARRIAGE NOTICES IN THE SOUTHERN CHURCHMAN WITH DATES OF PUBLICATION

youngest d. of Judge Richard H. Baker, by the Rev. N. A. Okeson, at the residence of R. H. Baker, Esq., in Norfolk. So. Ch., Nov. 13, 1873

Theodore S., and Mrs. Louisa Bowdoin, at Oak Grove, Northampton Co., Va. So. Ch., Aug. 13, 1885

GARRETT

Benj. F., and Pattie, d. of the late Alec. Cunningham, Esq., by the Rev. Geo. W. Dame, D.D., at Okolona, Pittsylvania Co. So. Ch., Dec. 12, 1889

Bessie J., d. of William H. Garrett of Blandford, and James W. Wells of Petersburg, Va., by the Rev. W. R. Savage, at Blandford, near Petersburg, Va. So. Ch., Oct. 5, 1893

Charles C., of Wilmington, Del., and Belle, d. of Charles S. Lee, Esq. of Clarke Co., Va., by the Rev. T. F. Martin, at "The Anchorage", the residence of the bride's father. So. Ch., Dec. 30, 1875

Laura Cunningham, d. of B. F. Garrett of Danville, Va., and Basil Kirke Watkins of Danville. Va., at 1008 Park Ave., Richmond, Va., the home of the Rev. W. M. Clark, the officiating clergyman. So. Ch., Jan. 4, 1913

GARRISON

John Marion, Director of Religious Education, Diocese of Southwestern Va., and Elizabeth Cheedell Porter, Teacher in Mission St. Stephen's, at Nora, Dickenson Co., in the Church of the Holy Comforter, Sumter, S.C. So. Ch., June 13, 1931

GARTH

Cellie, d. of Wm. Garth of Albemarle Co., Va., and Marshall Walker of Memphis, Tenn., by the Rev. D. C. T. Davie, at Birdwood, Albemarle Co., Va. So. Ch., Dec. 12, 1856

GARY

Mary E., d. of Adolphus Gary, Esq., and Herbert Jones, by the Rev. A. B. Tizzard, in Trinity Church, Clover Hill Pits.* So. Ch., Feb. 12, 1880

Minnie S., and John W. Bidgood, by the Rev. J. B. Craighill, at Suffolk, Va. So. Ch., Jan. 21, 1875

GASKINS

Wm. E. (Col.), and Hannah G. Blake, both of Fauquier Co., Va., by the Rev. Jno. S. Lindsay, at the bride's residence. So. Ch., Dec. 25, 1873

GASSAWAY

Alexander A., s. of John H. Gassaway, Esq. of Montgomery Co., Md., and Bettie F., only d. of the late Norman Miller of Martinsburg, W.Va., and gr.d. of the late Maj. Thomas Briscoe of Charles Town, W.Va., by the Rev. R. T. Brown, at Glenwood, Montgomery Co., Md. So. Ch., Mar. 2, 1882

Maria F. (Mrs.), oldest d. of Samuel C. Greenhow,** Esq. of Alexandria, Va., and the Rev. Francis M. Baker, rector of Grace Church, by the Rev. Dr. Peterkin, in St. James' Church, Richmond, Va. So. Ch., Nov. 30, 1871

---

* Given as printed
** A notice appears in the issue of Nov. 16, 1871, identical with this except that "Greenhow" is written "Greenwood"

MARRIAGE NOTICES IN THE SOUTHERN CHURCHMAN WITH DATES OF PUBLICATION

GATES
    Harold J., of Louisville, Ky., and Jane, d. of Col. Newland T. DePauw by the Rev. E. S. Hinks, at the home of the bride, "Waverley Farms", Haymarket, Va. So. Ch., Dec. 28, 1912

    Louisa W., d. of Joseph J. Gates, Esq. of Chesterfield Co., Va., and H. T. Sellers, C.S.A., by the Rev. A. B. Tizzard. So. Ch., Feb. 8, 1865

GATEWOOD
    Ann E., and B. Garnett, Esq. of Essex, Va., by the Rev. Mr. Carraway, at Linden Hall, the residence of the bride's father, Middlesex. So. Ch., Dec. 4, 1863

    Charles M., of Middlesex Co., and E. Harvie, d. of James R. Micow,* Esq. of Essex Co., Va., by the Rev. H. T. W. Temple assisted by the Rev. John P. McGuire, in St. John's Church, Tappahannock, Essex Co., Va. So. Ch., Aug. 9, 1866

    Ellen, and Thomas E. Sutton, both of Urbanna, Middlesex Co., Va., by the Rev. Thomas G. Addison, at Washington City. So. Ch., July 9, 1868

    Susan C., and Granville S. Healey, by the Rev. J. Hervey Hundley, in Christ Church, Middlesex Co. So. Ch., Oct. 30, 1873

    Wm. R., M.D., of Middlesex Co., Va., and Mary Mandville, d. of the late Col. Ro. McCandlish of Williamsburg, Va., by the Rev. E. C. Murdaugh, in Trinity Church, Fredericksburg, Va. So. Ch., Dec. 4, 1879

GATRIGHT**
    Sallie (Mrs.), and Ed. W. Moore of Washington, D.C., by the Rev. J. E. Hammond, at the residence of the bride's father, Wm. Martin, Manchester, Va. So. Ch., May 8, 1873

GAYLE
    Josiah P., of Spotsylvania, and Lottie E. Leavell, by the Rev. E. Meade, at Oakland, Essex Co., Va., the residence of the bride's mother, Mrs. Mary C. Leavell. So. Ch., Dec. 19, 1878

GAYLES
    Essie, youngest d. of Col. Levin Gayles, and William H. Wilson, Jr., all of Portsmouth, by the Rev. Thos. A. Tidball, in Trinity Church, Portsmouth. So. Ch., Nov. 8, 1877

GEARHART
    Kenneth M. (The Rev.). rector of Christ Church, Danville, Pa., and Phyllis G. Diotterick of Berwick, Pa., by Canon Clifford W. French, in Keferstein Memorial Chapel of the Holy Spirit, Bishopcourt, Harrisburg. So. Ch., Jan. 23, 1937

GEE
    Ann C., youngest d. of James Gee, deceased, and Capt. John A. Harris, by the Rev. William B. Rowzie, at Lunenburg Co. So. Ch., Sept. 18, 1835

    Martha, d. of the late Benjamin Gee of Lunenburg, and John H. McKinny, by the Rev. T. E. Locke. So. Ch., May 24, 1839

GEMENY
    Carrie E., and Morley Norris,

** Possibly Gathright, but given as printed
* Given as printed

MARRIAGE NOTICES IN THE SOUTHERN CHURCHMAN WITH DATES OF PUBLICATION

by the Rev. R. Castleman, at the residence of the bride's parents, near Kinsale, Westmoreland Co., Va. So. Ch., Jan. 10, 1889

GERHART
Willis (The Rev.), rector of the Church of the Heavenly Rest, Abilene, Tex., and Eleanor Deuel, by the Rt. Rev. E. Cecil Seaman, in Grace and Holy Trinity Cathedral, Kansas City. So. Ch., Nov. 16, 1940

GIBBONEY
Annie V., and Decatur B. Bear of Rockingham Co., Va., both deaf mutes, by the Rev. Job Turner assisted by the Rev. Mr. Preston as interpreter, at Wytheville, Va. So. Ch., Feb. 25, 1886

GIBBONS
Geo. A. (The Rev.), of Maryland, and Laura Whaley of Fairfax Co., Va., by the Rev. Wm. Sparrow, D.D., assisted by the Rev. John Ambler, in St. John's Church, West End. So. Ch., July 17, 1873
Margaret N., and Prof. James L. Cabell, by the Rev. R. K. Meade, at University of Virginia. So. Ch., Feb. 15, 1839

GIBBS
E. A. (Dr.), of Lexington, Va., and Mary L. Lewis, by the Rev. Dr. Wheat, at the residence of the bride's father, Lt. Gov. John F. Lewis, Lynwood, Rockingham Co., Va. So. Ch., Oct. 30 and Nov. 6, 1884
G. S. (The Rev.), of Virginia, now rector of St. Luke's and Mrs. Fannie Nowlan, by the Rev. J. C. Adams, in St. Luke's Church, Hot Springs, Ark. So. Ch., Jan. 25, 1883
Henry, and Rosa Bocock, both of Albemarle, by the Rev. T. E. Locke, at Woodstock, the residence of the bride's mother. So. Ch., Sept. 26, 1889
Jane, of South Carolina, and Addison T. Munsell, principal of Fleetwood Academy, by the Rev. T. F. Martin, at Fleetwood, Nelson Co., Va. So. Ch., Apr. 10, 1857

GIBSON
Adeline Douglas, only child and d. of W. D. Gibson, and Robert B. Green of Halifax, by the Rev. C. J. Gibson, in St. Paul's Church, Richmond. So. Ch., Dec. 17, 1858
Anna, and Dr. John Mitchell Willis, United States Army, by the Rev. John S. Gibson, D.D. and the Rev. Andrew J. Willis, fathers respectively of the bride and groom, in Trinity Church, Huntington, W.Va. So. Ch., July 15, 1911
Churchill Jones, and Gay Blackford Lloyd, by the Rt. Rev. Arthur Seldon Lloyd, D.D., assisted by the Rt. Rev. Robert Atkinson Gibson, D.D., in Christ Church, Short Hills, N.J. So. Ch., July 12, 1913
David E., of Kentucky, and Lily D. Mower, d. of the officiating minister, the Rev. B. F. Mower, at Florence, Ala. So. Ch., Nov. 28, 1878
Elizabeth M., oldest d. of the officiating minister, and VanLear Perry, M.D., of Cumberland, Md., by the Rev. C. J. Gibson, in Grace Church, Petersburg, Va. So. Ch.,

MARRIAGE NOTICES IN THE SOUTHERN CHURCHMAN WITH DATES OF PUBLICATION

Oct. 2, 1863
Fannie E., of Prince George's Co., Md., and James L. White, Esq. of Washington, D.C., by the Rev. John Collins McCabe, D.D., in St. Luke's Church, Bladensburg, Md. So. Ch., Oct. 25, 1866

George, Esq., and Mrs. A. E. J. Bartlett, by the Rev. C. Gibson, in Grace Church, Petersburg, Va. So. Ch., Aug. 29, 1856

Henrietta, d. of Dr. William Gibson, and John T. Cole, all of Alexandria, Va., by the Rev. Nathaniel L. Briggs, at the parsonage of Emmanuel P.E. Church, in Philadelphia. So. Ch., Feb. 8, 1883

Henry, of Roanoke, and Nannie May, d. of E. G. Higginbotham* of Henrico Co., by the Rev. Wyllys Rede, at the residence of Mrs. Bayley, Richmond, Va. So. Ch., Jan. 12, 1888

James Davis (The Rev.), rector of Christ Church, Wellsburg, W.Va., and Mary Leadbeater, by the Rev. John S. Gibson assisted by Wm. J. Morton, in Christ Church, Alexandria, Va. So. Ch., Dec. 18, 1909

John L. (The Rev.), of Bellaire, Ohio, and Ilicia W., d. of Dr. James M. Davis, by the Rev. Isaac Gibson assisted by the Rev. Wm. H. Neilson, Jr.,and the Rt. Rev.,the Bishop of the Diocese of New Jersey, in Trenton, at the residence of the bride's mother. So. Ch., Jan. 20, 1800

John T., Jr., and Bessie Thomson, d. of Wm. H. Moore, all of Jefferson Co., W.Va., by the Rev. Wm. H. Meade, in Zion Church, at Charles Town. So. Ch., Jan. 3, 1878

Lizzie Leigh, and J. Cowan Venable of Christiansburg, Ky., by the Rev. Bishop C. C. Penick, at Louisville, Ky. So. Ch., July 3, 1890

Mary Carr, d. of John Gibson of Chestnut Hill, Baltimore Co., Md., and the Rev. Richard Clarence Hall, pastor of St. Timothy's Church, New York, by the Rt. Rev. Bishop of Maryland, in St. John's Church, Huntington, near Baltimore. So. Ch., Jan. 13, 1860

Mary Walker, d. of the officiating clergyman, and Capt. J. H. Chamberlayne of the Norfolk "Virginian", by the Rev. Churchill Gibson assisted by the Rev. Robert Gibson, in Grace Church, Petersburg, Va. So. Ch., Oct. 30, 1873

Minnie Maude, d. of Dr. William Gibson of Alexandria, and David J. Howell of Charles Town, W.Va., by the Rev. Henderson Suter assisted by the Rev. Dr. Meade, in Christ Church, Alexandria. So. Ch., Dec. 10, 1885

P. H., Esq., and Margaret S., d. of John Williams, Esq., all of Petersburg, by the Rev. Churchill Gibson, in St. James' Church. So. Ch., Mar. 14, 1856

Robert A. (The Rev.), and Susan B., fourth d. of Hon. Alexandria H. H. Stuart, by the Rev. Churchill J. Gibson, in Trinity Church, Staunton. So. Ch., Nov. 28, 1872

S. Malone, of Galveston, Tex., and Marion Grieve, d. of the

* Given as printed

MARRIAGE NOTICES IN THE SOUTHERN CHURCHMAN WITH DATES OF PUBLICATION

late Dr. George S. Blackie of Nashville, Tenn., by the Rev. M. Cabell Martin, in St. Peter's Church, Nashville, Tenn. So. Ch., Dec. 2, 1886

T. Dabney, and Mary Long, oldest d. of Thomas W. Jones, all of Culpeper Co., Va., by the Rev. John McGill, at Mountain View, the residence of the bride's parents. So. Ch., Sept. 1, 1881

GIDDINGS
Ellen R., d. of Col. Wm. Giddings of Loudoun Co., and the Rev. Wm. G. Hammond of Middleburg, Va., by the Rev. Carter Page assisted by the Rev. Nelson Head, D.D. of the Methodist Church, in Christ Church, Geresville. So. Ch., July 17, 1890

GIFFORD
Charles L. C., of Newark, and Helen M., second d. of William Murray of Powhatan Co., Va., by the Rev. P. F. Berkeley, at Edge Hill. So. Ch., May 15, 1851

GILBERT
Cyrus S., of Newark, Ohio, and Mrs. Emilie Fontaine, by the Rev. Francis M. Whittle, at Pocahontas, Goochland Co., Va. So. Ch., July 10, 1851

GILDERSLEEVE
B. L. (Prof.), and E. F., d. of Raleigh Colston, Esq. of Albemarle, Va., by the Rev. Wm. M. Nelson, at Hillandale, Albemarle Co., Va. So. Ch., Oct. 4, 1866

GILDEY
Margaret Louise, and William Pratt Funsten, by the Rt. Rev. James Bowen Funsten, Bishop of Idaho, in St. John's Episcopal Church, Washington, D.C. So. Ch., Aug. 10, 1918

GILES
Lewis B., and Mrs. Elizabeth Perrin formerly of England, by the Rev. H. L. Derby, in St. Paul's Church, Suffolk, Va. So. Ch., Nov. 7, 1889

T. Peyton, gr.s. of the late Hon. Wm. B. Giles of Virginia, and Kate Randolph, d. of Egbert G. Leigh, Esq., by the Rev. A. B. Tizzard, at Richmond, Va. So. Ch., Sept. 22, 1887

GILL
Herbert A., and Monita W. Smith, both of Washington, by the Rev. E. H. Ingle, in Ascension Church, Washington, D.C. So. Ch., July 6, 1882

Mary Ellen, youngest d. of Thomas Gill of Berkeley Co., and Doct.* J. Brown of Gerrardstown, by the Rev. J. E. Jackson, of Winchester. So. Ch., Dec. 8, 1837

GILLESPIE
Frances E., of Jackson, Miss., and the Rev. Wallace Carnaham of San Marcos, Tex., at Jackson, Miss. So. Ch., Nov. 23, 1907

GILLIAM
Charles Macalister, of Petersburg, Va., and Blanche Bragg, d. of Andrew Syme, by the Rev. M. M. Marshall, D.D., in Christ Church, Raleigh, N.C. So. Ch., Jan. 19, 1893

Hannah S., d. of Col. J. S. Gilliam formerly of Petersburg, Va., and John E. McEnery, Esq. of Dinwiddie

* Given as printed

MARRIAGE NOTICES IN THE SOUTHERN CHURCHMAN WITH DATES OF PUBLICATION

Co., by the Rev. T. H. Lacy, in St. Luke's Church, Nottoway Co., Va. So. Ch., Apr. 10, 1873

James S. (Dr.), and Eliza Bates Hudnall, both of Lancaster Co., Va., by the Rev. Edmund Withers, in St. Stephen's Church, Baltimore. So. Ch., Oct. 25, 1866

Jarret Cleeman, youngest d. of the late Robt. Gilliam, and Joseph Pannill, by the Rev. Edmund Withers, at Petersburg. So. Ch., Oct. 16, 1851

Robert, Esq., of Prince George Co., and Charlotte Isabella, d. of Richard D. Sanxay, Esq. of Richmond, Va., by the Rev. Wm. H. Hart. So. Ch., Nov. 1, 1839

Thomas Howard, and Henrietta S., d. of Theodorick A. and Gertrude Williams, by the Rev. Walter Williams, D.D., of Christ Church, Baltimore, assisted by the Rev. Arthur S. Lloyd, in St. Luke's Protestant Episcopal Church, Norfolk, Va. So. Ch., June 18, 1891

Thomas M., and Martha Goodwyn, by the Rev. Luther W. Doggett assisted by the Rev. C. R. Hains, D.D., in St. Paul's Church, Petersburg, Va. So. Ch., June 12, 1890

GILLIES
J. Melville, of the U.S. Navy, and Rebecca S., d. of John Roberts, Esq. of Alexandria, D.C., by the Rev. C. B. Dana, in Christ Church. So. Ch., Dec. 15, 1837

GILLINGHAM
Rebecca V., of Fairfax Co., Va., and Clayton T. Scullin, by the Rev. Mr. Underhill, at the residence of the bride's grandmother, Hammonton, N.J. So. Ch., June 30, 1887

GILLIER
Anne H., and P. McGehee, both of Albemarle Co., Va., by the Rev. Wm. M. Nelson, at Edgefield. So. Ch., June 13, 1867

George H. (Judge), and Elizabeth C., d. of Henry Carrington, Esq. of Charlotte Co., Va., by the Rev. T. E. Locke, at Ingleside. So. Ch., Dec. 26, 1856

Louise E., eldest d. of the late Judge George H. Gilmer, and R. Holt Easley of Halifax C.H., Va., by the Rev. W. A. Alrich, in Emmanuel Church, Chatham, Pittsylvania Co., Va. So. Ch., Nov. 20, 1879

M. Peachy, of Chatham, Va., and John W. Craddock of Baltimore, Md., by the Rev. C. O. Pruden, rector, in Emmanuel Church, Chatham, Va. So. Ch., Dec. 30, 1886

Mary Peachy, d. of the late Peachy R. Gilmer, and the Rev. George T. Wilmer of Bototourt Co., Va., by the Rev. Richard K. Meade, at Leigh, Albemarle Co., Va. So. Ch., May 7, 1847

Willie C., d. of Z. Lee Gilmer of Albemarle Co., Va., and Alexander Caldwell Horsley of Buckingham Co., by the Rev. T. E. Locke, in St. John's Church, Scottsville, Va. So. Ch., Nov. 27, 1890

GILMORE
Estelle, eldest d. of Jas. H. Gilmore, Esq., and George E. Penn, Esq., all of Marion, Smyth Co., by

MARRIAGE NOTICES IN THE SOUTHERN CHURCHMAN WITH DATES OF PUBLICATION

the Rev. Robb White, in Christ Church, Marion, Smyth Co. So. Ch., Jan. 13, 1876

James C., U.S.N., and Mary Stuart, d. of Col. M. D. Ball of Alaska, formerly of Alexandria, at "The Castle", Sitka, Alaska. So. Ch., June 9, 1881

GINN
L. Holmes, and Meta Eugenia Cobb, both of Clarke Co., Va., by the Rev. John P. Tyler, rector, in Christ Church, Millwood, Va. So. Ch., May 19, 1892

GINNELLEY
Elizabeth H., and Geo. W. Boyce, by the Rev. Thos. Deane Lewis, at the residence of the bride's parents, Fairfax C.H., Va. So. Ch., Dec. 14, 1893

GISH
Robert E., of Liberty, Va., and Mary H., d. of Judge D. E. Spence, by the Rev. T. M. Carson, in St. Paul's Church, Lynchburg, Va. So. Ch., Nov. 13, 1873

Robert Ellis, of Lynchburg, Va., and Bessie Barbour, d. of John Jacquelin Ambler, by the Rev. A. P. Gray, at "Glen Ambler", Amherst Co., Va. So. Ch., Dec. 5, 1889

GITTINGS
Eleanor Addison, and William Armistead Hoale, by the Rev. J. S. B. Hodges, in St. Paul's Church, Baltimore. So. Ch., Dec. 30, 1880

GLASCOCK
Edwin Cook, and Nancy, third d. of Thos. Cockrill, Esq., all of Fauquier Co., Va., at the home of the bride's father. So. Ch., Feb. 22, 1872

Lou, and Willis W. Davenport, both of Lancaster Co., Va., by the Rev. H. L. Derby, at Lancaster C.H., Va. So. Ch., Nov. 17, 1881

GLASSELL
Susan T., only d. of Andrew Glassell of Mobile, and George S. Patton of Richmond, by the Rev. Philip Slaughter, in St. Paul's Church, Richmond. So. Ch., Nov. 16, 1855

GLENN
E. T. B., principal clerk of the C. F. & Y. V. R. R., and Mary E., d. of Col. John A. Pemberton, by the Rev. J. C. Huske, D.D., at Fayettesville, N.C. So. Ch., Jan. 3, 1884

John F., and Cornelia M., d. of George Watt, all of Richmond, Va., by the Rev. Chas. H. Read assisted by the Rev. Henry Wall, at the residence of the bride's father, Richmond, Va. So. Ch., Jan. 1, 1874

Wm. C. (Hon.), and Miriam M. Armstrong, by the Rev. R. S. Barrett, in St. Luke's Cathedral, Atlanta, Ga. So. Ch., Dec. 19, 1889

GLOVER
Fannie Perkins, eldest d. of Chapman Glover of Buckingham Co., Va., and Wylie W. Haskins, by the Rev. T. E. Locke, in Emmanuel Church, Glenmore. So. Ch., Dec. 6, 1888

John B., and C. Eugenia, d. of the late Thos. H. Crow of Berryville, Clarke Co., Va., by the Rev. T. F. Martin, in Grace Church, Berryville.

MARRIAGE NOTICES IN THE SOUTHERN CHURCHMAN WITH DATES OF PUBLICATION

So. Ch., Nov. 26, 1868
Lonnelle, of Smithfield, and Dr. W. F. Davison formerly of Richmond, Va., by the Rev. David Barr, at Smithfield, Va. So. Ch., Dec. 2, 1886
Sarah B., of Albemarle, and James W. Mason of Albemarle, by the Rev. Wm. M. Nelson, in Albemarle Co. So. Ch., Oct. 19, 1855

GODDARD
Mary Ege, d. of Isaac Goddard of Richmond, and Dr. William E. Harwood of Petersburg, by the Rev. C. J. Gibson, at Petersburg, the residence of John B. Ege, Esq. So. Ch., Nov. 12, 1885

GODWIN
Ella, d. of Thos. G. Godwin, Esq. of Fincastle, and Guy Whitten of Goodson, Va., by the Rev. Pendleton Brooke, in St. Mark's Church, Fincastle. So. Ch., May 14, 1874
Emma, d. of Col. Godwin of Linwood, Alexandria Co., and Gowin Tallaforro of Westmoreland Co., Va., by the Rt. Rev. Bishop Johns. So. Ch., Jan. 4, 1856
I. Robinson (Dr.), and Emma S. B., d. of Maj. Jno. T. Wilson, all of Fincastle, by the Rev. Edward H. Ingle of Roanoke, in St. Mark's Church, Fincastle, Botetourt Co. So. Ch., Nov. 7, 1867
James, of Baltimore, Md., and A. Eliza, d. of Col. D. Ammen of Botetourt Co., Va., by the Rev. Edmund W. Hubard, in St. Mark's Church, Fincastle. So. Ch., Dec. 15, 1870

GOFFIGON
Lucie E., d. of the late John Goffigon, and Edgar J. Spady, member of the House of Delegates, by the Rev. J. M. Chevers, at Abingdon,* Northampton Co. So. Ch., Mar. 7, 1856

GOGGIN
James M., of Memphis, Tenn., and Bettie Page of Gloucester, by the Rev. M. Mann, in Abingdon Church, Gloucester Co. So. Ch., Mar. 2, 1860
John O. L., Esq., Atty. at Law, of Christiansburg, Va., and Susan S., d. of Col. John W. Holt of Bedford, by the Rev. Jacob D. Mitchell. So. Ch., Nov. 24, 1837
Samuel C., of Bedford Co., and Lizzie D., d. of L. Moon, Esq., by the Rev. B. W. Moseley, near Leesville, Campbell Co. So. Ch., Mar. 21, 1878

GOING
Henry J., Esq., s. of the Venerable Archdeacon Going of Killaloe Co., Tipperary, Ireland, and Mary, d. of Henry Bowler of Richmond, Va., by the Rev. T. G. Dashiell, at Richmond, the home of the bride's father. So. Ch., Nov. 19, 1874

GOINGS
Elizabeth, of Alexandria Co., Va., and the Rev. E. J. Hall of Pocahontas Co., W.Va., by the Rev. D. F. Sprigg, in Alexandria Co. So. Ch., Oct. 18, 1877

GOLD
Lloyd O., of Florida, and Bertha, d. of Andrew J. and Belle Chunn, by the Rev. H. B. Lee, in Emmanuel Church, Fauquier Co., Va. So. Ch., Nov. 2, 1882

---

* "Abingdon" probably should be "Arlington"

MARRIAGE NOTICES IN THE SOUTHERN CHURCHMAN WITH DATES OF PUBLICATION

GOLDSBOROUGH
    Alice Lloyd, d. of Mrs. M. E. and the late Hon. W. T. Goldsborough, and Joseph Thruston Manning, by the Rev. Dr. W. W. Williams, in Christ Church, Baltimore. So. Ch., Dec. 4, 1884
    Edmund Kennedy (Dr.), and Mary Farr, d. of the late Fitzhugh Coyle, all of Washington, D.C., by the Rev. John B. Morgan, in the Church of the Holy Trinity in Paris, France. So. Ch., Sept. 26, 1878
    Nannie Lloyd, d. of the late Hon. Wm. T. Goldsborough, and Wm. Ross Hoff, by the Rev. W. W. Williams, D.D., in Christ Church, Baltimore. So. Ch., June 25, 1885
    Robert Lloyd (The Rev.), rector of St. Barnabas Church, Burlington, N.J., and Mrs. Ann Scott of Elkton, by the Rev. Wm. Schouler, in Trinity Church, Elkton, Md. So. Ch., July 20, 1882

GOLDSCHMIDT
    Otto, of Hamburg, one of the most accomplished pianists ever listened to in this country, and Jenny Lind, the melodious Swedish nightingale, by the Rev. Charles Mason assisted by Dr. Wainwright, at the residence of S. G. Ward, in Boston. So. Ch., Feb. 19, 1852

GOLDSMITH
    J. M., of St. Mary's Co., Md., and Mary J. Skinker, by the Rev. John McGill, at "Huntley", Fauquier Co., the residence of the bride's father. So. Ch., Jan. 6, 1870

GOOCH
    Bettie, d. of Dr. Wm. F. Gooch of Albemarle, and Wm. O. English of Westmoreland, by the Rev. D. C. T. Davis, in the Episcopal Church at Charlottesville. So. Ch., Aug. 12, 1859

GOOD
    Juliet Virginia, d. of the Hon. Wm. G. Good, and Dr. M. M. Jordan, by the Rev. E. M. Rodman, at Wheatland, Mecklenburg Co. So. Ch., Nov. 23, 1855

GOODE
    Agnes E., d. of the late John C. Goode of Mecklenburg, and James J. Williamson of Dinwiddie, by the Rev. Mr. Steele. So. Ch., Nov. 24, 1837
    Fannie C., of Bedford Co., Va., and Edward Scott of Lexington, Ky., by the Rev. Albert Ware, at the residence of Capt. Izzard. So. Ch., Oct. 19, 1876
    J. Thomas (Col.), of Mecklenburg, Va., and Bessie , d. of William Morton of Charlotte, Va., by the Rev. Thomas Wharey, at the residence of the bride's father. So. Ch., Oct. 12, 1876
    M. B., and Dr. M. M. Jordan, both of Mecklenburg, Va., by the Rev. Jno. Cosby, at Lombardy Grove. So. Ch., Feb. 17, 1860
    Richard Alexander, of Washington, D. C., and Jean Irvine, d. of F. H. Moss of Markham, Va., by the Rev. Herbert Scott Smith, D.D., in St. Margaret's Church, Washington, D.C. So. Ch., Nov. 17, 1917
    Richard Urquhart, and Sophie Jackson, d. of Marshall Parks of Norfolk, Va., by

MARRIAGE NOTICES IN THE SOUTHERN CHURCHMAN WITH DATES OF PUBLICATION

the Rev. Beverly D. Tucker, in St. Paul's Church, Norfolk, Va. So. Ch., Jan. 17, 1889

GOODHARD
Sallie R. W., d. of Wm. B. Goodhard, Esq. of Kent Island, Md., and Edward M. Legg, by the Rev. P. D. Thompson, at 547 Franklin Street, Baltimore. So. Ch., Oct. 2, 1879

GOODLOE
Cornelia R., and Granville S. P. Browne of North Carolina, by the Rev. Henry L. Derby, at the residence of the bride's mother, Suffolk, Va. So. Ch., Apr. 23, 1891
Tevis, Esq., of Louisville, Ky., and Harriet Gardner, d. of the Rt. Rev. Thomas Underwood Dudley, D.D., by the Rt. Rev. Bishop of Kentucky assisted by the Rev. William F. Gardner of Maryland, in Calvary Church, Louisville, Ky. So. Ch., Jan. 19, 1893

GOODNOW
J., of Hartford, Conn., and Elizabeth Nicolson, second d. of the Rev. George Woodbridge, D.D., at the residence of her father, in Richmond, Va. So. Ch., Apr. 12, 1877

GOODRICH
Lalla, and the Rev. R. K. Mosoley, by the Rev. J. W. Neill of San Antonio, assisted by the Rev. R. W. Laird of Gonzales, in the Presbyterian Church, Seguin, Tex. So. Ch., Dec. 9, 1886

GOODS
Victoria, and T. E. Harris, Esq., both of Bedford Co., Va., by the Rev. W. H. Pendleton, at the residence of the bride's father. So. Ch., Dec. 8, 1870

GOODWIN
Edward L. (The Rev.), of Franklin Co., and Maria L., d. of Margaret L. and the late Maj. J. Thomas Smith of Fauquier, by the Rev. C. Walker, D.D., assisted by the Rev. J. Harry Chesley, at the residence of the bride's mother, Seminary Hill, Fairfax Co., Va. So. Ch., Jan. 20, 1881
F. L. B. (The Hon.), of Vallejo, and Ella, d. of Dr. S. A. McMeans, by the Rev. Dr. Smith, at the residence of the bride's father, at Santa Rosa, Calif. So. Ch., Oct. 20, 1870
Fannie, and Thomas B. Winston, both of Louisa Co., Va., by the Rev. L. R. Combs, at the residence of the bride's mother. So. Ch., Jan. 15, 1885
Frederick D., rector of Trinity Church, Staunton, Va., and Mary F., d. of Dr. Robert Archer of the U.S. Army, by the Rev. Mr. Cheevers, at Fort Monroe, Va. So. Ch., Nov. 10, 1837
John T., of Louisa, and Bettie V. Terrill, by the Rev. W. T. Leavell, at Chestnut Hill, Orange Co., Va. So. Ch., Jan. 19, 1854
Mary B., of Wytheville, Va., and the Rev. T. H. Lacy of New Kent Co., Va., by the Rev. F. D. Goodwin assisted by the Rev. D. F. Forest, in St. John's Church, Wytheville, Va.

MARRIAGE NOTICES IN THE SOUTHERN CHURCHMAN WITH DATES OF PUBLICATION

So. Ch., Sept. 18, 1873
Mary Byrd, of Spotsylvania, and William P. Goodwin of Caroline Co., Va., by the Rev. Wm. W. Greene, at the residence of the bride's father. So. Ch., Nov. 30, 1871

R. A. (The Rev.), of Boyton, Va., and Sallie C., d. of the late Dr. William Crump of Culpeper, by the Rev. James G. Minnigerode, in St. Stephen's Church, Culpeper, Va. So. Ch., Nov. 1, 1877

Robert A. (The Rev.), of Salem, Roanoke Co., Va., and Mary Ambler, fifth d. of George F. Harrison of Longwood, by the Rev. B. T. Turner, in the Episcopal Church, Goochland C.H., Va. So. Ch., July 5, 1883

W. A. R., D.D. (The Rev.), rector of St. Paul's Church, Rochester, N.Y., and Ethel, d. of John C. Howard of Ashland, Va., by the Rev. E. L. Goodwin, D.D., assisted by the Rt. Rev. W. Cabell Brown, D.D., Bishop Coadjutor of the Diocese of Virginia, in St. James' Church, Ashland, Va. So. Ch., June 22, 1918

William P., of Caroline Co., Va., and Mary Byrd Goodwin of Spotsylvania, by the Rev. Wm. W. Greene, at the residence of the bride's father. So. Ch., Nov. 30, 1871

GOODWYN
A. Meade (Mrs.), d. of the late R. K. Meade of Brunswick Co., Va., and R. S. Montgomery, by the Rev. H. M. Galusha assisted by the Rev. Edmund Withers, at Greenwood, Greensville Co., Va. So. Ch., Apr. 4, 1862

D. Edward, and Fanny Hays, third d. of R. G. Montgomery, all of Greensville Co., Va., by the Rev. David Barr, in Christ Church, Hicksford, Va. So. Ch., Dec. 14, 1871

Elizabeth, eldest d. of W. S. Goodwyn, Esq. of Greensville Co., Va., and John William Ridley of Southampton Co., by the Rev. C. J. Gibson, in Greensville Co., Va. So. Ch., Dec. 30, 1875

George W., of Petersburg, and Bettie, d. of Dr. E. A. Morrison of Lawrenceville, by the Rev. Mr. Morrison of Baltimore, at Brunswick. So. Ch., Feb. 1, 1856

India Davis, d. of the late Judge Charles F. Goodwyn, and Sparrel Asa Wood, by the Rev. T. H. Lacy, D.D., at the home of the bride's mother, Nottoway, Va. So. Ch., Feb. 6, 1906

Lanetta Mason, d. of Mrs. Charles F. Goodwyn and the late Charles F. Goodwyn, and Gordon Gillette Harris of Culpeper Co., by the Rev. T. H. Lacy, at Nottoway, Va. So. Ch., June 26, 1909

Maria Meade, d. of the late Albert J. Goodwyn, Esq., and Charles Pannill of Petersburg, by the Rev. P. G. Robert, at Greenwood, Greensville Co. So. Ch., Sept. 11, 1857

Martha, and Thomas M. Gilliam, by the Rev. Luther W. Doggett assisted by the Rev. C. R. Haines, D.D., in St. Paul's Church, Peters-

MARRIAGE NOTICES IN THE SOUTHERN CHURCHMAN WITH DATES OF PUBLICATION

burg, Va. So. Ch., June 12, 1890

Mary Campbell, d. of Capt. and Mrs. J. A. Goodwyn, and Gaston Lake Aycock of Louisburg, N.C., by the Rev. J. C. Norton, rector of Emmanuel Church, Warrenton, N.C., at Elberon, N.C. So. Ch., Jan. 22, 1910

R. T., of Nottoway Co., Va., and Sallie B., oldest d. of Col. W. R. Aylett of King William Co., by the Rev. S. S. Hepbron, at the residence of the bride's father at Montville. So. Ch., July 9, 1891

Sallie A., d. of the late Dr. William B. Goodwyn, and Dr. Thomas H. Urquhart, by the Rev. P. G. Robert, at the residence of Mrs. E. N. Goodwyn, Southampton Co., Va. So. Ch., Apr. 11, 1856

GOOLRICK
Norah Elizabeth, and William Jones Lacy of Grand Junction, Col., by the Rt. Rev. C. K. Nelson, D.D., Bishop of Atlanta, assisted by Dr. J. Horace Lacy, at the home of her mother, Mrs. William Barber Goolrick, Fredericksburg, Va. So. Ch., Jan. 18, 1913

GORDON
Anna Campbell, only d. of Basil Gordon, Esq., of Falmouth, and John Hanson Thomas, M.D., of Baltimore, by the Rev. E. C. McGuire. So. Ch., Dec. 1, 1837

Boirne, of Savannah, and Elizabeth McKim, d. of Henry R. Hazlehurst, by the Rev. Hall Harrison, at Lilburn, Ellicott Co., Md. So. Ch., Nov. 16, 1882

Geo. S. (The Rev.), and Mary Jane, d. of the late Thomas Snowden, all of New York, by the Rev. Hugh Smith, D.D. So. Ch., July 19 and Aug. 2, 1839

Imogen, d. of J. N. Gordon, Esq., of Lynchburg, and William Minnigerode of Richmond, by the Rev. Chas. Minnigerode, D.D., father of the groom, assisted by the Rev. Dr. Hooper, in Second Presbyterian Church, Lynchburg, Va. So. Ch., Nov. 23, 1876

James R., of Richmond, and E. C. Croxton of Tappahannock, Va., by the Rev. J. B. Newton, in St. John's Church, Tappahannock. So. Ch., Apr. 2, 1874

Jessie, and W. O. English, by the Rev. Grayson Dashiell, at Richmond, Va. So. Ch., Sept. 11, 1879

Lucy W., oldest d. of Bazil Gordon, Esq., and Charles Herndon, Esq. of Caroline Co., by the Rev. Wm. Friend, at Prospect Hill, Caroline Co. So. Ch., Apr. 2, 1858

M. G. (Miss), of Essex Co., Va., and Dr. J. B. Hodgkin of Washington, D. C., by the Rev. Everard Meade, in St. John's Church, Tappahannock, Essex Co., Va. So. Ch., Nov. 25, 1880

Martha Harvey, d. of Dr. Thomas C. Gordon, and Henry W. Latane, by the Rev. H. W. L. Temple assisted by the Rev. J. A. Latane, in St. John's Church, Tappahannock, Essex Co., Va. So. Ch., June 3, 1870

Mary Long, d. of the late George Loyal Gordon of Albemarle, Va., and Dr. Richard Henry Lewis of Raleigh, N.C.,

MARRIAGE NOTICES IN THE SOUTHERN CHURCHMAN WITH DATES OF PUBLICATION

by the Rev. W. Q. Hullihen, at Staunton, Va. So. Ch., May 8, 1890

Nellie Hodge, youngest d. of Mr. and Mrs. John W. Gordon of 826 West Franklin Street, and Edmund Cooper Mayo, by the Rev. J. J. Gravatt and the Rt. Rev. Robert A. Gibson in Holy Trinity Church, Richmond, Va. So. Ch., Feb. 20, 1909

Rebecca C., d. of John M. Gordon, Esq. of Baltimore, and Eugene Blackfore of Lynchburg, Va., by the Rev. Randolph H. McKim of Portsmouth, assisted by the Rev. George Leeds, D.D., in Grace Church, Baltimore. So. Ch., July 4, 1867

Sallie T., eldest d. of Wm. and Charlotte M. Gordon, and the Rev. Thomson B. Maury, by the Rev. Thomas F. Martin, at Huntley, Nelson Co., Va. So. Ch., Dec. 25, 1863

Samuel, Jr., of St. Louis, Mo., and Alice D., d. of Thomas P. Yerby, Esq. of Spotsylvania Co., Va., by the Rev. James E. Poindexter, at Belle Voir, Spotsylvania Co., Va. So. Ch., Feb. 2, 1882

W. A., of Georgetown, D.C., and Harriet, d. of Hon. A. T. Caperton, by the Rev. Mr. Mason, at Union, W.Va. So. Ch., Jan. 21, 1875

GORE
Maggie, and Joseph Robbins, both of Dorchester Co., Md., by the Rev. William W. Greene, at the residence of Capt. L. Powell. So. Ch., May 20, 1880

GOSNELL
Mary Forrest, of Martinsburg, W.Va., and George Edward Talbott, by the rector, the Rev. W. D. Hanson, in Trinity Church, Martinsburg, W.Va. So. Ch., Dec. 18, 1873

GOSS
D. F., and Edith G. Garnett, by the Rev. Everard Meade, in St. John's Church, Tappahannock, Essex Co., Va. So. Ch., Nov. 25, 1880

Jane, d. of E. Goss, and R. R. Claiborne, rector of Emmanuel Church, Rapidan, by the Rev. J. S. Hansbrough of Orange, at the residence of the bride's father. So. Ch., Oct. 26, 1882

GOSSLING
Harry Johnson, of Philadelphia, and Ella L. Haines of Jefferson Co., W.Va., by the Rev. John McGill, in St. John's Church, Ripon, W.Va. So. Ch., Apr. 24, 1890

GOTT
Jas. P., of Montgomery Co., Md., and Anna Laura Covington of Bridgewater, by the Rev. O. S. Bunting, in the Baptist Church, Bridgewater, Rockingham Co. So. Ch., Nov. 11, 1886

GOUGH
Lucy Hayden, d. of the late Wilfred Gough of Chaptico, and the Rev. William John Wright of Washington, D.C., by the Bishop of Washington, at Chaptico, Md. So. Ch., Nov. 6, 1909

Richard, and Anne Lee Sothoron, d. of the officiating clergyman, the Rev. L. J. Sothoron, rector, in Trinity Church, Trinity parish, Charles Co., Md. So. Ch., Nov. 20, 1884

GOULD

MARRIAGE NOTICES IN THE SOUTHERN CHURCHMAN WITH DATES OF PUBLICATION

Anna D., d. of the late Horace Gould of St. Simon's Island, and the Rev. Anson G. P. Dodge, Jr., rector of Christ Church, Frederica, St. Simon's Island, Ga., by the Rev. Henry E. Lucas, rector, in St. Mark's Church, Brunswick, Ga. So. Ch., June 12, 1890

GOULDMAN
Izora, d. of H. B. Gouldman, Esq., and John Moore Stainback, M.D., of Brunswick Co., by the Rev. T. E. Locke, at White Point, Westmoreland Co. So. Ch., May 27, 1869

GOURDIN
Eloise, d. of Mrs. Harriet P. Gourdin and the late Theodore Gourdin, M.D., and the Rev. Frank G. Scott, rector of the parish, by the Rev. John Johnson, in the Episcopal Chapel, Eutawville, S.C. So. Ch., Oct. 14, 1880

GOWIN
Nellie Estelle, and Charles Andrews Jones, by the Rev. Jos. R. Jones assisted by the Rev. John P. Tyler, rector of Christ Church, in Christ Church, Milwood, Va. So. Ch., May 18, 1893

GRAEFF
Mary McKenzie, eldest d. of John E. Graeff, and Montgomery Wilcox, all of Philadelphia, by the Rev. Theodore S. Rumney, D.D., assisted by the Rev. Edward S. Watson, D.D., in Philadolphia. So. Ch., May 13, 1880

GRAHAM
Doddridge F., and Victoria, d. of Capt. Geo. W. Harrison (late U.S.A.), all of Deer Park, by the Rev. Herbert Assheton, at Deer Park. So. Ch., Jan. 11, 1883

James D. (Lt. Col.), U.S. Army, and Francis, d. of the late John Wickham, Esq., of Richmond, Va., by the Rev. Dr. Minnigerode, at Richmond. So. Ch., Feb. 20, 1857

Mary E. Lee (Mrs.), and Col. Robt. W. Ashlin, both of Fluvanna Co., by the Rev. S. C. Roberts, at Rivanna Mills, Fluvanna Co., Va. So. Ch., Mar. 9, 1871

W. H., of Hamilton, Canada, and Lucy Alfred Wood, by the Rev. A. B. Tizzard, at the residence of the bride's mother, Mrs. Henry Miller, in Richmond. So. Ch., Nov. 18, 1880

Wm. A., Jr. (Maj.), of North Carolina, and Julia H., d. of John W. Lane, Esq., of Amelia Co., Va., by the Rev. A. B. Tizzard, at the Oaks, the residence of the bride's father. So. Ch., June 17, 1864

William M. (Lt.), and Mary B., d. of Capt. James B. Ricketts, U.S. Army, by the Rev. M. L. Chevers, in Centurion Church, Old Point. So. Ch., Oct. 5, 1860

GRAMMER
Carl E. (The Rev.), Prof. of the Virginia Theological Seminary, and Mary Wallace, d. of the Rev. James J. Page, by the father of the bride assisted by the Rev. Dr. Julius E. Grammer and the Rev. Thomas Carter Page, in Holy Trinity Church, near Collington, Prince George's Co., Md. So. Ch., July 11, 1889

MARRIAGE NOTICES IN THE SOUTHERN CHURCHMAN WITH DATES OF PUBLICATION

Julius E. (The Rev.), and Bessie, d. of the officiating clergyman, the Rev. Wm. Sparrow, D.D., in the Chapel of the Theological Seminary. So. Ch., Dec. 28, 1855

Mary, d. of the Rev. John Grammer, and Nathaniel T. Green, Jr., all of Halifax Co., Va., by the Rev. John T. Clark, in St. John's Church, Antrim Parish.** So. Ch., Sept. 25, 1857

GRANT
Arthur Henry, and Eleanor C. Grubb, in St. Luke's Church, Live Oak, Fla. So. Ch., Oct. 28, 1911

James Benton, of Denver, Col., s. of the late James Benton Grant, ex-Governor of Colorado, and Mary Urquhart, d. of Mr. and Mrs. William Throckmorton Brooke, gr.d. of the late Hon. John Goode of Virginia, by the Rev. David W. Howard, in St. Luke's Church, Norfolk, Va. So. Ch., May 9, 1914*

Percival Stuart, and Avis, d. of Maj. D. N. Walker, by the Rev. Charles Minnigerode assisted by the Rev. Pike Powers, D.D., in St. Paul's Church, Richmond, Va. So. Ch., Oct. 29, 1885

GRANTLAND
Seaton (The Hon.), member of Congress from Georgia, and Catharine M., d. of Capt. George Dabney, by the Rev. George Woodbridge, in Hanover Co. So. Ch., Oct. 30, 1833

GRAVATT
Charles U. (Dr.), U.S. Navy, and Florence C., d. of F. F. Marshall of Erie, by the Rev. J. J. Gravatt assisted by the rector, the Rev. George A. Carstensen, in St. Paul's Church, Erie, Pa. So. Ch., Apr. 1, 1886

J. J. (The Rev.), and Judie W., second d. of W. S. Jones, Esq. of Elizabeth City Co., by the Rev. O. E. Herrick and the Rev. J. W. Ware, at Hampton, Va. So. Ch., May 8, 1879

Lucie J., d. of Dr. John J. Gravatt, and the Hon. Rees T. Bowen of Tazewell Co., Va., by the Rev. James E. Poindexter, at the residence of the bride's father, Port Royal, Va. So. Ch., Sept. 16, 1875

GRAVELY
J. Alberta, youngest d. of B. F. Gravely, Esq., and Lt. Wm. L. Fernald of Danville, by the Rev. Geo. W. Dame, at Leatherwood, Henry Co. So. Ch., Mar. 1, 1877

Willis L., and Roberta H. Tredway, by the Rev. Geo. W. Dame, in the Church of the Epiphany, Danville. So. Ch., Jan. 23, 1879

GRAVES
Dora, eldest d. of Mrs. Sarah and the late James W. Graves, and Edmund W. Scott, Esq., brother of the officiating minister, by the Rev. F. G. Scott, rector of Christ Church, Gordonsville, at the residence of the bride's mother. So. Ch., Nov. 1, 1877

J. C., and Elise C., youngest d. of B. Johnson Barbour, Esq., by the Rev. F. G. Scott, at the residence of the bride's father, Orange Co., Va. So. Ch., July 31, 1890

Joseph A. (The Rev.), of Raymond, Miss., and Florence A., d. of Mrs. S. V. Payne of St. Louis, Mo., by the Rev. John

---

* A notice appeared in the May 2, 1914 issue identical with this except that the groom's name was given as James Benton Grove, and he was not cited as the son of ex-Governor Grant of Colorado.

** Antrim Parish is in Halifax County, Virginia (Journal ... Diocese of Southern Virginia, Portsmouth, Va., 1941)

MARRIAGE NOTICES IN THE SOUTHERN CHURCHMAN WITH DATES OF PUBLICATION

G. Shopperson, at the residence of Dr. Hairston, Franklin Co., Va. So. Ch., Jan. 4, 1877

Margaret Copeland, d. of the late Mr. and Mrs. William B. Graves of Baltimore, and the Rev. Charles E. Botticher, Associate Editor of the Spirit of Missions, by the Rev. Hobart Smith, rector, in St. Thomas' Church, Garrison Forest, Md. So. Ch., May 4, 1918

R. F., Esq., of Powhatan Co., and Caroline N., oldest d. of Elgin Russel, Esq., by the Rev. R. P. Johnson, at Locus*Grove, Prince George Co., Va. So. Ch., Aug. 27, 1858

Richard M. (Capt.), C.S.A., and Mrs. Susan V. Boston of Fluvanna Co., Va., by the Rev. Wm. McGuire, at Buchanan, Botetourt Co. So. Ch., Dec. 4, 1863

William H., of Knoxville, Tenn., and Mary D., d. of the late Wm. Hankins, Esq., by the Rev. P. G. Robert, at Surry Co. So. Ch., Dec. 30, 1859

William S., of Liberty, Va., and Sallie E., d. of the late Dr. N. B. Cary, by the Rev. Dr. Minnigerode, at the residence of the bride's uncle, Col. John B. Cary, Richmond, Va. So. Ch., Sept. 27, 1883

GRAY
Arthur P. (The Rev.), of Prince William Co., Va., and Mina Myers, fourth d. of Mrs. Anne N. Radford of "Ashwood", Bedford Co., Va., by the Rev. E. W. Hubard, in St. Stephen's Church, Bedford Co., Va. So. Ch., Oct. 6, 1881

Arthur P., Jr. (The Rev.), rector of St. Andrew's Church, Lawrenceville, Va., and Elizabeth Stuart, youngest d. of the late Rev. Henry L. Derby, one time rector of St. Andrews, by the Rev. Arthur P. Gray, Sr., the Rev. Jeff. Ran. Taylor assisting, in the Episcopal Church, Accomac. So. Ch., Oct. 14, 1911

Bettie F., and Geo. Warren Fitzhugh, both of Fauquier, by the Rev. Jno. Lindsay, rector of St. James' Church, Warrenton. So. Ch., Dec. 7, 1871

Ellen, of Moundsville, W.Va., and the Rev. J. F. Woods, by the Rev. Thos. G. Addison, in Trinity Church, Washington, D.C. So. Ch., May 21, 1868

Ellen C., of Boston, and the Rev. Wm. H. Brooks, minister of St. Thomas' Church, Newark, Del., by the Rev. W. T. Smithett, in Trinity Church, Boston. So. Ch., Aug. 26, 1852

Ellen Douglas, only d. of the Rev. and Mrs. Arthur P. Gray, Sr., and Richard Barnes Tyler of Petersburg, Va., by the Rev. Arthur P. Gray, Jr., of Lawrenceville, Va., assisted by the Rev. A. P. Gray, Sr., in Trinity Church, Washington, Va. So. Ch., Jan. 11, 1913

Eliss E., and Helen M. Edmonds, both of Fauquier, by the Rev. Jno. Lindsay, rector of St. James Church, Warrenton, in Fauquier Co., Va. So. Ch., Dec. 7, 1871

Gertrude, d. of Mrs. J. M. Gray, and Wallace H. Hamilton of New York (formerly of Bristol, England), by the Rev. Magruder

* Given as printed

MARRIAGE NOTICES IN THE SOUTHERN CHURCHMAN WITH DATES OF PUBLICATION

Maury, at "Travellers' Rest", Stafford Co., Va. So. Ch., Jan. 12, 1871

Henrietta Henderson, d. of A. S. Gray of Harrisonburg, and Foxhall A. Daingerfield, 11th Regiment Virginia Cavalry, by the Rev. J. E. Latane, in the Presbyterian Church, Harrisonburg. So. Ch., Nov. 20, 1863

J. Bowie, of "Traveller's Rest", Stafford Co., Va., and Mary, d. of Maj. Bushrod W. Hunter of Alexandria, Va., by the Rev. R. H. McKim, at the residence of the bride's father. So. Ch., Nov. 17, 1870

J. C., of Newport, R.I., and E. Florence Parish of Virginia, by the Rev. J. Hervey Hundley, at Urbanna, Middlesex Co., Va. So. Ch., Mar. 6, 1879

John C. (The Rev.), rector of Trinity Church, Fredericksburg, and Frances, d. of the Rev. Dr. Southgate, by the Rt. Rev. Bishop Paret, at Annapolis, Md. So. Ch., Feb. 2, 1893

Julia R., of Buckingham Co., Va., and Col. John C. Page of Cumberland Co., by the Rev. B. H. Dupuy, at the residence of the bride's mother, in Buckingham Co., Va. So. Ch., Feb. 2, 1882

Lawrence B., and Marion L., d. of Mr. and Mrs. Henry A. Varn, at "Westwood", King and Queen Co., Va. So. Ch., Jan. 12, 1907

Lucie R., d. of the late J. B. Gray, and Dr. Joseph G. Alexander of Church Hill, Tenn., by the Rev. Dr. Murdaugh, at "Travellers' Rest." So. Ch., Dec. 2, 1875

Margarett, and William Dickerson, by the Rev. Mr. Randolph, at Travellers' Rest. So. Ch., Aug. 14, 1863

Orra H., d. of Algernon S. Gray of Harrisonburg, Va., and Thomas N. Langhorne of Lynchburg, by the Rev. A. W. Weddoll, at the residence of Foxhall A. Daingerfield, Harrisonburg. So. Ch., Oct. 26, 1871

R. Bentley, of St. Louis, Mo., and Lillie Pancoast of Leesburg, by the Rev. Theodore Reed, in St. James' Church, Leesburg. So. Ch., Nov. 16, 1876

Rhoda A., and Mason Kirkpatrick, by the Rev. A. S. Johns, at Landmark, Fauquier Co., Va. So. Ch., Jan. 5, 1882

Robert Aitcheson, of Stafford Co., Va., and Adelaide Getty, d. of the late William Hayman of Georgetown, D.C., by the Rev. J. I. Membert, D.D., in St. James' Church, Lancaster, Penn. So. Ch., Dec. 5, 1867

Victoria H., of Fauquier, and Thomas C. Thornton of Caroline Co., by the Rev. Jno. Lindsay of St. James' Church, Warrenton, in Fauquier Co., Va. So. Ch., Dec. 7, 1871

W. C. (The Rev.), of Bolivar, Tenn., and Fannie C. Bowers of Philadelphia, by the Rev. William V. Bowers, father of the bride, assisted by the Rev. Dr. Beaseley of Torresdale, in St. Andrew's Church, Philadelphia. So. Ch., Aug. 16, 1877

Wm. Ellzey, of Loudoun Co., and Rachel, d. of the late Dr. Sidney W. Smith of Alexandria, Va., by the Rt. Rev. Bishop

MARRIAGE NOTICES IN THE SOUTHERN CHURCHMAN WITH DATES OF PUBLICATION

Johns, in Christ Church, Alexandria. So. Ch., Nov. 30, 1860

GRAYSON
George M., Esq., and Lizzie Lee, d. of Henry T. Harrison, Esq., by the Rev. E. T. Perkins, in St. James' Church, Leesburg, Va. So. Ch., Sept. 26, 1867

George M., and Bessie P., d. of Dr. W. G. West, all of Loudoun Co., by the Rev. S. S. Ware, in Christ Church, Loudoun Co., Va. So. Ch., Jan. 1, 1880

J. C. (Dr.), of Culpeper Co., and Georgie, d. of the late Dr. Alfred Taliaferro of Culpeper Co., Va., by the Rev. W. T. Roberts, at "Fairmont." So. Ch., Jan. 13, 1887

Mary S., of Loudoun Co., Va., and the Rev. E. H. Harlow, rector of St. Marks, by the Rev. Charles H. Seymour of Dubuque, in St. Mark's Church, Fort Dodge, Ia. So. Ch., Dec. 8, 1870

Susan F., d. of the late George Grayson of Loudoun Co., and Henry Arthur Hall, Esq. of Upperville, Va., by the Rev. O. A. Kinsolving, at Newstead, Loudoun Co. So. Ch., Oct. 30, 1857

GREAVES
Alban (The Rev.), and Emily Norcom, d. of Samuel Smith, Esq. of Reidsville, by the Rev. H. O. Lacey, in the Episcopal Church, Reidsville, N.C. So. Ch., June 16, 1887

GREEN
Alexander R., and Lizzie R. Wanhop, by the Rev. O. A. Kinsolving, in St. John's Church, Halifax C.H. So. Ch., Nov. 16, 1871

Alice Bouldin, d. of Judge Boylan Green of Charlotte Co., Va., and Dr. Desausseur Preston of Burnwell, W.Va., at the home of Mr. and Mrs. Berryman Green, Theological Seminary, Va. So. Ch., Jan. 22, 1916

Boylan, Esq., s. of Col. Wm. E. Green of Charlotte Co., and Alice H., d. of the late Judge Wood Bouldin of the Court of Appeals, by the Rev. Davis M. Wood, at "Cleft Oak", Charlotte Co., Va. So. Ch., Sept. 15, 1881

Charles H., Esq., of Warren Co., Va., and Eloisa M. Castleman, by the Rev. F. M. Whittle, at Prospect Hill, the residence of the bride's mother, Clarke Co., Va. So. Ch., June 13, 1856

Edward R. A. (The Rev.), rector of St. Peter's Church, Tecumseh, and Fannie Nadler of Evanston, Ill., in the Anderson Memorial Chapel of Seabury Western Theological Seminary. So. Ch., July 7, 1935

Fanny, d. of John S. Green, Esq. of Rappahannock, Va., and Dr. George Crump of Vicksburg, Miss. formerly of Fredericksburg, Va., by the Rev. Mr. Woodville. So. Ch., Sept. 22, 1837

J. C., of Stafford Co., Va., and Josie M. Hendy of San Francisco, Cal., by the Rev. W. H. Platt, in San Francisco, Cal. So. Ch., Jan. 26, 1882

J. Mercier (The Rev.), rector of Christ Church, Charleston, and Margaret E., d. of the late Theodore Gaillard of St. John's Berkley,*by the Rev.

* Located in South Carolina

MARRIAGE NOTICES IN THE SOUTHERN CHURCHMAN WITH DATES OF PUBLICATION

W. B. W. Howe, in St. Philip's Church, Charleston. So. Ch., Nov. 11, 1859

Jno. A., and Margaret Fitchett, both of Warwick Co., Va., by the Rev. Henry Wall, D.D. So. Ch., Jan. 5, 1871

Julia, d. of the officiating clergyman, and Thomas B. Marshall of Baltimore, by the Rev. Thos. L. Green, in St. Luke's Church, Church Hill, Md. So. Ch., Feb. 15, 1883

Kate M., d. of Maj. John W. and Fannie Green, and the Rev. Louis L. Williams, by the Rev. G. H. Norton, D.D., in St. Paul's, Alexandria, Va. So. Ch., July 24, 1890

Mary S., d. of B. R. Green of Fauquier Co., Va., and Moses Showen of Shenandoah Co., by the Rev. H. B. Lee, at the residence of bride's father. So. Ch., Nov. 22, 1877

Mary V., and John T. Watson, Jr., both of Danville, by the Rev. O. S. Bunting of Trenton, N.J. assisted by the Rev. G. W. Dame, D.D., and the Rev. Alex Martin, D.D. of Danville, in Epiphany Church, Danville, Va. So. Ch., Dec. 24, 1891

Moses M., Esq., and Lily T. Marshall, d. of Mrs. Martin P. Brooke, all of Warrenton, by the Rev. John S. Lindsay, in St. James' Church, Warrenton, Va. So. Ch., Jan. 23, 1879

Robert B., of Halifax, and Adeline Douglas, only child and d. of W. D. Gibson, by the Rev. C. J. Gibson, in St. Paul's Church, Richmond. So. Ch., Dec. 17, 1858

Sarah Ann, and William S. Ashe, Esq., Attorney-at-Law, by the Rev. Thomas F. Davis, Jr., at Washington. So. Ch., Jan. 22, 1836

Sarah Virginia, third d. of James Green, and the Rev. Wm. F. M. Jacobs, by the Rev. J. T. Johnston, in St. Paul's Church. So. Ch., Aug. 6, 1858

William M. (The Rev.), and Charlotte I. Fleming, by the Rev. Philip B. Wiley, in St. Matthew's Church, Pittsborough. So. Ch., Jan. 8, 1836

Wm. W. (Dr.), and Lavinia Perry, both of Franklin Co., N.C., by the Rev. P. D. Thompson, at the residence of Charles Perry, Esq. So. Ch., Aug. 19, 1869

GREENE

B. H., of New Orleans, and Emmeline, d. of Thos. S. Dabney of Burleigh, by the Rt. Rev. J. P. B. Wilmer of the Diocese of Louisiana, assisted by the rector, the Rev. H. C. Harris, at Dry Grove, Miss., in the Church of the Holy Comforter. So. Ch., Nov. 18, 1869

Eliza T., d. of Maj. I. Greene, and Dr. J. W. Downer of Charles Town, by the Rev. T. F. Martin, at Berryville, Clarke Co., Va., at the residence of E. C. Marshall. So. Ch., May 8, 1879

J. Newport, Esq., formerly of Newtown House, Co. Kilkenney, Ireland, and Cloe Tyler, d. of Conway Whittle, Esq. of Norfolk, Va., by the Rev. N. A. Okeson assisted by the Rev. Julius Sans, in St. Paul's Church, Norfolk, Va.

MARRIAGE NOTICES IN THE SOUTHERN CHURCHMAN WITH DATES OF PUBLICATION

So. Ch., Sept. 7, 1876
Martha Wilson, d. of the officiating clergyman, and Robert M. Marshall, Jr., by the Rev. Wm. W. Greene, in Trinity Church, Church Creek, Dorchester Co., Md. So. Ch., Nov. 24, 1887

Mary Eliza, d. of the officiating minister, and Benjamin J. Linthicum of Church Creek, Dorchester Co., Md., by the Rev. Wm. W. Greene, in Calvary Church, Front Royal, Va. So. Ch., Oct. 30, 1890

Nathaniel T., Jr., and Mary, d. of the Rev. John Gramsier, all of Halifax Co., Va., by the Rev. John T. Clark, in St. John's Church, Antrim Parish.* So. Ch., Sept. 25, 1857

Thomas Evans, of Brooklyn, N.Y., s. of the officiating clergyman, and Virginia Vinton Yeakle of Baltimore, by the Rev. Wm. W. Greene, at the residence of the bride's mother, in the city of Baltimore. So. Ch., July 25, 1889

Wm. W. (The Rev.), of Spotsylvania Co., Va., and Henrietta H. Dance, by the Rev. John Cosby, at the residence of the bride's mother, Lunenburg Co., Va. So. Ch., Oct. 26, 1860

Willietta Woodbridge, d. of the officiating clergyman, and Charles Edgar Willis of Vicksburg, Miss., by the Rev. Wm. W. Greene, in Calvary Church, Front Royal, Va. So. Ch., Nov. 23, 1893

GREENFIELD
John M., of Salisbury, N.C., and Sallie L. Lindsay of Lexington, N.D., by the Rev. Geo. W. Dame, in the Church of the Epiphany, Danville. So. Ch., Mar. 22, 1877

GREENHOW
See also GASSAWAY, Maria F. (Mrs.)

GREENLAW
S. B., and Charlotte A., d. of G. M. Carter, Esq., all of Westmoreland Co., by the Rev. T. E. Locke, at the residence of the bride's father. So. Ch., Aug. 19, 1869

GREENWAY
Edward Capel, and Sadie Anna, youngest d. of Dr. Mix, by the Rev. T. E. Locke, at the residence of Dr. Oscar Gunnell Mix, near Warren, Albemarle Co., Va. So. Ch., June 21, 1888

Virginia, d. of J. Henry Greenway of Harford Co., Md., and Jacob Albert of Baltimore, by the Rt. Rev. T. B. Lyman, D.D., Bishop of North Carolina, assisted by the Rev. Chauncey B. Brewster, in Grace Church, Baltimore. So. Ch., Dec. 31, 1885

GREER
George H. T., of Franklin Co., and Mattie E., eldest d. of the late Pilip**Rahm of Richmond, by the Rev. George Woodbridge, D.D., at the residence of the bride's brother. So. Ch., Jan. 7, 1869

GREGG
Cephas, of Lagrange, Ky., and Mary M., d. of T. F. Newton, Esq., by the Rev. Francis M. Whittle, at Charleston, Kanawha Co., Va. So. Ch., Mar. 3, 1848

Henry S., of Merriam Park, Minn., and Estella Moore of New Martinsville, W.Va., by the Rev. Jacob Brittingham, in St. Ann's Church, New

---

** Given as printed
* Antrim Parish is in Halifax County, Virginia (Journal ... Diocese of Southern Virginia, Portsmouth, Va., 1941)

MARRIAGE NOTICES IN THE SOUTHERN CHURCHMAN WITH DATES OF PUBLICATION

Martinsville, W.Va. So. Ch., Dec. 12, 1889

Sarah N., of Wickliffe, Va., and the Rev. H. D. Page, rector of St. Stephens Church, Culpeper C.H., Va., by the Rev. J. J. Page, in Wickliffe Church, Clarke Co., Va. So. Ch., Jan. 11, 1883

Willis Ray, of Syracuse, N.Y., and Mary Chamberlayne Wall of Berryville, Va., by the Rev. Edward Wall, father of the bride, assisted by the Rt. Rev. W. L. Gravatt, D.D., Bishop Coadjutor of the Diocese of West Virginia, in Grace Episcopal Church, Berryville, Va. So. Ch., Oct. 31, 1914

GREGORY

Chas. A., and Bettie Thorp, both of Granville Co., N.C., by the Rev. P. D. Thompson, at the residence of the bride's father, Benj. P. Thorp. So. Ch., Dec. 19, 1872

Deucalion (Dr.), and Sallie P. Lewis, both of King William, by the Rev. J. Hervey Hundley, at Auburn, King William Co. So. Ch., Oct. 10, 1872

Ernest Trowbridge, of Brookline, Mass., and Mary Baldwin Brooke of Guthrie, Okla., by the Rt. Rev. Francis K. Brooke, father of the bride, and the Rev. Dr. George F. Smythe, in the Church of the Holy Spirit, Gambier, Ohio. So. Ch., Sept. 14, 1907

Isobel, d. of Wm. Gregory, and George Johnston, by the Rev. Dr. Bullock, at Alexandria, Va. So. Ch., Dec. 28, 1871

Jane T., d. of the late Dr. Thomas L. Gregory, and W. D. Cardwell, s. of the Hon. R. H. Cardwell, all of Hanover Co., Va., by the Rev. S. S. Hepbron, at Blenheim, the residence of the bride's mother. So. Ch., May 15, 1890

M. Alice, d. of the late Fendall Gregory, Esq. of Piping Tree, King William Co., and John B. Duvall of Charles City Co., by the Rev. S. S. Hepbron, in Acquintan Church, King William Co. So. Ch., Feb. 13, 1890

Martha T., and Dr. Nelson McP. Ferebee, U.S.N., by the Rev. P. D. Thompson, in Granville Co., N.C. So. Ch., Nov. 28, 1872

Mary, d. of Mrs. J. H. Gregory of Rochester, and the Rev. J. A. Massey, D.D., rector of Trinity Church, Mobile, by the Rt. Rev. J. P. B. Wilmer, D.D., Bishop of Louisiana, in Christ Church, Rochester, So. Ch., Aug. 16, 1877

W. F., of Petersburg, and Susie F. Norfleet, by the Rev. A. B. Tizzard, at the residence of the bride's mother, Amelia Co., Va. So. Ch., Jan. 31, 1878

William S., of Lunenburg Co., Va., and Rosa B., d. of Isaac O. Epes, Esq., by the Rev. William Herbert Assheton, at Bellefonte, Nottoway Co., Va. So. Ch., Feb. 16, 1882

GRESHAM

Alice M., eldest d. of Dr. Henry Gresham of Essex Co., Va., and John N. Temple of Fulton, Ark.,

MARRIAGE NOTICES IN THE SOUTHERN CHURCHMAN WITH DATES OF PUBLICATION

s. of the late Rev. H. W.
L. Temple of Essex Co., Va.,
by the Rev. E. Meade, in
St. John's Church, Tappa-
hannock, Va. So. Ch.,
Nov. 3, 1881

Mary B., of King and Queen
Co., Va., and Henry W.
Crane of Baltimore, at
Walkerton, King and Queen
Co., Va. So. Ch., Dec. 6,
1888

GRIFFIN
Lizzie P., and Dr. William
H. Ballard of Louisiana, by
the Rev. Edwin A. Penick, at
the residence of Dr. John H.
Griffin, Salem, Roanoke
Co., Va. So. Ch., Jan. 16,
1879

Mary, d. of Dr. John H.
Griffin of Salem, and Wm.
A. Johnson of New Orleans,
by the Rev. Edward H.
Ingle, at Salem, Roanoke
Co., Va. So. Ch., Dec.
31, 1868

Samuel, of Liberty, Va., and
Nannie R., d. of E. S.
Hutter, Esq., by the Rev.
Edward H. Ingle, at
"Poplar Forest", the resi-
dence of the bride's
father. So. Ch., Dec. 18,
1873

William I., and Camilla,
d. of the officiating
clergyman, the Rev.
M. H. Vaughan, in Christ
Church, Elizabeth City, N.C.
So. Ch., Nov. 16, 1882

GRIFFITH
David H., of Westmoreland Co.,
and Lucy Armistead, youngest
d. of the officiating
clergyman, the Rev. T. E.
Locke, in Christ Church, St.
Anne's parish, Albemarle Co.,
Va. So. Ch., June 11, 1885

Eleanor, and Dr. Wm. F. Fairfax of Tipton Co., Tenn.,
at Locust Farm, Westmore-
land Co. So. Ch., Mar.
14, 1867

Thos. W., of Loudoun, and
Martha A. Edwards, by the
Rev. F. M. Whittle, at
the residence of the bride's
father, Clarke Co. So.
Ch., Feb. 15, 1856

GRIGG
B. I., and Rosalie, d. of J.
C. and S. E. Blanton of
Cumberland Co., Va., by the
Rev. F. Stringfellow, in
Grace Church, Ca Ira, Va.
So. Ch., May 20, 1880

GRIGGS
Roscoe R., of Macon Co., N.C.,
and Mary Grace, d. of Nim-
rod M. Dobbin and Mary Duke
Hardin, his wife, of Watauga
Co., N.C., by the Rev. Hugh
A. Dobbin of Valley Crucis,
in Saint Matthews Church, Todd,
N.C. So. Ch., Sept. 30, 1911

GRILLEY
Edwin Warner, Jr. (The Rev.),
rector of the Church of
the Good Shepherd, Paw-
tucket, R.I., and Hazel,
d. of Mr. and Mrs. Clarence
Watson Scott of Conimicut,*
by the Rt. Rev. Granville
Gaylord Bennett, Suffragan-
Bishop of Rhode Island,
assisted by the Rev. Charles
Hosea Temple, rector of the
Church of the Transfiguration and the Rev. Irving
Andrew Evans, rector of St.
Andrews School, Barrington,
in the Church of the Transfiguration, Cranston, R.I.
So. Ch., Aug. 19, 1939

GRIMES
Charles E., Jr., and Augusta,
d. of the late Joseph T.
England, all of Baltimore,
by the Rev. Edward H. Ingle,

* Given as printed

MARRIAGE NOTICES IN THE SOUTHERN CHURCHMAN WITH DATES OF PUBLICATION

in St. Bartholomew's Church, Baltimore. So. Ch., Feb. 17, 1887

GRINNAN
A. S. (Doct*), of Madison Co., and Georgia I., second d. of John R. Bryan, Esq., by the Rev. C. Mann, at Eagle Point, Gloucester Co., Va. So. Ch., July 1, 1859

Frances Anne Cazemovo,** d. of the late Rev. Andrew Glassell Grinnan and his wife Anne Cazemore* Minor, and Edward Stuart, s. of Mr. and Mrs. Stuart Carter of Prince William Co., Va., by the Rev. R. Bryan Grinnan, at Brampton, near Orange, Va., at the home of her aunt, Nina S. Grinnan. So. Ch., Aug. 7, 1926

GRINNELLY
Ida J., and A. L. Cross of Centerville, by the Rev. R. A. Castleman, at residence near Fairfax C.H., Va. So. Ch., Feb. 23, 1893

GRINSTEAD
Robt. L., and Edna A. Smith, both of Frankfort, by the Rev. Henry T. Sharp, in the Church of the Ascension, Frankfort, Ky. So. Ch., Apr. 23, 1874

GRISWOLD
Mary Elizabeth, eldest d. of the late John B. Griswold of Goldsboro, and the Rev. J. Worrall Larmour, by the Rt. Rev. Theodore B. Lyman assisted by the Rev. Edward R. Rich, in St. Stephen's Church, Goldsboro, N.C. So. Ch., Feb. 21, 1878

GROOME
Charles Q., Esq., and Virginia Daingerfield, by the Rev. John C. McCabe, rector of the Church of the Ascension, in St. Peter's Church, Baltimore. So. Ch., Dec. 3, 1858

GROSER
Charlotte Lillian, d. of the late Thomas Wentworth Groser of Brookland, sister of A. S. Groser of Richmond, Va., and gr. niece and niece of the officiating clergymen, and Cecil Silas Pooley, by the Rev. S. M. Haskins, D.D., rector, assisted by the Rev. T. W. Haskins, D.D. of Los Angeles, Cal., in St. Mark's Church, Brooklyn, N.Y. So. Ch., Oct. 27, 1892

GROSS
William L., of Brunswick, Md., and Annie C. Housholder of Loudoun Co., Va., by the Rev. Edw. T. Helfenstein of St. Mark's parish, Frederick Co., Md., in the Lutheran Church, near Lovettsville, Va. So. Ch., Oct. 26, 1893

GRUBB
Curtis (The Rev.), and Annetta F. Schooley, both of Loudoun Co., Va., by the Rev. Theodore Reed, at Lovettsville. So. Ch., Oct. 17, 1878

Eleanor C., and Arthur Henry Grant, in St. Luke's Church, Live Oak, Fla. So. Ch., Oct. 28, 1911

Florence R., and Catlett C. Fitzhugh, at Cool Water, Hanover Co., the home of the bride's parents, J. F. and K. F. Grubb. So. Ch., Oct. 26, 1907

Joseph F., of Hanover Co., Va., formerly of Loudoun Co., Va., and Kate F. Schooley of

---

* Given as printed
** Given as printed, possibly "Cazenove"

MARRIAGE NOTICES IN THE SOUTHERN CHURCHMAN WITH DATES OF PUBLICATION

Loudoun Co., Va., by the Rev. Curtis Grubb assisted by the Rev. Carter Page, at Violet Hall, the residence of the bride's mother, Loudoun Co., Va. So. Ch., Nov. 27, 1884

Springer L., and Phoebe Brian, both of Newport, Del., by the Rev. W. D. Hanson. So. Ch., June 5, 1879

GRUBER

Martha J., d. of Jacob Gruber, and Richard Ryon, Esq., all of Jefferson Co., Va., by the Rev. Wm. McGuire, at the residence of the bride's father. So. Ch., Oct. 7, 1859

GRUNDY

Clara H., and Richard F. Boirne of Lewisburg, W.Va., by the Rev. Charles Morris, at the residence of the bride's father, J. B. Grundy, Ashland, Va. So. Ch., July 5, 1877

GRYMES

Annie, d. of Geo. E. Grymes, and John P. Washington, all of King George Co., by the Rev. Jas. W. Shields, at Mt. Stuart, King George Co. So. Ch., Dec. 23, 1875

Edmonia H., and Francis A. Tolson of Maryland, by the Rev. Arthur Johns, at the residence of the bride's mother, King George Co., Va. So. Ch., Nov. 13, 1873

H. C., of King George Co., and Mattie T., d. of Dr. Horace D. Ashton, by the Rev. Edward McGuire, at "Bleak Hill", the residence of the bride's father, King George Co. So. Ch., Dec. 9, 1880

Julia, d. of Geo. E. Grymes, Esq., and E. C. Hanway of Alleghany City, Pa., by the Rev. M. Hunter, at Mount Stuart, King George Co., Va. So. Ch., July 1, 1880

Lucy Fitzhugh, d. of the late Custis Grymes of King George Co., Va., and Edgar S. Meade, by the Rev. Jos. R. Jones, in Meade Memorial Church, White Post, Clarke Co., Va. So. Ch., Nov. 24, 1881

Nannie Atkinson, and H. Thacker Berry, by the Rev. John McNabb, at Woodstock, King George Co., Va. So. Ch., Jan. 12, 1893

Rosalie L., and Dr. Milton R. Stuart, by the Rev. Jos. R. Jones, in the Meade Memorial Church, White Post. So. Ch., Oct. 6, 1881

Susie, d. of Dr. R. P. Grymes, and Charles T. Honley, by the Rev. A. B. Tizzard, at Clover Hill, Chesterfield Co., Va. So. Ch., Jan. 4, 1883

W. D., and Mary, d. of Rosalie and the late S. P. Stuart, by the Rev. A. J. Willis, in St. Paul's Church, King George Co., Va. So. Ch., Nov. 25, 1886

See also TOLER, Ann N. (Mrs.)

GUERRAUT

John R. (Dr.), and Katharine Randolph Lee, both of Virginia, by the Rev. Frank Stringfellow, in Trinity Church, Rocky Mount. So. Ch., July 28, 1892

GUIGON

Alexander B., and Kate Empie, d. of the late James Sheppard and gr.d. of the Rev. Dr. Empie, first rector of St. James' Church, by the Rev.

MARRIAGE NOTICES IN THE SOUTHERN CHURCHMAN WITH DATES OF PUBLICATION

Joshua Peterkin, D.D., assisted by the Rev. Preston G. Nash, in St. James' Church, Richmond. So. Ch., Mar. 17, 1887

GUION

George S. (The Hon), of Louisiana, and Rosina C. Winder of Northampton Co., by the Rev. M. L. Chevers, at Eastville, Northampton Co. So. Ch., Oct. 16, 1857

Harriet Amelia, youngest d. of James Guion, Esq. of Westchester Co., N.Y., and the Rev. George Washington Cole of Tecumseh, Mich., by the Rev. Dr. Milnor, in New York. So. Ch., Oct. 11, 1839

GULICK

Greer R., of Loudoun Co., and Helen Wood, eldest d. of John S. and Alice J. Ewell of Prince William Co., by the Rev. A. P. Gray, at "Edge Hill", the residence of the bride's parents. So. Ch., Mar. 13, 1884

GUNN

E. Sterling (The Rev.), of Halifax Co., Va., and Susan Elwood (Ellie) Carter of Chatham, by the Rev. C. O. Pruden, assisted by the Rev. Mr. Amiss, Presiding Elder of the Methodist Church, Danville district, in Emmanuel Church, Chatham, Va. So. Ch., Jan. 1, 1891

George Purnell (The Rev.), of Alta Vista, Va., and Frances Hawkins Purnell of Charlotte, N.C., by the Rt. Rev. Robert C. Jett, assisted by the Rev. Berryman Green, in the Immanuel Chapel, Theological Seminary, Alexandria, Va. So. Ch., Sept. 6, 1930

GUNNELL

Mary N. R., and Donald Phillips, by the Rev. J. P. H. Mason, rector of St. Martin's Parish,* and the Rev. James W. Morris of the Epiphany Church, Washington, D.C., at Oakland, Hanover Co., Va. So. Ch., Aug. 10, 1925

GUTHRIE

George N., of Arkansas, and Ellen Cary Hobson of Powhatan Co., Va., by the Rev. J. D. Powell of Portsmouth, Va., at "Brooklyn", Powhatan Co., Va. So. Ch., Sept. 23, 1875

GUY

Mattie Wright, d. of Mattie W. and J. Emmett Guy, and Samuel Pride Daniel of Charlotte Co., Va., in St. John's Church, Marion, N.C. So. Ch., May 4, 1907

R. M., of Staunton, and Hallie G., d. of C. T. Wills, Esq., by the Rev. Mr. Suter, at Lynchburg. So. Ch., Oct. 10, 1867

GWATHMEY

Mary, d. of the late R. Carter and Emily Smith Gwathmey, and Fleming Saunders of Campbell Co., by the Rev. Charles Minnigerode, D.D., in the Church of "The Good Shepherd", Campbell Co. So. Ch., Aug. 20, 1874

Mary Ann, d. of Robert T. Gwathmey, Esq. of Richmond, and Charles R. Barney, by the Rt. Rev. Bishop Moore. So. Ch., June 7, 1839

R. C., Esq., of Richmond, and Emily, d. of Maj. Charles H. Smith of the U.S. Army, by the Rev. Mr. Parks. So. Ch., Dec. 1, 1837

W. W., Esq., of Richmond, Va.,

---

* St. Martin's Parish is in Hanover County, Virginia (<u>Journal ... Diocese of Virginia</u>, Richmond, 1941)

MARRIAGE NOTICES IN THE SOUTHERN CHURCHMAN WITH DATES OF PUBLICATION

and Mary L., d. of G. P. Tayloe, Esq., of Roanoke Co., Va., by the Rev. Mr. Pendleton. So. Ch., Oct. 17, 1856

GWATKIN
Lina, second d. of the late Charles A. Gwatkin of Richmond, Va., and F. L. Marshall of Washington, D.C., by the Rev. Chas. H. Road, of Richmond, Va., the residence of the bride's mother. So. Ch., Mar. 14, 1878

GWATKINS
Mary S., and Chas. P. Stokes, both of Richmond, Va., by the Rev. Wm. Norwood, D.D., at the residence of the bride's mother. So. Ch., Oct. 31, 1872

GWYN
Fanny Thurston, of Baltimore, Md., and Dr. John W. Harrison of Petersburg, Va., by the Rev. Dr. J. J. Sams, in Holy Trinity Church, Baltimore, Md. So. Ch., July 23, 1891

H

HABERSHAM
　Stephen E. (Dr.), of Aiken, S.C., and Lucy, d. of the late Maj. Richard Pollard of Albemarle Co., Va., by the Rev. Mr. Ambler, at Alta Vista, Va. So. Ch., Aug. 7, 1851

HABLISTON
　Sadie D., and Allen Madison Lyon, by the Rev. Dr. A. G. Brown, at the residence of the bride's father, Frederick H. Habliston. So. Ch., Apr. 30, 1891

HACK
　Sallie Upshur, and James K. Ayres, by the Rev. J. M. Chevers, at Fairview, Accomac Co. So. Ch., Dec. 5, 1856

HACKER
　Theodore, of New York, N.Y., and Hattie Cabell, d. of the late Thomas H. Blankenship of Richmond, by the Rev. Mr. Strong, in St. John's Episcopal Church, Savannah, Ga. So. Ch., Dec. 18, 1890

HACKETT
　S. H., and Cornelia L. Berkeley, d. of the officiating clergyman, the Rev. F. F. Berkeley, in Amelia Co., Va. So. Ch., Jan. 21, 1875

HACKLEY
　Eliza M., d. of the late Robert J. Hackley, Esq. of Florida, and Edward Scott, Esq. of Powhatan, by the Rev. A. B. Tizzard, at Mantua. So. Ch., Feb. 8, 1865

　Harriet Randolph, eldest d. of the late R. I. Hackley of Tallahassee, Fla., and Robt. I. Morrison of Lawrenceville, by the Rev. C. J. Gibson. So. Ch., Jan. 21, 1848

　Sallie F., second d. of the late Robt. Hackley of Tallahassee, Fla., and J. Wyckliffe Scott of Orange Co., by the Rev. Joseph Earnest, at Litchfield, Orange Co. So. Ch., Feb. 29, 1856

HADDEN
　Gavin, and Rebecca Selden, d. of the Rt. Rev. and Mrs. Arthur Selden Lloyd, by the Rt. Rev. Arthur Selden Lloyd assisted by the Rev. Theodore Sedgwick, rector, in Calvary Church, N.Y. So. Ch., Mar. 7, 1914

HADDOX
　Edrina C., d. of Mrs. S. D. and the late C. B. Haddox, and W. G. Davis of Fauquier Co., Va., by the Rev. F. B. Lee, at "Hillsboro", the residence of the bride's mother in Rappahannock Co. So. Ch., Jan. 1, 1885

HADEN
　M. Augusta, d. of Dr. Madison Haden, and John D. Harrison of Henry Co., by the Rev. Wm. W. Greene, at the residence of the bride's father, in Campbell Co. So. Ch., July 9, 1874

　William E., of Fluvanna Co., and Sarah A. Turner of Albemarle, by the Rev. T. E. Locke, at the residence of Mr. Hopkins, near Glendower. So. Ch.,

MARRIAGE NOTICES IN THE SOUTHERN CHURCHMAN WITH DATES OF PUBLICATION

HAGER
   Christopher, and Fredrica
   Cloak, both of Richmond,
   by the Rev. Mr. Hawley, in
   Washington, D.C. So. Ch.,
   Dec. 22, 1837
   Dorsey, of Los Angeles, Cal.,
   and Adelaide Tyler, d. of
   the late Frank and Isabel
   C. Myer of Norfolk, Va.,
   by the Rev. A. G. H.
   Bode, in St. Luke's
   Church, Long Beach, Cal.
   So. Ch., May 31, 1913
HAGNER
   Alexander B., of Annap-
   olis, Md., and Anna
   Louisa, d. of the late
   Randolph Harrison, Esq.,
   by the Rev. F. M. Whittle,
   at Elk Hill, Goochland
   Co., Va. So. Ch.,
   June 2, 1853
HAIGH
   William, s. of the late
   Ven. Henry Haigh, M.A.,
   Archdeacon of the "Isle
   of Wight" and Vicar of
   Newport, England, and
   Edmonia Louise, d. of
   Charles S. Lee, Esq. of
   Clarke Co., Va., by the
   Rev. P. P. Phillips, in
   Grace Church, Berryville,
   Va. So. Ch., Apr. 26,
   1888
HAIGHT
   Maggie A., only d. of
   Alex. Haight, Esq., and
   Thomas W. Lee, all of
   Fauquier Co., Va., by
   the Rev. Jno. McGill, at
   Sully, the residence of
   the bride's parents.
   So. Ch., Oct. 15, 1874
HAIL
   Leenell Virginia, only d.
   of Judge Stevadson A. Hail
   and Lucy Stewart Fitzhugh
   Feb. 12, 1885
   his wife, and Otto Kenton
   McAdams, all of Batesville,
   Ark., by the Rev. H. A.
   Stowell, in St. Paul's Epis-
   copal Church, Batesville, Ark.
   So. Ch., Feb. 11, 1911
HAILE
   Lizzie, of Essex Co., and
   Duncan L. McRae of Georgia,
   by the Rev. Everard Meade,
   in St. Paul's Church,
   Essex Co., Va. So. Ch.,
   Oct. 1, 1885
   Mollie M., of Essex Co.,
   Va., and Oscar O. Barr
   of Edgefield, by the Rev.
   E. T. Walker, at the resi-
   dence of the bride's brother-
   in-law, M. L. Holson, in
   Edgefield, S.C. So. Ch.,
   Jan. 6, 1881
   See also BOGARDUS, Ellen
   Haile
HAINES
   Claudia Marguerite, d. of
   Mr. and Mrs. J. B. Haines
   and sister of the Rev. E.
   S. Haines, missionary to
   Liberia now in this country
   on furlough, and the Rev.
   Jacob Ashton Winterstein,
   rector of Holy Trinity
   Church of West Chester, in
   the Diocese of Pennsylvania, at
   Swedesboro, N.J. So. Ch.,
   May 17, 1924
   Claudius R. (The Rev.), of
   the Diocese of South
   Carolina, and Cordelia
   Giles, d. of Jno. S. Hall,
   Esq. of Hartford Co., by
   the Rev. W. S. Crampton,
   in Spesutia Church, Hart-
   ford Co., Md. So. Ch.,
   Oct. 22, 1858
   Ella L., of Jefferson Co.,
   W.Va., and Harry Johnson
   Gossling of Philadelphia,
   by the Rev. John McGill,
   in St. John's Church,

MARRIAGE NOTICES IN THE SOUTHERN CHURCHMAN WITH DATES OF PUBLICATION

Ripon, W.Va. So. Ch., Apr. 24, 1890
John Taylor (Lt.), Fifth Cavalry, U.S. Army, and Annie, d. of Rear Admiral John J. Almy, U.S. Navy, by the Rev. David Barr, in the Church of the Epiphany, Washington, D.C. So. Ch., June 27, 1889

HAINS
Nannie, d. of the officiating clergyman, and Lilburn Wallace Spooner of Roanoke, Va., by the Rev. C. R. Hains, in St. Paul's Church, Petersburg. So. Ch., Jan. 29, 1885

HAIRSTON
George S., and Nannie W. Watkins, both of Henry Co., Va., by the Rev. Jno. R. Lee, at Shawnee, the residence of the bride's father. So. Ch., Jan. 6, 1870
Janie, d. of Dr. G. S. Hairston, deceased, of Henry Co., Va., and John S. Draper of Pulaski, Va., by the Rev. J. R. Lee, at Marrowbone, Henry Co., Va. So. Ch., May 11, 1871*

HAIST
Virginia Ethel, d. of the Rev. and Mrs. F. W. Haist of Henry, Ill., and the Rt. Rev. D. T. Huntington, D.D., Bishop of Anking, by Bishop Graves of Shanghai, in the Cathedral of Our Merciful Saviour, Anking, China. So. Ch., Feb. 3, 1917

HALE
Charles J., and Emily J. Moorsom, both lately of England, by the Rev. J. B. Craighill, in the rectory of St. Paul's Church, Suffolk. So. Ch., Jan. 15, 1874

HALES
Barksdale (Dr.), and Maggie, d. of Mrs. Susan Rowlett, all of Halifax Co., Va., by the Rev. O. A. Kinsolving, D.D., at the residence of Dabney Cosby. So. Ch., Sept. 10, 1885

HALL
Adelaide S., and Roger P. Annan, both of Clarke Co., Va., by the Rev. T. F. Martin, at the residence of Mrs. Catharine V. Hall. So. Ch., Nov. 7, 1867
Alexander Stuart, and Minnie M. Ellis, at "Afton", the Ellis home, Buckingham Co., Va. So. Ch., Mar. 14, 1908
Bessie Stuart, and R. O. Egerton of Petersburg, Va., by the Rev. J. K. Mason, at the residence of the bride's father, Horace B. Hall, Esq., at Fredericksburg, Va. So. Ch., May 1, 1884
Charles H. (The Rev.), rector of the Church of the Epiphany, and Lizzie M., d. of George C. Ames, Esq. of Washington, by the Rev. G. D. Cummins, D.D. So. Ch., Sept. 18, 1857
Cordelia Giles, d. of Jno. S. Hall, Esq. of Hartford Co., and the Rev. Claudius R. Haines of the Diocese of South Carolina, by the Rev. S. W. Crampton, in Spesutia Church, Hartford Co., Md. So. Ch., Oct. 22, 1858

---

* The original incorrect notice of this marriage published in the Southern Churchman May 4, 1871, and later corrected by the editor in the May 11th issue, is omitted from this volume

MARRIAGE NOTICES IN THE SOUTHERN CHURCHMAN WITH DATES OF PUBLICATION

E. G., and Louisa, d. of the late Dr. E. A. Currie, by the Rev. Henry L. Derby, at "Verville", the residence of the bride's mother, in Lancaster Co., Va. So. Ch., Dec. 29, 1881

E. J. (The Rev.), of Pocahontas Co., W.Va., and Elizabeth Goings of Alexandria Co., Va., by the Rev. D. F. Sprigg, in Alexandria Co. So. Ch., Oct. 18, 1877

Eliza S., of Portland, and the Rev. Douglass C. Peabody of Atlanta, Ga., by the Rev. Dr. Emery, former rector of the parish, assisted by the Rev. James F. Spaulding, in Trinity Church, Portland. So. Ch., Feb. 3, 1876

F. S. (Dr.), and Bessie, d. of the late Philip Slaughter of Rappahannock Co., Va., by the Rev. P. Slaughter, D.D., at Wellington, Culpeper Co., Va. So. Ch., Dec. 4, 1879

Fannie M., youngest d. of the late Richard C. Hall, and Walter M. Wren, all of Richmond, Va., by the Rev. Dr. Sprigg, at the residence of the bride's sister, Mrs. A. R. Yarbrough. So. Ch., Jan. 28, 1886

Hattie B., d. of Horace B. Hall of Fredericksburg, and W. R. Robertson of Culpeper Co., Va., by the Rev. R. J. McBryde, at the residence of the bride's father. So. Ch., June 17, 1880

Henry Arthur, Esq., of Upperville, Va., and Susan F., d. of the late George Grayson of Loudoun Co., by the Rev. O. A. Kinsolving, at Newstead, Loudoun Co. So. Co., Oct. 30, 1857

J. Leslie, Professor of English and History in the College of William and Mary, and Margaret F., d. of Mrs. E. Douglas Farland of Tappahannock, Va., in St. John's Church, Tappahannock. So. Ch., June 13, 1889

Jennie D., and James McCaw Fox, both of Richmond, Va., by the Rev. D. F. Sprigg assisted by the Rev. Joshua Peterkin, D.D., in Moore Memorial Church. So. Ch., Sept. 27, 1883

Marshall Carter, and Lily, d. of the late John S. Braxton of Norfolk, Va., by the Rev. R. J. McBryde, in St. George's Church, Fredericksburg, Va. So. Ch., Dec. 8, 1881

Mary, d. of Thomas J. Hall, Esq. of Anne Arundel Co., Md., and Ottomar Bremhe, Esq. of Baltimore, by the Rev. John C. McCabe, D.D., in St. James' Church, West River, Md. So. Ch., Nov. 16, 1860

Richard Clarence (The Rev.), pastor of St. Timothy's Church, New York, and Mary Carr, d. of John Gibson of Chestnut Hill, Baltimore Co., Md., by the Rt. Rev. Bishop of Maryland, in St. John's Church, Huntington, near Baltimore. So. Ch., Jan. 13, 1860

S. Cornelia, of Fairfax Co., Va., d. of the late Rev. Charles Hall of Newark,

MARRIAGE NOTICES IN THE SOUTHERN CHURCHMAN WITH DATES OF PUBLICATION

N.J., and the Rev. D. Otis Kellogg, Jr. of Bridgeport, Conn., by the Rev. W. Sparrow, D.D. assisted by the Rev. L. W. Bancroft of Connecticut, near Alexandria, Va. So. Ch., Apr. 26, 1861

Sophia C., d. of Horace B. Hall, and H. B. Lane, all of Fredericksburg, by the Rev. R. J. McBryde, at the residence of the bride's father. So. Ch., Jan. 19, 1882

Thomas M., and Emma Kendler, both of Chesterfield Co., Va., by the Rev. A. B. Tizzard, in Trinity Church, Clover Hill Mines. So. Ch., Oct. 2, 1873

Virginia, d. of Thomas I. Hall, Esq., and James C. Crane of Baltimore, by the Rev. Theodore Gambrall, in St. James' Church, Anne Arundel Co., Md. So. Ch., Apr. 29, 1875

HALLAM
Frank (The Rev.), of Calvary Church, Americus, Ga., and Virginia Hoge Hicks of Richmond, by the Rev. Joshua Peterkin, D.D., in Richmond, Va. So. Ch., Feb. 4, 1875

Frank (The Rev.), rector of Epiphany Parish, Prince George's Co., Md., and Emma B. Sullivan, by the Rev. F. G. Sears, rector of Christ Church, Holly Springs, at the residence of the bride's uncle, E. Virden, Jackson, Miss. So. Ch., May 19, 1892

HALPINE
Lucy J., d. of the late Gen. Charles G. Halpine, and John P. Faure of New York, by the Rev. J. B. Perry, in Washington. So. Ch., Oct. 11, 1888

HAMILTON
Hattie D., and Thomas S. Rutherfoord of Culpeper, Va., by the Rev. Charles Y. Steptoe, at the residence of the bride's father, George Hamilton of Culpeper, Va. So. Ch., Oct. 19, 1876

Isabella H., only d. of Dr. Hugh Hamilton, and Joseph Downman, Esq. of Layton Stone, by the Rev. Mr. Cole, at Oak Farm, Fauquier Co. So. Ch., Dec. 23, 1859

James C., and Ella A. McGilton, both of Uniontown, by the Rev. Henry T. Sharp, in St. John's Church, Uniontown, Ky. So. Ch., May 9, 1872

Janet S., third d. of Dr. Geo. S. Hamilton, and John D. Hamilton of Culpeper Co., by the Rev. John McGill, at "The Highlands", the residence of the bride's parents, Fauquier Co., Va. So. Ch., Dec. 11, 1884

John D., of Culpeper Co., and Janet S., third d. of Dr. Geo. S. Hamilton, by the Rev. John McGill, at "The Highlands", the residence of the bride's parents, Fauquier Co., Va. So. Ch., Dec. 11, 1884

Lewis Meyer, of New York, formerly of Baltimore, and Sarah Harriet, youngest d. of the late

MARRIAGE NOTICES IN THE SOUTHERN CHURCHMAN WITH DATES OF PUBLICATION

Thaddeus William Harris, M.D., by the Rev. Wm. Chancey Langdon, D.D., at Cambridge, Mass. So. Ch., Jan. 1, 1880

Lillias R., of Fauquier Co., and John F. Scott of Fredericksburg, at the residence of the bride's father, in Fauquier Co. So. Ch., Dec. 15, 1887

Nannie B., d. of Dr. Geo. S. Hamilton of Prince Wm. Co., Va., and Wilhelm H. Pratje, formerly of Germany, by the Rev. R. T. Brown, at "Burnside", near Haymarket. So. Ch., Nov. 21, 1872

Roberta W., d. of George Hamilton of Culpeper Co., Va., and John M. Cunningham of Nashville, Tenn., by the Rev. C. Y. Steptoe, in Christ Church. So. Ch., Oct. 1, 1874

W. Stanley, a native of Culpeper Co., Va., and Eva Petric, all of Jackson, Miss., by the Rev. John Hunter, at the residence of the bride's mother, Jackson, Miss. So. Ch., Feb. 3, 1876

Wallace H., of New York (formerly of Bristol, England), and Gertrude, d. of Mrs. J. M. Gray, by the Rev. Magruder Maury, at "Travellers Rest", Stafford Co., Va. So. Ch., Jan. 12, 1871

HAMLETT
Corlelia M., d. of Col. W. J. Hamlett of Oak Level, and Herrmann W. Schroeder of Charlotte, N.C., at Oak Level, Henry Co. So. Ch., May 4, 1871

HAMLIN

Thos., of Danville, Va., and Lucy Nelson, only d. of N. H. Massie, deceased, by the Rev. K. Nelson, D.D. assisted by the Rev. C. K. Nelson, D.D. and the Rev. J. S. Hanckle, D.D., in Christ Church, Charlottesville, Va. So. Ch., Feb. 18, 1886

Wood J., of Fluvanna, and Maggie H. Riddick of Brunswick, by the Rev. Otis A. Glazebrook, in St. Andrew's Church. So. Ch., Oct. 14, 1869

HAMMERSLOUGH
Reuben Warren, of Baltimore, and Sarah Champe Randolph, by the Rev. Frank Mezick, rector of the parish, at Markham, the residence of the bride's mother, Mrs. Louisa H. Randolph, Nelson Co., Va. So. Ch., July 25, 1908

HAMMOND
A. B., Esq., of Roanoke, Va., and Fanny Murray of Hagerstown, Md., by the Rev. D. M. Wood, at the residence of the bride's mother, in Hagerstown, Md. So. Ch., Oct. 23, 1884

Florinda J., of Berryville, Clarke Co., Va., and John B. Tilford of New York, by the Rev. T. F. Martin, at the residence of Mrs. Bushrod Taylor. So. Ch., Jan. 6, 1870

Frances W., and Alice B. Hankins, both of James City Co., by the Rev. L. B. Wharton, at Marlbrook, James City Co. So. Ch., Nov. 23, 1876

J. Pinkney (The Rev.), of Bangor, Me., and Nannie, d. of Washington C. Page,

MARRIAGE NOTICES IN THE SOUTHERN CHURCHMAN WITH DATES OF PUBLICATION

Esq. of Alexandria, by the Rev. C. B. Dana. So. Ch., Dec. 10, 1847

Jane B., d. of the late Thomas B. Hammond of Jefferson, and Dr. Geo. H. Pierce, by the Rev. C. E. Ambler, in the Episcopal Church, Charles Town. So. Ch., Oct. 17, 1856

Kensey Johns (The Rev.), and Florence Jones, by the Rev. Edmund L. Woodward of Shrine Mont, Orkney Springs, Va., assisted by the Rev. Robert E. Brown, rector of the Church of the Ascension and Prince of Peace, Baltimore, in the Bishop's Chapel in the Diocesan House, Baltimore, Md. So. Ch., May 1, 1937

Marie Louise, d. of Gen. John Hammond of New York, and William Tayloe Snyder of Georgetown, by the Rev. Albert Stuart of Christ Church, Georgetown, assisted by the Rev. Edward H. Ingle of the Church of the Ascension, in the Church of the Ascension, Washington, D.C. So. Ch., Apr. 5, 1883

Mary P., d. of Dr. Hammond of Shepherdstown, and G. F. Lloyd, Esq., by the Rev. C. W. Andrews, at Bedford, near Shepherdstown, Jefferson Co., Va. So. Ch., Oct. 31, 1856

Wm. G. (The Rev.), of Middleburg, Va., and Ellen R., d. of Col. Wm. Giddings of Loudoun Co., by the Rev. Carter Page assisted by the Rev. Nelson Head, D.D., of the Methodist Church, in Christ Church, Goresville. So. Ch., July 17, 1890

HAMPTON
Wm. H., and Maria J. Taylor, by the Rev. Henry T. Sharp, in the Church of the Ascension, Frankfort, Ky. So. Ch., Dec. 11, 1873

HANCKEL
Frances E., d. of the officiating minister, and Judge T. A. Lozier of Belleville, Canada, by the Rev. Dr. Hanckel, at Clifton Springs, N.Y. So. Ch., Nov. 29, 1883

HANCOCK
Nellie V., and D. G. Porter, both of Culpeper Co., Va., by the Rev. F. B. Lee, in St. Paul's Church, Culpeper Co., Va. So. Ch., Dec. 22, 1887

Wm. B., of Winchester, Va., and Lula L., d. of the late Jacob P. Effinger of Harrisonburg, Va., by the Rev. O. S. Bunting, in Emmanuel Church, Harrisonburg, Va. So. Ch., July 5, 1888

HANDCOCK
Stannue Henry, and Theodosia Violet, d. of M. M. and Mrs. F. Blacker, all of Amelia Co., Va., by the Rev. P. F. Berkeley, in St. John's Church, Grubb Hill, Amelia Co., Va. So. Ch., Oct. 4, 1883

HANDY
D. Claude (Dr.), of Annapolis, Md., and Annie D. Bagnall of Onancock, Accomac Co., Va., by the Rev. J. B. Craighill, in St. James' Church, Drummondtown.

MARRIAGE NOTICES IN THE SOUTHERN CHURCHMAN WITH DATES OF PUBLICATION

So. Ch., Dec. 2, 1869
Edward L., Com. U.S.N., and Mary Gallego, youngest d. of the late Peter J. Chevallie, by the Rev. George Woodbridge, in St. Paul's Church, in Richmond. So. Ch., Apr. 18, 1856
H. H. S., and Carrie T., eldest d. of Robert T. and Edlie H. Craighill, all of Lynchburg, by the Rev. T. M. Carson, rector of St. Paul's, at the residence of the bride's father, in Lynchburg, Va. So. Ch., Jan. 14, 1886

HANEWINCKLE
Ida Louise, d. of the late Fred'k Wm. Hanewinckle of Richmond, and Thomas Atkinson, Jr., by the Rt. Rev. Bishop of North Carolina, grandfather of the groom, in St. James' Church, Richmond, Va. So. Ch., Feb. 5, 1880
Meta M., d. of the late F. W. Hanewinckle, Esq. of Richmond, and Joseph Packard, Jr. of Baltimore, by the Rev. Joseph Packard, D.D., in Richmond, Va. So. Ch., Jan. 4, 1883
Roberta N., and William R. Trigg, both of Richmond, by the Rev. Joshua Peterkin, in Richmond. So. Ch., Jan. 17, 1884

HANFORD
M. E., of Society Hill, S.C., and Gregory A. Perdicaris, native of Greece and formerly Prof. in Washington College, Hartford, Conn., by the Rev. Mr. Forme, at Cheraw, S.C. So. Ch., June 2, 1837

HANKINS
Alice B., and Francis W. Hammond, both of James City Co., by the Rev. L. B. Wharton, at Marlbrook, James City Co. So. Ch., Nov. 23, 1876
Corilla P., eldest d. of Pryor Hankins, and George W. Taylor, Esq., all of James City Co., by the Rev. Mr. Ellett. So. Ch., Jan. 15, 1836
Emma, of Buchanan, W.Va., and W. E. Haymond, by the Rev. Samuel Steel, at the residence of the bride's father. So. Ch., Mar. 11, 1886
Harriet A., d. of George Hankins, Esq. of James City Co., Va., and Dr. Robert B. Richardson of Allenville, Todd Co., Ky., by the Rev. L. B. Wharton, at Marlbrook. So. Ch., Mar. 20, 1873
Mary D., d. of the late Wm. Hankins, Esq., and William H. Graves of Knoxville, Tenn., by the Rev. P. G. Robert, at Surry Co. So. Ch., Dec. 30, 1859
W. A., of Surry Co., Va., and Marcella C. Barret of Goochland Co., Va., by the Rev. P. M. Boyden, at Mt. Bernard in Goochland Co. So. Ch., Jan. 27, 1881

HANSBOROUGH
J. F., of Culpeper, and Anna Ophelia, d. of the late Edward Smith of King George Co., Va., by the Rev. John Cole, at "Zhu Hol", the residence of the bride's uncle, D. F. Slaughter, Esq. So. Ch., Jan. 31, 1867

MARRIAGE NOTICES IN THE SOUTHERN CHURCHMAN WITH DATES OF PUBLICATION

Lydia Gates, d. of the late David Hansborough of Albemarle Co., Va., and the Rev. S. Paxton Watters, rector of St. Stephen's Church, Culpeper, Va., by the Rev. A. T. Steele, in St. Mark's Church, Washington, D.C. So. Ch., Jan. 22, 1891

HANSBROUGH*
Charles A., and Mary C. Pannill, by the Rev. H. B. Lee, in St. Paul's Church, Culpeper Co., Va. So. Ch., Nov. 28, 1889

David, and V. L. Fretwell of Albemarle, by the Rev. Wm. N. Nelson assisted by the Rev. D. T. C. Davis. So. Ch., Mar. 14, 1862

Edwin M., of Culpeper Co., Va., and Margaret S., eldest d. of James F. and Anna O. Hansbrough, by the Rev. C. O. Pruden, at Motley's Depot, Pittsylvania Co., Va. So. Ch., Dec. 6, 1888

Georgie G., eldest d. of the officiating minister, and Lewis H. Lee, by the Rev. Jno. S. Hansbrough, in St. Thomas' Church, Orange Court House, Va. So. Ch., Nov. 9, 1876

John S., and Mary E., d. of the late Garland Ballard of Orange, by the Rev. J. Earnest, at Orange C.H. So. Ch., Aug. 15, 1856

Margaret S., eldest d. of James F. and Anna O. Hansbrough, and Edwin M. Hansbrough of Culpeper Co., Va., by the Rev. C. O. Pruden, at Motley's Depot, Pittsylvania Co., Va. So. Ch., Dec. 6, 1888

Roberta, and Wm. C. Williams, Esq., both of Orange Co., by the Rev. Joseph Earnest, at Orange Court House. So. Ch., Sept. 25, 1857

HANSBURY
Carrie E., of New York City, and Davidge Macgill of Hagerstown, Md., by the Rev. P. D. Thompson, at the residence of Sam'l P. Wilson, Pittsylvania Co., Va. So. Ch., May 14, 1868

HANSFORD
Judith W., and the Rev. Henry Wall, by the Rev. J. W. Chesley, at Green Height, King George Co., Va. So. Ch., Oct. 17, 1856

Julia, d. of the late Addison Hansford, Esq., of King George Co., Va., and the Rev. Henry Wall, by the Rev. H. R. Scott, at Green Height. So. Ch., Apr. 19, 1866

Mary B., d. of the late Addison Hansford, Esq., of King George Co., Va., and Samuel Wallace, Esq. of Stafford Co., by the Rev. Henry Wall, brother-in-law of the bride, at Green Height. So. Ch., Nov. 7, 1856

HANSON
T. Howard, of St. Louis, Mo., and Ada Morford of Deerwood, Minn., by the Rev. G. H. Davis, at the residence of the bride's father, in Deerwood, Minn. So. Ch., Sept. 27, 1888

William D. (The Rev.), and Fanny B., only d. of the late Rev. John Delaplane, by the Rev. Charles W. Andrews, D.D., in Trinity Church, Martinsburg. So.

* Given as printed

MARRIAGE NOTICES IN THE SOUTHERN CHURCHMAN WITH DATES OF PUBLICATION

Ch., May 10, 1866

HANWAY
E. C., of Allegheny City, Pa., and Julia, d. of Geo. E. Grymes, Esq., by the Rev. M. Hunter, at Mount Stuart, King George Co., Va. So. Ch., July 1, 1880

HARCUM
James O., and Adella J., d. of Dr. Porteus Towles, by the Rev. Edmund Withers, in Christ Church, Lancaster, Va. So. Ch., Dec. 25, 1857

HARDAWAY
Sallie A., only d. of the late John Hardaway, Esq., and the Rev. M. H. Galusha, by the Rev. W. H. Platt and the Rev. C. J. Gibson, at Mt. Pleasant, the residence of the bride's relations, Dinwiddie Co., Va. So. Ch., July 5, 1860

HARDGROVE
Joy Loree, of Westfield, N.J., and the Rev. Robert C. Clingman, rector of St. Peter's Church, Akron, Ohio, by the groom's father, the Bishop of Kentucky, at the residence of the bride. So. Ch., July 5, 1941

HARDIN
Lawrence Oscar, s. of William H. and Sarah Hardin of Blowing Rock, N.C., and Suma Bogle, only d. of Dr. H. McD. and Harriet A. Bogle Little, by the Rev. William R. Savage, at the home of the bride's parents, near Blowing Rock, N.C. So. Ch., Sept. 25, 1909

HARDING
C. R. (Dr.), Prof. of Greek at Davidson College, N.C., and Mildred, d. of Hon. Taylor Berry, by the Rev. Dr. Harding, at Edgewood, the residence of the bride's parents, Amherst, Va. So. Ch., Sept. 13, 1888

Cyrus, of Snowden Park, Northumberland, and V. Betty, d. of Capt. R. D. Carter of Fleets Bay, Northumberland, by the Rev. Edmund Withers, in Christ Church, Lancaster Co., Va. So. Ch., Dec. 14, 1855

Hopkins, of Northumberland Co., Va., and Fannie J., d. of Dr. Athwell Ball of Mississippi, by the Rev. H. L. Derby, at "Bewdley", the residence of Capt. James Ball, Lancaster, Va. So. Ch., Dec. 28, 1876

J. McAlpin (The Rev.), and Alice T. Hickey, both of Philadelphia, by the Rev. Dr. W. Bacon Stevens assisted by the Rev. J. P. Wilmer, in St. Andrew's Church. So. Ch., Nov. 12, 1858

Nathaniel (The Rev.), and Bettie, d. of the Rev. N. C. Hughes, by the Rev. N. Colin Hughes assisted by the Rev. Israel Harding, at Greenville, N.C. So. Ch., Mar. 12, 1874

Rawleigh W., and Julia Hurst, both of Northumberland, Va., by the Rev. Henry L. Derby, at the residence of Warner Hurst, Northumberland Co. So. Ch., Dec. 24, 1885

Sarah A., and Edgar Blackwell, both of Northumberland Co., Va., by the Rev. H. T. Bacon assisted by the Rev. H. L. Derby, in "Rehoboth Church." So.

MARRIAGE NOTICES IN THE SOUTHERN CHURCHMAN WITH DATES OF PUBLICATION

Ch., Dec. 16, 1880

HARDWICK
Samuel H., of Montgomery, Ala., and J. Algie C. Ware of Galveston, Texas, by the Rev. R. S. Barrett, in St. Paul's Church, Henderson, Ky. So. Ch., Oct. 25, 1883

HARDY
Charles W., Esq., of Norfolk, and Victoria, d. of Dr. Edmund P. Taliaferro, by the Rev. J. Earnest, at Orange Courthouse, Va. So. Ch., Nov. 2, 1865

HARFORD
Henry, and Mollie Lyell, both of Westmoreland, by the Rev. D. M. Wharton, in St. James' Church, Montross. So. Ch., Jan. 16, 1873

HARGRAVES
Wm. L. (The Rev.), rector of St. Mark's Church, Cocoa, Fla., and Minnie Frances Whittington of Merrett's Island, by Bishop Wing, in the church of Cocoa. So. Ch., Mar. 4, 1939

HARGROVE
Sallie Arthur, d. of James Hargrove, and Walter Jordan, all of Nansemond Co., by the rector, the Rev. Douglass Hooff, at the Glebe Church, Lower Suffolk Parish, Nansemond Co. So. Ch., Jan. 15, 1885

HARKINS
Judith, d. of P. J. Harkins of Powhatan Co., and Samuel Dennis of Albemarle, by the Rev. P. F. Berkeley, at the residence of the bride's father. So. Ch., Oct. 29, 1868

HARLEY
Anne C., and John Henson, both of Berkeley Co., W.Va., by the Rev. W. T. Leavell, at the residence of the bride's father, Dr. Thos. Harley, in Hedgesville. So. Ch., Dec. 23, 1880

Mary E., d. of Dr. T. J. Harley, and Charles Ellis, all of Berkeley Co., W.Va., by the Rev. George S. May, at Hedgesville. So. Ch., Nov. 26, 1874

Virginia, d. of Thomas J. Harley, and Benjamin S. Speck, by the Rev. George S. May, at the residence of the bride's father, in Hedgesville. So. Ch., Dec. 11, 1873

HARLLEE
C. Inez, and James C. Bell, by the Rev. Henry L. Derby, at the residence of the bride's mother, at Suffolk, Va. So. Ch., Feb. 26, 1891

HARLOW
E. H. (The Rev.), rector of St. Mark's, and Mary S. Grayson of Loudoun Co., Va., by the Rev. Charles H. Seymour of Dubuque, in St. Mark's Church, Fort Dodge, Iowa. So. Ch., Dec. 8, 1870

HARMAN
Wm. Everett, of Chicago, Ill., and Minnie R., d. of Dr. A. P. Burns of Maryland, by the Rev. Fritz Simons. So. Ch., Jan. 26, 1888*

HARNSBERGER
Annie V., d. of Henry B. Harnsberger, Esq., and John F. Lewis, Jr., s. of Lt. Governor, all of Rockingham Co., Va., by the Rev. Oscar S. Bunting, at the residence of the bride's father. So.

---

* A notice appears in the issue of Jan. 19, 1888 identical with this, except that "Fritz Simon" is written "Fitz Simon"

MARRIAGE NOTICES IN THE SOUTHERN CHURCHMAN WITH DATES OF PUBLICATION

Ch., Jan. 18, 1883
HARPER
   Howard (The Rev.), rector of Grace Church, Waycross, Ga., and Elizabeth, d. of the late Albert A. Lane of Cleveland, Ohio, by Bishop Reese, in Christ Church, Savannah. So. Ch., Dec. 21, 1935
   Minnie, d. of the late Joel Z. Harper, and Robert W. Briggs of Clarke Co., Va., by the Rev. O. A. Kinsolving, at "Rock Cliff", Fauquier Co., Va. So. Ch., Dec. 5, 1867
HARRELL
   Hattie E., d. of H. P. Harrell of Lewiston, and Junius B. Roane of Middlesex Co., Va., by the Rev. H. M. Jarvis, in Christ Church, near Lewiston, N.C. So. Ch., Nov. 10, 1887
   J. N., of Murfresborough*, N.C., and Susan A. Ruffin of Surry Co., Va., by the Rev. A. S. Smith of Norfolk. So. Ch., July 3, 1857
HARRIMAN
   Chester Karl, of Florence, Cal., and Charlotte, youngest d. of the Rev. J. H. and the late Charlotte Cox Townsend, by the bride's father, at the home of the bride, Smithtown, Long Island, N.Y. So. Ch., Aug. 28, 1920
   Frederick Wm. (The Rev.), rector of the parish, and Cora Elizabeth, d. of Charles A. Jarvis, Esq. of Portland, by the Rev. G. H. Deshon, D.D., of Meriden assisted by the Rev. F. D. Harriman, in Trinity Church, Portland, Conn.

So. Ch., Nov. 2, 1882
HARRINGTON
   Wm. W., and Ella E., d. of John R. Neild, all of Dorchester Co., Md., by the Rev. Wm. W. Greene, at the residence of the bride's father. So. Ch., Jan. 6, 1881
HARRIS
   Abner, Esq., of Powhatan Co., and Flora A., eldest d. of N. W. Harris, Esq. of Louisa Co., Va., by the Rev. G. D. E. Mortimer, at the residence of the bride's father, Fredericks Hall, Louisa Co. So. Ch., Feb. 8, 1865
   Abner T., of Amelia Co., and Julia V. Jones of Chesterfield Co., Va., by the Rev. A. B. Tizzard, at the residence of the bride's brother. So. Ch., Feb. 21, 1884
   Annie A., eldest d. of Hon. John T. Harris of Harrisonburg, Va., and S. W. Heard of McLeansboro, Ill., by the Rev. O. S. Bunting, at the residence of the bride's father. So. Ch., June 14, 1883
   B., d. of C. A. Harris of Versailles, and Arch. M. Robinson of Louisville, by the Rev. W. G. McCready, at the residence of the bride's uncle, Joseph Woolfolk, Lexington, Ky. So. Ch., Sept. 19, 1889
   Constance K., and James C. Robinson, by the Rev. C. C. Randolph, at Escalona, the home of the bride's father, Frank Harris. So. Ch., Nov. 30, 1907
   Elizabeth T., and Grenville Gaines, both of Warrenton,

---

* Given as printed

MARRIAGE NOTICES IN THE SOUTHERN CHURCHMAN WITH DATES OF PUBLICATION

Va., by the Rev. George W. Nelson, in St. James' Church, Warrenton, Va. So. Ch., Nov. 23, 1882

F. H., and Harriet, d. of Dr. W. Warren, formerly of Edenton, N.C., by the Rev. W. H. Pendleton, at Delecarlia, Bedford Co., Va. So. Ch., Dec. 8, 1870

Flora A., eldest d. of N. W. Harris, Esq. of Louisa Co., Va., and Abner Harris, Esq. of Powhatan Co., by the Rev. G. D. E. Mortimer, at Fredericks Hall, the residence of the bride's father, Louisa Co. So. Ch., Feb. 8, 1865

Gordon Gilette, of Culpeper Co., and Lanetta Mason, d. of Mrs. Charles F. Goodwyn and the late Charles F. Goodwyn, by the Rev. T. H. Lacy, at Nottoway, Va. So. Ch., June 26, 1909

Henrietta F., d. of the late John R. Harris of Brooklyn, N.Y., and the Rev. William J. Boone, by the Rev. Elliot H. Thomson, in the Chapel of the Nativity at Wuchang, China. So. Ch., Aug. 23, 1877

J. Andrew (The Rev.), and Anne Cole Wright, by the Rev. John Cole, in Philadelphia. So. Ch., Apr. 19, 1861

John A. (Capt.), and Ann C., youngest d. of James Gee, deceased, by the Rev. William B. Rowzie, in Lunenburg Co. So. Ch., Sept. 18, 1835

Lillie Tyson (nee Jolliffe) (Mrs.), of Washington, formerly of Frederick Co., Va., and Horatio Nelson Taplin of Montpelier, Vt., by the Rev. David Barr, in Washington, D.C. So. Ch., July 2, 1891

McMullen, and Mary J. Pane, both of Hanover, by the rector, the Rev. Rob't Douglas Roller, in Trinity Church, St. Martin's Parish. So. Ch., Jan. 3, 1878

Marshall L., and Mary N., d. of Capt. Henry A. Watkins, by the Rev. Andrew Hart. So. Ch., Mar. 1, 1839

N. B. (The Rev.), of Jacksonville, Fla., and Margaret Van Benthuysen, by the Rev. Dr. Kinsolving, at Houston, Va. So. Ch., May 4, 1893

Sarah Harriet, youngest d. of the late Thaddeus William Harris, M.D., and Lewis Meyer Hamilton of New York, formerly of Baltimore, by the Rev. Wm. Chancey Langdon, D.D., at Cambridge, Mass. So. Ch., Jan. 1, 1880

T. E., Esq., and Victoria Goods, both of Bedford Co., Va., by the Rev. W. H. Pendleton, at the residence of the bride's father. So. Ch., Dec. 8, 1870

W. B., Esq., of Clarke Co., Va., and Sarah E. Blackburn of Clarke Co., Va., by the Rev. Dr. Norton, in Alexandria. So. Ch., June 18, 1874

HARRISON

Amelia, d. of the late Charles W. Harrison, and Edward Robert Sharwood, all of Albemarle Co., by the Rev. T. E. Locke, in Christ Church, St. Ann's Parish, Albemarle Co., So. Ch., Oct. 1, 1874

Ann J. (Mrs.), and Ephraim J. Rawlings, both of Bruns-

MARRIAGE NOTICES IN THE SOUTHERN CHURCHMAN WITH DATES OF PUBLICATION

wick, by the Rev. Otis A. Glazebrook, at Brunswick. So. Ch., Jan. 5, 1871

Anna Byrd, eldest d. of William G. Harrison, Esq. of Lewis Co., and Ralph Wormley Norris of Charles Town, Jefferson Co., W.Va., by the Rev. T. H. Lacy, at the residence of the bride's father, near Weston, W.Va. So. Ch., Apr. 9, 1891

Anna Louisa, d. of the late Randolph Harrison, Esq., and Alexander B. Hagner of Annapolis, Md., by the Rev. F. M. Whittle, at Elk Hill, Goochland Co., Va. So. Ch., June 2, 1853

Anna M., d. of the late Wm. Harrison, Esq. of Maycox, James River*, and Wm. A. Christian of Alabama, by the Rev. Mr. Norwood, at Evergreen, seat of Lt. Cocke of the U.S. Navy. So. Ch., Aug. 2, 1839

Anna Maybury, third d. of Hon. M. W. and Mrs. Sarah Eliza Harrison, and Edwin George Davisson, by the Rev. T. H. Lacy, rector of St. Paul's Church, at the residence of the Hon. Matthew W. Harrison, Weston, W.Va. So. Ch., Dec. 29, 1892

Annie P., of Hanover, and Landon C. Berkely of Danville, by the Rev. Robert R. Claiborne, in Fork Church, Hanover Co., Va. So. Ch., Sept. 30, 1880

Archibald M., and Euphania C. Taylor, both of Fluvanna, by the Rev. James Doughen.
So. Ch., Dec. 1, 1837

Benjamin (Dr.), and Mattella C. Page of Clarke Co., Va., by the Rev. Mr. Hoff, at Saratoga, the residence of Mrs. R. Page. So. Ch., Feb. 12, 1858

Bessie Carr, second d. of George F. Harrison and gr. d. of the late D. Holmes Conrad of Martinsburg, W.Va., and Clarence V. Cavitt of Texas, by the Rev. Mr. McCoy of the Presbyterian Church assisted by the Rev. P. M. Boyden, at Longwood, Goochland Co., Va. So. Ch., May 22, 1879

Carrie Rivers, youngest d. of the late W. M. Harrison of Charles City Co., Va., and Jaquelin Marshall Douthat of Danville, Va., by the Rev. A. Wade, at Westover, the residence of the bride's brother-in-law. So. Ch., Nov. 20, 1879

Cora, d. of Philip Harrison, Esq., and Frederick Anderson, by the Rt. Rev. Richard C. Moore, at Richmond, Va. So. Ch., Nov. 6, 1835

Cornelia Rives (Mrs.), of Albemarle Co., Va., and Pardon Wilbur of Providence, R.I., by the Rev. T. E. Locke, at River Lawn. So. Ch., June 19, 1884

E. C., and Sue R. Willcox, by the Rev. Edward Valentine Jones, in Westover Church, Charles City Co., Va. So. Ch., July 16, 1891

E. J. (Dr.), of Cumberland Co., Va., and Susan M. Ficklen, at Redhouse, the residence of James B. Ficklen, Buckingham Co. So. Ch., June 11, 1868

---

* Given as printed

MARRIAGE NOTICES IN THE SOUTHERN CHURCHMAN WITH DATES OF PUBLICATION

Edmonia Churchill, of Danville, formerly of Hanover Co., Va., and James Grant Calhoun of Maryland, by the Rev. Geo. W. Dame, D.D., assisted by the Rt. Rev. A. M. Randolph, assistant Bishop of Virginia, and the Rev. J. Y. Downman, in the Church of the Epiphany, Danville, Va. So. Ch., Sept. 23, 1886

Edward Mortimer, and Lavinia Carter, by the Rev. Joseph Baker, rector of Westover, in Grace Church, Granville, Va. So. Ch., Feb. 28, 1914

Eliza C., d. of the late Thomas R. Harrison, and Archie C. Page of Goochland, by the Rev. J. Peterkin, in St. James' Church, Richmond. So. Ch., Jan. 6, 1860

Elizabeth A., d. of Mrs. Carter H. Harrison, and M. F. McLaurin of Rome, Ga., by the Rev. William C. Williams, D.D., at "Elkora", Cumberland Co., Va. So. Ch., Aug. 25, 1881

Elizabeth Gwynn, d. of Amana G. and James S. Harrison, M.D., lately of the University of Virginia, and Arthur St. Edmund Thorp of Somerset, England, by the Rev. A. P. Gray, at Gainesville, Prince William Co., Va. So. Ch., Mar. 24 and 31, 1887

Ella C., and R. B. Brooke, by the Rev. H. L. Derby, in White Chapel Church, Lancaster, Va. So. Ch., Nov. 25, 1886

Ellen, and George Darley, by the Rev. H. T. Sharp, in Grace Church, Alexandria, Va. So. Ch., Jan. 29, 1880

Elsie Chichester, and William Dade Hempstone, by the Rev. Walter P. Griggs of Poolesville, Md., in St. James' Church, Leesburg, Va. So. Ch., June 9, 1892

G. W., of Marion, Ala., and Mrs. S. G. Burruss of New Kent Co., Va., by the Rev. S. S. Hepbron, at Farmington, the residence of W. H. Macon, Esq. So. Ch., Jan. 31, 1899

Geo. F., of Goochland Co., and Mrs. Susan Mathews, second d. of the late Dr. B. H. Royall of Chesterfield, by the Rev. Edgar Woods, pastor of the Presbyterian Church, Charlottesville, at the University of Virginia. So. Ch., Feb. 14, 1867

George F., and Ida De Vere, youngest d. of Wm. Ayre of "Buena Vista", all of Fairfax Co., by the Rev. A. P. Gray, in St. John's Church, Centreville. So. Ch., Sept. 9, 1880

H. N. (Col.), and Willie J., d. of W. L. G. and Adelina C. Mitchell, by the Rev. H. L. Derby, at Nuttsville, Lancaster, Va. So. Ch., Nov. 22, 1877

Hall (The Rev.), of St. Paul's School, Concord, and Agnes Spottiswoode, only d. of the Hon. Anthony Kennedy, Ellerslie, Baltimore Co., Md., late United States Senator from Maryland, by the Rt. Rev. the Bishop of Pittsburgh, in St. Paul's

MARRIAGE NOTICES IN THE SOUTHERN CHURCHMAN WITH DATES OF PUBLICATION

Church, Baltimore, Md. So. Ch., Nov. 18, 1875
Hannah A., and Albert Wrenn, both of Fairfax, by the Rev. Frank Page, in Christ Church, Chantilly. So. Ch., May 24, 1883
Henrietta, d. of George F. Harrison of Goochland Co., Va., and William Herndon Barrett, by the Rev. R. A. Goodwin, brother-in-law of the bride and rector of the church, in St. John's Church, Petersburg, Va. So. Ch., Feb. 9, 1893
Henry T., Esq., one of the delegates to the General Assembly from Loudoun Co., and Mary E., d. of Gen. Walter Jones of Washington, by the Rev. Mr. Packard. So. Ch., Dec. 20, 1839
Holmes C., of Goochland Co., and Agnes M., d. of S. R. Thrower, Esq. of Boydton, by the Rev. B. T. Turner, in Boyiton, Mecklenburg Co., Va. So. Ch., Dec. 22, 1881
J. Prosser (Dr.), of Richmond, Va., and Willantina, d. of B. Temple, Esq. of Fredericksburg, Va., by the Rev. A. M. Randolph, in Fredericksburg. So. Ch., Feb. 3, 1860
James P., of Danville, and Mary Jane, eldest d. of Prof. John S. Davis, by the Rev. J. S. Hanckel, D.D., at the University of Virginia. So. Ch., Feb. 20, 1879
James P., of Danville, and Carrie Harrison Douthat of Charles City Co., by the Rev. John P. Tyler, rector, in Westover Church. So. Ch., Oct. 30, 1890
Jane Carey, d. of the late Thomas Harrison, Esq., and the Rev. Hugh Roy Scott, by the Rev. A. Empie, D.D., in St. James' Church, Richmond, Va. So. Ch., Oct. 7, 1852
Jannetta C., d. of Geo. F. Harrison, Esq. of Goochland Co., Va., and Walter H. P. Morris, Esq., of Richmond, by the Rev. J. D. Powell, at Longwood, Goochland Co. So. Ch., Nov. 1, 1866
Jennie Cary, d. of the late Wm. M. Harrison of Riverside, and John A. Ruffin, by the Rev. Edward Valentine Jones, at Westover, Charles City Co., Va. So. Ch., June 7, 1888
John, of Sussex Co., and Anne Clifton, d. of Edward S. Pegram of Albemarle Co., Va., by the Rev. E. Boyden, at Cismont, the residence of Mrs. Frances W. Meriwether. So. Ch., Nov. 28, 1872
John Caile, and Mary, eldest d. of Mrs. M. A. and the late Rev. A. J. Berger of Rolling Side, Catonsville, Md., by the Rev. J. S. B. Hodges, D.D., in St. Paul's Church, Baltimore. So. Ch., May 8, 1890
John D., of Henry Co., and M. Augusta, d. of Dr. Madison Haden, by the Rev. Wm. W. Greene, at the residence of the

MARRIAGE NOTICES IN THE SOUTHERN CHURCHMAN WITH DATES OF PUBLICATION

bride's father. So. Ch., July 9, 1874

John P., of Richmond, and Fannie, youngest d. of the Rev. John Cooke, by the Rev. Horace Stringfellow, at Dewberry, Hanover Co., Va. So. Ch., Nov. 16, 1855

John W. (Dr.), of Petersburg, Va., and Fanny Thurston Gwyn of Baltimore, Md., by the Rev. Dr. J. J. Sams, in Holy Trinity Church, Baltimore, Md. So. Ch., July 23, 1891

Julia, d. of Dr. Tom Harrison, and R. E. Richardson, all of New Kent Co., by the Rev. S. S. Hepbron, at the residence of the bride's father. So. Ch., Feb. 3, 1887

Lelia B., d. of Col. Randolph Harrison of Williamsburg, Va., and Edmund*Ruffin of Upper Marlburn, Hanover Co., Va., by the Rev. S. S. Hepbron, in Immanuel Church, Hanover Co., Va. So. Ch., Feb. 3, 1887

Lewis Carter (The Rev.), rector of St. Matthias Church, East Aurora, N.Y., and Ellen Harrison, d. of Kate H. and the late Powhatan Robertson of Virginia, by the Rev. H. de Wolf de Mauriac, rector, in St. Paul's Church, Lancaster, N.H. So. Ch., Oct. 19, 1912

Lizzie C., d. of the late W. M. Harrison of Charles City Co., Va., and R. Carter Wellford of Richmond Co., Va., by the Rev. Dr. A. Wade, at "Westover", the residence of the bride's brother-in-law. So. Ch., May 23 and 30, 1878

Lizzie Lee, d. of Henry T. Harrison, Esq., and George M. Grayson, Esq., by the Rev. E. T. Perkins, in St. James' Church, Leesburg, Va. So. Ch., Sept. 26, 1867

Lucia Cary, and Capt. Edmund Randolph Cocke of Oaklands, Cumberland Co., Va., by the Rev. Edmund C. Murdaugh, D.D., at Lower Brandon, James river. So. Ch., May 30, 1878

Lucius Ashton, and Irene Bankhead Waring, by the Rev. H. G. Lane of Newport News, in St. Mary's Chapel, Charles City Co., Va. So. Ch., Oct. 23, 1920

M. Leib, Esq., of Philadelphia, and Nannie T., d. of the late George W. Rothrock, Esq. of Fredericksburg, Va., by the Rev. E. C. Murdaugh, D.D., at the residence of the bride. So. Ch., Mar. 25, 1875

Mary, d. of the late Wm. M. Harrison, and Maj. A. Drewry, by the Rev. A. Wade assisted by the Rev. Joshua Peterkin, in Westover Church, Charles City Co., Va. So. Ch., Feb. 24, 1870

Mary A., d. of the late Carter H. Harrison of Cumberland, and Wm. H. Fitzhugh, Jr., Esq., of Fredericksburg, by the Rev. A. M. Randolph, at

* Given as printed

MARRIAGE NOTICES IN THE SOUTHERN CHURCHMAN WITH DATES OF PUBLICATION

"Longwood", the residence of the bride's brother, George F. Harrison, Goochland Co., Va. So. Ch., Apr. 1, 1859

Mary Ambler, fifth d. of George F. Harrison of Longwood, and the Rev. Robert A. Goodwin of Salem, Roanoke Co., Va., by the Rev. B. Turner, in the Episcopal Church, Goochland C.H., Va. So. Ch., July 5, 1883

Mary G., d. of Col. Randolph Harrison, and Gordon Webb of New Kent Co., by the Rev. W. C. Meredith assisted by the Rev. Lyman B. Wharton, in Bruton Parish Church, Williamsburg, Va. So. Ch., Feb. 22, 1877

Mary J., d. of the late Henry T. Harrison, and Frank E. Conrad, all of Leesburg, by the Rev. R. T. Davis, D.D., at home. So. Ch., Nov. 15, 1883

Mary M., eldest d. of M. W. Harrison, Esq. of Lewis Co., W.Va., and Allen A. Warren of Richmond, Va., by the Rev. W. H. H. Powers, in St. Paul's Church, Weston, W.Va. So. Ch., Dec. 25, 1879

Mary Virginia, d. of Jno. M. Harrison, Esq., and Douglass Tyler, Esq. of Leesburg, by the Rev. O. A. Kinsolving, at Windsor, Loudoun Co. So. Ch., July 1, 1869

Nanny Addison, fourth d. of George F. Harrison, and the Rev. B. Thornton Turner of Goochland Co., Va., at Longwood, Goochland Co., Va. So. Ch., Jan. 30, 1879

Olivia, d. of Joseph H. Harrison of Talbot Co., Md., and the Rev. Geo. W. Easter, rector of Hungars Parish, Northampton Co., Va., by the Rev. Ernest McGill, in Christ Church, St. Michael's, Talbot Co., Md. So. Ch., Oct. 20, 1887

R. Marshall (The Rev.), rector of St. Paul's Church, Bellingham, Wash., and Ella A. Wilkinson, Superintendent of St. Luke's Hospital, a parochial institution of Bellingham, Wash., by the Rev. Edgar M. Rodgers, in Trinity Church, Everett, Wash. So. Ch., Aug. 3, 1918

Rebecca Holmes, d. of Geo. F. Harrison of Longwood, Goochland Co., Va., and Norborne T. Johnson, by the Rev. Mr. Hullihen, in Trinity Church, Staunton, Va. So. Ch., Aug. 11, 1892

Richard Allen, s. of the late John N. Harrison of New Orleans, La., and Bessie May, d. of the late W. R. Knox of Birmingham, Ala., by the Rev. C. C. Randolph of the Episcopal Church, at "Lynnside", the residence of Col. W. L. Lewis, near Sweet Springs, W.Va. So. Ch., Jan. 24, 1889

Sara Roane, d. of Mr. and Mrs. E. C. Harrison of Elkord, Cumberland Co., Va., and George C. Ruffin, Jr. of Tar Bay,

MARRIAGE NOTICES IN THE SOUTHERN CHURCHMAN WITH DATES OF PUBLICATION

Prince George Co., Va., by the Rev. John Cornick of Onancock, at the home of the bride. So. Ch., May 11, 1912

Susie A., d. of Mr. and Mrs. William H. Harrison, and Charles James Faulkner, by the Rev. P. F. Berkeley, at the Wigwam, Amelia Co. So. Ch., Oct. 2, 1873

Thomas W., and Genevieve, second d. of E. and P. M. Ralston, all of Weston, by the Rev. T. H. Lacy, in St. Paul's Church, Weston, W.Va. So. Ch., May 15, 1890

Victoria, d. of Capt. Geo. W. Harrison (late U.S.A.), and Doddridge F. Graham, both of Deer Park, by the Rev. Herbert Assheton, at Deer Park. So. Ch., Jan. 11, 1883

Walter J., Esq., and Nannie W., d. of the late Dr. William L. Powell, by the Rev. E. T. Perkins, in St. James' Church, Leesburg, Va. So. Ch., Sept. 26, 1867

Wm. B., of Staunton, and Janet C., d. of the late Rev. Edmond Withers, by the Rev. F. G. Scott, in the rectory, Norwood, Nelson Co., Va. So. Ch., Oct. 9, 1879

Wm. G., clerk of the Circuit Court of Lewis Co., and Mrs. Eleanor Drusilla (Fleming) Davisson of Braxton Co., by the Rev. T. H. Lacy, in the church at Burnsville, Braxton Co., W.Va. So. Ch., Nov. 10, 1887

See also WEBB, Mary G. (Mrs.)

HARRISS

Fannie L., of Boydton, and Benj. L. Partlow, Esq., of Harrisonburg, Va., by the Rev. O. S. Bunting, in St. James' Church, Boydton, Va. So. Ch., Dec. 25, 1884

Jane Ann, d. of the late Capt. Benjamin Harriss, and Hardin Perkins, by the Rev. Isaac Paul, at Mountain Grove, Albemarle Co., Va. So. Ch., May 29, 1835

Mary P., eldest d. of Dr. S. G. Harriss of Boydton, Va., and Oscar S. Bunting of Amherst Co., Va., by the Rev. P. M. Boyden assisted by the Rev. R. A. Goodwin. So. Ch., Nov. 13, 1879

HART

Amelia H., d. of Elisha Hart, Esq., of Saybrook, Conn., and Joseph B. Hull, Lt. U.S. Navy, in New Haven, Conn. So. Ch., Aug. 2, 1839

Frances L., d. of the Rev. Wm. H. Hart of Richmond, and the Rev. Clement M. Butler of Syracuse, N.Y., by the Rt. Rev. Bishop Moore. So. Ch., Apr. 21, 1837

Margaret, d. of the late James Hart of Albemarle Co., and William C. Kean, Jr. of Louisa Co., by the Rev. C. H. Read, at the residence of A. P. Fox in Richmond. So. Ch., Dec. 6, 1877

Maude Pemberton (Mrs.), of Chattanooga, Tenn., and Peyton McGuire, s. of the

MARRIAGE NOTICES IN THE SOUTHERN CHURCHMAN WITH DATES OF PUBLICATION

Rev. and Mrs. Claudius F. Smith of Lynchburg, Va. So. Ch., Apr. 16, 1921

Wm. B., and Mattie P. Waller, both of Spotsylvania Co., Va., by the Rev. Wm. W. Greene, at "Cedar Point", the residence of the bride's father. So. Ch., Feb. 8, 1872

Wm. G., and Agnes Sanford, both of Spotsylvania Co., by the Rev. Wm. W. Greene, at Spotsylvania C.H. So. Ch., Dec. 31, 1868

HARTE
John Joseph Meakin (The Rev.), curate of Trinity Church, Tulsa, Okla., and Alice Eleanor Taylor of Brockway, Pa., by the Rev. W. O. Cross, rector of St. Paul's Church, Kittanning, Pa., at Grace Church, Ridgway, Pa. So. Ch., Oct. 18, 1941

HARTLEY
James H., and Sarah Jones, by the Rev. R. S. Barrett, at Richmond, Va. So. Ch., July 1, 1880

HARTMAN
St. Clair, and Jennie Tompkins, by the Rev. Wm. N. Nelson, at Stoney Point, Albemarle Co., Va. So. Ch., Mar. 9, 1854

HARVEY
Benson Heale (The Rev. Canon), and Eleanor C. T. Moss, both of Philippine Islands Mission, in St. John's Cathedral, Hongkong. So. Ch., Dec. 8, 1934

Chas., Publisher of "Our Church Work", Baltimore, and Virginia M. Pendleton of Clarke Co., Va., by the Rev. T. F. Martin assisted by the Rev. Hugh Roy Scott, at the residence of the bride's father, T. P. Pendleton, Esq. So. Ch., Nov. 13, 1873

Eliza A., d. of the late Lewis B. Harvey, and John W. Wertz, both of Franklin Co., Va., by the Rev. Edward H. Ingle, at the residence of Ira M. Hurst, Franklin Co., Va. So. Ch., Dec. 23, 1875

P. R., and Constance E. McKenney, by the Rev. D. M. Wharton, at the residence of the bride's mother, at Montross. So. Ch., Dec. 4, 1873

Robert (Col.), of Huntingdon, W.Va., and Charlotte E. Mitchell of Bedford City, by the Rev. T. W. Jones, at the residence of the late Judge Wingfield, near Bedford City, Va. So. Ch., Sept. 18, 1890*

HARVIE
Edwin J. (Lt.), U.S.A., and Mary Edmonia, d. of the late Hodejah Meade and gr. d. of Gen. Everard Meade, all of Amelia Co., by the Rev. P. F. Berkeley, at the Hermitage, the residence of Wm. E. Meade, Esq. So. Ch., Nov. 30, 1860

James B., and M. Lou, d. of W. W. Michaux, by the Rev. D. Barr, at "Beaumont", Powhatan Co., Va. So. Ch., May 6, 1875

Mary, d. of Dr. John B. Harvie of Powhatan Co., Va., and W. N. Ruffin of Richmond, Va., by the Rev. P. F. Berkeley, at Fighting Creek, the residence of the bride's

---

* A notice appears in the issue of Sept. 11, 1890, identical with this except that "Mitchell" is written "Wingfield"

MARRIAGE NOTICES IN THE SOUTHERN CHURCHMAN WITH DATES OF PUBLICATION

father. So. Ch., May 6, 1875
P. Blair, d. of Dr. John B. Harvie, and John L. Waring of Richmond, Va., by the Rev. Frank Stringfellow, in Immanuel Church, Powhatan Co., Va. So. Ch., May 18, 1882
Sarah H., d. of Dr. John B. Harvie of Powhatan Co., and Lt. Richard B. Chaffin late of the C.S. Army, by the Rev. Mr. Powell, at Fighting Creek, Powhatan Co. So. Ch., Nov. 29, 1866

HARWOOD
Samuel F., Esq., of King and Queen Co., and Betty Brockenbrough of Essex, by the Rev. P. W. Temple, in St. John's Church, at Tappahannock, Essex Co., Va. So. Ch., Apr. 8, 1869
William E. (Dr.), of Petersburg, and Mary Ege, d. of Isaac Goddard of Richmond, by the Rev. C. J. Gibson, at the residence of John B. Ege, Esq., in Petersburg. So. Ch., Nov. 12, 1885

HASKINS
Creed, of Powhatan Co., and V. R., d. of Dr. Benjamin and Charlotte W. Dennis of Amelia Co., Va., by the Rev. P. F. Berkeley, at Vauxcluse in Amelia Co. So. Ch., Feb. 20, 1868
T. C., of Brunswick Co., and Lulie T. Berkeley, d. of the officiating clergyman, the Rev. P. F. Berkeley, at Airwell, Amelia Co., Va. So. Ch., Sept. 28, 1882
Willard D., of Centre Cross, and Ella Garnett, d. of John T. T. Hundley, by the Rev. J. Hervey Hundley, in Rappahannock Christian Church, Dunnsville, Essex Co., Va. So. Ch., Oct. 18, 1888
Wylie W., and Fannie Perkins, eldest d. of Chapman Glover of Buckingham Co., Va., by the Rev. T. E. Locke, in Emmanuel Church, Glenmore. So. Ch., Dec. 6, 1888

HATCH
Ida B., d. of James H. Hatch, and T. A. Hatch of Orange Co., Va., by the Rev. Frank Page. So. Ch., Jan. 22, 1880
T. A., of Orange Co., Va., and Ida B., d. of James H. Hatch, by the Rev. Frank Page. So. Ch., Jan. 22, 1880

HATCHER
E. A., of Liberty, Va., and Jennie Vest of Charles City Co., Va., by the Rev. John P. Tyler, at Berkeley, Charles City Co., Va. So. Ch., Dec. 20, 1888
Emmie McC., and S. Wingfield Travers, by the Rev. Dr. J. Peterkin assisted by the Rev. Charles Minnigerode, at the residence of the bride's father, Thomas W. McCance, Richmond, Va. So. Ch., Jan. 21, 1886

HATTERSLEY
John, of the Albemarle Soap Stone Company, and Mary Shepherd, third d. of William H. Garland, all of Albemarle Co., by the Rev. Thomas E. Locke, at Ivy Hill. So. Ch., Oct. 28, 1886

HATTON
E. A., of Norfolk Co., and S. R. Nash, of Portsmouth, Va., by the Rev. J. Cosby,

MARRIAGE NOTICES IN THE SOUTHERN CHURCHMAN WITH DATES OF PUBLICATION

in St. John's Church, Portsmouth, Va. So. Ch., Oct. 28, 1859
Goodrich, and Mary Reed, d. of Judge Legh R. Watts, by the Rev. John D. Powell, at the residence of the bride's parents, 202 Middle St., Portsmouth, Va. So. Ch., Nov. 30, 1893

HAUSBROUGH*
L., of Orange Court House, and Albert B. Wooldridge of Richmond, Va., by the Rev. John S. Hausbrough*, at Orange Court House. So. Ch., Nov. 6, 1863

HAVENER
R. H., and Agnes, d. of Geo. McBurney, all of Alexandria, Va., by the Rev. Dr. Norton. So. Ch., Nov. 24, 1881

HAVENS
Frances M., d. of Rensselaer Havens, Esq., and the Rev. S. B. S. Bissell, by the Rev. Dr. Spring, in New York City. So. Ch., Dec. 20, 1839

HAVERSTICK
Mary, d. of the late Rev. and Mrs. Alexander C. Haverstick of Annapolis, Md., and Arthur Percival Heymond of Annapolis, Md., by the Rev. E. P. Dandridge, in the Church of the Incarnation, Ronceverte, W.Va. So. Ch., June 18, 1910

HAW
J. Osborn, and Claudia M., d. of the late Wm. T. and Mrs. Jane R. Blair, by the Rev. Joshua Peterkin, at the residence of Charles W. Goddin, 605 West Grace Street, Richmond. So. Ch., Apr. 26, 1883

HAWKINS
W. G. (The Rev.), of Centreville, Md., and Narcissa B., d. of Capt. Judah Simmons, by the Rev. S. Nash, in St. John's Church, Essex Co., Va. So. Ch., Oct. 9, 1851

HAWKS
Thomas H., of Cleveland, Ohio, and Sallie Shield, d. of R. J. McCandlish, by the Rev. C. H. Shield, at home, in Parkersburg, W.Va. So. Ch., July 1, 1886

HAXALL
Bolling W., Jr., of Baltimore, and Lena A., d. of B. P. Noland of Loudoun Co., Va., by the Rev. William M. Dame assisted by the Rev. Magruder Maury. So. Ch., Oct. 22, 1874
Charlotte, d. of R. Barton Haxall, Esq., and Robert E. Lee, by the Rev. George Woodbridge of Richmond, at "Rocklands", Orange Co., Va. So. Ch., Nov. 23, 1871
Hattie, d. of R. Barton Haxall, Esq. of Richmond, Va., and the Rev. Henry A. Wise, rector of the Church of the Saviour, Philadelphia, by the Rev. George Woodbridge, D.D., in Richmond, Va. So. Ch., Nov. 16, 1860
Richard B., Esq., and Octavia, d. of John Robinson, Esq., all of Richmond, Va., by the Rt. Rev. Bishop Moore, in Richmond, Va. So. Ch., Nov. 24, 1837
Robert W. (Dr.), of Richmond,

* Given as printed

MARRIAGE NOTICES IN THE SOUTHERN CHURCHMAN WITH DATES OF PUBLICATION

Va., and Mrs. Jane B. Macmurdo, d. of David Higginbotham, Esq., of Albemarle Co., by the Rev. Richard K. Meade, at Mowen. So. Ch., Nov. 22, 1839

Rosalie, youngest d. of R. Barton Haxall, Esq., and C. Powell Noland of Middleburg, Loudoun Co., Va., by the Rev. Arthur Johns assisted by the Rev. Mr. Joyce, in the Episcopal Church, in Gordonsville, Va. So. Ch., Nov. 6, 1879

William N., and Florence Isabella Reese, by the Rev. Randolph H. McKim, rector, in the Church of the Epiphany, Washington, D.C. So. Ch., Sept. 28, 1893

HAXHALL
Philip, and Mary Jenifer, d. of the late William S. Triplett, both of Richmond, by the Rev. Charles Minnigerode, D.D., at the residence of the bride's mother. So. Ch., Apr. 30, 1874

HAY
James and Constance, eldest d. of Dr. R. H. Tatum of Harrisonburg, by the Rev. David Barr, in Emmanuel Church, Harrisonburg, Va. So. Ch., Oct. 10, 1878

HAYDEN
Charles B., and Mrs. Julia A. Wilson, both of Smithfield, by the Rev. C. S. Roberts, at Smithfield, Va. So. Ch., Nov. 21, 1867

Horace Edwin (The Rev.), and Kate Elizabeth, d. of John A. Byers, Esq., all of Maryland, by the Rev. Joseph A. Nock, at Point Pleasant, W.Va. So. Ch., Dec. 10, 1868

Kate Hull, and William H. Cosby, both of Baltimore, by the Rev. Horace Edwin Hayden assisted by the Rev. J. Everest Cathell, rector of the Church of the Ascension, in the Church of the Ascension, Baltimore. So. Ch., June 11, 1874

HAYES
Gretta, of Missouri, and Robert G. Withers formerly of Nelson Co., Va., by the Rev. J. W. Ohl, in Christ Church, Aspen, Col. So. Ch., June 2, 1887

HAYMAN
Adelaide Getty, d. of the late William Hayman of Georgetown, D.C., and Robert Aitcheson of Stafford Co., Va., by the Rev. J. I. Membert, D.D., in St. James' Church, Lancaster, Penn. So. Ch., Dec. 5, 1867

HAYMOND
Julia A., sister of Alpheus Haymond, Judge of Supreme Court of West Virginia, and Charles Lisez of Jackson Co., W.Va., by the Rev. G. A. Gibbons, in Christ Church, Fairmont, W.Va. So. Ch., May 1, 1878

W. E., and Emma Hankins of Buchanan, W.Va., by the Rev. Samuel Steel, at the residence of the bride's father. So. Ch., Mar. 11, 1886

HAYNE
Adele Irvin, d. of Mr. and Mrs. Paul Trapier Hayne, and John Gordon Scott of Petersburg, Va., by the Rev. A. R. Mitchell, the rector, in Christ Church, Greenville, S.C. So.

MARRIAGE NOTICES IN THE SOUTHERN CHURCHMAN WITH DATES OF PUBLICATION

HAYNES
A. F., and Sue D. Jeffries, by the Rev. E. Meade, at Mattaponi Church, King and Queen Co., Va. So. Ch., Jan. 8, 1885

HAYWARD
Alexander F., Esq., of Florida, and Isabella, d. of Col. Geo. Willis, by the Rev. J. Earnest, at Woodpark, the residence of the bride's father, in Orange. So. Ch., June 10, 1859

HAZARD
Carleton B., and Marietta W., d. of Mrs. Elizabeth Watson, by the Rev. J. Green Shackelford, at Chatham, Fredericksburg, Va. So. Ch., May 3, 1888

HAZELHURST
Elizabeth McKim, d. of Henry R. Hazelhurst, and Beirne Gordon of Savannah, by the Rev. Hall Harrison, at Lilburn, Elliott Co., Md. So. Ch., Nov. 16, 1882

HAZELWOOD
Alice, and Capt. Peter Branch Jones, both of Lunenburg Co., by the Rev. Henry Wall, at the residence of Mr. Ingram. So. Ch., Apr. 6, 1860

HEAD
Margaret (Mrs.), and Benjamin Yeatman, both of Westmoreland Co., by the Rev. T. E. Locke. So. Ch., Feb. 8, 1861

Mary J., d. of George E. Head, Esq., and the Rt. Rev. Manton Eastburn, D.D., Bishop of Massachusetts, by the Rev. John Cotton Smith, in Trinity Church, Boston. So. Ch., Feb. 8, 1856

HEALEY
Granville S., and Susan C. Gatewood, by the Rev. J. Hervey Hundley, in Christ Church, Middlesex Co. So. Ch., Oct. 30, 1873

HEARD
S. W., of McLeansboro, Ill., and Annie A., eldest d. of Hon. John T. Harris of Harrisonburg, Va., by the Rev. O. S. Bunting, at the residence of the bride's father. So. Ch., June 14, 1883

HEARTWELL
Helen, and John J. Wyatt of Sussex Co., Va., at Elmwood, the residence of H. J. Heartwell. So. Ch., Feb. 14, 1884

HEATH
Caroline R., of Richmond, and Walter K. Marten, by the Rev. John Cole, in Culpeper Co., Va. So. Ch., Nov. 23, 1855

James E., and Indie A. Nottingham, by the Rev. J. B. Craighill, at "Pleasant Prospect", Northampton Co., Va. So. Ch., Dec. 17, 1868

Jesse H., of Petersburg, and Sallie E., youngest d. of Tarlton Fleming, Esq. of Mannsville, Goochland Co., Va., by the Rev. A. B. Tizzard. So. Ch., Dec. 1, 1853

HEATON
Katie, d. of the late Dr. J. D. Heaton, and R. Walter Braden of Loudoun Co., Va., by the Rev. S. S. Ware, in St. Paul's Church, Hamilton, Va. So.

MARRIAGE NOTICES IN THE SOUTHERN CHURCHMAN WITH DATES OF PUBLICATION

Ch., Feb. 3, 1881

HEBBERGER
  Gloria, d. of Mrs. Fred W. Hebberger of St. Louis, Mo., and the Rev. C. Horace Kehl formerly of Waco, Texas, by the Very Rev. Sidney E. Sweet, Dean of the Cathedral, assisted by the Rev. Everett H. Jones, rector of St. Mark's Church, San Antonio, Texas, in Christ Church Cathedral, St. Louis, Mo. So. Ch., Oct. 18, 1941

HEDGES
  Harry Slicer, M.D., of Moorefield, W.Va., and Mary Daniels Eicholberger, by the Rev. Robt. Douglas Roller, at Martinsburg, W.Va., So. Ch., Nov. 6, 1884
  Mary Lee, d. of the Rev. C. S. Hodges, rector of the parish, and the Rev. G. W. Stickney of Mobile, by the Rt. Rev. Bishop Polk, in St. Luke's Church, New Orleans. So. Ch., May 14, 1858

HEDLEY
  Anna Sterges, second d. of the late Hon. John Henry Hedley of Clifton, Staten Island, N.Y., and the Rev. Thomas Boone, rector of Christ Church, Savannah, Ga., by the Rev. John C. Eccleston, the rector of the parish, in St. John's Church, Clifton, Staten Island. So. Ch., Mar. 4, 1886

HEISKELL
  Susan Ann, d. of A. St. C. Heiskell of Charlottesville, and Geo. W. Craven, by the Rev. R. K. Meade, at Penn Park. So. Ch., Nov. 24, 1837

HELFENSTEIN
  Edward Trail (The Rev.), of Maryland, and Grace Fenton, eldest d. of the officiating clergyman, the Rev. Prof. Kinloch Nelson, D.D., assisted by the Rev. A. C. Hensley, in the Chapel of the Theological Seminary, near Alexandria, Va. So. Ch., Apr. 17, 1890

HELM
  William P., Esq., of New York city, and Agnes H., d. of Lewis Marshall, Esq., of Culpeper, Va., by the Rev. J. D. Powell, in St. John's Church, Portsmouth, Va. So. Ch., Nov. 10, 1881

HELMS
  Wm. T. (The Rev.), of Knoxville, Tenn., and Lucy H., d. of Robert A. Mayo, by the Rev. Wm. Norwood, at "Powhatan Seat", the residence of the bride's father. So. Ch., Sept. 14, 1865

HEMPHILL
  David, Esq., of South Carolina, and Lucy Everett, d. of Col. John C. Singleton of Columbia, S.C., by the rector, the Rev. James S. Hanckel, in the Episcopal Church, Charlottesville. So. Ch., Nov. 30, 1871

HEMPSTONE
  William Dade, and Elsie Chichester Harrison, by the Rev. Walter P. Griggs of Poolesville, Md., in St. James' Church, Leesburg, Va. So. Ch., June 9, 1892

HENDERSON
  Annie Thomas, only d. of Fenton M. Henderson, Esq. of Leesburg, and Joseph C. Millan of Jefferson, Texas, by the Rev. R. T. Davis, in St. James' Church, Leesburg. So. Ch., Sept. 25, 1873
  John H., Esq., and Lucy Garnett, d. of the late John H. Peyton, Esq., by the Rev. T. T. Castleman, at Staunton, Va. So. Ch.,

MARRIAGE NOTICES IN THE SOUTHERN CHURCHMAN WITH DATES OF PUBLICATION

Jan. 4, 1856
Mary (colored), of Gordonsville, and the Rev. Thomas W. Vaughan (colored), deacon in charge of the colored work, by the Rev. F. G. Scott, in St. Paul's Colored Mission Chapel, Gordonsville. So. Ch., Jan. 14, 1892

Mary X., and Wm. K. Lee, both of Lancaster, by the Rev. E. Withers. So. Ch., Dec. 12, 1856

HENDY
Josie M., of San Francisco, Cal., and J. C. Green of Stafford Co., Va., by the Rev. W. H. Platt, in San Francisco, Cal. So. Ch., Jan. 26, 1882

HENLEY
Charles T., and Susie, d. of Dr. R. P. Grymes, by the Rev. A. B. Tizzard, at Clover Hill, Chesterfield Co., Va. So. Ch., Jan. 4, 1883

Fanny Lear, oldest d. of the late Com. John D. Henley of the U.S. Navy, and the Rev. E. Y. Higbee of New York, by the Rev. Mr. Hawley. So. Ch., Dec. 22, 1837

HENLY
Indiana A., and Dr. Robert Emmet Robinson of Petersburg, by the Rev. Dr. Syme, at Bacons Castle, Surry Co., Va. So. Ch., Aug. 25, 1837

James C., and Nannie D. Garnett, by the Rev. E. Meade, in Rappahannock Church, Essex Co., Va. So. Ch., Jan. 8, 1885

HENNER
William Osborn (The Rev.), rector of St. Mark's Church, Geneva, Ill., and Rose Alice, d. of Mr. and Mrs. Alexander F. Kopp, by the Archdeacon W. H. Zeigler and the Rev. Dr. John Herbert Dennis, in St. Alban's Church, Norwood Park. So. Ch., Nov. 24, 1934

HENRIQUES
C. Amalia T., and Wm. M. Bartley, one of the principals of the Virginia and Tennessee College Institute, both of Bristol, by the Rev. F. T. Goodwin, at Bristol, Va. So. Ch., Oct. 2, 1857

HENRY
E. Winston, Jr., of Charlotte Co., Va., and Annie L. Ely of W. Carrianna, Fla., by the Rev. W. T. Saunders of the Episcopal Church, at W. Carrianna, Fla. So. Ch., Jan. 17, 1867

Jane C., d. of Dr. E. H. Henry of Fauquier, and Addison Taliaferro of Amherst, by the Rev. Mr. Kinsolving, in Upperville. So. Ch., Nov. 2, 1855

Lewis E., Esq., of Raleigh, N.C., and Jennie E., d. of Capt. George T. Massenburg of Hampton, by the Rev. John C. McCabe, rector of St. John's Church, in Hampton. So. Ch., Dec. 7, 1854

Susan R. (Mrs.), nee Burwell, and Dr. Archy Cary Randolph, by the Rev. C. Braxton Bryan, in Christ Church, Millwood, Clarke Co., Va. So. Ch., Oct. 13, 1881

HENSHAW

MARRIAGE NOTICES IN THE SOUTHERN CHURCHMAN WITH DATES OF PUBLICATION

Martha V., of Berkley, and Charles A. Taylor of Richmond, Va., by the Rev. A. Wade, at Berkley, Charles City Co., Va. So. Ch., Dec. 3, 1874

HENSON
John, and Anna C. Harley both of Berkeley Co., W. Va., by the Rev. W. T. Leavell, at the residence of the bride's father, Dr. Thos. Harley, in Hedgesville. So. Ch., Dec. 23, 1880

HEPBRON
E. W., of Kent Co., Md., and Alice Jackson of Loudoun Co., Va., by the Rev. S. S. Hepbron assisted by the Rev. Theo. Reed, at the residence of Wm. Jackson, Esq. of Loudoun. So. Ch., Dec. 31, 1874

Sewell S. (The Rev.), of Kent Co., Md., and Selina Lloyd, d. of Charles L. Powell, Esq. of Alexandria, by the Rev. R. H. McKim, in Christ Church, Alexandria. So. Ch., Apr. 20, 1871

HEPBURN
Annie Leake, d. of the late John M. Hepburn, Esq., and the Rev. John D. Powell, by the Rev. Mr. Tillinghast, in St. John's Church, in Georgetown. So. Ch., Oct. 12, 1854

Eliza J., of Georgetown, D. C., and Prof. M. Yarnall, U.S.N., by the Rev. N. P. Tillinghast. So. Ch., Nov. 2, 1855

HERBERT
Mr., and Henrietta Wray, both of Elizabeth City Co., Va., by the Rev. Dr. A. Wade, at the residence of John Selden, Shirley, Charles City Co. So. Ch., Feb. 9, 1871

Emma, d. of John C. Herbert, Esq. of Prince George's Co., Md., and the Rev. William Bryant, by the Rev. William Pinkney, in Prince George's Co., Md. So. Ch., Dec. 1, 1837

James R. (Col.), of Baltimore, and Elizabeth C., d. of Mark Alexander, Jr., Esq. of Mecklenburg, by the Rev. John T. Clark, at "Chester", the residence of the bride's grandfather, John Coleman, Esq. of Halifax. So. Ch., Nov. 26, 1868

Mary Lucretia, and Charles Bolling Wilson, by the Rev. James M. Owens, in St. Paul's Church, Norfolk, Va. So. Ch., May 11, 1912

May, d. of Col. Arthur Herbert of Muckross, Fairfax Co., Va., and John Daingerfield, s. of Capt. F. B. Hooe of Alexandria, by the Rev. George H. Norton, D.D., in the Chapel of the P. E. Theological Seminary of Virginia. So. Ch., June 12, 1890

HEREFORD
James S., of Dallas, Texas, and Jenny P., youngest d. of the late Capt. George Chichester of Fairfax Co., by the Rev. John McGill, in St. Paul's Church, Alexandria. So. Ch., Feb. 5, 1874

HERMAN
Jennie C., and J. Edward Bird, both of Baltimore,

MARRIAGE NOTICES IN THE SOUTHERN CHURCHMAN WITH DATES OF PUBLICATION

Md., by the Rev. Julius E. Grammer, D.D., at Baltimore. So. Ch., Nov. 13, 1884

HERNDON
Betty Hull, d. of Dr. B. S. Herndon, and Henry T. Botts, Esq., by the Rev. A. M. Randolph, in St. George's Church, Fredericksburg. So. Ch., July 27, 1860

Charles, Esq., of Caroline Co., and Lucy W., oldest d. of Bazil Gordon, Esq., by the Rev. Wm. Friend, at Prospect Hill, Caroline Co. So. Ch., Apr. 2, 1858

Lucy, third d. of Brodie Strachan Horndon, M.D. of Savannah, and Robt. Blackie, publisher, of Glasgow, Scotland, by the Rev. Thos. Boone, rector of Christ Church, at the residence of Capt. Mercor, Savannah, Ga. So. Ch., Nov. 29, 1877

Mary F., d. of Dr. B. S. Herndon, and Joseph Clay, Esq. of Georgia, by the Rev. M. Maury, at Fredericksburg. So. Ch., Dec. 7, 1865

HERR
Fannie, d. of A. H. Herr, Esq. of Georgetown, and Wm. C. Niblack, Esq. of Vincennes, Ind., by the Rev. John S. Lindsay, in St. John's Church, Georgetown, D.C. So. Ch., Feb. 19, 1880

HERRICK
James B., and Sophia, d. of Dr. A. T. Bledsoe of the University of Virginia, by the Rev. Dr. William Sparrow, in Christ Church, Charlottesville, Va. So. Ch., July 6, 1860

HERWIG
Henrich (Lt.), U.S.N., and Minnie A., d. of the late R. W. Wheat of Alexandria, Va., by the Rev. Dr. G. H. Norton, in St. Paul's Church, Alexandria, Va. So. Ch., Dec. 13, 1883

HESSER
James E., of Loudoun, and Emeline, d. of Squire Bell of Clarke Co., Va., by the Rev. F. M. Whittle, at Clarke Co., Va. So. Ch., Jan. 13, 1853

HESTER
Carrie Theresa, d. of Wm. Hester, and Eugene Simpson, all of Terry, Miss., by the Rev. Dr. Wm. C. Crane, in the Church of the Good Shepherd, Terry, Miss. So. Ch., July 13, 1876

Chas. A. (Capt.), C.S.A., and Pinkie, d. of Capt. John C. O'Grady late of New Orleans, by the Rev. Dr. Crane, at Rest Easy, near Jackson, Miss. So. Ch., June 17, 1864

Fannie, and Chas. T. Brown of Madison Co., by the Rev. Dr. Savage, at Rest Easy, the residence of the bride's father, near Jackson, Miss. So. Ch., June 17, 1864

Sallie A., and Dr. Chas. M. Adams of Madison Co., by the Rev. Mr. Woodall, at Rest Easy, near Jackson, Miss. So. Ch., June 17, 1864

HETH
Henry (Capt.), U.S.A., and Harriot C., d. of Miles C. Selden, Esq. of Norwood,

MARRIAGE NOTICES IN THE SOUTHERN CHURCHMAN WITH DATES OF PUBLICATION

Powhatan Co., Va., by the Rev. Erskine M. Rodman, at Norwood. So. Ch., Apr. 17, 1857
Mollie A., d. of the late Col. John Heth of Black Heth, Chesterfield Co., and the Rev. George D. E. Mortimer, rector of St. Paul's Church, Goochland Co., by the Rev. John D. Powell, at the residence of Edward Cunningham, Esq., in Powhatan Co. So. Ch., June 20, 1852

HEUSER
Wm. L., and M. Dora, d. of the late Frederick Foote, all of Prince William Co., Va., by the Rev. A. P. Gray, at the residence of the bride's family, at Waverly. So. Ch., Jan. 4, 1883

HEWITT
Anna K., oldest d. of Dr. R. N. and Mrs. Fannie D. Hewitt, and Thomas N. Langhorne, Jr. of Lynchburg, Va., by the Rev. B. W. Moseley, at Otter Hill, Campbell Co., Va. So. Ch., Oct. 17, 1878
Charles, and Evy L. Roberson, both of Falmouth, by the Rev. J. Green Shackelford of Trinity Church, Fredericksburg, at the residence of the bride's father, C. W. Roberson, Falmouth, Va. So. Ch., Nov. 22, 1888
Edwin L., and Elizabeth T. Brock, by the Rev. J. Y. Downman, at the residence of the bride's father, Dr. C. W. Brock. So. Ch., May 2, 1889
R. N. (Dr.), of Campbell Co., and Sarah H. Michie, by the Rev. H. B. Lee, in Christ Church, Charlottesville. So. Ch., Feb. 25, 1892
Thomas Marshall, and Josephine, d. of Jos. Allen, Esq. of Richmond, by the Rev. Joshua Peterkin, in Richmond. So. Ch., Apr. 16, 1858

HEYMOND
Arthur Percival, of Annapolis, Md., and Mary, d. of the late Rev. and Mrs. Alexander C. Haverstick of Annapolis, Md., by the Rev. E. P. Dandridge, in the Church of the Incarnation, Ronceverte, W.Va. So. Ch., June 18, 1910

HEYWARD
Benj. H., of Charleston, S.C., and Mariana Tabb, d. of Dr. Randolph Barksdale, by the Rev. Dr. Charles Minnigerode. So. Ch., Dec. 18, 1884

HICKEY
Alice T., and the Rev. J. McAlpin Harding, both of Philadelphia, by the Rev. Dr. W. Bacon Stevens assisted by the Rev. J. P. Wilmer, in St. Andrew's Church. So. Ch., Nov. 12, 1858

HICKS
Elizabeth A., only d. of Wm. E. Hicks of Mathews Co., Va., and John G. Davis, by the Rev. Peregrine Wroth, at the residence of the bride's father. So. Ch., Feb. 6, 1873
Imogen H., of Panola Co., Miss., and the Rev. Tullius C. Tupper, by the Rev. S. H. Green assisted by the Rev. G. White, D.D., of Memphis, in the Church

MARRIAGE NOTICES IN THE SOUTHERN CHURCHMAN WITH DATES OF PUBLICATION

of The Redeemer, Sardis, Miss. So. Ch., Sept. 17, 1874

Julia F., of Oxford, N.C., and William T. Brogden of Richmond Co., N.C., by the Rev. P. D. Thompson, at the residence of the bride's father, E. H. Hicks. So. Ch., June 18, 1874

Mattie M., only d. of Oliver Hicks, Esq. of Tiverton Four Corners, R.I., and W. H. Seabury of Norfolk, Va., by the Rev. Nelson Clarke, at Tiverton Four Corners, R.I. So. Ch., Sept. 23, 1859

Robert J. (Dr.), C. S. Army, and Nannie F. Randolph of Fauquier Co., Va., by the Rev. Richard Mason, in Columbia, Fluvanna Co., Va. So. Ch., Feb. 8, 1865

Virginia Hoge, of Richmond, and the Rev. Frank Hallam of Calvary Church, Americus, Ga., by the Rev. Joshua Peterkin, D.D., in Richmond, Va. So. Ch., Feb. 4, 1875

HICKSON
W. M., Esq., and Lizzie Tunstall Rives, by the Rev. Geo. W. Dame, in Danville. So. Ch., Oct. 27, 1870

William, and Elizabeth Gardiner, d. of Maj. B. C. Saunders of Campbell Co., Va., by the Rev. R. T. Davis assisted by the Rev. A. Jaeger, in the Church of the Good Shepherd, Campbell Co., Va. So. Ch., Aug. 13, 1885

HIGBEE
E. Y. (The Rev.), of New York, and Fanny Lear, eldest d. of the late Com. John D. Henley of the U.S. Navy, by the Rev. Mr. Hawley. So. Ch., Dec. 22, 1837

HIGGANBOTHAM*
Fanny, d. of E. G. Higganbotham of Henrico Co., Va., and John S. Knox, Jr., by the Rev. Joshua Peterkin, at 203 West Franklin St., Richmond, Va. So. Ch., July 27, 1882

HIGGINBOTHAM
Nannie May, d. of E. G. Higginbotham*, of Henrico Co., and Henry Gibson of Roanoke, by the Rev. Wyllys Rede, at the residence of Mrs. Bayley, Richmond, Va. So. Ch., Jan. 12, 1888

Rosa Bagby, d. of E. G. Higginbotham of Ravenswood, Henrico Co., and Collinson P. E. Burgwyn, by the Rev. Green Shackelford assisted by the Rev. Dr. Minnigerode, at the residence of the bride's grandmother, Mrs. Jane C. Bayly, 203 West Franklin St., Richmond, Va. So. Ch., Oct. 23, 1884

William Thomas, of Petersburg, and Mary Frances, youngest d. of the late Maj. Reuben Coleman of Amherst, by the Rev. Cleland Nelson. So. Ch., Sept. 6, 1839

See also MACMURDO, Jane B. (Mrs.)

HIGGINS
John S. (The Rev.), rector of the Church of the Advent, Chicago, and Marion Laird, by Bishop

* Given as printed

MARRIAGE NOTICES IN THE SOUTHERN CHURCHMAN WITH DATES OF PUBLICATION

Stewart assisted by the Rev. Walter C. Bihler, in Christ Church, Woodlawn. So. Ch., Sept. 23, 1933

HILL

Ellen T., and John B. Minor, Prof. of Law at the University of Virginia, by the Rev. Dr. Hanckel, at the residence of Dr. J. S. Davis. So. Ch., Nov. 20, 1884

Evelyn C., and John William Taylor, both of King William Co., Va., by the Rev. W. T. Roberts, at Edgeville, the residence of the bride's mother. So. Ch., Aug. 29, 1889

L. S. (Dr.), of South Carolina, and Lucie C., d. of the late William Deahl of Berryville, Clarke Co., Va., by the Rev. A. E. Cornish, at the residence of Capt. Clinton Ward, Edgeville Co., S.C. So. Ch., Aug. 14, 1890

Walker, of Richmond, Va., and Jeanie Morrison, d. of Angelica P. and the late R. J. Lockwood, by the Rt. Rev. Bishop Robertson, in Emmanuel Church, St. Louis Co., Mo. So. Ch., Nov. 12, 1885

William, and Elizabeth, d. of the late Christopher Johnson, Esq., at Canterbury, King William Co. So. Ch., Jan. 9, 1835

William, of Henderson, N.C., and Landonia M., d. of Maj. Ball, lately of Casanova, Fauquier Co., Va., by the Rev. David Barr of Epiphany Parish, Washington, at the residence of the bride, 2325 Pennsylvania Ave., Washington, D.C. So. Ch., Sept. 4, 1890

William L., of Balm, Ala., and Maria R., d. of James H. and Virginia Z. Wilson, and gr.d. of the late Gen. Felix Zollicoffer, by the Rev. Mayo Cabell Martin, rector of Holy Trinity Church, Nashville, Tenn., at the residence of the bride's parents, Nashville, Tenn. So. Ch., Sept. 13, 1888

HILLEARY

Mary Worthington, d. of Mrs. Clarence Hilleary, gr.d. of the late Gen. T. T. Wheeler, "Tudor Hall", Montgomery Co., Md., and the Rev. Robert W. Lewis of Mission Home, Va., by the Rev. E. E. Burgess assisted by Dr. E. T. Helfenstein, in St. Mark's Protestant Episcopal Church, "Merryland Tract", near Petersville. So. Ch., July 20, 1918*

Robert Brooks, of Washington, D.C., and Frances Shepherd, d. of Mr. and Mrs. Henry E. Wright of Centreville, Md., by the Venerable ** R. Bowden Shepherd, uncle of the bride, assisted by the Rev. A. Chamberlaine, rector of the church, in St. Paul's Church, Centreville, Md. So. Ch., Sept. 12, 1936

HILLIARD

Grafton, and Margaret Foreman, both of Smithfield, by the Rev. Alex. Jones. So. Ch., Dec. 15, 1837

HILYARD

Alva W. (Capt.), and Zillah Miller, by the Rev. W. D. Hansom, at the residence

---

* A notice appears in the issue of June 29, 1918 identical with this, except that "Mary Worthington Hilleary" is written "Mary Washington Hilleary"
** Title given to Archdeacon

MARRIAGE NOTICES IN THE SOUTHERN CHURCHMAN WITH DATES OF PUBLICATION

of the bride's father, in Newport, Del. So. Ch., Jan. 11, 1883

HINKS
Edwin S., of Baltimore, and Lizzie Lee, d. of the late Col. David Funsten, by the Rev. W. M. Dame assisted by the Rev. George M. Funsten, in Memorial Church, Baltimore. So. Ch., May 8, 1884
Lavinia, of Baltimore, and the Rev. George W. Dame, Jr., assistant minister of the Church of the Ascension, by the Rev. George W. Dame, Sr. assisted by the Rev. W. M. Dame and the Rev. Nelson Dame, in Memorial Church, Baltimore. So. Ch., June 12, 1884

HIPKINS
John, of Norfolk, Va., and Alice E., d. of the late Capt. Wentworth Parker of Halifax, N.S., by the Rev. Walter Williams, in St. George's Church, New York. So. Ch., Oct. 2, 1879

HIRSH
Elizabeth, d. of the late William L. Hirsh of Philadelphia, Pa., and James Keith Marshall, Jr. of Fauquier, by the Rev. Father Floyd, at the residence of the bride's mother, Washington, D.C. So. Ch., Jan. 29, 1891

HITE
Kedder Meade, and Susan Fitzhugh, d. of the late Robert S. Voss of Rappahannock Co., Va., by the Rev. James Hanckel, in Christ Church, Charlottesville. So. Ch., June 17, 1869
Susan Randolph Meade, d. of J. J. Hite, and Henry Baker, all of Nelson Co., by the Rev. Edmund Withers, at the residence of Mrs. Hopkins. So. Ch., Jan. 28, 1869
William Fowler, of Gainesville, Va., and Isabella Fairfax, youngest d. of the late Thomas R. Love of Fairfax Court House, Va., by the Rev. J. C. Hall, assisted by the Rev. W. A. Alrich, at Zion Episcopal Church, Fairfax C.H., Va. So. Ch., June 23, 1892

HOBBS
Hutoka, d. of the late Wm. T. Hobbs of Greensville Co., Va., and Richard T. Wilson of Sussex Co., Va., by the Rev. David Barr. So. Ch., Dec. 7, 1871
Wm. T., of Baltimore, Md., and Lula T., d. of Mary E. and the late Charles L. Ryan, by the Rev. A. P. Gray, in the Ascension Church, Amherst C.H. So. Ch., Dec. 5, 1889

HOBSON
Alexander Malem, of Richmond City, and Mary, eldest d. of the late John Pemberton of Goochland, by the Rev. Francis M. Whittle, at Goochland Co., Va. So. Ch., Feb. 13, 1851
Anna, eldest d. of the late Thomas L. Hobson, Esq. of Powhatan, and Mann Page of Albemarle, by the Rev. William H. Kinckle, in Powhatan Co. So. Ch., June 7, 1855
Anna C., eldest d. of W. W. Hobson, and Dr. Robert Page, all of Powhatan Co., Va., by the Rev. B. H.

MARRIAGE NOTICES IN THE SOUTHERN CHURCHMAN WITH DATES OF PUBLICATION

Dupuy, at the residence of the bride's father. So. Ch., Dec. 27, 1877

Ellen Cary, of Powhatan Co., Va., and George N. Guthrie of Arkansas, by the Rev. J. D. Powell of Portsmouth, Va., at "Brooklyn", Powhatan Co., Va. So. Ch., Sept. 23, 1875

J. Cannon, and Alice V. Pettitt, both of Goochland Co., Va., by the Rev. P. M. Boyden, at Hebron, Goochland Co., Va. So. Ch., June 5, 1879

J. Munford, and Jane, d. of Col. Ben. Jones of Amelia Co., Va., by the Rev. P. F. Berkeley, at the Oaks, the residence of the bride's father. So. Ch., Nov. 11, 1875

Mattie A., d. of Dr. J. V. Hobson, and Dr. E. A. Craighill of Lynchburg, in St. James' Church, Richmond. So. Ch., Apr. 23, 1874

S. Norvell, and Gen. J. Holmes Smith of Lynchburg, by the Rev. Joshua Peterkin, D.D., at the residence of the bride's parents, Dr. Joseph V. and Mrs. Mary E. Hobson, in Richmond. So. Ch., Mar. 21, 1878

Virginia K., d. of the late John B. Pemberton, and Thomas Mann Fleming, M.D., all of Goochland Co., by the Rev. Erskine M. Rodman, at Clover Forest. So. Ch., Mar. 13, 1857

Virginia Page, d. of the late Thomas L. Hobson, Esq., and Capt. Richard Archer, C.S. Army, all of Powhatan, by the Rev. J. D. Powell, in Emmanuel Church, Powhatan. So. Ch., Feb. 19, 1864

HODGE
Mary Robinson, d. of Mr. and Mrs. Hugh Bayard Hodge of 420 West Walnut Lane, Germantown, and the Rev. Percy L. Urban, assistant rector of St. Peter's Church, Germantown. So. Ch., July 23, 1921

HODGES
Carrie Seymour, d. of the officiating clergyman, and John L. Edwards, Esq. of Washington, D.C., by the Rev. Dr. Hodges, in Warrenton, N.C. So. Ch., Oct. 18, 1866

Cornelia L., third d. of the late John Hodges of Upper Marlboro, Md., and the Rev. William Hodges of Virginia, by the Rev. Mr. Marbury. So. Ch., Dec. 1, 1837

Nannie Ogle, d. of John Hodges, Esq., and Dr. Benjamin L. Bird, by the Rev. Wm. Hodges, at Omaha, Prince George's Co., Md. So. Ch., June 25, 1868

Philip A., of Bennettsville, S.C., and Ella M. Moseley of Richmond, Va., by the Rev. A. B. Tizzard assisted by the Rev. C. Minnigerode, D.D., in St. Paul's Church, Richmond, Va. So. Ch., May 12, 1887

William (The Rev.), of Virginia, and Cornelia L., third d. of the late John Hodges of Upper Marlboro, Md., by the Rev. Mr. Marbury. So. Ch., Dec. 1, 1837

HODGKIN
J. B. (Dr.), of Washing-

MARRIAGE NOTICES IN THE SOUTHERN CHURCHMAN WITH DATES OF PUBLICATION

ton, D.C., and Miss M. G. Gordon of Essex Co., Va., by the Rev. Everard Meade, in St. John's Church, Tappahannock, Essex Co., Va. So. Ch., Nov. 25, 1880

James B. (Dr.), of Alexandria, and Lizzie S., d. of John Rust of Westmoreland Co., by the Rev. Thomas E. Locke, in Oak Grove Church, Westmoreland Co. So. Ch., June 23, 1870

HODGSON

Jennie H., d. of Joseph Hodgson of Columbia, and Stephen B. Hughes, Esq. of Richmond, by the Rev. Erskine M. Rodman, at Columbia, Fluvanna Co. So. Ch., June 5, 1857

John Hamilton Potter (Dr.), and Harriette Saunders, d. of Enoch Ensley of Memphis, by the Rev. Telfair Hodgson, in the Calvary Church, Memphis, Tenn. So. Ch., Oct. 30, 1890

HOFF

E. W., and Jennie, d. of Judge George Blow of Norfolk, by the Rev. Dr. Barten, in Christ Church, at Norfolk, Va. So. Ch., Sept. 28, 1882

Francis H., and Emily Renshaw, d. of the late B. C. Presstman of Baltimore, by the Rev. A. M. Randolph, D.D., in Grace P. E. Church, Baltimore. So. Ch., Oct. 22, 1885

John F. (The Rev.), rector of Christ Church, Georgetown, D.C., and Juliana J., d. of Wm. Ross, Esq. of Fredericktown, Md., by the Rev. Upton Beall.
So. Ch., Nov. 15, 1839

Wm. Ross, and Nannie Lloyd, d. of the late Hon. Wm. T. Goldsborough, by the Rev. W. W. Williams, D.D., in Christ Church, Baltimore. So. Ch., June 25, 1885

HOFFECKER

J. H., Jr. of Wilmington, Del., and Bettie W. Meade, by the Rev. R. T. Davis, D.D., in St. James' Church, Leesburg, Va. So. Ch., Jan. 15, 1880

HOFFMAN

C. Colden (The Rev.), rector of St. Mark's Church, C. P., and Caroline M., d. of David M. Hogan of Philadelphia, by the Rt. Rev. J. Payne, Missionary Bishop at Cape Palmas, West Africa. So. Ch., May 21, 1858

Harriet Seton, youngest d. of the late Martin Hoffman, Esq. of New York, and the Rev. Henry H. Bean, rector of St. Stephen's Church, Harrisburg, Pa., by the Rev. J. T. Cushing, at Goshen, N.H.*
So. Ch., Oct. 14, 1852

Susan M., eldest d. of the officiating minister, and the Rev. J. Henry Watson, rector of the Church of the Good Shepherd, Hartford, Conn., by the Rev. Dr. E. A. Hoffman, dean of the General Theological Seminary, in Trinity Chapel, N.Y. So. Ch., Nov. 2, 1882

HOGAN

Caroline M., d. of David M. Hogan of Philadelphia, and the Rev. C. Colden Hoffman, rector of St. Mark's Church, C. P., by

* Possibly Goshen, N.Y., but given as printed

MARRIAGE NOTICES IN THE SOUTHERN CHURCHMAN WITH DATES OF PUBLICATION

the Rt. Rev. J. Payne, Missionary Bishop, at Cape Palmas, West Africa. So. Ch., May 21, 1858

William G., and Ida L. Royall, by the Rev. John C. Cornick, at the residence of Mr. Royall, Charles City Co., Va. So. Ch., Jan. 21, 1892

HOGE

Mary, d. of the late Isaac Hoge of Wheeling, and the Rt. Rev. Charles Clifton Penick, Bishop of Cape Palmas and Parts Adjacent, West Africa, by the Rt. Rev. George W. Peterkin, D.D., assisted by the Rev. P. R. Swope, at the residence of the bride's mother, Wheeling, W.Va. So. Ch., May 5, 1881

Nancy Hunter, only d. of Judge John Blair Hoge of Martinsburg, W.Va., and Arthur Percy, youngest s. of the late Capt. Archibald Blair Fairfax, U.S.N., by the Rev. Douglas F. Forrest, D.D., in Trinity Church, Washington, D.C. So. Ch., Feb. 9, 1882

Sallie M. (Mrs.), of Prince George's Co., Md., and James K. Edwards of Washington City, by the Rev. W. L. Hyland, D.D., rector, assisted by the Rev. J. M. E. McKee of Anacostia Parish, District of Columbia, in St. Barnabas' Chapel, St. John's Parish, Prince George's Co., Md. So. Ch., Aug. 31, 1882

HOLCOMBE

Elizabeth B., d. of Hon. James P. Holcombe of Bedford Co., Va., and Samuel M. Bolling of Fauquier Co., by the Rev. Edward H. Ingle of Roanoke, at "Bellvue", the residence of the bride's father. So. Ch., Sept. 12, 1872

Joseph Gales, of Washington, D.C., and Mary Eliza (Lily), d. of Benjamin and Sarah P. Brown, by the Rev. A. P. Gray, in Ascension Church, Amherst. So. Ch., Dec. 18, 1890

HOLDREN

Edmund, and Mary E. Browse, by the Rev. Jacob Brittingham, at Grape Island, W.Va. So. Ch., Feb. 23, 1882

HOLLADAY

Mary Minor, eldest d. of the late J. Z. Holladay of Charlottesville, and J. A. Latane of Essex, by the Rev. R. K. Meade. So. Ch., Nov. 16, 1855

Nannie, second d. of Mrs. Julia A. Holladay, and Dr. Wilson C. N. Randolph, all of Albemarle, by the Rev. R. K. Meade, at Northwood, near Charlottesville. So. Ch., Nov. 19, 1858

Sally W., youngest d. of Mrs. Julia A. Holladay of Charlottesville, Va., and T. Henry Johnston of Botetourt Co., by the Rev. R. K. Meade, at "Northwood." So. Ch., Apr. 27, 1860

Wm. A., of Orange Co., Va., and Affie F. Yerby, by the Rev. S. S. Ware, in Grace Church, Caroline Co., Va. So. Ch., Dec. 12, 1889

HOLLAR

Wm. H., of Pittsburgh, Pa., and Laura L. Rankin, by the Rev. John W. Lea, in Trinity Church, Martinsburg. So. Ch., Oct. 28,

MARRIAGE NOTICES IN THE SOUTHERN CHURCHMAN WITH DATES OF PUBLICATION

1875
HOLLEMAN
  Laura, d. of the late Hon.
  Joel Holleman of Isle of
  Wight Co., Va., and Jas. R.
  Carroll of Warren Co., by
  the Rev. John Wingfield, in
  Christ Church, Hicksford,
  Va. So. Ch., Mar. 8, 1865
HOLLEY
  Thomas D., and Eva M. Smith,
  both of Bertie Co., N.C.,
  by the Rev. Edward Wooten,
  in Coleraine, Bertie Co.,
  N.C. So. Ch., Mar. 4,
  1869
HOLLIDAY
  F. W. M. (Col.), of Winchester,
  Va., and Hannah T., eldest
  d. of Thos. McCormick, Esq.
  of Clarke Co., Va., by the
  Rev. T. F. Martin, at
  Elmington, the residence of
  the bride's father. So.
  Ch., Jan. 23, 1868
  Lewis H., and Jinnie P.
  Meredith, by the Rev.
  Charles C. Randolph, at the
  residence of Mrs. Lizzie
  Munford, Botetourt Co.,
  Va. So. Ch., July 14,
  1881
  Mary M., eldest d. of Dr.
  R. J. McK. Holliday of
  Winchester, and Thomas
  McCormick of Clarke, by the
  Rev. C. Walker. So. Ch.,
  Nov. 28, 1856
  Robert (Dr.), of Caroline
  Co., and Elvira Spindle, d.
  of Elijah Amiss of Rappa-
  hannock Co., by the Rev.
  P. Slaughter, at Melville,
  the seat of John Minor
  Leavell. So. Ch., Jan. 25,
  1866
HOLLINGSWORTH
  Charles M., M.D., and L.
  Josie Roller, by the Rev.
  R. D. Roller assisted by
  the Rev. O. S. Bunting,
  rector of the parish, at
  Inglewood, the residence of
  the bride's father, Rock-
  ingham Co., Va. So. Ch.,
  Nov. 6, 1884
  Sophia L., d. of Jessie
  Hollingsworth of Carroll
  Co., Md., and the Rev.
  Thos. J. Wyatt, by the Rev.
  Dr. Wyatt, in St. Paul's
  Church, Baltimore. So.
  Ch., Dec. 3, 1858
HOLLISTER
  Leone, and the Rev. Gordon V.
  Smith, by Bishop McCormick
  assisted by the rector, the
  Rev. L. B. Whittemore, in
  Grace Church, Grand Rapids.
  So. Ch., Feb. 23, 1935
HOLMAN
  George P., Jr., of Christians-
  burg, Va., and Ellie
  Josephine, d. of the late
  J. M. Quisenberry of
  Spotsylvania, by the Rev.
  Wm. W. Green, at Carter's
  Hall, Caroline Co. So. Ch.,
  Jan. 5, 1871
  Wm. H. (Capt.), of Bucking-
  ham, and Lucy M., d. of
  the late William Galt,
  Esq. of Fluvanna, by the
  Rev. James A. Latane, in
  Staunton. So. Ch., July
  15, 1864
HOLMES
  David Hull, of Baltimore,
  and Maude, youngest d. of
  Mr. and Mrs. F. L. Allen
  of Amherst, by the Rev. A.
  P. Gray of Ascension
  Church, at the home of the
  bride's parents. So. Ch.,
  Oct. 13, 1892
  Edward A., of Chatham Hill,
  Smyth Co., Va., and Annie
  P. Derrick of Houston, Va.,
  by the Rev. Mr. Raymond,
  at the home of the bride's

MARRIAGE NOTICES IN THE SOUTHERN CHURCHMAN WITH DATES OF PUBLICATION

brother, G. H. Derrick, in Pulaski, Va. So. Ch., Aug. 26, 1911

William Axford Benjamin (The Rev.), Chaplain, Pennsylvania Industrial School, and Laura Doris Wilkinson of Beaver, Pa., by the Rt. Rev. Bishop Wyatt Brown, in the Keferstein Chapel of the Holy Spirit, Bishopscourt, Harrisburg, Pa. So. Ch., July 17, 1937

HOLT
Charles J. (The Rev.), of Baltimore, Md., and Fannie Marshall of New York, by the Rev. A. M. Randolph of Baltimore, Md., in New York City. So. Ch., Oct. 21, 1875

Susan S., d. of Col. John W. Holt of Bedford, and John O. L. Goggin, Esq., Attorney-at-Law of Christiansburg, Va., by the Rev. Jacob D. Mitchell. So. Ch., Nov. 24, 1837

Taylor, of Leadville, Col., and Fannie Kyle of Amherst, Va., by the Rev. Arthur P. Gray, in Amherst, Va. So. Ch., June 5, 1890

HOLTZCLAW
Lucian D., and Bettie Shumate, both of Fauquier Co., Va., by the Rev. E. H. Ingle, in Washington, D.C. So. Ch., Aug. 23, 1883

HOLTZMAN
M. M., of Virginia, and the Rev. Charles McK. Callaway, by the Rev. Mr. McClark, in Christ Church, Alexandria. So. Ch., July 18, 1850

HOMER
Henrietta B., d. of Richard B. Homer of Fauquier Co., Va., and Frank H. Wyth of Philadelphia, by the Rev. John F. Hoff of Maryland, in the Church of The Holy Trinity, Philadelphia. So. Ch., May 9, 1862

HOMMAN
Wm. (The Rev.), and Fidella Smith, by the Rev. Mr. Burgess, at Hartford, Conn. So. Ch., Oct. 25, 1839

HONSHELL
Gus H., of Cincinati, Ohio, and Clara M. Stoddard of San Francisco, Cal., by the Rev. John W. Lea, at Huntington, W.Va. So. Ch., Dec. 25, 1879

HOOE
B. Howson, of Manassas, Va., and Edmonia Berkeley, by the Rev. W. A. Alrich, at the "White House", Hanover Co., Va. So. Ch., Oct. 7, 1880

John Daingerfield, s. of Capt. P. B. Hooe of Alexandria, and May, d. of Col. Arthur Herbert of Muckross, Fairfax Co., Va., by the Rev. George H. Norton, D.D., at the Chapel of the P.E. Theological Seminary of Virginia. So. Ch., June 12, 1890

Kate, d. of Howson and Catharine Hooe, and Dr. Wm. J. Jones of Gloucester C.H., Va., by the Rev. A. P. Gray, at "Longwood", the residence of the bride's brother, Fauquier Co., Va.

- 245 -

MARRIAGE NOTICES IN THE SOUTHERN CHURCHMAN WITH DATES OF PUBLICATION

So. Ch., Nov. 13, 1884
Mary B., d. of the late Abram B. Hooe of King George and Lewis A. Ashton, Esq., by the Rev. E. B. McGuire, in St. Paul's Church, King George Co. So. Ch., Dec. 8, 1870
Mary Jane, d. of Rice Hooe, Esq., and Robert Smith, Esq. of Fauquier Co., by the Rev. E. C. McGuire, D.D., at Bunker's Hill. So. Ch., Jan. 25, 1856
Philip B., and Mary H., d. of John B. Daingerfield, all of Alexandria, Va., by the Rev. George H. Norton, in Alexandria, Va. So. Ch., Oct. 24, 1867
Susie F., d. of Virginia and the late John Hooe of "Mayfield", Prince William Co., Va., and Wm. G. Iden of Fauquier Co., Va., by the Rev. A. P. Gray, at the residence of the bride's mother, Manassas, Va. So. Ch., Nov. 10, 1881
Virginia J., youngest d. of the late John Hooe, and Dr. Benjamin F. Iden of Manassas, by the Rev. Jno. McGill, at Mayfield, the residence of the bride's mother. So. Ch., Feb. 5, 1874

HOOF
Caroline, d. of Lewis Hoof, Esq. of Alexandria, Va., and Wm. L. Wallace of New York, by the Rev. James T. Johnston, in St. Paul's Church. So. Ch., June 26, 1851
Gurtrude* H., d. of P. H. Hoof of Alexandria, Va., and John R. Armistead of Charles City Co., Va., by the Rev. Wm. A. Stickney, at Weyanoke, the residence of Mrs. Mary H. Minge, Marengo Co., Ala. So. Ch., Dec. 6, 1883

HOOFF
Charles R., and Rebecca, d. of the late Abijah Janney of Alexandria, Va., by the Rev. Jas. T. Johnston, in St. Paul's Church. So. Ch., Oct. 2, 1851
Douglass (The Rev.), of Suffolk, Va., and Mary Douglass, d. of the late Rev. Chandler Robbins of Springfield, Ohio, by the rector, the Rev. George H. Norton, D.D., in St. Paul's Church, Alexandria, Va. So. Ch., Nov. 26, 1885
Ellen Douglass, d. of J. Wallace Hooff, and Benjamin Lawrence Wallace of Tarrytown, N.Y., by the Rev. Douglass Hooff, in St. Paul's Church, Alexandria, Va. So. Ch., June 18, 1890
John W., and Maria Ainsworth, both of Blue Ridge, Jefferson Co., W.Va., by the Rev. P. D. Thompson, at Wickliffe rectory. So. Ch., Apr. 13, 1893
Lewis, of Alexandria, and Mary A., d. of H. Z. Shackleford, Esq. of Rappahannock Co., Va., by the Rev. Douglass Hooff of Alexandria, at "Montpelier", the residence of the bride's father. So. Ch., Feb. 2, 1882
Mary Goulding, d. of J. Wallace Hooff of Alexandria, Va., and Edward S. Fawcett, by the Rev. Geo. H. Norton, D.D.,

* Given as printed

MARRIAGE NOTICES IN THE SOUTHERN CHURCHMAN WITH DATES OF PUBLICATION

in St. Paul's Church, Alexandria, Va. So. Ch., Oct. 28, 1875

Mattie B., d. of the late John Hooff of Alexandria, Va., and A. Brooke Beall of Norfolk, Va., by the Rev. A. M. Randolph, in Emmanuel Church, Baltimore. So. Ch., May 8, 1873

Philip H., of Alexandria, Va., and Bettie, d. of the late Samson Blincoe, Esq. of Leesburg, Loudoun Co., Va., by the Rev. George Adie. So. Ch., Feb. 19, 1847

HOOMES

Eliza Lewis, eldest d. of Richard B. Hoomes of Virginia, and Maj. James Parke Corbin of Mossneck, by the Rev. Thos. Addison, at Belle Hill, the residence of J. Edward Dickinson, Esq. So. Ch., Aug. 29, 1856

Hannah Battaile, only d. of H. B. Hoomes, Esq. of Alexandria, and W. F. Slaughter of Fredericksburg, Va., by the Rev. E. C. Murdaugh, D.D. So. Ch., Feb. 13, 1873

HOOPER

Matilda W., d. of the late John P. Hooper of Cambridge, Md., and Benjamin Cattell Presstman of Baltimore, by the Rt. Rev. A. M. Randolph, Assistant Bishop of Virginia, in Emmanuel Church, Baltimore. So. Ch., Oct. 16, 1884

HOPE

James Barron, Esq., and Annie B., d. of Kennon Whiting, Esq., by the Rev. John C. McCabe, rector of the Church of the Ascension, Baltimore, and former rector of the Church in Hampton, at Elmwood, near Hampton, Va. So. Ch., June 19, 1857

Jane Barron, d. of James Barron Hope, and Robert Marr of U.S. Coast and Geodetic Survey, by the Rev. Beverly D. Tucker of St. Paul's Church, at the residence of the bride's parents, in Norfolk, Va. So. Ch., Apr. 28, 1887

Nancy A., and James W. Nicholson, Esq., by the Rev. C. C. Randolph, in Emmanuel Church, Eagle Rock. So. Ch., Nov. 15, 1888

Nannie Mallory, youngest d. of James Barron Hope, Esq., and Richard H. Baker, Jr., by the Rev. Beverly D. Tucker, in St. Paul's Church, Norfolk. So. Ch., Nov. 5, 1885

HOPINS

Robert T., and Ada L. Martin, niece of the Rev. T. F. Martin, all of Nashville, by the Rev. T. F. Martin, rector of St. Ann's Church, assisted by the Rev. Jerry Witherspoon, pastor of the church in which the ceremony was performed, in First Presbyterian Church in Nashville, Tenn. So. Ch., Nov. 22, 1888

HOPKINS

Charles A. S., of Woodstock, Va., and Lilly, d. of Margaret and Wm. Temple Smith, by the Rev. A. P. Gray, in Trinity Church, Manassas. So. Ch., Nov.

MARRIAGE NOTICES IN THE SOUTHERN CHURCHMAN WITH DATES OF PUBLICATION

1, 1883
Harriotte Lee, youngest d. of the late John Hopkins, Esq. of Frederick Co., Va., and the Rev. Richard K. Meade of Charlottesville, Va., by the Rt. Rev. Bishop Meade, at Wheatland, Jefferson City, Va. So. Ch., Sept. 1, 1837

Mary, of Pittsylvania, and Christopher Lewis formerly of Brunswick Co., Va., by the Rev. C. O. Pruden, in Emmanuel Church, Chatham. So. Ch., Aug. 13, 1891

Mary A., d. of the late John Hopkins, Esq., and the Rev. William M. Jackson, by the Rev. Alexander Jones, at Winchester, Va. So. Ch., May 8, 1835

HORNER
Edna French, d. of the late Richard F. Horner of Fauquier, and Samuel Cooper Dawson, all of Alexandria, by the Rev. Prof. Berryman Green, D.D., at Alexandria, Va. So. Ch., Apr. 13, 1907

Elizabeth Welch, d. of Joseph Horner, Esq. of Warrenton, and John Somerville Knox of Alexandria, by the Rev. G. H. Norton, at Warrenton. So. Ch., Dec. 7, 1855

Ellen Ashton, d. of R. L. Horner, Esq. of Fauquier Co., Va., and Parker C. Wyeth of St. Joseph, Mo., by the Rev. G. W. Nelson, rector, in St. James' Church, Warrenton, Va. So. Ch., Oct. 2, 1890

Fanny Baylor, d. of Joseph Horner, Esq., and J. Blodget Britton of Philadelphia, by the Rev. John S. Lindsay, in St. James' Church, Warrenton, Va. So. Ch., Oct. 8, 1874

Fanny Scott, d. of Frederick Horner, and Robert H. Downman, by the Rev. G. H. Norton, in Warrenton. So. Ch., May 23, 1856

Frederick C., of Marshall, Va., and Miriam Glenn Ranson, by the Rev. William L. Glenn, at the residence of the bride's parents, Maj. and Mrs. A. R. H. Ranson, at Hilton, Md. So. Ch., Nov. 26, 1910

Minor C., of Midlothian, Va., and Bessie M. Archer of Vinita, Va., by the Rev. John G. Scott, rector of Manakin Church, Powhatan Co., Va., in Manakin Church, Powhatan Co., Va. So. Ch., Jan. 28, 1922

Richard Cary, of Bristol, Tenn., formerly of Fauquier Co., Va., and Daphne Jean Blackwell, in the Presbyterian Church, in Vicksburg, Miss. So. Ch., Feb. 6, 1909

Richard H., and Virgie A., d. of E. B. S. Cary, Esq., by the Rev. Charles Mann, at "Secluseval", Gloucester Co., Va. So. Ch., Jan. 25, 1872

Robt. L., and Ellen, youngest d. of H. W. Ashton, all of Fauquier, by the Rev. O. S. Barten, at "North Wales", the residence of the bride's father. So. Ch., Sept. 21, 1865

HORSELEY
Chas. Y., of Buckingham, and Jean, d. of the late

MARRIAGE NOTICES IN THE SOUTHERN CHURCHMAN WITH DATES OF PUBLICATION

Hugh Montgomerie of Lynchburg, by the Rev. Edmund Withers, at the parsonage, Norwood, Nelson Co., Va. So. Ch., Oct. 22, 1868

Irene Cooper, and the Rev. John J. Clopton, rector of Meade Memorial Church, Manchester, Va., by the Rev. George S. Somerville, in Trinity Church, Nelson Co., Va. So. Ch., Dec. 10, 1891

HORSELEY

Alexander Caldwell, of Buckingham Co., and Willie C., d. of Z. Lee Gilmer of Albemarle Co., Va., by the Rev. T. E. Locke, in St. John's Church, Scottsville, Va. So. Ch., Nov. 27, 1890

John, of Buckingham Co., Va., and Louisa L. Brady of Wheeling, Va., by the Rev. E. T. Perkins, in St. Matthew's Church, Wheeling. So. Ch., Jan. 11, 1861

John, of Buckingham Co., Va., and Mary Sue, eldest d. of the late John F. Stagg of Richmond, by the Rev. Moses D. Hoge, in Richmond, Va. So. Ch., Dec. 6, 1883

Nannie P., and Thomas P. Gantt, by the Rev. George Somerville, in Christ Church, Norwood, Nelson Co. So. Ch., July 9, 1891

HORTON

Susan Ophelia, d. of the late Caleb Horton, Esq. of New York, and the Rev. Alfred Louderback of Philadelphia, by the Rev. Dr. Milnor, New York, N.Y. So. Ch., Sept. 15, 1837

HOSKINS

Lucy K., and the Rev. John H. Scott, both of Miller's Tavern, Va., by the Rev. Thomas D. Lewis, in St. John's Church Rectory, Bethesda, Md. So. Ch., July 27, 1912

HOUNSHELL

David Stuart (Col.), and Annie Dunlop Werth, by the Rev. P. G. Robert, in the Church of the Holy Communion, St. Louis, Mo. So. Ch., Apr. 22, 1880

HOUSEHOLDER

Annie C., of Loudoun Co., Va., and William L. Gross of Brunswick, Md., by the Rev. Edw. T. Helfenstein of St. Mark's Parish, Frederick Co., Md., in the Lutheran Church, near Lovettsville, Va. So. Ch., Oct. 26, 1893

HOUSTON

Pugh B., C.E., and Emma B., d. of the late Robt. Allen, by the Rev. L. B. Johnston, at the residence of Dr. O. W. Kean, Goochland Co., Va. So. Ch., Oct. 31, 1878

Routez, d. of the late Dr. G. J. Houston of San Antonio, Texas, and Robert B. Minor, Esq. of Seguin, Texas, s. of the late Lucius H. Minor of Hanover Co., Va., by Dean Richardson, in St. Mark's Cathedral, San Antonio, Texas. So. Ch., Sept. 29, 1881

HOWARD

Ann Maria, eldest d. of William Howard, Esq. of Cooper Co., Mo., and the Rev. J. Dunn, rector of St. Mary's Church, Fayette, Mo., by the Rev. J. A. Harrison, in Christ Church, Boonville, Mo. So. Ch., Jan. 6, 1853

Edith, and R. Owen Allen,

MARRIAGE NOTICES IN THE SOUTHERN CHURCHMAN WITH DATES OF PUBLICATION

both of Clarke Co., Va., by the Rev. John McGill, rector of Piedmont Parish, Fauquier Co., Va., near Frederick, Md. So. Ch., Dec. 27, 1866

Elizabeth Key, eldest d. of Maj. Charles Howard, and James W. Tyson of Baltimore, Md., by the Rev. H. Melville Jackson, D.D. assisted by the Rev. Churchill J. Gibson, D.D., in Grace Church, Richmond, Va. So. Ch., Jan. 1, 1891

Ethel, d. of John C. Howard of Ashland, Va., and the Rev. W. A. R. Goodwin, D.D., rector of St. Paul's Church, Rochester, N.Y., by the Rev. E. L. Goodwin, D.D. assisted by the Rt. Rev. W. Cabell of the Diocese of Virginia, in St. James' Church, Ashland, Va. So. Ch., June 22, 1918

I. T., and Eliza Alice, d. of the late W. W. Coke of Norfolk, Va., by the Rev. Gabriel Johnson, in Dallas, Texas. So. Ch., Nov. 14, 1889

Julia L., d. of P. F. Howard of Richmond, Va., and J. R. Baylor, Jr. of Albemarle Co., Va., by the Rev. C. H. Read assisted by the Rev. Thomas Drew, at the residence of the bride's brother-in-law, A. C. Bruce, in Charlotte Co., Va. So. Ch., Dec. 6, 1883

Julian, and Eleanor Love, d. of the late Col. John A. Washington of Mount Vernon, Va., by the Rev. Dr. Meade and the Rev. Mr. Tucker, in the Zion Church, Charles Town, W.Va. So. Ch., May. 20, 1880

Lelia, of Clarke Co., Va., youngest d. of the late Douglas Howard of Baltimore, Md., and D. B. Morrison of Jefferson Co., W.Va., by the Rev. T. F. Martin, in Grace Church, Berryville. So. Ch., Oct. 10 and 17, 1872*

Mary Bullock, of Mount Sterling, Ky., and the Rev. W. Dudley Powers, minister-in-charge of the Church of the Nativity, Maysville, Ky., by the Rev. T. A. Tidball, D.D. assisted by the Rev. E. A. Penick, at the Church of the Ascension, Mount Sterling, Ky. So. Ch., Dec. 9, 1880

Mary E., d. of Philip F. Howard, and Albert C. Bruce of Charlotte Co., by the Rev. Charles H. Read, D.D., at the residence of the bride's father, in Richmond, Va. So. Ch., Dec. 10, 1874

Nannie Bruce, of Richmond, Va., and Orris A. Browne of Cape Charles City, by the Rev. Thomas Tidball, D.D. of Camden, N.J., assisted by the Rev. Landon R. Mason, rector of the church, in Grace Church, Richmond, Va. SO. Ch., Dec. 17, 1891

Norman de V. (Dr.), and Anna H. Skinker, by the Rev. W. H. H. Powers, at the residence of the bride's father, Fauquier Co. So. Ch., Apr. 23, 1874

Rebecca A. (Mrs.), of

---

* In the issue of Oct. 10, 1872 "Morrison" is written "Morison"

MARRIAGE NOTICES IN THE SOUTHERN CHURCHMAN WITH DATES OF PUBLICATION

Baltimore, and Dr. Alex.
H. Tyson of Baltimore Co.,
by the Rev. Dr. Johns. So.
Ch., Oct. 6, 1837

Thomas A., and Fannie C., d.
of Dr. R. Finley Hunt, by
the Rev. William Paret,
D.D., in the Church of the
Epiphany, Washington, D.C.
So. Ch., Nov. 9, 1882

Thos H. (Dr.), of Floyd Co.,
and Fannie J. Johnston of
Lynchburg, Va., by the
Rev. J. H. Williams, at
the residence of E. J.
Folkes, Lynchburg, Va.
So. Ch., Oct. 22, 1874

William H. (Dr.), of Hanover,
and Sarah C., d. of Maj. William Duval of Buckingham Co.,
by the Rev. Nicholas H. Cobbs.
So. Ch., Nov. 24, 1837

William R., of Baltimore, and E.
Mary, d. of the officiating
clergyman, the Rev. G. W.
Ridgely, at Wilmington, Del.
So. Ch., Dec. 4, 1873

HOWE
Fisher, of Princeton, N.J., and
Mary Willoughby Williams, at
the residence of the bride's
parents, Wilton, Westmoreland
Co., Va. So. Ch., Mar. 13,
1909

HOWELL
David, Jr., of Charles Town,
W.Va., and Mary Berkley,
only d. of the late Gen. Thos.
H. Botts of Frederick Co.,
by the Rev. Magruder Maury,
at the residence of T. B.
Barton, Esq. So. Ch., Nov.
19, 1868

David J., of Charles Town, W.Va.,
and Minnie Maude, d. of Dr.
William Gibson of Alexandria,
by the Rev. Henderson Suter
assisted by the Rev. Dr.
Meade, in Christ Church,
Alexandria. So. Ch., Dec.
10, 1885

Fleming (Dr.), of Clarksburg, and Gertrude, eldest
d. of the late Hon. J. M.
Bennett of Weston, formerly
Auditor of Virginia, by the
Rev. T. H. Lacy, in St.
Paul's Church, Weston, W.Va.
So. Ch., Oct. 8, 1891

Ruth A., and John H. Cocke
of Fluvanna Co., by the
Rev. Wm. H. Meade, in Zion
Church, Charles Town, W.Va.
So. Ch., Nov. 30, 1882

HOWELLS
Bertha Marie, of Pittsburgh, Pa., and the Rev.
E. Jeffery Jennings,
formerly of the Church
of the Ascension, Pittsburgh. So. Ch., June 8,
1918

Eliza Beulah, third d. of
Henry Charles Howells,
Esq. formerly of Bristol,
England, and the Rev.
Adam Elliot, Missionary
to the Six Nations Indians,
Upper Canada, by the Rev.
Dr. Upfold, Pittsburgh.
So. Ch., June 28, 1839

HOWISON
Ann M. Thorburn, d. of
Samuel Howison, Esq. of
Fredericksburg, Va., and
Lt. Thomas A. Dornin,
commanding U.S. Ship Relief
(an exploring vessel), by
the Rev. Mr. Wingfield, in
Christ Church, Norfolk, Va.
So. Ch., Aug. 4, 1837

Harriet E., and John S.
Love of Greenville,
Tenn., by the Rev.
John McGill, at
"Effingham", the
residence of the
bride, Prince William
Co., Va. So. Ch.,
July 13, 1876

MARRIAGE NOTICES IN THE SOUTHERN CHURCHMAN WITH DATES OF PUBLICATION

HOWLAND
- Bettie, and Charles Redding of Westmoreland Co., Va., by the Rev. Mr. McGuire, at the residence of the bride's father, in King George Co., Va. So. Ch., Jan. 14, 1875
- Kentie, d. of the late W. J. Howland, and Wm. Blackford Davis, Assistant Surgeon, U.S.N., by the Rev. J. D. Powell assisted by the Rev. J. S. Lindsay, at Portsmouth, Va. So. Ch., May 11, 1871

HOXTON
- Llewewelyn G. (Prof.), of the University of Virginia, and Helen G., d. of the late Philip R. Jones of Orange, by the Rev. Landon R. Mason, at the residence of Egbert G. Leigh, Esq., in Richmond. So. Ch., Sept. 26, 1908
- Llewelyn (Col.), of Baltimore Co., Md., and Fannie, d. of Mrs. A. K. and the late Archibald Robinson, Esq., by the Rev. A. M. Randolph, at Fruit Hill, the residence of the bride's mother, Jefferson Co., Va. So. Ch., Oct. 29, 1868
- Mary, of Baltimore, Md., and B. M. Randolph of York, Pa., both formerly of Virginia, by the Rev. A. M. Randolph, in Emmanuel Church, Baltimore, Md. So. Ch., Oct. 29, 1868
- Mary C., gr.d. of the Rev. Dr. Minnigerode, and Samuel Brooke of Prince George's Co., Md., by the Rev. Dr. Minnigerode and the Rev. Buckner Randolph, in St. Paul's Church, Alexandria. So. Ch., Oct. 26, 1893
- Sallie G., d. of the late Dr. Wm. Hoxton, and the Rev. Alfred M. Randolph, by the Rev. C. B. Dana, rector of Christ Church, Alexandria. So. Ch., May 6, 1859

HOY
- Frank D. (Lt.), and Helen V. Sterrett, both of Point Pleasant, by the Rev. T. H. Lacy, in Christ Church, Point Pleasant, W. Va. So. Ch., Dec. 12, 1878
- Lilly Berkley, d. of the late P. H. Hoy, and George Myer, by the Rev. Mr. Johns of the German Lutheran Church. So. Ch., Feb. 19, 1885

HOYT
- Clarissa C., and the Rev. Nathaniel P. Knapp, rector of Christ Church, Tuscaloosa, Ala., by the Rev. Dr. Cutler, at Brooklyn, N.Y. So. Ch., Sept. 27, 1839

HUBARD
- Bolling, of Buckingham, Va., and Felicia C., d. of Gov. Chapman of Alabama, by the Rev. J. M. Banister, D.D., in Huntsville. So. Ch., Mar. 5, 1874
- Isaetta Carter, of Arrington, Nelson Co., Va., and Beverly Landon Ambler of Amherst, Va., in the Church of the Advent, Spartansburg, S.C. So. Ch., Feb. 5, 1916
- James L. (Col.), of Buckingham Co., and Isaetta, d. of Dr. B. F. Randolph of Albemarle

MARRIAGE NOTICES IN THE SOUTHERN CHURCHMAN WITH DATES OF PUBLICATION

Co., Va., by the Rev. Samuel Ridout. So. Ch., Nov. 30, 1860

Louisa, d. of Robert T. Hubard, and Dr. Lewis C. Randolph of Albemarle, by the Rev. John S. Hansbrough, at Chellow, Buckingham Co. So. Ch., Feb. 7, 1867

M. Claiborne, d. of the late James R. Hubard of Norfolk, and Col. J. Douglas Bruce of Clarke Co., in Winchester. So. Ch., Nov. 5, 1868

Pocahontas Bolling, youngest d. of the late Mr. and Mrs. Robert Thruston Hubard, and Albert Johnston Torroll of Bear Garden, Buckingham Co., by the Rev. Lyttleton E. Huband of Elizabeth, N.J., assisted by the Rev. Plummer F. Jones, at Chollowe, the residence of the bride, in Buckingham Co. So. Ch., Nov. 5, 1921

Robert, Jr., of Buckingham Co., Va., and Sally, d. of John R. Edmunds of Halifax Co., Va., by the Rev. Edmund W. Hubard, at Rodfield. So. Ch., Nov. 10, 1870

Sallie Taylor, and Henry Northrup Castle, both of Norfolk, Va., by the Rev. Arthur Selden Lloyd, D.D. of Virginia, in New York City. So. Ch., Mar. 7, 1908

Sue M., d. of the late William B. Hubard, and the Rev. George S. Somervillo, rector of Nelson Parish,* by the Rev. C. J. Gibson, D.D., at Montezuma, the residence of the bride's mother. So. Ch., Nov. 13, 1890

Sue W., only d. of the late Hon. Edmund W. Hubard, and John T. Crow of Baltimore, by the Rev. Arthur Lloyd, at Saratoga, the residence of the bride, in Buckingham Co., Va. So. Ch., Feb. 10, 1881

Susan R., d. of Col. James F. Hubard of Nelson Co., Va., and John H. Slaughter of Amherst Co., Va., by the Rev. Davis M. Wood. So. Ch., Aug. 2, 1888

Wm. B., and Lila C., oldest d. of Dr. P. C. Callaway, all of Nelson Co., Va., by the Rev. T. F. Martin, at the residence of the bride's father. So. Ch., Feb. 8, 1865

HUBBALL
Mary Lilian, and James R. Branch, Jr., by the Rev. W. L. Gravatt, in St. Paul's Church, Richmond, Va. So. Ch., Nov. 5, 1885

HUBBARD
W. W. (The Rev.), of Brandon Parish,** and Julia L. Taylor of Louisa, by the Rev. E. Boyden assisted by the Rev. J. H. Williams, in St. John's Church, Louisa. So. Ch., Dec. 9, 1875

Ida, d. of Sterling J. Hubbard of London, Ohio, and Walter Whittlesey of Chelsea, Mass., by the Rev. Wm. Stevens Campbell, at the residence of the bride's father. So. Ch., Sept. 23, 1886

HUDGINS
Thos., of New York, and

---

* Nelson Parish is in Nelson County, Virginia.(Journal ... Diocese of Southwestern Virginia, /n.p./, 1940
** Martin's Brandon Parish is in Prince George County, Virginia (Journal ... Diocese of Southern Virginia, Portsmouth, Va., 1941)

MARRIAGE NOTICES IN THE SOUTHERN CHURCHMAN WITH DATES OF PUBLICATION

Adelade Crafton of Essex Co., Va., by the Rev. J. Horvey Hundley, at the home of the bride. So. Ch., Jan. 10, 1884

HUDNALL
Alfred, of Northumberland Co., and Mary P. Ball formerly of Mississippi, by the Rev. H. L. Derby, in Grace Church, Lancaster, Va. So. Ch., June 26, 1879

Eliza Bates, and Dr. James S. Gilliam, both of Lancaster Co., Va., by the Rev. Edmund Withers, in St. Stephen's Church, Baltimore. So. Ch., Oct. 25, 1866

HUDSON
Clement Wilson (Capt.), and Mary Elizabeth, d. of John Spilman of Westmoreland Co., Va., by the Rev. T. E. Locke, at the residence of Robert Spilman, Leedstown. So. Ch., June 18, 1868

Julius C., of Richmond, Va., and Mary Ann McHugh of Richmond, Va., by the Rev. Samuel R. Slack, in Richmond, Va. So. Ch., Dec. 26, 1862

Katie, d. of Dr. R. Hudson of Louisa Co., Va., and John Sawyer of St. Paul, Minn., by the Rev. L. R. Combs, at the residence of the bride's father. So. Ch., June 17, 1886

Mary Jane, of Northumberland Co., Va., and Foster Maynard, by the Rev. T. G. Dashiell, at Kinsale. So. Ch., July 22, 1859

O. R., and Mary E. Patton, both of Kanawha Co., W.Va., by the Rev. Pendleton Brooke, at the residence of the bride's father, Amandaville. So. Ch., Sept. 17, 1874

R. N. (Dr.), of Louisa Co., Va., and Helen S., d. of the late Rev. Hobart M. Bartlett, by the Rev. T. G. Dashiell, at the residence of P. H. Gibson, Esq., Richmond, Va. So. Ch., Oct. 13, 1881

HUGHES
Bettie, d. of the Rev. N. C. Hughes, and the Rev. Nathaniel Harding, by the Rev. N. Colin Hughes assisted by the Rev. Israel Harding, at Greenville, N.C. So. Ch., Mar. 12, 1874

Blackburn, of Martinsburg, and Sallie Pendleton, d. of A. S. Dandridge, Esq., by the Rev. James Grammer, at "The Bower", Jefferson Co., W.Va. So. Ch., Oct. 2, 1873

Charlotte, eldest d. of Lloyd G. Hughes, Esq. of Wheeling, Va., and the Rev. Thomas H. Smyth, by the Rev. Jas. D. McCabe, D.D., in St. John's Church, Wheeling. So. Ch., May 16, 1856

Floyd, Esq., of Norfolk, Va., and Virginia Allen, d. of Dr. C. W. P. Brock of Richmond, Va., by the Rev. J. Y. Downman assisted by the Rev. Dr. O. S. Barton, in All Saints' Church, Richmond, Va. So. Ch., Nov. 23, 1893

John H. G., and Annie M., d. of J. Preston Collins, all of Albemarle, Va.,

MARRIAGE NOTICES IN THE SOUTHERN CHURCHMAN WITH DATES OF PUBLICATION

by the Rev. T. E. Locke. So. Ch., Apr. 21, 1892

Mary Hudor, d. of E. B. M. Hughes, and the Rev. Edward Livingston Wells, both of New Haven, Conn., by the Rev. Edwin Harwood, Prof. in the Berkely Divinity School, Middletown, at New Haven, Conn. So. Ch., Oct. 22, 1858

Pattie, of Halifax, Va., and Wm. E. Cargill of New York, by the Rev. O. A. Kinsolving, at the residence of the bride's mother. So. Ch., Sept. 8, 1870

Thomas, of Rappahannock Co., and Bettie P. Tiffey, by the Rev. D. M. Wharton, at Montross. So. Ch., Jan. 21, 1869

Stephen B., Esq., of Richmond, and Jennie H., d. of Joseph Hodgson of Columbia, by the Rev. Erskine M. Rodman, at Columbia, Fluvanna Co. So. Ch., June 5, 1857

Woodson, Esq., attorney-at-law of Halifax Court House, Va., and Sally Page, second d. of William Nelson of Mecklenburg, Va., by the Rev. John T. Clark of the Episcopal Church, at Halifax Court House, Va. So. Ch., Dec. 20, 1839

HUGHEY
Thomas A., and Lucy C. Jones, both of Orange Co., by the Rev. James Harris, at Golden Lake, Orange Co., Fla. So. Ch., Apr. 18, 1878

HUIE
George William, M.D., of Louisville, Ky., and Sarah E., eldest d. of Hon. Robt. A. Thompson, by the Rev. Francis M. Whittle, at Charleston, Kanawha Co., Va. So. Ch., Oct. 26, 1848

HULETT
James, and Martha Flynn, by the Rev. Henry T. Sharp, in Frankfort, Ky. So. Ch., Aug. 27, 1874

HULL
Fannie, and Capt. J. B. Robinson, by the Rev. Andrew Fisher, at Edge Hill, Lancaster Co. So. Ch., Mar. 26, 1868

Joseph, Jr., of Savannah, Ga., and Minta Lockwood Jones of Charlotte, N. C., gr.d. of John Wilkes of Charlotte, N.C., by the Rev. Dr. G. C. F. Bratenahl, at the residence of the bride's great aunt, Jane Wilkes, Washington, D. C. So. Ch., May 8, 1915

Joseph B. (Lt.), U.S.Navy, and Amelia H., d. of Elisha Hart, Esq. of Saybrook, Conn., by the Rev. Dr. Croswell, at New Haven, Conn. So. Ch., Aug. 2, 1839

HUMPHREYS
Bettie H., d. of Mrs. M. W. and the late Judge Robert W. Humphreys of Clarksville, Tenn., and Cary N. Weisiger of Memphis, by the Rev. P. A. Fitts, in Trinity Church, Clarksville, Tenn. So. Ch., May 5, 1881

Fred H. (Dr.), of New York, and Louise Alfretta Parker of Washington, by the Rev. John S. Lindsay assisted by the Rev. Frank Humphreys of the

MARRIAGE NOTICES IN THE SOUTHERN CHURCHMAN WITH DATES OF PUBLICATION

Church of the Heavenly Rest, New York, in St. John's Church, Georgetown, D.C. So. Ch., Jan. 22, 1880
Kate, d. of the late Judge D. C. Humphreys of Washington, and the Rev. David May of Goshen, Va., by the Rev. Wm. A. Leonard, in St. John's Church, Washington, D.C. So. Ch., Dec. 18, 1884
Margaret A. (Mrs.), of Springfield, Ill., and H. E. C. Baskervill of Richmond, Va., in Springfield, Ill. So. Ch., Sept. 7, 1876

HUMPHRIES
Clarence Eli, of Gastonia, N.C., and Almeyda Tredway Purnell of Charlotte, N.C. and Winona, Miss., by the Rev. John Moore Walker, at the home of the bride's parents, Mr. and Mrs. James Carstaphen Purnell, Charlotte, N.C. So. Ch., Aug. 24, 1929

HUNDLEY
Amanda M., of Halifax, and Col. Thomas T. Boswell of Mecklenburg Co., by the Rev. John T. Clark, at Mount Laurel. So. Ch., Nov. 22, 1866
Eliza Boothe, d. of the Rev. J. Hervey Hundley, rector of Christ Church and St. David's, and William H. Farinholt, by the Rev. Beverly D. Tucker assisted by the father of the bride, at Rose Hill, Essex Co., Va. So. Ch., May 4, 1876
Ella Garnett, d. of John T. T. Hundley, and Willard D. Haskins of Centre Cross, by the Rev.
J. Hervey Hundley, in Rappahannock Christian Church, Dunnsville, Essex Co., Va. So. Ch., Oct. 18, 1888
J. Mason (Dr.), and Helen Murdoch, youngest d. of James Winslow Sweet of Baltimore, by the Rev. J. H. Hundley of Virginia, father of the groom, assisted by the rector, the Rev. Dr. Eccleston, in Emmanuel Church, Baltimore. So. Ch., Nov. 8, 1888
Lorena, and Edgar S. Dobyns, by the Rev. H. L. Derby, at the residence of Urvan Dunaway, Northumberland Co., Va. So. Ch., Jan. 25, 1883

HUNGERFORD
Philip C., and Amelia J. Spencer, by the Rev. J. W. Chesley, in St. James' Church, Montross, Westmoreland Co., Va. So. Ch., Nov. 2, 1855
Phillip C., and Lena, eldest d. of Col. Robert J. Washington, all of Westmoreland Co., Va., by the Rev. Alfred Harding, rector of St. Paul's Church, in Washington, D.C. So. Ch., Aug. 20, 1891
Virginia, d. of the late Col. John W. Hungerford of Westmoreland Co., Va., and the Rev. Dabney M. Wharton, by the Rev. T. E. Locke, at Twiford. So. Ch., June 25, 1868

HUNNICUTT
J. M., and Miss W. F. Thornton, by the Rev. Robt. R. Claiborne, at Sussex Court House. So. Ch., Mar. 4, 1880

HUNT

MARRIAGE NOTICES IN THE SOUTHERN CHURCHMAN WITH DATES OF PUBLICATION

Alice, d. of Mrs. and the late Henry B. Hunt of Cambridge, England, and Edmund Randolph, s. of Julia P. K. and the late Edmund Randolph Taylor of Charles Town, W.Va., by the Rev. Paca Kennedy, in St. Mark's Church, Washington, D.C. So. Ch., Jan. 10, 1925

Clara Jane, d. of Hon Wm. H. Hunt of Marietta, Ga., and Maj. C. A. Derby of the Georgia Military Institute, by the Rev. B. E. Habersham. So. Ch., Nov. 2, 1854

Eliza Stewart, d. of the late James Hunt, Esq. of Covington, Ky., and Robert Minor Moncure of Stafford Co., Va., by the Rev. John Moncure of Gallipolis, Ohio, at the home of the bride, 629 East Capitol Street, Washington, D.C. So. Ch., Jan. 8, 1891

Fannie C., d. of Dr. R. Finley Hunt, and Thomas A. Howard, by the Rev. William Paret, D.D., in the Church of the Epiphany, Washington, D.C. So. Ch., Nov. 9, 1882

James D., of Fredericksburg, and Ellen M., d. of Dr. S. Patrick, by the Rev. T. L. Smith, at "Forest Hill", the residence of the bride's father, Kanawha Co., Va. So. Ch., Nov. 5, 1858

Kate, and John W. Galusha, by the Rev. Robert R. Claiborne, at the residence of the bride's father in Sussex Co. So. Ch., Jan. 1, 1880

HUNTER

J. Harison (Dr.), and Sophie, d. of Dr. Summers of Virginia, by the Rev. Mr. Davis, at Martinsburg, Va. So. Ch., May 1, 1857

James, Esq., Principal Engineer on the Louisa Railroad, and Ellen D., eldest d. of Doct.* Charles Morris of Caroline, by the Rev. John McGuire, in Caroline Co., Va. So. Ch., Sept. 22, 1837

Martha C. Abell, d. of the late Edmund P. Hunter, and Henry A. Ridale, all of Martinsburg, W.Va., by the Rev. W. D. Hanson and the Rev. Dr. David H. Ridale, in Trinity Church. So. Ch., Aug. 20, 1874

Martha Forest, d. of Maj. R. W. Hunter, and Dr. John P. Campbell of the University of Georgia, Athens, by the Rev. Nelson P. Dame, in Christ Church, Winchester. So. Ch., Feb. 18, 1892

Mary, d. of Maj. Bushrod W. Hunter of Alexandria, Va., and J. Bowie Gray of "Traveller's Rest", Stafford Co., Va., by the Rev. R. H. McKim, at the residence of the bride's father. So. Ch., Nov. 17, 1870

Mary Louisa, youngest d. of the late Col. Edmund P. Hunter, and John Harlan Doll, by the Rev. Henry Thomas, in Trinity Church, Martinsburg, W.Va. So. Ch., July 16, 1891

Mary S., of Lacy Spring, and Robert A. Richard-

* Given as printed

MARRIAGE NOTICES IN THE SOUTHERN CHURCHMAN WITH DATES OF PUBLICATION

son of New Berne, N.C., by the Rev. O. S. Bunting, at Lacy Spring, Rockbridge Co., Va. So. Ch., Oct. 15, 1885

Mattie, d. of E. R. Hunter, Esq. of Portsmouth, and Henry V. Niemeyer, Jr. of Memphis, Tenn., by the Rev. J. D. Powell, at the residence of the bride's father. So. Ch., Sept. 17, 1874

Nathaniel C., and Amelia H., d. of the late George Terrett, Esq., by the Rev. W. F. Lockwood, at Oakland, Fairfax Co., Va. So. Ch., June 2, 1848

Robert W., of Winchester, and Margaret, d. of Dr. R. H. Stuart, by the Rev. Mr. Friend, at Cedar Grove, King Goerge Co., Va. So. Ch., Dec. 21, 1865

Susan Sumers, d. of Dr. J. H. Hunter, and Andrew Hutchins Mickle of New York, by the Rev. W. T. Leavell, rector, assisted by the Rev. Dr. Seabury of New York, in St. Mark's Church, Berkeley Springs. So. Ch., July 7, 1892

Susan T., d. of Dr. Thomas L. Hunter, and G. Ogle Tayloe, all of King George Co., by the Rev. E. B. McGuire, in St. John's Church, King George C.H., Va. So. Ch., Dec. 16, 1880

Taliaferro, and Lucy A., youngest d. of the late Dr. Alexander Tennent, by the Rev. E. C. McGuire, D.D. So. Ch., Nov. 15, 1839

Wilson G. (Dr.), of Norfolk, and Nannie W. Burwell, by the Rev. G. W. Dame, in Danville. So. Ch., Apr. 17, 1863

HUNTINGTON
D. T. (The Rt. Rev.), D.D., Bishop of Anking, and Virginia Ethel, d. of the Rev. and Mrs. F. W. Haist of Henry, Ill., by Bishop Graves of Shanghai, in the Cathedral of Our Merciful Saviour, Anking, China. So. Ch., Feb. 3, 1917

HUNTON
Eppa, Jr., and Erva W. Payne, both of Warrenton, Va., by the Rev. George W. Nelson assisted by the Rev. John S. Lindsay, D.D., in St. James' Church, Warrenton, Va. So. Ch., Jan. 1, 1885

Fannie W., d. of Charles H. Hunton, Esq., and Malcolm B. Washington, Esq. of Warrenton, by the Rev. W. A. Alrich, at "Cerro Gordo", Prince William Co., Va. So. Ch., Sept. 11, 1868

George W., M.D., and Rebecca A. Adams, both of Fauquier Co., Va., by the Rev. George W. Nelson, in Warrenton, Va. So. Ch., Jan. 1, 1885

James J., and Matilda C., d. of Hugh C. McNemara, by the Rev. Jno. Towles, at Anley, the residence of Charles J. Stovin, Fauquier Co. So. Ch., May 16, 1856

Logan, and Sarah A. Ball, by the Rev. W. A. Alrich, at the residence of the bride's father, near Buckland, Va. So. Ch., Apr. 8, 1869

Matilda B., d. of John

MARRIAGE NOTICES IN THE SOUTHERN CHURCHMAN WITH DATES OF PUBLICATION

B. Hunton, Esq., and Capt. A. Claxton Sorrel of Savannah, Ga., by the Rev. W. A. Alrich, at "Evergreen", the residence of the bride's father, in Fauquier Co., Va. So. Ch., Feb. 27, 1868

HURLEY
Mary A., and M. A. Canthorn, Esq. of Danville, by the Rev. George W. Dame, at Pittsylvania C.H. So. Ch., Dec. 29, 1870

HURST
Eva Adaline, of North Danville, Va., and Benjamin Harrison McGuire late of Halifax C.H., Va., by the Rev. P. A. Peterson, in Calvary Church, North Danville. So. Ch., Dec. 12, 1889

Julia, and Rawleigh W. Harding, both of Northumberland, Va., by the Rev. Henry L. Derby, at the residence of Warner Hurst, Northumberland Co. So. Ch., Dec. 24, 1885

Maria Louisa, d. of the late James Hurst of Norhtumberland, and Thomas Ball, by the Rev. E. Adams, in Northumberland Co. So. Ch., Dec. 11, 1835

HURT
Branch T., and Matilda F., d. of the late Richard N. Thweatt, by the Rev. P. F. Berkeley, at Mantua, Chesterfield Co. So. Ch., Oct. 18, 1839

Wm. B., and Ellen H. Carter, by the Rev. Geo. W. Dame, at Pittsylvania C.H. So. Ch., Feb. 10, 1870

HUSS
Anna S., of Chicago, and the Rev. Eri R. L. Peterson, late Roman Catholic priest received into the Episcopal ministry by Bishop Whipple of Minnesota, by the Rev. Henry G. Perry, in All Saints' Church, Chicago. So. Ch., Dec. 25, 1873

HUSTON
John H., of Comanche, Texas, and Nannie, d. of the late Thos. O. Blankingship of Manchester, by the Rev. J. J. Clopton, at Manchester, Va. So. Ch., Oct. 2, 1884

HUTCHERSON
Elizabeth Peyton, d. of Mr. and Mrs. N. B. Hutcherson of Rocky Mount, Va., and the Rev. Henry Johnston, Jr., by the Rt. Rev. Henry D. Phillips, D.D., Bishop of Southwestern Virginia, in St. John's Church, Roanoke, Va. So. Ch., July 5, 1941

HUTCHINSON
Arthur J., formerly of the British army, second s. of Gen. W. N. Hutchinson, Duke of Wellington's regiment, and Sadie Lindsay, d. of Col. J. M. Patton of Virginia, by the Rev. Garrett Scott, in Christ Church, Gordonsville, Va. So. Ch., Sept. 27, 1888

Mary A., and Samuel W. Hutchinson, both of Fairfax Co., Va., by the Rev. Frank Page, in Christ Church, Chantilly. So. Ch., Feb. 23, 1882

Mary L., of Richmond, and Benjamin J. Potter, organist of Monumental Church, Richmond, Va., by the Rev. J. Henning Nelms, D.D., in Ascension Church,

MARRIAGE NOTICES IN THE SOUTHERN CHURCHMAN WITH DATES OF PUBLICATION

Washington. So. Ch., Dec. 14, 1912

Mary Talcott, d. of the late Rev. E. C. Hutchinson of St. Louis and niece of Dr. Randolph of Millwood, and Robert A. Anderson of Edinburgh, Scotland, by the Rev. Joseph R. Jones, in Christ Church, Millwood, Clarke Co., Va. So. Ch., Apr. 22, 1880

Morton, of Sparrow's Point, Md., and Elizabeth G. Kanely, by the Rev. Alfred Harding, in St. Paul's Church, Washington, D.C. So. Ch., May 25, 1893

Samuel W., and Mary A. Hutchinson, both of Fairfax Co., Va., by the Rev. Frank Page, in Christ Church, Chantilly. So. Ch., Feb. 23, 1882

HUTCHISON

Sanford M., and Elizabeth M. Fitzhugh, both of Fairfax Co., Va., by the Rev. Frank Page, at the residence of the bride's mother. So. Ch., Jan. 20, 1881

HUTT

Edwin Brown, and Mary Elizabeth Omohundro, both of Westmoreland, by the Rev. R. A. Castleman, in St. Paul's, Nomini Grove, Westmoreland Co., Va. So. Ch., Jan. 30, 1890*

Lillie J., and William Coakley, by the Rev. D. M. Wharton, at the residence of the bride's father, Westmoreland Co., Va. So. Ch., Jan. 15, 1880

Neenah McClannahan, and Joseph Omohundro, in St. Paul's Chapel, Nomini Grove, Westmoreland, Va. So. Ch., Nov. 3, 1892

HUTTER

Charlotte S., of Bedford, and Col. J. Risque Hutter of Campbell, by the Rev. Albert Ware, at "Poplar Forest." So. Ch., Nov. 8, 1877

J. Risque (Col.), of Campbell, and Charlotte Hutter of Bedford, by the Rev. Albert Ware, at "Poplar Forest." So. Ch., Nov. 8, 1877

Nannie R., d. of E. S. Hutter, Esq. of Bedford Co., Va., and Samuel Griffin of Liberty, Va., by the Rev. Edward H. Ingle, at "Poplar Forest", the residence of the bride's father. So. Ch., Dec. 18, 1873

Nannie Scott, and Capt. Robert E. Craighill, both of Lynchburg, Va., by the Rev. T. M. Carson, rector, in St. Paul's Church, Lynchburg, Va. So. Ch., Nov. 23, 1893

HYDE

Meta Herbert, d. of the late Charles Keith Hyde, and Neville Herbert Whiting, by the Rev. George H. Norton, D.D., at the residence of Col. Arthur Herbert, Fairfax Co., Va. So. Ch., Nov. 3, 1881

HYLAND

William M., Esq., of Osceola, Clarke Co., Iowa, and Lizzie Kramer Potzman, by the Rev. W. L. Hyland, D.D. of St. John's Parish, Prince George's Co., Md., at the residence of the bride's father, in Morgantown, W.Va. So. Ch., Jan.

* A notice appears in the issue of Jan. 9, 1890 identical with this except that "Edwin" is written "Edwid"

MARRIAGE NOTICES IN THE SOUTHERN CHURCHMAN WITH DATES OF PUBLICATION

1, 1885
HYNSON
    Nathaniel, of Kent Co.,
      Md., and Lucy Weston
      Tiffey, formerly of King
      George Co., Va., by the

Rt. Rev. Bishop Pinckney
assisted by the Rev. Dr.
Elliott, associate rector,
in the Church of the
Ascension, Washington, D.C.
So. Ch., Feb. 8, 1877

IDEN
   Benjamin F. (Dr.), of Manassas, and Virginia J., youngest d. of the late John Hooe, by the Rev. Jno. McGill, at Mayfield, the residence of the bride's mother. So. Ch., Feb. 5, 1874

   Wm. G., of Fauquier Co., Va., and Susie F., d. of Virginia and the late John Hooe of "Mayfield", Prince William Co., Va., by the Rev. A. P. Gray, at the residence of the bride's mother, Manassas, Va. So. Ch., Nov. 10, 1881

IGLEHART
   W. T. (Lt.), C.S.A., of Annapolis, Md. and Kate Spotswood, d. of the late Dr. E. Berkeley of Staunton, by the Rev. J. A. Latane, at the residence of the bride's mother, in Staunton, Va. So. Ch., Aug. 7, 1863

IMBODEN
   J. D. (Gen.), and Annie H. Lockett, at Lombardy Grove, Mecklenburg Co., Va., the residence of the bride's father. So. Ch., Mar. 30, 1871

INGLE
   Adie, d. of the late Edward Ingle of Washington City, and Geo. G. Butler of Washington, by the Rev. Wm. Hodges, in Christ Church, Washington, D.C. So. Ch., Aug. 3, 1854

   Edward, of Washington, formerly of Baltimore and Richmond, and Mary Friend Mayo, d. of the late W. S. P. Mayo of Richmond, Va., by the Rev. John B. Newton assisted by the Rev. Ed. H. Ingle of Baltimore, in Monumental Church, Richmond. So. Ch., May 5, 1892

   Edward H. (The Rev.), of Roanoke, Va., and Imogen, d. of Col. Edward Tayloe of King George Co., Va., by the Rev. Charles Goodrich, D.D., at "Powhatan", the residence of the bride's father. So. Ch., Oct. 6, 1870

   J. Lowrie, M.D., and Rebecca C., d. of the late William Meade Addison, Esq., all of Baltimore, by the Rev. Edward H. Ingle assisted by the Rev. Campbell Fair, D.D., in the Church of the Ascension, Baltimore. Ch., Oct. 31, 1878

   Julian E., of Westmoreland, Md., and Annette Lewis, d. of G. W. Bassett, Esq. of Hanover Co., by the Rev. B. E. Habersham assisted by the Rev. E. A. Dalrymple, at Clover Lea, Hanover Co., Va. So. Ch., Feb. 13, 1873

   Julian Edward (The Rev.), of Henderson, N.C., and Amanda Pamela, d. of the late James and Ann Dent Dunlop of Richmond, by the Rev. Hartley Carmichael, in St. Paul's Church. So. Ch., May 19, 1892

INGRAM
   Mary Ann, and Robert Garner, all of Lancaster Co., by the Rev. H. L. Derby, at the residence of William N. Kirk, Lancaster, Va. So. Ch., Aug. 5, 1875

INNIS

MARRIAGE NOTICES IN THE SOUTHERN CHURCHMAN WITH DATES OF PUBLICATION

Alexander, of Rapides Parish, La., and Virginia, d. of the late Moreau Lemoine of Fairfax Co., Va., by the Rev. R. T. Brown, at Mount Wellington, Fairfax Co. So. Ch., Apr. 16, 1858

Fannie Chichester, and Robert Madison Slaughter, M.D., of Orange Co., Va., by the Rev. C. Walker, D.D., at "Wagram", the residence of the bride's mother, in Alexandria Co., Va. So. Ch., Sept. 18, 1884

INSCOE

George W., and Milly Trigger of King George Co., by the Rev. T. E. Locke, in the rectory of Washington Parish. So. Ch., Feb. 8, 1861

Mary, of King George Co., and James O. Mozingo, by the Rev. T. E. Locke, in the rectory of Washington Parish. So. Ch., Feb. 8, 1861

INSKEEP

Ida, eldest d. of J. W. Inskeep, and Angus M. Wood of Kentucky, by the Rev. G. A. Gibbons, at "Caledonia", the residence of the bride's father. So. Ch., Jan. 17, 1889

IREDELL

Annie, eldest d. of Hon. James Iredell, and Cadwallader Jones, Jr., Esq. of Hilsborough, by the Rev. George W. Freeman, rector of Christ Church, at Raleigh. So. Ch., Jan. 22, 1836

IRELAND

John Thomas, Esq., and Sarah E. C. Alcock, by the Rev. John C. McCabe, rector of the Church of the Ascension, Baltimore, in Baltimore. So. Ch., July 10, 1857

IRISH

Wm. N. (The Rev.), rector of St. John's Parish, Harper's Ferry, Va., and Emma Juliet, d. of Wm. Lewin, Esq. of Harper's Ferry, Va., by the Rev. Wm. Shelton, D.D., at Trinity Church, Buffalo. So. Ch., Nov. 8, 1849

IRVINE

A. Smith, of Baltimore, and Maysville A., only d. of the late Col. George F. Outten, of Norfolk, Va., by the Rev. Horace Edwin Hayden, rector of St. Peter's Church, at the residence of E. A. Outten, Esq., Plymouth, Luzerne Co., Pa. So. Ch., May 27, 1880

Alice Worthington, d. of Mrs. Wm. H. Irvine of Otter, Bedford Co., Va., and Jesse C. Saunders of McDowell, W.Va., by the Rev. Charles Woodson, at the rectory in Norfolk, Va. So. Ch., Nov. 30, 1907

George Todd, eldest s. of the late Rev. and Mrs. Edward D. Irvine, head of dep't of mathematics, Kemper Military School, Boonville, Mo., and Mrs. Mittie Gibson Mahon of Boonville, by the Rev. H. E. Martin, rector of Calvary Episcopal Church, Sedalia, Mo., in Christ Episcopal Church, Boonville, Mo. So. Ch., Aug. 23, 1919

Walter F., of New Orleans, and Margaret Soutter, only d. of the late Alexander Bell of Norfolk, by the Rev. O. S. Barten, at Christ Church. So. Ch., Nov. 19, 1868

IRVING

Charles R. (Lt.), of the First Virginia Medical Corps, and

MARRIAGE NOTICES IN THE SOUTHERN CHURCHMAN WITH DATES OF PUBLICATION

Elizabeth Logan, only d. of Mr. and Mrs. William C. Bentley, by the Rev. W. Russell Bowie, D.D., rector of St. Paul's Church, at the residence of the bride's parents, 2417 Park Avenue, Richmond, Va. So. Ch., Sept. 29, 1917

Joseph K., and Ida C., d. of Capt. John C. Turner, by the Rev. Thomas E. Locke, at Dunleith, Buckingham Co., Va. So. Ch., Nov. 10, 1881

Mary Carter, and Prof. Henry C. Brock of Kenmore University High School, by the Rev. R. J. McBryde, at the residence of R. K. Irving, near Buckingham C.H. So. Ch., Sept. 9, 1875

Millie Rose, and Dr. R. T. Coleman of Richmond, by the Rev. T. F. Martin, at Bellvotte, Nelson Co., Va. So. Ch., Nov. 9, 1855

Paulus A. (Dr.), and Lizzie Nash, both of Farmville, Va., by the Rev. A. S. Lloyd, at Richmond. So. Ch., Nov. 29, 1883

IRWIN

Chas. W., of New York, and Harriet P. Whiting formerly of Virginia, by the Rev. R. D. Brooke, in St. John's Church, Dubuque, Iowa. So. Ch., Aug. 14, 1851

Fairfax (Dr.), of Virginia, and Alice L., d. of the late Martin Paulsen of Christiansburg, Norway, by the Rev. Clinton Locke, D.D., in Chicago. So. Ch., Oct. 16, 1879

Frank P., of Oil City, Pa., and Virginia G. Farra of Mt. Jackson, by the Rev. John K. Mason, in St. Andrew's Church, Mt. Jackson, Va. So. Ch., Dec. 5, 1878

Grace, and Thomas Fleming, at the residence of the bride's father at Alexandria. So. Ch., Dec. 9, 1880

Ruth, d. of the late William H. Irwin of Alexandria, Va., and George D. Brookes, by the Rev. H. Suter assisted by the Rev. G. H. Norton, D.D., in Christ Church, Alexandria, Va. So. Ch., Dec. 1, 1881

ISAACS

Annie E., d. of Wm. B. Isaacs, and Rev. S. Sollay Moore of Herndon, Fairfax Co., by the Rev. Joshua Peterkin, D.D., in St. James' Church. So. Ch., Oct. 29, 1885

Wm. B., Jr., of Richmond, Va., and Mary W., d. of the late W. P. Lefebvre, by the Rev. J. S. B. Hodges, D.D., in Baltimore. So. Ch., Apr. 24, 1873

ISBELL

Ada, d. of the late T. M. Isbell of Jefferson Co., W.Va., and Armistead S. Lippitt, by the Rev. P. P. Phillips, at "Wortley", Jefferson Co., W.Va. So. Ch., May 3, 1883

JACKSON

Alice, of Loudoun Co., Va., and E. W. Hepbron of Kent Co., Md., by the Rev. S. S. Hepbron assisted by the Rev. Theo. Reed, at the residence of Wm. Jackson, Esq., of Loudoun. So. Ch., Dec. 31, 1874

Edgar, of Leesburg, Loudoun Co., and Evelyn A., d. of the late T. S. Pleasants, by the Rev. T. E. Locke, at Midwood, Fluvanna Co. So. Ch., Dec. 23, 1886

Elizabeth Duval, d. of the

MARRIAGE NOTICES IN THE SOUTHERN CHURCHMAN WITH DATES OF PUBLICATION

Rev. Wm. G. Jackson, D.D., of Maryland, and Emlen T. Littell of New York, by the Rt. Rev. Thomas Atkinson, Bishop of North Carolina, assisted by the Rev. T. Gardiner Littell, in Grace Church, Elk Ridge. So. Ch., June 16, 1870

Ella Bennett, d. of the late Col. Alfred Jackson, C.S.A., and Mrs. Mary Jackson, and Dr. Matthew Edmiston, by the Rev. T. H. Lacy, in St. Paul's Church, Weston, W.Va. So. Ch., May 15, 1890

Fannie Bell, and George Western Thompson, by the Rev. W. L. Hyland, rector of Trinity Parish, Wood Co., W.Va., at Parkersburg. So. Ch., May 13, 1869

Fannie K., eldest d. of the officiating clergyman, and Joseph A. Smoot of Maryland, by the Rev. L. E. Jackson, in Christ Church, Milford, Del. So. Ch., Jan. 18, 1883

Geo. W., Esq., of Gallipolis, Ohio, and Alfreda Tucker, d. of the late Chas. A. Smith of Winchester, Va., by the Rev. W. C. Meredith, in Christ Church, Winchester. So. Ch., Jan. 16, 1868

H. Melville (The Rev.), and Violet, eldest d. of James B. Pace, by the Rt. Rev. Bishop Whittle, in Richmond. So. Ch., Apr. 29, 1880

Harry M. Melville (The Rev.), of Norfolk, Va., and Rebecca, d. of the late John J. Lloyd, Esq., by the Rev. R. H. McKim, at Mount Ida, Alexandria Co. So. Ch., July 31, 1873

John, of Lunenburg Co., Va., and Helen, d. of Capt. Robert Turnbull, Lawrenceville, Va., by the Rev. Green Schackelford, at Lawrenceville, Va., at the residence of the bride's father. So. Ch., Jan. 26, 1882

John E., and Pattie Waller, d. of Charles L. Ellis, all of Amherst C.H., Va., by the Rev. A. P. Gray, in Ascension Church, Amherst C.H. So. Ch., Nov. 14, 1889

John T. (Dr.), of Prince Edward, and Eleanor, d. of D. Patrick H. Foster, by the Rev. J. T. Clark, at Red Level, Halifax Co., Va. So. Ch., Mar. 21, 1856

Malcolm, and Louise Fontaine, d. of Maj. Thomas L. and Mary M. Brown, all of Charleston, by Bishop Peterkin and the Rev. R. D. Roller, rector of the Church, in St. John's Church, Charleston, Kanawka Co., W.Va. So. Ch., Oct. 1, 1891

Mary Emma, and Francis Vinton Rathborne, by the Rev. W. L. Hyland, at the residence of the bride's father, Judge James M. Jackson, Parkersburg, W.Va. So. Ch., Dec. 4, 1873

Olive C., youngest d. of Dr. S. K. Jackson, and Francis T. Stribling of Staunton, by the Rev. H. M. Jackson and the Rev. Arthur Lloyd, in St. Luke's Church, in Norfolk. So. Ch., May 2, 1889

Sarah Jane, second d. of the Rev. J. E. Jackson of

MARRIAGE NOTICES IN THE SOUTHERN CHURCHMAN WITH DATES OF PUBLICATION.

Winchester, and the Rev. Thomas Estep Locke, rector of Cumberland Parish, Lunenburg Co., by the Rev. Alexander Jones. So. Ch., Oct. 6, 1837

Wm. G. (The Rev.), and Mary I., d. of John B. Sowers, Esq., by the Rev. Wm. M. Jackson, in Trinity Church, Staunton, Va. So. Ch., Apr. 29, 1836

William M. (The Rev.), and Mary A., d. of the late John Hopkins, Esq., by the Rev. Alexander Jones, at Winchester, Va. So. Ch., May 8, 1835

JACOB
Mary Hall, of Kentucky, and James Reeve Stuart, of South Carolina, by the Rev. Henry T. Sharp, at the old Mulholland House, Elizabethtown, Ky. So. Ch., Jan. 20, 1876

JACOBS
Eliza R., only d. of the late Samuel O. Jacobs, Esq., and the Rev. Henry C. Potter, by the Rt. Rev. Alonzo Potter, D.D., LL.D., at Spring Grove, Lancaster Co., Penn. So. Ch., Oct. 23, 1857

Louis D. (The Rev.), minister in charge of the Church of the Good Shepherd, Binghampton, N.Y., and Marie Mountain of New York City, in the Church of the Transfiguration. So. Ch., Sept. 28, 1935

Lucy E., and James Murray, both of Alexandria, Va., by the Rev. D. F. Sprigg, in Grace Church, Alexandria, Va. So. Ch., Apr. 8, 1869

Minnie R., d. of the late W. F. M. Jacobs of Fairfax Co., Va., and the Rev. Lawrence R. Combs of Gordonsville, formerly of Stafford Co., Va., by the Rev. Frank Stringfellow, at the Seminary Chapel. So. Ch., Dec. 20, 1883

Miriam N., and Wm. Jacqueline Taylor, both of Richmond, Va., by the Rev. Mr. Woodbridge. So. Ch., July 5, 1839

W. Fenton, formerly of Alexandria, Va., and Susie Stratton, by the Rev. L. R. Combs, at the residence of the bride's father, R. H. Stratton, Gordonsville, Va. So. Ch., Jan. 23, 1890

Wm. F. M. (The Rev.), and Sarah Virginia, third d. of James Green, by the Rev. J. T. Johnston, in St. Paul's Church. So. Ch., Aug. 6, 1858

JAMES
Charles D., of Judsonia, Ark., and Meta G., d. of the late Carter Shepherd of Clarke Co., Va., by the rector, the Rev. P. P. Phillips, in Grace Church, Berryville, Va. So. Ch., Oct. 10, 1889

E. Lee, M.D., and Martha Adams, d. of Charles Moran of New York, by the Rev. Reuben W. Howes, Jr., in the Church of the Transfiguration, New York. So. Ch., Sept. 18, 1873

E. P. (Dr.), of Goochland Co., Va., and Sarah Eliza, eldest d. of Robert G. Scott of Amherst Co., Va., by the Rev. J. P. Lawrence, at Riverside, the residence of the bride's father. So. Ch., May 22, 1879

Fanny Tebault, d. of the late Col. Edward James of Princess Anne, and Charles B. Barton, s. of the late Gen. Charles J. Barton of the English Army,

MARRIAGE NOTICES IN THE SOUTHERN CHURCHMAN WITH DATES OF PUBLICATION

by the Rev. William R. Savage, at the residence of the bride's mother, in Princess Anne Co., Va. So. Ch., Feb. 19, 1885

Fleming (The Rev.), rector of St. Mark's Church, and Mary E., d. of Henry Duvall, Esq., all of Baltimore, by the Rev. A. M. Randolph assisted by the Rev. T. V. Dudley, in St. Mark's Church, in Baltimore. So. Ch., May 9, 1872

Mary S., d. of Joseph S. James, Esq., and John Tabb, by the Rev. A. Y. Hundley, in Abingdon Church, Gloucester Co., Va. So. Ch., May 24, 1883

R. F., of Alabama, and Nannie E. Mayo of Cumberland Co., Va., by the Rev. John G. Anderson, at Cartersville, Va. So. Ch., Nov. 26, 1885

JAMESON
Cornelia L. T., d. of the late Wm. Taliaferro, Esq., Westmoreland Co., Va., and Brevet Maj. Louis A. Armistead, U.S.A., by the Rev. C. B. Dana, in Christ Church, Alexandria, Va. So. Ch., Apr. 7, 1853

Maggie, d. of M. M. Jameson, Esq. of Centreville, and George H. T. Macrae of Fairfax Co., by the Rev. W. A. Alrich, at the residence of the bride's father, Centreville, Fairfax Co., Va. So. Ch., Dec. 31, 1868

Ridia L., youngest d. of the late M. M. Jameson, Esq. of Fairfax Co., Va., and Richard B. Dear of Duluth, Minn., formerly of Virginia, by the Rev. C. P. Daucett, at La Crosse, Wis., at the residence of the bride's brother, Wm. Skeffington Jameson. So. Ch., Dec. 23, 1886

JAMISSON
Jean K., and William A. Daily, Esq. of Alleghany Co., Md., by the Rev. W. A. Alrich, at Centreville, Fairfax Co., Va. So. Ch., Feb. 27, 1868

JANNEY
Rebecca, d. of the late Abijah Janney of Alexandria, Va., and Charles R. Hooff, by the Rev. Jas. T. Johnston, in St. Paul's Church. So. Ch., Oct. 2, 1851

JAN-RHEIN
(Mr.), charge d'affaires for the Netherlands, and Caroline Wilding Boone, by the Rt. Rev. William J. Boone, D.D., father of the bride, at the Netherlands Consulate, Shanghai, China, and later in St. John's Memorial Church. So. Ch., June 26, 1890

J'ANSON
Richard W. (Dr.), of Surry, and Maria Theresa, d. of the late Wm. N. Edwards, Esq., by the Rev. Edward Valentine Jones, at Rosewood, Pr. George Co., Va., at the residence of Wm. Henry Harrison. So. Ch., Jan. 20, 1876

JANVIER
Edmund D. H., Esq., of Baltimore, and Juliet Gilmer, eldest d. of the late B. Franklin Minor, Esq., by the Rev. A. P. Stryker of Maryland, at the residence of the bride's mother, Ridgeway, Albemarle Co., Va. So. Ch., Nov. 19, 1868

JARVIS
Cora Elizabeth, d. of Charles A. Jarvis, Esq., of Portland, and the Rev. Frederick Wm. Harriman, rector of the parish, by the Rev. G. H. Deshon, D.D., of Meriden, assisted by the

MARRIAGE NOTICES IN THE SOUTHERN CHURCHMAN WITH DATES OF PUBLICATION

Rev. F. D. Harriman, in Trinity Church, Portland, Conn. So. Ch., Nov. 2, 1882

Ellen C., of Loudoun Co., Va., and George H. Denny of Boone Co., Mo., by the Rev. Theodore Reed, in St. James' Church, Leesburg. So. Ch., Nov. 16, 1876

JAY

Anna, eldest d. of Hon. William Jay, and the Rev. Lewis P. W. Balch, rector of St. Bartholomew's Church, New York, by the Rt. Rev. Bishop Onderdonk of New York Diocese. So. Ch., Apr. 19, 1839

JEFFERIES

Thomas E., and Redir Madeleine, second d. of Maj. D. DuBois, all of Charleston, W.Va., by the Rev. R. A. Cobbs, in St. John's Church, Charleston, W.Va. So. Ch., Oct. 30, 1884

JEFFERSON

J. Garland, and Harriett P., d. of the late John Y. Mason, Jr., and gr.d. of the Hon. John Y. Mason, deceased, by the Rev. P. F. Berkeley, in St. John's Church, Grub Hill, Amelia Co., Va. So. Ch., Mar. 6, 1884

JEFFERY

Aaron (Dr.), of Radford, Va., and Maimie Luck, by the Rev. E. L. Goodwin, at Buckingham C.H., Va. So. Ch., Nov. 6, 1890

JEFFERYS

William H., M.D., Supt. of the Philadelphia Protestant Episcopal City Mission, and Ann Prophet of Mt. Morris, N.Y. So. Ch., June 27, 1931

JEFFRESS

Fleming J. (Capt.), and Mary H., d. of George Terry, Esq. of Mecklenburg, by the Rev. Francis McGuire. So. Ch., Mar. 27, 1857

JEFFRIES

Florence G., of West Point, and Christopher C. Boykin of Buchanan, Va., by the Rev. E. Meade, in St. John's Church. So. Ch., Aug. 8, 1889

Lucie E., and Loren D. Warner, both of Richmond Co., by the Rev. Andrew Fisher, at the Glebe. So. Ch., Sept. 7, 1860

Lucy M., gr.d. of the late Judge James M. Jefferies, and James M. Dickenson, by the Rev. J. Hervey Hundley, in Bethel Methodist Church, Middlesex Co., Va. So. Ch., Oct. 29, 1891

Sue D., and A. F. Haynes, by the Rev. E. Meade, in Mattaponi Church, King and Queen Co., Va. So. Ch., Jan. 8, 1885

JELLIS

Thos. Deane, of Lynchburg, and Katherine, d. of the late P. St. George Ambler, by the Rev. J. P. Lawrence, at St. Moor, the residence of the bride's mother. So. Ch., Jan. 31, 1878

JENKINS

Benjamin F., and Bettie Brightwell, both of Spotsylvania Co., Va., by the Rev. Wm. W. Greene. So. Ch., Apr. 2, 1868

C. Taylor, of Baltimore, and Emily Moale, d. of the late Charles H. Dimmock of Richmond, Va., by the Rev. A. Y. Hundley, at "Sherwood", Gloucester Co. So. Ch.,

MARRIAGE NOTICES IN THE SOUTHERN CHURCHMAN WITH DATES OF PUBLICATION

Dec. 9, 1880
Evelyn Morton, d. of G. Taylor Jenkins, Esq. of Baltimore, and Eugene Worthington of Annapolis, by the Rev. John S. Lindsay, D.D., assisted by the Rev. Dr. Williams, in Christ Church, Baltimore. So. Ch., May 3, 1883

Mary L., and John Lewis, both of Spotsylvania Co., Va., by the Rev. Wm. W. Greene, at the residence of the bride's father, A. J. Jenkins. So. Ch., May 16, 1872

Mary McDonogh, d. of Geo. Taylor Jenkins of Baltimore, and Charles D. McCoy, by the Rev. James A. Latane, in Trinity Church, Staunton. So. Ch., Oct. 25, 1866

William M., of Louisville, Ky., and Angelica Lockwood, youngest d. of George R. and Anne R. P. Robinson, by the Rev. George H. Sterling, in Emmanuel Church, Old Orchard, Mo. So. Ch., Nov. 5, 1891

JENKS
James A., Esq., and Harriett C. Slaughter, by the Rev. W. H. Pendleton, at the residence of the bride's father, near New London, Campbell Co. So. Ch., Feb. 20, 1868

JENNINGS
Annie T. F., d. of the late John Jennings, Esq. and Mrs. Mary C. Jennings, and the Hon. Richard Shelton of Clay Co., W.Va., by the Rev. T. H. Lacy, at "Glen Hope", the beautiful country home of the bride's mother, near Weston, W.Va. So. Ch., June 8, 1893

E. Jeffery (The Rev.), formerly of the Church of the Ascension, Pittsburgh, and now a Y.M.C.A. Secretary in France, and Bertha Marie Howells of Pittsburgh, Pa. So. Ch., June 8, 1918

Katie L. (Mrs.), and William L. Schaeffer, by the Rev. Walter P. Griggs of Poolesville, Md., at Washington, D.C. So. Ch., Aug. 11, 1892

Mary Caroline, and Henry M. Ward, both of Lewis Co., W.Va., by the Rev. Andrew Fisher, at the home of the bride's father in Lewis Co., W.Va. So. Ch., Feb. 29, 1872

JERDONE
Maude M., of Charles City Co., Va., and Richard F. Coleman of Richmond, Va., by the Rev. John P. Tyler, at "Sterling", the home of the bride, in Charles City Co., Va. So. Ch., Dec. 4, 1890

JEREVEN
Alice A., third d. of the late Rev. N. B. Jereven, and the Rev. Roberts P. Johnson, all of Charleston, by the Rev. C. P. Gadsden, at St. Philip's Church, Charleston, S.C. So. Ch., June 27, 1856

JEROME
John A. (The Rev.), and Mary, d. of the Rev. Dr. Sparrow, by the Rev. William Sparrow, D.D., in the chapel of the Theological Seminary of Virginia. So. Ch., Sept. 25, 1851

JERVEY
Francis J., of Charleston, S. C., and Ida Beirne Morris of Arden, N.C., by the Rev.

MARRIAGE NOTICES IN THE SOUTHERN CHURCHMAN WITH DATES OF PUBLICATION

Thomas A. Morris, father of the bride, in Calvary Church, Henderson, N.C. So. Ch., Nov. 4, 1886

JETER

C. S., and the Rev. C. B. Walker, rector of Trinity Church, Edgefield, S.C., in Trinity Church, Edgefield, S.C. So. Ch., Feb. 18, 1848

JETT

Hannah C., d. of James Jett, of Rappahannock Co., Va., and Atchison Pollock of Stafford Co., by the Rev. A. M. Randolph, at the residence of the bride's father. So. Ch., Nov. 25, 1859

J. Bailey, of Westmoreland Co., and Lucy J., d. of the late John L. Chinn, Esq., by the Rev. E. C. McGuire, D.D. So. Ch., Feb. 15, 1856

Lulie Ethel, d. of Judge J. B. Jett of Stafford Co., Va., and Henry D. Locker of Rockbridge Co., by the Rev. Dr. Murdaugh, in Trinity Church, Fredericksburg, Va. So. Ch., Jan. 12, 1882

Mary J., d. of James Jett, Esq. of Westmoreland Co., and Dr. F. Fairfax of King George Co., by the Rev. Mr. Dashiell, at Loch Harbour, Westmoreland Co., Va. So. Ch., Dec. 7, 1855

Robert C., of Mount Jackson, Va., and Annie, youngest d. of the late Col. Oliver R. Funsten, by the Rev. R. Allen Castleman assisted by the Rev. James B. Funsten, at Emmanuel Church, Greenwood. So. Ch., Nov. 20, 1890

Wm. N. (Dr.), and Carrie M., d. of Carolinus Turner, Esq., all of King George Co., by the Rev. E. B. McGuire, in Immanuel Church, King George Co. So. Ch., Sept. 10, 1874

JEWETT

Bell F., and William P. Field, by the rector, in Moore Memorial Church, Richmond. So. Ch., May 2, 1889

Eliza Yonge, d. of the late Stephen Jewett of Wilmington, and the Rev. Edward Wooten, rector of St. Thomas' Church, Windsor, by the Rev. George Patterson, rector of St. John's Church, in St. James' Church, Wilmington, N.C. So. Ch., Nov. 18, 1875

JOHNS

A. B., Jr. (Dr.), and Lucinda Louisa, youngest d. of Thos. S. Galloway, Esq. of Rockingham Co., N.C., by the Rev. Jno. R. Lee, at Mount Vue. So. Ch., Nov. 18, 1869

Arthur S., and Eleanor, d. of Geo. M. Potts, Esq. of Frederick, Md., by the Rt. Rev. John Johns, Bishop of Virginia, at Frederick, Md. So. Ch., Oct. 24, 1867

Auther S. (The Rev.), and Helen Lane, by the Rt. Rev. John Johns and the Rev. E. C. Murdaugh, D.D., at Brompton, near Fredericksburg, Va. So. Ch., July 9, 1874

John (The Rt. Rev.), Assistant Bishop of the Diocese of Virginia, and Angelina E. Southgate of Norfolk, by the Rev. H. V. D. Johns, of Baltimore, at Norfolk. So. Ch., July 24, 1857

Kensey, s. of Bishop Johns of Maryland, and Laura, d. of the late C. C. Stuart, Esq., by the Rt. Rev. Bishop

MARRIAGE NOTICES IN THE SOUTHERN CHURCHMAN WITH DATES OF PUBLICATION

Johns of Virginia, in Chantilly, Fairfax Co., Va. So. Ch., Oct. 15, 1858

Lucy M. (Mrs.), of Washington, D. C., and Capt. W. P. S. Sanger, U.S.N., of Georgetown, by the Rev. Dr. Harris, in Trinity Church, Washington, D.C. So. Ch., July 26, 1877

Nannie M., d. of the late Dr. Montgomery Johns, and Horace Slingluff, by the Rev. A. M. Randolph, at the residence of the bride's mother. So. Ch., Jan. 26, 1882

Nannie V. D., youngest d. of the Rt. Rev. John Johns, D.D., and the Rev. Richard R. Mason, by the Rt. Rev. Wm. Meade, D.D., at Malvern, the residence of the bride's father. So. Ch., Apr. 16, 1858

JOHNSON

Alfred Edward, and Anne Robinson, both of Oilville, Goochland Co., Va., by the Rev. Wyllys Rede, in St. Mary's Church. So. Ch., Feb. 9, 1888

Ann E., d. of B. W. Johnson, and Dennis H. Frear of Dinwiddie, by the Rev. Mr. Ambler, at Brunswick. So. Ch., Jan. 18, 1856

Bettie F., d. of L. F. Johnson, Esq., and Eugene W. Crockett of Wythe Co., Va., by the Rev. Pendleton Brooke, at Bristol. So. Ch., Sept. 9, 1875

Bradley S., Esq., of Baltimore, and Ann Seddon, d. of the late John M. Rutherfoord, Esq., by the Rev. P. M. Boyden, at Rock Castle, the residence of the bride's mother, Mrs. Ann Roy Rutherfoord, in Goochland Co., Va. So. Ch., July 8, 1880

Charles Y., and Parthena Oliver of Amherst Co., by the Rev. W. H. Kinckle. So. Ch., June 27, 1856

Dagmar, and the Rev. James Cope Crosson, former rector of St. Jude and the Nativity, Philadelphia, by the Rev. Charles B. Dubell, rector of St. Simeon's, Philadelphia, and the Rev. Charles A. Jessup, Dean of St. Paul's Cathedral, Buffalo, N.Y. So. Ch., Oct. 24, 1925

Elizabeth, d. of the late Christopher Johnson, Esq., and William Hill, at Canterbury, King William Co. So. Ch., Jan. 9, 1835

Ellen, youngest d. of the Hon. Jas. F. Johnson, and Walter C. Douglass, by the Rev. T. W. Hooper, at the residence of the bride's father, Liberty, Va. So. Ch., Jan. 6, 1870

Emily, and Frank M. Lacy, by the Rev. Pendleton Brooke, at the residence of the bride's mother, Dresden, Ohio. So. Ch., May 2, 1878

Fannie, d. of the late Col. Wm. R. Johnson of Oakland, Chesterfield Co., Va., and John S. Caskie, Esq. of Richmond, by the Rev. A. B. Tizzard. So. Ch., Oct. 4, 1849

Frances E., of Herndon, and Emmerson A. Merriman of West Meridian, Conn., by the Rev. Jno. McGill, in St. Timothy's Hall, Herndon, Fairfax Co. So. Ch., Jan. 2, 1873

Frederick Foote, Bishop Coadjutor of Missouri, and

MARRIAGE NOTICES IN THE SOUTHERN CHURCHMAN WITH DATES OF PUBLICATION

Elizabeth Louise, d. of the late Daniel G. and Arabella Fitch Beers, of Newtown, by the Rev. James H. George, rector, assisted by the Rev. Charles J. Griffen of South Lee, Mass., in Trinity Church, Newtown, Conn. So. Ch., July 10, 1915

Geo. E., of Lynchburg, and Placie A. Carper of Botetourt, by the Rev. E. Hubbard, at Fincastle. So. Ch., June 22, 1871

Herbert L. (The Very Rev.), Dean of St. Paul's Cathedral, Detroit, and Marguerite M. Beale of Savannah, Ga., by the Rt. Rev. Herman Page, D.D., assisted by the Rev. R. W. Woodroofe, rector of St. John's Church, Detroit. So. Ch., Aug. 11, 1928

Hugh, Esq., and Louisa Perkins, both of Cumberland Co., Va., by the Rev. Wm. Hoxton, at Forkland, residence of Wm. A. Perkins. So. Ch., Jan. 16, 1873

I. L., of Uniontown, Penn., and Estelle V., third d. of the late Capt. Samuel T. Ashby, by the Rev. John McGill, at the residence of the Misses Kirkman, Culpeper, Va. So. Ch., Jan. 11, 1883

Joseph H., of Petersburg, and Mattie E. Lyzott of Greensville, by the Rev. Robert R. Clairborne, in Greensville Co. So. Ch., Jan. 8, 1880

Kate, of Concord, N.C., and J. Harry Werne of Richmond, Va., by the Rev. C. M. Payne, in the First Presbyterian Church, Concord, N.C. So. Ch., Oct. 23, 1890

Mary, d. of R. S. Johnson, Esq. of Philadelphia, and the Rev. J. Gordon Maxwell, by the Rev. Dr. Dorr. So. Ch., Oct. 25, 1839

Mary Brown, d. of R. B. Johnson, M.D., and gr.d. of the late Gov. McWillie, and the Rev. Wm. P. Browne, by the rector, the Rev. W. Prosbury, assisted by the Rev. V. B. Bowdon, in St. Philip's Church, Kirkwood, Miss. So. Ch., Aug. 23, 1883

Nannie Lou, only d. of Mrs. M. H. Johnson of Boydton, and John Cary Ambler, lately in charge of Emmanuel Church, Middleburg, and now attached to the Japan Mission, by the Rev. P. M. Boyden assisted by the Rev. John Ambler, in St. James' Church, Boydton, Mecklenburg Co., Va. So. Ch., June 27, 1889

Nicholas (Dr.), of Kanawha Falls, W.Va., and Sallie W. Langhorne of Botetourt Co., Va., by the Rev. Edward H. Ingle, at Cloverdale, Botetourt Co., Va. So. Ch., Feb. 17, 1876

Norborne T., and Rebecca Holmes, d. of Geo. F. Harrison of Longwood, Goochland Co., Va., by the Rev. Mr. Hullihen, in Trinity Church, Staunton, Va. So. Ch., Aug. 11, 1892

Richard R., and Emma Florence Armstrong, both of Albemarle Co., by the Rev. T. E. Locke. So. Ch., Oct. 15, 1885

Roberta, eldest d. of Judge

MARRIAGE NOTICES IN THE SOUTHERN CHURCHMAN WITH DATES OF PUBLICATION

Robert Johnson of Harrisonburg, Va., and Maj. John B. Brockenborough of Bedford Co., Va., by the Rev. O. S. Bunting, in Emmanuel Church, Harrisonburg, Va. So. Ch., Jan. 24, 1884

Roberts P. (The Rev.), and Alice A., third d. of the late Rev. N. B. Jereven, all of Charleston, by the Rev. C. P. Gadsden, in St. Philip's Church, Charleston, S.C. So. Ch., June 27, 1856

Rosalie, d. of the late Reuben Johnson, and Wm. H. Smith, all of Richmond, Va., by the Rev. Geo. Woodbridge. So. Ch., Apr. 8, 1836

Samuel, and Flora Bramble, both of Dorchester Co., Md., by the Rev. Wm. W. Greene, at Church Creek. So. Ch., Feb. 17, 1881

Sophia, and Solomon Fowthes, both of Petersburg, Va., by the Rev. Luther W. Doggett, at the residence of Joseph Carr. So. Ch., Oct. 3, 1889

Sue Fullerton, second d. of Hon. R. H. Johnson of Christiansburg, and Prof. Robert C. Price of Agricultural and Mechanical College, Blacksburg, Va., by the Rev. F. W. Hooper, D.D., and the Rev. John McGill, in the Presbyterian Church, Christiansburg, Va. So. Ch., Apr. 6, 1893

Thos. S., and Cora V. Maddux, by the Rev. Jno. McGill, in Trinity Church, Salem, Fauquier Co. So. Ch., July 15, 1869

Valentine M. (Lt.), of Marian, Ala., and Eliza H., d. of Lewis A. Boggs, Esq., by the Rev. William W. Greene, at Livingston, Spotsylvania Co., Va. So. Ch., May 10, 1861

W. J. (Maj.), of Richmond, and Nannie C. Friend of Port Royal, Va., by the Rev. Geo. Woodbridge, D.D., Richmond, Va., at the residence of Mrs. Tiffey, Washington, D.C. So. Ch., Oct. 26, 1876

Walter, and Maria Beverley, by the Rev. L. B. Combs, at the colored mission chapel, near Gordonsville. So. Ch., Dec. 3, 1885

Wentworth P., of Norfolk, Va., and Nannie Fassmann, d. of the late J. Shelby Williams and gr.d. of Mrs. Judge Phelan of "Fatherland", near Nashville, Tenn., by the Rev. T. T. Martin, rector, in St. Ann's Church, East Nashville, Tenn. So. Ch., Jan. 29, 1885

Wm. A., of New Orleans, and Mary, d. of Dr. John H. Griffin of Salem, by the Rev. Edwood H. Ingle, at Salem, Roanoke Co., Va. So. Ch., Dec. 31, 1868

Wm. R. (Capt.), of Crescent, Fayette, Co., W.Va., and Mary A., d. of the Rev. W. T. Leavell, by the Rev. Dallas Tucker assisted by the Rev. F. K. Leavell, in Zion Church, Charles Town, Jefferson Co., W.Va. So. Ch., Nov. 19, 1885

JOHNSTON

Bernard H., and Eleanor Marshall, eldest d. of the late Richard M. Scott, Esq., of

MARRIAGE NOTICES IN THE SOUTHERN CHURCHMAN WITH DATES OF PUBLICATION

"Bush Hill", Fairfax Co., Va., by the Rev. Dr. Elliot, rector of the Church of the Ascension, Washington, D.C. at "Bush Hill". So. Ch., Jan. 4, 1877

Fannie J., of Lynchburg, Va., and Dr. Thos. H. Howard of Floyd Co., by the Rev. J. H. Williams, at the residence of E. J. Folkes, Lynchburg, Va. So. Ch., Oct. 22, 1874

George, and Isobel, d. of Wm. Gregory, by the Rev. Dr. Bullock, at Alexandria, Va. So. Ch., Dec. 28, 1871

Helen G., and William H. Tinsley, of Big Lick, Roanoke Co., Va., by the Rev. Edwin A. Penick, at the residence of the bride's mother, Salem, Roanoke Co., Va. So. Ch., Nov. 7, 1878

Henrietta Ege, d. of George Johnston of Alexandria, and Nathaniel Clayton Manson, Jr., of Lynchburg, Va., by the Rev. Dr. Norton, in St. Paul's Church, Alexandria. So. Ch., Nov. 5, 1891

Henry, Jr. (The Rev.), and Elizabeth Peyton, d. of Mr. and Mrs. N. B. Hutcherson of Rocky Mount, Va., by the Rt. Rev. Henry D. Phillips, D.D., Bishop of Southwestern Virginia, in St. John's Church, Roanoke, Va. So. Ch., July 5, 1941

James B., and Virginia O., d. of the Rev. and Mrs. William E. Callender (Secretary of the Seaman's Institute of America), by the Rt. Rev. B. D. Tucker assisted by the Rev. F. C. Steinmetz, in Christ Church, Norfolk. So. Ch., July 30, 1921

James David, of Roanoke, Va., and Elizabeth Sinclair, d. of Judge and Mrs. Stafford Whittle of Virginia, by the rector, the Rev. Alfred W. Anson, in Christ Church, Martinsville, Va. So. Ch., June 14, 1913

Mario Lonnie, and Raymond Stony Pollister, at Nome, Alaska. So. Ch., July 26 and Aug. 2, 1918

Mary LeGrand, d. of Reuben Johnston, and Fielder C. Slingluff of Baltimore, Md., by the Rev. R. H. McKim assisted by the Rev. Reverdy Estill, in Christ Church, Alexandria, Va. So. Ch., Nov. 13, 1873

Nathaniel B., of Memphis, Tenn., and Mary Sayre, d. of Dr. W. H. Macon, by the Rev. L. Hepburn, at Immanuel Church, Hanover Co., Va. So. Ch., Feb. 2, 1882

Olivia M., and the Rev. M. T. Turner of Washington, Ga., by the Rev. J. B. Newton, D.D., assisted by the Rev. B. T. Turner, at the residence of A. Langstaff Johnston, Esq., Richmond, Va. So. Ch., Jan. 31, 1889

Rosa D., d. of Col. William Preston Johnston of Lexington, Va., and George A. Robinson of Louisville, Ky., by the Rev. W. N. Pendleton, at the residence of the bride's father. So. Ch., Oct. 14, 1880

MARRIAGE NOTICES IN THE SOUTHERN CHURCHMAN WITH DATES OF PUBLICATION

Samuel Richards, of Alexandria, Va., and Sara Campbell, d. of Judge Frederick Watts of Carlisle, by the Rev. W. C. Leverett, in St. John's Church, Carlisle, Pa. So. Ch., Oct. 14, 1886

T. Henry, of Botetourt Co., and Sally W., youngest d. of Mrs. Julia A. Holladay of Charlottesville, Va., by the Rev. R. K. Meade, at "Northwood." So. Ch., Apr. 27, 1860

JOLLIFFE

Helen Meredith, d. of the late Wm. H. Jolliffe of Baltimore, Md., and Charles Dana Sayres Clarkson of Haymarket, by the Rev. Cary Gamble, in St. Paul's Church, Haymarket, Va. So. Ch., Dec. 14, 1907

See also HARRIS, Lillie Tyson (Mrs.)

JOLLY

John, of Washington, D.C., and Christiana A. Smoot of Alexandria, by the Rev. D. F. Sprigg. So. Ch., June 14, 1866

JONES

A. Strachan (Dr.), of Warren Co., and Isabelle B. Daniel, gr.d. of the Hon. A. W. Venable of North Carolina, by the Rev. Taylor Martise, at the residence of the bride's grandfather. So. Ch., Dec. 28, 1871

Agnes Alexander, sister of the officiating clergyman, and Dr. W. W. S. Butler of Staunton, Va., by the Rev. W. Strother Jones, in Emmanuel Church, Fauquier Co., Va. So. Ch., Nov. 30, 1882

Alex. (The Rev.), D.D., and Ann H. Kearny of Perth Amboy, by the Rev. James Chapman, at Perth Amboy. So. Ch., Sept. 20, 1855

Alonzo B., and Mary A. Young, by the Rev. P. D. Thompson, at Bodkin Island* (where tradition says no marriage rite was ever performed before). So. Ch., Jan. 17, 1884

Cadwallader, Jr., Esq., of Hilsborough, and Annie, eldest d. of the Hon. James Iredell, by the Rev. George W. Freeman, rector of Christ Church, in Raleigh. So. Ch., Jan. 22, 1836

Calvin D., of Lynchburg, and Catharine M., d. of Dr. Henry L. Davies of Amherst, by the Rev. Mr. Martin. So. Ch., Feb. 29, 1856

Carrie C., and J. W. Falconer, both of Tappahannock, Va., by the rector, the Rev. T. W. Roberts, in St. John's Church, Tappahannock, Va. So. Ch., Jan. 3, 1889

Charles Andrews, and Nellie Estelle Gowin, by the Rev. Jas. R. Jones assisted by the Rev. John P. Tyler, rector of Christ Church, in Christ Church, Milwood, Va. So. Ch., May 18, 1893

Charles H. (Dr.), and Mary E. Morris, both of Baltimore, by the Rev. John Collins McCabe, D.D., rector of the Church of the Ascension, in St. Luke's Church, Baltimore. So. Ch., June 22, 1860

Charles R., and Mary B., only d. of Col. John C. Porter,

---

* Bodkin Island is in Chesapeake Bay. It is included in Queen Anne Co., Md.

MARRIAGE NOTICES IN THE SOUTHERN CHURCHMAN WITH DATES OF PUBLICATION

by the Rev. John McGill, in St. Paul's Church, Culpeper Co., Va. So. Ch., Nov. 23, 1882
Claggett, and Julia, d. of Bishop James A. Latane, by the Rev. J. M. Rawlings, at Bewdley, King and Queen Co., Va. So. Ch., Apr. 15, 1880
E. B., of Washington, Rappahannock Co., Va., and Alice L., only d. of Hon. P. C. Eastman, by the Rev. C. C. Pearson, near Point Pleasant, W.Va. So. Ch., Dec. 10, 1891
E. Lee (Dr.), of New York City, s. of the late Gen. Roger Jones, Adj. Gen., of U.S. Army, and Julia Calvert, d. of Dr. R. H. Stuart, by the Rev. Hugh Roy Scott, at Cedar Grove, King George Co., Va. So. Ch., June 1, 1860
E. Macon, of Huntington, W.Va., and Jennie M. Alford, by the Rev. John S. Gibson, at the residence of the bride, in Hamlin, Lincoln Co., W.Va. So. Ch., Mar. 16, 1893
Edward T., Esq., of Abingdon, and Minnie Bunting of Bristol - Goodson, by the Rev. O. S. Bunting, in Emmanuel Church, Bristol - Goodson, Va. So. Ch., Dec. 25, 1884
Edward Valentine (The Rev.), of the Diocese of Virginia, and Mary S., d. of Edmund Ruffin, Jr., Esq., by the Rev. B. E. Habersham assisted by the Rev. C. R. Page, at Upper Malbourne, Hanover Co. So. Ch., Dec. 4, 1873
Eliza, d. of F. Slaughter Jones, Esq., formerly of Culpeper Co., Va., and Samuel Barron Servant, by the Rev. Mr. Reed, at the residence of the bride's father, Jasper Co., Ill. So. Ch., June 26, 1857
Elizabeth F., youngest d. of Jesse Jones, of Bedford, and Wm. Dewitt, by the Rev. N. Sale. So. Ch., Dec. 22, 1837
Ella, d. of John W. Jones, and Richard B. Richardson, by the Rev. Edward Valentine Jones, at Mountain Gorge, near Buchanan, Va. So. Ch., Oct. 23, 1890
Elva M., and Dr. George E. Cooper, U.S. Army, by the Rev. M. L. Chevers. So. Ch., Oct. 5, 1860
Emilina, d. of Maj. Horace Jones of Hanover Academy, Va., and Abel J. Norwood of New Orleans, La., by the Rev. J. Green Shackelford of Trinity Church, Fredericksburg, in Fork Church, Hanover Co., Va. So. Ch., Jan. 5, 1888
Everett H. (The Rev.), rector of St. Marks, and Helen Miller Cameron, in St. Mark's Church, San Antonio, Tex. So. Ch., Dec. 7, 1940
F. John (Capt.), and Kate Cook, by the Rev. P. D. Thompson, in Christ Church, Kent Island, Md. So. Ch., Jan. 4, 1883
Fannie, d. of Dr. Francis D. Jones, and R. B. Taliaferro of Gloucester, by the Rev. Edmund Withers, at Ingleside, Lancaster Co. So. Ch., Feb. 15, 1856
Fannie B., and H. M. McIlhany of Staunton, Va., by the

MARRIAGE NOTICES IN THE SOUTHERN CHURCHMAN WITH DATES OF PUBLICATION

Rev. W. Strother Jones, in Emmanuel Church, Fauquier Co., Va. So. Ch., May 8, 1884

Fielding L., of the U.S. Signal Service, and Nellie C., d. of John Stanley, Esq. of Colorado Springs, by the Rev. W. Strother Jones of St. Thomas Parish, Baltimore Co., Md., in Grace Church, Colorado Springs, Col. So. Ch., Aug. 25, 1881

Florence, and the Rev. Kensey Johns Hammond, by the Rev. Edmund L. Woodward of Shrine Mont, Orkney Springs, Va., assisted by the Rev. Robert E. Brown, rector of the Church of the Ascension and Prince of Peace, Baltimore, in the Bishop's Chapel in the Diocesan House, Baltimore, Md. So. Ch., May 1, 1937

Frank Cazenove, of New York City, and Harriet Cazenove Lamar of Wellesley, by the Rev. Mr. Gardiner of Maryland, and Bishop Peterkin of the diocese of West Virginia, assisted by the Rev. J. T. Duryea, D.D., of Boston, at Wellesley, Mass., at the residence of Mrs. Henry Durant. So. Ch., July 12, 1883

Frank F., Esq., and Marion Stewart, d. of W. A. Powell, Esq. of Loudoun, by the Rev. Walter Williams, in St. James' Church, Leesburg. So. Ch., Nov. 18, 1859

Freeman W., sheriff of Brunswick Co., and Harriett R., d. of Dr. E. A. Morrison, by the Rev. J. H. Morrison, D.D., assisted by the Rev.

Mr. Glazebrook, at Lawrenceville, Va. So. Ch., Nov. 7, 1872

G. W. (Dr.), and Loisa A., d. of the late Dr. Carrington of Richmond, by the Rev. Joshua Peterkin, in the City of Richmond. So. Ch., June 13, 1856

Harvey E., and Marion, d. of the officiating clergyman, the Rev. Bishop Wilmer, in St. Paul's Church, Spring Hill, Ala. So. Ch., Dec. 16, 1869

Helen G., d. of the late Philip B. Jones of Orange, and Prof. Llewellyn G. Hoxton of the University of Virginia, by the Rev. Landon R. Mason, at the residence of Egbert G. Leigh, Esq., in Richmond. So. Ch., Sept. 26, 1908

Henry R., formerly of Richmond, and Helen Josephine, eldest d. of Col. W. C. Eggleston of Yallabusha Co., Miss., by the Rev. E. A. Taylor, at Grenada, Miss. So. Ch., July 28, 1881

Herbert, and Mary E., d. of Adolphus Gary, Esq., by the Rev. A. B. Tizzard, in Trinity Church, Clover Hill Pits.* So. Ch., Feb. 12, 1880

Irene Lewis, of Albemarle, and William David Ludisill, Jr., of Nelson Co., by the Rev. T. E. Locke, at the residence of B. H. Jones. So. Ch., Nov. 12, 1885

J. Fitzgerald, of Fauquier Co., Va., and Minna C. McGuire, by the Rev. W. Strother Jones, at the residence of Julian Ingle, Charles Co., Md. So. Ch.,

* Given as printed

MARRIAGE NOTICES IN THE SOUTHERN CHURCHMAN WITH DATES OF PUBLICATION

Aug. 10, 1893
Jane, d. of Col. Ben. Jones of Amelia Co., Va., and J. Mumford Hobson, by the Rev. P. F. Berkeley, at the Oaks, residence of the bride's father. So. Ch., Nov. 11, 1875

Jennie B., youngest d. of the late Dr. Oliver Jones of Fairfax Co., and Geo. R. Atkinson of Prince William Co., by the Rev. Dr. Addison, in Washington, D.C. So. Ch., Nov. 4, 1875

John Stevens, and Alverda Stuart, d. of Bessie Stuart and the late R. O. Egerton, by the Rev. Pembroke W. Reed, rector, in St. John's Church, Petersburg, Va. So. Ch., Feb. 24, 1912

John W., Esq., of Botetourt Co., and Marion S. Alexander of King George Co., Va., by the Rev. Wm. McGuire, in Trinity Church, Buchanan, Botetourt Co. So. Ch., Mar. 13, 1863

Joseph Courtney (The Rev.), of Baltimore, Md., and Edith Catharine, d. of the late C. J. B. Mitchell of Queen Anne Co., Md., by the Rev. B. T. Turner assisted by the Rev. Joseph R. Jones, in St. Luke's Church, Queenstown, Md. So. Ch., Oct. 12, 1893

Joseph R. (The Rev.), rector of Christ Church, Millwood, and Courtney B. Byrd, by the Rev. Dr. Andrews, in Trinity Church, Shepherdstown. So. Ch., Oct. 5, 1860

Judie W., second d. of W. S. Jones, Esq. of Elizabeth City Co., and the Rev. J. J. Gravatt, by the Rev. O. E. Herrick and the Rev. J. W. Ware, at Hampton, Va. So. Ch., May 8, 1879

Julia M., d. of John W. and Marion S. Jones, and Charles S. Mayo, by the Rev. C. C. Randolph, rector, assisted by the Rev. Edward Valentine Jones, in Trinity Church, Buchanan, Va. So. Ch., Oct. 16, 1890

Julia V., of Chesterfield Co., Va., and Abner T. Harris of Amelia Co., by the Rev. A. B. Tizzard, at the residence of the bride's brother. So. Ch., Feb. 21, 1884

Julianna M. J., d. of the Rev. Wm. G. H. Jones, rector of St. George's Parish, Accomac Co., Va., and Edmund Crosdale, by the Rev. William G. H. Jones, at Somerset Co., Md. So. Ch., Feb. 22, 1849

Lancy, Jr., of Hanover, and Nannie R., eldest d. of William H. Berkeley of King and Queen Co., by the Rev. Mr. Habersham, at Wanderer's Rest. So. Ch., Jan. 5, 1871

Lilian, d. of the late Henry R. Jones of Richmond, Va., and Fendall G. Winston of Minneapolis, Minn., by the Rev. J. C. Painter, at "Retreat", in Orange Co. So. Ch., Oct. 23 and 30, 1884

Lillie S., of Essex Co., Va., and Walter R. Smith of Richmond, by the Rev. Wm. Holden, assistant rector, in St. John's Church, Washington, D.C. So. Ch., Sept. 29, 1887

Lizzie Lee, and William Warfield

MARRIAGE NOTICES IN THE SOUTHERN CHURCHMAN WITH DATES OF PUBLICATION

Cockey, by the Rev. Henry L. Derby, at the residence of the bride, Suffolk, Va. So. Ch., Sept. 5, 1889

Lucy C., and Thomas A. Hughey, both of Orange Co., by the Rev. James Harris, at Golden Lake, Orange Co., Fla. So. Ch., Apr. 18, 1878

Marianna, d. of the late Dr. Elcon Jones of Fairfax C.H., Va., and P. L. W. Thornton, S.V.R.R., by the Rev. Dr. Addison, rector of Trinity Church, in Washington City. So. Ch., June 27, 1872

Mary E., d. of Gen. Walter Jones of Washington, and Henry T. Harrison, Esq., one of the delegates to the General Assembly, from London Co., Miss., by the Rev. Mr. Packard. So. Ch., Dec. 20, 1839

Mary Frances, d. of Putnam Jones of Westmoreland Co., and John H. Thomas, merchant and postmaster at Hillville, by the Rev. T. E. Locke. So. Ch., Feb. 8, 1861

Mary Jane, second d. of John Jones, Esq. of Pembroke, and Edward S. Russell, Esq. of York, by the Rev. John C. McCabe, rector of St. John's Church, Hampton, at Pembroke, Elizabeth City Co. So. Ch., Mar. 30, 1854

Mary L., of Mecklenburg, Va., and Ed. C. Walthall of Mississippi, by the Rev. Jno. Cosby, at St. Leon. So. Ch., Feb. 17, 1860

Mary Long, eldest d. of Thomas W. Jones, and T. Dabney Gibson, all of Culpeper Co., Va., by the Rev. John McGill, at Mountain View, the residence of the bride's parents. So. Ch., Sept. 1, 1881

Mary M., of King George Co., and William B. Deatley of Westmoreland Co., by the Rev. T. E. Locke, at Peach Hill, King George Co., Va. So. Ch., Nov. 19, 1868

Mary Ruffin, and the Rev. Roy Mason, by the Rev. Edw. Valentine Jones, father of the bride, and the Rev. E. Ruffin Jones, brother of the bride, in Christ Church, Middlesex Co., Va. So. Ch., July 20, 1912

Minta Lockwood, of Charlotte, N.C., gr.d. of John Wilkes of Charlotte, N.C., and Joseph Hull, Jr., of Savannah, Ga., by the Rev. Dr. G. C. F. Bratenahl, at the residence of the bride's great aunt, Miss Jane Wilkes, Washington, D.C. So. Ch., May 8, 1915

Monroe G., of Prince Edward, and Janet, youngest d. of Geo. D. Saunders of Buckingham Co., Va., by the Rev. A. S. Lloyd, in St. Paul's Church, Appomattox Co., Va. So. Ch., Mar. 22, 1883

Nannie M., second d. of Col. B. M. and Agnes P. Jones, and Dr. Thomas B. Pugh of Assumption Parish, La., by the Rev. George W. Dame, at Ruffin, N.C. So. Ch., Apr. 24, 1879

Pattie, only d. of the late Joel W. Jones, Esq. of Mobile, and the Rev. Chauncey C. Williams, by the Bishop of Alabama, in Christ Church, Mobile. So. Ch., Jan. 30, 1879

MARRIAGE NOTICES IN THE SOUTHERN CHURCHMAN WITH DATES OF PUBLICATION

Peter Branch (Capt.), and Alice Hazlewood, both of Lunenburg Co., by the Rev. Henry Wall, at the residence of Mr. Ingram. So. Ch., Apr. 6, 1860

R. M., Esq., and Mary E. French, both of Stafford Co., Va., by the Rev. J. H. Meredith, at the residence of the bride's father. So. Ch., Feb. 1, 1872

Rebecca Churchill, d. of the late Rev. Alexander Jones, D.D., and Col. W. C. Craighill, U.S.A., by the Rev. Joseph B. Jones of Virginia, in St. John's Church, Baltimore Co., Md. So. Ch., Oct. 1, 1874

Robert Lee, of Taylor, Tex., and Katharine Lawrence, d. of Col. N. L. Boyce of Clarke Co., Va., by the Rev. Jos. R. Jones, father of the groom, assisted by John P. Tyler, rector, in Christ Church, Millwood, Va. So. Ch., Oct. 29, 1891

Rosa T., d. of Jos. P. Jones, and Wm. J. Young, by the Rev. A. B. Tizzard, in Chesterfield Co. So. Ch., Nov. 13, 1863

Sarah, and James H. Hartley, by the Rev. R. S. Barrett, at Richmond, Va. So. Ch., July 1, 1880

Sarah Elizabeth, d. of Horatio Jones of Georgetown, and the Rev. Henry Major of Virginia, by the Rev. Dr. Harbury. So. Ch., Sept. 27, 1839

Susan Katherine, d. of W. Strother Jones of Virginia, and Jeffrey R. Brackett of Massachusetts, by the Rev. J. S. B. Hodges, S.T.D., in St. Paul's Church, Baltimore. So. Ch., June 24, 1886

Thomas Catesby, of New York, and Louisa, d. of the Bishop of Oklahoma, and Mrs. Francis Key Brooke, by the Rev. H. Percy Silver, chaplain of the Military Academy, West Point, assisted by the bride's father, at St. Saviour's Chapel, Cathedral of St. John the Divine, New York City. So. Ch., Sept. 9, 1916

Thomas Walker (The Rev.), rector of All Saint's Church, and Sallie Mitchell Campbell, in Christ Church, Roanoke, Va. So. Ch., Sept. 18, 1915

W. Strother (The Rev.), of Fauquier Co., and Kate A., d. of J. H. D. Smoot, Esq., at the residence of the bride's father, Alexandria, Va. So. Ch., Oct. 26, 1876

W. Strother (The Rev.), and and Minnie C., eldest d. of the late J. H. D. Smoot of Alexandria, by the Rev. Francis M. Burch. So. Ch., Nov. 29, 1888

Wm. J. (Dr.), of Gloucester C.H., Va., and Kate, d. of Howson and Catherine Hooe, by the Rev. A. P. Gray, at "Longwood", the residence of the bride's brother, Fauquier Co., Va. So. Ch., Nov. 13, 1884

William S., Esq., and Emily H., youngest d. of Thomas Lowry, Esq., by the Rev.

MARRIAGE NOTICES IN THE SOUTHERN CHURCHMAN WITH DATES OF PUBLICATION

John C. McCabe, rector of the Church of the Ascension, Baltimore, at Hampton, Va. So. Ch., Jan. 2, 1857

Winston, Jr., of New Kent Co., Va., and Irene S., d. of R. M. Bridges, Esq., Culpeper Co., Va., by the Rev. C. Y. Steptoe, in Culpeper Co., Va. So. Ch., Jan. 11, 1872

JORDAN

Ellen M., and Christopher C. Chalmers, by the Rev. David Barr, at Smithfield, Va. So. Ch., Oct. 22, 1885

Frances Westwood, d. of John O. Jordan and the late Alice Ellzey Jordan, and Dr. Harold H. Morris of Philadelphia, Pa., by the Rev. I. M. Greene, in St. Andrew's Church, Clifton Forge. So. Ch., Feb. 4, 1911

J. P., and H. M. Plain, both of Alexandria, Va., by Elder Wm. J. Purrington of Washington, at Alexandria, Va. So. Ch., Nov. 1, 1866

John O., Esq., of Richmond, Va., and Alice, third d. of Thomas Ellzey, Esq., by the Rev. R. T. Davis, at Mt. Middleton, Loudoun Co., Va. So. Ch., Nov. 6, 1873

Kate Banks, d. of the late Rix Jordan, Esq. of Hampton, Va., and Dr. Henry G. Davidson, resident physician at the Rockbridge Alum Springs, by the Rev. Edwin H. Harlow, in St. John's Church, Hampton, Va. So. Ch., June 25, 1858

Lafayette H. (Dr.), and Pamelia W., d. of Garrett Wynkoop, Esq., by the Rev. George S. May assisted by the Rev. W. D. Hanson, in Mt. Zion Church, Hedgesville. So. Ch., Dec. 21, 1871

Lizzie M., of Warrenton, Va., and DeLancy Evans of Washington, N.C., by the Rev. George W. Nelson, at Warrenton, Va. So. Ch., Jan. 1, 1885

M. M. (Dr.), and Juliet Virginia, d. of the Hon. Wm. G. Good, by the Rev. E. M. Rodman, at Wheatland, Mecklenburg Co. So. Ch., Nov. 23, 1855

M. M. (Dr.), and M. B. Goode, both of Mecklenburg, Va., by the Rev. Jno. Cosby, at Lombardy Grove. So. Ch., Feb. 17, 1860

Minnie L., d. of John F. Jordan, and Michael D. Cottrill, both of Lewis Co., by the Rev. T. H. Lacy, in St. Paul's rectory, Weston, W.Va. So. Ch., Oct. 13, 1887

Opie D., and Mary Eliza, d. of the late Robert Blackwell, all of Isle of Wight Co., by the Rev. David Barr, at Isle of Wight Co., Va. So. Ch., May 23, 1889

Walter, and Sallie Arthur, d. of James Hargrove, all of Nansemond Co., by the rector, the Rev. Douglass Hooff, in the Glebe Church, Lower Suffolk Parish, Nansemond Co. So. Ch., Jan. 15, 1885

William V., Esq., and Eliza M., d. of Col. John Crenshaw, deceased, by the Rev. John A. Wharton. So. Ch., Oct. 4, 1866

JOUBERT

Charles Alfred, de Ville-

MARRIAGE NOTICES IN THE SOUTHERN CHURCHMAN WITH DATES OF PUBLICATION

Marests, New Orleans, and Louise Montague Scott, eldest d. of Louise M. and C. Landon Scott, of Amherst, by the Rev. Arthur P. Gray, in Ascension Church, Amherst. So. Ch., Apr. 20, 1907

JOYNER
Henrietta, and George A. Revell, by the Rev. Dr. Burrows, at Norfolk, Va., in the First Baptist Church. So. Ch., June 11, 1885

John B. (The Rev.), of North Carolina, and Carrie F. Knapp of Virginia, by the Rev. P. J. Shand, rector, in Trinity Church, Columbia, S.C. So. Ch., Jan. 16, 1873

JOYNES
Edward S., professor in William and Mary College, and Eliza Waller, eldest d. of W. W. Vest, Esq. of Williamsburg, by the Rev. Dr. Minnigerode, at Williamsburg. So. Ch., Jan. 6, 1860

Levin, of Richmond, Va., and Ella Virginia, d. of the late Frederick Coggill of New York City, by the Rev. Dr. Houghton, in the Church of the Transfiguration, New York City. So. Ch., Nov. 25, 1886

Levin S. (Dr.), and Susan V., d. of Dr. Robert Archer, by the Rev. Charles Minnigerode, at Richmond. So. Ch., June 11, 1858

Sarah E., d. of Thomas R. Joynes of Montpelia, Accomac Co., Va., and Charles B. Duffield, Esq. of Drummondtown, by the Rev. Enoch Reed of Aberdeen. So. Ch., Aug. 18, 1853

Thomas R., Jr., and Sally W., d. of Dr. T. P. Bagwell, by the Rev. J. M. Chevers, at Onancock. So. Ch., Dec. 28, 1855

JULICK
Mary, of Point Pleasant, W.Va., and Jacob Uhrig of Gallipolis, Ohio, by the Rev. T. H. Lacy, at Point Pleasant, W.Va. So. Ch., Feb. 19, 1874

JUNIPER
Eliza, and Samuel Myers, by the Rev. Henry T. Sharp, at Frankfort, Ky. So. Ch., Jan. 1, 1874

JUNKIN
Elinor Jackson, d. of the officiating clergyman, and Lewis Berkeley Cox of Portland, Ore., by the Rev. William F. Junkin, in the First Presbyterian Church, Montclair, N.J. So. Ch., July 17, 1890

Evelyn, eldest d. of the officiating clergyman, and Lawrence Rust, by the Rev. Wm. F. Junkin, D.D., at Danville, Ky. So. Ch., April 13, 1876

K

KANELY
Elizabeth G., and Morton Hutchinson, of Sparrow's Point, Md., by the Rev. Alfred Harding, in St. Paul's Church, Washington, D.C. So. Ch., May 25, 1893

KATES
Frederick Ward (The Rev.), s. of Mrs. Roy C. Kates, and the late Mr. Kates of Rochester, rector of Trinity Church, Seneca Falls, N.Y., and Mary Harriet, d. of the Hon. and Mrs. William J. Maer of Seneca Falls, by the Rt. Rev. Malcom E. Peabody, D.D., Bishop Coadjutor of Central New York, assisted by the Rev. Jerome Kates, D.D., rector of St. Stephen's Church, Rochester, the groom's uncle, in Trinity Church, Seneca Falls, N.Y. So. Ch., Aug. 16, 1941

KEAN
Anne F., and Dr. Lewis S. Pendleton, all of Louisa Co., Va., by the Rev. H. P. R. McCoy, at the residence of the bride's father. So. Ch., Feb. 20, 1873

J. Margaret, youngest d. of the late Dr. O. W. Kean, of Goochland Co., Va., and R. H. Lawrence, by the Rev. P. M. Boydon, at Grape Ridge, the residence of the bride's mother. So. Ch., Jan. 24, 1889

Lizzie G., youngest d. of the late John V. Kean, Esq., and John J. Turner, by the Rev. H. Melville Jackson, in Grace Church, Richmond. So. Ch., Nov. 28, 1878

Nannie R., and Miller W. Michaux, Jr. of Powhatan Co., Va., by the Rev. Wm. W. Greene, at Olney, Caroline Co. So. Ch., Dec. 10, 1868

O. W. (Dr.), of Goochland Co., and Fannie J., d. of the late Hon. Robert Allen, by the Rev. J. A. Wharton, at Mt. Prospect, Bedford Co. So. Ch., Mar. 18, 1864

William C., Jr., of Louisa Co., and Margaret, d. of the late James Hart of Albemarle Co., by the Rev. C. H. Read, at the residence of A. P. Fox, at Richmond. So. Ch., Dec. 6, 1877

KEANE
Marie L., d. of Hugh Perry Keane, Esq., and T. T. Dabney of Gloucester Co., by the Rev. T. G. Dashiell, in St. Mark's Church, Richmond, Va. So. Ch., Dec. 6, 1889

KEARSLEY
Rebecca Ambler, d. of Maj. G. H. T. Kearsley, and Aubert Holt Reese of Savannah, Ga., by the Rev. Dallas Tucker, in Zion Church, Charles Town, W. Va. So. Ch., Feb. 7, 1889

Meta Burnett, fourth d. of Maj. G. W. F. Kearsley, and Andrew K. Polden, by the Rev. Dr.

MARRIAGE NOTICES IN THE SOUTHERN CHURCHMAN WITH DATES OF PUBLICATION

W. H. Meade, in Zion
Church, Charles Town, W.Va.
So. Ch., Dec. 4, 1879

KEARNY
Ann H., of Perth Amboy,
and the Rev. Alex Jones,
D.D., by the Rev. James
Chapman, at Perth Amboy.
So. Ch., Sept. 20, 1855

KEBLE
J. W. (The Rev.), of Kentucky, and Lucy R. Robinson of Essex, by the
Rev. John B. Newton, in
St. John's Church, Tappannock. So. Ch., Sept.
25, 1873

KEEBLER
Fannie K., and Dr. Chambers
L. Bunting, both of Bristol-
Goodson, by the Rev. O. S.
Bunting, at Bristol-Goodson, Va.-Tenn. So. Ch.,
Dec. 15, 1887

KEECH
Mary, and Robert Hall Turner,
by the Rev. L. J. Sothoron,
in Trinity Church, Trinity
Parish, Charles Co., Md.
So. Ch., Nov. 20, 1884

Nannie R., d. of the late
Mrs. Martha Keech of
Chesterfield, and Mortimer
M. Young, Esq. of Richmond, by the Rev. A. B.
Tizzard, at Oakland, Chesterfield Co. So. Ch., Nov.
23, 1860

KEELING
Robert J. (The Rev.), of
Newark, Del., formerly of
Norfolk, Va., and Elizabeth Bend, d. of the late
David P. Polk of Alexandria, by the Rev. Dr.
Johns, in Emmanuel Church,
Baltimore. So. Ch., Oct.
22, 1858

KEEN
Jennie (Mrs.), and John H.
Price, both of Queen Ann
Co., Md., by the Rev.
P. D. Thompson, in Christ's
Church, Kent Island, Md.
So. Ch., Jan. 17, 1884

KEHL
C. Horace (The Rev.), formerly
of Waco, Tex., and Gloria,
d. of Mrs. Fred W. Hebberger
of St. Louis, Md., by the
very Rev. Sidney E. Sweet,
dean of the Cathedral,
assisted by the Rev. Everett
H. Jones, rector of St.
Mark's Church, San Antonio,
Tex., in Christ Church
Cathedral, St. Louis, Mo.
So. Ch., Oct. 18, 1941

KEHLER
Crimora B., d. of the officiating clergyman, formerly
of Jefferson Co., Va., and
Henry J. Rogers, Esq., formerly of New York, by the
Rev. Mr. Kehler, at Denver
City, J. T.* So. Ch., Oct.
26, 1860

Mollie B., d. of the officiating clergyman, formerly of Jefferson Co.,
Va., and Thomas G. Wildman, Esq., formerly of
New York, by the Rev. Mr.
Kehler, at Denver City,
J. T.* So. Ch., Oct. 26,
1860

KEHR
V. Clarissa, d. of Charles
H. Kehr, and Wm. B. Gale,
all of Abingdon, by the
Rev. Edward H. Ingle, at
Abingdon. So. Ch., Aug.
9, 1866

KEISTER
Gertrude Helena, d. of Mr.
and Mrs. Keister, and
John Bolling Purcell of
Welch, W.Va., at Graham,
Va. So. Ch., Aug. 28,
1915

* Jefferson Territory became Colorado Territory in 1861

MARRIAGE NOTICES IN THE SOUTHERN CHURCHMAN WITH DATES OF PUBLICATION

KEITH
- C. (The Rev.), and C. P. Tenney, by the Rt. Rev. W. J. Boone, D.D., in the Mission Chapel of the Episcopal Church, Shanghai. So. Ch., Sept. 28, 1854
- James, judge of the 11th Judicial Circuit, and Lilias Gordon of Warrenton, d. of the late Arthur A. Morson, Esq. of Richmond, Va., by the Rev. Jno. S. Lindsay, in St. James' Church, Warrenton, Va. So. Ch., July 17, 1873
- James (The Hon.), and Frances B. Morson, both of Warrenton, Va., by the Rev. George W. Nelson, in St. James' Church, Warrenton, Va. So. Ch., Mar. 3, 1887
- John Randolph, M.D., of Augusta, Ky., and Mary Eliza, d. of the late John Contee, Esq. of Alexandria, Va., by the Rev. Charles B. Dana, in Christ Church, Alexandria, Va. So. Ch., June 22, 1860
- Margaret, and Robert W. Neilson, both of Fauquier Co., Va., by the Rev. George W. Nelson, in St. James' Church, Warrenton, Va. So. Ch., Nov. 23, 1882
- Mary Eliza, d. of the late John Contee Keith, Esq. of Alexandria, Va., and John Randolph Keith, M.D., of Augusta, Ky., by the Rev. Charles P. Dana, in Christ Church, at Alexandria, Va. So. Ch., June 22, 1860
- Reual (Prof.), U.S. Navy, and Martha B., d. of William Cleveland, Esq., by the Rev. Thomas S. Savage, in Trinity Church, at Pass Christian, Miss. So. Ch., Nov. 27, 1851

KELLAM
- John C., Esq., of Bellevue, Accomac Co., and Mary T., d. of Wm. P. Moore, Esq., by the Rev. Dr. Colton, at Horn Cliffs, Northampton Co. So. Ch., Feb. 8, 1861
- Lizzie M., and Geo. F. Dunton, by the rector of the parish, in Christ Church, Eastville. So. Ch., Jan. 27, 1870

KELLER
- George, Jr., and Virginia C. Dunn, by the Rev. Pendleton Brooke, at the residence of the bride's uncle, in Abingdon, Va. So. Ch., Nov. 30, 1871

KELLEY
- Belle, d. of Moses Kelley, Esq., of the National Metropolitan Bank, Washington, and Dr. F. A. Ashford, formerly of the 17th Va. Infantry, at Washington. So. Ch., Dec. 5, 1872
- Florence, third d. of Jas. S. Kelley, and Charles Allen, all of Hanover, by the Rev. S. S. Hepbron, at the residence of the bride's parents. So. Ch., Dec. 20, 1888

KELLOGG
- D. Otis, Jr. (The Rev.), of Bridgeport, Conn., and S. Cornelia, of Fairfax Co., Va., d. of the late Rev. Charles Hall of Newark, N.J., by the Rev. W. Sparrow, D.D. assisted by the Rev. L. W. Bancroft of Connecticut, near Alexandria, Va. So.

MARRIAGE NOTICES IN THE SOUTHERN CHURCHMAN WITH DATES OF PUBLICATION

Ch., Apr. 26, 1861

KELLY
Charles Vernon, rector of St. Stephen's Church, Harrisburg, Pa., and Elizabeth C., eldest d. of James Peacock, Esq., all of Harrisburg, Pa., by the Rt. Rev. H. V. Onderdonk. So. Ch., Jan. 25, 1839

KEMP
John H. O., of Maryland, and Virginia Washington, d. of the late Capt. James B. Lewis, U.S.N., by the Rev. W. T. Leavell, at "the Moorings", Jefferson Co., W. Va. So. Ch., Nov. 18, 1880

KENDLER
Emma, and Thomas M. Hall, both of Chesterfield Co., Va., by the Rev. A. B. Tizzard, in Trinity Church, Clover Hill Mines. So. Ch., Oct. 2, 1873

KENDRICK
Elizabeth Walter, and Howe Allen Williams, by the bride's father, the Bishop of New Mexico and Arizona, in Grace Church, Oceanside, Cal. So. Ch., Oct. 24, 1908

KENNARD
Mollie E., of Easton, Md., and the Rev. James A. Mitchell, rector of White Marsh Parish, by the Rev. Walter A. Mitchell assisted by the Bishop of the Diocese, in Christ Church, Easton, Md. So. Ch., Jan. 26, 1871

KENNEDY
Howard Angus, of Montreal, nephew of Prof. John Blackie of Edinburgh, and Louise Chapman, niece of Gen. B. F. Cheatham, by the Rev. William Graham, D.D., rector of Christ Church, assisted by the Rev. M. Cabell Martin, rector of St. Peter's, in St. Peter's Church, Nashville, Tenn. So. Ch., June 17, 1886

Mary Ellen, d. of the officiating clergyman, and John H. B. Lewis, Esq. of Jefferson Co., Va., by the Rev. G. W. Kennedy, at Oxford, Md. So. Ch., Oct. 19, 1860

Melissa, of New Castle, Pa., and L. Lamar McLeod, formerly of Richmond, by the Rev. Dr. Steel, rector of the Church, in the Church of St. Luke and Epiphany. So. Ch., Sept. 18, 1926

Robert M., of Camden, S.C., and Ann M., d. of Judge Joseph H. Sherrard, by the Rev. William C. Meredith, D.D., in Christ Church, Winchester. So. Ch., Mar. 25, 1875

KENNERLY
Wm. R. W., of Maryland, and Elizabeth Ward of Northampton Co., Va., by the Rev. J. B. Craighill, at "Occahannock Neck", So. Ch., Jan. 6, 1870

Richard B., of Richmond, and Louisiana B., d. of Col. Philip St. Geo. Cocke, by the Rev. J. D. Powell, at "Belmead", Powhatan Co., residence of the bride's father. So. Ch., June 29, 1860

KENT
Jonny Lewis, d. of Col. Joseph F. Kent, and H. F. Cochran of Richmond, Va., at "Bellefield", Wythe Co., Va. So. Ch., Jan. 22, 1880

Katharine E., of Roanoke, Va.,

MARRIAGE NOTICES IN THE SOUTHERN CHURCHMAN WITH DATES OF PUBLICATION

and Edmund Didier, Esq., late of Baltimore, by the Rev. D. M. Wood. So. Ch., Aug. 14, 1884

Joseph W., and Elizabeth, d. of George E. Yates, Esq., by the Rev. O. A. Kinsolving, D.D., at Halifax C.H. So. Ch., Sept. 10, 1885

McG. James (Dr.), of Montgomery Co., Va., and Lucy N. Oliver, by the Rev. Wm. H. Pendleton, at Monterey, Roanoke Co., Va. So. Ch., Sept. 14, 1854

Mary, d. of Chancellor Kent of New York, and the Rev. John S. Stone, D.D., of Boston, by the Rev. Dr. Milnor, at Chatham, N.Y. So. Ch., Sept. 20, 1839

KENTER
Kate (Mrs.), nee FEWELL, of Manassas, Va., and Jas. Warren Roberts of Richmond, by the Rev. A. P. Gray, in Trinity Church, Manassas. So. Ch., Jan. 4, 1883

KEPLER
Mary Grafton, d. of the Rev. H. S. Kepler of Richmond, and Walter D. Addison of New York, formerly of Alexandria, by the Rev. Dr. Peterkin, in St. James' Church, Richmond. So. Ch., June 20, 1867

Nannie, eldest d. of the officiating clergman, and J. VanLew McCreey, by the Rev. H. S. Kepler, in St. James' Church, Richmond. So. Ch., Oct. 26, 1865

KERCHEVAL
Adelaide, d. of W. A. Kercheval, both of Upperville, and Levin Powell, by the Rev. Mr. Kinsolving, at Upperville. So. Ch., Nov. 2, 1855

KERR
Lucy, of Clarksville, Tenn., and Thomas H. Levering of Toledo, Ohio, by the Rev. J. Hervey Hundley, at Locust Grove, Middlesex Co., Va. So. Ch., Oct. 29, 1891

KERSHAW
Henry Inglesby (The Rev.), rector of the parish, and Adaline*, d..of the late Thomas Clagett, by Bishop Pinckney assisted by the Rev. Dr. Lewin, the Rev. T. F. Billopp, and the Rev. R. S. Gordon, in Trinity Church, Upper Marlboro, Md. So. Ch., Dec. 24, 1874

KESSINGER
Janet Koe, of Alecandria, Va., and the Rev. Haskin V. Little of Tazewell, Va., in charge of Steas Memorial, at Tazewell, and Trinity at Richlands, by the Rev. Dr. Charles W. Lowry of the faculty of Virginia Seminary, in Emmanuel Chapel, at the Seminary. So. Ch., July 6, 1940

KEY
Alice, d. of the late Philip Barton Key, and Frank Hunter Potter of New York, by the Rev. Dr. H. C. and the Rev. Dr. E. N. Potter, in Grace Church, Baltimore. So. Ch., Mar. 2, 1882

KEYES
Susan W., and the Rev. Charles E. Ambler of Charles Town, by the Rev. Walter Williams of Leesburg, at the residence of the bride's father, H. Keyes, Esq., of Charles Town,

* Given as printed

MARRIAGE NOTICES IN THE SOUTHERN CHURCHMAN WITH DATES OF PUBLICATION

KEYS
    Rodney F., and Mary A. Smith, by the Rev. A. S. Johns, at Long Branch, Fauquier Co., Va. So. Ch., Jan. 5, 1882

KEYSER
    Ralph Stover (Maj.), United States Marine Corps, s. of Mr. and Mrs. Charles Eugene Keyser, and Charlotte P., d. of Mrs. John G. Capers of Washington, D.C., by the Rev. Walter B. Capers, the paternal uncle of Miss Capers, at the residence of Mrs. John G. Capers, Washington, D.C. So. Ch., Sept. 11, 1920

KIDD
    J. Burton (Miss), and E. Y. Loomis, late of Richmond, but now of Atlanta, Ga., by the Rev. Dr. Peterkin, at the residence of the bride's father, John B. Kidd, Richmond. So. Ch., Jan. 10, 1884

KIDWELL
    Sarah B., of Baltimore, and Benjamin T. Roberts, Jr., of Rochester, N.Y., by the Rev. Edward H. Ingle, in St. Bartholomew's Church, Baltimore. So. Ch., Feb. 17, 1887

KILGOUR
    Charles J. (The Rev.), of Frederick Co., Md., and Fannie Claiborne, youngest d. of the late Capt. Charles B. Beaufort, U.S.R.S., by the Rev. A. P. Stryker, in St. Barnabas' Church, Baltimore. So. Ch., Nov. 4, 1875

    Virginia, youngest d. of the late Alexander Kilgour, Esq. of Montgomery Co., Md., and Charles O. Vandervanter of Loudoun Co., Va., by the Rev. Charles J. Kilgour, at the residence of the bride. So. Ch., Oct. 28, 1875

KILLMAN
    Charlotte, and Jonathan Bryant, both of Westmoreland, by the Rev. D. M. Wharton. So. Ch., Dec. 31, 1868

KILMER
    Katie M., and Walter B. Lingamfelter, both of Berkeley Co., W.Va., by the rector, the Rev. W. T. Leavell, in Mount Zion Church, Hedgesville. So. Ch., Nov. 19, 1891

KIMBALL
    W. W. (The Rev.), and Violet Wrigley, both of Macon, Ga., by the Rev. James R. Winchester assisted by the Rev. W. Dudley Powers, in St. Barnabas' Chapel, Macon, Ga. So. Ch., June 13, 1889

KINCHELOE
    Jane, youngest d. of the late George Kincheloe of Parkersburg, Va., and Philip Doddridge Cambrill, Esq. of Marysville, Ky., by the Rev. W. L. Hylan, rector of Trinity Parish, Wood Co., Va. So. Ch., Dec. 28, 1860

KINCKLE
    Anna P., d. of the late Wm. H. Kinckle, and J. Peter Williams, all of Lynchburg, by the Rev. T. M. Carson, in St. Paul's Church, Lynchburg. So. Ch., Dec. 19, 1872

MARRIAGE NOTICES IN THE SOUTHERN CHURCHMAN WITH DATES OF PUBLICATION

Franklin A., of Lynchburg, and D. K. Daniel, by the Rev. E. W. Hubard, at Union Hill, Cumberland Co., Va. So. Ch., Dec. 16, 1869

Wm. H. (The Rev.), pastor of St. Paul's Church, and Deborah Davis, d. of the late Peter Dudley of Lynchburg, Va., by the Rt. Rev. Bishop Johns, in St. Paul's Church, Lynchburg. So. Ch., Oct. 26, 1865

KINDRED
E. T. (Capt.), of Texas, and Mary T., d. of Benj. T. Tinsley, Esq., by the Rev. J. Earnest, at the residence of the bride's father, Elmwood, Roanoke Co. So. Ch., Nov. 9, 1864

KING
Alice W., and Henry C. Wooldridge, by the Rev. A. B. Tizzard, in Manakin Church, Powhatan Co. So. Ch., Nov. 19, 1885

Benjamin (Dr.), of the U.S. Army, and Virginia, d. of the late Benjamin Price of Virginia, by the Rev. Ruel Keith, D.D., at Alexandria. So. Ch., June 2, 1837

Thompson Mason, and Ellen C. Robinson, in Trinity Church, Shepherdstown. So. Ch., Nov. 2, 1865

KINGSLEY
Kate, of Mansfield, Pa., and Francis Peyre Porcher, s. of the late Dr. Francis Peyre, and Margaret Ward Porcher, of Charleston, S.C., by the Rt. Rev. Dr. Howden, in the Episcopal Church, Albuquerque, N. M. So. Ch., June 26, 1915

KINNEY
Alexander F., of Staunton, and Jean Malcolm, d. of the late Wm. Galt of Glenarvon, Fluvanna Co., by the Rev. Mr. Latane, in Trinity Church, Staunton. So. Ch., Nov. 5, 1858

E., d. of William Kinney, Esq., and Edwin M. Taylor, Esq., by the Rev. Mr. Goodwin, at Staunton. So. Ch., June 28, 1839

Mary E., d. of Wm. Kinney, Esq. of Staunton, Augusta Co., and Alfred Chapman of Orange Co., by the Rev. F. D. Goodwin, at Staunton, Va. So. Ch., Dec. 15, 1837

KINSEY
George W., and Mary O. Fletcher, both of Rappahannock Co., Va., by the Rev. Walter P. Griggs, at "Rose Hill" the residence of the Bride's parents. So. Ch., Nov. 29, 1888

KINSOLVING
Chas. J., of Washington, and Rachel, d. of Thomas Clagett, Esq. of Prince George's Co., Md., by the Rev. O. A. Kinsolving of Virginia, in Trinity Church, Upper Marlboro. So. Ch., July 21, 1870

Lucien Lee (The Rev.), of Porto Alegre, Brazil, and Alice, youngest d. of the late Chas. Brown, Esq. of Mt. Holly, N. J., by the Rev. Prof. Angus Crawford of the Virginia Theological Seminary, brother-in-law of the bride, assisted by the Rev. O. A. Kinsolving, D.D., of the Diocese of Virginia, father of the groom, in Trinity Church, Mt. Holly, N.J. (the Rev. Martin Tignor, rector). So. Ch., Jan. 21, 1892

MARRIAGE NOTICES IN THE SOUTHERN CHURCHMAN WITH DATES OF PUBLICATION

O. A. (The Rev.), and Lucy
Lee, eldest d. of Gen.
A. Rogers. of Middleburg,
by the Rev. William Sparrow,
D.D., in Emanuel
Church, Middleburg. So.
Ch., Aug. 12, 1859

KINTZ
A. W., of Alexandria, and
Mollie C. McDonald, by
the Rev. H. L. Derby, at
Heathsville, Northumberland,
Va. So. Ch., Dec.
27, 1828

KIRBY
Annie H., d. of J. Thos.
Kirby of Talbot, and
the Rev. W. Y. Beaven,
rector of the parish, by
the Rev. George F. Beaven,
father of the groom, assisted by the Revs. E.
F. Dashiell, D.D., of St.
Michaels, Albert Ware, of
Wye, and Geo. S. Gassner
of Trinity Church, in
All Saints Church, Talbot
Co., Md. So. Ch., Feb.
5, 1885
Ella S., and John R. Pumphrey,
by the Rev. W. L. Hyland,
rector of St. John's parish,
in St. John's Church, Broad
Creek, Prince George's Co.,
Md. So. Ch., Dec. 18, 1879

KIRK
Edwin, of Washington, D.C.,
and Page, d. of Stevens M.
and Mary Mann Taylor, by
the Rev. H. B. Lee, rector
of Christ Church, Charlottesville,
Va., at "Lego" near
Charlottesville, Va. So.
Ch., July 19, 1913
Emily R., d. of James B. Kirk,
Esq. of Culpeper Co., Va.,
and Geo. T. Dunlop of Maryland,
by the Rev. R. H. Phillips,
at the residence of the
bride's father. So. Ch.,
Dec. 26, 1867
James B., and Isabella W.,
d. of the late Wm. Redin
of Georgetown, D.C., by
the Rev. John Cole, in
Culpeper Co. So. Ch.,
Sept. 26, 1867
Wm. M. (Dr.), of Lancaster,
Va., and Josephine, d. of
Mrs. Lucy Lewis, by the
Rev. John P. Newton, at
Langley, Essex Co., Va.
So. Ch., Dec. 14, 1871

KIRKBRIDE
J. J. (Dr.), and Sallie B.,
d. of the late Dr. H. B.
Davidson of Lexington,
by the Rev. R. J. McBryde,
D.D., at the
residence of the bride's
mother. So. Ch., June 18,
1885

KIRKHAM
Hannah Hower, and the Rev.
W. Nevin Elliott, rector
of St. James' Church,
Exchange, Penn., and s.
of Mrs. Mary C. Elliott,
by the Rev. J. Henry Lehn,
rector of St. John's Church,
in St. John's Church, Ashland,
Penn. So. Ch., July
30, 1932

KIRKPATRICK
Maria F., and Mason B. Dodd,
by the Rev. John McGill,
in Fauquier Co., Va. So.
Ch., Apr. 4, 1867
Mason, and Rhoda A. Gray,
by the Rev. A. S. Johns,
at Landmark, Fauquier Co.,
Va. So. Ch., Jan. 5, 1882

KIRWAN
Annie E., and John W. Denny,
both of Dorchester Co., Md.,
by the Rev. Wm. W. Greene,
at Church Creek. So. Ch.,
Jan. 4, 1883

KLAPP
E. Louise, d. of Dr. Joseph

MARRIAGE NOTICES IN THE SOUTHERN CHURCHMAN WITH DATES OF PUBLICATION

Klapp, of Philadelphia, and Dr. B. Franklin Nicholls, late of Spartansburg, S. C., by the Rev. W. F. Paddock, D.D., and the Rev. T. L. Franklin, D.D., in St. Andrew's Church, Philadelphia. So. Ch., Nov. 18, 1875

Carrie F., of Virginia, and the Rev. John B. Joyner, of North Carolina, by the Rev. P. J. Shand, rector, in Trinity Church, Columbia, S.C. So. Ch., Jan. 16, 1873

Nathaniel P. (The Rev.), rector of Christ Church, Tuscaloosa, Ala., and Clarissa C. Hoyt, by the Rev. Dr. Cutler, in Brooklyn, N.Y. So. Ch., Sept. 27, 1839

KNIGHT

Katie, d. of Wm. Knight, Esq. of Cecil Co., Md., and R. T. Barton, Esq. of Winchester, by the Rev. C. H. Shield, at "Essex Lodge." So. Ch., Mar. 5, 1868

Octavius, Jr. of New York City, and Helen Esther, eldest d. of Mrs. Jennie Franklin Wilson of Washington, and the late Whit Wilson of Washington, formerly of Augusta Co., Va., by the Rev. David Barr, at Washington, D.C. So. Ch., Feb. 9, 1907

R. (The Rev.), missionary for Frampton, and Sarah Phipps, by the Rt. Rev., The Lord Bishop of Montreal, at Quebec. So. Ch., Apr. 26, 1839

KNOX

Bessie May, d. of the late W. R. Knox of Birmingham, Ala., and Richard Allen, s. of the late John N. Harrison of New Orleans, La., by the Rev.

C. C. Randolph of the Episcopal Church, at "Lynnside" the residence of Col. W. L. Lewis near Sweet Springs, W. Va. So. Ch., Jan. 24, 1889

Douglas H., of Fredericksburg, Va., and Loula S., d. of Capt. Wm. A. Brockenbrough, by the Rev. A. B. Kinsolving, at Waveland, Richmond Co., Va. So. Ch., May 26, 1887

Janet Gordon, d. of the late John S. Knox of Fauquier Co., Va., and Dr. Samuel Nicholson of Wakefield, Sussex Co., Va., by the Rev. Henderson Suter, at the residence of the bride's sister in Alexandria, Va. So. Ch., Oct. 11, 1883

John (Dr.), and Sue C. Mayo, both of Richmond, Va., by the Rev. Dr. T. L. Preston assisted by the Rev. Dr. Chas. Minnigerode, at the residence of the bride's mother, Mrs. Rob't Mayo. So. Ch., Feb. 12 and 19, 1874

John S., Jr., and Fanny, d. of E. G. Higganbotham* of Henrico Co., Va., by the Rev. Joshua Peterkin, at 203 E. Franklin St., Richmond, Va. So. Ch., July 27, 1882

John Somerville, of Alexandria, and Elizabeth Welch, d. of Joseph Horner, Esq. of Warrenton, by the Rev. G. H. Norton, at Warrenton. So. Ch., Dec. 7, 1855

Mary Campbell, youngest d. of Thos. F. Knox, and Eustace W. Moncure of Stafford Co., by the Rev. D. Murdaugh assisted by the Rev. Arthur L. Johns, at the residence of the bride's father, Fredericksburg, Va. So. Ch.,

* Given as printed

MARRIAGE NOTICES IN THE SOUTHERN CHURCHMAN WITH DATES OF PUBLICATION

Nov. 27, 1873
Reuben B., and Mamie Heath, d. of Mrs. V. D. Upshaw, by the Rev. K. S. Nelson, at River Edge, Charles City Co., Va. So. Ch., Dec. 30, 1886

Rob't T., of Fredericksburg, and Etta, youngest d. of the late Col. M. F. Brockenbrough of Richmond Co., Va., by the Rev. Andrew Fisher, in St. John's Church, Warsaw, Richmond Co., Va. So. Ch., Nov. 19, 1868

Samuel G., formerly of Fredericksburg, now of Cedar Rapids, Iowa, and Vena C. Young, by the Rev. E. C. Murdaugh, D.D., at the residence of the bride's father, J. J. Young, in Fredericksburg, Va. So. Ch., Mar. 18, 1875

KOON
Abram L., and Jennie H., d. of the Hon. A. A. Freeman, by the Rev. Frank Page assisted by the Rev. John C. Fair, in Old Falls Church, Fairfax Co., Va. So. Ch., Apr. 24, 1884

J. C. (The Rev.), of Hancock, Md., and Mannie Moore Williams of Baltimore, by the Rev. Irving McElroy, in St. Luke's Church, Baltimore. So. Ch., Jan. 26, 1888

Jane Seymore, of Falls Church, and DeGraphen Freeman, of West Point, Miss., by the Rev. T. C. Koon, at the residence of the bride's mother near Falls Church, Va. So. Ch., Oct. 7, 1886

KOONTZ
Annie M., d. of Dr. P. H. H. Koontz, and Albertus A. Funkhauser, all of Shenandoah Co., by the Rev. W. W. Walker, at the residence of the bride's father, Mt. Jackson, Va. So. Ch., Jan. 6, 1881

KOPP
Rose Alice, d. of Mr. and Mrs. Alexander F. Kopp, and the Rev. William Osborn Henner, rector of St. Mark's Church, Geneva, Ill., by the Archdeacon W. H. Zeigler, and the Rev. Dr. John Herbert Dennis, in St. Alban's Church, Norwood Park. So. Ch., Nov. 24, 1934

KOPPER
John M., s. of Mr. and Mrs. Henry Kopper of Madison, N.J., and gr.s. of Gen. Thomas Trueman Wheeler of Maryland, and Sarah Genevieve, d. of the late Elizabeth West and Samuel Claggett, and great gr.d. of Bishop Thomas Claggett, by Archdeacon E. T. Helfenstein and the Rev. C. L. Atwater, at the home of the bride's brother, Dr. Samuel Claggett, Oakland, "the Merryland Tract", Md. So. Ch., May 20, 1911

KOUNSLAR
Lydia, youngest d. of the late Dr. Randolph Kounslar, and Edward M. Stribling, all of Clark Co., Va., by the Rev. F. F. Phillips, in Grace Church, Berryville, Va. So. Ch., Jan. 18, 1883

Randolph, and Alice M. Stribling of Clark Co. Va., by the Rev. T. F. Martin, in Grace Church, Berryville. So. Ch., Oct. 30, 1873

KOWNSLAR
Jane Blackburn, d. of the late

MARRIAGE NOTICES IN THE SOUTHERN CHURCHMAN WITH DATES OF PUBLICATION

Dr. Randolph Kownslar, and William Byrd Lee, rector of Emmanuel Church, Culpeper Co., Va., by the Rev. P. P. Phillips and the Rev. A. P. Gray, in Grace Church, Berryville, Va. So. Ch., Oct. 9, 1879

Lizzie, d. of the late Dr. Randolph Kownslar of Berryville, Clarke Co., Va., and Wm. Ludwell Baldwin of Frederick Co., by the Rev. P. P. Phillips, in Grace Church, Berryville. So. Ch., July 15, 1880

KRISE
Philip A., and M. Virginia Davis, by the Rev. Henderson Suter, at the residence of the bride's father, Lynchburg, Va. So. Ch., Nov. 19, 1868

KUBO
Tokutaro (Dr.), chief of staff in St. Luke's Hospital, Tokyo, and Iyo Araki, in Trinity Cathedral, Tokyo. So. Ch., Dec. 8, 1934

KUHN
Harding Wheeler, of Eustis, Fla., and Jeanette Wheeler, d. of the late Richard J. Ryon of Washington, D.C., by the Rt. Rev. George W. Peterkin, at the residence of the bride's mother, Mrs. A. I. Ryon, in Charleston, Kanawha Co., W.Va. So. Ch., Feb. 23, 1888

KURTZ
Kate B., d. of the late Lt. Col. John D. Kurtz, United States Engineers, and Allen Childs of Philadelphia, by the Rev. Dallas Tucker assisted by the Rev. D. B. Knickerbacker, D.D., at Gethsemane Church, Minneapolis, Minn. So. Ch., Oct. 10, 1878

Mary H., d. of the late Lt. Col. John D. Kurtz, U.S. Engineers, and Benjamin F. Mackall of Moorhead, Minn., by the Rev. Richard N. Thomas, in Trinity Church, West Philadelphia. So. Ch., Feb. 21, 1884

KUYKENDALL
William Johnson, and Nannie Lewis Miller, by the Rev. R. E. Strider, rector of Emmanuel Church, Keyser, W.Va., at the home of the parents of the bride, Mr. and Mrs. Charles M. Miller, of Keyser, W.Va. So. Ch., Apr. 26, 1913

KYLE
Fannie, of Amherst, Va., and Taylor Holt of Leadville, Col., by the Rev. Arthur P. Gray, at Amherst, Va. So. Ch., June 5, 1890

J. Warner, and Ella C. Agee, by the Rev. Mr. Burwell, near Columbia, Va., at the residence of B. H. Agee, Esq., father of the bride. So. Ch., Oct. 23, 1884

Thomas L., of Lynchburg, Va., and Tillie Watkins, by the Rev. A. S. Lloyd, at "Scotland", the home of the bride's parents in Appomattox Co., Va. So. Ch., Nov. 29, 1883

ADDENDA
A - K

-A-K-

ABBOT
    William R., Jr., of Bellevue, Bedford Co., Va., and Lucy Schoolfield, eldest d. of John Henry Lewis, Esq. of Lynchburg, Va., by the Rev. Albert M. Hilliker, in the Church of the Epiphany, Washington, D.C. So. Ch., Aug. 9, 1894

ACTON
    Mellie Greenough, d. of the late A. C. Acton of Alexandria, and the Rev. J. H. Griffith of Bristow, N.C., by the Rev. P. P. Phillips, in St. Paul's Church, Alexandria. So. Ch., May 13, 1897

ADDISON
    James A., and Grace Merryman Jolliffe, by the Rev. F. S. Stickney, at the residence of the bride's uncle, Dr. George W. Jones, Richmond, Va. So. Ch., June 25, 1896

ALRICH
    Anner* Moss, and Bailey Tyler of Haymarket, Prince William Co., Va., by the Rev. W. A. Alrich, father of the bride, in Spesutiae Church, Perryman, Harford Co., Md. So. Ch., Oct. 14, 1897

AMBLER
    Charles Edward, of New York, and Elsie, d. of the late William Williams, Esq. of London, England, by the Rev. J. W. Van Ingen, at St. Stephen's, Milburn, N.J. So. Ch., Oct. 15, 1904
    Edward B., and Virginia B. Pascoe, by the Rev. A. P. Gray, at Shirley, Va. So. Ch., June 18, 1895

ANDERSON
    John F. (Dr.), surgeon in the marine service, and Lucy Temple, youngest d. of the Rev. J. H. Hundley, D.D., by the Rt. Rev. F. M. Whittle, D.D., at the home of the bride's uncle, Dr. J. M. Hundley, Montague, Essex Co., Va. So. Ch., Nov. 16, 1899
    Mary Mason, and Francis Deane Williams, by the Rev. Hartley Carmichael, D.D., in St. Paul's Church, Richmond, Va. So. Ch., Dec. 3, 1896
    Mary S., and the Rev. J. H. Gibbons of Stafford Co., Va., by the Rev. Mr. Temple, in Washington, Rappahannock Co., Va. So. Ch., Dec. 2, 1897

APPLETON
    Edward W., D.D. (The Rev.), rector of St. Paul's Church, Cheltenham, Pa., and Mary, second d. of the late Rev. John Hewetson, M.A., former vicar of Measham, by the Rev. Joseph Hewetson, M.A., vicar, brother of the bride, assisted by the Rev. Henry C. Potter, D.D., Bishop of New York, in St. Lawrence's Church, Measham, Derbyshire, England. So. Ch., July 22, 1897

ARMSTRONG
    Louise Churchill, d. of the late Edward Armstrong of Philadelphia, and John W. Morris of Virginia, by the Rev. Edward Valentine Jones, in St. John's Chapel, Louisa Co., Va. So. Ch., May 7, 1896

ASSHETON
    William Herbert, of "Rock

* Given as printed

MARRIAGE NOTICES IN THE SOUTHERN CHURCHMAN WITH DATES OF PUBLICATION

Spring", Fauquier Co., Va., and Juliet Wilson, youngest d. of the late Jeremiah Wheelwright, Esq. of Baltimore, Md., by the Rev. J. S. B. Hodges, D.D. assisted by the Rev. W. F. Brand, D.D. and the Rev. George W. Nelson, in St. Paul's Church, Baltimore. So. Ch., Feb. 18, 1897

ATKINSON
Roger B., of Staunton, Va., and Ellen Louise, d. of the late Stephen M. Hopkins of Providence, R.I., by the Rev. Wm. J. Moody, in St. Philip's Church, Atlanta, Ga. So. Ch., Sept. 15, 1906

BAGBY
Parke Chamberlayne, and Charles E. Bolling, both of Richmond, by the Rev. John K. Mason, at the residence of the bride's mother, 311 E. Grace St., Richmond. So. Ch., Apr. 26, 1894

BAIRD
Banjamin Harrison, and Lucy Page Minor, d. of the officiating minister, the Rev. D. C. T. Davis, in Emmanuel Church, Albemarle Co., Va. So. Ch., Nov. 14, 1895

BAKER
Claiborne Barksdale, of the University of Virginia, and Cassie Moncure, by the Rev. James Nelson, at "Frascati", Orange Co., Va., the home of Mrs. Wm. H. Lyne. So. Ch., Jan. 13, 1900

BARBEE
John Preston, and Bessie, youngest d. of Prof. Charles L. Cocke, by the Rev. J. M. Luck assisted by the Rev. Collins Denny, D.D., at Hollins Institute. So. Ch., Aug. 12, 1897

BARBOUR
Caroline Homassel, eldest d. of the late Hon. B. Johnson Barbour, and Thomas Harding Ellis, M.D. of Powellton, W.Va., by the Rev. Josiah R. Ellis, at Barboursville, Orange Co., Va., at the old homestead. So. Ch., Jan. 24, 1895

BARKSDALE
John Woodson (Dr.), and Emily Meade, by the Rt. Rev. Hugh Miller Thompson, in St. Clement's Church, Vaiden, Miss. So. Ch., Apr. 28, 1900

BARNEY
Avis, d. of the late Dr. Charles Barney, and the Rev. I. Calvin Stewart, all of Richmond, Va., by the Rev. Mr. Gravatt assisted by the Rev. Dr. Hoge. So. Ch., Nov. 22, 1894

BARR
Elizabeth Beverley, d. of the officiating minister, and John Nichols Githens of Chicago, Ill., by the Rev. David Barr, in Washington, D.C. So. Ch., Sept. 15, 1900

BARTON
Joseph M., and Frankie B., d. of the late Maj. Francis B. Jones, C.S.A., and Mrs. Susan Peyton Jones, by the Rev. James Grammer, D.D., at Carysbrooke, Frederick Co., Va. So. Ch., May 25, 1899

BATEMAN
John M., of Columbia, S.C., and Edith, d. of the Hon. William A. Courtenay, by the Rt. Rev. Ellison Capers, D.D., Bishop of South Carolina, at "Innisfallen", Oconee Co., S.C.,

MARRIAGE NOTICES IN THE SOUTHERN CHURCHMAN WITH DATES OF PUBLICATION

the residence of the bride.
So. Ch., Dec. 10, 1896

BAYLOR
Sarah Evelyn, eldest d. of
James B. Baylor, Esq., and
Pelham Blackford, all of
Virginia, by the Rev. A,
S. Lloyd, D.D. assisted by
the Rev. A. B. Kinsolving,
D.D., at "Staunton Hill",
Halifax Co. So. Ch., July
2, 1904

BEALE
Mary Gordon, and the Rev. J.
F. Ribble, rector of the
church, by the Rev. Frederick Ribble, in St. Paul's
Church, Newport News, Va.
So. Ch., Dec. 10, 1896

BEAUMONT
Sarah A. (Mrs.), d. of the
late Dr. Sample Ford, and
the Rev. Jacob Brittingham,
all of Wheeling, W.Va., by
the Rt. Rev. Geo. W. Peterkin, in St. Luke's Church,
Wheeling, W.Va. So. Ch.,
May 4, 1896

BENNETT
Annie P. P., d. of Mrs. M. C.
P. and the late John C. F.
Bennett of Charleston, S.C.,
and George M. Nicol of Morristown, N.Y., by the Rt. Rev.
J. B. Newton, at the residence of the bride's mother,
104½ W. Grace St. So. Ch.,
July 19, 1894

BEST
Robin Saxon, of Cartersville,
Ga., and Mallie Hunter, d.
of Luther H. Ott of Harrisonburg, by the Rev. Robert N.
Brooking, rector of Emmanuel
Church, at the Ott residence,
S. Main St., Harrisonburg, Va.
So. Ch., Nov. 3, 1906

BIGGS
Dennis Simmons, of Williamston,
N.C., and Fannie Beeler Chase,
sister of Lt. Gilbert
Chase of the U.S. Navy, by
the Rev. Mr. Gamble of Tarboro, N.C., at the residence
of the Hon. Wilson G. Lamb.
So. Ch., Jan. 3, 1903

BLACKFORD
Charles Minor, Jr. (Dr.), of
Augusta, Ga., and Julia
Winifred, eldest d. of Wm.
G. and Stella B. Sears, by
the Rev. Dr. Angell, in St.
Stephen's Church, Harrisburg,
Pa. So. Ch., Sept. 23, 1897
Mary Berkeley, second d. of B.
Lewis Blackford, Esq. of
Washington, D.C., and Lt.
Charles Green Sawtelle, U.S.
Army, by the Rev. A. R.
Stuart, D.D., rector, in
Christ Church, Georgetown.
So. Ch., Apr. 29, 1897
Pelham, of Richmond, and Sarah
Evelyn, eldest d. of James
B. Baylor, Esq., all of
Virginia, by the Rev. A. S.
Lloyd, D.D. assisted by the
Rev. A. B. Kinsolving, D.D.,
at "Staunton Hill", Halifax
County. So. Ch., July 2,
1904
William S., and Julia, d. of
John A. Whitridge, by the
Rev. J. Houston Eccleston,
D.D. assisted by the Rev.
J. S. B. Hodges, D.D. of
St. Paul's Church, in
Emmanuel Church, Baltimore.
So. Ch., Apr. 27, 1899

BLAIR
John Mercer (The Rev.), of
Kiahing, China, formerly of
Virginia, and Claude Lacy
Grier of Tokushima, Japan,
formerly of North Carolina,
by the Rev. S. R. Hope assisted by the Rev. W. B. McIlvaine,
at Yokohama, Japan. So. Ch.,
Sept. 23, 1897

BOLLING

MARRIAGE NOTICES IN THE SOUTHERN CHURCHMAN WITH DATES OF PUBLICATION

Charles E., and Parke Chamberlayne Bagby, both of Richmond, by the Rev. John K. Mason, at the residence of the bride's mother, 311 E. Grace St., Richmond, Va. So. Ch., Apr. 26, 1894

Randolph, Esq., of Richmond, Va., and Sallie Bayly, d. of Mrs. W. B. Stokes, by the Rev. Dr. Carson, rector, in St. Paul's Church, Lynchburg, Va. So. Ch., Mar. 2, 1899

BOLTON
Belle Campbell, and John Thompson Brown, Jr., by the Rev. John H. Elliott, at "Branchland", the residence of the bride, in Albemarle Co., Va. So. Ch., Dec. 24, 1896

BOONE
Phoebe Elliott, second d. of the late Rt. Rev. Bishop Boone of China, and Albert Rhett Walker, eldest s. of the officiating clergyman, the Rev. Albert Walker, assisted by the Rt. Rev. Bishop Coleman, in Calvary Church, Wilmington, Del. So. Ch., Apr. 25, 1895

BOOTH
Lucy R., and Granville C. Medley, by the Rev. J. G. Shackelford, at Houston, Halifax Co., Va. So. Ch., Sept. 9, 1897

BOTTS
Thomas Hutchinson, and Lillian Word, d. of Henry Neeson, Esq., by the Rev. C. C. Griffith, in the Church of the Ascension, Lafayette Square, Baltimore, Md. So. Ch., Jan. 11, 1894

BOWIE
William, of Anne Arundel Co., Md., and Elizabeth Taylor,
d. of Mrs. Henry Starr Wattles, by the Rev. P. P. Philips, at the residence of the bride's mother, Alexandria, Va. So. Ch., July 6, 1899

BOXLEY
Frances Williams, d. of Dr. Claude Boxley of Markham, Va., and Dr. Peyton Hundley of Montague, Va., by the Rev. Thomas Atkinson, in St. Barnabas' Church, Baltimore. So. Ch., Apr. 28, 1900

BRAGG
Elise Calvin, d. of Mrs. William Albert Bragg, and Granville Gray Valentine, all of Richmond, Va., by the Rev. Robert Strange, in St. Paul's Church, Richmond, Va. So. Ch., Apr. 16, 1904

BRANDER
Louise, and Wm. Mayo Taliaferro, by the Rev. W. W. Brander, brother of the bride, assisted by the Rev. L. R. Mason and the Rev. R. P. Kerr, in Grace Church, Richmond, Va. So. Ch., Nov. 22, 1894

BRAYTON
Harriet A., d. of Michael Brayton, Esq. of Utica, and Lloyd Powell, s. of the Rev. S. S. Hepburn*, by the Rev. E. F. H. J. Massey, rector of St. Luke's P. E. Church, in Utica, N.Y. So. Ch., Aug. 20, 1904

BRINCKLE
William Draper, of Wilmington, Del., and Anna Hull Moncure of Fairfax, Va., by the Rev. Kinsey J. Hammond assisted by the Rev. W. H. K. Pendleton and the Rev. A. R. Walker, in Zion Church, Fairfax. So. Ch., July 15, 1901

BRITTINGHAM
Jacob (The Rev.), and Mrs.

* Given as printed

MARRIAGE NOTICES IN THE SOUTHERN CHURCHMAN WITH DATES OF PUBLICATION

Sarah A. Beaumont, d. of the late Dr. Sample Ford, all of Wheeling, W.Va., by the Rt. Rev. Geo. W. Peterkin, in St. Luke's Church, Wheeling, W.Va. So. Ch., May 4, 1896

BROWN

Edmund Fontaine, of Charleston, W.Va., and Sue Peyton, d. of Mrs. Joseph Ferdinand Kent of Wytheville, Va., by the Rev. Mercer P. Logan, D.D., in St. John's Episcopal Church, Wytheville, Va. So. Ch., Jan. 30, 1904

John Thompson, Jr., and Belle Campbell Bolton, by the Rev. John H. Elliott, at "Branchard", Albemarle Co., Va., the residence of the bride. So. Ch., Dec. 24, 1896

Lewis Pickett, of Malden, Mass, and Mrs. E. M. Moseley of Richmond, Va., by the Rev. Robert P. Kerr, at the residence of Dr. E. J. Moseley, in Richmond. So. Ch., Nov. 3, 1898

William Meade, s. of Theo. Brown and great gr.s. of Bishop Meade, and Letitier Field, d. of the late Capt. Edwin H. Moise of Louisville, Ky., at the residence of William Leachman, Walnut Hills, Cincinnati, Ohio. So. Ch., Nov. 22, 1894

BROWNE

Katherine H., and Benjamin Chew Howard, by the Rev. Edwin B. Niver, in Baltimore, Md. So. Ch., Apr. 28, 1898

Violet Hand, and Charles Worthington Hoff, both of Baltimore Co., Md., by the Rev. W. H. H. Powers, in Trinity Church, Towson, Md.

So. Ch., July 2, 1896

BRUCE

Philip Alexander, of Richmond, Va., and Mrs. Betty Taylor Newton, by the Rev. B. D. Tucker, at Beechwood Place, Norfolk, Va. So. Ch., Oct. 29, 1896

Sallie Archer, eldest d. of Thomas Seddon Bruce and gr.d. of the late Gen. Joseph R. Anderson and of Charles Bruce, and Arthur Barksdale Kinsolving, s. of the late Dr. O. A. Kinsolving and rector of Christ Church, Brooklyn, N.Y., in St. Paul's Church, Richmond. So. Ch., Feb. 13, 1896

BRYAN

Lucy White, of Memphis, Tenn., and Frederick W. Page, Librarian of the University of Virginia, at the University of Virginia. So. Ch., Sept. 27, 1902

BUNTING

John S., B.D. (The Rev.), assistant rector of Holy Apostle Episcopal Church, Philadelphia, Pa., and Mary Blair Horner of the "Moorings", Fauquier Co., Va., by the Rev. J. J. Norwood, rector of Whittle Parish*, and the Rev. Oscar Bunting of Petersburg, Va., in Trinity Church, Marshall, Fauquier Co., Va. So. Ch., June 16, 1898

BURR

Austin Hart, and Susan Moore, d. of John R. McMurdo, by the Rev. J. W. Ware, in St. James' Church, Ashland, Va. So. Ch., Oct. 29, 1896

BURROUGHS

Orion, d. of Edgar E. and Blanche McAlpine Burroughs,

---

* Whittle Parish is in Fauquier County, Virginia, (<u>Journal ... Diocese of Virginia</u>, Richmond, 1941)

MARRIAGE NOTICES IN THE SOUTHERN CHURCHMAN WITH DATES OF PUBLICATION

and Alonzo E. James, all of Princess Anne Co., Va., by the Rev. Wm. R. Savage, at Eastern Shore Chapel. So. Ch., May 27, 1897

BURWELL
Annie McCaleb, eldest d. of Mrs. Augusta and the late Elliott Burwell, and Sewell S. Hepburn Jr., M.D. of West River, by the Rev. Sewell S. Hepburn*, father of the groom, assisted by the Rev. Mr. Plummer, in St. John's Church, West River, Anne Arundel Co., Md. So. Ch., May 26, 1900

BUSHBY
Jennie, and H. Vernon Hackett, both of Hanover Co., Va., by the Rev. S. S. Hepbron, rector, in Fork Church. So. Ch., Oct. 14, 1897

BUTTS
Hallie M., and the Rev. Robert A. Goodwin, rector of St. John's Church, Richmond, Va., by the Rev. E. L. Goodwin, in Petersburg, Va. So. Ch., Nov. 10, 1900

CARDWELL
Charles Patteson, and Bessie Winston, d. of John Lee of Stafford Co., by the Rev. S. S. Hepbron, in St. Paul's Church. So. Ch., Dec. 15, 1900

CARHART
Eloise O., and Frank Suter of Washington, D.C., by the Rev. Charles Carhart, brother of the bride, at Dorset, Vt. So. Ch., Aug. 6, 1904

CARMICHAEL
Elizabeth Coalter, and the Rev. William D. Smith, rector of Christ Church, Winchester, Va., by the Rev. R. J. McBryde, D.D., the Rev. C. Braxton Bryan, D.D., and the Rev. James Carmichael, D.D., in Fredericksburg, Va. So. Ch., Dec. 16, 1905

CARR
Henry Hammond, of Baltimore, and Alice, d. of O. Mcp. Lyles, by the Rev. Alexander Galt, in St. James' Parish Church, Anne Arundel Co., Md. So. Ch., Jan. 18, 1894

CARTER
Anne Page, d. of Dr. C. Shirley and Mary M. Carter, and Dr. W. John Sheaff Stewart of Philadelphia, by the Rev. Berryman Green, in St. James' Church, Leesburg, Va. So. Ch., July 5, 1894

Frank, and Marion Clarkson Scott, by the Rev. William Short, rector, in St. Peter's Church, St. Louis, Mo. So. Ch., Feb. 28, 1895

CATLETT
John Breckenridge, M.D., of Staunton, Va., and Lizzie, d. of Capt. H. C. Michie, by the Rev. D. C. T. Davis, at "The Meadows", near Charlottesville, Va. So. Ch., Nov. 14, 1895

CHAPMAN
Elizabeth Power, d. of Col. and Mrs. Wm. H. Chapman, and the Rev. W. H. K. Pendleton of Fairfax, Va., by the Rt. Rev. A. M. Randolph, D.D., assisted by the Rev. Josiah R. Ellis, at "Clifton", the home of the bride's parents, Orange Co., Va. So. Ch., Aug. 19, 1897

CHASE
Fannie Beeler, sister of Lt. Gilbert Chase of the U.S. Navy, and Dennis Simmons Biggs of Williamston, N.C., by the Rev. Mr. Gamble of Tarboro, N.C., at the resi-

* Given as printed

MARRIAGE NOTICES IN THE SOUTHERN CHURCHMAN WITH DATES OF PUBLICATION

dence of the Hon. Wilson G. Lamb. So. Ch., Jan. 3, 1903

CHICHESTER
Esther M., of Fairfax Co., Va., and Edward H. Spindler of Washington, D.C., by the Rev. Mr. Niver, in Baltimore, Md. So. Ch., Mar. 17, 1898

CHURCHILL-SPENCER
Charles R., Duke of Marlborough, and Consuelo, d. of William Kissam Vanderbilt, Esq., by the Rt. Rev. Bishop of Long Island, the Rt. Rev. Bishop of New York, and the Rev. John W. Brown, in St. Thomas' Church, New York. So. Ch., Nov. 14, 1895

CLAIBORNE
Nena Bolling, d. of Sterling Claiborne, and Eldridge Herbert Hager of Max Meadows, Va., by the Rev. A. P. Gray, in St. Mark's Church, New Glasgow, Va. So. Ch., Dec. 12, 1895

CLARK
Frank Pinckney (The Rev.), minister-in-charge of the P. E. Hospital Mission, Philadelphia, Pa., and Maria, youngest d. of Capt. James Marshall of Happy Creek, Warren Co., Va., by the Rev. Charles Buck, rector of St. John's P. E. Church, at 3041 N Street, West Washington, D.C. So. Ch., Jan. 4, 1894

William Meade (The Rev.), rector of St. James' Church, Richmond, Va., and Mary Alice, d. of R. Tunstall Pierce, Esq., by the Rev. J. Y. Downman of All Saints' Church, Richmond, Va., at the home of the bride's parents, in Lancaster Co., Va. So. Ch., Dec. 21, 1899

CLARKE
Elizabeth Southall, and Douglas Huntley Gordon, by the Rev. John Francis Ribble, rector, assisted by the Rev. W. W. Brander of Baltimore, in St. Paul's Church, Newport News, Va. So. Ch., July 1, 1897

CLARKSON
Henry Bradford, and Mary Louise, d. of the Hon. William Sydney Laidley, by the Rev. Robert Douglas Roller, D.D., in St. John's Church, Charleston, Kanawha Co., W.Va. So. Ch., Jan. 20, 1898

CLAYBROOK
Sallie Bland, d. of the late Edwin C. and Judith Newton Claybrook of Westmoreland Co., Va., and Lt. Edward Murray Offley of the Twelfth Cavalry, U.S.A., by the Rev. Willoughby Newton Claybrook, brother of the bride and rector of Christ Church, at the residence of Ernest Griffith, Tyler, Tex. So. Ch., Feb. 8, 1902

COCHRAN
Wm. B. (Capt.), U.S.A., and Mathilda Hessler of Helena, Mont., by Bishop Brewer, at Helena, Mont. So. Ch., Sept. 24, 1904

COCKE
Bessie, youngest d. of Prof. Charles L. Cocke, and John Preston Barbee, by the Rev. J. M. Luck assisted by the Rev. Collins Denny, D.D., at Hollins Institute. So. Ch., Aug. 12, 1897

COLE
Kate, d. of Col. James Reid Cole of Dallas, Tex., and Edmund Pendleton Randolph

MARRIAGE NOTICES IN THE SOUTHERN CHURCHMAN WITH DATES OF PUBLICATION

Duval, of Lexington, Va., at the residence of the bride's father, Dallas, Tex. So. Ch., Aug. 12, 1905

COLEMAN
Alice McKenney (Mrs.), and Dr. Edward Willis Finch, by the Rev. Wm. Meade Clark, at 710 E. Leigh St., Richmond, Va. So. Ch., Dec. 3, 1896

Annie Josephine, d. of the late Judge Richard H. Coleman, and John Howard Southall of Richmond, Va., by the Rev. S. S. Ware, in Trinity Church, Bowling Green, Va. So. Ch., Dec. 17, 1896

Thomas Gordon, of News Ferry, Halifax Co., Va., and Marie, d. of Mr. and Mrs. Rhett of Brooklyn, N.Y., by the Rev. A. B. Kinsolving, rector, in Christ Church, Brooklyn, N.Y. So. Ch., Nov. 29, 1894

COLOMB
Brooks Amedee (Dr.), and Margaret Scott Gilmore, by the Rev. H. B. Lee assisted by the Rev. A. G. Grinnan, at the home of Prof. Gilmore, University of Virginia. So. Ch., Nov. 8, 1894

COLSTON
Eliza Pendleton, d. of Frederick M. Colston, Esq. of Baltimore, Md., and Wyatt William Randall, Ph.D., by the Rev. Percy F. Hall, in St. Timothy's Church, Catonsville, Md. So. Ch., July 7, 1898

CONNER
Sidney Nelson, of Quitman, Ga., and Sarah Annette Grubb of Live Oak, Fla., at St. Luke's Church, Live Oak, Fla. So. Ch., Sept. 22, 1906

COOKE
Giles B. (The Rev.), and Sarah Katherine, d. of Warren R. and Pauline Grosh, by the Rt. Rev. Dr. Wm. F. Adams, in St. Mary's Church, North East, Md. So. Ch., May 12, 1898

Lucy Landon, eldest d. of Churchill Cooke, Esq. of King William, and Fenton Noland of Hanover, by the Rev. S. S. Hepbron assisted by the Rev. C. L. Price, in St. James' Church, King William C.H., Va. So. Ch., Apr. 29, 1897

CORNER
Lillie K., and the Rev. Frank Mezick, rector of the Church of the Good Shepherd, Dinwiddie Co., by the Rev. Ridout, rector of Grace Church, Petersburg, assisted by the Rev. Alexander Galt, rector of St. Margaret's, in St. Margaret's Church, Anne Arundel Co., Md. So. Ch., Nov. 3, 1900

COUPLAND
Robert Saunders (The Rev.), rector of St. John's Church, Covington, Ky., and Cornelia Wickham, d. of Harry C. Whitehead of Norfolk, Va., by the Rev. A. S. Lloyd assisted by the Rev. Z. S. Farland, in St. Luke's Church, Norfolk, Va. So. Ch., Oct. 14, 1897

COURTENAY
Edith, d. of the Hon. William A. Courtenay, and John M. Bateman of Columbia, S.C., by the Rt. Rev. Ellison Capers, D.D., Bishop of South Carolina, at "Innisfallen", the residence of the bride, Oconee Co., S.C. So. Ch., Dec. 10, 1896

COWAN
Stephen G., and Mary E. Hopkins, by the Rev. P. F. Sprigg. So. Ch., Dec. 13, 1894

COX

MARRIAGE NOTICES IN THE SOUTHERN CHURCHMAN WITH DATES OF PUBLICATION

Jane Threlkeld, d. of Mrs. Thomas Campbell Cox, and Dr. Larkin White Glazebrook, all of Washington, D.C., by the Rev. Otis A. Glazebrook, D.D., father of the groom, assisted by the Rev. Alfred Harding, rector of the church, in St. Paul's Church, Washington, D.C. So. Ch., Feb. 7, 1895

Maude Robertson, and Clarence Gordon Montgomery, by the Rev. R. A. Goodwin, rector of St. John's Church, in Monumental Church, Richmond, Va. So. Ch., Mar. 25, 1905

COYNER
Luther T., of Augusta Co., Va., and Annette Kimbrough, d. of Dr. John Ligon, by the Rev. T. H. Lacy of Lynchburg, Va., at the home of the bride's father, Clover Lick, W.Va. So. Ch., June 29, 1899

CRAWFORD
A., Dr. (The Rev.), rector of St. Barnabas' Church, Tullahoma, Tenn., and Charlotte V. McIlvain of Little Rock, Ark., by the Rev. Charles H. Kues of Hot Springs, Ark., at the home of the bride's mother, Little Rock, Ark. So. Ch., Sept. 9, 1905

CRUTCHFIELD
Mattie Murton, d. of George Crutchfield and adopted d. of Mr. and Mrs. R. J. Murton of Richmond, Va., and William N. Hunter of Kansas City, Mo., by the Rev. Carroll M. Davis, D.D., Dean, in Christ Church Cathedral, St. Louis, Mo. So. Ch., Apr. 9, 1904

CULLEN
Mary Maben, of Richmond, Va., and William Temple Moseley, by the Rev. Dr. J. A. Aspinwall, rector, in St. Thomas' Chapel, Washington, D.C.
So. Ch., Nov. 26, 1896

CURTIS
William F., of Marietta, Ohio, and Mary A. Robinson, by the Rev. G. P. Sommerville, at the home of the bride, Willow Island, W.Va. So. Ch., Feb. 15, 1894

DABNEY
Richard Heath, Prof. of the University of Virginia, and Lily Heth, d. of the late I. M. M. Davis, by the Rev. D. C. T. Davis assisted by the Rev. H. B. Lee, at the chapel of the University of Virginia. So. Ch., Dec. 28, 1899

W. A., of Barton Heights, and Mary Bell Stuart of Virginia, by the Rev. S. S. Hepbron, at the residence of A. Spot. Wingfield, of Hanover Co. So. Ch., Dec. 10, 1904

DAINGERFIELD
Henrietta Henderson, and Norman Attilla Cox of Beattyville, Ky., by Dean Baker P. Lee of Christ Church Cathedral, Lexington assisted by the Rev. Alexander Patterson of Beattyville, Ky., at Castleton, the residence of the bride's father near Lexington, Ky. So. Ch., Feb. 13, 1904

Rebecca Fowle, and James Monroe Love, Jr. of Fairfax C.H., Va. by the Rev. P. P. Phillips assisted by the Rev. S. A. Wells, at the residence of the bride's parents, Alexandria, Va. So. Ch., Mar. 31, 1898

DALLAM
Corbin Braxton, and Nannie Poultney, d. of Charles D. Fisher, by the Rev. Edwin B. Niver, in Baltimore, Md. So. Ch., Mar. 3, 1898

DAVIS

MARRIAGE NOTICES IN THE SOUTHERN CHURCHMAN WITH DATES OF PUBLICATION

Dabney C. T., Jr., and Mary Miller, d. of Capt. Alexander F. Mathews, by the Rev. D. C. T. Davis assisted by the Rev. Wm. White, at Lewisburg, W.Va. So. Ch., Nov. 19, 1896

Lily Heth, d. of the late I. M. M. Davis, and Richard Heath Dabney, Prof. of the University of Virginia, by the Rev. D. C. T. Davis assisted by the Rev. H. B. Lee, at the chapel of the University of Virginia. So. Ch., Dec. 28, 1899

Lucy Page Minor, d. of the officiating minister, and Benjamin Harrison Baird, by the Rev. D. C. T. Davis, in Emmanuel Church, Albemarle Co., Va. So. Ch., Nov. 14, 1895

DeBELL
Annie V., and D. B. Gant, both of Centreville, Va., by the Rev. John McNabb, in the rectory at Herndon, Va. So. Ch., Oct. 12, 1901

DIMMOCK
Mary Lewis, and James H. Harris of Richmond, by the Rev. William Byrd Lee, at "Sherwood", Gloucester Co., Va. So. Ch., Apr. 30, 1896

DOSWELL
Paul Tillman, and Annie Dill, d. of W. C. Parkinson, all of Hanover Co., Va., by the Rev. S. S. Hepbron, in Taylorsville Baptist Church. So. Ch., Dec. 15, 1900

DOUGLAS
John S. (The Rev.), of Shenandoah, Va., and Elizabeth Power, d. of Henry C. McCauley of Washington, by the Rev. T. J. Packard of West River, Md., in Christ Church, Washington, D.C. So. Ch., Mar. 18, 1897

DuBOSE
William H. (The Rev.), M.A., of Sewanee, Tenn., and Dean, d. of Dr. H. N. Spencer, by the groom's father, the Rev. W. P. DuBose, S.T.D., dean of the theological dep't of the University of the South, at 2725 Washington Ave., St. Louis, Mo. So. Ch., Oct. 8, 1896

DUDLEY
May, d. of the Rt. Rev. Thomas U. Didlcy, D.D., and the Rev. James Kirkpatrick of Pittsburgh, Pa., by the Rt. Rev. the Bishop of Kentucky, in Emmanuel Church, Middleburg, Va. So. Ch., Sept. 12, 1895

DUKE
Evelyn, d. of Wm. Duke of Hanover Co., and John Page Trevillian, by the Rev. S. S. Hepbron, in Fork Church. So. Ch., Dec. 15, 1900

DUNLAP
Richard Alexander, and Mrs. Julia Anthony Warfield, d. of the late William Pleasants Anthony of Buchanan, Va., by the Rev. Julian E. Ingle assisted by the Rev. Robert Forsyth, in St. Paul's Church, Richmond, Va. So. Ch., May 19, 1906

DUNN
C. Irvin, of Baltimore, Md., and Emily Oliver, d. of the late Gustave Shiff of New York, by the Rev. Dr. C. George Currie assisted by the Rev. Dr. J. H. Eccleston, at Christ Church, Baltimore, Md. So. Ch., May 3, 1894

Jos. B. (The Rev.), and Martha C., d. of S. V. Southall, by the Rev. H. B. Lee, in Charlottesville, Va. So.

MARRIAGE NOTICES IN THE SOUTHERN CHURCHMAN WITH DATES OF PUBLICATION

Ch., Dec. 19, 1895

DuPONT
Philip Francis, s. of the late Dr. Alexis DuPont, and Elizabeth Braxton, d. of the late Dr. Frederick Horner, U.S. Navy, of Marshall, Va., in Christ Church rectory, Christiana Hundred, Del. So. Ch., June 17, 1905

DURAND
Herbert, and Mrs. Hortense Funsten Forbes, both of St. Louis, Mo., by the Rev. Jas. R. Winchester, D.D. So. Ch., July 23, 1905

DURRETTE
William Overton, of Albemarle Co., Va., and Annye M., second d. of Mr. and Mrs. Leverette S. Early, by the Rev. C. C. Randolph, in the Church of the Good Shepherd, near Evington, Va., at high noon. So. Ch., Dec. 15, 1900

DUVAL
Catherine Cooke, d. of the late Robert Randolph Duval of Richmond, Va., and Carter H. Harrison, by the Rev. R. C. Jett, at the residence of Mrs. J. E. B. Stuart, Staunton, Va. So. Ch., July 2, 1896

Edmund Pendleton Randolph, of Lexington, Va., and Kate, d. of Col. James Reid Cole of Dallas, Tex., at the residence of the bride's father, Dallas, Tex. So. Ch., Aug. 12, 1905

Lucy Waller, and P. Lightfoot Wormeley, Jr., by the Rev. Landon R. Mason, in Grace Episcopal Church, Fluvanna Co. So. Ch., June 25, 1904

Philip St. John, of Richmond, Va., and Sarah Louise, d. of Robert M. Payne of Danville, Va., by the Rev. W. R. Laird, at the residence of the Hon. A. J. Montague, Danville, Va. So. Ch., Aug. 12, 1897

EARLY
Annye M., second d. of Mr. and Mrs. Leverette S. Early, and William Overton Durrette of Albemarle Co., Va., by the Rev. C. C. Randolph, in the Church of the Good Shepherd, near Evington, Va., at high noon. So. Ch., Dec. 15, 1900

EDWARDS
W. F. C., and Pattie Valentine, youngest d. of Mr. and Mrs. W. M. Rawlings of Winfall, Perquimans Co., N.C., by the Rev. R. B. Drane, rector of St. Paul's, Edenton, N.C., at the residence of the bride's parents. So. Ch., July 26, 1894

ELLIS
Josiah R. (The Rev.), of Gordonsville, Va., and Lilly Archer, d. of Edward J. Warren of Richmond, by the Rt. Rev. F. M. Whittle assisted by the Rev. Landon R. Mason, in Grace Church, Richmond, Va. So. Ch., Dec. 13, 1894

Thomas Harding, M.D., of Powellton, W.Va., and Caroline Homassel, eldest d. of the late Hon. B. Johnson Barbour, by the Rev. Josiah R. Ellis, at the old homestead at Barboursville, Orange Co., Va. So. Ch., Jan. 24, 1895

EPPES
Agnes Horner, d. of Richard Eppes, M.D., and Aurelius Rives Shands, M.D. of Washington, D.C., by the Rev. C. R. Hains, D.D. assisted by the Rev. M. G. Cassell, in St.

MARRIAGE NOTICES IN THE SOUTHERN CHURCHMAN WITH DATES OF PUBLICATION

John's Church, City Point, Va. So. Ch., Jan. 9, 1896
Alfreda H., d. of the late Richard Eppes, M.D., and Herbert J. Maynard of London, England, by the Rev. W. R. Savage, at "Appomattox", the residence of the bride's mother. So. Ch., Aug. 13, 1896
Richard, of City Point, Va., and Mary F. Van Deusen, by the Rev. George W. Davenport, rector, in St. James' Church, Danbury, Conn. So. Ch., Apr. 16, 1904

EVANS
Maria Lee, d. of Dr. and Mrs. Jas. Evans of Florence, S.C., and Frank Boyd Gary of Abbeville, S.C., by the Rev. Wm. A. Guerry, chaplain of the University of the South, Sewanee, Tenn., assisted by the Rev. W. S. Holmes, rector, in St. John's Church, Florence, S.C. So. Ch., Jan. 28, 1897

FAIRFAX
Frederick Griffith, and Mary Fernando Fairfax Wharton, both of Westmoreland Co., Va., by the Rev. Richard P. Williams, pastor of Trinity Episcopal Church, at the residence of the bride's aunt, Mrs. Mittie Musser, Vermont Ave., Northwest Washington. So. Ch., May 9, 1903

FALCONER
William Armistead, and Annie Lyons Gilmore, by the Rev. H. B. Lee assisted by the Rev. A. G. Grinnan, at the home of Prof. Gilmore, University of Virginia. So. Ch., Nov. 8, 1894

FAUCETT
Ellen Daniel, and James Harrison Lassiter, Jr., both of Henderson, N.C., by the Rev. Junius Horner, at the residence of the bride's mother. So. Ch., Aug. 20, 1896

FAUNTLEROY
Betsy Todd, d. of the late Dr. S. G. and Mrs. F. E. Fauntleroy, and W. C. Foulds of Philadelphia, at "Marialva", in King and Queen Co., Va. So. Ch., Jan. 17, 1903

FEAST
Charles F., of Baltimore, Md., and Margaret Reid, d. of A. T. Herbert, Esq., by the Rev. William R. Savage, at "Sunnyside", near Kempsville, Princess Anne Co., Va. So. Ch., May 13, 1897

FENTON
Arthur F., (The Rev.), of Spruce Chapel, Upshur Co., W. Va., youngest s. of the late Kirkby Fenton, Esq. of Warwickshire, England, and Ella T., oldest d. of the late Col. John A. Gibbons of Point Pleasant, W.Va., by the Rev. A. G. Grinnan, rector, in Christ Church, Point Pleasant, W.Va. So. Ch., Sept. 23, 1897

FINCH
Edward Willis (Dr.), and Mrs. Alice McKenney Coleman, by the Rev. Wm. Meade Clark, at 710 E. Leigh St., Richmond, Va. So. Ch., Dec. 3, 1896

FINLEY
Augustus Clemens, and Agnes Langhorne, d. of Dr. Nicholas Johnson, by the Rev. Finley of Fishersville, Va., at Mammoth, W.Va. So. Ch., June 29, 1899

FISHER
Anne, d. of Robert Haxall Fisher, and Virginius Hall, by the Rev. F. S. Stickney, in Monumental Church, Richmond, Va.

MARRIAGE NOTICES IN THE SOUTHERN CHURCHMAN WITH DATES OF PUBLICATION

So. Ch., Aug. 15, 1895
Nannie Poultney, d. of Charles
D. Fisher, and Corbin Braxton Dallam, by the Rev. Edwin
B. Niver, in Baltimore, Md.
So. Ch., Mar. 3, 1898

FITZHUGH
Mary Brockenbrough, third d.
of Capt. R. H. and Agnes M.
Fitzhugh, formerly of
Virginia, and Harwell R.
Smith of St. Louis, Mo., by
the Rev. E. H. Ward, D.D.,
in Christ Church, Lexington, Ky. So. Ch., Nov. 15,
1894

FLORANCE
James Gardner, and Willie
Green, d. of Mrs. Angelina
Bassett Priddy, by the
Rev. L. B. Betty, at the
home of the bride's mother,
503 W. Clay St., Richmond,
Va. So. Ch., Dec. 1, 1906

FORBES
Hortense Funsten (Mrs.), and
Herbert Durand, both of St.
Louis, Mo., by the Rev. Jas.
R. Winchester, D.D. So. Ch.,
July 22, 1905

Jane D., youngest d. of Dr. I.
T. Forbes, and Jaquolin Marshall Robertson of Richmond,
Va., by the Rev. H. B. Lee,
at the residence of Capt.
Harrison Robertson, Charlottesville, Va. So. Ch., Dec. 12,
1895

FORD
See also BEAUMONT, Sarah A.
(Mrs.)

FOULDS
W. C., of Philadelphia, and
Betsy Todd, d. of the late Dr.
S. G. and Mrs. F. E. Fauntleroy, at "Marialva", in King and
Queen Co., Va. So. Ch., Jan.
17, 1903

FRED
Frank L., and Mattie Smith, by the
Rev. John D. LaMo[?]he, at
Locust Grove, Loudoun Co.,
Va. So. Ch., Apr. 14,
1900

FULLER
Robert Wright, of Atlanta,
Ga., and Bettie F., d. of
William A. Smoot, Esq. of
Alexandria, at Christ
Church, Alexandria, Va.
So. Ch., Feb. 16, 1899

FUNSTEN
Emily Ridgeway, d. of the
late Col. David Funsten of
Alexandria, and Robert M.
Ward, by the Rev. Dr. Dame,
in Memorial Church, Baltimore. So. Ch., Apr. 20,
1899

Oliver Herbert, of Richmond,
and Pessie Carter, d. of the
late Capt. Robert Dabney and
Landonia Minor, by the Rev.
James B. Funsten assisted by
the Rev. William Meade Clarke,
rector of the church, in St.
James' Church, Richmond.
So. Ch., Nov. 5, 1896

GAMBLE
Edward Watts (The Rev.), of
Florida, and Emily Arnold
Whitehead of Norfolk, by
the Rev. A. S. Lloyd, at the
residence of the bride's
parents, No. 57 Boush St.,
Norfolk, Va. So. Ch.,
June 11, 1896

GANT
D. B., and Annie V. DeBell,
both of Centreville, Va., by
the Rev. John McNabb, at the
rectory, Herndon, Va. So.
Ch., Oct. 12, 1901

GARNETT
Grace, d. of the Hon. Geo. Wm.
Garnett, and Dr. Larkin Hundley, s. of the officiating
clergyman, by the Rev. Dr.
Hundley, at "Cottage Park",

MARRIAGE NOTICES IN THE SOUTHERN CHURCHMAN WITH DATES OF PUBLICATION

Essex Co., Va., the home of the bride. So. Ch., Apr. 19 and 28, 1900

GARY
Frank Boyd, of Abbeville, S.C., and Maria Lee, d. of Dr. and Mrs. Jas. Evans of Florence, S.C., by the Rev. Wm. A. Guerry, chaplain of the University of the South, Sewannee, Tenn., assisted by the Rev. W. S. Holmes, rector, in St. John's Church, Florence, S.C. So. Ch., Jan. 23, 1897

GIBBONS
Ella T., eldest d. of the late Col. John A. Gibbons of Point Pleasant, W.Va., and the Rev. Arthur F. Fenton of Spruce Chapel, Upshur Co., W.Va., youngest s. of the late Kirkby Fenton, Esq. of Warwickshire, England, by the Rev. A. G. Grinnan, rector, in Christ Church, Point Pleasant, W.Va. So. Ch., Sept. 23, 1897

J. H. (The Rev.), of Stafford Co., Va., and Mary S. Anderson, by the Rev. Mr. Temple, in Washington, Rappahannock Co., Va. So. Ch., Dec. 2, 1897

James N., of Wilson, N.C., and Mary Ida, d. of the late William A. Scott of Isle of Wight Co., Va., by the Rev. Virginius Wronn of Norfolk, Va., at the residence of the bride's brother-in-law, Mr. Lofton J. Alley, Richmond, Va. So. Ch., Sept. 10, 1896

GILDERSLEEVE
Emma Louise, d. of Prof. and Mrs. Basil L. Gildersleeve, and Gardiner Martin Lane of Cambridge, Mass., by the Rev. Edwin B. Niver, in Christ Church, Baltimore, Md. So. Ch., June 16, 1898

GILMER
John Patton, of Kansas City, and Lucy Dabney Walker, by Rev. C. Breckinridge Wilmer assisted by Rev. W. A. Barr, at the residence of the Hon. E. W. Saunders of Rocky Mount, Va. So. Ch., Oct. 31, 1895

GILMORE
Annie Lyons, and William Armistead Falconer, by the Rev. H. B. Lee assisted by the Rev. A. G. Grinnan, at the home of Prof. Gilmore, University of Virginia. So. Ch., Nov. 8, 1894

Margaret Scott, and Dr. Brooks Amedee Colomb, by the Rev. H. B. Lee assisted by the Rev. A. G. Grinnan, at the home of Prof. Gilmore, University of Virginia. So. Ch., Nov. 8, 1894

GITHENS
John Nichols, of Chicago, Ill., and Elizabeth Beverley, d. of the officiating minister, the Rev. David Barr, in Washington, D.C. So. Ch., Sept. 15, 1900

GLAZEBROOK
Larkin White (Dr.), and Jane Throlkold, d. of Mrs. Thomas Campbell Cox, all of Washington, D.C., by the Rev. Otis A. Glazebrook, D.D., father of the groom, assisted by the Rev. Alfred Harding, rector of the church, in St. Paul's Church, Washington, D.C. So. Ch., Feb. 7, 1895

GOODWIN
Robert A. (The Rev.), rector of St. John's Church, Richmond, Va., and Hallie M. Butts, by the Rev. E. L. Goodwin, in Petersburg, Va. So. Ch., Nov. 10, 1900

Wm. A. R. (The Rev.), rector of

MARRIAGE NOTICES IN THE SOUTHERN CHURCHMAN WITH DATES OF PUBLICATION

St. John's Church, and Lizzie, d. of the late Major N. M. and Mrs. M. E. Tanner, by the Rt. Rev. Bishop Randolph, D.D. assisted by the Rev. R. A. Goodwin and the Rev. C. R. Hains, D.D., in St. Paul's Church, Petersburg. So. Ch., Feb. 28, 1895

GOODWYN
Mary Powell, d. of the Hon. Charles F. Goodwin, Judge of Nottoway County Court, and the Rev. C. R. Kuyk, by the Rev. Pike of Richmond assisted by the Rev. J. W. Ware of Farmville, in Christ Church. So. Ch., Apr. 16, 1896

GORDON
Douglas Huntly, and Elizabeth Southall Clarke, by the Rev. John Francis Ribble, rector, assisted by the Rev. W. W. Brander of Baltimore, in St. Paul's Church, Newport News, Va. So. Ch., July 1, 1897

GOWDEY
Lemuel Alston, of Paris, Tex., and Lucy Logan, only d. of the rector and Mrs. J. W. Keeble, by the Rt. Rev. Alexander Charles Garrett, D.D., LL.D., Bishop of the Diocese of Dallas, assisted by the bride's father, the Rev. James Walter Keeble, at Abilene, Tex. So. Ch., June 10, 1905

GRAMMER
Frederick Louis, and Anne, eldest d. of John T. and Katharine A. McKennan, all of Pittsburgh, Pa., by the Rev. Dr. Julius E. Grammer, in Pittsburgh, Pa. So. Ch., May 31, 1894
William S., formerly of Baltimore and now of Newfoundland, and Harriet Arnett, d. of the late John Thompson McKennan of Pittsburgh, by the Rev. Dr. Carl E. Grammer, the brother of the groom, at the home of James Hancock, the brother-in-law of the bride, at Wayne, Pa. So. Ch., Oct. 8, 1904

GRAVES
Richie Morris, d. of the late Capt. Richard Morris Graves and Susan Kean Graves of "Linden", Orange Co., Va., and John Peyton McGuire, Jr., by the Rev. Landon R. Mason, at "Forkfield", the residence of Dr. Lewis S. Pendleton, Louisa Co., Va. So. Ch., June 27, 1895

GREET
William Demont, late of Huntsville, Ala., and Eleanor Love, youngest d. of the Rev. T. F. and Cornelia Mayo Martin of Nashville, Tenn. and sister of the officiating clergyman, the Rev. Mayo Cabell Martin, rector of the parish, in St. Clement's Church, El Paso, Tex. So. Ch., May 12, 1900

GREGORY
Ellen, youngest d. of the late Dr. Thos. Gregory of Hanover Co., Va., and George Harrison, eldest s. of Janetta Carter and W. A. P. Morris of Richmond, Va., by the Rev. S. S. Hepbron, in St. Paul's Church, Hanover Co., Va. So. Ch., Apr. 29, 1897

GRIER
Claude Lacy, of Tokushima, Japan, formerly of North

MARRIAGE NOTICES IN THE SOUTHERN CHURCHMAN WITH DATES OF PUBLICATION

Carolina, and the Rev. John Mercer Blair of Kiahing, China, formerly of Virginia, by the Rev. S. K. Hope assisted by the Rev. W. B. McIlvaine, at Yokohama, Japan. So. Ch., Sept. 23, 1897

GRIFFITH
J. H. (The Rev.), of Bristow, N.C., and Mellie Greennough, d. of the late A. C. Acton of Alexandria, by the Rev. P. P. Phillips, in St. Paul's Church, Alexandria. So. Ch., May 13, 1897

GRINNAN
Andrew Glassell (The Rev.), rector of Christ Church, Point Pleasant, W.Va., and Anne Cazonove, youngest d. of Dr. Chas. L. C. Minor of Baltimore, Md., by the Rev. R. G. Jett, rector, assisted by the Rev. Wm. F. Gardner of Maryland, in Emmanuel Church, Staunton, Va. So. Ch., Oct. 24 and 31, 1895

Helen Glassell, and Jaquelin Smith Ware, by the Rev. S. S. and the Rev. J. W. Ware, at "Brampton", Madison Co., Va. So. Ch., Nov. 3, 1900

GROSH
Sarah Katherine, d. of Warren R. and Pauline Grosh, and the Rev. Giles B. Cooke, by the Rt. Rev. Dr. Wm. F. Adams, in St. Mary's Church, North East, Md. So. Ch., May 12, 1898

GRUBB
Sarah Annette, of Live Oak, Fla., and Sidney Nelson Conner of Quitman, Ga., in St. Luke's Church, Live Oak, Fla. So. Ch., Sept. 22, 1906

HACKETT
H. Vernon, and Jennie Bushby, both of Hanover Co., Va., by the Rev. S. S. Hepbron, rector, in Fork Church. So. Ch., Oct. 14, 1897

HAGER
Eldridge Herbert, of Max Meadows, Va., and Nona Bolling, d. of Sterling Claiborne, by the Rev. A. P. Gray, in St. Mark's Church, New Glasgow, Va. So. Ch., Dec. 12, 1895

HAILE
John R., and Eliza Clayborne, d. of the late B. E. and L. R. Wright of "Shelba", Essex Co., Va., by the Rev. Mr. Thompson, in St. Paul's Church, Essex Co., Va. So. Ch., Sept. 5, 1895

HALES
Susie Cosby, of Fredericksburg, Va., and N. A. Orr, M.D., of Belmont, N.C., by the Rev. F. Bouldin, at Houston, Va. So. Ch., Apr. 14, 1906

HALL
Virginius, and Anne, d. of Robert Haxall Fisher, by the Rev. F. S. Stickney, in Monumental Church, Richmond. So. Ch., Aug. 15, 1895

HAMMOND
Kensey John (The Rev.), of Wilmington, Del., and Carrie, d. of James P. Machen of Fairfax Co., Va., by the Rt. Rev. George W. Peterkin assisted by the Rev. R. A. Castleman of Bel Air, Md., in Emmanuel Church,

MARRIAGE NOTICES IN THE SOUTHERN CHURCHMAN WITH DATES OF PUBLICATION

HARRIS
    James H., of Richmond, and Mary Lewis Dimmock, by the Rev. William Byrd Lee, at "Sherwood", Gloucester Co., Va. So. Ch., Apr. 30, 1896

HARRISON
    Carter H., and Catherine Cooke, d. of the late Robert Randolph Duval of Richmond, Va., by the Rev. R. C. Jett, at the residence of Mrs. J. E. B. Stuart, Staunton, Va. So. Ch., July 2, 1896

    Susie R., of Hanover Co., Va., and James H. Murray of West River, Md., by the Rev. S. S. Hepbron, at the residence of the bride's aunt, Mrs. Mary E. Noland. So. Ch., Jan. 9, 1896

HEMINGWAY
    George S., of South Carolina, and Janie, d. of Mrs. E. M. and the late Edward Scott, by the Rev. A. B. Tizzard, at Manakin Farm, Powhatan Co., Va. So. Ch., Oct. 15, 1896

HENNEMAN
    John Bell (Prof.), of South Carolina, and Marion, d. of Col. Robert T. and Sallie E. Hubard, by the Rev. E. W. Hubard, at Chellowe, Buckingham Co., Va. So. Ch., Oct. 14, 1897

HEPBURN *
    Charles Lovin, s. of the officiating clergyman, and Elizabeth Ellerson Newport of Washington, D.C., by the Rev. S. S. Hepburn*, in Baltimore, at the residence of Mr. William Hull. So. Ch., Apr. 27, 1899

    Lloyd Powell, s. of the Rev. S. S. Hepburn*, and Harriott A., d. of Michael Brayton, Esq. of Utica, by the Rev. E. F. H. J. Massey, rector of St. Luke's P. E. Church, in Utica, N.Y. So. Ch., Aug. 20, 1904

    Selina Lloyd, only d. of the officiating clergyman, and Nicholas Snowden Hopkins of Waverly, Gloucester Co., Va., by the Rev. Sewell S. Hepburn*, in Fork Church, Hanover Co., Va. So. Ch., Jan. 20, 1900

    Sewell S., Jr., M.D., of West River, and Annie McCaleb, eldest d. of Mrs. Augusta and the late Elliott Burwell, by the Rev. Mr. Plummer, at St. John's Church, West River, Anne Arundel Co., Md. So. Ch., May 26, 1900

    Thomas Norval, of Virginia, s. of the officiating clergyman, and Katherine M., d. of the late A. A. Houghton, Esq. of Buffalo, N.Y., by the Rev. Sewell S. Hepburn* assisted by the Rev. Peregrine Wroth, in Christ Church, Baltimore, So. Ch., June 25, 1904**

HERBERT
    Margaret Reid, d. of A. T. Herbert, Esq., and Charles F. Feast of Baltimore, Md., by the Rev. William R. Savage, at "Sunnyside", near Kempsville, Princess Anne Co., Va. So. Ch., May 13, 1897

HESSLER
    Mathilde, of Helena, Mont., and Capt. Wm. B. Cochran, U.S.A., by Bishop Brewer, at Helena, Mont. So. Ch., Sept. 24, 1904

HEWETSON
    Mary, second d. of the late Rev. John Hewetson, M.A.,

* Given as printed
** This seems to be a correction of a notice which appeared in the issue of June 18, 1904

MARRIAGE NOTICES IN THE SOUTHERN CHURCHMAN WITH DATES OF PUBLICATION

former rector of Measham, and the Rev. Edward W. Appleton, D.D., rector of St. Paul's Church, Choltenham, Pa., by the Rev. Joseph Hewetson, M.A., vicar, brother of the bride, assisted by the Rev. Henry C. Potter, D.D., Bishop of New York, in St. Lawrence's Church, Measham, Derbyshire, England. So. Ch., July 22, 1897

HOFF
Charles Worthington, and Violet Hand Browne, both of Baltimore Co., Md., by the Rev. W. H. H. Powers, at Trinity Church, Towson, Md. So. Ch., July 2, 1896

HOPKINS
Ellen Louise, d. of the late Stephen M. Hopkins of Providence, R.I., and Roger B. Atkinson of Staunton, Va., by the Rev. Wm. J. Moody, in St. Philip's Church, Atlanta, Ga. So. Ch., Sept. 15, 1906

Mary E., and Stephen G. Cowan, by the Rev. P. F. Sprigg. So. Ch., Dec. 13, 1894

Nicholas Snowden, of Waverly, Gloucester Co., Va., and Selina Lloyd, only d. of the officiating clergyman, the Rev. Sewell S. Hepburn, at Fork Church, Hanover Co., Va. So. Ch., Jan. 20, 1900

HORNER
Elizabeth Braxton, d. of the late Dr. Frederick Horner, U.S. Navy, of Marshall, Va., and Philip Francis DuPont, s. of the late Dr. Aloxis DuPont, in Christ Church rectory, Christiana Hundred, Del. So. Ch., June 17, 1905

Francis Wyeth, formerly of Fauquier Co., Va., and Jean Eleanor, d. of the late Mr. James G. Howden of Montreal, Canada, at Derby Line, Vermont. So. Ch., Nov. 10, 1906

Mary Blair, of the "Moorings", Fauquier Co., Va., and the Rev. John S. Bunting, B.D., assistant rector of Holy Apostle Episcopal Church, Philadelphia, Pa., by the Rev. J. J. Norwood, rector of Whittle Parish*, and the Rev. Oscar Bunting of Petersburg, Va., in Trinity Church, Marshall, Fauquier Co., Va. So. Ch., June 16, 1898

HOUGHTON
Katherine M., d. of the late A. A. Houghton, Esq. of Buffalo, N.Y., and Thomas Norvel Hepburn** of Virginia, s. of the officiating clergyman, the Rev. Sewell S. Hepburn** assisted by the Rev. Peregrine Wroth, in Christ Church, Baltimore. So. Ch., June 25, 1904 ***

HOWARD
Benjamin Chow, and Katherine H. Brown, by the Rev. Edwin B. Niver, in Baltimore, Md. So. Ch., Apr. 28, 1898

Mary Eloise, of Richmond, Va., and Francis Elliott Shoup, by the Rt. Rev. Thomas F. Gailor, S.T.D., in St. Margaret's Chapel, Columbia Institute, Columbia, Tenn. So. Ch., Jan. 6, 1898

HOWDEN
Jean Eleanor, d. of the late James G. Howden of Montreal, Canada, and Francis Wyeth Horner formerly of Fauquier Co., Va., at Derby Line, Vermont. So. Ch., Nov. 10, 1906

---

* Whittle Parish is in Fauquier County, Virginia (Jour. Va., 1941, p. 17)
** Given as printed
*** This seems to be a correction of a notice which appeared in the issue of June 18, 1904

MARRIAGE NOTICES IN THE SOUTHERN CHURCHMAN WITH DATES OF PUBLICATION

HOXTON
    Archibald Robinson, of the Episcopal High School, and Sara Purvis, eldest d. of Charles S. Taylor, Esq. of Alexandria, by the Rt. Rev. A. M. Randolph, D.D., at St. Paul's Church, Alexandria. So. Ch., Jan. 2, 1904

    Eliza Griffith, of Alexandria, Va., gr.d. of the late Rev. Dr. Charles Minnigerode, and Legh Wilber Reid, also of Alexandria, Va., by the Rt. Rev. Alfred M. Randolph, uncle of the bride, in St. Paul's Church, Alexandria, Va. So. Ch., Dec. 6, 1894

HUBARD
    Lila C., and Clifford Cabell Robinson, by the Rev. G. S. Sommerville assisted by the Rev. Frank Stringfellow, in Christ Church, Norwood, Nelson Co., Va. So. Ch., July 8, 1897

    Marion, d. of Col. Robert T. and Sallie E. Hubard, and Prof. John Bell Honneman of South Carolina, by the Rev. E. W. Hubard, at Chellowe, Buckingham Co., Va. So. Ch., Oct. 14, 1897

    Mary Randolph, d. of Col. James L. Hubard of "Tyo Brooke", Nelson Co., Va., and Edward Miles Mathewes of Laurens, S.C., by the Rev. Frank Stringfellow, in Trinity Church, Nelson Co. So. Ch., Nov. 19, 1896

    Robert Thurston, of "Tye Brooke", Nelson Co., Va., and Lula Carleton, d. of Prof. James Moss of the University of Mississippi, by the Rev. Mr. McKnight, in St. Philip's Church, Atlanta, Ga. So. Ch., Mar. 4, 1897

HUDSON
    Robert Gibboney, of Pulaski, Va., and Margaret Douglas Scarburgh of Princess Anne, Md., by the Rev. David Barr of Rock Creek Parish, D.C., in Grace Church, Baltimore. So. Ch., June 25, 1896

HUFFMAN
    Ada Lena, only d. of James S. Huffman, and William C. Thacker, Jr., by the Rev. Thomas E. Locke, at Blenheim. So. Ch., Feb. 13, 1896

HUNDLEY
    Larkin (Dr.), s. of the officiating clergyman, and Grace, d. of the Hon. Geo. Wm. Garnett, by the Rev. Dr. Hundley, at "Cottage Park", Essex Co., Va., the home of the bride. So. Ch., Apr. 19 and 28, 1900

    Lucy Temple, youngest d. of the Rev. J. H. Hundley, D.D., and Dr. John F. Anderson, surgeon in the marine service, by the Rt. Rev. F. M. Whittle, D.D., at the home of the bride's uncle, Dr. J. M. Hundley, at Montague, Essex Co., Va. So. Ch., Nov. 16, 1899

    Poyton (Dr.), of Montague, Va., and Frances Williams, d. of Dr. Claude Boxley of Markham, Va., by the Rev. Thomas Atkinson, at St. Barnabas' Church, Baltimore. So. Ch., Apr. 28, 1900

HUNTER
    Solomon Keeling, and Mary Arlington James, both of Princess Anne Co., Va., by the Rev. William R. Savage, by candle-light, in Eastern Shore Chapel, near Virginia Beach. So. Ch., Sept. 14, 1899

    William N., of Kansas City, Mo.,

MARRIAGE NOTICES IN THE SOUTHERN CHURCHMAN WITH DATES OF PUBLICATION

and Mattie Murton, d. of George Crutchfield and adopted d. of Mr. and Mrs. R. J. Murton of Richmond, Va., by the Rev. Carroll M. Davis, D.D., Dean, in Christ Church Cathedral, St. Louis, Mo. So. Ch., Apr. 9, 1904

HUNTING
George C. (The Rev.), rector of St. Paul's Church, Virginia City, Nev., and Mary G. Pullman of Washington, D.C., by the Rev. Samuel Unsworth, in Trinity Church, Reno, Nev. So. Ch., Nov. 1, 1894

HUTSON
Bertha Stanyarne, d. of Mr. and Mrs. John C. Hutson, and the Rev. William Boo Sams, rector of Trinity Church, Abbeville, S.C., by the Rev. A. E. Cornish assisted by the Rev. T. W. Clift, rector of the parish, at Aiken, S.C. So. Ch., June 24, 1905

INGRAM
Anne Elizabeth (Mrs.), and Timothy Ward Wood, both of Manchester, Va., by the Rev. Edgar N. Dickerson, in St. Luke's, Blackstone, Va. So. Ch., Sept. 26, 1903

IRVINE
G. Sinkler (Dr.), and Eva S., d. of Capt. Fleming Saunders, by the Rev. Chiswell Dabney, at the residence of the bride's parents. So. Ch., Dec. 3, 1896

JAMES
Alonzo E., and Orion, d. of Edgar E. and Blanche McAlpine Burroughs, all of Princess Anne Co., Va., by the Rev. Wm. R. Savage, at Eastern Shore Chapel. So. Ch., May 27, 1897
Mary Arlington, and Solomon Keeling Hunter, both of Princess Anne Co., Va., by the Rev. William R. Savage, by candle-light, in Eastern Shore Chapel, near Virginia Beach. So. Ch., Sept. 14, 1899

JOHNSON
Agnes Langhorne, d. of Dr. Nicholas Johnson, and Augustus Clemons Finley, by the Rev. Dr. Finley of Fishersville, Va., at Mammoth, W.Va. So. Ch., June 29, 1899

JOHNSTON
Christopher (Dr.), and Madeline Tasker, d. of the late Capt. Richard Lloyd Tilghman, U.S. Navy, of "Grosses", Talbot Co., Md., by the Rev. J. S. B. Hodges, in Emmanuel Church, Baltimore, Md. So. Ch., June 10, 1897

JOLLIFFE
Grace Merryman, and James A. Addison, by the Rev. F. S. Stickney, at the residence of the bride's uncle, Dr. George W. Jones, in Richmond, Va. So. Ch., June 25, 1896

JONES
Alexander T., of Frederick Co., Va., and Emily C., d. of the officiating minister, the Rev. Bishop F. M. Whittle, at the home of the bride, in Richmond. So. Ch., Oct. 20, 1898
Blair, of Chicago, Ill., and Alice Page, d. of Thomas Walker Lewis of Albemarle Co., Va., by the Rev. E. Valentine Jones, brother of the groom, assisted by the Rev. Mr. Smoot, rector of Christ Church, Alexandria, Va.

MARRIAGE NOTICES IN THE SOUTHERN CHURCHMAN WITH DATES OF PUBLICATION

So. Ch., Nov. 14, 1903
Edmund, Jr., of Lenoir, N.C., and Joan Honry Wilcox, by the Rov. William R. Savage of Blowing Rock, N.C., at Dresden, the home of the bride, in Ashe County, N.C. So. Ch., June 23, 1906

Frankie B., d. of the late Maj. Francis B. Jones, C.S.A. and Mrs. Susan Peyton Jones, and Joseph M. Barton, by the Rev. James Grammer, D.D., at Carysbrooke, Frederick Co., Va. So. Ch., May 25, 1899

Mabel Frances, d. of Fielding Lewis and Nellie Stanley Jones, and William Arthur Liptrap of Ramah, Colorado, by the Rev. W. Strother Jones, D.D., at Woodside, near Fruita, Colorado. So. Ch., Sept. 12, 1903

Norvell Caskie, d. of Philip B. Jones, and Egbert G. Leigh of Richmond, Va., by the Rev. Le Bas Cross of Rapidan, at Piedmont, the home of the bride, Orange Co., Va. So. Ch., July 26, 1902

JOYNER
Wilmer, of Dover, N.J., and Lena K., d. of the late Dr. M. A. Pinckard of Virginia, by the Rev. J. R. Joyner, father of the groom, at St. Bartholomew's Church, Baltimore, Md. So. Ch., Jan. 14, 1905

KEEBLE
Lucy Logan, only d. of the rector and Mrs. J. W. Keeble, and Lemuel Alston Gowdy of Paris, Tex., by the Rt. Rev. Alexander Charles Garrett, D.D., LL.D., Bishop of the Diocese of Dallas, assisted by the bride's father, the Rev. James Walter Keeble, at Abilene, Tex. So. Ch., June 10, 1905

KEFERSTEIN
Carl B., of Washington, D.C., and Elizabeth Taylor, d. of Mrs. John Boyle Tilford, by the Rev. R. L. Howell, rector of St. Margaret's Church, assisted by the Rev. W. H. Milton, rector of Henshaw Memorial Church, Baltimore, at the residence of the bride's mother, No. 1336 New Hampshire Ave., Washington, D.C. So. Ch., Feb. 20, 1896

KENNEDY
Alvis (Dr.), and Nella Allen, eldest d. of Mr. and Mrs. George A. Preston, by the Bishop of Dallas assisted by the rector of the parish, the Rev. J. B. C. Beaubien, at Trinity Church, Bonham, Tex. So. Ch., Dec. 5, 1903

S. R. Mullorg, of New Orleans, and Sarah Strother, d. of Col. R. H. Logan of Salem, Va., by the Rev. Berryman Green, rector of Christ Church, in Alexandria, Va. So. Ch., May 25, 1899

KENT
Sue Payton, d. of Mrs. Joseph Ferdinand Kent of Wytheville, Va., and Edmund Fontaine Broun of Charleston, W.Va., by the Rev. Mercer P. Logan, D.D., in St. John's Episcopal Church, Wytheville, Va. So. Ch., Jan. 30, 1904

KIMBER
Robert Bootman (The Rev.), and Genevieve Louise, d. of Vernon A. Tylor, by the Rev. Joshua Kimber, father of the groom, assisted by the Bishop of Long Island, in the Church of the Resurrection, Richmond Hill, L.I. So. Ch., June 28,

MARRIAGE NOTICES IN THE SOUTHERN CHURCHMAN WITH DATES OF PUBLICATION

1894
KINSOLVING
  Arthur Barksdale, s. of the late Dr. O. A. Kinsolving and rector of Christ Church, Brooklyn, N.Y., and Sallie Archer Bruce, eldest d. of Mr. Thomas Seddon Bruce and gr.d. of the late General Joseph R. Anderson and of Charles Bruce, in St. Paul's Church, Richmond. So. Ch., Feb. 13, 1896
KIRKPATRICK
  James (The Rev.), of Pittsburgh, Pa., and May, d. of the Rt. Rev. Thomas U. Dudley, D.D., by the Rt. Rev. the Bishop of Kentucky, in Emmanuel Church, Middleburg, Va. So. Ch., Sept. 12, 1895
KUYK
  C. R. (The Rev.), and Mary Powell, d. of the Hon. Charles F. Goodwyn, Judge of Nottoway Co. Court, by the Rev. Pike Powers of Richmond, assisted by the Rev. J. W. Ware of Farmville, in Christ Church. So. Ch., Apr. 16, 1896

ANNOUNCEMENTS OF APPROACHING MARRIAGES
1915 - 1940

ANNOUNCEMENTS OF APPROACHING MARRIAGES RECORDED IN THE SOUTHERN CHURCHMAN, 1915-1940

BETTICHER
    Charles E. (The Rev.), editor of the *Spirit of Missions*, and Margaret C. Graves of Baltimore. Dec. 22, 1917

BLANDFORD
    Virginia Hayden, and the Rev. Arthur Machen Lewis, rector of St. James' Church, Oskaloosa, Iowa, by the Rt. Rev. Harry Sherman Langley, in the Church of the Atonement, Philadelphia. So. Ch., Aug. 12, 1916

DORST
    Thomas C., D.D. (The Rt. Rev.), Bishop of the Diocese of East Carolina, and Lauriston, d. of Mr. and Mrs. J. H. Hardin of Wilmington, N.C., in Wilmington. So. Ch., Dec. 4, 1915

GRAVES
    Margaret C., of Baltimore, and the Rev. Charles E. Betticher, editor of the *Spirit of Missions*. So. Ch., Dec. 22, 1917

HARDIN
    Lauriston, d. of Mr. and Mrs. J. H. Hardin of Wilmington, N.C., and the Rt. Rev. Thomas C. Dorst, D.D., Bishop of the Diocese of East Carolina, in Wilmington. So. Ch., Dec. 4, 1915

HEMINGWAY
    Honora Mary of Sherbourne, Vermont, and the Rev. George Putnam Huntington of Providence, R.I. So. Ch., Apr. 30, 1938

HUNTINGTON
    George Putnam (The Rev.), of Providence, R.I., and Honora Mary Hemingway of Sherbourne, Vermont. So. Ch., Apr. 30, 1938

KELL
    Robert C. (The Rev.), and Janet, d. of the Rev. and Mrs. Arlington A. McCallam of Washington. So. Ch., July 20, 1940

INDEX TO MARRIAGE NOTICES
IN
THE SOUTHERN CHURCHMAN
1835 - 1941

Prepared by

The Historical Records Survey of Virginia,
Service Division
Work Projects Administration

Sponsored by

The Virginia Conservation Commission

VOLUME II
L - Z

Richmond, Virginia
The Historical Records Survey of Virginia
May 1942

The Historical Records Survey Projects

    Sargent B. Child, Director
    Kathleen Bruce, State Supervisor

Research and Records Programs

    Harvey E. Becknell, Director
    Milton W. Blanton, Regional Supervisor
    James A. McAleer, State Supervisor

Service Division

    Florence Kerr, Assistant Commissioner
    Blanche M. Ralston, Chief Regional Supervisor
    Ella G. Agnew, State Director

WORK PROJECTS ADMINISTRATION

    Howard O. Hunter, Commissioner
    Roy Schroder, Regional Director
    Russell S. Hummel, State Administrator

PREFACE

In January 1936 the Historical Records Survey, a nation-wide project of the Works Progress Administration now the Work Projects Administration, was organized by Dr. Luther H. Evans who served as director until March 1, 1940, when he was succeeded by Mr. Sargeant B. Child.

The survey began to function in Virginia in March 1936 as part of the Federal Writers' Project of which Dr. H. J. Eckenrode was State Director, and Dr. Lester J. Cappon of the University of Virginia part-time Technical Assistant. In November 1936, when the Historical Records Survey became independent of the Federal Writers' Project, Dr. Cappon was appointed part-time State Director. At the same time Miss Elizabeth B. Parker, a former supervisor of the Survey, was appointed Assistant State Director. On September 5, 1939, the Historical Records Survey of Virginia became a Statewide non-Federal project, with Miss Parker as State Supervisor.

The Historical Records Survey was consolidated with the Survey of Federal Archives in Virginia on January 1, 1940, to constitute a new Historical Records Survey project. Dr. Kathleen Bruce, who had been in charge of Federal Archives work in Virginia since September 16, 1936, was appointed State Supervisor and Miss Parker, Assistant State Supervisor. Miss Parker resigned from the Historical Records Survey on April 29, 1940. Mrs. Helen D. Bullock was appointed Assistant State Supervisor on June 24, 1940. Mrs. Bullock, who resigned on September 19, 1940, was succeeded on January 20, 1941, by Dr. Katharine Elizabeth Crane.

The Historical Records Survey of Virginia has published indexes to vital statistics as well as inventories of county, church, and Federal archives. The INDEX TO MARRIAGE NOTICES IN THE SOUTHERN CHURCHMAN is the third index to vital statistics, recorded in religious weeklies, which the project has published. The preceding volumes were the INDEX TO OBITUARY NOTICES IN THE RELIGIOUS HERALD, 1828-1938, December 1940, and the INDEX TO MARRIAGE NOTICES IN THE RELIGIOUS HERALD, Vol. I, A-L, August 1941, and Vol. II, M-Z, September 1941. The RELIGIOUS HERALD is a Baptist weekly published in Richmond. Indexes to vital statistics in religious papers have not commonly been undertaken by the Historical Records Survey projects; the volumes compiled in Virginia had to be specially authorized. The importance of making available to the public vital statistics in religious journals published in Virginia is better understood when one knows something of the history of the recording of marriages in Virginia and the fate of some of the older marriage records.

In the colonial period an official register of marriages, births, and deaths was kept in every Virginia parish, and copies of each registration were returned to the county clerk of the parish vestry and the head of the family. The official registrations of births and deaths ceased with the separation of Church and State in Virginia, not long after the establishment of the Commonwealth, and were not resumed until the middle of the nineteenth century. The official registration of marriages, however, never lapsed. This was because the Commonwealth made provision for maintaining the same sort of paper record as that which had been required under the colonial government, apart from the official register of marriages kept by the parish vestry. According to the State Bureau of Vital Statistics at Richmond, hundreds of these scraps of papers which testify to marriages celebrated in Virginia are still

i

Preface

extant, but it has not been determined whether they are the licenses that were required, or a marriage bond, or a combined license and marriage bond.

Under the code of 1849, the clerk of the county court and the clerk of the corporation court were required to register in books to be kept for that purpose every marriage license which they issued. These books are known as the registers of marriages. By an act of April 11, 1853, which became effective July 1, 1853, the clerk of the county court and the clerk of the corporation court were each required to "transmit to the auditor of public accounts a copy of his register of marriages during the preceding year, and on or before the first day of March in each year." In 1853, also, the General Assembly passed an act to take effect January 1, 1854, which ordered every minister to record every marriage celebrated by him and to return the certificate to the clerk of the county court or of the corporation court of the county or city in which the marriage was celebrated. At the same time, the clerk of the county court and the clerk of the corporation court were required to record in special volumes a note of the licenses which they issued, and to report to the commonwealth's attorney for prosecution any minister who failed to return the licenses. Finally in 1919 the marriage certificates and licenses were combined. Since then the note of licenses issued has been recorded in the marriage register, as is also the detailed information that is given in the combined marriage certificates and licenses. This information constitutes the permanent record of marriages.

Under the act effective July 1, 1853, which ordered the clerk of the county court and the clerk of the corporation court each to send annually to the auditor of public accounts a copy of his register of marriages, the first concentration of marriage records was brought about in Virginia. An act of 1918, approved March 9, 1918, required the auditor of public accounts to turn over to the newly created State Bureau of Vital Statistics all copies of the register of marriages which had been filed with him. Thereafter the clerk of the county court and the clerk of the corporation court were required to send copies of their registers of marriages direct to the State Bureau of Vital Statistics on or before March first in each year. An act of 1938, approved March 10, 1938, required that a duplicate of each combined license and certificate instead of a copy of each register of marriages be sent to the State Bureau of Vital Statistics. In this bureau are now concentrated the records of marriages celebrated in Virginia since June 30, 1853, although on account of inadequate storage, theft, fire, and other calamities which occured before the State Bureau of Vital Statistics was created, a number of these official records of marriages are missing. There is now being prepared under the sponsorship of the State Bureau of Vital Statistics an index to the marriage records dating from 1870 which are in its custody. In due course the index will probably be extended back to 1853. The Historical Records Survey has had no part in this index, which is not being constructed for publication but for use in the office of the State Bureau of Vital Statistics.

The INDEX TO MARRIAGE NOTICES IN THE SOUTHERN CHURCHMAN points to a recording of the marriages, over a period of 106 years, of approximately between six and seven thousand persons, most of whom were either members of the Protestant Episcopal Church in Virginia, or otherwise directly connected with it, or connected with it through descent from Virginia Episcopalians. The indexes to marriage notices published by the Historical Records Survey make amends in part for the lack of concentration of official records of marriages in Virginia prior to 1853. They provide a means for obtaining information on

Preface

some of the marriages celebrated from 26 to 35 years prior to 1861 in those eastern counties whose records were removed to the state courthouse at Richmond during the War for Southern Independence and destroyed when the courthouse was burned in the evacuation fire. Thus they point to substitute records for some of those early official marriage records dating from 1853 which are missing from the file of the State Bureau of Vital Statistics. The file of the SOUTHERN CHURCHMAN on which the index is based belongs, except the volume for 1900, to the Southern Churchman Publishing Company which maintains an office in the basement of the Mayo Memorial Church House, Richmond. That part of the file for the years, January 2, 1835-1893 and 1907 to 1942, was placed by the Company in the custody of the Virginia State Library. These volumes are available to searchers in the reading room of the State Library. Bound volumes for 1894-1899 and 1901-1906 are in the office of the Company, but steps are being taken to place them also in the custody of the State Library. Meanwhile they were made available to Historical Records Survey workers through the courtesy of Mrs. Tate Irvine, news editor of the weekly. Through the kindness of the family of the Rev. Meade Clark, D.D., rector of St. James' Church and editor of the SOUTHERN CHURCHMAN when he died in 1914, a project worker was permitted to collect the marriage notices in Dr. Clark's bound volume for 1900. Thus there are no gaps in the volumes for 1894-1906. Two workers specially assigned to the task checked the file in the custody of the Virginia State Library and found the following gaps: 1840-January 15, 1847; January 1, 8, 22, and 29, 1852; May 31-November 15, 1861 (apparently not published); March 14, 1862; June 10 and 24, 1864; July 8 and 22, 1864; August 5 and 19, 1864; September 2, 9, 16, and 30, 1864; October 7, 14, and 28, 1864; November 2, 1864; and March 22-August 24, 1865 (unknown whether any issues published). The number for November 4, 1842, and that for May 29, 1842, are in the SOUTHERN CHURCHMAN file of the College of William and Mary. The librarian, Dr. E. G. Swem, kindly had the marriage notices in these numbers copied for the Historical Records Survey.

In the volume January 17, 1850-January 6, 1853, in the custody of the State Library, the numbers for January 2 and 9, 1851, are bound immediately after the number for December 25, 1851, instead of at the beginning of 1851. Immediately following January 9, 1851, is January 15, 1852, then consecutively January 20 and 27, 1853. Then comes February 5, 1852. From this date, the numbers for 1852 are complete and are arranged in chronological order. As has already been stated in the list of gaps in the file, the numbers for January 1, 8, 22, and 29, 1852, are missing. These errors in binding are mentioned to save the time of students who are unfamiliar with the file.

Many workers by their alertness, their precision, and their energy have made it possible to complete the INDEX TO MARRIAGE NOTICES IN THE SOUTHERN CHURCHMAN before there becomes effective a reorganization of the Historical Records Survey with other statewide projects to form a clerical project under the War Services Program of the Work Projects Administration. The entry of the United States into the second World War caused a turnover of WPA workers so rapid that it is impracticable to list the names of all who took part in the work. The greater part of it on both Volume I and Volume II was checked, edited, and compiled under the supervision of Mrs. Neva Thompson. When Mrs. Thompson resigned on April 15, 1942, to accept a clerical position under the War Department, Mrs. Jennette A. Walls was assigned to take her post. The index was completed under the supervision of Mrs. Walls, who as a successful clerical worker is herself a product of the Historical Records Survey, since

Preface

she had never been trained or gainfully employed until she was assigned to the project's Richmond office. Mrs. Anne R. Morrison served as chief proofreader, and Mr. Ernest E. Williams as foreman of field work.

As in the INDEX TO MARRIAGE NOTICES IN THE RELIGIOUS HERALD, no attempt has been made to correct any name, spelling, date, or statement made in the printed notice except in the rare case of the spelling of the name of a well known rector, such, for instance, as the name Minnigerode, or in cases where names of Virginia counties were misspelled. In all other cases, names, dates, and statements have been reproduced exactly as they are printed in the SOUTHERN CHURCHMAN. When a second notice of the same marriage appeared, however, the notice which seemed to be the correct notice was indexed, and a reference to the other notice made in a footnote. This symbol * is also used to point out anything in an entry so unusual that it might appear to be an error of the copyist, the typist, or the editor. In certain cases, such as that of a parish for which no geographical location is cited, or of a name like "Big Lick", the settlement which later became the city of Roanoke, an explanatory footnote is given. In four major respects does editorial procedure depart from that employed in the INDEX TO MARRIAGE NOTICES IN THE RELIGIOUS HERALD. The first of these is the inclusion in each entry of the name of the paper immediately before the date of the issue in which the marriage notice appeared. The second is the inclusion of all facts given in the printed notice. The third is the inclusion of Marriage Announcements, A-K, in Volume I. The fourth is a cross reference printed under the maiden name of a widow to the entry which records her re-marriage. By citing "So. Ch." before the date of each issue, the possibility of one's assuming that the date cited is the date on which the marriage was celebrated is done away with. By citing all facts, it is believed that much additional pertinent information is furnished, such as the name of the domicile of the bride and of the groom before marriage, or the name of the place where the marriage was celebrated. In a number of cases the names of members of the families other than those of the parents are also cited. The advantage of having the marriage announcements, A-K, in Volume I and the cross references relative to widows does not have to be explained.

For clarity, as in the earlier index, a double entry is given for every marriage notice, one under the name of the groom, the other under the maiden name of the bride. In seeking a name, the searcher should be sure to look for the letter under "Addenda", if he has failed to find it under the letter alphabetically arranged in the body of the text. As all facts in the printed marriage notices are included in the entries, which number approximately between three thousand and thirty-five hundred, it was absolutely necessary to publish the index in two volumes.

The brief historical sketch which traces the founding of the weekly and the names and dates of service of its editors was written by Dr. Bruce.

Kathleen Bruce

Kathleen Bruce
State Supervisor
Historical Records Survey

Richmond, Virginia
May 29, 1942

THE SOUTHERN CHURCHMAN

The SOUTHERN CHURCHMAN, a weekly, representing the evangelical thought within the Protestant Episcopal Church in the United States of America, is published in Richmond, Virginia, by the Southern Churchman Publishing Company, an independent, unincorporated company. The paper was founded, however, by an individual, one hundred and six years ago. The founder was the Rev. William Fitzhugh Lee, rector of St. John's Church, Richmond, September 1828-December 21, 1829, and afterward rector of Christ Church, Richmond.

According to the bishop of the Protestant Episcopal Church in Virginia who was the assistant bishop in 1835, William Fitzhugh Lee through his mother, Sally Lee, who married Edmund I. Lee of Alexandria, was the grandson of Richard Henry Lee of Chantilly, Westmoreland County, one of the outstanding Virginians of the American Revolution (Bishop /William/ Meade, OLD CHURCHES, MINISTERS, AND FAMILIES OF VIRGINIA, 1857, II, 143). Young Lee was compelled to give up his rectorship on account of his health. "As to body", wrote Bishop Meade, "Mr. Lee being little more than thin air, or a light feather ... his horse felt not the rider on his back but the people felt the weight and power of a strong mind ... he devoted himself to the press, and was the first editor of the Southern Churchman, establishing it at Richmond. He continued to edit the same until his part of the work was performed. When lying on a sick-bed, his proof sheets corrected, his selections made and editorials written, while propped up with bolsters and pillows thus to the last spending and being spent ..." (IBID, I, 460-61). Lee published the first issue of the SOUTHERN CHURCHMAN on January 2, 1835. He was only in his thirty-third year when he died on Friday, May 19, 1837, in Alexandria which was then in the District of Columbia. The weekly issue due on the day he died and on Friday, May 26, 1837, appeared as usual. Lee's indomitable spirit, his mind, and his energy had triumphed. He had established a journal which would live.

There was no break in the immediately succeeding issues. Beginning on June 2, and running through September 1, 1837, the space in which "William F. Lee, editor", had formerly been printed carried "Rev. Lucius M. Purdy, editor." Beginning with the issue of September 8, however, the space for the editor's name is blank until November 17, 1837, when "Rev. Z. Meade, editor", fills the blank. On leaving his congregation in Boston, Meade sought the restoration of his health "in the milder climate of Richmond and in the editorial chair" (IBID, II, 53). Without a break also, the paper is headed "Richmond", and the Richmond office address is given through December 31, 1839, although it has been said that when Lee left Richmond for Alexandria, he "moved his office with him" (The Editors ...", SO. CH., Jan. 5, 1935).

Because of a gap, 1840-January 15, 1847, in the only available files of this paper, the change in editors during these years, and the date of the removal of the office of the editor from Richmond could not be traced. The next available issue is dated January 22, 1847; it is headed "Alexandria, Va.", and the usual space for the editor's name shows "Rev. E. R. Lippitt, editor." Nine years later Lippitt was advertizing in the SOUTHERN CHURCHMAN (Sept. 26, 1856) his "Family School for Boys" in Alexandria. In 1846 the United States Government had retroceded to Virginia the territory in the District of Columbia which the General Assembly by an act of December 3, 1789, had ceded

The SOUTHERN CHURCHMAN

to the United States for the permanent seat of the Government. Lippitt's name as that of editor of the SOUTHERN CHURCHMAN appears for the last time in the issue of Friday, March 31, 1848. The issue of April 7, cites no editor's name but gives the names of the printers. In the issue of June 2, 1848, the "Rev. George A. Smith, editor", is recorded. Meanwhile, Bishop Meade wrote in the issue of May 26, 1848, "The editorial care of the Southern Churchman, our Diocesan paper, has recently, as you all know, been transferred to another editor. The Rev. George A. Smith, one of our esteemed ministers, has undertaken the charge of it." The significance of the paper for the diocese is implied in the bishop's words, "our Diocesan paper."

Smith edited the SOUTHERN CHURCHMAN for seven years; he published his farewell editorial in the issue of September 27, 1855. But the Rev. D. Francis Sprigg was to edit it for forty-four years. At the head of the issue of Friday, October 5, 1855, appears the new editor's motto, carried thereafter under his editorship, "Nisi Dominus Frustra" which he explained were "the first words of the 127th Psalm in the Vulgate version. The whole verse reads: 'Except the Lord build the house, they labor in vain that build it: except the Lord keep the city, the watchman waketh but in vain.'"

Having taken charge in 1855, Sprigg was editor of the SOUTHERN CHURCHMAN during the War for Southern Independence. When United States troops occupied Alexandria, he moved the paper to Richmond. No issue appeared after that which is headed Alexandria, May 24, 1861, until that of November 22, 1861, which was the earliest war issue printed in Richmond. The last known issue which appeared during the war is dated March 15, 1865. Each war issue printed in Richmond was cut to a single sheet until November 9, 1864, when the single sheet which had been shortened on April 8, 1864, was folded over, thus making two small sheets. When the war ended Sprigg returned to Alexandria, and started afresh with "New Series, Vol. I, No. 1," August 31, 1865. The paper was printed in Alexandria until he was called to Richmond in 1879 to be rector of the Moore Memorial Church, the forerunner of the present Grace and Holy Trinity. Sprigg moved the paper with him, and the first issue of the new series to be headed Richmond appeared on April 17, 1879. The office of the SOUTHERN CHURCHMAN remained thereafter in Richmond. In the issue of September 28, 1899, Sprigg wrote: "With this number of the Southern Churchman my connection with it ceases. I have no pecuniary interest in it, or responsibility; no editorial management of it. Its good-will has been bought by the 'Protestant Episcopal Churchman Company' who have appointed Rev. William Meade Clark of St. James' Church, Richmond, its editor. In taking leave of its subscribers, some of whom are my friends and have been, I do so with more or less sorrow. I have been connected with it for forty-four years."

The name of the editor and that of the publishing company is not printed in the issues of 1899. Beginning with the issue of March 3, 1900, the Southern Churchman Publishing Company is cited as the publisher.

The Rev. Meade Clark served as editor until his death in 1914. His successors were the Rev. Edward L. Goodwin, D.D., 1914-1920, the Rev. W. Russell Bowie, D.D., 1920-1923, the Rev. Joseph B. Dunn, D.D., 1924-1927, Langbourne M. Williams, 1927-1931, the first layman to serve as editor, the Rev. Charles W. Sherrin, D.D., 1931-September 10, 1938, the Rev. Samuel B. Chilton, September 10, 1938-May 1940, and the Rev. Beverley M. Boyd, May 1940---.

ABBREVIATIONS

Com.	....	Commodore
Co.	....	County
d. of	....	daughter of
gr.d.	....	granddaughter
gr.s.	....	grandson
Rev.	....	Reverend
Rt. Rev.	....	Right Reverend
s. of	....	son of
So. Ch.	....	Southern Churchman
Ven.	....	Venerable

CONTENTS

	Page
Preface	i
The Southern Churchman	v
Abbreviations	vii
Letter L	1
Letter M	32
Letter N	87
Letter O	99
Letter P	103
Letter Q	138
Letter R	139
Letter S	163
Letter T	211
Letters UV	240
Letter W	245
Letters XYZ	295
Addenda: Letters L - Z	301
Announcements of Approaching Marriages, 1915 - 1940	327

INDEX TO MARRIAGE NOTICES
IN
THE SOUTHERN CHURCHMAN
1835 - 1941

LACKLAND
  Charlotte S., d. of the late
  Samuel Lackland, Esq. of
  Jefferson Co., and Thomas
  E. Sublett formerly of
  Powhatan Co., Va., by the
  Rev. Mr. Ambler, in the
  Episcopal Church, Charles
  Town. So. Ch., Apr. 22,
  1859
  Fanny, d. of the late Thomas
  Lackland of Jefferson Co.,
  and Lawrence Washington of
  "Wareland", Fauquier Co.,
  by the Rev. Wm. H. Meade,
  in Zion Church, Charles Town,
  Jefferson Co., Va. So.
  Ch., Aug. 3, 1876
LACY
  Cora Virginia, of Lynchburg,
  and Thomas M. Fendley of
  Chesterfield Co., by the
  Rev. T. M. Carson, in St.
  Paul's Church, Lynchburg.
  So. Ch., Apr. 28, 1870
  Edward N., and Olivia B.
  Noble, by the Rev. A. B.
  Tizzard, at the residence
  of Edward Gates, Esq.,
  Chesterfield Co., Va. So.
  Ch., May 12, 1887
  Frank M., and Emily Johnson,
  by the Rev. Pendleton
  Brooke, at the residence of
  the bride's mother, Dresden,
  Ohio. So. Ch., May 2,
  1878
  Richmond T., Esq., and
  Ellen, eldest d. of Mrs.
  Sarah Lane, by the Rev.
  Park Farley Berkeley, at
  Vaucluse, Amelia. So.
  Ch., May 8, 1835
  Richmond T., Jr. of New
  Kent Co., Va., and Lizzie
  Winston of Caroline Co.,
  Va., by the Rev. T. H.
  Lacy, at Shepherd's Hill,
  the residence of the
  bride's mother. So. Ch.,
  Oct. 19, 1876
  T. H. (The Rev.), of New
  Kent Co., Va., and Mary B.
  Goodwin of Wytheville, Va.,
  by the Rev. F. D. Goodwin
  assisted by the Rev. D. F.
  Forest, in St. John's
  Church, Wytheville, Va.
  So. Ch., Sept. 18, 1873
  William Jones, of Grand
  Junction, Col., and
  Norah Elizabeth Goolrick,
  by the Rt. Rev. C. K.
  Nelson, D.D., Bishop of
  Atlanta, assisted by Dr. J.
  Horace Lacy, at the home of
  the bride's mother, Mrs.
  William Barber Goolrick, in
  Fredericksburg, Va. So.
  Ch., Jan. 18, 1913
LAIN
  William M., of Washington,
  D.C., and Maria Louisa,
  d. of John G. Mosby, Esq.
  of Richmond, Va., by the
  Rev. Wm. H. Hart, in
  Richmond, Va. So. Ch.,
  Aug. 11, 1837
LAIRD
  Marion, and the Rev. John S.
  Higgins, rector of the
  Church of the Advent,
  Chicago, by Bishop Stewart
  assisted by the Rev. Walter
  C. Bihler, in Christ Church,
  Woodlawn. So. Ch., Sept.
  23, 1933
  Philip D., and Ella G.
  Magruder, by the Rev. Wm.
  H. Laird, in St. John's
  Church, Olney, Montgomery
  Co., Md. So. Ch., Dec.
  31, 1885
  William, Jr., and Anna Key,

MARRIAGE NOTICES IN THE SOUTHERN CHURCHMAN WITH DATES OF PUBLICATION

d. of the late Wm. G. Ridgely, Esq., by the Rev. S. Ridout, in Georgetown, D.C. So. Ch., June 21, 1866

William H. (The Rev.), of Mecklenburg Co., Va., and Rosa I., d. of the Rev. Dr. Packard of Fairfax Co., by Bishop Johns, in the chapel of the Theological Seminary, Fairfax Co., Va. So. Ch., Sept. 9, 1869

LAKIN
Frances A., of Princess Anne Co., Va., formerly of Augusta, Me., and Benj. F. Lownsbery, Jr. of Norfolk, formerly of Jamestown, N. Y., by the Rev. W. R. Savage, in Emmanuel Church, Kempsville, Va. So. Ch., Oct. 10, 1889

LAMAR
Harriet Cazenove, of Wellesley, and Frank Cazenove Jones of New York City, by the Rev. Mr. Gardiner of Maryland and Bishop Peterkin of the Diocese of West Virginia, assisted by the Rev. J. T. Duryea, D.D. of Boston, at the residence of Mrs. Henry Durant, in Wellesley, Mass. So. Ch., July 12, 1883

LAMB
James C., Esq., of Richmond, and Loula Gray, d. of the late George L. Brockenbrough of Florida, by the Rev. Everard Meade, at the residence of Thomas W. Brockenbrough of Richmond Co. So. Ch., Mar. 3, 1881

Jas. C., of Richmond, Va., and Saide, eldest d. of Wm. F. Brockenbrough, Esq. of "Belleville", Richmond Co., Va., by the Rev. M. Johnson assisted by the Rev. B. D. Tucker of Norfolk, Va., in St. John's Church, Warsaw, Va. So. Ch., Jan. 7 and 14, 1886

John (Capt.), of Charles City Co., and Mattie R., d. of the officiating clergyman, the Rev. Dr. A. Wade, in the rectory, Charles City Co. So. Ch., Dec. 16, 1869

Mary Content, and John Donnell of Washington City, by the Rev. Thos. Gallaudet of St. Ann's, New York, assisted by the Rev. B. D. Tucker, at the residence of the bride's brother, Col. William Lamb, Norfolk. So. Ch., Apr. 28, 1887

LAMBERT
Lola Naomi, and Fitz-Hugh Ball Marshall, by the Rev. Norman Fitz-Hugh Marshall, at the home of the bride's parents, Mr. and Mrs. Walter Lambert, Monticello, Ark. So. Ch., June 24, 1911

LAMBETH
William Meredith, of New Orleans, and Georgianna Slacum of Alexandria, by the Rev. Chas. Dana. So. Ch., Aug. 16, 1839

LAMBIRE
Maurice W., of Georgetown, D.C., and Blanche, d. of Sam'l T. Ashby, Esq., of Culpeper Co., Va., by the Rev. Jno. S. Lindsay, in St. Stephen's Church, Culpeper C.H., Va. So. Ch., Dec. 25, 1873

LAMON
George M., and Alvernon H., d. of Daniel Anderson, Esq., all of Berkely Co., Va.,

MARRIAGE NOTICES IN THE SOUTHERN CHURCHMAN WITH DATES OF PUBLICATION

by the Rev. Wm. McGuire, at the residence of Franklin Bowley, Esq. So. Ch., Apr. 8, 1859

Robort*, and Bessie Keyes Burkhart, both of Martinsburg, by the Rev. Henry Thomas assisted by the Rev. Walter Q. Hullihen, in Trinity Church, Martinsburg. So. Ch., May 2, 1889

LANCASTER
J. J., and Phronia L., d. of Horace J. Moody, Esq., by the Rev. William S. Langford, in St. John's Church, Yonkers, N.Y. So. Ch., Dec. 9, 1875

LANE
Charles S., s. of Gen. C. S. Lane of the English Army, and Mrs. Alice F. Sandys, d. of the late Hon. R. N. Thweatt of Chesterfield Co., Va., by the Rev. A. B. Tizzard, in Trinity Church, Dale Parish, Chesterfield Co., Va. So. Ch., May 1, 1890

Elizabeth, d. of the late Albert A. Lane of Cleveland, Ohio, and the Rev. Howard Harper, rector of Grace Church, Waycross, Ga., by Bishop Reese, in Christ Church, Savannah. So. Ch., Dec. 21, 1935

Ellen, eldest d. of Mrs. Sarah Lane, and Richmond T. Lacy, Esq., by the Rev. Park Farley Berkeley, at Vaucluse, Amelia. So. Ch., May 8, 1835

H. B., and Sophie C., d. of Horace B. Hall, all of Fredericksburg, by the Rev. R. J. McBryde, at the residence of the bride's father. So. Ch., Jan. 19, 1882

Josephine J., and Joseph W. Chinn, both of Richmond Co., Va., by the Rev. Campbell Fair, D.D., at 384 Lauvale St., Baltimore, Md. So. Ch., Oct. 1, 1885

Julia H., d. of John W. Lane, Esq., of Amelia Co., Va., and Maj. Wm. A. Graham, Jr. of North Carolina, by the Rev. A. B. Tizzard, at the Oaks, the residence of the bride's father. So. Ch., June 17, 1864

Lizzie J., d. of the late John G. Lane, and William S. Daniel of Richmond, by the Rev. W. M. Clark, at the residence of the bride's brother, H. B. Lane, Fredericksburg, Va. So. Ch., Oct. 22, 1891

S. Helen, and the Rev. Auther S. Johns, by the Rt. Rev. John Johns and the Rev. E. C. Murdaugh, D.D., at Brompton, near Fredericksburg, Va. So. Ch., July 9, 1874

Sidney, and Mrs. Jane Ann McCarty, both of Richmond Co., by the Rev. Andrew Fisher, at Laurel Grove. So. Ch., Sept. 16, 1859

Thomas B. (Dr.), and Ellen Randolph Tabb, by the Rev. Jno. McGill, in Christ Church, Matthews Co. So. Ch., May 5, 1870

Wm. L., and Georgeanna Staton, both of Berlin, Worcester Co., Md., by the Rev. George S. Fitzhugh. So. Ch., Jan. 15, 1874

* Given as printed

MARRIAGE NOTICES IN THE SOUTHERN CHURCHMAN WITH DATES OF PUBLICATION

LANGHORNE
C. W., and Lou Belle, d. of Dr. Wm. S. Morris, all of Lynchburg, Va., by the Rev. T. M. Carson, in St. Paul's Church. So. Ch., Nov. 25, 1875

Charles M., of Richmond, Va., and Mrs. Llewellyn Johnson Eubank of Waco, Tex., at Roanoke, Va. So. Ch., Oct. 21, 1911

John D., and Nannie C., d. of George P. Tayloe of Roanoke Co., Va., by the Rev. Peter Tinsley. So. Ch., Jan. 8, 1864

Lydia, and George P. Craighill, both of Lynchburg, by the Rev. James P. Craighill and the Rev. T. M. Carson, in St. Paul's Church, Lynchburg, Va. So. Ch., Oct. 28, 1875

Nellie, d. of Col. Morris S. and Elizabeth C. Langhorne, and Arthur T. Powell, by the Rev. T. M. Carson, in St. Paul's Church, Lynchburg, Va. So. Ch., Oct. 14, 1880

Sallie W., of Botetourt Co., Va., and Dr. Nicholas Johnson of Kanawha Falls, W.Va., by the Rev. Edward H. Ingle, at Cloverdale, Botetourt Co., Va. So. Ch., Feb. 17, 1876

Thomas N., of Lynchburg, and Orra H., d. of Algernon S. Gray of Harrisonburg, Va., by the Rev. A. W. Weddell, at the residence of Foxhall A. Daingerfield, in Harrisonburg. So. Ch., Oct. 26, 1871

Thomas N., Jr., of Lynchburg, Va., and Anna K., eldest d. of Dr. R. N. and Mrs. Fannie D. Hewitt, by the Rev. B. W. Moseley, at Otter Hill, Campbell Co., Va. So. Ch., Oct. 17, 1878

LARMOUR
J. Worrall (The Rev.), and Mary Elizabeth, eldest d. of the late John B. Griswold of Goldsboro, by the Rt. Rev. Theodore B. Lyman, D.D., assisted by the Rev. Edward R. Rich, in St. Stephen's Church, Goldsboro, N.C. So. Ch., Feb. 21, 1878

LARSEN
Julia Louise, and R. Price Patterson, by the Rev. Thomas P. Baker, in Christ Church, Adam's Run, S.C. So. Ch., Nov. 25, 1911

LATANE
Henry W., and Martha Harvey, d. of Dr. Thomas C. Gordon, by the Rev. H. W. L. Temple assisted by the Rev. J. A. Latane, in St. John's Church, Tappahannock, Essex Co., Va. So. Ch., June 3, 1870

J. A., of Essex, and Mary Minor, eldest d. of the late J. Z. Holladay of Charlottesville, by the Rev. R. K. Meade. So. Ch., Nov. 16, 1855

Janet R. R., and Wm. Campbell, both of Essex Co., Va., by the Rev. H. W. L. Temple, in Essex Co. So. Ch., Jan. 2, 1868

Julia, d. of Bishop James A. Latane, and Clagget Jones, by the Rev. J. M. Rawlings, at Bewdley, King and Queen Co., Va. So. Ch., Apr. 15, 1880

Mary Susan, d. of Dr. James

MARRIAGE NOTICES IN THE SOUTHERN CHURCHMAN WITH DATES OF PUBLICATION

H. Latane, and Charles J. Sale, all of Essex Co., Va., by the Rev. John B. Newton, in St. John's Church, Tappahannock. So. Ch., Dec. 14, 1871

Nannie R., d. of Dr. James H. Latane, and R. L. Ware, all of Essex, by the Rev. H. W. L. Temple, at Mahockany. So. Ch., Dec. 7, 1860

William C. (The Rev.), rector of Washington Parish, and Susan, d. of John E. Wilson, Esq. of "Wakefield", Westmoreland Co., Va., by the Rev. Beverly D. Tucker, in St. Peter's Church, Oak Grove. So. Ch., Nov. 9, 1876

LATHAM
George Woodville, of Lynchburg, Va., and Louise C., d. of P. Calhoun, Esq. of Bridgeport, by the Rev. G. S. Coit, D.D., at Bridgeport, Conn. So. Ch., Sept. 30, 1859

LATROBE
B. H., Jr. (The Rev.), and Jennie Estelle, d. of the late G. W. Yates, Esq., by the Rev. A. M. Randolph assisted by the Rev. J. E. Cathell, in the Church of Our Savier, Baltimore. So. Ch., Dec. 11, 1873

Ferdinand C., of Baltimore, and Ellen Swann, d. of the late John R. Penrose of Philadelphia, by the Rev. J. Andrew Harris, at "Hillside", the residence of the bride's mother, at Chestnut Hill, Philadelphia. So. Ch., July 15, 1880

LAURIE
Lizziedelle, d. of the late Dr. Shepherd Laurie of Little Rock, Ark., and Geo. E. Pegram formerly of Albemarle Co., Va., by the Rev. F. R. Hanson, in Demopolis, Ala. So. Ch., May 12, 1870

LAUSTER
Ruth E., and the Rev. William Christian Roberts, rector of St. James' Parish, Monkton, Md., by Bishop Helfenstein assisted by the Rev. James A. Mitchell, in the Church of the Messiah, Hamilton, Baltimore, Md. So. Ch., Dec. 7, 1929

LAWRENCE
Bessie Allen, youngest d. of Capt. George and Mary R. Lawrence of Goochland C.H., and Oscar D. Derr, Esq., of Roanoke, Va., by the Rev. P. M. Boyden, in Grace Episcopal Church, at Goochland C.H., Va. So. Ch., June 17, 1886

Cassius M., of North Bingham, Pa., and Addie May, second d. of C. T. Shear, Esq., by the Rev. R. A. Castleman, at Sully, the residence of the bride's parents, near Chantilly, Fairfax Co., Va. So. Ch., June 29, 1893

J. P. (The Rev.), and Edmonia, fourth d. of the late Wm. H. Berkeley of King and Queen Co., Va., by the Rev. H. M. Jackson assisted by the Rev. Pike Powers, in Grace Church, Richmond, Va. So. Ch., Jan. 5, 1888

Juner P. (The Rev.), of St. Luke's Church, Petlar, Amherst Co., and Maggie L. Nevitt of Pohick, Fairfax

MARRIAGE NOTICES IN THE SOUTHERN CHURCHMAN WITH DATES OF PUBLICATION

Co., Va., by the Rev. Richard Ellerby, in Pohick Church. So. Ch., Feb. 3, 1876

R. H., and J. Margaret, youngest d. of the late Dr. O. W. Kean of Goochland Co., Va., by the Rev. P. M. Boyden, at Grape Ridge, the residence of the bride's mother. So. Ch., Jan. 24, 1889

Thomas Nevitt (The Rev.), rector of Nottoway Parish, Southampton Co., Va., and Virginia Elligood, d. of Mr. and Mrs. William Wyatt, by the Rev. John Cornick, in the Presbyterian Church at Belle Haven, Accomac Co., Va., the home of the bride. So. Ch., Nov. 13, 1909

William T., and Mary F. M., d. of the late R. S. Coxe, Esq. of Richmond, Va., and gr.d. of the late Dr. Wm. Smith Coxe of Burlington, N.J., by the Rev. R. S. Barrett, at the residence of the bride's mother, in Henrico Co., Va. So. Ch., Feb. 26, 1880

LAWSON
John W., M.D. (The Hon.), of Isle of Wight Co., Va., and Maggie Norfleet, youngest d. of Mrs. Louisa R. Urquhart, by the Rev. Edw. W. Wroth, at Warrique, the residence of the bride's mother, Southampton Co., Va. So. Ch., Feb. 15, 1877

LAY
Henry C. (The Rev.), and Eliza W., d. of Roger B. Atkinson of Lunenburg Co., Va., by the Rev. Edmund Withers, at Sherwood. So. Ch., May 28, 1847

LEA
John W. (The Rev.), rector of St. Mark's Church, St. Albans, W.Va. and Trinity Church, Huntington, W.Va., and Mrs. K. H. W. Wilson, d. of the late Col. R. W. Wyatt, by the Rev. J. S. Hanckel, D.D., at the residence of the bride's mother, Clifton, Va. So. Ch., June 5, 1884

LEACH
Charles H., Esq. of Fauquier Co., and Hortensia Tyler of Front Royal, by the Rev. R. T. Berry, at Front Royal. So. Ch., Oct. 12, 1865

LEACHMAN
Mary Lewis, d. of J. T. Leachman of Prince William Co., Va., and R. Carey Buck, M.D. of Fauquier Co., by the Rev. Arthur P. Gray, at the residence of the bride's parents. So. Ch., Dec. 1, 1881

LEADBEATER
Faith M., of Alexandria, and the Rev. John Ridout of Grace Church, Petersburg, by the Rev. Ernest M. Stires of West Point, Va. and the Rev. Theron Rice of Alexandria, at Alexandria, Va. So. Ch., Nov. 17, 1892

Mary, and the Rev. James Davis Gibson, rector of Christ Church, Wellsburg, W.Va., by the Rev. John S. Gibson assisted by the Rev. Wm. J. Morton, in Christ Church, Alexandria, Va. So. Ch., Dec. 18, 1909

LEAKE
Fannie Kean, and the Rev.

MARRIAGE NOTICES IN THE SOUTHERN CHURCHMAN WITH DATES OF PUBLICATION

J. Lindsay Patton of Ashland, by the Rev. T. M. Ambler, at the residence of the bride's father, William J. Leake, Ashland, Va. So. Ch., July 3, 1890

Shelton F., of Terrell, Tex., and Kate D. Nelson of Culpeper, Va., by the Rev. W. T. Roberts, in St. Stephen's Church, Culpeper. So. Ch., Dec. 4, 1884

LEARY
David, and Betty Booker, both of Amelia Co., Va., by the Rev. P. F. Berkeley, at the residence of the bride's mother. So. Ch., Dec. 12, 1872

LEATHEM
Mary, youngest d. of Robert H. Leathem, Esq., and the Rev. J. Dudley Ferguson, rector of Trinity Church, Canaseraga, Diocese of Western New York, by the Rev. Erskine M. Rodman, D.D., rector of Grace Church, Plainfield, N.J., and Dean of Convocation. So. Ch., July 6, 1882

LEATHERBURY
Edward R. (Dr.), and Elizabeth M., d. of Dr. T. P. Bagwell, by the Rev. J. M. Chevers, in Onancock. So. Ch., Dec. 28, 1855

Thomas E., of Northampton, and Joanna T. West of Accomac, by the Rev. J. B. Craighill, in Northampton Co., Va. So. Ch., Feb. 11, 1869*

LEATON
Jane, of Canada East, and the Rev. Charles H. Page of Hedgesville, Berkeley Co., W.Va., by the Rev. R. K. Meade, in Charlottesville. So. Ch., June 23, 1870

LEAVELL
Anne E., of Jefferson Co., W.Va., and John Moncure Daniel, Esq. of Louisville, Ky., by the Rev. W. H. Meade assisted by the Rev. C. E. Ambler and the Rev. W. T. Leavell, at Media, Jefferson Co., W.Va. So. Ch., Nov. 5, 1874

Edmund S., and Harriet A. Spindle, by the Rev. E. C. McGuire, in Spotsylvania Co. So. Ch., Sept. 22, 1837

Elizabeth H. T., and J. W. Ware, Jr., by the Rev. J. W. Ware and the Rev. P. N. McDonald, at "Media", Jefferson Co., W.Va. So. Ch., Mar. 18, 1916

Francis K. (The Rev.), of Coal Valley, and Lillie, eldest d. of Mrs. Charles B. Thurston of Cumberland, by the rector, the Rev. P. Nelson Meade assisted by the Rev. W. T. Leavell, in Emmanuel Church, Cumberland. So. Ch., Feb. 4, 1886

Julia Yates, and Maj. Edward H. McDonald of Louisville, Ky., formerly of Virginia, by the Rev. W. T. Leavell assisted by the Rev. J. E. Poindexter, at Media, near Charles Town, Va. So. Ch., Oct. 21, 1869

Lottie E., and Josiah P. Gayle of Spotsylvania, by the Rev. E. Meade, at Oakland, the residence of the bride's mother, Mrs. Mary C. Leavell, Essex Co., Va.

---

* A notice appears in the issue of Feb. 4, 1869 identical with this, except that "Leatherbury" is written "Leatherburt"

MARRIAGE NOTICES IN THE SOUTHERN CHURCHMAN WITH DATES OF PUBLICATION

So. Ch., Dec. 19, 1878
Mary A., d. of the Rev. W. T. Leavell, and Capt. Wm. R. Johnson of Cresent, Fayette Co., W.Va., by the Rev. Dallas Tucker assisted by the Rev. F. K. Leavell, in Zion Church, Charles Town, Jefferson Co., W.Va. So. Ch., Nov. 19, 1885

Nannie S., and Edwin Blackwell, professor in Bethel Academy, by the Rev. W. T. Leavell assisted by the Rt. Rev. Bishop Peterkin, in St. Stephen's Church, Culpeper C.H. So. Ch., Nov. 28, 1878

W. T. (The Rev.), and Emma, d. of Garrett Wynkoop, Esq., of Hedgesville, by the Rev. J. Owen Darsey assisted by the Rev. R. D. Roller, in Mt. Zion Church, Hedgesville, Berkeley Co., W.Va. So. Ch., June 7, 1883

Wm. T. (The Rev.), rector of Westover Parish, Charles City Co., and Anne, d. of John Yates, Esq. of Jefferson Co., by the Rev. Richard T. Brown. So. Ch., Nov. 26, 1847

LECKIE

George W., of Rockbridge Co., and Ella M., d. of Richard M. Cleveland of Albemarle Co., Va., by the Rev. T. E. Locke, at the residence of the bride's father. So. Ch., Apr. 18, 1889

LEE

Alice C., of Fredericksburg, and Dabney J. Waller of Caroline Co., by the Rev. J. G. Shackelford of Trinity Church, at the residence of A. H. Conway, Fredericksburg, Va. So. Ch., Nov. 7, 1889

Alice Dandridge, d. of the Rev. Dr. and Mrs. Charles H. Lee, and Lt. Dwight Harvey, U.S.N., s. of Mr. and Mrs. Carlyle Harwood Day of St. Paul, Minn., by the Rev. David Cady Wright, D.D., rector of Christ Church, Savannah, Ga., assisted by the Rev. Robb White, Jr., rector of St. Thomas' Church, Thomasville, Ga., in historic Christ Church, Frederica, St. Simons Island, Ga. So. Ch., Aug. 4, 1934

Annie E., youngest d. of Cassius F. Lee, Esq. of Fairfax Co., and J. Thompson Cole of the Japan Mission, by the Rev. William F. Gardner assisted by the Rt. Rev. George W. Peterkin, D.D., in the Chapel of the Theological Seminary near Alexandria, Va. So. Ch., May 6, 1886

Annie E., of Fredericksburg, and John P. Seaman of Caroline Co., by the Rev. J. G. Shackelford of Trinity Church, at the residence of A. H. Conway, Fredericksburg, Va. So. Ch., Nov. 7, 1889

Belle, d. of Charles S. Lee, Esq. of Clarke Co., Va., and Charles C. Garrett of Wilmington, Del., by the Rev. T. F. Martin, at "The Anchorage", the residence of the bride's father. So.

MARRIAGE NOTICES IN THE SOUTHERN CHURCHMAN WITH DATES OF PUBLICATION

Ch., Dec. 30, 1875
Cassius F., Jr., and Mary, eldest d. of Richard Loyd, Esq., by the Rev. Wm. F. Meade, at Belmont, Alexandria Co., Va. So. Ch., June 5, 1873
Cazenove G., of Fairfax Co., Va., and Marguerite L., youngest d. of the late E. Irenie Du Pont of Brandywine, by the Rt. Rev. G. W. Peterkin of West Virginia assisted by the Rev. D. D. Smith, in Christ Church, Brandywine, Del. So. Ch., Sept. 29, 1881
Charles Henry, Jr. (The Rev.), and Susan Randolph Cooke, by the Rev. John P. Tyler and the Rev. William R. Lee, in Christ Church, Millwood, Clarke Co., Va. So. Ch., Oct. 5, 1893
Constance Gardner, d. of Cassius F. Lee, Esq., and the Rev. Geo. W. Peterkin of Richmond, by the Rev. Dr. Peterkin, at Monokin, Fairfax Co., Va. So. Ch., Nov. 5, 1868
Daniel Murray, and Nannie E., d. of the late J. B. Ficklin*, Esq. of Falmouth, by the Rev. Dr. Murdaugh, in St. George's Church, Fredericksburg, Va. So. Ch., Oct. 21, 1875
Edmonia Louise, d. of Charles S. Lee, Esq. of Clarke Co., Va., and William, s. of the late Henry Haigh, M.A., Archdeacon of the "Isle of Wight" and Vicar of Newport, England, by the Rev. P. P. Phillips, in Grace Church, Berryville, Va. So. Ch., Apr. 26, 1888

Edmund I., Jr., of Jefferson Co., W.Va., and Rebecca L., d. of Col. A. T. M. Rust, by the Rev. H. B. Lee assisted by the Rev. R. T. Davis, at Rockland, Loudoun Co., Va. So. Ch., Sept. 30, 1875
Edmund J., Jr., Esq., and Henrietta, d. of the late Daniel Bedinger, by the Rev. E. Cornwall, at Southport, Conn. So. Ch., Sept. 18, 1835
Edmund J. (Dr.), and Mary, d. of Charles Smith, Esq. of Philadelphia, by the Rt. Rev. Geo. W. Peterkin assisted by the Rev. Francis D. Lee, in the Church of the Holy Trinity, Philadelphia. So. Ch., Dec. 18, 1879
Edward Henry, of Chicago, and Ruth Sheldon, d. of the Bishop of Oklahoma and Mrs. Francis Key Brooke, by the Rt. Rev. Dr. Daniel Sylvester Tuttle, Presiding Bishop of the Church, in the chapel of St. Luke's Church, Evanston, Ill. So. Ch., Oct. 7, 1916
Edward Jennings, and Bessie R. Neilson, by the Rev. Dr. W. H. Neilson, father of the bride, assisted by the Rev. J. H. Aspinwall of Washington, D.C., in Trinity Church, Shepherdstown. So. Ch., Oct. 5, 1893
Eliza Atkinson, d. of Col. R. H. Lee of Clarke Co., Va., and the Rev. James R. Winchester of Maryland, by the Rev. Wm. B.

* Given as printed

MARRIAGE NOTICES IN THE SOUTHERN CHURCHMAN WITH DATES OF PUBLICATION

Lee and the Rev. Joseph R. Jones, in Christ Church, Millwood, Clarke Co., Va. So. Ch., Sept. 26 and Oct. 10, 1878

Elizabeth G., and the Rev. A. D. Pollock, pastor of the Presbyterian Church on Shockoe Hill, Richmond, Va., by the Rev. Mr. Wilson, at Presque Isle, Culpeper Co. So. Ch., Dec. 3, 1835

Fannie, d. of Maj. Baker P. Lee, and Henry Wise Booker, by the Rev. J. J. Gravatt, in St. John's Church, Hampton, Va. So. Ch., June 29, 1882

Fitzhugh (Gen.), of Richlands, Va., and Ellen Bernard, d. of the late George D. Fowle of Alexandria, by the Rev. Geo. H. Norton, D.D., at the residence of the bride's uncle, Philip B. Hooe, Esq. So. Ch., Apr. 27, 1871

Francis D. (The Rev.), and Annie Henderson, d. of the late H. Allen Taylor, by the Rev. Dr. Norton, at Alexandria, Va. So. Ch., May 6, 1880

Francis P. (The Rev.), and Sarah Ann, only d. of the late B. B. Cooper, Esq., by the Rev. John Woart, at Camden. So. Ch., Oct. 27, 1837

Frank A. (Dr.), of Lynchburg, Va., and Kate J., d. of Maj. S. T. Peters, by the Rev. W. L. Dolly, at "Delacarlia", in Bedford Co., Va. So. Ch., Oct. 8, 1891

H. B. (The Rev.), and Lucy J., only d. of J. Keith and F. L. Marshall and great gr.d. of Chief Justice Marshall, all of Fauquier Co., Va., by the Rev. Robb White assisted by the Rev. James R. Winchester, at Marven, the residence of the bride's parents. So. Ch., Sept. 27, 1877

Harriotte Hopkins, d. of Cassius F. Lee, and Thomas S. Taliaferro, Esq., of Gloucester Co., Va., by the Rev. C. B. Dana, in Alexandria. So. Ch., Dec. 7, 1860

Helen S., d. of Geo. W. Lee, and A. J. Skinner, by the Rev. Frank Page, at the residence of the bride's father in Fairfax Co. So. Ch., June 7, 1883

Henry Tucker (The Rev.), of Winchester, Va., rector of Trinity Church, Society Hill, S.C., and Fannie Fraser, d. of J. C. Whaley, Esq. of Edisto, by the Rt. Rev. W. B. W. Howe, D.D. assisted by the Rev. John Johnson, rector of St. Philip's Church, in St. Philip's Church, Charleston, S.C. So. Ch., Apr. 30, 1874

Henry W. (The Rev.), minister of Christ Church, Springfield, and Lydia M., d. of the Hon. Marcus Morton of Taunton, by the Rt. Rev. Bishop Griswold, at Taunton, Mass. So. Ch., Apr. 26, 1839

Hortensia H., d. of Judge Lee of New Lexington, Ohio, and

MARRIAGE NOTICES IN THE SOUTHERN CHURCHMAN WITH DATES OF PUBLICATION

the Rev. Henry Beeman of New Lexington, Ohio, by the Rev. Pendleton Brooke, at Clarksburg, W.Va. So. Ch., Oct. 20, 1870

Ida, d. of Edmund I. Lee Esq., and Armstead T. M. Rust, Esq., of Loudoun, by the Rev. C. W. Andrews, D.D., at Bedford, near Shepherdstown. So. Ch., Oct. 5, 1860

John M. (Maj.), and Nora, youngest d. of Dr. Wm. Bankhead of Caroline Co., by the Rev. B. E. Habersham, at Signal Hill (the residence of B. L. Winston, Esq., in Hanover Co.) So. Ch., Nov. 16, 1871

John R., Esq., and Elizabeth Mann P. Nelson, both of Halifax, Va., by the Rev. Charles Dresser, at the parsonage of Antrim Parish. So. Ch., Jan. 15, 1836

Katharine Randolph, and Dr. John R. Guerrant, both of Virginia, by the Rev. Frank Stringfellow, in Trinity Church, Rocky Mount. So. Ch., July 28, 1892

Laura, only d. of Mrs. Lillie Lee and the late Lt. Col. Wm. F. Lee, C.S. A., and gr.d. of the late Rev. W. F. Lee of Richmond, Va., and Lt. Wm. A. Simpson of the Second Artillery, U.S.A., by the Rev. Mr. Hubbard, at Shepherdstown, W. Va. So. Ch., May 20, 1880

Laura D., d. of Maj. Charles H. Lee of Loudoun Co., and George H. Burwell of Richmond, by the Rev. W. H. Johnson, at "Dunbarton", the residence of the bride's father. So. Ch., Oct. 4, 1877

Lewis H., and Georgie G., eldest d. of the officiating minister, the Rev. Jno. S. Hansbrough, in St. Thomas' Church, Orange C. H., Va. So. Ch., Nov. 9, 1876

Mary A. M., and James E. Caldwell, Esq., both of Petersburg, Va., by the Rev. C. J. Gibson, in Grace Church, Petersburg, Va. So. Ch., Dec. 12, 1856

Mary Morrison, d. of the late Rev. Wm. F. Lee, and the Rev. Robert A. Castleman, by the Rev. Dr. Sparrow, in the chapel of the Theological Seminary. So. Ch., July 29, 1852

Matilda T., only d. of the late Lt. John Hite Lee, U.S. Navy, and John Roy Alcombe, Esq., by the Rev. Wm. H. Kinckle, at Lynchburg, Va. So. Ch., Jan. 4, 1856

Maud, d. of Judge Geo. H. Lee, and J. J. Ducan, by the Rev. J. F. Woods, at Clarksburg, W.Va. So. Ch., Nov. 2, 1871

Mildred, d. of the late Charles Carter Lee of Windsor, Powhatan Co., and Dr. John T. Francis of Norfolk, by the Rev. Martin Johnson, in St. Luke's Church, Powhatan Co. So. Ch., Feb. 23, 1888

Philip De Catesby, and

MARRIAGE NOTICES IN THE SOUTHERN CHURCHMAN WITH DATES OF PUBLICATION

Zelia R. Baden, both of Fairfax Co., by the Rev. R. A. Castleman, at the residence of Mr. Yates, near Chantilly, Va. So. Ch., Oct. 26, 1893

Richard H., of Jefferson Co., Va., and Evelyne, d. of the late Wm. B. Page of Clarke Co., Va., by the Rev. J. T. Hooff, at Milwood, Clarke Co., Va. So. Ch., June 30, 1848

Robert E., and Charlotte, d. of R. Barton Haxall, Esq., by the Rev. George Woodbridge of Richmond, at "Rocklands", Orange Co., Va. So. Ch., Nov. 23, 1871

Thomas A., of Staunton, Va., and Caroline C., d. of H. S. Wattles of Alexandria, Va., by the Rev. Dr. George H. Norton assisted by the Rev. Reverdy Estill and the Rev. Frank Stringfellow, in St. Paul's Church, Alexandria, Va. So. Ch., July 7, 1881

Thomas W., and Maggie A., only d. of Alex. Haight, Esq., all of Fauquier Co., Va., by the Rev. Jno. McGill, at Sully, the residence of the bride's parents. So. Ch., Oct. 15, 1874

William Byrd (The Rev.), rector of Emmanuel Church, Culpeper Co., Va., and Jane Blackburn, d. of the late Dr. Randolph Kownslar, by the Rev. P. P. Phillips and the Rev. A. P. Gray, in Grace Church, Berryville, Va. So. Ch., Oct. 9, 1879

Wm. F. (Lt.), U.S. Army, and Lillie M., d. of the late Dr. Richard Parran of Jefferson Co., Va., by the Rev. C. W. Andrews, D.D., in Trinity Church, Shepherdstown, Va. So. Ch., Sept. 23, 1859

Wm. H. Fitzhugh (Lt.), of U.S. Army, and Georgianna, d. of the late George Weckham of U. S. Navy, by the Rev. Dr. Wade, at Shirley, in Charles City Co. So. Ch., Apr. 15, 1859

Wm. K., and Mary X. Henderson, both of Lancaster, Va., by the Rev. E. Withers. So. Ch., Dec. 12, 1856

Wm. K., Jr., and Nannie L. Munday, by the Rev. H. L. Derby, in Grace Church, Lancaster, Va. So. Ch., Mar. 31, 1881

LEFEBVRE
Mary W., d. of the late H. P. Lefebvre, and Wm. B. Isaacs, Jr. of Richmond, Va., by the Rev. J. S. B. Hodges, D.D., in Baltimore. So. Ch., Apr. 24, 1873

LEFROY
J. Arthur, of County Down, Ireland, and Sallie Watson, d. of Jno. H. Montague, by the Rev. J. Peterkin, in St. James' Church, Richmond, Va. So. Ch., Apr. 19, 1877

LEFTWICH
Maria L., d. of the late John O. Leftwich, and J. Morton Speece, M.D., all of Bedford Co., by the Rev. Richard H. Wilmer, So. Ch., Feb. 27, 1857

MARRIAGE NOTICES IN THE SOUTHERN CHURCHMAN WITH DATES OF PUBLICATION

W. Blanche, and J. Thompson Coles, both of Pittsylvania Co., Va., by the Rev. C. O. Pruden, at "Forest Grove", the residence of the bride's mother, Mrs. M. B. Coles, Pittsylvania Co., Va. So. Ch., Feb. 5, 1885

LEGG
Edward C., and Louise B. Price, both of Kent Island, Md., by the Rev. P. D. Thompson, in Christ Church, Kent Island, Md. So. Ch., June 19, 1884

Edward M., and Sallie R. W., d. of Wm. B. Goodhard, Esq. of Kent Island, Md., by the Rev. P. D. Thompson, at 547 Franklin St., Baltimore. So. Ch., Oct. 2, 1879

Wm. H., and Ida M. Thompson, both of Kent Island, Md., by the Rev. P. D. Thompson, in Christ Church Rectory, Kent Island, Md. So. Ch., Nov. 21, 1889

LEIBERMAN
Charles D., of Washington, D.C., and Jonnie D. Ferrall of Prince George's, by the Rev. Jno. Collins McCabe, D.D., at the residence of the bride's grandfather, Robert Clark, Esq., in Prince George's Co., Md. So. Ch., Nov. 7, 1867

LEIGH
B. W., Martinsburg, W.Va., and Olive, youngest d. of the late E. F. Buckingham, Washington, D.C., by the Rev. Wallace Carnahan, Little Rock, Ark., at the home of Mr. and Mrs. Warren Taylor, Bastrop, La. So. Ch., Oct. 5, 1893

Chapman Johnson, of New York City, and Anne Campbell, youngest d. of Hill Carter, Esq., by the Rev. A. M. Randolph, at Shirley, Charles City Co., Va. So. Ch., June 29, 1860

John P., Jr., and Fannie P., d. of Dr. G. W. Cowdery, all of Norfolk, by the Rev. N. A. Oakeson, in St. Paul's Church. So. Ch., May 3, 1861

Kate Randolph, d. of Egbert G. Leigh, Esq., and T. Poyton Giles, gr.s. of the late Hon. Wm. B. Giles of Virginia, by the Rev. A. B. Tizzard, in Richmond, Va. So. Ch., Sept. 22, 1887

Lottie, of Aylett, King William Co., Va., and Argyle Carneal of Richmond, by the Rev. W. T. Roberts, at the residence of the bride's mother. So. Ch., Jan. 3, 1889

Lucy Amelia, and William J. P. Whitlock, by the rector, the Rev. John London, in St. James' Church, Louisa, Va. So. Ch., Mar. 18, 1911

Mary Grammer, and John Charles Randolph Taylor, at Houston, Va. So. Ch., July 20, 1907

Mary Page, of Aylett, King William Co., Va., and Frederick T. Nason of San Angelo, Tex., by the Rev. Pendleton Brooke, in St. David's Church, King William Co., Va. So. Ch., Feb. 24, 1887

Mary W., d. of Dr. J. R. Leigh, and William H. Talliferro, by the Rev.

MARRIAGE NOTICES IN THE SOUTHERN CHURCHMAN WITH DATES OF PUBLICATION

F. N. Whaley, in Clarksville, Va. So. Ch., Feb. 23, 1888

Pattie K., of Aylett, Va., and Matthew M. Puller of Baltimore, Md., by the Rev. Pendleton Brooke, in St. David's Church, King William Co., Va. So. Ch., Aug. 2, 1888

Rebecca, d. of the late Judge William Leigh, and George W. Williams of Richmond, by the Rev. William H. Laird, at the residence of Benjamin Watkins Leigh, Esq., in Mecklenburg Co., Va. So. Ch., Jan. 14, 1875

Sue W. (Mrs.), and the Rev. Charles Morris of Ashland, Va., by the Rev. W. A. Alrich, at the residence of the bride's father, Dr. Lemmon, near Castle Craig, Campbell Co., Va. So. Ch., Sept. 7, 1876

Wm., of Halifax C.H., Va., and Louise C. Carrington, by the Rev. D. M. Wood, at the residence of the bride's father, Col. H. A. Carrington. So. Ch., Oct. 11, 1883

Williams, and Mary White, d. of the late Edward Colston, Esq., by the Rev. D. Francis Sprigg, at Honeywood, Berkeley Co., Va. So. Ch., Nov. 23, 1854

LEITH
Willie, of Loudoun Co., and James C. Crane of Jefferson Co., W.Va., by the Rev. T. F. Martin, at the residence of Dr. Plaster, Snickersville. So. Ch., June 5, 1873

LEMMON
Flora T., d. of Dr. R. T. Lemmon, and Eugene D. Saunders of New Orleans, by the Rev. W. A. Alrich, at Green Meadows, the residence of the bride's father. So. Ch., Apr. 8, 1880

Geo. E., of Lynchburg, and Priscilla S. Clark of Martinsville, Va., by the Rev. J. T. Clark assisted by the Rev. W. M. Clark and the Rev. Thomas J. Packard, in St. Luke's Church, Clover. So. Ch., Feb. 7, 1884

Lucy Paxton, and N. H. Massie, both of Danville, by the Rev. R. C. Jett, at the Arlington Hotel, Danville, Va. So. Ch., Sept. 12, 1889

LEMOINE
Josephine, d. of the late Fereol Lemoine, and Chas. W. Smith, by the Rev. Edmund Withers, in Richmond Co. So. Ch., July 2, 1858

Oscar M., and Maria G., d. of John S. and Olivia J. Braxton, all of Emmerton, Va., by the Rev. A. M. Randolph, in Emmanuel Church, Baltimore. So. Ch., Aug. 3, 1876

Virginia, second d. of the late Moreau Lemoine of Fairfax Co., Va., and Alexander Innis of Rapidan Parish, La., by the Rev. R. T. Brown, at Mount Wellington, Fairfax Co. So. Ch., Apr. 16, 1858

LESTER
Sallie P., d. of John Lester, Esq., and Matthew W. Yarrington,

MARRIAGE NOTICES IN THE SOUTHERN CHURCHMAN WITH DATES OF PUBLICATION

 all of Richmond, by the
 Rev. Mr. Kepler, in St.
 John's Church, Richmond,
 Va. So. Ch., Nov. 28,
 1856
LETCHER
 John Davidson, of Lexington,
 Va., and Louisa Leonard,
 d. of the late Tazewell
 Taylor, Esq., of Norfolk,
 Va., by the Rt. Rev. A. M.
 Randolph, D.D., LL.D.,
 assisted by the Rev. John
 J. Lloyd, D.D., at Norfolk,
 Va. So. Ch., May 30, 1908
 Margaret K., d. of the late
 ex-Governor Letcher of Vir-
 ginia, and Robert J. Showell
 of Maryland, by the Rev.
 Dr. McBryde, at the resi-
 dence of the bride's mother,
 at Lexington, Va. So. Ch.,
 Mar. 6, 1884
 Marguerite Robertson, d. of
 Mrs. Anna Meade and the
 late Dr. Robert P. Letcher
 of Henderson and gr.d. of
 the late Hon. Tucker
 Woodson of "Churchland",
 Jassamine Co., Ky., and
 N. L. Bronaugh of Nicholas-
 ville, Ky., by the Rev.
 Russell Cecil. So. Ch.,
 Jan. 1, 1885
LEVERING
 Thomas H., of Toledo,
 Ohio, and Lucy Kerr of
 Clarksville, Tenn., by
 the Rev. J. Hervey
 Hundley, at Locust
 Grove, Middlesex Co., Va.
 So. Ch., Oct. 29, 1891
LEVIN
 Thomasine Gist, d. of the Hon.
 Lewis C. Levin, and the Rev.
 George E. Thrall, all of
 Philadelphia, by the Rev.
 Dudley A. Tyng. So. Ch.,
 June 14, 1855
LEWELLYN
 Albinia W., d. of Richard
 Lewellyn of Albemarle
 Co., Va., and Wm. M.
 Owens, by the Rev. W. M.
 Nelson. So. Ch., Nov. 30,
 1855
LEWIN
 Emma Juliet, d. of Wm.
 Lewin, Esq. of Harper's
 Ferry, Va., and the Rev.
 Wm. N. Irish, rector of
 St. John's Parish, Harper's
 Ferry, Va., by the Rev.
 Wm. Shelton, D.D., in
 Trinity Church, Buffalo.
 So. Ch., Nov. 8, 1849
LEWIS
 Agnes Stewart, third d. of
 John S. Lewis, Esq., and
 Columbus Sehon, Esq., all
 of Mason Co., W.Va., by
 the Rev. T. H. Lacy, at
 Spring Hill, the resi-
 dence of the bride's
 father, near Point
 Pleasant, W.Va. So.
 Ch., June 29, 1876
 Catesby L., and Lucy E.,
 second d. of the late H.
 L. W. Temple, all of
 Essex, by the Rev. J. B.
 Newton, in St. Paul's
 Church, Essex, Va. So.
 Ch., Oct. 3, 1872
 Christopher, formerly of
 Brunswick Co., Va., and
 Mary Hopkins of Pittsyl-
 vania, by the Rev. C. O.
 Pruden, in Emmanuel
 Church, Chatham. So.
 Ch., Aug. 13, 1891
 Cora Barksdale, second d.
 of John O. Lewis of Albe-
 marle, and Roderick
 Chilli McIntosh of
 Quitman, Ga., by the Rev.
 T. E. Locke, at Cliffside,
 near Scottsville, Albe-
 marle Co., Va. So. Ch.,
 Oct. 24, 1878

MARRIAGE NOTICES IN THE SOUTHERN CHURCHMAN WITH DATES OF PUBLICATION

Dangerfield, Esq. of Cleve, King George Co., Va., and Belle Fauntleroy, eldest d. of John A. Browning, Esq. of Greenfield, Rappahannock Co., Va., by the Rev. James Carmichael, D.D. assisted by the Rev. John McGill, in Trinity Church, Bloomfield Parish. So. Ch., Nov. 18, 1880

Edward P. C., and Lucy B., d. of Col. S. W. Ware, all of Clarke Co., Va., by the Rev. H. Suter, at the residence of the bride's father, in Clarke Co., Va. So. Ch., Apr. 1, 1859

Elizabeth, eldest d. of Gen. S. H. Lewis of Rockingham, and the Rev. James C. Wheat of Staunton, by the Rev. T. T. Castleman, in Rockingham Co., Va. So. Ch., Aug. 9, 1855

Emily Contee, d. of G. W. Lewis, Esq., and E. A. Stevens of Hoboken, N.J., by the Rev. P. P. Phillips, in Grace Church, Berryville, Va. So. Ch., Nov. 6, 1879

Estelle, d. of Fielding Lewis of King George Co., and John G. Pollock, by the Rev. E. B. McGuire, at "Marmion", the residence of the bride's father. So. Ch., Dec. 17, 1868

Esther, d. of G. Washington Lewis, and Samuel McCormick, all of Clarke Co., Va., by the Rev. P. P. Phillips, in Grace Church, Berryville, Va. So. Ch., Dec. 14, 1882

Flora Temple, d. of William S. Lewis, Esq., and Frederick Kinloch Page, by the Rev. P. M. Boyden, in Grace Church, Albemarle Co., Va. So. Ch., Nov. 28, 1878

George F., and Lulie F., d. of Dr. Nelson G. and Virginia T. West, by the Rev. Carter Page, at the residence of the bride's father in Goresville, Loudoun Co. So. Ch., Jan. 15, 1885

Granville R. (Dr.), of Prince Edward Co., and Nannie E., d. of Dr. Thomas J. Williams of Charlotte Co., Va., by the Rev. James A. Mitchell, in Charlotte Co. So. Ch., Nov. 8, 1866

H. L. D., Esq., of Clarke Co., Va., and Carter Penn, third d. of John Freeland, Esq. of Richmond, Va., by the Rev. Dr. Minnigerode, in St. Paul's Church, Richmond, Va. So. Ch., May 11, 1871

J. S. (Dr.), of Weston, and Jessie, only d. of Dr. T. B. Camden of Wheeling, by the Rev. R. R. Swope, in St. Matthew's Church. So. Ch., Feb. 15, 1883

Jane Vivian, d. of the late Judge G. W. Lewis of Westmoreland Co., Va., and Joseph Miller Long of Frederick Co., Va., by the Rev. Joseph R. Jones, in Trinity Church, Washington, D.C. So. Ch., June 24, 1886

Jefferson (The Rev.), of the Philadelphia Conference, and Louisa S., d. of Dr. E. W. Skelton of Powhatan Co., Va., by the Rev.

MARRIAGE NOTICES IN THE SOUTHERN CHURCHMAN WITH DATES OF PUBLICATION

P. F. Berkeley. So. Ch., Mar. 20, 1835

John, and Mary L. Jenkins, both of Spotsylvania Co., Va., by the Rev. Wm. W. Greene, at the residence of the bride's father, A. J. Jenkins. So. Ch., May 16, 1872

John F., Jr., s. of the Lt. Governor, and Annie V., d. of Henry B. Harnsberger, Esq., all of Rockingham Co., Va., by the Rev. Oscar S. Bunting, at the residence of the bride's father. So. Ch., Jan. 18, 1883

John H. B., Esq., of Jefferson Co., Va., and Mary Ellen, d. of the officiating clergyman, the Rev. G. W. Kennedy, at Oxford, Md. So. Ch., Oct. 19, 1860

Josephine, d. of Mrs. Lucy Lewis, and Dr. Wm. M. Kirk of Lancaster, Va., by the Rev. John B. Newton, at Langley, Essex Co., Va. So. Ch., Dec. 14, 1871

Kate, of Essex Co., Va., and Nathan Morris of Arkansas, by the Rev. Joseph Lewis assisted by the Rev. E. Meade, in St. Paul's Church, Essex Co., Va. So. Ch., Sept. 25, 1890

Kate D., d. of Fielding Lewis, Esq. of King George Co., and Matthew B. Pollock of Stafford Co., Va., by the Rev. Edward McGuire, at "Marmion", the residence of the bride's father, in King George Co. Va. So. Ch., Nov. 17, 1870

Libbie E., and Samuel L. Smith of Mt. Airy, Pittsylvania Co., Va., by the Rev. C. O. Pruden, at the residence of the bride's father, Ephraim Lewis, near Straight Stone, Pittsylvania Co., Va. So. Ch., Feb. 2, 1888

Lorenzo, and Rose E., d. of the late Francis McCormick, all of Clarke Co., Va., by the Rev. P. P. Phillips, at Frankford, Clarke Co., Va. So. Ch., May 21, 1885

Lucy Pratt, d. of Geo. W. Lewis of Westmoreland Co., Va., and Oliver Ridgeway Funsten of Clarke Co., by the Rev. T. E. Locke, at Claymont, the residence of the bride's father. So. Ch., June 18, 1868

Lydia L., and Henry L. Smith of West Virginia by the Rev. Robb White, at the residence of Capt. John Fry, Keswick, Va. So. Ch., Jan. 25, 1883

Mary B., d. of John B. Lewis, Esq., and Henry B. Fitzhugh, Esq., of "Sherwood Forest", Stafford Co., Va., by the Rev. Henry Wall, at "Shellfield", Westmoreland Co., Va. So. Ch., Feb. 21, 1867

Mary G., d. of Z. R. Lewis, Esq. of Nelson Co., Va., and F T. Anderson of Howardsville, Albemarle Co., Va., by the Rev. G. S. Somerville, in Christ Church, Norwood, Nelson Co., Va. So. Ch., Feb. 26, 1891

Mary L., and Dr. E. A. Gibbs of Lexington, Va., by the Rev. Dr. Wheat, at the residence of the

MARRIAGE NOTICES IN THE SOUTHERN CHURCHMAN WITH DATES OF PUBLICATION

bride's father, Lt. Governor John F. Lewis, Lynwood, Rockingham Co., Va. So. Ch., Oct. 30 and Nov. 6, 1884

Mary W., d. of Daingerfield Lewis of King George Co., and John Tayloe of King George Co., by the Rev. Joseph A. Russell, at Marmion, King George Co., Va. So. Ch., Nov. 9, 1854

Maude, d. of the late G. Washington Lewis of Clarke Co., Va., and Fenton P. Whiting of Roanoke, Va., by the rector, the Rev. P. P. Phillips, in Grace Church, Berryville, Va. So. Ch., Sept. 10, 1891

Minnie Claiborne, d. of John C. Lewis of Albemarle Co., Va., and Samuel Stevens Rountree of Quitman, Ga., by the Rev. Thos. E. Locke, at Cliffside. So. Ch., Feb. 20, 1890

Phoebe Waln, d. of David Lewis, Esq., and the Rev. John B. Clemson, rector of the Church of the Ascension, Philadelphia, by the Rev. John Coleman. So. Ch., Aug. 2, 1839

Reverdy Johnson, s. of the late G. Washington Lewis and gr.s. of the late Lorenzo Lewis, and Alice Burnett, d. of the late Maj. Philip H. Powers and gr.d. of the late Edward Jaquelin Smith, all of Clarke Co., Va., at "Auburn", the home of the bride. So. Ch., May 9, 1908

Richard Henry (Dr.), of Raleigh, N.C., and Mary Long, d. of the late George Loyal Gordon of Albemarle, Va., by the Rev. W. Q. Hullihen, at Staunton, Va. So. Ch., May 8, 1890

Robert W. (The Rev.), of Mission Home, Va., and Mary Worthington, d. of Mrs. Clarence Hilleary and gr.d. of the late Gen. T. T. Wheeler, "Tudor Hall", Montgomery Co., Md., by the Rev. E. E. Burgess assisted by Dr. E. T. Helfenstein, in St. Mark's Protestant Episcopal Church, "Merryland Tract", near Petersville. So. Ch., July 20, 1918*

Sallie P., and Dr. Deucalion Gregory, both of King William, by the Rev. J. Hervey Hundley, at Auburn, King William Co. So. Ch., Oct. 10, 1872

Sally P., second d. of John O. Lewis of Albemarle Co., Va., and Robert C. Strudwick of Durham, N.C., by the Rev. T. E. Locke, at Cliffside, the residence of the bride's father. So. Ch., May 22, 1884

Sally Perkins, of Nelson Co., Va., and Wingfield L. Brown of Montana, by the Rev. T. E. Locke, at Avon Hill, the residence of Z. R. Lewis. So. Ch., Jan. 26, 1888

Susan, and Cesley Smoot, by the Rev. Everard Meade, in St. Paul's Church, Essex Co., Va. So. Ch., May 3, 1888

Thos. M., M.D., of Westmoreland, and Alice A., d. of the late Charles Tayloe of King George

---

* A Notice appears in the issue of June 29, 1918 identical with this, except that "Mary Worthington Hilleary" is written "Mary Washington Hilleary"

MARRIAGE NOTICES IN THE SOUTHERN CHURCHMAN WITH DATES OF PUBLICATION

Co., Va., by the Rev. T. E. Locke, at Oaken Brow. So. Ch., June 3, 1859

Thomas M. (Dr.), of Clarke Co., and Jennie, d. of the late Edgar Snowden, by the Rev. H. Suter, at the residence of the bride's mother, at Alexandria. So. Ch., Dec. 30, 1880

Thomas W., Esq., and Jane Walker, d. of Frederick W. Page, Esq., all of Albemarle Co., Va., by the Rev. E. Boyden, in Grace Church, Walker's Parish, Albemarle Co., Va. So. Ch., Jan. 21, 1875

Virginia Washington, d. of the late Capt. James B. Lewis, U.S.N., and John H. O. Kemp of Maryland, by the Rev. W. T. Leavell, at "The Moorings", Jefferson Co., W.Va. So. Ch., Nov. 18, 1880

Warner (Dr.), of New Kent, and Mary, d. of the late H. L. W. Temple, by the Rev. J. B. Newton, in St. Paul's Church, Essex, Va. So. Ch., Oct. 3, 1872

William Meade, and Fannie Bathurst, second d. of the late Charles Scott, all of Albemarle Co., Va., by the Rev. T. E. Locke, in St. John's Church, Scottsville. So. Ch., Nov. 1, 1877

Z. B., Jr., of Nelson Co., and Nannie Langhorn, youngest d. of the late Charles Scott of Albemarle Co., by the Rev. T. E. Locke, in St. John's Church, Scottsville, Albemarle Co., Va. So. Ch., Sept. 24, 1885

LIGGETT
Jennie R., d. of J. N. Liggett, Esq. of Harrisonburg, and N. W. Shuler of New Market, by the Rev. O. S. Bunting, in Emmanuel Church, Harrisonburg, Va. So. Ch., Nov. 29, 1883

LIGHT
Florence H., and Dr. Alexander Watson Williams, by the Ven. Richard P. Williams, Canon of Washington, father of the groom, at the Bethlehem Chapel of the Nativity, Washington, D.C. So. Ch., Aug. 21, 1915

LIGHTFOOT
Harriet A., d. of John B. Lightfoot, Esq. of Port Royal, and Dr. Francis S. Brooke of Spotsylvania Co., by the Rev. William Friend, in St. Peter's Church, Port Royal, Va. So. Ch., Nov. 7, 1867

LIGON
Belle G., d. of Dr. John and Mrs. Sallie G. Ligon, and the Hon. C. P. Door of Webster Co., by the Rev. T. H. Lacy, at Clover Lick, Pocahontas Co., W.Va. So. Ch., Oct. 1, 1885

Hannah Elizabeth, second d. of Dr. John and Mrs. Sallie G. Ligon, and Dr. F. T. McClintic, all of Pocahontas Co., W.Va., by the Rev. T. H. Lacy, in Clover Lick Church, Pocahontas Co., W.Va. So. Ch., Nov. 28, 1889

M. Maude, of Nelson Co.,

MARRIAGE NOTICES IN THE SOUTHERN CHURCHMAN WITH DATES OF PUBLICATION

Va., and Thomas C. Peek of New York City, by the Rev. J. W. Ware, at the residence of the bride's father. So. Ch., Dec. 29, 1881

Mary Louisa, third d. of Dr. John and Mrs. Sallie G. Ligon of Pocahontas Co., W.Va., and Julius Jackson Coyner of Basic City, Va., by the Rev. T. H. Lacy, in Emmanuel Church, Clover Lick, Pocahontas Co., W.Va. So. Ch., Oct. 1, 1891

LILE
Eleanor, d. of Prof. and Mrs. William Minor Lile of the University of Virginia, and the Rev. Beverly Dandridge Tucker, Jr., second s. of the officiating bishop, the Rt. Rev. Beverly D. Tucker, bishop-coadjutor of the Diocese of Southern Virginia, in St. Paul's Memorial Church, University of Virginia. So. Ch., May 8, 1915

William Minor, and Maude Lee, d. of the officiating clergyman, the Rev. T. M. Carson, in St. Paul's Church, Lynchburg. So. Ch., Feb. 2, 1888

LIMESTRONG
Charles R., late of England, and Catherine M., d. of Emma G. and the late Capt. Wm. Adamson of Dundee, Scotland, by the Rev. A. P. Gray, in Trinity Church, Manassas. So. Ch., Oct. 2, 1884

LIND
Jenny, the melodious Swedish Nightingale, and Otto Goldschmidt of Hamburg, one of the most accomplished pianists ever listened to in this country, by the Rev. Charles Mason assisted by Dr. Wainwright, at the residence of S. G. Ward, in Boston. So. Ch., Feb. 19, 1852

LINDSAY
John S. (The Rev.), rector of St. James' Church, Warrenton, Va., and Carrie W., d. of Mrs. Mary H. Smith of Baltimore, by the Rev. A. M. Randolph, D.D., assisted by the Rev. George W. Peterkin, in Emmanuel Church, Baltimore, Md. So. Ch., June 21, 1877

Sallie L., of Lexington, N.C., and John M. Greenfield of Salisbury, N.C., by the Rev. Geo. W. Dame, in the Church of the Epiphany, Danville. So. Ch., Mar. 22, 1877

LINGAMFELTER
Walter B., and Katie M. Kilmer, both of Berkeley Co., W.Va., by the rector, the Rev. W. T. Leavell, at Mount Zion Church, Hedgesville. So. Ch., Nov. 19, 1891

LINTHICUM
Benjamin J., of Church Creek, Dorchester Co., Md., and Mary Eliza, d. of the Rev. Wm. W. Greene, the officiating clergyman, in Calvary Church, Front Royal, Va. So. Ch., Oct. 30, 1890

LINTON
Wm. A., of Washington, D.C., and Sallie C. Chichester of Fauquier Co., Va., by the Rev.

MARRIAGE NOTICES IN THE SOUTHERN CHURCHMAN WITH DATES OF PUBLICATION

George W. Nelson, in "Baldwin's Ridge" Church. So. Ch., Mar. 4, 1886

LION
Thomas H., and Ethel Adamson, by the Rev. A. P. Gray, in Trinity Church, Manassas. So. Ch., June 28, 1888

LIONBERGER
Ann Megguire, of Pilot Grove, Mo., d. of Lt. John Lionberger (deceased, originally of Virginia), and Charles L., s. of Mrs. Joseph Minor Crane of Charles Town, W.Va., at the residence of the bride's sister, Mrs. R. R. Kimball, Ormond, Fla. So. Ch., May 8, 1909

LIPPITT
Armistead S., and Ada, d. of the late T. M. Isbell of Jefferson Co., W.Va., by the Rev. P. P. Phillips, at "Wartley", Jefferson Co., W.Va. So. Ch., May 3, 1883

C. E. (Dr.), and Nannie, d. of Thomas McCormick, Esq., all of Clarke Co., Va., by the Rev. T. F. Martin, at the residence of the bride's father, Elmington. So. Ch., Jan. 28, 1869

Laura Alexandria, d. of the late Rev. E. R. Lippitt, and Wm. B. Page, all of Clarke Co., Va., by the Rev. T. F. Martin, at "Elsinore", the residence of the bride's mother. So. Ch., June 5, 1873

W. F. (Dr.), of Washington, D.C., and M. Louisa, d. of the Hon. Thomas Perry, by the Rev. E. R. Lippitt, at Cumberland, Md. So. Ch., Nov. 18, 1859

W. F., Jr. (Dr.), of Charles Town, Jefferson Co., W.Va., and Mary, d. of Col. W. P. Craighill, by the Rev. Dallas Tucker. So. Ch., Aug. 11, 1887

LIPSCOMB
Mary V., only d. of N. G. Lipscomb, and James R. Apperson, all of New Kent, by the Rev. S. S. Hepbron, in St. Peter's Church. So. Ch., Dec. 13, 1888

LISEZ
Charles, of Jackson Co., W.Va., and Julia A., sister of Alpheus Haymond, the Judge of the Supreme Court of West Virginia, by the Rev. G. A. Gibbons, in Christ Church, Fairmont, W.Va. So. Ch., May 1, 1878

LIST
Eugene, of Wheeling, and Mary Lavinia, d. of C. I. Neal, Esq. of Parkersburg, Va., by the Rev. W. L. Hyland, in Trinity Church, Parkersburg. So. Ch., Mar. 29, 1861

LITCHFIELD
Anna, and James McDonald, by the Rev. D. M. Wharton, at the residence of the bride's father, Heathsville, Northumberland Co., Va. So. Ch., May 7, 1868

LITTELL
Emlen T., of New York, and Elizabeth Duval, d. of the Rev. Wm. G. Jackson,

MARRIAGE NOTICES IN THE SOUTHERN CHURCHMAN WITH DATES OF PUBLICATION

D.D. of Maryland, by the Rt. Rev. Thomas Atkinson, Bishop of North Carolina, assisted by the Rev. T. Gardner Littell, in Grace Church, Elk Ridge. So. Ch., June 16, 1870

John S. (The Rev.), D.D., rector of St. James' Church, West Hartford, Conn., and Estelle M., d. of the late Henry H. Sherman of New York, by the Rev. Eliot White, B.D., at Grace Chantry, New York. So. Ch., May 19, 1923

LITTLE

Haskin V. (The Rev.), of Tazewell, Va., in charge of Stras Memorial at Tazewell and Trinity at Richlands, and Janet Koe Kessinger of Alexandria, Va., by the Rev. Dr. Charles W. Lowry of the faculty of Virginia Seminary, in Emmanuel Chapel at the Seminary. So. Ch., July 6, 1940

John P., M.D., of Richmond, and Zettie, youngest d. of the late Judge Beverly Tucker of Williamsburg, by the Rev. Chas. Minnigerode, D.D., at Williamsburg, Va. So. Ch., June 6, 1867

Lou Fitzhugh, d. of Wm. A. Little, Esq. of Fredericksburg, Va., and Edward Arney Price of Richmond, by the Rev. R. J. McBryde assisted by the Rev. E. C. Murdaugh, D.D., in St. George's Church, Fredericksburg. So. Ch., Dec. 20, 1877

Robert C., and Emma W. Pendleton, both formerly of Richmond, Va., at the residence of the bride's brother, S. H. Pendleton, in Elizabeth, N.J. So. Ch., Sept. 14, 1882

Suma Bogle, only d. of Dr. H. McD. and Harriet A. Bogle Little, and Lawrence Oscar, s. of William H. and Sarah Hardin of Blowing Rock, N.C., by the Rev. William R. Savage, at the home of the bride's parents, near Blowing Rock, N.C. So. Ch., Sept. 25, 1909

LITTLEJOHN

Bettie M., of Oxford, and Capt. Frederick Nash of Charlotte, N.C., by the Rev. P. D. Thompson, in Oxford, N.C. So. Ch., Nov. 20, 1873

Sophia D., of Oxford, N.C., and John F. Brown of Minneapolis, by the Rev. P. D. Thompson, at the residence of the bride's father, Maj. J. T. Littlejohn. So. Ch., July 2, 1874

LIVINGSTON

Athenia, d. of the late Anthony Rutgers Livingston, and Gen. James Bowen of Hastings upon Hudson, by the Rev. Wm. Paret, D.D., in the Church of the Epiphany, Washington, D.C. So. Ch., Apr. 3, 1879

Esther Margaretta, d. of Mrs. Moncrief Livingston, and the Rev. Hobart Smith, rector of St. Thomas' Parish, Baltimore Co., Md., by the Rt. Rev. William Paret, D.D., in St. John's Church, Kingston, N.Y. So. Ch., Oct. 10, 1889

LLEWELLYN

MARRIAGE NOTICES IN THE SOUTHERN CHURCHMAN WITH DATES OF PUBLICATION

Charles Marshall, and Bernard Joseph, d. of the late Col. William M. Peyton, formerly of Roanoke Co., lately of Albemarle, by the Rev. T. E. Locke, at the residence of the bride's mother, Alta Vista. So. Ch., Dec. 14, 1871

LLOYD
Anne H., d. of John Lloyd, Esq. of Alexandria, Va., and the Rev. John Stearns of New York, by the Rev. C. B. Dana. So. Ch., July 28, 1848

Arthur Selden, and Lizzie Robertson Blackford, by the Rev. John J. Lloyd assisted by the Rev. Wm. M. Clark, in St. Thomas' Church, Abingdon, Va. So. Ch., July 15, 1880

C. Howard, and Mary C., d. of the late Wm. Donnell, by the Rev. Dr. J. H. Eccleston, at the residence of the bride's mother, in Baltimore. So. Ch., Nov. 29, 1888

Eliza F., d. of the late John J. Lloyd of Alexandria Co., Va., and Rowland Burks of Liberty, Va., by the Rev. Arthur S. Lloyd, at Farmville, Va. So. Ch., Feb. 17, 1881

Elizabeth Blackford, d. of Arthur Selden and Lizzie Robertson Blackford Lloyd, and Charles Junior* Symington of New York, by the bride's father, the Rev. Arthur Selden Lloyd, assisted by the Rev. W. H. H. Powers, D.D., of Towson, Md., at Madison, Conn. So. Ch., Oct. 12, 1912

G. F., Esq., and Mary P., d. of Dr. Thos. Hammond of Shepherdstown, by the Rev. C. W. Andrews, at Bedford, near Shepherdstown, Jefferson Co., Va. So. Ch., Oct. 31, 1856

Gay Blackford, and Churchill Jones Gibson, by the Rt. Rev. Arthur Selden Lloyd, D.D., assisted by the Rt. Rev. Robert Atkinson Gibson, D.D., in Christ Church, Short Hills, N.J. So. Ch., July 12, 1913

Harrison, and Ann Eliza Beavers, by the Rev. F. M. Whittle. So. Ch., Aug. 3, 1854

Mary Robertson, d. of Arthur Selden and Lizzie Blackford Lloyd, and the Rev. Edmund Pendleton Dandridge, by the Rev. A. S. Lloyd, D.D., and the Bishop of West Virginia, in Christ Church, Alexandria, Va. So. Ch., Oct. 16, 1909

Rebecca, d. of the late John J. Lloyd, Esq., and the Rev. Harry M. Melville Jackson of Norfolk, Va., by the Rev. R. H. McKim, at Mount Ida, Alexandria Co. So. Ch., July 31, 1873

Rebecca Selden, d. of the Rt. Rev. and Mrs. Arthur Selden Lloyd, and Gavin Hadden, by the Rt. Rev. Arthur Selden Lloyd assisted by the Rev. Theodore Sedgwick, rector, in Calvary Church, New York. So. Ch., Mar. 7, 1914

LOBBEND
Mary, and N. C. McGehee, Esq., by the Rev. Wm. M. Nelson, in St.

* Given as printed

MARRIAGE NOTICES IN THE SOUTHERN CHURCHMAN WITH DATES OF PUBLICATION

LOCHER
    Harry O., of Rockbridge Co., and Lulie Ethel, d. of Judge J. B. Jett of Stafford Co., Va., by the Rev. Dr. Murdaugh, in Trinity Church, Fredericksburg, Va. So. Ch., Jan. 12, 1882

LOCKE
    Belle Nelson, eldest d. of the officiating clergyman, and John Taylor, by the Rev. T. E. Locke, at the rectory in Washington Parish, Westmoreland Co., Va. So. Ch., Mar. 7, 1867

    Ella M., and John S. Richey, by the Rev. T. F. Martin, at "Green Hill", the residence of the bride's father. So. Ch., Nov. 1, 1877

    Georgie T., d. of Capt. J. M. Locke, and Wm. A. Campbell, all of Berryville, Va., by the Rev. P. P. Phillips, in Grace Church, Berryville, Va. So. Ch., Apr. 26, 1888

    Lucy Armistead, youngest d. of the officiating clergyman, and David H. Griffith of Westmoreland Co., by the Rev. T. E. Locke, in Christ Church, St. Anne's Parish, Albemarle Co., Va. So. Ch., June 11, 1885

    Mary E., d. of the Rev. Thos. E. Locke, and Dr. David N. Rust of Alexandria, Va., by the Rev. Thos. E. Locke assisted by the Rev. Edmund Withers, in Christ Church, St. Ann's Parish, Albemarle Co., Va. So. Ch., Oct. 19, 1876

    Rosa Van Doren, d. of the officiating clergyman, and Thos. Leiper Taylor, by the Rev. T. E. Locke, at the rectory, Washington Parish, Westmoreland Co., Va. So. Ch., Nov. 12, 1868

    Thomas Estep (The Rev.), rector of Cumberland Parish, Lunenburg Co., and Sarah Jane, second d. of the Rev. J. E. Jackson of Winchester, by the Rev. Alexander Jones. So. Ch., Oct. 6, 1837

LOCKERT
    Mattie, of Norfolk, Va., and Monroe Robinson of Baltimore, by the Rev. Dr. Hodges, in St. Paul's Church, Baltimore, Md. So. Ch., Dec. 6, 1877

LOCKETT
    Annie H., and Gen. J. D. Imboden, at Lombardy Grove, the residence of the bride's father, Mecklenburg Co., Va. So. Ch., Mar. 30, 1871

    James B. L., of Clarksville, Tenn., and Mary C. Thompson of Kanawha Co., W.Va., by the Rev. W. G. Stewart, at Belleville, the residence of the late Col. Frank Thompson. So. Ch., Jan. 2, 1868

    John W., Esq., and Belle Atkinson, by the Rev. J. Maxwell Pringle, at the residence of the bride's father, John C. Atkinson, Esq., at Henderson, Ky. So. Ch., Dec. 3, 1874

MARRIAGE NOTICES IN THE SOUTHERN CHURCHMAN WITH DATES OF PUBLICATION

LOCKRIDGE
    Florence, and J. W. Milligan of Clermont, Iowa, by the Rev. R. H. Mason, at Meadow Dale, Pocahontas Co., W. Va. So. Ch., June 13, 1878

LOCKWOOD
    Alison, third d. of Joshua Lockwood, Esq., of Charleston, S.C., and the Rev. R. C. Webb of St. Luke's Parish, by the Rt. Rev. Dr. Bowen. So. Ch., Mar. 11, 1836

    Jeanie Morrison, d. of Angelica P. and the late R. J. Lockwood, and Walker Hill of Richmond, Va., by the Rt. Rev. Bishop Robertson, in Emmanuel Church, St. Louis Co., Mo. So. Ch., Nov. 12, 1885

    Louise Saunders, d. of Mr. and Mrs. George R. Lockwood of St. Louis, and Gray Carroll Stribling of Spokane, Wash., by the Rev. A. A. V. Binnington, rector, in the Church of the Ascension, St. Louis, Mo. So. Ch., July 22, 1911

    Wm. F. (The Rev.), of Fairfax Co., Va., and Sally Champe, d. of Samuel Slaughter, Esq., by the Rev. Mr. Cole, at Western View, Culpeper Co. So. Ch., Nov. 7, 1850

LOEHR
    Louisa, of Culpeper, and Joseph Nunn of Louisa Co., Va., by the Rev. W. T. Roberts, at the residence of Charles Schuman, Culpeper, Va. So. Ch., Dec. 4, 1884

LOFLIN
    Walter Lee (The Rev.), and Daisy Garland Sowers, by the Rev. Dr. F. J. Mallett, in St. Luke's Rectory, Salisbury, N.C. So. Ch., Nov. 16, 1912

LOFSTROM
    Mabel Collins (Mrs.), and the Rt. Rev. Frank Arthur McElwain, D.D., Bishop of Minnesota, by the Rt. Rev. Irving P. Johnson, D.D., in the Church of the Good Shepherd, Windom, Minn. So. Ch., Aug. 14, 1920

LOGAN
    Anna C., d. of James W. Logan, Esq., of Salem, formerly of "Dungeness", Goochland Co., Va., and Col. Robert H. Logan of Salem, by the Rev. Edward H. Ingle, in St. Paul's Chapel, Salem. So. Ch., Jan. 18, 1872

    J. Lewis (Prof.), of the Agricultural and Mechanical College, Lexington, Ky., and Mattie B. Welch, by the Rev. W. R. Laird, at the residence of the bride's father, Dr. S. D. Welch, near Nicholasville, Ky. So. Ch., Dec. 31, 1891

    Jennie D., d. of Jas. W. Logan, Esq., late of Goochland Co., and Samuel White of Roanoke, by the Rev. Edward H. Ingle, in St. Paul's Chapel, Salem, Roanoke Co. So. Ch., Jan. 6, 1870

    Joseph D., of West Virginia, and Georgine, youngest d. of the late Col. Geo. Willis, by the Rev. Mercer P. Logan assisted by the Rev. R. R. Claiborne, in Emmanuel Church, Rapidan, Va. So. Ch., May 27, 1886

MARRIAGE NOTICES IN THE SOUTHERN CHURCHMAN WITH DATES OF PUBLICATION

Lulu, youngest d. of the late Joseph Logan of Louisiana, and William Chamberlayne Bentley of Richmond, Va., by the Rev. Novell Logan of Vicksburg, Miss., at the country residence of the bride's uncle, Gen. T. M. Logan, Algoma,* Buckingham Co., Va. So. Ch., Dec. 10, 1891

Martha Webb, and Arthur Lawrence Eubank of Greenville Co., by the Rev. F. A. Juhan, at Greenville, S.C. So. Ch., Feb. 23, 1918

Mercer P., D.D., and Eliza Huger Dunkin, by the Rt. Rev. William A. Guerry, D.D., in St. Paul's Church, Radcliffeboro, Charleston, S.C. So. Ch., Oct. 22, 1921

Robert H. (Col.), of Salem, and Anna C., d. of James W. Logan, Esq. of Salem, formerly of "Dungeness", Goochland Co., Va., by the Rev. Edward H. Ingle, in St. Paul's Chapel, Salem. So. Ch., Jan. 18, 1872

LOGUE
Wm. P., of Jackson, Tenn., and Mary E., eldest d. of Thompson Coleman, Esq., by the Rev. Geo. W. Dame, in Pittsylvania. So. Ch., Aug. 1, 1862

LOMAX
Kate R., d. of the late Dr. R. Stuart Lomax, and the Rev. Theodore Reed of Loudoun Co., by the Rev. Melville Boyd of Brooklyn, N.Y., at Cedar Grove, the residence of Dr. R. H. Stuart, King George Co., Va. So. Ch., Oct. 31, 1878

L. L. (Gen.), and Bettie W., eldest d. of Dr. Allen S. Payne, by the Rev. Kinloch Nelson, at Markham Station, Fauquier Co., Va. So. Ch., Feb. 27, 1873

R. Stuart (Dr.), of King George, and Jeannie, d. of Frederick Foote, Esq., of Prince William Co., by the Rev. John Towles, at Waverley. So. Ch., Dec. 7, 1855

LONG
Ione Elizabeth, d. of the Rev. Wm. H. C. and Mary Long, and Francis Haughton Wilshire, by the Rev. H. L. Derby, in Christ Church, Lancaster, Va. So. Ch., Sept. 24, 1873

Joseph Miller, of Frederick Co., Va., and Jane Vivian, d. of the late Judge G. W. Lewis of Westmoreland Co., Va., by the Rev. Joseph R. Jones, in Trinity Church, Washington, D.C. So. Ch., June 24, 1886

Lucy Lewis, and Lucian Dade Winston, by the Rev. Parnell LeBas Cross of Emmanuel Episcopal Church, Rapidan, in Winston Memorial Chapel, Winston, Va. So. Ch., Nov. 6, 1909

Mary Mercer, only child of the late Dr. Reuben Long, and Henry Somerville, M.D., all of Culpeper Co., Va., by the Rev. Dr. Slaughter, at

* Given as printed

MARRIAGE NOTICES IN THE SOUTHERN CHURCHMAN WITH DATES OF PUBLICATION

the home of the bride's mother, Wellington. So. Ch., May 6, 1880

LORENTZ
Landonia, d. of John Lorentz of Lewis Co., W.Va., and the Rev. J. Curtis, pastor of St. Paul's Church, by the Rev. D. Greer of Clarksburg, in St. Paul's Church, Weston, W.Va. So. Ch., Apr. 23, 1868

LOOMIS
E. Y., late of Richmond but now of Atlanta, Ga., and J. Burton Kidd, by the Rev. Dr. Peterkin, at the residence of the bride's father, John B. Kidd, Richmond. So. Ch., Jan. 10, 1884

LOUDERBACK
Alfred (The Rev.), of Philadelphia, and Susan Ophelia, d. of the late Caleb Horton, Esq., of New York, by the Rev. Dr. Milnor, in New York, N.Y. So. Ch., Sept. 15, 1837

LOUNSBERY
Mary G., eldest d. of the late Samuel G. Lounsbery of New York, and the Rev. Jacob Rambo of the African Mission, by the Rev. Edward Lounsbery, in St. Jude's Church, Philadelphia. So. Ch., Oct. 29, 1858

LOUTHAN
James T., and Emoline F., d. of Wm. A. Castleman, Esq., all of Clarke Co., Va., by the Rev. F. M. Whittle. So. Ch., Apr. 17, 1857

LOVE
Isabella Fairfax, youngest d. of the late Thomas R. Love of Fairfax Court House, Va., and William Fowler Hite of Gainsville, Va., by the Rev. J. C. Hall assisted by the Rev. W. A. Alrich, in Zion Episcopal Church, Fairfax C.H., Va. So. Ch., June 23, 1892

Jane M., d. of T. R. Love, Esq., of Fairfax Court House, and Bloden T. Dulany, late of Fauquier Co., by the Rev. R. T. Brown, pastor of Zion Church, Fairfax C.H., Va., in Trinity Church, Washington, D.C. So. Ch., Apr. 15, 1859

John S., of Greenville, Tenn., and Harriet E. Howison, by the Rev. John McGill, at "Effingham", the residence of the bride, in Prince William Co., Va. So. Ch., July 13, 1876

Mary J., d. of Thomas R. Love, Esq. of Fairfax Courthouse, and the Rev. Wm. A. Alrich, rector of St. Martin's Parish, Hanover Co., Va., by the Rev. O. A. Kinsolving, at the residence of the bride's father. So. Ch., May 13, 1869

Thomas R., Esq., and Sallie B., d. of Col. Henry B. Tyler, by the Rev. O. A. Kinsolving, at Fairfax Court House. So. Ch., Dec. 16, 1869

LOVELL
John P., of Franklin, and Sally C., d. of the late Lewis Wingfield, Esq., of Bedford Co., by the Rev. N. Sale. So. Ch., Nov.

MARRIAGE NOTICES IN THE SOUTHERN CHURCHMAN WITH DATES OF PUBLICATION

30, 1855

LOVING
    Fanny Pate, d. of the Hon. Henry Loving of Amherst Co., Va., and Dan T. Mitchell of Lynchburg, by the Rev. Wm M. Clark, at "Brooklyne",* Amherst Co., Va. So. Ch., Aug. 20, 1885

    Sallie W., d. of Henry Loving, Esq. of Amherst, and C. H. Sutton, Esq. of Richmond, Va., by the Rev. Oscar Bunting, at "Brooklyn"*, the residence of the bride's father, Amherst Co., Va. So. Ch., May 13, 1880

LOWE
    Julia M., of Alexandria, Va., and G. A. McGaw of Baltimore, by the Rev. Thomas G. Addison, in Trinity Church, Washington, D.C. So. Ch., July 22, 1875

LOWMAN
    John H., of Roanoke, Va., and Fannie Allen Armistead of Farmville, Va., by the Rev. Dr. Harding, in the Presbyterian Church, Farmville, Va. So. Ch., Oct. 20, 1892

LOWNSBERY
    Benj. F., Jr., of Norfolk, formerly of Jamestown, N.Y., and Frances A. Larkin of Princess Anne Co., Va., formerly of Augusta, Me., by the Rev. W. R. Savage, in Emmanuel Church, Kempsville, Va. So. Ch., Oct. 10, 1889

LOWRY
    Emily H., youngest d. of Thomas Lowry, Esq., and William S. Jones, Esq., by the Rev. John C. McCabe, rector of the Church of the Ascension, Baltimore, at Hampton, Va. So. Ch., Jan. 2, 1857

    Mary E., eldest d. of A. J. Lowry of Madison Parish, La., and Richard Bruce, Esq. of Halifax Co., Va., by the Rev. C. K. Marshall, in Madison Parish, La. So. Ch., Feb. 27, 1857

LOYALL
    B. P., and Nina Taylor, by the Rev. Dr. O. S. Barten, at the residence of the bride's mother. So. Ch., Nov. 30, 1882

LOYD
    Mary, eldest d. of Richard Loyd, Esq., and Cassius F. Lee, Jr., by the Rev. Wm. F. Meade, at Belmont, Alexandria Co. So. Ch., June 5, 1873

LOZIER
    T. A. (Judge), of Belleville, Canada, and Frances E., d. of the officiating minister, the Rev. Dr. Hanckel, at Clifton Springs, N.Y. So. Ch., Nov. 29, 1883

LUARD
    Walter Montague, s. of the Rev. O. Luard, rector of Aunsby, Lincolnshire, England, and Eleanor Louise, youngest d. of William Assheton, Esq., by the Rev. Herbert Assheton, at Rock Spring, Fauquier Co., Va. So. Ch., Jan. 11, 1883

LUCAS
    Harleston Toomer, d. of

---

* Given as printed

MARRIAGE NOTICES IN THE SOUTHERN CHURCHMAN WITH DATES OF PUBLICATION

Mr. and Mrs. T. G. S. Lucas, and Alleine Williamson Newton of Richmond, Va., s. of the late Rt. Rev. John B. Newton of Virginia, by the Rev. Mr. Way, at Charleston, S. C. So. Ch., Feb. 9, 1907

Joseph W., and Emma Capers, d. of Capt. C. C. Tracy, by the Rev. Thomas P. Baker, in Jude's Church, Walterboro, S.C. So. Ch., Dec. 18, 1909

LUCK
Felix A., and Sallie Ann, second d. of Thompson Coleman, Esq., by the Rev. Geo. W. Dame, near Ringgold in Pittsylvania. So. Ch., Mar. 18, 1864

Maimie, and Dr. Aaron Jeffery of Radford, Va., by the Rev. E. L. Goodwin, Buckingham C.H., Va. So. Ch., Nov. 6, 1890

LUCKE
Sallie C., and Ross Carter, by the Rev. Geo. W. Dame assisted by the Rev. Wm. Hoxton, Pittsylvania Courthouse. So. Ch., July 15, 1869

LUCKETT
Dinwiddie Johnston, of Rockville, Md., and Julia W., d. of the late Horace P. Edmond, by the Rev. James W. Morris, at the residence of the bride's aunt, Miss Woodbridge. So. Ch., June 24, 1911

LUDISILL
William David, Jr. of Nelson Co., and Irene Lewis Jones of Albemarle, by the Rev. T. E. Locke, at the residence of B. H. Jones. So. Ch., Nov. 12, 1885

LUDLAM
Frances A. (Mrs.), d. of Richard Anderson, Esq., and Jacob Michaux, Esq., all of Powhatan Co., by the Rev. Andrew Fisher, in St. Luke's Church, Powhatan Parish.**So. Ch., Nov. 28, 1856

LUDLOW
Cora Harrison, and Waddy Thompson Michaux, by the Rev. P. F. Berkeley, at the residence of the bride's mother, Mrs. Jacob Michaux*, Powhatan Co. So. Ch., May 18, 1876

LUKE
Catharine, of Snickersville, Loudoun Co., Va., and Jacob Enders of Clarke, by the Rev. F. M. Whittle, at Snickersville, Loudoun Co., Va. So. Ch., July 7, 1853

LUMPKIN
K. D. W. (Mrs.), of Columbus, and Gen. Robert Ransom of New Berne, N.C., by the Rev. William A. Carter, at Columbus, Ga. So. Ch., Sept. 25, 1884

V. M. (Miss), and T. J. Fogg, both of Essex Co., Va., by the Rev. H. H. Jones. So. Ch., Oct. 29, 1885

LUNDQUIST
Albert Edward of New York, and Helen Defebaugh, youngest d. of Mr. and Mrs. Henry Morris, by the Rev. Robert Burton, at the Church of the Ascension, Norfolk, Va. So. Ch., Aug. 2, 1924

* Given as printed
** Powhatan Parish is in Powhatan County, Virginia (Journal ... Diocese of Southern Va., Portsmouth, Va., 1941)

MARRIAGE NOTICES IN THE SOUTHERN CHURCHMAN WITH DATES OF PUBLICATION

LUNN
  Maurice Johnston, of Pittsburg, Pa., and Elizabeth Todd Robins of Richmond. So. Ch., July 4, 1908

LUNSFORD
  Charles, of Petersburg, Va., and Rose, eldest d. of Taylor Berry, Esq. of Amherst C.H., Va., by the Rev. O. S. Bunting, at the residence of the bride's father. So. Ch., May 12, 1881

LUSTGARTEN
  Regina B., and Dr. John Wilson Wood, at the Church of the Transfiguration, New York. So. Ch., Aug. 26, 1939

LYELL
  Mollie, and Henry Harford, both of Westmoreland, by the Rev. D. M. Wharton, in St. James' Church, Montross. So. Ch., Jan. 16, 1873
  Nannie T., only d. of Samuel Lyell, Esq., and James V. Garland, all of Richmond Co., Va., by the Rev. Beverly D. Tucker, at Forest Home, the residence of the bride's So. Ch., Dec. 28, 1876

LYKE
  Florence E., oldest d. of Wm. S. Lyke of King and Queen Co., Va., and Wm. H. Richardson, Jr. of Richmond, Va., by the Rev. J. Hervey Hundley, at the residence of the bride's father. So. Ch., June 28, 1888

LYMAN
  Alice, eldest d. of George T. Lyman of Bellport, L.I., and William Platt Pepper of Philadelphia, by the Rev. Morgan Dix, D.D., in Trinity Chapel, New York. So. Ch., May 15, 1879
  Augustus Julian, of Asheville, N.C., youngest s. of the Rt. Rev. Theodore B. Lyman, Bishop of North Carolina, and gr.s. of the late Jacob Albert Merchant of Baltimore, and Julia, eldest d. of P. W. Ellsworth, Esq., M.D., and great gr.d. of the late Chief Justice Ellsworth of the U. S. Supreme Court, by the Rt. Rev. John Williams, Bishop of Connecticut, assisted by the father of the groom, at the residence of the bride's father, at Hartford, Conn. So. Ch., Dec. 28, 1882
  Maria Ellen D. S., youngest d. of the late Hon. J. H. Lyman of Northampton, Mass., and T. J. Trist of Philadelphia, by the Rev. T. H. Gallaudet assisted by the Rev. P. P. Irving, in Christ Church, New Brighton, N.Y. So. Ch., Oct. 22, 1858
  Theodore Benedict, D.D. (The Rt. Rev.), Bishop of North Carolina, and Susan Boone, d. of the late Alexander Robertson of Charleston, S.C., by the Rev. Charles C. Pinckney, D.D., in St. Michael's Church, Charleston, S.C. So. Ch., Mar. 16, 1893

LYNCH
  Hattie C., d. of Amos Lynch, Esq., residing near Middletown, and Samuel L. Pratt, Esq. of Queen Ann's Co., Md., by the Rev. John

MARRIAGE NOTICES IN THE SOUTHERN CHURCHMAN WITH DATES OF PUBLICATION

Collins McCabe, D.D., in Saint Ann's Church, Middletown, Del. So. Ch., Oct. 15, 1868

LYNE

Henry, Esq., of Henderson, and Nelly, youngest d. of the late Col. Angus W. McDonald of Winchester, Va., by the Rev. J. G. Minnigerode, at the residence of the bride's mother. So. Ch., May 10, 1893

LYNN

David, of Cumberland, Md., and Mary J. Acheson of Wheeling, Va., by the Rev. E. T. Perkins, at the residence of the bride's father. So. Ch., Jan. 11, 1861

Sarah A., and Richard C. Crosson, by the Rev. F. M. Whittle. So. Ch., Apr. 17, 1857

LYON

Allen Madison, and Sadie D. Habliston, by the Dr. A. G. Brown, at the residence of the bride's father, Frederick H. Habliston. So. Ch., Apr. 30, 1891

James William, of Baltimore, and Fanny Moncure, d. of Dr. William A. Nelson of Stafford Co., Va., by the Rev. J. M. Meredith, in Aquia Church. So. Ch., May 11, 1876

Mollie, only d. of Wm. S. Lyon, Esq., and Wm. F. Chesley, Esq., all of St. Mary's Co., Md., by the Rev. J. W. Chesley, at "The Heights", St. Mary's Co., Md. So. Ch., July 25, 1878

LYZOTT

Mattie E., of Greensville, and Joseph H. Johnson of Petersburg, by the Rev. Robert R. Claiborne, in Greensville Co. So. Ch., Jan. 8, 1880

M

McADAMS
    Otto Kenton, and Leenell Virginia, only d. of Judge Stevadson A. Hail and Lucy Stuart Fitzhugh, his wife, all of Batesville, Ark., by the Rev. H. A. Stowell, in St. Paul's Episcopal Church, Batesville, Ark. So. Ch., Feb. 11, 1911

McALLISTER
    Joseph, of Covington, Va., and Virginia Anderson of Bath Co., Va., by the Rev. L. R. Combs assisted by the Rev. Mr. White (Presbyterian), in Grace Church, Warm Springs, Bath Co., Va. So. Ch., Apr. 27, 1893

McBRIDE
    Anna Maria, and Robert James Davidson of Liverpool, England, by the Rev. John McGill, at the residence of the bride's father, Blacksburg, Va. So. Ch., May 12, 1892

McBRYDE
    R. J. (The Rev.), of Amherst, and Ellen D., d. of the late Rev. David Caldwell, by the Rev. Edmund Withers assisted by the Rev. Henderson Suter, at Hazelwood, Nelson Co. So. Ch., June 8, 1871

McBURNEY
    Agnes, d. of Geo. McBurney, and R. H. Havener, all of Alexandria, Va., by the Rev. Dr. Norton. So. Ch., Nov. 24, 1881
    Alexander, of Alexandria, and Florence M., d. of the late Benj. Thomas, by the Rev. Henry Nice, at the residence of Joshua Thomas, Baltimore. So. Ch., Feb. 24, 1881

McCABE
    Alice, d. of the late Rev. James D. McCabe, D.D. of Baltimore, and James E. Thomas of Richmond, Ind., by the Rev. George W. Peterkin, in Memorial Church, Baltimore. So. Ch., Nov. 25, 1875
    Emily A. H., d. of the officiating clergyman, and Alfred Shield, Esq., by the Rev. John C. McCabe, rector of the Church of the Ascension, Baltimore, in St. James' Church, Richmond, Va. So. Ch., Jan. 9, 1857*
    Jennie L. Smith, d. of the officiating clergyman, and Gill A. Carey, Esq. of Hampton, Va., by the Rev. John C. McCabe, rector of the Church of the Ascension, at Baltimore. So. Ch., Oct. 3, 1856
    John Collins, D.D. (The Rev.), rector of St. Ann's Church, Middletown, Del., and Virginia, youngest d. of the late Henry C. Mackall, Esq. of Elkton, by the Rev. R. H. B. Mitchell assisted by the Rev. Doane Mitchell, in Trinity Church, Elkton, Md. So. Ch., Oct. 15, 1868
    W. Gordon, Esq., s. of the officiating clergyman, and Jennie, d. of Edmund Osborne, Esq., by the Rev. John Collins McCabe, D.D., rector of St. Luke's Church, Bladensburg, Md., at Petersburg, Va. So. Ch., Apr. 18, 1867

McCANCE
    See also HATCHER, Emmie McC. (Mrs.)

McCANDLISH
    Chas. S., of Parkersburg, W.Va., and Lizzie W., d. of Douglas Putnam, by the Rev.

---

*The notice in issue of Jan. 2, 1857, announcing Miss McCabe's marriage "to Alfred Smith" is evidently incorrect. The Parish register of St. James' Church records the marriage as printed in issue of Jan. 9, 1857, given here.

MARRIAGE NOTICES IN THE SOUTHERN CHURCHMAN WITH DATES OF PUBLICATION

H. C. Haskell, at the residence of the bride's father, Harmar, Ohio. So. Ch., May 10, 1883

Mary Mandville, d. of the late Col. Ro. McCandlish of Williamsburg, Va., and Wm. R. Gatewood, M.D. of Middlesex Co., Va., by the Rev. E. C. Murdaugh, in Trinity Church, Fredericksburg, Va. So. Ch., Dec. 4, 1879

Sallie Shield, d. of R. J. McCandlish, and Thomas H. Hawks of Cleveland, Ohio, by the Rev. C. H. Shield, at Parkersburg, W.Va. So. Ch., July 1, 1886

McCARTEY
Sally, only d. of the late John M. McCartey of Loudoun Co., Va., and Frederick W. Pleasants, Esq. of New York, by the Rev. R. H. Phillips. So. Ch., Nov. 30, 1855

McCARTHY
Edward (Dr.), of Richmond, and Deborah Couch, d. of the late William H. and Mary D. Anthony of Botetourt Co., Va., by the Rev. Joshua Peterkin assisted by the Rev. L. W. Burton, in St. James' Church. So. Ch., Oct. 23, 1890

McCARTY
Alverta B., and Joseph C. Palmer, by the Rev. Henry L. Derby, in White Chapel Church, Lancaster, Va. So. Ch., Dec. 27, 1883

Cornelia A., and John C. Tapscott, both of Lancaster, Va., by the Rev. H. L. Derby, in White Chapel Church, Lancaster, Va. So. Ch., Sept. 24, 1885

Jane Ann (Mrs.), and Sidney Lane, both of Richmond, by the Rev. Andrew Fisher, at Laurel Grove. So. Ch., Sept. 16, 1859

John M., of Richmond Co., and Mrs. Susan J. Chilton of Lancaster, by the Rev. H. L. Derby, at Norwood, Lancaster, Va. So. Ch., Nov. 18, 1875

William Mason, and Mary Champe, d. of Edgar M. Garnett, all of Richmond, Va., by the Rev. Joshua Peterkin, D.D. So. Ch., Aug. 18, 1881

Winifred E., of Middlesex Co., Va., and Dr. Samuel B. Carey of Gloucester, by the Rev. Mr. Carraway, in Christ Church. So. Ch., Feb. 1, 1856

McCAW
Ellen T., d. of Dr. J. B. McCaw, and Charles Davenport, all of Richmond, Va., by the Rev. Dr. Minnigerode, at the residence of the bride's father. So. Ch., Dec. 11, 1879

Georgina, youngest d. of the late David McCaw, M.D., and Thomas A. Patteson, Esq. of New York, by the Rev. Lewis Walke, at "Millwood" in Powhatan Co. So. Ch., Mar. 2, 1860

McCLAIN
Jackson (Col.), and Mrs. Helen Trafton, by the Rev. R. S. Barrett, at Henderson, Ky. So. Ch., Oct. 25, 1883

Sarah Catherine, and the Rev. Arthur G. W. Pfaffko, rector of the Church of the Transfiguration, Blue Ridge Summit, Pa., by the Rev. Dr. S. Tagart Steele, vicar of the Intercession, in the Chapel of the Intercession, Trinity Parish, New York City. So. Ch., Oct. 18, 1941

McCLANAHAN
Mary Scott, of Roanoke Co., Va., and Quin M. Word of Richmond, by the Rev. W. H. Pendleton, at Locust Grove, Roanoke Co., Va. So. Ch., Jan. 4, 1856

McCLAY
Alice Minnette, d. of the Rev. R. S. McClay, D.D., of Yokohama, and the Rev. Wm. B. Cooper of the Protestant Episcopal Mission, Yedo, by

MARRIAGE NOTICES IN THE SOUTHERN CHURCHMAN WITH DATES OF PUBLICATION

the Rt. Rev. C. M. Williams, D.D., in Christ Church, Yokohama, Japan. So. Ch., Apr. 12, 1877

McCLELLAND
Edmond L., of the Episcopal High School, near Alexandria, Va., and Lucy Eleanor, second d. of D. Robert Barclay, Esq., by the Rev. George C. Betts, rector in Trinity Church, St. Louis. So. Ch., July 20, 1882

James Bruce, of Clarendon, Tex. (formerly of Virginia), and Kate Ellerbe, second d. of Dr. H. J. Winn of Birmingham, by the Rev. T. J. Beard, in the Church of the Advent, Birmingham, Ala. So. Ch., July 15, 1886

Robert, of Chattanooga, and Mollie C. Payne of Roanoke, by the Rev. Edward H. Ingle, at the residence of J. M. Terry, Esq., Roanoke Co. So. Ch., Oct. 29, 1868

McCLENAHAN
Robert W., of Chestnut Hills, Philadelphia, and Sally Howes, d. of the Rev. Z. B. Phillips, D.D., rector of Epiphany Church and chaplain of the Senate of the United States, by the bride's father, the Rev. Z. B. Phillips, in Epiphany Church, Washington, D.C. So. Ch., Jan. 27, 1934

McCLINTIC
F. T. (Dr.), and Hannah Elizabeth, second d. of Dr. John and Mrs. Sallie G. Ligon, all of Pocahontas Co., by the Rev. T. H. Lacy, in Clover Lick Church, Pocahontas Co., W.Va. So. Ch., Nov. 28, 1889

McCLINTOCK
Mattie C., and John E. Wharton, both of Liberty, by the Rev. John K. Mason, at the residence of the Rev. John A. Wharton. So. Ch., Jan. 25, 1883

M'COLLOUCH
S. E. (Mrs.), d. of Maj. John DeWitt of Society Hill, S.C., and the Rev. U. M. Wheeler. So. Ch., Nov. 11, 1836

McCOLLUM
Mary Bell, and George W. Schlosser, M.D., by the Rev. F. G. Scott, at the residence of the bride's uncle, near Gordonsville, Va. So. Ch., Oct. 19, 1876

McCONNEL
Mabel Helen, d. of Mr. and Mrs. E. H. McConnell of Williamsport, Pa., and the Rev. Arthur James, s. of Mr. and Mrs. R. A. Mackie of Renova, Pa., by the Rt. Rev. Hiram R. Hulse, D.D., Bishop of Cuba, in All Saints' Church, Guantanamo, Cuba, where the groom is rector. So. Ch., Apr. 5, 1924

McCORKLE
John Macon, of Newton, N.C., and Matt Whitaker, d. of Gen. Robert Ransom, by the Rev. T. M. N. George, in Christ Church, Newborn, N.C. So. Ch., Dec. 18, 1890

Samuel W., of Lynchburg, Va., and Mary C. Sale of Liberty, Va., by the Rev. John K. Mason, in St. John's Church, Liberty, Va. So. Ch., Jan. 25, 1883

McCORMICK
Augustine (The Rev.), and Helen Smith, by the Rt. Rev. John N. McCormick, Bishop of Western Michigan and father of the groom, in St. Mark's Pro-Cathedral, Grand Rapids, Diocese of Western Michigan. So. Ch., Aug. 30, 1924

Bessie T., and Province McCormick, Jr., both of Clarke Co., Va., by the Rev. T. F. Martin, in Grace Church, Berryville. So. Ch., Dec. 21, 1871

Dawson, and Margaretta Mess, d. of the late Dr. J. C. Broun, all of Clarke Co., Va., by the Rt. Rev.

MARRIAGE NOTICES IN THE SOUTHERN CHURCHMAN WITH DATES OF PUBLICATION

R. H. Wilmer, D.D., Bishop of Alabama, and the Rev. P. P. Phillips, rector in Grace Church, Berryville, Va. So. Ch., Sept. 13, 1883

Frank, and Edith Ramsay, both of Virginia, by the Rev. Wm. Jackson Morton, at Alexandria, Va. So. Ch., June 20, 1908

Hannah T., eldest d. of Thos. McCormick, Esq. of Clarke Co., Va., and Col. F. W. M. Holliday of Winchester, Va., by the Rev. T. F. Martin, at Elmington, residence of bride's father. So. Ch., Jan. 23, 1868

John, and Virginia S. Newton formerly of Alexandria, Va., by the Rev. Mr. Cole, at Culpeper C.H. So. Ch., Feb. 21, 1862

M. T. (The Rev.), of Petersburg, Va., and Helen, eldest d. of Charles W. Cornwall, Esq., by the Rev. John Downie, M.A., at Colchester, Ontario, Canada. So. Ch., Oct. 2, 1873

Mary E., oldest d. of Col. Francis McCormick of Clarke Co., Va., and Col. Marshall McDonald of the Virginia Military Institute, by the Rev. T. F. Martin, at Frankford, Clarke Co., Va. So. Ch., Jan. 23, 1868

Nannie, d. of Thomas McCormick, Esq., and Dr. C. E. Lippitt, all of Clarke Co., Va., by the Rev. T. F. Martin, at Elmington, residence of the bride's father. So. Ch., Jan. 28, 1869

Nannie, second d. of Col. Francis McCormick, and Thomas McCormick, all of Clarke Co., Va., by the Rev. T. F. Martin, at "Frankford", residence of the bride's father. So. Ch., Jan. 4, 1872

Nannie H., d. of the late Edward McCormick, and Goodwin H. Williams, all of Clarke Co., Va., by the rector, the Rev. P. P. Phillips, assisted by the Rev. S. S. Moore, in Grace Church, Berryville, Va. So. Ch., Mar. 25, 1886

Province, Jr., and Bessie T. McCormick, both of Clarke Co., Va., by the Rev. T. F. Martin, in Grace Church, Berryville. So. Ch., Dec. 21, 1871

Rose E., d. of the late Francis McCormick, and Lorenzo Lewis, all of Clarke Co., Va., by the Rev. P. P. Phillips, at Frankford, Clarke Co., Va. So. Ch., May 21, 1885

Samuel, and Esther, d. of G. Washington Lewis, all of Clarke Co., Va., by the Rev. P. P. Phillips, in Grace Church, Berryville, Va. So. Ch., Dec. 14, 1882

Thomas, of Clarke Co., and Mary M., oldest d. of Dr. R. J. McK. Holliday of Winchester, by the Rev. C. Walker. So. Ch., Nov. 28, 1856

Thomas, and Nannie, second d. of Col. Francis McCormick, all of Clarke Co., Va., by the Rev. T. F. Martin, at "Frankford", residence of the bride's father. So. Ch., Jan. 4, 1872

McCOY

Charles D., and Mary McDonogh, d. of Geo. Taylor Jenkins of Baltimore, by the Rev. James A. Latane, in Trinity Church, Staunton. So. Ch., Oct. 25, 1866

James, of Warren Co., Va., and Elizabeth Clothilde Wood of Clarke Co., Va., by the Rev. John Lindsay, D.D., at Washington, D.C. So. Ch., Nov. 5, 1885

Thomas J., and Josephine I. Norris, by the Rev. P. N. McDonald, in St. Paul's Church, Sistersville, W.Va. So. Ch., July 11, 1908

McCRAE

MARRIAGE NOTICES IN THE SOUTHERN CHURCHMAN WITH DATES OF PUBLICATION

Colin, of Virginia, and Maria H., d. of Judge F. R. Thompson of San Francisco, by the Rev. Dr. Gallaudet, in New York City. So. Ch., July 2, 1874

McCRAVEN
Bonner N., of Houston, Texas, and Sarah Amelia Pringle, by the Rev. J. M. Pringle, father of the bride, at the house of her brother-in-law, Robert C. Soaper, Henderson, Ky. So. Ch., Oct. 27, 1887

McCRAW
Otho L., of Henderson, N.C., and Belle, d. of Dr. Thomas L. and Annie E. Scott, by the Rev. W. B. Williams, at the residence of the late Dr. Thos. L. Scott, Caroline Co., Va. So. Ch., July 19, 1888

McCREA
Wythe, Esq., of New Orleans, and Fanny M., d. of Col. John D. Morris, by the Rev. Mr. Ringgold, in Trinity Church, Clarksville, Tenn. So. Ch., Oct. 4, 1866

McCREERY
J. Van Lew, and Nannie, oldest d. of the officiating clergyman, the Rev. H. S. Kepler, in St. James' Church, Richmond. So. Ch., Oct. 26, 1865

McCRINDLE
Elizabeth C., and Wiley R. Phillips, both of Richmond, by the Rev. D. F. Sprigg, in Richmond, Va. So. Ch., Mar. 3, 1881

McCUE
Lina L., d. of John H. McCue of Staunton, Va., and Walter S. Sublett of Richmond, by the Rev. Walter Q. Hullihen, in the Episcopal Church, Staunton. So. Ch., Jan. 10, 1878

Massie L. (Dr.), and Emma F., d. of C. W. Purcell, Esq. of Alton Park, Albemarle Co., Va., by the Rev. Mr. Greaves, at the residence of the bride's father. So. Ch., Nov. 27, 1879

Otelia S., d. of Hon. J. H. McCue, and Gabriel Santini of New Orleans, by the Rev. Edmund Withers, at Lovingston, Nelson Co., Va. So. Ch., Feb. 12, 1874

McCULLOCH
Duncan (The Rev.), and Mary Sterett, d. of Henry Hill Carroll of Baltimore Co., Md., by the Rev. Landon R. Mason, at Clymalera Manor. So. Ch., Jan. 5, 1888

John, Jr., of Point Pleasant, and Cordelia Agnes, d. of the late John A. Byers, C.E., of Hancock, Md., by the Rev. Horace Edwin Hayden, rector of St. John's Church, West Brownsville, Pa., assisted by the Rev. T. Hugo Lacy, rector of the parish, in Christ's Church, Point Pleasant, W.Va. So. Ch., Nov. 13, 1873

M'CULLOCH
John A., and Kate Barbee, both of Macon Co., W.Va., by the Rev. T. H. Lacy, at the residence of bride's father, Dr. Andrew Barbee, at Point Pleasant, W. Va. So. Ch., Nov. 1, 1877

McDaniel
Frances Minor, only d. of John T. McDaniel, and Robert W. Byrd of Roanoke City, by the Rev. John McGill, at the residence of the bride's parents, in Montgomery Co., Va. So. Ch., Feb. 16, 1893

J. W., and Mary Louisa Croxton, both of Tappahannock, by the Rev. H. W. L. Temple, at Tappahannock, Essex Co. So. Ch., Jan. 2, 1868

Lelia, and Dr. Thos. W. Nelson, both of Bedford Co., Va., by the Rev. Wm. Henry Pendleton, at the residence of Saml. McDaniel, Esq. of Bedford Co., Va. So.

MARRIAGE NOTICES IN THE SOUTHERN CHURCHMAN WITH DATES OF PUBLICATION

Ch., Nov. 18, 1869
R. E., and Delia, d. of the late John Richeson of Essex Co., by the Rev. A. Broadus, in Essex Co. So. Ch., Jan. 9, 1835

McDONALD
Donald, of Louisville, Ky., and Betsy Breckenbridge, d. of Col. G. W. Carr of "Hawksdale", Roanoke Co., Va., by the Rev. W. H. Meade, D.D., in St. John's P. E. Church, Roanoke. So. Ch., Nov. 3, 1887

Edward H. (Maj.), of Louisville, Ky., formerly of Virginia, and Julia Yates Leavell, by the Rev. W. T. Leavell assisted by the Rev. J. E. Poindexter, at Medin, near Charles Town, Va. So. Ch., Oct. 21, 1869

James, and Anna Litchfield, by the Rev. D. M. Wharton, at the residence of the bride's father, Heathsville, Northumberland Co., Va. So. Ch., May 7, 1868

Marshall (Col.), of the Virginia Military Institute, and Mary E., oldest d. of Col. Francis McCormick of Clarke Co., Va., by the Rev. T. F. Martin, at Frankford, Clarke Co., Va. So. Ch., Jan. 23, 1868

Mollie C., and A. W. Kintz of Alexandria, by the Rev. H. L. Derby, at Heathsville, Northumberland Co., Va. So. Ch., Dec. 27, 1888

Molly, youngest d. of the late Col. Angus W. McDonald of Winchester, Va., and Henry Lyne, Esq. of Henderson, by the Rev. J. G. Minnigerode, at the residence of the bride's mother, So. Ch., May 10, 1883

Pearce Naylor (The Rev.), of Anchorage, Ky., and Frances Louise Browse, by the Rt. Rev. George W. Peterkin assisted by the Rev. J. L. Fish of Sistersville, at the home of the bride's mother, Mrs. Robert Browse, Raven Rock, Pleasants Co., W.Va. So. Ch., July 2, 1910

Sue L., d. of Col. Angus McDonald of Hampshire Co., and Maj. John B. Stanard, ex-mayor of Culpeper, by the Rev. Dr. Pratt, at Lexington, Va. So. Ch., Aug. 15, 1872

Susan Ida, and Hiram T. Cornnell, Esq., both of Clarke Co., Va., by the Rev. John P. Tyler, rector, in Christ Church, Millwood, Va. So. Ch., Dec. 31, 1891

McDONOUGH
A. A. (The Rev.), and Florence, d. of Judge John Brenon of Weston, by the Rev. J. F. Woods, at Weston, W.Va. So. Ch., June 29, 1876

McDOWELL
Thomas P., and L. Constance, d. of Wm. S. Warwick, by the Rev. Thomas Ambler, in Powhatan Co., Va. So. Ch., Feb. 27, 1857

William Adair, Esq. of Clay City, Ky., and Alice Harrison, third d. of the Rt. Rev. Thomas Underwood Dudley, D.D., by the Bishop of the Diocese of Kentucky, in Calvary Church, Louisville, Ky. So. Ch., Nov. 3, 1887

MACE
Willie Amelia, d. of Wm. W. Mace, and Luther P. Martin, all of Dorchester Co., Md., by the Rev. William W. Greene, at the residence of the bride's father. So. Ch., Dec. 23, 1880

McELWAIN
Frank Arthur, D.D. (The Rt. Rev.), Bishop of Minnesota, and

MARRIAGE NOTICES IN THE SOUTHERN CHURCHMAN WITH DATES OF PUBLICATION

Mrs. Mabel Collins Lofstrom, by the Rt. Rev. Irving P. Johnston, D.D., in the Church of the Good Shepherd, Windom, Minn. So. Ch., Aug. 14, 1920

McELWEE
Samuel (The Rev.), of Dover, Del. (formerly of Washington, D.C.), and Mary, eldest d. of the late John and Catharine Elliott of Baltimore, by the Rt. Rev. Alfred Lee, D.D., at Wilmington, Del. So. Ch., Dec. 14, 1871

McENERY
John E., Esq., of Dinwiddie Co., and Hannah S., d. of Col. J. S. Gilliam, formerly of Petersburg, Va., by the Rev. T. H. Lacy, in St. Luke's Church, Nottoway Co., Va. So. Ch., Apr. 10, 1873

MACFARLAND
Elizabeth B., d. of Wm. H. MacFarland, Esq., and Dr. Randolph Barksdale, all of Richmond, by the Rev. Chas. Minnigerode, in St. Paul's Church, Richmond, Va. So. Ch., June 11, 1858

John Montgomery, and Agnes Lyle, d. of the late Samuel Forrest, Purser, U.S. Navy, by the Rev. Wm. H. Meade, at Charles Town, W.Va., at the residence of the bride's mother. So. Ch., Jan. 2, 1879

Nannie Beirne, d. of the late William MacFarland of Richmond, Va., and Frank Donaldson, Jr., by the Rev. Dr. C. W. Rankin, in St. Paul's Church, Baltimore. So. Ch., Apr. 29, 1880

McGARY
Charles, and Isabel Stuart, d. of Dr. J. C. and Mrs. M. C. Mercer, all of Durham, N.C., at the residence of W. L. Wall, on Chapel Hill St., Durham, N.C. So. Ch., Nov. 1, 1888

McGAVOCK
Cynthia, second d. of the late Ephraim McGavock, and Judge John H. Fulton, all of Wytheville, Va., by the Rev. Robb White, at the residence of the bride's mother. So. Ch., June 15, 1876

McGAW
G. A., of Baltimore, and Julia M. Lowe of Alexandria, Va., by the Rev. Thomas G. Addison, in Trinity Church, Washington, D.C. So. Ch., July 22, 1875

McGEHEE
J. R., Esq., of Kentucky, and Matilda, d. of the late Charles Middleton of Chesterfield Co., Va., by the Rev. A. B. Tizzard, at Woodstock Farm. So. Ch., Oct. 17, 1872

N. C., Esq., and Mary Lobbend, by the Rev. Wm. M. Nelson, in St. Paul's Church, Albemarle Co., Va. So. Ch., Dec. 5, 1867

P., and Anne H. Gilmer, both of Albemarle Co., Va., by the Rev. Wm. M. Nelson, at Edgefield. So. Ch., June 13, 1867

McGHEE
William G., Esq., of Bedford Co., Va., and Anna, d. of Nelson Sprinkel, Esq. of Harrisonburg, Va., by the Rev. T. U. Dudley, at the residence of the bride's father. So. Ch., Dec. 5, 1867

MACGILL
Davidge, of Hagerstown, Md., and Carrie E. Hansbury of New York City, by the Rev.

MARRIAGE NOTICES IN THE SOUTHERN CHURCHMAN WITH DATES OF PUBLICATION

P. D. Thompson, at the residence of Sam'l P. Wilson, Pittsylvania Co., Va. So. Ch., May 14, 1868

Mollie Ragan, d. of the late Dr. Chas. Macgill of Richmond, formerly of Hagerstown, Md., and Henry Rosenberg of Galveston, Texas, by the Rev. Hartley Carmichael of St. Paul's Church, in Grace Church, Richmond. So. Ch., Nov. 28, 1889

Wm. D., and Agnes H., d. of Samuel P. Wilson, Esq., all of Pittsylvania Co., by the Rev. P. D. Thompson, in Pittsylvania Co. So. Ch., Oct. 24, 1867

McGILL

Eleanor W., eldest d. of Dr. T. J. McGill of Frederick, Md., and Jos. A. Williamson, by the Rev. Jno. McGill assisted by the rector of the parish, the Rev. O. Ingle, at the residence of the bride's father. So. Ch., Nov. 16, 1871

John (The Rev.), and Virginia, third d. of Robt. Beverly, Esq. of Fauquier Co., by the Rev. R. M. McKim, in the Episcopal Church, at The Plains, Fauquier Co. So. Ch., July 3, 1873

Lizzie R., second d. of Dr. T. J. McGill of Frederick, Md., and Wm. Pinckney Mason, by the Rev. Jno. McGill, at the residence of the bride's father. So. Ch., Jan. 2, 1873

S. (Dr.), of Fauquier Co., Va., and Lizzie Randolph, eldest d. of Dr. John Faunt-Le-Roy, formerly of Clarke Co., by the Rev. John McGill, assistant

minister of St. James' Church, and the Rev. Richard T. Davis, in St. James' Church, Leesburg. So. Ch., May 11, 1871

Thomas J. (Dr.), of Jefferson, Mo., and Julia Ann, d. of Samuel Phillips, Esq. of Fredericksburg, Va., by the Rev. Richard H. Phillips. So. Ch., Dec. 15, 1837

McGILTON

Ella A., and James C. Hamilton, both of Uniontown, by the Rev. Henry T. Sharp, in St. John's Church, Uniontown. Ky. So. Ch., May 9, 1872

McGILVRA

Seth Curtis (Dr.), and Annie Kittredge Scott of Richmond, by the Rev. D. F. Sprigg, at No. 909 Park Ave., Richmond, the residence of Robert S. Chamberlayne, Esq., a cousin of the bride. So. Ch., Oct. 8, 1891

McGLASSON

Jennie, and Samuel B. Shaw, both of Fairfax Co., by the Rev. W. A. Alrich, at the residence of Wm. T. Ramsey, Esq., Fairfax C.H. So. Ch., Dec. 31, 1868

McGRATH

Fanny, of Ireland, and Joseph Bishop of Albemarle, by the Rev. Wm. M. Nelson, at the residence of the Rev. Joseph Wilmer, Albemarle Co. So. Ch., Nov. 5, 1858

McGUIRE

Benjamin Harrison, late of Halifax C.H., Va., and Eva Adaline Hurst of North Danville, Va., by the Rev. F. A. Peterson, in Calvary Church, North Danville. So. Ch., Dec. 12, 1889

Betty Burnet, d. of the Rev.

MARRIAGE NOTICES IN THE SOUTHERN CHURCHMAN WITH DATES OF PUBLICATION

Dr. E. C. McGuire, and the Rev. Charles E. Ambler, rector of St. Ann's Church, Albemarle Co., Va., in St. George's Church, Fredericksburg. So. Ch., Aug. 7, 1851

Betty C., d. of the Rev. William McGuire, and William A. Smoot, Esq. of Alexandria, Va., by the Rev. William McGuire, in Trinity Church, Washington, D.C. So. Ch., Oct. 23, 1873

Edward B. (The Rev.), and Sarah N., d. of Austin W. Fitzhugh, Esq., by the Rev. T. E. Locke, at Mill Bank, King George Co. So. Ch., July 15, 1869

Emily Page, youngest d. of the late Rev. John P. McGuire, and Philip W. Nelson of Albemarle, by the Rev. J. B. Newton, in St. John's Church, Tappahannock. So. Ch., July 10, 1873

F. H., and Helen, eldest d. of Emil O. Nolting, by the Rev. Mr. Oehlschlager, at the residence of the bride's father, in Richmond. So. Ch., Nov. 26, 1885.

James Mercer Garnett, M.D., of Berryville, Va., and Mrs. Elizabeth Alexandria Ware Britton, d. of the late Josiah W. Ware, Esq. of Berryville, Va., by the Rev. Horace Edwin Hayden assisted by the Rev. Henry L. Jones, at Plymouth, Pa. So. Ch., May 8, 1884

Janie M., d. of the rector, and George Turner of Belle Grove, by the Rev. Edward McGuire, in St. John's Church, King George C.H. So. Ch., Oct. 26, 1876

John P., and S. R. Morris, by the Rev. Joshua Peterkin, in St. James' Church. So. Ch., July 7, 1881

Lucy E. H., eldest d. of David H. McGuire, Esq., and Treadwell Smith, Jr., all of Clarke Co., Va., by the Rev. H. Suter, at Berryville. So. Ch., Nov. 25, 1859

Mary M., youngest d. of the late D. H. McGuire of Clarke Co., Va., and John Stevens of Hobokem, by the rector, the Rev. P. P. Phillips, assisted by the Rev. G. C. Houghton, rector of Trinity Church, Hobokem, N.J., in Grace Church, Berryville, Va. So. Ch., June 28, 1883

Minna C., and J. Fitzgerald Jones of Fauquier Co., Va., by the Rev. W. Strother Jones, at the residence of Julian Ingle, Charles Co., Md. So. Ch., Aug. 10, 1893

Sallie B., and the Rev. Charles C. Randolph, by the Rev. William McGuire assisted by the Rev. Henderson Suter, in Christ Church, Alexandria, Va. So. Ch., May 22, 1884

Sallie Nelson, d. of William H. McGuire, and gr.d. of the late Woodson Hughes, Esq., of Halifax C.H., Va., and Joseph Trueman Clark of Prince Edward Co., by the Rev. Dr. O. A. Kinsolving, in St. John's Church, Halifax C.H. So. Ch., Feb. 7, 1889

William (The Rev.), of Westmoreland, and Mariette, d. of Gustavus B. Alexander, Esq., by the Rev. B. B. Leacock, in St. Paul's Church, King George Co., Va.

MARRIAGE NOTICES IN THE SOUTHERN CHURCHMAN WITH DATES OF PUBLICATION

So. Ch., Mar. 25, 1852
Wm. (The Rev.), of Essex Co., Va., and Mary Wilson Beadles of Richmond, Va., by the Rev. Joshua Peterkin, D.D., in St. James' Church, Richmond, Va. So. Ch., Oct. 11, 1883

McHUGH
Mary Ann, of Richmond, Va., and Julius C. Hudson of Richmond, Va., by the Rev. Samuel R. Slack, in Richmond, Va. So. Ch., Dec. 26, 1862

McILHANY
H. M., of Staunton, Va., and Fannie B. Jones, by the Rev. W. Strother Jones, in Emmanuel Church, Fauquier Co., Va. So. Ch., May 8, 1884

John W. (Dr.), of Greenville, Miss., and Margaret B., eldest d. of James K. Skinker, Esq. of Fauquier, by the Rev. O. A. Kinsolving, at Huntley, Fauquier Co., Va. So. Ch., Mar. 8, 1861

McINTOSH
D. G. (Col.), of South Carolina, and Virginia J. Pegram of Richmond, by the Rev. Charles Minnigerode, D.D., at Linden Square, Richmond, Va. So. Ch., Nov. 30, 1865

Jas. (Capt.), of the U.S. Army, and Judith Brockenbrough, d. of the late Jefferson Phelps of Covington, Ky., and gr. d. of the late Judge Wm. Brockenbrough of Richmond, Va., by the Rev. R. T. Davis, in Trinity Church, Martinsburg, Va. So. Ch., Mar. 4, 1859

Roderick Chilli, of Quitman, Ga., and Cora Barksdale, second d. of John O. Lewis of Albemarle, by the Rev. T. E. Locke, at Cliffside, near Scottsville, Albemarle Co., Va. So. Ch., Oct. 24, 1878

McKAIG
Thomas J., Jr., and Ada, d. of M. S. Norman, by the Rev. Julius E. Grammer, in St. Peter's Church, Baltimore. So. Ch., May 18, 1882

MACKALL
Anna W., d. of the late Henry C. Mackall, Esq. of "Wilna", Cecil Co., and niece of the officiating clergyman, and Capt. William H. May of Elkton, Md., by the Rev. John Collins McCabe, D.D., in St. Luke's Church, Bladensburg, Md. So. Ch., Oct. 17, 1867

Benjamin F., of Moorhead, Minn., and Mary H., d. of the late Lt. Col. John D. Kurtz, U.S. Engineers, by the Rev. Richard N. Thomas, in Trinity Church, West Philadelphia. So. Ch., Feb. 21, 1884

Robert McGill, and Alice Ashby, by the Rev. Jno. McGill, at "Sunny Side", the residence of the bride's father, in Fauquier Co. So. Ch., Jan. 30, 1868

Virginia, youngest d. of the late Henry C. Mackall, Esq. of Elkton, and the Rev. John Collins McCabe, D.D., rector of St. Ann's Church, Middletown, Del., by the Rev. R. H. B. Mitchell assisted by the Rev. Doane Mitchell, in Trinity Church, Elkton, Md. So. Ch., Oct. 15, 1868

McKAY
G. D. (The Rev.), formerly of

MARRIAGE NOTICES IN THE SOUTHERN CHURCHMAN WITH DATES OF PUBLICATION

the Valley of Virginia, Presbyterian Missionary, and Chang Mia Tsong, a puella Formosa, at Formosa, China. So. Ch., Nov. 28, 1878

McKENNEY
Constance E., and P. R. Harvey, by the Rev. D. M. Wharton, at the residence of the bride's mother, Montross. So. Ch., Dec. 4, 1873

MACKENZIE
Edmund Lyons, and Julia Stricker, only d. of Peyton S. Coles of Albemarle Co., by the Rev. T. E. Locke assisted by the Rev. Robert Coles, in Christ Church, St. Anne's Parish, Albemarle Co., Va. So. Ch., July 26, 1888

Ella B., d. of the late Thos. Mackenzie of Baltimore, and the Rev. Ogle Marbury of Howard Co., by the Rev. Bishop Pinckney assisted by the Rev. Dr. Leeds and the Rev. Dr. Lewin, in Grace Church, Baltimore. So. Ch., Apr. 15, 1880

MACKIE
Arthur James (The Rev.), s. of Mr. and Mrs. R. A. Mackie of Renova, Pa., and Mabel Helen, d. of Mr. and Mrs. E. H. McConnell of Williamsport, Pa., by the Rt. Rev. Hiram R. Hulse, D.D., Bishop of Cuba, in All Saints' Church, Guantanamo, Cuba, where the groom is rector. So. Ch., Apr. 5, 1924

McKIM
Haslett (The Rev.), and Harriet R., d. of Henry R. Winthrop, Esq., all of New York, by the Rev. George S. Converse, at the residence of the bride's parents.
So. Ch., Sept. 22, 1870

John Leighton (The Rev.), of Philadelphia, and Sarah F., d. of Henry F. Rodney of Lewes, by the Rev. George Seymour Lewis, in St. Peter's Church, Lewes, Del. So. Ch., Dec. 21, 1860

Randolph H. (Lt.), P.A.C.S., of Baltimore, and Agnes Grey, eldest d. of the officiating clergyman, the Rev. R. H. Phillips, assisted by the Rev. J. A. Latane, in Trinity Church, Staunton, Va. So. Ch., Mar. 20, 1863

Randolph Harrison (The Rev.), D.D., and Mrs. A. M. C. Brooke, d. of the late Hon. Daniel R. Clymer of Reading, Pa., by the Rt. Rev. Wm. Paret, D.D., Bishop of Maryland, assisted by the Rev. Halstead McKim, in St. Thomas' Church, New York. So. Ch., July 31, 1890

McKINNEY
Ellen Dupuy, youngest d. of the late Thomas McKinney of Lynchburg, Va., and John T. Berry of Paris, Texas, by the Rev. George Beckett, in St. Peter's Church, Columbia, Tenn. So. Ch., Nov. 21, 1872

McKINNY
John H., and Martha, d. of the late Benjamin Gee, by the Rev. T. E. Locke. So. Ch., May 24, 1839

McKNIGHT
Kate P., d. of Wm. H. McKnight, Esq. of Alexandria, Va., and Prof. J. M. Fischer of Washington, Ga., by the Rev. D. F. Sprigg, at Alexandria, Va.

MARRIAGE NOTICES IN THE SOUTHERN CHURCHMAN WITH DATES OF PUBLICATION

McLAURIN
M. F., of Rome, Ga., and Elizabeth A., d. of Mrs. Carter H. Harrison, by the Rev. William C. Williams, at "Elkora", Cumberland Co., Va. So. Ch., Aug. 25, 1881

McLEAN
Donald, of New York, and Emily Nelson, d. of Judge John Ritchie, and gr. d. of Judge William Maulsby, by the Rev. Osborn Ingle and the Rt. Rev. William Pinckney, Bishop of Maryland, in All Saints' Church, Frederick, Md. So. Ch., May 3, 1883

Donald, of Joana, Fairfax Co., and Lucy M. Tebbs of Alexandria, Va., by the Rev. George H. Norton, D.D., in St. Paul's Church, Alexandria, Va. So. Ch., July 8, 1886

Lucretia, formerly of Alexandria, Va., and W. H. Snyder of Alton, by the Rev. R. D. Brooke, at Galena, Ill. So. Ch., Aug. 14, 1851

Malcolm, of Alexandria, Va., and Olive Dunbar, d. of the Rev. Robert D. Brooke of Iowa, by the Rev. R. H. McKim, in Christ Church, Alexandria, Va. So. Ch., Nov. 20, 1873

MACLEAN
W. L., and Nannie Mayo, d. of R. H. and Agnes Dade Fitzhugh, at the residence of the bride's father, in Lexington, Ky. So. Ch., Sept. 28, 1893

McLEOD
James Edward, of Washington, and Helen Virginia Martin formerly of Buchanan, Va., by the Rev. David Barr, in the Church of the Epiphany, Washington, D.C. So. Ch., July 2, 1891

L. Lamar, formerly of Richmond, and Melissa Kennedy of New Castle, Pa., by the Rev. Dr. Steel, rector of the church, in the Church of St. Luke and the Epiphany. So. Ch., Sept. 18, 1926

MACLIN
William Henry, of Tennessee, and Mary Aletha, d. of Lancelot Minor, Esq. of Amherst Co., Va., by the Rev. R. L. Dabney, D.D., of the U. T. Seminary, at Briery Tenowho. So. Ch., Sept. 26, 1872

McMEANS
Ella, d. of Dr. S. A. McMeans, and the Hon. F. L. B. Goodwin of Vallejo, by the Rev. Dr. Smith, at the residence of the bride's father at Santa Rosa, Cal. So. Ch., Oct. 20, 1870

McMILLAN
Harriet Harrington, d. of the Rev. and Mrs. Alexander McMillan of Carlisle, Pa., and the Rev. Samuel Blackwell Chilton, rector of St. Paul's Church, Carlisle, Pa. So. Ch., Sept. 26, 1925

McMINN
Kate C., second d. of John A. McMinn, Esq. of Hanover Co., and R. Temple Southall of New Kent, by the Rev. S. S. Hepbron, at the residence of the bride's father. So. Ch., Jan. 1, 1891

Omega, eldest d. of John A. McMinn of Hanover Co., and Delaware B. Gardner, by the Rev. S. S. Hepbron, at the residence of the bride's father. So. Ch., Dec. 1, 1887

McMULLEN
Harris, and Mary J. Pane, both of Hanover, by the Rev. Robt. Douglas Roller, in Trinity Church, St. Martin's Parish.* So. Ch., Jan. 3, 1878

McMULLIN
Andrew J., of Kentucky, and

---

* St. Martin's Parish is in Hanover County, Virginia (Journal ... Diocese of Virginia, Richmond, Va., 1941)

MARRIAGE NOTICES IN THE SOUTHERN CHURCHMAN WITH DATES OF PUBLICATION

Sallie A., d. of the late Kinney Stribling of Staunton, Va., by the Rev. Horace E. Hayden, at the residence of John W. English, Esq., Point Pleasant, W.Va. So. Ch., Nov. 21, 1867

MACMURDO
Jane B. (Mrs.), d. of David Higginbotham, Esq. of Albemarle Co., and Dr. Robert W. Haxall of Richmond, Va., by the Rev. Richard K. Meade, at Mowen. So. Ch., Nov. 22, 1839

Kathleen M., of Ashland, Va., and F. S. Williams of Baltimore, by the Rev. G. W. Easter. So. Ch., Mar. 26, 1868

Mary E., d. of C. W. MacMurdo of Alexandria, Va., and Thomas Pemberton of Goochland Co., Va., by the Rev. George W. Woodbridge. So. Ch., Dec. 14, 1855

Rose, of Richmond, Va., and the Rev. Geo. W. Easter of Baltimore, Md., by the Rev. Geo. Woodbridge, D.D., at Ashland, Hanover Co., Va. So. Ch., Mar. 21, 1867

Sadie C., only d. of James B. Macmurdo and gr.d. of the late Bishop Moore, and Alfred, s. of the Hon. Wm. C. Rives, by the Rev. Dr. Minnigerode, in St. Paul's Church, Richmond, Va. So. Ch., Feb. 11, 1859

McMURDO
Rebecca K., and Charles Stebbins, by the Rev. John McGill, at the residence of the bride's brother, Col. John McMurdo, Ashland, Va. So. Ch., Feb. 3, 1887

McNEELY
Thomson W., and Mary Henrietta, d. of Devin Derickson, by the Rev. Geo. S. Fitzhugh, in St. Paul's Church, Berlin, Md. So. Ch., Dec. 12, 1872

McNEILEY
J. S. (Capt.), of Greenville, Miss., and Mary M., d. of Col. Edmund and Mary Berkeley of Prince William Co., Va., by the Rev. A. P. Gray assisted by the Rev. H. T. Sharp, at "Evergreen." So. Ch., June 30, 1881

McNEMARA
Matilda C., d. of Hugh C. McNemara, and James J. Hunton, by the Rev. Jno. Towles, at Anley, the residence of Charles J. Stovin, Fauquier Co. So. Ch., May 16, 1856

McNUTT
James M. (Dr.), of Bedford, and Mollie L. Fisher of Northampton Co., Va., by the Rev. J. B. Craighill, in Christ Church, Eastville. So. Ch., Mar. 24, 1870

MACON
Annie L., d. of E. B. Macon of Princess Anne, and the Rev. John Cornick, by the Rev. Mr. Lloyd and the Rev. Mr. Anson, rector, in the Old Chapel, Princess Anne. So. Ch., Nov. 2, 1893

Charlotte N., and Frank M. Randolph, by the Rev. Robb White, in Grace Church, Albemarle Co., Va. So. Ch., Jan. 25, 1883

Lucy S., d. of the late Miles Macon of Richmond, Va., and John J. Clarke, Civil Engineer, Rockingham Co., N.C., by the Rev. H. S. Kepler. So. Ch., Apr. 13, 1860

Mary Sayre, d. of Dr. W. H. Macon, and Nathaniel B. Johnston of Memphis, Tenn., by the Rev. L. Hepburn, in Immanuel Church, Hanover Co., Va. So. Ch., Feb. 2, 1882

MARRIAGE NOTICES IN THE SOUTHERN CHURCHMAN WITH DATES OF PUBLICATION

Randolph Harrison, and Katheryne E. Whitby, both of St. Louis, Mo. So. Ch., Dec. 11, 1915
Sallie, d. of E. B. Macon of Princess Anne Co., and John C. Maupin of Portsmouth, Va., by the Rev. Reverdy Estill, pastor of Trinity Church, Portsmouth, assisted by the Rev. C. B. Bryan, in the old Eastern Shore Chapel, Princess Anne Co., Va. So. Ch., Mar. 4, 1880
Wm. Hartwell, of Hanover Co., and Mrs. Mary G. Webb, d. of Col. R. Harrison of Williamsburg, by the Rev. S. S. Hopbrow, in the Protestant Episcopal Church, Williamsburg, Va. So. Ch., Dec. 24, 1885

MACRAE
Alice, oldest d. of the late Henry and Elizabeth S. MacRae of Chuckatuck, Nansemond Co., Va., and Jesse John Vann of Monroe, Union Co., N.C., by the Rev. Douglass Hooff, at the residence of the bride's mother. So. Ch., Apr. 21, 1887
Emily, only d. of Alexander MacRae, Esq., and James F. Payne of Virginia, by the Rev. T. M. Ambler of Wilmington, at Argyle, the residence of the bride's father, in Robeson Co., N.C. So. Ch., Nov. 19, 1874
George H. T., of Fairfax Co., and Maggie, d. of M. M. Jamesson, Esq. of Centerville, by the Rev. W. A. Alrich, at Centerville, the residence of the bride's father, Fairfax Co., Va. So. Ch., Dec. 31, 1868
Louisa V., of Fairfax Co., and Albert G. Gardner of Alexandria Co., by the Rev. W.

F. Lockwood, in the chapel of the Theological Seminary of Virginia. So. Ch., Jan. 18, 1851
Samuel, s. of Judge MacRae of North Carolina, and Evelynn, d. of Robert and Mary Clayter of Bedford City, Va., by the Rev. T. W. Jones, in St. John's Church, Bedford City, Va. So. Ch., Dec. 25, 1890
Sheldena, of Upperville, Fauquier Co., Va., and the Rev. Maurice Clarke of England, by the Rev. R. W. Trapnell, in St. Andrew's-on-the-Mountain, near Charles Town, W.Va. So. Ch., June 22, 1907

McRAE
Cameron Farquhar, of North Carolina, and Sarah Nicoll Woodward of New Jersey, by the Rt. Rev. F. R. Graves, D.D., in St. John's Church, Pro-Cathedral, Shanghai, China. So. Ch., Apr. 11, 1908
Duncan L., of Georgia, and Lizzie Haile of Essex Co., by the Rev. Everard Meade, in St. Paul's Church, Essex Co., Va. So. Ch., Oct. 1, 1885

MACREA
Mary, and M. Filmore Pinner, both of Chuckatuck, Nansemond Co., Va., by the Rev. Douglass Hooff, at home. So. Ch., Dec. 6, 1883

McREE
Joseph H., of Wilmington, N.C., and Catherine Cameron Buxton, by the Rev. J. Buxton, D.D., assisted by the Rev. D. Hillhouse Buel, at Asheville, N.C. So. Ch., Nov. 11, 1875

McVEIGH
Benjamin Franklin, of Alexandria, and Sarah E. Lane, d. of Edward Fearneyhough, Esq. of

MARRIAGE NOTICES IN THE SOUTHERN CHURCHMAN WITH DATES OF PUBLICATION

Albemarle Co., by the Rev. S. R. Slack, at Mt. Airy, Albemarle Co., Va. So. Ch., Mar. 3, 1853
L. W., and Charlotte R. Skelton, both of Richmond, by the Rev. P. F. Berkeley, in The Monumental Church, Richmond. So. Ch., Oct. 14, 1869

MADDOX
Alfred (Capt.), of Baltimore, and Charlotte, d. of Henry Ayres, Esq., by the Rev. J. B. Craighill, at "Salt Grove", Northampton Co., Va. So. Ch., Jan. 27, 1870
Clifford M., of Baltimore, Md., and Charlotte F. Butler of Harrisonburg, Va., by the Rev. D. M. Wood, at the residence of the bride's brother, Dr. W. S. Butler, Roanoke City, Va. So. Ch., Apr. 23, 1885
W. C. H., of Richmond, Va., and Martha P. Weisiger, by the Rev. Jas. H. Williams, at Highland Lodge, Nelson Co., the bride's home. So. Ch., Nov. 14, 1908

MADDUX
Cora V., and Thos. S. Johnson, by the Rev. Jno. McGill, in Trinity Church, Salem, Fauquier Co. So. Ch., July 15, 1869

MADISON
Edward Cooper, of Orange Co., Md., and Lizzie Fox, youngest d. of the late John F. Stagg of Richmond, by the Rev. M. D. Hoge, D.D., in Richmond, Va. So. Ch., July 22, 1886
Lelia B., youngest d. of the late Ambrose Madison of Madison, and Wm. Pope Dabney of Powhatan, by the Rev. J. Earnest, at Woodbury Forest, Madison, Va. So. Ch., Jan. 15, 1857

Robt. L., M.D., of Lexington, Va., and Helen T., youngest d. of the late John Monro* Banister, Esq., by the Rev. Mr. Platt, in St. Paul's Church, Petersburg, Va. So. Ch., Feb. 10, 1860
Wm. Randolph, and Margaret Gray Dickenson, by the Rev. J. K. Mason, in St. George's Church, Fredericksburg, Va. So. Ch., Oct. 9, 1890

MAER
Mary Harriet, d. of the Hon. and Mrs. William J. Maer of Seneca Falls, and the Rev. Frederick Ward, s. of Mrs. Roy C. Kates and the late Mr. Kates of Rochester, rector of Trinity Church, Seneca Falls, N.Y., by the Rt. Rev. Malcolm E. Peabody, D.D., Bishop Coadjutor of Central New York, assisted by the Rev. Jerome Kates, D.D., rector of St. Stephen's Church, Rochester, the groom's uncle, in Trinity Church, Seneca Falls, N.Y. So. Ch., Aug. 16, 1941

MAGILL
Nannie Temple, d. of the late Dr. Henry D. Magill of Leesburg, Va., and Leonard K. Sparrow of Baltimore, by the Rev. Dr. J. E. Grammer, in St. Peter's Church, Baltimore. So. Ch., Feb. 22, 1877

MAGRUDER
Ella G., and Philip D. Laird, by the Rev. Wm. H. Laird, in St. John's Church, Olney, Montgomery Co., Md. So. Ch., Dec. 31, 1885
Emily C. B., of Prince George's Co., Md., and Edson E. Ferris of New York, by the Rev. J. H. Elliot, D.D., in Ascension Parsonage, Washington, D.C.

* Given as printed

MARRIAGE NOTICES IN THE SOUTHERN CHURCHMAN WITH DATES OF PUBLICATION

Randolph Harrison, and Katheryne E. Whitby, both of St. Louis, Mo. So. Ch., Dec. 11, 1915

Sallie, d. of E. B. Macon of Princess Anne Co., and John C. Maupin of Portsmouth, Va., by the Rev. Reverdy Estill, pastor of Trinity Church, Portsmouth, assisted by the Rev. C. B. Bryan, in the old Eastern Shore Chapel, Princess Anne Co., Va. So. Ch., Mar. 4, 1880

Wm. Hartwell, of Hanover Co., and Mrs. Mary G. Webb, d. of Col. R. Harrison of Williamsburg, by the Rev. S. S. Hepbren, in the Protestant Episcopal Church, Williamsburg, Va. So. Ch., Dec. 24, 1885

MACRAE

Alice, oldest d. of the late Henry and Elizabeth S. MacRae of Chuckatuck, Nansemond Co., Va., and Jesse John Vann of Monroe, Union Co., N.C., by the Rev. Douglass Hooff, at the residence of the bride's mother. So. Ch., Apr. 21, 1887

Emily, only d. of Alexander MacRae, Esq., and James F. Payne of Virginia, by the Rev. T. M. Ambler of Wilmington, at Argyle, the residence of the bride's father, in Robeson Co., N.C. So. Ch., Nov. 19, 1874

George H. T., of Fairfax Co., and Maggie, d. of M. M. Jamesson, Esq. of Centerville, by the Rev. W. A. Alrich, at Centerville, the residence of the bride's father, Fairfax Co., Va. So. Ch., Dec. 31, 1868

Louisa V., of Fairfax Co., and Albert G. Gardner of Alexandria Co., by the Rev. W. F. Lockwood, in the chapel of the Theological Seminary of Virginia. So. Ch., Jan. 18, 1851

Samuel, s. of Judge MacRae of North Carolina, and Evelynn, d. of Robert and Mary Clayter of Bedford City, Va., by the Rev. T. W. Jones, in St. John's Church, Bedford City, Va. So. Ch., Dec. 25, 1890

Sheldona, of Upperville, Fauquier Co., Va., and the Rev. Maurice Clarke of England, by the Rev. R. W. Trapnell, in St. Andrew's-on-the-Mountain, near Charles Town, W.Va. So. Ch., June 22, 1907

McRAE

Cameron Farquhar, of North Carolina, and Sarah Nicoll Woodward of New Jersey, by the Rt. Rev. F. R. Graves, D.D., in St. John's Church, Pro-Cathedral, Shanghai, China. So. Ch., Apr. 11, 1908

Duncan L., of Georgia, and Lizzie Haile of Essex Co., by the Rev. Everard Meade, in St. Paul's Church, Essex Co., Va. So. Ch., Oct. 1, 1885

MACREA

Mary, and M. Filmore Finner, both of Chuckatuck, Nansemond Co., Va., by the Rev. Douglass Hooff, at home. So. Ch., Dec. 6, 1883

McREE

Joseph H., of Wilmington, N.C., and Catherine Cameron Buxton, by the Rev. J. Buxton, D.D., assisted by the Rev. D. Hillhouse Buel, at Asheville, N.C. So. Ch., Nov. 11, 1875

McVEIGH

Benjamin Franklin, of Alexandria, and Sarah E. Lane, d. of Edward Fearneyhough, Esq. of

MARRIAGE NOTICES IN THE SOUTHERN CHURCHMAN WITH DATES OF PUBLICATION

Albemarle Co., by the Rev. S. R. Slack, at Mt. Airy, Albemarle Co., Va. So. Ch., Mar. 3, 1853

L. W., and Charlotte R. Skelton, both of Richmond, by the Rev. P. F. Berkeley, in The Monumental Church, Richmond. So. Ch., Oct. 14, 1869

MADDOX

Alfred (Capt.), of Baltimore, and Charlotte, d. of Henry Ayres, Esq., by the Rev. J. B. Craighill, at "Salt Grove", Northampton Co., Va. So. Ch., Jan. 27, 1870

Clifford M., of Baltimore, Md., and Charlotte F. Butler of Harrisonburg, Va., by the Rev. D. M. Wood, at the residence of the bride's brother, Dr. W. S. Butler, Roanoke City, Va. So. Ch., Apr. 23, 1885

W. C. H., of Richmond, Va., and Martha P. Weisiger, by the Rev. Jas. H. Williams, at Highland Lodge, Nelson Co., the bride's home. So. Ch., Nov. 14, 1908

MADDUX

Cora V., and Thos. S. Johnson, by the Rev. Jno. McGill, in Trinity Church, Salem, Fauquier Co. So. Ch., July 15, 1869

MADISON

Edward Cooper, of Orange Co., Md., and Lizzie Fox, youngest d. of the late John F. Stagg of Richmond, by the Rev. M. D. Hoge, D.D., in Richmond, Va. So. Ch., July 22, 1886

Lelia B., youngest d. of the late Ambrose Madison of Madison, and Wm. Pope Dabney of Powhatan, by the Rev. J. Earnest, at Woodbury Forest, Madison, Va. So. Ch., Jan. 15, 1857

Robt. L., M.D., of Lexington, Va., and Helen T., youngest d. of the late John Monro* Banister, Esq., by the Rev. Mr. Platt, in St. Paul's Church, Petersburg, Va. So. Ch., Feb. 10, 1860

Wm. Randolph, and Margaret Gray Dickenson, by the Rev. J. K. Mason, in St. George's Church, Fredericksburg, Va. So. Ch., Oct. 9, 1890

MAER

Mary Harriet, d. of the Hon. and Mrs. William J. Maer of Seneca Falls, and the Rev. Frederick Ward, s. of Mrs. Roy C. Kates and the late Mr. Kates of Rochester, rector of Trinity Church, Seneca Falls, N.Y., by the Rt. Rev. Malcolm E. Peabody, D.D., Bishop Coadjutor of Central New York, assisted by the Rev. Jerome Kates, D.D., rector of St. Stephen's Church, Rochester, the groom's uncle, in Trinity Church, Seneca Falls, N.Y. So. Ch., Aug. 15, 1941

MAGILL

Nannie Temple, d. of the late Dr. Henry D. Magill of Leesburg, Va., and Leonard K. Sparrow of Baltimore, by the Rev. Dr. J. E. Grammer, in St. Peter's Church, Baltimore. So. Ch., Feb. 22, 1877

MAGRUDER

Ella G., and Philip D. Laird, by the Rev. Wm. H. Laird, in St. John's Church, Olney, Montgomery Co., Md. So. Ch., Dec. 31, 1885

Emily C. B., of Prince George's Co., Md., and Edson E. Ferris of New York, by the Rev. J. H. Elliot, D.D., in Ascension Parsonage, Washington, D.C.

* Given as printed

MARRIAGE NOTICES IN THE SOUTHERN CHURCHMAN WITH DATES OF PUBLICATION

So. Ch., Jan. 31, 1889
Henry M., and Sallie G. Minor, both of Albemarle Co., by the Rev. Mr. Hanckel of Christ Church, at Ridgeway, the residence of the bride's mother. So. Ch., Apr. 22, 1869

MAHAN
John T., and Kate C. Mitchell, both of Pittsylvania Co., Va., by the Rev. C. D. Pruden, at the residence of the bride's father, H. C. Mitchell, Pittsylvania Co. So. Ch., Jan. 22, 1885

MAHON
Mittie Gibson (Mrs.), of Boonville, and George Todd, eldest s. of the late Rev. and Mrs. Edward D. Irvine, head of dep't of mathematics, Kemper Military School, Boonville, Mo., by the Rev. H. E. Martin, rector of Calvary Episcopal Church, Sedalia, Mo., in Christ Episcopal Church, Boonville, Mo. So. Ch., Aug. 23, 1919

MAITLAND
Benjamin** Jr., Esq., and Estelle, d. of C. M. Deshon, Esq., all of Baltimore, by the Rev. Jno. C. McCabe, D.D., rector of the Church of the Ascension, in Baltimore. So. Ch., Aug. 17, 1860

MAJOR
Henry (The Rev.), of Virginia, and Sarah Elizabeth, d. of Horatio Jones of Georgetown, by the Rev. Dr. Marbury. So. Ch., Sept. 27, 1839
William Jr., and Laura M., eldest d. of J. M. Spindle, Esq., all of Culpeper Co., Va., by the Rev. John McGill, at the residence of the bride's father. So. Ch., Nov. 7, 1878

MALLABY
Thomas (The Rev.), and Catherine Kortright, d. of the late Capt. John Seaman of Staten Island, by the Rev. W. H. Walter, in St. Paul's Church, Tomkinsville, R.I. So. Ch., Aug. 11, 1837

MALLORY
Edmund S., and Jennie Parker, by the Rev. J. A. Harrison, at Jackson, Tenn. So. Ch., Oct. 3, 1872
George S., D.D. (The Rev.), and Ellen Haile Bogardus, d. of the late John J. Haile, Esq. of Plattsburg, N.J., by the Rev. J. H. Chesley, in St. John's Church, Hampton, Va. So. Ch., Dec. 21, 1882

MANLY
Helen A., d. of the late Gov. Charles Manly of North Carolina, and Daniel Sprigg Pickrell, by the Rev. J. B. Perry, at Washington. So. Ch., Oct. 11, 1888

MANN
Charles, and Emerline J. Banton of Richmond, by the Rev. W. H. Kinckle. So. Ch., June 27, 1856
Nannie H., third d. of the Rev. C. Mann, and Wm. M. Peyton of Albemarle Co., by the Rev. Wm. G. Jackson, D.D., of Maryland, in Ware Church. So. Ch., Nov. 10, 1870

MANNING
Eliza Sinkler, d. of the late Hon. Richard J. Manning, and Richard C. Richardson, Jr., all of Clarendon, by the Rev. Edward R. Miles, at the residence of the bride's mother, in Sumter Co., S.C. So. Ch., Jan. 29, 1880*
Frank J., Esq., of Jefferson Co.,

---

* A notice appears in the issue of Jan. 15, 1880, identical with this except that "Richard I. Manning" is written "Richard J. Manning"
** Given as printed

MARRIAGE NOTICES IN THE SOUTHERN CHURCHMAN WITH DATES OF PUBLICATION

Va., and Louisa Antoinette, d. of Jacob N. Cowan*, Esq., by the Rev. T. U. Dudley, at "Belmont", Rockingham Co., Va. So. Ch., Jan. 30, 1868

John, of Prince George's Co., Md., and Mary Eliza, d. of Dr. Thomas R. Ditty of Westmoreland Co., Va., by the Rev. T. E. Locke, at Eltham, Westmoreland Co., Va. So. Ch., June 18, 1858

Joseph Thruston, and Alice Lloyd, d. of Mrs. M. E. and the late Hon. W. T. Goldsborough, by the Rev. Dr. W. W. Williams, in Christ Church, Baltimore. So. Ch., Dec. 4, 1884

William J., of Winchester, Va., and Rosa W. Bradford of Clarke Co., Va., by the Rev. Jas. R. Hubard assisted by the Rev. John P. Tyler, at "Abbeyville", Clarke Co., Va. So. Ch., May 19, 1892

Wm. L., of Clarendon, and Margaret C., d. of the late Wm. Adger, Esq. of Charleston, by the Rev. G. R. Brackett, in Second Presbyterian Church. So. Ch., Feb. 22, 1877

MANSON
Nathaniel Clayton, Jr., of Lynchburg, Va., and Henrietta Ege, d. of George Johnston of Alexandria, by the Rev. Dr. Norton, in St. Paul's Church, Alexandria. So. Ch., Nov. 5, 1891

MANTLO
Bettie V., d. of John G. Mantlo of Hanover Co., Va., and Capt. Benjamin F. Moore, by the Rev. S. S. Hepbron, at the residence of the bride's father. So. Ch., Jan. 24, 1884

MAPP
Gabriella S., and Dr. George L. Ames, by the Rev. Henry L. Derby, in St. George's Church, Pungoteague, Accomac, Va. So. Ch., Dec. 14, 1893

MARBURY
Elizabeth Marshall, of Prince George's Co., Md., and the Rev. William Christian of Washington, D.C., by the Rev. Dr. Pinckney, in St. Luke's Church, Bladensburg, Md. So. Ch., Oct. 1, 1858

Fannie S., d. of the late Rev. J. Somerville Marbury of Alabama, and Dr. J. L. Beale of Washington, D.C., by the Rev. C. K. Nelson, D.D., at Georgetown, D.C., residence of the bride's gr. father, John Marbury, Esq. So. Ch., Dec. 11, 1873

Ogle (The Rev.), of Howard Co., and Ella B., d. of the late Thos. Mackenzie of Baltimore, by Bishop Pinckney, assisted by the Rev. Dr. Leeds and the Rev. Dr. Lewin, in Grace Church, Baltimore. So. Ch., Apr. 15, 1880

MARCHANT
John R., and Virginia E. Blackburn, by the Rev. J. Hervey Hundley, at "Barn Elms", Middlesex Co., Va. So. Ch., Feb. 29, 1872

MARDERS
Ida E., and J. W. Willcoxen, both of Prince William Co., Va., by the Rev. A. P. Gray, at the residence of the bride's mother. So. Ch., Jan. 4, 1883

MARINER
Lillie A., of Fauquier Co., Va., and Dr. Leslie R. Quackenbush of Florida, by the Rev.

* Given as printed

MARRIAGE NOTICES IN THE SOUTHERN CHURCHMAN WITH DATES OF PUBLICATION

H. B. Lee, at Rappahannock Station, Fauquier Co., Va. So. Ch., Dec. 22, 1887

MARKOE
Emily Maxey, d. of the late Francis Markoe, and David Caldwell F. Rivinus of Philadelphia, by the Rev. Wm. Hodges, D.D., at Tulip Hill, the residence of the bride, in Anne Arundel Co. So. Ch., Nov. 13, 1873

MARKS
Mary Ella, d. of the late John Marks, Esq., and Richard H. Peterson, Esq., all of Prince George, by the Rev. R. P. Johnson, at Old Town, Prince George Co., Va. So. Ch., Nov. 5, 1858

MARMADUKE
Lydia Ann, and Dr. R. A. Stuart, both of Westmoreland, by the Rev. D. M. Wharton. So. Ch., Feb. 8, 1883

MARNER
Eleanor, and George E. Nelson of Baltimore, (lately of Culpeper, Va.), at Annandale, the residence of the bride's father, in Culpeper Co., Va. So. Ch., Dec. 21, 1871

MARR
Robert, of U.S. Coast and Geodetic Survey, and Jane Barron, d. of James Barron Hope, by the Rev. Beverly D. Tucker of St. Paul's Church, at the residence of the bride's parents, Norfolk, Va. So. Ch., Apr. 28, 1887

MARSHALL
Agnes H., d. of Lewis Marshall, Esq. of Culpeper, Va., and William P. Helm, Esq. of New York City, by the Rev. J. D. Powell, in St. John's Church, Portsmouth, Va. So. Ch., Nov. 10, 1881

Agnes Robb, d. of the late Alexander Marshall, and Dr. S. C. Chew, by the Rev. Mr. Paine, in Mount Calvary Church, Baltimore. So. Ch., June 12, 1884

Edward C., Jr. of Fauquier Co., Va., and Virginia E., d. of Dr. Samuel Taylor of Berryville, by the Rev. F. M. Whittle, at Berryville, Va. So. Ch., Dec. 26, 1856

Eliza, d. of the late Dr. Jaqueline A. Marshall of Fauquier Co., and Harrison Robertson of Norfolk, by the Rev. Thomas Duncan, at Prospect Hill, Fauquier Co. So. Ch., Oct. 28, 1859

Eliza G., of Lunenburg Co., Va., and A. W. Thompson of Tennessee, by the Rev. L. J. Sothoron, at Rose Hill, Lunenburg Co., Va. So. Ch., Aug. 21, 1879

Elizabeth A. M., eldest d. of the late James Edward Marshall, and Joseph Reading of Maryland, by the Rev. H. B. Lee, at Mt. Blanc, the residence of the bride's mother, Fauquier Co., Va. So. Ch., Oct. 24, 1878

Elizabeth Lewis, d. of Henry M. Marshall, and Bowles E. Armistead, by the Rev. Kinloch Nelson, at Fairfield, Fauquier Co. So. Ch., Dec. 7, 1871

Ella, and Sam'l Atwell, both of King George Co., Va., by the Rev. T. E. Locke, at Shiloh, King George Co. So. Ch., Sept. 7, 1860

Ellen H., of Fauquier, d. of the late Dr. Jaqueline A. Marshall, and C. Marshall Barton of Frederick, Va., by

MARRIAGE NOTICES IN THE SOUTHERN CHURCHMAN WITH DATES OF PUBLICATION

the Rev. Ch. H. Sheilds, at Prospect Hill, Fauquier Co. So. Ch., Oct. 7, 1859

Emmy W., and Frederick H. Moss, at the home of Mrs. William Marshall, 2009 Eye St., N.W., Washington, D.C. So. Ch., Dec. 27, 1924

F. L., of Washington, D.C., and Lina, second d. of the late Charles A. Gwatkin of Richmond, Va., by the Rev. Chas. H. Read, in Richmond, Va., at the residence of the bride's mother. So. Ch., Mar. 14, 1878

Fannie, of New York, and the Rev. Charles J. Holt of Baltimore, Md., by the Rev. A. M. Randolph of Baltimore, Md., in New York City. So. Ch., Oct. 21, 1875

Fitz-Hugh Ball, and Lola Naomi Lambert, by the Rev. Norman Fitz-Hugh Marshall, at the home of the bride's parents, Mr. and Mrs. Walter Lambert, Monticello, Ark. So. Ch., June 24, 1911

Florence C., d. of F. F. Marshall of Erie, and Dr. Charles V. Gravatt, U.S. Navy, by the Rev. J. J. Gravatt assisted by the rector, the Rev. George A. Carstensen, in St. Paul's Church, Erie, Pa. So. Ch., Apr. 1, 1886

Jakqueline (Dr.), of Fauquier Co., Va., and Mary, d. of Maj. R. Douhtut* of Charles City Co., by the Rev. A. Wade, at "Lower Weyanoke." So. Ch., Dec. 16, 1869

James E., and Mary M., eldest d. of Henry M. Marshall, Esq. of Fauquier Co., Va., by the Rev. C. M. Callaway, at Fairfield, the residence of her father. So. Ch., Mar. 21, 1856

James Keith, Jr., of Fauquier, and Elizabeth, d. of the late William L. Hirsh of Philadelphia, Pa., by the Rev. Father Floyd, in Washington, D.C., at the residence of the bride's mother. So. Ch., Jan. 29, 1891

Jaqueline A., and Eliza R., d. of Edward C. Turner, Esq., by the Rev. W. H. H. Powers, in Grace Church, The Plains. So. Ch., Oct. 31, 1878

Joel W., and Agnes G., d. of Henry Carrington, Esq., by the Rev. J. A. Mitchell, at Ingleside, Charlotte Co., Va. So. Ch., Dec. 14, 1865

John, of Markham, and Lucretia, d. of the late Norman R. Fitzhugh of Alexandria, by the Rev. James T. Johnson, in St. Paul's Church, Alexandria, Va. So. Ch., Feb. 16, 1854

Llewellyn B., and Mary D. Banta, by the Rev. Henry T. Sharp, in the Church of the Ascension, Frankfort, Ky. So. Ch., Dec. 23, 1875

Lottie, and Robert Burnham, by the Rev. Robb White, in Grace Church, Albemarle Co., Va. So. Ch., Jan. 10, 1884

Lucy J., only d. of J. Keith and F. L. Marshall and great gr.d. of Chief Justice Marshall, and the Rev. H. B. Lee, all of Fauquier Co., Va., by the Rev. Robb White assisted by the Rev. James R. Winchester, at Marven, the residence of the bride's parents. So. Ch., Sept. 27, 1877

Madge L., d. of the late Col.

* Given as printed

MARRIAGE NOTICES IN THE SOUTHERN CHURCHMAN WITH DATES OF PUBLICATION

Thomas Marshall of Fauquier Co., Va., and A. Adgate Duer of Baltimore, by the Rev. Wm. Meredith, at Springdale, Va. So. Ch., Nov. 7, 1872

Mary M., eldest d. of Henry M. Marshall, Esq. of Fauquier Co., Va., and James E. Marshall, by the Rev. C. M. Callaway, at Fairfield, the residence of the bride's father. So. Ch., Mar. 21, 1856

N. F. (The Rev.), and Mary V. Ball of Norfolk Co., Va., by the Rev. A. S. Lloyd, in St. Luke's Church, Norfolk. So. Ch., Dec. 23, 1886

Nannie Burwell, d. of Hon. James K. Marshall, and the Rev. George Hatley Norton, by the Rev. Wm. H. Pendleton, at Fauquier Co., Va. So. Ch., June 8, 1854

Rebecca C., of Fauquier Co., Va., and William H. Perry of Lunenburg Co., by the Rev. Alexander Overby, rector, in the Church of the Holy Innocents, Burkeville, Va. So. Ch., Nov. 13, 1890

Rebecca F., d. of F. Lewis Marshall, Esq., formerly of Fauquier Co., Va., and Charles R. Nash, by the Rev. Reverdy Estill assisted by the Rev. J. D. Powell, at Portsmouth, Va., at the residence of the bride's brother, R. C. Marshall, Esq. So. Ch., Nov. 28, 1878

Rebecca P., d. of J. A. and Rebecca Marshall, and Robert Douthat, Jr., all of Fauquier Co., by the Rev. H. B. Lee, at "The Craig", the residence of the bride's parents. So. Ch., Jan. 3, 1884

Robert M., Jr., and Martha Wilson, d. of the officiating clergyman, the Rev. Wm. W. Greene, in Trinity Church, Church Creek, Dorchester Co., Md. So. Ch., Nov. 24, 1887

Robert T., of Kentucky, and Rebekah L. Taylor of Richmond, Va., by the Rev. Joshua Peterkin, D.D. So. Ch., Oct. 14, 1880

Susan Lewis, and Bowles Ed. Armistead, by the Rev. Jno. McGill, at "Ivanhoe", the residence of the bride's father. So. Ch., Oct. 31, 1867

Thomas B., of Baltimore, and Julia, d. of the officiating clergyman, the Rev. Thos. L. Green, in St. Luke's Church, Church Hill, Md. So. Ch., Feb. 15, 1883

Thomas Richie, of Richmond, and Nannie Maury, d. of S. Wellford and Nannie Maury Corbin of Farley Vale, King George Co., Va., by the Rev. J. K. Mason, in St. George's Church, Fredericksburg, Va. So. Ch., July 8, 1886

William C., of Fauquier Co., Va., and Lucy P., d. of the late W. C. Meredith, in Leeds Church, Fauquier Co., Va. So. Ch., Oct. 29, 1885

MARSTELLAR
A. A. (Dr.), of Washington, D.C., and Emma, d. of Anderson Smith, Esq., in Grace Church, The Plains, Fauquier Co., Va. So. Ch., Jan. 3, 1878

MARSTELLER
E. M., M.D., and Marianne C., d. of the late Maynadier Mason, Esq. of Fairfax Co., by the Rt. Rev. Bishop Johns, at the residence of the late James M. Mason. So. Ch., Dec. 4, 1873

MARRIAGE NOTICES IN THE SOUTHERN CHURCHMAN WITH DATES OF PUBLICATION

Llera Corine, and James
Clinton Milburn of Alexandria, by the Rev. John
Towles of Prince George's
Co., Md., at Arelton, the
residence of Arell Marsteller, Esq., Prince
William Co., Va. So. Ch.,
Jan. 23, 1868

MARTEN
Walter K., and Caroline R.
Heath of Richmond, by the
Rev. John Cole, at Culpeper Co., Va. So. Ch.,
Nov. 23, 1855

MARTIN
Ada L., niece of the Rev. T.
F. Martin, and Robert T.
Hopkins, all of Nashville,
by the Rev. T. F. Martin,
rector of St. Ann's Church,
assisted by the Rev. Jerry
Witherspoon, pastor of the
church in which the ceremony
was performed, in First
Presbyterian Church, Nashville, Tenn. So. Ch., Nov.
22, 1888

Charles S., and Mamie R.
Tenison, both of Nashville,
by the rector, the Rev. W. C.
Gray, D.D., assisted by the
Rev. T. F. Martin and the
Rev. Cabell Martin, father
and brother of the groom,
at the Church of the Advent,
Nashville, Tenn. So. Ch.,
Dec. 20, 1883

Daniel D., of Cass Co., Me.,
and Emma B., d. of James V.
Weir of Clarke Co., Va., by
the Rev. J. F. Hoff. So.
Ch., June 11, 1858

Elizabeth, and Wm. H. Boteler,
both of Fauquier Co., Va.,
by the Rev. Geo. Lemmon.
So. Ch., Oct. 6, 1837

Helen Virginia, formerly of
Buchanan, Va., and James
Edward McLeod of Washington,
by the Rev. David Barr, in
the Church of the Epiphany,
Washington, D.C. So. Ch.,
July 2, 1891

J. Evans, of South Carolina,
and Empsie, d. of Dr. R. B.
Rennolds of Fredericksburg,
Va., by the Rev. R. J.
McBryde, in St. George's
Episcopal Church, Fredericksburg, Va. So. Ch., Nov. 3,
1881

Luther P., and Willis Amelia,
d. of Wm. W. Mace, all of
Dorchester Co., Md., by the
Rev. William W. Greene, at
the residence of the bride's
father. So. Ch., Dec. 23,
1880

Mary Cornelia Briscoe, third d.
of the officiating clergyman,
and Charles O'Reilly Armstrong,
by the Rev. T. F. Martin,
rector of the church, assisted
by the Rt. Rev. C. T. Quintard,
in St. Ann's Church, Nashville. So. Ch., Jan. 23,
1890

Mayo Cabell (The Rev.), rector
of St. Clement's Church, El
Paso, Tex., and Laura M., d.
of B. J. Farrar of Nashville,
Tenn., by the Rev. T. F.
Martin assisted by the Rev.
James R. Winchester and the
Rev. W. C. Gray, D.D., in
Woodland Street Presbyterian
Church, Nashville. So. Ch.,
Nov. 17, 1892

MARTS
Samuel T., and Ann Maria Furr,
both of Clarke Co., Va., by the
Rev. F. M. Whittle. So. Ch.,
Aug. 3, 1854

MARYE
J. L., Jr., of Newport News, Va.,
and Kate C. Dickinson of "Moss
Side", by the rector of the
parish, in Grace Church,
Caroline Co., Va. So. Ch.,

MARRIAGE NOTICES IN THE SOUTHERN CHURCHMAN WITH DATES OF PUBLICATION

Dec. 25, 1890
Mary Thornton, only d. of Col. Morton and C. Hommassel Marye, and J. S. Barbour Thompson, all of Alexandria, Va., by the Rev. G. H. Norton, D.D., in St. Paul's Church, Alexandria, Va. So. Ch., Feb. 21, 1884

MASON
Anna, d. of the late Col. Thomas Mason of Albemarle Co., Va., and William E. Clarke, Esq. of Baltimore, by the Rev. Richard K. Meade, at Tafton. So. Ch., Nov. 28, 1857

Anna Harrison, d. of Dr. John R. Mason of Sussex Co., Va., and George W. Williams of Prince George Co., by the Rev. C. J. Gibson, at "Oak Spring." So. Ch., Dec. 30, 1875

Augustine S. (Dr.), of Falmouth, Va., and Mary M. Eliason, by the Rev. O. A. Kinsolving, at "Oakley", Fauquier Co., the residence of Henry G. Dulaney, Esq. So. Ch., Nov. 12, 1858

Bettie S., d. of the late Dr. Alexander H. Mason, and Lt. Edward P. Alexander, U.S. Army, by the Rev. T. E. Locke, at Cleveland, King George Co. So. Ch., Apr. 13, 1860

Beverly R., of Fairfax Co., and Bettie Harrison, d. of K. S. Nelson of Culpeper, by the Rev. J. G. Minnigerode assisted by the Rev. C. K. Nelson, D.D., in St. Stephen's Church, Culpeper, Va. So. Ch., Sept. 16, 1875

Cornelia, d. of W. Roy Mason, Esq., and John Stephenson, Esq. of Frederick Co., Va., by the Rev. Henry Wall, at Cleivland*, King George Co. So. Ch., July 23, 1858

Florence P., formerly of Virginia, and Benjamin T. Fendall of Maryland, by the Rev. W. A. Leonard, D.D., in St. John's Church, Washington, D.C. So. Ch., May 12, 1887

Harriet P., d. of the late John Y. Mason, Jr., and gr.d. of the Hon. John Y. Mason, deceased, and J. Garland Jefferson, by the Rev. P. F. Berkeley, in St. John's Church, Grub Hill, Amelia Co., Va. So. Ch., Mar. 6, 1884

J. K. (The Rev.), and Claudia Hamilton, eldest d. of the Rev. G. H. Norton, by the Rev. D. F. Sprigg, in St. Paul's Church, Alexandria, Va. So. Ch., Nov. 27, 1879

James E. (Lt.), of Accomac Co., Va., and Bettie S., eldest d. of Joseph H. Turner, Esq., by the Rev. R. R. Mason, at Columbia, Fluvanna Co., Va. So. Ch., Mar. 8, 1865

James E., of Richmond, Va., and Mary F., d. of William H. and M. V. Anthony of Botetourt Co., Va., by the Rev. C. C. Randolph, in Trinity Church, Buchanan. So. Ch., Jan. 8, 1885

James M., and Madge, d. of Maj. John H. Chichester, by the Rev. Kinloch Nelson, D.D., in Old Falls Church, Fairfax Co., Va. So. Ch., Oct. 30, 1884

James W., and Sarah B. Glover, both of Albemarle, by the Rev. Wm. M. Nelson, in Albemarle Co. So. Ch., Oct. 19, 1855

John G., Esq., of Fredericksburg,

* Given as printed

MARRIAGE NOTICES IN THE SOUTHERN CHURCHMAN WITH DATES OF PUBLICATION

and Mary M. Boteler, by the Rev. C. W. Andrews, D.D. and the Rev. C. R. Hains, in Trinity Church, Shepherdstown. So. Ch., Mar. 24, 1870

John K., and Roberta K., d. of the Rev. E. C. Murdaugh, D.D., former rector of Trinity Church, by the Rev. J. Green Shackelford, at the residence of the bride's mother, Fredericksburg, Va. So. Ch., May 3, 1888

Joseph G., of Clarke Co., Va., and Gertrude M. Carr, by the Rev. Pendleton Brooke, at the residence of the bride's father, Dr. J. L. Carr, Clarksburg, W.Va. So. Ch., Nov. 25, 1869

L. R. (The Rev.), and Lucy, eldest d. of the Rev. John Ambler, by the Rt. Rev. John Johns assisted by the Rev. R. R. Mason, at Clarens, the residence of the late Hon. James M. Mason, near Alexandria, Va. So. Ch., Nov. 25, 1875

Lambert, of St. Joseph, Mo., and Corinne, d. of Col. John J. Riley of Clarke Co., Va., by the rector, the Rev. P. P. Phillips, in Grace Church, Berryville, Va. So. Ch., July 10, 1890

Louise, d. of Mrs. John K. Mason and the late Dr. John K. Mason, and Edwin Wright of Ardmore, Pa., at Elkton, Va. So. Ch., Sept. 13, 1913

Lucy Wiley, only d. of Charles Mason, and Edward Jaqueline Smith, all of King George, by the Rev. Moses H. Hunter, in St. John's Church, King George C.H., Va. So. Ch., June 16, 1881

Margaret B., d. of W. R. Mason, Esq., and Alfred N. Bernard, Esq., by the Rev. Mr. Friend, at Cleveland, King George Co., Va. So. Ch., Nov. 23, 1855

Marianna C., d. of the late Maynadier Mason, Esq. of Fairfax Co., and E. M. Marsteller, M.D., by the Rt. Rev. Bishop Johns, at the residence of the late Hon. James M. Mason. So. Ch., Dec. 4, 1873

Mary, d. of the late John Y. Mason, and gr.d. of Judge John Y. Mason, former Minister to France, and P. J. Berkeley, by the Rev. P. F. Berkeley, in St. John's Church, Grub Hill, Amelia Co., Va. So. Ch., Nov. 10, 1881

Mary K., d. of the late Richard Mason of Georgetown, Md., and the Rev. Hanson T. Wilcoxsen, by the Rev. J. Campbell White, in St. Andrew's Church, Washington Co., Md. So. Ch., Mar. 1, 1855

Richard R. (The Rev.), and Nannie V. D., youngest d. of the Rt. Rev. John Johns, D.D., by the Rt. Rev. Wm. Meade, D.D., at Malvern, the residence of the bride's father. So. Ch., Apr. 16, 1858

Thompson B., of Philadelphia, and Sarah C., d. of John B. Taylor, Esq., by the Rev. F. M. Whittle, at Rockland, Jefferson Co., Va. So. Ch., Nov. 2, 1855

W. Douglas, of Virginia, and Loulie, d. of Hon. W. E. Clarke of Demopolis, by the Rev. R. W. Barnwell, in Trinity Church, Demopolis, Ala. So. Ch., June 17, 1880

W. Roy (The Rev.), and Mary

MARRIAGE NOTICES IN THE SOUTHERN CHURCHMAN WITH DATES OF PUBLICATION

Ruffin Jones, by the Rev. Edw. Valentine Jones, father, and the Rev. E. Fuffin Jones, brother of the bride, in Christ Church, Middlesex Co., Va. So. Ch., July 20, 1912

Wm. Pinckney, and Lizzie R., second d. of Dr. T. J. McGill of Frederick, Md., by the Rev. Jno. McGill, at the residence of the bride's father. So. Ch., Jan. 29, 1873

MASSENBURG

Jennie E., d. of Capt. George T. Massenburg of Hampton, and Lewis E. Henry, Esq., of Raleigh, N.C., by the Rev. John C. McCabe, rector of St. John's Church, at Hampton. So. Ch., Dec. 7, 1854

MASSEY

J. A. (The Rev.), D.D., rector of Trinity Church, Mobile, and Mary, d. of Mrs. J. H. Gregory of Rochester, by the Rt. Rev. J. P. B. Wilmer, D.D., Bishop of Louisiana, in Christ Church, Rochester. So. Ch., Aug. 16, 1877

Lizzie, d. of the late E. W. Massey, Esq., and Grymes Meade, all of Clarke Co., Va., by the Rev. Mr. Eggleston assisted by the Rev. J. R. Jones, at White Post. So. Ch., July 22, 1875

Thomas Niven, of Westmoreland, and Mary Stevenson, d. of Mr. and Mrs. Edward Newton, by the Rev. Arthur P. Gray, in Hague Chapel, Cople Parish, Westmoreland Co. So. Ch., Feb. 19, 1910

MASSIE

Florence L., d. of the late Wm. Massie of Nelson, and John L., of Lynchburg, Va., s. of W. P. Tunstall, by the Rev. Edmund Withers, at Pharsalia, Nelson Co. So. Ch., Dec. 31, 1868

Lucy Nelson, only d. of N. H. Massie, deceased, and Thos. Hamlin of Danville, by the Rev. K. Nelson, D.D., assisted by the Rev. C. K. Nelson, D.D., and the Rev. J. S. Hanckle, D.D., in Christ Church, Charlottesville, Va. So. Ch., Feb. 18, 1886

Mary (Mrs.), and Capt. John L. Cochran, both of Charlottesville, by the Rev. Edmund Withers, at the residence of P. C. Massie, Nelson Co. So. Ch., Sept. 17, 1868

Mary Stuart, only d. of the late Dr. William F. Massie formerly of Alexandria, Va., and Gustavus B. Quarrier, Esq. of Kanawha Co., W.Va., by the Rev. R. A. Cobbs, in St. Mark's Church, St. Albans, W.Va. So. Ch., Oct. 25, 1877

N. H., of Charlottesville, and Eliza K., d. of Thos. F. Nelson, Esq., by the Rev. F. M. Whittle, at Wheehaw*, Clarke Co., Va. So. Ch., Apr. 18, 1856

N. H., and Lucy Paxton Lemmon, both of Danville, by the Rev. R. C. Jett, at the Arlington Hotel, Danville, Va. So. Ch., Sept. 12, 1889

Patrick Cabell, Esq., of Nelson Co., and Susan C., youngest d. of Dr. Robt. W. Withers of Campbell Co., by the Rev. T. E. Locke, at Rock Castle, Campbell Co. So. Ch., June 26, 1857

Robert Kinloch (The Rev.), of Charlottesville, Va., and Harrietta Ross, d. of W. Taylor Milton of Clarke Co.,

---

* Given as printed

MARRIAGE NOTICES IN THE SOUTHERN CHURCHMAN WITH DATES OF PUBLICATION

Va., by the Rev. P. P. Phillips, rector, assisted by the Rev. Kinloch Nelson, D.D., in Grace Church, Berryville, Va. So. Ch., July 23, 1891

Sue W., and Stuart B. Whitehead, by the Rev. J. W. Ware, in Grace Church, Nelson Co., Va. So. Ch., June 29, 1893

Wm. Foote, M.D., and Maria Catharine Smith of Fauquier, by the Rev. Wm. F. Lockwood, at Orlean, Fauquier Co., Va. So. Ch., Mar. 6, 1851

MASSON
Edward, Esq., counsellor-at-law in Napoli di Romania and former Attorney General of the Kingdom, and E. Mulligan, missionary of the Protestant Episcopal Church, at Athens, Greece. So. Ch., Feb. 1, 1839

MASTERS
Bessie, and Laurence Stabler, both of Alexandria, by the Rev. George H. Norton, D.D., in St. Paul's Church, Alexandria. So. Ch., Oct. 1, 1885

MATHEUS*
Nathaniel, and Kate L., youngest d. of William L. Neblett, all of Lunenburg Co., by the Rev. Mr. Sothoron, in St. John's Church, Lunenburg, Va. So. Ch., Dec. 19, 1878

MATHEWS
Susan (Mrs.), second d. of the late Dr. S. H. Royall of Chesterfield, and Geo. F. Harrison of Goochland Co., by the Rev. Edgar Woods, pastor of the Presbyterian Church, Charlottesville, at the University of Virginia. So. Ch., Feb. 14, 1867

MATTHEWS
M. Bruce, d. of Maj. Wm. B. Matthews of Port Tobacco, Md., and the Rev. C. K. Nelson, Jr. of Virginia, by the Rev. Meyer Lewin, in Christ Church, Port Tobacco, Md. So. Ch., June 21, 1877

Mary Sydnie, d. of the late Rev. James A. Matthews, and John Goldsborough White formerly of Haymarket, Va., but now residing in El Paso, Tex., by the Rev. Mr. Thompson of Trinity Episcopal Church, Van Buren, Ark. So. Ch., Oct. 30, 1909

Nannie O., and L. S. Neblett, both of Lunenburg Co., Va., by the Rev. L. J. Sothoron, at the residence of the bride's father. So. Ch., Nov. 23, 1876

MAUPIN
Chapman, of the University of Virginia, and Margaret Lewis, d. of Col. Alexander G. Taliaferro of Culpeper Co., Va., by the Rev. J. S. Hansbrough, at Annandale. So. Ch., Jan. 5, 1871

James F., of Norfolk, and Edmonia Fitzhugh, d. of the late R. W. Tomlin, Esq. of Hanover, by the Rev. S. S. Hepbron, in Immanuel Church, Hanover. So. Ch., Nov. 22, 1888

John C., of Portsmouth, Va., and Sallie, d. of E. B. Macon of Princess Anne Co., by the Rev. Reverdy Estill, pastor of Trinity Church, Portsmouth, assisted by the Rev. C. B. Bryan, in the old

---

* Given as printed

MARRIAGE NOTICES IN THE SOUTHERN CHURCHMAN WITH DATES OF PUBLICATION

Eastern Shore Chapel, Princess Anne Co., Va. So. Ch., Mar. 4, 1880

Ro. W., of Baltimore, and Agnes Marshall, youngest d. of Col. A. G. Taliaferro, by the Rev. Philip Slaughter assisted by the Rev. C. Y. Steptoe and the Rev. Dr. B. Franklin, in Emmanuel Church, Rapidan, Va. So. Ch., Dec. 24, 1874

Sallie C., and Joseph Perkins, Esq. of Albemarle, by the Rev. Wm. M. Nelson, at the residence of the bride's mother, Mrs. Sarah M. Maupin, Albemarle Co., Va. So. Ch., Dec. 10, 1868

Socrates (Dr.), and Sally Hay Washington, by the Rev. Richard Channing Moore. So. Ch., Dec. 22, 1837

MAURY

Anne H., d. of R. H. Maury, and Poitiaux Robinson, by the Rev. Joshua Peterkin, at the residence of the bride's father, Richmond. So. Ch., Feb. 7, 1878

Eliza, d. of the late Com. Matthew F. Maury, and Thomas Withers, acting chief engineer of the Denver and South Park Railroad, Colorado, by the Rev. Edmund Withers, in Richmond. So. Ch., Sept. 26, 1878

Lucy Minor, youngest d. of the late Com. M. F. Maury, and Meverell L. Van Doren of Blenheim, Albemarle Co., Va., by the Rev. Dr. Woodbridge, in Monumental Church. So. Ch., July 12, 1877

Magruder (The Rev.), rector of St. George's Church, Fredericksburg, and Lila, d. of the officiating clergyman, the Rev. C. W. Andrews, D.D., in Trinity Church, Shepherdstown. So. Ch., Nov. 2, 1865

Mary Herndon, d. of the late Com. M. F. Maury, and James R. Werth, by the Rev. Dr. Woodbridge, at the residence of the bride's mother, in Richmond. So. Ch., July 12, 1877

Matthew Fontaine, of Richmond, and Sophie C. Bruce of South Bend, Halifax Co., by the Rev. C. B. Bryan assisted by the rector, the Rev. Dr. G. W. Dame, in the Church of the Epiphany, Danville. So. Ch., June 23, 1892

Sarah Ann S., only d. of the late Francis F. Maury, and the Rev. Edward F. Berkeley, minister of Christ Church, Lexington, Ky., by the Rev. M. F. Maury, at Bath Co., Ky. So. Ch., May 24, 1839

Thomson B. (The Rev.), and Sallie T., eldest d. of Wm. and Charlotte M. Gordon, by the Rev. Thomas F. Martin, at Huntley, Nelson Co., Va. So. Ch., Dec. 25, 1863

William Lewis, of St. Louis, Mo., formerly of Virginia, and Cora Wells Sears of Myrtle Lake, by the Rev. F. R. Holeman, at Myrtle Lake, Orange Co., Fla. So. Ch., Jan. 6, 1887

MAUZY

Mary P., d. of the late Fayette Mauzy, and Dr. Samuel R. Rixey, all of Culpeper C.H., Va., by the Rev. Geo. W. Peterkin, at Culpeper. So. Ch., Sept. 25, 1873

MAXWELL

J. Gordon (The Rev.), and Mary, d. of R. S. Johnson, Esq., all of Philadelphia, by the Rev. Dr. Dorr. So. Ch., Oct. 25, 1839

J. Gordon (The Rev), and

MARRIAGE NOTICES IN THE SOUTHERN CHURCHMAN WITH DATES OF PUBLICATION

Mary Hamilton, d. of the late James Willett Turner, by the Rev. G. Emlen Hare, D.D., in Emmanuel Church. So. Ch., Sept. 10, 1858

Samuel Meredith, of New York, and Mary V. Taliaferro of Orange Co., Va., by the Rev. James L. Maxwell, rector of St. Luke's Church, Montclair, N.J., at the residence of John Taliaferro, Orange Co., Va. So. Ch., Nov. 7, 1878

William, Esq., President of Hampden-Sydney College, and Mary Frances Robertson of Norfolk, Va., by the Rev. Wm. Neil. So. Ch., June 14, 1839

See also GOODWYN, A. Meade (Mrs.)

MAY

David (The Rev.), of Goshen, Va., and Kate, d. of the late Judge D. C. Humphreys of Washington, by the Rev. Wm. A. Leonard, in St. John's Church, Washington, D.C. So. Ch., Dec. 18, 1884

Venetia Morrill, and Harry Lee Roberts, by the Rev. T. A. Cheatham, at Farmville, N.C. So. Ch., May 9, 1908

William H. (Capt.), of Elkton, Md., and Anna W., d. of the late Henry C. Mackall, Esq. of "Wilma", Cecil Co., and niece of the officiating clergyman, the Rev. John Collins McCabe, D.D., in St. Luke's Church, Bladensburg, Md. So. Ch., Oct. 17, 1867

MAYER

Anna, d. of John A. Mayer, Esq. of Norfolk Co., and Hugh, s. of the late Gen. Charles J. Barton of the English Army, by the Rev. W. R. Savage, in Emmanuel Church, Kempsville, Va. So. Ch., June 14, 1888

Sarah Newell, youngest d. of the late George Louis Mayer, Esq., and the Rev. Edward Webster Appleton of St. John's Church, all of Lancaster, by the Rt. Rev. Samuel Bowman, D.D., Assistant Bishop of the Diocese, in St. John's (Free) Church, Lancaster. So. Ch., Oct. 15, 1858

MAYNARD

Foster, and Mary Jane Hudson of Northumberland Co., Va., by the Rev. T. E. Dashiell, at Kinsale. So. Ch., July 22, 1859

MAYO

Agnes Atkinson, and Thomas Nelson Carter, by the Rev. Robert A. Mayo assisted by the Rev. John B. Newton, in Monumental Church, Richmond. So. Ch., Dec. 8, 1887

Charles J. S. (The Rev.), and Mary Reynolds, eldest d. of the late Gen. J. C. Webber, U.S. Vol.,* and gr.s. of the late Maj. Wm. P. Bainbridge, U.S.A., by the Rev. J. J. Gravatt assisted by the Rev. J. B. Newton, in St. John's Church, Hampton, Va. So. Ch., Oct. 12, 1882

Charles S., and Julia M., d. of John W. and Marion S. Jones, by the Rev. C. C. Randolph, rector, assisted by the Rev. Edward Valentine Jones, in Trinity Church, Buchanan, Va. So. Ch., Oct. 16, 1890

Edmund Cooper, and Nellie Hodge, youngest d. of Mr. and Mrs. John W. Gordon of 826 Franklin Street, by the Rev. J. J. Gravatt and the Rt. Rev. Robert A.

---

* Given as printed

MARRIAGE NOTICES IN THE SOUTHERN CHURCHMAN WITH DATES OF PUBLICATION

Gibson, in Holy Trinity Church, Richmond, Va. So. Ch., Feb. 20, 1909

Elizabeth Bland, and Charles L. Stovin, by the Rev. Wm. F. Lee. So. Ch., May 8, 1835

John Campbell (Dr.), of Westmoreland Co., Va., and Mary Lewis, d. of Charles J. Stovin, Esq., by the Rev. John C. McCabe, rector of the Church of the Ascension, Baltimore, at "Airley", Fauquier Co., Va. So. Ch., June 19, 1857

Joseph, Jr. (Col.), and Mary Armistead, second d. of Dr. Wat H. Tyler, all of Westmoreland Co., Va., by the Rev. Andrew Fisher, at "Locust Farm", Westmoreland Co., Va. So. Ch., Mar. 19 and 26, 1868

Kate Friend, and Edward V. Valentine, in Monumental Church. So. Ch., Jan. 7, 1892

Lucy H., d. of Robert A. Mayo, and the Rev. Wm. T. Helms of Knoxville, Tenn., by the Rev. Wm. Norwood, at "Powhatan Seat", the residence of the bride's father. So. Ch., Sept. 14, 1865

Mary Friend, d. of the late W. S. P. Mayo of Richmond, Va., and Edward Ingle of Washington, formerly of Baltimore and Richmond, by the Rev. John B. Newton assisted by the Rev. Ed. H. Ingle of Baltimore, in Monumental Church, Richmond. So. Ch., May 5, 1892

Nannie E., of Cumberland Co., Va., and R. F. James of Alabama, by the Rev. John G. Anderson, at Cartersville, Va. So. Ch., Nov. 26, 1885

Nannie S., d. of Dr. L. W. Mayo of Bedford Co., Va., and Walter J. Brodie of Forfarshire, Scotland, by the Rev. G. A. Gibbons, at the residence of the bride's father. So. Ch., Jan. 14, 1875

Sallie Taliaferro, d. of Mr. and Mrs. P. H. Mayo, and Benneham Cameron of North Carolina, in All Saints Church, Richmond, Va. So. Ch., Nov. 19, 1891

Sue C., and Dr. John Knox, both of Richmond, Va., by the Rev. Dr. T. L. Preston assisted by the Rev. Dr. Chas. Minnigerode, at the residence of the bride's mother, Mrs. Robt. Mayo. So. Ch., Feb. 12 and 19, 1874

William, and Lizzie Brown, both of Westmoreland, by the Rev. D. M. Wharton, at the residence of the bride's father, Col. Thomas Brown. So. Ch., Jan. 16, 1873

Wyndham R. (Capt.), of Virginia, and Maria S., d. of Com. Stephen Decatur, United States Navy, by the Rev. Pelham Williams, in the Church of the Messiah, Boston, Mass. So. Ch., Apr. 30, 1874

MEADE

Alexander Brown, of Roanoke, Va., s. of the Rev. R. K. Meade of Virginia and gr.s. of Bishop Meade, and Fannie Lee, d. of the late Richard H. B. and Martha J. Day of Buckhannon, W.Va., by the Rev. T. H. Lacy, in the Church of the Transfiguration, Buckhannon, W.Va. So. Ch., Nov. 13, 1890

Anna Maria (Mrs.), of Richmond, and David Chalmers, Esq. of Halifax Co., by the Rev. George Woodbridge, in St.

MARRIAGE NOTICES IN THE SOUTHERN CHURCHMAN WITH DATES OF PUBLICATION

Paul's Church. So. Ch., Jan. 18, 1856

Bessie R., d. of Drayton G. and Annie B. Meade of Virginia and gr.d. of the late Joseph Sands of New York, and David Randolph Meade of Texas, by the Rev. James Grammer, at The Plains, Fauquier Co., Va. So. Ch., Oct. 12, 1882

Bettie W., and J. H. Hoffecker, Jr. of Wilmington, Del., by the Rev. R. T. Davis, D.D., in St. James' Church, Leesburg, Va. So. Ch., Jan. 15, 1880

Catharine Mackey, eldest d. of John N. Meade, Esq. of Frederick Co., Va., and James W. Fletcher of Rappahannock Co., by the Rev. Wm. C. Meredith, at Shady Oak, the residence of the bride's father. So. Ch., Feb. 3, 1870

David, of Clarke Co., Va., and Nannie, d. of Edgar Snowden, Esq., the veteran editor of the Alexandria "Gazette", by the Rev. J. T. Johnston, D.D., in St. Paul's Church, Alexandria. So. Ch., Dec. 28, 1865

David Randolph, of Texas, and Bessie R., d. of Drayton G. and Annie B. Meade of Virginia, and gr.d. of the late Joseph Sands of New York, by the Rev. James Grammer, at The Plains, Fauquier Co., Va. So. Ch., Oct. 12, 1882

Edgar S., and Lucy Fitzhugh, d. of the late Custis Grymes of King George Co., Va., by the Rev. Jos. R. Jones, in Meade Memorial Church, White Post, Clarke Co., Va. So. Ch., Nov. 24, 1881

Edward N., rector of St. Paul's Church, Sing Sing, and Jane, eldest d. of the Rev. Wm. Creighton, D.D., by the Rt. Rev. Benj. T. Onderdonk, D.D., at Mount Pleasant, Westchester Co., N.Y. So. Ch., Jan. 11, 1839

Eleanor B., d. of the late John E. Meade of Prince George Co., Va., and the Rev. William H. Platt, rector of St. Paul's Church, Petersburg, by the Rt. Rev. J. Johns, D.D., Assistant Bishop of Virginia, at the residence of David Callender, Esq., Petersburg. So. Ch., July 3, 1857

Everard Kidder, s. of Francis Key Meade and the late Mrs. Sarah Manson Calloway Meade, and Margaret Della, d. of the late Judge T. R. B. Wright and Mrs. Della Preston Wright, by the Rev. William Nelson Meade, uncle of the groom, in St. John's Church, Tappahannock. So. Ch., Dec. 18, 1915

Francis Key, of Clarke, an associate principle of Norwood School, and Sarah B., d. of Dr. P. Carrington Callaway of Nelson, by the Rev. Edmund Withers, at Montezuma, Nelson Co., Va. So. Ch., Sept. 24, 1874

Geo. W., Esq., formerly of Clarke Co., Va., and Sallie K. Callaway of Spotsylvania Co., Va., by the Rev. C. M. Callaway, at Topeka, Kan. So. Ch., June 4, 1858

Grymes, and Lizzie, d. of the late E. W. Massey, Esq., all of Clarke Co., Va., by the Rev. Mr. Eggleston assisted by the Rev. J. R. Jones, at White Post. So. Ch., July 22, 1875

MARRIAGE NOTICES IN THE SOUTHERN CHURCHMAN WITH DATES OF PUBLICATION

Harriet Hairston, d. of the late Sarah Knight Callaway and William Washington Meade, and Newland G. De Pauw of Haymarket, Va., by the Rev. A. G. Grinnan, at the home of the bride's brother, Stasius Meade, Braddock Heights, Alexandria, Va. So. Ch., May 6 and 13, 1911

Josephine, eldest d. of the late Elizabeth Randolph and David Randolph Meade of Virginia, and Theodore Davis of Globe, Ariz., by the Rev. Henry Easter, in St. Clement's Church, El Paso, Tex. So. Ch., July 31, 1909

Lila Hardaway, d. of the late Richard H. Meade, and Benjamin Batchelder, s. of Mann S. Valentine, all of Richmond, by the Rev. Dr. Newton, in Monumental Church, Richmond. So. Ch., Nov. 4, 1886

Lizzie Brockenbrough, d. of the Rev. Everard Meade, D.D., and the Rev. Charles William Sydnor of Pocahontas, Va., in old Pohick Church, Fairfax Co., Va. So. Ch., Sept. 17, 1910

Mary, eldest d. of John Macky Meade, and Torrance J. Ewart, all of Topeka, Kans., by the Rev. Bishop F. R. Millspaugh assisted by Dean Kay, in Grace Cathedral, Topeka, Kans. So. Ch., July 24, 1909. [Miss Meade belongs to the Virginia family and finished her education at Winchester, Va., at the Episcopal Female Institute.]

Mary Edmonia, d. of the late Hodejah Meade, and gr.d. of Gen. Everard Meade, and Lt. Edwin J. Harvie, U.S.A., by the Rev. P. F. Berkeley, at the Hermitage, residence of Wm. E. Meade, Esq. So. Ch., Nov. 30, 1860

Mary Mann, and Archibald Buchanan Bevan, both of Clarke Co., Va., by the Rev. Edward H. Ingle, in the Church of the Epiphany, Washington, D.C. So. Ch., Feb. 6, 1909

Mary N., gr.d. of the late Bishop Wm. Meade, D.D., of the P. E. Church of Virginia, and William L. Valentine of Windsor, N.C., by the Rev. J. H. Kasler, in the Methodist Church, Windsor, N.C. So. Ch., Sept. 1, 1887

Mary Virginia, d. of the late Dr. Theo. Meade, and Dr. J. Blackwood Strachan, by the Rev. Wm. H. Platt, D.D., at the residence of the Hon. R. K. Meade. So. Ch., May 15, 1857

Richard Hardaway, and Nellie Prior Atkins, both of Richmond, Va., by the Rev. Moses D. Hoge, pastor, and the Rev. J. B. Newton, rector of Monumental Church, in the Second Presbyterian Church, Richmond, Va. So. Ch., Nov. 23, 1893

Richard K. (The Rev.), of Charlottesville, Va., and Harriotte Lee, youngest d. of the late John Hopkins, Esq., of Frederick Co., Va., by the Rt. Rev. Bishop Meade, at Wheatland, Jefferson City, Va. So. Ch., Sept. 1, 1837

Stasius, s. of the late Wm. W. Meade of Clarke Co., Va., and Anna Marguerite, eldest d. of Mr. and Mrs. Francis B. Mohun, by the Rev. Father Boland, at the home of the bride, Washington, D.C. So. Ch., July 6, 1893

MARRIAGE NOTICES IN THE SOUTHERN CHURCHMAN WITH DATES OF PUBLICATION

Wm. H., of Charlottesville, and Pattie S., d. of Pike and Lelia Powers of Halifax, Va., by the Rev. R. K. Meade, Halifax Co. So. Ch., July 24, 1863

Wm. Nelson (The Rev.), of Virginia, and Louise Porcher, by the Rev. Benjamin Allston, at Badwell, Abbeville Co., S.C. So. Ch., Oct. 13, 1887

See also PANNILL, Indiana (Mrs.)

MEECH

Richard, of England, and Ellen Douglas, d. of the late James O. Pollard of King William Co., by the Rev. J. Hervey Hundley, in St. David's Church, King William Co., Va. So. Ch., Mar. 16, 1876

MEETZE

Edward B., Esq., and Susan Scott, d. of Mrs. E. J. Williamson, by the Rev. W. Strother Jones, at "Greenhill", Fauquier Co., Va. So. Ch., Dec. 14, 1876

MERCER

Corbin Waller, s. of Dr. John C. Mercer formerly of U.S. Navy, and gr.s. of Gen. Hugh Mercer who fell at battle of Princeton during the Revolutionary War, and Fannie Burwell, d. of the Hon. William Nelson of Yorktown, Va. and gr.d. of President Nelson of Revolutionary fame,* in Durham, N.C. So. Ch., Dec. 10, 1885

Eliza C., d. of Dr. John Mercer, and Dr. B. St. George Tucker, by the Rev. Mr. Ambler, in Williamsburg. So. Ch., Dec. 6, 1861

Isabel Stuart, d. of Dr. J. C. and Mrs. M. C. Mercer, and Charles McGary, all of Durham, N.C., at the residence of W. L. Wall, on Chapel Hill St., Durham, N.C. So. Ch., Nov. 1, 1888

Mary Louise, d. of Dr. John C. Mercer, and the Rev. Daniel Blain, by the Rev. S. W. Blain, at Williamsburg, Va. So. Ch., Feb. 7, 1867

MERCHANT

Annie E., and Ronald J. Adamson, by the Rev. A. P. Gray, in Trinity Church, Manassas. So. Ch., Oct. 2, 1884

MEREDITH

Clyde Robe, and Eugenie du Maurier, by the Rev. Page Dame, D.D., at Memorial Church Rectory, Baltimore, Md. So. Ch., Oct. 17, 1925

Jacqueline M., of Stafford Co., and Ellen M. Bankhead of Orange, by the Rev. Joseph Earnest, at Edgemont, Orange Co. So. Ch., Jan. 15, 1858

Jennie P., and Lewis H. Holliday, by the Rev. Charles C. Randolph, at the residence of Mrs. Lizzie Munford, Botetourt Co., Va. So. Ch., July 14, 1881

Lewly (Mrs.), d. of H. M. Bowyer, Esq., of Botetourt Co., Va., by the Rev. Pendleton Brooke, at Valveide, the residence of Col. R. W. Hughes. So. Ch., Apr. 6, 1871

Lucy P., d. of the late W. C. Meredith, and William C. Marshall of Fauquier Co., Va., in Leeds Church, Fauquier Co., Va. So. Ch., Oct. 29, 1885

Mary Bolling, d. of the Rev. W. C. Meredith, and A. Magill Smith, Esq., all of Winchester, Va., by the Rev. W. C. Meredith, in Christ Church, Winchester, Va. So. Ch., Jan. 16, 1868

* Possibly not granddaughter but great granddaughter of William Nelson, 1711-1772, who served as president of the Governor's council and was generally known as President Nelson

MARRIAGE NOTICES IN THE SOUTHERN CHURCHMAN WITH DATES OF PUBLICATION

W. C. (The Rev.), and Pocahontas, d. of Robert Bolling, Esq. of Buckingham Co., Va., by the Rev. Olcott Bulkley, at Chellou. So. Ch., June 11, 1847

W. C., D.D. (The Rev.), rector of Christ Church, Winchester, Va., and Fanny Randolph, d. of Wm. N. Page, Esq. of Cumberland Co., Va., by the Rev. T. U. Dudley, in Christ Church, Baltimore, Md. So. Ch., June 12, 1873

Wm. C. (The Rev.), and Bettie Hanson, d. of the late J. P. Cushman, former President of Hampden-Sydney College, by the Rev. Geo. W. Dame, at The Fork, residence of Mrs. Carter Page, in Cumberland Co. So. Ch., Jan. 27, 1860

MERIWETHER

Margaret Douglas, d. of C. J. Meriwether, and Eldon Dawson, by the Rev. A. Ware, at Broadview, the residence of the bride's father, Bedford Co., Va. So. Ch., Jan. 29, 1880

Mary C., d. of James A. Meriwether, and Cyrus B. Clay, all of Belford, by the Rev. R. H. Wilmer. So. Ch., Dec. 21, 1855

Wm. D. (Dr.), of Albemarle Co., and Nannie W., d. of John E. Page, Esq., by the Rev. Mr. Jones, at Pagebrook, Clarke Co. So. Ch., Feb. 19, 1864

MERRIMAN

Emmerson A., of West Meridian, Conn., and Frances E. Johnson of Herndon, by the Rev. Jno. McGill, at St. Timothy's Hall, Herndon, Fairfax Co. So. Ch., Jan. 2, 1873

MERRITT

Frank, and Bettie Crutchfield, both of Tazewell Co., by the Rev. W. R. Savage, in Stras Memorial Church, Tazewell C.H. So. Ch., May 25, 1893

MEYER

Henry U., of New York, and Melvina A. Rayner, by the Rev. H. Wall, D.D., at Rocketts. So. Ch., Dec. 15, 1870

MICHAELS

A. H., of Reidsville, N.C., and Augusta Norfleet of Amelia Co., Va., by the Rev. A. B. Tizzard, at the residence of the bride's mother. So. Ch., Feb. 21, 1884

Thomas S. (Dr.), of Henrico Co., and Margaret V. Walters of Richmond, by the Rev. Geo. C. Sutton, in Richmond, Va. So. Ch., July 1, 1880

MICHAUX

Jacob, Esq., and Mrs. Frances A. Ludlam, d. of Richard Anderson, Esq., all of Powhatan Co., by the Rev. Andrew Fisher, in St. Luke's Church, Powhatan Parish.* So. Ch., Nov. 28, 1856

M. Lou, d. of W. M. Michaux, and James B. Harvie, all of Powhatan Co., Va. So. Ch., May 6, 1875

Miller W., Jr., of Powhatan Co., Va., and Nannie R. Kean, by the Rev. Wm. W. Greene, at Olney, Caroline Co. So. Ch., Dec. 10, 1868

Waddey Thompson, and Cora Harrison Ludlow of Powhatan, by the Rev. P. F. Berkeley, in Powhatan Co., at the residence of the bride's mother, Mrs. Jacob

---

* Powhatan Parish is in Powhatan County, Virginia (Journal ... Diocese of Southern Virginia, Portsmouth, Va., 1941)

MARRIAGE NOTICES IN THE SOUTHERN CHURCHMAN WITH DATES OF PUBLICATION

Michaux. So. Ch., May 18, 1876

MICHEL
Sue H., and Maj. Wm. M. Taliaferro, by the Rev. L. B. Wharton, at the residence of the bride's mother, in Abingdon, Va. So. Ch., Nov. 7, 1867

MICHIE
Octavus G., and Sarah A. M., d. of Capt. James Michie, by the Rev. Mr. Stack, at Belle Air, Albemarle Co. So. Ch., Nov. 9, 1848

Sarah A. M., d. of Capt. James Michie, and Octavus G. Michie, by the Rev. Mr. Stack, at Belle Air, Albemarle Co. So. Ch., Nov. 9, 1848

Sarah H., and Dr. R. N. Hewitt, of Campbell Co., by the Rev. H. B. Lee, in Christ Church, Charlottesville. So. Ch., Feb. 25, 1892

Theodore A. (Dr.), of Charlottesville, Albemarle Co., Va., and J. Annie, d. of the late Col. Edward Colston of Berkeley Co., W.Va., by the Rev. R. D. Roller, in Trinity Church, Martinsburg, W.Va. So. Ch., Oct. 23 and Nov. 6, 1884

MICKLE
Andrew Hutchins, of New York, and Susan Sumers, d. of Dr. J. H. Hunter, by the Rev. W. T. Leavell, rector, assisted by Dr. Seabury of New York, in St. Mark's Church, Berkeley Springs. So. Ch., July 7, 1892

Andrew, merchant of Hillsborough, and Helen Mary, d. of the Hon. William Norwood, by the Rev. Henry Prout. So. Ch., Dec. 20, 1839

MICOU
Margaret, and John Moncure Daniel, Jr., by the Rev. R. W. Micou, father of the bride, in the chapel of the Theological Seminary. So. Ch., Dec. 26, 1908

Paul (The Rev.), and Janet Sayce, d. of Allen Childs, by the Rev. Dr. Louis C. Washburn, the rector, and the Rev. Dr. William E. Gardner, in Old Christ Church, Philadelphia. So. Ch., Dec. 24, 1921

Rosalie G., d. of J. R. Micon*, Esq. of Essex, and George D. Nicholson of Middlesex, by the Rev. J. B. Newton assisted by the Rev. W. A. Baynham, in St. John's Church, Tappahannock. So. Ch., Jan. 13, 1876

MICOW
E. Herbie, d. of James R. Micow, Esq., of Essex Co., Va., and Charles M. Gatewood of Middlesex Co., by the Rev. H. T. W. Temple assisted by the Rev. John P. McGuire, in St. John's, Tappahannock, Essex Co., Va. So. Ch., Aug. 9, 1866

Fannie B. M., d. of James Roy Micow, Esq., and Thos. S. Roy, Esq. of Fauquier Co., by the Rev. H. W. L. Temple, at Tappahannock. So. Ch., Dec. 25, 1857

MIDDLETON
Benjamin Arthur, M.D., of Richmond Co., Va., and Mary Elizabeth, d. of John L. Barnett, Esq.

* Given as printed

MARRIAGE NOTICES IN THE SOUTHERN CHURCHMAN WITH DATES OF PUBLICATION

of Salem, Va., by the Rev. E. C. Gordon, at Salem, Va. So. Ch., Dec. 24, 1881

Henry C., of Farmville, and Juliet B., d. of Ferdinand Woltz, Esq., Clerk of Botetourt County Court, by the Rev. T. F. Martin of Nelson Co., at Fincastle. So. Ch., Oct. 29, 1858

Kate Hyatt, d. of Reuben Middleton, Esq., and Lemuel Clark, Esq. of Baltimore, by the Rev. John Collins McCabe, D.D., at Hyattsville, near Bladensburg, Md. So. Ch., May 31, 1866

Maria Louisa, youngest d. of the late Charles Middleton, Esq. of England, and W. W. Davies of Richmond, Va., by the Rev. A. B. Tizzard, at Eppington, Chesterfield Co., Va. So. Ch., Dec. 22, 1887

Matilda, d. of the late Charles Middleton of Chesterfield Co., Va., and J. R. McGehee, Esq. of Kentucky, by the Rev. A. B. Tizzard, at Woodstock Farm. So. Ch., Oct. 17, 1872

Thomas Allston, Esq., of Charleston, S.C., and Mary Gray, d. of Andrew Beirne, Esq., by the Rev. Wm. McGuire, at Linden Grove, Monroe Co., W.Va. So. Ch., July 26, 1866

MILLAN

Emily Virginia, d. of Dr. L. Millan of Rappahannock Co., and Lewis B. Brown of Madison Co., by the Rev. R. T. Brown, at Woodville, Va. So. Ch., April 21, 1870

Joseph C., of Jefferson, Tex., and Annie Thomas, only d. of Fenton M. Henderson of Leesburg, by the Rev. R. T. Davis, in St. James' Church, Leesburg. So. Ch., Sept. 25, 1873

Lucy Lee, and Wm. Mason Stuart, both of Rappahannock Co., Va., by the Rev. Charles S. Harrison, in St. Paul's Church, Woodville, Va. So. Ch., Nov. 10, 1892

MILLER

Ann Lewis, eldest d. of Narcissus W. and Kitty Miller, and Dr. Wm. Morris, all of Goochland Co., by the Rev. Geo. D. E. Mortimer, in Goochland Co. So. Ch., Jan. 22, 1864

Bettie F., only d. of the late Norman Miller of Martinsburg, W.Va., gr.d. of the late Maj. Thomas Briscoe of Charleston, W.Va., and Alexander, s. of John H. Gassaway, Esq. of Montgomery Co., Md., by the Rev. R. T. Brown, at Glenwood, Montgomery Co., Md. So. Ch., Mar. 2, 1882

Blanchard C., of Grayson, Carter Co., Ky., and Maria Ann, d. of Capt. W. P. Blakey of Richmond, Va., by the Rev. T. G. Dashiell, at the residence of the bride's father. So. Ch., Dec. 23, 1880

Blanche Cantrell, and Capt. Rankin Wiley, Jr., by the Rev. T. M. Lacey, at the residence of the bride's father, C.C. Miller, Esq., near Point Pleasant, W.Va. So. Ch., Oct. 9, 1879

MARRIAGE NOTICES IN THE SOUTHERN CHURCHMAN WITH DATES OF PUBLICATION

Eva, and Ephriam Myers, by the Rev. W. D. Hanson, at the residence of the bride's father, Newport, Del. So. Ch., Feb. 20, 1879

John, of Washington, D.C., and Sarah B., d. of Samuel Pulman, Esq., by the Rev. W. Strother Jones, rector of Grace Church, Fauquier, at Mount Erin, Fairfax Co., Va. So. Ch., Dec. 20, 1877

Judith Fauntleroy, and Preston Stoddard Avery of Pensacola, Fla., by the Rev. K. J. Hammond, in Trinity Church, Washington, Va. So. Ch., Nov. 6, 1920

Margaret E. F., d. of Charles G. Miller, Esq., of Mason Co., W.Va., and John J. Dashner of Monroe Co., Mo., by the Rev. Horace E. Hayden, at the residence of the bride's father. So. Ch., Oct. 8, 1868

Mary E., d. of Charles M. and Mrs. Lizzie L. Miller of Keyser, W.Va., and Dr. Henry B. Potter of Providence, R.I., by the rector, the Rev. R. E. L. Strider, in Emmanuel Church, Keyser, W.Va. So. Ch., Oct. 5, 1912

Mary Maud, d. of Mr. and Mrs. Harry J. Miller of Washington, Va., and Cecil Ambrey Speake of Luray, Va., by the Rev. Churchill J. Gibson, pastor of Calvary Church, Luray, in Trinity Church. So. Ch., June 13, 1917

Nannie Lewis, and William Johnson Kuykendall, by the Rev. R. E. Strider, rector of Emmanuel Church, Keyser, W.Va., at the home of the bride's parents, Mr. and Mrs. Charles M. Miller, at Keyser, W.Va. So. Ch., Apr. 26, 1913

Susan A., d. of R. R. Miller, and Wm. G. Williams, both of Richmond, by the Rev. Wm. S. Plummer. So. Ch., Dec. 30, 1836

Walter Gideon, formerly of Washington, Va., and Katherine E. Ostrander of Westwood, Cal., by the Rev. C. W. Pogue, at Susanville, Cal. So. Ch., July 24, 1915

William, and Sarah, d. of John Warrock, Esq., both of Richmond, Va., by the Rev. George Woodbridge. So. Ch., Dec. 1, 1837

Wm. H., Esq., attorney-at-law, of Parkville, Mo., and Mary Frances Adams of Weston, Mo., by the Rev. W. Norman Irish, at Weston, Mo. So. Ch., Nov. 9, 1855

Zillah, and Capt. Alva W. Hilyard, in Newport, Del., at the residence of the bride's father. So. Ch., Jan. 11, 1883

MILLIGAN
J. W., of Clermont, Iowa, and Florence Lockridge, by the Rev. R. H. Mason, at Meadow Dale, Pocahontas Co., W.Va. So. Ch., June 13, 1878

MILLS
Charles S., M.D., and Claudia, d. of Col. Crozet, by the Rev. Dr. Empie, in Richmond, Va. So. Ch., Oct. 25, 1839

Martha Virginia, Superintendent of Burlington County Hospital, Mt. Holly, N.J.,

MARRIAGE NOTICES IN THE SOUTHERN CHURCHMAN WITH DATES OF PUBLICATION

and the Rev. Dr. David McConnel Steele, rector of the Church of St. Luke and the Epiphany, Philadelphia. So. Ch., June 7, 1930

Henry W., Esq., of Nelson Co., and Ella Rose, d. of S. Meredith Garland, Esq. of Amherst C.H., by the Rev. J. D. Powell, at the residence of the bride's father. So. Ch., Aug. 5, 1858

MILTON

Harietta Ross, d. of W. Taylor Milton of Clarke Co., Va., and the Rev. Robert Kinloch Massie of Charlottesville, Va., by the Rev. P. P. Phillips, rector, assisted by the Rev. Kinloch Nelson, D.D., in Grace Church, Berryville, Va. So. Ch., July 23, 1891

Lizzie, d. of the late John and Louisa A. Milton, and Philip S. Campbell, by the Rev. John L. McKee, at the residence of R. M. Cunningham, in Louisville, Ky. So. Ch., Oct. 20, 1870

W. Taylor, of Clarke Co., Va., and Fannie C., youngest d. of the late Stephen Duncan of Louisiana, by the Rev. T. F. Martin, in Grace Church, Berryville, Va. So. Ch., Nov. 14, 1867

William Byrd Lee (The Rev.), rector of Christ Church Parish, Lancaster Co., Va., and Frances Gordon, d. of Mr. and Mrs. Arthur Presley Thornton, by the Rev. Churchill J. Gibson assisted by the rector, the Rev. Dudley Boogher, and the Rt. Rev. Henry St. George Tucker, in St. George's Church, Fredericksburg, Va. So. Ch., Dec. 22, 1934

MILWARD

Henry Kavanaugh, s. of Mrs. Kate Adams and the late Col. Hubbard Kavanaugh Milward of Lexington, Ky., and Sarah Louise, d. of the Rt. Rev. and Mrs. Lewis W. Burton of Lexington, by the Bishop of Lexington assisted by the Very Rev. W. T. Capers, Dean of the Cathedral, in Christ Church Cathedral, Lexington, Ky. So. Ch., July 9, 1910

MINGE

David, of Alabama, and Elvira, d. of the late Dr. John Adams of Richmond, Va., by the Rev. Wm. H. Hart, at Richmond, Va. So. Ch., Oct. 13, 1837

MINNIGERODE

Emsie, of Richmond, and James A. Duckworth of Mosely Hill, England, by the Rev. Charles Minnigerode, D.D., father of the bride, in St. Paul's Church, Richmond, Va. So. Ch., May 19, 1881

James G. (The Rev.), rector of Calvary Church, Louisville, Ky., and Annie, d. of George G. Thompson of Culpeper, by the Rev. Dr. Charles Minnigerode of St. Paul's Church, Richmond, Va., assisted by the Rev. George W. Peterkin, D.D., Bishop-elect of West Virginia, in St. Stephen's Church, Culpeper. So. Ch., May 23, 1878

Jas. Gibbon (The Rev.), of Rappahannock Co., Va., and Mary V., d. of J. Madison Slaughter, Esq. late of Baltimore,

MARRIAGE NOTICES IN THE SOUTHERN CHURCHMAN WITH DATES OF PUBLICATION

by the Rev. C. Minnigerode, rector of the church, assisted by the Rev. A. M. Randolph, in Emmanuel Church, Baltimore. So. Ch., Oct. 23, 1873

William, of Richmond, and Imogen, d. of J. H. Gordon, Esq. of Lynchburg, by the Rev. Chas. Minnigerode, D.D., father of the groom, assisted by the Rev. Dr. Hooper, in the Second Presbyterian Church, Lynchburg, Va. So. Ch., Nov. 23, 1876

MINOR

Berkely, and Susan W., d. of the late James Fontaine, Esq. of Hanover, by the Rev. George W. Nelson, at Rock Castle, Hanover Co., Va. So. Ch., Sept. 16, 1875

Bettie, d. of Lancelot Minor, Esq., and the Rev. Thomas Mowbray formerly of Edinburgh, Scotland, by the Rev. David Teese, at "Briery Knowl", in Amherst Co., Va. So. Ch., Oct. 28, 1886

Carrie, d. of Launcelot and Mary Minor, and Andrew J. Richison, all of Amherst Co., Va., by the Rev. J. P. Lawrence, in St. Luke's Church, Pedlar Mills. So. Ch., Nov. 21, 1878

Charles L. C., of Hanover Co., and Fanny A., d. of the late Louis A. Cazenove of Alexandria, by the Rev. C. Walker, D.D., at Alexandria. So. Ch., Jan. 18, 1861

Charles Launcelot, M.D., of New York, and Mary McLowell, d. of Prof. Charles S. Venable of the University, by the Rev. G. L. Petrie assisted by the Rev. J. S. Hanckel, D.D., in the chapel of the University of Virginia. So. Ch., Dec. 18, 1890

Elizabeth, d. of Judge Robert Minor of San Antonio, Tex., and Walter T., s. of John Tabb, Esq. of Gloucester Co., Va., in the Church of the Messiah, in New York. So. Ch., June 21, 1919

Fanny C., d. of Lancelot Minor, Esq. of Amherst, and Robert C. Berkeley of Hanover Co., by the Rev. Wm. H. Kinckle of Lynchburg, at "Briery Knowl", Amherst Co., Va. So. Ch., May 8, 1863

Geo. Gilmer, and Ophelia Yarbrough, by the Rev. A. W. Weddell, D.D., in St. John's Church, Richmond, Va. So. Ch., Dec. 9, 1880

Helen Willis, fourth d. of the late Dr. Jones M. Minor formerly of Virginia, and the Rev. N. C. S. Poyntz of Gloucestershire, England, by the Rev. Geo. H. Houghton, D.D., assisted by the Rev. T. McKee Brown, in the Church of the Transfiguration, New York. So. Ch., Jan. 4, 1883

John, and Lucy Lee Trice, by the Rev. E. L. Goodwin assisted by the Rev. P. H. Gwinn, at Wiloughby, Albemarle Co., Va. So. Ch., June 18, 1891

John (Dr.), of Washington, D.C., s. of Dr. and Mrs. Charles L. Minor of Asheville, N.C., and

MARRIAGE NOTICES IN THE SOUTHERN CHURCHMAN WITH DATES OF PUBLICATION

Mildred, d. of Mrs. Edward Truslow of Summit, N.J., by the Rev. W. O. Kinsolving, rector of the church, and the Rev. Elmore McKee of Waterbury, Conn., brother-in-law of the bride, in Christ Church, Summit, N.J. So. Ch., Apr. 29, 1922

John B. (Prof.), of the University of Virginia, and Nannie F., d. of the late Thomas M. Colston of Fauquier, by the Rev. D. C. T. Davis, at Hillandale, the residence of Raleigh Colston. So. Ch., Mar. 11, 1859

John B., Prof. of Law at the University of Virginia, and Ellen L. Hill, by the Rev. Dr. Hanckel, at the residence of Dr. J. S. Davis. So. Ch., Nov. 20, 1884

Juliet Gilmer, eldest d. of the late B. Franklin Minor, Esq., and Edmund D. H. Janvier, Esq. of Baltimore, by the Rev. A. P. Stryker of Maryland, at the residence of the bride's mother, at Ridgeway, Albemarle Co., Va. So. Ch., Nov. 19, 1868

Kate Meade, third d. of the late Lucius H. Minor, and Richard Morris Fontaine, all of Hanover, Va., by the Rev. W. A. Alrich, in Trinity Church, St. Martin's Parish, Hanover. So. Ch., June 4, 1874

Kitty, d. of Launcelot Minor, Esq., and Maj. John D. Rogers, by the Rev. Robert J. McBryde assisted by the Rev. Mr. Lawrence, rector of the parish, at "Briery Knowl", Amherst Co., Va. So. Ch., Oct. 26, 1882

Landonia R., second d. of the late Capt. Robert D. Minor, and William S. Dashiell assisted by the Rev. Dr. Peterkin, in Richmond, Va. So. Ch., Dec. 20, 1883

Lucy Landon, d. of Dr. Charles L. and Mary Venable Minor, and Lt. Paul B. Barringer of Virginia, by the Rev. W. G. Clark, in Trinity Church, Asheville, N.C. So. Ch., Dec. 22, 1917

Maria W., youngest d. of the late Warner W. Minor, Esq., and Wm. H. R. Worlman of South Carolina, by the Rev. Jacob S. Scott, chaplain of the University of Virginia, at Wertland. So. Ch., Nov. 9, 1848

Mary Aletha, d. of Lancelot Minor, Esq. of Amherst Co., Va., and William Henry Maclin of Tennessee, by the Rev. R. L. Dabney, D.D. of the Union Theological Seminary, at "Briery Tenowho."* So. Ch., Sept. 26, 1872

Mary Ann, of King William Co., and Thomas Wheeley of Richmond, Va., by the Rev. G. W. Trice. So. Ch., Dec. 30, 1836

Mattie M., d. of Prof. John B. Minor of the University of Virginia, and Conway Whittle Sams of Norfolk, Va., by the Rev. J. S. Hanckel, D.D., assisted by the Rev. Julius Sams, D.D., of Baltimore, in the University Chapel. So. Ch., Nov. 13, 1890

* Given as printed

MARRIAGE NOTICES IN THE SOUTHERN CHURCHMAN WITH DATES OF PUBLICATION

Robert B., Esq., of Sequin, Texas, s. of the late Lucius H. Minor of Hanover Co., Va., and Routez, d. of the late Dr. G. J. Houston of San Antonio, Tex., by Dean Richardson, in St. Mark's Cathedral, San Antonio, Tex. So. Ch., Sept. 29, 1881

Sallie G., and Henry M. Magruder, both of Albemarle Co., by the Rev. Mr. Hanckel of Christ Church, at Ridgeway, the residence of the bride's mother. So. Ch., Apr. 22, 1869

MITCHELL

Adelina, d. of Wm. L. G. and Adelina Mitchell of Nuttsville, Lancaster Co., Va., and Frank W. Motley of Richmond Co., by the Rev. Henry L. Derby, in White Chapel Church, Lancaster, Va. So. Ch., Dec. 20, 1888

Alfred, and Martha Jane Starke, by the Rev. Dr. Empie, in Richmond, Va. So. Ch., Dec. 20, 1839

Charles T., Esq., of Charleston, S.C., and Frances Carter, d. of G. W. Bassett, Esq., by the Rev. Mr. Carraway, at "Clover Lea", the residence of the bride's father, in Hanover. So. Ch., Dec. 11, 1863

Charlotte E., of Bedford City, and Col. Robert Harvey of Huntington, W.Va., by the Rev. T. W. Jones, at the residence of the late Judge Wingfield, near Bedford City, Va. So. Ch., Sept. 18, 1890*

Dan. T., of Lynchburg, and Fanny Pate, d. of Hon. Henry Loving of Amherst Co., Va., by the Rev. W. M. Clark, at "Brooklyne", Amherst Co., Va. So. Ch., Aug. 20, 1885

Dorothy, d. of George W. Mitchell of Williamsport, Pa., and T. R. B., s. of the late Judge T. R. B. Wright and Della Preston Wright of Tappahannock, Va., in the home of the Rev. James M. Wallace, Baltimore, Md. So. Ch., Dec. 18, 1915

Edith Catharine, d. of the late C. J. B. Mitchell of Queen Anne Co., Md., and the Rev. Joseph Courtney Jones of Baltimore, Md., by the Rev. B. T. Turner assisted by the Rev. Joseph R. Jones, in St. Luke's Church, Queenstown, Md. So. Ch., Oct. 12, 1893

James A. (The Rev.), rector of White Marsh Parish, and Mollie E. Kennard of Easton, Md., by the Rev. Walter A. Mitchell assisted by the Bishop of the Diocese, in Christ Church, Easton, Md. So. Ch., Jan. 26, 1871

John, Esq., of Des Moines, Iowa, and Rebecca, second d. of the late C. P. Anshutz, by the Rev. Wm. F. M. Jacobs, at Moundsville. So. Ch., Jan. 14, 1859

John M. (The Rev.), rector of St. John's Church, Montgomery, Ala., and Mattie M., d. of the late Judge John B. Christian of Virginia, by the Rt. Rev. Richard H. Wilmer, D.D., at Wakefield, Perry Co.,

---

* A notice appears in the issue of Sept. 11, 1890, identical with this, except that "Mitchell" is written "Wingfield"

MARRIAGE NOTICES IN THE SOUTHERN CHURCHMAN WITH DATES OF PUBLICATION

Ala. So. Ch., Dec. 26, 1862

John R., Esq., of Washington, and Fannie F., d. of Dr. John Gantt of Albemarle Co., by the Rev. Wm. M. Nelson, in Albemarle Co., Va. So. Ch., Oct. 26, 1854

Kate C., and John T. Mahan, both of Pittsylvania Co., Va., by the Rev. C. D. Pruden, at the residence of the bride's father, H. C. Mitchell, Pittsylvania Co. So. Ch., Jan. 22, 1885

L. C., of Lancaster Co., Va., and Lola H., d. of Henry Fitzhugh, Esq. of Sherwood Forest, by the Rev. R. J. McBryde, at the residence of John Tayloe, Esq., Fredericksburg, Va. So. Ch., Jan. 11, 1883

Margaret W., d. of W. L. G. and Adalina Mitchell, and the Rev. A. J. Willis of King George, by the Rev. H. L. Derby assisted by the Rev. Mr. Johnson and the Rev. Mr. Mason, at White Chapel, Lancaster, Va. So. Ch., Nov. 26, 1885

Myrtle, of Negaunee, Mich., and the Rt. Rev. Walter Taylor Sumner, Bishop of Oregon, by Bishop Anderson, in the Cathedral of Sts. Peter and Paul, Chicago. So. Ch., Jan. 19, 1918

R. Sommerville, and Annie Newcomb, both of Lancaster Co., Va., by the Rev. H. L. Derby, at "White Chapel." So. Ch., Dec. 23, 1880

Robert, and Nannie Key Tyson of Baltimore, Md., by the Rev. C. Clifton Pennick, at Oakland, Md. So. Ch., Dec. 5, 1872

Robert Fairfax, of Richmond Co., and Mrs. M. Victoria Tapscott formerly of Baltimore, Md., by the Rev. H. L. Derby, at "Oakley", Lancaster, Va. So. Ch., Mar. 2, 1876

S. F., and Mrs. Julia E. Zimmer, d. of C. M. Nimmo, Esq., all of Richmond, by the Rev. F. M. Baker, in Grace Church. So. Ch., Jan. 9, 1863

William, and Lizzie Alston, d. of L. J. Beall, all of Richmond, by the Rev. Joshua Peterkin, in St. James' Church, Richmond. So. Ch., Dec. 2, 1875

Willie J., d. of W. L. G. and Adalina C. Mitchell, and Col. H. H. Harrison, by the Rev. H. L. Derby, at Nuttsville, Lancaster, Va. So. Ch., Nov. 22, 1877

MIX

Bettie Lewis, eldest d. of Dr. Mix, and John Lucas Follit, by the Rev. T. E. Locke, at the residence of Dr. Oscar Gunnell Mix, near Warren, Albemarle Co., Va. So. Ch., June 21, 1888

E. Katie, third d. of Dr. Mix, and Sidney Barnett, all of Albemarle Co., by the Rev. T. E. Locke. So. Ch., Oct. 15, 1885

Sadie Anna, youngest d. of Dr. Mix, and Edward Capel Greenway, by the Rev. T. E. Locke, at the residence of Dr. Oscar Gunnell Mix, near Warren, Albemarle Co., Va. So. Ch., June 21, 1888

MOALE

William Armistead, and Eleanor Addison Gittings, by the

MARRIAGE NOTICES IN THE SOUTHERN CHURCHMAN WITH DATES OF PUBLICATION

Rev. J. S. B. Hodges in St. Paul's Church, Baltimore. So. Ch., Dec. 30, 1880

MOHLER
 M. C. J., and Sallie J. Robinson, by the Rev. Jno. McGill, in Christ Church, Fairfax Co. So. Ch., Jan. 4, 1877

MOHUN
 Anna Marguerite, eldest d. of Mr. and Mrs. Francis B. Mohun, and Stasius, s. of the late Wm. W. Meade of Clarke Co., Va., by the Rev. Father Boland, at the home of the bride, in Washington, D.C. So. Ch., July 6, 1893

MONCURE
 Dora Ashley, d. of Mr. and Mrs. Powhatan Moncure of "Oakenwold", Stafford Co., Va., and the Rev. Wm. Jackson Morton of Richmond, Va., by the Rev. John K. Mason, D.D. assisted by the rector, the Rev. Wm. M. Clark, in St. George's Church, Fredericksburg, Va. So. Ch., May 18, 1893

 Eustace W., of Stafford Co., Va., and Mary Campbell, youngest d. of Thos. F. Knox, by the Rev. Dr. Murdaugh assisted by the Rev. Arthur L. Johns, at the residence of the bride's father, in Fredericksburg, Va. So. Ch., Nov. 27, 1873

 Fannie W., d. of the Hon. R. C. L. Moncure of Stafford Co., Va., and Thomas J. Moncure of Richmond City, by the Rev. A. M. Randolph, in Stafford Co. So. Ch., Dec. 16, 1859

 George V., Jr., and Lizzie Allen, d. of the late N. W. Ford, Esq., all of Stafford Co., Va., by the Rev. John Moncure assisted by the Rev. G. H. Appleton, at Aquia Church, Va. So. Ch., Jan. 11, 1883

 Hallie E., d. of Judge R. C. L. Moncure and his wife of Stafford Co., Va., and Thomas Wallace, Esq., by the Rev. Mr. McBryde, in Stafford Co., Va. So. Ch., Jan. 27, 1881

 Hallie Wallace, d. of Dr. and Mrs. W. Peyton Moncure of Fairfax, Va., and Franklin Packard Sagendorf, by the Rev. Thomas A. Houghton-Burke, in the rectory of Christ Church, Rockville, Md. So. Ch., July 12, 1913

 J. Jacquelin (Dr.), and Edith, d. of Dr. Orlando Fairfax, at the residence of the father, in Richmond. So. Ch., Nov. 15, 1877

 John (The Rev.), rector of the parish, and Lalla M., d. of A. Vance, Esq. of Gallipolis, by the Rev. Jacob Brittingham of Clarksburg, W.Va. assisted by the Rev. J. Cowpland of Point Pleasant, W.Va., in St. Peter's Church, Gallipolis, Ohio. So. Ch., Mar. 6, 1884

 Mary B., d. of R. C. L. Moncure, Jr., and James Ashby, by the Rev. J. M. Meredith, at Aquia Church, Stafford Co., Va. So. Ch., Jan. 2, 1879

 Mary C., and the Rev. W. R. D. Moncure, both of Stafford Co., Va., by the Rev.

MARRIAGE NOTICES IN THE SOUTHERN CHURCHMAN WITH DATES OF PUBLICATION

Samuel B. Barber, at Glencairne, the residence of Judge R. C. L. Moncure. So. Ch., Dec. 10, 1868

Robert Minor, of Stafford Co., Va., and Eliza Stewart, d. of the late James Hunt, Esq. of Covington, Ky., by the Rev. John Moncure of Gallipolis, Ohio, at the home of the bride, No. 629 East Capital Street, Washington, D.C. So. Ch., Jan. 8, 1891

Thomas J., of Richmond City, and Fannie W., d. of the Hon. R. C. L. Moncure of Stafford Co., Va., by the Rev. A. M. Randolph, in Stafford Co. So. Ch., Dec. 16, 1859

Travers D., and Bessie, d. of the late Hon. B. B. Douglas, by the Rev. E. Meade, at "Cownes", King William Co., Va. So. Ch., July 20, 1882

W. R. D. (The Rev.), and Mary C. Moncure, both of Stafford Co., Va., by the Rev. Samuel B. Barber, at Glencairne, the residence of Judge R. C. L. Moncure. So. Ch., Dec. 10, 1868

William W., eldest s. of the officiating clergyman, and Alice, youngest d. of Asa Stewart, Esq. of Bennington, Vt., by the rector, the Rev. William H. Monroe, in Christ Church, Boston. So. Ch., Feb. 22, 1883

MONEY
Ernle George (Elder), s. of the late Wm. Taylor Money of the Madras Army, and Susie Stanford, only child of James T. and Susan S. Bacon of Stanford Hall, Albemarle Co., Va., by the Rev. Edward Valentine Jones, in Grace Church, Albemarle Co., Va. So. Ch., Oct. 22, 1891

MONTAGUE
Bessie Douglas, d. of Dr. T. B. Montague, and Hugh Whiting of Clarke Co., Va., by the Rev. Mr. Meredith, at Rose Dale, Stafford Co., Va. So. Ch., Oct. 31, 1889

Edgar B., and Sarah Virginia, d. of Joseph Ewbank, by the Rev. Edmund Withers, at Nesting, Middlesex Co. So. Ch., Dec. 24, 1858

Meredith F., and Emily Louisa, d. of Mrs. Nannie J. and the late William Stone Triplett, by the Rev. Charles Minnigerode, D.D., assisted by the Rev. Joshua Peterkin, D.D., in St. Paul's Church, Richmond, Va. So. Ch., Jan. 17, 1884

Percy, and Inez, d. of Dr. W. M. Withers, all of Richmond, by the Rev. Moses D. Hoge assisted by the Rev. Dr. Peterkin, in the Second Presbyterian Church. So. Ch., Aug. 11, 1881

Sallie Watson, d. of Jno. H. Montague, and J. Arthur Lefroy of County Down, Ireland, by the Rev. J. Peterkin, in St. James' Church, Richmond, Va. So. Ch., Apr. 19, 1877

William Ivanhoe, and Virginia W., d. of the late Gen. Henry A. Thompson, all of Baltimore, by the Rev. A. M. Randolph, rector, assisted by the Rev. W. W. Williams of the Church of the Holy Innocents, in Emmanuel Church, Baltimore. So. Ch., Dec. 1, 1881

MONTGOMERIE
Jean, d. of the late Hugh Montgomerie of Lynchburg, and Chas. V. Horseley of Buckingham, by the Rev.

MARRIAGE NOTICES IN THE SOUTHERN CHURCHMAN WITH DATES OF PUBLICATION

Edmund Withers, at the parsonage, Norwood, Nelson Co., Va. So. Ch., Oct. 22, 1868

MONTGOMERY

Fanny Hays, third d. of R. C. Montgomery, and D. Edward Goodwyn, all of Greensville Co., Va., by the Rev. David Barr, in Christ Church, Hicksford, Va. So. Ch., Dec. 14, 1871

R. S., and Mrs. A. Meade Goodwyn, d. of the late R. K. Meade of Brunswick Co., Va., by the Rev. H. M. Galusha assisted by the Rev. Edmund Withers, at Greenwood, in Greensville Co., Va. So. Ch., Apr. 4, 1862

Robert, Esq., and Bell Farrar, both of Point Coupee Parish, La., by the Rev. Jno. R. Lee, at Bleak Hill, the residence of Peter Saunders, Jr., Esq., Franklin Co., Va. So. Ch., Jan. 6, 1870

Robert H., of King George Co., and Branch Brockenbrough of Richmond Co., Va., by the Rev. Beverly Tucker, at Wareland. So. Ch., Dec. 27, 1877

Walter A., of Warrenton, N.C., and Lizzie, d. of Dr. Thomas E. Wilson of Roanoke Co., Va., by the Rev. Edward H. Ingle, in St. John's Church, Roanoke Co. So. Ch., Oct. 5, 1871

MOODY

Lellie Wingfield, second d. of George W. Moody of Surry, and Joel Flournoy Whitley of Surry, by the Rev. David Barr, near Surry C.H., Va. So. Ch., Oct. 13, 1887

Phronia L., d. of Horace J. Moody, Esq., and J. J. Lancaster, by the Rev. William S. Langford, in St. John's Church, Yonkers, N.Y. So. Ch., Dec. 9, 1875

MOOERS

Alice E., and Chas. M. Southall, both of Charles City Co., by the Rev. W. B. Everett, in Mapisco Church, Charles City Co., Va. So. Ch., Jan. 4, 1883

MOON

Lizzie D., d. of L. Moon, Esq., and Samuel C. Goggin of Bedford Co., by the Rev. B. W. Moseley, near Leesville, Campbell Co. So. Ch., Mar. 21, 1878

MOORE

A., Jr., of Clarke Co., and Cornelia Daniel, eldest d. of Col. Charles Ellet of Pennsylvania, by the Rev. Edmund Withers, at Norwood, Nelson Co., Va. So. Ch., Sept. 18, 1873

Alexander B., of Loudoun, and Lucy Beverley, d. of Maj. William N. Berkeley of Albemarle Co., formerly of Loudoun, by the Rev. J. S. Hanckle, D.D., in Christ Church, Charlottesville, Va. So. Ch., Feb. 24, 1881

Alfred (Dr.), of Huntsville, Ala., and Mary Jane, d. of Matthew Watson, Esq., by the Rev. Richard Channing Moore, at the residence of George L. Thompson. So. Ch., Sept. 30, 1836

Benjamin F. (Capt.), and Bettie V., d. of John G. Mantlo, by the Rev. S. S. Hepbron, at the residence of the bride's father. So. Ch., Jan. 24, 1884

MARRIAGE NOTICES IN THE SOUTHERN CHURCHMAN WITH DATES OF PUBLICATION

Bessie Thomson, d. of Wm. H. Moore, and John T. Gibson, Jr., by the Rev. Wm. H. Meade, in Zion Church, in Charles Town. So. Ch., Jan. 3, 1878

Ed. W., of Washington, D.C., and Mrs. Sallie M. Gatright, by the Rev. J. E. Hammond, at the residence of the bride's father, Wm. Martin, Manchester, Va. So. Ch., May 8, 1873

Edward A., of Rockbridge Co., Va., and Mary Watts, d. of Judge John J. Allen of Botetourt Co., Va., by the Rev. Edward H. Ingle, at "Beaver Dam", the residence of the bride's father. So. Ch., Dec. 6, 1877

Elizabeth Jane, of Princess Anne, and the Rev. J. B. Colhoun, by the Rev. James Moore, father of the bride, and the Rev. Meyer Lewin, in St. Andrew's Church, Princess Anne, Somerset Co., Md. So. Ch., Oct. 22, 1858

Estella, of New Martinsville, W.Va., and Henry S. Gregg of Merriam Park, Minn., by the Rev. Jacob Brittingham, in St. Ann's Church, New Martinsville. So. Ch., Dec. 12, 1889

George D., and Louise H. Blume, both of Charles Town, W.Va., by the Rev. R. J. McBryde, D.D., in St. George's rectory, Fredericksburg, Va. So. Ch., June 8, 1907

Gertrude, niece of Thomas Moore, Esq., and Alfred H. Taylor of Washington, D.C., by the Rev. Frank Page, in Zion Church, Fairfax C.H., Va. So. Ch., June 24, 1886

J. S., Esq., and Jane, d. of Samuel R. Owens, Esq. of Chesterfield Co., by the Rev. A. B. Tizzard, at Chestnut Cottage. So. Ch., Apr. 4, 1867

Jane J., d. of Alexander Moore, Esq. of Alexandria, and Randolph Coyle, by the Rev. Mr. Dana, at Alexandria, D.C. So. Ch., Dec. 22, 1837

John H. (Dr.), and Ella B. Mount, both of Waterford, Loudoun Co., Va., by the Rev. Theo. Reed, in Waterford Church. So. Ch., Nov. 18, 1875

John Randolph, and Sallie A. Sprouse, by the Rev. Robt. White, at the residence of the bride's father, in Albemarle Co. So. Ch., Jan. 10, 1884

Lizzie, and Allen Apperson of Richmond, Va., by the Rev. A. Wade, at Kittawan, the residence of the bride's father. So. Ch., Mar. 19, 1874

Mary A. (Mrs.), and J. W. Rudd, by the Rev. A. B. Tizzard, at the residence of G. W. Bartlum, Chesterfield Co., Va. So. Ch., Feb. 18, 1886

Mary M., of Mason Co., and Shepard W. Moore of Missouri, by the Rev. C. C. Pearson, at Verona, the residence of Col. C. T. Beale, Mason Co., W.Va. So. Ch., Nov. 7, 1889

Mary T., d. of Wm. P. Moore, Esq., and John C. Kellam, Esq. of Bellevue, Accomac Co., by the Rev. Dr. Colton, at Horn Cliffs, Northampton

MARRIAGE NOTICES IN THE SOUTHERN CHURCHMAN WITH DATES OF PUBLICATION

Co. So. Ch., Feb. 8, 1861
Milly (Mrs.), and Thos. Wilson, by the Rev. W. H. Pendleton, in Bedford Co., Va., at the home of Mr. Bartee. So. Ch., Feb. 20, 1868
P. T. (Gen.), and Mrs. Bettie Strother, both of Richmond, by the Rev. James Hanckle, D.D., at Charlottesville, Va. So. Ch., Feb. 10, 1881
Preston B., and Maria P., d. of John O. Steger, all of Baltimore, by the Rev. Joshua Peterkin, at the residence of the bride's father. So. Ch., Nov. 28, 1872
S. Sollay (The Rev.), of Herndon, Fairfax Co., Va., by the Rev. Joshua Peterkin, D.D., in St. James' Church. So. Ch., Oct. 29, 1885
Shepard W., of Missouri, and Mary M. Moore of Mason Co., by the Rev. C. C. Pearson, at Verona, the residence of Col. C. T. Beale, Mason Co., W.Va. So. Ch., Nov. 7, 1889
Susan Lindsay, d. of Thomas Moore, and S. Rozell Donohoe, editor of the Fairfax Herald, by the Rev. Frank Page, in Zion Church, Fairfax C.H., Va. So. Ch., May 29, 1884
Wm. Cabell (Dr.), of Washington City, and Elizabeth, d. of John Fox, Sr., at the home of the bride's parents, at Big Stone Gap, Va. So. Ch., Sept. 21, 1907

MOORMAN
Bessie A., of Campbell Co., Va., and Ruffin Dillard of North Carolina, by the Rev. W. W. Kimball, at the home of the bride. So. Ch., Oct. 6, 1881

MOORSON
Emily J., and Charles J. Hale, both lately of England, by the Rev. J. B. Craighill, in the rectory of St. Paul's Church, Suffolk. So. Ch., Jan. 15, 1874

MOPPS
Dorotha W. (Mrs.), of Baltimore, and the Rev. Joseph S. Collins of Alexandria, Va., by the Rev. T. B. Lemon. So. Ch., Jan. 3, 1850

MORAN
F. Berger, of Charlottesville (formerly of New York), and Jane W., d. of the late Dr. R. S. Blackburn of Clarke Co., Va., by the Rev. T. F. Martin assisted by the Rev. H. Sutter, at Weehaw*, the residence of the bride's mother. So. Ch., July 13, 1871
Martha Adams, d. of Charles Moran of New York, and E. Lee James, M.D., by the Rev. Reuben W. Howes, Jr., in the Church of the Transfiguration, New York. So. Ch., Sept. 18, 1873

MORDECAI
Wm. Y., of Henrico Co., and Helen Alves, d. of the officiating clergyman, the Rev. Wm. Norwood, D.D., in Emmanuel Church, Henrico Co., Va. So. Ch., Dec. 23, 1875

* Given as printed

MARRIAGE NOTICES IN THE SOUTHERN CHURCHMAN WITH DATES OF PUBLICATION

MORFORD
  Ada, of Deerwood, Minn., and T. Howard Hanson of St. Louis, Mo., by the Rev. G. H. Davis, at the residence of the bride's father, at Deerwood, Minn. So. Ch., Sept. 27, 1888

MORGAN
  Artelia, of Amelia Co., and George Pickett of Richmond, by the Rev. P. F. Berkeley, at the residence of the bride's father. So. Ch., Feb. 19, 1874
  Caroline A., of Fauquier Co., Va., and Edward W. Blodgett of Pawtucket, R.I., by the Rev. George W. Nelson, in St. James' Church, Warrenton, Va. So. Ch., Mar. 3, 1887
  Edward L., and Mary L. Welty, both of Fairmont, by the Rev. G. A. Gibbons, at the residence of the bride's sister, Mrs. Annie Turney. So. Ch., Jan. 2, 1879
  Ella C., d. of Col. Benjamin Morgan, and Geo. C. Shepherd, all of Clarke Co., Va., by the Rev. T. F. Martin, in Grace Church, Berryville. So. Ch., Jan. 15, 1874
  Emeline M., d. of Col. Benj. Morgan, and James H. Vandeventer, all of Clarke Co., Va., by the Rev. James T. F. Martin, at the residence of the bride's father. So. Ch., Nov. 5, 1868
  Frank C., of the Channel Islands, and Mary, d. of John Alexander of Albemarle Co., Va., by the Rev. William J. Morton of Richmond, at Warren, Albemarle Co., Va. So. Ch., Dec. 15, 1893
  Jennie L., and Richard S. Woodson, both of Isle of Wight Co., by the Rev. R. S. Barrett, at Richmond, Va. So. Ch., July 8, 1880
  Lillie B., d. of the late Jacob Morgan of Jefferson Co., and Augustine J. Smith of Alexandria, by the Rev. Mr. Andrews, near Shepherdstown. So. Ch., Dec. 14, 1855
  Margaret Johnston, d. of the Rev. Gilbert Morgan, D.D., of South Carolina, and E. Delafield Smith of New York, by the rector, the Rev. LeGrand Guerry, in St. Philip's Church, Bradford Springs, S.C. So. Ch., July 23, 1874
  Sarah Ann, d. of Richard Morgan, deceased, and Jesse Watkins, by George Thomas, Esq., in Richmond Co. So. Ch., Jan. 22, 1836
  Yelverton Peyton (The Rev.), and Mary Hilliard, d. of Dr. Elisha Sterling, by the Rev. G. T. Bedell, Bishop of Ohio, assisted by the Rev. James Bolles, D.D., at Cleveland, Ohio. So. Ch., June 18, 1885

MORRILL
  Annie J., d. of the late Capt. Morrill of Alexandria, and the Rev. Theodore S. Rumney, rector of Cople Parish, West-

MARRIAGE NOTICES IN THE SOUTHERN CHURCHMAN WITH DATES OF PUBLICATION

moreland Co., by the Rev. Charles B. Dana, in Westmoreland Co. So. Ch., Dec. 27, 1849

MORRIS

Alice W. (Mrs.), d. of the late Gen. Edward Watts, and Judge Wm. J. Robertson, by the Rev. J. Earnest, at Oaklands, Roanoke Co. So. Ch., July 24, 1863

Charles (The Rev.), of Ashland, Va., and Mrs. Sue W. Leigh, by the Rev. W. A. Alrich, at the residence of Dr. Lemmon, the bride's father, near Castle Craig, Campbell Co., Va. So. Ch., Sept. 7, 1876

Ellen B., of Caroline Co., Va., and T. Bernard Doswell of Hanover Co., by the Rev. Curtis Grubb, in St. Martin's Church, Hanover Co., Va. So. Ch., Dec. 25, 1884

Ellen D., eldest d. of Doct.* Charles Morris of Caroline, and James Hunter, Esq., Principal Engineer on the Louisa Railroad, by the Rev. John McGuire, in Caroline Co., Va. So. Ch., Sept. 22, 1837

Fanny M., d. of Col. John D. Morris, and Wythe McCrea, Esq., of New Orleans, by the Rev. Mr. Ringgold, in Trinity Church, Clarksville, Tenn. So. Ch., Oct. 4, 1866

Governeur, of Huntington, W.Va., and Florence Walton, ward of the Hon. S. A. Miller, by the Rev. C. M. Callan, rector, assisted by the Rev. Edward Valentine Jones, in St. John's Church, Charleston, W.Va. So. Ch., Dec. 5, 1872

H. P., of Richmond, Va., and Maria D. Allen of Jefferson Co., W.Va., by the Rev. H. J. Willis, in the Church of the Holy Spirit, Summit Point, Jefferson Co., W.Va. So. Ch., Dec. 22, 1892

Harold H. (Dr.), of Philadelphia, Pa., and Frances Westwood, d. of John O. and the late Alice Ellzey Jordan, by the Rev. I. M. Greene, in St. Andrew's Church, Clifton Forge, Va. So. Ch., Feb. 4, 1911

Helen Defebaugh, youngest d. of Mr. and Mrs. Robert Henry Morris, and Albert Lundquist of New York, by the Rev. Robert Burton, in the Church of the Ascension, Norfolk, Va. So. Ch., Aug. 2, 1924

Ida Beirne, of Arden, N.C., and Francis J. Jervey of Charleston, S.C., by the Rev. Thomas A. Morris, father of the bride, in Calvary Church, Henderson, N.C. So. Ch., Nov. 4, 1886

James M., of Louisa Co., and Victoria E., d. of the late John Philips, Esq., of Fauquier Co., Va., by the Rev. J. Earnest, at Meadow Farm, the residence of Erasmus Taylor, Esq. So. Ch., Dec. 14, 1860

John M'Quisten, of Portsmouth, Ohio, and Clara F. Cartwright of Mason Co., W.Va., by the Rev. T. H. Lacy, at the residence of Judge John Cartwright, the bride's father, near Mason City, Mason Co., W.Va. So. Ch., Sept. 18, 1879

Lettie, d. of E. G. Morris

---

* Given as printed

MARRIAGE NOTICES IN THE SOUTHERN CHURCHMAN WITH DATES OF PUBLICATION

of Hanover Co., and the Rev. Frank Page, by the Rev. Curtis Grubb assisted by the Rev. John McGill, in St. James' Church, Ashland. So. Ch., Oct. 28, 1886

Lou Belle, d. of Dr. Wm. S. Morris, and C. W. Langhorne, all of Lynchburg, Va., by the Rev. T. M. Carson, in St. Paul's Church. So. Ch., Nov. 25, 1875

Maria S., d. of the late Com. Morris of Washington, D.C., and the Rev. Thomas Duncan of Fauquier, by the Rev. Geo. D. Cummins, in Trinity Church, Washington, D.C. So. Ch., June 12, 1857

Mary Love, d. of Col. John D. Morris, and Thomas M. Barker of Christian Co., Ky., by the Rev. Mr. Ringgold, at Clarksville, Tenn. So. Ch., Jan. 24, 1857

Mary W., eldest d. of Edward W. Morris of Hanover Co., Va., and James N., eldest s. of the Rev. Robert Nelson, missionary to China, of Huntington, W.Va., by the Rev. W. A. Alrich, at Claymont, the residence of the bride's father. So. Ch., Feb. 20, 1873

Maury, and Susan D. Morris, by the Rev. Moses D. Hoge, D.D.,assisted by the Rev. Robb White, at Sylvania, the residence of the bride's mother. So. Ch., Jan. 25, 1883

Nathan, of Arkansas, and Kate Lewis of Essex Co., Va., by the Rev. Joseph Lewis assisted by the Rev. E. Meade, in St. Paul's Church, Essex Co., Va. So. Ch., Sept. 25, 1890

R. P. W. (Prof.), of Bryan, Tex., and Lizzie, eldest d. of Chas. W. and V. Statham, by the Rev. Chas. Morris, at the residence of the bride's father, Lynchburg, Va. So. Ch., Mar. 1, 1877

Rose Irving, d. of Edward W. Morris of Claremont, Hanover Co., Va., and Dr. John Whitehead of Salisbury, N.C., by the Rev. Frank Page, in Zion Church, Fairfax C.H. So. Ch., Nov. 7, 1889

S. R., and John F. McGuire, by the Rev. Joshua Peterkin, in St. James' Church. So. Ch., July 7, 1881

Sue W., d. of Mrs. Anne C. Morris of Charlottesville, and Joseph W. Anderson of Botetourt Co., by the Rev. R. K. Meade, in Christ Church, Charlottesville. So. Ch., July 8, 1859

Susan D., and Maury Morris, by the Rev. Moses D. Hoge, D.D.,assisted by the Rev. Robo White, at Sylvania, the residence of the bride's mother. So. Ch., Jan. 25, 1883

Susie D., youngest d. of Edward W. Morris of Claremont, Hanover Co., Va., and Rosewell Page of Danville, Va., by the Rev. Frank Page, brother of the groom, at Ashland. So. Ch., Jan. 27, 1887

Thomas A. (The Rev.), rector of the parish, and Mrs. Emma E. Rice, d. of the late Jacob Farney, by the Rev. Henry C. Lay, D.D., in St. Luke's Church, Jack-

MARRIAGE NOTICES IN THE SOUTHERN CHURCHMAN WITH DATES OF PUBLICATION

 sonville, Ala. So. Ch., Feb. 12, 1858
Walter H. P., Esq., of Richmond, and Jannetta C., d. of Geo. F. Harrison, Esq.,of Goochland Co., Va., by the Rev. J. D. Powell, at Longwood, Goochland Co. So. Ch., Nov. 1, 1866
Wm. (Dr.), and Ann Lewis, eldest d. of Narcissus W. and Kitty Miller, all of Goochland Co., by the Rev. Geo. D. E. Mortimer, in Goochland Co. So. Ch., Jan. 22, 1864

MORRISON
A. (Prof.), of Virginia, and Irene Tiernage of Fayette Co., Tenn., by the Rev. J. B. Canada, at "Walnut Grove", the residence of the bride's mother, in Fayette Co., Tenn. So. Ch., June 14, 1877
Alice S., d. of the late Rev. J. H. Morrison, D.D., of Virginia, and F. P. Flippen of Cumberland Co., Va., by Chaplain Wm. F. Morrison, U.S.N., assisted by the Rev. Henry Thomas, in St. Peter's Church, Poolesville, Md. So. Ch., Jan. 20, 1887
Anna, d. of the Rev. J. H. Morrison, D.D., and Dr. T. M. Fleming, by the Rev. J. H. Morrison, D.D., at the rectory, Goochland Co. So. Ch., Jan. 19, 1871
Archibald M. (The Rev.), and Margaret Caldwell, d. of James S. Shapter, Esq., by the Rev. Dr. Stone, in Christ Church, South Brooklyn. So. Ch., Aug. 26, 1852
Bertha Lee, d. of the late Rev. G. H. Morrison, D.D., and Armstrong Tate of Burlington, N.C., by the Rev. W. F. Morrison, U.S.N., in Memorial Church, Baltimore. So. Ch., June 22, 1893
Bettie, d. of Dr. E. A. Morrison of Lawrenceville, and George W. Goodwyn of Petersburg, by the Rev. Mr. Morrison of Baltimore, in Brunswick. So. Ch., Feb. 1, 1856
Brownie M., and Dr. J. H. Neff, both of Harrisonburg, Va., by the Rev. O. S. Bunting. So. Ch., Nov. 15, 1883
D. B., of Jefferson Co., W.Va., and Leila Howard of Clarke Co., Va., youngest d. of the late Douglas Howard of Baltimore, Md., by the Rev. T. F. Martin, in Grace Church, Berryville. So. Ch., Oct. 10 and 17, 1872*
Hariett R., d. of Dr. E. A. Morrison, and Freeman W. Jones, Sheriff of Brunswick Co., by the Rev. J. H. Morrison, D.D. assisted by the Rev. Mr. Glazebrook, in Lawrenceville, Va. So. Ch., Nov. 7, 1872
Lucia B., and D. Meade Bernard, Jr., Esq., by the Rev. Dr. J. H. Morrison and the Rev. Otis A. Glazebrook, in St. Andrew's Church, Brunswick Co., Va. So. Ch., Jan. 26, 1871
Robert I., of Lawrenceville, and Harriet Randolph, eldest d. of the late R. I. Hackley of Tallahassee, Fla., by the Rev. C. J. Gibson. So. Ch., Jan. 21, 1848

* In the issue of Oct. 10, 1872, "Morrison" is written "Morison"

MARRIAGE NOTICES IN THE SOUTHERN CHURCHMAN WITH DATES OF PUBLICATION

Wm. Foster (The Rev.), Chaplain U.S. Navy, and Julia, d. of the late George Pomeroy, Esq. of Madison, N.J., by the Rt. Rev. H. C. Potter, D.D., in Grace Church, New York. So. Ch., Nov. 26, 1885

MORSELL
W. F. C., and Sallie Upshur Beasley, d. of the officiating clergyman, the Rev. Dr. Beasley assisted by the Rev. Dr. Morsell, in All Saints' Church, Torresdale, Philadelphia. So. Ch., July 10, 1873

MORSE
Edwin Augustus, and Victoria Ellen Evans, by the Rev. R. A. Castleman, in the Cople rectory, Hague, Westmoreland Co., Va. So. Ch., Mar. 3, 1892

MORSON
Frances B., and the Hon. James Keith, both of Warrenton, Va., by the Rev. George W. Nelson, in St. James' Church, Warrenton, Va. So. Ch., Mar. 3, 1887

Hugh, of Raleigh, N.C., and Sallie T. Field of Port Royal, by the Rev. James E. Poindexter, in St. Peter's Church, Port Royal, Va. So. Ch., May 15, 1879

Lilias Gordon, of Warrenton, d. of the late Arthur Morson, Esq. of Richmond, Va., and James Keith, Judge of the 11th Judicial Circuit, by the Rev. Jno. S. Lindsay, in St. James' Church, Warrenton, Va. So. Ch., July 17, 1873

MORTIMER
George D. E. (The Rev.), rector of St. Paul's Church, Goochland Co., and Mollie A., d. of the late Col. John Heth of Black Heth, Chesterfield Co., by the Rev. John D. Powell, at the residence of Edward Cunningham, Esq., in Powhatan Co. So. Ch., June 20, 1862

MORTON
Bessie, d. of William Morton of Charlotte, Va., and Col. J. Thomas Goode of Mecklenburg, Va., by the Rev. Thomas Wharey, at the residence of the bride's father. So. Ch., Oct. 12, 1876

Lydia M., d. of the Hon. Marcus Morton of Taunton, Mass., and the Rev. Henry W. Lee, minister of Christ Church, Springfield, by the Rt. Rev. Bishop Griswold, in St. Thomas' Church, Taunton, Mass. So. Ch., Apr. 26, 1839

Samuel, and Rebecca Tarry, by the Rev. R. D. Brooke, in St. Luke's Church, Mecklenburg Co., Va. So. Ch., Sept. 12, 1850

Wm. Jackson (The Rev.), of Richmond, Va., and Dora Ashley, d. of Mr. and Mrs. Powhatan Moncure, of "Oakenwold", Stafford Co., Va., by the Rev. John K. Mason, D.D., assisted by the rector, the Rev. Wm. M. Clark, in St. George's Church, Fredericksburg, Va. So. Ch., May 18, 1893

MOSBY
Alice J., eldest d. of John W. Mosby, Esq., and Dr. J.

MARRIAGE NOTICES IN THE SOUTHERN CHURCHMAN WITH DATES OF PUBLICATION

F. Gardner, all of Nelson Co., Va., by the Rev. T. F. Martin, at Valley Farm, Nelson Co., Va. So. Ch., Jan. 24, 1867

Maria Louisa, d. of John G. Mosby, Esq. of Richmond, Va., and William M. Luin of Washington, D.C., by the Rev. Wm. H. Hart, Richmond, Va. So. Ch., Aug. 11, 1837

MOSELEY

Ella M., of Richmond, Va., and Philip A. Hodges of Bennettsville, S.C., by the Rev. A. B. Tizzard assisted by the Rev. C. Minnigerode, D.D., in St. Paul's Church, Richmond, Va. So. Ch., May 12, 1887

R. K. (The Rev.), and Lalla Goodrich, by the Rev. J. W. Neill of San Antonio assisted by the Rev. R. W. Laird of Gonzales, in the Presbyterian Church, Sequin, Texas. So. Ch., Dec. 9, 1886

Susan, d. of the late Mrs. Mary T. Moseley of Powhatan Co., and Richard F. Archer, by the Rev. A. B. Tizzard, in St. James' Church, Richmond. So. Ch., Feb. 2, 1871

MOSELY

Bettie F., and James C. Slaughter, by the Rev. R. H. Wilmer, at the residence of Spottswood Brown. So. Ch., Apr. 18, 1856

MOSS

Charlotte A., d. of J. T. Moss of Powhatan, and F. T. Dunsten of Richmond, by the Rev. A. B. Tizzard, at Manakintown. So. Ch., Jan. 25, 1861

Eleanor C. T., and the Rev. Canon Benson Heale Harvey, both of Philippine Islands Mission, in St. John's Cathedral, Hongkong. So. Ch., Dec. 8, 1934

Frederick H., of Fauquier Co., Va., and Kitty M., d. of Robert Whitehead, Esq. of Nelson Co., Va., by the Rev. B. T. Turner assisted by the Rev. Paul Whitehead, D.D., at Forkland. So. Ch., Oct. 23, 1884

Frederick H., and Emmy W. Marshall, at the home of Mrs. William Marshall, 2009 Eye St., N.W., Washington, D.C. SO. Ch., Dec. 27, 1924

Harry Parker, and Ana* Randolph, youngest d. of the Hon. Wm. Nelson Chancellor, at Parkersburg, W.Va. So. Ch., May 8, 1890

Jean Irvine, d. of F. H. Moss of Markham, Va., and Richard Alexander Goode of Washington, D.C., by the Rev. Herbert Scott Smith, D.D., in St. Margaret's Church, Washington, D.C., So. Ch., Nov. 17, 1917

Margaret Baldwin, and John Taylor Stephenson of Alexandria, Va., at Forkland, the home of the bride's aunt, Miss Mary B. Whitehead. So. Ch., Nov. 8, 1919

Wm. G., of Westmoreland Co., and Homoiselle R. Cox of Heathsville, Northumberland Co., by the Rev. H. L.

* Given as printed

MARRIAGE NOTICES IN THE SOUTHERN CHURCHMAN WITH DATES OF PUBLICATION

Derby, in St. Stephen's Church, Heathsville, Northumberland Co., Va. So. Ch., Sept. 7, 1882

Wm. G., and Sallie G., eldest d. of the Rev. E. L. Baptist, by the Rev. P. M. Boyden, in Mecklenburg Co., Va., at the residence of the bride's father. So. Ch., Mar. 31, 1892

MOTHERSHEAD
Harriet S., and James F. Reynolds, both of Westmoreland Co., Va., by the Rev. T. E. Dashiell, at Mt. Pleasant. So. Ch., July 22, 1859

MOTLEY
Frank W., of Richmond Co., and Adelina, d. of Wm. L. G. and Adelina Mitchell, of Nuttsville, Lancaster Co., Va., by the Rev. Henry L. Derby, in White Chapel Church, Lancaster, Va., So. Ch., Dec. 20, 1888

James W., and Ella J. Dalton, by the Rev. C. O. Pruden, in St. John's P. E. Church, Mt. Airy, Pittsylvania Co., Va. So. Ch., July 14, 1892

MOUNT
Ella B., and Dr. John E. Moore, both of Waterford, Loudoun Co., Va., by the Rev. Theo. Reed, in Waterford Church. So. Ch., Nov. 18, 1875

MOUNTAIN
Marie, of New York City, and the Rev. Louis D. Jacobs, minister-in-charge of the church of the Good Shepherd, Binghamton, N.Y., in the Church of the Transfiguration. So. Ch., Sept. 28, 1935

MOWBRAY
Thomas (The Rev.), formerly of Edinburgh, Scotland, and Bettie, d. of Lancelot Minor, Esq., by the Rev. David Teese, at "Briery Knowl", in Amherst Co., Va. So. Ch., Oct. 28, 1886

MOWER
Lily D., d. of the officiating minister, and David E. Gibson of Kentucky, by the Rev. B. F. Mower, in Florence, Ala. So. Ch., Nov. 28, 1878

MOZINGO
James O., and Mary Inscoe of King George Co., by the Rev. T. E. Locke, in the Rectory of Washington Parish. So. Ch., Feb. 8, 1861

MUDGE
Lizzie E., d. of D. C. Mudge, Esq. of Volcano, and John Reed of New York, by the Rev. S. D. Thompkins, in Emmanuel Church, Volcano, Wood Co., W.Va. So. Ch., Nov. 20, 1873

MUIR
Carrie Cousins, and James Spencer Smith, both of Petersburg, by the Rev. Luther W. Doggett, in Grace Church, Petersburg, Va. So. Ch., Oct. 3, 1889

MULCHAHEY
James (The Rev.), rector of St. Mary's Church, Portsmouth, and Mary, d. of Capt. John Watson of Warren, R.I., by the Rev. Mr. Hathaway, in St. Mark's Church, Warren, R.I. So. Ch., Dec. 17, 1847

MULLIGAN
E., missionary of the Protestant Episcopal Church, and Edward Masson, Esq., Coun-

MARRIAGE NOTICES IN THE SOUTHERN CHURCHMAN WITH DATES OF PUBLICATION

sellor-at-law in Napoli di Romania and formerly Attorney General of the Kingdom, in Athens, Greece. So. Ch., Feb. 1, 1839

MUNDAY
Lizzie, and Henry W. Stamper, by the Rev. H. W. L. Temple, at Lewis Level, Essex. So. Ch., Jan. 7, 1869

Nannie L., and Wm. K. Lee, Jr., by the Rev. H. L. Derby, in Grace Church, Lancaster, Va. So. Ch., Mar. 31, 1881

MUNDY
Johnson M., of Rochester, N.Y., and Frances L. Colvin of Suffolk, Va., by the Rev. Douglass Hoff, in Trinity Church, Portsmouth, Va. So. Ch., Oct. 9 and 16, 1884

MUNFORD
John D. (Col.), of Williamsburg, and Mrs. Elizabeth R. Preston of Washington Co., Va., by the Rev. L. B. Wharton, in St. Thomas' Church, Abingdon, Va. So. Ch., Nov. 7, 1867

Rosalie, d. of the late Col. G. W. and Elizabeth T. Munford, and William Rhett of Charleston, S.C., by the Rev. Beverly D. Tucker, at the residence of the bride's mother, in Richmond, Va. So. Ch., July 27, 1882

Thomas T. (Gen.), and Emma, d. of W. H. Tayloe, Esq., all of Virginia, at Georgetown, D.C. So. Ch., May 3, 1866

MUNSELL
Addison T., principal of Fleetwood Academy, and Jane Gibbs of South Carolina, by the Rev. T. F. Martin, at Fleetwood, Nelson Co., Va. So. Ch., Apr. 10, 1857

MURDAUGH
Edmund C. (The Rev.), of Alabama, and Roberta, d. of the late Col. Robert Sheild, by the Rev. Henry M. Denison, at Williamsburg. So. Ch., May 3, 1849

Roberta K., d. of the Rev. E. C. Murdaugh, D.D., former rector of Trinity Church, and John K. Mason, by the Rev. J. Green Shackelford, at the residence of the bride's mother, Fredericksburg, Va. So. Ch., May 3, 1888

MURDOCK
Catharine M. (Mrs.), d. of the late Hon. J. M. H. Beale, and Col. Charles B. Waggoner, all of Mason Co., by the Rev. Horace Edwin Hayden, at the residence of Charles T. Beale, Mason Co., W.Va. So. Ch., Sept. 16, 1869

Esther, and the Rev. George H. Boyd, rector of historic St. Peter's Church, Perth Amboy, N.J., by the Rt. Rev. Francis M. Taitt, Bishop of Pennsylvania, assisted by the Rev. John R. McCrory, rector of St. Bartholomew's Episcopal Church, Wissisnoming. So. Ch., July 7, 1935

James W. (Dr.), of Parkersburg, Va., and Mary L., d. of the late Wm. Steenberger of Shenandoah, by the Rev. A. R. Rude. So. Ch.,

MARRIAGE NOTICES IN THE SOUTHERN CHURCHMAN WITH DATES OF PUBLICATION

Jan. 21, 1859
Laura V., d. of W. C. Murdock, and Joseph B. Church, all of Washington, by the Rev. Edward H. Ingle, in the Church of the Ascension, Washington, D.C. So. Ch., June 15, 1882

MURPHY
Ella Laurence, d. of Thomas N. Murphy, Esq. of Iowa, and Gilbert Jefferson Cox of Alexandria, Va., by the Rev. R. A. Castleman, in Cople Chapel, Westmoreland Co., Va. So. Ch., Jan. 7, 1892

John, Esq., of Westmoreland, Va., and Mary L., d. of Geo. Fred. and M. Fenton Brown, by the Rev. John M. Rogers of New Jersey, at Peckatone, the residence of the bride's father. So. Ch., Nov. 30, 1860

Lillie B., eldest d. of John N. Murphy, Esq., and B. Frank Brown, all of Westmoreland Co., Va., by the Rev. Wm. Dame, in Baltimore, Md. So. Ch., June 17, 1886

MURRAY
Fanny, of Hagerstown, Md., and A. B. Hammond, Esq. of Roanoke, Va., by the Rev. D. M. Wood, at the residence of the bride's mother in Hagerstown, Md. So. Ch., Oct. 23, 1884

Gay, d. of William Murray of Powhatan, and Mr. Rawlings of Mecklenburg, by the Rev. P. F. Berkeley, at Genito, in Powhatan Co. So. Ch., Jan. 8, 1864

Helen M., second d. of William Murray of Powhatan Co., Va., and Charles L. C. Gifford of Newark, by the Rev. P. F. Berkeley, at Edge Hill. So. Ch., May 15, 1851

James, and Lucy E. Jacobs, both of Alexandria, Va., by the Rev. D. F. Sprigg, in Grace Church, Alexandria, Va. So. Ch., Apr. 8, 1869

Margaret, d. of Wm. Murray of Wilson, and Harry R. Nottingham of Northampton Co., Va., by the Rev. J. H. Guinne, at Wilson, N.C. So. Ch., Oct. 25, 1883

Nannie G., d. of Capt. William Murray of Powhatan Co., Va., and Dr. John B. Wyley of Amelia, by the Rev. P. F. Berkeley, in St. Paul's Church, Richmond, Va. So. Ch., Mar. 18, 1859

MURRELL
Fannie B., of Bedford Co., and Newton J. Farmer of Campbell Co., by the Rev. W. W. Kimball, near New London, Bedford Co., Va. So. Ch., Mar. 2, 1882

Wm. M., and Flora Scott, d. of Col. Robert W. Withers, all of Campbell Co., Va., by the Rev. W. W. Kimball, in Trinity Church, Rustburg. So. Ch., Nov. 29, 1883

MUSE
G. M., and Frances Merriweather Belfield, by the Rev. D. M. Wharton, at the residence of the bride's father. So. Ch., Jan. 21, 1869

MUSSER
Wm. H., of Maryland, and Mary Jett Fairfax, by the Rev. D. M. Wharton, in St. James' Church, Westmoreland. So.

MARRIAGE NOTICES IN THE SOUTHERN CHURCHMAN WITH DATES OF PUBLICATION

Ch., June 14, 1883

MUTTER
Euphemia Kate, of Scotland, and John Henry Gain of Loudoun, by the Rev. A. B. Tizzard, at Mantua, Chesterfield Co., Va. So. Ch., Mar. 13, 1879

MYER
Adelaide Tyler, d. of the late Frank and Isabel C. Myer of Norfolk, Va., and Dorsey Hager of Los Angeles, Cal., by the Rev. A. G. H. Bode, in St. Luke's Church, Long Beach, Cal. So. Ch., May 31, 1913

George, and Lilly Berkley, d. of the late P. H. Hoy, by the Rev. Mr. Johns of the German Lutheran Church. So. Ch., Feb. 19, 1885

MYERS
Barton, of Norfolk, and Kate M. Baldwin of Winchester, by the Rev. James Hubard assisted by the Rev. Walter Q. Hullihen, at Winchester, Va. So. Ch., Jan. 11, 1883

Elizabeth K., and W. C. Preston, by the Rev. D. F. Sprigg assisted by the Rev. Dr. Preston, father of the groom, at the residence of the bride's father, Maj. E. F. D. Myers. So. Ch., Jan. 26, 1888

Ephraim, and Eva Miller, by the Rev. W. D. Hanson, in Newport, Del., at the residence of the bride's father. So. Ch., Feb. 20, 1879

Kate, and Joseph Stucky, Esq., both of Berkeley Co., W.Va., by the Rev. George S. May, at the residence of Jeter M. French, Esq. So. Ch., Jan. 15, 1874

Louis Cash (Mrs.), of Memphis, Tenn., and the Rt. Rev. Wm. Theodotus Capers, D.D., Bishop of West Texas, by the Rev. Dr. Walter B. Capers, brother of the groom and rector of St. Andrew's Church, Jackson, Miss., assisted by the Rev. W. D. Britton, in Grace Church, Memphis. So. Ch., June 13, 1936

Samuel, and Eliza Juniper, by the Rev. Henry T. Sharp, at Frankfort, Ky. So. Ch., Jan. 1, 1874

N

NADLER
- Fannie, of Evanston, Ill., and the Rev. Edward R. A. Green, rector of St. Peter's Church, Tecumseh, in the Alderson Memorial Chapel of Seabury Western Theological Seminary. So. Ch., July 7, 1935

NALLE
- Fannie Wallace, d. of P. P. Nalle of Culpeper Co., and Charles Yancey Steptoe, by the Rev. P. Slaughter, in St. Paul's Church, Culpeper Co. So. Ch., Oct. 24, 1872
- G. B. Wallace, of Culpeper, and Nannie H. Porter of Orange, by the Rev. C. Y. Steptoe, at Riverside, Orange Co. So. Ch., Jan. 16, 1873
- H. B., and May Bresee, by the Rev. R. R. Claiborne, in Emmanuel Church, Rapidan. So. Ch., Dec. 18, 1884
- M. Fenton, second d. of P. P. Nalle, Sr., and Douglas G. Somerville, all of Culpeper Co., by the Rev. John McGill assisted by the Rev. J. P. Strider, in St. Paul's Church, Culpeper Co., Va. So. Ch., Dec. 28, 1882

NANCE
- Addington G., of Mississippi, and Margaret W., d. of Mary W. and Edmund Berkeley of Prince William Co., Va., by the Rev. A. P. Gray, at "Evergreen", the residence of the bride's parents. So. Ch., Sept. 25, 1884

NASH
- Charles R., and Rebecca F., d. of F. Lewis Marshall, Esq. formerly of Fauquier Co., Va., by the Rev. Reverdy Estill assisted by the Rev. J. D. Powell, at the residence of the bride's brother, R. C. Marshall, Esq., in Portsmouth, Va. So. Ch., Nov. 28, 1878
- Frederick (Capt.), of Charlotte, N.C., and Bettie M. Littlejohn of Oxford, by the Rev. P. D. Thompson. So. Ch., Nov. 20, 1873
- Lizzie, d. of Dr. John W. Nash, and Dr. Paulus A. Irving, all of Farmville, Va., by the Rev. A. S. Lloyd, in Richmond. So. Ch., Nov. 29, 1883
- S. R. (Miss), of Portsmouth, Va., and E. A. Hatton of Norfolk Co., by the Rev. J. Cosby, in St. John's Church, Portsmouth, Va. So. Ch., Oct. 28, 1859

NASON
- Frederick T., of San Angelo, Tex., and Mary Page Leigh of Aylett, King William Co., Va., by the Rev. Pendleton Brooke, in St. David's Church, King William Co., Va. So. Ch., Feb. 24, 1887

NAUDAIN
- Laura E., and Merit Williams, Esq., both of New Castle Co., Del., by the Rev. Jno. Collins McCabe, D.D. assisted by the Rev. Jno. W. Brown of Philadelphia, in St. Ann's Church, Middletown, Del. So. Ch., Oct. 21, 1869

MARRIAGE NOTICES IN THE SOUTHERN CHURCHMAN WITH DATES OF PUBLICATION

NAYLOR
    F. Y., and Ann E. Brightwell, both of the District of Columbia, by the Rev. Wm. Pinckney. So. Ch., Dec. 22, 1837

NEAL
    Anna Rockwell, of Marion, N.C., and John Nicholas Ambler of Buckingham Co., Va., by the Rev. R. L. Abernethy, D.D., in the Methodist Episcopal Church, Marion, N.C. So. Ch., July 14, 1892

    Laura, d. of J. S. Neal, Esq., and John B. Newton, Jr., resident engineer of French Broad Valley Railroad, by the Rev. J. B. Newton, rector of Monumental Church, Richmond, in Marion, N.C., So. Ch., Nov. 6, 1880

    Mary Lavinia, d. of C. I. Neal, Esq. of Parkersburg, Va., and Eugene List of Wheeling, by the Rev. W. L. Hyland, in Trinity Church, Parkersburg. So. Ch., Mar. 29, 1861

NEALE
    Edwin Lewis, and Attarah Beall, d. of Col. Charles B. Waggener, all of Mason Co., by the Rev. Horace Edwin Hayden, at Edge Hill, Mason Co., W. Va. So. Ch., Jan. 12, 1871

NEBLETT
    Annie McFarland, d. of Colin Neblett, and E. D. Winstead of North Carolina, by the Rev. E. B. Jones, at the residence of the bride's father, Greenock, Lunenburg Co. So. Ch., Jan. 24, 1884

    Belle G., d. of Colin Neblett, Esq., and Thomas G. Epes, all of Lunenburg Co., Va., by the Rev. L. J. Sothoron, at the residence of the bride's father. So. Ch., June 17, 1875

    Clara R., and Colin S. Bagly, by the Rev. L. J. Sothoron, in St. John's Church, Cumberland Parish.**So. Ch., Nov. 27, 1879

    Henry M. (Dr.), of Virginia, and Anna, d. of Dr. Benjamin Wilkins, at "Forest Home", Louisiana. So. Ch., Apr. 13, 1871

    Kate L., youngest d. of William L. Neblett, and Nathaniel Matheus*all of Lunenburg Co., by the Rev. Mr. Sothoron, in St. John's Church, Lunenburg, Va. So. Ch., Dec. 19, 1878

    L. S., and Nannie O. Matthews,* both of Lunenburg Co., Va., by the Rev. L. J. Sothoron, at the residence of the bride's father. So. Ch., Nov. 23, 1876

NEEDLES
    Charles E., of Baltimore, and Kate B., youngest d. of Jacob Senseney, by the Rev. Cornelius Walker, at Edgehill, near Winchester. So. Ch., Nov. 30, 1855

NEELY
    Floyd (Hon.), of West Union, W. Va., and Nannie M., d. of the Rev. Thomas Smith, deceased (first rector of Trinity Parish) and Mrs. Ann M. Smith of Parkersburg, W.Va., by the Rev. Robert A. Gibson assisted by the Rev. Geo. W. Peterkin, in Trinity Church, Parkersburg, W.Va. So. Ch., Apr. 12, 1883

NEFF
    H. (Dr.), and Brownie M.

---

* Given as printed
** Cumberland Parish is in Lunenburg County, Virginia (Journal ... Diocese of Southern Virginia, Portsmouth, Va., 1941)

MARRIAGE NOTICES IN THE SOUTHERN CHURCHMAN WITH DATES OF PUBLICATION

Morrison, both of Harrisonburg, Va., by the Rev. O. S. Bunting. So. Ch., Nov. 15, 1883

NEILD
Ella E., d. of John R. Neild, and Wm. W. Harrington, all of Dorchester Co., Md., by the Rev. Wm. W. Greene, at the residence of the bride's father. So. Ch., Jan. 6, 1881

NEILL
Mary, of Clarke Co., and Joseph M. Barton of Frederick Co., Va., by the Rev. F. M. Whittle. So. Ch., Feb. 27, 1857

NEILSON
Bessie R., and Edward Jennings Lee, by the Rev. Dr. W. H. Neilson, father of the bride, assisted by the Rev. J. H. Aspinwall of Washington, D.C., in Trinity Church, Shepherdstown. So. Ch., Oct. 5, 1893

John, Esq., of New York, and Augusta, eldest d. of the Rev. Dr. Balch, by the Rev. Dr. Balch assisted by the Rt. Revs. the Bishops of Vermont and Delaware, in Newport, R.I. So. Ch., Feb. 16, 1861

Robert W., and Margaret Keith, both of Fauquier Co., by the Rev. George W. Nelson, in St. James' Church, Warrenton, Va. So. Ch., Nov. 23, 1882

See also BYRD, Emily (Mrs.)

NELSON
Alice Coleman, d. of Mr. and Mrs. Hugh Nelson of 924 W. Grace St., Richmond, Va., and Duncan Smith of New York, s. of Dr. and Mrs. Francis Smith of the University, by the Rev. Wm.

Meade Clark, D.D. So. Ch., Jan. 3, 1914

Alice Page, d. of Wm. A. Nelson, former surgeon of the U.S. Navy, and Thomas J., s. of Col. Thos. Waller of Stafford, by the Rev. T. C. Page assisted by the Rev. John Moncure, in Clifton Chapel, Stafford Co., Va. So. Ch., Feb. 7, 1889

Bettie Harrison, d. of K. S. Nelson of Culpeper, and Beverly R. Mason of Fairfax Co., by the Rev. J. C. Minnigerode assisted by the Rev. C. K. Nelson, D.D., in St. Stephen's Church, Culpeper, Va. So. Ch., Sept. 16, 1875

C. K., Jr. (The Rev.), of Virginia, and M. Bruce Matthews of Port Tobacco, Md., by the Rev. Meyer Levin, in Christ Church, Port Tobacco, Md. So. Ch., June 21, 1877

Carolyn Peyton, d. of the late Rev. George Washington Nelson, and John R. Britton of Trenton, N.J., by the Rev. E. S. Hinks, in St. James' Church, Warrenton, Va. So. Ch., Sept. 24, 1910

Eliza A., d. of Wm. N. and Mary A. Nelson of Clarke Co., Va., and John C. Woolfolk of Columbus, Ga., by the Rev. Jos. R. Jones, in Christ Church, Millwood. So. Ch., Jan. 3, 1878

Eliza K., d. of Thos. F. Nelson, Esq., and N. H. Massie of Charlottesville, by the Rev. F. M. Whittle, at Wheehaw*, Clarke Co., Va. So. Ch., Apr. 18, 1856

Eliza K., and Dr. James Bowyer,

* Given as printed

MARRIAGE NOTICES IN THE SOUTHERN CHURCHMAN WITH DATES OF PUBLICATION

by the Rev. W. H. Pendleton, at the residence of Dr. Thos. H. Nelson, Elk Hill, Bedford Co. So. Ch., Sept. 21, 1860

Elizabeth Mann P., and John R. Lee, Esq., both of Halifax, Va., by the Rev. Charles Dresser, at the parsonage of Antrim Parish. So. Ch., Jan. 15, 1836

Emily Goggin, d. of the late Dr. Thomas N. Nelson of Bedford, and William Albert Dabney, Esq. of Lynchburg, Va., by the Rev. Albert Ware, at the residence of the bride's mother, Elk Hill, Bedford Co., Va. So. Ch., Nov. 8 and 29, 1877

Evelyn Willing, d. of Wm. N. and Mary A. Nelson, and Wm. C. Turpin of Macon, Ga., by the Rev. C. B. Bryan, in Christ Church, Millwood, Clarke Co., Va. So. Ch., Apr. 10, 1884

Fannie Burwell, d. of the Hon. William Nelson of Yorktown, Va. and gr.d. of President Nelson of Revolutionary fame*, and Corbin Waller, s. of Dr. John C. Mercer formerly of the U.S. Navy, and gr.s. of Gen. Hugh Mercer who fell in the battle of Princeton during the Revolutionary War, in Durham, N.C. So. Ch., Dec. 10, 1885

Fanny Moncure, eldest d. of Dr. William A. Nelson of Stafford Co., Va., and James William Lyon of Baltimore, by the Rev. J. M. Meredith, in Aquia Church. So. Ch., May 11, 1876

Fanny N., d. of the Rev. C. R. Nelson, D.D. of Rockville, Md., and R. S. Worthington of Kansas, by the Rev. Kinloch Nelson assisted by the rector, the Rev. A. Johns, in Christ Church, Rockville. So. Ch., July 11, 1889

Frank, and Ida, d. of Col. Robt. W. Withers, by the Rev. G. W. Nelson assisted by the Rev. Frank Page and the Rev. W. W. Kimball, in Trinity Church, Rustburg, Va. So. Ch., Dec. 23, 1880

George E., of Baltimore (lately of Culpeper, Va.), and Eleanor Warner, at the residence of the bride's father, Annandale, Culpeper Co., Va. So. Ch., Dec. 21, 1871

Grace Fenton, eldest d. of the officiating clergyman, and the Rev. Edward Trail Helfenstein of Maryland, by the Rev. Prof. Kinloch Nelson, D.D. assisted by the Rev. A. C. Hensley, in the chapel of the Theological Seminary, near Alexandria, Va. So. Ch., Apr. 17, 1890

Hugh M., of Clarke Co., Va., and Sallie Page Nelson, d. of the officiating clergyman, the Rev. Geo. W. Nelson, in St. James' Church, Warrenton. So. Ch., May 7, 1885

Isabella C., d. of F. K. Nelson, Esq., and Dr. John F. Gardner of Richmond, by the Rev. E. Borden, at Clover Fields, Albemarle Co. So. Ch., Oct. 31, 1856

---

* Possibly not granddaughter but great granddaughter of William Nelson, 1711-1772, who served as president of the Governor's council and was generally known as President Nelson

MARRIAGE NOTICES IN THE SOUTHERN CHURCHMAN WITH DATES OF PUBLICATION

James N., of Huntington, W.Va., eldest s. of the Rev. Robert Nelson, missionary to China, and Mary W., eldest d. of Edward W. Morris of Hanover Co., Va., by the Rev. W. A. Alrich, at Claymont, residence of the bride's father. So. Ch., Feb. 20, 1873

Kate, of Boydton, Va., and the Rev. Thomas C. Thackston of Farmville, by the Rev. Dr. Wm. A. Smith, at Boydton, Va. So. Ch., July 20, 1854

Kate D., of Culpeper, Va., and Shelton F. Leake of Terrell, Tex., by the Rev. W. T. Roberts, in St. Stephen's Church, Culpeper. So. Ch., Dec. 4, 1884

Mary Scollay, d. of the late Rev. George W. and Mary Scollay Nelson, and Lowell Laurence Decker of New York, in St. James' Church, Warrenton, Va. So. Ch., Oct. 19, 1912

Nannie E., d. of the late Wm. D. Nelson, and Dr. James Thomas, by the Rev. D. M. Wharton, in Nomini Church, Westmoreland Co. So. Ch., Dec. 31, 1868

Philip W., of Albemarle, and Emily Page, youngest d. of the late Rev. John P. McGuire, by the Rev. J. B. Newton, in St. John's Church, Tappahannock. So. Ch., July 10, 1873

Sallie Berkeley, and Col. William T. Robins, all of Gloucester Co., by the Rev. A. Y. Hundley, in Abingdon Church. So. Ch., June 6, 1878

Sallie Page, d. of the officiating clergyman, and Hugh M. Nelson of Clarke Co., Va., by the Rev. Geo. W. Nelson, in St. James' Church, Warrenton. So. Ch., May 7, 1885

Sally Page, second d. of William Nelson of Mecklenburg, and Woodson Hughes, Esq., attorney-at-law of Halifax Court House, Va., by the Rev. John T. Clark of the Episcopal Church, at Halifax Court House, Va. So. Ch., Dec. 20, 1839

Thomas M., of Clarke Co., Va., and Susie H., d. of Dr. Robert Atkinson of Baltimore, by the Rev. Jos. R. Jones, rector of Christ Church, Millwood, Va., in Grace Church, Baltimore. So. Ch., Jan. 3, 1876

Thos. W. (Dr.), and Lelia Mc-Daniel, both of Bedford Co., Va., by the Rev. Wm. Henry Pendleton, at the residence of Sam I. McDaniel, Esq., Bedford Co., Va. So. Ch., Nov. 18, 1869

Virginia Duncan, d. of Mr. and Mrs. F. W. Nelson, and George, s. of Mr. and Mrs. J. G. Campbell of Mobile, Ala., by the Rev. B. Nelson, a cousin of the bride, in Richmond. So. Ch., Sept. 25, 1920

NEVE

Frederick W. (The Rev.), and Fannie G., only d. of Dr. Taylor of Albemarle Co., Va., by the Rev. T. E. Locke assisted by the Rev. H. B. Lee, in St. Paul's Church, Fredericksville Parish, Albemarle Co., Va. So. Ch., June 29, 1893

NEVITT

Emily R., d. of Dr. Thomas Nevitt of Fairfax Co., Va., and Hugh Cox Nevitt of Maryland,

MARRIAGE NOTICES IN THE SOUTHERN CHURCHMAN WITH DATES OF PUBLICATION

by the Rev. J. P. Lawrence in St. Luke's Church, Pedlar Valley, Amherst Co., Va. So. Ch., Jan. 4, 1877

Hugh Cox, of Maryland, and Emily R., d. of Dr. Thomas Nevitt of Fairfax Co., Va., by the Rev. J. P. Lawrence, in St. Luke's Church, Pedlar Valley, Amherst Co., Va. So. Ch., Jan. 4, 1877

Maggie L., of Pohick, Fairfax Co., Va., and the Rev. Juner P. Lawrence of St. Luke's Church, Pedlar Amherst Co., by the Rev. Richard Ellerby, in Pohick Church. So. Ch., Feb. 3, 1876

NEWBOLD

William A. (The Rev.), assistant minister of St. Andrew's Church, Wilmington, Del., and Emily, d. of John Boulton, Esq. of Philadelphia, by the Rt. Rev. Alfred Lee, D.D., in the Church of the Epiphany. So. Ch., Oct. 15, 1858

NEWCOMB

Annie, and R. Sommerville Mitchell, both of Lancaster Co., Va., by the Rev. H. L. Derby, at "White Chapel." So. Ch., Dec. 23, 1880

NEWMAN

J. B., of Burlington, Orange Co., and Mrs. Mary F. Seib of Fredericksburg, by the Rev. E. Bryden, at the home of G. S. Conway, Esq. So. Ch., Mar. 8, 1866

NEWSOM

Mary Cornelia, of Petersburg, and Robert H. Davis, Esq. of St. Louis, by the Rev. W. H. Platt, at Petersburg, Va. So. Ch., Feb. 13, 1857

NEWTON

Alleine Williamson, of Richmond, Va., s. of the late Rt. Rev. John B. Newton of Virginia, and Harleston Toomer, d. of Mr. and Mrs. T. G. S. Lucas, by the Rev. Mr. Way, at Charleston, S.C. So. Ch., Feb. 9, 1907

Edward A., Esq., and Susan C., d. of the late Hon. Dudley A. Tyng, by the Rev. Dr. Tyng of Philadelphia, in Grace Church, Boston. So. Ch., July 21, 1837

Edward Colston, and Lucy Yates, youngest d. of the late Dr. Wat H. Tyler, by the Rev. John B. Newton, at Kelvin Grove, Westmoreland Co., Va. So. Ch., Dec. 2, 1875*

Emma E., and Robert E. S. Skinner, by the Rev. R. A. Castleman, at Arcola, Loudoun Co., Va. So. Ch., Feb. 23, 1893

James Harry, formerly of England, and Annie May Brinkley of Suffolk, Va., by the Rev. Henry L. Derby, in St. Paul's Church, Suffolk, Va. So. Ch., Nov. 28, 1889

John B., Jr., resident engineer of French Broad Valley railroad, and Laura, d. of J. S. Neal, Esq., by the Rev. J. B. Newton, rector of Monumental Church, Richmond, at Marion, N.C. So. Ch., Nov. 6, 1890

Judith W., and Edwin C. Claybrook, by the Rev. Andrew Fisher, at Lindew, the residence of the bride's father, in Westmoreland Co. So. Ch., Jan. 31, 1867

* This seems to be a correction of a notice which appeared in the issue of Nov. 18, 1875

MARRIAGE NOTICES IN THE SOUTHERN CHURCHMAN WITH DATES OF PUBLICATION

Kate B., and Walter Christian of Richmond, Va., by the Rev. John B. Newton assisted by the Rev. S. S. Hepbron, at Summer Hill, Hanover Co., Va. So. Ch., Dec. 4 and 11, 1884

Mary M., d. of T. F. Newton, Esq., and Cephas Gregg of Lagrange, Ky., by the Rev. Francis M. Whittle, at Charleston, Kanawha Co., Va. So. Ch., Mar. 4, 1848

Mary Stevenson, d. of Mr. and Mrs. Edward Newton, and Thomas Niven Massey of Westmoreland, by the Rev. Arthur P. Gray, in Hague Chapel, Cople Parish, Westmoreland Co. So. Ch., Feb. 19, 1910

Robert, and A. E. Arnest, both of Westmoreland, by the Rev. D. M. Wharton, at Westmoreland Co., Va. So. Ch., May 7, 1868

Virginia S., formerly of Alexandria, Va., and John McCormick, by the Rev. Mr. Cole, at Culpeper C.H. So. Ch., Feb. 21, 1862

William B., and Mary E. Shields, both of Norfolk, Va., by the Rev. J. B. Newton assisted by the Rev. T. C. Jones, at the home of the bride. So. Ch., Sept. 24, 1891

Willoughby, of Bristol, Va., formerly of Richmond, s. of the late Rt. Rev. John B. Newton of Virginia, and Alice Oliver, by the Rev. J. K. Mason, at Louisville, Ky. So. Ch., Feb. 9, 1907

NIBLACK
Wm. C., Esq., of Vincennes, Ind., and Fannie, d. of of A. H. Herr, Esq. of Georgetown, by the Rev. John S. Lindsay, in St. John's Church, Georgetown, D.C. So. Ch., Feb. 19, 1880

NICHOLAS
Maria Byrd, youngest d. of R. C. Nicholas of Baltimore, and the Rev. Henry T. Sharp of the Diocese of Kentucky, by the Rev. J. S. B. Hodges, in St. Paul's Church, Baltimore, Md. So. Ch., July 27, 1871

NICHOLLS
B. Franklin (Dr.), late of Spartanburg, S.C., and E. Louise, d. of Dr. Joseph Klapp of Philadelphia, by the Rev. W. F. Paddock, D.D. and the Rev. T. L. Franklin, D.D., in St. Andrew's Church, Philadelphia. So. Ch., Nov. 18, 1875

Mary Lee, of Louisville, Ky., and William B. Whiting, former midshipman of the U.S. Navy, by the Rev. Mr. Jackson, at Louisville, Ky. So. Ch., Dec. 27, 1839

NICHOLS
George H., of Buckingham Co., Va., and Florence Reeve, gr.d. of the late Capt. James Edwin Pleasants of Goochland, by the Rev. P. H. Boydon, at "Spring Dale", Goochland Co., Va. So. Ch., Jan. 3, 1884

S. Jennie, and Col. Frank J. Bramshall, by the Rev. John McNabb, at the residence of the bride's parents. So. Ch., June 14, 1877

NICHOLSON
George D., of Middlesex, and Rosalie G. Micou,* d. of

---

* Given as printed

MARRIAGE NOTICES IN THE SOUTHERN CHURCHMAN WITH DATES OF PUBLICATION

J. R. Micon,* Esq., of Essex, by the Rev. J. B. Newton assisted by the Rev. W. A. Baynham, in St. John's Church, Tappahannock. So. Ch., Jan. 13, 1876

Isaac (The Rev.), rector of St. Mark's Church, Philadelphia, and Adele Ellicott of Baltimore, by the Rev. J. S. B. Hodges, in St. Paul's Church, Baltimore. So. Ch., Apr. 29, 1880

Isaac F., of Baltimore, and Rosa, d. of the late Archibald Robinson of Fruit Hill, Jefferson Co., W.Va., by the Rev. Dr. Andrews, at Fruit Hill, Jefferson Co., W.Va. So. Ch., Oct. 12, 1871

James D. (The Rev.), of Maryland, and Frances Henrietta, d. of W. W. Dougherty, Esq., by the Rev. John M. Forbes, in St. Luke's Church, New York. So. Ch., Apr. 21, 1837

James W., Esq., and Nancy A. Hope, by the Rev. C. C. Randolph, in Emmanuel Church, Eagle Rock. So. Ch., Nov. 15, 1888

Laura L., and John E. Crawford, both of Lynchburg, by the Rev. W. H. Pendleton, at Salem, Roanoke Co., Va. So. Ch., Feb. 15, 1855

Rebecca, youngest d. of Andrew Nicholson, Esq., deceased, and the Rev. George Woodbridge, rector of Christ Church, by the Rt. Rev. Richard Channing Moore, D.D., at Richmond, Va. So. Ch., Oct. 30, 1835

Samuel (Dr.), of Wakefield, Sussex Co., Va., and Janet Gordon, d. of the late John S. Knox of Fauquier Co., Va., by the Rev. Henderson Suter, at the residence of the bride's sister, Alexandria, Va. So. Ch., Oct. 11, 1883

Tweed, and Alfred Lee Sacrey, by the Rev. J. Green Shackelford, at the residence of the bride's parents, Fredericksburg. So. Ch., Oct. 24, 1889

NICKLIN
Blanche H., of Alexandria, Va., and the Rev. H. J. Beagen of Norfolk, Va., by the Rev. George H. Norton, D.D., in St. Paul's Church, Alexandria, Va. So. Ch., Nov. 1, 1888

NICOL
Chas. Edgar, and M. Louise, eldest d. of Prof. Ezra and Julia C. Bauder, by the Rev. A. P. Gray, at the residence of the bride's parents, Brentsville, Va. So. Ch., Nov. 25, 1880

NICOLSON
Sallie B., eldest d. of Dr. G. Nicolson, and G. Thurston Williams of London, England, by the Rev. J. Hervey Hundley, in Christ Church, Middlesex Co., Va. So. Ch., May 11, 1876

NIEMEYER
Henry V., Jr., of Memphis, Tenn., and Mattie, d. of E. R. Hunter, Esq. of Portsmouth, Va., by the Rev. J. D. Powell, at the residence of the bride's father. So. Ch., Sept. 17, 1874

NILES
Charles Martin, D.D., and

* Given as printed

MARRIAGE NOTICES IN THE SOUTHERN CHURCHMAN WITH DATES OF PUBLICATION

Mary Francis, d. of Ida C. and the late George W. Doyle of Wilmington, N.C., by the Rev. Edmund Banks Smith, chaplain U.S.A. headquarters, Governor's Island, N.Y., in the Church of the Saviour, Philadelphia, Pa. So. Ch., Oct. 24, 1908

NIMMO
Julia Ellis, of Alexandria, Va., and the Rev. Wm. J. Zimmer of Atlanta, Ga., by the Rev. Mr. Woodbridge, in Monumental Church. So. Ch., Oct. 16, 1851

NOBLE
Olivia B., and Edward N. Lacy, by the Rev. A. B. Tizzard, at the residence of Edward Gates, Esq., Chesterfield Co., Va. So. Ch., May 12, 1887

NOBLIT
James B. (The Rev.), rector of St. Mark's Church, Lewistown, Penn., and Ellen, eldest d. of the late Richard Ross of Glenn Ross, Montgomery Co., Md., by the Rev. Mr. Hoff. So. Ch., June 14, 1839

NOLAN
Margaret, and Anderson Q. Gaines, by the Rev. Henry T. Sharp, at Frankfort, Ky. So. Ch., Sept. 3, 1874

NOLAND
Anna W., d. of Maj. Burr P. Noland of Middleburg, and Virginius Dabney, Esq., by the Rev. O. A. Kinsolving. So. Ch., Feb. 28, 1867
Bessie Lloyd, d. of the late Maj. Burr P. Noland, and the Rev. Robert S. Carter of Virginia, by the Rt. Rev. T. W. Dudley, D.D., in Immanuel Church, Middleburg, Loudoun Co. So. Ch., Sept. 10 and 17, 1891
C. Powell, of Middleburg, Loudoun Co., Va., and Rosalie, youngest d. of R. Barton Haxall, Esq., by the Rev. Arthur Jones assisted by the Rev. Mr. Joyce, in the Episcopal Church at Gordonsville, Va. So. Ch., Nov. 6, 1879
Kate Huntington, second d. of Maj. Burr P. Noland of Loudoun, and James M. Garnett, president of St. John's College, Annapolis, Md., by the Rev. Wm. M. Dame, at Middleburg, Va. So. Ch., Apr. 27, 1871
Lena A., d. of B. P. Noland of Loudoun Co., Va., and Bolling W. Haxall, Jr. of Baltimore, by the Rev. William M. Dame assisted by the Rev. Magruder Maury. So. Ch., Oct. 22, 1874

NOLTING
Helen, eldest d. of Emil O. Nolting, and F. H. McGuire, by the Rev. Mr. Oehlschlager, at the residence of the bride's father, in Richmond. So. Ch., Nov. 26, 1885

NORFLEET
Augusta, of Amelia Co., Va., and A. H. Michaels of Reidsville, N.C., by the Rev. A. B. Tizzard, at the residence of the bride's mother. So. Ch., Feb. 21, 1884
Susie F., and W. F. Gregory of Petersburg, by the Rev. A. B. Tizzard, at the residence of the bride's mother,

MARRIAGE NOTICES IN THE SOUTHERN CHURCHMAN WITH DATES OF PUBLICATION

NORMAN
  Ada, d. of M. S. Norman, and Thomas J. McKaig, Jr., by the Rev. Julius E. Grammer, in St. Peter's Church, Baltimore. So. Ch., May 18, 1882

NORRIS
  Edith, d. of James L. Norris of Washington, and the Rev. P. P. Phillips, rector of Grace Church, Berryville, Va., by the Rev. B. Sunderland, D.D., and the Rev. Dallas Tucker, rector of Zion Church, Charleston, W.Va., at Washington, D.C. So. Ch., Feb. 9, 1893

  Elizabeth Wormely, d. of John B. and Alice Norris, and Ed. S. Cordoza of Richmond, Va., by the Rev. J. E. Hammond, in Memorial Church, Manchester, Va. So. Ch., Dec. 14, 1871

  John C., and Susanna D. Rogers, both of Baltimore, by the Rev. John C. McCabe, D.D., rector of St. James' Parish, Anne Arundel Co., Md., at Baltimore. So. Ch., Dec. 7, 1860

  Josephine I., and Thomas J. McCoy, by the Rev. P. N. McDonald, in St. Paul's Church, Sistersville, W.Va. So. Ch., July 11, 1908

  Mary E., and Dr. Charles H. Jones, all of Baltimore, by the Rev. John Collins McCabe, D.D., rector of the Church of the Ascension, in St. Luke's Church, Baltimore. So. Ch., June 22, 1860

  Morley, and Carrie E. Gemeny, Amelia Co., Va. So. Ch., Jan. 31, 1878

  by the Rev. R. Castleman, at the residence of the bride's parents, near Kinsale, Westmoreland Co., Va. So. Ch., Jan. 10, 1889

  Ralph Wormley, of Charles Town, Jefferson Co., and Anna Byrd, eldest d. of William G. Harrison, Esq. of Lewis Co., W.Va., by the Rev. T. H. Lacy, at the residence of the bride's father, near Weston, W.Va. So. Ch., Apr. 9, 1891

NORTH
  Nannie J., and Charles H. Fontaine, by the Rev. Albert Walker, at Oak Grove, the residence of Mrs. Parham Moon, in Halifax Co., Va. So. Ch., Apr. 2, 1868

NORTHAM
  Blanche A., of Onancock, and Claudius N. Wyant formerly of Rockingham Co., Va., by the Rev. Henry L. Derby, in Trinity Church, Onancock, Accomac, Va. So. Ch., July 28, 1892

NORTON
  Claudia Hamilton, eldest d. of the Rev. G. H. Norton, and the Rev. J. K. Mason, by the Rev. D. F. Sprigg, in St. Paul's Church, Alexandria, Va. So. Ch., Nov. 27, 1879

  George Hatley (The Rev.), and Nannie Burwell, d. of Hon. James K. Marshall, by the Rev. Wm. H. Pendleton, at Fauquier Co., Va. So. Ch., June 8, 1854

NORVELL
  Sallie R., of Lynchburg, and Wm. H. Barney of Mobile, Ala., by the Rev. W. H. Pendleton, in St. Stephen's Church, Bedford, Va. So. Ch., Oct. 31, 1867

MARRIAGE NOTICES IN THE SOUTHERN CHURCHMAN WITH DATES OF PUBLICATION

NORWOOD
  Abel J., of New Orleans, La., and Emelina, d. of Maj. Horace Jones of Hanover Academy, Va., by the Rev. J. Green Shackelford of Trinity Church, Fredericksburg, in Fork Church, Hanover Co., Va. So. Ch., Jan. 5, 1888
  Helen Alves, d. of the officiating clergyman, and Wm. Y. Mordecai of Henrico Co., by the Rev. Wm. Norwood, D.D., in Emmanuel Church, Henrico Co., Va. So. Ch., Dec. 23, 1875
  Helen Mary, d. of the Hon. William Norwood, and Andrew Mickle, merchant of Hillsborough, by the Rev. Henry Prout. So. Ch., Dec. 20, 1839
  Thomas Hill, and Ellen Moore, d. of the late Thos. R. Price, all of Richmond, by the Rev. Wm. Norwood, D.D. So. Ch., Jan. 4, 1872

NOTTINGHAM
  Annie S., d. of John Nottingham, Esq. of Northampton Co., Va., and the Rev. J. W. Ware, by the Rev. S. S. Ware assisted by the Rev. J. J. Gravatt, in Christ Church, Eastville, Northampton Co., Va. So. Ch., Nov. 6, 1879
  Benjamin S., of Northampton Co., and Cornelia Page Parker of Accomac Co., by the Rev. John McNabb, in St. George's Church, Pungoteague. So. Ch., Feb. 2, 1888
  Henry B., of Northampton Co., Va., and Margaret, d. of Wm. Murray of Wilson, by the Rev. J. H. Guinne, at Wilson, N.C. So. Ch., Oct. 25, 1883
  Indie A., and James E. Heath, by the Rev. J. B. Craighill, at "Pleasant Prospect", Northampton Co., Va. So. Ch., Dec. 17, 1868
  Levin W., and Alice, d. of Dr. A. W. Downing, by the Rev. J. B. Craighill, at "Chatham", Northampton Co., Va. So. Ch., May 12, 1870
  Lottie Y., d. of Dr. Thomas J. L. L. Nottingham, and George F. Wilkins, Esq., M.D., by the Rev. J. J. Clemens, at Mt. Lebanon, Northampton Co., Va. So. Ch., Oct. 27, 1870
  Robinson, and Rebecca M. Byrd, both of Northampton Co., Va., by the Rev. Dr. Colton, in Christ Church, Eastville, Va. So. Ch., Nov. 23, 1860
  Severn M., and Jaqueline Ware, by the Rev. J. W. Ware, in St. Stephen's Church, Culpeper, Va. So. Ch., June 22, 1912
  Severn P. (Dr.), and Annie K., d. of the late R. Wise of Northampton Co., by the Rev. J. D. Powell of Portsmouth, in Christ Church, Eastville, Northampton Co. So. Ch., July 7, 1870

NOURSE
  Charles J., Esq., of Fauquier Co., and Annie C. Simpson of Smithfield, by the Rev. David Barr, at Christ Church, Smithfield, Va. So. Ch., Aug. 20, 1885

NOWLAN
  Fannie (Mrs.), and the Rev. G. S. Gibbs of Virginia, now rector of St. Luke's, by the Rev. J. C. Adams,

MARRIAGE NOTICES IN THE SOUTHERN CHURCHMAN WITH DATES OF PUBLICATION

in St. Luke's Church,
Hot Springs, Ark. So.
Ch., Jan. 25, 1883
NUCKOLS
Hartwell McKendree, and
Verna Vest, eldest d.
of Abner C. Nuckols
and gr.d. of J. J.
English of Richmond,
at Oak Grove, Goochland
Co., the residence of
the bride's parents.
So. Ch., Nov. 30, 1893
Verna Vest, eldest d. of
Abner C. Nuckols, and
gr.d. of J. J. English
of Richmond, and Hartwell
McKendree Nuckols, at
Oak Grove, Goochland
Co., the residence
of the bride's parents.
So. Ch., Nov. 30,

1893
NUNN
Joseph, of Louisa Co., Va.,
and Louisa Loehr of Culpeper, by the Rev. W. T.
Roberts, at the residence
of Charles Schuman, Culpeper, Va. So. Ch., Dec.
4, 1884
NUTT
James, and Jane Middleton
Walker, by the Rev.
Ephraim Adams, at Level
Fields, Lancaster Co.
So. Ch., Dec. 11, 1835
NUTTALL
Wm. L. (Dr.), and Mary
Alice Chestnutt, by the
Rev. Henry T. Sharp, in
the Church of the Ascension, Frankfort, Ky.
So. Ch., May 11, 1876

– O –

ODEN
　Mary, of Martinsburg, and Philip Fry of Orange C.H., by the Rev. R. R. Mason assisted by the Rev. W. C. Meredith, D.D., in Christ Church, Winchester, Va. So. Ch., Aug. 21, 1873

OGLE
　Louisa, d. of Benj. Ogle, Esq., and the Rev. Upton Beall, by the Rev. Dr. Marbury, at Bel-Air, Prince George's Co., Md. So. Ch., Oct. 27, 1837

O'GRADY
　Pinkie, d. of Capt. John C. O'Grady of North Dakota, and Capt. Chas. A. Hester, C.S.A., by the Rev. Dr. Crane, at Rest Easy, near Jackson, Miss. So. Ch., June 17, 1864

OLD
　Alice Leigh, d. of Maj. Charles and Anne C. Old of Powhatan Co., and Stuart Lee Dance of Richmond, Va., by the Rev. C. O. Pruden, at Emanuel Church, Powhatan Co., Va. So. Ch., Jan. 1, 1891
　Ellen Alice, d. of William W. Old and Alice Herbert his wife, and William Morton Dey, by the Rev. Francis C. Steinmetz, S.T.D., rector, in Christ Church, Norfolk, Va. So. Ch., Jan. 7, 1911
　Julia Wickham, d. of Maj. Charles and Annie C. Old of Powhatan Co., Va., and the Rev. Clevius Olando Pruden of Chatham, Va., by the Rev. B. M. Randolph of Emmanuel Church, Henrico Co., Va., at the residence of Maj. Charles Old, Powhatan Co., Va. So. Ch., Oct. 27, 1887
　Margaret Nash, d. of William W. Old and Alice Herbert his wife, and John Stone Stump, Jr. formerly of Maryland, by the Rev. Francis C. Steinmetz, in Christ Church, Norfolk, Va. So. Ch., Nov. 13, 1909
　William, youngest s. of Maj. Charles Old, and Bessie Abbott, eldest d. of Ryland R. Weisiger, Esq., both of Powhatan Co., by the Rev. C. C. Pruden, in Grace Church, Powhatan Co., Va. So. Ch., Aug. 17, 1893

OLDHAM
　Charles Russell, of Moundesville, W.Va., and Callie, d. of Edward C. Bruce of Winchester, by the Rev. Nelson P. Dame, in Christ Church, Winchester. So. Ch., July 5, 1888

OLEY
　Octavia, and Clinton Dewitt, Esq., both of Alexandria, Va., by the Rev. T. M. Carson, in St. Paul's Church, Lynchburg. So. Ch., Aug. 27, 1874

OLIFFE
　Helen R., and Addison Butler Atkins, s. of the officiating clergyman, the Rev. A. B. Atkins, D.D., rector of St. John's Church, Yonkers, at the residence of the bride's mother, in New York. So. Ch., Feb. 13, 1879

OLIVER
　Alice, and Willoughby Newton of Bristol, Va. formerly of Richmond, s. of the late Rt. Rev. John B. Newton of

MARRIAGE NOTICES IN THE SOUTHERN CHURCHMAN WITH DATES OF PUBLICATION

Virginia, by the Rev. J. K. Mason, at Louisville, Ky. So. Ch., Feb. 9, 1907

Charles, and Mattie, d. of Thomas L. Dyke of King and Queen Co., Va., by the Rev. J. H. Hundley, at the residence of the bride's father. So. Ch., Feb. 6, 1890

Jas. W. (Dr.), of Mecklenburg, and Anna E. Crichton of Brunswick Co., Va., by the Rev. Theo. Pryor, D.D., at the residence of the bride's father. So. Ch., June 13, 1867

Lucy N., and Dr. McG. James Kent of Montgomery Co., Va., by the Rev. Wm. H. Pendleton, at Monterey, Roanoke Co., Va. So. Ch., Sept. 14, 1854

Parthena, of Amherst Co., and Charles Y. Johnson, by the Rev. W. H. Kinckle. So. Ch., June 27, 1856

OLIVIER
Louise Norton, and Capt. Henry Parham, both of Petersburg, Va., by the Rev. Mr. Hullihen, at the residence of Warner Lewis Olivier, Esq., Staunton. So. Ch., Mar. 14, 1878

OLTROGGE
Henry Carl, and Margaret Winstead Worsham, by the Rev. Melville E. Johnson assisted by the Rev. C. A. Ashby, in the Church of the Good Shepherd, Jacksonville, Fla. So. Ch., Oct. 21, 1922

OMOHUNDRA
Willie, d. of T. T. Omohundra of Albemarle Co., Va., and Wm. D. Staples of Fluvanna Co., by the Rev. T. E. Locke, at the residence of the bride's father. So. Ch., Dec. 7, 1882

OMOHUNDRO
James T., and Sallie R. Fitzhugh, both of Pittsylvania Co., Va., by the Rev. C. O. Pruden, in Pittsylvania Co., Va. So. Ch., Jan. 1, 1885

Joseph, and Neenah McClannahan Hutt, in St. Paul's Chapel, Nomini Grove, Westmoreland, Va. So. Ch., Nov. 3, 1892

Mary Elizabeth, and Edwin Brown Hutt, both of Westmoreland, by the Rev. R. A. Castleman, in St. Paul's, Nomini Grove, Westmoreland Co., Va. So. Ch., Jan. 30, 1890*

Tipton Tiptoe, Jr., of Albemarle, and Mrs. Laura A. Sheppard of Halifax Co., Va., by the Rev. Thomas E. Locke, at the rectory, St. Anne's Parish.**So. Ch., Dec. 28, 1893

O'NEIL
Francis J., of Washington, D.C., and Jeanie Cabell, youngest d. of Capt. and Mrs. N. H. Van Zandt of Virginia, by the Rev. Dr. George H. Houghton, at the Church of the Transfiguration, New York. So. Ch., May 18, 1893

ORDWAY
Charles F., of Nashville, Tenn., and Mary Lewis, d. of Prof. Wm. Leroy Broun of Vanderbilt University, by the Rev. Wm. Graham, rector of Christ Church, at the residence of the bride's father. So. Ch., July 21, 1881

ORGAIN
Bettie C., of Berkeley, Charles City Co., and Powhatan B. Stark, M.D., by the Rev. Wm. H. Platt, in St. Paul's Church, Petersburg. So. Ch., May 21, 1858

OSBORNE

---

* A notice appears in the issue of Jan. 9, 1890, identical with this except that "Edwin" is written "Edwid"

** St. Anne's Parish is in Albemarle County, Virginia (**Journal ... Diocese of Virginia**, Richmond, Va., 1941)

MARRIAGE NOTICES IN THE SOUTHERN CHURCHMAN WITH DATES OF PUBLICATION

Dorothy, youngest d. of Barry Baldwin Osborne, Esq., and Lt. Lloyd W. Townsend, U.S.N., by the Rev. J. H. Townsend, at St. Paul's Church, Willimantic, Conn. So. Ch., Feb. 11, 1911

Jennie, d. of Edmund Osborne, Esq., and W. Gordon McCabe, Esq., s. of the officiating clergyman, the Rev. John Collins McCabe, D.D., rector of St. Luke's Church, Bladensburg, Md., at Petersburg, Va. So. Ch., Apr. 18, 1867

Phoebe, of Castile, Genessee Co., N.Y., (a pupil of the Institution for the Deaf and Dumb), and J. R. Burnett of Livingston, N.J., by the Rev. Dr. Milnor, president of the Institution, at the Institution for the Deaf and Dumb, Richmond, Va. So. Ch., Aug. 16, 1839

OSBURN
Abner (Dr.), of Loudoun, and Elizabeth Osburn, by the Rev. Wm. D. Hanson, in Jefferson Co., Va. So. Ch., Feb. 24, 1853

Elizabeth, and Dr. Abner Osburn of Loudoun, by the Rev. Wm. D. Hanson, in Jefferson Co., Va. So. Ch., Feb. 24, 1853

OST
Charles J., Esq., and Sallie J., d. of James Burcher, Esq., by the Rev. John C. McCabe of Hampton. So. Ch., Dec. 28, 1855

Elizabeth Burcher, and William Fillmore Turnbull, by the Rev. J. J. Gravatt, in St. John's Church, Hampton, Va. So. Ch., Oct. 12, 1882

OSTRANDER
Katherine E., of Westwood, Cal., and Walter Gideon Miller formerly of Washington, Va., by the Rev. C. W. Pogue, at Susanville, Cal. So. Ch., July 24, 1915

OTEY
Kate, gr.d. of the late Bishop Otey, and William Arthur, s. of Gen. Alex. Yerger, by the Rev. Ralph H. Prosser, in Grace Church, Rosedale, Miss. So. Ch., Oct. 2, 1879

OTT
George Hunter, and Frances Gertrude Compton, both of Harrisonburg, Va., by the Rev. Dr. Addison, at Washington City. So. Ch., Nov. 7, 1889

OUTTEN
Maysville A., only d. of the late Col. George F. Outten of Norfolk, Va., and A. Smith Irvine of Baltimore, Md., by the Rev. Horace Edwin Hayden, rector of St. Peter's Church, at the residence of E. A. Outten, Esq., Plymouth, Luzerne Co., Pa. So. Ch., May 27, 1880

OVERBY
Daniel A., of Mossingford, Charlotte Co., Va., and Sallie E., youngest d. of Maj. Wm. E. Shepherd, by the Rev. W. Dame, at Danville. So. Ch., Feb. 3, 1876

OWEN
Mattie F., d. of Dr. Thomas J. Owen of Prince Edward Co., Va., and Capt. David L. Sublett, by the Rev. Daniel Witt. So. Ch., July 6, 1871

Wm. E., and Mattie H. Easley, d. of the late Dr. Henry Easley of Halifax, by the Rev. O. A. Kinsolving, D.D., at the Presbyterian Church, Black Walnut, Halifax Co.

MARRIAGE NOTICES IN THE SOUTHERN CHURCHMAN WITH DATES OF PUBLICATION

OWENS
    Harriett H., youngest d. of Samuel R. Owens, Esq., and William Richards, by the Rev. A. B. Tizzard, at Chestnut Cottage, Chesterfield Co. So. Ch., Mar. 9, 1860
    Jane, d. of Samuel R. Owens, Esq., of Chesterfield Co., and J. S. Moore, Esq., by the Rev. A. B. Tizzard, at Chestnut Cottage. So. Ch., Apr. 4, 1867
    Wm. M., and Albinia W., d. of Richard Lewellyn of Albemarle Co., Va., by the Rev. W. M. Nelson. So. Ch., Nov. 30, 1855

OYLER
    James Morgan, and Belia Scott Richards, by the Rev. F. G. Scott, at Lynchburg, Va. So. Ch., Nov. 26, 1885

So. Ch., Oct. 23, 1884

PACE
    Sidney Willard, of Fluvanna Co., Va., and Virginia Adoline Ancell, by the Rev. T. E. Locke, at the rectory of St. Anne's Parish, Albemarle Co., Va. So. Ch., Jan. 1, 1885
    Violet, eldest d. of James B. Pace, and the Rev. H. Melville Jackson, by the Rt. Rev. Bishop Whittle, at Richmond. So. Ch., Apr. 29, 1880

PACKARD
    Joseph, Jr., of Virginia, and Laura Dillon, eldest d. of William Bennet, Esq. of Burke Co., Ga., by the Rt. Rev. John W. Beckwith, D.D., in Savannah, Ga. So. Ch., Apr. 23, 1868
    Joseph, Jr., of Baltimore, and Meta M., d. of the late F. W. Hanewinckle, Esq. of Richmond, by the Rev. Joseph Packard, D.D., in Richmond, Va. So. Ch., Jan. 4, 1883
    Rosa I., d. of the Rev. Dr. Packard of Fairfax Co., and the Rev. William H. Laird of Mecklenburg Co., Va., by Bishop Johns, in the chapel of the Theological Seminary, Fairfax Co., Va. So. Ch., Sept. 9, 1869
    Thomas J. (The Rev.), of Halifax Co., Va., and Hattie, d. of John W. Cunningham, Esq. of Person Co., N.C., by the Rev. O. A. Kinsolving, D.D. assisted by the Rev. B. S. Bronson, in Cunningham Chapel, N.C. So. Ch., June 11, 1885

PACKWOOD
    George H., of Maitland, Fla., and Lalivesia H. P., d. of the late Col. Wm. A. Caruthers formerly of Lexington, Va., by the Rev. Wm. W. Greene, at the residence of the bride's mother, in Nottoway Co., Va. So. Ch., July 8, 1880

PADGETT
    Chas. O., and Mrs. Sarah A. Campbell, by the Rev. W. H. Pendleton, at the residence of the bride's mother in Bedford Co. So. Ch., Feb. 20, 1868
    Matris C., and Joseph M. Wilson, by the Rev. W. H. Pendleton, at the residence of the bride's father in Bedford Co., Va. So. Ch., Jan. 16, 1868

PAGE
    Ann Willing, d. of the late William Byrd Page, and Thomas Carter, Esq., by the Rev. Mr. Stringfellow, at Page-Brook, the residence of Jno. Page, Esq. So. Ch., Dec. 11, 1835
    Annie Nelson, d. of Frederick W. Page, Esq. of Albemarle Co., Va., and Nathaniel R. Coleman, Esq. of Halifax Co., Va., by the Rev. E. Boyden, in Grace Church, Walker's Parish, Albemarle Co., Va. So. Ch., Jan. 21, 1875
    Archie C., of Goochland, and Eliza C., d. of

MARRIAGE NOTICES IN THE SOUTHERN CHURCHMAN WITH DATES OF PUBLICATION

the late Thomas R. Harrison, by the Rev. J. Peterkin, in St. James' Church, Richmond. So. Ch., Jan. 6, 1860

Bettie, of Gloucester, and James M. Goggin of Memphis, Tenn., by the Rev. M. Mann, in Abingdon Church, Gloucester Co. So. Ch., Mar. 2, 1860

C. B. (The Rev.), rector of Trinity Church, Danville, Ky., and Ella, eldest d. of W. B. Baker, Esq. of Winchester, Va., by the Rev. George W. Peterkin, rector of Memorial Church, Baltimore, Md., assisted by the Rev. Mr. Gilbert, at the residence of the bride's father. So. Ch., Dec. 23, 1875

Carter B., and Mary Lewis Stumph of Washington, D.C., by the Rev. J. B. Funsten, at Portsmouth, Va. So. Ch., Nov. 10, 1892

Charles H. (The Rev.), of Hodgesville, Berkeley Co., W.Va., and Jane Loaton of Canada East, by the Rev. R. K. Meade, in Charlottesville. So. Ch., June 23, 1870

Edmonia R., youngest d. of the late E. R. Page, Esq. of Campbell C.H., Va., and Thomas A. Bledsoe, Esq. of Staunton, Va., by the Rev. R. A. Cobbs, at "Austed", near "Hawks Nest", Fayette Co., W.Va. So. Ch., May 1, 1879

Elizabeth Calvert, eldest d. of Gen. R. L. and Alexina Page, and Capt.

William C. Whittle, Jr., by the Rev. Dr. O. S. Barten, in Christ Church, Norfolk. So. Ch., Nov. 21, 1872

Evelyn Byrd, d. of Frederick W. Page of Albemarle Co., Va., and John Mabry Coleman, by the Rev. O. A. Kinsolving, in Grace Church, Halifax Co., Va. So. Ch., July 27, 1882

Evelyn Byrd, d. of R. P. Page, M.D. of Berryville, Va., and Charles Gordon Van-Hook of Washington, D.C., by the Rev. P. P. Phillips, rector, in Grace Church, Berryville, Va. So. Ch., Sept. 29, 1892

Evelyne, d. of the late Wm. B. Page of Clarke Co., Va., and Richard H. Lee of Jefferson Co., Va., by the Rev. J. T. Hooff, at Melwood, Clarke Co., Va. So. Ch., June 30, 1848

Fanny Randolph, d. of Wm. N. Page, Esq. of Cumberland Co., Va., and the Rev. W. C. Meredith, D.D., rector of Christ Church, Winchester, Va., by the Rev. T. U. Dudley, in Christ Church, Baltimore, Md. So. Ch., June 12, 1873

Frank (The Rev.), and Lettie, d. of E. G. Morris of Hanover Co., by the Rev. Curtis Grubb assisted by the Rev. John McGill, in St. James' Church, Ashland. So. Ch., Oct. 28, 1886

Frederick Kinloch, and Flora Temple, d. of

MARRIAGE NOTICES IN THE SOUTHERN CHURCHMAN WITH DATES OF PUBLICATION

William S. Lewis, Esq., by the Rev. P. M. Boyden, in Grace Church, Albemarle Co., Va. So. Ch., Nov. 28, 1878

Frederick W., of Albemarle Co., Va., and Lucy C. Brent of Fredericksburg, Va., by the Rev. G. L. Petrie, at the residence of Prof. Dennington, University of Virginia. So. Ch., Dec. 6, 1883

H. D. (The Rev.), rector of St. Stephen's Church, Culpeper C.H., Va., and Sarah N. Gregg of Wickliffe, Va., by the Rev. J. J. Page, in Wickliffe Church, Clarke Co., Va. So. Ch., Jan. 11, 1883

Harriet R., d. of the late John C. Page of Cumberland, and David Coupland Randolph of Richmond, by the Rev. W. H. Kinckle, at Union Hill. So. Ch., May 15, 1857

Jane Byrd, d. of John W. Page, Esq. of Clarke Co., Va., and the Rev. Jas. Chisholm, rector of Norborne Parish, Berkeley Co., by the Rev. Wm. G. H. Jones, in Christ Church, Millwood. So. Ch., Sept. 3, 1847

Jane Byrd, d. of Mann R. Page, Esq., and Gurdon H. Pendleton of Jefferson Co., by the Rev. Francis M. Whittle, at Mannsfield, Clarke Co., Va. So. Ch., May 25, 1854

Jane Walker, d. of Frederick W. Page, Esq., and Thomas W. Lewis, Esq., all of Albemarle Co., Va., by the Rev. E. Boyden, in Grace Church, Walker's Parish, Albemarle Co., Va. So. Ch., Jan. 21, 1875

John A., of Roanoke, Va., and C. Belle Bibb of Nelson Co., Va., by the Rev. Davis M. Wood, in Trinity Church, Nelson Co., Va. So. Ch., Dec. 16, 1886

John C. (Col.), of Cumberland Co., and Julia R. Gray of Buckingham Co., Va., by the Rev. B. H. Dupuy, at the residence of the bride's mother, in Buckingham Co., Va. So. Ch., Feb. 2, 1882

Mann, of Albemarle, and Anna, eldest d. of the late Thomas L. Hobson, Esq. of Powhatan, by the Rev. William H. Kinckle, in Powhatan Co. So. Ch., June 7, 1855

Maria Vidal, d. of Dr. Wm. Byrd Page of Natchez, Miss., formerly of Virginia, and Thomas C. Bowie of Tensas Parish, La., by the Rev. Dr. Dana, rector of Trinity Church, Natchez, Miss. So. Ch., June 7, 1866

Mary Bowdoin, youngest d. of Carter H. and Lelia G. Page, of Albemarle Co., Va., and Gilbert Bonham, s. of the late Robert Bird, deputy Surgeon Gen. of the East India Medical Service, by the Rev. J. S. Hanckel assisted by the Rev. H. B. Lee, at the residence of the bride's father. So. Ch., Mar. 10, 1892

Mary Wallace, d. of the Rev. James J. Page, and the Rev. Carl E.

MARRIAGE NOTICES IN THE SOUTHERN CHURCHMAN WITH DATES OF PUBLICATION

Grammer, Prof. of the Virginia Theological Seminary, by the father of the bride assisted by the Rev. Dr. Julius E. Grammer and the Rev. Thomas Carter Page, in Holy Trinity Church, near Collington, Prince George's Co., Md. So. Ch., July 11, 1889

Mattella C., of Clarke Co., Va., and Dr. Benjamin Harrison, by the Rev. Mr. Hoff, at Saratoga, the residence of Mrs. R. Page. So. Ch., Feb. 12, 1858

Mattie H., d. and only child of the late Alex. and Martha E. Page, and W. Douglass Stuart of Alexandria, by the Rev. James Grammer, at Northfield, Cumberland Co., Va. So. Ch., June 20, 1867

Nannie, d. of Washington C. Page, Esq. of Alexandria, and the Rev. J. Pinckney Hammond of Bangor, Me., by the Rev. C. B. Dana. So. Ch., Dec. 10, 1847

Nannie W., d. of John E. Page, Esq., and Dr. Wm. D. Meriwether of Albemarle Co., by the Rev. Mr. Jones, at Pagebrook, Clarke Co. So. Ch., Feb. 19, 1864

Philip Powers, and Mrs. Alleyne Castleman, by the Rev. C. T. Page, father of the groom, of Altavista, Va., in Chicago, Ill. So. Ch., Feb. 18, 1922

Powhatan R., of Gloucester Co., and Lizzie, d. of Dr. Sam'l Scollay of Smithfield, Jefferson Co., Va., by the Rev. Julius E. Grammer, at Smithfield, Jefferson Co., Va. So. Ch., Nov. 28, 1856

Richard Mann, and Kate Mallory Wray, by the Rev. A. Y. Hundley, in Abingdon Church, Gloucester Co., Va. So. Ch., Oct. 24, 1878

Robert (Dr.), and Anna G., eldest d. of W. W. Hobson, all of Powhatan Co., Va., by the Rev. B. H. Dupuy, at the residence of the bride's father. So. Ch., Dec. 27, 1877

Rosewell, of Danville, Va., and Susie D., youngest d. of Edward W. Morris of Claremount, Hanover Co., Va., by the Rev. Frank Page, brother of the groom, in Ashland. So. Ch., Jan. 27, 1887

Sally, second d. of John W. Page of Clarke Co., Va., and Thomas Page, Esq. of Powhatan, by the Rev. Wm. Jackson, in Janeville, Va. So. Ch., Dec. 20, 1839

Sarah B., d. of the officiating clergyman, and John M. Bowie, by the Rev. James J. Page, in Holy Trinity Church, Prince George's Co., Md. So. Ch., Nov. 1, 1888

T. Carter (The Rev.), of Stafford Co., Va., and Fanny Ballard, d. of the late P. H. Powers and Roberta M. Powers, by the Rev. J. J. Page, at Auburn, Clarke Co., Va. So. Ch., Dec.

MARRIAGE NOTICES IN THE SOUTHERN CHURCHMAN WITH DATES OF PUBLICATION

22, 1887
Thomas, Esq., of Powhatan, and Sally, second d. of John W. Page of Clarke Co., Va., by the Rev. Wm. M. Jackson, at Janeville, Va. So. Ch., Dec. 20, 1839

Thos. Nelson, of Richmond, and Annie Seddon, d. of Charles Bruce, Esq. of Charlotte Co., Va., by the Rev. Frank Page, at Staunton Hill. So. Ch., Aug. 12, 1886

Thos. Nelson, of Virginia, and Mrs. Henry Field of Chicago, by the Rev. Frank Page of Waco, Tex. assisted by the Rev. Mr. Anderson of Elmhurst, at the home of the bride's mother, Elmhurst, Ill. So. Ch., June 15, 1893

Walker Y., formerly of Virginia, and Nannie C., youngest d. of Dr. Wm. Tyler, Sr. of Frederick, Md., by the Rev. Chas. Seymour, in All Saints' Church, Frederick, Md. So. Ch., June 11, 1858

Wm. B., and Laura Alexander, d. of the late Rev. E. R. Lippitt, all of Clarke Co., Va., by the Rev. T. F. Martin, at "Elsinore", the residence of the bride's mother. So. Ch., June 5, 1873

PALMER
Alfred Copeland (Dr.), of Norfolk, and Susan Catharine, d. of Judge and Mrs. W. S. Barton, by the Rev. J. Green Shackelford, the rector, in Trinity Church, Fredericksburg. So. Ch., Dec. 8, 1887

Arthur W., of Baltimore, Md., and Elizabeth James Thackara, by the Rev. Owen P. Thackara, father of the bride, in St. Peter's Church, Fernandina, Fla. So. Ch., July 23, 1874

Giles Buckner (The Rev.), and Elizabeth Read Barksdale, by the Rev. Giles B. Cooke, uncle of the groom, at Durham, N.C. So. Ch., Oct. 24, 1914

Joseph C., and Alverta B. McCarty, by the Rev. Henry L. Derby, in White Chapel Church, Lancaster, Va. So. Ch., Dec. 27, 1883

Leize, of Richmond, Va., and Arthur P. Gaillard of South Carolina, by the Rev. J. Peterkin, at the residence of W. Fletcher Richardson. So. Ch., Jan. 23, 1890

Wm. H., and Lillie, second d. of John S. Barnes, all of Fairfax Co., by the Rev. Jno. McGill, in Zion Church, Fairfax Court House. So. Ch., Feb. 8, 1877

PANCOAST
Lillie, of Leesburg, and R. Bentley Gray of St. Louis, Mo., by the Rev. Theodore Reed, in St. James' Church, Leesburg. So. Ch., Nov. 16, 1876

PANE
Mary J., and Harris McMullen, both of Hanover, by the rector, the Rev. Robt. Douglas Roller, in Trinity Church, St. Martin's Parish.* So. Ch., Jan. 3,

---

* St. Martin's Parish is in Hanover County, Virginia (Journal ... Diocese of Virginia, Richmond, Va., 1941)

MARRIAGE NOTICES IN THE SOUTHERN CHURCHMAN WITH DATES OF PUBLICATION

1878
PANNELL
Joseph B., of Orange Co., and Frances B., d. of Dr. Williams of Culpeper Co., Va., by the Rev. Mr. Woodville, near Culpeper Court House, Va. So. Ch., Sept. 22, 1837

PANNILL
Annie P., eldest d. of P. P. Pannill of "Green Level", Orange Co., and Lee Pannill, by the Rev. John McGill, in St. Paul's Church, Culpeper Co., Va. So. Ch., Oct. 30, 1884
Charles, of Petersburg, and Maria Meade, d. of the late Albert J. Goodwyn, Esq., by the Rev. P. G. Robert, at Greenwood, Greensville Co. So. Ch., Sept. 11, 1857
D. H., Esq., of Pittsylvania Co., and Augusta Hunter Roberts of Northampton Co., Va., by the Rev. J. J. Gravatt, rector of St. John's Church, Hampton, Va., at the residence of the bride's father. So. Ch., Oct. 11, 1877
Indiana (Mrs.), d. of the late Hon. Richard K. Meade, and the Rev. Wm. H. Platt, rector of Calvary Church, Louisville, Ky., by the Rev. C. J. Gibson, in St. Paul's Church, Petersburg, Va. So. Ch., Feb. 27, 1868
Joseph, and Jarret, youngest d. of the late Robt. Gilliam, by the Rev. Edmund Withers, at Petersburg, Va. So. Ch., Oct. 16, 1851
Lee, and Annie P., eldest d. of P. P. Pannill of "Green Level", Orange Co., by the Rev. John McGill, in St. Paul's Church, Culpeper Co., Va. So. Ch., Oct. 30, 1884
Mary C., and Charles A. Hansbrough, by the Rev. H. B. Lee, in St. Paul's Church, Culpeper Co., Va. So. Ch., Nov. 28, 1889

PARHAM
Henry (Capt.), and Louise Norton Oliver, both of Petersburg, Va., by the Rev. Mr. Hullihen, at the residence of Warner Lewis Oliver, Esq., in Staunton. So. Ch., Mar. 14, 1878

PARISH
E. Florence, of Virginia, and J. C. Gray of Newport, R.I., by the Rev. J. Harvey Hundley, at Urbanna, Middlesex Co., Va. So. Ch., Mar. 6, 1879

PARKE
Annie P., second d. of the late Rev. P. Parke, D.D., and the Rev. Hobart Chetwood, rector of Burlington College, by the Rev. Lewis Walke, in Christ Church, Norfolk. So. Ch., May 1, 1857

PARKER
Alice E., d. of the late Capt. Wentworth Parker of Halifax, N.S., and John Hipkins of Norfolk, Va., by the Rev. Walter Williams, in St. George's Church, New York. So. Ch., Oct. 2, 1879
Cornelia Page, of Accomac Co., and Benjamin S. Nottingham of Northampton

MARRIAGE NOTICES IN THE SOUTHERN CHURCHMAN WITH DATES OF PUBLICATION

Co., by the Rev. John McNabb, in St. George's Church, Pungoteague. So. Ch., Feb. 2, 1888

Eva Wills, oldest d. of Henry R. Parker, Esq. of Smithfield, and Robert A. Edwards, Esq., sheriff of Isle of Wight Co., by the Rev. David Barr, in Christ Church, Smithfield. So. Ch., Feb. 2, 1888

Jennie, and Edmund S. Mallory, by the Rev. J. A. Harrison, at Jackson, Tenn. So. Ch., Oct. 3, 1872

Louise Alfretta, of Washington, and Dr. Fred. H. Humphreys of New York, by the Rev. John S. Lindsay assisted by the Rev. Frank Humphreys of the Church of the Heavenly Rest, New York, in St. John's Church, Georgetown, D.C. So. Ch., Jan. 22, 1880

Mary Dorsey, d. of the late Com. F. A. Parker, U.S. Navy and gr.d. of the late Thomas Donaldson, and Edward Lloyd, s. of the late Gen. Charles S. Winder, by the Rev. W. D. Powers, in Grace Church, Elk Ridge, Md. So. Ch., Oct. 30, 1884

PARKS
Sophie Jackson, d. of Marshall Parks of Norfolk, Va., and Richard Urquhart Goode, by the Rev. Beverly D. Tucker, in St. Paul's Church, Norfolk, Va. So. Ch., Jan. 17, 1889

PARR
Ella, d. of Israel M. Parr, and the Rev. Frederick F. Reese, all of Baltimore, by the Rt. Rev. George W. Peterkin, D.D., Bishop of West Virginia, assisted by the Rev. Wm. M. Dame and the Rev. Campbell Fair, D.D., in Memorial Church, Baltimore. So. Ch., Nov. 27, 1879

Gretchen, and Orville Clifton Bell, both of Bedford City, by the Rev. T. W. Jones, in St. John's, Bedford City, Va. So. Ch., Nov. 6, 1890

PARRAN
Lillie M., d. of the late Dr. Richard Parrin of Jefferson Co., Va., and Lt. Wm. F. Lee, U.S. Army, by the Rev. C. W. Andrews, D.D., in Trinity Church, Shepherdstown, Va. So. Ch., Sept. 23, 1859

PARRISH
Philip Percy (Dr.), oldest s. of R. L. Parrish of Covington, Va., and Sarah Cabell, d. of James A. August of Hot Springs, Va., by the Rev. L. R. Combs, in the Episcopal Church at Warm Springs, Va. So. Ch., Oct. 19, 1893

PARSONS
Kittie Bell, and Charles C. Bowyer, Esq., by the Rev. T. H. Lacy, in Christ Church, Point Pleasant, W.Va. So. Ch., Oct. 9, 1879

PARTLOW
Benj. L., Esq., of Harrisonburg, Va., and Fannie L. Harriss of Boydton, by the Rev. O. S. Bunting, in St.

MARRIAGE NOTICES IN THE SOUTHERN CHURCHMAN WITH DATES OF PUBLICATION

PARVIN
 Robert J. (The Rev.), rector of Christ Church, Tawanda, Pa., and Adelaide R., d. of Capt. Thomas Singer of Alexandria, by the Rev. John Coleman, D.D., in Trinity Church. So. Ch., Dec. 17, 1847

PATE
 C. (Maj.), of Bedford Co., and Lizzie Stagg of Richmond, by the Rev. A. B. Tizzard, in Richmond. So. Ch., Nov. 23, 1860
 Joseph A., and Maggie E. Conway, by the Rev. R. S. Barrett, in Richmond, Va. So. Ch., July 1, 1880

PATRICK
 Ellen M., d. of Dr. S. Patrick, and James D. Hunt of Fredericksburg, by the Rev. T. L. Smith, at "Forest Hill", the residence of the bride's father, Kanawha Co., Va. So. Ch., Nov. 5, 1858

PATTERSON
 Charles H., and Mary J. Cooper, by the Rev. Henry T. Sharp, in St. John's Church, Uniontown, Ky. So. Ch., Nov. 28, 1872
 John Oliver (The Rev.), priest-in-charge of St. Ansgarius Church, Chicago, and Elizabeth Andrews. So. Ch., Aug. 15, 1936
 Mary L., d. of Thomas Leiper Patterson of Cumberland, and William L. Venable of Petersburg, Va., by the Rev. James W. Robins of Philadelphia, Pa., in Emmanuel Church, Cumberland, Md. So. Ch., May 16, 1872
 Mattie L., d. of Dr. Wm. Patterson of Richmond, and Jas. R. Branch of Petersburg, by the Rev. Horace Stringfellow, in St. Paul's Church, Richmond. So. Ch., Dec. 12, 1856
 R. Price, and Julia Louise Larsen, by the Rev. Thomas P. Baker, in Christ Church, Adams Run, S.C. So. Ch., Nov. 25, 1911

PATTESON
 Anna Mills, d. of Capt. Camm Patteson, and James D. Duval, by the Rev. T. E. Locke, at Sunnyside, Buckingham Co., Va. So. Ch., May 31, 1888
 George W., and Kate, youngest d. of the late Dr. David Patteson of Buckingham Co., Va., by the Rev. T. E. Locke, at Repton, the residence of Capt. Camm Patteson, the brother of the bride. So. Ch., Dec. 10, 1885
 Kate, youngest d. of the late Dr. David Patteson of Buckingham Co., Va., and George W. Patteson, by the Rev. T. E. Locke, at Repton, the residence of Capt. Camm Patteson, the brother of the bride. So. Ch., Dec. 10, 1885
 Thomas A., Esq., of New York, and Georgina, youngest d. of the late David McCaw, M.D., by the Rev. Lewis Walke, at "Millwood", in Powhatan Co. So. Ch., Mar. 2, 1860

PATTISON
 Everard K., and Fanny, d. of the late Dr. William Maffitt Post, by the

MARRIAGE NOTICES IN THE SOUTHERN CHURCHMAN WITH DATES OF PUBLICATION

Rev. Campbell Fair, D.D., in Ascension Church, Baltimore. So. Ch., Feb. 23, 1882

PATTON
Anthony B., and Virginia B., d. of the late Horace Cookley of Fredericksburg, Va., by the Rev. R. J. McBryde, at the residence of the bride's mother. So. Ch., Jan. 19, 1882

George S., of Richmond, and Susan T., only d. of Andrew Glassell of Mobile, by the Rev. Philip Slaughter, in St. Paul's Church, Richmond, Va. So. Ch., Nov. 16, 1855

George T., and V. R. Pemberton, both formerly of Ashland, Va., by the Rev. Mr. Chapham assisted by the Rev. J. L. Patton, at Bakersfield, Cal. So. Ch., Dec. 25, 1890

J. Lindsay (The Rev.), of Ashland, and Fannie Kean Leake, by the Rev. T. M. Ambler, at the residence of William J. Leake, father of the bride, at Ashland, Va. So. Ch., July 3, 1890

James Boyd, and May Beverley Williams, by the Rev. Preston Nash, in St. James' Church, Richmond. So. Ch., Nov. 7, 1889

John M., of Virginia, and Lucy A., d. of the late John P. Crump of Dinwiddie Co., Va., by the Rev. William M. Dame, in Memorial Church, Baltimore. So. Ch., Oct. 24, 1878

Mary E., and O. R. Hudson, both of Kanawha Co., W.Va., by the Rev. Pendleton Brooke, at the residence of the bride's father, Amandaville. So. Ch., Sept. 17, 1874

Mary H., of Richmond, and Alexander R. Dearborn of Atlanta, Ga., by the Rev. Dr. Eccleston of Baltimore, in St. James' Church, Richmond, Va. So. Ch., July 8, 1886

Sadie Lindsay, d. of Col. J. M. Patton of Virginia, and Arthur J. Hutchinson formerly of the British Army, second s. of Gen. W. N. Hutchinson, Duke of Wellington's regiment, by the Rev. Garrett Scott, in Christ Church, Gordonsville, Va. So. Ch., Sept. 27, 1888

PAUL
M. Catherine, and Beverley Douglas Causey, in Christ Church, La Crosse, Wis. So. Ch., July 25, 1908

Samuel, of Springfield, Mo., and Mary Abell of Martinsburg, by the Rev. Henry Thomas, in Trinity Church, Martinsburg. So. Ch., May 2, 1889

PAULSEN
Alice L., d. of the late Martin Paulsen of Christiansburg, Norway, and Dr. Fairfax Irwin of Virginia, by the Rev. Clinton Locke, D.D., in Chicago. So. Ch., Oct. 16, 1879

PAXTON
John, Esq., of Scottsburg, Halifax Co., Va., and Rebecca Robinson, by the Rev. Charles Randolph,

MARRIAGE NOTICES IN THE SOUTHERN CHURCHMAN WITH DATES OF PUBLICATION

at the residence of Starkey Robinson, Esq., at Shepherd's Island, Botetourt Co., Va. So. Ch., Mar. 1, 1883

PAYNE

Bettie W., eldest d. of Dr. Allen S. Payne, and Gen. L. L. Lomax, by the Rev. Kinsloch Nelson, at Markham Station, Fauquier Co., Va. So. Ch., Feb. 27, 1873

Cornelia C., d. of Col. Samuel S. Payne, and John L. Boyden, by the Rev. P. M. Boyden assisted by the Rev. Oscar Bunting, at Mountain Home, Amherst Co., Va. So. Ch., Sept. 11, 1879

Erva W., and Eppa Hunton, Jr., both of Warrenton, Va., by the Rev. George W. Nelson assisted by the Rev. John S. Lindsay, D.D., in St. James' Church, Warrenton, Va. So. Ch., Jan. 1, 1885

Fairinda C., and Charles W. Forster of South Carolina, by the Rev. Dr. Pendleton, in Grace Church, Lexington, Va. So. Ch., Nov. 27, 1879

Florence A., d. of Mrs. S. V. Payne of St. Louis, Mo., and the Rev. Joseph A. Graves of Raymond, Miss., by the Rev. John G. Shepperson, at the residence of Dr. Hairston, Franklin Co., Va. So. Ch., Jan. 4, 1877

George (Dr.), of Scottsville, Albemarle, and Catherine, d. of Capt. E. Penn, by the Rev. Mr. Sale, at Laneville, Amherst Co. So. Ch., Oct. 25, 1839

James F., of Virginia, and Emily, only d. of Alexander MacRae, Esq., by the Rev. T. M. Ambler of Wilmington, at Argyle, the residence of the bride's father, Robeson Co., N.C. So. Ch., Nov. 19, 1874

John, D.D., (The Rt. Rev.), of King George Co., Va., missionary appointed by the Episcopal Church to Cape Palmas, Africa, and Anna Matilda Barroll, by the Rev. C. F. Jones, in Chestertown, Md. So. Ch., Apr. 21, 1837

John (Rt. Rev.), D.D., and Martha Williford, by the Rev. C. C. Hoffman, at Covalla, West Africa. So. Ch., Oct. 15, 1858

Mollie C., of Roanoke, and Robert McClelland of Chattanooga, by the Rev. Edward H. Ingle, at the residence of J. M. Terry, Esq., in Roanoke Co. So. Ch., Oct. 29, 1868

William T., of Georgetown, D.C., and Priscila Richards, d. of James Entwisle, Sr. of Alexandria, Va., by the Rev. D. F. Sprigg, in Grace Church. So. Ch., Dec. 17, 1858

PEABODY

Douglass C. (The Rev.), of Atlanta, Ga., and Eliza S. Hall of Portland, by the Rev. Dr. Emery, former rector of the parish, assisted by the Rev. James F. Spaulding, in Trinity Church, Portland. So. Ch., Feb. 3, 1876

PEACE

Washington, Jr., of Watha,

MARRIAGE NOTICES IN THE SOUTHERN CHURCHMAN WITH DATES OF PUBLICATION

N.C., and Mollie Brockinton, at West Andrews, S.C. So. Ch., June 4, 1910
Washington F., of Warrenton, Va., and Nannie M. Baron Fitzhugh of Culpeper, Va., by the Rev. C. O. Pruden, at the residence of the bride's brother, Wm. F. Fitzhugh, in Pittsylvania Co., Va. So. Ch., Feb. 19, 1885

PEACHY
Augusta, youngest d. of the late John Peachy, and Conway Barksdale, all of Amelia Co., by the Rev. P. F. Berkeley, in the parish church of Raleigh Parish. So. Ch., May 4, 1860
Mary Blair, eldest d. of the late John Peachy of Florida, and Lt. John Wilkinson of U.S. Navy, by the Rev. P. Berkeley, at Osmore, the residence of Mrs. Banister, in Amelia Co. So. Ch., Jan. 15, 1858

PEACOCK
Elizabeth C., oldest d. of James Peacock, Esq., and the Rev. Charles Vernon Kelly, rector of St. Stephen's Church, all of Harrisburg, Pa., by the Rt. Rev. H. V. Onderdonk. So. Ch., Jan. 25, 1839

PEARCE
George B., of Key Port, N.J., and Rosa Sargent formerly of New York, by the Rev. H. L. Derby, in Bethel Church, Lancaster Co. So. Ch., Oct. 24, 1878
Thomas Butler, III (Lt.), of Quantico Marine Base, Va., and Frances Robertson, only d. of Mr. and Mrs. Eugene Bates Smith of Greenville, S.C., by the Rev. Sam B. Chilton, in Trinity Episcopal Church, Fredericksburg, Va. So. Ch., Oct. 4, 1941
Washington, Esq., and Eliza W., d. of the late George Fitzhugh, Esq., by the Rev. J. Cole, at Milton, Culpeper Co., Va. So. Ch., June 27, 1856

PECK
Francis (The Rev.), rector of the Church of the Ascension, Baltimore, and Francis* Augustie Folix of San Andres, Island of Cuba, by the Rev. Mr. Guion, at Kensington, Conn. So. Ch., Sept. 17, 1847

PEDIN
James W., of Suffolk, Va., and Ellen P., d. of Richard H. Whitlock of Richmond, by the Rev. H. S. Kepler. So. Ch., Apr. 25, 1856

PEEK
Thomas C., of New York City, and M. Maude Ligon of Nelson Co., Va., by the Rev. J. W. Ware, at the residence of the bride's father. So. Ch., Dec. 29, 1881

PEGRAM
Anne Clifton, d. of Edward S. Pegram of Albemarle Co., Va., and John Harrison of Sussex Co., by the Rev. E. Boyden, at Cismont, the residence of Mrs. Frances W. Meriwether. So. Ch., Nov. 28, 1872
Blair, Esq., and Minerva J., d. of John Wilson, Esq., by the Rev. John

---

* Given as printed

MARRIAGE NOTICES IN THE SOUTHERN CHURCHMAN WITH DATES OF PUBLICATION

C. McCabe, at Woodland, Surry Co., Va. So. Ch., June 21, 1855

Geo. E., formerly of Albemarle Co., Va., and Lizziedelle, d. of the late Dr. Shepherd Laurie of Little Rock, Ark., by the Rev. F. R. Hanson, in Demopolis, Ala. So. Ch., May 12, 1870

Mary E., d. of the late Gen. James W. Pegram, and Gen. Jos. R. Anderson of Richmond, Va., by the Rev. William Dame, at the residence of D. G. McIntosh, Towsontown. So. Ch., Nov. 9, 1882

Virginia J., of Richmond, and Col. D. G. McIntosh of South Carolina, by the Rev. Charles Minnigerode, D.D., at Linden Square, Richmond, Va. So. Ch., Nov. 30, 1865

PEIRCE
C. T. (Dr.), of Lancaster Co., and Elizabeth Edmington Combs, by the Rev. L. R. Combs, father of the bride, assisted by the Rev. W. M. Clark of St. James' Church, Richmond, in Trinity Church, Lancaster Co., Va. So. Ch., Mar. 23, 1907

PEMBERTON
Mary, eldest d. of the late John Pemberton of Goochland, and Alexander Malem Hobson of Richmond City, by the Rev. Francis M. Whittle, in Goochland Co. So. Ch., Feb. 13, 1851

Mary E., d. of Col. John A. Pemberton, and E. T. B. Glenn, principal clerk of the C. F. & Y. V. R. R., by the Rev. C. J. Huske, D.D., at Fayetteville, N.C. So. Ch., Jan. 3, 1884

Pattie, d. of Gen. John C. Pemberton of Fauquier Co., Va., and Dr. Jno. C. Baylor of Norfolk, Va., by the Rev. John S. Lindsay, in St. James' Church, Warrenton, Va. So. Ch., Jan. 15, 1874

Thomas, of Goochland Co., Va., and Mary E., d. of C. W. Macmurdo of Alexandria, Va., by the Rev. George W. Woodbridge. So. Ch., Dec. 14, 1855

V. R., and George T. Patton, both formerly of Ashland, Va., by the Rev. Mr. Chapham assisted by the Rev. J. L. Patton, at Bakersfield, Cal. So. Ch., Dec. 25, 1890

See also HOBSON, Virginia K.

PENDLETON
Agnes Roy, and Edward Christian, by the Rev. E. Meade, in St. John's Church, Tappahannock, Va. So. Ch., Jan. 7, 1886

Dudley D. (Capt.), and Helen M., d. of the Hon. Alexander R. Boteler, by the Rev. Charles W. Andrews, D.D., in Trinity Church, Sphepherdstown.* So. Ch., May 3, 1866

Ellie S., d. of Mrs. Henrietta R. Pendleton of Fauquier Co., and L. B. Perry Ayscough of England, by the Rev. E. S. Hinks, in Emmanuel Church, Fauquier Co. So. Ch., Sept. 29, 1892

Emma W., and Robert C. Little, both formerly of Richmond, Va., at the

---

* Possibly Shepherdstown, W.Va.

MARRIAGE NOTICES IN THE SOUTHERN CHURCHMAN WITH DATES OF PUBLICATION

residence of the bride's brother, S. H. Pendleton, in Elizabeth, N.J. So. Ch., Sept. 14, 1882

Gurdon H., of Jefferson Co., and Jane Byrd, d. of Mann R. Page, Esq., by the Rev. Francis M. Whittle, at Mannsfield, Clarke Co., Va. So. Ch., May 25, 1854

Julia Nelson, only d. of Hugh N. Pendleton of Jefferson, and James W. Allen of Bedford, by the Rev. Mr. Pendleton, at Westwood. So. Ch., Mar. 28, 1856

Kate C., and Capt. John M. Brooke of Virginia Military Institute, by the Rev. M. Maury, in St. George's Episcopal Church, Fredericksburg, Va. So. Ch., Mar. 30, 1871

Lolla Page, d. of the late Rev. Dr. Pendleton, and Edward Miles Gadsen of Washington, D.C., by the Rev. Frank Page and the Rev. Robert J. McBryde, D.D., rector of the parish, at the residence of the bride's family, Lexington, Va. So. Ch., Feb. 19, 1885

Lewis S. (Dr.), and Anne F. Kean, both of Louisa Co., Va., by the Rev. H. P. R. McCoy, at the residence of the bride's father. So. Ch., Feb. 20, 1873

Lizzie C., and Dr. Walter Coles of St. Louis, by the Rev. E. W. Hubard, in Trinity Church, Buchanan, Va. So. Ch., July 18, 1872

Martha C., formerly of Richmond, Va., and Joseph M. Fourqurean of Richmond, Va., by the Rev. Robert Lowry, in Trinity Church, Elizabeth, N.J. So. Ch., Mar. 2, 1871

Mildred Edmonia, and Tasker Carter Crabb, by the Rev. Andrew Fisher, at Warsaw, Richmond Co. So. Ch., Oct. 31, 1867

Robert G., of Clarke Co., and Sophie R. Rust of Westmoreland, Va., by the Rev. Wm. C. Latane, in St. Peter's Church, Oak Grove, Va. So. Ch., Nov. 19, 1885

Virginia M., of Clarke Co., Va., and Chas. Harvey, publisher of "Our Church Work", Baltimore, by the Rev. T. F. Martin assisted by the Rev. Hugh Roy Scott, at the residence of the bride's father, T. P. Pendleton, Esq. So. Ch., Nov. 13, 1873

William Walter, Esq., formerly of Louisa Co. but now of Clifton Forge, Va., and Mary Blanche, eldest d. of George W. Cargill, Esq. of Winfield, Putnam Co., W.Va., by the Rev. R. A. Cobbs of Charleston, at the residence of the bride's father. So. Ch., Nov. 13, 1884

Willie D., only d. of Dr. J. D. Pendleton, and J. Morton Spence, Esq. of Bedford City, by the Rev. F. G. Scott, in Christ Church, Gordonsville. So. Ch., Jan. 14, 1892

PENICK
E. A. (The Rev.), rector of the parish, and May R.,

MARRIAGE NOTICES IN THE SOUTHERN CHURCHMAN WITH DATES OF PUBLICATION

d. of George B. Shipman, by the Rt. Rev. Thomas U. Dudley, D.D., Bishop of Kentucky, assisted by the Rt. Rev. C. C. Penick, D.D., rector of St. Andrew's Parish, Louisville, in the Church of the Ascension, Frankfort, Ky. So. Ch., Nov. 6, 1884

Maurice H., and Louisa R. Easley, by the Rev. O. A. Kinsolving, D.D., at "Wilbon", near South Boston, Halifax Co., Va. So. Ch., Oct. 8, 1885

PENICKE
Charles Clifton, D.D., (The Rt. Rev.), Bishop of Cape Palmas and Parts Adjacent, West Africa, and Mary, d. of the late Isaac Hoge of Wheeling, by the Rt. Rev. George W. Peterkin, D.D. assisted by the Rev. P. R. Swope, at the residence of the bride's mother, Wheeling, W.Va. So. Ch., May 5, 1881

PENN
Catherine, d. of Capt. E. Penn, and Dr. George Payne of Scottsville, Albemarle, by the Rev. Mr. Sale, at Lanevillo, Amherst Co. So. Ch., Oct. 25, 1839

George E., Esq., and Estelle, eldest d. of Jas. H. Gilmore, Esq., all of Marion, Smyth Co., by the Rev. Robb White, in Christ Church, Marion, Smyth Co. So. Ch., Jan. 13, 1876

PENNINGTON
Edgar L. (The Rev.), rector of Holy Cross Church, Miami, Fla., and Gertrude Guerry Barnett, by Bishop Wing of South Florida, in St. Barnabas' Church, DeLand, Fla. So. Ch., July 6, 1940

PENROSE
Ellen Swann, d. of the late John R. Penrose of Philadelphia, and Ferdinand C. Latrobe of Baltimore, by the Rev. J. Andrew Harris, at "Hillside", the residence of the bride's mother, Chestnut Hill, Philadelphia. So. Ch., July 15, 1880

Wilkinson (Lt.), C.S.A., of New Orleans, and Jenny V., d. of the late John H. Butler of Norfolk, Va., by the Rev. Wm. C. Butler, in Norfolk, Va. So. Ch., Mar. 7, 1862

PEPPER
William Platt, of Philadelphia, and Alice, eldest d. of George T. Lyman of Bellport, L.I., by the Rev. Morgan Dix, D.D., in Trinity Chapel, New York. So. Ch., May 15, 1879

PERCHER
Julius T., of South Carolina, and Mary Fanning, d. of the late E. F. Wickham, by the Rev. Mr. Peterkin, at the residence of W. F. Wickham, Hanover Co. So. Ch., Feb. 6, 1857

PERDICARIS
Gregory A., native of Greece and formerly professor in Washington College, Hartford, Conn., and M. E. Hanford of Society Hill, S.C., by the Rev. Mr. Forme,

MARRIAGE NOTICES IN THE SOUTHERN CHURCHMAN WITH DATES OF PUBLICATION

at Cheraw, S.C. So. Ch., June 2, 1837

PERKINS
Hardin, and Jane Ann, d. of the late Capt. Benjamin Harriss, by the Rev. Isaac Paul, at Mountain Grove, Albemarle Co., Va. So. Ch., May 29, 1835

Ida A., of Louisville, d. of the officiating minister, and Dr. Chas. G. Edwards, Leesburg, Va., by the Rev. E. T. Perkins, in St. Paul's Church, Louisville, Ky. So. Ch., Dec. 19, 1872

Joseph, Esq., of Albemarle, and Sallie C. Maupin, by the Rev. Wm. M. Nelson, at the residence of the bride's mother, Mrs. Sarah M. Maupin, Albemarle Co., Va. So. Ch., Dec. 10, 1868

Louisa H., and Hugh Johnson, Esq., both of Cumberland Co., Va., by the Rev. Wm. Hoxton, at Forkland, the residence of Wm. A. Perkins. So. Ch., Jan. 16, 1873

Mary A., of Cumberland Co., Va., and Capt. H. G. Richardson of Farmville, Va., by the Rev. Wm. Hoxton, at Forkland, the residence of Wm. A. Perkins. So. Ch., Jan. 16, 1873

Mary Sydnor, youngest d. of the officiating clergyman, and Walter Walker, by the Rev. E. T. Perkins, D.D., in St. Paul's Church, Louisville. So. Ch., May 31, 1883

Samuel R., of Richmond, and Kate, youngest d. of A. G. Elam, Esq. of Chesterfield Co., Va., by the Rev. A. B. Tizzard, at the residence of the bride's parents. So. Ch., Sept. 9, 1880

PEROE
Leonora, and J. Edward Creery, both of Richmond, in Christ Church, Richmond, Va. So. Ch., May 3, 1877

PERRIN
Elizabeth (Mrs.), formerly of England, and Lewis B. Giles, by the Rev. H. L. Derby, in St. Paul's Church, Suffolk, Va. So. Ch., Nov. 7, 1889

PERRY
George P., and Ida M. Smith, both of Henrico Co., Va., by the Rev. R. S. Barrett, in Richmond, Va. So. Ch., Nov. 22, 1877

J. B. (The Rev.), of South Carolina, and Fannie E., d. of the Rev. D. F. Sprigg, by the Rev. Dr. Norton assisted by the Rev. Dr. Lewin, in Alexandria. So. Ch., Jan. 18, 1877

James De Wolf, Jr. (The Rev.), s. of the Rt. Rev. James De Wolf Perry of the Diocese of Rhode Island, and Adela Carter, d. of Mr. and Mrs. John Haigh Daingerfield of Norfolk, by the bridegroom's father assisted by the rector, the Rev. W. Taylor Willis, in Christ and St. Luke's Church. So. Ch., Oct. 7, 1939

Lavinia, and Dr. Wm. W. Green, both of Franklin Co., N.C., by the Rev.

MARRIAGE NOTICES IN THE SOUTHERN CHURCHMAN WITH DATES OF PUBLICATION

P. D. Thompson, at the residence of Charles Perry, Esq. So. Ch., Aug. 19, 1869

M. Louisa, d. of the Hon. Thomas Perry, and Dr. W. F. Lippitt of Washington, D.C., by the Rev. E. R. Lippitt, at Cumberland, Md. So. Ch., Nov. 18, 1859

Van Lear, M.D., of Cumberland, Md., and Elizabeth M., eldest d. of the officiating minister, the Rev. C. J. Gibson, in Grace Church, Petersburg, Va. So. Ch., Oct. 2, 1863

Wm. E., and Lucy Powers, both of Stafford Co., Va., by the Rev. Robert S. Barrett, at the residence of the bride's mother. So. Ch., Feb. 22, 1877

William H., of Lunenburg Co., and Rebecca C. Marshall of Fauquier Co., Va., by the Rev. Alexander Overby, rector, in the Church of the Holy Innocents, Burkeville, Va. So. Ch., Nov. 13, 1890

PERRY-AYSCOUGH
L. B., of England, and Ellie S., d. of Mrs. Henrietta R. Pendleton of Fauquier Co., by the Rev. E. S. Hinks, in Emmanuel Church, Fauquier Co. So. Ch., Sept. 29, 1892

PERSON
Samuel J. (The Hon.), of Wilmington, N.C., Judge of Superior Court of that state, and Ellen, only d. of the late Rev. Joseph D. Tyler, principal of the Institution for the Education of the Deaf and Dumb at Staunton, Va., by the Rev. C. B. Dana of Alexandria, in Trinity Church, Staunton. So. Ch., June 25, 1858

PERVIS
Mary Earle, d. of the late Wm. Pervis of Mobile, Ala., and Chas. S. Taylor, Jr. of Alexandria, by the Rev. Edward H. Ingle, at Salem, Roanoke Co., Va. So. Ch., Nov. 15, 1877

PETERKIN
Elizabeth Spencer, d. of William S. Peterkin of Baltimore, and Dr. John N. Upshur, by the Rt. Rev. Geo. William Peterkin, D.D., in Richmond, Va. So. Ch., Dec. 18, 1879

Geo. W. (The Rev.), of Richmond, and Constance Gardner, d. of Cassius F. Lee, Esq., by the Rev. Dr. Peterkin, at Menokin, Fairfax Co., Va. So. Ch., Nov. 5, 1868

George W., D.D. (The Rt. Rev.), Bishop of West Virginia, and Marion Macintosh, d. of John Stewart, Esq. of Brook Hill, near Richmond, by the Rev. Dr. Norwood, rector of the church, assisted by the Rev. Dr. Peterkin, in Emmanuel Church, Henrico Co., Va. So. Ch., June 19, 1884

PETERS
Kate J., d. of Maj. S. T. Peters, and Dr. Frank A. Lee of Lynchburg, Va., by the Rev. W. L. Dolly, at "Delacarlia", in Bedford Co., Va. So. Ch., Oct. 8, 1891

Mattie W., and Legh R. Watts, Esq., both of

MARRIAGE NOTICES IN THE SOUTHERN CHURCHMAN WITH DATES OF PUBLICATION

at Cheraw, S.C. So. Ch., June 2, 1837

PERKINS
  Hardin, and Jane Ann, d. of the late Capt. Benjamin Harriss, by the Rev. Isaac Paul, at Mountain Grove, Albemarle Co., Va. So. Ch., May 29, 1835
  Ida A., of Louisville, d. of the officiating minister, and Dr. Chas. G. Edwards, Leesburg, Va., by the Rev. E. T. Perkins, in St. Paul's Church, Louisville, Ky. So. Ch., Dec. 19, 1872
  Joseph, Esq., of Albemarle, and Sallie C. Maupin, by the Rev. Wm. M. Nelson, at the residence of the bride's mother, Mrs. Sarah M. Maupin, Albemarle Co., Va. So. Ch., Dec. 10, 1868
  Louisa H., and Hugh Johnson, Esq., both of Cumberland Co., Va., by the Rev. Wm. Hoxton, at Forkland, the residence of Wm. A. Perkins. So. Ch., Jan. 16, 1873
  Mary A., of Cumberland Co., Va., and Capt. H. G. Richardson of Farmville, Va., by the Rev. Wm. Hoxton, at Forkland, the residence of Wm. A. Perkins. So. Ch., Jan. 16, 1873
  Mary Sydnor, youngest d. of the officiating clergyman, and Walter Walker, by the Rev. E. T. Perkins, D.D., in St. Paul's Church, Louisville. So. Ch., May 31, 1883
  Samuel R., of Richmond, and Kate, youngest d. of A. G. Elam, Esq. of Chesterfield Co., Va., by the Rev. A. B. Tizzard, at the residence of the bride's parents. So. Ch., Sept. 9, 1880

PEROE
  Leonora, and J. Edward Creery, both of Richmond, in Christ Church, Richmond, Va. So. Ch., May 3, 1877

PERRIN
  Elizabeth (Mrs.), formerly of England, and Lewis B. Giles, by the Rev. H. L. Derby, in St. Paul's Church, Suffolk, Va. So. Ch., Nov. 7, 1889

PERRY
  George P., and Ida M. Smith, both of Henrico Co., Va., by the Rev. R. S. Barrett, in Richmond, Va. So. Ch., Nov. 22, 1877
  J. B. (The Rev.), of South Carolina, and Fannie E., d. of the Rev. D. F. Sprigg, by the Rev. Dr. Norton assisted by the Rev. Dr. Lewin, in Alexandria. So. Ch., Jan. 18, 1877
  James De Wolf, Jr. (The Rev.), s. of the Rt. Rev. James De Wolf Perry of the Diocese of Rhode Island, and Adela Carter, d. of Mr. and Mrs. John Haigh Daingerfield of Norfolk, by the bridegroom's father assisted by the rector, the Rev. W. Taylor Willis, in Christ and St. Luke's Church. So. Ch., Oct. 7, 1939
  Lavinia, and Dr. Wm. W. Green, both of Franklin Co., N.C., by the Rev.

MARRIAGE NOTICES IN THE SOUTHERN CHURCHMAN WITH DATES OF PUBLICATION

P. D. Thompson, at the residence of Charles Perry, Esq. So. Ch., Aug. 19, 1869

M. Louisa, d. of the Hon. Thomas Perry, and Dr. W. F. Lippitt of Washington, D.C., by the Rev. E. R. Lippitt, at Cumberland, Md. So. Ch., Nov. 18, 1859

Van Lear, M.D., of Cumberland, Md., and Elizabeth M., eldest d. of the officiating minister, the Rev. C. J. Gibson, in Grace Church, Petersburg, Va. So. Ch., Oct. 2, 1863

Wm. E., and Lucy Powers, both of Stafford Co., Va., by the Rev. Robert S. Barrett, at the residence of the bride's mother. So. Ch., Feb. 22, 1877

William H., of Lunenburg Co., and Rebecca C. Marshall of Fauquier Co., Va., by the Rev. Alexander Overby, rector, in the Church of the Holy Innocents, Burkeville, Va. So. Ch., Nov. 13, 1890

PERRY-AYSCOUGH

L. B., of England, and Ellie S., d. of Mrs. Henrietta R. Pendleton of Fauquier Co., by the Rev. E. S. Hinks, in Emmanuel Church, Fauquier Co. So. Ch., Sept. 29, 1892

PERSON

Samuel J. (The Hon.), of Wilmington, N.C., Judge of Superior Court of that state, and Ellen, only d. of the late Rev. Joseph D. Tyler, principal of the Institution for the Education of the Deaf and Dumb at Staunton, Va., by the Rev. C. B. Dana of Alexandria, in Trinity Church, Staunton. So. Ch., June 25, 1858

PERVIS

Mary Earle, d. of the late Wm. Pervis of Mobile, Ala., and Chas. S. Taylor, Jr. of Alexandria, by the Rev. Edward H. Ingle, at Salem, Roanoke Co., Va. So. Ch., Nov. 15, 1877

PETERKIN

Elizabeth Spencer, d. of William S. Peterkin of Baltimore, and Dr. John N. Upshur, by the Rt. Rev. Geo. William Peterkin, D.D., in Richmond, Va. So. Ch., Dec. 18, 1879

Geo. W. (The Rev.), of Richmond, and Constance Gardner, d. of Cassius F. Lee, Esq., by the Rev. Dr. Peterkin, at Menokin, Fairfax Co., Va. So. Ch., Nov. 5, 1868

George W., D.D. (The Rt. Rev.), Bishop of West Virginia, and Marion Macintosh, d. of John Stewart, Esq. of Brook Hill, near Richmond, by the Rev. Dr. Norwood, rector of the church, assisted by the Rev. Dr. Peterkin, in Emmanuel Church, Henrico Co., Va. So. Ch., June 19, 1884

PETERS

Kate J., d. of Maj. S. T. Peters, and Dr. Frank A. Lee of Lynchburg, Va., by the Rev. W. L. Dolly, at "Delacarlia", in Bedford Co., Va. So. Ch., Oct. 8, 1891

Mattie W., and Legh R. Watts, Esq., both of

MARRIAGE NOTICES IN THE SOUTHERN CHURCHMAN WITH DATES OF PUBLICATION

Portsmouth, Va., by the Rev. R. H. McKim, at the residence of the bride's father. So. Ch., Dec. 3, 1868

Thomas McClure (The Rev.), and Alice Clarissa, d. of the Rev. William Richmond, the officiating minister, in St. Michael's Church, Bloomingdale. So. Ch., July 16, 1847

PETERSON
Eri R. L. (The Rev.), late Roman Catholic Priest received into the Episcopal Ministry by Bishop Whittle of Minnesota, and Anna S. Huss of Chicago, by the Rev. Henry G. Perry, in All Saints' Church, Chicago. So. Ch., Dec. 25, 1873

John A., Jr., of Prince George Co., and Mary R. F., d. of the late Robert Epes of Prince George Co., by the Rev. A. B. Tizzard, in Petersburg, Va. So. Ch., May 18, 1854

Richard H., Esq., and Mary Ella, d. of the late John Marks, Esq., all of Prince George, by the Rev. R. P. Johnson, at Old Town, Prince George Co., Va. So. Ch., Nov. 5, 1853

PETRIC
Eva, and W. Stanley Hamilton, a native of Culpeper Co., Va., both of Jackson, Miss., by the Rev. John Hunter, at the residence of the bride's mother, Jackson, Miss. So. Ch., Feb. 3, 1876

PETTIGREW
Thomas (Maj.), formerly of North Carolina, now resident of West Virginia, and Mary Thomazine, second d. of D. M. Bailey, Esq., cashier of National Exchange Bank of Weston, by the Rev. T. H. Lacy, at the residence of the bride's parents, Weston, W.Va. So. Ch., Feb. 5, 1891

PETTITT
Alice V., and J. Cannon Hobson, both of Goochland Co., Va., by the Rev. P. M. Boyden, at Hebron, Goochland Co., Va. So. Ch., June 5, 1879

PETTUS
John C. (Prof.), late of Iuka, Miss., and Emma J. Turner of Richmond, Va., by the Rev. H. McDonald. So. Ch., July 28, 1881

PEYTON
Agatha Garnett, d. of Col. Wm. M. Peyton, and Walter Preston, Esq. of Abingdon, Washington Co., Va., by the Rev. W. H. Pendleton, at Elmwood, the residence of Col. Wm. M. Peyton. So. Ch., Sept. 27, 1855

Bernard Joseph, d. of the late Col. William M. Peyton formerly of Roanoke Co., now of Albemarle, and Charles Marshall Llewellyn, by the Rev. T. E. Locke, at the residence of the bride's mother, at Altavista. So. Ch., Dec. 14, 1871

John Lewis, Esq., of Staunton, Va., and Betty, d. of John C. Washington, Esq. of Vernon, by the Rev. Frederick Fitzgerald, at Vernon, Lenoir Co., N.C.

MARRIAGE NOTICES IN THE SOUTHERN CHURCHMAN WITH DATES OF PUBLICATION

So. Ch., Jan. 4, 1856
Lucy Garnett, d. of the late John H. Peyton, Esq., and John H. Henderson, Esq., by the Rev. T. T. Castleman, at Staunton, Va. So. Ch., Jan. 4, 1856
Robert E., Jr., and Carrie G. Foster, by the Rev. Jno. McGill, in Trinity Church, Salem, Fauquier. So. Ch., Apr. 28, 1870
Wm. M., of Albemarle Co., and Nannie H., third d. of the Rev. C. Mann, by the Rev. Wm. G. Jackson, D.D. of Maryland, in Ware Church. So. Ch., Nov. 10, 1870

PFAFFKO
Arthur G. W. (The Rev.), rector of the Church of the Transfiguration, Blue Ridge Summit, Pa. and founder of the Greek Letter societies, Pi Alpha and Tau Delta Alpha, and Sarah Catherine Mc-Clain, by the Rev. Dr. S. Tagart Steele, vicar of the Intercession, in the Chapel of the Intercession, Trinity Parish, New York City. So. Ch., Oct. 18, 1941

PHAUP
Fannie, d. of A. A. Phaup, of Chesterfield Co., Va., and James W. Smart, Esq. of London, England, by the Rev. A. B. Tizzard, at the residence of the bride's parents. So. Ch., Sept. 17, 1891

PHELPS
E. Randolph, and Sally B. Field, by the Rev. Everard Meade, at Walnut Grove, Greensville Co., Va. So. Ch., Nov. 17, 1892

Judith Brockenbrough, d. of the late Jefferson Phelps of Covington, Ky. and gr.d. of the late Judge Wm. Brockenbrough of Richmond, Va., and Capt. Jas. McIntosh of the U.S. Army, by the Rev. R. T. Davis, in Trinity Church, Martinsburg, Va. So. Ch., Mar. 4, 1859

PHENIX
Lucy, and William A. Warner, by the Rev. Dr. Grammer assisted by the Rev. Mr. Kaze, at the home of Joseph A. Sprigg, Baltimore. So. Ch., Nov. 8, 1877

PHILIPS
Victoria E., d. of the late John Philips, Esq. of Fauquier Co., Va., and James M. Morris of Louisa Co., by the Rev. J. Earnest, at Meador Farm, the residence of Erasmus Taylor, Esq. So. Ch., Dec. 14, 1860

PHILLIPS
A. K., Esq., of Fredericksburg, and Annie Douglass, d. of Col. Hamilton Rodgers of Loudoun Co., by the Rev. Mr. Kinsolving, at Oakham. So. Ch., Mar. 2, 1860
Agnes Grey, eldest d. of the officiating clergyman, and Lt. Randolph McKim, P.A.C.S.* of Baltimore, by the Rev. R. H. Phillips assisted by the Rev. J. A. Latane, in Trinity Church, Staunton, Va. So. Ch., Mar. 20, 1863
D. B., (Surgeon U.S.N.), and Mary Frances, d. of Wm. Walden, Esq., all

* Provisional Army Confederate States

MARRIAGE NOTICES IN THE SOUTHERN CHURCHMAN WITH DATES OF PUBLICATION

of Virginia, by the Rev. Wm. T. Leavell, at Glen Farm, Rappahannock Co., Va. So. Ch., Mar. 13, 1857

Donald (Lt.), and Mary N. R. Gunnell, by the Rev. J. P. H. Mason, rector of St. Martin's Parish,* and the Rev. James W. Morris of the Epiphany Church, Washington, D.C., at Oakland, Hanover Co., Va. So. Ch., Aug. 18, 1928

James, Esq., of Greensville Co., Va., and Bettie Buford, by the Rev. Otis A. Glazebrook, at the residence of the bride's mother in Brunswick. So. Ch., May 4, 1871

Joe, d. of the late Col. Joe Phillips, Confederate States Army, of Hampton, Va., and J. E. B. Stuart, Jr. of Larned, Kan., formerly of Virginia, by the Rev. J. J. Gravatt assisted by the Rev. Mr. Meade, in St. John's Church, Hampton, Va. So. Ch., July 29, 1886

Julia Ann, d. of Samuel Phillips, Esq. of Fredericksburg, Va., and Dr. Thomas J. McGill of Jefferson, Mo., by the Rev. Richard H. Phillips. So. Ch., Dec. 15, 1837

Nannie D., d. of A. K. Phillips, Esq., and Courtland H. Smith of Alexandria, by the Rev. J. R. Mason, at the residence of the bride's father, in Fredericksburg. So. Ch., May 2, 1889

P. P. (The Rev.), rector of Grace Church, Berryville, Va., and Edith, d. of James L. Norris of Washington, by the Rev. B. Sunderland, D.D. and the Rev. Dallas Tucker, rector of Zion Church, Charleston, W.Va. So. Ch., Feb. 9, 1893

Sally Hewes, d. of the Rev. Z. B. Phillips, D.D., rector of Epiphany Church and chaplain of the Senate of the United States, and Robert W. McClenahan of Chestnut Hill, Philadelphia, by the bride's father, the Rev. Z. B. Phillips, in Epiphany Church, Washington, D.C. So. Ch., Jan. 27, 1934

Wiley R., and Elizabeth C. McCrindle, both of Richmond, by the Rev. D. F. Sprigg, in Richmond, Va. So. Ch., Mar. 3, 1881

PHILPOT
Harry T., and Esther W. Swenson, by the Rev. W. H. Pettis, in St. James' Church, West Somerville, Mass. So. Ch., May 10, 1913

PHIPPS
Sarah, and the Rev. R. Knight, missionary for Frampton, by the Rt. Rev. the Lord Bishop of Montreal, at Quebec. So. Ch., Apr. 26, 1839

PICKERELL
J. M., U.S.N., of Richmond, Va., and Evaline Putnam, at Honolulu, H.I. So. Ch., July 11, 1889

PICKETT
George, of Richmond, and Artelia Morgan of Amelia

---

* St. Martin's Parish is in Hanover County, Virginia (<u>Journal ... Diocese of Virginia</u>, Richmond, Va., 1941)

MARRIAGE NOTICES IN THE SOUTHERN CHURCHMAN WITH DATES OF PUBLICATION

Co., by the Rev. P. F. Berkeley, at the residence of the bride's father. So. Ch., Feb. 19, 1874

PICKRELL
Daniel Sprigg, and Helen A., d. of the late Gov. Charles Manly of North Carolina, by the Rev. J. B. Perry, in Washington. So. Ch., Oct. 11, 1888

Ida, d. of John F. and the late Violetta Pickrell, and Lt. Victor M. Bridgeman, U.S.A., by the Rev. J. B. Perry, in Washington, D.C. So. Ch., Oct. 6, 1887

Kate K., of Alexandria, Va., and Noble Dement of Charles Co., Md., by the Rev. J. T. Johnston. So. Ch., Jan. 11, 1856

PIERCE
Geo. H. (Dr.), and Jane B., d. of the late Thomas B. Hammond of Jefferson, by the Rev. C. E. Ambler, in the Episcopal Church, Charles Town. So. Ch., Oct. 17, 1856

Roberta, of New Kent Co., Va., and Joseph Veal of Rome, Ga., by the Rev. John P. Tyler assisted by the Rev. C. J. Gibson, in Petersburg, Va. So. Ch., May 29, 1890

PIERREPONT
Frances Matilda, d. of the late H. B. Pierrepont, and the Rev. Frederick S. Wiley, rector of Grace Church, Honesdale, by the Rev. Dr. Cutler, in St. Anne's Church, Brooklyn. So. Ch., Nov. 1, 1849

PILLAR
John, and Martha Ann, d. of David Smith of Lunenburg, by the Rev. Thomas E. Locke. So. Ch., July 5, 1839

PINCKNEY
Thomas, of Charleston, S.C., and Mary, d. of Jno. Stewart, Esq. of Brook Hill, by the rector, the Rev. Wm. Norwood, D.D., in Emmanuel Church, Henrico Parish. So. Ch., May 12, 1870

Thomas, and Camilla, d. of the late Robert E. Scott of Fauquier Co., Va., by the Rev. John K. Mason, D.D., at the residence of Maj. R. Taylor Scott, Warrenton, Va. So. Ch., July 21, 1892

PINNER
Arthur J., and Nannie T., d. of Benjamin C. Eley, all of Chuckatuck, Va., by the Rev. Douglass Hooff, at the residence of the bride's father. So. Ch., Dec. 27, 1883

M. Filmore, and Mary MacRea, both of Chuckatuck, Nansemond Co., Va., by the Rev. Douglass Hooff, at home. So. Ch., Dec. 6, 1883

PLAIN
M. M. (Mrs.), and J. P. Jordan, both of Alexandria, Va., by Elder Wm. J. Purrington of Washington, in Alexandria, Va. So. Ch., Nov. 1, 1866

PLATT
Franklin, Esq., of Newark, Del., and Ella A. B., d. of the late Richard J.

MARRIAGE NOTICES IN THE SOUTHERN CHURCHMAN WITH DATES OF PUBLICATION

Foard, Esq. of Bohemia
Manor, by the Rev. Jno.
Collins McCabe, D.D.,
rector of St. Ann's
Church, Middletown, Del.,
in St. Augustine Church,
Bohemia Manor, Md. So.
Ch., Feb. 3, 1870
William H. (The Rev.),
rector of St. Paul's
Church, Petersburg, and
Eleanor B., d. of the
late John E. Meade of
Prince George Co., Va.,
by the Rt. Rev. J. Johns,
D.D., Assistant Bishop
of Virginia, at the
residence of David
Callender, Esq., in
Petersburg. So. Ch.,
July 3, 1857
Wm. H. (The Rev.), rector
of Calvary Church,
Louisville, Ky., and
Mrs. Indiana Pannill,
d. of the late Hon.
Richard K. Meade, by
the Rev. C. J. Gibson,
in St. Paul's Church,
Petersburg, Va. So. Ch.,
Feb. 27, 1868
PLEASANTS
Charles E. (The Rev.),
of Philadelphia, and
Caroline, d. of
Nathaniel Wattles,
Esq., by the Rev. John
T. Johnston. So. Ch.,
Jan. 15, 1836
Evelyn A., d. of the late
T. S. Pleasants, and
Edgar Jackson of Lees-
burg, Loudoun Co., by
the Rev. T. E. Locke,
at Midwood, Fluvanna
Co. So. Ch., Dec. 23,
1886
Frederick W., Esq., of
New York, and Sally,
only d. of the late John
M. McCartoy of Loudoun
Co., Va., by the Rev. R.
E. Phillips. So. Ch.,
Nov. 30, 1855
H. Clay, of Clinton, Tex.,
formerly of Goochland
Co., Va., and Anne Eliza
Atkinson, by the Rev.
Mr. Jones of the Episcopal
Church, near Gonzales,
Tex. So. Ch., Feb. 5,
1858
John H. (Dr.), of Din-
widdie Co., and Laura
Townes, only d. of the
late Robert Birchett of
Petersburg, by the Rev.
C. J. Gibson, in Grace
Church, Petersburg. So.
Ch., July 3, 1857
Randolph R., Esq., and
Annie H. Thompson, by
the Rev. T. E. Locke,
at Midwood, Fluvanna
Co., Va., So. Ch., Mar.
27, 1890*
PLUMMER
Julia M., third d. of Mrs.
Lucy D. Plummer of
Fairfax Co., and John B.
Trott, by the Rev. W. F.
Lockwood, at Centerville.
So. Ch., Nov. 16, 1848
POAGUE
F. B., and Roberta
Robinson, by the Rev.
C. C. Randolph, at Mrs.
Mary Robinson's,
"Beaver Dam", Botetourt
Co., Va. So. Ch., Oct.
13, 1881
POINDEXTER
Eliza G., and Lt. H. L.
Carter of the 53d
Virginia Regiment, by
the Rev. George T.
Wilmer, D.D., at
Pittsylvania C.H. So.
Ch., Feb. 27, 1863
Fannie S., and Hugh D.

---

* A notice appears in the issue of Mar. 20, 1890 identical with this, except that it is written Pleasants, Randolph L.

MARRIAGE NOTICES IN THE SOUTHERN CHURCHMAN WITH DATES OF PUBLICATION

Poindexter, both of Bedford Co., Va., by the Rev. G. A. Gibbons, at the residence of the bride's father. So. Ch., Nov. 26, 1874

Hugh D., and Fannie S. Poindexter, both of Bedford Co., Va., by the Rev. G. A. Gibbons, at the residence of the bride's father. So. Ch., Nov. 26, 1874

James Edward (The Rev.), rector of St. Mary's Parish, Caroline Co., Va., and Katharine Gordon, d. of the late Dr. J. Gordon Wallace, by the Rev. E. C. Murdaugh, D.D., at the residence of the bride's mother, at Fredericksburg, Va. So. Ch., Nov. 1, 1883

Sallie R., sister of the officiating minister, and Dr. Roger G. B. Broome of Louisa Co., Va., by the Rev. James E. Poindexter, in St. Peter's Church, Port Royal, Caroline Co. So. Ch., Dec. 18, 1884

William Bowyer, of Greenlee, Va., and Lucy Page, sister of the Rev. Dr. C. B. Wilmer of Atlanta and d. of the late Rev. Dr. G. T. Wilmer, by the Rev. J. W. Cantey Johnson of St. John's Church, Roanoke, at "Briar Hill", near Amsterdam, Va. So. Ch., July 12, 1913

POINTS
Bettie B., d. of Dr. Wm. J. Points of Harrisonburg, and Robert P. Stone of Washington, D.C., by the Rev. O. S. Bunting, in Emmanuel Church, Harrisonburg, Va. So. Ch., Feb. 26, 1885

John T. (The Rev.), of New Kent Co., and Bettie G., d. of Dr. Wat. H. Tyler, by the Rev. G. S. Carroway, at Tarwood, Hanover Co. So. Ch., Apr. 16, 1858

POLK
Catherine, of New Orleans, second d. of the Rt. Rev. L. Polk, D.D., Bishop of Louisiana, and William D. Gale of Tennessee, by the Rt. Rev. L. Polk, D.D., Bishop of Louisiana, in Trinity Church, New Orleans. So. Ch., Jan. 14, 1859

Elizabeth Bend, d. of the late David P. Polk of Alexandria, and the Rev. Robert J. Keeling of Newark, Del., formerly of Norfolk, Va., by the Rev. Dr. Johns, in Emmanuel Church, Baltimore. So. Ch., Oct. 22, 1858

POLLARD
Ellen Douglas, oldest d. of the late James O. Pollard of King William Co., and Richard Meech of England, by the Rev. J. Hervey Hundley, in St. David's Church, King William Co. So. Ch., Mar. 16, 1876

Lizzie R., d. of Mrs. Georgeanna Pollard of King William Co., Va., and George Eppes of Richmond, by the Rev. S. S. Hepbron, at Octogon, the residence of the bride's mother. So. Ch., Nov. 26, 1891

Lucy, d. of the late Maj. Richard Pollard of Albe-

MARRIAGE NOTICES IN THE SOUTHERN CHURCHMAN WITH DATES OF PUBLICATION

marle Co., Va., and Dr. Stephen E. Habersham of Aiken, S.C., by the Rev. Mr. Ambler, at Altavista. So. Ch., Aug. 7, 1851

M. Spottswood, of King William Co., and Richard S. Wood of Goochland, by the Rev. S. S. Hepbron, at Octogon, King William Co. So. Ch., Oct. 27, 1892

POLLISTER

Raymond Stony, and Marie Lonnie Johnston, at Nome, Alaska. So. Ch., July 26, 1913

POLLITT

Drucilla Amanda, youngest d. of William Pollitt, Esq. of Somerset Co., Md., and Whitty M. Sasser of Louisiana, by the Rev. George W. Woodbridge, in Richmond, Va. So. Ch., Sept. 30, 1836

POLLOCK

A. D. (The Rev.), pastor of the Presbyterian Church on Shockoe Hill, Richmond, Va., and Elizabeth G. Lee, by the Rev. Mr. Wilson, at Presque Isle, Culpeper Co. So. Ch., Dec. 3, 1835

Atchison, of Stafford Co., and Hannah C., d. of James Jett of Rappahannock Co., Va., by the Rev. A. M. Randolph, at the residence of the bride's father. So. Ch., Nov. 25, 1859

John G., and Estelle, d. of Fielding Lewis of King George Co., by the Rev. E. B. McGuire, at "Marmion", the residence of the bride's father. So. Ch., Dec. 17, 1868

Margaret Aitcheson, d. of the late Rev. Jno. Pollock, D.D., minister of the Parish of Govan, Scotland, and the Rev. Horatio Potter, D.D., rector of St. Peter's Church, Albany, by the Rt. Rev. Bishop Potter, D.D., in Trinity Church, New York. So. Ch., Oct. 11, 1849

Matthew B., of Stafford Co., Va., and Kate D., d. of Fielding Lewis, Esq. of King George Co., by the Rev. Edward McGuire, at "Marmion", the residence of the bride's father, in King George Co., Va. So. Ch., Nov. 17, 1870

Matthew B., of Stafford Co., and Lucy Daingerfield, eldest d. of the late Col. John Tayloe of Chatterton, by the Rev. James W. Shields assisted by the Rev. Melville Boyd, at Chatterton, King George Co. So. Ch., Dec. 23, 1875

POLSLEY

Eliza Margaret, d. of Hon. Daniel Polsley of Point Pleasant, and George B. Crow of Jackson Co., by the Rev. Horace Edward Hayden, at Point Pleasant, W.Va. So. Ch., Apr. 28, 1870

Harriet Burton, d. of Hon. Daniel Polsley, and William Smith, all of Mason Co., by the Rev. Horace Edwin Hayden, at Point Pleasant, W.Va. So. Ch., Sept. 16, 1869

POMEROY

MARRIAGE NOTICES IN THE SOUTHERN CHURCHMAN WITH DATES OF PUBLICATION

Julia, d. of the late George Pomeroy, Esq. of Madison, N.J., and the Rev. Wm. Foster Morrison, chaplain in U.S. Navy, by the Rt. Rev. H. C. Potter, D.D., in Grace Church, New York. So. Ch., Nov. 26, 1885

POOLE
Anna Cost, d. of Mrs. Richard Poole, and the Rev. Walter Williams, rector of Grace Church, Georgetown, by Bishop Alfred Harding assisted by the Rev. J. W. Blake, in Christ Church, Georgetown, D.C. So. Ch., Oct. 23, 1909

E. A., of Washington, and Ella C., d. of the officiating clergyman, the Rev. John Towles, assisted by the Rev. E. A. Dalrymple, S.T.D., of Baltimore, in Christ Church, Accokeek. So. Ch., Jan. 22, 1880

Minnie W., of Poolesville, and Alfred Wilson of Bethesda, Md., by the Rev. Walter P. Griggs, in St. Peter's Church, Poolesville, Md. So. Ch., June 30, 1892

Rosalie, d. of Judge W. W. Poole, and the Rev. Henry Thomas of Poolesville, Md., by the Rev. Dr. Lewis, in St. Peter's Church, Dickerson, Md. So. Ch., Dec. 3, 1885

POOLEY
Cecil Silas, and Charlotte Lillian, d. of the late Thomas Wentworth Groser of Brookland, sister of A. S. Groser of Richmond, Va. and g. niece and niece of the officiating clergymen, the Rev. S. M. Haskins, D.D., rector, and the Rev. T. W. Haskins, D.D. of Los Angeles, Cal., in St. Mark's Church, Brooklyn, N.Y. So. Ch., Oct. 27, 1892

POORE
Robbie M., and R. G. Sutton, by the Rev. A. H. Hamilton, at Canicello, the residence of Blackford Harris in Rockbridge Co. So. Ch., Mar. 8, 1888

POPE
Benjamin Franklin, of Baltimore, and Mary Gertrude Fyffe of Poolesville, by the Rev. Walter P. Griggs, in St. Peter's Church, Poolesville, Md. So. Ch., June 30, 1892

James Turner, of Brunswick, and Margaret, d. of the late Rev. Geo. Adie of Leesburg, Loudoun Co., Va., by the Rev. James Grammer, at the residence of Mrs. B. H. Harrison in Cumberland Co. So. Ch., Oct. 21, 1864

Willard S., and Martha E. Patterson, d. of the Rt. Rev. Dr. Bissell of Burlington, Vt., by the Rev. Rufus Clarke, Jr., rector of St. Paul's Church, at Detroit, Mich. So. Ch., Nov. 2, 1882

PORCHER
Francis Peyre, s. of the late Dr. Francis Peyre and Margaret

MARRIAGE NOTICES IN THE SOUTHERN CHURCHMAN WITH DATES OF PUBLICATION

Ward Porcher of Charleston, S.C., and Kate Kingsley of Mansfield, Pa., by the Rt. Rev. Dr. Howden, in the Episcopal Church, Albuquerque, N.M. So. Ch., June 26, 1915

Laura E., d. of the late Dr. Edward Porcher of Charleston, S.C., and Maj. Thomas H. Allen of Charlotte, N.C., by the Rev. Edward H. Ingle, in St. Paul's Chapel, Salem. So. Ch., July 16, 1874

PORTER

D. G., and Nellie V. Hancock, both of Culpeper Co., Va., by the Rev. H. B. Lee, in St. Paul's Church, Culpeper Co., Va. So. Ch., Dec. 22, 1887

Elizabeth Cheadell, teacher in St. Stephen's Mission at Nora, Dickenson Co., and John Marion Garrison, Director of Religious Education, Diocese of Southwestern Virginia, in the Church of the Holy Comforter, Sumter, S.C. So. Ch., June 13, 1931

Mary B., only d. of Col. John C. Porter, and Charles R. Jones, by the Rev. John McGill, in St. Paul's Church, Culpeper Co., Va. So. Ch., Nov. 23, 1882

Mary Jane, d. of Col. John A. Porter, and James W. Walker, Jr., all of Orange Co., by the Rev. John Cole. So. Ch., Sept. 5, 1856

Mary Maxwell, d. of Mrs. Caroline Porter and the late Charles B. Porter, and Albert Williams of Kansas City, at the family residence in St. Joseph, Mo. So. Ch., Oct. 22, 1910

Nannie K., of Orange, and G. B. Wallace Nalle of Culpeper, by the Rev. C. Y. Steptoe, at Riverside, Orange Co. So. Ch., Jan. 16, 1873

PORTERFIELD

Emily Serena, d. of Col. Geo. A. Porterfield, and Geo. Washington, all of Charles Town, Jefferson Co., W.Va., by the Rev. Dallas Tucker, in Zion Church. So. Ch., Feb. 25, 1886

POST

Fanny, d. of the late Dr. William Maffitt Post, and Everard K. Pattison, by the Rev. Campbell Fair, D.D., in Ascension Church, Baltimore. So. Ch., Feb. 23, 1882

POTTER

Benjamin J., organist of Monumental Church, Richmond, Va., and Mary L. Hutchinson, also of Richmond, by the Rev. J. Henning Nelms, D.D., in Ascension Church, Washington. So. Ch., Dec. 14, 1912

Charles, and Elizabeth Ann, d. of R. P. Trice, all of Fairfax Co., by the Rev. R. T. Brown, near Pohick. So. Ch., Apr. 22, 1859

Dexter (The Rev.), and Uleyetta, d. of the Rev. James Sabine, by the Rev. Henry Blackaller, at Clappville, Mass. So. Ch., Dec.

MARRIAGE NOTICES IN THE SOUTHERN CHURCHMAN WITH DATES OF PUBLICATION

15, 1837
Frank Hunter, of New York, and Alice, d. of the late Philip Barton Key, by the Rev. Dr. H. C. Potter and the Rev. Dr. E. N. Potter, in Grace Church, Baltimore. So. Ch., Mar. 2, 1882

Henry B. (Dr.), of Providence, R.I., and Mary E., d. of Charles M. and Mrs. Lizzie L. Miller of Keyser, W.Va., by the rector, the Rev. R. E. L. Strider, in Emmanuel Church, Keyser, W.Va. So. Ch., Oct. 5, 1912

Henry C. (The Rev.), and Eliza R., only d. of the late Samuel O. Jacobs, Esq., by the Rt. Rev. Alonzo Potter, D.D., LL.D., at Spring Grove, Lancaster Co., Pa. So. Ch., Oct. 23, 1857

Horatio (The Rev.), D.D., rector of St. Peter's Church, Albany, and Margaret Aitcheson, d. of the late Rev. Jno. Pollock, D.D., minister of the Parish of Govan, Scotland, by the Rt. Rev. Bishop Potter, D.D., in Trinity Church, New York. So. Ch., Oct. 11, 1849

Sallie T., and the Rev. Jno. Tennent, by the Rev. Dr. Cotton of Hungar's Parish, Northampton, in St. James' Church, Accomac Co. So. Ch., June 25, 1858

POTTS
Eleanor, d. of Geo. M. Potts, Esq. of Frederick, Md., and Arthur S. Johns, by the Rt. Rev. John Johns, Bishop of Virginia, at Frederick, Md. So. Ch., Oct. 24, 1867

Henry W., of Pottstown, Pa., and Eleanor S. Powell of Shepherdstown, W.Va., by the Rev. Landon Mason, in Trinity Church, Shepherdstown, W.Va. So. Ch., Oct. 6, 1881

Joseph S., of Richmond, and Isabel Gertrude, d. of Mrs. Kate E. and the late James Sheppard, and gr.d. of the late Rev. Dr. Empie, by the Rev. Joshua Peterkin, D.D., at the residence of the bride's mother, in Richmond, Va. So. Ch., Apr. 17, 1884

Netta, of Richmond, Va., and Robert Ranlet of Holyoke, Mass., by the Rev. John B. Newton, rector of Monumental Church, and the Rev. Hartley Carmichael, D.D., of St. Paul's Church, in Monumental Church, Richmond, Va. So. Ch., Nov. 16, 1893

POTZMAN
Lizzie Kramer, and William M. Hyland, Esq. of Osceola, Clarke Co., Iowa, by the Rev. W. L. Hyland, D.D. of St. John's Parish, Prince George Co., Md., at the residence of the bride's father, in Morgantown, W.Va. So. Ch., Jan. 1, 1885

POULTNEY
Arthur E., of Baltimore, and Emily Chapman, only d. of Col. Eugene Blackford of Baltimore Co., Md., by the Rev.

MARRIAGE NOTICES IN THE SOUTHERN CHURCHMAN WITH DATES OF PUBLICATION

E. Lawrence, rector, assisted by the Rev. J. S. Lindsay, D.D. of Boston, Mass., in St. Mark's Church, Pikesville, Md. So. Ch., June 16, 1892

POWELL

Arthur T., and Nellie, d. of Col. Morris S. and Elizabeth C. Langhorne, by the Rev. T. M. Carson, in St. Paul's Church, Lynchburg, Va. So. Ch., Oct. 14, 1880

Bettie W., d. of Dr. F. W. Powell of Middleburg, Va., and John M. Strother of the University of Virginia, by the Rev. O. A. Kinsolving. So. Ch., Mar. 1, 1861

Eleanor S., of Shepherdstown, W.Va., and Henry W. Potts of Pottstown, Pa., by the Rev. Landon Mason, in Trinity Church, Shepherdstown, W.Va. So. Ch., Oct. 6, 1881

Ella, d. of Cuthbert Powell formerly of Alexandria, now of Danville, Va., and John Lloyd Stearns of Elizabeth, N.J., by the Rev. Henderson Suter, in Christ Church, Alexandria. So. Ch., Oct. 17, 1878

Eloise Hepburn, oldest d. of the Rev. J. D. Powell, and John Ravenscroft Eoff, Esq., by the Rev. J. D. Powell, rector, in St. John's Church, Portsmouth, Va. So. Ch., June 27, 1889

Florence, of Richmond, and William F. Brooks of Alexandria, Va., by the Rev. J. D. Powell, at the residence of Col. D. Lee Powell, in Richmond. So. Ch., Jan. 26, 1871

Harriett H., eldest d. of Dr. F. W. Powell of Middleburg, Va., and William Carmichael, Esq. of Maryland, by the Rev. C. A. Kinsolving. So. Ch., Nov. 9, 1860

Ida, d. of the late George Cuthbert Powell of Loudoun Co., Va., and Henry Grafton Dulany, by the Rev. O. A. Kinsolving, in Emmanuel Church, Middleburg. So. Ch., June 14, 1855

John D. (The Rev.), and Annie Leake, d. of the late John M. Hepburn, Esq., by the Rev. Mr. Tillinghast, in St. John's Church, Georgetown. So. Ch., Oct. 12, 1854

Laura Stuart, of Shepherdstown, W.Va., and Wm. Thomas Roberts, rector of St. Stephen's Church, Culpeper, Va., by the rector, the Rev. L. R. Mason, in Trinity Church, Shepherdstown, W.Va. So. Ch., May 20, 1886

Legh, of Richmond, s. of the officiating clergyman, and Cora Maupin Eastwood of Portsmouth, Va., by the Rev. J. D. Powell assisted by the Rev. O. S. Barten, D.D., in St. John's Church, Portsmouth. So. Ch., Nov. 2, 1882

Levin, and Adelaide, d. of W. A. Kercheval, both of Upperville, by the Rev. Mr. Kinsolving,

MARRIAGE NOTICES IN THE SOUTHERN CHURCHMAN WITH DATES OF PUBLICATION

in Upperville. So. Ch., Nov. 2, 1855

Llewellyn Lee, and Eulalia Rorer, both of Roanoke, Va., by the Rev. John D. Powell assisted by the Rev. W. H. Meade, in St. John's Church, Roanoke, Va. So. Ch., Nov. 17, 1887

M. Antoinette, d. of Wm. A. Powell, Esq. of Leesburg, Va., and James Evans, Surgeon, C.S.A., of Marion Dist., So. Ca.,* by the Rev. J. D. Powell, in Richmond City. So. Ch., Jan. 11, 1865

Marion Steuart, d. of W. A. Powell, Esq. of Loudoun, and Frank F. Jones, Esq., by the Rev. Walter Williams, in St. James' Church, Leesburg. So. Ch., Nov. 18, 1859

Mary (Mrs.), and the Rev. Geo. Adie, rector of Shelburn Parish, by the Rev. C. W. Andrews, at Longholler, Loudoun Co., Va. So. Ch., Jan. 8, 1836

Nannie W., d. of the late Dr. William L. Powell, and Walter J. Harrison, Esq., by the Rev. E. T. Perkins, in St. James' Church, Leesburg. So. Ch., Sept. 26, 1867

Selina Lloyd, d. of Charles L. Powell, Esq. of Alexandria, and the Rev. Sewell S. Hepbron of Kent Co., Md., by the Rev. R. H. McKim, in Christ Church, Alexandria. So. Ch., Apr. 20, 1871

Virginia, and Benjamin Probasco of Freehold, N.J., by the Rev. Wyllys Rede, rector of St. Mary's Church, at the residence of Richard Powell, Goochland Co., Va. So. Ch., Dec. 23, 1886

POWERS

Alice Burnett, d. of the late Maj. Philip H. Powers and gr.d. of the late Edward Jacquelin Smith, and Reverdy Johnson Lewis, s. of the late G. Washington Lewis and gr.s. of the late Lorenzo Lewis, all of Clarke Co., Va., at "Auburn", the home of the bride. So. Ch., May 9, 1908

David B., and Mary Rosina, d. of Champe B. Thornton, all of Port Royal, Caroline Co., Va., by the Rev. James E. Poindexter, at the residence of the bride's father. So. Ch., Nov. 2, 1871

E. C., and George A. Barksdale, both of Richmond, by the Rev. Pike Powers assisted by the Rev. W. H. H. Powers of Maryland, in St. Andrew's Church, Richmond. So. Ch., Oct. 12, 1882

Fanny Ballard, d. of the late P. K. and Roberta M. Powers, and the Rev. T. Carter Page of Stafford Co., Va., by the Rev. J. J. Page, at Auburn, Clarke Co., Va. So. Ch., Dec. 22, 1887

H. H., of Roanoke, Va., and Bettie M. Taylor of Christiansburg, by the Rev. W. Dudley Powers of the Diocese of Maryland, at the residence of the bride's father at Christiansburg. So. Ch.,

* Given as printed

MARRIAGE NOTICES IN THE SOUTHERN CHURCHMAN WITH DATES OF PUBLICATION

May 10, 1883
Lucy, and Wm. E. Perry, both of Stafford Co., Va., by the Rev. Robert S. Barrett, at the residence of the bride's mother. So. Ch., Feb. 22, 1877

Mattie, and Dr. John H. Price of Charles Co., Md., at the residence of the bride, Stafford Co. So. Ch., Nov. 14, 1889

Pattie S., d. of Pike and Lelia Powers of Halifax, Va., and Wm. H. Meade of Charlottesville, by the Rev. R. K. Meade, in Halifax Co. So. Ch., July 24, 1863

Philip H., of Charles Town, and Roberta M., d. of E. J. Smith, by the Rev. F. M. Whittle, Smithfield, Clarke Co., Va. So. Ch., Jan. 13, 1853

Philip S., of Richmond, and Ann Conway, d. of Maj. Thomas L. and Mary M. Broun, by Bishop Peterkin and the Rev. R. D. Roller, rector of the Church, in St. John's Church in Charleston, Kanawha Co., W.Va. So. Ch., Oct. 1, 1891

W. Dudley (The Rev.), minister-in-charge of the Church of the Nativity, Maysville, Ky., and Mary Bullock Howard of Mount Sterling, Ky., by the Rev. T. A. Tidball, D.D. assisted by the Rev. E. A. Penick, in the Church of the Ascension, Mount Sterling, Ky. So. Ch., Dec. 9, 1880

Wm. H. H. (The Rev.), and Louise, adopted d. of Judge Sheffey, by the Rev. Walter Q. Hullihen, in Trinity Church, Staunton, Va. So. Ch., Oct. 31, 1872

POWLES
P. L. (The Rev.), M.A., B.D., and M. V. Rhodes of Clarendon, Va., by Bishop Brown of Virginia, in Washington Cathedral. So. Ch., July 18, 1925

POYNTZ
N. C. S. (The Rev.), of Gloustershire,*England, and Helen Willis, fourth d. of the late Dr. James M. Minor formerly of Virginia, by the Rev. Geo. H. Houghton, D.D. assisted by the Rev. T. McKee Brown, in the Church of the Transfiguration, New York. So. Ch., Jan. 4, 1883

POYTHERESS
Marie Josephine, nee Brouse, and James Chandler Dorst formerly of Salem, Va., by the Rev. W. R. Savage assisted by the Rev. W. H. Burkhardt of Bluefield, W.Va., in Stras Memorial Church, Tazewell C.H. So. Ch., May 25, 1893

PRATJE
Wilhelm H., formerly of Germany, and Nannie B., d. of Dr. Geo. S. Hamilton of Prince William Co., Va., by the Rev. R. T. Brown, at "Burnside", near

* Given as printed

MARRIAGE NOTICES IN THE SOUTHERN CHURCHMAN WITH DATES OF PUBLICATION

PRATT
　Ida Virginia, youngest d. of W. C. and Eliza Pratt, and the Rev. J. B. Funsten, by the Rev. J. E. Poindexter, at Camden, near Port Royal, Caroline Co., Va. So. Ch., Dec. 23, 1886
　Samuel L., Esq., of Queen Anne's Co., Md., and Hattie C., d. of Amos Lynch, Esq., residing near Middletown, by the Rev. John Collins McCabe, D.D., in Saint Ann's Church, Middletown, Del. So. Ch., Oct. 15, 1868
　William C., of Caroline, and Eliza H., d. of Richard Turner of King George Co., by the Rev. J. E. Locke, at Woodlawn. So. Ch., May 18, 1860

PRENTISS
　John J., and Elizabeth Wells Wilson, by the Rev. Thomas P. Baker, in the Episcopal Church, Yonges Island, S.C. So. Ch., Nov. 25, 1911
　Richard Robert, M.D., and Claudia Wilkinson, by the Rev. Thomas P. Baker, in Christ Church Chapel, Yonges Island, S.C. So. Ch., Jan. 28, 1911

PRESCOTT
　Caroline, d. of the late Oliver Prescott, M.D. of Newberryport, Mass., and the Rev. Charles West Thompson, rector of St. John's Church, York, Pa., by the Rev. Charles Mason, in Grace Church, Boston, Mass. So. Ch., May 3, 1849
　Haymarket. So. Ch., Nov. 21, 1872

PRESSTMAN
　Benjamin Cattell, of Baltimore, and Matilda W., d. of the late John P. Hooper of Cambridge, Md., by the Rt. Rev. A. M. Randolph, Assistant Bishop of Virginia, in Emmanuel Church, Baltimore. So. Ch., Oct. 16, 1884
　Emily Renshaw, d. of the late B. C. Presstman of Baltimore, and Francis H. Hoff, by the Rev. A. M. Randolph, D.D., in Grace P. E. Church, Baltimore. So. Ch., Oct. 22, 1885

PRESTON
　A. A., Esq., of Charleston, W.Va., and Sallie, eldest d. of Maj. N. Fitzhugh, by the Rev. C. M. Callaway, rector, assisted by the Rev. Edward Valentine Jones, in St. John's Church, Charleston, W.Va. So. Ch., Dec. 5, 1872
　Bettie F., and Harrison W. Fendley, by the Rev. Henry Wall, D.D., in St. John's Church, Richmond. So. Ch., Nov. 10, 1870
　Davidella, and T. R. B. Wright of Tappahannock, Essex Co., Va., by the Rev. G. H. Denny, at the residence of Dr. J. R. Woods, Albemarle Co., Va. So. Ch., Dec. 14, 1876
　Desaussour (Dr.), of Burnwell, W.Va., and Alice Bouldin, d. of Judge Boylan Green of Charlotte Co., Va., at the home of Dr. and Mrs. Berryman Green,

MARRIAGE NOTICES IN THE SOUTHERN CHURCHMAN WITH DATES OF PUBLICATION

Theological Seminary, Va. - So. Ch., Jan. 22, 1916

E. R., d. of Col. J. T. L. Preston of Lexington, Va., and Col. William Allan of Baltimore, by the Rev. Thomas L. Preston, D.D., in Lexington, Va. So. Ch., June 4, 1874

Elizabeth R. (Mrs.), of Washington Co., and Col. John D. Munford of Williamsburg, by the Rev. L. B. Wharton, in St. Thomas' Church, Abingdon. So. Ch., Nov. 7, 1867

Geo. A., recently of Virginia, and Martha S. Alexander of Bonham, by the Rev. Francis R. Starr, at Bonham, Fannin Co., Tex. So. Ch., Oct. 24, 1872

Jane Grace, d. of the late Gov. W. Ballard Preston of Virginia, and Aubin L. Boulware of Richmond, by the Rev. Nelson P. Dame, at Smithfield, the residence of the bride's mother, in Montgomery Co. So. Ch., Nov. 21, 1878

L. A. C., second d. of the late Hon. Walter Preston, and Geo. W. Ward, Jr. of Abingdon, Va., by the Rev. Thos. W. Humes, D.D., at the residence of the bride's mother, Mrs. A. Garnett Preston, in Knoxville, Tenn. So. Ch., Dec. 26, 1878

W. C., and Elizabeth K. Myers, by the Rev. D. F. Sprigg assisted by the Rev. Dr. Preston, father of the groom, at the residence of the bride's father, Maj. E. T. D. Myers. So. Ch., Jan. 26, 1888

Walter, Esq., of Abingdon, Washington Co., Va., and Agatha Garnett, d. of Col. Wm. M. Peyton, by the Rev. W. H. Pendleton, at Elmwood, the residence of Col. Wm. M. Peyton. So. Ch., Sept. 27, 1855

PRETLOW
Susan E., eldest d. of R. Henley Pretlow of "Little Surry", Va., and Richard S. Boykin of Southampton Co., by the Rev. David Barr, in the Church of Our Saviour, Ivor, Va. So. Ch., Apr. 14, 1887

PREWITT
Elizabeth Sheffer, and Alfred Rives Shands, M.D. of Washington, D.C., at "Dunreath", Lexington, Ky. So. Ch., Aug. 14, 1926

PRICE
Bayard R., of Philadelphia, and Edulia G. Smith of West Point, by the Rev. J. Y. Downman, in the Episcopal Church, West Point, Va. So. Ch., Dec. 28, 1882

Bell, and R. P. Quesenbury, by the Rev. A. J. Willis assisted by the Rev. J. K. Mason of Fredericksburg, at Edge Hill, King George Co. So. Ch., Nov. 1, 1888

Charles W., Esq., of Missouri, and Virginia L., d. of John L. Cobbs,

MARRIAGE NOTICES IN THE SOUTHERN CHURCHMAN WITH DATES OF PUBLICATION

Esq. of Bedford, by the Rev. O. A. Kinsolving, in Bedford Co., Va. So. Ch., Nov. 23, 1848

Edward Arney, of Richmond, and Lou Fitzhugh, d. of Wm. A. Little, Esq. of Fredericksburg, Va., by the Rev. R. J. McBryde assisted by the Rev. E. C. Murdaugh, D.D., in St. George's Church, Fredericksburg. So. Ch., Dec. 20, 1877

Ellen Moore, d. of the late Thos. R. Price, and Thomas Hill Norwood, by the Rev. Wm. Norwood, D.D. So. Ch., Jan. 4, 1872

John H., and Mrs. Jennie Keen, both of Queen Anne's Co., Md., by the Rev. P. D. Thompson, in Christ Church, Kent Island, Md. So. Ch., Jan. 17, 1884

John H. (Dr.), of Charles Co., Md., and Mattie Powers, at the residence of the bride, Stafford Co. So. Ch., Nov. 14, 1889

John W. (Dr.), of Mt. Airy, Pittsylvania Co., Va., and Jeanie B. Wilkinson of Brandon, Miss., by the Rev. C. O. Pruden, in Epiphany Church, Danville. So. Ch., May 31, 1888

Louise B. (Mrs.), and Edward C. Legg, both of Kent Island, Md., by the Rev. P. D. Thompson, in Christ Church, Kent Island, Md. So. Ch., June 19, 1884

Parham F., and Mattie B., d. of William A. and Alice Withers, by the Rev. W. W. Kimball, at the residence of the bride's father, in Campbell Co. So. Ch., Nov. 2, 1882

Robert C. (Prof.), of the Agricultural and Mechanical College, Blacksburg, Va., and Sue Fullerton, second d. of Hon. R. H. Johnson, all of Christiansburg, by the Rev. F. W. Hooper, D.D. and the Rev. John McGill, in the Presbyterian Church, Christiansburg, Va. So. Ch., Apr. 6, 1893

Virginia, d. of the late Benjamin Price of Virginia, and Dr. Benjamin King of the U.S. Army, by the Rev. Ruel Keith, D.D., in Alexandria. So. Ch., June 2, 1837

Virginia F., and Wm. J. Black, both of Lynchburg, by the Rev. T. M. Carson, in St. Paul's Church, Lynchburg. So. Ch., Mar. 14, 1872

PRICHETT
John W., Esq., of Amelia Co., and Mary D., d. of William Wilkinson, Esq. of Chesterfield, by the Rev. A. B. Tizzard. So. Ch., Dec. 17, 1858

PRIDE
Emma, d. of the late John Pride, and Philip S. Wood, all of Amelia Co., Va., by the Rev. P. F. Berkely, at Lucerne, the residence of the bride's mother, Amelia Co. So. Ch., Mar. 9, 1876

PRINGLE
Annie E., second d. of the Rev. J. M. and the

MARRIAGE NOTICES IN THE SOUTHERN CHURCHMAN WITH DATES OF PUBLICATION

late J. E. Pringle, and Robt. C. Soaper, by the rector of St. Paul's Church, in St. Paul's Church, Henderson, Ky. So. Ch., Dec. 4, 1873

Clara A., d. of the officiating minister, the Rev. J. M. Pringle, and T. T. Barret, all of Henderson, Ky., in St. Paul's Church, Henderson, Ky. So. Ch., Dec. 14, 1876

Sarah Amelia, and Bonner N. McCraven of Houston, Tex., by the Rev. J. M. Pringle, father of the bride, at the residence of the bride's brother-in-law, Robert C. Soaper, Henderson, Ky. So. Ch., Oct. 27, 1887

PRITCHETT
John H., and Nonie Carter, by the Rev. H. L. Derby, at the residence of the bride's mother, in Lancaster, Va. So. Ch., July 22, 1880

PROBASCO
Benjamin, of Freehold, N.J., and Virginia Powell, by the Rev. Wyllys Rede, rector of St. Mary's Church, at the residence of Richard Powell, Goochland Co., Va. So. Ch., Dec. 23, 1886

PROPHET
Ann, of Mt. Morris, N.Y., and William H. Jefferys, M.D., Supt. of the Philadelphia Protestant Episcopal City Mission. So. Ch., June 27, 1931

Anna, of New Orleans, and the Rev. Wm. Taylor Douglas, rector of Grace Church, Lake Providence, La., by the Rev. Wm. K. Douglas, D.D. assisted by the Rev. C. S. Hedges, D.D., the Bishop of Louisiana pronouncing the blessing, in Calvary Church, New Orleans. So. Ch., Feb. 26, 1885

PRUDEN
Clevius Orlando (The Rev.), of Chatham, Va., and Julia Wickham, d. of Maj. Charles and Annie C. Old of Powhatan Co., Va., by the Rev. B. M. Randolph of Emmanuel Church, Henrico Co., Va., at the residence of Maj. Charles Old, Powhatan Co., Va. So. Ch., Oct. 27, 1887

PRYOR
Richard S. (Dr.), and Lucy Barbour Sthreshley, both of Vicksburg, Miss., by Bishop Adams, at the residence of H. M. Goff, near Bovina, Miss. So. Ch., Dec. 7, 1882

PUCKETTE
Charles McD., and Charlotte Barnwell Elliott, by the Rt. Rev. R. W. Elliott, Bishop of Western Texas, assisted by the Rt. Rev. Bishop of Tennessee and the Rt. Rev. Bishop of Mississippi, in St. Paul's-on-the-Mountain, Sewanee, Tenn. So. Ch., Jan. 17, 1884

PUGH
Thomas B. (Dr.), of Assumption Parish, La., and Nannie M., second d. of Col. B. H. and Agnes P. Jones, by the Rev. George W. Dame, at Ruffin, N.C. So. Ch., Apr. 24, 1879

PUGIN

MARRIAGE NOTICES IN THE SOUTHERN CHURCHMAN WITH DATES OF PUBLICATION

Byron A., and Jennie Lynd Collins, both of Albemarle, by the Rev. T. E. Locke, at the residence of Wm. Collins. So. Ch., Nov. 12, 1885

PULLER
Matthew M., of Baltimore, Md., and Pattie K. Leigh of Aylett, Va., by the Rev. Pendleton Brooke, in St. David's Church, King William Co., Va. So. Ch., Aug. 2, 1888

PULLIAM
Lucy A., of Powhatan Co., and Jefferson P. Archer, Esq. of Richmond, by the Rev. Andrew Fisher, in St. Luke's Church, Powhatan Co. So. Ch., Jan. 8, 1858

William E., of Pocahontas, Ark., and Leah, d. of Dr. R. Summers of Martinsburg, by the Rev. Mr. Davis. So. Ch., Sept. 7, 1860

PULMAN
Sarah B., d. of Samuel Pulman, Esq., and John Miller of Washington, D.C., by the Rev. W. Strother Jones, rector of Grace Church, Fauquier, at Mount Erin, Fairfax Co., Va. So. Ch., Dec. 20, 1877

PUMPHREY
John R., and Ella S. Kirby, by the Rev. W. L. Hyland, rector of St. John's Parish, in St. John's Church, Broad Creek, Prince George's Co., Md. So. Ch., Dec. 18, 1879

PURCELL
Emma F., d. of C. W. Purcell, Esq. of Alton Park, Albemarle Co., Va., and Dr. Massie L. McCue, by the Rev. Mr. Greaves, at the residence of the bride's father. So. Ch., Nov. 27, 1879

Jas. Bryant (The Rev.), rector of St. John's Church, Mount Washington, Baltimore Co., and Mary Ann E., d. of the late Edward Cowcher of Dartmouth, England, by the Rev. A. M. Randolph, D.D., rector, assisted by the Rev. Dr. Dalrymple, in Emmanuel Church, Baltimore. So. Ch., Nov. 28, 1878

John Bolling, of Welch, W.Va., and Helena Gertrude, d. of Mr. and Mrs. Keister, at Graham, Va. So. Ch., Aug. 28, 1915

PURDIE
Sue A. (Mrs.), of Chesterfield Co., Va., and J. T. Crump, by the Rev. A. B. Tizzard, at Clover Hill, Chesterfield Co., Va. So. Ch., Jan. 10, 1889

PURNELL
Almeyda Tredway, of Charlotte, N.C. and Winona, Miss., and Clarence Eli Humphries of Gastonia, N.C., by the Rev. John Moore Walker, at the home of the bride's parents, Mr. and Mrs. James Carstaphen Purnell, Charlotte, N.C. So. Ch., Aug. 24, 1929

Angeline B., and the Rev. Georges Fitzhugh, by the Rt. Rev. Henry C. Lay, D.D., LL.D., in St. Paul's Church, Berlin, Worcester Co., Md. So. Ch., June 18, 1874

MARRIAGE NOTICES IN THE SOUTHERN CHURCHMAN WITH DATES OF PUBLICATION

Francis Hawkins, of Charlotte, N.C., and the Rev. George Purnell Gunn of Altavista, Va., by the Rt. Rev. Robert C. Jett assisted by the Rev. Berryman Green, in the Immanuel Chapel, Theological Seminary, Alexandria, Va. So. Ch., Sept. 6, 1930

Jessie Tredway, and Mallory King Cannon, both of Charlotte, N.C., by the Rev. Willis Gaylord Clark, rector, in St. Peter's Episcopal Church, Charlotte, N.C. So. Ch., June 5, 1937

PURVIS
William Reginald (Dr.), and Eloise Bartleman, d. of the late F. Westwood Ashby, by the Rev. Dr. Suter, in Christ Church, Alexandria, Va. So. Ch., June 23, 1892

PUTNAM
Evaline, and J. M. Pickerell, U.S.N., of Richmond, Va., at Honolulu, H.I. So. Ch., July 11, 1889

Lizzie W., d. of Douglas Putnam, and Chas. S. McCandlish of Parkersburg, W.Va., by the Rev. H. C. Haskell, at the residence of the bride's father, at Harmar, O. So. Ch., May 10, 1883

Solon G. (The Rev.), of Guilford, Chenango Co., and Eunice Amarida De Forest of Dover, Dutchess Co., N.Y., by the Rev. Mr. Kellogg, at Clinton, Oneida Co., N.Y. So. Ch., Jan. 11, 1839

Q

QUACKENBUSH
Leslie R. (Dr.), of Florida, and Lillie A. Mariner of Fauquier Co., Va., by the Rev. H. B. Lee, at Rappahannock Station, Fauquier Co., Va. So. Ch., Dec. 22, 1887

QUARRIER
Gustavus B., Esq., of Kanawha Co., W.Va., and Mary Stuart, only d. of the late Dr. William F. Massie formerly of Alexandria, Va., by the Rev. R. A. Cobbs, in St. Mark's Church, St. Albans, W.Va. So. Ch., Oct. 25, 1877

QUESENBURY
R. P., and Bell Price, by the Rev. A. J. Willis assisted by the Rev. J. K. Mason of Fredericksburg, at Edge Hill, King George Co. So. Ch., Nov. 1, 1888

QUIGLEY
Jane Morrison, and Charles W. Andrews of Shephordstown, at the residence of Henry C. Page, Charles Town, W.Va. So. Ch., May 8, 1909

QUILLEN
Jane E. (Mrs.), and Wm. M. Freeman, all of Berlin, Worcester Co., Md., by the Rev. George S. Fitzhugh. So. Ch., Jan. 15, 1874

QUISENBERRY
Ellie Josephine, d. of the late J. M. Quisenberry of Spotsylvania, and George P. Holman, Jr. of Christiansburg, Va., by the Rev. Wm. W. Green, at Carter's Hall, Caroline Co. So. Ch., Jan. 5, 1871

R

RADCLIFFE
    Emma L., d. of Quinton Radcliffe, Esq., and Robert Spencer, Esq., all of Baltimore, by the Rev. John Collins McCabe, D.D., rector of St. Matthews Parish, Bladensburg, Md., in the Church of the Ascension, Baltimore. So. Ch., Aug. 2, 1866

RADFORD
    Emma N., of Bedford, and Wm. M. Chalmers, Esq. of Lynchburg, by the Rev. W. H. Pendleton, at Ashwood, Bedford Co., Va. So. Ch., Dec. 17, 1868

    Francis, Esq., of Meigs Co., Ohio, and Fannie Gallagher of Mason Co., W.Va., by the Rev. T. H. Lacy, at the residence of the bride's mother, in West Columbia, W.Va. So. Ch., Feb. 1, 1877

    Kate L., youngest d. of the late Capt. Winston Radford, and Louis T. Eggleston of Giles Co., by the Rev. E. W. Hubbard,* at Ashwood, Bedford Co., Va. So. Ch., Dec. 1, 1887

    Lizzie C., d. of Dr. John B. Radford, and Capt. Richard H. Adams, all of Montgomery Co., Va., by the Rev. Edward H. Ingle, at "Arnheim", the residence of the bride's father. So. Ch., Nov. 9, 1871

    Mary M., d. of Dr. Jno. B. Radford of Montgomery Co., Va., and Wm. T. Yancey, Jr. of Lynchburg, by the Rev. Edward H. Ingle, at "Arnheim", the residence of the bride's father. So. Ch., Nov. 25, 1869

    Mina Myers, fourth d. of Mrs. Anne N. Radford of "Ashwood", Bedford Co., Va., and the Rev. Arthur P. Gray of Prince William Co., Va., by the Rev. E. W. Hubard,* in St. Stephen's Church, Bedford Co., Va. So. Ch., Oct. 6, 1881

    R. C. W. (Col.), of Bedford Co., and Fanny C., d. of Thomas Steptoe, by the Rev. T. M. Carson, at the residence of the bride's father, L'Esperance, near Lynchburg, Va. So. Ch., Apr. 22, 1880

RAHM
    Emma, and V. S. Carleton, both of Richmond, Va., by the Rt. Rev. F. M. Whittle, at Trinity Church, Rocky Mount, Va. So. Ch., Nov. 30, 1876

    Mattie E., eldest d. of the late Philip Rahm of Richmond, and George H. T. Green of Franklin Co., by the Rev. George Woodbridge, D.D., at the residence of the bride's brother. So. Ch., Jan. 7, 1869

    Philip, and Anna S., second d. of Thomas Foster, all of Richmond, by the Rev. Geo. Woodbridge, in the Monumental Church. So. Ch., Mar. 1, 1861

RALSTON
    Genovieve, second d. of Mr. E. and Mrs. P. M. Ralston, and Thomas W. Harrison, all of Weston, by the Rev. T. H. Lacy, in St. Paul's

---

* Given as printed

MARRIAGE NOTICES IN THE SOUTHERN CHURCHMAN WITH DATES OF PUBLICATION

Church, Weston, W.Va. So. Ch., May 15, 1890

RAMBO
Jacob (The Rev.), of the African Mission, and Mary G., eldest d. of the late Samuel G. Lounsbery of New York, by the Rev. Edward Lounsbery, in St. Jude's Church, Philadelphia. So. Ch., Oct. 29, 1858

RAMSAY
Edith, and Frank McCormick, both of Virginia, by the Rev. Wm. Jackson Morton, in Alexandria, Va. So. Ch., June 20, 1908

RAMSEY
Julia L., d. of G. H. Ramsey of Jackson, Tenn., and Edmund Berkeley late of Virginia, by the Rev. N. B. Jones, at Jackson, Tenn. So. Ch., Oct. 23, 1879

RANDOLPH
Alfred M. (The Rev.), and Sallie G., d. of the late Dr. Wm. Hoxton, by the Rev. C. B. Dana, rector of Christ Church, Alexandria. So. Ch., May 6, 1859

Archy Cary (Dr.), and Mrs. Susan R. Henry (nee Burwell), by the Rev. C. Braxton Bryan, at Christ Church, Millwood, Clarke Co., Va. So. Ch., Oct. 13, 1881

B. M., of York, Pa., and Mary Hoxton of Baltimore, Md., both formerly of Virginia, by the Rev. A. M. Randolph, in Emmanuel Church, Baltimore, Md. So. Ch., Oct. 29, 1868

C. C. (The Rev.), and S. T., d. of Wm. H. and Mrs. Mary V. Anthony, by the Rev. H. M. Jackson, in Trinity Church, Buchanan, Botetourt Co., Va. So. Ch., Oct. 23, 1879

Charles C. (The Rev.), and Sallie B. McGuire, by the Rev. William McGuire assisted by the Rev. Henderson Suter, in Christ Church, Alexandria, Va. So. Ch., May 22, 1884

David Coupland, of Richmond, and Harriet R., d. of the late John C. Page of Cumberland, by the Rev. W. H. Kinckle, at Union Hill. So. Ch., May 15, 1857

Eliza Llewellyn, eldest d. of the officiating clergyman, and James Murray Ambler of Baltimore, by the Rt. Rev. A. M. Randolph, D.D., in St. Paul's Church, Richmond, Va. So. Ch., Jan. 21, 1886

Eva F., and R. H. Dulany, Jr., both of Loudoun Co., by the Rev. W. H. Johnson, in Trinity Church, Upperville. So. Ch., Oct. 4, 1877

Frank M., and Charlotte N. Macon, by the Rev. Robb White, in Grace Church, Albemarle Co., Va. So. Ch., Jan. 25, 1883

Isaetta, d. of Dr. B. F. Randolph of Albemarle Co., and Col. James L. Hubard of Buckingham Co., by the Rev. Samuel Ridout. So. Ch., Nov. 30, 1860

Isham, of Clarke Co., Va., and Mary Taylor of Lewisburg, Greenbrier Co., W.Va., by Canon Knowles, in the Cathedral of Sts. Peter and Paul, Chicago. So. Ch., June 29, 1882

Kate Whitcomb, youngest d. of the late Mr. j. Peyton

MARRIAGE NOTICES IN THE SOUTHERN CHURCHMAN WITH DATES OF PUBLICATION

Randolph of Virginia, and Charles Landon Scott, Jr. of Amherst, by the Rev. J. W. Ware of Culpeper, at Amherst, in Ascension Episcopal Church. So. Ch., Jan. 15, 1910

Lewis C. (Dr.), of Albemarle, and Louisa, d. of Robert T. Hubard, by the Rev. John S. Hansborough, at Chellow, Buckingham Co. So. Ch., Feb. 7, 1867

M. Lewis, Esq., of Albemarle, and Anna T. Daniel of Cumberland, by the Rev. R. J. McBryde, in St. Paul's Church, Lynchburg. So. Ch., Feb. 10, 1870

Martha L., of Suffolk, and Nicholas Constantine formerly of Satista, Greece, now of Norfolk, Va., by the Rev. H. L. Derby, in St. Paul's Church, Suffolk, Va. So. Ch., June 6, 1889

Mary E., d. of the late Maj. Peyton Randolph, and Otto L. Evans of Amherst C.H., by the Rev. G. H. Norton, Alexandria. So. Ch., Dec. 17, 1891

Nannie F., of Fauquier Co., and Dr. J. Robert Hicks, C.S. Army, by the Rev. Richard Mason, in Columbia, Fluvanna Co., Va. So. Ch., Feb. 8, 1865

Norman V., and Janet Henderson, d. of the late Arel Weaver, by the Rev. Charles K. Jenkins, at Warrenton, Fauquier Co. So. Ch., June 17, 1880

Robert L., of Baltimore, and S. B. Garnett of King George Co., Va., by the Rev. Percy Gordon, D.D. of Alabama, at the residence of the bride's mother. So. Ch., Jan. 22, 1880

Sarah Champe, and Reuben Warren Hammerslough of Baltimore, by the Rev. Frank Mezick, rector of the parish, at Markham, Nelson Co., Va., the home of the bride's mother, Mrs. Louisa H. Randolph. So. Ch., July 25, 1908

Virginia, d. of Dr. Wilson J. Randolph of Charlottesville, and George S. Shackelford of Orange, by the Rev. J. S. Hanckel, D.D. and the Rev. Green Shackelford, at the residence of the bride's father. So. Ch., July 10, 1884

Wm. L., Esq., of Albemarle Co., and Agnes Dillon of Savannah, Ga., by the Rev. J. D. Powell, at "Oakland", Cumberland Co. So. Ch., Mar. 1, 1866

Wilson C. N. (Dr.), and Nannie, second d. of Mrs. Julia A. Holladay, all of Albemarle, by the Rev. R. K. Meade, at Northwood, near Charlottesville. So. Ch., Nov. 19, 1858

RANKIN

Laura L., and Wm. H. Hollar of Pittsburgh, Pa., by the Rev. John W. Lea, in Trinity Church, Martinsburg. So. Ch., Oct. 28, 1875

Mary Hart, and B. L. Tabler, by the Rev. W. D. Hanson, in Trinity Church, Martinsburg. So. Ch., Aug. 18, 1870

RANLET

Robert, of Holyoke, Mass., and Netta Potts of Richmond, Va., by the Rev. John B. Newton, rector of Monumental Church, and the Rev.

MARRIAGE NOTICES IN THE SOUTHERN CHURCHMAN WITH DATES OF PUBLICATION

Hartley Carmichael, D.D., of St. Paul's Church, in Monumental Church, Richmond, Va. So. Ch., Nov. 16, 1893

RANNEY
Edward Ellicott, of Louisville, Ky., and Margaret Hamilton Thornton, at the residence of the bride's father, George W. Thornton, M.D. So. Ch., Jan. 5, 1882

RANSOM
Matt Whitaker, d. of Gen. Robert Ransom, and John Macon McCorkle of Newton, N.C., by the Rev. T. M. N. George, in Christ Church, New Bern, N.C. So. Ch., Dec. 18, 1890

Robert (Gen.), of New Bern, N.C., and Mrs. K. D. W. Lumpkin of Columbus, by the Rev. William A. Carter, at Columbus, Ga. So. Ch., Sept. 25, 1884

Miriam Glenn, and Frederick C. Horner of Marshall, Va., by the Rev. William L. Glenn, at the residence of the bride's parents, Major and Mrs. A. R. H. Ransom, at Hilton, Md. So. Ch., Nov. 26, 1910

RATHBORNE
Francis Vinton, and Mary Emma Jackson, by the Rev. Mr. Hyland, at the residence of the bride's father, Judge James M. Jackson, Parkersburg, W.Va. So. Ch., Dec. 4, 1873

RAVENEL
Charles Jervey, and Emily Lagare, d. of Mr. and Mrs. Morton Waring Simmons, by the Rev. Thomas P. Baker, at the residence of the bride's parents, Adam's Run, S.C. So. Ch., Dec. 18, 1909

Helen Lowndes, youngest d. of the late Dr. St. Julian Ravenel, and James Daniel Evans of Philadelphia, by the Rev. John Kershaw, D.D., rector of St. Michael's Church, Charleston, S.C., at home. So. Ch., Apr. 27, 1907

RAWLES
H. O., of Baltimore, and Nannie E., d. of the late John H. Butler of Norfolk, Va., by the Rev. Wm. C. Butler, in the Church of the Holy Innocents, Henderson, N.C. So. Ch., Jan. 15, 1864

RAWLINGS
(Mr.), of Mecklenburg, and Gay, d. of William Murray of Powhatan, by the Rev. P. F. Berkeley, at Genito, Powhatan Co. So. Ch., Jan. 8, 1864

Ephraim J., and Mrs. Ann J. Harrison, both of Brunswick, by the Rev. Otis A. Glazebrook, at Brunswick. So. Ch., Jan. 5, 1871

RAWLINS
James L., and Clara L. Boggs, both of Spotsylvania Co., Va., by the Rev. Wm. Greene, at "Livingston", Spotsylvania Co. So. Ch., Feb. 15, 1872

RAWLINSON
Lionel Seymour, of Herringstone, Augusta Co., Va., s. of Canon Rawlinson of Canterbury, and Anna Elizabeth, d. of Col. James C. and Elizabeth Brooke Cochran of Folly, Augusta Co., Va. and gr.d. of the late Judge Brooke of St. Julien, Spotsylvania Co., Va., by the Rev. W.

MARRIAGE NOTICES IN THE SOUTHERN CHURCHMAN WITH DATES OF PUBLICATION

Q. Hullihen, in Trinity Church, Staunton, Va. So. Ch., June 22, 1893

RAYNER
Melvina A., and Henry U. Meyer of New York, by the Rev. H. Wall, D.D., at Rocketts. So. Ch., Dec. 15, 1870

READ
Bettie Sims, d. of the late Thomas C. Read of Roanoke Co., Va., and Wm. W. Berkeley of King and Queen Co., by the Rev. L. B. Wharton, at Alta Monte, the residence of Mrs. Walter Preston. So. Ch., Sept. 8, 1870

David S., Esq., of Roanoke Co., and Emma B. Camp of Norfolk, by the Rev. O. S. Barton, D.D., rector, in Christ Church, Norfolk. So. Ch., Aug. 18, 1870

READING
Joseph, of Maryland, and Elizabeth A. M., oldest d. of the late James Edward Marshall, by the Rev. H. B. Lee, at Mt. Blanc, residence of the bride's mother, Fauquier Co., Va. So. Ch., Oct. 24, 1878

REDD
Eugene M., of Hanover, Hanover Co., Va., and Jennie Claiborne, by the Rev. Oscar S. Bunting, at Geddes, Amherst Co., Va. So. Ch., Jan. 1, 1880

REDDING
C. C., of King George Co., Va., and W. S. Chambers of Caroline Co., Va., by the Rev. Dr. W. A. Baynham, at the residence of J. M. Garret. So. Ch., Mar. 1, 1883*

Charles, of Westmoreland Co., Va., and Bettie Howland, by the Rev. Mr. McGuire, at the residence of the bride's father, King George Co., Va. So. Ch., Jan. 14, 1875

REDIN
Isabella W., d. of the late Wm. Rodin of Georgetown, D.C., and James B. Kirk, by the Rev. John Cole, in Culpeper Co. So. Ch., Sept. 26, 1867

REDMAN
W. F. (Dr.), and Mary H. Rives, by the Rev. R. S. Barrett, at Henderson, Ky. So. Ch., Oct. 11, 1883

REDWOOD
Virginia Caroline, d. of Wm. E. Redwood, Esq., and A. Carlyle Fairfax, both of Baltimore, by the Rev. A. S. Randolph, in Emmanuel Church, Baltimore. So. Ch., May 8, 1873

REED
David Henry, of Richmond, Va., and Susan, d. of Elias Reed, by the Rev. Mr. Christian, at Mitchell, Prince George Co. So. Ch., Nov. 22, 1839

John, of New York, and Lizzie E., d. of D. C. Mudge, Esq. of Volcano, by the Rev. S. D. Thompkins, in Emmanuel Church, Volcano, Wood Co., W.Va. So. Ch., Nov. 20, 1873

Katharine Lomax, youngest d. of Mrs. Kate Lomax and the late Rev. Theodore Reed, rector of the churches at Bladensburg and Hyattsville, Md., and Nelson Chancellor, s. of Dr. William Burwell of Parkersburg, W.Va., by the

---

* It is impossible to discern in this case which is the husband and which the wife, except by the custom of the editor of the Southern Churchman to publish the name of the husband first, which would make the husband C. C. Redding

MARRIAGE NOTICES IN THE SOUTHERN CHURCHMAN WITH DATES OF PUBLICATION

Rev. R. P. Williams, at Trinity Chapel, Washington, D.C. So. Ch., Jan. 30, 30, 1909

Margaret M., and Issac Bowman, both of Berryville, Clarke Co., Va., by the Rev. T. F. Hartin, at the residence of Mr. Leiday. So. Ch., Feb. 20, 1868

Susan, d. of Elias Reed, and David Henry Reed of Richmond, Va., by the Rev. Mr. Christian, at Mitchell, Prince George Co. So. Ch., Nov. 22, 1839

Theodore (The Rev.), of Loudoun Co., and Kate R., d. of the late Dr. R. Stuart Lomax, by the Rev. Melville Boyd of Brooklyn, N.Y., at Cedar Grove, the residence of Dr. R. H. Stuart, King George Co., Va. So. Ch., Oct. 31, 1878

REESE
Aubert Holt, of Savannah, Ga., and Rebecca Ambler, d. of Maj. G. H. T. Kearsley, by the Rev. Dallas Tucker, at Zion Church, Charles Town, W.Va. So. Ch., Feb. 7, 1889

Eleanor Fisher, and John Milton Reifsnider of Westminster, Md., by the Rev. James W. Reese, in St. John's Church. So. Ch., Nov. 4, 1886

Florence Isabella, and William N. Haxall, by the Rev. Randolph H. McKim, rector, in the Church of the Epiphany, Washington, D.C. So. Ch., Sept. 28, 1893

Frederick F. (The Rev.), and Ella, d. of Israel M. Parr, all of Baltimore, by the Rt. Rev. George W. Peterkin, D.D., Bishop of West Virginia, assisted by the Rev. Wm. H. Dame and the Rev. Campbell Fair, D.D., in Memorial Church, Baltimore. So. Ch., Nov. 27, 1879

REEVE
Florence, gr.d. of the late Capt. James Edwin Pleasants of Goochland, and George H. Nichols of Buckingham Co., Va., by the Rev. P. H. Boydon, at "Spring Dale", Goochland Co., Va. So. Ch., Jan. 3, 1884

REID
Allen, of Owensboro, Ky., and Marion Hamilton, d. of Wm. Dickson formerly of Scotland, now of Albemarle, by the Rev. T. E. Locke, at Oakland Grove, Albemarle Co., Va. So. Ch., Dec. 2, 1886

John I., of Rappahannock Co., and Lucy P., d. of the the late Gen. David Rodes, by the Rev. Dr. Mitchell, at Lynchburg. So. Ch., Oct. 10, 1867

Lucretia M., youngest d. of Col. John Reid, and Col. James Thrift, all of Fairfax, by the Rev. W. F. Lockwood, at Fruit Vale. So. Ch., Nov. 16, 1848

Mary Cassandra, d. of Col. L. Wilber Reid, and Emmett Clarke Dunn, by the Rev. William Hullihen Burkhardt, brother-in-law of the groom, in St. Paul's Church, Alexandria, Va. So. Ch., Nov. 23, 1893

REIFSNIDER
John Milton, of Westminster, Md., and Eleanor Fisher Reese, by the Rev. James W. Reese, in St. John's Church. So. Ch., Nov. 4,

MARRIAGE NOTICES IN THE SOUTHERN CHURCHMAN WITH DATES OF PUBLICATION

1886
RENISON
    Marjorie Mae, d. of the Rev. and Mrs. George E. Renison of Eagle Rock, Cal., and the Rev. Samuel Hunting Sayre, rector of St. Mary's Church, Williamsport, Pa., by the Rev. Theodore St. Clair Will, rector, assisted by the Rev. Edwin Royal Carter of Petersburg, Va., in St. John's Church, Hampton, Va. So. Ch., Jan. 20, 1934

REYNOLDS
    Empsie, d. of Dr. R. B. Rennolds of Fredericksburg, Va., and J. Evans Martin of South Carolina, by the Rev. R. J. McBryde, in St. George's Episcopal Church, Fredericksburg, Va. So. Ch., Nov. 3, 1881

    Robert G., and Nellie C. Addison, both of Richmond, by the Rev. Dr. Peterkin, in St. James' Church. So. Ch., Jan. 22, 1885

RENSHAW
    Robert H., of Baltimore, and Anne Carter, d. of Gen. Wm. C. Wickham, by the Rev. Charles Minnigerode, at Hickory Hill, Va. So. Ch., Nov. 17, 1881

REVELL
    George A., and Henrietta Joyner, by the Rev. Dr. Burrows, in First Baptist Church, Norfolk, Va. So. Ch., June 11, 1885

REYNOLDS
    James F., and Harriet S. Mothershead, both of Westmoreland Co., by the Rev. T. E. Dashiell, at Mt. Pleasant. So. Ch., July 22, 1859

    Mary Susan, and George Hamilton Fones, both of Westmoreland, by the Rev. R. A. Castleman, at Cople rectory, Hague, Westmoreland Co., Va. So. Ch., Jan. 23, 1890

    P. W., of Roanoke, and Sallie T. Word of Roanoke, by the Rev. D. M. Wood, in St. John's Church, Roanoke, Va. So. Ch., Dec. 3, 1885

RHETT
    William, of Charleston, S.C., and Rosalie, d. of the late Col. G. W. and Elizabeth T. Lunford, by the Rev. Beverly D. Tucker, at the residence of the bride's mother in Richmond, Va. So. Ch., July 27, 1882

RHODES
    M. V., of Clarendon, Va., and the Rev. P. L. Powles, M.A., B.D., by Bishop Brown of Virginia, in Washington Cathedral. So. Ch., July 18, 1925

RICE
    Emma, d. of John T. Rice, Esq., and Benedict Walker, Jr., by the Rev. T. Grayson Dashiell, at Laurel Spring, Westmoreland Co. So. Ch., Dec. 17, 1858

    Emma E. (Mrs.), d. of the late Jacob Farney, and the Rev. Thomas A. Morris, rector of the parish, by the Rev. Henry C. Lay, D.D., in St. Luke's Church, Jacksonville, Ala. So. Ch., Feb. 12, 1858

RICHARDS
    Delia Scott, and James Morgan Oyler, by the Rev. F. G. Scott, at Lynchburg, Va. So. Ch., Nov. 26, 1885

    Sarah (Mrs.), of Washington, D.C., and Col. John M. Fessenden of Boston, by the Rev. D. M. Wharton,

MARRIAGE NOTICES IN THE SOUTHERN CHURCHMAN WITH DATES OF PUBLICATION

at Spring Grove, the residence of the bride's mother, Westmoreland, Va. So. Ch., July 16, 1868

Sarah G., d. of the late George B. Richards, and Joseph M. Adams of Rockbridge Co., by the Rev. R. H. Mason, at Jay Cliff, near Warm Springs, Va. So. Ch., July 9, 1868

William, and Harriett H., youngest d. of Samuel R. Owens, Esq., by the Rev. A. B. Tizzard, at Chestnut Cottage, Chesterfield Co. So. Ch., Mar. 9, 1860

RICHARDSON

Cornelia A., of Clarke Co., Va., and Horace Beall, by the rector, the Rev. P. P. Phillips, in Grace Church, Berryville, Va. So. Ch., Oct. 27, 1881

H. G. (Capt.), of Farmville, Va., and Mary A. Perkins of Cumberland Co., Va., by the Rev. Wm. Hoxton, at the residence of Wm. A. Perkins, Forkland, Va. So. Ch., Jan. 16, 1873

Jesse C., and Annie E. Byus, both of Church Creek, Dorchester Co., Md., by the Rev. Wm. W. Greene. So. Ch., Apr. 7, 1881

Mary E., eldest d. of Maj. Jno. D. Richardson of Clarke Co., Va., and Ernest Blum of Richmond, by the Rev. T. F. Martin, at Fairfield, the residence of the bride's father. So. Ch., Apr. 8, 1869

R. E., and Julia, d. of Dr. Tom Harrison, all of New Kent Co., by the Rev. S. S. Hepbron, at the residence of the bride's father. So. Ch., Feb. 3, 1887

Richard B., and Ella, d. of John W. Jones, by the Rev. Edward Valentine Jones, at Mountain Gorge, near Buchanan, Va. So. Ch., Oct. 23, 1890

Richard C., Jr., of Clarendon, and Eliza Sinkler, d. of the late Hon. Richard I. Manning* of Clarendon, by the Rev. Edward R. Miles, at "Homesley", the residence of the bride's mother, in Sumter Co., S.C. So. Ch., Jan. 29, 1880

Robert A., of New Bern, N.C., and Mary S. Hunter of Lacy Spring, by the Rev. O. S. Bunting, at Lacy Spring, Rockbridge Co., Va. So. Ch., Oct. 15, 1885

Robert B. (Dr.), of Allensville, Todd Co., Ky., and Harriet A., d. of George Hankins, Esq. of James City Co., by the Rev. L. B. Wharton, at Marlbrooke. So. Ch., Mar. 20, 1873

Virgil Holman, and Mary Elizabeth Cocke, both of Columbia, Fluvanna Co., Va., by the Rev. J. H. Morrison, D.D., in St. John's Church, Columbia, Va. So. Ch., July 20, 1876

Wm. H., Jr., of Richmond, Va., and Florence E., eldest d. of Wm. S. Syke of King and Queen Co., Va., by the Rev. J. Hervey Hundley, at the residence of the bride's father. So. Ch., June 28, 1888

RICHESON

Delia, d. of the late John Richeson of Essex Co., and R. E. McDaniel, by

---

* A notice appears in the issue of Jan. 15, 1880, identical with this except that "Richard I. Manning" is written "Richard J. Manning"

MARRIAGE NOTICES IN THE SOUTHERN CHURCHMAN WITH DATES OF PUBLICATION

the Rev. A. Broadus, in Essex Co. So. Ch., Jan. 9, 1835

RICHEY
John S., and Ella M. Locke, by the Rev. T. F. Martin, at "Green Hill", the residence of the bride's father. So. Ch., Nov. 1, 1877

Thos. (The Rev.), and Emma Cecilia Bacot, by the Rev. Dr. Mahan, in Grace Church, Jersey City. So. Ch., Oct. 22, 1858

RICHISON
Andrew J., and Carrie, d. of Launcelot and Mary Minor, all of Amherst Co., Va., by the Rev. J. P. Lawrence, in St. Luke's Church, Pedlar Mills. So. Ch., Nov. 21, 1878

RICHMOND
Alice Clarissa, d. of the Rev. William Richmond, and the Rev. Thomas McClure Peters, by the Rev. William Richmond, in St. Michael's Church, Bloomingdale. So. Ch., July 16, 1847

RICKETTS
Mary B., d. of Capt. James B. Ricketts, U.S. Army, and Lt. William M. Graham, by the Rev. M. L. Chevers, at the Centurion Church, Old Point. So. Ch., Oct. 5, 1860

RIDALE
Henry A., and Martha C. Abell, d. of the late Edmund P. Hunter, all of Martinsburg, W.Va., by the Rev. W. D. Hanson and the Rev. Dr. David H. Ridale, in Trinity Church. So. Ch., Aug. 20, 1874

RIDDICK
John H., Esq., of Suffolk, and Julia D. Allen, youngest d. of Wm. D. Roberts, Esq. of Norfolk City, by the Rev. Dr. Minnigerode, at Norfolk. So. Ch., Jan. 18, 1856

Lillian S., youngest d. of the late Rich. H. Riddick, Esq., and Dr. Anthony R. Boykin of Smithfield, by the Rev. J. B. Craighill, at the residence of the bride's mother, in Isle of Wight Co., Va. So. Ch., Oct. 12, 1876

Maggie H., of Brunswick, and Wood J. Hamlin of Fluvanna, by the Rev. Otis A. Glazebrook, in St. Andrew's Church. So. Ch., Oct. 14, 1869

RIDDLE
Charles Morton, of Petersburg, Va., and Mildred Carter, d. of Maj. Robt. Douthat, at "Westbury", the residence of the bride's parents, Charles City Co., Va. So. Ch., July 6, 1893

RIDGELY
Anna Key, d. of the late Wm. G. Ridgely, Esq., and William Laird, Jr., by the Rev. S. Ridout, in Georgetown, D.C. So. Ch., June 21, 1866

E. Mary, d. of the officiating clergyman, and William R. Howard of Baltimore, by the Rev. G. W. Ridgely, at Wilmington, Del. So. Ch., Dec. 4, 1873

Edith, d. of J. Randolph Ridgely, and William H. Fisher, by the Rev. J. H. Eccleston, D.D., in Emmanuel Church, Baltimore. So. Ch., Nov. 27, 1884

Juliana Elizabeth Howard,

MARRIAGE NOTICES IN THE SOUTHERN CHURCHMAN WITH DATES OF PUBLICATION

and J. Southgate Yeaton, by the Rev. W. H. H. Powers, at Hampton, Baltimore Co., Md. So. Ch., Oct. 9, 1884
Sophia, and William Tayloe of King George Co., Va., by the Rev. Charles Goodrich, D.D., at Nottingham, Md. So. Ch., Nov. 28, 1872

RIDLEY
John William, of Southampton Co., and Elizabeth, eldest d. of W. S. Goodwyn, Esq. of Greensville Co., Va., by the Rev. C. J. Gibson, in Greensville Co., Va. So. Ch., Dec. 30, 1875

RIDOUT
Charles D., and Carrie J. Corner, by the Rev. Samuel Ridout, in St. Margaret's Church, Anne Arundel Co., Md. So. Ch., Nov. 29, 1883
John (The Rev.), of Grace Church, Petersburg, and Faith M. Leadbeater of Alexandria, by the Rev. Ernest M. Stires of West Point, Va. and the Rev. Theron Rice of Alexandria, at Alexandria, Va. So. Ch., Nov. 17, 1892

RIELY
Corrine Taylor, d. of Col. John J. Riely of Clarke Co., Va., and Lambert Mason of St. Joseph, Mo., by the rector, the Rev. P. P. Phillips, in Grace Church, Berryville, Va. So. Ch., July 10, 1890
John J., of Clarke Co., and Lucy O., d. of John B. Taylor, Esq.,by the Rev. F. M. Whittle of Jefferson Co., in Jefferson Co., Va. So. Ch., Dec. 5, 1856
John W., of Fredericksburg, and Emma Carrington of Charlotte Co., Va., by the Rev. James A. Mitchell, at "Ingleside", the residence of the bride's father. So. Ch., Nov. 7, 1867

RILEY
Juliet Marie, d. of the late Dr. John C. Riley, and Charles Phelps Williams, all of Georgetown, by the Rev. John S. Lindsay, D.D., in St. John's Church, Georgetown, D.C. So. Ch., May 3, 1883

RION
Holbrook,* Esq., of Winnsboro, S.C., and Helen J., second d. of the Hon. Taylor Berry of Amherst, by the Rev. Wm. Meade Clark, in Ascension Church, Amherst C.H., Va. So. Ch., May 21, 1885

RISON
John W., of Richmond, and Sarah A., d. of Col. Robert W. Ashlin of Fluvanna Co., by the Rev. T. C. Roberts, at Rivanna Hall, Fluvanna Co., Va. So. Ch., Feb. 24, 1870

RISQUE
John P., of Silver City, N.M., and Jeannie S., d. of George R. Robinson, by the Rev. A. Batte, in Emmanuel Church, St. Louis Co., Mo. So. Ch., Aug. 7, 1879

RITCHIE
Albert, of Baltimore, and Lizzie Caskie, d. of Dr. Robert G. Cabell of Richmond, by the Rev. Thomas G. Addison, D.D. assisted by the Rev. Charles Minni-

* A notice appears in the issue of May 14, 1885 identical with this, except that "Holbrook" is written "Holbrooke"

MARRIAGE NOTICES IN THE SOUTHERN CHURCHMAN WITH DATES OF PUBLICATION

gerode, D.D., in St. Paul's Church, Richmond, Va. So. Ch., Nov. 18, 1875

Emily Nelson, d. of Judge John Ritchie and gr.d. of Judge William Maulsby, and Donald McLean of New York, by the Rev. Osborn Ingle and the Rt. Rev. William Pinckney, Bishop of Maryland, in All Saints Church, Frederick, Md. So. Ch., May 3, 1883

RIVES
Alfred, s. of the Hon. Wm. C. Rives, and Sadie C., d. of James Macmurdo and gr.d. of the late Bishop Moore, by the Rev. Dr. Minnigerode, in St. Paul's Church, Richmond, Va. So. Ch., Feb. 11, 1859

Amelie, d. of Alfred Landon and S. C. Rives, and John Armstrong Chanler, by the Rev. E. L. Goodwin, at Castle Hill, Albemarle Co., Va. So. Ch., June 21, 1888

Isabella, d. of Alexander Rives of Albemarle, and T. Gordon Coleman, Jr., by the Rev. R. K. Meade, at Carlton. So. Ch., Dec. 12, 1856

Lizzie Tunstall, and W. M. Hickson, Esq., by the Rev. Geo. W. Dame, at Danville. So. Ch., Oct. 27, 1870

Lucy B., d. of Alexander Rives, Esq., and Prof. DeVere M. Schele of the University of Virginia, by the Rev. R. K. Meade, at Carlton, near Charlottesville. So. Ch., Mar. 30, 1860

Mary H., and Dr. W. F. Redman, by the Rev. R. S. Barrott, at Henderson, Ky. So. Ch., Oct. 11, 1883

Sallie Evolyn, only d. of Edwin W. and Indiana V. Rives of Sussex Co., Va., and William Daniel, by the Rev. Richard McIlwain, in the Presbyterian Church, Farmville. So. Ch., Nov. 23, 1865

RIVINUS
David Caldwell F., of Philadelphia, and Emily Maxey, d. of the late Francis Markoe, by the Rev. Wm. Hodges, D.D., at Tulip Hill, the residence of the bride, Anne Arundel Co. So. Ch., Nov. 13, 1873

RIXEY
Eppa, and Miss Willie Walton, both of Culpeper Co., by the Rev. John McGill, in Christ Church, Brandy Station, So. Ch., July 6, 1882

Saml. R. (Dr.), and Mary P., d. of the late Fayette Mauzy, all of Culpeper C.H., Va., by the Rev. Geo. W. Peterkin, at Culpeper. So. Ch., Sept. 25, 1873

ROANE
Junius B., of Middlesex Co., Va., and Hattie E., d. of H. P. Harrell of Lewiston, by the Rev. H. M. Jarvis, in Christ Church, near Lewiston, N.C. So. Ch., Nov. 10, 1887

ROBB
Mattie F., only d. of Capt. Robt. G. Robb formerly of the U.S. Navy, and W. Augustine Smith of King George Co., Va., by the Rev. Wm.

- 150 -

MARRIAGE NOTICES IN THE SOUTHERN CHURCHMAN WITH DATES OF PUBLICATION

Friend, in St. Peter's Church, Port Royal, Va. So. Ch., Jan. 6, 1870

ROBBINS

Joseph, and Maggie Gore, both of Dorchester Co., Md., by the Rev. William W. Greene, at the residence of Capt. L. Powell. So. Ch., May 20, 1880

Mary Douglas, d. of the late Rev. Chandler Robbins of Springfield, Ohio, and the Rev. Douglass Hooff of Suffolk, Va., by the rector, the Rev. George H. Norton, D.D., in St. Paul's Church, Alexandria, Va. So. Ch., Nov. 26, 1885

ROBERSON

Evy L., and Charles Hewitt, both of Falmouth, by the Rev. J. Green Shackelford of Trinity Church, Fredericksburg, Va., at the residence of the bride's father, C. W. Roberson, Falmouth, Va. So. Ch., Nov. 22, 1888

ROBERT

J. D., M.D., of St. Louis, Mo., and Minnie Thweatt, d. of G. M. Wilson and gr.d. of the late Hon. R. N. Thweatt of Chesterfield Co., Va., by the Rev. A. B. Tizzard assisted by the Rev. H. M. Jackson, D.D., in Grace Church, Richmond. So. Ch., Jan. 10, 1889

P. G. (The Rev.), rector of Meherrin Parish,* and Bettie, eldest d. of Dr. Edward P. Scott of Greensville Co., by the Rev. C. J. Gibson, at Oakland, Greensville Co. So. Ch., Oct. 26, 1854

ROBERTS

Augusta Hunter, of Northampton Co., Va., and D. H. Pannill, Esq. of Pittsylvania Co., by the Rev. J. J. Gravatt, rector of St. John's Church, Hampton, Va., at the residence of the bride's father. So. Ch., Oct. 11, 1877

Benjamin T., Jr., of Rochester, N.Y., and Sarah B. Kidwell of Baltimore, by the Rev. Edward H. Ingle, in St. Bartholomew's Church, Baltimore. So. Ch., Feb. 17, 1887

Harry Lee, and Venetia Morrill May, by the Rev. T. A. Cheatham, at Farmville, N.C. So. Ch., May 9, 1908

Jas. Warren, of Richmond, and Mrs. Kate Kenter (nee Fewell) of Manassas, Va., by the Rev. A. P. Gray, in Trinity Church, Manassas. So. Ch., Jan. 4, 1883

Joseph (Capt.), U.S.A., and Adeline C., d. of Col. J. Dimick, U.S.A., by the Rev. M. L. Chevers, in the Centurion Church, Old Point. So. Ch., Oct. 19, 1860

Rebecca S., d. of John Roberts, Esq. of Alexandria, D.C., and J. Melville Gillies of the U.S. Navy, by the Rev. C. B. Dana, in Christ Church. So. Ch., Dec. 15, 1837

William Christian (The Rev.), rector of St. James Parish, Monkton, Md., and Ruth E. Lauster, by Bishop Helfenstein assisted by

* Meherrin Parish is in Greensville County, Virginia (Journal ... Diocese of Southern Virginia, Portsmouth, Va., 1941)

MARRIAGE NOTICES IN THE SOUTHERN CHURCHMAN WITH DATES OF PUBLICATION

the Rev. James A. Mitchell, in the Church of the Messiah, Hamilton, Baltimore, Md. So. Ch., Dec. 7, 1929
Wm. Thomas, rector of St. Stephen's Church, Culpeper, Va., and Laura Stuart Powell of Shepherdstown, W.Va., by the rector, the Rev. L. R. Mason, in Trinity Church, Shepherdstown, W.Va. So. Ch., May 20, 1886
See also ALLEN, Julia D. (Mrs.)

ROBERTSON
Duncan, and Lillie Payne Todd, both of Norfolk, Va., by the Rev. F. C. Steinmetz, rector of Christ Church, at the home of Mr. and Mrs. John D. Letcher, Norfolk. So. Ch., Jan. 23, 1909
Ellen Harrison, d. of Kate H. and the late Powhatan Robertson of Virginia, and the Rev. Lewis Carter Harrison, rector of St. Matthias Church, East Aurora, N.Y., by the Rev. H. deWolf de Mauriac, rector, in St. Paul's Church, Lancaster, N.H. So. Ch., Oct. 19, 1912
Gay Bernard, and A. Walton Fleming of Washington, D.C., by the Rev. S. S. Ware, in St. Peter's Church, Port Royal. So. Ch., Nov. 26, 1891
George W., of Richmond, and Anna E., only d. of the late Dr. Austin Watkins of Nottoway, by the Rev. C. J. Gibson, at Rosewood, Nottoway Co. So. Ch., Feb. 5, 1858
H. C., of Greensborough, Ala., and Julia O., d. of the late Francis G. Yancey, Esq., by the Rev. Mr. Bartlett, at Petersburg, Va. So. Ch., Aug. 25, 1837
Harrison, of Norfolk, and Eliza, d. of the late Dr. Jaqueline A. Marshall of Fauquier Co., by the Rev. Thomas Duncan, at Prospect Hill, Fauquier Co. So. Ch., Oct. 28, 1859
Harrison, Esq., of Danville, Va., and Laura V., d. of Dr. J. T. Forbes, by the Rev. Wm. M. Dame, at the residence of the bride's father, Baltimore, Md. So. Ch., Nov. 18, 1880
Horace C., and Virgie B., d. of the late Wm. B. Robertson, by the Rev. A. B. Tizzard, at Clover Hill, Chesterfield Co., Va. So. Ch., Jan. 10, 1889
Huling P., of Salado, Bell Co., Tex., and Mary Gatlin, eldest d. of Chas. Cooke, at Gainsville, Sumter Co., Ala. So. Ch., Mar. 5, 1885
Julia, and J. Marsden Smith, both of Norfolk, by the Rev. Beverly D. Tucker, at the residence of the bride's father, Duncan Robertson, Esq. So. Ch., Oct. 14, 1886
Kate M., and James L. White, by the Rev. L. B. Wharton, at "The Meadows", the residence of the Hon. Wyndham Robertson. So. Ch., Nov. 7, 1867
Mary, eldest d. of Wyndham Robertson, Esq., and Wm. W. Blackford, by the Rev. Mr. Woodbridge, in St. Paul's Church, Richmond. So. Ch., Jan. 18, 1856
Mary Frances, of Norfolk, Va., and William Maxwell,

MARRIAGE NOTICES IN THE SOUTHERN CHURCHMAN WITH DATES OF PUBLICATION

Esq., president of Hampden-Sydney College, by the Rev. Wm. Neil. So. Ch., June 14, 1839

Octavia H., d. of William Robertson, Esq. of Culpeper, Va., and Dr. Edmund P. Taliaferro of Green Co., Ala., by the Rev. William C. H. Jones, at Delorain. So. Ch., Dec. 1, 1837

Sarah Ann, d. of Mrs. Ann Robertson of Willington, Culpeper Co., and Edmund L. Taylor of Taylorsville, Hanover Co., by the Rev. John W. Woodville. So. Ch., Dec. 15, 1837

Susan Boone, d. of the late Alexander Robertson of Charleston, S.C., and the Rt. Rev. Theodore Benedict Lyman, D.D., Bishop of North Carolina, by the Rev. Charles C. Pinckney, D.D., in St. Michael's Church, Charleston, S.C. So. Ch., Mar. 16, 1893

Victor James, of San Francisco, Cal., and Sarah White, d. of the late Samuel M. Bailey, by the Rev. Frank Woods Baker, in Covington, Ky. So. Ch., Oct. 31, 1889

Virgie B., d. of the late Wm. B. Robertson, and Horace C. Robertson, by the Rev. A. B. Tizzard, at Clover Hill, Chesterfield Co., Va. So. Ch., Jan. 10, 1889

W. R., of Culpeper Co., Va., and Hattie B., second d. of Horace B. Hall of Fredericksburg, by the Rev. R. J. McBryde, at the residence of the bride's father. So. Ch., June 17, 1880

Wm. Gordon, of Roanoke, Va., and Nannie A., d. of Mrs. Peachy Gilmer Breckinbridge of Botetourt Co., Va., by the Rev. C. C. Randolph, at Grove Hill, Botetourt Co. So. Ch., Nov. 23, 1882

Wm. J. (Judge), and Mrs. Alice W. Morris, d. of the late Gen. Edward Watts, by the Rev. J. Earnest, at Oaklands, Roanoke Co. So. Ch., July 24, 1863

ROBINS

Elizabeth Todd, of Richmond, and Maurice Johnston Lunn of Pittsburgh, Pa. So. Ch., July 4, 1908

Helen, and Emmet Nelson White, formerly of Haymarket, Va., by the Rev. W. W. Wyckoff, in Christ Episcopal Church, Gary, Ind. So. Ch., July 5, 1913

Ruth R., and Lemuel L. Dirding, both of Berkeley Co., W.Va., by the Rev. W. T. Leavell, rector of Mt. Zion Church, Hedgesville, Va., at North Mountain, Berkeley Co., W.Va. So. Ch., Jan. 4, 1883

William T. (Col.), and Sallie Berkeley Nelson, both of Gloucester Co., by the Rev. A. Y. Hundley, in Abingdon Church. So. Ch., June 6, 1878

ROBINSON

Alice B., niece of Mrs. Haxall, and Charles S. Carpender of New Brunswick, N.J., by the Rev. Charles Minnigerode, in Richmond, at the residence of W. H. Haxall. So. Ch., June 24, 1875

Angelica Lockwood, youngest d. of George R. and Anne

MARRIAGE NOTICES IN THE SOUTHERN CHURCHMAN WITH DATES OF PUBLICATION

R. P. Robinson, and William M. Jenkins of Louisville, Ky., by the Rev. George H. Sterling, in Emmanuel Church, Old Orchard, Mo. So. Ch., Nov. 5, 1891

Anne, and Alfred Edward Johnson, both of Oilville, Goochland Co., Va., by the Rev. Wyllys Rede, in St. Mary's Church. So. Ch., Feb. 9, 1888

Arch. M., of Louisville, and B., d. of C. A. Harris of Versailles, by the Rev. W. G. McCready, at the residence of the bride's uncle, Joseph Woolfolk, Lexington, Ky. So. Ch., Sept. 19, 1889

Chas. Andrews, and Fannie S. Annan, both of St. Louis, by the Rev. P. G. Robert, in St. Louis, Mo. So. Ch., Jan. 15, 1885

Ellen C., and Thompson Mason King, in Trinity Church, Shepherdstown. So. Ch., Nov. 2, 1865

Ellgean, d. of the late John M. Robinson, Esq. of Botetourt Co., Va., and Lt. George B. St. Clair, C.S.A. of Texas, by the Rev. Wm. McGuire, at the residence of the bride's mother, Beaverdam. So. Ch., Feb. 8, 1865

Fannie, d. of Mrs. A. K. and the late Archibald Robinson, Esq., and Col. Llewelyn Hoxton of Baltimore Co., Md., by the Rev. A. M. Randolph, at Fruit Hill, the residence of the bride's mother, Jefferson Co., Va. So. Ch., Oct. 29, 1868

George A., of Louisville, Ky., and Rosa D., d. of Col. William Preston Johnston of Lexington, Va., by the Rev. W. N. Pendleton, at the residence of the bride's father. So. Ch., Oct. 14, 1880

Geo. R., and Annie, d. of the officiating clergyman, the Rev. C. W. Andrews, D.D., in the Episcopal Church, Shepherdstown. So. Ch., Oct. 5, 1855

J. B. (Capt.), and Fannie Hull, by the Rev. Andrew Fisher, at Edge Hill, Lancaster Co. So. Ch., Mar. 26, 1868

James C., and Constance K. Harris, by the Rev. C. C. Randolph, at Escalona, the home of the bride's father, Frank Harris. So. Ch., Nov. 30, 1907

Jas. J., of West Virginia, and Kathleen B., youngest d. of the late P. A. L. Smith of Fauquier Co., by the Rev. A. P. Gray, at the residence of Capt. Brookefield, near New Baltimore, Fauquier Co. So. Ch., Sept. 27, 1883

Jeannie S., d. of George R. Robinson, and John P. Risque of Silver City, N.M., by the Rev. A. Batte, in Emmanuel Church, St. Louis Co., Mo. So. Ch., Aug. 7, 1879

John S., and Lizzette G., oldest d. of P. A. L. Smith of Fauquier Co., by the Rev. Jno. McGill, at the residence of the bride's father. So. Ch., Nov. 13, 1873

Lila Andrews, d. of George R. Robinson of St. Louis, and Walter Checkley

MARRIAGE NOTICES IN THE SOUTHERN CHURCHMAN WITH DATES OF PUBLICATION

Tiffany of Minneapolis, by the Rev. George Sterling, in Emmanuel Church, near St. Louis, Mo. So. Ch., May 10, 1888

Lizzie B., formerly of Baltimore Co., and Alexander R. Claytor of West River, by the Rev. William F. Gardner, at "Clifton." So. Ch., Nov. 13, 1884

Lucy R., of Essex, and the Rev. J. W. Keble of Kentucky, by the Rev. John B. Newton, in St. John's Church, Tappahannock. So. Ch., Sept. 25, 1873

Mary Alice, and James Burton Simmonds, both of Lancaster, Va., by the Rev. H. L. Derby, in Trinity Church, Lancaster C.H., Va. So. Ch., Sept. 16, 1886

Monroe, of Baltimore, and Mattie Lockert of Norfolk, Va., by the Rev. Dr. Hodges, in St. Paul's Church, Baltimore, Md. So. Ch., Dec. 6, 1877

Octavia, d. of John Robinson, Esq., and Richard B. Haxall, Esq., all of Richmond, Va., by the Rt. Rev. Bishop Moore, in Richmond, Va. So. Ch., Nov. 24, 1837

Poitiaux, and Anne H., d. of R. H. Maury, by the Rev. Joshua Peterkin, at the residence of the bride's father, Richmond. So. Ch., Feb. 7, 1878

Rebecca, and John Paxton, Esq. of Scottsburg, Halifax Co., Va., by the Rev. Charles Randolph, at Shepherd's Island, Botetourt Co., Va., the residence of Starkey Robinson, Esq. So. Ch., Mar. 1, 1883

Robert Emmet (Dr.), of Petersburg, and Indiana A. Henly, by the Rev. Dr. Syme, at Bacons Castle, Surry Co., Va. So. Ch., Aug. 25, 1837

Roberta, and F. B. Poague, by the Rev. C. C. Randolph, at Mrs. Mary Robinson's, "Beaver Dam", Botetourt Co., Va. So. Ch., Oct. 13, 1881

Rosa, d. of the late Archibald Robinson of Fruit Hill, Jefferson Co., W.Va., and Isaac F. Nicholson of Baltimore, by the Rev. Dr. Andrews, at Fruit Hill, Jefferson Co., W.Va. So. Ch., Oct. 12, 1871

Sallie J., and M. C. J. Mohler, by the Rev. Jno. McGill, in Christ Church, Fairfax Co. So. Ch., Jan. 4, 1877

ROCKE
Frank T., Esq., formerly of Hampton, Va., now of Austin, Tex., and Josephine Wingfield of Elizabeth City Co., by the Rev. J. J. Gravatt, at Back River, Elizabeth City Co., Va. So. Ch., Jan. 12, 1882

RODES
Lafayette Penn, brother of the late Maj. Gen. R. E. Rodes, C.S.A., and Laura Carter, eldest d. of J. J. Ambler, Esq. and gr.d. of the late Hon. Philip Pendleton Barbour, for many years Associate Justice of the Supreme Court of the U.S., by the Rev. E. S.

MARRIAGE NOTICES IN THE SOUTHERN CHURCHMAN WITH DATES OF PUBLICATION

Gregory, rector of the Church of the Epiphany, at the residence of the bride's parents, Lynchburg, Va. So. Ch., July 19, 1883

Lucy P., d. of the late Gen. David Rodes, and John I. Reid of Rappahannock Co., by the Rev. Dr. Mitchell, at Lynchburg. So. Ch., Oct. 10, 1867

RODGERS

Annie Douglass, d. of Col. Hamilton Rodgers of Loudoun Co., and A. K. Phillips, Esq., of Fredericksburg, by the Rev. Mr. Kinsolving, at Oakham. So. Ch., Mar. 2, 1860

C. L. (The Rev.), of Osmond, Neb., formerly of North Carolina, and Elizabeth H. Chrisman, by the Rev. Wilson P. Chrisman of Moundsville, W.Va., brother of the bride, at the home of the bride in Martinsburg, W.Va. So. Ch., Jan. 12, 1907

John D. (Maj.), and Kitty, d. of Launcelot Minor, Esq., by the Rev. Robert J. McBryde assisted by the Rev. Mr. Lawrence, rector of the parish, at Briery Knowe, Amherst Co., Va. So. Ch., Oct. 26, 1882

RODMAN

Erskine M. (The Rev.), and Sarah Wickham, d. of W. F. Sharpe, Esq. of Goshen, N.Y., by the Rev. W. De L. Granniss assisted by the Rev. Washington Rodman, rector of Grace Church, Plainfield, N.J., at the residence of the bride's father. So. Ch., June 22, 1871

Erskine Mason (The Rev.), and Nannie, youngest d. of Miles C. Seldon, Esq. of Norwood, Powhatan Co., Va., by the Rev. Washington Rodman, at Norwood, Powhatan Co., Va. So. Ch., Nov. 21, 1856

RODNEY

Sarah F., d. of Henry F. Rodney of Lewes, and the Rev. John Leighton McKim of Philadelphia, by the Rev. George Seymour Lewis, in St. Peter's Church, Lewes, Del. So. Ch., Dec. 21, 1860

ROESER

Thekla, d. of Carl Roeser, and Richard Coleman, by the Rev. Frank Page, at the residence of the bride's father, near Dranesville. So. Ch., Feb. 8, 1883

ROGERS

Alexander H., and Julia, only d. of Dr. Thomas H. Clagett, all of Loudoun Co., Va., by the Rev. O. A. Kinsolving, at Leesburg. So. Ch., Nov. 5, 1858

Ferdinand (The Rev.), of Brownville, Jefferson Co., N.Y., and Angelina, youngest d. of Silas Stone, Esq. of Hudson, N.Y., by the Rev. Isaac Pardee, in Christ Church, Hudson, N.Y. So. Ch., June 14, 1839

G. A., of Richmond, Va., and Annie Cosby of Hanover, by the Rev. R. S. Barrett, in Hanover Co. So. Ch., June 3, 1880

Henry J., Esq., formerly of New York, and Crimora B. Kohler, d. of the

MARRIAGE NOTICES IN THE SOUTHERN CHURCHMAN WITH DATES OF PUBLICATION

officiating clergyman formerly of Jefferson Co., Va., by the Rev. Mr. Kehler, in Denver City, J.T.,* So. Ch., Oct. 26, 1860

Joseph, and Elizabeth Crump, in Richmond, Va. So. Ch., Jan. 9, 1835

Lucy H., only d. of James H. Rogers, Esq. of Charleston, and Edward Galatti, Esq. of Louisville, Ky., by the Rev. R. A. Cobbs, the rector, in St. John's Church, Charleston, W.Va. So. Ch., Mar. 26, 1885

Lucy Lee, eldest d. of Gen. A. Rogers of Middleburg, and the Rev. O. A. Kinsolving, by the Rev. William Sparrow, D.D., in Emanuel Church, Middleburg. So. Ch., Aug. 12, 1859

Mortimer M., of Baltimore, Md., and Jennie, youngest d. of George P. Tayloe of Roanoke Co., Va., by the Rev. Edward H. Ingle, at "Buena Vista", the residence of the bride's father. So. Ch., Nov. 25, 1875

Susanna D., and John C. Norris, both of Baltimore, by the Rev. John C. McCabe, D.D., rector of St. James' Parish, Anne Arundel Co., Md., in Baltimore. So. Ch., Dec. 7, 1860

ROLLER
L. Josie, and Charles M. Hollingsworth, M.D., by the Rev. R. D. Roller assisted by the Rev. O. S. Bunting, rector of the parish, at Inglewood, Rockingham Co., Va., the residence of the bride's father. So. Ch., Nov. 6, 1884

Robert Douglas (The Rev.), of St. Martin's Parish, Hanover Co., Va., formerly of Rockingham Co., Va., and Carrie, d. of the late George T. Booker of Richmond, by the Rev. Charles Minnigerode, D.D., in Richmond, at the residence of the bride's father. So. Ch., Nov. 1, 1877

RORER
Eulalia, and Llewellyn Lee Powell, both of Roanoke, Va., by the Rev. John D. Powell assisted by the Rev. W. H. Meade, in St. John's Church, Roanoke, Va. So. Ch., Nov. 17, 1887

ROSE
Anna M., and Clinton W. Russell, both of Richmond, at Claremont, Va. So. Ch., Apr. 28, 1892

John Taylor (The Rev.), and Linda, d. of the late Charles and Mary Dows Stebbins, by the Rev. Dr. H. G. Coddington, rector of Grace Church, Syracuse, N.Y., in St. Peter's Church, Cazenovia, N.Y. So. Ch., Dec. 6, 1919

L. W. (The Rev.), of Boydton, Va., and Mrs. Bessie E. Walker, d. of Charles Zogbaum, Esq., by the Rev. Richard Newton, D.D., rector of the Church of the Covenant, at Germantown, Philadelphia. So. Ch., Dec. 18, 1884

Wm. W. (Dr.), of King George, and Kate Corbin, youngest d. of the late Wm. F. and Mary W. Taliaferro of Peckatone, Westmoreland, Va., by the Rev. E. B. McGuire, at

---

* Jefferson Territory became Colorado Territory in 1861

MARRIAGE NOTICES IN THE SOUTHERN CHURCHMAN WITH DATES OF PUBLICATION

Peckatone. So. Ch., Nov. 30, 1860

ROSENBERG
Henry, of Galveston, Tex., and Mollie Ragan, d. of the late Dr. Chas. Macgill of Richmond, formerly of Hagerstown, Md., by the Rev. Hartley Carmichael of St. Paul's Church, at Grace Church, Richmond. So. Ch., Nov. 28, 1889

ROSS
Ellen, eldest d. of the late Richard Ross of Glen Ross, Montgomery Co., Md., and the Rev. James B. Noblit, rector of St. Mark's Church, Lewistown, Pa., by the Rev. Mr. Hoff. So. Ch., June 14, 1839

Juliana J., d. of Wm. Ross, Esq. of Frederickstown, Md., and the Rev. John F. Hoff, rector of Christ Church, Georgetown, D.C., by the Rev. Upton Beall. So. Ch., Nov. 15, 1839

William B., and Elizabeth Mayo, d. of Col. John Thom, by the Rev. Walker Woodville, at Berry Hill. So. Ch., Oct. 27, 1837

ROTHACKER
Margaret Ruth, and George Craig Stewart, Jr., s. of the officiating clergyman, by Bishop George Craig Stewart, in the Lady Chapel of St. Luke's Pro-Cathedral. So. Ch., July 20, 1935

ROTHROCK
Nannie T., d. of the late George W. Rothrock, Esq. of Fredericksburg, Va., and M. Leib Harrison, Esq. of Philadelphia, by the Rev. E. C. Murdaugh, D.D., at the residence of the bride. So. Ch., Mar. 25, 1875

ROULHAC
J. G. P. (Dr.), of Hickman, Ky., and Mildred, d. of the late Lewis Dupree, Esq., by the Rev. P. G. Robert, at "Retirement", Southampton Co. So. Ch., Mar. 20, 1857

ROUNDTREE
Samuel Stevens, of Quitman, Ga., and Minnie Claiborne, d. of John C. Lewis of Albemarle Co., Va., by the Rev. Thos. E. Locke, at Cliffside. So. Ch., Feb. 20, 1890

ROWE
Peter Trimble, D.D. (The Rt. Rev.), Bishop of Alaska, and Rose Fullerton, by the Rev. E. V. Shayler, in St. Mark's Church, Seattle, Wash. So. Ch., Nov. 20, 1915

ROWLAND
Harriet C., d. of John H. Rowland, Esq. of Norfolk, and Rev. W. F. Gardner, by the Rev. Mr. Barten, in Christ Church, Norfolk, Va. So. Ch., Apr. 30, 1868

Virginia, second d. of John H. Rowland, Esq., and Thos. U. Dudley, rector of Christ Church, Baltimore, by the Rev. O. S. Barten, in Christ Church, Norfolk, Va. So. Ch., Apr. 15 and May 13, 1869

ROWLETT
Maggie, d. of Mrs. Susan Rowlett, and Dr. Barksdale Hales, all of Halifax Co., Va., by the Rev. O. A. Kinsolving, D.D., at the residence of Dabney Cosby.

MARRIAGE NOTICES IN THE SOUTHERN CHURCHMAN WITH DATES OF PUBLICATION

ROY
Ann S., d. of Wm. H. Roy, Esq., and John C. Rutherford, Esq. of Goochland Co., Va., by the Rev. G. S. Carraway, Green Plains, Mathews Co., Va. So. Ch., Oct. 31, 1856

Susan, d. of Wm. H. Roy, Esq. of Mathews Co., Va., and Dr. Thos. H. Carter of King William Co., Va., by the Rev. Mr. Carraway, at Green Plains. So. Ch., Dec. 14, 1855

Thos. S., Esq., of Fauquier Co., and Fannie B. M., d. of James Roy Micow, Esq., by the Rev. H. W. L. Temple, at Tappahannock. So. Ch., Dec. 25, 1857

ROYALL
Ida L., and William G. Hogan, by the Rev. John C. Cornick, at the residence of Mr. Royall, Charles City Co., Va. So. Ch., Jan. 21, 1892

Mary G., and Thos. J. Turpin, both of Powhatan Co., Va., by the Rev. John D. Powell, at the residence of Joseph W. Royall, Esq., the bride's father. So. Ch., Dec. 2, 1859

W. R., and Laura Holmes, youngest d. of Raleigh Colston, all of Richmond, Va., by the Rev. Dr. Peterkin assisted by the Rev. Dr. Kerr, in St. James' Church. So. Ch., Feb. 24, 1887

See also MATHEWS, Susan (Mrs.)

ROYSTER
Harriet R., of New Kent, Va., and Charles E. Yeatman, Esq. of Mathews Co., Va., by the Rev. G. S. Carraway, at the residence of the bride's mother, Mrs. E. Royster. So. Ch., Nov. 16, 1860

ROYSTON
Sally F., and C. W. Tompkins of Spotsylvania, Va., by the Rev. Jas. E. Poindexter, at Ormsby, Caroline Co., Va. So. Ch., Nov. 28, 1872

RUCKER
H. Scott, of Pocahontas Co., W.Va., and Lizzie C. Scott of Virginia, by the Rev. T. N. Lacy, at the residence of Dr. Wm. P. Rucker, near Lewisburg, W.Va. So. Ch., Mar. 16, 1882

RUDD
Everett W., and Ella C., d. of Thomas Womack, Esq., by the Rev. A. B. Tizzard, at Eppington, Chesterfield Co., Va. So. Ch., Feb. 12, 1880

J. W., and Mrs. Mary A. Moore, by the Rev. A. B. Tizzard, at the residence of Mr. G. W. Bartlam, Chesterfield Co., Va. So. Ch., Feb. 18, 1886

RUFFIN
Annie C., and W. B. Sims of Halifax Co., Va., by the Rev. B. S. Bronson, at the residence of the bride's father, Dr. John K. Ruffin, Wilson, N.C. So. Ch., July 5, 1883

Bessie C., second d. of Mrs. L. M. Ruffin, and Roland F. Broaddus, Esq., all of Hanover, by the Rev. S. S. Hepbron, in Immanuel Church, Hanover. So. Ch., May 2, 1889

MARRIAGE NOTICES IN THE SOUTHERN CHURCHMAN WITH DATES OF PUBLICATION

Edmond, of Upper Marlburn, Hanover Co., Va., and Lelia B., d. of Col. Randolph Harrison of Williamsburg, by the Rev. S. S. Hepbron, in Immanuel Church, Hanover Co., Va. So. Ch., Feb. 3, 1887

George C., Jr., of Tar Bay, Prince George Co., Va., and Sara Roane, d. of Mr. and Mrs. E. C. Harrison of Elkord, Cumberland Co., Va., by the Rev. John Cormick of Onancock, at the home of the bride. So. Ch., May 11, 1912

John A., and Jennie Cary, d. of the late Wm. M. Harrison of Riverside, by the Rev. Edward Valentine Jones, at Westover, Charles City Co., Va. So. Ch., June 7, 1888

Julian Meade, and Mary Ruffin, both grandchildren of the late Edmund Ruffin, Sr., one of Virginia's distinguished agriculturists, by the Rev. T. W. Jones, at Elmwood, home of the bride. So. Ch., July 28, 1887

M. C., d. of Edmund Ruffin, Esq. of Hanover Co., Va., and B. B. Sayre, Esq. of Frankfort, Ky., by the Rev. G. S. Carraway, at Marlbourne. So. Ch., Oct. 28, 1859

Mary, and Julian Meade Ruffin, both grandchildren of the late Edmund Ruffin, Sr., one of Virginia's distinguished agriculturists, by the Rev. T. W. Jones, at Elmwood, the home of the bride. So. Ch., July 28, 1887

Mary H. Willians, d. of the late Col. Ruffin of North Carolina, and Rev. J. Preston Fugitt, by the Rt. Rev. W. R. Whittingham, Bishop of Maryland, in Mt. Calvary Church, Baltimore City. So. Ch., Sept. 30, 1859

Mary S., d. of Edmund Ruffin, Jr., Esq., and the Rev. Edward Valentine Jones of the Diocese of Virginia, by the Rev. B. E. Habersham assisted by the Rev. C. R. Page, at Upper Marlbourne, Hanover Co. So. Ch., Dec. 4, 1873

Susan A., of Surry Co., Va., and J. N. Harrell of Murfreesboro, N.C., by the Rev. A. S. Smith of Norfolk. So. Ch., July 3, 1857

W. N., of Richmond, Va., and Mary, d. of Dr. John B. Harvie of Powhatan Co., Va., by the Rev. P. F. Berkeley, at Fighting Creek, the residence of the bride's father. So. Ch., May 6, 1875

RULON-MILLER
Caroline, d. of Mr. and Mrs. John Rulon-Miller, Newton Square, Pa., and Capt. Alexander Rives, First Missouri Infantry, s. of Mr. and Mrs. Thomas Keith Skinker of St. Louis, by the Rt. Rev. James R. Winchester, Bishop of Arkansas, at 63 Vandeventer Place, St. Louis. So. Ch., Aug. 25, 1917

RUMNEY
Theodore S. (The Rev.), rector of Cople Parish, Westmoreland Co., Va., and Annie J., d. of the late Capt. Wm. Morrill of Alex-

MARRIAGE NOTICES IN THE SOUTHERN CHURCHMAN WITH DATES OF PUBLICATION

andria, by the Rev. Charles B. Dana, in Westmoreland Co. So. Ch., Dec. 27, 1849

Theodore Stanwood, and Annie V. Denison, s. and d. of the officiating clergymen, the Rev. Dr. Rumney and the Rev. Dr. Denison, in the Church of the Heavenly Rest, New York. So. Ch., Apr. 18, 1872

RUSH

Madison, s. of Richard H. Rush of Philadelphia, and Catherine, d. of Robert and Catherine Costin, by the Rev. George W. Easter, at the residence of the bride's parents, Kendall Grove, Eastville, Va. So. Ch., Oct. 9, 1884

Murray, of Philadelphia, and Louisa, d. of George E. Bowdoin of Baltimore, by the Rt. Rev. John Johns, in Christ Church, Baltimore. So. Ch., Jan. 13, 1876

RUSSELL

Caroline N., eldest d. of Elgin Russell, Esq., and R. F. Graves, Esq. of Powhatan Co., by the Rev. R. P. Johnson, Locus* Grove, Prince George Co., Va. So. Ch., Aug. 27, 1858

Clinton W., and Anna M. Rose, both of Richmond, at Claremont, Va. So. Ch., Apr. 28, 1892

Edward S., Esq., of York, and Jane, second d. of John Jones, Esq. of Pembroke, by the Rev. John C. McCabe, rector of St. John's Church, Hampton, at Pembroke, Elizabeth City Co. So. Ch., Mar. 30, 1854

Julia B., and William A. Dade, by the Rev. Curtis Grubb, in St. John's Church, Pittman, Lake Co., Fla. So. Ch., May 26, 1892

Virginia Ann, only d. of the late Thomas C. Russell, Esq., and Robert Cooke, Esq. late of Louisiana, by the Rev. John C. McCabe, rector of St. John's Church, Hampton, at "Half-Way House", York Co. So. Ch., Feb. 2, 1854

William C. (The Rev.), rector of St. Andrew's Church, Wilmington, Del., and Margaret Ann Barclay, d. of the late John D. Brown, by the Rev. James T. Johnston, at Alexandria, D.C. So. Ch., Dec. 3, 1835

RUST

Armstead T. M., Esq., of Loudoun, and Ida, d. of Edmund I. Lee, Esq., by the Rev. C. W. Andrews, D.D., at Bedford, near Shepherdstown. So. Ch., Oct. 5, 1860

David N. (Dr.), of Alexandria, Va., and Mary E., d. of the officiating clergyman, the Rev. Thos. E. Locke, assisted by the Rev. Edmund Withers, in Christ Church, St. Ann's Parish, Albemarle Co., Va. So. Ch., Oct. 19, 1876

Ella, of Westmoreland, Va., and Jas. M. Smith, Esq. of Charlottesville, Va., by the Rev. Wm. C. Latane, in Trinity Church, Washington, D.C. So. Ch., May 5, 1881

Julia, eldest d. of the late

* Given as printed

MARRIAGE NOTICES IN THE SOUTHERN CHURCHMAN WITH DATES OF PUBLICATION

Gen. Albert Rust, former member of Congress from the State of Arkansas, and John McLellan Tutwiler, Esq. of Lexington, Va., by the Rev. John Ambler, at the residence of the bride's mother, Mrs. Nannie B. Rust, Luray, Page Co., Va. So. Ch., Apr. 9, 1874

Lawrence, and Evelyn, d. of the officiating clergyman, by the Rev. Wm. F. Junkin, D.D., at Danville, Ky. So. Ch., Apr. 13, 1876

Lily Southgate, and Thos. W. Edwards, Jr., all of Loudoun Co., by the Rev. H. B. Lee assisted by the Rev. R. T. Davis, D.D., at Rockland, the home of the bride, near Leesburg, Va. So. Ch., Sept. 19, 1889

Lizzie S., d. of John Rust of Westmoreland Co., and Dr. James B. Hodgkin of Alexandria, by the Rev. Thomas E. Locke, at Oak Grove Church, Westmoreland Co. So. Ch., June 23, 1870

Rebecca L., d. of Col. A. T. M. Rust, and Edmund I. Lee, Jr. of Jefferson Co., W.Va., by the Rev. H. B. Lee assisted by the Rev. R. T. Davis, at Rockland, Loudoun Co., Va. So. Ch., Sept. 30, 1875

Sophie R., of Westmoreland, Va., and Robert G. Pendleton of Clarke Co., by the Rev. Wm. C. Latane, in St. Peter's Church, Oak Grove, Va. So. Ch., Nov. 19, 1885

RUTHERFOARD

Mary, and Edwin D. Sampson, by the Rev. P. F. Berkeley, in Amelia Co. So. Ch., Nov. 7, 1867

RUTHERFOORD

Ann Seddon, d. of the late John M. Rutherfoord, Esq. of Baltimore, by the Rev. P. M. Boyden, at Rock Castle, the residence of the bride's mother, Mrs. Ann Roy Rutherfoord, in Goochland Co., Va. So. Ch., July 8, 1880

Anna, d. of the late William Rutherfoord of Richmond, Va., and J. Ryland Fleet of King and Queen Co., Va., by the Rev. Joshua Peterkin, D.D., in Richmond, Va. So. Ch., Feb. 12, 1880

Fanny, d. of Samuel J. Rutherfoord of Amelia Co., and George S. Bernard, by the Rev. P. F. Berkely, at Cassels, the residence of the bride's father. So. Ch., June 30, 1870

Thomas S., of Culpeper, Va., and Hattie D. Hamilton, by the Rev. Charles Y. Steptoe, at the residence of the bride's father, George Hamilton, Culpeper, Va. So. Ch., Oct. 19, 1876

RUTHERFORD

Ella W., d. of the late Samuel J. Rutherford, and Dr. Lewis Wheat, by the Rev. J. C. Wheat, D.D., assisted by the Rev. Charles Minnigerode, in St. Paul's Church, Richmond. So. Ch., Nov. 11, 1886

John C., Esq., of Goochland Co., Va., and Ann S., d. of Wm. H. Roy, Esq., by the Rev. G. S. Carraway, at Green Plains, Mathews Co., Va. So. Ch., Oct. 31, 1856

MARRIAGE NOTICES IN THE SOUTHERN CHURCHMAN WITH DATES OF PUBLICATION

Sallie W., d. of William Rutherford, Esq. of Richmond, Va., and Rev. Douglas French Forrest, by the Rev. J. Peterkin, D.D., at the residence of the bride's father. So. Ch., Jan. 30, 1873

RYAN
John Francis (Capt.), R.A.M.C., of Kingston, Ontario, and Pauline Crane, d. of Dr. and Mrs. Thomas Rutherford Savage of New York City, by the Very Rev. Dean Starr, in St. George's Cathedral, Kingston, Ontario, Canada. So. Ch., Mar. 30, 1918

Lula T., d. of Mary E., and the late Charles L. Ryan, and Wm. T. Hobbs of Baltimore, Md., by the Rev. A. P. Gray, in the Ascension Church, Amherst C.H. So. Ch., Dec. 5, 1889

RYON
Jeannette Wheeler, d. of the late Richard J. Ryon of Washington, D.C., and Harding Wheeler Kuhn of Eustis, Fla., by the Rt. Rev. George W. Peterkin, at the residence of the bride's mother, Mrs. A. I. Ryon, Charleston, Kanawha Co., W.Va. So. Ch., Feb. 23, 1888

Richard, Esq., and Martha J., d. of Jacob Gruber, all of Jefferson Co., Va., by the Rev. Wm. McGuire, at the residence of the bride's father. So. Ch., Oct. 7, 1859

S

SABINE
Uleyetta, d. of the Rev. James Sabine, and the Rev. Dexter Potter, by the Rev. Henry Blackaller, at Clappville, Mass. So. Ch., Dec. 15, 1837

SACREY
Alfred Lee, and Tweed Nicholson, by the Rev. J. Green Shackelford, at the residence of the bride's parents, Fredericksburg. So. Ch., Oct. 24, 1889

SAGENDORF
Franklin Packard, and Hallie Wallace, d. of Dr. and Mrs. W. Peyton Moncure of Fairfax, Va., by the Rev. Thomas A. Houghton-Burke, at the rectory of Christ Church, Rockville, Md. So. Ch., July 12, 1913

ST. CLAIR
George B. (Lt.), C.S.A., of Texas, and Ellegean, d. of the late John M. Robinson, Esq. of Botetourt Co., Va., by the Rev. Wm. McGuire, at Beaverdam, the residence of the bride's mother. So. Ch., Feb. 8, 1865

SALE
Charles I., of Tappahannock, Va., and Fanny Bruce Beale, in St. George's Church, Fredericksburg, Va. So. Ch., Oct. 17, 1914

Charles J., and Susan, d. of Dr. James H. Latane, all of Essex Co., Va., by the Rev. John B. Newton, in St. John's Church, Tappahannock. So. Ch., Dec. 14, 1871

Mary C., of Liberty, Va., and Samuel W. McCorkle of Lynchburg, Va., by the Rev. John K. Mason, in St. John's Church, Liberty, Va. So. Ch., Jan. 25, 1883

SALISBURY
John, of Pittsburgh, Pa., and Isabella M. Blackburn of Volcano, by the Rev. S. D. Tomkins, in Emmanuel Church, Volcano, Wood, W.Va. So. Ch., Sept. 17, 1874

SAMPSON
Edwin D., and Mary Rutherfoord, by the Rev. F. F. Berkeley, in Amelia Co. So. Ch., Nov. 7, 1867

SAMS
Conway Whittle, of Norfolk, Va., and Mattie M., d. of Prof. John B. Minor of the University of Virginia, by the Rev. J. S. Hanckel, D.D. assisted by the Rev. Julius Sams, D.D., in the University Chapel. So. Ch., Nov. 13, 1890

F. Julius (The Rev.), rector of Trinity Church, Black Oak, S.C., and Mary E., d. of Conway Whittle, Esq., by the Rev. E. M. Rodman, rector of Christ Church, at the residence of the bride's father, Norfolk, Va. So. Ch., Feb. 11, 1859

Mary Lewis, of Baltimore, and J. Addison Cooke of Staunton, Va., by the Rev. Dr. J. J. Sams, in Holy Trinity Church, Baltimore. So. Ch., May 8, 1890

SANCHEZ
Lizzie M., of Augusta, and Lewis T. Taliaferro formerly of Richmond, Va.,

MARRIAGE NOTICES IN THE SOUTHERN CHURCHMAN WITH DATES OF PUBLICATION

now of Augusta, by the Rev. C. C. Williams, in St. Paul's Church, Augusta, Ga. So. Ch., Mar. 24, 1881

SANDERSON
Mary A., d. of the late John Y. Sanderson of New Kent, and Alexander Thurman of Lynchburg, by the Rev. Mr. Hepbron, in St. Peter's Church, New Kent Co. So. Ch., Nov. 17, 1887

SANDYS
Alice F. (Mrs.), d. of the late Hon. R. N. Thweatt of Chesterfield Co., Va., and Charles S., s. of Gen. C. S. Lane of the English Army, by the Rev. A. B. Tizzard, in Trinity Church, Dale Parish, Chesterfield Co., Va. So. Ch., May 1, 1890

Arthur, of Calcutta, and Alice F., d. of the late R. N. Thweatt of Chesterfield, by the Rev. A. B. Tizzard, at the residence of the bride's mother, Mount Ida, Chesterfield Co., Va. So. Ch., May 26, 1881

SANFORD
Agnes, and Wm. G. Hart, both of Spotsylvania Co., Va., by the Rev. Wm. W. Greene, at Spotsylvania C.H. So. Ch., Dec. 31, 1868

Lawrence, and Louisa A. Frazer, both of Spotsylvania Co., Va., by the Rev. Wm. W. Greene. So. Ch., Nov. 27, 1863

Oscar Davenport, and Lucy Ann Davis, all of Westmoreland Co., by the Rev. Pendleton Brooke, at the residence of the bride's father, at Oldham's Cross Roads, Westmoreland Co., Va. So. Ch., Jan. 17, 1884

Robert Conway, of Westmoreland Co., and Nannie Lee, d. of James Flexmer and Mariah Bell, by the Rev. H. L. Derby, at the residence of the bride's parents, Ditchley, Northumberland Co., Va. So. Ch., Mar. 27, 1884

SANGER
W. P. S. (Capt.), U.S.N., of Georgetown, and Mrs. Lucy M. Johns of Washington, D.C., by the Rev. Dr. Harris, in Trinity Church, Washington, D.C. So. Ch., July 26, 1877

SANTINI
Gabriel, of New Orleans, and Olelia S., d. of Hon. J. H. McCue, by the Rev. Edmund Withers, at Lovingston, Nelson Co., Va. So. Ch., Feb. 12, 1874

SANXAY
Charlotte Isabella, d. of Richard D. Sanxay, Esq. of Richmond, Va., and Robert Gilliam, Esq. of Prince George Co., by the Rev. Wm. H. Hart. So. Ch., Nov. 1, 1839

SARGENT
Rosa, formerly of New York, and George B. Pearce of Key Port, N.J., by the Rev. H. L. Derby, in Bethel Church, Lancaster Co. So. Ch., Oct. 24, 1878

SASSER
Whitty M., of Louisiana, and Drucilla Amanda, youngest d. of William Pollitt, Esq. of Somerset Co., Md., by the Rev. George W. Woodbridge, in Richmond, Va. So. Ch., Sept. 30, 1836

SAUNDERS

MARRIAGE NOTICES IN THE SOUTHERN CHURCHMAN WITH DATES OF PUBLICATION

Alice F., d. of Maj. Robert C. Saunders, and James M. M. Davis of Richmond, Va., by the Rev. Wm. W. Greene, in the Church of the Good Shepherd, Campbell Co., Va. So. Ch., Jan. 15, 1874

E. A., Jr., and Martha A., second d. of Richard L. Brown, Esq., by the Rev. L. W. Burton, in St. John's Church, Richmond, Va. So. Ch., May 1, 1884

Elizabeth Gardiner, d. of Maj. B. C. Saunders of Campbell Co., Va., and William Hickson, by the Rev. R. T. Davis assisted by the Rev. A. Jaeger, in the Church of the Good Shepherd, Campbell Co., Va. So. Ch., Aug. 13, 1885

Eugene D., of New Orleans, and Flora T., d. of Dr. R. T. Lemmon, by the Rev. W. A. Aldrich, at Green Meadows, the residence of the bride's father. So. Ch., Apr. 8, 1880

Fleming, of Campbell Co., and Mary, d. of the late R. Carter and Emily Smith Gwathmey, by the Rev. Charles Minnigerode, D.D., in the Church of the Good Shepherd, Campbell Co. So. Ch., Aug. 20, 1874

Herbert S., formerly of Richmond, Va., and Rosalie M. Bell of Charles City, Va., by the Rev. John P. Tyler, at the Glebe, Charles City Co., Va. So. Ch., Nov. 21, 1889

Janet, youngest d. of Geo. D. Saunders of Buckingham Co., Va., and Monroe G. Jones of Prince Edward, by the Rev. A. S. Floyd, in St. Paul's Church, Appomattox Co., Va. So. Ch., Mar. 22, 1883

Jesse C., of McDowell, W.Va., and Alice Worthington, d. of Mrs. Wm. H. Irvine of Otter, Bedford Co., Va., by the Rev. Charles Woodson, at the rectory, in Norfolk, Va. So. Ch., Nov. 30, 1907

Marianna B., eldest d. of Robert Saunders, Esq., and the Rev. George T. Wilmer, all of Williamsburg, Va., by the Rev. Richard H. Wilmer of Bedford Co., Va. So. Ch., Oct. 12, 1855

Mary, and Joseph H. Blackwell of Charlottesville, by the Rev. J. Y. Downman, at the residence of the bride's brother-in-law, Charles W. Green. So. Ch., May 2, 1889

Mary Elsie, and Henry Fenton Day, by the Rev. C. C. Randolph, in the Church of the Good Shepherd, Campbell Co., Va. So. Ch., July 5, 1913

Minnie E., and E. C. Dame of Covington, Ky., by the Rev. Dr. George Dame assisted by the Rev. George W. Dame, at the residence of Mrs. William O. Saunders, South Pine Street, Richmond. So. Ch., Sept. 15, 1887

Walton (Dr.), of Essex Co., Va., and Mary F., d. of B. C. Bibb, Esq. of Baltimore, by the Rev. A. M. Randolph, at the residence of the bride's parents, in Baltimore. So. Ch., Nov. 16, 1882

William E., Jr., of Lynchburg, and Columbia E. Swann, by the Rev. William W. Greene, at the

MARRIAGE NOTICES IN THE SOUTHERN CHURCHMAN WITH DATES OF PUBLICATION

residence of the bride's father, in Caroline Co. So. Ch., Dec. 4, 1863

SAVAGE
Jessie D., d. of the late Thomas D. Savage of New York, and the Rev. Thomas L. Cole of Rhinecliff, N.Y., by the Rev. J. H. Eccleston, D.D. assisted by the Rev. Samuel A. Wallis, in Emmanuel Church, Baltimore, Md. So. Ch., July 3, 1884

Juliet T., of Mason Co., Ky., and Julius L. Anderson of Ironton, Ohio, by the Rev. J. B. Craighill, near Mayesville. So. Ch., Nov. 2, 1871

M. Parker, youngest d. of the late Nathaniel L. Savage of New Kent Co., Va., and Cyrus Bossieux, by the Rev. Wm. Norwood, D.D., in Richmond, Va. So. Ch., Aug. 10, 1871

Pauline Crane, d. of Dr. and Mrs. Thomas Rutherford Savage of New York City, and Capt. John Francis Ryan, R.A.M.C., of Kingston, Ontario, by the Very Rev. Dean Starr, in St. George's Cathedral, Kingston, Ontario, Canada. So. Ch., Mar. 30, 1918

Thomas S. (The Rev.), M.D., and M. V. Chapin of the Episcopal Mission, at Cape Palmas, Western Africa. So. Ch., Nov. 4, 1842

SAWYER
Edward A., M.D., of Gardiner, Mass., and Myra B., d. of Alfred G. Tebault, M.D., by the Rev. Wm. R. Savage, at the residence of the bride's parents, Norfolk, Va. So. Ch., May 21, 1885

John, of St. Paul, Minn., and Katie, d. of Dr. Hudson of Louisa Co., Va., by the Rev. L. R. Combs, at the residence of the bride's father. So. Ch., June 17, 1886

SAYLES
Nancy Nye, and Lee Garnett Day, by the Rev. Frederic S. Penfold, at Pawtucket, R.I. So. Ch., Oct. 3, 1925

SAYRE
B. B., Esq., of Frankfort, Ky., and M. C., d. of Edmund Ruffin, Esq. of Hanover Co., Va., by the Rev. G. S. Carraway, at Marlbourne. So. Ch., Oct. 28, 1859

Samuel Hunting (The Rev.), rector of St. Mary's Church, Williamsport, Pa., and Marjorie Mae, d. of the Rev. and Mrs. George E. Renison of Eagle Rock, Cal., by the Rev. Theodore St. Clair Will, rector, assisted by the Rev. Edwin Royal Carter of Petersburg, Va., in St. John's Church, Hampton, Va. So. Ch., Jan. 20, 1934

Wm., formerly of Virginia, and Jane D., d. of the late Rt. Rev. C. E. Gadsden, by the Rev. T. F. Gadsden, at Mt. Pleasant, Charleston, S.C. So. Ch., Nov. 28, 1872

SAYRS
Jeanie Irwin, youngest d. of the late John J. Sayrs of Alexandria, Va., and Dr. Henry M. Clarkson, Surgeon, P.A.C.S., of South Carolina, by the Rev. R. R. Mason, of Fluvanna Co., Va., at the residence of the bride's

MARRIAGE NOTICES IN THE SOUTHERN CHURCHMAN WITH DATES OF PUBLICATION

brother-in-law, W. S. Boswell, Esq. So. Ch., Oct. 2, 1863

SCATCHERD
Ethelwolf, s. of the late Thomas Scatcherd, Esq., M.P. of London, Canada, and Mary S., d. of the late Rev. Thomas H. Smyth, rector of St. Paul's Church, Weston, W.Va., by the Rev. Horace Edwin Hayden, rector of St. John's Church, West Brownsville, in Christ Church, Brownsville, Pa. So. Ch., Sept. 13, 1877

SCATES
Lucy A. E., and Richard H. Smith, by the Rev. D. M. Wharton, at the residence of the bride's father. So. Ch., Jan. 15, 1880

SCHAEFFER
William L., and Mrs. Katie L. Jennings, by the Rev. Walter P. Griggs of Poolesville, Md., in Washington, D.C. So. Ch., Aug. 11, 1892

SCHENCK
Grace Fitz-Randolph, d. of the Rev. Dr. Schenck, and Erastus Corning, Jr. of Albany, by the Bishop of Long Island, in St. Ann's Church, Brooklyn. So. Ch., Jan. 23, 1879

SCHLOSSER
George W., M.D., and Mary Bell McCollum, by the Rev. F. G. Scott, at the residence of the bride's uncle, near Gordonsville, Va. So. Ch., Oct. 19, 1876

SCHOOLER
Mary O., of Hanover Co., Va., and John Ambler of Louisa Co., Va., at Shantilly,* in Hanover Co., Va. So. Ch., Jan. 3, 1884

SCHOOLEY
Annetta F., and the Rev. Curtis Grubb, both of Loudoun Co., Va., by the Rev. Theodore Reed, in Lovettsville. So. Ch., Oct. 17, 1878
Kate F., of Loudoun Co., Va., and Joseph F. Grubb of Hanover Co., Va., formerly of Loudoun Co., Va., by the Rev. Curtis Grubb assisted by the Rev. Carter Page, at Violet Hall, the residence of the bride's mother, Loudoun Co., Va. So. Ch., Nov. 27, 1884

SCHROEDER
Herrmann W., of Charlotte, N.C., and Corlelia M., d. of Col. Wm. J. Hamlett of Oak Level, at Oak Level, Henry Co. So. Ch., May 4, 1871

SCOLLARY
Lizzie, d. of Dr. Sam'l Scollary of Smithfield, Jefferson Co., Va., and Powhatan R. Page of Gloucester Co., by the Rev. Julius E. Grammer, at Smithfield, Jefferson Co., Va. So. Ch., Nov. 28, 1856

SCOTT
Ann (Mrs.), of Elkton, and the Rev. Robert Lloyd Goldsborough, rector of St. Barnabas Church, Burlington, N.J., by the Rev. Wm. Schouler, in Trinity Church, Elkton, Md. So. Ch., July 20, 1882
Annie Kittredge, of Richmond, and Dr. Seth Curtis McGilvra, by the Rev. D. F. Sprigg, at the residence of Robert S. Chamberlayne, Esq., a cousin of the bride, No. 909 Park Ave., Richmond. So. Ch., Oct. 8, 1891
Belle, d. of Dr. Thomas L. and

* Given as printed

MARRIAGE NOTICES IN THE SOUTHERN CHURCHMAN WITH DATES OF PUBLICATION

Annie E. Scott, and Otho L. McCraw of Henderson, N.C., by the Rev. W. B. Williams, at the residence of the late Dr. Thos. L. Scott, Caroline Co., Va. So. Ch., July 19, 1888

Bettie, eldest d. of Dr. Edward P. Scott of Greensville Co., and the Rev. P. G. Robert, rector of Meherrin Parish,* by the Rev. C. J. Gibson, at Oakland, Greensville Co. So. Ch., Oct. 26, 1854

Bettie Lane, d. of the late John F. Scott of Fredericksburg, Va., and William V. R. Watson of Houston, Tex., by the Rev. P. G. Robert, at the residence of Frank Carter, St. Louis. So. Ch., Mar. 7, 1878

Camilla, d. of the late Robert E. Scott of Fauquier Co., Va., and Thomas Pinkney, by the Rev. John K. Mason, D.D., at the residence of Maj. R. Taylor Scott, Warrenton, Va. So. Ch., July 21, 1892

Charles Landon, and Louise Montague Everett, both of Albemarle, by the Rev. W. H. Williams, at Belmont, the residence of the bride's mother. So. Ch., Oct. 16, 1879

Charles Landon, Jr., of Amherst, Va., and Kate Whitcomb, youngest d. of the late Maj. Peyton Randolph of Virginia, by the Rev. J. W. Ware of Culpeper, Va., in Ascension Episcopal Church, Amherst, Va. So. Ch., Jan. 15, 1910

Cornelia, d. of Mr. and Mrs. Edmund Willis Scott and niece of the officiating clergyman, and Robert Alexander Smith of Fauquier Co., Va., by the Rev. F. G. Scott, at Spring Forest, the home of the bride's parents, near Somerset, Va. So. Ch., Sept. 19, 1908

Edmund W., Esq., brother of the officiating minister, and Dora, eldest d. of Mrs. Sarah and the late James W. Graves, by the Rev. F. G. Scott, rector of Christ Church, Gordonsville, at the residence of the bride's mother. So. Ch., Nov. 1, 1877

Edward, of Powhatan, and Mary Scott of Albemarle Co., by the Rev. Wm. M. Nelson, at the residence of Chas. Scott, in Albemarle Co. So. Ch., Nov. 5, 1858

Edward, Esq., of Powhatan, and Eliza M., d. of the late Robert J. Hackley, Esq. of Florida, by the Rev. A. B. Tizzard, at Mantua. So. Ch., Feb. 8, 1865

Edward, of Lexington, Ky., and Fannie C. Goode of Bedford Co., Va., by the Rev. Albert Ware, at the residence of Capt. Izzard. So. Ch., Oct. 19, 1876

Eleanor Marshall, eldest d. of the late Richard M. Scott, Esq. of "Bush Hill", Fairfax Co., Va., and Bernard H. Johnston, by the Rev. Dr. Elliot, rector of the Church of the Ascension, Washington, D.C., at "Bush Hill." So. Ch., Jan. 4, 1877

Elizabeth H., of Buckingham Co., and Gunnell H. Ashlin of Fluvanna, by the Rev. Wm. M. Nelson, in Buckingham

---

* Meherrin Parish is in Greensville County, Virginia (Journal ... Diocese of Southern Virginia, Portsmouth, Va., 1941)

MARRIAGE NOTICES IN THE SOUTHERN CHURCHMAN WITH DATES OF PUBLICATION

Co. So. Ch., Oct. 19, 1855

Emma, d. of the late William H. Scott, and J. Fenton Taylor, by the Rev. John G. Scott of Hot Springs, Va., brother of the bride, assisted by the Rev. Meade Clark, D.D., rector of St. James' Church, at the home of the bride, 10 E. Franklin St., Richmond, Va. So. Ch., July 2, 1910

F.G., Jr., M.D., of Orange, Va., and Charlotte Barnes, d. of Judge and Mrs. T. R. B. Wright, by the Rev. F. G. Scott, D.D. assisted by the Rev. Wm. Nelson Meade, in St. John's Church, Tappahannock, Va. So. Ch., Jan. 4, 1913

Fannie Bathurst, second d. of the late Charles Scott, and William Meade Lewis, all of Albemarle Co., Va., by the Rev. T. E. Locke, in St. John's Church, Scottsville. So. Ch., Nov. 1, 1877

Frank G. (The Rev.), rector of the parish, and Eloise, d. of Mrs. Harriet P. and the late Theodore Gourdin, M.D., by the Rev. John Johnson, in the Episcopal Chapel, Eutawville, S.C. Oct. 14, 1880

Frederic William, and Elizabeth Mayo Strother, both of Richmond, Va., by the Rev. Hartley Carmichael, in St. Paul's Church, Richmond, Va. So. Ch., Nov. 2, 1893

G. R., of Corpus Christi, Tex., and Ella R. Dickinson of Houston, by the Rev. J. J. Clemens, in Christ Church, Houston, Tex. So. Ch., May 12, 1881

Genevieve, d. of Dr. Thos. L. and Annie E. Scott, and John E. Wright, Jr., of Nansemond Co., Va., by the Rev. W. B. Williams, at the residence of the late Dr. Thos. L. Scott, Caroline Co., Va. So. Ch., July 19, 1888

Hazel, d. of Mr. and Mrs. Clarence Watson Scott of Conimicut*, and the Rev. Edwin Warner Grilley, Jr., rector of the Church of the Good Shepherd, Pawtucket, R.I., by the Rt. Rev. Granville Gaylord Bennett, Suffragan Bishop of Rhode Island, assisted by the Rev. Charles Hosea Temple, rector of the Church of the Transfiguration, and the Rev. Irving Andrew Evans, rector of St. Andrew's School, Barrington, in the Church of the Transfiguration, Cranston, R.I. So. Ch., Aug. 19, 1939

Hugh Roy (The Rev.), and Jane Carey, d. of the late Thomas Harrison, Esq., by the Rev. A. Empie, D.D., in St. James' Church, Richmond, Va. So. Ch., Oct. 7, 1852

Hugh Roy (The Rev.), rector of St. Mark's Church, Cape Palmas, and Anna M. Steele of Cavalla, near Cape Plamas, Western Africa. So. Ch., Oct. 26, 1854

J. Wycliffe, of Orange Co., and Sallie F., d. of the late Rob't Hackley of Tallahassee, Fla., by the Rev. Joseph Earnest, at Litchfield, in Orange Co. So. Ch., Feb. 29, 1856

James Hamilton, of Richmond, Va., and Mary, d. of the officiating clergyman, the Rt. Rev. Bishop Wingfield, at Benicia, Cal. So. Ch., Nov. 2, 1893

John F., of Fredericksburg,

* Given as printed

MARRIAGE NOTICES IN THE SOUTHERN CHURCHMAN WITH DATES OF PUBLICATION

and Lillias R. Hamilton of Fauquier Co., at the residence of the bride's father, in Fauquier Co. So. Ch., Dec. 15, 1887

John Gordon, of Petersburg, Va., and Adele Irvine, d. of Mr. and Mrs. Paul Trapier Hayne, by the Rev. A. A. Mitchell, the rector, of Greenville, S.C., in Christ Church, Greenville, S.C. So. Ch., May 10, 1913

John H. (The Rev.), and Lucy K. Hoskins, both of Miller's Tavern, Va., by the Rev. Thomas D. Lewis, in St. John's Church rectory, Bethesda, Md. So. Ch., July 27, 1912

Lizzie C., of Virginia, and H. Scott Rucker of Pocahontas Co., W.Va., by the Rev. T. N. Lacy, at the residence of Dr. Wm. P. Rucker, near Lewisburg, W.Va. So. Ch., Mar. 16, 1882

Lizzie Rose, eldest d. of the late Charles Scott, and Thomas Perkins Gantt, all of Albemarle Co., by the Rev. T. E. Locke. So. Ch., Nov. 19, 1874

Louise Montague, oldest d. of Louise M. and C. Landon Scott of Amherst, and Charles Alfred Joubert de Ville-Marests, New Orleans, by the Rev. Arthur P. Gray, in Ascension Church, Amherst, Va. So. Ch., Apr. 20, 1907

Mary, of Albemarle Co., and Edward Scott of Powhatan, by the Rev. Wm. M. Nelson, at the residence of Chas. Scott, Albemarle Co. So. Ch., Nov. 5, 1858

Mary, d. of Dr. W. W. Scott of Lenoir, N.C., and the Rev. C. B. Bryan of Virginia, by the Rev. F. L. Bush. So. Ch., Mar. 9, 1882

Mary Jane, d. of Mr. and Mrs. Edmund Willie Scott, and Cary Marcellus Crafton of Orange, by the Rev. F. G. Scott, D.D. of Petersburg, uncle of the bride, in Epiphany Chapel, Somerset, Va. So. Ch., June 14, 1913

Minna J., d. of the late Wm. A. Scott of Buckingham Co., Va., and Alfred F. Brady of New Orleans, La., by the Rev. B. M. Wales. So. Ch., Oct. 8, 1874

Nannie Langhorn, youngest d. of the late Charles A. Scott of Albemarle Co., and Z. B. Lewis, Jr. of Nelson Co., by the Rev. T. E. Locke, in St. John's Church, Scottsville, Albemarle Co., Va. So. Ch., Sept. 24, 1885

Sallie W., of Gordonsville, and Richard F. Berkeley, by the Rev. L. R. Combs, at the residence of the bride's brother, J. W. Scott, M.D., Gordonsville, Va. So. Ch., Nov. 26, 1885

Sarah Eliza, eldest d. of Robert G. Scott of Amherst Co., Va., and Dr. E. P. James of Goochland Co., Va., by the Rev. J. P. Lawrence, at Riverside, the residence of the bride's father. So. Ch., May 22, 1879

Sue G., youngest d. of the late John F. Scott, and the Rev. J. J. Clemens of Eastville, Va., by the Rev. A. M. Randolph, at the residence of the bride's mother, Fredericksburg, Va.

MARRIAGE NOTICES IN THE SOUTHERN CHURCHMAN WITH DATES OF PUBLICATION

So. Ch., Sept. 21, 1871
William C., Jr., and Susan Emma, d. of E. Festus Cowherd, Esq., by the Rev. F. G. Scott, at the residence of the bride's father, near Gordonsville, Va. So. Ch., June 1, 1876

SCULLIN
Clayton R., and Rebecca V. Gillingham of Fairfax Co., Va., by the Rev. Mr. Underhill, at the residence of the bride's grandmother, at Hammonton, N.J. So. Ch., June 30, 1887

SEABURY
W. H., of Norfolk, Va., and Mattie M., only d. of Oliver Hicks, Esq., of Tiverton Four Corners, R.I., by the Rev. Nelson Clarke, at Tiverton Four Corners, R.I. So. Ch., Sept. 23, 1859

SEAMAN
Catherine Kortright, d. of the late Capt. John Seaman, Staten Island, and the Rev. Thomas Wallaby by the Rev. W. H. Walter, in St. Paul's Church, Thompkinsville, R.I. So. Ch., Aug. 11, 1837

Isabel Gordon, d. of Mr. and Mrs. William H. Seaman, and Dr. H. C. Chalmers of Charlotte Co., Va., at the residence of Maj. and Mrs. Owen, Washington, D.C. So. Ch., Dec. 25, 1915

John P., of Caroline Co., and Annie E. Lee of Fredericksburg, by the Rev. J. G. Shackelford of Trinity Church, at the residence of A. H. Conway, Fredericksburg, Va. So. Ch., Nov. 7, 1889

SEARS
Charles E., and Sallie E. Faunt LeRoy, at Oakenham, Middlesex Co., Va. So. Ch., July 20, 1876

Cora Wells, of Myrtle Lake, and William Lewis Maury of St. Louis, Mo. (formerly of Virginia), by the Rev. F. R. Holeman, at Myrtle Lake, Orange Co., Fla. So. Ch., Jan. 6, 1887

SEARSON
William B., and Ethel Towles, by the Rev. Thos. P. Baker, at Yonge's Island, S.C. So. Ch., Jan. 16, 1909

SEBRELL
J. N., and Romine Darden, by the Rev. H. L. Derby, at Jerusalem, Southampton, Va. So. Ch., Apr. 18, 1872

SEDDON
Thos. A., of Fredericksburg, Va., and Ella Bruce, d. of the late Mayo Cabell, Esq., by the Rev. Edmund Withers, at Union Hill, Nelson Co., Va. So. Ch., Jan. 6, 1876

SEGAR
Mary Minor, d. of Jno. R. Segar, Esq., and Andrew S. Browne of Norfolk, Va., by the Rev. J. Hervey Hundley, at the residence of the bride's father in Middlesex Co., Va. So. Ch., Oct. 6, 1887

Sarah C., of Middlesex, Va., and Thos. M. Wiatt, Esq. of Gloucester, Va., by the Rev. C. S. Carraway, in Urbanna Church. So. Ch., Feb. 15, 1855

SEHON
Columbus, Esq., and Agnes Stuart, d. of John S. Lewis, Esq., all of Mason Co., W.Va., by the Rev. T. H. Lacy, at Spring Hill, the residence of the

MARRIAGE NOTICES IN THE SOUTHERN CHURCHMAN WITH DATES OF PUBLICATION

bride's father, near Point Pleasant, W. Va. So. Ch., June 29, 1876

SEIB
John, U.S. Topographical Engineer, and Mary Frances, d. of the late Dr. George Fitzhugh of King George Co., Va., by the Rev. E. C. McGuire, D.D. So. Ch., Nov. 23, 1854

Mary F. (Mrs.), of Fredericksburg, and J. B. Newman of Burlington, Orange Co., by the Rev. E. Bryden, at the home of G. S. Conway, Esq. So. Ch., Mar. 8, 1866

SELDEN
Andrew K., and Meta Burnett, fourth d. of Maj. G. W. F. Kearsley, by the Rev. Dr. W. H. Meade, in Zion Church, Charles Town, W.Va. So. Ch., Dec. 4, 1879

Harriet C., d. of Miles C. Selden, Esq. of Norwood, Powhatan Co., Va., and Capt. Henry Heath, U.S.A., by the Rev. Erskine M. Rodman, at Norwood. So. Ch., Apr. 17, 1857

Mary Byrd, second d. of R. C. and C. W. Selden, and William Courtney Dimmock of Richmond, Va., by the Rev. A. Y. Hundley, at Sherwood, the residence of the bride's father, Gloucester Co., Va. So. Ch., Dec. 10, 1874

Samuel M., of Lynchburg, Va., and Emma Randolph, second d. of John D. Bland, by the Rev. J. C. Dinwiddie, at the residence of the bride's father, Orange C.H. So. Ch., July 10, 1873

Sarah Ann, second d. of Charles Selden, and Dr. Richard H. Tatum, by the Rev. P. F. Berkeley, in Powhatan Co., So. Ch., Jan. 15, 1852

Susie, and J. Lloyd Tabb of Baltimore, by the Rev. A. Y. Hundley, at Sherwood, Gloucester Co., Va. So. Ch., Mar. 22, 1877

Vinna P., d. of Maj. John A. Selden, Esq., and Walter D., s. of Garret F. Watson, Esq., all of Richmond, by the Rev. J. G. Armstrong, D.D., in Monumental Church. So. Ch., Apr. 24, 1884

SELDON
Nannie, youngest d. of Miles C. Seldon, Esq. of Norwood, Powhatan Co., Va., and the Rev. Erskine Mason Rodman, by the Rev. Washington Rodman, at Norwood, Powhatan Co., Va. So. Ch., Nov. 21, 1856

SELLERS
H. T., C.S.A., and Louisa W., d. of Joseph J. Gates, Esq. of Chesterfield Co., Va., by the Rev. A. B. Tizzard. So. Ch., Feb. 8, 1865

SEMMES
Mary Anna, d. of D. R. Semmes, Esq., and G. M. Bastable, Jr. of Fauquier Co., Va., by the Rev. H. Suter, in Christ Church, Alexandria, Va. So. Ch., Dec. 13, 1883

Thomas, of Alexandria, D.C., and Eliza Frances, d. of the late William Bernard, Jr., Esq. of Belle Grove, King George Co., Va., by the Rev. Mr. Friend, at Port Royal, Va. So. Ch., Dec. 6, 1839

Thomas, of Alexandria, Va., and Margaret Byrd, d. of Col. O. R. Funsten, by the Rev. James B. Funsten, at "Mirador", Albemarle Co., Va. So. Ch., June 9, 1887

MARRIAGE NOTICES IN THE SOUTHERN CHURCHMAN WITH DATES OF PUBLICATION

SEMPLE
　Bettie B., second d. of Dr. Geo. Semple, and Welson Q. Walthall, Esq. of Alabama, by the Rev. Wm. F. M. Jacobs, in St. John's Church, Hampton. So. Ch., June 15, 1860
　James A., and Letitia, d. of the Hon. John Tyler of Williamsburg, Va., by the Rev. Wm. Hodges. So. Ch., Mar. 1, 1839

SENSENEY
　Kate B., youngest d. of Jacob Senseney, and Charles E. Needles of Baltimore, by the Rev. Cornelius Walker, at Edgehill, near Winchester. So. Ch., Nov. 30, 1855

SERVANT
　Samuel Barron, and Eliza, d. of F. Slaughter Jones, Esq. formerly of Culpeper Co., Va., by the Rev. Mr. Reed, at the residence of the bride's father, Jasper Co., Ill. So. Ch., June 26, 1857

SESSOUS
　J. W. (Dr.), of North Carolina, and Nannie M., d. of Wm. P. Underwood, Esq., Clerk of the Court of Surry County, by the Rev. John C. McCabe, rector of St. John's Church, Hampton, at Surry C.H. So. Ch., Nov. 30, 1855

SETTLE
　Joseph A., of Rappahannock Co., and Bessie Gardner Wells of Fairfax Co., by the Rev. John McGill, in St. John's Church, Centreville, Fairfax Co. So. Ch., Mar. 1, 1877

SEWARD
　Clara Brooke, and George M. Trible, by the rector, the Rev. D. Hundley, in St. Luke's P. E. Church, Essex Co., Va. So. Ch., Mar. 9, 1893

SHACKELFORD
　George S., of Orange, Va., and Virginia, d. of Dr. Wilson J. Randolph of Charlottesville, Va., by the Rev. J. S. Hanchel, D.D. and the Rev. Green Shackelford, at the residence of the bride's father. So. Ch., July 10, 1884
　J. Green (The Rev.), rector of Trinity Church, Fredericksburg, Va., and Anna W. Fassman, gr.d. of Mrs. Judge Phelan of "Fatherland Place", East Nashville, by the Rev. T. F. Martin, rector, assisted by the Rev. M. Cabell Martin, in St. Ann's Church, Nashville, Tenn. So. Ch., Nov. 10, 1887
　Lucy, of Charlottesville, and Charles C. Walker of Richmond, Va., by the Rev. Green Shackelford assisted by the Rev. Frank Stringfellow, in Christ Church, Charlottesville, Va. So. Ch., Oct. 25, 1883

SHACKLEFORD
　Hudson Z., of Albemarle, and Harriet V., d. of the late Henry Barnes of Madison Co., Va., by the Rev. James T. Johnston, in St. Paul's Church. So. Ch., May 29, 1857
　Mary A., d. of H. Z. Shackleford, Esq. of Rappahannock Co., Va., and Lewis Hooff of Alexandria, at "Montpelier", the residence of the bride's father. So.

MARRIAGE NOTICES IN THE SOUTHERN CHURCHMAN WITH DATES OF PUBLICATION

SHACKLETT
Mattie Glenn, d. of Abner Shacklett, and D. Newton Bear, all of Harrisonburg, by the Rev. O. S. Bunting, in Emmanuel Church, Harrisonburg, Va. So. Ch., Dec. 28, 1882

SHADGETT
Sarah (Mrs.), of Quebec, Canada, and Edward B. Barber of London, by the Rev. Dr. Empie, at Richmond, Va. So. Ch., Dec. 1, 1837

SHAFFER
M. Virginia, and David H. Dodd, both of Berkeley Co., W.Va., by the Rev. W. T. Leavell, in Mt. Zion Church, Hedgesville. So. Ch., July 7, 1892

SHANDS
Alfred Rives, M.D., of Washington, D.C., and Elisabeth Sheffer Prewitt, at "Dunreath", Lexington, Ky. So. Ch., Aug. 14, 1926

Mary S., oldest d. of the late Elverton A. Shands of Harrisonburg, Va., and James R. Bowen, Esq. of Bedford Co., Va., by the Rev. T. U. Dudley, at Harrisonburg, Va. So. Ch., June 11, 1868

SHAFTER
Margaret Caldwell, eldest d. of James S. Shapter, Esq., and the Rev. Archibald M. Anderson, by the Rev. Dr. Stone, in Christ Church, South Brooklyn. So. Ch., Aug. 26, 1852

SHARP
Eliza F., youngest d. of W. W. Sharp, Esq. of Norfolk, and James C. Southall, editor of The Richmond Enquirer and Examiner, by the Rev. N. A. Okeson

Ch., Feb. 2, 1882

assisted by the Rev. T. M. Ambler, at the residence of the bride's father. So. Ch., Dec. 9, 1869

Henry T. (The Rev.), of the Diocese of Kentucky, and Maria Byrd, youngest d. of R. C. Nicholas of Baltimore, by the Rev. J. S. B. Hodges, in St. Paul's Church, Baltimore. So. Ch., July 27, 1871

Virginia M., d. of W. W. Sharp, Esq. of Norfolk, and the Rev. Thomas M. Ambler, by the Rev. E. M. Rodman assisted by the Rev. J. J. Sams, in Christ Church, Norfolk. So. Ch., Oct. 26, 1860

SHARPE
Sarah Wickham, d. of W. F. Sharpe, Esq. of Goshen, N.Y., and the Rev. Erskine M. Rodman, by the Rev. W. De L. Granniss assisted by the Rev. Washington Rodman, rector of Grace Church, Plainfield, N.J., at the residence of the bride's father. So. Ch., June 22, 1871

Virginia, d. of the late Jesse Sharpe, Esq., and Thomas H. Burwell of Virginia, by the Rev. Dr. H. B. Martin, at Wilmington, Del. So. Ch., Nov. 16, 1882

SHARWOOD
Edward Robert, and Amelia, d. of the late Charles W. Harrison, all of Albemarle Co., by the Rev. T. E. Locke, in Christ Church, St. Ann's Parish, Albemarle Co., Va. So. Ch., Oct. 1, 1874

SHAW
(Mr.), of Texas and Eliza-

MARRIAGE NOTICES IN THE SOUTHERN CHURCHMAN WITH DATES OF PUBLICATION

beth, d. of Austin Ferguson,* Esq., by the Rev. Dr. A. Wade, at Northwood, Charles City Co. So. Ch., Feb. 9, 1871

Samuel B., and Jennie McGlasson, both of Fairfax Co., by the Rev. W. A. Alrich, at the residence of Wm. T. Rumsey, Esq. of Fairfax C.H. So. Ch., Dec. 31, 1868

SHEAR
Addie May, second d. of C. T. Shear, Esq., and Cassius M. Lawrence of North Bingham, Pa., by the Rev. R. A. Castleman, at Sully, the residence of the bride's parents, near Chantilly, Fairfax Co., Va. So. Ch., June 29, 1893

SHEARER
Florence V., of Moorefield, W.Va., and the Rev. Jacob Brittingham of Parkersburg, by the Rt. Rev. George W. Peterkin, in Immanuel Church, Moorefield, W.Va. So. Ch., Sept. 21, 1882

SHEARMAN
C. B., and Tazewell Edmonds, both of Lancaster, by the Rev. H. L. Derby, at the residence of Thomas Smither, Kilmarnock, Lancaster, Va. So. Ch., Jan. 31, 1878

SHEFFEY
Eliza Lee, and Oliver P. Baldwin, Esq., by the Rev. Mr. Boyden, at Staunton. So. Ch., June 28, 1839

Louise, adopted d. of Judge Shoffey, and the Rev. Wm. H. H. Powers, by the Rev. Walter Q. Hullihen, in Trinity Church, Staunton, Va. So. Ch., Oct. 31, 1872

SHEILD
Roberta, d. of the late Col. Robert Sheild, and the Rev. Edmund C. Murdaugh of Alabama, by the Rev. Henry M. Denison, at Williamsburg. So. Ch., May 3, 1849

SHELTON
Eleanor A., d. of D. R. Shelton of Louisa Co., Va., and Francis Breathed of Goochland Co., Va., by the Rev. H. P. R. McCoy, at Roseneath, the residence of the bride's father. So. Ch., Mar. 11, 1880

Hallie W. (Mrs.), d. of Jos. H. Turner, Esq., and Chas. E. Cosby of Halifax, by the Rev. John Cosby, at Columbia, Fluvanna Co., Va. So. Ch., July 29, 1869

Richard (The Hon.), of Clay Co., W.Va., and Annie T. F., d. of the late John, Esq., and Mrs. Mary C. Jennings, by the Rev. T. H. Lacy, at "Glen Hope", the beautiful country home of the bride's mother, near Urston, W.Va. So. Ch., June 8, 1893

SHEPARD
Lyman W., of Ontario, Canada, and Mary, d. of the late Thomas L. Ellzey, by the Rev. R. T. Davis, D.D., at Westwood Grove, Loudoun Co., Va. So. Ch., Oct. 9, 1879

SHEPHERD
Fanny, only d. of the late R. D. and Elizabeth Stockton Shepherd, and Hugh P. Allen, by the Rev. L. R. Mason, in Trinity Church, Shepherdstown. So. Ch., Feb. 2,

* Given as printed

MARRIAGE NOTICES IN THE SOUTHERN CHURCHMAN WITH DATES OF PUBLICATION

1888
Geo. C., and Ella C., d. of Col. Benjamin Morgan, all of Clarke Co., Va., by the Rev. T. F. Martin, in Grace Church, Berryville. So. Ch., Jan. 15, 1874

Hambleton, of Irvington, Ce., and Mary Gertrude, d. of Edward Fant of Fauquier, by the Rev. O. S. Barten, in the Episcopal Church, at Warrenton. So. Ch., Dec. 23, 1859

Meta G., d. of the late Carter Shepherd of Clarke Co., Va., and Charles D. James of Judsonia, Ark., by the rector, the Rev. P. P. Phillips, in Grace Church, Berryville, Va. So. Ch., Oct. 10, 1989

S. Smith, and Rosa, youngest d. of the late Thomas Courtney of King and Queen Co., Va., by the Rev. J. Hervey Hundley, at the residence of Bird Courtney. So. Ch., Dec. 20, 1888

Sallie E., youngest d. of Maj. Wm. E. Shepherd, and Daniel A. Overby of Mossingford, Charlotte Co., Va., by the Rev. Geo. W. Dame, at Danville. So. Ch., Feb. 3, 1876

Thomas Martin, of Batopilas, Mexico, and Charlotte Moncure Blackburn of Alexandria, Va., by the Rev. Henry Easter, in St. Clement's Episcopal Church, El Paso, Tex. So. Ch., Jan. 8, 1910

SHEPPARD
Isabel Gertrude, d. of Mrs. Kate E. and the late James Sheppard and gr.d. of the late Rev. Dr. Empie, and Joseph S. Potts of Richmond, by the Rev. Joshua Peterkin, D.D., at the residence of the bride's mother, in Richmond, Va. So. Ch., Apr. 17, 1884

Kate Empie, d. of the late James Sheppard and gr.d. of the Rev. Dr. Empie, first rector of St. James' Church, and Alexander B. Guigon, by the Rev. Joshua Peterkin, D.D. assisted by the Rev. Preston G. Nash, in St. James' Church, Richmond. So. Ch., Mar. 17, 1887

Laura A., of Halifax Co., Va., and Tipton Tiptoe Omohundro, Jr. of Albemarle, by the Rev. Thomas E. Locke, at the rectory, St. Anne's Parish.* So. Ch., Dec. 28, 1893

Mary Adeline, d. of William F. Sheppard of Savannah, Ga., and the Rev. Armand Tice Eyler, vicar of Christ Church, Valdosta, and St. James' Church, Quitman, Ga., by the Rev. Bishop Reese and the Rev. C. C. J. Carpenter, rector of St. John's Church, in St. John's Church, Savannah, Ga. So. Ch., Mar. 4, 1933

Thomas, and Mrs. Elizabeth Auld, both of Richmond, by the Rev. R. S. Barrett, in Richmond, Va. So. Ch., June 3, 1880

SHEPPARD
Mary F., and Wm. B. Williamson, both of Warrenton, Va., by the Rev. George W. Nelson, in St. James' Church, Warrenton, Va. So. Ch., Mar. 4, 1886

SHEPPERSON
Nannie, d. of Josiah Shep-

---

* St. Anne's Parish is in Albemarle County, Virginia (Journal ... Diocese of Virginia, Richmond, Va., 1941)

MARRIAGE NOTICES IN THE SOUTHERN CHURCHMAN WITH DATES OF PUBLICATION

person, Esq. of Campbell Co., and John Booker of Prince Edward, by the Rev. T. E. Locke, at Cottage Hill, Charlotte Co. So. Ch., June 26, 1857

SHERMAN
Estelle M., d. of the late Henry H. Sherman of New York, and the Rev. John S. Littell, D.D., rector of St. James' Church, West Hartford, Conn., by the Rev. Eliot White, B.D.; in Grace Chantry, New York. So. Ch., May 19, 1923

SHERRARD
Ann M., d. of Judge Joseph H. Sherrard, and Robert M. Kennedy of Camden, S.C., by the Rev. William C. Meredith, D.D., in Christ Church, Winchester. So. Ch., Mar. 25, 1875

SHERWOOD
Arthur E., of Clifton Forge, Va., formerly of Derbyshire, England, and M. Alice, d. of the late Capt. Edward Echols of Rockbridge Co., Va., by the Rev. D. W. Shanks, at Mountain Home, Va. So. Ch., Jan. 8, 1880

SHIELD
Alfred, Esq., and Emily A. H., d. of the officiating clergyman, the Rev. John C. McCabe, rector of the Church of the Ascension, Baltimore, in St. James' Church, Richmond, Va. So. Ch., Jan. 9, 1857.
C. H. (The Rev.), and Mrs. M. W. Baldwin, by the Rev. C. E. Ambler, at Springfield. So. Ch., Oct. 13, 1870
Nannie C., and John M. Willis, Esq., both of Hampton, Va., by the Rev. J. J. Gravatt, in St. John's Church, Hampton, Va. So. Ch., Nov. 15, 1877

SHIELDS
A. W., Esq., of Richmond, and Eliza C., d. of William H. Clark, Esq. of Halifax Co., Va., by the Rev. John T. Clark, at Banister Lodge. So. Ch., Dec. 5, 1867
James W. (The Rev.), of Richmond, Va., and Grace Hamilton, youngest d. of the late S. C. Elliott of Norfolk, Va., by the Rev. Wm. M. Dame assisted by the Rev. O. S. Barton, in St. Luke's Church, Norfolk, Va. So. Ch., July 22, 1875
Mary E., and William B. Newton, both of Norfolk, Va., by the Rev. J. B. Newton assisted by the Rev. T. G. Jones, at the home of the bride. So. Ch., Sept. 24, 1891

SHIFF
Lucy M., of Baltimore, and the Rev. Dr. B. Franklin of Shrewsbury, N.J., by the Rt. Rev. John Scarborough, D.D., Bishop of New Jersey, assisted by the Rev. William Kirkus of Baltimore, in Grace Church, Baltimore. So. Ch., Sept. 23, 1886

SHIPMAN
May R., d. of George B. Shipman, and the Rev. A. Penick, rector of the parish, by the Rt. Rev. Thomas W. Dudley, D.D., Bishop of Kentucky, assisted by the Rt. Rev. C. C. Penick, D.D., rector of St. Andrew's Parish, Louisville, in the Church

MARRIAGE NOTICES IN THE SOUTHERN CHURCHMAN WITH DATES OF PUBLICATION

of the Ascension, Frankfort, Ky. So. Ch., Nov. 6, 1884

SHIRLEY
Annie, d. of George Shirley, and Henry B. Baylor, all of Jefferson Co., by the Rev. J. W. Blake, in Grace Church, Smithfield, Jefferson Co., W.Va. So. Ch., Nov. 4, 1880

SHOBER
Francis E., Jr., of North Carolina, and Helen Lloyd, d. of J. L. Aspinwall of Barrytown, N.Y., by the Rev. J. T. Wheat, D.D. assisted by the Rev. G. B. Hopson, at the residence of the bride's mother. So. Ch., May 4, 1882

SHOEMAKER
Blanche, d. of Augusta C. E., and the late Samuel M. Shoemaker, and Frederick William Bruno, by the Rev. J. H. Eccleston, in Emmanuel Church, Baltimore, Md. So. Ch., May 7, 1885

Leila, and R. J. Walker Brewster, by the Rev. John Lindsay, D.D., in West Washington, D.C. So. Ch., Nov. 5, 1885

Samuel M., and Ellen Ward, d. of John A. Whitridge, Esq., by the Rev. J. H. Eccleston, D.D., in Emmanuel Church, Baltimore. So. Ch., Nov. 27, 1884

SHORES
Lucie Perkins, d. of Chastain Shores, deceased, and Maj. Wm. D. Clopton of Cumberland, by the Rev. Wm. C. Meredith, at Seven Islands, Buckingham Co. So. Ch., Aug. 27, 1858

SHOWELL
John Letcher (The Rev.), gr.s. of the late ex-Governor John Letcher of Virginia, and Virginia Craft, by the Rt. Rev. William Forbes Adams, D.D., LL.D., D.C.L., assisted by the rector of the parish, at Vienna, Md. So. Ch., Sept. 27, 1913

Robert J., of Maryland, and Margaret K., d. of the late ex-Governor Letcher of Virginia, by the Rev. Dr. McBride, at the residence of the bride's mother, Lexington, Va. So. Ch., Mar. 6, 1884

SHOWEN
Moses, of Shenandoah Co., and Mary S., d. of B. R. Green of Fauquier Co., Va., by the Rev. H. B. Lee, at the residence of the bride's father. So. Ch., Nov. 22, 1877

SHULER
N. W., of New Market, and Jennie R., d. of J. N. Liggett, Esq. of Harrisonburg, by the Rev. O. S. Bunting, in Emmanuel Church, Harrisonburg, Va. So. Ch., Nov. 29, 1883

SHUMATE
Bettie, and Lucian D. Holtzclaw, both of Fauquier Co., Va., by the Rev. E. H. Ingle, in Washington, D.C. So. Ch., Aug. 23, 1883

SIBLEY
See also STOKES, Helen Sibley (Mrs.)

SIGOURNEY
Jane Carter, d. of Charles Sigourney, Esq. of Hartford, Conn., and Michael Burnham of New York, by the Rt. Rev. Bishop Griswold, in Boston. So. Ch.,

MARRIAGE NOTICES IN THE SOUTHERN CHURCHMAN WITH DATES OF PUBLICATION

SILAS
Augustus Ramon, of Savannah, and Valeria Berrien, youngest d. of the late Hon. Jno. Whitehead of Burke Co., Ga. and gr. d. of Maj. John Berrien of the Continental Army, by the Rev. William A. Leonard, in St. John's Church, Washington, D.C. So. Ch., Jan. 1, 1885

SIMMONDS
James Burton, and Mary Alice Robinson, both of Lancaster Va., by the Rev. H. L. Derby, in Trinity Church, Lancaster C.H., Va. So. Ch., Sept. 16, 1886

SIMMONS
Emily Lagore, d. of Mr. and Mrs. Morton Waring Simmons, and Charles Jervey Ravenel, by the Rev. Thomas P. Baker, at the residence of the bride's parents, Adams Run, S.C. So. Ch., Dec. 18, 1909

Narcissa B., d. of Capt. Judah Simmons, and the Rev. W. G. Hawkins of Centerville, Md., by the Rev. S. Nash, in St. John's Church, Essex Co., Va. So. Ch., Oct. 9, 1851

SIMPSON
Annie C., of Smithfield, and Charles J. Nourse, Esq. of Fauquier Co., by the Rev. David Barr, in Christ Church, Smithfield, Va. So. Ch., Aug. 20, 1885

Eugene, and Carrie Theresa, d. of Wm. Hester, all of Terry, Miss., by the Rev. Dr. Wm. C. Crane, in the Church of the Good Shephord, Torry, Miss. So. Ch., July 13, 1876

Wm. A. (Lt.), Second Artillery, U.S.A., and Laura Loo, only d. of Mrs. Lillie and Lt. Col. Wm. F. Lee, C.S.A., and gr. d. of the late Rev. W. F. Lee of Richmond, Va., by the Rev. Mr. Hubbard, at Shepherdstown, W.Va. So. Ch., May 20, 1880

SIMS
Eliza B., eldest d. of Wm. H. and Sallie J. Sims, and Jno. W. Timberlake of Albemarle Co., by the Rev. John T. Clark, at "Black Walnut", Halifax Co. So. Ch., Dec. 23, 1869

J. W., Esq., and E. M. Brown, by the Rev. A. B. Tizzard, in Chesterfield Co., Va. So. Ch., Oct. 17, 1872

W. B., of Halifax Co., Va., and Annie C. Ruffin, by the Rev. B. S. Bronson, at the residence of the bride's father, Dr. John K. Ruffin, Wilson, N.C. So. Ch., July 5, 1883

SINCLAIR
William W., s. of the late Com. Arthur Sinclair, U.S.N., of Norfolk, Va., and Corine, d. of the late Charles Alexander Swann of Alexandria, Va., by the Rev. Geo. W. Peterkin, rector, bishop-elect of West Virginia, in the Memorial P. E. Church, So. Ch., May 16, 1878

SINGER
Adelaide R., d. of Capt. Thomas Singer of Alexandria, and Rev. J. Parvin, rector of Christ Church, Towanda, Pa., by the Rev. John Coleman, D.D., in Trinity Church. So. Ch., Dec. 17, 1847

SINGLETON
Lucy Everett, d. of Col. John C. Singleton of Columbia, S.C., and David Hemphill, Esq. of South

MARRIAGE NOTICES IN THE SOUTHERN CHURCHMAN WITH DATES OF PUBLICATION

Carolina, by the rector, the Rev. James S. Hanckel, in the Episcopal Church, Charlottesville. So. Ch., Nov. 30, 1871

SIPE
Conrad A., of Waynesburg, Pa., and Mary R., d. of Otis Watson, Esq. of Marion Co., W. Va., by the Rev. G. A. Gibbons, at the residence of the bride's father. So. Ch., Dec. 5, 1878

SKELDING
Joseph, and Emily Fletcher, at the bride's residence, Lowmoor. So. Ch., Nov. 14, 1889

Mary Elizabeth, of Alleghany Co., Va., and Alfred Francis Davidson of London, England, by the Rev. L. R. Combs, at the residence of the bride's brother-in-law, Dr. O. L. Rogers, Covington, Va. So. Ch., Apr. 27, 1893

SKELTON
Charlotte R., and L. W. McVeigh, both of Richmond, by the Rev. P. F. Berkley, in Monumental Church, Richmond. So. Ch., Oct. 14, 1869

E. M., d. of Dr. John G. Skelton, and P. Hamilton Baskerville, all of Richmond, by the Rev. George Woodbridge assisted by the Rev. Charles Minnigerode, in the Monumental Church, Richmond, Va. So. Ch., June 24, 1875

Louisa S., d. of Dr. E. W. Skelton of Powhatan Co., and the Rev. Jefferson Lewis of the Philadelphia Conference, by the Rev. P. F. Berkley. So. Ch., Mar. 20, 1835

Maria W., eldest d. of Dr. John G. Skelton of Powhatan Co., and John L. Williams of Richmond, by the Rev. P. F. Berkley, in Grace Church, Powhatan Co. So. Ch., Nov. 9, 1864

SKINKER
Alexander Rives (Capt.), First Missouri Infantry, s. of Mr. and Mrs. Thomas Keith Skinker of St. Louis, and Caroline, d. of Mr. and Mrs. John Rulon-Miller, Newtown Square, Pa., by the Rt. Rev. James R. Winchester, Bishop of Arkansas, at Vandeventer Place, St. Louis. So. Ch., Aug. 25, 1917

Anna H., and Dr. Norman de V. Howard, by the Rev. W. H. H. Powers, at the residence of the bride's father, Fauquier Co. So. Ch., Apr. 23, 1874

Margaret R., eldest d. of James K. Skinker, Esq. of Fauquier, and Dr. John W. McIlhany of Greenville, Miss., by the Rev. O. A. Kinsolving, at Huntley, Fauquier Co., Va. So. Ch., Mar. 8, 1861

Mary J., and J. M. Goldsmith of St. Mary's Co., Md., by the Rev. John McGill, at "Huntley", Fauquier Co., the residence of the bride's father. So. Ch., Jan. 6, 1870

SKINNER
A. J., and Helen S., d. of Geo. W. Lee, by the Rev. Frank Page, at the residence of the bride's father, in Fairfax Co. So. Ch., June 7, 1883

Robert E. S., and Emma E. Newton, by the Rev. R. A. Castleman, at Arcola, Loudoun Co., Va. So. Ch., Feb. 23, 1893

MARRIAGE NOTICES IN THE SOUTHERN CHURCHMAN WITH DATES OF PUBLICATION

SKIPPER
    Augusta, of Baltimore Co., Md., and G. Edwin Entwisle of Alexandria, by the Rev. D. F. Sprigg, in Grace Church, Alexandria. So. Ch., Dec. 9, 1869

SKIPWITH
    Robert, and Jane Rolfe, d. of the late Col. Wm. Bolling, by the Rev. J. P. B. Wilmer, at Bolling Hall, Goochland Co., Va. So. Ch., July 16, 1847
    Thos. B., and Emma S. Derrieux, both of Powhatan Co., Va., by the Rev. P. F. Berkeley, at Edge Hill, the residence of M. L. Waring. So. Ch., Dec. 7, 1871

SLACK
    Mary R., d. of the officiating clergyman and formerly of Albemarle Co., Va., and Alfred Wyman, by the Rev. Samuel R. Slack, in Trinity Church, Weymouth, Mass. So. Ch., Nov. 3, 1881
    Samuel R. (The Rev.), and Helen M. Dunbar, both of Weymouth, by the Rev. John Wright, rector of St. Matthew's Church, Boston, in Trinity Church, Weymouth, Mass. So. Ch., Jan. 18, 1877

SLACUM
    Georgianna, of Alexandria, and William Meredith Lambeth of New Orleans, by the Rev. Chas. Dana. So. Ch., Aug. 16, 1839

SLADE
    Cooke F., and Sarah E., d. of the late Wm. M. Fitzhugh, all of Fairfax, Va., by the Rev. Frank Page, in Zion Church, Fairfax C.H. So. Ch., July 21, 1887

    Selina M., of Fairfax Co., and Philip M. Edmonds of Fauquier Co., by the Rev. Jno. McGill, in "The Falls" Church. So. Ch., Nov. 1, 1877

SLAUGHTER
    Bessie, d. of the late Philip Slaughter of Rappahannock Co., Va., and Dr. F. S. Hall, by the Rev. P. Slaughter, D.D., at Wellington, Culpeper Co., Va. So. Ch., Dec. 4, 1879
    Eliza Lane, d. of Judge Montgomery Slaughter, and John Strother Berryman, by the Rev. D. E. C. Murdaugh, in Trinity Church, Fredericksburg, Va. So. Ch., Feb. 21, 1884
    Harriet C., and James A. Jenks, Esq., by the Rev. W. H. Pendleton, at the residence of the bride's father, near New London, Campbell Co. So. Ch., Feb. 20, 1868
    Hattie, and Charles E. Thackett, by the Rev. John K. Mason, in St. George's Church, Fredericksburg, Va. So. Ch., Nov. 15, 1888
    J. A., of Little Rock, Ark., and Gary, d. of the late David Funsten of Alexandria, Va., by the Rev. Wm. M. Dame, in St. Luke's Church, Norfolk. So. Ch., Dec. 24, 1874
    James C., and Mrs. Bettie F. Mosely, both of Bedford Co., by the Rev. R. H. Wilmer, at the residence of Spottswood Brown. So. Ch., Apr. 18, 1856
    John B., Jr., and Mary W.,

MARRIAGE NOTICES IN THE SOUTHERN CHURCHMAN WITH DATES OF PUBLICATION

d. of John R. Triplett, Esq., by the Rev. Montgomery Schuyler, D.D., the Rt. Rev. Bishop of the Diocese pronouncing the benediction, in Christ Church, St. Louis. So. Ch., Dec. 23, 1875

John H., of Amherst Co., Va., and Susan B., d. of Col. James F. Hubard of Nelson Co., Va., by the Rev. Davis M. Wood. So. Ch., Aug. 2, 1888

Mary V., d. of J. Madison Slaughter, Esq. late of Baltimore, and the Rev. Jas. Gibbon Minnigerode of Rappahannock Co., Va., by the Rev. C. Minnigerode, rector of the church, assisted by the Rev. A. M. Randolph, in Emmanuel Church, Baltimore. So. Ch., Oct. 23, 1873

Robert Madison, M.D., of Orange Co., Va., and Fannie Chichester Innis, by the Rev. C. Walker, D.D., at "Wagram", the residence of the bride's mother, in Alexandria Co., Va. So. Ch., Sept. 18, 1884

Sally Champe, d. of Samuel Slaughter, Esq., and the Rev. Wm. F. Lockwood of Fairfax Co., by the Rev. Mr. Cole, at Western View, Culpeper Co. So. Ch., Nov. 7, 1850

Sophia Mercer, d. of the officiating clergyman, and Thomas Towles Slaughter, by the Rev. P. Slaughter, at Clover Hill, Rappahannock Co. So. Ch., Feb. 15, 1866

Susan A. S., and Geo. H. Cox of Buckingham, by the Rev. R. H. Wilmer, at the residence of J. A. Clay, Esq. of Bedford Co., Va. So. Ch., Apr. 4, 1856

Thomas Towles, and Sophia Mercer, d. of the officiating clergyman, the Rev. P. Slaughter, at Clover Hill, Rappahannock Co. So. Ch., Feb. 15, 1866

W. F., of Fredericksburg, Va., and Hannah Battaile, only d. of H. B. Hoomes, Esq. of Alexandria, by the Rev. E. C. Murdaugh, D.D. So. Ch., Feb. 13, 1873

SLEET

Ellen T., d. of Yancey Sleet of Mathews Co., Va., and James W. Bonnett of Middlesex Co., Va., by the Rev. Peregrine Wroth, at Mathews C.H., Va. So. Ch., Mar. 18, 1875

SLINGLUFF

Fielder C., of Baltimore, Md., and Mary LeGrand, d. of Reuben Johnston, by the Rev. R. H. McKim assisted by the Rev. Reverdy Estill, in Christ Church, Alexandria, Va. So. Ch., Nov. 13, 1873

Horace, and Nannie M., d. of the late Dr. Montgomery Johns, by the Rev. A. M. Randolph, at the residence of the bride's mother. So. Ch., Jan. 26, 1882

SMART

James W., Esq., of London, England, and Fannie, d. of A. A. Phaup of Chesterfield Co., Va., by the Rev. A. B. Tizzard, at the residence of the bride's parents. So. Ch.,

MARRIAGE NOTICES IN THE SOUTHERN CHURCHMAN WITH DATES OF PUBLICATION

Sept. 17, 1891
Wm. R., of Gloucester, and A. Rosalie Carter, by the Rev. Edmund Withers, in White Chapel Church, Lancaster Co., Va. So. Ch., Sept. 18, 1857

SMEDLY
Matilda F., of Chicago, and the Rev. W. M. A. Broadnax, rector of St. Paul's Church, Lee Center, by the Rev. H. N. Shenck, in Trinity Church, Chicago. So. Ch., June 17, 1859

SMITH
A. Magill, Esq., and Mary Bolling, d. of the Rev. W. C. Meredith, all of Winchester, Va., by the Rev. W. C. Meredith, in Christ Church, Winchester, Va. So. Ch., Jan. 16, 1868

Agnes M., and Capt. Samuel Barron, Jr., both of Richmond Co., by the rector, in St. John's Church, Lunenburg Parish, Richmond Co. So. Ch., May 20, 1869

Alfreda Tucker, d. of the late Chas. A. Smith of Winchester, Va., and Geo. W. Jackson, Esq. of Gallipolis, Ohio, by the Rev. W. C. Meredith, in Christ Church, Winchester. So. Ch., Jan. 16, 1868

Algernon (Dr.), of Maryland, and A. T. Taylor of Hillsboro, by the Rev. Theodore Reed, at the residence of Dr. Taylor, in Hillsboro, Va. So. Ch., June 28, 1877

Alice Corbyn, d. of Francis L. Smith, Esq. of Alexandria, Va., and William E. Strong of New York, by the Rev. Dr. Horton, rector of St. Paul's Church, at the residence of the bride's father. So. Ch., Dec. 5, 1872

Allen, and Cornelia Lee Stuart, at "Cedar Grove", King George Co., the residence of the bride's mother. So. Ch., Nov. 7, 1889

Amanda M., d. of A. G. Smith of Middleburg, and Edward S. Duffey, by the Rev. O. A. Kinsolving. So. Ch., Mar. 18, 1869

Anna Ophelia, d. of the late Edward Smith of King George Co., Va., and J. F. Hansborough of Culpeper, by the Rev. John Cole, at "Zhu Hol", the residence of the bride's uncle, Dr. D. F. Slaughter, Esq. So. Ch., Jan. 31, 1867

Annie F., d. of Dr. Washington A. Smith of Taylor's Island, and Dr. Thomas A. Corroll, by the Rev. Dr. Wm. W. Greene, in Grace Church, Taylor's Island, Dorchester, Md. So. Ch., Dec. 25, 1879

Augustine J., of Alexandria, and Lillie B., youngest d. of the late Jacob Morgan of Jefferson Co., by the Rev. Mr. Andrews, near Shepherdstown. So. Ch., Dec. 14, 1855

Benj. B. (The Rt. Rev.), and Harriot L. Douglass of New York, by the Rt. Rev. Bishop Onderdonk, in St. Thomas' Church, New York. So. Ch., Sept. 18, 1835

Beverly, Esq., and Mrs. Virginia S. Snodgrass, both of Parkersburg, by the Rev. W. L. Hyland, rector of Trinity Church, Parkersburg, Va., in Trinity Church, Parkersburg, Va. So. Ch., Dec. 23, 1859

C. P., and Addie J., only

MARRIAGE NOTICES IN THE SOUTHERN CHURCHMAN WITH DATES OF PUBLICATION

d. of W. L. Waring of Bendour, Goochland Co., Va., by the Rev. P. M. Boyden, at the residence of the bride's father. So. Ch., Nov. 4, 1886

C. S., and Lalla R. Wright, both of Essex Co., Va., by the Rev. Everard Meade, in St. Paul's Church, South Farnham Parish, Essex Co., Va. So. Ch., Dec. 1, 1881

Carrie W., d. of Mrs. Mary H. Smith of Baltimore, and the Rev. John S. Lindsay, rector of St. James' Church, Warrenton, Va., by the Rev. A. M. Randolph, D.D. assisted by the Rev. George W. Peterkin, in Emmanuel Church, Baltimore, Md. So. Ch., June 21, 1877

Chas. W., and Josephine, d. of the late Fereol Lemoine, by the Rev. Edmund Withers, in Richmond Co. So. Ch., July 2, 1858

Charles W. F.* (The Rev.), assistant minister of St. Paul's Church, Richmond, Va., and Ivy Watkins of London, England, by the Rev. Beverly D. Tucker, D.D., rector of St. Paul's Church, Richmond, assisted by the Rev. Vincent L. Bennett, rector of St. Michael's, and the Rev. James DeWolf Hubbard, in St. Michael's Church, Milton, Mass. So. Ch., Dec. 22, 1934

Claudia W., d. of Margaret L. and the late Maj. J. Thomas Smith of Fauquier Co., Va., and the Rev. J. Harry Chesley of Maryland, by the Rev. J. W. Chesley assisted by the Rev. C. Walker, D.D., at the residence of the bride's mother, on Seminary Hill. So. Ch., July 25, 1878

Courtland H., of Alexandria, and Nannie D., d. of A. K. Phillips, Esq., by the Rev. J. R. Mason, at the residence of the bride's father, in Fredericksburg. So. Ch., May 2, 1889

Dudley D., and Susan J., d. of the officiating clergyman, the Rev. Wm. Sparrow, D.D., in the chapel of the Theological Seminary. So. Ch., June 24, 1859

Duncan, of New York City, s. of Dr. and Mrs. Francis Smith of University of Virginia, and Alice Coleman, d. of Mr. and Mrs. Hugh Nelson of 924 W. Grace St., Richmond, Va. by the Rev. Wm. Meade Clark, D.D. So. Ch., Jan. 3, 1914

E. Dolafield, of New York, and Margaret Johnston, d. of the Rev. Gilbert Morgan, D. D. of South Carolina, by the rector, the Rev. Le Grand F. Guerry, in St. Philip's Church, Bradford Springs, S.C. So. Ch., July 23, 1874

Edna A., and Robt. L. Grinstead, both of Frankfort, by the Rev. Henry T. Sharp, in the Church of The Ascension, Frankfort, Ky. So. Ch., Apr. 23, 1874

Edulia G., of West Point, and Bayard R. Price of Philadelphia, by the Rev. J. Y. Downman, in the Episcopal Church, West Point, Va. So. Ch., Dec. 28, 1882

Edward Jaquelin, and Lucy

---

* Not recorded in the Vestry Minutes of St. Paul's Church, Richmond, Va., as having any connection with that church

MARRIAGE NOTICES IN THE SOUTHERN CHURCHMAN WITH DATES OF PUBLICATION

Wiley, only d. of Charles Mason, all of King George, by the Rev. Moses H. Hunter, in St. John's Church, King George C.H., Va. So. Ch., June 16, 1881

Ella J., of Spotsylvania, and James B. Dabney of Caroline Co., Va., by the Rev. Wm. W. Greene, at the residence of the bride's father. So. Ch., Feb. 8, 1872

Ella W., d. of the late William M. Smith, M.D., and the Rev. P. M. Boyden, rector of St. James Parish, Northam, by the Rev. Frank Stringfellow, in Hebron Church, Goochland Co. So. Ch., Sept. 4, 1879

Emily, d. of Maj. Charles H. Smith of the U.S. Army, and R. C. Gwathmey, Esq. of Richmond, by the Rev. Mr. Parks. So. Ch., Dec. 1, 1837

Emily Norcom, d. of Samuel Smith, Esq. of Reidsville, and the Rev. Alban Greaves, by the Rev. H. O. Lacey, in the Episcopal Church, Reidsville, N.C. So. Ch., June 16, 1887

Emma, d. of Anderson Smith, Esq., and Dr. A. A. Marsteller of Washington, D.C., in Grace Church, The Plains, Fauquier Co., Va. So. Ch., Jan. 3, 1878

Eugenia C., d. of the late George D. Smith of Loudoun Co., Va., and Frank L. Fred of Indian Territory, by the Rev. Carter Page, at Locust Grove, the home of the bride. So. Ch., Oct. 20, 1887

Eva M., and Thomas D. Holley, all of Bertie Co., N.C., by the Rev. Edward Wooten, in Coleraine, Bertie Co., N.C. So. Ch., Mar. 4, 1869

Fidella, and the Rev. Wm. Homman, by the Rev. Mr. Burgess, at Hartford, Conn. So. Ch., Oct. 25, 1839

Frances Anne, of the Woman's Union Missionary Society of New York, d. of the Rev. Dudley D. Smith, rector of Emmanuel Protestant Episcopal Church, Kensington, Philadelphia, and Edgar Wood, Jr., M.D. of the American Southern Presbyterian Mission, by the Rev. E. H. Thomson of the American Episcopal Mission, at Bridgman Memorial Home, Shanghai, China. So. Ch., June 2, 1892

Frances Robertson, only d. of Mr. and Mrs. Eugene Bates Smith of Greenville, S.C., and Lt. Thomas Butler Pearce, 3rd of Quantico Marine Base, Va., by the Rev. Sam. B. Chilton, in Trinity Episcopal Church, Fredericksburg, Va. So. Ch., Oct. 4, 1941

George A., of Richmond, Va., and May Taylor, by the Rev. J. Green Shackelford, at the home of the bride in Orange Co., Va. So. Ch., Dec. 3, 1885

George R., of Scotland, and Sally P. Cheatwood of Russell Parish, Bedford Co., Va., by the Rev. Albert Ware, at the residence of the bride's father. So. Ch., Oct. 26, 1876

Gordon V. (The Rev.), and Leone Hollister, by Bishop McCormick assisted by the rector, the Rev. L. B. Whittemore, in Grace Church, Grand Rapids. So. Ch.,

MARRIAGE NOTICES IN THE SOUTHERN CHURCHMAN WITH DATES OF PUBLICATION

Feb. 23, 1935
Hariot Taylor, d. of the late D. Boyd Smith of Alexandria, and Rev. George H. Edwards of New Jersey, by the Rev. D. J. Edwards, in St. Paul's Church, Alexandria. So. Ch., Nov. 16, 1882

Helen, and the Rev. Augustine McCormick, by the Rt. Rev. John N. McCormick, Bishop of Western Michigan and father of the groom, in St. Mark's Pro-Cathedral, Grand Rapids, Diocese of Western Michigan. So. Ch., Aug. 30, 1924

Henry L., of West Virginia, and Lydia L. Lewis, by the Rev. Robb White, at the residence of Capt. John Fry, Keswick, Va. So. Ch., Jan. 25, 1883

Hobart (The Rev.), rector of St. Thomas' Parish, Baltimore Co., Md., and Esther Margerotta, d. of Mrs. Moncrief Livingston, by the Rt. Rev. William Paret, D.D., in St. John's Church, Kingston, N.Y. So. Ch., Oct. 10, 1889

Ida M., and George P. Perry, both of Henrico Co., Va., by the Rev. R. S. Barrett, in Richmond, Va. So. Ch., Nov. 22, 1877

J. H., Esq., of the firm of Smith & Powzie, Philadelphia, and Mattie, youngest d. of the late William Tyler, Esq. of Virginia, by the Rev. John Collins McCabe, D.D., rector of the Church of the Ascension, Baltimore, at Sherwood Forest, Charles City Co., Va., the county seat of the bride's uncle, the Hon. John Tyler, ex-President of the United States. So. Ch., June 1, 1860

J. Holmes (Gen.), of Lynchburg, and S. Norvell Hobson, by the Rev. Joshua Peterkin, D.D., at the residence of the bride's parents, Dr. Joseph V. and Mrs. Mary E. Hobson, Richmond, Va. So. Ch., Mar. 21, 1878

J. Marsden, and Julia Robertson, both of Norfolk, by the Rev. Beverly D. Tucker, at the residence of the bride's father, Duncan Robertson, Esq. So. Ch., Oct. 14, 1886

James E., and Wilholmina Wood, both of Caroline Co., Va., by the Rev. Wm. W. Green, at Rose Hill, the residence of the bride's father, Col. Fleming Wood. So. Ch., Dec. 26, 1872

James Henderson, and Natalie Churchill, d. of the late Charles Friend, Esq. of Petersburg, Va., by the Rev. Churchill J. Gibson, D.D. of Petersburg, at the residence of the bride's great uncle, the Rev. J. M. Atkinson, D.D., Hampden-Sidney College, Va. So. Ch., Dec. 26, 1878

James M., Esq., and Mary Miller Northana, youngest d. of Capt. James M. Bell, by the Rev. Mr. Lamon. So. Ch., Jan. 9, 1835

Jas. M., Esq., of Charlottesville, Va., and Ella Rust of Westmoreland, Va., by the Rev. Wm. C. Latane, in Trinity Church, Washington, D.C. So. Ch., May 5, 1881

James Spencer, and Carrie Cousins Muir, both of Petersburg, by the Rev. Luther W. Doggett, in Grace Church, Petersburg, Va.

MARRIAGE NOTICES IN THE SOUTHERN CHURCHMAN WITH DATES OF PUBLICATION

So. Ch., Oct. 3, 1889
Jane K., d. of the late James Smith, Esq. of Richmond, and /the name of the groom was omitted_/, by the Rev. William Gadsby of Washington, at Aldie, Va. So. Ch., Dec. 15, 1837

John Rutledge, Esq., and Sophia Gordon, d. of the late James Taylor, by the Rev. Mr. Hanckell, in St. Paul's Church, Charleston, S.C. So. Ch., Nov. 6, 1835

Kathleen B., youngest d. of the late P. A. L. Smith of Fauquier Co., and Jas. J. Robinson of West Virginia, by the Rev. A. P. Gray, at the residence of Capt. Brookfield, near New Baltimore, Fauquier Co. So. Ch., Sept. 27, 1883

Leonidas S. (The Rev.), and Sarah Jane, youngest d. of William P. Stewart, Esq., by the Rt. Rev. Dr. Johns, in Norfolk, Va. So. Ch., Jan. 2, 1851

Lewis Stirling, and Addie C., second d. of the late W. W. Coke of Princess Anne Co., Va., by the Rt. Rev. Alexander Garrett, in St. Matthew's Cathedral, Dallas, Tex. So. Ch., Oct. 22, 1891

Lillie D., d. of Margaret and Wm. Temple Smith, and Charles A. S. Hopkins of Woodstock, Va., by the Rev. A. P. Gray, in Trinity Church, Manassas. So. Ch., Nov. 1, 1883

Lizzette G., eldest d. of P. A. L. Smith of Fauquier Co., and John S. Robinson, by the Rev. Jno. McGill, at the residence of the bride's father. So. Ch., Nov. 13, 1873

Lizzie M., and Walter J. Suthon of Louisiana, by the Rev. Nelson P. Dame, in Christ Church, Winchester, Va. So. Ch., Mar. 24, 1893

Lucy E., d. of the Rev. George A. Smith, and J. D. Corse, by the Rev. R. D. Brooke, in Christ Church, Alexandria. So. Ch., June 21, 1855

Madge W., d. of Mrs. M. L. Smith, and the Rev. Robert W. Forsyth, by the Rev. Dr. Walker assisted by the Rev. Peregrine Wroth, in Emmanuel Church, Theological Seminary, Va. So. Ch., Dec. 20, 1883

Maggie S., d. of Dr. G. W. Smith of "Ingleside", Eastville, Va., and the Rev. James B. Craighill of Maysville, Ky., by the Rev. J. J. Clemens, in Carist Church, Northampton Co. So. Ch., Dec. 8, 1870

Margaret A., eldest d. of O. M. Smith, Esq., and Richard H. Wilson, by the Rev. Thomas W. White, at Glenbrook, Lunenburg, Va. So. Ch., Feb. 27, 1863

Margaret Farlie, of Hanover Co., Va., and Wm. Robert Boyd, Esq. of Alabama, by the Rev. G. S. Carraway, in Immanuel Church, Hanover Co., Va. So. Ch., Oct. 28, 1859

Maria Catharine, and Wm. Foote Massie, M.D., both of Fauquier, by the Rev. Wm. F. Lockwood, at Orlean, Fauquier Co., Va. So. Ch., Mar. 6, 1851

Maria L., d. of Margaret L. and the late Maj. J. Thomas Smith of Fauquier, and the Rev. Edward L. Goodwin of Franklin Co., by the Rev.

MARRIAGE NOTICES IN THE SOUTHERN CHURCHMAN WITH DATES OF PUBLICATION

C. Walker, D.D. assisted by the Rev. J. Harry Chesley, at the residence of the bride's mother, Seminary Hill, Fairfax Co., Va. So. Ch., Jan. 20, 1881

Maria Louisa, d. of Jabez Smith of Chesterfield Co., and Thomas M. Buford of Petersburg, Va., by the Rev. Andrew Syme, at Petersburg, Va. So. Ch., Dec. 1, 1837

Marina Bishop, d. of the late Jacob Smith, Esq. of East Haven, and the Rev. Lorenzo T. Bennett, assistant minister of the Parish of Trinity Church, by the Rev. Dr. Croswell, at New Haven, Conn. So. Ch., Aug. 9, 1839

Martha Ann, d. of David Smith of Lunenburg, and John Pillar, by the Rev. Thomas E. Locke. So. Ch., July 5, 1839

Mary, d. of the late Dr. Sidney W. Smith, and Dr. S. W. Everett of Quincy, Ill., by the Rev. C. B. Dana, at Alexandria. So. Ch., July 16, 1858

Mary, d. of Charles Smith, Esq. of Philadelphia, and Dr. Edmund J. Lee, by the Rt. Rev. Geo. W. Peterkin assisted by the Rev. Francis D. Lee, at the Church of the Holy Trinity, Philadelphia. So. Ch., Dec. 18, 1879

Mary A., and Rodney F. Keys, by the Rev. A. S. Johns, at Long Branch, Fauquier Co., Va. So. Ch., Jan. 5, 1882

Mary Brockenbrough, d. of the late Dr. John Philip Smith of Clarke Co., and Thomas D. Addison of Fairfax Co., by the Rev. John B. Newton, in Monumental Church, Richmond, Va. So. Ch., Feb. 24, 1887

Mary W., eldest d. of the late Rev. Thos. Smith, former rector of the Episcopal Church in Parkersburg, and Mathias M. Ward of New York, by the Rev. E. T. Perkins. So. Ch., Aug. 11, 1848

Mary W., eldest d. of the Rev. George A. Smith of Clarens, Fairfax Co., and the Rev. Robert D. Brooke of Dubuque, Iowa, by the Rev. C. B. Dana. So. Ch., Oct. 25, 1850

Mary W., of Weston, d. of Mrs. S. A. V. and the late Isaac Smith of Williamsburg, Va. and niece of Hon. W. E. Lively of Weston, and Prof. J. W. Bonnor of Marion Co., W.Va., by the Rev. T. H. Lacy, in St. Paul's Church, Weston, W.Va. So. Ch., June 28, 1888

Monita W., and Herbert A. Gill, both of Washington, by the Rev. E. H. Ingle, in Ascension Church, Washington, D.C. So. Ch., July 6, 1882

Nannie M., d. of Rev. Thomas Smith, deceased, first rector of Trinity Parish, and Mrs. Ann M. Smith of Parkersburg, W.Va., and the Hon. Floyd Neely of West Union, W.Va., by the Rev. Robert A. Gibson assisted by the Rt. Rev. Geo. W. Peterkin, in Trinity Church, Parkersburg, W.Va. So. Ch., Apr. 12, 1883

Nannie W., and J. H. Whit-

MARRIAGE NOTICES IN THE SOUTHERN CHURCHMAN WITH DATES OF PUBLICATION

low, both of Campbell Co., by the Rev. W. E. Webb. So. Ch., July 1, 1859

Orlando, Esq., of Lunenburg C.H., and Louisa W., d. of Roger B. Atkinson, Esq., by the Rev. Henry Wall assisted by the Rt. Rev. Henry C. Lay, D.D., brother-in-law of the bride, at Sherwood, Lunenburg Co., Va. So. Ch., May 4, 1860

Peyton McGuire, s. of the Rev. and Mrs. Claudius F. Smith of Lynchburg, Va., and Mrs. Maude Pemberton Hart of Chattanooga, Tenn. So. Ch., Apr. 16, 1921

R. T., and Mollie J. Thorp of Granville Co., N.C., by the Rev. P. D. Thompson, at the residence of the bride's father. So. Ch., Nov. 9, 1871

Rachel, d. of the late Dr. Sidney W. Smith of Alexandria, Va., and Wm. Ellzey Gray of Loudoun Co., by the Rt. Rev. Bishop Johns, in Christ Church, Alexandria. So. Ch., Nov. 30, 1860

Rebekah Daingerfield, d. of the late David Boyd Smith of Alexandria, Va., and the Rev. George H. Fullerton of Philadelphia, by the Rev. George H. Norton, at the residence of the bride's father, Alexandria, Va. So. Ch., Jan. 3, 1884

Richard H., and Lucy A. E. Scates, by the Rev. D. M. Wharton, at the residence of the bride's father. So. Ch., Jan. 15, 1880

Richard H., and Mary D., d. of Ellen H. and the late Charles M. Barton, by the Rev. H. B. Lee, at the residence of the bride's mother, at Markham, Fauquier Co., Va. So. Ch., Nov. 2, 1882

Robert, Esq., of Fauquier Co., and Mary Jane, d. of Rice Hooe, Esq., by the Rev. E. C. McGuire, D.D., at Bunker's Hill. So. Ch., Jan. 25, 1856

Robert Alexander, of Fauquier Co., Va., and Cornelia, d. of Mr. and Mrs. Edmund Willis Scott and niece of the officiating clergyman, by the Rev. F. G. Scott, at Spring Forest, the home of the bride's parents, near Somerset, Va. So. Ch., Sept. 19, 1903

Roberta M., d. of E. J. Smith, and Philip H. Powers of Charles Town, by the Rev. F. M. Whittle, at Smithfield, Clarke Co., Va. So. Ch., Jan. 13, 1853

Sadie J., and John O. Crown, editor of "Clarke Courier", both of Berryville, by the Rev. T. F. Martin, in Grace Church, Berryville. So. Ch., Oct. 30, 1873

Sallie V., and Edward Lonsdale Daingerfield, by the Rev. Dr. Norton, at the residence of the bride's father, F. L. Smith, Esq. So. Ch., Oct. 21, 1875

Samuel L., of Mt. Airy, Pittsylvania Co., Va., and Libbie E. Lewis, by the Rev. C. O. Pruden, at the residence of the bride's father, Ephraim Lewis, near Straight Stone, Pittsylvania Co., Va. So. Ch., Feb. 2, 1888

Sarah Ellen, and A. Judson Crane of Richmond, by the

MARRIAGE NOTICES IN THE SOUTHERN CHURCHMAN WITH DATES OF PUBLICATION

Rev. Mr. Temple, in King and Queen Co. So. Ch., Dec. 21, 1855

Thomas W., and Mary J. Blackwell, both of Fauquier Co., by the Rev. G. W. Nelson, at the home of the bride. So. Ch., Sept. 23, 1886

Treadwell, Jr., and Lucy E. H., eldest d. of David H. McGuire, Esq., all of Clarke Co., Va., by the Rev. H. Suter, at Berryville. So. Ch., Nov. 25, 1859

W. Augustine, of King George Co., Va., and Mattie F., only d. of Capt. Robt. G. Robb formerly of U.S. Navy, by the Rev. Wm. Friend, in St. Peter's Church, Port Royal, Va. So. Ch., Jan. 6, 1870

Walter R., of Richmond, and Lillie S. Jones of Essex Co., Va., by the Rev. Wm. Holden, assistant rector, in St. John's Church, Washington, D.C. So. Ch., Sept. 29, 1887

William, and Harriet Burton, d. of the Hon. Daniel Polsley, all of Mason Co., by the Rev. Horace Edwin Hayden, at Point Pleasant, W.Va. So. Ch., Sept. 16, 1869

Wm. H., and Rosalie, d. of the late Reuben Johnson, by the Rev. Geo. Woodbridge. So. Ch., Apr. 8, 1836

SMOAK
Chester Leo, and Elizabeth Behling, by the Rev. Thomas P. Baker, at the residence of the bride's parents, near Meggett, S.C. So. Ch., Mar. 23, 1912

SMOOT
Anthony Egerton, and Virginia, d. of the late Maris Taylor, Esq. all of Alexandria, Va., at the residence of the bride's mother. So. Ch., Aug. 6, 1885

Cesley, and Susan Lewis, by the Rev. Everard Meade, at St. Paul's Church, Essex Co., Va. So. Ch., May 3, 1888

Christiana A., of Alexandria, and John Jolly of Washington, D.C., by the Rev. D. F. Sprigg. So. Ch., June 14, 1866

Fanny, d. of J. Rector Smoot, Esq., and Washington Danenhower, by the Rev. Mr. Suter, at the residence of the bride's father, Alexandria, Va. So. Ch., Oct. 25, 1883

James Rector, of Alexandria, and Anna Irvine, d. of Robert Whitehead, Esq. of Nelson Co., Va., by the Rev. Paul Whitehead, D.D., at the residence of the bride's father. So. Ch., Aug. 26, 1880

Joseph A., of Maryland, and Fannie K. Jackson, eldest d. of the officiating clergyman, by the Rev. L. H. Jackson, in Christ Church, Milford, Del. So. Ch., Jan. 18, 1883

Kate A., d. of J. H. D. Smoot, Esq., and the Rev. W. Strother Jones of Fauquier Co., at the residence of the bride's father, Alexandria, Va. So. Ch., Oct. 26, 1876

MARRIAGE NOTICES IN THE SOUTHERN CHURCHMAN WITH DATES OF PUBLICATION

Mary C., and the Rev. F. M. Burch, by the Rev. W. Strother Jones assisted by the Rev. James H. Williams, at the residence of the bride's father, J. H. D. Smoot, Alexandria, Va. So. Ch., Nov. 16, 1882

Minnie C., oldest d. of the late J. H. D. Smoot of Alexandria, and the Rev. W. Strother Jones, by the Rev. Francis M. Burch. So. Ch., Nov. 29, 1888

William A., Esq., of Alexandria, Va., and Betty C., d. of the officiating clergyman, by the Rev. William McGuire, in Trinity Church, Washington, D.C. So. Ch., Oct. 23, 1873

SMUTZGER*
Frederick Charles, of Denver, Col., and Raymonde Virginia, d. of Mrs. Mildred Middleton and the late Ralph Hastings Cutter* of Savannah, Ga., by the Rev. Percy Grant, in the Church of the Ascension, Fifth Avenue, New York City. So. Ch., Feb. 15, 1908

SMYTH
Thomas H. (The Rev.), and Charlotte, oldest d. of Lloyd G. Hughes, Esq. of Wheeling, by the Rev. Jas. D. McCabe, D.D., in St. John's Church, Wheeling. So. Ch., May 16, 1856

SMYTHE
Mary S., d. of the late Rev. Thomas H. Smythe, rector of St. Paul's Church, Weston, W.Va., and Ethelwolf, s. of the late Thomas Scatcherd, Esq., M.P. of London, Canada, by the Rev. Horace Edwin Hayden, rector of St. John's Church, West Brownsville, in Christ Church, Brownsville, Pa. So. Ch., Sept. 13, 1877

SNEAD
Edwin B., of Richmond, Va., and Louisa Atkinson, d. of the officiating clergyman, by the Rev. Lewis Walke, in St. Stephen's Church, Cecil Co., Md. So. Ch., Jan. 24, 1884

SNODGRASS
Virginia S. (Mrs.), and Beverley Smith, Esq., both of Parkersburg, by the Rev. W. L. Hyland, rector of Trinity Church, Parkersburg, Va., in Trinity Church, Parkersburg, Va. So. Ch., Dec. 23, 1859

SNOW
Julian F., and Mattie A. Derby, by the Rev. B. D. Tucker assisted by the Rev. H. L. Derby, in Grace Church, Lancaster, Va. So. Ch., Feb. 13, 1879

Kate C., d. of David R. Snow, Esq., and Joel T. Adams of Algoma, W.Va., by the Rev. C. O. Pruden, at Snowdown, the home of the bride's father, in Pittsylvania Co., Va. So. Ch., Apr. 14, 1892

William C., formerly of Northumberland but now of Greensboro, N.C., and Ella, d. of Maj. Henry Deshield of Northumberland Co., Va., by the Rev. John Mancure assisted by the Rev. H. L. Derby, in St. Stephen's Church, Heathsville, Va. So. Ch., Dec. 8, 1881

SNOWDEN
Charles D. (The Rev.), rector

---

* A notice appears in the issue of Feb. 1, 1908, identical with this except that "Smutzger" is written "Sweetzer" and "Cutter" is written "Cutler"

MARRIAGE NOTICES IN THE SOUTHERN CHURCHMAN WITH DATES OF PUBLICATION

of St. Margaret's Church, Menands, N.Y., and Charlotte C. White of Cincinnati, Ohio, in the chapel of the Diocesan House. So. Ch., Oct. 5, 1940

Hubert, and Edith T. Ashby, by the Rev. H. Suter, in Christ Church, Alexandria. So. Ch., June 19, 1879

Jennie, d. of the late Edgar Snowden, and Dr. Thomas M. Lewis of Clarke Co., by the Rev. H. Suter, at the residence of the bride's mother, Alexandria. So. Ch., Dec. 30, 1880

Mary, d. of the late Edgar Snowden, and Rev. Samuel A. Wallis of Fairfax Co., by the Rev. H. Suter, at the residence of the bride's mother, Alexandria. So. Ch., May 8, 1890

Mary Jane, d. of the late Thomas Snowden of New York, and the Rev. Geo. S. Gordon, by the Rev. Hugh Smith, D.D. So. Ch., July 19 and Aug. 2, 1839

Nannie, d. of Edgar Snowden, Esq., the veteran editor of the <u>Alexandria "Gazette"</u>, and David Meade of Clarke Co., Va., by the Rev. J. T. Johnston, D.D., in St. Paul's Church, Alexandria. So. Ch., Dec. 28, 1865

SNYDER
W. H., of Alton, and Lucretia McLean formerly of Alexandria, Va., by the Rev. R. D. Brooke, at Galena, Ill. So. Ch., Aug. 14, 1851

William Tayloe, of Georgetown, and Marie Louise, d. of Gen. John Hammond of New York, by the Rev. Albert Stuart of Christ Church, Georgetown, assisted by the Rev. Edward H. Ingle of the Church of the Ascension, in the Church of The Ascension, Washington, D.C. So. Ch., Apr. 5, 1883

SOAMES
Florence Amelia, youngest d. of the late Aldurm Soames of Tramoke Lodge, Brighton, and the Rev. Herbert Guildford Sprigg, Vicar of Shelford, near Nottingham, at the parish church in Brighton, England. So. Ch., Sept. 4, 1879

SOAPER
Robt. C., and Annie E., second d. of the Rev. J. M. and the late J. E. Pringle, by the rector of St. Paul's Church, in St. Paul's Church, Henderson, Ky. So. Ch., Dec. 4, 1873

Susan H., of Henderson, and Haydon M. Young of Louisville, by the Rev. R. S. Barrott, in St. Paul's Church, Henderson, Ky. So. Ch., Feb. 21, 1884

SOMERS
Charles L. (The Rev.), /colored rector of colored churches in Lynchburg, Bedford, and Roanoke/, and Mrs. Helena J. Barnes /colored/, of Lynchburg, Va., by the Rev. Robert A. Magill, rector of St. John's Episcopal Church, Lynchburg, at Lynchburg, Va. So. Ch., Jan. 18, 1936

Daniel M., of Brooklyn, N.Y., formerly of Virginia, and Alice S. Davis, by the Rev. Henderson Suter, at the residence of the bride's father, Lynchburg, Va. So. Ch., Nov. 19, 1868

MARRIAGE NOTICES IN THE SOUTHERN CHURCHMAN WITH DATES OF PUBLICATION

Joseph R., of Fairfax Co., Va., and Mary Carloton, oldest d. of the late Guy Atkinson, Esq. of Alexandria, D.C., by the Rev. E. R. Lippet, at Alexandria. So. Ch., Oct. 6, 1837

SOMERVILLE

Atwell, and Mary, d. of the late Capt. R. Staunton Stringfellow, all of Culpeper Co., Va., by the Rev. John McGill, at "Church View", the residence of the bride's mother. So. Ch., Dec. 25, 1884

Douglas G., and M. Fenton, second d. of P. P. Nalle, Sr., all of Culpeper Co., by the Rev. John McGill assisted by the Rev. J. P. Strider, in St. Paul's Church, Culpeper Co., Va. So. Ch., Dec. 28, 1882

George S. (The Rev.), rector of Nelson Parish,*and Sue M., d. of the late William B. Hubard, by the Rev. C. J. Gibson, D.D., at Montezuma, the residence of the bride's mother. So. Ch., Nov. 13, 1890

Henry, M.D., and Mary Mercer, only child of the late Dr. Reuben Long, all of Culpeper Co., Va., by the Rev. Dr. Slaughter, at Wellington, the home of the bride's mother. So. Ch., May 6, 1880

SOMMERVILLE

E. L., and Dr. Wm. B. Bowen, by the Rev. Joseph R. Jones, in Meade Memorial Church, White Post, Va. So. Ch., Oct. 20, 1881

SORREL

A. Claxton (Capt.), of Savannah, Ga., and Matilda B., d. of John B. Hunton, Esq., by the Rev. W. A. Alrich, at "Evergreen", the residence of the bride's father, in Fauquier Co., Va. So. Ch., Feb. 27, 1868

SOTHORON

Annie Lee, d. of the officiating clergyman, and Richard Gough, by the rector, the Rev. L. J. Sothoron, in Trinity Church, Trinity Parish, Charles Co., Md. So. Ch., Nov. 20, 1884

SOUTH

F. G., of Colorado, and H. E. Coghill of King George, by the Rev. A. J. Willis, at "Lothian", the residence of the bride's father, in King George Co., Va. So. Ch., Mar. 17, 1877

SOUTHALL

Chas. M., and Alice E. Moorers, both of Charles City Co., by the Rev. W. B. Everett, at Mapisco Church, Charles City Co., Va. So. Ch., Jan. 4, 1883

James C., editor of the Richmond Enquirer and Examiner, and Eliza F., youngest d. of W. W. Sharp, Esq. of Norfolk, by the Rev. N. A. Okeson assisted by the Rev. T. M. Ambler, at the residence of the bride's father. So. Ch., Dec. 9, 1869

R. Temple, of New Kent, and Kate C., second d. of John A. McMinn, Esq. of Hanover Co., by the Rev. S. S. Hepbron, at the

---

* Nelson Parish is in Nelson County, Virginia (<u>Journal ... Diocese of Southwestern Va.</u>, 1940)

MARRIAGE NOTICES IN THE SOUTHERN CHURCHMAN WITH DATES OF PUBLICATION

residence of the bride's father. So. Ch., Jan. 1, 1891

SOUTHGATE

Angeline E. (Mrs.), of Norfolk, and the Rt. Rev. John Johns, by the Rev. H. V. D. Johns of Baltimore, in Norfolk. So. Ch., July 24, 1857

Frances, d. of the Rev. Dr. Southgate, and the Rev. John C. Gray, rector of Trinity Church, Fredericksburg, by the Rt. Rev. Bishop Paret, at Annapolis, Md. So. Ch., Feb. 2, 1893

SOWERS

Daisy Garland, and the Rev. Walter Lee Loflin, by the Rev. Dr. F. J. Mallett, at St. Luke's rectory, Salisbury, N.C. So. Ch., Nov. 16, 1912

Mary I., d. of John B. Sowers, Esq., and the Rev. Wm. G. Jackson, in Trinity Church, Staunton, Va. So. Ch., Apr. 29, 1836

SPADY

Edgar J., member of the House of Delegates, and Lucie E., d. of the late John Goffigon, by the Rev. J. M. Chevers, at Abingdon,*Northampton Co., Va. So. Ch., Mar. 7, 1856

SPARHAWK

Edward V., editor of the *Petersburg Intelligencer*, and Eloise Warrell of Richmond, Va., by the Rev. Wm. H. Hart, in Richmond, Va. So. Ch., Aug. 11, 1837

SPARROW

Bessie, d. of the officiating clergyman, and the Rev. Julius E. Grammer, by the Rev. Wm. Sparrow, D.D., in the chapel of the Theological Seminary. So. Ch., Dec. 28, 1855

Kate, youngest d. of the officiating clergyman, and the Rev. T. G. Dashiel of Richmond, by the Rev. Wm. Sparrow, D.D., at Staunton. So. Ch., Jan. 11, 1865

Leonard K., of Baltimore, and Nannie Temple, d. of the late Dr. Henry D. Magill of Leesburg, Va., by the Rev. Dr. J. E. Grammer, in St. Peter's Church, Baltimore. So. Ch., Feb. 22, 1877

Mary, d. of the Rev. Dr. Sparrow, and the Rev. John A. Jerome, by the Rev. Wm. Sparrow, D.D., in the chapel of the Theological Seminary of Virginia. So. Ch., Sept. 25, 1851

Samuel L., of Middlesex Co., and Anna E., oldest d. of James Burch of Essex Co., Va., by the Rev. J. H. Hundley, at the residence of the bride's father. So. Ch., Oct. 31, 1889

Susan J., d. of the officiating clergyman, and Dudley D. Smith, by the Rev. Wm. Sparrow, D.D., in the chapel of the Theological Seminary. So. Ch., June 24, 1859

Wilhemina, d. of the Rev. Dr. Sparrow, and the Rev. T. Grayson Dashiell, by the Rev. Dr. Sparrow, in the chapel of the Theological Seminary of Virginia. So. Ch., July 27, 1854

SPAULDING

Henry F., Esq. of New York, and Catherine Devereux, d. of Dr. John Beckwith of

---

* Given as printed. "Abingdon" probably should be "Arlington".

MARRIAGE NOTICES IN THE SOUTHERN CHURCHMAN WITH DATES OF PUBLICATION

the Diocese of Maryland, in St. Paul's Church, Petersburg. So. Ch., July 3, 1857

SPEAKE
Cecil Ambrey, of Luray, Va., and Mary Maud, d. of Mr. and Mrs. Harry J. Miller of Washington, Va., by the Rev. Churchill J. Gibson, pastor of Calvary Church, Luray, in Trinity Church. So. Ch., June 16, 1917

SPEARS
Martha E., d. of Thos. A. Spears, Esq. of Powhatan Co., and Robert B. Foster of Charlotte Co., by the Rev. A. B. Tizzard, at Alexandria, Va. So. Ch., Nov. 7, 1856

SPECK
Benjamin S., and Virginia, d. of Thomas J. Hardy, by the Rev. George S. May, at the residence of the bride's father, in Hedgesville. So. Ch., Dec. 11, 1873

SPEECE
J. Morton, M.D., and Maria L., d. of the late John O. Loftwich, all of Bedford Co., by the Rev. Richard H. Wilmer. So. Ch., Feb. 27, 1857

SPEED
John W., and Catherine Waller, by the Rev. William Hodges, at Williamsburg. So. Ch., May 24, 1839

SPEER
William F., and Elizabeth C. Cook, both of Petersburg, by the Rev. Dr. Andrew Symm. So. Ch., Nov. 3, 1837

SPENCE
J. Morton, Esq., of Bedford City, and Willie D., only d. of Dr. J. D. Pendleton, by the Rev. F. G. Scott, in Christ Church, Gordonsville. So. Ch., Jan. 14, 1892

Mary H., d. of Judge D. E. Spence, and Robert E. Gish of Liberty, Va., by the Rev. T. M. Carson, in St. Paul's Church, Lynchburg, Va. So. Ch., Nov. 13, 1873

SPENCER
Amelia J., and Philip C. Hungerford, by the Rev. J. W. Chesley, in St. James' Church, Montross, Westmoreland Co., Va. So. Ch., Nov. 2, 1855

Caroline, d. of Reuben Spencer of Richmond, Va., and Rev. George Benton, Missionary to Crete, by the Rev. Bird Wilson, D.D., in St. Peter's Church. So. Ch., Sept. 9, 1836

John B., of Halifax Co., Va., and Zella Maud, d. of John J. and Elizabeth M. Barksdale, by the Rev. C. O. Pruden, at the home of the bride's parents, "Little Nook" farm, near Mt. Airy, Pittsylvania Co., Va. So. Ch., Dec. 6, 1888

Robert, Esq., and Emma L., d. of Quinton Radcliffe, Esq., all of Baltimore, by the Rev. John Collins McCabe, D.D., rector of St. Matthew's Parish, Bladensburg, Md., in the Church of the Ascension, Baltimore. So. Ch., Aug. 2, 1866

SPIERS
Richard Percy, of Halifax, N.C., and Mary Elizabeth, eldest d. of John S. Buckner of Rappahannock Co., by the Rev. R. T.

MARRIAGE NOTICES IN THE SOUTHERN CHURCHMAN WITH DATES OF PUBLICATION

Brown, near Sperryville, Va. So. Ch., Feb. 9, 1871

SPILMAN
Anne Camden, eldest d. of Mr. and Mrs. Baldwin D. Spilman of "Elway Hall", and Richard Rice Barrett of Concord, Mass., at Warrenton, Va. So. Ch., Jan. 25, 1913

James W., and Martha L. Baggott, by the Rev. Edw. C. McGuire. So. Ch., Sept. 13, 1839

Mary Elizabeth, d. of John Spilman of Westmoreland Co., Va., and Capt. Clement Wilson Hudson, by the Rev. T. E. Locke, at the residence of Robert Spilman, Leedstown. So. Ch., June 18, 1868

SPINDLE
Harriet A., and Edmund S. Leavell, by the Rev. E. C. McGuire, in Spotsylvania Co. So. Ch., Sept. 22, 1837

Laura M., eldest d. of J. M. Spindle, Esq., and William Major, Jr., all of Culpeper Co., Va., by the Rev. John McGill, at the residence of the bride's father. So. Ch., Nov. 7, 1878

Lizzie M., and George F. Stringfellow of Caroline Co., by the Rev. John McGill, in St. Paul's Church, Culpeper Co., Va. So. Ch., June 19, 1884

SPOONER
Lilburn Wallace, of Roanoke, Va., and Nannie, d. of the the officiating clergyman, by the Rev. C. R. Hains, in St. Paul's Church, Petersburg. So. Ch., Jan. 29, 1885

SPRIGG
Fannie E., d. of the Rev. D. F. Sprigg, and the Rev. J. B. Perry of South Carolina, by the Rev. Dr. Norton assisted by the Rev. Dr. Lewin, at Alexandria. So. Ch., Jan. 18, 1877

Herbert Guilford (The Rev.), Vicar of Shelford, near Nottingham, and Florence Amelia, youngest d. of the late Aldurm Soames, of Tramoke Lodge, Brighton, in the parish church, Brighton, England. So. Ch., Sept. 4, 1879

Mary Elizabeth, d. of D. Sprigg, Esq., and William Donnell, Esq., all of Baltimore, by the Rev. D. F. Sprigg, in Emanuel Church, Baltimore. So. Ch., Apr. 1, 1859

Sally C., d. of Daniel Sprigg, and Oliver Beirne of Virginia, by the Rev. D. F. Sprigg, at the residence of the bride's father, Baltimore, Md. So. Ch., Jan. 7, 1869

SPRINKEL
Anna, d. of Nelson Sprinkel, Esq. of Harrisonburg, Va., and William G. McGhee, Esq. of Bedford Co., Va., by the Rev. T. U. Dudley, at the residence of the bride's father. So. Ch., Dec. 5, 1867

Willett, d. of Charles A. Sprinkel of Harrisonburg, Va., and Dr. James M. Warren of New Hope, Augusta Co., Va., by the Rev. O. S. Bunting, at the residence of the bride's father.

MARRIAGE NOTICES IN THE SOUTHERN CHURCHMAN WITH DATES OF PUBLICATION

So. Ch., June 14, 1883
SPROUSE
　Sallie A., and John Randolph Moore, by the Rev. Robb White, at the residence of the bride's parents, Albemarle Co. So. Ch., Jan. 10, 1884
STABLER
　Laurence, and Bessie Masters, both of Alexandria, by the Rev. George H. Norton, D.D., in St. Paul's Church, Alexandria. So. Ch., Oct. 1, 1885
STAGG
　Lizzie, of Richmond, and Maj. C. Pate of Bedford Co., by the Rev. A. B. Tizzard, in Richmond. So. Ch., Nov. 23, 1860
　Lizzie Fox, youngest d. of the late John F. Stagg of Richmond, and Edward Cooper Madison of Orange Co., by the Rev. M. D. Hoge, D.D., in Richmond, Va. So. Ch., July 22, 1886
　Mary Sue, eldest d. of the late John F. Stagg of Richmond, and John Horsley of Buckingham Co., Va., by the Rev. Moses D. Hoge, in Richmond, Va. So. Ch., Dec. 6, 1883
STAINBACK
　John Moore, M.D., of Brunswick Co., and Izora, d. of H. B. Gouldman, Esq., by the Rev. T. E. Locke, at White Point, Westmoreland Co., Va. So. Ch., May 27, 1869
STALLARD
　Mary, d. of D. P. Stallard, and Norman Ashby, all of Culpeper, Va., by the Rev. J. Green Shackelford and the Rev. Wm. T. Roberts, in Ascension Church, Washington, D.C. So. Ch., Nov. 12, 1885
STAMPER
　Henry W., and Lizzie Munday, by the Rev. H. W. L. Temple, at Lewis Level, Essex. So. Ch., Jan. 7, 1869
STANARD
　John B., (Maj.), ex-mayor of Culpeper, and Sue L., d. of Col. Angus McDonald of Hampshire Co., by the Rev. Dr. Pratt, Lexington, Va. So. Ch., Aug. 15, 1872
STANHOPE
　John, of Hagerstown, Md., and Carrie Courtney of Baltimore, by the Rev. Dr. Hodges of St. Paul's Church, Baltimore. So. Ch., Nov. 27, 1884
STANLEY
　Nellie C., d. of John Stanley, Esq., of Colorado Springs, and Fielding L. Jones of the U.S. Signal Service, by the Rev. W. Strother Jones of St. Thomas Parish, Baltimore Co., Md., in Grace Church, Colorado Springs, Col. So. Ch., Aug. 25, 1881
STANSBURY
　James Edward, of Baltimore, Md., and Edmonia Churchill, youngest d. of Mr. and Mrs. James Churchill Cooke, by the Rev. J. Y. Downman, D.D. of All Saints' Church, Richmond, at Foxleigh, the residence of Mr. and Mrs. James Churchill Cooke. So. Ch., Dec. 24, 1910
　Julia Bell, second d. of

MARRIAGE NOTICES IN THE SOUTHERN CHURCHMAN WITH DATES OF PUBLICATION

Capt. John L. Stansbury of Snowden, near Fredericksburg, and William F. Ficklin, Esq., by the Rev. E. C. Murdaugh, D.D., in St. George's Church, Fredericksburg, Va. So. Ch., Oct. 28, 1874

STANWOOD
Eliza Mary, and Richard Beaman of Nansemond Co., Va., by the Rev. Douglass Hooff, at the residence of the bride, Portsmouth. So. Ch., Dec. 27, 1883

STAPLES
Harriet L. Douglas, d. of Seth P. Staples, Esq. of New York, and the Rt. Rev. Benj. B. Smith, by the Rt. Rev. Bishop Onderdonk, in St. Thomas' Church, New York. So. Ch., Sept. 18, 1835

Mary Alice, and J. B. Weedon, by the Rev. A. J. Willis, at "Poplar Hill", King George Co., Va. So. Ch., Nov. 1, 1888

Wm. D., of Fluvanna Co., and Willie, d. of T. T. Omohundra of Albemarle Co., Va., by the Rev. T. E. Locke, at the residence of the bride's father. So. Ch., Dec. 7, 1882

STARK
Powhatan B., M.D., and Bettie C. Orgain of Berkeley, Charles City Co., by the Rev. Wm. H. Platt, in St. Paul's Church, Petersburg. So. Ch., May 21, 1858

William E. (Lt.), of the U.S. Marine Corps, and Elizabeth W., youngest d. of Alexander Wilson, Esq., by the Rev. Mr. Atkinson, in Norfolk, Va. So. Ch., Dec. 8, 1837

STARKE
Martha Jane, and Alfred Mitchell, by the Rev. Dr. Empie, in Richmond, Va. So. Ch., Dec. 20, 1839

Sallie Stuart, youngest d. of the late Gen. Wm. E. Starke of New Orleans, and Dr. Wm. M. Eggleston, by the Rt. Rev. Bishop Adams, in the Church of the Holy Trinity, Vicksburg, Miss. So. Ch., Dec. 29, 1881

STATAN
Georgeanna, and Wm. L. Lane, both of Berlin, Worcester Co., Md., by the Rev. George S. Fitzhugh. So. Ch., Jan. 15, 1874

STATHAM
Lizzie, eldest d. of Chas. W. and V. Statham, and Prof. R. P. W. Morris of Bryan, Tex., by the Rev. Chas. Morris, at the residence of the bride's father, Lynchburg, Va. So. Ch., Mar. 1, 1877

STATON
James Grist, and Fannie Chase Biggs, by the Rt. Rev. Robert Strange, Bishop of East Carolina, at the Church of the Advent, Williamston, N.C. So. Ch., Sept. 12, 1908

STEARNS
John (The Rev.), of New York, and Anne H., d. of John Lloyd, Esq. of Alexandria, Va., by the Rev. C. B. Dana. So. Ch., July 28, 1848

MARRIAGE NOTICES IN THE SOUTHERN CHURCHMAN WITH DATES OF PUBLICATION

John Lloyd, of Elizabeth, N.J., and Ella, d. of Cuthbert Powell formerly of Alexandria, Va., by the Rev. Henderson Suter, in Christ Church, Alexandria. So. Ch., Oct. 17, 1878

STEBBINS
Charles, and Rebecca K. McMurdo, by the Rev. John McGill, at the residence of the bride's brother, Col. John McMurdo, Ashland, Va. So. Ch., Feb. 3, 1887

Linda, d. of the late Charles and Mary Dows Stebbins, and the Rev. John Taylor Rose, by the Rev. Dr. H. G. Coddington, rector of Grace Church, Syracuse, N.Y., in St. Peter's Church, Cazenovia, N.Y. So. Ch., Dec. 6, 1919

STEDMAN
Nathan A., Esq., Comptroller of the State of North Carolina, and Euphania W., d. of T. W. White, by the Rev. William S. Plumer. So. Ch., Jan. 15, 1836

STEED
Carrie V., and Abram H. Symth*, Esq. of Alexandria, Va., by the Rev. J. Owen Dorsey, at the residence of the bride's father, James M. Steed, Prince George Co. So. Ch., Nov. 25, 1875

STEEL
Alice Lawrason, d. of the Ven. W. W. Steel, Archdeacon of Havana, and Edward Davis, First Lt. Eleventh Cavalry, U.S. Army, in Holy Trinity Chapel, Havana, Cuba. So. Ch., Nov. 30, 1907

STEELE
Anna M., of Cavalla, and the Rev. Hugh Roy Scott, rector of St. Mark's Church, Cape Palmas, by the Rt. Rev. John Payne, D.D., at Cavalla, near Cape Palmas, Western Africa. So. Ch., Oct. 26, 1854

David McConnel (The Rev. Dr.), rector of the Church of St. Luke and the Epiphany, Philadelphia, and Martha Virginia Mills, Superintendent of Brulington * County Hospital, Mt. Holly, N.J. So. Ch., June 7, 1930

Mattie Paxton, d. of J. P. Steele, Esq., and Dr. J. Hammond Campbell of Athens, Ga., by the Rev. Mr. Irwin of the Presbyterian Church, in Lexington, Va. So. Ch., Jan. 4, 1883

STEENBERGEN
Alice B. Potter, d. of the late J. B. Steenbergen of Virginia, and William Blackford formerly of Lynchburg, by the Rev. M. Mahan, D.D., in St. Paul's Church, Baltimore. So. Ch., Oct. 14, 1869

Nannie Beirne, youngest d. of the late J. B. Steenbergen of Virginia, and B. Lewis Blackford of Washington City (late of Va.), by the Rt. Rev. H. C. Lay, D.D., Bishop of Easton, in St. Paul's Church, Baltimore. So. Ch., July 29, 1869

STEENBERGER*
Mary E., d. of the late Wm. Steenberger*, of Shenandoah, and Dr. James W. Mur-

* Given as printed

MARRIAGE NOTICES IN THE SOUTHERN CHURCHMAN WITH DATES OF PUBLICATION

dock of Parkersburg, Va., by the Rev. A. R. Rude, at Shenandoah. So. Ch., Jan. 21, 1859

STEGER
Maria P., d. of John O. Steger, and Preston B. Moore, all of Baltimore, by the Rev. Joshua Peterkin, at the residence of the bride's father. So. Ch., Nov. 28, 1872

STEM
Cordelia, and Dr. Geo. W. Cox, both of Lunenburg Co., by the Rev. Henry Wall, at the residence of G. W. Geo. So. Ch., Apr. 6, 1860

STEPHENS
Saml. M., of Baltimore, and Hattie A., d. of J. A. Byers, Esq., of Hancock, Md., by the Rev. Horace E. Hayden, at the residence of Taliaferro Stribling, Esq., Point Pleasant, W.Va. So. Ch., Dec. 26, 1867

Sarah L., of "Oakwood", Theological Seminary, formerly of Fauquier Co., and George C. Caton of Fauquier Co., Va., by the Rev. Prof. Samuel A. Wallis, at "Oakwood", Theological Seminary, Va. So. Ch., Jan. 8, 1916

STEPHENSON
John, Esq., of Frederick Co., Va., and Cornelia, d. of W. Roy Mason, Esq., by the Rev. Henry Wall, at Cleivland, King George Co. So. Ch., July 23, 1858

John Taylor, of Alexandria, Va., and Margaret Baldwin Moss, at Forkland, home of the bride's aunt, Miss Mary B. Whitehead. So. Ch., Nov. 8, 1919

John W., Esq., and Eliza G., d. of James W. Warwick, Esq., all of Bath Co., by the Rev. George L. Brown, at "Warwickton", the residence of the bride's father, in Bath Co., Va. So. Ch., Nov. 21, 1878

Philip D. (The Rev.), pastor of the Presbyterian Church, Trenton, Tenn., and Jane Mingo, second d. of the late Charles Friend, Esq. of Prince George Co., Va., by the Rev. Churchill J. Gibson, in the chapel of the Union Theological Seminary, Prince Edward Co. So. Ch., Jan. 13, 1876

Sarah (Mrs.), d. of Bolton Brown of Southampton Co., Va., and Walter L. Wade of Lynchburg, Va., by the Rev. John Ridout, at Blandford, near Petersburg, Va. So. Ch., Oct. 5, 1893

Wm., of Washington, Penn., and Mary Cornelia, d. of Wm. C. Cabell Martin, by the Rev. Mayo Cabell, rector of the Church of the Holy Trinity, Nashville, Tenn., at Norwood, the home of the bride's father, Nelson Co., Va. So. Ch., Aug. 11, 1887

STEPTOE
Charles Yancey, and Fannie Wallace, d. of P. P. Nalle of Culpeper Co., by the Rev. P. Slaughter, in St. Paul's Church, Culpeper Co. So. Ch., Oct. 24, 1872

Edward J. (Col.), of the U.S.

MARRIAGE NOTICES IN THE SOUTHERN CHURCHMAN WITH DATES OF PUBLICATION

John Lloyd, of Elizabeth, N.J., and Ella, d. of Cuthbert Powell formerly of Alexandria, Va., by the Rev. Henderson Suter, in Christ Church, Alexandria. So. Ch., Oct. 17, 1878

STEBBINS
Charles, and Rebecca K. McMurdo, by the Rev. John McGill, at the residence of the bride's brother, Col. John McMurdo, Ashland, Va. So. Ch., Feb. 3, 1887

Linda, d. of the late Charles and Mary Dows Stebbins, and the Rev. John Taylor Rose, by the Rev. Dr. H. G. Coddington, rector of Grace Church, Syracuse, N.Y., in St. Peter's Church, Cazenovia, N.Y. So. Ch., Dec. 6, 1919

STEDMAN
Nathan A., Esq., Comptroller of the State of North Carolina, and Euphania W., d. of T. W. White, by the Rev. William S. Plumer. So. Ch., Jan. 15, 1836

STEED
Carrie V., and Abram H. Symth*, Esq. of Alexandria, Va., by the Rev. J. Owen Dorsey, at the residence of the bride's father, James M. Steed, Prince George Co. So. Ch., Nov. 25, 1875

STEEL
Alice Lawrason, d. of the Ven. W. W. Steel, Archdeacon of Havana, and Edward Davis, First Lt. Eleventh Cavalry, U.S. Army, in Holy Trinity Chapel, Havana, Cuba. So. Ch., Nov. 30, 1907

STEELE
Anna M., of Cavalla, and the Rev. Hugh Roy Scott, rector of St. Mark's Church, Cape Palmas, by the Rt. Rev. John Payne, D.D., at Cavalla, near Cape Palmas, Western Africa. So. Ch., Oct. 26, 1854

David McConnel (The Rev. Dr.), rector of the Church of St. Luke and the Epiphany, Philadelphia, and Martha Virginia Mills, Superintendent of Brulington * County Hospital, Mt. Holly, N.J. So. Ch., June 7, 1930

Mattie Paxton, d. of J. P. Steele, Esq., and Dr. J. Hammond Campbell of Athens, Ga., by the Rev. Mr. Irwin of the Presbyterian Church, in Lexington, Va. So. Ch., Jan. 4, 1883

STEENBERGEN
Alice B. Potter, d. of the late J. B. Steenbergen of Virginia, and William Blackford formerly of Lynchburg, by the Rev. M. Mahan, D.D., in St. Paul's Church, Baltimore. So. Ch., Oct. 14, 1869

Nannie Beirne, youngest d. of the late J. B. Steenbergen of Virginia, and B. Lewis Blackford of Washington City (late of Va.), by the Rt. Rev. H. C. Lay, D.D., Bishop of Easton, in St. Paul's Church, Baltimore. So. Ch., July 29, 1869

STEENBERGER*
Mary E., d. of the late Wm. Steenberger*, of Shenandoah, and Dr. James W. Mur-

* Given as printed

MARRIAGE NOTICES IN THE SOUTHERN CHURCHMAN WITH DATES OF PUBLICATION

dock of Parkersburg, Va., by the Rev. A. R. Rude, at Shenandoah. So. Ch., Jan. 21, 1859

STEGER

Maria P., d. of John O. Steger, and Preston B. Moore, all of Baltimore, by the Rev. Joshua Peterkin, at the residence of the bride's father. So. Ch., Nov. 28, 1872

STEM

Cordelia, and Dr. Geo. W. Cox, both of Lunenburg Co., by the Rev. Henry Wall, at the residence of G. W. Geo. So. Ch., Apr. 6, 1860

STEPHENS

Saml. M., of Baltimore, and Hattie A., d. of J. A. Byers, Esq., of Hancock, Md., by the Rev. Horace E. Hayden, at the residence of Taliaferro Stribling, Esq., Point Pleasant, W.Va. So. Ch., Dec. 26, 1867

Sarah L., of "Oakwood", Theological Seminary, formerly of Fauquier Co., and George C. Caton of Fauquier Co., Va., by the Rev. Prof. Samuel A. Wallis, at "Oakwood", Theological Seminary, Va. So. Ch., Jan. 8, 1916

STEPHENSON

John, Esq., of Frederick Co., Va., and Cornelia, d. of W. Roy Mason, Esq., by the Rev. Henry Wall, at Cleivland, King George Co. So. Ch., July 23, 1858

John Taylor, of Alexandria, Va., and Margaret Baldwin Moss, at Forkland, home of the bride's aunt, Miss Mary B. Whitehead. So. Ch., Nov. 8, 1919

John W., Esq., and Eliza G., d. of James W. Warwick, Esq., all of Bath Co., by the Rev. George L. Brown, at "Warwickton", the residence of the bride's father, in Bath Co., Va. So. Ch., Nov. 21, 1878

Philip D. (The Rev.), pastor of the Presbyterian Church, Trenton, Tenn., and Jane Mingo, second d. of the late Charles Friend, Esq. of Prince George Co., Va., by the Rev. Churchill J. Gibson, in the chapel of the Union Theological Seminary, Prince Edward Co. So. Ch., Jan. 13, 1876

Sarah (Mrs.), d. of Bolton Brown of Southampton Co., Va., and Walter L. Wade of Lynchburg, Va., by the Rev. John Ridout, at Blandford, near Petersburg, Va. So. Ch., Oct. 5, 1893

Wm., of Washington, Penn., and Mary Cornelia, d. of Wm. C. Cabell Martin. by the Rev. Mayo Cabell, rector of the Church of the Holy Trinity, Nashville, Tenn., at Norwood, the home of the bride's father, Nelson Co., Va. So. Ch., Aug. 11, 1887

STEPTOE

Charles Yancey, and Fannie Wallace, d. of P. P. Nalle of Culpeper Co., by the Rev. P. Slaughter, in St. Paul's Church, Culpeper Co. So. Ch., Oct. 24, 1872

Edward J. (Col.), of the U.S.

MARRIAGE NOTICES IN THE SOUTHERN CHURCHMAN WITH DATES OF PUBLICATION

Army, and Mary R. Claytor of Lynchburg, by the Rev. W. H. Kinckle, at Lynchburg. So. Ch., Jan. 27, 1860

Fanny C., d. of Thomas Steptoe, and Col. R. C. Radford of Bedford Co., by the Rev. T. M. Carson, at L'Esperance, the residence of the bride's father, near Lynchburg, Va. So. Ch., Apr. 22, 1880

STERLING
Mary Hilliard, d. of Dr. Elisha Sterling, D.D., and the Rev. Yelverton Peyton Morgan, by the Rt. Rev. G. T. Bedell, D.D., Bishop of Ohio, assisted by the Rev. James A. Bolles, D.D., in Cleveland, Ohio. So. Ch., June 18, 1885

STERRETT
Helen V., and Lt. Frank D. Hoy, both of Point Pleasant, by the Rev. T. H. Lacy, in Christ Church, Point Pleasant, W.Va. So. Ch., Dec. 12, 1878

STEVENS
E. A., Hoboken, N.J., and Emily Contee, d. of G. W. Lewis, Esq., by the Rev. P. P. Phillips, in Grace Church, Berryville, Va. So. Ch., Nov. 6, 1879

John, of Hoboken, and Mary M., youngest d. of the late D. H. McGuire of Clarke Co., Va., by the rector, the Rev. P. P. Phillips, assisted by the Rev. G. C. Haughton, rector of Trinity Church, Hoboken, N.J., in Grace Church, Berryville, Va. So. Ch., June 28, 1883

Mary Gertrude, and Wm. C. Bailey, by the Rev. A. E. Evison, in Trinity Church, Edisto Island, S.C. So. Ch., Sept. 14, 1907

STEVENSON
Emily, d. of the late Crooke Stevenson, Esq. of Philadelphia, and the Rev. James W. Cooke, assistant minister of St. George's Church, New York, by the Rev. Stephen H. Tyng, D.D., in Philadelphia. So. Ch., Aug. 23, 1839

James B., and Julia M. Cramer, both of Harrisonburg, Va., by the Rev. O. S. Bunting. So. Ch., Nov. 20, 1884

STEWART
Alice, youngest d. of Asa Stewart, Esq. of Bennington, Vt., and William W. Monroe, eldest s. of the officiating clergyman, by the rector, the Rev. William H. Monroe, in Christ Church, Boston. So. Ch., Feb. 22, 1883

George Craig, Jr., s. of the officiating clergyman, and Margaret Ruth Rothacker, by the Rev. Bishop George Craig Stewart, in the Lady Chapel of St. Luke's Pro-Cathedral. So. Ch., July 20, 1935

Isabel Lamont, second d. of John Stewart, Esq. of Brook Hill, and Joseph Bryan, Esq. of Richmond, by the Rev. Wm. Norwood, D.D., in Emmanuel Church, Henrico Co. So. Ch., Feb. 16, 1871

Marion Macintosh, d. of John Stewart, Esq. of

MARRIAGE NOTICES IN THE SOUTHERN CHURCHMAN WITH DATES OF PUBLICATION

Brook Hill, near Richmond, and the Rt. Rev. George W. Peterkin, D.D., Bishop of West Virginia, by the Rev. Dr. Norwood, rector of the church, assisted by the Rev. Dr. Peterkin, in Emmanuel Church, Henrico Co., Va. So. Ch., June 19, 1884

Mary, d. of the officiating clergyman, and W. Minor Woodward of Richmond, by the Rev. K. J. Stewart, at Gordonsville, Va. So. Ch., Nov. 4, 1869

Mary, d. of Jno. Stewart, Esq. of Brook Hill, and Thomas Pinckney of Charleston, S.C., by the rector, the Rev. Wm. Norwood, D.D., in Emmanuel Church, Henrico Parish. So. Ch., May 12, 1870

Sarah Jane, youngest d. of William P. Stewart, Esq., and the Rev. Leonidas S. Smith, by the Rt. Rev. Dr. Johns, at Norfolk, Va. So. Ch., Jan. 2, 1851

Virginia, d. of W. C. Stewart, and the Rev. William Stevens Campbell of Trinity Church, Bellaire, by the Rev. J. M. Kendrick, D.D., at the residence of the bride's parents, in Bellaire, Ohio. So. Ch., Aug. 16, 1888

STHRESHLEY
Lucy Barbour, and Dr. Richard S. Pryor, both of Vicksburg, Miss., by the Rev. Bishop Adams, at the home of H. M. Goff, near Bovina, Miss. So. Ch., Dec. 7, 1882

STICKNEY
G. W. (The Rev.), of Mobile, and Mary Lee, d. of the Rev. C. S. Hodges, rector of the parish, by the Rt. Rev. Bishop Polk, in St. Luke's Church, New Orleans. So. Ch., May 14, 1858

STICKNY
Charles L., of Greensboro, Ala., and Euretta B., d. of the late John Munro Banister, by the Rev. Mr. Platt, in St. Paul's Church, Petersburg, Va. So. Ch., Oct. 5, 1860

STILES
Robert, of Richmond, and Lolia, d. of the Hon. A. T. Caperton, by the Rev. Mr. Phillips of Staunton, at the residence of the bride's father, near Union, Monroe Co., W.Va. So. Ch., July 23, 1874

STOCKTON
Emma Matilda, d. of the late William T. Stockton, Esq. of Pennsylvania, and Lt. John Wentworth Cox, U.S. Navy, by the Rev. Mr. Meade, in Albemarle Co. So. Ch., Nov. 24, 1837

STODDARD
Clara M., of San Francisco, Cal., and Gus H. Honshell of Cincinnati, Ohio, by the Rev. John W. Lea, at Huntington, W.Va. So. Ch., Dec. 25, 1879

STOKES
Chas. P., and Mary S. Gwatkins, both of Richmond, Va., by the Rev. Wm. Norwood, D.D., at the residence of the bride's mother. So. Ch., Oct. 31, 1872

Geo. S., of Danville, Va., and Willie A., d. of Dr. P. F. Browne of Accomac, by the Rev. T. A. Tidball, in St. James' Church, Drummondtown, Va. So. Ch., June 20, 1872

Helen Sibley (Mrs.), d. of

MARRIAGE NOTICES IN THE SOUTHERN CHURCHMAN WITH DATES OF PUBLICATION

the late Gen. Sibley of the U.S. Army, and William Seymour White, Commonwealth's Attorney of Stafford Co., and secretary of the Fredericksburg Improvement Company, by the rector, the Rev. W. M. Clark, in St. George's Church, Fredericksburg, Va. So. Ch., Feb. 12, 1891
Wyndham, of Welch, W.Va., and Inez C. Tench of Washington, by the Rev. Edward H. Ingle, in the Church of the Epiphany, Washington, D.C. So. Ch., Feb. 22, 1908

STONE
Angelina, youngest d. of Silas Stone, Esq. of Hudson, N.Y. and the Rev. Ferdinand Rogers, of Brownville, Jefferson Co., N.Y., by the Rev. Isaac Pardee, in Christ Church, Hudson, N.Y. So. Ch., June 14, 1839
John S., D.D. (The Rev.), of Boston, and Mary, d. of Chancellor Kent of New York, by the Rev. Dr. Milnor, at Chatham, N.J. So. Ch., Sept. 20, 1839
Robert P., of Washington, D.C., and Bettie B., d. of Dr. Wm. J. Points of Harrisonburg, by the Rev. O. S. Bunting, in Emmanuel Church, Harrisonburg, Va. So. Ch., Feb. 26, 1885
Walter S., of Hanover Co., Va., and Mary L. Brooks of Caroline Co., Va., by the Rev. Curtis Grubb, at St. Martin's Church, Hanover Co., Va. So. Ch., Jan. 11, 1883

STONEHAM
Hartwell, and Lizzie Webster, both of Lancaster, by the Rev. Henry L. Derby, at Merry Point, Lancaster, Va. So. Ch., Dec. 11, 1884

STONNELL
Richard, Esq., of Prince William Co., Va., and Emmott F., d. of the late James Atkinson of Alexandria, Va., by the Rev. Dr. R. H. McKim, in Christ Church, Alexandria, Va. So. Ch., Nov. 26, 1874

STORRS
Betty P., of Marengo Co., and the Rev. R. A. Cobbs, rector of the parish, by the Rt. Rev. N. H. Cobbs, D.D., in the Church of the Holy Cross, Uniontown, Ala. So. Ch., Sept. 17, 1858

STOUTENBURGH
Kate M., oldest d. of James A. S. Stoutenburgh of Alexandria, and Stephen Woolls of Richmond, by the Rev. Dennis O'Kane, in St. Mary's Church, Alexandria. So. Ch., Sept. 16, 1880
Phebe J., and Charles J. Deahl, by the Rev. H. T. Sharp, at Alexandria. So. Ch., Oct. 18, 1888

STOVER
Ethel Knorr, d. of Mr. and Mrs. Bruce Emerick Stover of Wheeling, a graduate of Swarthmore College, and the Rt. Rev. Robert E. L. Strider, Bishop of West Virginia, in St. Matthew's Church, Wheeling. So. Ch., Jan. 11, 1941

STOVIN
Charles L., and Elizabeth Bland Mayo, by the Rev. Wm. F. Lee. So. Ch., May 8, 1835

MARRIAGE NOTICES IN THE SOUTHERN CHURCHMAN WITH DATES OF PUBLICATION

Mary Lewis, d. of Charles J. Stovin, Esq., and Dr. John Campbell Mayo of Westmoreland Co., Va., by the Rev. John C. McCabe, rector of the Church of the Ascension, Baltimore, at "Airley", Fauquier Co., Va. So. Ch., June 19, 1857

STRACHAN

J. Blackwood (Dr.), and Mary Virginia, d. of the late Dr. Theo. Meade, by the Rev. Wm. H. Platt, D.D., at the residence of the Hon. R. K. Meade. So. Ch., May 15, 1857

STRATTON

Susie, and W. Fenton Jacobs formerly of Alexandria, Va., by the Rev. L. R. Combs, at the residence of the bride's father, R. H. Stratton, Gordonsville, Va. So. Ch., Jan. 23, 1890

STRIBLING

Alice M., of Clarke Co., Va., and Randolph Kounslar, by the Rev. T. F. Martin, in Grace Church, Berryville. So. Ch., Oct. 30, 1873

Edward M., and Lydia, youngest d. of the late Dr. Randolph Kounslar, all of Clarke Co., Va., by the Rev. P. P. Phillips, in Grace Church, Berryville, Va. So. Ch., Jan. 18, 1883

Fannie C., d. of Dr. F. Stribling of Staunton, Va., and Richard F. Foster of Richmond, by the Rev. Mr. Latane, at the residence of the bride's father. So. Ch., Mar. 2, 1860

Francis T., of Staunton, and Olive C., youngest d. of Dr. S. K. Jackson, by the Rev. H. M. Jackson and the Rev. Arthur Lloyd, in St. Luke's Church, Norfolk. So. Ch., May 2, 1889

Gray Carroll, and Louise Saunders, d. of Mr. and Mrs. George R. Lockwood of St. Louis, by the Rev. A. A. V. Binnington, rector, in the Church of the Ascension, St. Louis, Mo. So. Ch., July 22, 1911

Lizzie, d. of Mrs. Mildred and the late Dr. Wm. C. Stribling, and John H. Foster, all of Fauquier Co., by the Rev. H. B. Lee, at "Hartlands", Fauquier Co. So. Ch., June 30, 1881

R. (Col.), of Fauquier Co., and Agnes, d. of Maj. R. Douthat, by the Rev. A. Wade, at Wyanoke, Charles City Co. So. Ch., Sept. 1, 1870

Robt. M., Jr. (Dr.), and Mary Cary, d. of Maj. Thos. M. Ambler, by the Rev. Thos. E. Duncan, at Morvon, Fauquier Co. So. Ch., Sept. 4, 1857

Sallie A., d. of the late Kinney Stribling of Staunton, Va., and Andrew J. McMullin of Kentucky, by the Rev. Horace E. Haydon, at the residence of John W. English, Esq., Pt. Pleasant, W.Va. So. Ch., Nov, 21, 1867

STRIDER

Robert E. L. (The Rt. Rev.), bishop of West Virginia, and Ethel Knorr, d. of Mr. and Mrs. Bruce Emerick Stover of Wheeling,

MARRIAGE NOTICES IN THE SOUTHERN CHURCHMAN WITH DATES OF PUBLICATION

a graduate of Swarthmore College, in St. Matthew's Church, Wheeling. So. Ch., Jan. 11, 1941

STRIEFF
John R., of Cincinnati, Ohio, and Sarah Farrar, only d. of the late Thomas Wood of Linden, Ohio, by the Rev. Wm. S. Campbell, in Trinity Church, Linden, Ohio. So. Ch., Mar. 11, 1886

STRINGFELLOW
Ann Wallace, of Culpeper Co., Va., and John Jacquelin Taylor of Richmond, by the Rev. Carter Page, in St. Paul's Church, Raccoon Ford. So. Ch., Oct. 12, 1893

George F., of Caroline Co., and Lizzie M. Spindle, by the Rev. John McGill, in St. Paul's Church, Culpeper Co., Va. So. Ch., June 19, 1884

Ida Herndon, and the Rev. W. A. Barr, by the Rev. F. Stringfellow, the bride's father, at the rectory, Martinsville, Va. So. Ch., Feb. 9, 1893

Mary, d. of the late Capt. R. Staunton Stringfellow, and Atwell Somerville, all of Culpeper Co., Va., by the Rev. John McGill, at "Church View", the residence of the bride's mother. So. Ch., Dec. 25, 1884

STRODE
H. A., Prin. of University High School, and Millie J., d. of the late Col. Thomas J. Ellis, 19th Virginia Infantry, by the Rev. R. J. McBryde, in Ascension Church, Amherst C.H., Va. So. Ch., Oct. 31, 1872

STRONG
Samuel B., of Chattanooga, and Fanny S. Thornton of Fredericksburg, Va., by the Rev. E. C. Murdaugh, in Trinity Church, Fredericksburg, Va. So. Ch., Dec. 4, 1879

William E., of New York, and Alice Corbyn, d. of Francis L. Smith, Esq., of Alexandria, Va., by the Rev. Dr. Norton, rector of St. Paul's Church, at the residence of the bride's father. So. Ch., Dec. 5, 1872

STROTHER
Bettie P. (Mrs.), and Gen. P. T. Moore, both of Richmond, by the Rev. James Hanckle, D.D., at Charlottesville, Va. So. Ch., Feb. 10, 1881

Elizabeth Kendall, eldest d. of the late John M. Strother, and Methven T. Freeman of Macon, Va., by the Rev. Joshua Peterkin, D.D., in St. James' Church. So. Ch., Feb. 4, 1886

Elizabeth Mayo, and Frederic William Scott, both of Richmond, Va., by the Rev. Hartley Carmichael, in St. Paul's Church, Richmond, Va. So. Ch., Nov. 2, 1893

James F., of Madison Co., and Mary Eppes Thweatt of Chesterfield Co., Va., by the Rev. A. B. Tizzard, in Trinity Church, Chesterfield Co., Va. So. Ch., June 14, 1888

John M., of the University of Virginia, and Bettie W.,

MARRIAGE NOTICES IN THE SOUTHERN CHURCHMAN WITH DATES OF PUBLICATION

d. of Dr. F. W. Powell of Middleburg, Va., by the Rev. O. A. Kinsolving. So. Ch., Mar. 1, 1861

STRUDWICK
Robert C., of Durham, N.C., and Sally P., second d. of John O. Lewis of Albemarle Co., Va., by the Rev. T. E. Locke, at Cliffside, the residence of the bride's father. So. Ch., May 22, 1884

STRYKER
A. P. (The Rev.), and Phobe K., d. of J. Mason Campbell, Esq. of Baltimore, by the Rt. Rev. W. R. Whittingham, D.D., in Grace Church, Baltimore, Md. So. Ch., Oct. 12, 1865

STUART
Cornelia Lee, and Allen Smith, at "Cedar Grove", King George Co., the residence of the bride's mother. So. Ch., Nov. 7, 1889

Ellen Calvert, d. of the late C. C. Stuart, Esq., and the Rev. Addison B. Atkins, rector of Christ Church, Germantown, Philadelphia, by the Rev. R. T. Brown, rector of Zion Church, Fairfax C.H., at Chantilly, Fairfax Co., Va. So. Ch., Nov. 30, 1854

H. L., of Alexandria, Va., and Lucie Laurie, d. of Wm. G. Carr of Albemarle Co., Va., by the Rev. J. Stuart Hanckle, D.D., at Bentivar, the residence of the bride's father. So. Ch., July 1, 1875

Julia Calvert, d. of Dr. R. H. Stuart, and Dr. E. Lee Jones, s. of the late Gen. Roger Jones, Adj. Gen. U.S. Army, of New York City, by the Rev. Hugh Roy Scott, at Cedar Grove, King George Co., Va. So. Ch., June 1, 1860

J. E. B., Jr., of Larned, Kan., formerly of Virginia, and Joe, d. of the late Col. Joe Phillips, C.S. Army, of Hampton, Va., by the Rev. J. J. Gravatt assisted by the Rev. Mr. Meade, in St. John's Church, Hampton, Va. So. Ch., July 29, 1886

James Reeve, of South Carolina, and Mary Hall Jacob of Kentucky, by the Rev. Henry T. Sharp, at the old Mulholland House, Elizabethtown, Ky. So. Ch., Jan. 20, 1876

Laura, d. of the late C. C. Stuart, Esq., and Kensey, s. of Bishop Johns, by the Rt. Rev. Bishop Johns of Virginia, at Chantilly, Fairfax Co., Va. So. Ch., Oct. 15, 1858

Margaret, d. of Dr. R. H. Stuart, and Robert W. Hunter of Winchester, by the Rev. Mr. Friend, at Cedar Grove, King George Co., Va. So. Ch., Dec. 21, 1865

Mary, d. of Rosalie and the late S. P. Stuart, and W. D. Grymes, by the Rev. A. J. Willis, in St. Paul's Church, King George Co., Va. So. Ch., Nov. 25, 1886

Mary Johnson, of Staunton, and Capt. Wm. L. Clarke, Jr., by the Rev. Mr. Baker, at Staunton, Va. So. Ch., May 16, 1862

MARRIAGE NOTICES IN THE SOUTHERN CHURCHMAN WITH DATES OF PUBLICATION

Metá, d. of the late Col. Charles Stuart of Alexandria, and Bartlett Bolling of Petersburg, by the Rev. Henderson Suter, in Christ Church, Alexandria. So. Ch., June 23, 1881

Milton R. (Dr.), and Rosalie L. Grymes, by the Rev. Jos. R. Jones, in the Meade Memorial Church, White Post. So. Ch., Oct. 6, 1881

R. A. (Dr.), and Lydia Ann Marmaduke, both of Westmoreland, by the Rev. D. M. Wharton. So. Ch., Feb. 8, 1883

Rosalie Eugenia, eldest d. of Dr. R. H. Stuart, and S. T. Stuart of Fairfax Co., by the Rev. Kensey Stewart, at Cedar Grove, King George Co. So. Ch., Nov. 18, 1859

S. T., of Fairfax Co., and Rosalie Eugenia, eldest d. of Dr. R. H. Stuart, by the Rev. Kensey Stewart, at Cedar Grove, King George Co., Va. So. Ch., Nov. 18, 1859

Susan B., fourth d. of the Hon. Alexandria H. H. Stuart, and the Rev. Robert A. Gibson, by the Rev. Churchill J. Gibson, in Trinity Church, Staunton. So. Ch., Nov. 28, 1872

Virginia Pelham, only d. of Mrs. Gen. J. E. B. Stuart*, and Robert Page Waller of Norfolk, by the Rev. W. Q. Hullihen assisted by the Rev. O. S. Barten, in Staunton. So. Ch., Jan. 20, 1887

W. D., of Hagerstown, Md., s. of Col. W. D. Stuart of Virginia, and Bettie B. Wood of Roanoke, by the Rev. R. A. Goodwin, in St. John's Church, Roanoke. So. Ch., July 3, 1884

W. Douglass, of Alexandria, and Mattie H., d. and only child of the late Alex. T. and Martha E. Page, by the Rev. James Grammar, at Northfield, Cumberland Co., Va. So. Ch., June 20, 1867

Wm. Mason, and Lucy Lee Millan, both of Rappahannock Co., Va., by the Rev. Charles S. Harrison, in St. Paul's Church, Woodville, Va. So. Ch., Nov. 10, 1892

STUCKY
Joseph, Esq., and Kate Myers, both of Berkeley Co., W.Va., by the Rev. George S. May, at the residence of Jeter M. French, Esq. So. Ch., Jan. 15, 1874

STUMP
John Stone, Jr., formerly of Maryland, and Margaret Nash, d. of William W. Old and Alice Herbert his wife, by the Rev. Francis C. Steinmetz, in Christ Church, Norfolk, Va. So. Ch., Nov. 13, 1909

STUMPH
Mary Lewis, of Washington, D.C., and Carter B. Page, by the Rev. J. B. Funsten, at Portsmouth, Va. So. Ch., Nov. 10, 1892

STURGEON
Nannie, of Louisville, and Richard B. Washington, Jr. of Silver City, N.M., formerly of Jefferson Co., W.Va., by the Rev. Dr. Perkins, in St. Paul's Church, Louisville, Ky.

* Given as printed

MARRIAGE NOTICES IN THE SOUTHERN CHURCHMAN WITH DATES OF PUBLICATION

SUBLETT
David L. (Capt.), and Mattie F., d. of Dr. Thomas J. Owen of Prince Edward Co., Va., by the Rev. Daniel Witt. So. Ch., Dec. 4, 1884

Mary Carter, and John White Arrington, by the Rev. J. J. Clopton, in Meade Memorial Church, Manchester, Va. So. Ch., July 6, 1871

Thomas E., formerly of Powhatan Co., Va., and Charlotte E., d. of the late Samuel Lackland, Esq. of Jefferson Co., by the Rev. Mr. Ambler, in the Episcopal Church, Charles Town. So. Ch., May 30, 1889

Walter S., of Richmond, and Lina L., d. of Judge John H. McCue of Staunton, Va., by the Rev. Walter Q. Hullihen, in the Episcopal Church, Staunton. So. Ch., Apr. 22, 1859

Walter S., of Richmond, Va., and Jennie R. Wills of Nelson Co., Va., by the Rev. D. M. Wood, in Trinity Church, Nelson Co. So. Ch., Jan. 10, 1878

SUDDARDS
W. L. (The Rev.), and Rebecca G., d. of the late Samuel P. Wetherill, Esq., by the Rev. E. Neville, in Grace Church, Philadelphia. So. Ch., Nov. 22, 1888

SUDLER
J. E. (Capt.), of Maryland, and Sarah A., d. of Jno. M. E. Valk, by the Rev. Edmund Withers, at "Summerfield", Northumberland Co. So. Ch., May 14, 1847

SULLIVAN
Emma B., and the Rev. Frank Hallam, rector of Epiphany Parish, Prince George's Co., Md., by the Rev. P. G. Sears, rector of Christ Church, Holly Springs, at the residence of the bride's uncle, E. Virden, Jackson, Miss. So. Ch., Feb. 21, 1867

Fannie M., d. of James V. Sullivan of Lancaster Co., Va., and James K. Ball, by the Rev. H. L. Derby assisted by the Rev. John Moncure, at "Riverside", Lancaster Co., Va. So. Ch., May 19, 1892

Marian A., of Lancaster Co., and Dr. Felix E. Brown of Baltimore, Md., by the Rev. H. L. Derby, at "Riverside", Lancaster Co., Va. So. Ch., Dec. 15, 1881

SULLY
Julia, of Alexandria, Va., and D. Conway Chichester of Fairfax, by the Rev. C. B. Dana, in Christ Church. So. Ch., Aug. 24, 1882

SUMMERS
Leah, d. of Dr. R. Summers of Martinsburg, and William E. Pulliam of Pocahontas, Ark., by the Rev. Mr. Davis. So. Ch., May 4, 1860

Minnie, d. of Dr. R. Summers of Martinsburg, Va., and Capt. Wm. B. Colston of the "Stonewall Brigade", by the Rev. W. D. Hanson. So. Ch., Sept. 7, 1860

Sophie, d. of Dr. Summers of Virginia, and Dr. J. Harison Hunter, by the Rev. Mr. Davis, at Martinsburg,

MARRIAGE NOTICES IN THE SOUTHERN CHURCHMAN WITH DATES OF PUBLICATION

Va. So. Ch., May 1, 1857

SUMNER
Walter Taylor (The Rt. Rev.), Bishop of Oregon, and Myrtle Mitchell of Negaunee, Mich., by the Rev. Bishop Anderson, in the Cathedral of Sts. Peter and Paul, Chicago. So. Ch., Jan. 19, 1918

SUTHON
Walter J., of Louisiana, and Lizzie M. Smith, by the Rev. Nelson P. Dame, in Christ Church, Winchester, Va. So. Ch., Mar. 24, 1892

SUTTON
C. H., Esq., of Richmond, Va., and Sallie W., d. of Henry Loving, Esq. of Amherst, by the Rev. Oscar Bunting, at "Brooklyn", the residence of the bride's father, Amherst Co., Va. So. Ch., May 13, 1880

R. G., and Robbie M. Poore, by the Rev. A. H. Hamilton, at Canicello, the residence of Blackford Harris, in Rockbridge Co. So. Ch., Mar. 8, 1888

Thomas E., and Ellen Gatewood, both of Urbanna, Middlesex Co., Va., by the Rev. Thomas G. Addison, in Washington. So. Ch., July 9, 1868

SWANN
Ann Jane, and Dr. Wesley Wright, both of Caroline Co., by the Rev. Wm. W. Greene, in Caroline Co., Va. So. Ch., Jan. 18, 1861

Clare B., and Richard R. Banks, both of Wilmington, Del., by the Rev. W. D. Hanson, at Wilmington, Del. So. Ch., Aug. 28, 1884

Columbia E., and William E. Saunders, Jr. of Lynchburg, by the Rev. William W. Greene, at the residence of the bride's father, in Caroline Co. So. Ch., Dec. 4, 1863

Corinne, d. of the late Charles Alexander Swann of Alexandria, Va., and William W. Sinclair, s. of the late Com. Arthur Sinclair, U.S.N.,of Norfolk, Va., by the Rev. Geo. W. Peterkin, rector, bishop-elect of West Virginia, in the Memorial P. E. Church. So. Ch., May 16, 1878

Lydia A., and Cyrus Carson, both of Caroline Co., Va., by the Rev. W. W. Greene, So. Ch., Feb. 1, 1861

SWEET
Emily Winslow, d. of James W. Sweet, and Henry A. Walker of Staunton, Va., by the Rev. Maltbie D. Babcock, at the residence of the bride's parents. So. Ch., Oct. 3, 1889

Helen Murdoch, youngest d. of James Winslow Sweet of Baltimore, and Dr. J. Mason Hundley, by the Rev. J. H. Hundley of Virginia, father of the groom, assisted by the rector, the Rev. Dr. Eccleston, in Emmanuel Church, Baltimore. So. Ch., Nov. 8, 1888

Lucy Arline, d. of Edwin J. Sweet of Washington, D.C., and Edwin Spottswood Clark formerly of The Plains, Va.,

MARRIAGE NOTICES IN THE SOUTHERN CHURCHMAN WITH DATES OF PUBLICATION

  by the Rev. David Barr, in the Church of the Epiphany, Washington, D.C. So. Ch., Sept. 12, 1889

SWENSON
  Eric Pierson, of New York, and Maud, d. of the late Gen. Lloyd Tilghman, by the Rev. Henry Mason Smyth of Plattsburg, N.Y. assisted by the Rev. Dr. Greer of St. Bartholomew's Church, New York, in St. James' Church, New York. So. Ch., June 20, 1889

  Esther W., and Harry T. Philpot, by the Rev. W. H. Pettus, in St. James' Church, West Somerville, Mass. So. Ch., May 10, 1913

SWOPE
  R. Rush (The Rev.), rector of St. Matthew's Church, Wheeling, W. Va., and Mary, d. of R. P. Brown, M.D. of Cleveland, by the Rev. J. W. Brown, D.D. assisted by the Rev. G. W. Hinkle, in Trinity Church, Cleveland, Ohio. So. Ch., Jan. 30, 1879

SYDNOR
  Charles William (The Rev.), of Pocahontas, Va., and Lizzie Brockenbrough, d. of the Rev. Everard Meade, D.D., in Old Pohick Church, Fairfax Co., Va. Sept. 17, 1910

SYME
  Blanche Bragg, d. of Andrew Syme, and Charles Macalister Gilliam of Petersburg, Va., by the Rev. M. M. Marshall, D.D., in Christ Church, Raleigh, N.C. So. Ch., Jan. 19, 1893

SYMINGTON
  Charles Junior,* of New York, and Elizabeth Blackford, d. of Arthur Selden and Lizzie Robertson Blackford Lloyd, by the bride's father assisted by the Rev. W. H. H. Powers, D.D. of Towsen, Md., at Madison, Conn. So. Ch., Oct. 12, 1912

SYMTH*
  Abram H., Esq., of Alexandria, Va., and Carrie V. Steed, by the Rev. J. Owen Dorsey, at the residence of the bride's father, James M. Steed, Prince George Co. So. Ch., Nov. 25, 1875

* Given as printed

TABB
    Cynthia, d. of the late Dr. J. Henry Tabb, of "Auburn", Mathews Co., Va., and Capt. John N. Tabb of Gloucester Co., by the Rev. R. J. McBryde, in St. George's Church, Fredericksburg. So. Ch., Feb. 1, 1883

    Ellen Randolph, and Dr. Thomas B. Lane, by the Rev. Jno. McGill, at Christ Church, Mathews Co. So. Ch., May 5, 1870

    Emiline M., youngest d. of the late Capt. P. E. Tabb, of Waverly, Gloucester Co., Va., and Dr. J. Spottswood Wellford, of Fredericksburg, by the Rev. Chas. Minnigerode, in Richmond, at the residence of Judge W. W. Crump. So. Ch., Apr. 16 and 23, 1858

    G. R., and Juliet J. Tabb, by the Rev. E. Meade, in Mattaponi Church, King and Queen Co., Va. So. Ch., Jan. 7, 1886

    J. Lloyd, of Baltimore, and Susie Seldon, by the Rev. A. Y. Hundley, Sherwood, Gloucester Co., Va. So. Ch., Mar. 22, 1877

    John, and Mary S., d. of Joseph S. James, Esq., by the Rev. A. Y. Hundley, in Abingdon Church, Gloucester Co., Va. So. Ch., May 24, 1883

    John N. (Capt.), of Gloucester Co., Va., and Cynthia, d. of the late Dr. J. Henry Tabb of "Auburn", Mathews Co., Va., by Rev. R. J. McBryde, in St. George's Church, Fredericksburg. So. Ch., Feb. 1, 1883

    Juliet J., and G. R. Tabb, by the Rev. E. Meade, in Mattaponi Church, King and Queen Co., Va. So. Ch., Jan. 7, 1886

    Lucia Cary, and Dr. John Wilkins, C.S.A., by the Rev. G. S. Carraway, at Auburn, Mathews Co. So. Ch., Feb. 21, 1862

    Lucy H., d. of the late Thomas Tabb of Toddsburg,* Gloucester Co., Va., and George Brower, Esq., by the Rev. C. Mann, at Exchange, the residence of James K. Dabney, Esq. So. Ch., Mar. 19, 1858

    Philip, of Baltimore, and Hester V. T., d. of Austin Fergusson,* Esq., by the Rev. A. Wade, at Northwood, Charles City Co., Va. So. Ch., Feb. 24, 1870

    Thos. S., Esq., of Taddsburg,* Gloucester Co., Va., and Mary Adelaide Billups of Mathews Co., Va., by the Rev. Mr. Carraway, in Trinity Church, Kingston Parish** So. Ch., Nov. 23, 1854

    Walter T., s. of John Tabb, Esq. of Gloucester Co., Va., and Elizabeth, d. of Judge Robert B. Minor of San Antonio, Tex., in the Church of the Messiah, in New York. So. Ch., June 21, 1919

    Yelvarton, of Amelia, and Mary M., d. of E. R. Turnbull, Esq., by the Rev. Otis A. Glazebrook, at the

---

* Given as printed
** Kingston Parish is in Mathews County, Virginia (Journal ... Diocese of Virginia, Richmond, Va., 1941)

MARRIAGE NOTICES IN THE SOUTHERN CHURCHMAN WITH DATES OF PUBLICATION

residence of the bride's father, in Lawrenceville, Va. So. Ch., Dec. 14, 1871

TABLER
B. L., and Mary Hart Rankin, by the Rev. W. D. Hanson, in Trinity Church, Martinsburg. So. Ch., Aug. 18, 1870

TACKETT
Charles E., and Hattie Slaughter, by the Rev. John K. Mason, in St. George's Church, Fredericksburg, Va. So. Ch., Nov. 15, 1888

John F., and Nannie, d. of T. D. Fendall, Esq., all of Alexandria, Va., by the Rev. J. B. Perry, in St. Paul's Church, Alexandria, Va. So. Ch., Oct. 25, 1883

TALBOT
Helen M., second d. of E. A. Talbot, Esq. of Bedford Co., Va., and John F. Terry, Esq. of Lynchburg, by the Rev. R. H. Wilmer. So. Ch., May 16, 1856

TALBOTT
George Edwards, and Mary Forrest Gosnell of Martinsburg, W.Va., by the rector, the Rev. W. D. Hanson, in Trinity Church, Martinsburg, W. Va. So. Ch., Dec. 18, 1873

TALIAFERRO
Addison, of Amherst, and Jane C., d. of Dr. E. H. Henry of Fauquier, by the Rev. Mr. Kinsolving, at Upperville. So. Ch., Nov. 2, 1855

Agnes Marshall, youngest d. of Col. A. G. Taliaferro, and Ro. W. Maupin of Baltimore, by the Rev. Philip Slaughter assisted by the Rev. C. Y. Steptoe and the Rev. Dr. B. Franklin, in Emanuel Church, Rapidan, Va. So. Ch., Dec. 24, 1874

Chas. C. (The Rev.), rector of Cumberland Parish, Lunenburg Co., Va., and Louisa G. Armistead of Fauquier Co., by the Rev. C. W. Andrews, near Upperville, Fauquier Co., Va. So. Ch., June 3, 1836

Edmund P. (Dr.), of Green Co., Ala., and Octavia H., d. of William Robertson, Esq. of Culpeper, Va., by the Rev. William C. H. Jones [at Delorain]. So. Ch., Dec. 1, 1837

Georgie, d. of the late Dr. Alfred Taliaferro of Culpeper Co., Va., and Dr. J. C. Grayson of Culpeper Co., by the Rev. W. T. Roberts, at "Fairmont." So. Ch., Jan. 13, 1887

Jane A., d. of the late Rev. Charles Taliaferro, and Dr. Cassius Carter of Fairfax, by the Rev. J. Earnest, at Mount Sharon, in Orange, Va. So. Ch., June 27, 1856

Janie A., d. of the late Rev. C. C. Taliaferro of Virginia, and Henry Coit Day of Georgia, by the Rev. M. Hansborough, at Mt. Sharon, Va. So. Ch., Sept. 29, 1870

Kate Corbin, youngest d. of the late Wm. F. and Mary W. Taliaferro of Peckatone, Westmoreland, Va., and Dr. Wm. W. Rose of King George, by the Rev. E. B. McGuire, at Peckatone. So. Ch., Nov. 30, 1860

Lawrence, of Hazley, Esq.,* and Mary Austin, d. of the late Hay Taliaferro, Esq. of King George Co., by the Rev. Henry Wall, at Freidland. So. Ch., July 12, 1866

* Given as printed

MARRIAGE NOTICES IN THE SOUTHERN CHURCHMAN WITH DATES OF PUBLICATION

Lucy W., d. of the late Hay Taliaferro of Orange, Va., and Edwin B. Bradley, Esq. of Baltimore, by the Rev. J. Earnest, in St. Thomas' Church, Orange C.H. So. Ch., Sept. 16, 1859

Margaret Lewis, d. of Col. Alexander G. Taliaferro of Culpeper Co., Va., and Chapman Maupin of the University of Virginia, by the Rev. J. S. Hansbrough, at Annandale. So. Ch., Jan. 5, 1871

Mary Austin, d. of the late Hay Taliaferro, Esq. of King George Co., Va., and Lawrence Taliaferro, Esq. of Hazley, by the Rev. Henry Wall, at Freidland. So. Ch., July 12, 1860

Mary E., d. of Dr. Edmund P. Taliaferro, and George Cullen, all of Orange C.H., Va., by the Rev. J. Earnest, rector of Zion Parish, Prince George's Co., Md., in Emmanuel Church, Baltimore. So. Ch., Dec. 13, 1866

Mary V., of Orange Co., Va., and Samuel Meredith Maxwell of New York, by the Rev. James L. Maxwell, rector of St. Luke's Church, Montclair, N.J., at the residence of John Taliaferro, Orange Co., Va. So. Ch., Nov. 7, 1878

Melville, of Henrico Co., Va., and Annie Meriwether, eldest d. of John J. Woods, Esq. of Ivy Depot, Albemarle Co., Va., by the Rev. J. A. Greaves, M.A., at the residence of the bride's parents. So. Ch., Oct. 13, 1881

Nannie Leftwich, d. of Richard M. Taliaferro of New York, and H. J. Wadley, Esq. of Wayne Co., Ga., by the Rev. Robb White, in St. John's Church, Wytheville, Va. So. Ch., Sept. 21, 1876

R. B., of Gloucester, and Fannie, d. of Dr. Francis D. Jones, by the Rev. Edmund Withers, at Ingle-Side, Lancaster Co. So. Ch., Feb. 15, 1856

Susan S., only d. of Warren T. Taliaferro, Esq., and Beverly R. Wellford, Esq. of Richmond, by the Rev. C. Mann, at Belleville, the residence of the bride's father. So. Ch., Mar. 19, 1858

Thomas S., Esq. of Gloucester Co., Va., and Harriotte Hopkins, d. of Cassius F. Lee, by the Rev. C. B. Dana, in Alexandria. So. Ch., Dec. 7, 1860

Victoria, d. of Dr. Edmund P. Taliaferro, and Charles W. Hardy, Esq. of Norfolk, by the Rev. J. Earnest, at Orange C.H., Va. So. Ch., Nov. 2, 1865

Wm. M. (Maj.), and Sue H. Michel, by the Rev. L. B. Wharton, at the residence of the bride's mother, Abingdon, Va. So. Ch., Nov. 7, 1867

See also Jamesson, Cornelia L. T. (Mrs.)

TALIFERRO

Lewis T., formerly of Richmond, Va., now of Augusta, and Lizzie M. Sanchez of Augusta, by the Rev. C. C. Williams, in St. Paul's Church, Augusta, Ga. So. Ch., Mar. 24, 1881

TALLAFERRO

Gowin of Westmoreland Co., Va., and Emma, d. of Col.

MARRIAGE NOTICES IN THE SOUTHERN CHURCHMAN WITH DATES OF PUBLICATION

Godwin of Linwood, Alexandria Co., by the Rt. Rev. Bishop Johns. So. Ch., Jan. 4, 1856

TALLIFERRO
William H., and Mary W., d. of Dr. J. B. Leigh, by the Rev. F. N. Whaley, at Clarksville, Va. So. Ch., Feb. 23, 1888

TAMS
Margaret A., eldest d. of Sampson Tams, Esq., and the Rev. Richard B. Duane, rector of Grace Church, Honesdale, Penn., by the Rev. J. B. Fowles, in St. Andrew's Church, Philadelphia. So. Ch., Oct. 24, 1850

TANNER
Cornelia F., and Robert H. Withers, both of Campbell Co., Va., by the Rev. W. W. Kimball. So. Ch., Nov. 3, 1881

TAPLIN
Horatio Nelson, of Montpelier, Vt., and Mrs. Lillie Tyson (Jolliffee) Harris of Washington, formerly of Frederick Co., Va., by the Rev. David Barr, in Washington, D.C. So. Ch., July 2, 1891

TAPSCOTT
John C., and Cornelia A. McCarty, both of Lancaster, Va., by the Rev. H. L. Derby, in White Chapel Church, Lancaster, Va. So. Ch., Sept. 24, 1885

M. Victoria (Mrs.), formerly of Baltimore, Md., and Robert Fairfax Mitchell of Richmond Co., by the Rev. H. L. Derby, at "Oakley", Lancaster, Va. So. Ch., Mar. 2, 1876

Nannie Douglas, of Amherst C.H., Va., and the Rev. W. M. Clark, rector of the parish, by the Rev. John T. Clark of North Carolina assisted by the Rev. A. S. Lloyd of St. Luke's Church, Norfolk, Va., in the Ascension Church, Amherst C.H., Va. So. Ch., Oct. 15, 1885

TARRY
Mary H., d. of George Tarry, Esq. of Mecklenburg, and Capt. Fleming J. Jefferess, by the Rev. Francis McGuire. So. Ch., Mar. 27, 1857

Rebecca, and Samuel Morton, by the Rev. R. D. Brooke, in St. Luke's Church, Mecklenburg Co. So. Ch., Sept. 12, 1850

TATASPAUGH
Edwin Francis, and Julia Dixon, both of Alexandria, by the Rev. John Aiken. So. Ch., Nov. 16, 1848

TATE
Armstrong, of Burlington, N.C., and Bertha Lee, d. of the late Rev. G. H. Morrison, D.D., by the Rev. W. F. Morrison, U.S.N., in Memorial Church, Baltimore. So. Ch., June 22, 1893

TATUM
Constance, eldest d. of Dr. R. H. Tatum of Harrisonburg, and James Hay, by the Rev. David Barr, in Emmanuel Church, Harrisonburg, Va. So. Ch., Oct. 10, 1878

Lucian B., of Richmond, Va., and Mary Seldon, d. of Dr. R. H. Tatum of Harrisonburg, Va., by the Rev. O. S. Bunting, at the residence of the bride's father. So. Ch., June 15, 1882

Mary Seldon, d. of Dr. R. H. Tatum of Harrisonburg, Va., and Lucian B. Tatum of

- 215 -

MARRIAGE NOTICES IN THE SOUTHERN CHURCHMAN WITH DATES OF PUBLICATION

Richmond, Va., by the Rev. O. S. Bunting, at the residence of the bride's father. So. Ch., June 15, 1882

Richard H. (Dr.), and Sarah Ann, second d. of Charles Seldon, by the Rev. P. F. Berkeley, in Powhatan Co., Va. So. Ch., Jan. 15, 1852

TAYLOE

Alice A., d. of the late Charles Tayloe of King George Co., Va., and Thos. M. Lewis, M.D. of Westmoreland, by the Rev. T. E. Locke, at Oaken Brow. So. Ch., June 3, 1859

Bladen Tasker, of King George, and Fannie Lightfoot, d. of William H. Fowle, Esq. of Alexandria, by the Rev. D. Francis Sprigg, rector of Grace Church. So. Ch., May 6, 1859

E. Thornton (Capt.), of Marengo Co., Ala., and Rosa A., d. of George P. Tayloe, Esq. of Roanoke Co., Va., by the Rev. Edward H. Ingle, at "Buena Vista", the residence of the bride's father. So. Ch., Nov. 10, 1870

Emma, d. of W. H. Tayloe, Esq., and Gen. Thomas T. Munford (late C.S.A.), all of Virginia, at Georgetown, D.C. So. Ch., May 3, 1866

Etta O., d. of Henry A. Tayloe, Esq., and Beverly T. Crump of Richmond, by the Rev. M. Johnson, at "Mount Airy", Richmond Co., Va. So. Ch., Oct. 23, 1884

G. Ogle, and Susan T., d. of Dr. Thomas L. Hunter, all of King George Co., by the Rev. E. B. McGuire, in St. John's Church, at King George C.H., Va. So. Ch., Dec. 16, 1880

Imogen, d. of Col. Edward Tayloe of King George Co., Va., and Rev. Edward H. Ingle of Roanoke Co., Va., by the Rev. Charles Goodrich, D.D., at "Powhatan", the residence of the bride's father. So. Ch., Oct. 6, 1870

Jennie, youngest d. of George P. Tayloe of Roanoke Co., Va., and Mortimer M. Rogers of Baltimore, Md., by the Rev. Edward H. Ingle, at Buena Vista, residence of the bride's father. So. Ch., Nov. 25, 1875

John, of King George Co., and Mary W., d. of Daingerfield Lewis of King George Co., by the Rev. Joseph A. Russell, at Marmion, King George Co., Va. So. Ch., Nov. 9, 1854

John, Jr., Esq., of "Cloverdale", King George Co., Va., and Jane Elizabeth, d. of Henry Fitzhugh, Esq., by the Rev. Henry Wall, at "Sherwood Forest", Stafford Co., Va. So. Ch., Jan. 17, 1867

Kate A., and Daniel P. Wirt of Westmoreland Co., by the Rev. Mr. Shields, at Chatterton, King George Co., Va. So. Ch., Dec. 6, 1877

Lucy Daingerfield, eldest d. of the late Col. John Tayloe, of Chatterton, and Matthew B. Pollock of Stafford Co., by the Rev. James W. Shields assisted by the Rev. Melville Boyd, at Chatterton, King George Co. So. Ch., Dec. 23, 1875

Mary L., d. of G. P. Tayloe, Esq. of Roanoke Co., Va. and W. W. Gwathmey, Esq. of

MARRIAGE NOTICES IN THE SOUTHERN CHURCHMAN WITH DATES OF PUBLICATION

Richmond, Va., by the Rev. Mr. Pendleton. So. Ch., Oct. 17, 1856

Nannie C., d. of George P. Tayloe of Roanoke Co., Va., and John D. Langhorne, by the Rev. Peter Tinsley. So. Ch., Jan. 8, 1864

Rosa M., d. of George P. Tayloe, Esq. of Roanoke Co., Va., and Capt. E. Thornton Tayloe of Marengo Co., Ala., by the Rev. Edward H. Ingle, at "Buena Vista", the residence of the bride's father. So. Ch., Nov. 10, 1870

Sallie, d. of Henry A. Tayloe, Esq., and Key Compton of Norfolk, by the Rev. A. B. Kinsolving, at "Mount Airy", Richmond Co., Va. So. Ch., Nov. 22, 1888

William, of King George Co., Va., and Sophia Ridgely, by the Rev. Charles Goodrich, D.D., at Nottingham, Md. So. Ch., Nov. 28, 1872

TAYLOR

A. T., of Hillsboro, and Dr. Algernon Smith of Maryland, by the Rev. Theodore Reed, in Hillsboro, Va., at the residence of Dr. Taylor. So. Ch., June 28, 1877

Agness Marion, d. of the late Dr. John Taylor of Caroline Co., and Dr. J. Washington Ashby, by the Rev. John Cole, at the residence of her brother in Culpeper Co. So. Ch., May 13, 1859

Alfred H., of Washington, D.C., and Gertrude Moore, niece of Thomas Moore, Esq., by the Rev. Frank Page, in Zion Church, Fairfax C.H., Va. So. Ch., June 24, 1886

Alice Eleanor of Brockway, Pa., and Rev. John Joseph Meaken Harte, curate of Trinity Church, Tulsa, Okla., by the Rev. W. O. Cross, rector of St. Paul's Church, Kittanning, Pa., in Grace Church, Ridgway, Pa. So. Ch., Oct. 18, 1941

Alice Marshall, d. of James M. Taylor, Esq. of Richmond, Va., and Walter Armistead Williams, by the Rev. T. G. Dashiell assisted by the Rev. W. B. Williams, in St. James' Church. So. Ch., Feb. 24, 1887

Annie Henderson, d. of the late H. Allen Taylor, and the Rev. Francis D. Lee, by the Rev. Dr. Norton, at Alexandria, Va. So. Ch., May 6, 1880

Bennett, of Albemarle Co., Va., and Lucy, d. of the late Edward Colston of Honeywood, Berkeley Co., Va., by Rev. W. D. Hanson. So. Ch., July 12, 1866

Bettie F., d. of the late Dr. Edward P. Taylor, and Rev. Joseph Earnest, rector of St. Thomas', by the Rev. E. Boydon, in St. Thomas' Church, Orange, Va. So. Ch., Jan. 15, 1852

Bettie M., of Christiansburg, and H. H. Powers of Roanoke, Va., by the Rev. W. Dudley Powers of the Diocese of Maryland, at the residence of the bride's father, at Christiansburg. So. Ch., May 10, 1883

Charles A., of Richmond, Va., and Martha V. Henshaw of Berkley, by Rev. A. Wade, at Berkley, Charles City Co., Va. So. Ch., Dec. 3, 1874

Chas. S., Jr., of Alexandria, and Mary Earle, d. of the

MARRIAGE NOTICES IN THE SOUTHERN CHURCHMAN WITH DATES OF PUBLICATION

late Wm. Pervis of Mobile, Ala., by the Rev. Edward H. Ingle, at Salem, Roanoke Co., Va. So. Ch., Nov. 15, 1877

Edmund L., of Taylorsville, Hanover Co., and Sarah Ann, d. of Mrs. Ann Robertson of Willington, Culpeper Co., by the Rev. John W. Woodville. So. Ch., Dec. 15, 1837

Edmund Randolph, s. of Julia P. K. and the late Edmund Randolph Taylor of Charles Town, W.Va., and Alice, d. of Mrs. and the late Henry B. Hunt of Cambridge, England, by the Rev. Paca Kennedy, in St. Mark's Church, Washington, D.C. So. Ch., Jan. 10, 1925

Edwin M., Esq., and Miss E., d. of William Kinney, Esq., by the Rev. Mr. Goodwin, at Staunton. So. Ch., June 28, 1839

Eliza, and Dr. Alfred B. Tucker of Winchester, by the Rev. F. M. Whittle, at Springberry, Clarke Co., Va. So. Ch., Aug. 29, 1856

Erasmus, and Roberta S., d. of the late John Ashby, Esq., by the Rev. J. Earnest, at Mount Independence in Fauquier Co. So. Ch., Jan. 15, 1852

Esther D., d. of Charles S. Taylor, Esq., and Julian T. Burke, all of Alexandria, by the Rev. D. F. Sprigg, in St. Paul's Church, Alexandria. So. Ch., Oct. 25, 1877

Euphania C., and Archibald M. Harrison, both of Fluvanna, by the Rev. James Doughen. So. Ch., Dec. 1, 1837

Fannie G., only d. of Dr. Taylor of Albemarle Co., Va., and the Rev. Frederick W. Neve, by the Rev. T. E. Locke assisted by the Rev. H. B. Leo, in St. Paul's Church, Fredericksville Parish, Albemarle Co., Va. So. Ch., June 29, 1893

Frances Virginia, d. of John B. Taylor, Esq., and Josiah R. White of Loudoun Co., Va., by the Rev. F. M. Whittle, at Clifton, Clarke Co., Va. So. Ch., Sept. 13, 1855

George Braxton (Rev.), of Chapel Hill, N.C., and Jessie Cabell of Norwood, Nelson Co., Va., by the Rev. J. B. Taylor, D.D. assisted by the Rev. Davis M. Wood, in Christ Church, Norwood. So. Ch., Jan. 3, 1889

George W., Esq., and Corilla P., eldest d. of Pryor Hankins, all of James City Co., by the Rev. Mr. Ellett. So. Ch., Jan. 15, 1836

Hattie M., of Fredericksburg, and William B. Daingerfield of Alexandria, by the Rev. Dr. Murdaugh, in St. George's Church, Fredericksburg, Va. So. Ch., Oct. 22, 1874

Henry, Jr., and Virginia, eldest d. of the late Dr. George W. Bagby, by the Rev. Joshua Peterkin assisted by the Rt. Rev. A. M. Randolph. So. Ch., June 17, 1886

J. Fenton, and Emma, d. of the late William H. Scott, by the Rev. John G. Scott of Hot Springs, Va., brother of the bride, assisted by the Rev. Meade Clark, D.D., rector of St. James'

MARRIAGE NOTICES IN THE SOUTHERN CHURCHMAN WITH DATES OF PUBLICATION

Church, at the home of the bride, 10 E. Franklin St., Richmond, Va. So. Ch., July 2, 1910

James W., of Ashland, and Mrs. R. A. Apperson of Richmond, by the Rev. T. G. Dashiell, at the residence of P. P. Winston. So. Ch., Aug. 7, 1884

Jefferson Randolph (The Rev.), rector of Trinity Church, Moundsville, W.Va., and Mary Hubbard, d. of Edward C. Bruce, Esq. of Winchester, by the Rev. Nelson P. Dame, rector of the parish, in Christ Church, Winchester, Va. So. Ch., Jan. 29, 1891

John, and Belle Nelson Locke, eldest d. of the officiating clergyman, by the Rev. T. E. Locke, in the rectory, Washington Parish, Westmoreland Co., Va. So. Ch., Mar. 7, 1867

John Charles Randolph, and Mary Grammer Leigh, at Houston, Va. So. Ch., July 20, 1907

John Jacquelin, of Richmond, and Ann Wallace Stringfellow of Culpeper Co., Va., by the Rev. Carter Page, in St. Paul's Church, Raccoon Ford. So. Ch., Oct. 12, 1893

John William, and Evelyn C. Hill, both of King William Co., Va., by the Rev. W. T. Roberts, at Edgehill, the residence of the bride's mother. So. Ch., Aug. 29, 1889

Julia L., of Louisa, and Rev. E. W. Hubbard of Brandon Parish**by the Rev. E. Boyden assisted by the Rev. J. H. Williams, in St. John's Church, Louisa. So. Ch., Dec. 9, 1875

Julian, of Alexandria, Va., and Mrs. Mary Eggleston Wailes, by the Rev. Charles White, D.D., at Hampden-Sidney,* Va. So. Ch., Nov. 12, 1891

Louisa Leonard, d. of the late Tazewell Taylor, Esq. of Norfolk, Va., and John Davidson Letcher of Lexington, Va., by the Rt. Rev. A. M. Randolph, D.D., LL.D. assisted by the Rev. John J. Lloyd, D.D., at Norfolk, Va. So. Ch., May 30, 1908

Lucy O., d. of John B. Taylor, Esq., and John J. Riely of Clarke Co., by the Rev. F. M. Whittle, in Jefferson Co. So. Ch., Dec. 5, 1856

M. E., d. of E. C. Taylor, and William Bird, by the Rev. P. F. Berkeley, at Green Wood, Hanover Co. So. Ch., Nov. 29, 1866

Maria J., and Wm. H. Hampton, by the Rev. Henry T. Sharp, in the Church of the Ascension, Frankfort, Ky. So. Ch., Dec. 11, 1873

Mary, of Lewisburg, Greenbriar Co., W.Va., and Isham Randolph of Clarke Co., Va., by Canon Knowles, at the Cathedral of Sts. Peter and Paul, Chicago. So. Ch., June 29, 1882

Mary E., and Wm. H. Wilson, all of Bedford, by the Rev. N. Sale. So. Ch., Feb. 22, 1856

Mary E., d. of Mrs. S. H. Taylor, and Benjamin R.

---

* Given as printed
** Brandon Parish is in Prince George County, Virginia (<u>Journal ... Diocese of Southern Virginia</u>, Portsmouth, Va., 1941)

MARRIAGE NOTICES IN THE SOUTHERN CHURCHMAN WITH DATES OF PUBLICATION

R. Brown, all of Norfolk, Va., by the Rev. A. S. Lloyd, at St. Luke's Church, Norfolk, Va. So. Ch., Jan. 13, 1887

Mary Louisa, d. of Maj. R. C. Taylor of Norfolk, Va., and Richard W. Gamble of Savannah, Ga., by the Rev. A. S. Lloyd, rector of St. Luke's Episcopal Church, Norfolk, Va. So. Ch., June 16, 1892

May, and George A. Smith of Richmond, Va., by the Rev. J. Green Shackelford, at the home of the bride, in Orange Co., Va. So. Ch., Dec. 3, 1885

Nina, and B. P. Loyall, by the Rev. Dr. O. S. Barten, at the residence of the bride's mother. So. Ch., Nov. 30, 1882

Page, d. of Steven M. and Mary Mann Taylor, and Edwin Kirk of Washington, D.C., by the Rev. H. B. Lee, rector of Christ Church, at "Lego," Charlottesville, Va. So. Ch., July 19, 1913

Pulina, d. of H. Porterfield Taylor of Richmond, and Rev. L. B. Wharton of William and Mary College, Williamsburg, Va., by the Rev. J. A. Wharton, at the residence of the bride's parents. So. Ch., Jan. 17, 1878

R. Innes, of Spotsylvania Co., and Nannie H., d. of the late W. Yates Downman, by the Rev. E. C. Murdaugh, D.D., at Idlewild, the residence of the bride's mother, near Fredericksburg. So. Ch., Oct. 26, 1876

Rebecca Porterfield, second d. of Edwin M. Taylor, Esq., and James J. Foster of Richmond, by the Rev. James A. Latine, at the residence of the bride's father, at Staunton, Va. So. Ch., Dec. 5, 1867

Rebekah L., of Richmond, Va., and Robert T. Marshall of Kentucky, by the Rev. Joshua Peterkin, D.D. So. Ch., Oct. 14, 1880

Roberta B., d. of John R. and Sallie E. Taylor, and Benjamin R. Coward, by the Rev. Curtis Grubb, at the residence of the bride's parents, Taylorsville, Hanover Co., Va. So. Ch., Feb. 15, 1883

Rosalie V., d. of the late Charles Taylor of King George Co., Va., and William L. Waring of Essex Co., by the Rev. T. E. Locke, at Oaken Brow. So. Ch., Nov. 12, 1858

Sarah C., d. of John B. Taylor, Esq., and Thompson B. Mason of Philadelphia, by the Rev. F. M. Whittle, at Rockland, Jefferson Co., Va. So. Ch., Nov. 2, 1855

Sidney, of Cumberland, Md., and Mary M., eldest d. of John C. and Sarah Bronaugh, by the Rev. A. P. Gray, at the residence of the bride's sister, in Prince William Co. So. Ch., Mar. 13, 1884

Sophia Gordon, d. of the late James Taylor, and John Rutledge Smith, Esq., by the Rev. Mr. Hanckell, in St.

MARRIAGE NOTICES IN THE SOUTHERN CHURCHMAN WITH DATES OF PUBLICATION

Paul's Church, Charleston, S.C. So. Ch., Nov. 6, 1835

T. P. (Maj.), and Mrs. Mary Walker Flood, by the Rev. W. H. Pendleton, in St. Paul's Church, Lynchburg. So. Ch., Apr. 14, 1870

Thos. Leiper, and Rosa Van Doren, d. of the officiating clergyman, by the Rev. T. E. Locke, at the rectory, Washington Parish, Westmoreland Co., Va. So. Ch., Nov. 12, 1868

Virginia, d. of the late Maris Taylor, Esq., and Anthony Egerton Smoot, all of Alexandria, Va., at the residence of the bride's mother. So. Ch., Aug. 6, 1885

Virginia E., d. of Dr. Samuel Taylor of Berryville, and Edward C. Marshall, Jr. of Fauquier Co., Va., by the Rev. F. M. Whittle, at Berryville, Va. So. Ch., Dec. 26, 1856

Virginia S., d. of Thomas S. Taylor, and James H. Harris, all of Alexandria,* by the Rev. J. Peterkin, in St. James' Church, Richmond, Va. So. Ch., Apr. 25, 1856

Wm. B., of Richmond, and Bessie M'C., elder d. of Gen. Wm. R. Boggs of the Virginia Agricultural and Mechanical College, by the Rev. Nelson P. Dame, at the Episcopal Church in Blacksburg, Va. So. Ch., Dec. 18, 1879

Wm. Jaqueline, and Miriam N. Jacobs, both of Richmond, Va., by the Rev. Mr. Woodbridge. So. Ch., July 5, 1839

Wm. Marshall, and Lelia Madison, eldest d. of Judge Wm. Pope Dabney, by the Rev. Frank Stringfellow, in Powhatan Co., Va. So. Ch., Oct. 19, 1882

Wm. P., and Florence Ida, d. of Geo. M. Carter, by Bishop Payne, at Oak Grove, Westmoreland Co., Va. So. Ch., May 15, 1873

TEBAULT

Myra B., d. of Alfred G. Tebault, M.D., and Edward A. Sawyer, M.D. of Gardiner, Mass., by the Rev. Wm. R. Savage, in Norfolk, Va., at the residence of the bride's parents. So. Ch., May 21, 1885

V. C., only d. of Mrs. C. H. Tebault of New Orleans, and Joseph K. Anderson of Montgomery Co., Va., by the Rev. J. P. Lawrence, at Oak Grove, Amherst Co., Va., at the residence of Mrs. Col. E. R. Long. So. Ch., Dec. 2, 1886

W. Paul, (M.D.), and Mary A., d. of James P. Wright, M.D., all of Princess Anne Co., Va., by the Rev. Wm. R. Savage, in Eastern Shore Chapel, Princess Anne Co., Va. So. Ch., May 21, 1885

TEBBS

Lucy M., of Alexandria, Va., and Donald McLean of Joanna, Fairfax Co., by the Rev. George H. Norton, D.D., in St. Paul's Church, Alexandria, Va. So. Ch., July 8, 1886

Sallie Tyler, of Loudoun Co., Va., and William H. Garber, Esq. of Staunton, by the Rev. O. A. Kinsolving, in Emanuel Church, Middleburg. So. Ch., Nov. 23, 1854

TEMPLE

---

* A notice appears in the issue of Mar. 28, 1856 identical with this except that "all of Alexandria" is written "all of Richmond"

MARRIAGE NOTICES IN THE SOUTHERN CHURCHMAN WITH DATES OF PUBLICATION

John N., of Fulton, Ark., s. of the late Rev. H. W. L. Temple of Essex Co., Va., and Alice M., eldest d. of Dr. Henry Gresham of Essex Co., Va., by the Rev. E. Meade, in St. John's Church, Tappahannock, Va. So. Ch., Nov. 3, 1881

Lucy E., second d. of the late H. L. W. Temple, and Catesby L. Lewis, all of Essex, by the Rev. J. B. Newton, in St. Paul's Church, Essex, Va. So. Ch., Oct. 3, 1872

Mary, d. of the late H. L. W. Temple, and Dr. Warner Lewis, of New Kent, by the Rev. J. B. Newton, at St. Paul's Church, Essex, Va. So. Ch., Oct. 3, 1872

Mary L., and Henry C. Varn of South Carolina, by the Rev. Everard Meade, in St. Paul's Church. So. Ch., Oct. 1, 1885

Willantina, d. of B. Temple, Esq. of Fredericksburg, Va., and Dr. Prosser J. Harrison of Richmond, Va., by the Rev. A. M. Randolph, at Fredericksburg. So. Ch., Feb. 3, 1860

TENCH
Inez C., of Washington, and Wyndham Stokes of Welch, W.Va., by the Rev. Edward H. Ingle, in the Church of the Epiphany, Washington, D.C. So. Ch., Feb. 22, 1908

TENISON
Mamie R., and Charles S. Martin, both of the City of Nashville, by the rector, the Rev. W. C. Gray, D.D., assisted by the Revs. T. F. and M. Cabell Martin, father and brother of the groom, in the Church of the Advent, Nashville, Tenn. So. Ch., Dec. 20, 1883

TENNENT
Jno. (The Rev.), and Sallie T. Potter, by the Rev. Dr. Colton of Hungar's Parish, Northampton, in St. James' Church, Accomac Co. So. Ch., June 25, 1858

Lucy A., youngest d. of the late Dr. Alexander Tennent, and Taliaferro Hunter, by the Rev. E. C. McGuire, D.D. So. Ch., Nov. 15, 1839

TENNEY
C. P., and the Rev. C. Keith, by the Rt. Rev. W. J. Boone, D.D., in the Mission Chapel of the Episcopal Church, Shanghai. So. Ch., Sept. 28, 1854

TERRELL
Albert Johnston, of Bear Garden, Buckingham Co., and Pocahontas Bolling, youngest d. of the late Mr. and Mrs. Robert Thurston Hubard, by the Rev. Lyttleton E. Hubard of Elizabeth, N.J. assisted by the Rev. Plummer F. Jones, at the bride's home, Chellowe, in Buckingham Co. So. Ch., Nov. 5, 1921

M. D. (Miss), of Hanover, Va., and W. H. Walker of Ontario, Canada, by the Rev. Robert R. Claiborne, at East View, Hanover Co., Va. So. Ch., Dec. 23, 1880

TERRETT
Amelia H., d. of the late George Terrett, Esq., and Nathaniel C. Hunter, by the Rev. W. F. Lockwood, at Oakland, Fairfax Co., Va. So. Ch., June 2, 1848

Grace A., second d. of F. A. C. Terrett of Fairfax Co., and A. C. Bleight of Fauquier Co., by the Rev. John McGill, in Zion Church, Fairfax Co. So. Ch., Oct. 4, 1877

TERRILL
Bettie V., and John T.

MARRIAGE NOTICES IN THE SOUTHERN CHURCHMAN WITH DATES OF PUBLICATION

Goodwin of Louisa, by the Rev. W. T. Leavell, at Chestnut Hill, Orange Co., Va. So. Ch., Jan. 19, 1854

TERRY

Annie E., d. of the late Thos. W. Terry, and William L. Carpenter of Albemarle, by the Rev. Robt. Douglas Roller, at the residence of H. C. Doswell, Esq., Hanover Co., Va. So. Ch., Nov. 9, 1876

J. Coles, of Roanoke Co., Va., and Lizzie B., d. of Com. W. Whittle, by the Rev. Pendleton Brooke, in Trinity Church, Buchanan. So. Ch., May 1, 1873

Jno. F., Esq., of Lynchburg, and Helen M., second d. of E. A. Talbot, Esq. of Bedford Co., Va., by the Rev. R. H. Wilmer. So. Ch., May 16, 1856

THACKARA

Elizabeth James, and Arthur W. Palmer of Baltimore, Md., by the Rev. Owen P. Thackara, father of the bride, in St. Peter's Church, Fernandina, Fla. So. Ch., July 23, 1874

THACKSTON

Thomas C. (The Rev.), of Farmville, and Kate Nelson of Boydton, Va., by the Rev. Dr. Wm. A. Smith, at Boydton, Va. So. Ch., July 20, 1854

THOM

Elizabeth Mayo, d. of Col. John Thom, and William B. Ross, all of Culpeper Co., by the Rev. Walker Woodsville, at Berry Hill. So. Ch., Oct. 27, 1837

William A., Jr., and Kate Brooke, d. of the late Richard Baylor, Esq. of Essex Co., Va., by the Rev. B. D. Tucker assisted by the Rev. Arthur Lloyd, in St. Paul's Church, Norfolk, Va. So. Ch., Jan. 20, 1887

THOMAS

Florence M., d. of the late Benj. Thomas, and Alexander McBurney of Alexandria, by the Rev. Henry Nice, at the residence of Joshua Thomas, Baltimore. So. Ch., Feb. 24, 1881

Grace A., d. of George C. Thomas of Berryville, Va., and Judson H. Booker, M.D. of Northumberland Co., by the Rev. P. P. Phillips, at Berryville, Va. So. Ch., Dec. 10, 1885

Henry (The Rev.), of Poolesville, Md., and Rosalie, d. of Judge W. W. Poole, by the Rev. Dr. Lewin, in St. Peter's Church, Dickerson, Md. So. Ch., Dec. 3, 1885

James (Dr.), and Nannie E., d. of the late Wm. D. Nelson, by the Rev. D. M. Wharton, in Nomini Church, Westmoreland Co. So. Ch., 1868

James E., of Richmond, Ind., and Alice, d. of the late Rev. James D. McCabe, D.D. of Baltimore, by the Rev. George W. Peterkin, in Memorial Church, Baltimore. So. Ch., Nov. 25, 1875

John H., merchant and postmaster at Milleville, and Mary Frances, d. of Putnam Jones of Westmore-

MARRIAGE NOTICES IN THE SOUTHERN CHURCHMAN WITH DATES OF PUBLICATION

land Co., by the Rev. T. E. Locke. So. Ch., Feb. 8, 1861

John Hanson, M.D., of Baltimore, and Anna Campbell, only d. of Basil Gordon, Esq. of Falmouth, by the Rev. E. C. McGuire. So. Ch., Dec. 1, 1837

Lizzie W., of Richmond, and Algernon Gray Daingerfield of Harrisonburg, Va., by the Rev. T. G. Addison, D.D., at the rectory of Trinity Church, 219 C. St., N.W., Washington, D.C. So. Ch., Sept. 2, 1886

Mary C., d. of D. C. Thomas of Nelson Co., Va., and Wm. Tyler Tompkins of Albemarle Co., by the Rev. T. F. Martin, at the residence of the bride's father. So. Ch., Nov. 27, 1863

Mary L., and James Blackiston, both of Kent Island, Queen Anne's Co., by the Rev. P. D. Thompson, in Kingsley Chapel, Kent Island, Md. So. Ch., Oct. 8, 1885

Mary R., d. of Dr. J. Hanson Thomas of Baltimore, and John N. Carroll of the "Caves", Baltimore Co., by the Rev. Dr. Mahan, in Grace Church, Baltimore. So. Ch., April 28, 1870

Nanny, eldest d. of Judge H. W. Thomas, and Benjamin Eglin of Washington City, by the Rev. John McGill, at Fairfax C.H. So. Ch., Jan. 2, 1873

Recton P., Esq., of Maryland, and Bettie R., d. of William Ayre, by the Rev. W. A. Alrich, at the residence of the bride's father, in Fairfax Co. So. Ch., Feb. 27, 1868

Robert J., of Louisville, Ky., and Ella, d. of John A. Dixon of Alexandria, by the Rev. G. H. Norton, D.D., at the residence of the bride's parents. So. Ch., June 1, 1871

THOMPSON

A. W., of Tennessee, and Eliza G. Marshall of Lunenburg Co., Va., by the Rev. L. J. Sothoron, at Rose Hill, Lunenburg Co., Va. So. Ch., Aug. 21, 1879

A. Judson (Dr.), of South Carolina, and Bettie R. Easley, by the Rev. O. A. Kinsolving, D.D., at "Wilbon", near South Boston, Halifax Co., Va. So. Ch., Oct. 8, 1885

Annie, d. of George G. Thompson of Culpeper, and the Rev. James G. Minnigerode, rector of Calvary Church, Louisville, Ky., by the Rev. Dr. Charles Minnigerode of St. Paul's Church, Richmond, Va. assisted by the Rev. George W. Peterkin, D.D., Bishop-elect of West Virginia, in St. Stephen's Church, Culpeper. So. Ch., May 23, 1878

Annie H., and Randolph R. Pleasants, Esq.,* by the Rev. T. E. Locke, at Midwood, Fluvanna Co., Va. So. Ch., Mar. 27, 1890

Caroline Homozelle, of Kanawha Co., W.Va., and Geo. E. Cook of Clarksville, Tenn., by the Rev. W. G. Stewart, at Belleville, the residence of the late Col. Frank Thompson.

* A notice appears in the issue of Mar. 20, 1890 identical with this except that it is written Pleasants, Randolph L.

MARRIAGE NOTICES IN THE SOUTHERN CHURCHMAN WITH DATES OF PUBLICATION

So. Ch., Jan. 2, 1868
Charles West (The Rev.),
rector of St. John's
Church, York, Pa., and
Caroline, d. of the late
Oliver Prescott, M.D. of
Newberryport, Mass., by
the Rev. Charles Mason, in
Grace Church, Boston,
Mass. So. Ch., May 3,
1849
Elizabeth C., d. of the
rector of Leeds Church,*
and the Rev. R. C. Cowling
of Wickliffe, Va., by
the Rev. P. D. Thompson
assisted by the Rev.
E. W. Cowling, in Leeds
Church, Fauquier Co., Va.
So. Ch., Aug. 14, 1909
Emily M., d. of C. J.
Thompson, Esq., of Louisa
Co., Va., and Wm. T. Ellis,
Esq. of Vicksburg, Miss.,
by the Rev. J. D. Powell,
at "Edgwood", Louisa Co.,
Va. So. Ch., Sept. 27,
1866
Fanny E., d. of the late
John Thompson of Cul-
popor Co., and the Rev.
John Cole, rector
of St. Stephen's Church,
Culpopor Co., by the Rev.
Wm. F. Lockwood, rector
of St. Thomas' Parish,
Md., at Culpopor C.H.,
Va. So. Ch., Apr. 19,
1855
Frank A. (Miss), and Wilson
H. Thompson, by the Rev.
John McGill, at the
residence of the bride's
parents. So. Ch., Jan.
22, 1874 *
George Western, and Fannie
Bell Jackson, by the Rev.
W. L. Hyland, rector of
Trinity Parish, Wood Co.,
W.Va., at Parkersburg.

So. Ch., May 13, 1869
Ida M., and Wm. H. Legg,
both of Kent Island, Md.,
by the Rev. P. D. Thomp-
son, at Christ Church
rectory, Kent Island, Md.
So. Ch., Nov. 21, 1889
J. S. Barbour, and Mary
Thornton, only d. of Col.
Morton and C. Homassel
Marye, all of Alexandria,
Va., by the Rev. G. H.
Norton, D.D., in St.
Paul's Church, Alexandria,
Va. So. Ch., Feb. 21,
1884
Lucas P. (Judge), of Staun-
ton, and Arabella White
of Romney, by the Rev.
T. T. Castleman, at Rom-
ney. So. Ch., Nov. 16,
1855
Maria Farley, d. of the late
John Thompson, Esq. of
Culpepor C.H., and Dr.
John N. Buffington of
Cabell Co., by the Rev.
John Cole, in Culpepor Co.
So. Ch., Mar. 20, 1857
Maria H., d. of Judge P.
R. Thompson of San
Francisco, and Colin
McCrae of Virginia, by
the Rev. Dr. Gallaudet,
in New York City. So.
Ch., July 2, 1874
Mary C., of Kanawha Co.,
W.Va., and James B. L.
Lockett of Clarksville,
Tenn., by the Rev. W. G.
Stewart, at Belleville,
the residence of the late
Col. Frank Thompson.
So. Ch., Jan. 2, 1868
P. D. (The Rev.), of Halifax,
and Lucy Carter, eldest d.
of the officiating clergy-
man, by the Rev. Geo. W.
Dame, in the Church of the
Epiphany, in Danville, Va.

* Given as printed

MARRIAGE NOTICES IN THE SOUTHERN CHURCHMAN WITH DATES OF PUBLICATION

Apr. 8, 1864
Sarah E., eldest d. of the Hon. Robt. A. Thompson, and George William Huie, M.D. of Louisville, Ky., by the Rev. Francis M. Whittle, at Charleston, Kanawha Co., Va. So. Ch., Oct. 26, 1848

Virginia W., d. of the late Gen. Henry A. Thompson, and William Ivanhoe Montague, all of Baltimore, by the Rev. A. M. Randolph, rector, assisted by the Rev. W. W. Williams of Christ Church and the Rev. C. J. Holt of the Church of the Holy Innocents, in Emanuel Church, Baltimore. So. Ch., Dec. 1, 1881

Willia, d. of Mrs. E. H. Thompson of Louisville and the late William Henry Thompson, U.S. Navy, and the Rev. Anselan Buchanan, rector of St. John's P. E. Church, Bayonne, N.J., by the Rev. Dr. Craik, in Christ Church. So. Ch., July 1, 1875

Wilson H., and Miss Frank A. Thompson, by the Rev. John McGill, at the residence of the bride's parents. So. Ch., Jan. 22, 1874

THOMSON
Clara H., d. of John A. Thomson, Esq. of Jefferson Co., W.Va., and Dr. Edwin G. Booth of Nottoway Co., Va., by the Rev. T. F. Martin, in Grace Church, Berryville, Va. So. Ch., Oct. 20, 1870

George Napier, of Richmond, and Jemima, d. of John Dickson formerly of Scotland, now of Albemarle Co., Va., by the Rev. T. D. Bell, pastor of the Presbyterian Church in Scottsville, assisted by the Rev. T. E. Locke, rector of St. Ann's Parish, at Oakland Grove, Albemarle Co. So. Ch., Oct. 24, 1878

THORNTON
Ada S., d. of W. H. Thornton, Esq., and Geo. Lee R. Tuberville, all of Fairfax Co., Va., by the Rev. Frank Page, in St. John's Church, Centerville. So. Ch., Feb. 27, 1879

Anna Ratcliffe, d. of the late Maj. W. W. Thornton of Brentsville, and J. Boyd Washington of Caroline Co., by the Rev. A. P. Gray, in St. James' Church. Brentsville, Va. So. Ch., Aug. 21, 1890

Antoinette Virginia, eldest d. of N. A. Thornton, Esq. of Richmond, and Miles K. Crenshaw of Charles City Co., by the Rev. Dr. Minnigerode, in St. Paul's Church, Richmond, Va. So. Ch., Nov. 28, 1856

Fannie Hawes, d. of Howard F. Thornton, Esq., and Isaac Tyson, 3rd of Baltimore, by the Rev. F. M. Whittle, at Rosemont, Clarke Co., Va. So. Ch., Oct. 12, 1854

Fanny S., of Fredericksburg, Va., and Samuel B. Strong of Chattanooga, by the Rev. E.

MARRIAGE NOTICES IN THE SOUTHERN CHURCHMAN WITH DATES OF PUBLICATION

C. Murdaugh, in Trinity Church, Fredericksburg, Va. So. Ch., Dec. 4, 1879

Frances Gordon, d. of Mr. and and Mrs. Arthur Presley Thornton, and the Rev. William Byrd Lee Milton, rector of Christ Church Parish, Lancaster Co., Va., by the Rev. Churchill J. Gibson assisted by the rector, the Rev. Dudley Boogher, and the Rt. Rev. Henry St. George Tucker, in St. George's Church, Fredericksburg, Va. So. Ch., Dec. 22, 1934

J. Bankhead T., and Fannie Caro, second d. of Prof. Ezra and Julia C. Bauder, all of Brentsville, by the Rev. A. P. Gray, in St. James Church, Brentsville. So. Ch., Nov. 19, 1885

Margaret Hamilton, and Edward Ellicott Ramey of Louisville, Ky., at the residence of the bride's father, George W. Thornton, M.D. So. Ch., Jan. 5, 1882

Mary, d. of Dr. Philip Thornton, and Robert S. Voss, Esq., at Montpelier, Rappahannock Co. So. Ch., Jan. 9, 1835

Mary Rosina, d. of Champe B. Thornton, and David B. Powers, all of Port Royal, Caroline Co., Va., by the Rev. James E. Poindexter, at the residence of the bride's father. So. Ch., Nov. 2, 1871

Mildred H., eldest d. of Maj. W. W. Thornton of Brentsville, Va., and James J. Davies, by the Rev. Jno. McGill, at the residence of the bride's father. So. Ch., Apr. 17, 1873

Nina, second d. of Chas. A. Thornton, Esq. of Mississippi, and Edward Cunningham, Jr. of St. Louis, by the Rev. Aristides Smith, at the residence of P. B. Key, Esq., in Enfield, N.C. So. Ch., Jan. 4, 1877

P. L. W., S.V.R.R., of Richmond, and Marianna, d. of the late Dr. Elcon Jones of Fairfax C.H., Va., by the Rev. Addison, rector of Trinity Church, in Washington City. So. Ch., June 27, 1872

Robert H. (Dr.), of Newport, Ky., and Susy Bacon of Richmond, Va., by the Rev. Mr. Craighill, in the Episcopal Church, Dalton, Ga. So. Ch., Nov. 19, 1891

Thomas C., of Caroline Co., Va., and Victoria H. Gray of Fauquier, by the Rev. Jno. Lindsay of St. James Church, Warrenton, in Fauquier Co., Va. So. Ch., Dec. 7, 1871

W. F., and J. M. Hunnicutt, by the Rev. Robt. R. Claiborne, at Sussex C.H. So. Ch., Mar. 4, 1880

Wm. H., of Fairfax Co., Va., and Mary M. Whedbie formerly of North Carolina, now of Prince William Co., Va., by the Rev. Arthur P. Gray, in St. Paul's Church, Haymarket. So. Ch., Jan. 5, 1888

THORP

Arthur St. Edmund, of Somerset, England, and Elizabeth Gwynn, d. of Amana G.

MARRIAGE NOTICES IN THE SOUTHERN CHURCHMAN WITH DATES OF PUBLICATION

and James S. Harrison, M.D. lately of the University of Virginia, by the Rev. A. P. Gray, at Gainesville, Prince William Co., Va. So. Ch., Mar. 24 and 31, 1887

Bettie, and Chas. A. Gregory, both of Granville Co., N.C., by the Rev. P. D. Thompson, at the residence of the bride's father, Benj. P. Thorp. So. Ch., Dec. 19, 1872

F. G., of Henrico Co., Va., and Evelyn V. Carter of Nelson Co., Va., by the Rev. Edmund Withers, at the residence of Wm. Carter, in Nelson Co. So. Ch., Dec. 5, 1867

Mollie J., of Granville Co., N.C., and R. T. Smith, by the Rev. P. D. Thompson, at the residence of the bride's father. So. Ch., Nov. 9, 1871

THRALL
George E. (The Rev.), and Thomasine Gist, d. of the Hon. Lewis C. Levin of Philadelphia, by the Rev. Dudley A. Tyng. So. Ch., June 14, 1855

THRIFT
James (Col.), and Lucretia M., d. of Col. John Reid, all of Fairfax, by the Rev. W. F. Lockwood, at Fruit Vale. So. Ch., Nov. 16, 1848

THROWER
Agnes M., d. of S. R. Thrower, Esq. of Boydton, and Holmes C. Harrison of Goochland Co., by the Rev. B. T. Turner, at Boydton, Mecklenburg Co., Va. So. Ch., Dec. 22, 1881

THURSTON
Agnes, d. of Edward T. Thurston, Esq., and Samuel V. Corbell, all of Gloucester Co., by the Rev. Wm. B. Lee, in Abingdon Church, Gloucester Co., Va. So. Ch., Oct. 22, 1885

THURMAN
Alexander, of Lynchburg, and Mary A., d. of the late John Y. Sanderson of New Kent, by the Rev. Mr. Hepbron, in St. Peter's Church, New Kent Co. So. Ch., Nov. 17, 1887

THURSTON
Lillie, eldest d. of Mrs. Charles P. Thurston of Cumberland, and the Rev. Francis K. Leavell of Coal Valley, by the rector, the Rev. P. Nelson Meade, assisted by the Rev. W. T. Leavell, in Emmanuel Church, Cumberland. So. Ch., Feb. 4, 1886

THWEATE *
Mary Eppes, second d. of the late Richard N. Thweate, and Rev. P. E. Berkley, by the Rev. Wm. V. Bowers, at Mantua, Chesterfield Co., Va. So. Ch., Sept. 15, 1837

THWEATT
Alfred F., Esq., and Louisa E., d. of Wm. H. Wilson of Amelia Co., by the Rev. A. B. Tizzard, in Trinity Church, Chesterfield Co. So. Ch., Apr. 4, 1867

Alice F., d. of the late R. N. Thweatt of Chesterfield, and Arthur Sandys of Calcutta, by the Rev. A. B. Tizzard, at Mount Ida, the residence of the bride's mother, in Chesterfield Co., Va. So. Ch., May 26, 1881

Julia, d. of the late Richard Thweatt, Esq. of Chesterfield Co., Va., and the Rev.

* Given as printed

MARRIAGE NOTICES IN THE SOUTHERN CHURCHMAN WITH DATES OF PUBLICATION

A. B. Tizzard, by the Rev.
F. P. Berkley, at Mantua.
So. Ch., Jan. 3, 1850
Mary E., d. of the late R.
N. Thweatt, Esq. of Chesterfield, Va., and George M.
Wilson of Amelia Co., by
the Rev. A. B. Tizzard, at
Mount Ida. So. Ch., Feb.
8, 1865
Mary Eppes, of Chesterfield
Co., and James F. Strother
of Madison Co., by the
Rev. A. B. Tizzard, in
Trinity Church, Chesterfield Co., Va. So. Ch.,
June 14, 1888
Matilda F., d. of the late
Richard N. Thweatt, and
Branch T. Hurt, by the
Rev. P. F. Berkley, at
Mantua, Chesterfield Co.
So. Ch., Oct. 18, 1839
See also SANDYS, Alice F.
(Mrs.)

TIDBALL
T. A. (The Rev.), rector of
Trinity, Portsmouth, and
Josephine, eldest d. of
Dr. P. T. Browne of Accomack Co., Va., by the Rev.
Alexander S. Berkley, in
St. James' Church, Drummondtown. So. Ch., Oct.
31, 1872

TIERNAGE
Irene, of Fayette Co.,
Tenn., and Prof. A. Morrison of Virginia, by
the Rev. J. B. Canada, at
"Walnut Grove", at the
residence of the bride's
mother, Fayette Co., Tenn.
So. Ch., June 14, 1877

TIFFANY
Emily, and the Rev. Carter
Beverly, rector of the
church at Ivy, Va., by
the Rt. Rev. H. St. George
Tucker, D.D., Bishop of
Virginia, at Warrenton, Va.
So. Ch., Sept. 24, 1932
Walter Checkley, of Minneapolis, and Lila Andrews, d.
of George R. Robinson of
St. Louis, by the Rev.
George Sterling, in
Emmanuel Church, near St.
Louis, Mo. So. Ch.,
May 10, 1888

TIFFEY
Anna C., d. of Richard V.
Tiffey, Esq., and Rev.
Wm. Friend of Port
Royal, by the Rev. George
Woodbridge of Richmond, at Office Hall,
King George Co. So. Ch.,
Feb. 27, 1857
Bettie P., and Thomas Hughes
of Rappahannock, by the
Rev. D. M. Wharton, at
Montross, Va. So. Ch.,
Jan. 21, 1869
Lucy Weston, formerly of
King George Co., Va.,
and Nathaniel Hynson of
Kent Co., Md., by the
Rt. Rev. Bishop Pinckney
assisted by the Rev. Dr.
Elliott, associate rector, in
the Church of the Ascension,
Washington, D.C. So. Ch.,
Feb. 8, 1877

TILDEN
C. Henry, of Philadelphia,
and Kate Davis of Essex Co.,
Va., by the Rev. Mr. Keeble,
in St. John's, Tappahannock.
So. Ch., Aug. 10, 1876

TILFORD
John B., of New York, and
Florinda J. Hammond of
Berryville, Clarke Co.,
Va., by the Rev. T. F.
Martin, at the residence
of Mrs. Bushrod Taylor.
So. Ch., Jan. 6, 1870
Lottie J., of Hampton, and
John B. Clay of Newport

MARRIAGE NOTICES OF THE SOUTHERN CHURCHMAN WITH DATES OF PUBLICATION

News, by the Rev. J. J. Gravatt, in St. John's Church, Hampton, Va. So. Ch., Jan. 12, 1882

TILGHMAN
Charles H., of Talbot Co., Md., and Elizabeth, d. of William Donnell, Esq., by the Rev. A. M. Randolph, D.D., at the residence of the bride's father, in Baltimore. So. Ch., Dec. 8, 1881

Maud, d. of the late Gen. Lloyd Tilghman, and Eric Pierson Swenson of New York City, by the Rev. Henry Mason Smyth of Plattsburg, N.Y., assisted by the Rev. Dr. Greer of St. Bartholomew's Church, New York, at St. James' Church, New York. So. Ch., June 20, 1889

TILLER
Thomas M., and Virginia Isabella, d. of David W. Burns, all of Richmond, by the Rev. Mr. Peterkin, in St. James' Church, Richmond, Va. So. Ch., Nov. 28, 1856

TILLINGHAST
John Huske (The Rev.), of St. Paul's, Clinton, and Sarah Jane, d. of John Wilkins, Esq., of Rutherford, N.C., by the Rev. J. D. McCullough of the Diocese of South Carolina, in St. John's Church, Rutherford, N.C. So. Ch., Nov. 9, 1865

TIMBERLAKE
Jno. W., of Albemarle Co., and Eliza B., eldest d. of Wm. H. and Sallie J. Sims, by the Rev. John T. Clark, at "Black Walnut", Halifax Co. So. Ch., Dec. 23, 1869

Martha V. (Mrs.), nee Crane, of Jefferson Co., W.Va., and Maj. H. M. Bell of Staunton, Va., by the Rev. Dallas Tucker, rector of Zion Church, Charles Town, assisted by the Rev. Walter O. Hullihen, rector of Trinity Church, Staunton, Va., at the residence of the bride's mother, Mrs. Margaret S. Crane, near Charles Town, Jefferson Co., W. Va. So. Ch., Nov. 11, 1886

Richard N., and Maggie L. Watson, both of Spotsylvania Co., by the Rev. J. Green Shackelford, rector of Trinity Church, Fredericksburg, in St. George's Chapel, Spotsylvania Co. So. Ch., Jan. 26, 1888

Wayt Bell, of Staunton, Va., and Frances Stuart, eldest d. of Mrs. Emma K. and the late John Orfeur Yates of Jefferson Co., W.Va., by the Rev. John S. Alfriend assisted by the Rev. P. N. McDonald, in Zion Episcopal Church, Charles Town, W.Va. So. Ch., Jan. 26, 1907

TINSLEY
David C., of Amherst, and J. Alice Achree of Bedford, by the Rev. R. J. McBryde, at Forest Home, Bedford Co. So. Ch., Dec. 23, 1869

Mary T., d. of Benj. T. Tinsley, Esq., and Capt. E. T. Kindred of Texas, by the Rev. J. Earnest, at Elmwood, Roanoke Co., the residence of the bride's father. So. Ch., Nov. 9, 1864

William H., of Big Lick, Roanoke Co., Va., and

MARRIAGE NOTICES IN THE SOUTHERN CHURCHMAN WITH DATES OF PUBLICATION

Helen G. Johnston, by the Rev. Edwin A. Penick, at the residence of the bride's mother, Salem, Roanoke Co., Va. So. Ch., Nov. 7, 1878

Z. D., Esq., of Amherst Co., and Mary Ann, d. of the late Capt. Pleasant Dawson, by the Rev. Mr. Cofer, in Bedford Co. So. Ch., Nov. 24, 1837

TIZZARD
A. B. (The Rev.), and Julia, d. of the late Richard Thweatt, Esq. of Chesterfield Co., Va., by the Rev. F. P. Berkley, at Mantua. So. Ch., Jan. 3, 1850

TODD
Everard M. (Maj.), and Mrs. Julia W. Carroll, both of Smithfield, Va., by the Rev. David Barr, in Christ Church, Norfolk, Va. So. Ch., Nov. 3, 1887

James, of Wheeling, and Ann Devoe of Parkersburg, by the Rev. E. T. Perkins. So. Ch., Aug. 11, 1848

John W., and Everallan Carroll, both of Smithfield, Isle of Wight Co., Va., by the Rev. Edw. W. Wroth, in Christ Church, Smithfield, Va. So. Ch., Jan. 11, 1877

Lillie Payne, and Duncan Robertson, both of Norfolk Va., by the Rev. F. C. Steinmetz, rector of Christ Church, at the home of Mr. and Mrs. John D. Letcher, Norfolk, Va. So. Ch., Jan. 23, 1909

TOLER
Ann N. (Mrs.), d. of the late George N. Grymes of King George Co., Va., and Roger B. Atkinson, Esq. of Sherwood, by the Rev. C. T. Gibson, at Kinderwood, Lunenburg Co. So. Ch., June 15, 1860

TOLFORD
David W. (The Rev.), of Gambier, Ohio, and Priscilla M. Waring, late of Prince George's Co., Md., by the Rev. Ethan Allen, in Dayton, Ohio. So. Ch., Nov. 22, 1839

TOLLE
Henry C., and Elizabeth Fyffe, by the Rev. T. E. Locke, in St. John's Church, Scottsville, Va. So. Ch., Nov. 27, 1890

TOLSON
Francis A., of Maryland, and Edmonia H. Grymes, by the Rev. Arthur Johns, at the residence of the bride's mother, in King George Co., Va. So. Ch., Nov. 13, 1873

TOMLIN
Edmonia Fitzhugh, d. of the late R. W. Tomlin, Esq. of Hanover, and James F. Maupin of Norfolk, by the Rev. S. S. Hepbron, in Immanuel Church, Hanover. So. Ch., Nov. 22, 1888

Mary L., d. of the late Williamson Tomlin, Esq., and Wm. C. Eustace of Lancaster Co., by the Rev. E. C. McGuire. So. Ch., Dec. 15, 1837

TOMPKINS
C. W., of Spotsylvania, Va., and Sally F. Royston, by the Rev. Jas. E. Poindexter, at Ormsby, Caroline Co., Va. So. Ch., Nov. 28, 1872

Evelina W., and John H. Abell of St. Mary's Co., Md., by the Rev. J. E. Poindexter, at Ormsby, Caroline Co., Va.

- 231 -

MARRIAGE NOTICES IN THE SOUTHERN CHURCHMAN WITH DATES OF PUBLICATION

So. Ch., Sept. 28, 1882
Henderson F., of Fauquier, and Lizzie B., d. of R. C. and Mary Weir of Manassas, by the Rev. A. P. Gray, in Trinity Church, Manassas.
So. Ch., Feb. 1, 1883
Jennie, and St. Clair Hartman, by the Rev. Wm. N. Nelson, at Stony Point, Albemarle Co., Va. So. Ch., Mar. 9, 1854
Mary Agnes, of Spotsylvania Co., Va., and Henry F. Turnipseed of Montgomery Co., Ala., by the Rev. J. E. Poindexter, at Ormsby, Caroline Co., Va. So. Ch., Sept. 28, 1882
Robert R., formerly of Fauquier Co., Va., and Evelina S. Wellford, late of Fredericksburg, by the Rev. Wm. W. Greene, at the residence of the bride's uncle, C. C. Wellford, in Spotsylvania Co. So. Ch., Feb. 19, 1864
Samuel Woods, of Richmond, and Sarah Nellie, second d. of the late James Tompkins of Albemarle Co., by the Rev. T. E. Locke, at Locust Shades, the residence of the bride's mother. So. Ch., Dec. 7, 1893
Sarah Nellie, second d. of the late James Tompkins of Albemarle Co., and Samuel Woods Tompkins of Richmond, by the Rev. T. E. Locke, at Locust Shades, the residence of the bride's mother. So. Ch., Dec. 7, 1893
Wm. Tyler, of Albemarle Co., and Mary C., d. of D. C. Thomas of Nelson Co., Va., by the Rev. T. F. Martin, at the residence of the bride's father. So. Ch., Nov. 27, 1863

TUNRY
Barbara Ellen, of Westernport, and George R. Cole of Piedmont, W.Va., by the Rev. W. Herbert of Assheton, at Westernport, Md. So. Ch., Jan. 11, 1883

TOOT
Sallie F., and John Mattaner Carrington, by the Rev. Albert R. Walker, in St. John's Church, Halifax C.H., Va. So. Ch., Mar. 10, 1870

TORRENCE
George J., and Fannie Washington Brown, by the Rt. Rev. A. M. Randolph assisted by the Rev. J. Lumbley Lough, in Emmanuel Church, Baltimore. So. Ch., Nov. 8, 1883

TOWLES
Adella J., d. of Dr. Porteus Towles, and James O. Harcum, by the Rev. Edmund Withers, in Christ Church, Lancaster, Va. So. Ch., Dec. 25, 1857
Edwin L., formerly of Fredericksburg, and Willie, d. of Dr. Porteus Towles, at the residence of the bride's father, Lancaster, Va. So. Ch., Jan. 28, 1875
Ella C., d. of the rector, and E. A. Poole of Washington, by the Rev. John Towles, rector, assisted by the Rev. E. A. Dalrymple, S.T.D., of Baltimore, in Christ Church, Accokeek. So. Ch., Jan. 22, 1880
Ethel, and William B. Searson, by the Rev. Thos. P. Baker, at Yonge's Island,

MARRIAGE NOTICES IN THE SOUTHERN CHURCHMAN WITH DATES OF PUBLICATION

S.C. So. Ch., Jan. 16, 1909
John, and Sophronia Elizabeth, youngest d. of Col. John Chowning, by the Rev. Ephraim Adams, in White Chapel, Lancaster Co. So. Ch., Aug. 21, 1835
Louisa, and H. M. Lagley lately from Virginia, by the Rev. R. S. Barrett, at the residence of the bride's mother, in Henderson, Ky. So. Ch., Feb. 21, 1884
Willie, d. of Dr. Porteus Towles, and Edwin L. Towles formerly of Fredericksburg, at the residence of the bride's father, Lancaster, Va. So. Ch., Jan. 28, 1875

TOWNES
William, Jr., of Mecklenburg, and Nannie E. Barksdale of Charlotte, by the Rev. H. A. Brown, at the residence of Henry E. Edmunds, Charlotte Co., Va. So. Ch., Dec. 14, 1864

TOWNSEND
Charlotte, youngest d. of the Rev. J. H. and the late Charlotte Cox Townsend, and Chester Karl Harriman of Florence, Cal., by the bride's father, at her home, Smithtown, Long Island, N.Y. So. Ch., Aug. 28, 1920
J. H. (The Rev.), rector of St. John's Church, Camden, N.J., and Elizabeth Wilmer Wilson Edwards, by the Rev. W. T. Snyder, rector of the Church of the Incarnation, at the residence of the bride's brother, Admiral Henry B. Wilson, Washington, D.C. So. Ch., Nov. 10, 1917
J. H., Jr. (Capt.), American Red Cross, and Mary Rose Weber of Portland, Ore., in St. George's English Church, Paris, France. So. Ch., Nov. 1, 1919
Lloyd W. (Lt.), U.S.N., and Dorothy, youngest d. of Harry Baldwin Osborne, Esq., by the Rev J. H. Townsend, in St. Paul's Church, Willimantic, Conn. So. Ch., Feb. 11, 1911

TRACY
Emma Capers, d. of Capt. C. C. Tracy, and Joseph W. Lucas, by the Rev. Thomas P. Baker, in Jude's Church, Walterboro, S.C. So. Ch., Dec. 18, 1909

TRAFTON
Helen, and Col. McClain Jackson, by the Rev. R. S. Barrett, at Henderson, Ky. So. Ch., Oct. 25, 1883

TRAPNELL
Joseph, Esq., s. of the officiating clergyman, and Rebecca H., d. of N. S. White, Esq., by the Rev. Jos. Trapnell, Jr. assisted by the Rev. M. Ambler, at Charles Town, Jefferson Co., W.Va. So. Ch., Nov. 29, 1866

TRAVERS
S. Wingfield, and Emmie McC. Hatcher, by the Rev. Dr. J. Peterkin assisted by the Rev. Charles Minnigerode, at the residence of the bride's father, Thomas W. McCance, Richmond, Va. So. Ch., Jan. 21, 1886

TREDWAY
Roberta H., and Willis L. Gravely, by the Rev. Geo. W. Dame, in the Church of the Epiphany, Danville. So. Ch., Jan. 23, 1879

TRENT

MARRIAGE NOTICES IN THE SOUTHERN CHURCHMAN WITH DATES OF PUBLICATION

P. (Dr.), of Richmond, Va., and Lucy C., d. of Col. Thos. N. Burwell of Botetourt Co., Va., by the Rev. F. M. Baker, at Rustic Lodge. So. Ch., Oct. 26, 1855

TRIBBLE
John S. (Dr.), of Essex Co., and Mrs. Anna J. Dillard formerly of Gloucester, by the Rev. H. L. Derby, at "Midway", Lancaster Co., Va. So. Ch., Mar. 1, 1877

TRIBLE
George M., and Clara Brooke Seward, by the rector, the Rev. Dr. Hundley, in St. Luke's P. E. Church, Essex Co., Va. So. Ch., Mar. 9, 1883

TRICE
Elizabeth Ann, d. of R. P. Trice, and Charles Potter, all of Fairfax Co., by the Rev. R. T. Brown, near Pohick. So. Ch., Apr. 22, 1859

Lucy Lee, and John Minor, by the Rev. E. L. Goodwin assisted by the Rev. P. H. Gwinn, at Wiloughby, Albemarle Co., Va. So. Ch., June 18, 1891

TRIGG
William R., and Mrs. Roberta N. Hanewinckel, both of Richmond, by the Rev. Joshua Peterkin, in Richmond. So. Ch., Jan. 17, 1884

TRIGGER
Milly, of King George Co., and George W. Inscove, by the Rev. T. E. Locke, at the rectory of Washington Parish.* So. Ch., Feb. 8, 1861

TRIPLETT
Emily Louisa, d. of Mrs. Nannie J. and the late William Stone Triplett, and Meredith F. Montague, by the Rev. Charles Minnigerode, D.D. assisted by the Rev. Joshua Peterkin, D.D., in St. Paul's Church, Richmond, Va. So. Ch., Jan. 17, 1884

John B., and Sarah S., d. of the late James Cox of Pleasants Co., Va. formerly of Hedgesville, Berkeley Co., by the Rev. W. L. Hyland, at the residence of the bride's brother, in Pleasants Co. So. Ch., Mar. 29, 1861

Mary Jenifer, d. of the late William S. Triplett, and Philip Haxhall, both of Richmond, by the Rev. Charles Minnigerode, D.D., at the residence of the bride's mother. So. Ch., Apr. 30, 1874

Mary W., d. of John R. Triplett, Esq., and John B. Slaughter, Jr., by the Rev. Montgomery Schuyler, D.D., the Rt. Rev. Bishop of the Diocese pronouncing the benediction, in Christ Church, St. Louis. So. Ch., Dec. 23, 1875

TRIST
T. J., of Philadelphia, and Maria Ellen D. S., youngest d. of the late Hon. J. H. Lyman of Northampton, Mass., by the Rev. T. H. Gallaudet assisted by the Rev. P. P. Irving, in Christ Church, New Brighton, N.Y. So. Ch., Oct. 22, 1858

TROTT

---

* Washington Parish is in Westmoreland County, Virginia (<u>Journal ... Diocese of Virginia</u>, Richmond, 1941)

MARRIAGE NOTICES IN THE SOUTHERN CHURCHMAN WITH DATES OF PUBLICATION

John B., and Julia M., third
d. of Mrs. Lucy D. Plummer
of Fairfax Co., by the Rev.
W. F. Lockwood, at Centerville. So. Ch., Nov. 16, 1848

TRUSLOW
Mildred, d. of Mrs.
Edward Truslow of Summit,
N.J., and Dr. John
Minor of Washington, D.C.,
s. of Dr. and Mrs. Charles
L. Minor of Asheville,
N.C., by the Rev. W. O.
Kinsolving, rector
of the church, and the Rev.
Elmore McKee of Waterbury,
Conn., brother-in-law
of the bride, in
Christ Church, Summit,
N.J. So. Ch., Apr. 29, 1922

TSONG
Chang Mia, a puella
Formosa, and the Rev. G. D.
McKay formerly of the
Valley of Virginia,
Presbyterian Missionary,
at Formosa, China. So.
Ch., Nov. 28, 1878

TUBMAN
Mary, of Charles Co., and
the Rev. Simon Wilmer, rector
of Christ Church, Prince
George's and Charles Counties, Md., by the Rt. Rev.
Wm. H. Stone, D.D., at
Mulberry Grove. So. Ch.,
Aug. 4, 1837

TUCKER
Alfred B. (Dr.), of Winchester, and Eliza Taylor, by
the Rev. F. M. Whittle,
at Springberry, Clarke
Co., Va. So. Ch., Aug. 29, 1856

Alonzo F., and Annie E.
West, both of Hanover Co.,
Va., by the Rev. S. S.
Hepbron, at Gethsemane
(Campbellite) Church. So.
Ch., May 15, 1890

Annie B., of Charlottesville,
Va., and Prof. Lyon G. Tyler of Memphis, Tenn., by
the Rev. G. H. Gilmer, at
the residence of the minister, in Pulaski Co., Va.
So. Ch., Nov. 28, 1878

B. St. George (Dr.), and
Eliza C., second d. of
Dr. John Mercer, by the
Rev. Mr. Ambler, at
Williamsburg. So. Ch.,
Dec. 6, 1861

Beverly D. (The Rev.), of Warsaw, Va., and Anna Maria,
d. of the late Col. John
A. Washington of Mount
Vernon, by the Rev. Mr.
Leavell, in Zion Church,
Charles Town, W.Va. So.
Ch., July 31, 1873

Beverly Dandridge, Jr. (The
Rev.), second s. of the
officiating bishop, and
Eleanor, d. of Prof. and
Mrs. William Minor Lile
of the University of Virginia,
by the Rt. Rev. Beverly D.
Tucker, Bishop Coadjutor
of the Diocese of Southern
Virginia, in St. Paul's
Memorial Church, University
of Virginia. So. Ch.,
May 8, 1915

Cassie D., and J. Thompson
Brown, both of Virginia,
by the Rev. Dallas Tucker,
in St. James' Episcopal
Church, Wooster, Ohio.
So. Ch., Oct. 26, 1882

Dallas (The Rev.), and Harriett
E., d. of the late Algernon E. Ashburner of Philadelphia, by the Rev. L. S.
Osborne, at Trinity Church,
West Philadelphia. So. Ch.,
July 1, 1880

Emma Beverly, d. of the late

MARRIAGE NOTICES IN THE SOUTHERN CHURCHMAN WITH DATES OF PUBLICATION

David H. Tucker of Richmond, Va., and Forrest W. Brown, Commonwealth's Attorney, Charles Town, W.Va., by the Rev. Dallas Tucker, in Zion Church, Charles Town, W.Va. So. Ch., June 25, 1885

J. Randolph, of Charleston, W.Va., and Fanny B., youngest d. of Judge William W. Crump of Richmond, by the Rev. Dr. Minnigerode assisted by the Rev. Dallas Tucker, in Richmond. So. Ch., May 15, 1873

Thomas S. B. (Capt.), of Williamsburg, Va., and Julia, d. of the late William L. Clark, Esq. of Winchester, Va., by the Rev. William C. Meredith, at Carysbrook, Frederick Co., Va. So. Ch., Dec. 20, 1866

Zettie, youngest d. of the late Judge Beverly Tucker of Williamsburg, and John P. Little, M.D. of Richmond, by the Rev. Chas. Minnigerode, D.D., at Williamsburg, Va. So. Ch., June 6, 1867

TUGGLE
Florence Lacy, and Harry Stanard Beverly, by the Rev. T. P. Eppes assisted by the Rev. W. H. Milton, at "The Grove", the residence of the bride's father, in Nottoway Co., Va. So. Ch., Dec. 28, 1893

TULLOSS
Joseph D., and Annie Campbell, by the Rev. Jno. McGill, at the residence of S. Welsh, the bride's uncle. So. Ch., Dec. 9, 1869

William R. (Dr.), of Haymarket, Prince William Co., Va., and Fannie Walker, d. of Dr. E. P. Clark of The Plains, Fauquier Co., Va., by the Rev. David Barr, in Washington, D.C. So. Ch., Feb. 9, 1907

TUNSTALL
John B., of Marshall Co., Miss., and Grace D., d. of the late Richard R. Watson, Esq. of Albemarle Co., Va., by the Rev. Edward H. Ingle, at Coyners Spring, Va. So. Ch., Feb. 22, 1877

John L., of Lynchburg, Va., s. of W. P. Tunstall, and Florence L., d. of the late Wm. Massie of Nelson, by the Rev. Edward Withers, at Pharsalia, Nelson Co. So. Ch., Dec. 31, 1868

Mary E., and Joseph J. Dillard, by the Rev. H. L. Derby, at "Spring Hill", Sussex, Va. So. Ch., Sept. 4, 1873

Mary M., of Lynchburg, and Jas. G. Brooks of Richmond, by the Rev. W. H. Kinckle, in St. Paul's Church, Lynchburg. So. Ch., June 12, 1857

TUNSTILL
Sallie, only d. of E. M. and Christine Tunstill, and E. M. Vandervort, both of Lewis Co., by the Rev. T. H. Lacy, rector of St. Paul's Church, at the residence of the bride's parents, in Weston, W.Va. So. Ch., July 15, 1886

TUPPER
Tullius C. (The Rev.), and Imogen H. Hicks of Panola Co., Miss., by the Rev. S. H. Green assisted by the Rev. G. White, D.D. of Memphis, in the Church of The Redeemer, Sardis, Miss.

MARRIAGE NOTICES IN THE SOUTHERN CHURCHMAN WITH DATES OF PUBLICATION

TURBERVILLE
Geo. Lee R., and Ada S., d. of W. H. Thornton, Esq., all of Fairfax Co., Va., by the Rev. Frank Page, in St. John's Church, Centreville. So. Ch., Feb. 27, 1879

TURNBULL
Helen, d. of Capt. Robert Turnbull, Lawrenceville, Va., and John Jackson of Lunenburg Co., Va., by the Rev. Green Shackelford, in Lawrenceville, Va., at the residence of the bride's father. So. Ch., Jan. 26, 1882

Mary M., d. of E. R. Turnbull, Esq., and Yelverton Tabb of Amelia, by the Rev. Otis A. Glazebrook, at the residence of the bride's father, in Lawrenceville, Va. So. Ch., Dec. 14, 1871

Virginia, d. of R. D. Turnbull, Esq., and George Claiborne, Esq., by the Rev. R. A. Castleman, in Lawrenceville, Brunswick Co., Va. So. Ch., Feb. 6, 1863

William Fillmore, and Elizabeth Burcher Ost, by the Rev. J. J. Gravatt, in St. John's Church, Hampton, Va. So. Ch., Oct. 12, 1882

TURNER
B. Thornton (The Rev.), of Goochland Co., Va., and Nanny Addison, fourth d. of George F. Harrison, at Longwood, Goochland Co. So. Ch., Jan. 30, 1879

Bettie S., eldest d. of Joseph H. Turner, Esq., and Lt. James E. Mason of Accomac Co., Va., by the Rev. R. R. Mason, at Columbia, Fluvanna Co., Va. So. Ch., Mar. 8, 1865

Carrie M., d. of Carolinus Turner, Esq., and Dr. Wm. N. Jett, all of King George Co., by the Rev. E. B. McGuire, in Immanuel Church, King George Co. So. Ch., Sept. 10, 1874

Charles L., of Prince George's Co., Md., and Lillie, d. of A. P. Burns of Baltimore, by the Rev. J. B. Perry, in St. Andrew's Church, Washington, D.C. So. Ch., July 30, 1885

Eliza H., d. of Richard Turner of King George Co., and William C. Pratt of Caroline, by the Rev. J. E. Locke, at Woodlawn. So. Ch., May 18, 1860

Eliza R., d. of Edward C. Turner, Esq., and Jacqueline A. Marshall, by the Rev. W. H. H. Powers, in Grace Church, The Plains. So. Ch., Oct. 31, 1878

Emma J., of Richmond, Va., and Prof. John C. Pettus late of Iuka, Miss., by the Rev. H. McDonald. So. Ch., July 28, 1881

George, and Jane C. W., d. of Austin Fitzhugh, Esq., all of King George Co., by the Rev. E. B. McGuire, at the residence of the bride's father, Mill Bank. So. Ch., May 30, 1872

George, of Belle Grove, and Janie M. McGuire, d. of the rector, by the Rev. Edward McGuire, in St. John's Church, King George C.H. So. Ch., Oct. 26, 1876

Ida C., d. of Capt. John C. Turner, and Joseph K. Irving, by the Rev. Thomas

MARRIAGE NOTICES IN THE SOUTHERN CHURCHMAN WITH DATES OF PUBLICATION

E. Locke, at Dunleith, Buckingham Co., Va. So. Ch., Nov. 10, 1881

Jeanie, and Capt. Edward Carter, by the Rev. John McGill. So. Ch., Sept. 26, 1867

John J., and Lizzie G., youngest d. of the late John V. Kean, Esq., by the Rev. H. Melville Jackson, in Grace Church, Richmond. So. Ch., Nov. 28, 1878

M. T. (The Rev.), of Washington, Ga., and Olivia M. Johnston, by the Rev. J. B. Newton, D.D. assisted by the Rev. B. T. Turner, at the residence of A. Langstaff Johnston, Esq., Richmond, Va. So, Ch., Jan. 31, 1889

Mary Hamilton, d. of the late James Willett Turner, and the Rev. J. Gordon Maxwell, by the Rev. G. Emlen Hare, D.D., in Emmanuel Church, So. Ch., Sept. 10, 1858

Mary Welby, and Capt. I. H. Cochran, Coast Artillery Corps, U.S.A., in Grace Church, The Plains, Va. So. Ch., Oct. 27, 1917

Robert Hall, and Mary Keech, by the Rev. L. J. Sothoron, in Trinity Church, Trinity Parish, Charles Co., Md. So. Ch., Nov. 20, 1884

Sarah A., of Albemarle, and William E. Haden of Fluvanna Co., by the Rev. T. E. Locke, at the residence of Mr. Hopkins, near Glendower. So. Ch., Feb. 12, 1885

See also **SHELTON**, Hallie W. (Mrs.)

TURNIPSEED

Henry F., of Montgomery Co., Ala., and Mary Agnes Tompkins of Spotsylvania Co., Va., by the Rev. J. E. Poindexter, at Ormsby, Caroline Co., Va. So. Ch., Sept. 28, 1882

TURPIN

Jackson, Esq., and Susan Latane, d. of E. A. J. Clopton, Esq., by the Rev. Henry Wall, D.D., in St. John's Church, Richmond, Va. So. Ch., June 1, 1871

Thos. J., and Mary G. Royall, both of Powhatan Co., Va., by the Rev. John D. Powell, at the residence of the bride's father, Joseph W. Royall, Esq. So. Ch., Dec. 2, 1859

Wm. C., of Macon, Ga., and Evelyn Willing, d. of Wm. N. and Mary A. Nelson, by the Rev. C. B. Bryan, in Christ Church, Millwood, Clarke Co., Va. So. Ch., Apr. 10, 1884

TUTWILER

John McLellan, Esq. of Lexington, Va., and Julia, eldest d. of the late Gen. Albert Rust, former member of Congress from the State of Arkansas, by the Rev. John Ambler, at the residence of the bride's mother, Mrs. Nannie B. Rust, Luray, Page Co., Va. So. Ch., Apr. 9, 1874

TWING

A. T., D.D. (The Rev.), of New York City, and Mary Abbot, d. of Charles Emery, Esq. of Dorchester, by the Rt. Rev. the Bishop of the Diocese, in St. Mary's Church, Dorchester, Mass. So. Ch., June 22, 1876

TILER

Adele, and Dr. Wm. Armendt, by the Rev. R. S. Barrett,

MARRIAGE NOTICES IN THE SOUTHERN CHURCHMAN WITH DATES OF PUBLICATION

in Trinity Church, Owensboro, Ky. So. Ch., Feb. 21, 1884

Alice, d. of ex-President Tyler of Sherwood Forest, Charles City Co., and the Rev. Henry Mandeville Denison of Brooklyn, N.Y., by the Rev. W. T. Leavell, at Sherwood Forest, Charles City Co., Va. So. Ch., July 18, 1850

Bettie G., d. of Dr. Wat H. Tyler, and the Rev. John T. Points of New Kent Co., by the Rev. G. S. Carroway, at Tarwood, Hanover Co. So. Ch., Apr. 16, 1858

Cassie M., d. of Col. Nat. Tyler formerly of Richmond, Va., and Robert L. Armstrong of Baltimore, by the Rev. Wm. Kirkus, in the Church of Saint Michael and All Angels. So. Ch., July 8, 1880

Douglass, Esq., of Leesburg, and Mary Virginia, d. of Jno. M. Harrison, Esq., by the Rev. O. A. Kinsolving, at Windsor, Loudoun Co. So. Ch., July 1, 1869

Ellen, only d. of the late Rev. Joseph D. Tyler, Principal of the Institution for the Education of the Deaf and Dumb, at Staunton, Va., and the Hon. Samuel J. Person of Wilmington, N.C., Judge of the Superior Court of that state, by the Rev. C. B. Dana of Alexandria, in Trinity Church, Staunton. So. Ch., June 25, 1858

Hortensia, of Front Royal, and Charles H. Leach, Esq. of Fauquier Co., by the Rev. R. T. Berry, at Front Royal. So. Ch., Oct. 12, 1865

Letitia, d. of the Hon. John Tyler of Williamsburg, Va., and James A. Semple, by the Rev. Wm. Hodges. So. Ch., Mar. 1, 1839

Lucy Yates, youngest d. of the late Dr. Wat H. Tyler, and Edward Colston Newton, by the Rev. John B. Newton, at Kelvin Grove, Westmoreland Co., Va. So. Ch., Dec. 2, 1875*

Lyon G. (Prof.), of Memphis, Tenn., and Annie B. Tucker of Charlottesville, Va., by the Rev. G. H. Gilmer, at the residence of the officiating minister, in Pulaski Co., Va. So. Ch., Nov. 28, 1878

Mary Armistead, second d. of Dr. Wat H. Tyler, and Col. Joseph Mayo, Jr., all of Westmoreland Co., Va., by the Rev. Andrew Fisher, at Locust Farm, Westmoreland Co., Va. So. Ch., Mar. 19 and 26, 1868

Mary E., d. of the late Edmund Tyler of Loudoun Co., and Jos. T. Watson, by the Rev. O. A. Kinsolving, in the church at Aldie. So. Ch., Dec. 16, 1869

Mary Lyon, d. of Judge and Mrs. David Gardiner Tyler, and George Peterkin Gamble, by the Rev. Cary Gamble of the Church of the Nativity, Huntsville, Ala., and the Rev. E. W. Gamble of St. Paul's Church, Selma, Ala.,

---

* This seems to be a correction of a notice which appeared in the issue of Nov. 18, 1875

MARRIAGE NOTICES IN THE SOUTHERN CHURCHMAN WITH DATES OF PUBLICATION

father and uncle of the groom, at "Sherwood Forest", Charles City Co., Va., the home of the bride's parents. So. Ch., Oct. 23, 1926

Mattie, youngest d. of the late William Tyler, Esq. of Virginia, and J. H. Smith, Esq. of the firm of Smith and Powzie, Philadelphia, by the Rev. John Collins McCabe, D.D., rector of the Church of the Ascension, Baltimore, at "Sherwood Forest", Charles City Co., Va., the county seat of the bride's uncle, the Hon. John Tyler, ex-President of the United States. So. Ch., June 1, 1860

Nannie C., youngest d. of Dr. Wm. Tyler, Sr. of Frederick, Md., and Walker Y. Page formerly of Virginia, by the Rev. Chas. Seymour, in All Saints' Church, Frederick, Md. So. Ch., June 11, 1858

Richard Barnes, of Petersburg, Va., and Ellen Douglass, only d. of the Rev. and Mrs. Arthur P. Gray, Sr., by the Rev. Arthur P. Gray, Jr. of Lawrenceville, Va. assisted by the Rev. Arthur P. Gray, Sr., in Trinity Church, Washington, Va. So. Ch., Jan. 11, 1913

Robert H. (Capt.), and Sallie S. Chinn, both of Prince William Co., Va., by the Rev. H. W. L. Temple, at Tappahannock, Essex Co. So. Ch., Feb. 27, 1863

Sallie B., d. of Col. Henry B. Tyler, and Thomas R. Love, Esq., by the Rev. O. A. Kinsolving, at Fairfax C.H. So. Ch., Dec. 16, 1869

TYNG

Susan C., d. of the late Hon. Dudley A. Tyng, and Edward A. Newton, Esq. of Pittsfield, by the Rev. Dr. Tyng of Philadelphia, in Grace Church, Boston. So. Ch., July 21, 1837

TYSON

Alex. H. (Dr.), of Baltimore Co., and Mrs. Rebecca A. Howard of Baltimore, by the Rev. Dr. Johns. So. Ch., Oct. 6, 1837

Isaac, 3rd of Baltimore, and Fannie Hawes, d. of Howard F. Thornton, Esq., by the Rev. F. M. Whittle, at Rosemont, Clarke Co., Va. So. Ch., Oct. 12, 1854

James W., of Baltimore, Md., and Elizabeth Key, eldest d. of Maj. Charles Howard, by the Rev. H. Melville Jackson, D.D. assisted by the Rev. Churchill J. Gibson, D.D., in Grace Church, Richmond, Va. So. Ch., Jan. 1, 1891

Nannie Key, and Robert Mitchell, both of Baltimore, Md., by the Rev. C. Clifton Pennick, at Oakland, Md. So. Ch., Dec. 5, 1872

-UV-

UHRIG
    Jacob, of Gallipolis, Ohio, and Mary Julick of Point Pleasant, W.Va., by the Rev. T. H. Lacy, at Point Pleasant, W.Va. So. Ch., Feb. 19, 1874

UNDERWOOD
    Nannie M., d. of Wm. P. Underwood, Esq., Clerk of the Court of Surry Co., and Dr. J. W. Sessous of North Carolina, by the Rev. John C. McCabe, rector of St. John's Church, Hampton, at Surry C.H. So. Ch., Nov. 30, 1855

UNRUH
    Georgianna, and Bushrod E. Courtney, by the Rev. T. Grayson Dashiell, in Yeocomico Church. So. Ch., Dec. 17, 1858

UPHAM
    Benjamin N., of Vermont, and Fannie Scott, d. of George H. Dameron of Amherst Co., by the Rev. J. P. Lawrence, at the residence of the bride's father. So. Ch., Nov. 7, 1878

UPSHAW
    Mamie Heath, d. of Mrs. V. D. Upshaw, and Reuben B. Knox, by the Rev. K. S. Nelson, at River Edge, Charles City Co., Va. So. Ch., Dec. 30, 1886

UPSHUR
    Abel B., Esq., and Columbia W., d. of the late Capt. W. G. Williams of the Corps of Topographical Engineers, U.S. Army, by the Rev. A. Stryker, in Baltimore. So. Ch., June 27, 1872
    John N. (Dr.), and Lucy P., d. of the officiating clergyman, the Rev. Bishop F. M. Whittle, in St. James' Church, Richmond, Va. So. Ch., Nov. 27, 1873
    John N. (Dr.), and Elizabeth Spencer, d. of William S. Peterkin of Baltimore, by the Rt. Rev. Geo. William Peterkin, D.D., in Richmond, Va. So. Ch., Dec. 18, 1879
    Sallie Parker, only d. of Mrs. Sarah A. P. Upshur, and Thomas C. Walston, Esq., by the Rev. Arthur Johns, in Christ Church, Eastville, Va. So. Ch., Apr. 12, 1877

URBAN
    Percy L. (The Rev.), assistant rector of St. Peter's Church, Germantown, and Mary Robinson, d. of Mr. and Mrs. Hugh Bayard Hodge of 420 West Walnut Lane, Germantown. So. Ch., July 23, 1921

URQUHART
    Maggie Norfleet, youngest d. of Mrs. Louisa R. Urquhart, and the Hon. John W. Lawson, M.D. of Isle of Wight Co., Va., by the Rev. Edw. W. Wroth, at Warrique, the residence of the bride's mother, Southampton Co., Va. So. Ch., Feb. 15, 1877
    Margaret Ada, and J. E. L. Delk, M.D., both of Isle of Wight Co., Va., by the Rev. E. W. Wroth, in the Church of our Saviour, Ivor, Va. So. Ch., May 10, 1877
    Murdock M., of Southampton Co., and Henrietta E. Anthony, d. of George H. Dillard, Esq., of Sussex Co., Va., by the

MARRIAGE NOTICES IN THE SOUTHERN CHURCHMAN WITH DATES OF PUBLICATION

Rev. C. J. Gibson, at "Inglewood." So. Ch., Dec. 30, 1875

Thomas H. (Dr.), and Sallie A., d. of the late Dr. William B. Goodwyn, by the Rev. P. G. Robert, at the residence of Mrs. E. N. Goodwyn, in Southampton Co., Va. So. Ch., Apr. 11, 1856

Thomas N., and Mrs. Ann E. Delk, both of Isle of Wight Co., Va., by the Rev. David Barr assisted by the Rev. Mr. Pearson, at Smithfield, Va. So. Ch., Dec. 30, 1886

VALENTINE

Benjamin Batchelder, s. of Mann S. Valentine, and Lila Hardaway, d. of the late Richard H. Meade, all of Richmond, by the Rev. Dr. Newton, in Monumental Church, Richmond. So. Ch., Nov. 4, 1886

Cary, d. of Mr. and Mrs. Mann S. Valentine, Jr., and Louis E., s. of Col. and Mrs. Sol. Cutchins of Richmond, Va., by the Rev. Robert Williams. So. Ch., Jan. 22, 1910

Edward Pleasants, of Richmond, Va., and Martha Dabney, d. of John Hampden Chamberlayne and gr.d. of the Rev. Churchill J. Gibson, D.D., by the Rev. Robert H. Gibson, rector of Christ Church, Cincinnati, Ohio, in Grace Church, Petersburg, Va. So. Ch., Nov. 23, 1893

Edward V., and Kate Friend Mayo, in Monumental Church. So. Ch., Jan. 7, 1892

Mann S., Jr., of Richmond, Va., and Sally Cary, d. of James M. Finch, Esq., by the Rev. Frank Stringfellow, at Belle Nemus, Powhatan Co., Va. So. Ch., Mar. 23, 1882

Mann S., and Elizabeth M., d. of Jas. M. Finch, Esq., by the Rev. Preston Nash, at Belle Nemus, Powhatan Co., Va. So. Ch., Dec. 8, 1887

Mary M., d. of the late Mann S. Valentine of Richmond, and J. Warwick Woods of Albemarle Co., by the Rev. J. Peterkin, D.D. So. Ch., June 28, 1866

William L., of Windsor, N.C., and Mary N., gr.d. of the late Bishop Wm. Meade, D.D. of the P. E. Church of Virginia, by the Rev. J. H. Kabler, in the Methodist Church, Windsor, N.C. So. Ch., Sept. 1, 1887

VALK

Sarah A., d. of Jno. M. E. Valk, and Capt. J. E. Sudler of Maryland, by the Rev. Edmund Withers, at "Summerfield", Northumberland Co. So. Ch., Feb. 21, 1867

VAN BENTHUYSEN

J. D. (Capt.), of New Orleans, and Camelia C. Cosby of Halifax Co., Va., by the Rev. John Cosby, at "Woodside", the residence of the bride's father. So. Ch., Dec. 19, 1867

Margaret, and the Rev. N. B. Harris of Jacksonville, Fla., by the Rev. Dr. Kinsolving, at Houston, Va. So. Ch., May 4, 1893

VANCE

Isabelle Dudley, and John Herbert Brotbeck, by the Rev. Joseph Baker, in Mapisco Church, Charles City Co., Va. So. Ch., Feb. 28, 1914

Lalla M., d. of A. Vance, Esq. of Gallipolis, and the Rev. John Moncure, rector of the parish, by the Rev. Jacob Brittingham of Clarksburg, W.Va. assisted by the Rev. J. Cowpland of Point Pleasant, W.Va., in St.

MARRIAGE NOTICES IN THE SOUTHERN CHURCHMAN WITH DATES OF PUBLICATION

Peter's Church, Gallipolis, Ohio. So. Ch., Mar. 6, 1884

VANDERVORT
E. M., and Sallie, only d. of E. M. and Christine Tunstill, all of Lewis Co., by the Rev. T. H. Lacy, rector of St. Paul's Church, at the residence of the bride's parents, in Weston, W.Va. So. Ch., July 15, 1886

VANDEVANTER
Charles O., of Loudoun Co., Va., and Virginia, youngest d. of the late Alexander Kilgour, Esq. of Montgomery Co., Md., by the Rev. Charles J. Kilgour, at the residence of the bride. So. Ch., Oct. 28, 1875

VAN DEVANTER
Mary N., d. of the late Cornelius Van Devanter of Clarke Co., Va., and W. Benton Crisp of Baltimore, by the rector, the Rev. P. P. Phillips, in Grace Church, Berryville, Va. So. Ch., Aug. 5, 1886

VANDEVENTER
James H., and Emeline M., d. of Col. Benj. Morgan, all of Clarke Co., Va., by the Rev. James T. F. Martin, at the residence of the bride's father. So. Ch., Nov. 5, 1868

VAN DORAN
Jacob, Jr., and Mary, d. of the late Robt. P. Bryarly, by the Rev. Wm. McGuire, at Federal Hill, Berkeley Co. So. Ch., Oct. 9, 1857

VAN DOREN
Meverell L., of Blenheim, Albemarle Co., Va., and Lucy Minor, youngest d. of the late Com. M. F. Maury, by the Rev. Dr. Woodbridge, in Monumental Church. So. Ch., July 12, 1877

VAN-HOOK
Charles Gordon, of Washington, D.C., and Evelyn Byrd, d. of R. P. Page, M.D. of Berryville, Va., by the Rev. P. P. Phillips, rector, in Grace Church, Berryville, Va. So. Ch., Sept. 29, 1892

VANN
Jesse John, of Monroe, Union Co., N.C., and Alice, eldest d. of the late Henry and Elizabeth S. MacRae of Chuckatuck, Nansemond Co., Va., by the Rev. Douglas Hooff, at the residence of the bride's mother. So. Ch., Apr. 21, 1887

VAN RENSSELAER
Cornelia, oldest d. of Cornelius G. Van Rensselaer of Greenbush, and Rev. Cornelius Winter Bolton, rector of Christ Church, Pelham, by the Rev. Alexander Dickson, at Greenbush. So. Ch., Sept. 26, 1856

VANWYCK
John C. (Dr.), of Baltimore, and Rosalie T., d. of Henry Berry, Esq. of Shepherdstown, Va., by the Rev. Dr. Andrews. So. Ch., Apr. 23, 1858

VAN ZANDT
Jeanie Cabell, youngest d. of Capt. and Mrs. N. H. Van Zandt of Virginia, and Francis J. O'Neill of Washington, D.C., by the Rev. Dr. George H. Houghton, in the Church of the

MARRIAGE NOTICES IN THE SOUTHERN CHURCHMAN WITH DATES OF PUBLICATION

    Transfiguration, New York. So. Ch., May 18, 1893

VARN
    Henry C., of South Carolina, and Mary L. Temple, by the Rev. Everard Meade, in St. Paul's Church. So. Ch., Oct. 1, 1885
    Marion L., d. of Mr. and Mrs. Henry A. Varn, and Lawrence B. Gray, at "Westwood", King and Queen Co., Va. So. Ch., Jan. 12, 1907

VASS
    Henry F., and Minnie H. France, by the Rev. Geo. W. Dame, in the Church of the Epiphany, Danville. So. Ch., Feb. 13, 1879
    James, of Culpeper Co., Va., and Anna E. Digges of Warrenton, Va., by the Rev. George W. Nelson, in St. James' Church, Warrenton, Va. So. Ch., Nov. 23, 1882

VAUGHAN
    Camilla, d. of the officiating clergyman, and William I. Griffin, by the Rev. M. H. Vaughan, in Christ Church, Elizabeth City, N.C. So. Ch., Nov. 16, 1882
    Mary L., d. of Dr. John N., deceased, and Henrietta Vaughan, and Edwin D. Bell, Esq. of Staunton, by the Rev. C. J. Gibson, at "Virginia Villa", the residence of Mrs. Vaughan, near Petersburg. So. Ch., Nov. 12, 1885
    Thomas W. (The Rev.), (colored), deacon in charge of the colored work, and Mary Henderson of Gordonsville, by the Rev. F. G. Scott, in St. Paul's Colored Mission Chapel, Gordonsville. So. Ch., Jan. 14, 1892

VEAL
    Joseph, of Rome, Ga., and Roberta Pierce of New Kent Co., Va., by the Rev. John P. Tyler assisted by the Rev. C. J. Gibson, at Petersburg, Va. So. Ch., May 29, 1890

VEALE
    Caroline Cordelia, and the Rev. R. H. Weller, rector of St. John's Church, Jacksonville, by the Rev. O. P. Thackara, in St. Peter's Church, Fernandina, Fla. So. Ch., Sept. 24, 1874

VENABLE
    Arthur Orr, of Atlanta, Ga., and Blanche B., d. of the late Wm. Ronald Cocke, by the Rev. Edward Valentine Jones, at Red Hills, in Fluvanna Co., Va. So. Ch., June 18, 1890
    Charles Woodson, formerly of Prince Edward Co., and Mary, second d. of Dr. N. H. and Susan W. Wooding of Pittsylvania Co., by the Rev. C. O. Prudon, in St. John's Church, at Mt. Airy, Pittsylvania Co., Va. So. Ch., Oct. 2, 1890
    Edward C., of Petersburg, Va., and Helen Skipwith Wilmer, by the Rt. Rev. J. P. B. Wilmer and the Rev. Dr. Slaughter, in Emmanuel Church, in Culpeper Co., Va. So. Ch., Jan. 3, 1878
    J. Cowan, of Christiansburg, Ky., and Lizzie Leigh Gibson, by the Rev. Bishop C. C. Penick, at Louisville, Ky. So. Ch., July 3, 1890

MARRIAGE NOTICES IN THE SOUTHERN CHURCHMAN WITH DATES OF PUBLICATION

Mary McLowoll, oldest d. of Prof. Charles S. Venable of the University, and Charles Launcelot Minor, M.D. of New York, by the Rev. G. L. Petrie assisted by the Rev. J. S. Hanckel, D.D., in the chapel of the University of Virginia. So. Ch., Dec. 18, 1890

William L., of Petersburg, Va., and Mary L., d. of Thomas Leiper Patterson of Cumberland, by the Rev. James W. Robins of Philadelphia, Pa., in Emanuel Church, at Cumberland, Md. So. Ch., May 16, 1872

VEST

Eliza Waller, eldest d. of W. W. Vest, Esq. of Williamsburg, and Edward S. Joynes, professor in William and Mary College, by the Rev. Dr. Minnigerode, at Williamsburg. So. Ch., Jan. 6, 1860

Jennie (Mrs.), of Charles City Co., Va., and E. A. Hatcher of Liberty, Va., by the Rev. John P. Tyler, at Berkeley, Charles City Co., Va. So. Ch., Dec. 20, 1888

VILES

John, and Mrs. Sarah A. Bradley, by the Rev. H. Wall, D.D.. So. Ch., Mar. 16, 1871

VOSE

Henry J., of New Orleans, and Fanny, d. of the late Littleton T. Waller of Williamsburg, Va., by the Rev. Moses D. Hoge, D.D., in Baltimore. So. Ch., Nov. 25, 1880

VOSS

Mary Thornton, second d. of Robert S. Voss, Esq., and Rev. Julius M. Dashiell, Vice-Rector of the College of St. James, Maryland, by the Rev. Dr. Kerfoot, at Hawthorne, the residence of the bride's father, in Rappahannock County, Va. So. Ch., Aug. 25, 1859

Robert S., Esq., and Mary, d. of Dr. Philip Thornton, at Montpellier, Rappahannock Co. So. Ch., Jan. 9, 1835

Susan Fitzhugh, d. of the late Robert S. Voss of Rappahannock Co., Va., and Keddor Meade Hite, by the Rev. James Hanckel, in Christ Church, Charlottesville. So. Ch., June 17, 1869

W

WADDEY
Eliza, and John T. W. Custis, both of Northampton Co., Va., by the Rev. John M. Chevers, in Christ Church, Eastville. So. Ch., June 5, 1857

WADDY
Frederick, and Maggie H. Downing, both of Northampton Co., Va., by the Rev. J. B. Craighill, at Chatham, the residence of the bride's father. So. Ch., Apr. 29, 1869

WADE
Mattie R., d. of the officiating clergyman, and Capt. John Lamb of Charles City Co., by the Rev. Dr. A. Wade, in the rectory at Charles City Co. So. Ch., Dec. 16, 1869

Walter L., of Lynchburg, Va., and Mrs. Sarah Stephenson, d. of Balton Brown of Southampton Co., Va., by the Rev. John Ridout, at Blandford, near Petersburg, Va. So. Ch., Oct. 5, 1893

WADLEY
H. J., Esq., of Wayne Co., Ga., and Nannie Leftwich, d. of Richard M. Taliaferro of New York, by the Rev. Robb White, in St. John's, Wytheville, Va. So. Ch., Sept. 21, 1876

WAGENER
Frances H., d. of the late Abraham N. Wagener, Esq. of Pen Yan, and the Rev. E. Folsom Baker, by the Rev. Dr. Mahan, in St. Stephen's Church, Olean, N.Y. So. Ch., Oct. 22, 1858

WAGGENER
Attarah Beall, d. of Col. Charles B. Waggener, and Edwin Lewis Neale, all of Mason Co., by the Rev. Horace Edwin Hayden, at Edge Hill, Mason Co., W.Va. So. Ch., Jan. 12, 1871

Charles B. (Col.), and Mrs. Catharine M. Murdock, d. of the late Hon. J. M. H. Beale, all of Mason Co., by the Rev. Horace Edwin Hayden, at the residence of Charles T. Beale, Mason Co., W.Va. So. Ch., Sept. 16, 1869

WAILES
Mary Eggleston (Mrs.), and Julian Taylor of Alexandria, Va., by the Rev. Charles White, D.D., at Hampden-Sydney, Va. So. Ch., Nov. 12, 1891

WAINWRIGHT
S. D., and Mrs. Hattie S. Carter, both of Norwood, Nelson Co., Va., by the Rev. Davis M. Wood, at Norwood, Va. So. Ch., Nov. 22, 1888

WALDEN
Mary Frances, d. of Wm. Walden, Esq., and D. B. Phillips, Surgeon U.S.N., all of Virginia, by the Rev. Wm. T. Leavell, at Glen Farm, Rappahannock Co., Va. So. Ch., Mar. 13, 1857

WALDHAUER
David (Capt.), of Savannah, Ga., (late Confederate service), and Janie P., second d. of Bickerton L.

MARRIAGE NOTICES IN THE SOUTHERN CHURCHMAN WITH DATES OF PUBLICATION

Winston, Esq., by the Rev. B. E. Habersham, at Signal Hill, Hanover Co., Va. So. Ch., Oct. 18, 1877

WALDRON

Susan E., of Berryville, Va., d. of the late Francis Waldron, and Thomas P. Cooke of Gloucester Co., by the Rev. P. P. Phillips, rector of Grace Church, in Berryville, Va. So. Ch., Jan. 29, 1891

WALKE

Caroline L., and Francis M. Whittle, Jr., by the Rt. Rev. F. M. Whittle and the Rev. Lewis Walke, in St. Stephen's Church, Cecil Co., Md. So. Ch., Dec. 9, 1880

Elizabeth L., eldest d. of the Rev. Lewis Walke, and Capt. Thomas A. Brander, P.A.C.S., by the Rev. F. M. Baker, in St. Luke's Church, Powhatan Co. So. Ch., Feb. 15, 1865

Lewis (The Rev.), and Mary T., second d. of Roger B. Atkinson, Esq., by the Rev. F. M. Baker, at Sherwood, Lunenburg Co., Va. So. Ch., Oct. 8, 1858

Louisa Atkinson, d. of the officiating clergyman, and Edwin B. Snead of Richmond, Va., by the Rev. Lewis Walke, in St. Stephen's Church, Cecil Co., Md. So. Ch., Jan. 24, 1884

Lucy H., d. of the Rev. Lewis Walke, and Thomas C. Cruikshank, Jr., by the Rev. Lewis Walke assisted by the Rev. F. M. Baker, in St. Stephen's Church, Cecil Co., Md. So. Ch., Dec. 23, 1875

WALKER

Avis, d. of Maj. D. N. Walker, and Percival Stuart Grant, by the Rev. Charles Minnigerode assisted by the Rev. Pike Powers, D.D., in St. Paul's Church, Richmond, Va. So. Ch., Oct. 29, 1885

B. F. (Dr.), of Augusta Co., Va., and Mattie Wright, by the Rev. G. H. Denny, at "The Forest", the residence of the bride's mother, Essex Co., Va. So. Ch., Nov. 2, 1876

Benedict, Jr., and Emma, d. of John T. Rice, Esq., by the Rev. T. Grayson Dashiell, at Laurel Spring, Westmoreland Co. So. Ch., Dec. 17, 1858

Bessie E. (Mrs.), d. of Charles Zogbaum, Esq., and the Rev. L. W. Rose of Boydton, Va., by the Rev. Richard Newton, D.D., at Germantown, Philadelphia. So. Ch., Dec. 18, 1884

C. B. (The Rev.), rector of Trinity Church, Edgefield, S.C., and C. S. Jeter, in Trinity Church, Edgefield, S.C. So. Ch., Feb. 18, 1848

C. Baldwin, of Baltimore, and Belle T. Willis, by the Rev. E. J. Willis, father of the bride, at Clarksburg, W.Va. So. Ch., Apr. 24, 1884

Charles C., of Richmond, Va., and Lucy Shackelford of Charlottesville, by the Rev. Green Shackelford assisted by the Rev. Frank Stringfellow, in Christ Church, Charlottesville, Va. So. Ch., Oct. 25, 1883

Charles D. (The Rev.), of

MARRIAGE NOTICES IN THE SOUTHERN CHURCHMAN WITH DATES OF PUBLICATION

Virginia, and Bessie Edmondston, d. of C. Zogbaum, Esq. of Germantown, by the Rev. T. S. Rumney, D.D. assisted by the Rev. C. Walker, D.D., in St. Peter's Church, Germantown, Pa. So. Ch., Sept. 16, 1875

Cornelius (The Rev.), and Margaret J., d. of James Fisher, Jr. of Richmond, by the Rev. Andrew Fisher. So. Ch., Dec. 24, 1847

Florence O., eldest d. of Thomas H. Walker, Esq., and William Ayre, Jr., all of Fairfax Co., by the Rev. John McGill, at the residence of the bride's parents. So. Ch., Feb. 7, 1878

Henry A., of Staunton, Va., and Emily Winslow, d. of James W. Sweet of Baltimore, Md., by the Rev. Maltbie D. Babcock, at the residence of the bride's parents. So. Ch., Oct. 3, 1889

James Pickens, of Barbour Co., W.Va., and Amy Perry Fitzsimons, by the Rev. Thos. P. Baker, at Adams Run, S.C. So. Ch., Oct. 31, 1908

James W., Jr., and Mary Jane, d. of Col. John A. Porter, all of Orange Co., by the Rev. John Cole. So. Ch., Sept. 5, 1856

Jane Middleton, and James Nutt, by the Rev. Ephraim Adams, at Level Fields, Lancaster Co. So. Ch., Dec. 11, 1835

Laura M., and the Rev. Wm. Meade Clarke of Mecklenburg Co., Va., by the Rev. John T. Clarke assisted by the Rev. C. Walker, D.D., in the Seminary Chapel, near Alexandria, Va. So. Ch., June 16, 1881

Lizzie M., and the Rev. S. S. Ware, by the Rev. C. Walker, D.D. assisted by the Rev. Nelson P. Dame, in the chapel of the Theological Seminary near Alexandria. So. Ch., Jan. 9, 1879

Margaret P., d. of the late Judge Richard W. Walker, and John M. Bolling of New York City, by the Rev. J. M. Bannister, D.D., at the residence of the bride's mother, at Huntsville, Ala. So. Ch., Nov. 24, 1881

Marshall, of Memphis, Tenn., and Cellie, d. of Wm. Garth, Esq. of Albemarle Co., Va., by the Rev. D. C. T. Davis, at Birdwood, Va. So. Ch., Dec. 12, 1856

Mary L., and J. Otis Fitchette, by the Rev. T. W. Jones, in the Episcopal Rectory, Liberty, Va. So. Ch., May 24, 1888

Mary N., d. of the Rev. C. Walker, D.D. of the Theological Seminary of Virginia, and the Rev. Nelson P. Dame of Blacksburg, Va., by the Rev. George W. Dame assisted by the Rev. W. W. Walker, in the chapel on Seminary Hill. So. Ch., July 4, 1878

Thomas L. (Dr.), and Kitty M., d. of Chiswell Dabney, Esq., all of Lynchburg, by the Rev. W. H. Kinckle, in St. Paul's Church. So.

MARRIAGE NOTICES IN THE SOUTHERN CHURCHMAN WITH DATES OF PUBLICATION

Ch., Aug. 22, 1856
W. H., of Ontario, Canada, and Miss M. D. Terrell of Hanover, Va., by the Rev. Robert R. Claiborne, at East View, Hanover Co., Va. So. Ch., Dec. 25, 1880

W. Woodson (The Rev.), of Mt. Jackson, Va., and Elizabeth P. G. Williams of Clarke Co., Va., by the Rev. W. T. Leavell assisted by the Rev. C. Walker, D.D., at "Smithfield", Clarke Co., Va. So. Ch., July 8, 1880

Walter, and Mary Sydnor, youngest d. of the officiating clergyman, the Rev. E. T. Perkins, D.D., in St. Paul's Church, Louisville. So. Ch., May 31, 1883

WALL

A. Newton (Mrs.), and Daniel A. Brooks, Jr., by the Rev. Henry T. Sharp, in St. Paul's Church, Caseyville, Ky. So. Ch., Mar. 2, 1871

Edward (The Rev.), and Mary S., d. of E. H. Chamberlayne, all of Richmond, by the Rev. J. Peterkin, D.D. So. Ch., May 11, 1876

Henry (The Rev.), and Judith W. Hansford, by the Rev. J. W. Chesley, at Green Height, King George Co., Va. So. Ch., Oct. 17, 1856

Henry (The Rev.), and Julia, d. of the late Addison Hansford, Esq. of King George Co., Va., by the Rev. H. R. Scott, at Green Height. So. Ch., Apr. 19, 1866

Julia, d. and sister of the officiating clergymen, and George Bell, by the Rev. Dr. Wall assisted by his son, the Rev. Edward Wall, in St. Paul's Church, Kent Co., Md. So. Ch., Dec. 25, 1884

Mary Chamberlayne, of Berryville, Va., and Willis Ray Gregg of Syracuse, N.Y., by the Rev. Edward Wall, father of the bride, assisted by the Rt. Rev. W. L. Gravatt, D.D., Bishop Coadjutor of the Diocese of West Virginia, in Grace Episcopal Church, Berryville, Va. So. Ch., Oct. 31, 1914

WALLACE

Benjamin Lawrence, of Tarrytown, N.Y., and Ellen Douglass, d. of J. Wallace Hooff, by the Rev. Douglass Hooff, in St. Paul's Church, Alexandria, Va. So. Ch., June 18, 1890

Carrie, and Dr. C. G. Wilson, both of Clarksville, Tenn., by the Rev. J. T. Hargrave, at the residence of the bride's mother. So. Ch., Oct. 20, 1887

Katharine Gordon, d. of the late Dr. J. Gordon Wallace, and the Rev. James Edward Poindexter, rector of St. Mary's Parish, Caroline Co., Va., by the Rev. E. C. Murdaugh, D.D., at the residence of the bride's mother, at Fredericksburg, Va. So. Ch., Nov. 1, 1883

Lucille, d. of Dr. John H. Wallace of Freder-

MARRIAGE NOTICES IN THE SOUTHERN CHURCHMAN WITH DATES OF PUBLICATION

icksburg, and James Carmichael, by the Rev. A. M. Randolph, in Fredericksburg. So. Ch., Dec. 13, 1861

Lucille, d. of the late Dr. J. Gordon and Elizabeth G. Wallace, and Thomas Pratt Yerby, Jr. of Spotsylvania Co., Va., by the Rev. John K. Mason, at the residence of the bride's mother, Fredericksburg, Va. So. Ch., May 26, 1887

Samuel, Esq. of Stafford Co., and Mary B., d. of the late Addison Hansford, Esq. of King George Co., Va., by the Rev. Henry Wall, brother-in-law of the bride, at Green Height. So. Ch., Nov. 7, 1856

Thomas, Esq., and Hallie E., d. of Judge R. C. L. and Mrs. Moncure of Stafford Co., Va., by the Rev. Mr. McBryde, in Stafford Co., Va. So. Ch., Jan. 27, 1881

Wm. L., of New York, and Caroline, d. of Lewis Hooff, Esq. of Alexandria, Va., by the Rev. James T. Johnston, in St. Paul's Church. So. Ch., June 26, 1851

WALLER

Caroline S., d. of Withers Waller, and J. North Caldwell of Greenbrier Co., W.Va., by the Rev. T. C. Page, in Clifton Chapel, Stafford Co., Va. So. Ch., May 5, 1887

Catherine, and John W. Speed, by the Rev. Wm. Hodges, at Williamsburg. So. Ch., May 24, 1839

Dabney J., of Caroline Co., and Alice C. Lee of Fredericksburg, by the Rev. J. G. Shackelford of Trinity Church, at A. H. Conway's, Fredericksburg, Va. So. Ch., Nov. 7, 1889

Eliza M., d. of Wm. M. Waller, Esq., and Alexander Duval, Esq., by the Rev. Mr. Sale, at Forest Hill, Amherst Co., Va. So. Ch., May 10, 1839

Fanny, d. of the late Littleton T. Waller of Williamsburg, Va., and Henry J. Vose of New Orleans, by the Rev. Moses D. Hoge, D.D., in Baltimore. So. Ch., Nov. 25, 1880

G. C. (The Rev.), rector of Zion Church, Louisville, and Kate M., d. of Mrs. Elizabeth H. Blackburn of Bowling Green, by the Rev. E. T. Perkins, D.D., rector of St. Paul's Church, Louisville, in Christ Church, Bowling Green, Ky. So. Ch., Mar. 16, 1876

Mattie P., and Wm. B. Hart, both of Spotsylvania Co., Va., by the Rev. Wm. W. Greene, at "Cedar Point", the residence of the bride's father. So. Ch., Feb. 8, 1872

Olivia D., and Capt. Wm. D. Waller, both of Spotsylvania Co., by the Rev. Wm. W. Greene, at "Cedar Point", Spotsylvania Co., Va. So. Ch., Oct. 31, 1867

Robert Page, of Norfolk, and Virginia Pelham, only d. of Mrs. Gen. J. E. B. Stuart*, by the Rev. W. Q. Hullihen assisted by the Rev. O. S.

* Given as printed

MARRIAGE NOTICES IN THE SOUTHERN CHURCHMAN WITH DATES OF PUBLICATION

Barten, in Staunton. So. Ch., Jan. 20, 1887
Thomas J., s. of Col. Thos. Waller of Stafford, and Alice Page, d. of Wm. A. Nelson, former surgeon of the U.S. Navy, by the Rev. T. C. Page assisted by the Rev. John Moncure, in Clifton Chapel, Stafford Co., Va. So. Ch., Feb. 7, 1889
Wm. D. (Capt.), and Olivia D. Waller, both of Spotsylvania Co., by the Rev. Wm. W. Greene, at "Cedar Point", Spotsylvania Co., Va. So. Ch., Oct. 31, 1867

WALLIS
Samuel A. (The Rev.), of Fairfax Co., and Mary, d. of the late Edgar Snowden, by the Rev. H. Suter, at the residence of the bride's mother, in Alexandria. So. Ch., May 8, 1890

WALPOLE
Clare H., and Nina Nelson Gardner, by the Rev. Mr. Clark, at Meadowbrook, Nelson Co., Va. So. Ch., Sept. 18, 1884

WALSTON
Thomas C., Esq., and Sallie Parker, only d. of Mrs. Sarah A. P. Upshur, by the Rev. Arthur Johns, in Christ Church, Eastville, Va. So. Ch., Apr. 12, 1877

WALTERS
Margaret V., of Richmond, and Dr. Thomas S. Michaels of Henrico Co., by the Rev. Geo. C. Sutton, at Richmond, Va. So. Ch., July 1, 1880

WALTHALL
Ed. C., of Mississippi, and Mary L. Jones of Mecklenburg, Va., by the Rev. Jno. Cosby, at St. Leon. So. Ch., Feb. 10, 1860
Welson Q., Esq., of Alabama, and Bettie B., second d. of Dr. Geo. Semple, by the Rev. Wm. F. M. Jacobs, in St. John's Church, Hampton. So. Ch., June 15, 1860

WALTHOUR
Robert H., and Anna Wilhelmina, eldest d. of Wm. S. Bogart, all of Savannah, by the Rev. Charles H. Strong, in St. John's Church, Savannah, Ga. So. Ch., Mar. 1, 1883

WALTON
Florence, a ward of the Hon. S. A. Miller, and Governeur Morris of Huntington, W.Va., by the Rev. C. M. Callaway assisted by the Rev. Edward Valentine Jones, in St. John's Church, Charleston, W.Va. So. Ch., Dec. 5, 1872
Richard Lee, of Norfolk, Va., and Laura Virginia de Lony, by the Rev. R. T. Davis, D.D., at the residence of the bride's uncle, Maj. Charles H. Lee of Leesburg, Va. So. Ch., Apr. 11, 1889
Willie (Miss), and Eppa Rixey, both of Culpeper Co., by the Rev. John McGill, in Christ Church, Brandy Station, Va. So. Ch., July 6, 1882

WANHOP
Lizzie R., and Alexander R. Green, by the Rev. O. A. Kinsolving, in St. John's Church, Halifax C.H. So. Ch., Nov. 16,

MARRIAGE NOTICES IN THE SOUTHERN CHURCHMAN WITH DATES OF PUBLICATION

1871
WARD
Eddie K., d. of the officiating minister, and Dr. Pearson Chapman of Maryland, by the Rev. Wm. N. Ward, at Bladensfield, Westmoreland Co., Va. So. Ch., Nov. 30, 1876

Elizabeth, of Northampton Co., Va., and Wm. R. W. Kennedy of Maryland, by the Rev. J. B. Craighill, at "Occahannock Neck." So. Ch., Jan. 6, 1870

Geo. W., Jr., of Abingdon, Va., and L. A. C. Preston, second d. of the late Hon. Walter Preston, by the Rev. Thos. W. Humes, D.D., at the residence of the bride's mother, Mrs. A. Garnett Preston, in Knoxville, Tenn. So. Ch., Dec. 26, 1878

Henry M., and Mary Caroline Jennings, both of Lewis Co., W.Va., by the Rev. Andrew Fisher, at the residence of the bride's father, in Lewis Co., W.Va. So. Ch., Feb. 29, 1872

Julian F. (Dr.), of Baltimore, Md., and Mrs. Nellie Wirt of Cecil Co., Md., by the Rev. J. R. Hubard, D.D., at the residence of the bride's brother-in-law, R. T. Barton, Winchester, Va. So. Ch., Feb. 4, 1886

Martha, d. of the Rev. Wm. N. Ward, and James Cary, Jr. of Baltimore, Md., at Bladensfield, Richmond Co., Va. So. Ch., July 1, 1869

Mary A., and P. H. Bool, by the Rev. J. B. Craighill, at the residence of Mrs. Tabitha Ward, Northampton Co. So. Ch., Apr. 22, 1869

Mathias M., of New York, and Mary W., eldest d. of the late Rev. Thos. Smith, former rector of the Episcopal Church in Parkersburg, by the Rev. E. T. Perkins. So. Ch., Aug. 11, 1848

William N. (The Rev.), of Bowling Green, Caroline Co., Va., and Mary Blincoe, by the Rev. George Adie, at Leesburg, Va. So. Ch., Aug. 26, 1836

WARDWELL
Margaret, of New York, and Maxwell Wyeth of Philadelphia, by the Rev. Dr. Neilson McVicar, at South Orange, N.J. So. Ch., Oct. 3, 1889

WARE
J. Algie C., of Galveston, Tex., and Samuel H. Hardwick of Montgomery, Ala., by the Rev. R. S. Barrett, in St. Paul's Church, Henderson, Ky. So. Ch., Oct. 25, 1883

J. W. (The Rev.), and Annie S., d. of John Nottingham, Esq. of Northampton Co., Va., by the Rev. S. S. Ware assisted by the Rev. J. J. Gravatt, in Christ Church, Eastville, Northampton Co., Va. So. Ch., Nov. 6, 1879

J. W., Jr., and Elizabeth H. T. Leavell, by the Rev. J. W. Ware and the Rev. P. N. McDonald, at "Media", Jefferson Co., W.Va. So. Ch., Mar. 18, 1916

Jaqueline, and Severn M. Nottingham, by the Rev. J. W. Ware, in St. Stephen's Church,

MARRIAGE NOTICES IN THE SOUTHERN CHURCHMAN WITH DATES OF PUBLICATION

Culpeper, Va. So. Ch., June 22, 1912
Lucy B., d. of Col. S. W. Ware, and Edward P. C. Lewis, all of Clarke Co., Va., by the Rev. H. Suter, at the residence of the bride's father, Clarke Co., Va. So. Ch., Apr. 1, 1859
R. L., and Nannie R., d. of Dr. James H. Latane, all of Essex, by the Rev. H. W. L. Temple, at Mahockany. So. Ch., Dec. 7, 1860
S. S. (The Rev.), and Lizzie M. Walker, by the Rev. C. Walker, D.D, assisted by the Rev. Nelson P. Dame, in the chapel of the Theological Seminary near Alexandria. So. Ch., Jan. 9, 1879
See also BRITTON, Elizabeth Alexander Ware (Mrs.)

WARFIELD
Evan W. (Dr.), of Maryland, and Julia Gilmer, youngest d. of Col. Wm. H. Anthony, by the Rt. Rev. A. M. Randolph, at the home of the bride, 403 E. Main St., Richmond, Va. So. Ch., July 10, 1890

WARING
Addie J., only d. of W. L. Waring of Bendour, Goochland Co., Va., and C. P. Smith, by the Rev. P. M. Boyden, at the residence of the bride's father. So. Ch., Nov. 4, 1886
Irene Bankhead, and Lucius Ashton Harrison, by the Rev. H. G. Lane of Newport News, in St. Mary's Chapel, Charles City Co., Va. So. Ch., Oct. 23, 1920
John L., of Richmond, Va., and P. Blair, d. of Dr. John B. Harvie, by the Rev. Frank Stringfellow, in Immanuel Church, Powhatan Co., Va. So. Ch., May 18, 1882
Priscilla M., late of Prince George's Co., Md., and the Rev. David W. Tolford of Gambier, Ohio, by the Rev. Ethan Allen, Dayton, Ohio. So. Ch., Nov. 22, 1839
William L., of Essex Co., and Rosalie V., d. of the late Charles Taylor of King George Co., Va., by the Rev. T. E. Locke, at Oaken Brow. So. Ch., Nov. 12, 1858

WARNER
Loren D., and Lucie E. Jeffries, both of Richmond Co., by the Rev. Andrew Fisher, at the Glebe. So. Ch., Sept. 7, 1860
Virginia Craddock, of Portsmouth, Va., and Joseph Eager Caldwell of Wytheville, Va., by the Rev. Braxton Bryan, in Grace Church, Petersburg, Va. So. Ch., May 22, 1915
William A., and Lucy Phenix, by the Rev. Dr. Grammer assisted by the Rev. Mr. Kaze, at the home of Joseph A. Sprigg, Baltimore. So. Ch., Nov. 8, 1877

WARRELL
Eloise, of Richmond, Va., and Edward V. Sparhawk, editor of the Petersburg Intelligencer, by the Rev. Wm. H. Hart, Richmond, Va. So. Ch., Aug. 11, 1837

WARREN

MARRIAGE NOTICES IN THE SOUTHERN CHURCHMAN WITH DATES OF PUBLICATION

Allen A., of Richmond, Va., and Mary M., eldest d. of M. W. Harrison, Esq. of Lewis Co., W.Va., by the Rev. W. H. H. Powers, in St. Paul's Church, Weston, W.Va. So. Ch., Dec. 25, 1879

Harriet, d. of Dr. W. Warren formerly of Edenton, N.C., and F. H. Harris, by the Rev. W. H. Pendleton, at Delecarlia, Bedford Co., Va. So. Ch., Dec. 8, 1870

James M. (Dr.), of New Hope, Augusta Co., Va., and Willett, d. of Charles A. Sprinkel of Harrisonburg, Va., by the Rev. O. S. Bunting, at the residence of the bride's father. So. Ch., June 14, 1883

John A. (Dr.), of Coahoma Co., Miss., and Mrs. Martha B. Washington, d. of the late Jona. Bliss, Esq. of Gainesville, by the Rev. A. A. Morse, in Gainesville, Ala. So. Ch., Dec. 25, 1879

Sallie A., youngest d. of William R. Warren, Esq., and the Rev. Robb White of Wytheville, Va., by the Rev. A. W. Weddell assisted by the Rev. H. B. Lee, in Harrisonburg, Va. So. Ch., Dec. 2, 1875

WARRINER
S.S., and James Bedsu of England, by the Rev. P. F. Berkeley, at Oaklevel, the residence of the bride in the county of Amelia. So. Ch., Mar. 25, 1880

WARROCK
Sarah, d. of John Warrock, Esq., and William Miller, all of Richmond, Va., by the Rev. George Woodbridge. So. Ch., Dec. 1, 1837

WARWICK
Eliza G., d. of James W. Warwick, Esq., and John W. Stephenson, Esq., all of Bath Co., by the Rev. George L. Brown, at "Warwickton", the residence of the bride's father, Bath Co., Va. So. Ch., Nov. 21, 1878

Elsie Florence, eldest d. of A. Warwick, and Geo. A. Barksdale, all of Richmond, by the Rev. Chas. Minnigerode, at the residence of the bride's father. So. Ch., Jan. 27, 1860

L. Constance, d. of Wm. S. Warwick, and Thomas P. McDowell, by the Rev. Thomas Ambler, Powhatan Co., Va. So. Ch., Feb. 27, 1857

WASHINGTON
Anna Maria, d. of the late Col. John A. Washington of Mount Vernon, and the Rev. Beverly D. Tucker of Warsaw, Va., by the Rev. Mr. Leavell, in Zion Church, Charles Town, W.Va. So. Ch., July 31, 1873

Anne Maria, d. of the late Thomas Blackburn Washington, Esq. of Claymont, Jefferson Co., W.Va., and James Alfred Ewing, by the Rev. John Piper assisted by the Rev. E. W. Syle, D.D., at the British Legation, Yedo, Japan, before Sir Harry Parkes, K.C.B. So. Ch., June 19, 1879

Betty, d. of John C.

MARRIAGE NOTICES IN THE SOUTHERN CHURCHMAN WITH DATES OF PUBLICATION

Washington, Esq. of Vernon, and John Lewis Peyton, Esq. of Staunton, Va., by the Rev. Frederick Fitzgerald, at Vernon, Lenoir Co., N.C. So. Ch., Jan. 4, 1856

Bushrod C., Jr. of Charles Town, W.Va., and Emma, youngest d. of Wm. T. Allen of Clarke Co., Va., by the Rev. P. P. Phillips, rector of Grace Church, Berryville, Va., at Balclutha, Clarke Co., Va. So. Ch., Oct. 20, 1887

Bushrod Corbin, Esq. of Jefferson Co., and Emma Edwards, youngest d. of Thos. H. Willis, Esq. of Charles Town, by the Rev. W. H. Meade, in Zion Church, Charles Town. So. Ch., Nov. 28, 1878

Eleanor Love, d. of the late Col. John A. Washington of Mount Vernon, Va., and Julian Howard, by the Rev. Dr. Meade and the Rev. Mr. Tucker, in Zion Church, Charles Town, W.Va. So. Ch., May 20, 1880

Geo., and Emily Serena, d. of Col. Geo. A. Porterfield, all of Charles Town, Jefferson Co., W.Va., by the Rev. Dallas Tucker, in Zion Church. So. Ch., Feb. 25, 1886

George, and Agnes W. Wirt, both of Westmoreland, Va., by the Rev. Wm. C. Latane, in St. Peter's Church, Oak Grove, Va. So. Ch., July 20, 1893

J. Augusta, and Dabney E. Wirt, by the Rev. J. W. Chesley, in St. Peter's Church, Westmoreland Co., Va. So. Ch., Nov. 30, 1855

J. Boyd, of Caroline Co., and Anna Ratcliffe, d. of the late Maj. W. W. Thornton of Brentsville, by the Rev. A. P. Gray, in St. James' Church, Brentsville, Va. So. Ch., Aug. 21, 1890

John Augustine, and Jeannie K., d. of Mrs. Susan W. and the late Rev. Charles E. Ambler, by the Rev. Dallas Tucker, at the residence of the bride's mother, Charles Town, W.Va. So. Ch., Dec. 18, 1890

John H., and Selina D., third d. of Maj. Richard H. Carter, all of Fauquier Co., Va., by the Rev. Jno. McGill, at "Glenn Welby", the residence of the bride's father. So. Ch., Nov. 16, 1871

John P., and Annie, d. of Geo. E. Grymes, all of King George Co., by the Rev. Jas. W. Shields, at Mt. Stuart, King George Co. So. Ch., Dec. 23, 1875

L. W. (Col.), of Jefferson Co., Va., and Ella M., d. of G. W. Bassett, Esq., by the Rev. G. S. Carraway, at Clover Lea, Hanover Co., Va. So. Ch., Nov. 16, 1860

Lawrence, of "Wareland", Fauquier Co., and Fanny, d. of the late Thomas Lackland of Jefferson Co., by the Rev. Wm. H. Meade, in Zion Church, Charles Town, Jefferson Co., Va. So. Ch., Aug. 3, 1876

Lena, eldest d. of Col.

- 255 -

MARRIAGE NOTICES IN THE SOUTHERN CHURCHMAN WITH DATES OF PUBLICATION

Robert J. Washington, and Phillip C. Hungerford, all of Westmoreland Co., Va., by the Rev. Alfred Harding, rector of St. Paul's Church, Washington, D.C. So. Ch., Aug. 20, 1891

Louisa Fontaine, and Philip Dawson of Lynchburg, s. of the late Nicholas Dawson of Fairfax Co., Va., by the Rt. Rev. B. D. Tucker of Southern Virginia, uncle of the bride, and the Rev. William G. Pendleton, D.D., rector of the Virginia Episcopal School and brother-in-law of the groom, at the home of the bride's mother, Mrs. Lawrence Washington, at Washington, D.C. So. Ch., July 9, 1921

Malcolm B., Esq., of Warrenton, and Fannie W., d. of Charles H. Hunton, Esq., by the Rev. W. A. Alrich, at "Cerro Gordo", Prince William Co., Va. So. Ch., Sept. 17, 1868

Martha B. (Mrs.), d. of the late Jona. Bliss, Esq. of Gainesville, and Dr. John A. Warren of Coahoma Co., Miss., by the Rev. W. A. Morse, in Gainsville, Ala. So. Ch., Dec. 25, 1879

Mary, d. of Lawrence Washington, Esq. of Westmoreland, and Dr. Walker Washington of Caroline Co., by the Rev. J. W. Chesley, at Blenham, Westmoreland Co., Va. So. Ch., Jan. 9, 1857

Mary A., and Andrew C. Fisher, by the Rev. Wm. C. Latane, in St. Peter's Church, Oak Grove, Va. So. Ch., Oct. 6, 1881

R. J., and Bettie P. Wirt, both of Westmoreland Co., Va., by the Rev. William C. Chesley, at Wirtland, the residence of the bride's father. So. Ch., Dec. 5, 1867

Richard B., Jr., now of Silver City, N.M., formerly of Jefferson Co., W.Va., and Nannie Sturgeon of Louisville, by the Rev. Dr. Perkins, in St. Paul's Church, Louisville, Ky. So. Ch., Dec. 4, 1884

Sallie Hay, and Dr. Socrates Maupin, by the Rt. Rev. Richard Channing Moore. So. Ch., Dec. 22, 1837

Thomas B., of Jefferson Co., W.Va., and Ellen T., d. of the late Dr. R. S. Blackburn of Clarke Co., Va., by the Rev. Dr. G. H. Norton, D.D., in Alexandria. So. Ch., Nov. 12, 1874

Walker (Dr.), of Caroline Co., and Mary, d. of Lawrence Washington, Esq. of Westmoreland, by the Rev. J. W. Chesley, at Blenham, Westmoreland Co., Va. So. Ch., Jan. 9, 1857

WATKINS

Agnes Tenable, of Richmond, Va., and Hugh Cabell Winfree of Drewry's Bluff, Va., by the Rev. G. Otis Mead, at the residence of Mr. Allen Harless, in Christiansburg, Va. So. Ch., Mar. 29, 1913

Anna A., of Louisa Co., and Thomas Wayant of Albemarle

MARRIAGE NOTICES IN THE SOUTHERN CHURCHMAN WITH DATES OF PUBLICATION

Co., by the Rev. L. R. Combs, at the residence of the bride's mother. So. Ch., July 1, 1886

Anna E., only d. of the late Dr. Austin Watkins of Nottoway, and George W. Robertson of Richmond, by the Rev. C. J. Gibson, at Rosewood, Nottoway Co. So. Ch., Feb. 5, 1858

Basil Kirke, of Danville, Va., and Laura Cunningham, d. of B. F. Garrett of Danville, Va., by the Rev. W. M. Clark, at the home of the Rev. W. M. Clark, 1008 Park avenue, Richmond, Va. So. Ch., Jan. 4, 1913

Claiborne, and Virginia T., d. of the late J. B. Abbott, all of Richmond, by the Rev. Joshua Peterkin, in St. James' Church, Richmond. So. Ch., Mar. 14, 1856

Ivy, of London, England, and the Rev. Charles W. F. Smith,* assistant minister, St. Paul's Church, Richmond, Va., by the Rev. Beverly D. Tucker, D.D., rector of St. Paul's Church, Richmond, assisted by the Rev. Vincent L. Bennett, rector of St. Michael's, and by the Rev. James DeWolf Hubbard, in St. Michael's Church, Milton, Mass. So. Ch., Dec. 22, 1934

Jesse, and Sarah Ann, d. of Robert Morgan, deceased, by George Thomas, Esq., in Richmond Co. So. Ch., Jan. 22, 1836

Mary L., d. of Edward O. Watkins, Esq., and Capt. Paul A. Clay of Bedford Co., by the Rev. William H. Hart, at Presque Isle, Chesterfield Co., Va. So. Ch., Dec. 1, 1837

Mary N., d. of Capt. Henry A. Watkins, all of Charlotte, Va., and Marshall L. Harris, by the Rev. Andrew Hart. So. Ch., Mar. 1, 1839

Nannie W., and George S. Hairston, both of Henry Co., Va., by the Rev. Jno. R. Lee, at "Shawnee", the residence of the bride's father. So. Ch., Jan. 6, 1870

Tillie, and Thomas L. Kyle of Lynchburg, Va., by the Rev. A. S. Lloyd, at "Scotland", the home of the bride's parents in Appomattox Co., Va. So. Ch., Nov. 29, 1883

WATSON

Ann Virginia, d. of the late Dr. Geo. Watson, and Robert S. Archer, all of Richmond, by the Rev. F. D. Goodwin, in St. Paul's Church, Richmond, Va. So. Ch., Dec. 5, 1856

Frank C., of Jacksonville, Fla., and Margaret Chalmers of Smithfield, by the Rev. David Barr, in Christ Church, Smithfield, Va. So. Ch., Dec. 2, 1886

Grace D., d. of the late Richard R. Watson, Esq. of Albemarle Co., Va., and John B. Tunstall of Marshall Co., Miss., by the Rev. Edward W. Ingle, at Coyners Spring, Va. So. Ch., Feb. 22, 1877

J. Henry (The Rev.), rector of the Church of the Good

---

* Not recorded in the Vestry Minutes of St. Paul's Church, Richmond, Va., as having any connection with that church

MARRIAGE NOTICES IN THE SOUTHERN CHURCHMAN WITH DATES OF PUBLICATION

Shepherd, Hartford, Conn., and Susan M., eldest d. of the officiating clergyman, the Rev. Dr. E. A. Hoffman, dean of the General Theological Seminary, in Trinity Chapel, New York. So. Ch., Nov. 2, 1882

John T., Jr., and Mary V. Green, both of Danville, by the Rev. O. S. Bunting of Trenton, N.J. assisted by the Rev. G. W. Damo, D.D. and the Rev. Alex. Martin, D.D. of Danville, in Epiphany Church, Danville, Va. So. Ch., Dec. 24, 1891

Jos. T., and Mary E. Tyler, d. of the late Edmund Tyler of Loudoun Co., by the Rev. O. A. Kinsolving, in the church at Aldie. So. Ch., Dec. 16, 1869

Maggie L., and Richard N. Timberlake, both of Spotsylvania Co., by the Rev. J. Green Shackelford, rector of Trinity Church, Fredericksburg, in St. George's Chapel, Spotsylvania Co. So. Ch., Jan. 26, 1888

Manie F., and Marcellus N. Barnes, both of Fairmont, by the Rev. G. A. Gibbons, in Christ Church, Fairmont, W.Va. So. Ch., Jan. 2, 1879

Margaret F., and Richard P. Williams of New York, by the Rev. Dr. Minnigerode, at the residence of the bride's father, corner of Franklin and Adams Streets, Richmond. So. Ch., June 21, 1883

Marietta W., d. of Mrs. Elizabeth Watson, and Carleton B. Hazard, by the Rev. J. Green Shackelford, at Chatham, Fredericksburg, Va. So. Ch., May 3, 1888

Mary, d. of Capt. John Watson of Warren, R.I., and the Rev. James Mulchahey, rector of St. Mary's Church, Portsmouth, by the Rev. Mr. Hathaway, in St. Mark's Church, Warren, R.I. So. Ch., Dec. 17, 1847

Mary Jane, d. of Matthew Watson, Esq., and Dr. Alfred Moore of Huntsville, Ala., by the Rt. Rev. Richard Channing Moore, at the residence of George L. Sampson. So. Ch., Sept. 30, 1836

Mary R., d. of Otis Watson, Esq., of Marion Co., W.Va., and Conrad A. Sipe of Waynesburg, Pa., by the Rev. G. A. Gibbons, at the residence of the bride's father. So. Ch., Dec. 5, 1878

Virginia M., d. of Thomas S. Watson, and Charles M. Barker of Clarksville, Tenn., by the Rev. J. M. Rawlings, at Brackett's, Louisa Co., Va. So. Ch., Dec. 25, 1879

Walter D., s. of Garret F. Watson, Esq., and Vinna P. Seldon, d. of Maj. John A. Seldon, Esq., all of Richmond, by the Rev. J. G. Armstrong, D.D., in Monumental Church. So. Ch., Apr. 24, 1884

William V. R., of Houston, Tex., and Bettie Lane, d. of the late John F. Scott of Fredericksburg, Va., by the Rev. P. G. Robert, at the residence of Frank Carter, in St. Louis. So. Ch., Mar. 7,

MARRIAGE NOTICES IN THE SOUTHERN CHURCHMAN WITH DATES OF PUBLICATION

1878

WATT
- Cornelia M., d. of George Watt, and John F. Glenn, all of Richmond, Va., by the Rev. Chas. H. Read assisted by the Rev. Henry Wall, at the residence of the bride's father, Richmond, Va. So. Ch., Jan. 1, 1874
- Norman Randolph, and Dorothy, d. of Mr. and Mrs. Eugene Cushing Dame of Richmond, Va., by the Rev. Wm. M. Clark, D.D., in St. James' Church, Richmond, Va. So. Ch., June 29, 1912

WATTERS
- S. Paxson (The Rev.), rector of St. Stephen's Church, Culpeper, Va., and Lydia Gates, d. of the late David Hansborough of Albemarle Co., Va., by the Rev. A. T. Steele, in St. Mark's Church, Washington, D.C. So. Ch., Jan. 22, 1891

WATTLES
- Caroline, d. of Nathaniel Wattles, Esq., and the Rev. Charles E. Pleasants of Philadelphia, by the Rev. John T. Johnston. So. Ch., Jan. 15, 1836
- Caroline C., d. of H. S. Wattles of Alexandria, Va., and Thomas A. Lee of Staunton, Va., by the Rev. Dr. George H. Norton assisted by the Rev. Reverdy Estill and the Rev. Frank Stringfellow, in St. Paul's Church, Alexandria, Va. So. Ch., July 7, 1881

WATTS
- Emma Gilmer, d. of the late Gen. Edward Watts, and Lt. Geo. Watson Carr, 9th Infantry, U.S.A., by the Rev. P. Tinsley, in St. John's Church, Roanoke Co. So. Ch., Dec. 7, 1860
- Legh R., Esq., and Mattie W. Peters, both of Portsmouth, Va., by the Rev. R. H. McKim, at the residence of the bride's father. So. Ch., Dec. 3, 1868
- Mary Reed, d. of Judge Legh R. Watts, and Goodrich Hatton, by the Rev. John D. Powell, at 202 Middle St., Portsmouth, Va., the residence of the bride's parents. So. Ch., Nov. 30, 1893
- Sara Campbell, d. of Judge Frederick Watts of Carlisle, and Samuel Richards Johnston of Alexandria, Va., by the Rev. W. C. Leverett, in St. John's Church, Carlisle, Pa. So. Ch., Oct. 14, 1886
- Winifred Washington, d. of Judge Legh Richmond and Mrs. Mattie Peters Watts of Portsmouth, Va., and the Rt. Rev. William Ambrose Brown, D.D., LL.D., Bishop of Southern Virginia, by the Rt. Rev. Robert C. Jett, D.D., retired Bishop of Southwestern Virginia, assisted by Philip DuMond Davis, in St. John's Church, Portsmouth. So. Ch., Sept. 16, 1939

See also MORRIS, Alice W. (Mrs.)

WAUGH
- Isabella J., only d. of Pom-

MARRIAGE NOTICES IN THE SOUTHERN CHURCHMAN WITH DATES OF PUBLICATION

broke E. Waugh of Amherst Co., and James Woods, s. of Col. Thomas D. Woods of Amherst Co., Va., by the Rev. J. P. Laurence, at the residence of the bride's father. So. Ch., Nov. 7, 1878

WAYANT
Thomas, of Albemarle Co., and Anna A. Watkins of Louisa Co., by the Rev. L. R. Combs, at the residence of the bride's mother. So. Ch., July 1, 1886

WAYLAND
J. F., of Albemarle Co., Va., and Lillie M., d. of Dr. A. T. Bledsoe of Baltimore, by the Rev. T. U. Dudley, in Baltimore. So. Ch., July 21, 1870

WEADON
William Lee (Dr.), of Fauquier Co., Va., and Mabel C. Faulconer of Low Moor, Va., by the Rev. P. N. McDonald, at Mt. Carbon, W.Va. So. Ch., June 5, 1909

WEATHERS
William, of Kentucky, and Mary Ellen Douglass, youngest d. of the late Hon. Beverly Douglass of King William Co., by the Rev. S. S. Hepbron, at Coons, King William Co. So. Ch., Nov. 5, 1891

WEAVER
Janet Henderson, d. of the late Arel Weaver, and Norman Randolph, by the Rev. Charles K. Jenkins, at Warrenton, Fauquier Co. So. Ch., June 17, 1880
Robert C., of Warren Co., Va., and Nannie L. Dodd, by the Rev. Mr. Turbin, at the residence of the bride's father, near Bealton, Fauquier Co., Va. So. Ch., Nov. 8, 1883
Virgil Gardner, of Solma, Ala., and Rosa Burnet Doans of Gloucester Co., Va., by the Rev. Y. Hundley, in Abingdon Church, Gloucester Co., Va. So. Ch., July 22, 1875

WEBB
B. C. (The Rev.), of St. Luke's Parish, and Alison, d. of Joshua Lockwood, Esq. of Charleston, S.C., by the Rt. Rev. Dr. Bowen. So. Ch., Mar. 11, 1836
Gordon, of New Kent Co., and Mary G. Harrison, d. of Col. Randolph Harrison, by the Rev. W. C. Meredith assisted by the Rev. Lyman B. Wharton, in Bruton Parish Church, Williamsburg, Va. So. Ch., Feb. 22, 1877
Joseph P., and Annie J., eldest d. of A. S. Darden, Esq. of Suffolk, Va., by the Rev. James Murray, at the residence of the bride's father. So. Ch., Feb. 10, 1881
Louisa E., d. of the Rev. Wellington E. Webb, and the Rev. T. Lewis Bannister, rector of St. Thomas' Church, Greenville, Ala., by the rector of St. Paul's Church, Borgen, N.J., in St. Paul's Church, Borgen, N.J. So. Ch., Nov. 16, 1871
Mary G. (Mrs.), eldest d. of Col. R. Harrison of Williamsburg, and Wm. Hartwell Macon of Hanover Co., by the Rev. S. S. Hepbron, in the Protestant Episcopal Church, Williamsburg, Va. So. Ch., Dec. 24, 1885

MARRIAGE NOTICES IN THE SOUTHERN CHURCHMAN WITH DATES OF PUBLICATION

WEBBER
Mary Reynolds, eldest d. of the late Gen. J. C. Webber, U.S.Vol. and gr.d. of the late Maj. Wm. P. Bainbridge, U.S.A., and the Rev. Charles J. S. Mayo, by the Rev. J. J. Gravatt assisted by the Rev. J. B. Newton, in St. John's Church, Hampton, Va. So. Ch., Oct. 12, 1892

WEBER
Mary Rose, of Portland, Ore., and Capt. J. H. Townsend, Jr. of the American Red Cross, in St. George's English Church, Paris, France. So. Ch., Nov. 1, 1919

WEBSTER
Lizzie, and Hartwell Stoneham, both of Lancaster, by the Rev. Henry L. Derby, at Merry Point, Lancaster, Va. So. Ch., Dec. 11, 1884

WECKHAM
Georgianna, d. of the late George Weckham of U.S. Navy, and Lt. Wm. H. Fitzhugh Lee of U.S. Army, by the Rev. Dr. Wade, at Shirley, in Charles City Co. So. Ch., Apr. 15, 1859

WEED
Hannah Elizabeth, d. of Joseph A. Weed, and Dr. Richard D. Addington, all of Richmond, Va., by the Rev. J. Ambler Weed, in Monumental Church, Richmond, Va. So. Ch., Nov. 9, 1855

WEEDON
J. B., and Mary Alice Staples, by the Rev. A. J. Willis, at "Poplar Hill", King George Co., Va. So. Ch., Nov. 1, 1888

WEIR
Edna Vaulx, d. of Edgar V. and Eugenia A. Weir of Prince William Co., Va., and James W. Birkett of England, by the Rev. A. P. Gray, in Trinity Church, Manassas, Va. So. Ch., Dec. 29, 1881

Emma B., d. of James V. Weir of Clarke Co., Va., and Daniel D. Martin of Cass Co., Mo., by the Rev. J. F. Hoff. So. Ch., June 11, 1858

Joan D. (Mrs.), nee Douglas, and Joseph D. Dixon of Lancastershire, England, by the Rev. A. P. Gray, at "Liberia", Prince William Co., Va. So. Ch., Oct. 23, 1879

Julia E., and Josiah Wilcoxon, both of Prince William Co., Va., by the Rev. John Towles. So. Ch., Feb. 27, 1857

Lizzie B., d. of R. C. and Mary Weir of Manassas, and Henderson F. Tompkins of Fauquier, by the Rev. A. P. Gray, in Trinity Church, Manassas. So. Ch., Feb. 1, 1883

Walter, of Prince William Co., and Elizabeth Joan Douglass of Williamsburg, by the Rev. Andrew Fisher, at Zoar, King William Co. So. Ch., Oct. 24, 1867

WEISIGER
Bessie Abbott, eldest d. of Ryland R. Weisiger, Esq., and William, youngest s. of Maj. Charles Old, all of Powhatan Co., by the Rev. C. O. Pruden, in Grace Church, Powhatan Co., Va. So. Ch., Aug. 17, 1893

Cary N., of Memphis, and

MARRIAGE NOTICES IN THE SOUTHERN CHURCHMAN WITH DATES OF PUBLICATION

Bettie H., d. of Mrs. M. W. and the late Judge Robert W. Humphreys of Clarksville, Tenn., by the Rev. P. A. Fitts, in Trinity Church, Clarksville, Tenn. So. Ch., May 5, 1881

Lucy Page, youngest d. of Wm. B. and Sally N. Weisiger, and Lee A. Coulter, by the Rev. Davis Sessums, in Calvary Church, Memphis, Tenn. So. Ch., June 25, 1885

Martha P., and W. C. H. Haddox of Richmond, Va., by the Rev. Jas. H. Williams, at Highland Lodge, Nelson Co., the bride's home. So. Ch., Nov. 14, 1908

Nannie M., second d. of W. B. and S. M. Weisiger formerly of Virginia, and E. F. Adams of Memphis, Tenn., by the rector, the Rev. D. Sessums, in Calvary Church, Memphis, Tenn. So. Ch., Sept. 10, 1885

Wm. B., Jr., recently of Virginia, and Annie, eldest d. of John Brown, Esq. of Memphis, Tenn., by the Rev. Mr. Taylor, in Court Street Presbyterian Church. So. Ch., Oct. 22, 1874

WELBOURN

John Armstead (The Rev.), of Tokyo, Japan, and Margaret Lynn, d. of Dr. and Mrs. R. B. Fishburne, by the Rev. Hullihen Burkhardt assisted by the Rev. Edwin B. Nivor, D.D., in St. James' Church, Leesburg, Va. So. Ch., Jan. 2, 1915

John E., of Baltimore, and Lucy F. Armistead, by the Rev. Dr. A. Wade, at Tommahind, Charles City Co., Va. So. Ch., Feb. 12, 1874

WELCH

Ida B., and Chas. H. Ashton of King George Co., by the Rev. Jno. M. Gill, at the residence of the bride's father, S. Welch, near "The Plains", Fauquier Co. So. Ch., Dec. 15, 1869

Mattie B., and Prof. J. Lewis Logan of the Agricultural and Mechanical College, Lexington, Ky., by the Rev. W. R. Laird, at the residence of the bride's father, Dr. S. D. Welch, near Nicholasville, Ky., So. Ch., Dec. 31, 1891

WELFARE

Thomas S., and Mary J. Wilson, by the Rev. Geo. W. Dame, in Lexington, N.C. So. Ch., Mar. 16, 1876

WELLER

R. H. (The Rev.), rector of St. John's Church, Jacksonville, and Caroline Cordelia Veale, by the Rev. O. P. Thackara, in St. Paul's Church, Fernandina, Fla. So. Ch., Sept. 24, 1874

WELLFORD

Beverly R., Esq., of Richmond, and Susan S., only d. of Warner T. Taliaferro, Esq., by the Rev. C. Mann, at Belleville, the residence of the bride's father. So. Ch., Mar. 19, 1858

Evelina S., late of Fredericksburg, and Robert R. Tompkins formerly of

MARRIAGE NOTICES IN THE SOUTHERN CHURCHMAN WITH DATES OF PUBLICATION

Fauquier Co., Va., by the Rev. Wm. W. Greene, in Spotsylvania Co., at the residence of the bride's uncle, C. C. Wellford. So. Ch., Feb. 19, 1864

J. Spotswood (Dr.), of Fredericksburg, and Emiline M., youngest d. of the late Capt. P. E. Tabb of Waverly, Gloucester Co., Va., by the Rev. Chas. Minnigerode, at the residence of Judge W. W. Crump, in Richmond. So. Ch., Apr. 16 and 23, 1859

R. Carter, of Richmond Co., and Lizzie C. Harrison, d. of the late W. M. Harrison of Charles City Co., by the Rev. Dr. A. Wade, at "Westover", the residence of the bride's brother-in-law. So. Ch., May 23, and 30, 1878

WELLS

Bessie Gardner, of Fairfax Co., and Joseph A. Settle of Rappahannock Co., by the Rev. John McGill, in St. John's Church, Centreville, Fairfax Co. So. Ch., Mar. 1, 1877

Edward Livingston (The Rev.), and Mary Huder, d. of E. B. M. Hughes, both of New Haven, Ct., by the Rev. Edwin Harwood, Professor in the Berkely Divinity School, Middletown, at New Haven, Ct. So. Ch., Oct. 22, 1858

James W., of Petersburg, Va., and Bessie J., d. of William H. Garrett of Blandford, by the Rev. W. R. Savage, at Blandford, near Petersburg, Va. So. Ch., Oct. 5, 1893

WELTY

Mary E., and Edward L. Morgan, both of Fairmont, by the Rev. G. A. Gibbons, at the residence of the bride's sister, Mrs. Annie Turney. So. Ch., Jan. 2, 1879

WERNE

J. Harry, of Richmond, Va., and Kate Johnson of Concord, N.C., by the Rev. C. M. Payne, in the First Presbyterian Church, Concord, N.C. So. Ch., Oct. 23, 1890

WERNER

Lucile, and the Rev. Charles E. Woodson, rector of Christ Church, Vicksburg, Miss., in Christ Church, Tuscaloosa, Ala. So. Ch., July 11, 1931

WERTH

Annie Dunlap, and Col. David Stuart Hounshell, by the Rev. P. G. Robert, in the Church of the Holy Communion, St. Louis, Mo. So. Ch., Apr. 22, 1880

James R., and Mary Herndon, d. of the late Com. M. F. Maury, by the Rev. Dr. Woodbridge, at the residence of the bride's mother in Richmond. So. Ch., July 12, 1877

WERTZ

John W., and Eliza A. Harvey, d. of the late Lewis B. Harvey, all of Franklin Co., Va., by the Rev. Edward H. Ingle, at the residence of Ira M. Hurst, Franklin Co., Va. So. Ch., Dec. 23, 1875

WEST

A. J., and Ann E. Campbell, both of Jefferson, by the Rev. J. D. Powell. So. Ch.,

MARRIAGE NOTICES IN THE SOUTHERN CHURCHMAN WITH DATES OF PUBLICATION

Feb. 15, 1856

Annie E., and Alonzo F. Tucker, both of Hanover Co., Va., by the Rev. S. S. Hepbron, in the Campbellite Church, at Gethsemane. So. Ch., May 15, 1890

Bessie P., d. of Dr. W. G. West, and George M. Grayson, both of Loudoun Co., by the Rev. S. S. Ware, in Christ Church, Loudoun Co. So. Ch., Jan. 1, 1880

Eugene, from Frederick Co., Md., of Company G, 7th Virginia Cavalry, Rosser's Brigade, and Annie L., d. of J. N. Cowen of Rockingham Co., Va., by the Rev. J. C. Wheat, at Belmont Hall, the residence of the bride's father. So. Ch., Apr. 29, 1864

George W., of Richmond, and Susie G. Braxton, d. of the late Dr. W. P. Braxton of Hanover, by the Rev. S. S. Hepbron, in Immanuel Church, Hanover Co. So. Ch., Oct. 16, 1890

Joanna T., of Accomac, and Thomas E. Leatherbury of Northampton, by the Rev. J. B. Craighill, in Northampton Co., Va. So. Ch., Feb. 11, 1869 *

Lulie F., d. of Dr. Nelson G. and Virginia T. West, and George F. Lewis, by the Rev. Carter Page, at the residence of the bride's father in Goresville, Loudoun Co. So. Ch., Jan. 15, 1885

Mary L., d. of Dr. W. G. West of Loudoun Co., Va., and J. Wilson Bowie, by the Rev. S. S. Ware, in Christ Church, Loudoun Co., Va. So. Ch., Jan. 8, 1880

WETHERILL

Rebecca G., d. of the late Samuel P. Wetherill, and the Rev. W. L. Suddards, by the Rev. E. Neville, in Grace Church, Philadelphia. So. Ch., May 14, 1847

WETMORE

George Badger, D.D. (The Rev.), and Pattie Helen, d. of the late Lewis B. Banner, Esq., by the Rev. James A. Weston, at Banner Elk, Watauga Co., N.C. So. Ch., Apr. 16, 1885

WHALEY

Fannie Fraser, d. of J. C. Whaley, Esq. of Edisto, and the Rev. Henry Tucker Lee of Winchester, Va., rector of Trinity Church, Society Hill, S.C., by the Rt. Rev. W. B. W. Howe, D.D., assisted by the Rev. John Johnson, rector of the church, in St. Philip's Church, Charleston, S.C. So. Ch., Apr. 30, 1874

Laura, of Fairfax Co., Va., and the Rev. Geo. A. Gibbons of Maryland, by the Rev. Wm. Sparrow, D.D. assisted by the Rev. John Ambler, in St. John's Church, West End. So. Ch., July 17, 1873

WHARTON

Bettie, of Mississippi, and the Rev. Heber O. Crane, by the Rev. J. Francis Girault, rector of St. Anne's Church, New Orleans, at the residence of Gen. J. Wharton, brother of the bride, in New Orleans. So. Ch., Mar. 23, 1876

---

* This notice appears in the issue of Feb. 4, 1869 except that "Leatherbury" is written "Leatherburt"

MARRIAGE NOTICES IN THE SOUTHERN CHURCHMAN WITH DATES OF PUBLICATION

Dabney M. (The Rev.), and Virginia Hungerford, d. of the late Col. John W. Hungerford of Westmoreland Co., Va., by the Rev. T. E. Locke, at Twiford. So. Ch., June 25, 1868

E. L. (Capt.), and Ella Louise Fairfax, both of Westmoreland, Va., by the Rev. D. M. Wharton. So. Ch., Jan. 13, 1881

John E., and Mattie C. McClintock, both of Liberty, by the Rev. John K. Mason, at the residence of the Rev. John A. Wharton. So. Ch., Jan. 25, 1883

L. B. (The Rev.), of William and Mary College, Williamsburg, Va., and Paulina, d. of H. Porterfield Taylor of Richmond, by the Rev. J. A. Wharton, at the residence of the bride's parents. So. Ch., Jan. 17, 1878

WHEAT

J. J., and Emily E. Dixon, by the Rev. James T. Johnston, in St. Paul's Church. So. Ch., Nov. 4, 1842

James C. (The Rev.), and Elizabeth, eldest d. of Gen. S. H. Lewis of Rockingham, by the Rev. T. T. Castleman, Rockingham Co., Va. So. Ch., Aug. 9, 1855

Lewis (Dr.), and Ella W. Rutherford, d. of the late Samuel J. Rutherford, by the Rev. J. C. Wheat, D.D. assisted by the Rev. Charles Minnigerode, in St. Paul's Church, Richmond. So. Ch., Nov. 11, 1886

Minnie A., d. of the late R. W. Wheat of Alexandria, Va., and Lt. Henrich Herwig, U.S.N., by the Rev. Dr. G. H. Norton, in St. Paul's Church, Alexandria, Va. So. Ch., Dec. 13, 1883

WHEATLY

Elvira A., of Virginia, and Arthur H. Edey of South Carolina, by the Rev. C. Y. Steptoe, in Christ Church, Culpeper Co. So. Ch., Aug. 21, 1873

WHEDBIE

Mary M., formerly of North Carolina, now of Prince William Co., Va., and Wm. H. Thornton of Fairfax Co., Va., by the Rev. Arthur P. Gray, in St. Paul's Church, Haymarket. So. Ch., Jan. 5, 1888

WHEELER

Mary Bawman, d. of Charles Wheeler, Esq., and the Rev. Henry A. Coit of Concord, N.H., by the Rev. Dr. Bawman, in the Church of the Epiphany, Philadelphia. So. Ch., Apr. 11, 1856

U. M. (The Rev.), and Mrs. S. E. M'Collough, d. of Maj. John DeWitt of Society Hill, S.C. So. Ch., Nov. 11, 1836

WHEELEY

Thomas, of Richmond, Va., and Mary Ann Minor of King William Co., by the Rev. G. W. Trice. So. Ch., Dec. 30, 1836

WHITBY

Katheryne E., and Randolph Harrison Macon, both of St. Louis, Mo. So. Ch., Dec. 11, 1915

WHITCHER

Benjamin W. (The Rev.), rector of St. Peter's Church,

MARRIAGE NOTICES IN THE SOUTHERN CHURCHMAN WITH DATES OF PUBLICATION

Oriskany, and Francis *
Miriam, d. of Lewis Berry,
Esq. of Whitesborough,
by the Rev. Mr. Hull, in
St. Peter's Church, Oriskany. So. Ch., Jan. 29,
1847

WHITE
Agnes Almeda, of Isle of
Wight Co., and Thomas
Atkinson, Esq., by the
Rev. James Chisholm, at
Smithfield, Va. So. Ch.,
Jan. 19, 1854

Anne D., of Washington,
D.C., and William B. Everette, III of Marshall,
Va., by Dean Powell and
the Rev. B. D. Chambers,
cousin of the bride, in
Bethlehem Chapel of the
National Cathedral. So.
Ch., Apr. 27, 1940

Arabella, of Romney, and
Judge Lucas P. Thompson
of Staunton, by the Rev.
T. T. Castleman, at Romney. So. Ch., Nov. 16,
1855

Charlotte C., of Cincinnati,
Ohio, and the Rev. Charles
D. Snowden, rector of St.
Margaret's Church, Menands, N.Y., in the Chapel
of the Diocesan House. So.
Ch., Oct. 5, 1940

Emmet Nelson, formerly of
Haymarket, Va., and Helen
Robins, by the Rev. W. W.
Wyckoff, in Christ
Episcopal Church, Gary,
Ind. So. Ch., July 5,
1913

Euphania W., d. of T. W.
White, and Nathan A.
Stedman, Esq., Comptroller of the State of North
Carolina, by the Rev.
William S. Plumer. So.
Ch., Jan. 15, 1836

Fannie, eldest d. of Dr.
J. W. White, and Geo. P.
Ball formerly of Spotsylvania Co., by the Rev.
Geo. W. Dame, at the residence of the bride's father,
near Laurel Grove, Spotsylvania Co. So. Ch., Jan.
11, 1877

James G., of Albemarle Co.,
Va., and Mary, only d. of
W. J. Carpenter of Ashland,
Va., by the Rev. John McGill, at the residence of
the bride's parents. So.
Ch., Dec. 15, 1887

James L., Esq., of Washington,
D.C., and Fannie E. Gibson
of Prince George's Co., Md.,
by the Rev. John Collins
McCabe, D.D., in St. Luke's
Church, Bladensburg, Md.
So. Ch., Oct. 25, 1866

James L., and Kate M. Robertson, by the Rev. L. B. Wharton, at "The Meadows", the
residence of the Hon. Wyndham Robertson. So. Ch.,
Nov. 7, 1867

John G., of Fauquier, and
Seignora C., d. of Winston
Carter of Prince William Co., by the Rev. R. T.
Brown, in St. Paul's
Church, Haymarket. So. Ch.,
Nov. 21, 1872

John Goldsborough, of El Paso,
Tex., formerly of Haymarket,
Va., and Mary Sydnie, d. of
the late Rev. James A. Matthews, by the Rev. Mr. Thompson of Trinity Episcopal
Church, Van Buren, Ark. So.
Ch., Oct. 30, 1909

Josiah R., of Loudoun Co.,
Va., and Frances Virginia,
d. of John B. Taylor, by
the Rev. F. M. Whittle, at
Clifton, Clarke Co., Va.
So. Ch., Sept. 13, 1855

* Given as printed

MARRIAGE NOTICES IN THE SOUTHERN CHURCHMAN WITH DATES OF PUBLICATION

Katherine Douglas, and Chiles Mason Ferrell, by the Rev. D. A. Cunningham, D.D., in the First Presbyterian Church, Wheeling, W.Va. So. Ch., Mar. 12, 1891

L. B., of Norfolk, and Miss C. H. Bell of Mathews, by the Rev. Jno. McGill, in Trinity Church, Mathews Co. So. Ch., Jan. 13, 1870

Mansfield, of Maryland, and Ella R., d. of John H. and Elizabeth Whitmore, by the Rev. Carter Page, in Christ Church, Goresville, Loudoun Co., Va. So. Ch., Feb. 5, 1885

Nellie Smith, and Harry McGill Williams, by the rector, the Rev. Walter P. Griggs, in St. Peter's Church, Poolesville, Md. So. Ch., Nov. 27, 1890

Rebecca H., d. of N. S. White, Esq., and Joseph Trapnell, Esq., s. of the officiating clergyman, the Rev. Jos. Trapnell, Jr. assisted by the Rev. Mr. Ambler, at Charles Town, W.Va. So. Ch., Nov. 29, 1866

Robb (The Rev.), of Wytheville, Va., and Sallie A., youngest d. of William R. Warren, Esq., by the Rev. A. W. Weddell assisted by the Rev. H. B. Lee, at Harrisonburg, Va. So. Ch., Dec. 2, 1875

Samuel, of Roanoke, and Jennie D. Logan, d. of Jas. W. Logan, Esq. late of Goochland Co., by the Rev. Edward H. Ingle, in St. Paul's Chapel, Salem, Roanoke Co. So. Ch., Jan. 6, 1870

Thos. Ward (The Rev.), and Alice Fleming, d. of Richard K. Cralle, Esq., by the Rev. T. V. Moore, D.D., in the First Presbyterian Church, Richmond, Va. So. Ch., Oct. 24, 1862

William Seymour, Commonwealth's Attorney of Stafford Co. and Secretary of the Fredericksburg Improvement Company, and Mrs. Helen Sibley Stokes, d. of the late General Sibley of the United States Army, by the rector, the Rev. W. M. Clark, in St. George's Church, Fredericksburg, Va. So. Ch., Feb. 12, 1891

WHITEHEAD

Anna Irvine, d. of Robert Whitehead, Esq. of Nelson Co., Va., and James Rector Smoot of Alexandria, by the Rev. Paul Whitehead, D.D., at the residence of the bride's father. So. Ch., Aug. 26, 1880

Cabell, assistant assayer of the United States Mint, at Boise City, Ida., and Bena Ayres, d. of Col. E. W. Ayres, the well known Washington correspondent, by the Rev. Dr. Mott, assistant rector of Epiphany Church, Washington, D.C. So. Ch., Oct. 11, 1888

John (Dr.), of Salisbury, N.C., and Rose Irving, d. of Edward W. Morris of Clazemont, Hanover Co., Va., by the Rev. Frank Page, in Zion Church, Fairfax C.H. So. Ch., Nov. 7, 1889

Kitty M., d. of Robert Whitehead, Esq. of Nelson Co., Va., and Frederick H. Moss of Fauquier Co., Va., by the

MARRIAGE NOTICES IN THE SOUTHERN CHURCHMAN WITH DATES OF PUBLICATION

Rev. B. T. Turner assisted by the Rev. Paul Whitehead, D.D., at Forkland. So. Ch., Oct. 23, 1884

Robert Lee of Roanoke, Va., and Fanny Lea, d. of Carl Zogbaum, by the Rev. T. S. Rumney assisted by the Rev. Mr. Bryan, at Germantown, Pa. So. Ch., Nov. 14, 1889

Stuart B., and Sue W. Massie, by the Rev. J. W. Ware, in Grace Church, Nelson Co., Va. So. Ch., June 29, 1893

Valeria Berrien, youngest d. of the late Hon. Jn. Whitehead of Burke Co. and gr.d. of Maj. John Berrien of the Continental Army, and Augustas Ramon Silas of Savannah, formerly of Charleston, S.C., by the Rev. William A. Leonard, in St. John's Church, Washington, D.C. So. Ch., Jan. 1, 1885

Wm. E., and Mattie Cheadle, both of Appomattox Co., Va., by the Rev. A. S. Lloyd, at the home of the bride's father. So. Ch., Dec. 28, 1882

WHITING

Annie B., d. of Kennon Whiting, Esq., and James Barron Hope, Esq., by the Rev. John C. McCabe, rector of the Church of the Ascension, Baltimore (and former rector of the church in Hampton), at Elmwood, near Hampton, Va. So. Ch., June 19, 1857

Fenton P., of Roanoke, Va., and Maude, d. of the late G. Washington Lewis of Clarke Co., Va., by the rector, the Rev. P. P. Phillips, in Grace Church, Borryville, Va. So. Ch., Sept. 10, 1891

Hannah B., of Hampton, and Richard M. Cary, Esq. of Petersburg, by the Rev. John C. McCabe, at Hampton. So. Ch., Aug. 30, 1855

Harriet P., formerly of Virginia, and Chas. W. Irwin of New York, by the Rev. R. D. Brooke, in St. John's Church, Dubuque, Iowa. So. Ch., Aug. 14, 1851

Hugh, of Clarke Co., Va., and Bessie Douglas, d. of Dr. T. B. Montague, by the Rev. Mr. Meredith, at Rosedale, Stafford Co., Va. So. Ch., Oct. 31, 1889

Kate C., d. of H. C. Whiting, Esq. of Hampton, Va., and William Green Young, by the Rev. J. J. Gravatt, in St. John's Church, Hampton, Va. So. Ch., June 29, 1882

Lizzie, second d. of Kenon * Whiting, Esq., and John Critchler, Esq. of Westmoreland Co., Va., by the Rev. E. H. Harlow, at Hampton, Elizabeth City Co. So. Ch., Nov. 20, 1857

Neville Herbert, and Meta Herbert, d. of the late Charles Keith Hyde, by the Rev. George H. Norton, D.D., at the residence of Col. Arthur Herbert, Fairfax Co., Va. So. Ch., Nov. 3, 1881

William B., former midshipman of the U.S. Navy, and Mary Lee Nicholls of Louisville, Ky., by the Rev. Mr. Jackson, at Louisville, Ky. So. Ch., Dec. 27, 1839

WHITLEY

Joel Flournoy, of Surry, and Lollie Wingfield, second d.

* Given as printed

MARRIAGE NOTICES IN THE SOUTHERN CHURCHMAN WITH DATES OF PUBLICATION

of George W. Moody of Surry, by the Rev. David Barr, near Surry C.H., Va. So. Ch., Oct. 13, 1887

WHITLOCK

Ellen P., d. of Richard H. Whitlock of Richmond, and James W. Pedin of Suffolk, Va., by the Rev. H. S. Kepler. So. Ch., Apr. 25, 1856

John T., and Elizabeth Gertrude Whitworth, by the Rev. J. E. Hammond, in Memorial Church, Manchester, Va. So. Ch., Dec. 21, 1871

William J. P., and Lucy Amelia Leigh, by the rector, the Rev. John London, in St. James' Church, Louisa, Va. So. Ch., Mar. 18, 1911

WHITLOW

J. H., and Nannie W. Smith, both of Campbell Co., by the Rev. W. E. Webb. So. Ch., July 1, 1859

WHITMORE

Ella R., d. of John H. and Elizabeth Whitmore, and Mansfield White of Maryland, by the Rev. Carter Page, in Christ Church, Goresville, Loudoun Co., Va. So. Ch., Feb. 5, 1885

WHITNEY

Chas. B., of Campbell Court House, and Sarah Coles of Lancaster, by the Rev. Edmund Withers, at Locust Green, Lancaster Co., Va. So. Ch., May 16, 1856

WHITRIDGE

Ellen Ward, d. of John A. Whitridge, Esq., and Samuel M. Shoemaker, by the Rev. J. H. Eccleston, D.D., in Emmanuel Church, Baltimore. So. Ch., Nov. 27, 1884

WHITTEN

Guy, of Goodson, Va., and Ella, d. of Thos. G. Godwin, Esq., of Fincastle, by the Rev. Pendleton Brooke, in St. Mark's Church, Fincastle. So. Ch., May 14, 1874

WHITTINGHAM

Edward T., M.D., and Martha, d. of Israel D. Condit, all of Milburn, by the Bishop of Maryland assisted by the Bishop of New Jersey, in St. Stephen's Church, Milburn, N.J. So. Ch., Jan. 21, 1859

WHITTINGTON

Charles H., and Margaret L. Fewell, by the Rev. Jno. McGill, at Manassas. So. Ch., Dec. 21, 1871

Minnie Frances, of Merrett's Island, and the Rev. Wm. L. Hargraves, rector of St. Mark's Church, Cocoa, Fla., in the church, at Cocoa. So. Ch., Mar. 4, 1939

WHITTLE

Cloe Tyler, d. of Conway Whittle, Esq. of Norfolk, Va., and J. Newport Greene, Esq. formerly of Newton House, County Kilkenney, Ireland, by the Rev. N. A. Okeson assisted by the Rev. Julius Sams, in St. Paul's Church, Norfolk, Va. So. Ch., Sept. 7, 1876

Elizabeth Sinclair, d. of Judge and Mrs. Stafford G. Whittle of Virginia, and James David Johnston of Roanoke, Va., by the rector, the Rev. Alfred W. Anson, in Christ Church, Martinsville, Va. So. Ch., June 14, 1913

Francis M. (The Rev.), of Ka-

MARRIAGE NOTICES IN THE SOUTHERN CHURCHMAN WITH DATES OF PUBLICATION

nawha Co., Va., and Emily C., eldest d. of W. M. C. Fairfax, Esq., by the Rev. C. M. Butler, D.D., at Washington, D.C. So. Ch., June 23, 1848

Francis M., Jr., and Caroline L. Walke, by the Rt. Rev. F. M. Whittle and the Rev. Lewis Walke, in St. Stephen's Church, Cecil Co., Md. So. Ch., Dec. 9, 1880

Jeanie, d. of Com. Wm. C. Whittle of Buchanan, and the Rev. David Barr, rector of Meherrin Parish, Greensville Co., Va., by the Rev. Pendleton Brooke, in Trinity Church, Buchanan, Va. So. Ch., Feb. 13, 1873

Lizzie, d. of Com. W. Whittle, and J. Coles Terry of Roanoke Co., Va., by the Rev. Pendleton Brooke, in Trinity Church, Buchanan. So. Ch., May 1, 1873

Lucy P., d. of the officiating clergyman, and Dr. John N. Upshur, by Bishop F. M. Whittle, in St. James' Church, Richmond, Va. So. Ch., Nov. 27, 1873

Mary E., d. of Conway Whittle, Esq., and the Rev. F. Julius Sams, rector of Trinity Church, Black Oak, S.C., by the Rev. E. M. Rodman, rector of Christ Church, Norfolk, Va., at the residence of the bride's father, Norfolk, Va. So. Ch., Feb. 11, 1859

Wm. C. (Capt.), U.S. Navy, and Ann E. Hanner, d. of the late Samuel Anthony, Esq., by the Rev. T. M. Ambler, at the residence of the bride's uncle, at Buchanan. So. Ch., Aug. 12, 1859

William C., Jr. (Capt.), and Elizabeth Calvert, eldest d. of Gen. R. L. and Alexina Page, by the Rev. Dr. O. S. Barten, in Christ Church, Norfolk. So. Ch., Nov. 21, 1872

Zillah M., d. of L. N. Whittle, Esq., and Ferdinand Emmel, Esq., by the Rev. Benjamin Johnson, in Christ Church, Macon, Ga. So. Ch., Apr. 23, 1874

WHITTLESEY
Walter, of Chelsea, Mass., and Ida, d. of Sterling J. Hubbard of London, Ohio, by the Rev. Wm. Stevens Campbell, at the residence of the bride's father. So. Ch., Sept. 23, 1886

WHITWORTH
Elizabeth Gertrude, and John T. Whitlock, by the Rev. J. E. Hammond, in Memorial Church, Manchester, Va. So. Ch., Dec. 21, 1871

WIATT
Hannah More, of Spotsylvania Co., Va., and J. T. Ashton of King George, by the Rev. A. M. Randolph, in Spotsylvania Co., Va. So. Ch., Nov. 25, 1859

Maria S., and Peter P. Burr of Fredericksburg, by the Rev. W. W. Green, at the residence of the bride's brother-in-law, in Spotsylvania Co. So. Ch., Dec. 18, 1863

Thos. M., Esq., of Gloucester, Va., and Sarah C. Segar of Middlesex, Va., by the Rev. G. S. Carraway, in the Urbanna Church. So. Ch., Feb. 15, 1855

WICKER
Virginia L., d. of the late Col. Francis Wicker of Richmond, and Benj.

MARRIAGE NOTICES IN THE SOUTHERN CHURCHMAN WITH DATES OF PUBLICATION

W. B. Blanton of Cumberland Co., by the Rev. H. S. Kepler, rector of St. John's Church, Richmond. So. Ch., Feb. 22, 1856

WICKHAM
Anne Carter, d. of Gen. Wm. C. Wickham, and Robert H. Renshaw of Baltimore, by the Rev. Charles Minnigerode, at Hickory Hill, Va. So. Ch., Nov. 17, 1881

Elizabeth, d. of L. E. T. Wickham of Henrico Co., Va., and Parke Fitzhugh of Pittsylvania Co., Va., by the Rev. Green Shackelford, at the residence of the bride's father. So. Ch., Jan. 24, 1884

Francis, d. of the late John Wickham, Esq. of Richmond, Va., and Lt. Col. James D. Graham, U.S. Army, by the Rev. Dr. Minnigerode, Richmond. So. Ch., Feb. 20, 1857

George, s. of the late John Wickham, Esq., and Charlotte F. Carter, d. of William Carter, Esq. of Hanover Co., by the Rt. Rev. R. C. Moore, in Richmond, Va. So. Ch., Oct. 25, 1839

Henry T., of Hanover Co., Va., and Elise W., d. of George A. Barksdale, Esq. of Richmond, Va., by the Rev. Charles Minnigerode, D.D., in St. Paul's Church, in Richmond, Va. So. Ch., Dec. 24, 1885

John, of Henrico, and Elizabeth Hill Carter, eldest d. of Hill Carter, Esq. of Charles City, by the Rev. Dr. Okesen, at Shirley. So. Ch., Dec. 9, 1859

Lucy Carter, d. of the late E. F. Wickham, and Geo. H. Byrd of Baltimore, by the Rev. Mr. Peterkin, at the residence of W. F. Wickham, Hanover Co. So. Ch., Feb. 6, 1857

Mary Fanning, d. of the late E. F. Wickham, and Julius T. Percher of South Carolina, by the Rev. Mr. Peterkin, at the residence of W. F. Wickham, Hanover Co. So. Ch., Feb. 6, 1857

WIESE*
George F. (Capt.), and M. Elizabeth Comer, by the Rev. J. Jacquelin Ambler, Jr., in St. Mark's Church, Dento, Va. So. Ch., May 9, 1931

WIGGINS
James A., of Madison Co., Ala., and Mary A. Floyd, by the Rev. Geo. W. Dame, at Brookfield, Campbell Co. So. Ch., Sept. 24, 1858

WILBUR
Pardon, of Providence, R.I., and Mrs. Cornelia Rives Harrison of Albemarle Co., Va., by the Rev. T. E. Locke, at River Lawn. So. Ch., June 19, 1884

WILBURN
James Clinton, of Alexandria, and Llora Corine Marsteller, by the Rev. John Towles of Prince George's Co., Md., at Arelton, the residence of Arell Marsteller, Esq. So. Ch., Jan. 23, 1868

WILCHEN
Sarah J., and Richard Witt, by the Rev. R. J. McBryde, in Amherst Co., Va. So. Ch., Feb. 10, 1870

WILCOX
E. Sherred, d. of Col. James

---

* Probably "Weise," but given as printed

MARRIAGE NOTICES IN THE SOUTHERN CHURCHMAN WITH DATES OF PUBLICATION

M. Wilcox of Charles City Co., Va., and Wm. W. Adams of Potersburg, by the Rev. Dr. Wade, at Buckland, the residence of the bride's father. So. Ch., Nov. 14, 1872

Montgomery, and Mary McKenzie, eldest d. of John E. Graeff, all of Philadelphia, by the Rev. Theodore S. Rumney, D.D., assisted by the Rev. Edward S. Watson, D.D., in Philadelphia. So. Ch., May 13, 1880

WILCOXON
Josiah, and Julia E., both of Prince William Co., Va., by the Rev. John Towles. So. Ch., Feb. 27, 1857

WILCOXSEN
Hanson T. (The Rev.), and Mary K., d. of the late Richard Mason of Georgetown, Md., by the Rev. J. Campbell White, in St. Andrew's Church, Washington Co., Md. So. Ch., Mar. 1, 1855

WILDMAN
Thomas G., Esq., formerly of New York, and Mollie B. Kehler, d. of the officiating clergyman, formerly of Jefferson Co., Va., by the Rev. Mr. Kehler, in Denver City, J.T.* So. Ch., Oct. 26, 1860

WILEY
Frederick S. (The Rev.), rector of Grace Church, Honesdale, and Frances Matilda, d. of the late H. B. Pierrepont, by the Rev. Dr. Cutler, in St. Anne's Church, Brooklyn. So. Ch., Nov. 1, 1849

Rankin, Jr. (Capt.), and Blanche Cantrell Miller, by the Rev. T. H. Lacy, at the residence of the bride's father, C. C. Miller, Esq., near Point Pleasant, W.Va. So. Ch., Oct. 9, 1879

WILKERSON
N. A., of Rockingham Co., N.C., and Malissa T. Coppridge of Pittsylvania Co., Va., by the Rev. C. O. Pruden, at the residence of the bride's mother, in Pittsylvania. So. Ch., Jan. 1, 1885

WILKINS
Anna, d. of Dr. Benjamin Wilkins, and Dr. Henry M. Neblett of Virginia, at "Forest Home", Louisiana. So. Ch., Apr. 13, 1871

George F., M.D., and Lottie Y. Nottingham, d. of Dr. Thomas J. L. L. Nottingham, by the Rev. J. J. Clemens, at Mt. Lebanon, Northampton Co., Va. So. Ch., Oct. 27, 1870

Isabella of Drummondtown, Accomac Co., Va., and Robert F. Williams of Richmond, by the Rev. Wm. C. Williams of Georgia, in St. James' Church, Drummondtown, Accomac Co., Va. So. Ch., Nov. 14, 1856

John (Dr.), C.S.A., and Lucia Cary Tabb, by the Rev. G. S. Carraway, at Auburn, Mathews Co. So. Ch., Feb. 21, 1862

O. Edward, cashier of the Henrietta Mills, and Loula A., d. of the late John T. Ball of Meridian, Miss., by the Rev. E. A. Osborne of Charlotte, at the residence of Mr. Fred S. Mosher, Supt. of Henrietta Mills, Rutherford

---

* Jefferson Territory became Colorado Territory in 1861

MARRIAGE NOTICES IN THE SOUTHERN CHURCHMAN WITH DATES OF PUBLICATION

Co., N.C. So. Ch., Oct. 2, 1890
Sarah Jane, d. of John Wilkins, Esq. of Rutherford, N.C., and the Rev. John Huske Tillinghast of St. Paul's, Clinton, by the Rev. J. D. McCullough of the Diocese of South Carolina, in St. John's Church, Rutherford, N.C. So. Ch., Nov. 9, 1865
William W., of Brunswick Co., and Rosa Clark of Halifax, by the Rev. John T. Clark, at Bannister Lodge. So. Ch., Nov. 22, 1866

WILKINSON
Claudia, and Richard Robert Prentiss, M.D., by the Rev. Thomas P. Baker, in Christ Church Chapel, Yonge's Island, S.C. So. Ch., Jan. 28, 1911
David M. (Dr.), of Chesterfield, and Nannie Jane, d. of the late Alfred Wood, Esq. of Amelia, by the Rev. A. B. Tizzard, at Oldenplace, Amelia Co. So. Ch., May 8, 1857
Ella A., superintendent of St. Luke's Hospital, a parochial institution of Bellingham, Wash., and the Rev. R. Marshall Harrison of St. Paul's Church, Bellingham, Wash., by the Rev. Edgar M. Rodgers, in Trinity Church, Everett, Wash. So. Ch., Aug. 3, 1918
Jeanie B., of Brandon, Miss., and Dr. John W. Price of Mt. Airy, Pittsylvania Co., Va., by the Rev. C. O. Pruden, in Epiphany Church, Danville. So. Ch., May 31, 1888
John (Lt.), U.S. Navy, and Mary Blair, d. of the late John Peachy of Florida, by the Rev. P. Berkeley, at Osmore, the residence of Mrs. Banister, in Amelia Co. So. Ch., Jan. 15, 1858
Laura Doris, of Beaver, Pa., and the Rev. William Axford Benjamin Holmes, chaplain of Pennsylvania Industrial School, by the Rt. Rev. Bishop Wyatt Brown, in the Keferstein Chapel of the Holy Spirit, Bishops Court, Harrisburg, Penn. So. Ch., July 17, 1938
Mary D., of William Wilkinson, Esq., and John W. Prickett, Esq., of Amelia Co., by the Rev. A. B. Tizzard. So. Ch., Dec. 17, 1858
Mary Hannah, d. of E. Wilkinson, Esq., Mayor of West Point, and Chas. A. W. Barham formerly of Durham, N.C., by the Rev. Pendleton Brooke, in St. John's Church, West Point, Va. So. Ch., Mar. 7, 1889
Telia H., of Powhatan Co., Va., and Charles J. Beattie of "Marlboro", S.C., by the Rev. R. N. Pratt, at "Belone", S.C. So. Ch., Mar. 17, 1885

WILLCOX
Sue R., and E. C. Harrison, by the Rev. Edward Valentine Jones, in Westover Church, Charles City Co., Va. So. Ch., July 16, 1891
Thomas H., and Mary Cary Ambler, d. of the Rev. T. M. Ambler of Wilmington, N.C., by the Rev. A. S. Lloyd assisted by the

MARRIAGE NOTICES IN THE SOUTHERN CHURCHMAN WITH DATES OF PUBLICATION

Rev. R. R. Claiborne, in St. Luke's Church, Norfolk, Va. So. Ch., Nov. 12, 1885

Thomas W., Esq., of Charles City Co., and Mattie A., d. of Dr. Wm. S. Claiborne, by the Rev. J. D. Powell, in Saint Mark's Church, New Glasgow. So. Ch., Dec. 17, 1858

WILLCOXEN

J. W., and Ida E. Marders, both of Prince William Co., Va., by the Rev. A. P. Gray, at the residence of the bride's mother. So. Ch., Jan. 4, 1883

WILLIAMS

Albert, of Kansas City, and Mary Maxwell Porter, d. of Mrs. Caroline Porter and the late Charles B. Porter, at the family residence in St. Joseph, Mo. So. Ch., Oct. 22, 1910

Alexander Watson (Dr.), U.S.A., and Florence H. Light, by the Ven. Richard P. Williams, Canon of Washington, father of the groom, in the Bethlehem Chapel of the Nativity, Washington, D.C. So. Ch., Aug. 21, 1915

Charles B., and Kate M. Daniel, both of Culpeper Co., by the Rev. John B. McGill, at the residence of the bride's mother. So. Ch., Dec. 28, 1882

Charles D. (The Rev.), and Lucy V. Benedict, by the Rev. Dr. Benedict, father of the bride and rector of St. Paul's, assisted by the Rev. Dr. Pise and the Rev. Dr. Jaeger formerly of Gambier, in St. Paul's Church, Cincinnati. So. Ch., Oct. 21, 1886

Charles Phelps, and Juliet Marie Riley, d. of the late Dr. John C. Riley, all of Georgetown, by the Rev. John S. Lindsay, D.D., in St. John's Church, Georgetown, D.C. So. Ch., May 3, 1883

Chauncey C. (The Rev.), and Pattie, only d. of the late Joel W. Jones, Esq., of Mobile, by the Bishop of Alabama, in Christ Church, Mobile. So. Ch., Jan. 30, 1879

Columbia W., d. of the late Capt. W. G. Williams of the Corps of Topographical Engineers, United States Army, and Abel B. Upshur, Esq., by the Rev. A. Stryker, in Baltimore. So. Ch., June 27, 1872

Cyane Dandridge, of Alexandria, Va., and Eli Lockert Bemis of New Orleans, by the Rev. T. G. Dashiell assisted by the Rev. Joshua Peterkin, in St. James' Church, Richmond. So. Ch., Jan. 16, 1890

Elizabeth P. G., of Clarke Co., Va., and the Rev. W. Woodson Walker of Mt. Jackson, Va., by the Rev. W. T. Leavell assisted by the Rev. C. Walker, D.D., at "Smithfield", Clarke Co., Va. So. Ch., July 8, 1880

F. S., of Baltimore, and Kathleen M. Macmurdo of Ashland, Va., by the Rev. G. W. Easter. So. Ch., Mar. 26, 1868

Frances B., d. of Dr. Wil-

MARRIAGE NOTICES IN THE SOUTHERN CHURCHMAN WITH DATES OF PUBLICATION

liams of Culpeper Co., Va., and Joseph B. Pannell, by the Rev. Mr. Woodville, near Culpeper C.H., Va. So. Ch., Sept. 22, 1837

G. Thurston, of London, England, and Sallie B. Nicolson, d. of Dr. G. Nicolson, by the Rev. J. Hervey Hundley, in Christ Church, Middlesex Co., Va. So. Ch., May 11, 1876

George W., of Richmond, and Rebecca, d. of the late Judge William Leigh, by the Rev. William H. Laird, at the residence of Benjamin Watkins Leigh, Esq., in Mecklenburg Co., Va. So. Ch., Jan. 14, 1875

George W., of Prince George Co., and Anna Harrison, d. of Dr. John R. Mason of Sussex Co., Va., by the Rev. C. J. Gibson, at "Oak Spring". So. Ch., Dec. 30, 1875

Goodwin H., and Nannie H., d. of the late Edward McCormick, all of Clarke Co., Va., by the rector, the Rev. P. P. Phillips, assisted by the Rev. S. S. Moore, in Grace Church, Berryville, Va. So. Ch., Mar. 25, 1886

Hannah Maria, third d. of Allen Williams, Esq., and Henry Buchanan Bird of Delaware, by the Rev. F. M. Whittle, at Mount Hebron, Clarke Co., Va. So. Ch., Feb. 8, 1855

Harry McGill, and Nellie Smith White, by the rector, the Rev. Walter P. Griggs, in St. Peter's Church, Poolesville, Md. So. Ch., Nov. 27, 1890

Hattie, d. of Allen Williams, Esq. of Clarke Co., Va., and Col. Wm. T. Dortch of Goldsborough, N.C., by the Rev. J. F. Martin, at the residence of the bride's father. So. Ch., Jan. 11, 1872

Hazeal (Dr.), and Julia C. Diggs, both of Virginia, by the Rev. H. M. Wharton. So. Ch., Apr. 13, 1882

Henry Horton (The Rev.), of Charlottesville, Va., formerly of Birkenhead, England, and Frances Callender, youngest d. of the late Maj. William N. Berkeley of the University of Virginia, formerly of Aldie, Loudoun Co., by the Rev. W. R. Mason. So. Ch., Oct. 9, 1909

Harry S. (Lt.), of Mecklenburg, and Susan Dabney, second d. of Col. R. Withers, by the Rev. Geo. W. Dame, in the Church of the Epiphany, Danville. So. Ch., Jan. 4, 1866

Howe Allen, and Elizabeth Walter Kendrick, by the bride's father, the Bishop of New Mexico and Arizona, in Grace Church, Oceanside, Calif. So. Ch., Oct. 24, 1908

J. Peter, and Anna P., d. of the late Wm. H. Kinckle, all of Lynchburg, by the Rev. T. M. Carson, in St. Paul's Church, Lynchburg. So. Ch., Dec. 19, 1872

James A. (The Rev.), rector of St. Mark's Church, Orange, N.J., and Elizabeth Ann, d. of Ichabod Condit also of Orange, N.J., by the Rev. Richard Cox, at Orange, N.J. So. Ch., Oct. 27, 1837

MARRIAGE NOTICES IN THE SOUTHERN CHURCHMAN WITH DATES OF PUBLICATION

James H. (The Rev.), of Nashville, former rector of Grace Church, Lynchburg, and Mrs. Elizabeth Denison Allen, gr.d. of President Tyler and d. of the late Rev. Henry Denison, by the Rev. Mr. Hubard of Salem assisted by the Rev. Mr. Hullihen, in Trinity Church, Staunton. So. Ch., Apr. 27, 1893

James Henry (The Rev.), of New York City, and Indiana Fletcher of Amherst, Va., by the Rev. Wm. H. Kinckle, in St. Paul's Church, Lynchburg, Va. So. Ch., Sept. 14, 1865

Jessie Bryan, d. of the Rev. John B. Williams, rector of the parish, and John Elliot Bull, by the Rev. Dr. Ellison Capers, in Prince George's Winjah Episcopal Church, Georgetown, S.C. So. Ch., Jan. 12, 1893

John L., of Richmond, and Maria W., eldest d. of John G. Skelton of Powhatan Co., by the Rev. F. F. Berkeley, in Grace Church, Powhatan Co. So. Ch., Nov. 9, 1864

Louis L. (The Rev.), and Kate M., d. of Maj. John W. and Fannie Green, by the Rev. G. H. Norton, D.D., in St. Paul's Church, Alexandria, Va. So. Ch., July 24, 1890

Margaret S., d. of John Williams, Esq., and P. H. Gibson, Esq., all of Petersburg, by the Rev. Churchill Gibson, in St. James' Church. So. Ch., Mar. 14, 1856

Mary L. D., d. of Philip Williams, Esq. of Winchester, and the Rev. Jas. A. Averitt of Alabama, by the Rev. Mr. Meredith, in Christ Church, Winchester. So. Ch., Mar. 14, 1862

Mary Willoughby, and Fisher Howe of Princeton, N.J., at the home of her parents, Wilton, Westmoreland Co., Va. So. Ch., Mar. 13, 1909

May Beverley, and James Boyd Patton, by the Rev. Preston Nash, in St. James Church, Richmond. So. Ch., Nov. 7, 1889

Morritt F. (The Rev.), priest-in-charge of St. Stephen's Mission, Fort Yukon, Alaska, s. of Mr. and Mrs. Leonard O. Williams of St. Louis, Mo., and Lucy Ogden Cornell, nurse in the Hudson Stuck Memorial Hospital at Fort Yukon, Alaska, d. of the late Dr. William P. Cornell of Charleston, S.C. and of Mrs. William P. Cornell, Executive Secretary of the Diocese of Florida, by the Rt. Rev. John Boyd Bentley, Bishop Suffragan of Alaska, at Fort Yukon, Alaska. So. Ch., Aug. 6, Dec. 3 and 10, 1932

Nannie E., d. of Dr. Thomas J. Williams. of Charlotte Co., Va., and Dr. Granville R. Lewis of Prince Edward Co., by the Rev. James A. Mitchell, in Charlotte Co. So. Ch., Nov. 8, 1866

Nannie Fassman, d. of the late J. Shelby Williams and gr.d. of Mrs. Judge* Pholan of "Fatherland", near Nashville, Tenn., and Wentworth P. Johnson

* Given as printed

MARRIAGE NOTICES IN THE SOUTHERN CHURCHMAN WITH DATES OF PUBLICATION

of Norfolk, Va., by the Rev. L. T. Martin, rector, in St. Ann's Church, East Nashville, Tenn. So. Ch., Jan. 29, 1885

Nannie H., d. of Capt. E. Peachy Williams formerly of Clarke Co., Va., and Frank Dunklie of Giles Co., Va., by the Rev. Woodson Walker of Mt. Jackson, Shenandoah Co., Va., in Grace Church, Berryville. So. Ch., May 19, 1881

Nannie Moore, of Baltimore, and the Rev. J. C. Koon of Hancock, Md., by the Rev. Irving McElroy, in St. Luke's Church, in Baltimore. So. Ch., Jan. 26, 1888

Richard P., of New York, and Margaret F. Watson, by the Rev. Dr. Minnigerode assisted by the Rev. Dr. Shackelford, at the residence of the bride's father, corner of Franklin and Adams streets, Richmond, Va. So. Ch., June 21, 1883

Robert F., of Richmond, and Isabella Wilkins of Drummondtown, Accomac Co., Va., by the Rev. Wm. C. Williams of Georgia, in St. James' Church, Drummondtown, Accomac Co., Va. So. Ch., Nov. 14, 1856

Henrietta S., d. of Theodorick A. and Gertrude Williams, and Thomas Howard Gilliam, by the Rev. Walter Williams, D.D., of Christ Church, Baltimore, assisted by the Rev. Arthur S. Lloyd, in St. Luke's Protestant Episcopal Church, Norfolk, Va. So. Ch., June 18, 1891

Walter (The Rev.), of Leesburg, Va., and Alice, youngest d. of Joseph H. Bradley, Esq. of Washington, by the Rev. George D. Cummins, D.D. of Baltimore, in Trinity Church. So. Ch., Mar. 4, 1859

Walter (The Rev.), rector of Grace Church, Georgetown, and Anna Cost Poole, d. of Mrs. Richard Poole, by the Rev. Bishop Alfred Harding assisted by the Rev. J. W. Blake, in Christ Church, Georgetown, D.C. So. Ch., Oct. 23, 1909

Walter Armistead, and Alice Marshall, d. of James M. Taylor, Esq. of Richmond, Va., by the Rev. T. G. Dashiell assisted by the Rev. W. B. Williams, in St. James' Church. So. Ch., Feb. 24, 1887

Wm. C., Esq., and Roberta Hansbrough, both of Orange Co., by the Rev. Joseph Earnest, at Orange C.H. So. Ch., Sept. 25, 1857

Wm. G., and Susan A., d. of R. R. Miller, all of Richmond, by the Rev. Wm. S. Plummer. So. Ch., Dec. 30, 1836

WILLIAMSON

James J., of Dinwiddie, and Agnes E., d. of the late John C. Goode of Mecklenburg, by the Rev. Mr. Steele. So. Ch., Nov. 24, 1837

Jos. A., and Eleanor W., eldest d. of Dr. T. J. McGill of Frederick, Md., by the Rev. Jno. McGill assisted by the rector of the parish, the Rev. O. Ingle, at the residence of the bride's father. So. Ch., Nov. 16, 1871

MARRIAGE NOTICES IN THE SOUTHERN CHURCHMAN WITH DATES OF PUBLICATION

Susan Scott, d. of Mrs. E. J. Williamson, and Edward B. Meetze, Esq., by the Rev. W. Strother Jones, at "Greenhill", Fauquier Co., Va. So. Ch., Dec. 14, 1876

W. G. (Capt.), and Bettie M. Cralle, both of Virginia, by the Rev. Edward Valentine, at Huntington, W.Va. So. Ch., Oct. 24, 1872

Wm. B., and Mary F. Shepperd, both of Warrenton, Va., by the Rev. George W. Nelson, in St. James' Church, Warrenton, Va. So. Ch., Mar. 4, 1886

WILLIFORD
Martha, and the Rt. Rev. John Payne, D.D., by the Rev. C. C. Hoffman, at Cavella, West Africa. So. Ch., Oct. 15, 1858

WILLIS
A. J. (The Rev.), of King George, and Margaret W., d. of W. L. G. and Adalina Mitchell, by the Rev. H. L. Derby assisted by the Rev. Mr. Johnson and the Rev. Mr. Mason, at White Chapel, Lancastor, Va. So. Ch., Nov. 26, 1885

Achille Murat, of Rappahannock, Va., and Sopha B. Dickinson of King George Co., Va., by the Rev. A. J. Willis, at Berry Plain, the residence of the bride's father, King George Co., Va. So. Ch., Mar. 19, 1885

Belle T., and C. Baldwin Walker of Baltimore, by the Rev. E. J. Willis, father of the bride, in Clarksburg, W.Va. So. Ch., Apr. 24, 1884

Charles Edgar, of Vicksburg, Miss., and Willietta Woodbridge Greene, d. of the officiating clergyman, the Rev. Wm. W. Greene, in Calvary Church, Front Royal, Va. So. Ch., Nov. 23, 1893

Emma Edwards, youngest d. of Thos. H. Willis, Esq. of Charles Town, and Bushrod Corbin Washington, Esq. of Jefferson Co., by the Rev. W. H. Meade, in Zion Church, Charles Town. So. Ch., Nov. 28, 1878

Georgine, youngest d. of the late Col. Geo. Willis, and Joseph D. Logan of West Virginia, by the Rev. R. R. Claiborne, in Emmanuel Church, Rapidan, Va. So. Ch., May 27, 1886

Henry G., of Orange Co., and Leah Seddon, d. of C. W. Chancellor, M.D. of Baltimore and gr.d. of the late Gen. A. G. Taliaferro and Mrs. A. H. M. Taliaferro of "Annandale", Culpeper Co., Va., by the Rev. George Murray, the rector, in Emmanuel Church, Culpeper Co. So. Ch., Dec. 15, 1887

Isabella, d. of Col. Geo. Willis, and Alexander F. Hayward, Esq. of Florida, by the Rev. J. Earnest, at Wood Park, the residence of the bride's father, in Orange. So. Ch., June 10, 1859

John M., Esq., and Nannie C. Shield, both of Hampton, Va., by the Rev. J. J. Gravatt, in St. John's Church, Hampton, Va. So. Ch., Nov. 15, 1877

MARRIAGE NOTICES IN THE SOUTHERN CHURCHMAN WITH DATES OF PUBLICATION

John Mitchell (Dr.), U.S. Army, and Anna Gibson, by the Rev. John S. Gibson, D.D., father of the bride, and the Rev. Andrew J. Willis, father of the groom, in Trinity Church, Huntington, W.Va. So. Ch., July 15, 1911

Nellie C., and W. Byrd Willis, both of Orange Co., by the Rev. T. F. Martin, at "Fairfield", the residence of Maj. John D. Richardson, in Clarke Co., Va. So. Ch., May 9, 1878

Virginia C., d. of the late Col. George Willis, and Charles E. Cary of Gloucester, Va., by the Rev. John S. Hansbrough, at Wood Park, Orange Co., Va. So. Ch., June 11, 1885

W. Byrd, and Nellie C. Willis, both of Orange Co., Va., by the Rev. T. F. Martin, at "Fairfield", the residence of Maj. John D. Richardson, in Clarke Co., Va. So. Ch., May 9, 1878

WILLITTS
Morit, Esq., and Laura E. Naudain, both of New Castle Co., Del., by the Rev. Jno. Collins McCabe, D.D. assisted by the Rev. Jno. W. Brown of Philadelphia, in St. Ann's Church, Middletown, Del. So. Ch., Oct. 21, 1869

WILLMETH
W. A., and Dora Beck, both of Roanoke, by the Rev. D. M. Wood, in Roanoke, Va. So. Ch., Dec. 3, 1885

WILLS
Annie M., d. of Thomas H. Wills, Esq., and R. J. Ambler, by the Rev. Charles E. Ambler, at Rock Hall, Jefferson Co. So. Ch., Aug. 21, 1857

Hallie G., d. of C. T. Wills, Esq., and R. M. Guy of Staunton, by the Rev. Mr. Suter, at Lynchburg. So. Ch., Oct. 10, 1867

Jennie R., of Nelson Co., and Walter S. Sublett of Richmond, Va., by the Rev. D. M. Wood, in Trinity Church, Nelson Co. So. Ch., Nov. 22, 1888

WILLSON
Maria, d. of the late T. C. Willson of Amelia Co., Va., and Carthous Archer of Henrico, by the Rev. P. F. Berkeley, at Selma, the residence of Richard Anderson of Amelia Co. So. Ch., Oct. 29, 1868

WILMER
George T. (The Rev.), of Botetourt Co., Va., and Mary Peachy, d. of the late Peachy R. Gilmer, by the Rev. Richard K. Meade, at Leigh, Albemarle Co., Va. So. Ch., May 7, 1847

George T. (The Rev.), and Marianna B., eldest d. of Robert Saunders, Esq., all of Williamsburg, Va., by the Rev. Richard H. Wilmer of Bedford Co., Va. So. Ch., Oct. 12, 1855

Helen Skipwith, and Edward C. Venable of Petersburg, Va., by the Rt. Rev. J. P. B. Wilmer and the Rev. Dr. Slaughter, in Emmanuel Church, Culpeper Co., Va.

MARRIAGE NOTICES IN THE SOUTHERN CHURCHMAN WITH DATES OF PUBLICATION

So. Ch., Jan. 3, 1878
Lucy Page, sister of the Rev. Dr. C. B. Wilmer of Atlanta and d. of the late Rev. Dr. G. T. Wilmer, and William Bowyer Poindexter of Greenlee, Va., by the Rev. J. W. Cantey Johnson of St. John's Church, Roanoke, at "Brier Hill", near Amsterdam, Va. So. Ch., July 12, 1913

Marion, d. of the officiating Bishop, and Harvey E. Jones, by Bishop Wilmer, in St. Paul's Church, Spring Hill, Ala. So. Ch., Dec. 16, 1869

Simon (The Rev.), rector of Christ Church, Prince George's and Charles counties, Md., and Mrs. Mary Tubman of Charles Co., by the Rt. Rev. Wm. M. Stone, D. D., at Mulberry Grove. So. Ch., Aug. 4, 1837

WILSHIRE
Francis Haughton, and Ione Elizabeth, d. of the Rev. Wm. H. C. and Mary Long, by the Rev. H. L. Derby, in Christ Church, at Lancaster, Va. So. Ch., Sept. 24, 1874

WILSON
Adella J., and Reuben A. Bellen, both of Nansemond Co., Va. but originally from Schoharie Co., N.Y., by the Rev. J. B. Craighill, in the rectory of St. Paul's Church, in Suffolk. So. Ch., Jan. 11, 1877

Agnes H., d. of Samuel P. Wilson, Esq., and Wm. D. Macgill, all of Pittsylvania Co., by the Rev. P. D. Thompson, in Pittsylvania Co. So. Ch.,

Oct. 24, 1867
Alfred, of Bethesda, Md., and Minnie W. Poole of Poolesville, by the Rev. Walter P. Griggs, in St. Peter's Church, Poolesville, Md. So. Ch., June 30, 1892

Anna L., d. of the late John S. Wilson, and Robert E. Allen, all of Buchanan, by the Rev. Edward H. Ingle, in Trinity Church, Buchanan. So. Ch., Nov. 15, 1877

C. G. (Dr.), and Carrie Wallace, both of Clarksville, Tenn., by the Rev. J. T. Hargrave, at the residence of the bride's mother. So. Ch., Oct. 20, 1887

Charles Bolling, and Mary Lucretia Herbert, by the Rev. James M. Owens, in St. Paul's Church, Norfolk, Va. So. Ch., May 11, 1912

Eliza G., youngest d. of the late Thos. C. Wilson, and G. T. Crallis, by the Rev. P. F. Berkeley, at Selma, Amelia Co. So. Ch., Mar. 29, 1866

Elizabeth W., youngest d. of Alexander Wilson, Esq., and Lt. William E. Stark of the U.S. Marine Corps, by the Rev. Mr. Atkinson, at Norfolk, Va. So. Ch., Dec. 8, 1837

Elizabeth Wells, and John J. Prentiss, by the Rev. Thomas P. Baker, in the Episcopal Church, Yonges Island, S.C. So. Ch., Nov. 25, 1911

Emma S. B., d. of Maj. Jno. T. Wilson, and Dr. I. Robinson Godwin, all of Fin-

MARRIAGE NOTICES IN THE SOUTHERN CHURCHMAN WITH DATES OF PUBLICATION

castle, by the Rev. Edward H. Ingle of Roanoke, in St. Mark's Church, Fincastle, Botetourt Co. So. Ch., Nov. 7, 1867

George M., of Amelia Co., and Mary E., d. of the late R. N. Thweatt, Esq. of Chesterfield, Va., by the Rev. A. B. Tizzard, at Mount Ida. So. Ch., Feb. 8, 1865

Helen Esther, eldest d. of Mrs. Jonnie Franklin Wilson of Washington and the late Whit Wilson of Washington, formerly of Augusta Co., Va., and Octavius Knight, Jr. of New York City, by the Rev. David Barr, in Washington, D.C. So. Ch., Feb. 9, 1907

Jessie, eldest d. of Dr. John R. Wilson, and John R. Wood of Danville, formerly of Atlanta, Ga., by the Rev. George W. Dame, at Oak Ridge, the residence of the bride's father in Pittsylvania Co. So. Ch., Feb. 3, 1876

John H., Esq., Commonwealth's Attorney of Greensville Co., and Lizzie, eldest d. of Maj. Wm. F. Avent of Oxford, Miss., by the Rev. David Barr, at the residence of Tamlin Avent, the bride's grandfather, Greensville Co. So. Ch., Oct. 3, 1872

Joseph M., and Matris C. Padgett, by the Rev. W. H. Pendleton, at the residence of the bride's father, in Bedford Co., Va. So. Ch., Jan. 16, 1868

Julia A. (Mrs.), and Charles B. Haydon, by the Rev. C. S. Roberts, at Smithfield, Va. So. Ch., Nov. 21, 1867

Julian Moseley, s. of Calvin Wilson, and Alys Landon, d. of Mrs. Annie Guy Clemmitt, by the Rev. G. Freeland Peter assisted by the Rev. J. Calvin Stewart, at the home of the bride's mother, in Richmond, Va. So. Ch., Jan. 27, 1917

K. H. W. (Mrs.), d. of the late Col. R. W. Wyatt, and the Rev. John W. Lea, rector of St. Mark's Church, St. Albans, W.Va., and Trinity Church, Huntington, W.Va., by the Rev. J. S. Hanckel, D.D., at the residence of the bride's mother, at Clifton, Va. So. Ch., June 5, 1884

Lizzie, d. of Dr. Thomas E. Wilson of Roanoke Co., Va., and Walter A. Montgomery of Warrenton, N.C., by the Rev. Edward H. Ingle, in St. John's Church, Roanoke Co. So. Ch., Oct. 5, 1871

Louise E., d. of Wm. H. Wilson, and Alfred F. Thweatt, by the Rev. A. B. Tizzard, in Trinity Church, Chesterfield Co. So. Ch., Apr. 4, 1867

Maria R., d. of James H. and Virginia Z. Wilson and gr.d. of the late Felix Zollicoffer, and William L. Hill of Balm, Ala., by the Rev. Mayo Cabell Martin, rector of Holy Trinity Church, Nashville, Tenn., at the residence of the bride's parents, Nashville, Tenn. So. Ch., Sept. 13, 1888

MARRIAGE NOTICES IN THE SOUTHERN CHURCHMAN WITH DATES OF PUBLICATION

Mary E., of Botetourt Co., Va., and J. J. Carper of Franklin Co., Va., by the Rev. E. W. Hubard, in St. Mark's Church, Fincastle. So. Ch., Dec. 28, 1871

Mary J., and Thomas S. Welfare, by the Rev. Geo. W. Dame, at Loxington, N.C. So. Ch., Mar. 16, 1876

Minorva J., d. of John Wilson, Esq., and Blair Pogram, Esq., by the Rev. John C. McCabe, at Woodland, Surry Co. So. Ch., June 21, 1855

Minnie Pogram, and Richard Elliott Boykin, Esq. of Smithfield, Va., by the Rev. J. W. Keeble, at Mantura, Surry Co., Va. So. Ch., Nov. 22, 1877

Minnie Thweatt, d. of G. M. Wilson and gr.d. of the late Hon. R. N. Thweatt of Chesterfield Co., Va., and J. D. Robert, M.D. of St. Louis, Mo., by the Rev. A. B. Tizzard assisted by the Rev. H. M. Jackson, D.D., in Grace Church, Richmond. So. Ch., Jan. 10, 1889

Richard H., and Margaret A., eldest d. of O. M. Smith, Esq., by the Rev. Thomas W. White, at Glenbrook, Lunenburg, Va. So. Ch., Feb. 27, 1863

Richard T., of Sussex Co., Va., and Hutoka, d. of the late Wm. F. Hobbs of Greensville Co., Va., by the Rev. David Barr. So. Ch., Dec. 7, 1871

Robert T., M.D., and Mabel, only d. of the late Dr. James Chinn, all of Baltimore, by the Rt. Rev. Alfred Randolph, D.D., in Emanuel Church, Baltimore. So. Ch., Jan. 17, 1884

S. E., of Terrell, Tex., and Kate H. Wyatt of Albemarle Co., by the Rev. Wm. Paret, D.D. assisted by the Rev. J. S. Lindsay, D.D., in the Church of the Epiphany, Washington, D.C. So. Ch., Oct. 14, 1880

Samuel M., Esq., of Norfolk Co., and Sallie B., d. of the late Gen. Philip St. George Cocke of Powhatan, by the Rev. J. D. Powell, at "Bellmead", Powhatan Co. So. Ch., Mar. 1, 1866

Susan, d. of John E. Wilson, Esq. of "Wakefield", Westmoreland Co., Va., and the Rev. William C. Latane, rector of Washington Parish, by the Rev. Beverly D. Tucker, in St. Peter's Church, Oak Grove. So. Ch., Nov. 9, 1876

Thos., and Mrs. Milly Moore, by the Rev. W. H. Pendleton, at the home of Mr. Bartee, in Bedford Co., Va. So. Ch., Feb. 20, 1868

William H., and Mary E. Taylor, both of Bedford, by the Rev. N. Sale. So. Ch., Feb. 22, 1856

William H., Jr., and Essie, youngest d. of Col. Levin Gayles, all of Portsmouth, by the Rev. Thos. A. Tidball, in Trinity Church, Portsmouth. So. Ch., Nov. 8, 1877

See also EDWARDS, Elizabeth Wilmer Wilson

WINCHESTER

James R. (The Rev.), of Maryland, and Eliza Atkinson, d. of Col. R. H. Lee of Clarke Co., Va., by the Rev. Wm. B. Lee and the Rev. Joseph R. Jones, in Christ Church, Millwood, Clarke Co., Va. So. Ch., Sept. 26 and Oct. 10, 1878

MARRIAGE NOTICES IN THE SOUTHERN CHURCHMAN WITH DATES OF PUBLICATION

WINDER
    Edward Lloyd, s. of the late Gen. Charles S. Winder, and Mary Dorsey, d. of the late Com. F. A. Parker, U.S. Navy, and gr.d. of the late Thomas Donaldson, by the Rev. W. D. Powers, in Grace Church, Elk Ridge, Md. So. Ch., Oct. 30, 1884

    Rosina C., of Northampton, and the Hon. George S. Guion of Louisiana, by the Rev. N. L. Chevers, at Eastville, Northampton Co. So. Ch., Oct. 16, 1857

WINFREE
    Hugh Cabell, of Drewry's Bluff, Va., and Agnes Tenable Watkins of Richmond, Va., by the Rev. G. Otis Mead, at the residence of Allen Harless, in Christiansburg, Va. So. Ch., Mar. 29, 1913

WINGFIELD
    J. H. D., D.D. (The Rev.), and Mrs. Anne Garland, in St. Paul's Church, Petersburg. So. Ch., June 25, 1874

    John H. D., and Mary J., d. of the late John R. Chandler, M.D., U.S.N., by the Rev. John H. Wingfield, in Trinity Church, Portsmouth, Va. So. Ch., Sept. 2, 1859

    Josephine, of Elizabeth City Co., and Frank T. Roche, Esq., formerly of Hampton, Va., now of Austin, Tex., by the Rev. J. J. Gravatt, at Back River, Elizabeth City Co., Va. So. Ch., Jan. 12, 1882

    Mary, d. of the officiating clergyman, and James Hamilton Scott of Richmond, Va. by the Rt. Rev. Bishop Wingfield, at Benicia, Cal. So. Ch., Nov. 2, 1893

    Sally C., d. of the late Lewis Wingfield, Esq. of Bedford Co., and John P. Lovell of Franklin, by the Rev. N. Sale. So. Ch., Nov. 30, 1855

WINN
    D. Watson (The Rev.), of Richmond, Va., and Bettie Carter, d. of the late Josiah L. Deans of Gloucester Co., Va., by the Rev. R. H. Paine, in Mt. Calvary Church, Baltimore, Md. So. Ch., Jan. 6, 1887

    Kate Ellerbe, second d. of Dr. H. J. Winn of Birmingham, and James Bruce McClelland of Clarendon, Tex., formerly of Virginia, by the Rev. T. J. Beard, in the Church of the Advent, Birmingham, Ala. So. Ch., July 15, 1886

WINSTEAD
    E. D., of North Carolina, and Annie Macfarland Neblett, d. of Colin Neblett, by the Rev. E. B. Jones, at Greenock, Lunenburg Co., the residence of the bride's father. So. Ch., Jan. 24, 1884

WINSTON
    B. L., of Hanover, and Bettie, d. of Dr. Wm. Bankhead of Orange, by the Rev. Joseph Earnest, at Edgemont, Orange Co. So. Ch., June 11, 1858

    Fendall G., of Minneapolis, Minn., and Lilian, d. of the late Henry R. Jones of Richmond, Va., by the Rev. J. C. Painter, at "Retreat", the residence of Mrs. E. A. T. Jones, in Orange Co. So. Ch., Oct. 23 and 30, 1884

MARRIAGE NOTICES IN THE SOUTHERN CHURCHMAN WITH DATES OF PUBLICATION

Janie P., second d. of Bickorton L. Winston, Esq., and Capt. David Waldhaner of Savannah, Ga., by the Rev. B. E. Habersham, at Signal Hill, Hanover Co., Va. So. Ch., Oct. 18, 1877

Lizzie, of Caroline Co., Va., and Richmond T. Lacy, Jr. of New Kent Co., Va., by the Rev. T. H. Lacy, at Shepherd's Hill, the residence of the bride's mother. So. Ch., Oct. 19, 1876

Lucian Dade, and Lucy Lewis Long, by the Rev. Parnell LeBas Cross of Emmanuel Episcopal Church, Rapidan, in Winston Memorial Chapel, Winston, Va. So. Ch., Nov. 6, 1909

Maida W., eldest d. of O. P. Winston formerly of Louisa Co., Va., and J. Thomas Black of Bastross Co., Tex., by the Rev. J. W. Phillips of Austin, in Bastross Co., Tex. So. Ch., Feb. 18, 1875

Richard M., of Hanover, and Rosalie Stuart Bankhead, d. of Dr. Wm. Bankhead of Orange Co., by the Rev. Joseph Earnest, at Edgemont. So. Ch., Nov. 20, 1857

Thomas B., and Fannie Goodwin, both of Louisa Co., Va., by the Rev. L. R. Combs, at the residence of the bride's mother. So. Ch., Jan. 15, 1885

WINTERSTEIN

Jacob Ashton (The Rev.), rector of Holy Trinity Church, Westchester, in the Diocese of Pennsylvania, and Claudia Marguerite, d. of Mr. and Mrs. J. B. Haines and sister of the Rev. E. S. Haines, missionary to Liberia, now in this country on furlough, at Swedesboro, N.J. So. Ch., May 17, 1924

WINTHROP

Edward (The Rev.), Professor of Sacred Literature in the Theological Seminary, Kentucky, and Elizabeth, d. of John Andras, Esq. of Bath, England, by the Rev. John Ward, at Lexington. So. Ch., June 28, 1839

Harriet R., d. of Henry R. Winthrop, Esq., and the Rev. Haslett McKim, all of New York, by the Rev. George S. Converse, at the residence of the bride's parents. So. Ch., Sept. 22, 1870

WIRT

Agnes W., and George Washington, both of Westmoreland, Va., by the Rev. Wm. C. Latane, in St. Peter's Church, Oak Grove, Va. So. Ch., July 20, 1893

Bettie P., and R. J. Washington, both of Westmoreland Co., by the Rev. William C. Chesley, at Wirtland, the residence of the bride's father. So. Ch., Dec. 5, 1867

Dabney E., and J. Augusta Washington, by the Rev. J. W. Chesley, in St. Peter's Church, Westmoreland Co., Va. So. Ch., Nov. 30, 1855

Daniel P., of Westmoreland Co., and Kate A. Taylos, by the Rev. Mr. Shields, at Chatterton, King George Co., Va. So. Ch., Dec. 6, 1877

Nellie (Mrs.), of Cecil Co., Md.,

MARRIAGE NOTICES IN THE SOUTHERN CHURCHMAN WITH DATES OF PUBLICATION

and Dr. Julian F. Ward of Baltimore, Md., by the Rev. J. R. Hubard, D.D., at the residence of the bride's brother-in-law, R. T. Barton, Winchester, Va. So. Ch., Feb. 4, 1886

WISE
Annie K., d. of the late Tully R. Wise of Northampton Co., and Dr. Severn P. Nottingham, by the Rev. J. D. Powell of Portsmouth, in Christ Church, Eastville, Northampton Co. So. Ch., July 7, 1870

George D., Esq., of Accomac Co., and Marietta Atkinson, d. of the Hon. Archibald of Smithfield, by the Rev. Henry A. Wise, at Smithfield, Isle of Wight Co. So. Ch., Dec. 23, 1859

Henry A. (The Rev.), rector of the Church of The Saviour, Philadelphia, and Hattie, d. of R. Barton Haxall, Esq. of Richmond, Va., by the Rev. George Woodbridge, D.D., in Richmond, Va. So. Ch., Nov. 16, 1860

James Madison, and Ann Dent, d. of the late James and Ann Dent Dunlop, all of Richmond, by the Rev. Dr. Minnigerode, in St. Paul's Church, Richmond, Va. So. Ch., Dec. 2, 1880

John C. (Dr.), United States Navy, and Agnes T. Brooke formerly of Fauquier Co., Va., by the Rev. A. Y. Hundley, in Abingdon Church, Gloucester Co., Va. So. Ch., May 15, 1879

WITHERS
Flora Scott, d. of Col. Robert W. Withers, and Wm. M. Murrell, all of Campbell Co., Va., by the Rev. W. W. Kimball, in Trinity Church, Rustburg. So. Ch., Nov. 29, 1883

Ida, d. of Col. Robt. W. Withers, and Frank Nelson, by the Rev. G. W. Nelson assisted by the Rev. Frank Page and the Rev. W. W. Kimball, in Trinity Church, Rustburg, Va. So. Ch., Dec. 23, 1880

Inez, d. of Dr. W. M. Withers, and Percy Montague, all of Richmond, by the Rev. Moses D. Hoge assisted by the Rev. Dr. Peterkin, in the Second Presbyterian Church. So. Ch., Aug. 11, 1881

Janet C., d. of the late Rev. Edmund Withers, and Wm. B. Harrison of Staunton, by the Rev. F. G. Scott, in the rectory at Norwood, Nelson Co., Va. So. Ch., Oct. 9, 1879

Jannet T., and Robert E. Garbee, both of Campbell Co., Va., by the Rev. W. W. Kimball, at the home of the bride. So. Ch., Oct. 6, 1881

Louise, youngest d. of the late Rev. Edmund Withers, and Richard H. Cabell of Lovingston, by the Rev. B. T. Turner, in Christ Church, Norwood. So. Ch., July 3, 1884

Mattie B., d. of William A. and Alice Withers, and Parham F. Price, by the Rev. W. W. Kimball, at the residence of the bride's father, in Campbell Co. So. Ch., Nov. 2, 1882

Robert G., formerly of Nelson Co., Va., and Gretta Hayes of Missouri, by the

MARRIAGE NOTICES IN THE SOUTHERN CHURCHMAN WITH DATES OF PUBLICATION

Rev. J. W. Ohl, in Christ Church, at Aspen, Col. So. Ch., June 2, 1887

Robert H., and Cornelia F. Tanner, both of Campbell Co., Va., by the Rev. W. W. Kimball. So. Ch., Nov. 3, 1881

Robert W., of Alabama, and Josephine P. Burks, by the Rev. John K. Mason, at the residence of O. P. Bell, at Liberty, Va. So. Ch., June 15, 1882

Samuel T., and Nannie C. Blackford, only d. of Charles M. Blackford, Esq., all of Lynchburg, Va., by the Rev. T. M. Carson, in St. Paul's Church, at Lynchburg, Va. So. Ch., Feb. 22, 1883

Susan C., youngest d. of Dr. Robt. W. Withers of Campbell Co., and Patrick Cabell Massie, Esq., of Nelson Co., by the Rev. T. E. Locke, at Rock Castle, Campbell Co. So. Ch., June 26, 1857

Susan Dabney, second d. of Col. R. Withers, and Lt. Henry S. Williams of Mecklenburg, by the Rev. Geo. W. Dame, in the Church of the Epiphany, at Danville. So. Ch., Jan. 4, 1866

Thomas, acting chief enginoer of the Denver and South Park Railroad, Col., and Eliza, d. of the late Com. Matthew F. Maury, by the Rev. Edmund Withers, in Richmond. So. Ch., Sept. 26, 1878

WITHROW
Clara Bell, and Joseph D. Battle formerly of North Carolina, by the Rev. Mr. Bird of Trinity Church, at the residence of the bride's mother, in Galveston, Tex. So. Ch., Sept. 23, 1886

WITT
Richard, and Sarah J. Wilchen, by the Rev. R. J. McBryde, in Amherst Co., Va. So. Ch., Feb. 10, 1870

WITTICHEN
Otto, late of Germany, now of Prince William Co., Va., and Kate Ramsay, d. of John Murray Forbes, Esq. of Fauquier, by the Rev. Philip Slaughter, D.D. assisted by the Rev. John S. Lindsay, in St. James' Church, Warrenton, Va. So. Ch., Nov. 28, 1878

WOLTZ
E. Ann, d. of Ferdinand Woltz, Esq., Clerk of Botetourt County Court, and Woodville Bowyer of Fincastle, by the Rev. T. F. Martin of Nelson Co., at Fincastle. So. Ch., Oct. 29, 1858

Juliet B., d. of Ferdinand Woltz, Esq., Clerk of Botetourt County Court, and Henry C. Middleton of Farmville, by the Rev. T. F. Martin of Nelson Co., at Fincastle. So. Ch., Oct. 29, 1858

WOMACK
Ella C., d. of Thomas Womack, Esq., and Everett W. Rudd, by the Rev. A. B. Tizzard, at Eppington, Chesterfield Co., Va. So. Ch., Feb. 12, 1880

WOMBWELL
L. B., Esq., of Florida, and J. L. Curd, by the

MARRIAGE NOTICES IN THE SOUTHERN CHURCHMAN WITH DATES OF PUBLICATION

Rev. Lewis W. Burton of St. John's Church, at the residence of the bride's parents, 1920 E. Broad St. Richmond. So. Ch., Dec. 27, 1888

WOOD

Angus M., of Kentucky, and Ida, eldest d. of J. W. Inskeep, Esq., by the Rev. G. A. Gibbons, at "Caledonia", the residence of the bride's father. So. Ch., Jan. 17, 1889

Bettie B., of Roanoke, and W. D. Stuart of Hagerstown, Md., s. of Col. W. D. Stuart of Virginia, by the Rev. R. A. Goodwin, in St. John's Church, Roanoke. So. Ch., July 3, 1884

Edwin (Dr.), and Evy Allen, by the Rev. Pendleton Brooke, at the residence of the bride's mother, Botetourt Co., Va. So. Ch., Jan. 22, 1874

Elizabeth Clothilde, of Clarke Co., Va., and James McCoy of Warren Co., Va., by the Rev. John Lindsay, D. D., at Washington, D.C. So. Ch., Nov. 5, 1885

John R., of Danville, formerly of Atlanta, Ga., and Jesse, eldest d. of Dr. John R. Wilson, by the Rev. George W. Dame, at Oak Ridge, the residence of the bride's father, in Pittsylvania Co., Va. So. Ch., Feb. 3, 1876

John Wilson (Dr.), and Regina B. Lustgarten, in the Church of the Transfiguration, New York. So. Ch., Aug. 26, 1939

Lucy Alfred, and W. H. Graham of Hamilton, Canada, by the Rev. A. B. Tizzard, at the residence of the bride's mother, Mrs. Henry Miller, in Richmond. So. Ch., Nov. 18, 1880

Nannie Jane, d. of the late Alfred Wood, Esq. of Amelia, and Dr. David M. Wilkinson of Chesterfield, by the Rev. A. B. Tizzard, at Oldenplace, Amelia Co. So. Ch., May 8, 1857

Philip S., and Emma Pride, d. of the late John Pride, all of Amelia Co., Va., by the Rev. P. F. Berkeley, at Lucerne, the residence of the bride's mother, in Amelia Co. So. Ch., Mar. 9, 1876

Rebecca Benneham, of Edenton, N.C., and the Rev. Frederick Blount Drane, Archdeacon of Alaska, at Seattle, Wash. So. Ch., Oct. 11, 1924

Richard S., of Goochland, and M. Spottswood Pollard of King William Co., by the Rev. S. S. Hepbron, at Octogon, King William Co. So. Ch., Oct. 27, 1892

Sarah Farrar, only d. of the late Thomas Wood of Lindon, Ohio, and John R. Strieff of Cincinnati, Ohio, by the Rev. Wm. S. Campbell, in Trinity Church, Lindon, Ohio. So. Ch., Mar. 11, 1886

Sparrel Asa, and India Davies Goodwyn, d. of the late Judge Charles F. Goodwyn, by the Rev. T. H. Lacy, D.D., at the home of her mother, in Nottoway, Va. So. Ch., Feb. 6 and 13, 1909

Warner, of Farmington, and Margaret Lynn, d. of the late Dr. John R. Woods of Albemarle Co., Va., by the Rev. Robb White, at Holkham, the residence of the

MARRIAGE NOTICES IN THE SOUTHERN CHURCHMAN WITH DATES OF PUBLICATION

bride's mother. So. Ch., Jan. 20, 1887

Wilhemina, and James E. Smith, both of Caroline Co., Va., by the Rev. Wm. W. Green, at "Rosehill", the residence of the bride's father, Col. Fleming Wood. So. Ch., Dec. 26, 1872

WOODBRIDGE

Elizabeth Nicolson, second d. of the Rev. George Woodbridge, D.D., and J. Goodnow of Hartford, Conn., by the Rev. George Woodbridge, D.D., at the residence of her father in Richmond, Va. So. Ch., Apr. 12, 1877

George (The Rev.), rector of Christ Church, and Rebecca Nicholson, d. of Andrew Nicholson, Esq., deceased, by the Rt. Rev. Richard Channing Moore, D.D., at Richmond, Va. So. Ch., Oct. 30, 1835

Geo. N., and Martha A., youngest d. of Robert Edmond, Esq., by the Rev. George Woodbridge, in the Monumental Church in Richmond. So. Ch., Dec. 15, 1870

J. Edwards, and Louisa, d. of John O. Doshong, by the Rev. Geo. Woodbridge, D.D. of Richmond assisted by the Rev. Henry Brown, at Chester, Pa. So. Ch., June 8, 1876

Julia C., d. of the late Rev. Geo. Woodbridge, D.D., and W. Pierce Bell of Washington, D.C., by the Rt. Rev. Wm. Pinckney assisted by the Rev. Dr. Elliott of Washington, D.C., at the residence of the bride's mother, in Richmond. So. Ch., Feb. 27, 1879

Sarah E., d. of the officiating clergyman, and Horace P. Edwards, by the Rev. Geo. Woodbridge, D.D., in the Monumental Church, Richmond. So. Ch., Nov. 19, 1858

WOODHOUSE

Minnie Lee, and William Avery, by the Rev. John C. Cornick, in Eastern Shore Chapel, Princess Anne Co., Va. So. Ch., Sept. 17, 1891

Nellie L., and George L. Bonney, both of Princess Anne, by the Rev. W. R. Savage, in Eastern Shore Chapel, Princess Anne Co., Va. So. Ch., Jan. 28, 1886

WOODING

Mary, second d. of Dr. N. H. and Susan W. Wooding of Pittsylvania Co., and Charles Woodson Venable formerly of Prince Edward Co., by the Rev. C. O. Pruden, in St. John's Church, Mt. Airy, Pittsylvania Co., Va. So. Ch., Oct. 2, 1890

WOODMAN

Frank, and Nannie M., second d. of Dr. John T. Cotton, all of Charleston, by the Rev. R. A. Cobbs, at the residence of the bride. So. Ch., Oct. 30, 1884

WOODS

Annie Meriwether, eldest d. of John J. Woods, Esq. of Ivy Depot, Albemarle Co., Va., and Melville Taliaferro of Henrico Co., Va., by the Rev. J. A. Greaves, M. A., at the residence of

MARRIAGE NOTICES IN THE SOUTHERN CHURCHMAN WITH DATES OF PUBLICATION

the bride's parents. So. Ch., Oct. 13, 1881

Edgar, Jr., M.D., of the American Southern Presbyterian Mission, and Frances Anne Smith of the Woman's Union Missionary Society of New York, d. of the Rev. Dudley D. Smith, rector of Emmanuel Protestant Episcopal Church, Kensington, Philadelphia, by the Rev. E. H. Thomson of the American Episcopal Mission, in Bridgman Memorial Home, Shanghai, China. So. Ch., June 2, 1892

Fanny, of Albemarle Co., Va., and the Rev. Wm. C. Butler of Halifax C.H., Va., by the Rev. R. K. Meade, in Christ Church, Charlottesville. So. Ch., Dec. 30, 1859

J. F. (The Rev.), and Ellen Gray of Moundsville, W. Va., by the Rev. Thos. G. Addison, in Trinity Church, Washington, D.C. So. Ch., May 21, 1868

J. Warwick, of Albemarle Co., and Mary M., d. of the late Mann S. Valentine of Richmond, by the Rev. J. Peterkin, D.D. So. Ch., June 28, 1866

James, s. of Col. Thomas D. Woods of Amherst Co., Va., and Isabella J. Waugh, only d. of Pembroke E. Waugh of Amherst Co., by the Rev. J. P. Lawrence, at the residence of the bride's father. So. Ch., Nov. 7, 1878

Margaret Lynn, d. of the late Dr. John R. Woods of Albemarle Co., Va., and Warner Wood of Farmington, by the Rev. Robb White, at Holkham, the residence of the bride's mother. So. Ch., Jan. 20, 1887

Robert Harris, of Albemarle Co., Va., and Margaret Warfield, d. of Joshua W. Dorsey of Ellicott City, Md., by the Rev. R. A. Poole, in St. Stephen's Church, Ellicott City, Md. So. Ch., Nov. 29, 1888

WOODSON

Blake L. (Maj.), of Craig Co., and Leila W., d. of Col. W. E. M. Word of Fincastle, by the Rev. H. Ingle assisted by the Rev. E. W. Hubard, in St. Mark's Church, Fincastle. So. Ch., Dec. 15, 1870

C. E. (The Rev.), of Franklin, Va., and Janet McG., d. of Col. T. W. Ashby, by the Rev. Dr. Suter assisted by the Rev. Dr. Walker, in Christ Church, Alexandria, Va. So. Ch., Nov. 27, 1890

Charles E. (The Rev.), rector of Christ Church, Vicksburg, Miss., and Lucile Werner, in Christ Church, Tuscaloosa, Ala. So. Ch., July 11, 1931

Richard S., and Jennie L. Morgan, both of Isle of Wight Co., by the Rev. R. S. Barrett, in Richmond, Va. So. Ch., July 8, 1880

WOODWARD

Harry Reamer, Esq., of New Albany, Ind., and Fanny Berkeley Cochran, d. of the Rt. Rev. Thomas

MARRIAGE NOTICES IN THE SOUTHERN CHURCHMAN WITH DATES OF PUBLICATION

Underwood Dudley, D.D., by the Rt. Revs. the Bishops of Kentucky and Louisiana,* in Calvary Church, Louisville, Ky. So. Ch., June 10, 1886

Sarah Nicoll, of New Jersey, and Cameron Farquhar McRae of North Carolina, by the Rt. Rev. F. R. Graves, D.D., in St. John's Church, Pro-Cathedral, Shanghai, China. So. Ch., Apr. 11, 1908

W. Minor, of Richmond, and Mary, d. of the officiating clergyman, the Rev. K. J. Stewart, at Gordonsville, Va. So. Ch., Nov. 4, 1869

WOOLDRIDGE
Albert B., of Richmond, Va., and L. Hausbrough* of Orange Court House, by the Rev. John S. Hausbrough at Orange Court House. So. Ch., Nov. 6, 1863

Henry C., and Alice W. King, by the Rev. A. B. Tizzard, in Manakin Church, Powhatan Co. So. Ch., Nov. 19, 1885

WOOLF
Robt. D., and Mary K., oldest d. of Wm. Ayre of Fairfax Co., Va., by the Rev. Jno. McGill, at Buena Vista. So. Ch., Feb. 12, 1874

WOOLFOLK
John C., of Columbus, Ga., and Eliza A. Nelson, d. of Wm. N. and Mary A. Nelson of Clarke Co., Va., by the Rev. Jos. R. Jones, in Christ Church, Millwood. So. Ch., Jan. 3, 1878

WOOLFORD
Joseph E., and Margaret T. Yates, both of Dorchester Co., Md., by the Rev.
Wm. W. Greene, at Church Creek. So. Ch., Apr. 14, 1881

WOOLLS
Stephen, of Richmond, and Kate M., oldest d. of James A. S. Stoutenburgh of Alexandria, by the Rev. Dennis O'Kane, in St. Mary's Church, Alexandria. So. Ch., Sept. 16, 1880

WOOLSEY
Emily, and the Rev. Morgan Dix, S.T.D., rector of Trinity Church, by the Rt. Rev. H. Potter, D.D., at the residence of the bride's mother, in New York. So. Ch., June 11, 1874

WOCSTER
Susan Nash,** d. of the Hon. Henry K. Nash, and Hill Burgwin, Esq. of Pittsburgh, by the Rev. Joseph W. Murphy, at Hillsboro, N.C. So. Ch., Nov. 1, 1888

WOOTEN
Edward (The Rev.), rector of St. Thomas' Church, Windsor, and Eliza Yonge, d. of the late Stephen Jewett of Wilmington, by the Rev. George Patterson, rector of St. John's Church, in St. James' Church, Wilmington, N.C. So. Ch., Nov. 18, 1875

WOOTON
Martha, d. of the late Dr. Turner Wooton and Mrs. Caroline Wooton, and Thomas Anderson, Esq. (Vestryman), by the Rev. W. A. Avirett, in Christ Church, Rockville, Montgomery Co., Md. So. Ch., Feb. 20, 1873

* Given as printed
** Possibly Mrs.

MARRIAGE NOTICES IN THE SOUTHERN CHURCHMAN WITH DATES OF PUBLICATION

WORD
- Loila W., d. of Col. W. E. M. Word of Fincastle, and Maj. Blake L. Woodson of Craig Co., by the Rev. Edward H. Ingle assisted by the Rev. E. W. Hubard, in St. Mark's Church, Fincastle. So. Ch., Dec. 15, 1870
- Quin M., of Richmond, and Mary Scott McClanahan of Roanoke Co., Va., by the Rev. W. H. Pendleton, at Locust Grove, Roanoke Co., Va. So. Ch., Jan. 4, 1856
- Sallie T., of Roanoke, and P. W. Reynolds of Roanoke, by the Rev. D. M. Wood, in St. John's Church, Roanoke, Va. So. Ch., Dec. 3, 1885

WORLMAN
- Wm. H. R., of South Carolina, and Maria W., d. of the late Warner W. Minor, Esq., by the Rev. Jacob S. Scott, chaplain of the University of Virginia, at Wertland. So. Ch., Nov. 9, 1848

WORMELY
- P. Lightfoot, and Lucy Waller Duval, by the Rev. Dr. Peterkin, in St. James' Church, Richmond, Va. So. Ch., Oct. 23, 1873

WORSHAM
- Alice, and Thomas H. Booker, both of Amelia Co., Va., by the Rev. P. F. Berkeley, at the bride's residence. So. Ch., Dec. 12, 1872
- Emma, and Edmond Clarke, both of West Point, Va., by the Rev. Pendleton Brooke, at the residence of the bride's father. So. Ch., Sept. 6, 1888
- M. R. (The Rev.), and Ethel Armstrong of Shelbyville, Ky., by the Rev. Dr. John K. Mason, in St. Andrew's Church, Louisville, Ky. So. Ch., May 9, 1908
- Margaret Winstead, and Henry Carl Oltrogge, by the Rev. Melville E. Johnson assisted by the Rev. C. A. Ashby, in the Church of the Good Shepherd, Jacksonville, Fla. So. Ch., Oct. 21, 1922

WORTHAM
- Samuel R., and Mary Jane Cox, both of Amherst, by the Rev. W. H. Kinckle. So. Ch., Nov. 9, 1855

WORTHINGTON
- Eugene, of Annapolis, and Evelyn Morton Jenkins, d. of G. Taylor Jenkins, Esq. of Baltimore, by the Rev. John S. Lindsay, D.D. assisted by the Rev. Dr. Williams, in Christ Church, Baltimore. So. Ch., May 3, 1883
- Geo. Y., Jr., of Fauquier Co., Va., and Nannie T., d. of the late William E. Coleman of Virginia, by the Rev. W. C. Williams, at Summerville, Ga. So. Ch., Nov. 28, 1878
- R. S., of Kansas, and Fanny N., d. of the Rev. C. R. Nelson, D.D., of Rockville, Md., by the Rev. Kinloch Nelson of Pennsylvania assisted by the rector, the Rev. A. Johns, in Christ Church, Rockville. So. Ch., July 11, 1889

WRAY
- Henrietta, and Mr. Herbert, both of Elizabeth City Co., Va., by the Rev. Dr. A. Wade, at Shirley, the res-

MARRIAGE NOTICES IN THE SOUTHERN CHURCHMAN WITH DATES OF PUBLICATION

idence of John Selden, in Charles City Co. So. Ch., Feb. 9, 1871

Kate Mallory, and Richard Mann Page, by the Rev. A. Y. Hundley, in Abingdon Church, Gloucester Co., Va. So. Ch., Oct. 24, 1878

WREN

Mary W., youngest d. of the late Maj. John F. Wren, and Robert R. Field, by the Rev. Dr. Peterkin, in St. James' Church, Richmond. So. Ch., Dec. 17, 1885

Walter M., and Fannie M., youngest d. of the late Richard C. Hall, all of Richmond, Va., by the Rev. Dr. Sprigg, at the residence of the bride's sister, Mrs. A. R. Yarbrough. So. Ch., Jan. 28, 1886

William D., of Richmond, and Fanny L. Dunn of Powhatan Co., Va., by the Rev. F. Stringfellow, in Emmanuel Church, Powhatan Co. So. Ch., Nov. 16, 1876

WRENN

Albert, and Hannah A. Harrison, both of Fairfax, by the Rev. Frank Page, in Christ Church, Chantilly. So. Ch., May 24, 1883

WRIGHT

(The Rev. Mr.), and Mildred Woodward Cochran, by Bishop Jett assisted by the Rev. Dr. David Cady Wright of Christ Church, Savannah, and the Rev. John J. Gravatt, rector of Trinity Church, in Trinity Church, Staunton, Va. So. Ch., Sept. 23, 1933

Anne Cole, and the Rev. J. Andrew Harris, by the Rev. John Cole, in Philadelphia. So. Ch., Apr. 19, 1861

Betty C., second d. of the late Col. Robt. L. Wright of Loudoun Co., and R. N. Breckinridge of Staunton, by the Rev. J. R. Hubard, in Christ Church, Winchester, Va. So. Ch., June 15, 1876

Charlotte Barnes, d. of Judge and Mrs. T. R. B. Wright, and F. G. Scott, Jr., M.D. of Orange, Va., by the Rev. F. G. Scott, D.D. assisted by the Rev. Wm. Nelson Meade, in St. John's Church, Tappahannock, Va. So. Ch., Jan. 4, 1913

Edwin, of Ardmore, Pa., and Louise, d. of Mrs. John K. Mason and the late Dr. John K. Mason, at Elkton, Va. So. Ch., Sept. 13, 1913

Ellen C., d. of James M. Wright, Esq., and James S. Cowan of Baltimore, by the Rev. Jno. Collins McCabe, D.D., rector of St. Luke's Church, Bladensburg, in Prince George's Co., Md. So. Ch., July 4, 1867

Frances Shepherd, d. of Mr. and Mrs. Henry E. Wright of Centreville, Md., and Robert Brooks Hilleary of Washington, D.C., by the Ven. R. Bowden Shepherd, uncle of the bride, assisted by the Rev. A. Chamberlaine, rector of the church, in St. Paul's Church, Centreville, Md. So. Ch., Sept. 12, 1936

Henry Ennels, and Fanny Shepherd, only d. of Mrs. William B. Earle and the late William Brundige Earle, all of Queen Anne's Co., Md., by the Ven. R. Bowden Shepherd, Archdeacon

MARRIAGE NOTICES IN THE SOUTHERN CHURCHMAN WITH DATES OF PUBLICATION

of the Diocese of New Jersey, in St. Paul's Church, Centreville, Md. So. Ch., Jan. 25, 1913

John E., Jr., of Nansemond Co., Va., and Genevieve, d. of Dr. Thos. L. and Annie E. Scott, by the Rev. W. B. Williams, at the residence of the late Dr. Thos. L. Scott, Caroline Co., Va. So. Ch., July 19, 1888

Lalla R., and C. S. Smith, both of Essex Co., Va., by the Rev. Everard Meade, in St. Paul's Church, South Farnham Parish, Essex Co., Va. So. Ch., Dec. 1, 1881

Margaret Della, d. of the late Judge T. R. B. Wright and Mrs. Della Preston Wright, and Everard Kidder, s. of Frances* Key Meade and the late Mrs. Sarah Manson Calloway Meade, by the Rev. William Nelson Meade, uncle of the groom, in St. John's Church, Tappahannock. So. Ch., Dec. 18, 1915

Mary A., d. of James P. Wright, M.D., and W. Paul Tebault, M.D., all of Princess Anne Co., Va., by the Rev. Wm. R. Savage, in Eastern Shore Chapel, Princess Anne Co., Va. So. Ch., May 21, 1885

Mattie, and Dr. B. F. Walker of Augusta Co., Va., by the Rev. G. H. Denny, at "The Forest", the residence of the bride's mother, Essex Co., Va. So. Ch., Nov. 2, 1876

Robert Braden, of Williamsport, Md., and Mrs. Anne Ambler Eyster, by her rector, the Rev. Conrad Goodwin, and the Rev. F. W. Ambler of Summerville, S.C., brother of the bride, at Charles Town, W.Va., at the home of the bride. So. Ch., Sept. 3, 1921

Sallie U., of Williamsburg, and M. Dulany Ball, Esq. of Fairfax Co., Va., by the Rev. R. T. Brown, in the chapel of William and Mary College. So. Ch., Oct. 26, 1860

T. R. B., of Tappahannock, Essex Co., Va., and Davidella Preston, by the Rev. G. H. Denny, at the residence of Dr. J. R. Woods, Albemarle Co., Va. So. Ch., Dec. 14, 1876

T. R. B., s. of the late Judge T. R. B. Wright and his wife, Della Preston Wright of Tappahannock, Va., and Dorothy, d. of George W. Mitchell of Williamsport, Pa., in Baltimore, Md., in the home of the Rev. James M. Wallace. So. Ch., Dec. 18, 1918

Wesley (Dr.), and Ann Jane Swann, both of Caroline Co., by the Rev. Wm. W. Greene, in Caroline Co., Va. So. Ch., Jan. 18, 1861

William John (The Rev.), of Washington, D.C., and Lucy Hayden, d. of the late Wilfred Gaugh of Chaptico, by the Bishop of Washington, at Chaptico, Md. So. Ch., Nov. 6, 1909

WRIGLEY

Violet, and the Rev. W. W. Kimball, both of Macon, Ga., by the Rev. James

---

* Given as printed

MARRIAGE NOTICES IN THE SOUTHERN CHURCHMAN WITH DATES OF PUBLICATION

R. Winchester assisted by the Rev. W. Dudley Powers, in St. Barnabas' Chapel, Macon, Ga. So. Ch., June 13, 1889

WROTH
Peregrine (The Rev.), rector of the church, and Minnie, eldest d. of L. W. and M. A. Counselman of Baltimore, by the Rt. Rev. Wm. Pinckney, D.D., in the Church of the Messiah, Baltimore, Md. So. Ch., Feb. 26, 1880

WYANT
Claudius N., formerly of Rockingham Co., Va., and Blanche A. Northam of Onancock, by the Rev. Henry L. Derby, in Trinity Church, Onancock, Accomack, Va. So. Ch., July 28, 1892

WYATT
John J., of Sussex Co., Va., and Helen Heartwell, at Elmwood, the residence of H. J. Heartwell. So. Ch., Feb. 14, 1884

Kate H., of Albemarle Co., Va., and S. E. Wilson of Terrell, Tex., by the Rev. Wm. Paret, D.D. assisted by the Rev. J. S. Lindsay, D.D., at the Church of the Epiphany, Washington, D.C. So. Ch., Oct. 14, 1880

Thos. J. (The Rev.), and Sophia L., d. of Jessie Hollinsworth of Carroll Co., Md., by the Rev. Dr. Wyatt, in St. Paul's Church, Baltimore. So. Ch., Dec. 3, 1858

Virginia Elligood, d. of Mr. and Mrs. William Wyatt of Belle Haven, Accomac Co., Va., and the Rev. Thomas Nevitt Lawrence, rector of Nottoway Parish, Southampton Co., Va., by the Rev. John Cornick, in the Presbyterian Church, Belle Haven, Accomac Co., Va. So. Ch., Nov. 13, 1909
See also WILSON, K. H. W. (Mrs.)

WYETH
Maxwell, of Philadelphia, and Margaret Wardwell of New York, by the Rev. Dr. Neilson McVicar, at South Orange, N.J. So. Ch., Oct. 3, 1889

Parker C., of St. Joseph, Mo., and Ellen Ashton Horner, d. of R. L. Horner, Esq. of Fauquier Co., Va., by the Rev. G. W. Nelson, the rector, in St. James' Church, Warrenton, Va. So. Ch., Oct. 2, 1890

WYLEY
John B. (Dr.), of Amelia, and Nannie G., d. of Capt. William Murray of Powhatan Co., Va., by the Rev. P. F. Berkeley, in St. Paul's Church, Richmond, Va. So. Ch., Mar. 18, 1859

WYLIE
A. M. (The Rev.), and Margaret F., d. of Henry N. Conklin, Esq., all of Brooklyn, by the Rev. B. C. Cutler, D.D., at the residence of the bride's parents. So. Ch., Dec. 21, 1860

WYMAN
Alfred, and Mary R. Slack, d. of the officiating clergyman and formerly of Albemarle Co., Va., by

MARRIAGE NOTICES IN THE SOUTHERN CHURCHMAN WITH DATES OF PUBLICATION

the Rev. Samuel R. Slack, in Trinity Church, at Weymouth, Mass. So. Ch., Nov. 3, 1881

WYNCOOP*
C. Virginia, d. of Garrett Wyncoop*, of Hodgesville, and the Rev. Owen J. Dorsey of Maryland, by the Rev. John W. Lea, at Hedgesville, W.Va. So. Ch., Apr. 27, 1876

WYNKOOP
Addie, d. of Garrett Wynkoop*, of Hedgesville, W.Va., and Dr. D. D. Carter of Hancock, Md., by the Rev. W. D. Hanson, in Mount Zion Church, at Hedgesville. So. Ch., Oct. 28, 1869

Adrian G., of Woodstock, Va., and Mary Brooke Yates, d. of Col. Francis Yates of Flowing Springs, Jefferson Co., W.Va., by the Rev. Dallas Tucker assisted by the Rev. Frank Aglionby of London, England, the bride's cousin, and by the Rev. J. Owen Dorsey, at the home of the bride. So. Ch., Oct. 22, 1891

Emma, d. of Garrett Wynkoop*, Esq., of Hodgesville, and the Rev. W. T. Leavell, by the Rev. J. Owen Dorsey assisted by the Rev. R. D. Roller, in Mt. Zion Church, at Hedgesville, Berkeley Co., W.Va. So. Ch., June 7, 1883

Pamelia W., d. of Garrett Wynkoop*, Esq., and Dr. Lafayette H. Jordon, by the Rev. George S. May assisted by the Rev. W. D. Hanson, in Mt. Zion Church, at Hedgesville. So. Ch., Dec. 21, 1871

WYTH
Frank H., of Philadelphia, and Henrietta B., d. of Richard B. Homor of Fauquier Co., Va., by the Rev. John F. Hoff of Maryland, in the Church of the Holy Trinity, in Philadelphia. So. Ch., May 9, 1862

* Given as printed

YANCEY

Julia O., d. of the late Francis G. Yancey, Esq., and H. C. Robertson of Greensborough, Ala., by the Rev. Mr. Bartlett, at Petersburg, Va. So. Ch., Aug. 25, 1857

Wm. T., Jr. of Lynchburg, and Mary M., d. of Dr. Jno. B. Radford of Montgomery Co., Va., by the Rev. Edward H. Ingle, at "Arnheim", the residence of the bride's father. So. Ch., Nov. 25, 1869

YARBROUGH

Ophelia, and Geo. Gilmer Minor, by the Rev. A. W. Weddell, D.D., in St. John's Church, Richmond, Va. So. Ch., Dec. 9, 1880

YARNALL

M. (Prof.), U.S.N., and Eliza J. Hepburn of Georgetown, D.C., by the Rev. N. P. Tillinghast. So. Ch., Nov. 2, 1855

YARRINGTON

Matthew W., and Sallie P., d. of John Lester, Esq., all of Richmond, Va., by the Rev. Mr. Kepler, in St. John's Church, Richmond. So. Ch., Nov. 28, 1856

YATES

Anne, d. of John Yates, Esq. of Jefferson Co., and the Rev. Wm. T. Leavell, rector of Westover Parish, Charles City Co., by the Rev. Richard T. Brown. So. Ch., Nov. 26, 1847

Elizabeth, d. of George E. Yates, Esq., and Joseph W. Kent, by the Rev. O. A. Kinsolving, D.D., at Halifax C.H. So. Ch., Sept. 10, 1885

Frances Stuart, eldest d. of Mrs. Emma K. and the late John Orfeur Yates of Jefferson Co., and Wayt Bell Timberlake of Staunton, Va., by the Rev. John S. Alfriend assisted by the Rev. P. N. McDonald, in Zion Episcopal Church, Charles Town, W.Va. So. Ch., Jan. 26, 1907

Jennie Estelle, d. of the late G. W. Yates, Esq., and the Rev. B. H. Latrobe, Jr., by the Rev. A. M. Randolph assisted by the Rev. J. E. Catnell, in the Church of Our Savior, Baltimore. So. Ch., Dec. 11, 1873

Margaret T., and Joseph E. Woolford, both of Dorchester Co., Md., by the Rev. Wm. W. Green, at Church Creek. So. Ch., Apr. 14, 1881

Mary Brooke, d. of Col. Francis Yates of Flowing Springs, Jefferson Co., W.Va., and Adrian G. Wynkoop of Woodstock, Va., by the Rev. Dallas Tucker assisted by the bride's cousin, the Rev. Frank Aglionby of London, England, and the Rev. J. Owen Dorsey, at the home of the bride. So. Ch., Oct. 22, 1891

Mary Ella, d. of Lewis A. Yates, and Archibald M. Aiken, all of Danville, by the Rev. Geo. W. Dame, at the residence of the bride's father, Danville,

MARRIAGE NOTICES IN THE SOUTHERN CHURCHMAN WITH DATES OF PUBLICATION

Va. So. Ch., Jan. 12, 1882

YEAKLE
Virginia Vinton, of Baltimore, and Thomas Evans Greene of Brooklyn, N.Y., s. of the officiating clergyman, by the Rev. Wm. W. Greene, at the residence of the bride's mother, in Baltimore. So. Ch., July 25, 1889

YEATMAN
Benjamin, and Mrs. Margaret Head, both of Westmoreland Co., by the Rev. T. E. Locke. So. Ch., Feb. 8, 1861

Charles E., Esq. of Mathews Co., Va., and Harriet R. Royster of New Kent, Va., by the Rev. G. S. Carraway, at the residence of the bride's mother, Mrs. E. Royster. So. Ch., Nov. 16, 1860

YEATON
J. Southgate, and Juliana Elizabeth Howard Ridgely, by the Rev. W. H. H. Powers, at Hampton, Baltimore Co., Md. So. Ch., Oct. 9, 1884

YERBY
Affie F., and Wm. A. Holladay of Orange Co., Va., by the Rev. S. S. Ware, in Grace Church, in Caroline Co., Va. So. Ch., Dec. 12, 1889

Alice D., d. of Thomas P. Yerby, Esq. of Spotsylvania Co., Va., and Samuel Gordon, Jr., of St. Louis, Mo., by the Rev. James E. Poindexter, at Belle Voir, in Spotsylvania Co. So. Ch., Feb. 2, 1882

Thomas I., and Jane H., d. of Wm. I. Dickinson, all of Spotsylvania, by the Rev. Mr. Friend, at "Nottingham", the residence of the bride's father in Spotsylvania Co. So. Ch., July 27, 1860

Thomas Pratt, Jr., of Spotsylvania Co., Va., and Lucille, d. of the late Dr. J. Gordon and Elizabeth G. Wallace, by the Rev. John K. Mason, at the residence of the bride's mother, at Fredericksburg, Va. So. Ch., May 26, 1887

YERGER
Marie Louisa (Mrs.), and the Rev. William Porcher, S.T.D., Professor of Exegesis, Chaplain in the University of the South, by the Rt. Rev., the Assist. Bishop of Kentucky, at Moffat, Tenn. So. Ch., Jan. 30, 1879

William Arthur, s. of Gen. Alex. Yerger, and Kate Otey, gr.d. of the late Bishop Otey, by the Rev. Ralph H. Prosser, in Grace Church, Rosedale, Miss. So. Ch., Oct. 2, 1879

YOUNG
Hayden M., of Louisville, and Susan H. Soaper, of Henderson, by the Rev. R. S. Barrett, in St. Paul's Church, at Henderson, Ky. So. Ch., Feb. 21, 1884

Karl (Dr.), of the University of Wisconsin, and Frances Campbell, only d. of Mr. and Mrs. Robert Carter Berkeley, by the Rev. G. McClaren Brydon, rector of Trinity Church, at Ellembrie, the residence of the bride's father, at Morgantown, W.Va. So. Ch.,

MARRIAGE NOTICES IN THE SOUTHERN CHURCHMAN WITH DATES OF PUBLICATION

Aug. 26, 1911
Mary A., and Alonzo B. Jones, by the Rev. P. D. Thompson, on Bodkin Island* (where tradition says no marriage was ever performed before.) So. Ch., Jan. 17, 1884

Mortimer M., Esq., of Richmond, and Nannie R., d. of the late Mrs. Martha Keech of Chesterfield, by the Rev. A. B. Tizzard, at Oakland, Chesterfield Co. So. Ch., Nov. 23, 1860

Vena C., and Samuel G. Knox of Cedar Rapids, Iowa, formerly of Fredericksburg, by the Rev. E. C. Murdaugh, D.D., at the residence of the bride's father, J. J. Young, at Fredericksburg, Va. So. Ch., Mar. 18, 1875

William Green, and Kate C., d. of H. C. Whiting, Esq. of Hampton, Va., by the Rev. J. J. Gravatt, in St. John's Church, at Hampton, Va. So. Ch., June 29, 1882

Wm. J., and Rosa T., d. of Jos. P. Jones, by the Rev. A. B. Tizzard, in Chesterfield Co. So. Ch., Nov. 13, 1863

ZIMMER
Julia E. (Mrs.), d. of C. M. Nimmo, Esq., and S. P. Mitchell, all of Richmond, Va., by the Rev. F. M. Baker, in Grace Church. So. Ch., Jan. 9, 1863

Wm. J. (The Rev.), of Atlanta, Ga., and Julia Ellis Nimmo of Alexandria, Va., by the Rev. Mr. Woodbridge, in Monumental Church. So. Ch., Oct. 16, 1851

ZOGBAUM
Bessie Edmondston, d. of C. Zogbaum, Esq. of Germantown, and the Rev. Charles Walker of Virginia, by the Rev. T. S. Rumney, D.D. assisted by the Rev. C. Walker, D.D., in St. Peter's Church, at Germantown, Pa. So. Ch., Sept. 16, 1875

Fanny Lea, d. of Carl Zogbaum, and Robert Lee Whitehead of Roanoke, Va., by the Rev. T. S. Rumney assisted by the Rev. Mr. Bryan, at Germantown, Pa. So. Ch., Nov. 14, 1889
See also WALKER, Bessie E. (Mrs.)

* Bodkin Island is in Chesapeake Bay. It is included in Queen Anne Co., Md.

ADDENDA
L - Z

- L-Z -

LAIDLEY
　Mary Louise, d. of the Hon. William Sydney Laidley, and Henry Bradford Clarkson, by the Rev. Robert Douglas Roller, D.D., in St. John's Church, Charleston, Kanawha, W.Va. So. Ch., Jan. 20, 1898

LAIRD
　Wilhemina Goldsborough, of Albemarle Co., Va., and Caleb Stabler of Montgomery Co., Md., by the Rev. Wm. H. Laird, in Christ Church, St. Ann's Parish, Albemarle Co., Va. So. Ch., Aug. 4, 1898

LAMARCH
　John Victor, of Brooklyn, N.Y., and Rose, d. of the late Rev. Robert Nelson, D.D., for many years missionary to China, by the Rt. Rev. Dr. Van DeVyer, Roman Catholic Bishop of Richmond, at Oakland, the residence of Maj. John Page, in Hanover Co. So. Ch., Nov. 21, 1895

LAMOTHE
　John D. (The Rev.), and Margaret M., d. of the Rev. Cornelius Walker, D.D., by the Rev. William M. Walker assisted by the Rev. Nelson P. Dame, in the Seminary chapel of Virginia. So. Ch., Sept. 20, 1894

LANE
　Gardiner Martin, of Cambridge, Mass., and Emma Louise, d. of Prof. and Mrs. Basil L. Gildersleeve, by the Rev. Edwin B. Niver, in Christ Church, Baltimore, Md. So. Ch., June 16, 1898

LASSITER
　James Harri[s]on, Jr., and Ellen Daniel Faucett, both of Henderson, N.C., by the Rev. Junius Horner, at the residence of the bride's mother. So. Ch., Aug. 20, 1896

LEE
　Baker P., Jr. (The Rev.), of Farmville, and Lulu Lee Skinner of Danville, by the Rt. Rev. Alfred M. Randolph, D.D., assisted by the Rev. George W. Nelson and the Rev. W. H. K. Pendleton, at the residence of Mrs. P. W. Charrington, near Warrenton, Va. So. Ch., Aug. 27, 1896
　Bessie Winston, d. of John Lee of Stafford Co., and Charles Patteson Cardwell, by the Rev. S. S. Hepbron, in St. Paul's Church. So. Ca., Dec. 15, 1900
　John Penn, and Isabella Gilmer Walker, by the Rev. S. O. Southall, at the residence of Edward Saunders. So. Ch., Dec. 10, 1896
　Robert E., and Sarah Elizabeth, d. of Joseph Patten, Esq., by the Rev. R. A. Castleman, in Christ Church, Chantilly, Fairfax Co., Va. So. Ch., June 20, 1895

LEIGH
　Egbert G., of Richmond, Va., and Norvell Caskie, d. of Philip B. Jones, by the Rev. Le Bas Cross of Rapi-

MARRIAGE NOTICES IN THE SOUTHERN CHURCHMAN WITH DATES OF PUBLICATION

dan, at "Piedmont", the home of the bride, in Orange Co., Va. So. Ch., July 26, 1902

LEWIS

Alice Page, d. of Thomas Walker Lewis of Albemarle Co., Va., and Blair Jones of Chicago, Ill., by the Rev. Valentine Jones, brother of the groom, assisted by the Rev. Mr. Smoot, rector of Christ Ashton, in Christ Church, Alexandria, Va. So. Ch., Nov. 14, 1903

Howell Carr, of Charlottesville, Va., and Elizabeth Johnson, d. of the late R. Worthy Smith, Esq. of Norfolk, Va., by the Rev. William Rutherford Savage, rector of East Lynnhaven Parish*, in Emmanuel Church, Kempsville, Princess Anne Co., Va. So. Ch., Dec. 8, 1898

Lucy Schoolfield, eldest d. of John Henry Lewis, Esq. of Lynchburg, Va., and William R. Abbot, Jr. of Bellevue, Bedford Co., Va., by the Rev. Albert M. Hilliker, in the Church of the Epiphany, Washington, D.C. So. Ch., Aug. 9, 1894

Wm. H. T., of Jefferson Co., W.Va., and Katherine Stuart, d. of the late Dr. S. S. Neill of Berryville, by the Rev. Edward Wall, at the residence of the bride, in Berryville, Va. So. Ch., Nov. 3, 1898

LIGON

Annette Kimbrough, d. of Dr. John Ligon, and Luther T. Coyner of Augusta Co., Va., by the Rev. T. H. Lacy

of Lynchburg, Va., at the home of the bride's father, at Clover Lick, W.Va. So. Ch., June 29, 1899

LIPTRAP

William Arthur, of Ramah, Col., and Mabel Frances, d. of Fielding Lewis and Nellie Stanley Jones, by the Rev. W. Strother Jones, D.D., at Woodside, near Fruita, Col. So. Ch., Sept. 12, 1903

LOGAN

Sarah Strother, d. of Col. R. H. Logan of Salem, Va., and S. R. Mullorg Kennedy of New Orleans, by the Rev. Berryman Green, rector of Christ Church, in Alexandria, Va. So. Ch., May 25, 1899

LONG

Nanny Williams, of North Carolina, and Thomas Burks Yuille of Virginia, by the Rev. Julian Ingle, rector, assisted by the Rev. E. S. Gunn of Brandon, Va., in the Church of the Holy Innocents, Henderson, N.C. So. Ch., Nov. 8, 1894

LOVE

James Monroe, Jr., of Fairfax C.H., Va., and Rebecca Fowle Daingerfield, by the Rev. P. P. Phillips assisted by the Rev. S. A. Walls, at the residence of the bride's parents, Alexandria, Va. So. Ch., Mar. 31, 1898

LYLES

Alice, d. of O. Mcp. Lyles, and Henry Hammond Carr of Baltimore, by the Rev. Alexander Galt, in St.

---

* East Lynnhaven Parish is in Princess Anne County, Virginia, (*Journal ... Diocese of Southern Va.*, (Portsmouth, Va., 1941)

MARRIAGE NOTICES IN THE SOUTHERN CHURCHMAN WITH DATES OF PUBLICATION

James' Parish Church, Anne Arundel Co., Md. So. Ch., Jan. 18, 1894

LYMAN
Alice, and William P. Trent of the University of the South, at the residence of the bride's mother, No. 101 Harrison St., East Orange, N.J. So. Ch., Dec. 17, 1896
Lillian Forbes, and James Fontaine Minor, both of Charlottesville, by the Rev. H. B. Lee assisted by the Rev. R. C. Jett of Emmanuel Church, Staunton, Va., in Christ Church, Charlottesville, Va. So. Ch., Nov. 17, 1906

McBEE
Silas, and Louisa Jugger Post, by the rector, the Rev. Kirkland Huske, in All Saints' Church, Great Neck, L.I. So. Ch., Dec. 29, 1900

McCAULEY
Elizabeth Power, d. of Henry C. McCauley of Washington, and the Rev. John S. Douglas of Shenandoah, Va., by the Rev. T. J. Packard of West River, Md., in Christ Church, Washington, D.C. So. Ch., Mar. 18, 1897

McGUFFEY
Charles Drake, and Mary Byrd, d. of Mrs. Glover and the late Dr. G. Perin, Assistant Surgeon General, U.S. Army, and gr.d. of the late Charles H. Page, in St. Paul's Church, St. Paul, Minn. So. Ch., July 9, 1896

McGUIRE
John Peyton, Jr., and Richie Morris, d. of the late Capt. Richard Morris Graves and Susan Koan Graves his wife of "Linden", Orange Co., Va., by the Rev. Landon R. Mason, at "Forkfield", Louisa Co., Va., the residence of Dr. Lewis S. Pendleton. So. Ch., June 27, 1895
Muncey Mason, and Mary, d. of the late Capt. Jefferson Davis Van Benthuysen of New Orleans, by the Rev. O. A. Kinsolving, at Houston, Halifax Co., Va. So. Ch., June 21 and 28, 1894

McILVAIN
Charlotte V., of Little Rock, Ark., and the Rev. Dr. A. Crawford, rector of St. Barnabas' Church, Tullahoma, Tenn., by the Rev. Charles H. Kues of Hot Springs, Ark., at the home of the bride's mother, Little Rock, Ark. So. Ch., Sept. 9, 1905

McKENNAN
Anne, eldest d. of John T. and Katharine A. McKennan, and Frederick Louis Grammer, all of Pittsburgh, Pa., by the Rev. Dr. Julius E. Grammer, in Pittsburgh, Pa. So. Ch., May 31, 1894
Harriet Arnett, d. of the late John Thompson McKennan of Pittsburgh, and William S. Grammer formerly of Baltimore and now of Newfoundland, by the Rev. Dr. Carl E. Grammer, brother of the groom, at the home of James Hancock, brother-in-law of the bride, at Wayne, Pa. So. Ch., Oct. 8, 1904

McMURDO
Susan Moore, d. of John R. McMurdo, and Austin Hart Burr, by the Rev. J. W.

MARRIAGE NOTICES IN THE SOUTHERN CHURCHMAN WITH DATES OF PUBLICATION

Ware, in St. James' Church, Ashland, Va. So. Ch., Oct. 29, 1896

MACHEN
Carrie, d. of James P. Machen of Fairfax Co., Va., and the Rev. Kensey John Hammond of Wilmington, Del., by the Rt. Rev. George W. Peterkin assisted by the Rev. R. A. Castleman of Bel Air, Md., in Emmanuel Church, Baltimore, Md. So. Ch., Dec. 3, 1896

MARLBOROUGH
See also, CHURCHILL-SPENCER, Charles R., Duke of Marlborough

MARSHALL
Caroline Stribling, d. of Mrs. Mildred P. Marshall, and the Rev. Frederick Goodwin Ribble of Lawrenceville, Va., by the Rev. J. F. Ribble, brother of the groom, assisted by the Rev. Charles Lee, rector of Leeds Parish*, and the Rev. Edwin L. Goodwin, uncle of the groom, at "Glendale", Fauquier Co., Va. So. Ch., July 12, 1894

Maria, youngest d. of Capt. James Marshall of Happy Creek, Warren Co., Va., and the Rev. Frank Pinckney Clark, minister-in-charge of the P. E. Hospital Mission, Philadelphia, Pa., by the Rev. Charles Buck, rector of St. John's P. E. Church, at 3041 N Street, West Washington, D.C. So. Ch., Jan. 4, 1894

MARTIN
Eleanor Love, youngest d. of the Rev. T. F. and Cornelia Mayo Martin of Nashville, Tenn. and sister of the officiating clergyman, and William Demont Greet, late of Huntsville, Ala., by the Rev. Mayo Cabell Martin, rector of the parish, in St. Clement's Church, El Paso, Tex. So. Ch., May 12, 1900

Katherine Neill, d. of the Rev. T. F. Martin, rector of St. Ann's Church, Nashville, Tenn., and Frank H. Seamon of El Paso, by the Rev. Mayo Cabell Martin, rector of the parish and brother of the bride, in St. Clement's Church, El Paso, Tex. So. Ch., Sept. 22, 1900

MATHEWES
Edward Miles, of Laurens, S. C., and Mary Randolph, d. of Col. James L. Hubard of "Tye Brooke", Nelson Co., Va., by the Rev. Frank Stringfellow, in Trinity Church, Nelson Co., Va. So. Ch., Nov. 19, 1896

MATHEWS
Mary Miller, d. of Capt. Alexander F. Mathews, and Debney C. T. Davis, Jr., by the Rev. D. C. T. Davis assisted by the Rev. Wm. White, at Lewisburg, W.Va. So. Ch., Nov. 19, 1896

MAUPIN
Edward Watts, Jr., and Marjorie Peters, d. of Logh R. and Mattie P. Watts, by Bishop A. M. Randolph and the Rev. W. A. Brown, rector of St. John's Church, at the residence of the bride's parents, No. 202 Middle Street, Portsmouth, Va. So. Ch., May 12, 1906

MAYNARD
Herbert J., of London,

* Leeds Parish is in Fauquier County, Virginia (Journal ... Diocese of Virginia, Richmond, Va., 1941)

MARRIAGE NOTICES IN THE SOUTHERN CHURCHMAN WITH DATES OF PUBLICATION

England, and Alfreda H., d. of the late Richard Eppes, M.D., by the Rev. W. R. Savage, at "Appomattox", the residence of the bride's mother, at City Point, Va. So. Ch., Aug. 13, 1896

MEAD
George Otis (The Rev.), of Casanova, Va., and Lilian, fourth d. of Gen. and Mrs. R. H. G. Minty, by the Rev. A. B. Chinn, assistant rector of Grace Church, Chicago, Ill., assisted by the Rev. Charles Scadding, rector of Emmanuel Church, La Grange, Ill. So. Ch., Dec. 2, 1897

MEADE
Emily, and Dr. John Woodson Barksdale, by the Rt. Rev. Hugh Miller Thompson, in St. Clemont's Church, Vaiden, Miss. So. Ch., Apr. 28, 1900

MEARS
Eugenia, d. of J. W. Mears, and J. H. Tompkins of Roanoke, Va., s. of Frank Tompkins of Spotsylvania Co., Va., by the Rev. Charles H. Boggs, at the residence of the bride's father, near Norfolk, Va. So. Ch., May 3, 1894

MEDLEY
Granville C., and Lucy R. Booth, by the Rev. J. G. Shackelford, at Houston, Halifax Co., Va. So. Ch., Sept. 9, 1897

MEZICK
Frank (The Rev.), rector of the Church of the Good Shepherd, Dinwiddie Co., and Lillie K. Corner, by the Rev. John Ridout, rector of Grace Church, Petersburg, assisted by the Rev. Alexander Galt, rector of St. Margaret's, in St. Margaret's Church, Anne Arundel Co., Md. So. Ch., Nov. 3, 1900

MICHIE
Lizzie, d. of Capt. H. C. Michie, and John Breckenridge, M.D. of Staunton, Va., by the Rev. D. C. T. Davis, at "The Meadows", near Charlottesville, Va. So. Ch., Nov. 14, 1895

MILLS
Ellis, and Cora Ritchie, d. of Benjamin Franklin Nalle, Esq., by the Rev. Parnell Le Bas Cross, at Bellvue, Rapidan, Va. So. Ch., Nov. 21, 1895

MINOR
Anne Cazenove, youngest d. of Dr. Chas. L. C. Minor of Baltimore, Md., and the Rev. Andrew Glassell Grinnan, rector of Christ Church, Point Pleasant, W.Va., by the Rev. R. C. Jett, rector, assisted by the Rev. Wm. F. Gardner of Maryland, in Emmanuel Church, Staunton, Va. So. Ch., Oct. 24 and 31, 1895

Bessie Carter, d. of the late Capt. Robert Dabney and Landonia Minor, and Oliver Herbert Funsten of Richmond, by the Rev. James B. Funsten assisted by the Rev. William Meade Clark, rector of the church, in St. James' Church, Richmond. So. Ch., Nov. 5, 1896

Fanny Ansley, d. of Dr. Charles L. C. Minor of Baltimore, Md., and the Rev. James F. Plummer, rector of St. Stephen's Oxford, N.C., by the Rev.

MARRIAGE NOTICES IN THE SOUTHERN CHURCHMAN WITH DATES OF PUBLICATION

Wm. F. Gardner of Maryland assisted by the Rev. R. C. Jett, in Emmanuel Church, Staunton, Va. So. Ch., Oct. 24 and 31, 1895

James Fontaine, and Lillian Forbes Lyman, both of Charlottesville, by the Rev. H. B. Lee assisted by the Rev. R. C. Jott of Emmanuel Church, Staunton, Va., in Christ Church, Charlottesville, Va. So. Ch., Nov. 17, 1906

MINTY

Lilian, fourth d. of Gen. and Mrs. R. H. G. Minty, and the Rev. George Otis Mead of Casenove, Va., by the Rev. A. B. Chinn, assistant rector of Grace Church, Chicago, Ill., assisted by the Rev. Charles Scadding, rector of Emmanuel Church, La Grange, Ill., in Emmanuel Church, La Grange, Ill. So. Ch., Dec. 2, 1897

MOISE

Letitier Field, d. of the late Capt. Edwin H. Moise of Louisville, Ky., and William Meade, s. of Theo. Brown and great gr.s. of Bishop Meade, at the residence of William Loachman, Walnut Hills, Cincinnati, Ohio. So. Ch., Nov. 22, 1894

MONCURE

Anna Hull, of Fairfax, Va., and William Draper Brinckle of Wilmington, Del., by the Rev. Kensey J. Hammond, assisted by the Rev. W. H. K. Pendleton and the Rev. A. R. Walker, in Zion Church, Fairfax. So. Ch., July 13, 1901

Cassie, and Claiborne Barksdale Baker of the University of Virginia, by the Rev. James Nelson, at "Frascati", the home of Mrs. Wm. H. Lyne, in Orange Co., Va. So. Ch., Jan. 13, 1900

John G., of Stafford, and Marie Louise Pollard of King William Co., Va., by the Rev. Dr. Hundley, the rector, in St. David's Church, Aylott, Va. So. Ch., July 26, 1894

MONTGOMERY

Clarence Gordon, and Maude Robertson Cox, by the Rev. R. A. Goodwin, rector of St. John's Church, in Monumental Church, Richmond, Va. So. Ch., Mar. 25, 1905

MORRIS

George Harrison, eldest s. of Janette Carter and W. A. P. Morris of Richmond, Va., and Ellen, youngest d. of the late Dr. Thos. Gregory of Hanover Co., Va., by the Rev. S. S. Hopbron, in St. Paul's Church, Hanover Co., Va. So. Ch., Apr. 29, 1897

John W., of Virginia, and Louise Churchill, d. of the late Edward Armstrong of Philadelphia, by the Rev. Edward Valentine Jones, in St. John's Chapel, Louisa Co., Va. So. Ch., May 7, 1896

MOSELEY

E. M. (Mrs.), of Richmond, Va., and Lewis Pickett Brown of Malden, Mass., by the Rev. Robert P. Kerr, at the residence

MARRIAGE NOTICES IN THE SOUTHERN CHURCHMAN WITH DATES OF PUBLICATION

of Dr. E. J. Moseley, in Richmond. So.Ch., Nov. 3, 1898

William Tample, and Mary Maben Cullon of Richmond, Va., by the Rev. Dr. J. A. Aspinwall, rector, in St. Thomas' Chapel, Washington, D.C. So. Ch., Nov. 26, 1896

MOSS
Lula Carleton, d. of Prof. James Moss of the University of Mississippi, and Robert Thruston Hubard of "Tye Brook", Nelson Co., Va., by the Rev. Mr. McKnight, in St. Philip's Church, Atlanta, Ga. So. Ch., Mar. 4, 1897

MUNFORD
Annie Bland, and William S. Robertson, by the Rev. Beverly D. Tucker, D.D., at the residence of the bride's mother, Mrs. G. W. Munford, in Richmond. So. Ch., Aug. 27, 1896

Lucy Taylor, d. of the late Rev. William Munford, and Lt. William Peterkin, s. of Dr. and Mrs. J. N. Upshur of Richmond, by the Rt. Rev. George W. Peterkin, Bishop of West Virginia, assisted by the Rev. Joseph P. McComas, rector of St. Anne's, in St. Anne's Church, Annapolis, Md. So. Ch., Jan. 7, 1905

MURRAY
James H., of West River, Md., and Susie R. Harrison of Hanover Co., Va., by the Rev. S. S. Hepbron, at the residence of the bride's aunt, Mrs. Mary E. Noland. So. Ch., Jan. 9, 1896

NALLE
Cora Ritchie, d. of Benjamin Franklin Nalle, Esq., and Ellis Mills, by the Rev. Parnell Le Bas Cross, at Bellevue, Rapidan, Va. So. Ch., Nov. 21, 1895

William Camp, and Augusta Dabney, d. of Daniel Payne Wirt of Westmoreland Co., Va. and great gr.d. of Attorney-General William Wirt, by the Rev. W. Page Dame, rector of St. Bartholomew's Church, Baltimore, Md., at the home of Dr. Edward M. L. Engle, at Merion, Pa. So. Ch., Nov. 3, 1906

NEESON
Lillian Word, d. of Henry Neeson, Esq., and Thomas Hutchinson Botts, by the Rev. C. C. Griffith, in the Church of the Ascension, Lafayette Square, Baltimore, Md. So. Ch., Jan. 11, 1894

NEILL
Katherine Stuart, d. of the late Dr. S. S. Neill of Berryville, and Wm. H. T. Lewis of Jefferson Co., W.Va., by the Rev. Edward Wall, at the residence of the bride, in Berryville, Va. So. Ch., Nov. 3, 1898

NELSON
Rose, d. of the late Rev. Robert Nelson, D.D., for many years missionary to China, and John Victor Lamarch of Brooklyn, N.Y., by the Rt. Rev. Dr. Van DeVyver, Roman Catholic Bishop of Richmond, at Oakland, the residence of Maj. John Page, Hanover Co. So. Ch., Nov. 21, 1895

Ruth, d. of the late Rev. Robert Nelson, D.D., and

MARRIAGE NOTICES IN THE SOUTHERN CHURCHMAN WITH DATES OF PUBLICATION

Rosewell Page of Richmond, by the Rev. S. S. Hepbron, at "Oakland", Hanover Co., Va. So. Ch., Feb. 24, 1898

NEWPORT
Elizabeth Ellerson, of Washington, D.C., and Charles Levin Hepburn*, s. of the officiating clergyman, the Rev. S. S. Hepburn, at the residence of William Hull. So. Ch., Apr. 27, 1899

NEWTON
Betty Taylor (Mrs.), and Philip Alexander Bruce of Richmond, Va., by the Rev. B. D. Tucker, at Beechwood Place, Norfolk, Va. So. Ch., Oct. 29, 1896

NICOL
George M., of Morristown, N.Y., and Annie P. P., d. of Mrs. M. C. P. and the late John C. F. Bennett of Charleston, S.C., by the Rt. Rev. J. B. Newton, at the residence of the bride's mother, 104½ W. Grace St., Richmond. So. Ch., July 19, 1894

NOLAND
Fenton, of Hanover, and Lucy Landon, eldest d. of J. Churchill Cooke, Esq. of King William, by the Rev. S. S. Hepbron assisted by the Rev. C. L. Price, in St. James' Church, King William C.H., Va. So. Ch., Apr. 29, 1897

NORMAN
Attilla Cox, of Beattyville, Ky., and Henrietta Henderson Daingerfield, by Dean Baker P. Lee of Christ Church Cathedral, Lexington, assisted by the Rev. Alexander Patterson of Beattyville, Ky., at Castleton, the residence of the bride's father, near Lexington, Ky.
So. Ch., Feb. 15, 1904

OFFLEY
Edward Murray (Lt.), of the Twelfth Cavalry, U.S.A., and Sallie Bland, d. of the late Edwin C. and Judith Newton Claybrook of Westmoreland Co., Va., by the Rev. Willoughby Newton Claybrook, brother of the bride and rector of Christ Church, at the residence of Ernest Griffith, at Tyler, Tex. So. Ch., Feb. 8, 1902

OLD
Anne, eldest d. of Wm. W. and Alice Herbert Old, and Ensign Charles Webster, U.S. Navy, of Stockbridge, Mass., by the Rev. O. S. Barten, D.D., rector of Christ Church, Norfolk, Va., at the residence of the bride's parents, 260 Freemason St., Norfolk, Va. So. Ch., Apr. 29, 1897

Annie Carter Leigh, d. of Maj. Charles Old of Powhatan Co., and William Fanning Wickham, by the Rev. C. O. Pruden, in Grace Church, Powhatan Co. So. Ch., May 14, 1896

ORR
N. A., M.D., of Belmont, N.C., and Susie Cosby Hales of Fredericksburg, Va., by the Rev. F. Bouldin, at Houston, Va. So. Ch., Apr. 14, 1906

OTT
Mallie Hunter, d. of Luther H. Ott of Harrisonburg, and Robin Saxon Best of Cartersville, Ga., by the Rev. Robert N. Brooking, rector of Emmanuel Church,

* Given as printed

MARRIAGE NOTICES IN THE SOUTHERN CHURCHMAN WITH DATES OF PUBLICATION

of the Ott residence, S. Main St., Harrisonburg, Va. So. Ch., Nov. 3, 1906

PAGE
Frederick W., librarian of the University of Virginia, and Lucy White Bryan of Memphis, Tenn., at the University of Virginia. So. Ch., Sept. 27, 1902
Rosewell, of Richmond, and Ruth, d. of the late Rev. Robert Nelson, D.D., by the Rev. S. S. Hepbron, at "Oakland", Hanover Co., Va. So. Ch., Feb. 24, 1898

PARKINSON
Annie Dill, d. of W. C. Parkinson, and Paul Tillman Doswell, all of Hanover Co., Va., by the Rev. S. S. Hepbron, in Taylorsville Baptist Church. So. Ch., Dec. 15, 1900

PARRAN
William Seymour, and Sallie Fitzhugh Welch, by the Rev. Josiah R. Ellis, at "Burlington", the residence of James Barbour Newman, in Orange Co., Va. So. Ch., Dec. 10, 1896

PASCOE
Virginia B., and Edward B. Ambler, by the Rev. A. P. Gray, at Shirley, Va. So. Ch., June 18, 1895

PATTEN
Sarah Elizabeth, d. of Joseph Patton, Esq., and Robert E. Lee, by the Rev. R. A. Castleman, in Christ Church, Chantilly, Fairfax Co. So. Ch., June 20, 1895

PAYNE
Sarah Louise, d. of Robert M. Payne of Danville, Va., and Philip St. John Duval of Richmond, Va., by the Rev. W. R. Laird, at the residence of the Hon. A. J. Montague, Danville, Va. So. Ch., Aug. 12, 1897

PENDLETON
Garnet Payton, d. of the late Rev. Wm. H. and Henrietta Randolph Pendleton of Fauquier Co., Va., and William Dabney Wirt of Westmoreland Co., Va., by the Rev. E. S. Hinks assisted by the Rev. Chas. H. Lee and the Rev. G. W. Nelson, in St. James' Church, Warrenton, Va. So. Ch., Nov. 29, 1894
W. H. K. (The Rev.), of Fairfax, Va., and Elizabeth Power, d. of Col. and Mrs. Wm. H. Chapman, by the Rt. Rev. A. M. Randolph, D.D. assisted by the Rev. Josiah R. Ellis, at "Clifton", the home of the bride's parents, in Orange Co., Va. So. Ch., Aug. 19, 1897

PERIN
Mary Byrd, d. of Mrs. Glover and the late Dr. G. Perin, Assistant Surgeon General, U.S. Army, and gr.d. of the late Charles H. Page, and Charles Drake McGuffey, in St. Paul's Church, St. Paul, Minn. So. Ch., July 9, 1896

PIERCE
Mary Alice, d. of R. Tunstall Pierce, Esq., and the Rev. William Meade Clark, rector of St. James' Church, Richmond, Va., by the Rev. J. Y. Downman of All Saints' Church, Richmond, Va., assisted by the Rev. Preston Nash of Christ Church, Richmond, Va., at the home of the bride's parents, in Lancaster Co., Va. So. Ch.,

MARRIAGE NOTICES IN THE SOUTHERN CHURCHMAN WITH DATES OF PUBLICATION

Dec. 21, 1899
PINCKARD
    Lena K., d. of the late Dr. M. A. Pinckard of Virginia, and Wilmer Joyner of Dover, N.J., by the Rev. J. R. Joyner, father of the groom, in St. Bartholomew's Church, Baltimore, Md. So. Ch., Jan. 14, 1905

PLUMMER
    James F. (The Rev.), rector of St. Stephen's, Oxford, N.C., and Fanny Ansley, d. of Dr. Charles L. C. Minor of Baltimore, Md., by the Rev. Wm. F. Gardner of Maryland assisted by the Rev. R. C. Jett, in Emmanuel Church, Staunton, Va. So. Ch., Oct. 24 and 31, 1895

POINDEXTER
    Elizabeth Wallace, d. of the Rev. James Edward and Katherine Gordon Poindexter, and Dr. William Woodruff Taylor of Warrenton, N.C., by the father of the bride, in Emmanuel Church, Warrenton, N.C. So. Ch., July 22, 1905

POLLARD
    Marie Louise, of King William Co., Va., and John G. Moncure of Stafford, by the rector, the Rev. Dr. Hundley, in St. David's Church, Aylett, Va. So. Ch., July 26, 1894

PORCHER
    Julia Wickham, d. of the late Dr. J. Peyre Porcher of Charleston, S.C., and Thomas Ashby Wickham, by the Rev. John Korshaw, in St. Michael's Church, Charleston, S.C. So. Ch., Dec. 16, 1897

POST
    Louise Jagger, and Silas McBee, by the rector, the Rev. Kirkland Huske, in All Saints' Church, Great Neck, L.I. So. Ch., Dec. 29, 1900

POTTS
    Allen, and Gertrude, d. of Col. A. L. Rives of Castle Hill, Albemarle Co., Va., by the Rev. E. Valentine Jones assisted by the Rev. Hartley Carmichael, D.D. of St. Paul's Church, Richmond, Va., in Grace Church, Albemarle Co., Va. So. Ch., Oct. 29, 1896

POWELL
    Carrie Henderson, and William Reid Williams, both of Richmond, Va., by the Rev. W. B. Williams, at the home of the bride's father, Richmond. So. Ch., Jan. 4, 1894

POWERS
    Edmonia Ware, d. of the late Maj. Philip H. Powers of Clarke Co., Va., and Robert Frederick Whitehead of Washington, D.C., at "Auburn", the home of the bride. So. Ch., Jan. 7, 1905

PRESTON
    Nella Allen, eldest d. of Mr. and Mrs. George A. Preston, and Dr. Alvis Kennedy, by the Bishop of Dallas assisted by the rector of the parish, the Rev. J. B. C. Beaubien, in Trinity Church, Bonham, Tex. So. Ch., Dec. 5, 1903

PRIDDY
    Willie Green, d. of Mrs. Angelina Bassett Priddy, and James Gardner Florance, by the Rev. L. B. Botty, at the home of the bride's mother, 503 W. Clay St.,

MARRIAGE NOTICES IN THE SOUTHERN CHURCHMAN WITH DATES OF PUBLICATION

Richmond, Va. So. Ch., Dec. 1, 1906

PULLMAN
Mary G., of Washington, D.C., and the Rev. George C. Hunting, rector of St. Paul's Church, Virginia City, Nev., by the Rev. Samuel Unsworth, in Trinity Church, Reno, Nev. So. Ch., Nov. 1, 1894

RAMSAY
Lucy, d. of G. Wm. Ramsay, and T. Seddon Taliaferro, Jr., of Green River City, Wyo., by the Rev. Berryman Green assisted by the Rev. J. Thompson Cole, in Christ Church, Alexandria. So. Ch., Apr. 30, May 7, 1896

RANDALL
Wyatt William, Ph.D., and Eliza Pendleton, d. of Frederick M. Colston, Esq. of Baltimore, Md., by the Rev. Percy F. Hall, in St. Timothy's Church, Catonsville, Md. So. Ch., July 7, 1898

RAWLINGS
Pattie Valentine, youngest d. of Mr. and Mrs. W. M. Rawlings of Winfall, Perquimans Co., N.C., and W. F. C. Edwards, by the Rev. R. B. Drane, rector of St. Paul's, Edenton, N.C., at the residence of the bride's parents. So. Ch., July 26, 1894

REID
Legh Wilber, of Alexandria, Va., and Eliza Griffith Hoxton, also of Alexandria, Va., gr. d. of the late Rev. Dr. Charles Minnigerode, by the Rt. Rev. Alfred M. Randolph, uncle of the bride, in St. Paul's Church, Alexandria, Va. So. Ch., Dec. 6, 1894

RHETT
Mario, d. of Mr. and Mrs. Roland Rhett of Brooklyn, N.Y., and Thomas Gordon Coleman of News Ferry, Halifax Co., Va., by the Rev. A. B. Kinsolving, rector, in Christ Church, Brooklyn, N.Y. So. Ch., Nov. 29, 1894

RIBBLE
Frederick Goodwin (The Rev.), of Lawrenceville, Va., and Caroline Stribling, d. of Mrs. Mildred P. Marshall, by the Rev. J. F. Ribble, brother of the groom, assisted by the Rev. Charles Loo, rector of Leeds Parish, and the Rev. Edward L. Goodwin, uncle of the groom, at "Glendale", Fauquier Co., Va. So. Ch., July 12, 1894

J. F. (The Rev.), rector of the church, and Mary Gordon Beale, by the Rev. Frederick Ribble, in St. Paul's Church, Newport News, Va. So. Ch., Dec. 10, 1896

RICH
Fannie Miller, and William Edward Wyatt, by the Revs. E. R. and A. M. Rich, in St. Michael's Church, Baltimore Co., Md. So. Ch., Oct. 22, 1896

RICHARDSON
Edward Andrews, and Francis* Byrd Winston, by the Rev. S. S. Hepbron, in St. Paul's Church, Hanover Co., Va. So. Ch., Apr. 27, 1899

RIVES
Gertrude, d. of Col. A. L. Rives of Castle Hill, Albemarle Co., Va., and Allen Potts, by the Rev. E. Valentine Jones assisted by the Rev. Hartley Carmichael, D.D. of St. Paul's Church,

---

* Given as printed

MARRIAGE NOTICES IN THE SOUTHERN CHURCHMAN WITH DATES OF PUBLICATION

Richmond, Va., in Grace Church, Albemarle Co., Va. So. Ch., Oct. 29, 1896

ROANE
James Keith, and Virginia McRae Waring, by the Rev. Everard Meade, in St. David's Church, Aylett, Va. So. Ch., Mar. 11, 1897

ROBERTSON
Jaquolin Marshall, of Richmond, Va., and Jane D., youngest d. of Dr. I. T. Forbes, by the Rev. H. B. Lee, at the residence of Capt. Harrison Robertson, Charlottesville, Va. So. Ch., Dec. 12, 1895

William S., and Annie Bland Munford, by the Rev. Beverly D. Tucker, D.D., at the residence of the bride's mother, Mrs. G. W. Munford, in Richmond. So. Ch., Aug. 27, 1896

ROBINSON
Clifford Cabell, and Lila C. Hubard, by the Rev. G. S. Sommerville assisted by the Rev. Frank Stringfellow, in Christ Church, Norwood, Nelson Co., Va. So. Ch., July 8, 1897

Mary A., and William F. Curtis of Marietta, Ohio, by the Rev. G. P. Sommerville, at the home of the bride, Willow Island, W.Va. So. Ch., Feb. 15, 1894

SAMS
William Boo (The Rev.), rector of Trinity Church, Abbevillo, S.C., and Bertha Stanyarne, d. of Mr. and Mrs. John C. Hutson, by the Rev. A. E. Cornish assisted by the Rev. T. W. Clift, rector of the parish, at Aiken, S.C. So. Ch., June 24, 1905

SAUNDERS
Eva S., d. of Capt. Fleming Saunders, and Dr. G. Sinkler Irvine, by the Rev. Chiswell Dabney, at the residence of the bride's parents. So. Ch., Dec. 3, 1896

SAWTELLE
Charles Green (Lt.), U.S. Army, and Mary Berkoloy, second d. of B. Lewis Blackford, Esq. of Washington, D.C., by the Rev. A. R. Stuart, D.D., rector, in Christ Church, Georgetown. So. Ch., Apr. 29, 1897

SCARBURGH
Margaret Douglas, of Princess Anne, Md., and Robert Gibboney Hudson of Pulaski, Va., by the Rev. David Barr of Rock Creek Parish, D.C., in Grace Church, Baltimore. So. Ch., June 25, 1896

SCHLEY
Mary, d. of George Schley, and J. Alex. Stouart, all of Baltimore, by the Rev. Peregrine Wroth, in Baltimore. So. Ch., Oct. 22, 1896

SCOTT
Janie, d. of Mrs. E. M. and the late Edward Scott, and George S. Hemingway of South Carolina, by the Rev. A. B. Tizzard, at Manakin Farm, Powhatan Co., Va. So. Ch., Oct. 15, 1896

Marion Clarkson, and Frank Carter, by the Rev. William Short, rector, in St. Peter's Church, St. Louis, Mo. So. Ch., Feb. 28, 1895

SEAMON

MARRIAGE NOTICES IN THE SOUTHERN CHURCHMAN WITH DATES OF PUBLICATION

Frank H., of El Paso, and Katherine Neill, d. of the Rev. T. F. Martin, rector of St. Ann's Church, Nashville, Tenn., by the Rev. Mayo Cabell Martin, rector of the parish and brother of the bride, in St. Clement's Church, El Paso, Tex. So. Ch., Sept. 22, 1900

SEARS
Julia Winifred, eldest d. of Wm. G. and Stella B. Sears, and Dr. Charles Minor Blackford, Jr. of Augusta, Ga., by the Rev. Dr. Angell, in St. Stephen's Church, Harrisburg, Pa. So. Ch., Sept. 23, 1897

SETTLE
Caroline, d. of the late Hon. Thomas Settle, and James Renwick Wilkes of Charlotte, N.C., by the Rt. Rev. Joseph Blunt Choshire, Jr., Bishop of North Carolina, at Greensboro, N.C. So. Ch., Dec. 10, 1896

SHACKELFORD
Annie B., of Richmond, Va., and R. B. Smithey of Ashland, Va., by the Rev. J. Green Shackelford. So. Ch., Aug. 20, 1896

SHANDS
Aurelius Rives, M.D. of Washington, D.C., and Agnes Hornor, d. of Richard Eppes, M.D., by the Rev. C. R. Haines, D.D. assisted by the Rev. M. G. Cassell, in St. John's Church, City Point, Va. So. Ch., Jan. 9, 1896

SHIFF
Emily Oliver, d. of the late Gustave Shiff of New York, and C. Irwin Dunn of Baltimore, Md., by the Rev. Dr. C. George Currie assisted by the Rev. Dr. J. H. Eccleston, in Christ Church, Baltimore, Md. So. Ch., May 3, 1894

SHOUP
Francis Elliott, and Mary Eloise Howard of Richmond, Va., by the Rt. Rev. Thomas F. Gailor, S.T.D., in St. Margaret's Chapel, Columbia Institute, Columbia, Tenn. So. Ch., Jan. 6, 1898

SKINNER
Lula Lee, of Danville, and the Rev. Baker P. Lee, Jr. of Farmville, by the Rt. Rev. Alfred M. Randolph, D.D. assisted by the Rev. George W. Nelson and the Rev. W. H. K. Pendleton, at the residence of Mrs. P. W. Charrington, near Warrenton, Va. So. Ch., Aug. 27, 1896

SMITH
Bettie M., and Robert R. Smith, both of Wickliffe, Clarke Co., Va., by the Rev. W. D. Smith, brother of the bride, assisted by the Rev. P. D. Thompson, at "Smithfield", the residence of the bride. So. Ch., Jan. 7, 1897

Edward Jaquelin, of Clarke Co., Va., and Mary Page Thompson of Jefferson Co., W.Va., by the Rev. P. D. Thompson, father of the bride, assisted by the Rev. G. W. Dame, D.D. of Danville, Va., grandfather of the bride, and the Rev. W. D. Smith of Norfolk, Va., brother of the groom, in Wickliffe Church. So. Ch., Nov. 8, 1894

MARRIAGE NOTICES IN THE SOUTHERN CHURCHMAN WITH DATES OF PUBLICATION

Elizabeth Johnson, d. of the late R. Worthy Smith, Esq. of Norfolk, Va., and Howell Carr Lewis of Charlottesville, Va., by the Rev. William Rutherford Savage, rector of East Lynnhaven Parish,* in Emmanuel Church, Kempsville, Princess Anne Co., Va. So. Ch., Dec. 8, 1898

Frances L., and Wm. L. Zimmer of Petersburg, Va., at the home of the bride, Waterford, Loudoun Co., Va. So. Ch., Nov. 4, 1897

Harwell R., of St. Louis, Mo., and Mary Brockenbrough, third d. of Capt. R. H. and Agnes M. Fitzhugh formerly of Virginia, by the Rev. E. H. Ward, D.D., in Christ Church, Lexington, Ky. So. Ch., Nov. 15, 1894

Mattie, and Frank L. Fred, by the Rev. John D. Lamothe, at Locust Grove, Loudoun Co., Va. So. Ch., Apr. 14, 1900

Robert R., and Bettie M. Smith, both of Wickliffe, Clarke Co., Va., by the Rev. W. D. Smith, brother of the bride, assisted by the Rev. P. D. Thompson, at "Smithfield", the residence of the bride. So. Ch., Jan. 7, 1897

William D. (The Rev.), rector of Christ Church, Winchester, Va., and Elizabeth Coalter Carmichael, by the Rev. R. J. McBryde, D.D., the Rev. C. Braxton Bryan, D.D., and the Rev. James Carmichael, D.D., in Fredericksburg, Va. So. Ch., Dec. 16, 1905

SMITHEY
R. B., of Ashland, Va., and Annie B. Shackelford of Richmond, Va., by the Rev. J. Green Shackelford. So. Ch., Aug. 20, 1896

SMOOT
Bettie F., d. of William A. Smoot, Esq. of Alexandria, and Robert Waight Fuller of Atlanta, Ga., in Christ Church, Alexandria, Va. So. Ch., Feb. 16, 1899

SOUTHALL
John Howard, of Richmond, Va., and Annie Josephine, d. of the late Judge Richard H. Coleman, by the Rev. S. S. Ware, in Trinity Church, Bowling Green, Va. So. Ch., Nov. 26 and Dec. 17, 1896

Martha C., d. of S. V. Southall, and the Rev. Jos. B. Dunn, by the Rev. H. B. Lee, in Charlottesville, Va. So. Ch., Dec. 19, 1895

Stephen O. (The Rev.), of Rocky Mount, Va., rector of Franklin Parish,** and Julia Pride, d. of the late Philip S. and Emma P. Wood of Amelia C.H., Va., by the Rev. V. Wrenn, rector of Raleigh Parish,*** in Christ Church, Amelia C.H., Va. So. Ch., May 4, 1899

SPENCER
Dean, d. of Dr. H. N. Spencer, and the Rev. William H. DuBose, M.A. of Sewanee, Tenn., by the Rev. W. P. DuBose, S.T.D., father of the groom and dean of the theological dep't of the University of the South, at 2725 Washington Ave., St. Louis, Mo. So. Ch., Oct. 8, 1896

SPINDLER
Edward H., of Washington, D.C., and Esther M. Chichester of Fairfax Co., Va.,

---

*East Lynnhaven Parish is in Princess Anne County (Journal ... Diocese of Southern Virginia, Portsmouth, Va., 1941)
**Franklin Parish is in Franklin County (Journal ... Diocese of Southwestern Virginia, 1940)
***Raleigh Parish is in Amelia County (Journal ... Diocese of Southern Virginia, Portsmouth, Va., 1941)

MARRIAGE NOTICES IN THE SOUTHERN CHURCHMAN WITH DATES OF PUBLICATION

by the Rev. Mr. Niver, in Baltimore, Md. So. Ch., Mar. 17, 1898

SPRATLEY
Tazewell Taylor, of Smithfield, Va., and Helen Moore, d. of Maj. Everard Moore Todd of Smithfield, by the Rev. F. G. Scott, former rector of the parish, and the Rev. John M. Todd of Maryland, uncle of the bride, in Christ Church, Smithfield, Va. So. Ch., Oct. 13, 1900

STABLER
Caleb, of Montgomery Co., Md., and Wilhemina Goldsborough Laird of Albemarle Co., Va., by the Rev. Wm. H. Laird, in Christ Church, St. Anne's Parish, Albemarle Co., Va. So. Ch., Aug. 4, 1898

STEUART
J. Alex., and Mary, d. of George Schley, all of Baltimore, by the Rev. Peregrine Wroth, in Baltimore. So. Ch., Oct. 22, 1896

STEWART
I. Calvin (The Rev.), and Avis, d. of the late Dr. Charles Barney, all of Richmond, Va., by the Rev. M. Gravatt assisted by the Rev. Dr. Hoge. So. Ch., Nov. 22, 1894

Juliet Roy Bradford, of Washington, D.C., and John H. Windoler of Blenheim, N.Y., by the Rev. Alex. Mackay-Smith, D.D. assisted by the Rev. Kensey Johns Stewart, D.D., in St. John's Church, Washington, D.C. So. Ch., June 17, 1897

W. John Shoaff (Dr.), of Philadelphia, and Anne Page, d. of Dr. C. Shirley and Mary M. Carter, by the Rev. Berryman Green, in St. James' Church, Leesburg, Va. So. Ch., July 5, 1894

STOKES
Sallie Bayly, d. of Mrs. W. B. Stokes, and Randolph Bolling, Esq. of Richmond, Va., by the Rev. Dr. Carson, rector of St. Paul's Church, Lynchburg, Va. So. Ch., Mar. 2, 1899

STOTT
Mary Ida, d. of the late William A. Scott of Isle of Wight Co., Va., and James N. Gibbons of Wilson, N.C., by the Rev. Virginius Wronn of Norfolk, Va., at the residence of the bride's brother-in-law, Lofton J. Alley, Richmond, Va. So. Ch., Sept. 10, 1896

STUART
Mary Bell, of Virginia, and W. A. Dabney of Barton Heights, by the Rev. S. S. Hepbron, at the residence of Mr. A. Spot. Wingfield of Hanover Co. So. Ch., Dec. 10, 1904

SUHLING
Wilhelm Gerhard, and Mary Leigh, d. of Anna Page and the late J. Peter Williams, by the Rev. John J. Lloyd, in Grace Memorial Church, Lynchburg, Va. So. Ch., Oct. 22, 1896

SUTER
Frank, of Washington, D.C., and Eloise O. Carhart, by the Rev. Charles Carhart, brother of the bride, at Dorset, Vt. So. Ch., Aug. 6, 1904

MARRIAGE NOTICES IN THE SOUTHERN CHURCHMAN WITH DATES OF PUBLICATION

TALIAFERRO
  Chas. C., and Mary S., d. of the late Thomas M. Wilkinson of Bedford Co., Va., by the Rev. John S. Hansborough, at Mount Sharon, Orange Co., Va. So. Ch., Oct. 10, 1895
  Philippa Ludwell, d. of Thomas S. Taliaferro of Gloucester Co. and gr.d. of the late Cassius F. Lee of Alexandria, Va., and Thomas J. Wyche of Wyoming, by the Rt. Rev. Ethelbert Talbot, D.D., at Green River, Wyo. So. Ch., Dec. 27, 1894
  T. Seddon, Jr., of Green River City, Wyo., and Lucy, d. of G. Wm. Ramsay, by the Rev. Berryman Green assisted by the Rev. J. Thompson Cole, in Christ Church, Alexandria. So. Ch., Apr. 30 and May 7, 1896
  Wm. Mayo, and Louise Brander, by the Rev. W. W. Brander, brother of the bride, assisted by the Revs. L. R. and R. P. Kerr, in Grace Church, Richmond, Va. So. Ch., Nov. 22, 1894

TANNER
  Lizzie, d. of the late Maj. N. M. and Mrs. M. E. Tanner, and the Rev. Wm. A. R. Goodwin, rector of St. John's Church, by the Rt. Rev. Bishop Randolph, D.D. assisted by the Rev. R. A. Goodwin and the Rev. C. R. Hains, D.D., in St. Paul's Church, Petersburg. So. Ch., Feb. 28, 1895

TAYLOR
  Margaret Locke, youngest d. of Mr. and Mrs. John Taylor of Oak Grove, and Richard Vivian Turner of King George Co., Va., by the Rev. B. T. Turner of King George Co., in St. Peter's P. E. Church, Oak Grove, Va. So. Ch., Nov. 3, 1906
  Sara Purvis, eldest d. of Charles S. Taylor, Esq. of Alexandria, and Hoxton Archibald Robinson of the Episcopal High School, by the Rt. Rev. A. M. Randolph, D.D., in St. Paul's Church, Alexandria. So. Ch., Jan. 2, 1904
  William Woodruff (Dr.), of Warrenton, N.C., and Elizabeth Wallace, d. of the Rev. James Edward and Katherine Gordon Poindexter, the father of the bride officiating, in Emmanuel Church, Warrenton, N.C. So. Ch., July 22, 1905

THACKER
  William C., Jr., and Ada Lena, only d. of James S. Huffman, by the Rev. Thomas E. Locke, at Blenheim. So. Ch., Feb. 13, 1896

THOMPSON
  Mary Page, of Jefferson Co., W.Va., and Edward Jaquelin Smith of Clarke Co., Va., by the Rev. P. D. Thompson, father of the bride, assisted by the Rev. G. W. Dame, D.D. of Danville, Va., grandfather of the bride, and the Rev. W. D. Smith of Norfolk, Va., brother of the groom, in Wickliffe Church. So. Ch., Nov. 8, 1894

THOMSON
  Anne Leslie, d. of the Rev. Elliot H. Thomson of

MARRIAGE NOTICES IN THE SOUTHERN CHURCHMAN WITH DATES OF PUBLICATION

Shanghai, China, and Arthur Presley Thornton of Port Royal, Va., by the Rev. Arthur C. Thomson, brother of the bride, at Tappahannock, Essex Co., Va. So. Ch., Jan. 31, 1895

THORNTON
Arthur Presley, of Port Royal, Va., and Anne Leslie, d. of the Rev. Elliot H. Thomson of Shanghai, China, by the Rev. Arthur C. Thomson, brother of the bride, at Tappahannock, Essex Co., Va. So. Ch., Jan. 31, 1895

TILFORD
Elizabeth Taylor, d. of Mrs. John Boyle Tilford, and Carl B. Keferstein of Washington, D.C., by the Rev. R. L. Howell, rector of St. Margaret's Church, assisted by the Rev. W. H. Milton, rector of Henshaw Memorial Church, Baltimore, at the residence of the bride's mother, No. 1336 New Hampshire Ave., Washington, D.C. So. Ch., Feb. 20, 1896

TILGHMAN
Madeline Tasker, d. of the late Capt. Richard Lloyd Tilghman, U.S. Navy, of "Grosses", Talbot Co., Md., and Dr. Christopher Johnston, by the Rev. J. H. Eccleston assisted by the Rev. J. S. B. Hodges, in Emmanuel Church, Baltimore, Md. So. Ch., June 10, 1897

TODD
Helen Moore, d. of Maj. Everard Moore Todd of Smithfield, Va., and Tazewell Taylor Spratley of Smithfield, Va., by the Rev. F. G. Scott, former rector of the parish, and the Rev. John M. Todd of Maryland, uncle of the bride, in Christ Church, Smithfield, Va. So. Ch., Oct. 13, 1900

TOMPKINS
J. H., of Roanoke, Va., s. of Frank Thompkins of Spotsylvania Co., Va., and Eugenia, d. of J. W. Mears, by the Rev. Charles H. Boggs, at the residence of the bride's father, near Norfolk, Va. So. Ch., May 3, 1894

TRENT
William P., of the University of the South, and Alice Lyman, at the residence of the bride's mother, No. 101 Harrison St., East Orange, N.J. So. Ch., Dec. 17, 1896

TREVILLIAN
John Page, and Evelyn, d. of Wm. Duke of Hanover Co., by the Rev. S. S. Hepbron, in Fork Church. So. Ch., Dec. 15, 1900

TUNSTALL
Belle Waller, and Dr. Frank Walke, by the Rev. A. S. Lloyd assisted by the Rev. B. D. Tucker, at home, Norfolk, Va. So. Ch., Nov. 12, 1896

TURNER
Beauregard, and Annie Wattington, both of King William Co., by the Rev. S. S. Hepbron of Hanover, in the Baptist Church, at West Point. So. Ch., Oct. 10, 1895

Richard Vivian, of King George Co., Va., and Margaret Locke, youngest

MARRIAGE NOTICES IN THE SOUTHERN CHURCHMAN WITH DATES OF PUBLICATION

d. of Mr. and Mrs. John Taylor of Oak Grove, by the Rev. B. T. Turner of King George Co., in St. Peter's P. E. Church, Oak Grove, Va. So. Ch., Nov. 3, 1906

TYLER
Bailey, of Haymarket, Prince William Co., Va., and Anner* Moss Alrich, by the Rev. W. A. Alrich, father of the bride, in Spesutiae Church, Perryman, Harford Co., Md. So. Ch., Oct. 14, 1897

Genevieve Louise, d. of Vernon A. Tyler, and the Rev. Robert Bootman Kimber, by the Rev. Joshua Kimber, father of the groom, assisted by the Bishop of Long Island, in the Church of the Resurrection, Richmond Hill, L.I. So. Ch., June 28, 1894

UPSHUR
William Peterkin (Lt.), s. of Dr. and Mrs. J. N. Upshur of Richmond, and Lucy Taylor, d. of the late Rev. William Munford, by the Rt. Rev. George W. Peterkin, Bishop of West Virginia, assisted by the Rev. Joseph P. Mc-Comas, rector of St. Anne's, in St. Anne's Church, Annapolis, Md. So. Ch., Jan. 7, 1905

VALENTINE
Granville Gray, and Elise Calvin, d. of Mrs. William Albert Bragg, all of Richmond, Va., by the Rev. Robert Strange, in St. Paul's Church, Richmond, Va. So. Ch., Apr. 16, 1904

Richard Roane, of Richmond, and Julia Elizabeth, only d. of the late Walter Weir of Prince William Co., Va. and Mrs. J. D. Dixon of King William Co., Va., by the Rev. Dr. Hundley, at Canterbury, the home of the bride's mother, in King William Co., Va. So. Ch., Nov. 29, 1894

VAN BENTHUYSEN
Mary, d. of the late Capt. Jefferson Davis Van Benthuysen of New Orleans, and Muncey Mason McGuiro, by the Rov. O. A. Kinsolving, at Houston, Halifax Co., Va. So. Ch., June 21 and 28, 1894

VANDERBILT
Consuelo, d. of William Kissam Vanderbilt, Esq., and Charles R. Churchill-Spencer, Duke of Marlborough, by the Rt. Rev. Bishop of Long Island, the Rt. Rev. Bishop of Now York, and the Rev. John W. Brown, in St. Thomas' Church, N.Y. So. Ch., Nov. 14, 1895

VAN DEUSEN
Mary F., and Richard Eppes of City Point, Va., by the Rev. George W. Davenport, rector, in St. James' Church, Danbury, Conn. So. Ch., Apr. 16, 1904

WADDELL
Maude, d. of Legh R. Waddell, Esq., and L. Marsh Walker of "The Brook", Albemarle Co., Va., s. of the late Gen. Walker of Tennessee, by the Rev. G. Mosley Murray assisted by the Rev. J. C. Painter, at Chestnut Ridge, the home of the bride's father, in Albemarle Co. So. Ch., Apr. 12,

* Given as printed

MARRIAGE NOTICES IN THE SOUTHERN CHURCHMAN WITH DATES OF PUBLICATION

1894
WAGNER
Hancke Frederic (Dr.), of
Charleston, S.C., and
Lucia Chauncey Yeaton of
Alexandria, Va., by the
Rev. H. H. Phelps, in
Calvary Church, Fletcher,
N.C. So. Ch., July 21,
1898
WALKE
Frank Anthony (Dr.), and
Belle Waller Tunstall, by
the Rev. A. S. Lloyd assisted
by the Rev. B. D. Tucker, at
home, in Norfolk, Va. So.
Ch., Nov. 12, 1896
WALKER
Albert Rhett, eldest s. of
the officiating clergyman,
and Phoebe Elliott, second
d. of the late Rt. Rev.
Bishop Boone of China, by
the Rev. Albert Walker assisted
by the Rt. Rev. Bishop Coleman, in Calvary Church,
Wilmington, Del. So. Ch.,
Apr. 25, 1895
Isabella Gilmer, and John
Penn Lee, by the Rev.
S. O. Southall, at the
residence of Edward Saunders.
So. Ch., Dec. 10, 1896
L. Marsh, of "The Brook",
Albemarle Co., Va., s. of
the late Gen. Walker of
Tennessee, and Maude, d.
of Legh R. Waddell, Esq.,
by the Rev. G. Mosley
Murray assisted by the
Rev. J. C. Painter, at
Chestnut Ridge, the home
of the bride's father,
Albemarle Co. So. Ch.,
Apr. 12, 1894
Lucy Dabney, and John Patton
Gilmer of Kansas City, by
the Rev. C. Breckinridge
Wilmer assisted by the Rev.
W. A. Barr, at the residence
of the Hon. E. W. Saunders
of Rocky Mount, Va. So.
Ch., Oct. 31, 1895
Margaret M., d. of the Rev.
Cornelius Walker, D.D.,
and the Rev. John D.
Lamothe, by the Rev. William M. Walker assisted by
the Rev. Nelson P. Dame,
in the Seminary Chapel of
Virginia. So. Ch., Sept.
20, 1894
WARD
Robert M., and Emily Ridgeway, d. of the late Col.
David Funsten of Alexandria, by the Rev. Dr.
Dame, in Memorial Church,
Baltimore. So. Ch., Apr.
20, 1899
WARE
Jaquelin Smith, and Helen
Glassell Grinnan, by the
Revs. S. S. and J. W. Ware,
at "Brampton", Madison Co.,
Va. So. Ch., Nov. 3, 1900
WARFIELD
Julia Anthony (Mrs.), d. of
the late William Pleasants
Anthony of Buchanan, Va.,
and Richard Alexander Dunlap, by the Rev. Julian E.
Ingle asisted by the Rev.
Robert Forsyth, in St.
Paul's Church, Richmond,
Va. So. Ch., May 19,
1906
WARING
Virginia McRae, and James
Keith Roane, by the Rev.
Everard Meade, in St.
David's Church, Aylett,
Va. So. Ch., Mar. 11,
1897
WARREN
George William, and Lilian
Moore Yarbrough, both of
Richmond, by the Rev. Fennor S. Stickney, in Monumental Church, Richmond,

MARRIAGE NOTICES IN THE SOUTHERN CHURCHMAN WITH DATES OF PUBLICATION

Va. So. Ch., Jan. 28, 1897
Lilly Archer, d. of Edward J. Warren of Richmond, and the Rev. Josiah R. Ellis of Gordonsville, Va., by the Rt. Rev. F. M. Whittle assisted by the Rev. Landon R. Mason, in Grace Church, Richmond, Va. So. Ch., Dec. 13, 1894

WASHINGTON
Samuel Walter, of Charles Town, W.Va., and Elizabeth Ryland, d. of N. H. Willis, by the Rev. Andrew Willis assisted by the Rev. Beverly D. Tucker, at Rock Hall, Jefferson Co., W.Va. So. Ch., Nov. 3, 1900

WATKINS
Rebekah Gustavia, and Robert Lancaster Williams, by the Rev. Donald Guthrie assisted by the Rev. W. B. Williams, at the residence of the bride's mother, Mrs. Charles Watkins. So. Ch., Dec. 21, 1899

WATTINGTON
Annie, and Beauregard Turner, both of King William Co., by the Rev. S. S. Hepbron of Hanover, in the Baptist Church at West Point. So. Ch., Oct. 10, 1895

WATTLES
Elizabeth Taylor, d. of Mrs. Henry Starr Wattles, and William Bowie of Anne Arundel Co., Md., by the Rev. P. P. Phillips, at the residence of the bride's mother, Alexandria, Va. So. Ch., July 6, 1899

WATTS
Marjorie Peters, d. of Legh R. and Mattie P. Watts, and Edward Watts Maupin, Jr., by Bishop A. M. Randolph and the Rev. W. A. Brown, rector of St. John's Church, at the residence of the bride's parents, No. 202 Middle St., Portsmouth, Va. So. Ch., May 12, 1906

WEBSTER
Charles (Ensign), U.S.N., of Stockbridge, Mass., and Anne, eldest d. of Wm. W. and Alice Herbert Old, by the Rev. O. S. Barten, D.D., rector of Christ Church, Norfolk, Va., at the residence of the bride's parents, 260 Freemason St., Norfolk, Va. So. Ch., Apr. 29, 1897

WEIR
Julia Elizabeth, only d. of the late Walter Weir of Prince William Co., Va. and Mrs. J. D. Dixon of King William Co., Va., and Richard Roane Valentine of Richmond, by the Rev. Dr. Hundley, at Canterbury, the home of the bride's mother, King William Co., Va. So. Ch., Nov. 29, 1894

WELCH
Sallie Fitzhugh, and William Seymour Parran, by the Rev. Josiah R. Ellis, at "Burlington", Orange Co., Va., the residence of James Barbour Newman. So. Ch., Dec. 10, 1896

WHARTON
Mary Fernando Fairfax, and Frederick Griffith Fairfax, both of Westmoreland Co., Va., by the Rev. Richard P. Williams, pastor of Trinity Episcopal Church, at the residence of the bride's aunt, Mrs. Mittie

MARRIAGE NOTICES IN THE SOUTHERN CHURCHMAN WITH DATES OF PUBLICATION

Musser, Vermont Ave., Northwest Washington. So. Ch., May 9, 1903

WHEELWRIGHT
Juliet Wilson, youngest d. of the late Jeremiah Wheelwright, Esq. of Baltimore, Md., and William Herbert Assheton of "Rock Spring", Fauquier Co., Va., by the Rev. J. S. B. Hodges, D.D. assisted by the Rev. W. F. Bland, D.D. and the Rev. George W. Nelson, in St. Paul's Church, Baltimore. So. Ch., Feb. 18, 1897

WHITEHEAD
Cornelia Wickham, d. of Harry C. Whitehead of Norfolk, Va., and the Rev. Robert Saunders Coupland, rector of St. John's Church, Covington, Ky., by the Rev. A. S. Lloyd assisted by the Rev. Z. S. Farland, in St. Luke's Church, Norfolk, Va. So. Ch., Oct. 14, 1897

Emily Arnold, of Norfolk, and the Rev. Edward Watts Gamble of Florida, by the Rev. A. S. Lloyd, at the residence of the bride's parents, No. 57 Boush St., Norfolk, Va. So. Ch., June 11, 1896

Robert Frederick, of Washington, D.C., and Edmonia Ware, d. of the late Maj. Philip H. Powers of Clarke Co., Va., at "Auburn", the home of the bride. So. Ch., Jan. 7, 1905

WHITRIDGE
Julia, d. of John A. Whitridge, and William S. Blackford, by the Rev. J. Houston Eccleston, D.D. assisted by the Rev. J. S. B. Hodges, D.D. of St. Paul's Church, in Emmanuel Church, Baltimore. So. Ch., Apr. 27, 1899

WHITTLE
Emily C., d. of the officiating minister, the Rev. Bishop F. M. Whittle, and Alexander T. Jones of Frederick Co., Va., at the home of the bride in Richmond. So. Ch., Oct. 20, 1898

WICKHAM
Thomas Ashby, and Julia Wickham, d. of the late Dr. J. Peyre Porcher of Charleston, S.C., by the Rev. John Kershaw, in St. Michael's Church, Charleston, S.C. So. Ch., Dec. 16, 1897

William Fanning, and Annie Carter Leigh, d. of Maj. Charles Old of Powhatan Co., by the Rev. C. O. Pruden, in Grace Church, Powhatan Co. So. Ch., May 14, 1896

WILCOX
Jean Henry, and Edmund Jones, Jr. of Lenoir, N.C., by the Rev. William R. Savage of Blowing Rock, N.C., at Dresden, the home of the bride, in Ashe Co., N.C. So. Ch., June 23, 1906

WILKES
James Fenwick, of Charlotte, N.C., and Caroline, d. of the late Hon. Thomas Settle, by the Rt. Rev. Joseph Blunt Cheshire, Jr., Bishop of North Carolina, at Greensboro, N.C. So. Ch., Dec. 10, 1896

WILKINSON
Mary S., d. of the late Thomas M. Wilkinson of Bedford Co., Va., and Chas. C. Taliaferro, by the Rev. John S. Hans-

MARRIAGE NOTICES IN THE SOUTHERN CHURCHMAN WITH DATES OF PUBLICATION

borough, at Mount Sharon, Orange Co., Va. So. Ch., Oct. 10, 1895

WILLIAMS

Elsie, d. of the late William Williams, Esq. of London, England, and Charles Edward Ambler of New York, by the Rev. J. W. Van Ingen, at St. Stephen's, Milburn, N.J. So. Ch., Oct. 15, 1904

Francis Deane, and Mary Mason Anderson, by the Rev. Hartley Carmichael, D.D., in St. Paul's Church, Richmond, Va. So. Ch., Dec. 3, 1896

Mary Leigh, d. of Anna Page and the late J. Peter Williams, and Wilhelm Gerhard Suhling, by the Rev. John J. Lloyd, in Grace Memorial Church, Lynchburg, Va. So. Ch., Oct. 22, 1896

Robert Lancaster, and Robekah Gustavia Watkins, by the Rev. Donald Guthrie assisted by the Rev. W. B. Williams, at the residence of the bride's mother, Mrs. Charles Watkins. So. Ch., Dec. 21, 1899

William Reid, and Carrie Henderson Powell, both of Richmond, Va., by the Rev. W. B. Williams, at the home of the bride's father, Richmond. So. Ch., Jan. 4, 1894

WILLIS

Elizabeth Ryland, d. of N. H. Willis, and Samuel Walter Washington of Charles Town, W.Va., by the Rev. Andrew Willis assisted by the Rev. Beverly D. Tucker, at Rock Hall, Jefferson Co., W.Va. So. Ch., Nov. 3, 1900

WILSON

Martha Allen (Mrs.), and Lewis Warrington Wise, at No. 805 W. Franklin St., Richmond, Va. So. Ch., Dec. 3, 1896

WINDELER

John H., of Blenheim, N.Y., and Juliet Rey Bradford Stewart of Washington, D.C., by the Rev. Alex. Mackay-Smith, D.D. assisted by the Rev. Kensey Johns Stewart, D.D., in St. John's Church, Washington, D.C. So. Ch., June 17, 1897

WINSTON

Francis* Byrd, and Edward Andrews Richardson, by the Rev. S. S. Hepbron, in St. Paul's Church, Hanover Co., Va. So. Ch., Apr. 27, 1899

WIRT

Augusta Dabney, d. of Daniel Payne Wirt of Westmoreland Co., Va. and great gr.d. of Attorney-General William Wirt, and William Camp Nalle, by the Rev. W. Page Dame, rector of St. Bartholomew's Church, Baltimore, Md., at the home of Dr. Edward M. L. Engle at Morion, Pa. So. Ch., Nov. 3, 1906

William Dabney, of Westmoreland Co., Va., and Garnet Poyton, d. of the late Rev. Wm. H. and Henrietta Randolph Pendleton of Fauquier Co., Va., by the Rev. E. S. Hinks assisted by the Rev. Chas. H. Lee and the Rev. G. W. Nelson, in St. James' Church, Warrenton, Va. So. Ch., Nov. 29, 1894

WISE

* Given as printed

MARRIAGE NOTICES IN THE SOUTHERN CHURCHMAN WITH DATES OF PUBLICATION

Lewis Warrington, and Mrs. Martha Allen Wilson, at No. 805 W. Franklin St., Richmond, Va. So. Ch., Dec. 3, 1896

WOOD
Julia Pride, d. of the late Philip S. and Emma P. Wood of Amelia C.H., Va., and the Rev. Stephen O. Southall of Rocky Mount, Va., rector of Franklin Parish*, by the Rev. V. Wrenn, rector of Raleigh Parish**, in Christ Church, Amelia C.H., Va. So. Ch., May 4, 1899

Timothy Ward, and Mrs. Anna Elizabeth Ingram, both of Manchester, Va., by the Rev. Edgar N. Dickerson, in St. Luke's, Blackstone, Va. So. Ch., Sept. 26, 1903

WORMELEY
P. Lightfoot, Jr., and Lucy Waller Duval, by the Rev. Landon R. Mason, in Grace Episcopal Church, Fluvanna Co. So. Ch., June 25, 1904

WRIGHT
Eliza Clayborne, d. of the late B. E. and L. R. Wright of "Shelba", Essex Co., Va., and John R. Haile, by the Rev. Mr. Thompson, in St. Paul's Church, Essex Co., Va. So. Ch., Sept. 5, 1895

WYATT
William Edward, and Fannie Miller Rich, by the Rev. E. R. Rich and the Rev. A. M. Rich, in St. Michael's Church, Baltimore Co., Md. So. Ch., Oct. 22, 1896

WYCHE
Thomas J., of Wyoming, and Philippa Ludwell, d. of Thomas S. Taliaferro of Gloucester Co. and gr.d. of the late Cassius F. Lee of Alexandria, Va., by the Rt. Rev. Ethelbert Talbot, D.D., at Green River, Wyo. So. Ch., Dec. 27, 1894

YARBROUGH
Lilian Moore, and George William Warren, both of Richmond, by the Rev. Fenner S. Stickney, in Monumental Church, Richmond, Va. So. Ch., Jan. 28, 1897

YEATON
Lucia Chauncey, of Alexandria, Va., and Dr. Hancke Frederic Wagner of Charleston, S.C., by the Rev. H. H. Phelps, in Calvary Church, Fletcher, N.C. So. Ch., July 21, 1898

YUILLE
Thomas Burks, of Virginia, and Nanny Williams Long of North Carolina, by the Rev. Julian Ingle, rector, assisted by the Rev. E. S. Gunn of Brandon, Va., in the Church of the Holy Innocents, Henderson, N.C. So. Ch., Nov. 8, 1894

ZIMMER
Wm. L., of Petersburg, Va., and Frances L. Smith, at the home of the bride, Waterford, Loudoun Co., Va. So. Ch., Nov. 4, 1897

* Franklin Parish is in Franklin County, Va. (Journal ... Diocese of Southwestern Virginia, 1940)
** Raleigh Parish is in Amelia County, Va. (Journal ... Diocese of Southern Virginia, Portsmouth, 1941)

ANNOUNCEMENTS OF APPROACHING MARRIAGES
1915 - 1940

ANNOUNCEMENTS OF APPROACHING MARRIAGES RECORDED IN THE SOUTHERN CHURCHMAN, 1915-1940

LAWRENCE
Alfred Stratton, Jr. (The Rev.), of Durham, N.C., manager of Vade Mecum and minister-in-charge of St. Joseph's and St. Andrew's Church in Durham, N.C., and of St. Mark's, Roxbury, N.C., and Alma Lee, diocesan Y.P.S.L. executive, d. of Mr. and Mrs. R. H. Roney of Rocky Mount and Burlington, N.C., in the Church of the Holy Comforter, Burlington. So. Ch., Sept. 24, 1938

LEWIS
Arthur Machen (The Rev.), rector of St. James' Church, Oskaloosa, Iowa, and Virginia Hayden Blandford, by the Rt. Rev. Harry Sherman Langley, in the Church of the Atonement, Philadelphia. So. Ch., Aug. 12, 1916

McCALLAM
Janet, d. of the Rev. and Mrs. Arlington A. McCallam of Washington, and the Rev. Robert C. Kell. So. Ch., July 20, 1940

PHILLIPS
Ella Parr, d. of the Rt. Rev. and Mrs. Henry Disbron Phillips, and Samuel Jordan Slate, at White Plains, N.Y. So. Ch., Mar. 11, 1939

RONEY
Alma Lee, diocesan Y.P.S.L. executive, d. of Mr. and Mrs. R. H. Roney of Rocky Mount and Burlington, N.C., and Rev. Alfred Stratton Lawrence, Jr. of Durham, N.C., manager of Vade Mecum and minister-in-charge of St. Joseph's and St. Andrew's churches in Durham, N.C., and of St. Mark's, Roxbury, N.C., in the Church of the Holy Comforter, Burlington. So. Ch., Sept. 24, 1938

SLATE
Samuel Jordan, and Ella Parr, d. of the Rt. Rev. and Mrs. Henry Disbron Phillips, at White Plains, N.Y. So. Ch., Mar. 11, 1939

www.ingramcontent.com/pod-product-compliance
Lightning Source LLC
Chambersburg PA
CBHW071230300426
44116CB00008B/973